KU-304-595

The **Rough Guide** to

Andalucía

written and researched by

Geoff Garvey and Mark Ellingham

with additional contributions by
Pam Lalonde, Pau Sandham and Chris Stewart

ROUGH GUIDES

NEW YORK · LONDON · DELHI
www.roughguides.com

Contents

◄◄ Osborne bull, Cádiz province ◄ Street, Almonaster La Real

Introduction to

Andalucía

Andalucía is the southernmost territory of Spain and the part of the Iberian peninsula that is most quintessentially Spanish. The popular image of Spain as a land of bullfights, flamenco, sherry and ruined castles derives from this spectacularly beautiful region. The influences that have washed over Andalucía since the first paintings were etched on cave walls here more than 25,000 years ago are many – Phoenicians, Carthaginians, Greeks, Romans, Visigoths and Vandals all came and left their mark. And the most influential invaders of all, the Moors, who ruled the region for seven centuries and named it *al-Andalus*, have left an enduring imprint on Andalucian culture and customs.

 The heartland of Andalucía is the fertile valley of the mighty **Río Guadalquivir**, flowing across the region from its source in the Cazorla mountains in the northeast through the magnificent cities of Córdoba and Seville, before draining into the marshes and wetlands of the Doñana National Park and the Gulf of Cádiz. North of this great artery rise the undulating hills of the **Sierra Morena**, from where was gouged the mineral wealth – silver, lead and tin – sought by successive waves of invaders from Phoenicians to Romans. The **Moors**, who arrived in the eighth century, were more interested in harvesting Andalucía's natural wealth and turned the region into an orchard rich in olives, citrus fruits, almonds, saffron, figs and vines – still the major products of the land today. In 1492 the Christian reconquest, after centuries of struggle, finally succeeded in wresting Spain from its Moorish occupiers, the victors symbolically planting their flags on the towers of the Alhambra, the emblematic monument of Andalucía.

The **Moorish legacy** is the most striking feature of Andalucía today, not only in the dazzling historical monuments such as those of Seville, Córdoba and Granada but also in the whitewashed houses of many of its smaller medieval towns such as Ronda or the flat-roofed villages of Las Alpujarras. The Moorish love of water is to be seen in the pleasure gardens of the Alhambra, and the typical Andalucian patio – tiled plant-bedecked courtyards often with a central fountain – is another Arab legacy as are the ubiquitous wrought-iron window grilles which lend character to any village street. The dances and music of **flamenco**,

Fact file

• Andalucía's **land area** of 90,000 square kilometres is about the size of Ireland or Indiana. With a population of seven million, it is the second largest of Spain's seventeen autonomous regions, with its own administration and parliament based in the regional capital, Seville.

• Physically, Andalucía is a land of stark contrasts. To the west the **dunes** and **wetlands** of the Coto de Doñana National Park comprise the largest roadless area in western Europe, whilst in the east the province of Almería has Europe's only **desert**. The province of Granada has the Iberian peninsula's **highest peak**, the 3483m Mulhacén.

• Andalucía's **economy** is based on tourism and agriculture, the main products of which – sherry, olive oil and *jamón serrano* (cured ham) – are prized throughout Spain.

• Despite its sunny image Andalucía contains an area with the **highest rainfall** on the Spanish peninsula, the natural park of **Grazalema**.

• Love it or hate it, Andalucía is devoted to the **bullfight**. This multi-billion euro business employs thousands of workers both in the rings and on the ranches where the fearsome *toro bravo*, a beast descended from an ancient species of fighting bull, is raised. In the poverty-ridden backstreets of Seville and Málaga, the route to fame in the *corrida* is a fabulous temptation for young men (and sometimes women) and big name *toreros* are idolized and wealthy.

◄ Feria de Córdoba

5

Canary Islands

whilst probably not of Moorish origin, display the soul of Andalucía and can be an electrifying spectacle when dancers in brilliantly coloured dresses drill their heels into the floorboards in a frenzy of emotion or, in *cante jondo* (deep song), turn the art form into a blues-style lament. The Muslim influence on speech and vocabulary, a stoical fatalism in the face of adversity, and an obsession with the drama of death – publicly displayed in the spectacle of the bullfight – are also facets of the modern Andalucian character. Contrastingly, the *andaluzes* also love nothing more than a party, and the colour and sheer energy of the region's countless and legendary **fiestas** – always in traditional flamenco costume worn with pride – make them among the most exciting in the world. The **romerías**, wild and semi-religious pilgrimages to honour local saints at country shrines, are yet another excuse for a jamboree.

Despite the region's abundant natural wealth, poverty is widespread, a legacy of the repressive **latifundia** landholding system of large estates with absentee landlords. The Christian monarchs who ousted the Moorish

7

farmers doled out the conquered land to the Church, the military orders and individual nobles. These new proprietors often had little interest in the land nor personal contact with those who worked their estates, often leaving an overseer in charge, and an atmosphere of resentment built up towards the wretched pay and miserable conditions that this system entailed. It is perhaps not surprising that many inhabitants emigrated to find work in northern Spain or abroad, or that anarchism found many converts among the desperate *braceros* (farmhands) of Andalucía before the Spanish Civil War. Two percent of the landowners still possess fifty percent of the land today, and in the 1960s alone a million Andalucians left their native region to seek a better life elsewhere.

Whilst life for many in the countryside remains hard, new industries, particularly tourism, have had a major impact on the region's **economy**. Apart from the petrochemical industry around Algeciras, mining in Huelva and aircraft manufacture in Sevilla, Andalucía has little heavy industry and those not employed in agriculture are usually working in fishing or tourism. One growth industry of recent years is servicing the population of mainly northern European emigrants who have come to the south of Spain to live, retire or do business. Now numbering close to half of a million, these expatriates have funded much building and development particularly along the coastal strip of the Costa del Sol, earning this zone its new nickname, the "California of Spain".

Where to go

Andalucía's manageable size makes it easy to take in something of each of its elements – inland cities, extensive coastline and mountainous sierras – even on a brief visit. The region's eight provinces take their names from the **provincial capitals**, which are both compellingly individual cultural centres and vibrant cosmopolitan beehives in their own right. The most important is **Seville**, Andalucía's stylishly exuberant capital city, home of *Carmen* and all the clichés of the Spanish south with beautiful *barrios* (quarters), major Christian and Moorish monuments, fine museums and extraordinary **festivals** at Easter and at the April *feria*. Close behind comes **Granada** whose Alhambra palace has a fair claim to being the most sensual building in Europe, whilst at **Córdoba**, the exquisite Mezquita, a former mosque, is another breathtakingly beautiful building left behind by the Moors. Coastal **Málaga** boasts a fine Moorish fort and a good museum stuffed with artworks by its most famous son, **Picasso**, and further down the coast sea-locked **Cádiz** is one of the most atmospheric cities of the south and Andalucía's seafood capital. Whilst they do not always attract the attention lavished on their more immediately appealing neighbours, the cities of **Huelva**, **Jaén** and **Almería** also all have sights well worthy

Ancient Andalucía

Andalucía's rich and varied history has resulted in a great number of ancient sites, many unique in Europe. The dolmens at **Antequera** and the third-millenium BC settlement at **Los Millares** in Almería are remarkable vestiges from the prehistoric age.

Roman sites are scattered across the region, but the excavated towns at **Baelo Claudia** near Tarifa and **Itálica** near Seville plus a fascinating necropolis at **Carmona** are worth making an effort to get to. Two sites in superb locations are the Roman villa at **Bruñel** on the fringe of the Cazorla natural park in Jaén, and **Ocuri**, atop a bluff to the north of Ubrique in Cádiz. One sensational discovery of recent years is the Roman villa at **Almedinilla**, complete with a spectacular cascade feature in its dining room.

of a visit. Inland, small-scale towns and villages, once grand, now hardly significant, are an Andalucian speciality. **Baeza** and **Úbeda** in Jaén are remarkable treasure-houses of Renaissance architecture, while **Ronda** and the **Pueblos Blancos** (White Towns) to the west are among the most picturesque hill villages in Spain.

Not that Andalucía is predominantly about cities and monuments. Few places in the world can boast such a wealth of **natural wonders** in so compact an area. The 400km-long Río Guadalquivir, which crosses and irrigates the region, reaches the sea at the dune-fringed beaches and *marismas* (wetlands/marshes) of the **Coto Doñana National Park**, Europe's largest and most important wildlife sanctuary. To the east and towering above Granada are the peaks of the **Sierra Nevada National Park**, snowcapped for most of the year, and only thirty or so kilometres from the sweltering coastal beaches. Nestling in the folds of the same mountains are the valleys of the **Alpujarras**, a wildly picturesque region dotted with dozens of mountain villages, many of them little changed since Moorish times. Further east come the gulch-ridden badlands and lunar landscapes of Almería's **deserts**, sought out by film-makers and astronomers for the clearest skies in Europe.

Andalucía's rural areas are a paradise for hikers and naturalists and the Sierra Nevada and Las Alpujarras are excellent places for **trekking**, as are the densely wooded hills of the **Sierra de Cazorla** and the **Sierra de Morena** – including the latter's less well-known offshoot, the **Sierra de Aracena**, to the north of Huelva. The region also has a score of other *parques naturales* (natural parks), all located in areas of great natural beauty and detailed throughout the *Guide*.

▲ Plaza de Toros, Ronda

On **the coast** it's often easy to despair. Extending to the west of **Málaga** is the **Costa del Sol**, Europe's most developed coastline, with its beaches hidden behind a remorseless density of concrete hotels and apartment complexes. This is Andalucía's summer playground, famous for its in-your-face brashness and the unlimited nightlife on offer at every resort. Despite the fact that many places such as **Torremolinos** have given themselves a thorough makeover with new theme parks and improved facilities, the Costa del Sol's appeal is not to everyone's taste. Thankfully though, even here the other Andalucía is still to be found if you're prepared to seek it out: go merely a few kilometres inland and you'll encounter the timeless Spain of high sierras, white villages and wholehearted country fiestas.

Offbeat Andalucía

Among the more bizarre things to see in Andalucía are a museum at Mijas in Málaga displaying the world's tiniest things, including a copy of the *Last Supper* painted on a grain of rice, and a rosary museum at Aroche in Huelva with displays of beads once owned by the famous (and infamous). Other curiosities include a nineteenth-century English-designed housing estate in the middle of the city of Huelva, a still-functioning sulphur spa at Carratraca in Málaga once used by Lord Byron, and a communist village run on Utopian principles at Marinaleda in Seville. Andalucía's oldest inn dating from the thirteenth century, complete with highwayman's cell, is located at Alfarnate in the rugged Axarquía district of Málaga whilst Spain's first donkey sanctuary is to be found at Rute in the south of Córdoba province.

Alternatively, travel further both east and west along the coast and you'll find some of the best beaches in all Spain: the **Costa de la Luz** to the west, where Atlantic breakers wash the white-sand strands of **Tarifa**, **Conil de la Frontera** and **Isla Cristina**; in the centre at the less frenzied resorts of **Nerja** and **Almuñecar** on the **Costa Tropical**; and to the east along the **Costa de Almería** where appealing resorts like **San José, Agua Amarga and Mojácar** all hark back to pre-Costa del Sol tranquillity.

Wherever you go in Andalucía you can't fail to notice the *andaluzes'* infectious enthusiasm for life. This is always ebulliently evident in the countless celebrations, **ferias** and **fiestas** that happen almost daily at one town or village or another throughout the summer months. But at other times too, and even in the smallest towns, there will always be good food, drink and a surprising range of nightlife and entertainment to be enjoyed. And there are few greater pleasures than joining the regulars at a local bar to wind down over a glass of **fino** (dry sherry from Jerez) while nibbling **tapas** – Andalucía's great titbit invention.

When to go

In terms of climate the question is mainly one of how much heat you can take. During the **summer** months of July and August temperatures of over 40°C (104°F) on the coast are normal and inland they can rise even higher in cities such as Seville, generally reckoned to be the hottest in Spain. The solution here is to follow the natives and get about in the relative

▼ Carnaval, Cádiz

cool of the mornings and late afternoons, finding somewhere shady to rest up as the city roasts in the midday furnace. The major resorts are busy in July and packed in August (the Spanish holiday month) when prices also are at their highest.

Better times to visit are the **spring** months of April, May and early June when lower temperatures combine with a greener landscape awash with wild flowers. **Autumn** is good, too, although by late October much of the coastal landscape looks parched and the resorts have begun to wind down; in hilly and mountainous areas, however, such as the sierras of Cazorla, Nevada and Aracena and the high valleys of Las Alpujarras, the splendours of autumn can be especially scenic. The **winter** months – particularly December and January – can often be dismal and wet as well as cold at high altitude, although the past decade, when the extended drought of the 1990s was followed by some

The olive and its oil

Spain is the world's largest producer of olive oil, an enormous quantity of which is harvested in Andalucía. Vast areas of the provinces of Seville, Córdoba and especially Jaén are given over to the orderly lines of trees, many a thousand years old and more. The finest extra-virgin oils have near-zero acidities, the mark of the crème de la crème of the oil world, and these qualities have gained the product a reputation as a vital aid to health – Spaniards' markedly low susceptibility to conditions such as coronary disease is attributed to their olive-oil-rich, low-cholesterol diet.

In these days of energy conservation the olive is also coming into its own as a major provider of electricity. The waste squeezed fruit from the production process used to be turned into dried-out "briquettes" by farmers to throw on to the fire in winter. This has now been taken a stage further and the many millions of tons of waste that were formerly dumped is now being transformed into fuel to supply power generating stations in Córdoba and Jaén – and more are in the pipeline.

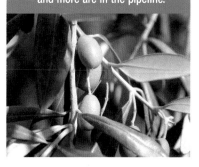

unusually wet winters, has tended to throw the normal weather patterns into confusion. The winter, of course, is a good time to visit the museums and monuments of Seville, Málaga, Córdoba and Granada when they are far less crowded and

– should you be lucky with the weather – the cities themselves can look wonderful, too. The desert province of Almería sees only one day of rain a year on average and in winter has many days of perfect crystal visibility.

Average daily temperatures (C/F)

	Feb	Apr	Jun	Aug	Oct	Dec
Almería						
av. max temp	16/61	20/68	26/79	29/84	23/73	17/63
av. min temp	8/46	12/54	18/64	22/72	16/61	9/48
Cádiz						
av. max temp	16/61	21/70	27/80	30/86	23/73	16/61
av. min temp	9/48	12/54	18/64	20/68	16/61	9/48
Córdoba						
av. max temp	16/61	23/73	32/90	36/97	24/75	14/57
av. min temp	5/41	10/50	17/63	20/68	13/55	5/41
Granada						
av. max temp	14/57	20/68	30/86	34/93	22/72	12/54
av. min temp	2/36	7/45	14/57	17/63	9/48	2/36
Huelva						
av. max temp	18/64	22/72	29/84	32/90	25/77	17/63
av. min temp	7/45	11/52	16/61	18/64	14/57	7/45
Jaén						
av. max temp	14/57	20/68	30/86	34/93	22/72	12/54
av. min temp	5/41	10/50	17/63	21/70	13/55	5/41
Málaga						
av. max temp	17/63	21/70	28/82	30/86	24/75	17/63
av. min temp	8/46	11/52	17/63	20/68	15/59	9/48
Seville						
av. max temp	17/63	23/73	32/90	36/97	26/79	16/61
av. min temp	6/43	11/52	17/63	20/68	14/57	7/45
Tarifa						
av. max temp	17/63	20/68	24/75	27/80	23/73	17/63
av. min temp	11/52	13/55	17/63	20/68	17/63	11/52

things not to miss

It's not possible to see everything Andalucía has to offer in one trip – and we don't suggest you try. What follows is a selective list of the region's highlights from outstanding buildings and natural wonders to vibrant festivals and tasty food. They're arranged in five colour-coded categories which you can browse through to find the very best things to see and experience. All highlights have a page reference to take you straight into the guide, where you can find out more.

01 **Cabo de Gata, Almería** Page **552** • The Cabo de Gata natural park is famous for its salt marshes and its birdlife including storks, egrets and magnificent pink flamingos.

02 Sherry Page **234** & *Andalucian cuisine* colour section • Andalucía's great wine comes from the "sherry triangle" towns of Jerez, El Puerto de Santa María and Sanlúcar de Barrameda, each with plenty of *bodegas* to visit.

04 Parque Nacional de Coto de Doñana Page **331** • The vast wilderness of Spain's biggest wildlife reserve is home to the endangered Spanish lynx, imperial eagle and exotic flamingoes.

03 El Rocío Page **334** • On the edge of the Doñana national park and surrounded by wetlands this village's church holds a venerated image of the Virgin, the focus of one of the most extraordinary pilgrimages in Spain.

05 Mezquita, Córdoba Page **382** & *Moorish Andalucía* colour section • Nothing can prepare you for the beauty of Córdoba's medieval mosque, one of the greatest Islamic buildings of all time.

06 Cathedral, Seville Page **257** • The world's largest Gothic church is a treasure house full of artistic riches. Its astonishingly beautiful Moorish minaret, the Giralda, is now its bell-tower and can be climbed for a stunning view.

07 Tapas Page **42** & *Andalucian cuisine* colour section • Dine Andalucian style, sampling plates of delicious tapas in a variety of bars.

08 Sierra de Grazalema Page **170** • The pretty white village of Grazalema lends it's name to the surrounding *parque natural* where soaring limestone peaks are swathed in forests of oak and fir.

17

09 **Hiking** Page **511** & **521** • Andalucía is prime hiking territory and the walks around Spain's highest mountain, the Mulhacén, can be both challenging and rewarding.

10 **Museo Picasso, Málaga**
Page **79** • Málaga's most famous son has a spectacular new museum in the heart of the old quarter displaying hundreds of his works.

11 **Jamón** Page **363** & *Andalucian cuisine* colour section • Delicious, mouthwatering mountain-cured ham is one of Andalucía's specialities.

12 **Gibraltar** Page **141** • This colonial hangover with its pubs, sterling currency and Barbary apes makes a bizarre contrast with the rest of Andalucía.

13 Castillo de Santa Catalina, Jaén Page 434 •
Formerly an impregnable Moorish fort, this monument now houses Andalucía's most spectacularly sited parador.

14 Plaza Vázquez de Molina, Úbeda Page 444 •
Along with nearby Baeza, Úbeda has a cornucopia of ravishing Renaissance buildings and this square, at its heart, is one of the most beautiful in Andalucía.

15 Encierro Page 155 •
No village fiesta is complete without an *encierro*, when a fierce *toro bravo* roams the streets looking for an encounter with anyone who thinks they're brave enough.

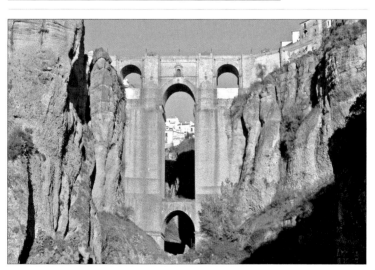

16 Ronda Page 156 •
Ringed by mountains and perched astride the yawning El Tajo gorge, irresistible Ronda is one of the most dramatically sited towns in Andalucía.

17 **Flamenco** Page **591** • The soul of Andalucía, flamenco dance, music and song are widely performed and express the *alegría y dolor* (happiness and pain) of andaluz life.

18 **Baelo Claudia** Page **191** • Many civilizations have left their mark on Andalucía, including the Romans, who raised the fishing town of Baelo Claudia on the coast near Cádiz.

19 **Parque Natural Sierra de Cazorla** Page **456** • Andalucía's largest natural park is a vast area of rugged mountains and forested valleys inhabited by a feast of wildlife including ibex, wild boar, golden eagles and griffon vultures.

20 Las Alpujarras Page **511** • Ancient cobble-streeted villages situated in a dramatically beautiful area of woodland and gushing mountain streams.

22 Museo Bellas Artes, Seville Page **275** • An eighteenth-century former convent provides a magnificent setting for Seville's fine arts museum, filled with major works.

21 Alhambra, Granada Page **477** & *Moorish Andalucía* colour section • One of the most sensual palaces ever built, the magical Alhambra is the supreme legacy of Islamic Spain.

23 Seafood Page **43** • An *andaluz* passion, the freshest and tastiest fish and shellfish are to be found in all coastal regions.

24 Medina Azahara Page **398** & *Moorish Andalucía* colour section • The ruins of Caliph Abd ar-Rahman III's palace-city, named after his favourite wife az-Zahra, evoke the splendour of the Cordoban caliphate.

25 Semana Santa, Seville Page **296** & *Semana Santa* colour section • Holy Week is the most important date in the religious calendar and is celebrated in every town and village, while cities such as Seville, Granada, Córdoba and Málaga stage spectacular processions.

26 Alcázar, Seville Page **263** • This fabulous Mudéjar palace with enchanting gardens and dazzling *artesonado* ceilings, tiles and stuccowork is one of the glories of the city.

27 Cádiz Page **201** • Steeped in history, sealocked Cádiz is one of the great cities of the Spanish south and serves up the best seafood in Andalucía.

28 **Costa de la Luz beaches** Page **184** • Stunning beaches are to be found all along Andalucía's coastline, and the Costa de la Luz has some of the region's best.

29 **The Albaicín** Page **488** • Granada's atmospheric old Moorish quarter stands on the Sacromonte hill and its sinuous alleys and cobbled streets are a delight to explore.

31 Écija Page **308** • Famed for its dazzling collection of colourful Baroque church towers, Éjica also has some fine mansions and an excellent museum.

30 Priego de Córdoba Page **414** • A jewel of Córdoba province, Priego has a collection of spectacular Baroque churches and a flower-bedecked old Moorish quarter, the Barrio de la Villa.

33 Jardín de la Concepción, Málaga Page **84** • Among many magnificent gardens in Andalucía, Málaga's Jardín Botanico de la Concepción is a spectacular natural wonder.

32 Mini Hollywood Page **567** • Clint Eastwood, Yul Brynner and Steve McQueen all faced gunfighters on the streets of Mini Hollywood in the Almerian desert, where the film sets of many famous Westerns are preserved.

Basics

Basics

Getting there

Flying is the quickest way of getting to Andalucía, with by far the widest choice of routes being from the UK and Ireland. Málaga is the usual point of entry for most visitors, though the summer holiday trade to the areas beyond the costas, and the rapid growth of European budget airlines, has opened up regional airports right across the region from Seville and Jerez in the west to Granada and Almería in the east. However, Málaga's rapidly expanding airport retains its status as Andalucía's busiest and now has direct flights to New York. Alternatively, taking the train from London to Andalucía is no longer the endurance test it was, with the possibility of a Eurostar service to Paris, a comfortable overnight journey on the "train-hotel" to Madrid followed by a lightning-fast trip to Seville or Málaga on the superlative new AVE high-speed train in a little over two hours. Driving is a bit more of an adventure, but there are several routes that can save you time, like the direct ferry services from Plymouth to Santander and from Portsmouth to Bilbao.

Air, train and ferry fares are seasonal, at their highest in summer (June to end Sept) and around Christmas/New Year and Easter week. You should always book as far in advance as possible to get the best deals. The **cheapest flights** from the UK and Ireland are usually with budget and charter airlines, which are sold direct (by phone or online) on a one-way basis, so you may find one leg of your journey considerably more expensive depending on demand. Be aware, too, that **airport taxes** can cost more than the flight itself, while increasingly things like in-flight meals and luggage allowances are being charged as extra. Cheap flights tend to have fixed dates and are non-changeable and non-refundable, while tickets with holiday charter airlines may limit your stay to one month. Major **scheduled airlines** are usually (though not always) more expensive, but tickets remain valid for three months or more and normally have a degree of flexibility should you need to change dates after booking. You may be able to cut costs by going through a specialist **flight, discount or online agent**, who may also offer special student and youth fares plus a range of other travel-related services.

Flights from the UK and Ireland

Flight time to Andalucía is two to three hours, depending on the route, and usually the cheapest flights are with the no-frills **budget airlines** such as bmibaby (www.bmibaby .com), easyJet (www.easyjet.com) and Ryanair (www.ryanair.com), who between them fly from over twenty regional UK and Irish airports direct to destinations all over Andalucía. London flights tend to depart from Stansted or Luton; other budget airlines, including Jet2 (from Leeds/Bradford, Manchester, Newcastle and Blackpool; www.jet2.com) or flybe (from Exeter and Southampton; www.flybe.com), concentrate on flights out of particular British regions, while easyJet also flies out of Belfast. In any case, you should be able to find a route that suits you, and not just to the main cities either – many budget airlines offer direct access to smaller regional airports in Andalucía. **Fares** for flights on all routes start at around £9.99 each way, or sometimes (depending on the airline) even free with just the taxes to pay. However, book last minute in the summer and you can expect to pay considerably more, up to £100 each way depending on the route.

For convenient flights to the **Costa del Sol**, you can also check the websites of holiday and charter companies such as Monarch (www.flymonarch.com), First Choice (www.firstchoice.co.uk), Thomas Cook (www.flythomascook.com) and Thomson (www.thomsonfly.com). You might not get the rock-bottom deals of the budget airlines, as schedules and prices are geared towards the summer holiday season, but flights depart from regional airports right around the UK.

Iberia (@www.iberia.com), Spain's national airline, and British Airways (@www.britishairways.com) have the widest range of **scheduled flights**, with direct services from London Gatwick or Heathrow to Málaga and Seville. You'll also be able to arrange add-on sections to London from regional UK airports such as Manchester or Newcastle or from Scotland. Special offers mean prices start at around £100 return, though again a typical late-booking summer rate can be more like £200 return.

From Ireland, you can fly with Iberia from Dublin to Madrid, or with Aer Lingus (@www.aerlingus.com) from Dublin or Cork to up to eight Spanish airports (including Málaga). Ryanair also connects Dublin and Shannon with Málaga, plus Seville and Almería. Prices are highly flexible, starting at around €40 each way, though these rise sharply for last-minute bookings or to popular summer destinations.

Flights from the US and Canada

The widest choice of scheduled flights **from the United States** to Spain is with the national carrier Iberia (@www.iberia.com), which flies direct, non-stop from New York to Madrid or Barcelona, and from Miami and Chicago to Madrid. Journey time (typically overnight) is between seven hours ten minutes and eight hours thirty minutes, depending on the route. Fares start at around $600 return, though high-season supplements and taxes can push this up to $1000 or so. The advantage of flying with Iberia is that it offers connecting flights to six airports throughout Andalucía, which can be very good value if booked with your transatlantic flight. However, there are other airlines offering Spanish routes (some on a code-share basis with Iberia or other airlines), including American Airlines (@www.aa.com), Continental (@www.continental.com), Spanair (@www.spanair.com) and United (@www.united.com). Delta (@www.delta.com) also offer a **direct flight** four days a week from New York to Málaga.

Fly less – stay longer! Travel and climate change

Climate change is perhaps the single biggest issue facing our planet. It is caused by a build-up in the atmosphere of carbon dioxide and other greenhouse gases, which are emitted by many sources – including planes. Already, **flights** account for three to four percent of human-induced global warming: that figure may sound small, but it is rising year on year and threatens to counteract the progress made by reducing greenhouse emissions in other areas.

Rough Guides regard travel as a **global benefit**, and feel strongly that the advantages to developing economies are important, as are the opportunities for greater contact and awareness among peoples. But we also believe in travelling responsibly, which includes giving thought to how often we fly and what we can do to redress any harm that our trips may create.

We can travel less or simply reduce the amount we travel by air (taking fewer trips and staying longer, or taking the train if there is one); we can avoid night flights (which are more damaging); and we can make the trips we do take "climate neutral" via a carbon offset scheme. **Offset schemes** run by climatecare.org, carbonneutral.com and others allow you to "neutralize" the greenhouse gases that you are responsible for releasing. Their websites have simple calculators that let you work out the impact of any flight – as does our own. Once that's done, you can pay to fund projects that will reduce future emissions by an equivalent amount. Please take the time to visit our website and make your trip climate neutral, or get a copy of the *Rough Guide to Climate Change* for more detail on the subject.

www.roughguides.com/climatechange

You can also fly to Spain with airlines such as Air France, KLM, Lufthansa, TAP or British Airways which tend to fly via their respective European hubs – in which case, you can add three to fours hours to your total travel time, depending on the connection.

From Canada, there's a direct, non-stop route from Toronto to Madrid with Air Canada (🌐www.aircanada.com), with onward connections across Spain with their partner Spanair. Fares start from CAN$545 one way from Toronto, Montreal or Ottawa, CAN$715 from Calgary or Vancouver. Otherwise, you'll be able to find a route using one of the major European airlines via their respective hubs, with fares starting at around CAN$1100 return.

Flights from Australia, New Zealand and South Africa

There are no direct flights to Spain **from Australia or New Zealand**, but many airlines offer through-tickets with their partners via their European or Asian hubs. Flights via Asia are generally the cheaper option, but fares don't vary as much between airlines as you might think, and in the end you'll be basing your choice on things like flight timings, routes and possible stop offs on the way. If you're seeing Spain as part of a wider European trip, you might want to aim first for the UK, since there's a wide choice of cheap flights to Spain once there. Or consider a Round-the-World fare, with most basic options able to offer Madrid or Barcelona as standard stopovers.

From **South Africa**, there are direct flights with Iberia (🌐www.iberia.com) from Johannesburg to Madrid, which take around ten hours.

Package holidays, tours and city breaks

The basic, mass-market **package holidays** to the traditional resorts on the Costa del Sol and elsewhere are not to everyone's taste, but bargains can be found online or at any UK high-street travel agent, from as little as £99 for a seven-night flight-and-hotel package. There are often really good deals for families, either in hotels or in self-catering apartments, though the time of year you visit can increase prices significantly (school holidays are always most expensive).

A huge number of **specialist tour operators** offer a wider range of activity holidays or tours, from hiking in the Alpujarras to touring the artistic highlights of Andalucía. We've given a flavour of what's available in the listings at the end of this section, but the options are almost endless. Prices vary wildly depending on the quality of accommodation offered and whether the tours are fully inclusive or not. Many cycle tours, for example, can either be guided or done on a more independent (and cheaper) self-guided basis. Spanish-based tour operators offer some of the more interesting, off-the-beaten-track options, but for these you'll usually have to arrange your own flights to Spain, while some foreign-based operators also tend to quote for their holidays exclusive of airfares.

Some operators and websites specialize in **city breaks**, with destinations including Seville, Córdoba and Granada. UK prices start at around £200 for three-day (two-night) breaks, including return flights, airport transfer and B&B in a centrally located one-, two- or three-star hotel. Adding extra nights or upgrading your hotel is possible, too, usually at a fairly reasonable cost. The bigger US operators, such as American Express and Delta Vacations, can also easily organize short city breaks to Spain on a flight-and-hotel basis, while from Australia Iberian specialist Ibertours (🌐www.ibertours.com.au) can arrange two- or three-night packages in most Spanish cities.

Other package deals worth considering are **fly-drive** offers, where you'll get a flight, accommodation and car rental arranged through your tour operator. Some companies specialize in villas and apartments, or off-the-beaten-track farmhouses and the like, while on other holiday packages you can tour the country's historic paradores, with car rental included.

Trains

Travelling by train from the UK to Andalucía is a viable option, with total journey times from London of around twenty hours to Seville or Málaga travelling via Madrid. You

take the afternoon **Eurostar** (ⓦwww
.eurostar.com) from London St Pancras
International to Paris and change there for
the overnight "train-hotel" for Madrid with an
onward connection using the AVE high-
speed train to Andalucía. **Fares** start at £59
return for the Eurostar to Paris (through-
tickets available from UK towns and cities),
plus £51 each way for the cheapest sleeper
accommodation on the overnight train. The
cheapest pre-booked one-way ticket for the
AVE high-speed train from Madrid to Seville
or Málaga costs around €70 (no discount for
return). You'll have to book well in advance
on all services to get the lowest prices. There
are alternative daytime services through
France and Spain, though they don't save
you any money.

The best first stop for information
about train travel to Spain is the excellent
ⓦ**www.seat61.com**, which provides full
route, ticket, timetable and contact information. You can book the whole journey
online with Rail Europe (ⓣ0844/848 5848,
ⓦwww.raileurope.co.uk) or call a specialist
rail agent such as Ffestiniog Travel
(ⓣ01766/772 050, ⓦwww.ffestiniogtravel
.co.uk) or the Spanish Rail Service
(ⓣ020/7725 7063, ⓦwww.spanish-rail.co
.uk). If you live outside the UK, you can book
Eurostar and "train-hotel" tickets through
ⓦwww.raileurope.com. These contacts can
also advise about **rail passes** (principally
InterRail and Eurail), which have to be
bought before leaving home – see p.35 for
more details.

Buses

You can reach most major cities in Andalucía
by bus from the UK with **Eurolines** services
(ⓣ08705/808080, ⓦwww.eurolines.co.uk).
The main routes are from London (though
add-on fares are available from any British
city) to Barcelona (25hr), Madrid (27hr) and
Valencia (30hr), with connections to
Andalucía adding an additional five to six
hours, but it's a long time to spend cooped
up in a bus. Standard return fares are around
£145–192 to Málaga, £122–160 to Seville
depending upon season and when booked.
You'll get better deals if you book seven,
fifteen or thirty days in advance or check the
website for special offers. You can book

tickets online or at any British National
Express bus terminal.

Driving to Spain

Provided you're not in a hurry, **driving to
Spain** from the UK is an interesting way to
get there, but with fuel, toll and overnight
costs it doesn't compare in terms of price
with flying or taking the train. It's about
2500km from London to Málaga, for
example, which, with stops, takes almost
two full days to drive.

Many people use the conventional **cross-
Channel ferry links**, principally Dover–Calais,
though services to Brittany or Normandy
might be more convenient depending on
where you live (and they cut out the trek
around Paris). However, the quickest way of
crossing the Channel is to use the **Eurotunnel**
(ⓣ08705/353 535, ⓦwww.eurotunnel.com),
which operates drive-on-drive-off shuttle
trains between Folkestone and Calais/
Coquelles. The 24-hour service runs every
twenty minutes throughout the day; though
you can just turn up, booking is advised,
especially at weekends and in the summer
holidays, or if you want the best deals (from
£49 one way). French railways run a **Motorail**
service (mid-May to mid-Sept; 1–2 departures
a week; from £190) from Calais or Paris,
where your car is loaded on to the train and
you sleep overnight in a couchette, but it only
runs as far as Narbonne, on the French
Mediterranean side of the Pyrenees, so is a
pricey way to save a few hours' driving time.

The best way to cut driving time is to use
either of the direct UK–Spain ferry crossings.
Brittany Ferries (ⓣ0871/244 0744, ⓦwww
.brittany-ferries.co.uk) operates a car and
passenger ferry from **Plymouth to
Santander** in Cantabria (twice weekly; 20hr),
or there's a P&O service (ⓣ0871/664 5645,
ⓦwww.poferries.com) from **Portsmouth to
Bilbao** (twice weekly; 34hr; restricted
services Dec & Jan), east of Santander in the
Basque Country. Both services are very
expensive, especially in summer, when return
fares can cost as much as £800 (it's cheaper
for foot-passengers, though everyone has to
book some form of seating or cabin accommodation). From the Basque country to the
northern border of Andalucía is a journey of
around 650km or a day's drive.

Any ferry company or travel agent can supply up-to-date schedules and ticket information, or you can consult the encyclopedic ⓦ www.directferries.com, which has details about, and links to, every European ferry service. For driving requirements and regulations in Spain, see p.35.

Online booking

ⓦ www.cheapflights.com,
ⓦ www.ebookers.com, ⓦ www.ebookers.ie,
ⓦ www.expedia.co.uk, ⓦ www.expedia.com,
ⓦ www.expedia.ca,
ⓦ www.lastminute.com, ⓦ www.us
.lastminute.com, ⓦ www.lastminute.com.au,
ⓦ www.travelocity.co.uk, ⓦ www.travelocity
.com, ⓦ www.travelocity.ca,
ⓦ www.zuji.com.au

Discount travel agents

North South Travel UK ☏ 01245/608291, ⓦ www.northsouthtravel.co.uk. Friendly, competitive travel agency, offering discounted fares. Profits are used to support projects in the developing world, especially the promotion of sustainable tourism.
STA Travel UK ☏ 0871/230 0040, ⓦ www .statravel.co.uk; US ☏ 1-800/781-4040, ⓦ www .statravel.com; Australia ☏ 134 782, ⓦ www .statravel.com.au. Worldwide specialists in low-cost flights, and tours for students and under 26s. Also student IDs, travel insurance, car rental, rail passes and more.
Trailfinders UK ☏ 0845/058 5858, ⓦ www .trailfinders.com; Republic of Ireland ☏ 01/677 7888, ⓦ www.trailfinders.ie; Australia ☏ 1300/780 212, ⓦ www.trailfinders.com.au. One of the best-informed and most efficient agents for independent travellers.

Tour operators

Backpacker travel

Busabout UK ☏ 020/7950 1661, ⓦ www .busabout.com. The European backpacker bus service also offers a seven-day Spain/Portugal bus tour (basically Andalucía and the Portuguese Algarve; £399); prices include hostel accommodation, guides, transport, surf lessons and so on all aimed at a young, party crowd.

Birdwatching, painting and dance holidays

Andalucian Guides Spain ☏ 956 43 23 16 ⓦ www.andalucianguides.com. Guided

birdwatching trips in Cádiz by the week or the day. Day trips around €35 or less depending on number of people.
Andalucian Painting Holidays UK ☏ 01382/553 736, ⓦ www.langeart.co.uk. Painting holidays with Scottish artist based in the pretty Málaga hill village of Ojén.
Dance Holiday Company UK ☏ 020/7099 4816, ⓦ www.danceholidays.com. Flamenco, salsa and Argentinian tango holiday courses in Seville, Córdoba and Granada. From £500 per week including tuition but excluding flights.
Limosa Holidays UK ☏ 01263/578 143, ⓦ www .limosaholidays.co.uk. Bird-watching tours to the Strait of Gibraltar. See the great spring and autumn migrations accompanied by knowledgeable guides.

Cycling

Bravobike Spain ☏ 917 582 945, ⓦ www .bravobike.com. Offers a variety of cycle tours including one covering Córdoba, Granada, Priego, Zuheros and Rute. Prices are variable, ranging from €30 for a short day trip, €650 self-guided per week and from €1000 guided.
Easy Rider Tours US ☏ 1-800/488 8332, ⓦ www .easyridertours.com. Guided cycling and sightseeing tours in Andalucía and elsewhere. One trip takes in Carmona and Córdoba. Tours are all-inclusive and fully supported, from around $3000 for a week, though airfares are extra.
Explore! UK ☏ 0845/013 0537, ⓦ www.explore .co.uk. Walking and cycling holidays in Axarquía and Alpujarras.
Iberocycle Spain ☏ 942 581 085, ⓦ www .iberocycle.com. An English-run, Spain-based company specializing in supported or self-guided cycling tours, which include a White Town tour taking in Ronda, Zahara and Vejer. Short five-night trips start at around €430.

Food and drink

Arblaster & Clarke UK ☏ 01730/263 111, ⓦ www.arblasterandclarke.com. The most notable wine-tour specialist, with quality trips to all of Spain's wine-producing regions, including tour of *bodegas* in the sherry triangle. Around £1500 for five-night all-included trip.
A Taste of Spain Spain ☏ 856 079 626, ⓦ www .atasteofspain.com. Organizes gourmet Iberian culinary tours incuding *fino* tasting in Jerez, *jamón serrano* in Jabugo and olive oil in the province of Córdoba. Andalucía and central Spain, with tastings, meals and cookery lessons. Prices for six nights all included start at €3000.
Winetrails UK ☏ 01306/712 111, ⓦ www .winetrails.co.uk. Wine-based tours of Andalucía.

History, art and culture

Abercrombie and Kent UK ☎0845/618 2203, ⓦ www.abercrombieandkent.co.uk; US ☎1-800/554 7016, ⓦ www.abercrombieandkent .com. Pricey, upmarket independent or fully escorted tours, with the ten-day "Signature Spain" trip (Córdoba, Granada, Seville) typically providing a private guide for monument visits.

Kirker Travel UK ☎020/7593 1899, ⓦ www .kirkerholidays.com. Short breaks and holiday packages in Andalucían towns and cities. Twelve-day tour of Moorish Seville, Córdoba and Granada costs £2200 per person.

Martin Randall Travel UK ☎020/8742 3355, ⓦ www.martinrandall.com. Small group cultural tours to Seville and elsewhere, led by experts on art, archeology or music. Departures several times a year on various trips and themes, from around £1800.

Horseriding

Fantasia Adventure Holidays Spain ⓦ www .fantasiaadventureholidays.com. British-run company offering riding breaks on the Costa de la Luz, from full-board weekends to week-long holidays (from £655 excluding flights). Contact is best by email.

Surfing

Surf Spain UK ☎01691/648514, ⓦ www .surfspain.co.uk. Surf camps, short-break and tailor-made surfing holidays based at El Palmar on the Costa de la Luz, with a typical seven-night break costing from £340 per person (excluding flights).

Walking, cycling and adventure

Adventure Center US ☎1-800/228 8747, ⓦ www.adventurecenter.com. Active vacations in Andalucía and the Sierra Nevada.

Exodus Travels UK ☎020/8675 5550, ⓦ www .exodus.co.uk. Walking and cycling in Andalucía, as well as cultural and sightseeing trips. There's

a big range of trips at all prices, but typical is a week's walking or cycling priced from around £800 including flights.

Inntravel UK ☎01653/617 945, ⓦ www.inntravel .co.uk. Experienced and reliable company offering self-guided cycling tours (Sierra de Grazalema and Ronda) and walking tours (Sierras de Aracena and Grazalema, Las Alpujarras, Cabo de Gata etc) on which your baggage is moved to the next destination. A week's walking in the Alpujarras starts at £515 (excluding airfares).

Olé Spain US ☎1-888/869 7156, ⓦ www .olespain.com. Small-group cultural walking tours in Seville, Córdoba and Granada provinces with a mixture of city sightseeing and open country trekking. Prices starting at $3300 for an eight-day tour (excluding airfares).

Ramblers Worldwide Holidays UK ☎01707/331 133, ⓦ www.ramblersholidays.co.uk. Long-established walking tour operator, offering walking and hiking holidays throughout Spain including tours of classical Andalucía. From around £527 for an all-inclusive week in the Sierra Nevada.

Rustic Blue Spain ☎958 76 33 81, ⓦ www .rusticblue.com. Alpujarras-based company (see p.520) specializing in rural and activity holidays (rambling and horse trekking) and renting traditional village houses.

Sherpa Expeditions UK ☎020/8577 2717, ⓦ www.sherpa-walking-holidays.co.uk. Trekking in the Sierra Nevada and the Alpujarras.

Spirit of Adventure UK ☎01822/880 277, ⓦ www.spirit-of-adventure.com. Multi-activity holidays throughout Spain including a week's trekking based in the Sierra de Grazalema. From £450 per person, excluding flights.

Walkalpujarra Spain Spain ☎958 85 85 80, ⓦ www.walkalpujarra.com. Founded by Alpujarras-based writer and walking guide Jeremy Rabjohns, this company offers guided or self-led hikes (from one day upwards) with maps and information provided. Also offers painting holidays.

Getting around

Most of Andalucía is well covered by public transport. The rail network reaches all the provincial capitals and the main towns along the inter-city lines and high-speed trains now connect the cities of Málaga and Seville with Madrid. Inter-city bus services are often more frequent, cheaper and just as fast as the regular trains, and will usually take you closer to your destination, as some train stations are a few kilometres from the town or village they serve (see map, p.34). Driving a car, meanwhile, will give you the freedom to head away from the major tourist routes and take in some of the spectacular scenery at your own pace.

Approximate journey times and frequencies can be found in the "Travel details" at the end of each chapter, and local peculiarities are pointed out in the text of the *Guide*. One important point to remember is that all public transport, and the bus service especially, is drastically reduced on Sundays and public holidays – don't even consider travelling to out-of-the-way places on these days. The words to look out for on timetables are *diario* (daily), *laborables* (workdays, including Sat), and *domingos y festivos* (Sun and public holidays).

By train

Andalucía's trains, operated by **RENFE** (☎902 240 202, ⓦwww.renfe.es), tend to be efficient and comfortable, and nearly always run on time. There's a confusing array of services, though the website has a useful English-language version on which you can check timetables and even buy tickets with a credit card (printing them out at home before you travel).

Cercanías are local commuter trains in and around the major cities, while **media distancia** (regional) and **larga distancia** (long-distance) trains go under a bewildering number of names, including Intercity (IC), Regionales and Talgo services. The difference is speed, service and number of stops, and you'll always pay more on the quickest routes (sometimes quite a lot more). The premier services are the high-speed trains, such as the expanding **AVE** (Alta Velocidad Española) network from Madrid to Seville and Málaga. The AVE trains have cut travelling times dramatically, with Madrid to Seville,

for example, taking two and a half hours compared with six to nine hours on the slower trains. One great feature of Andalucía's train network is that it still takes in a wide variety of inviting rural destinations including the Sierra de Aracena, the Sierra Norte, the Serranía de Ronda, and the Parque Natural de los Alcornocales with many small rural stations set in the midst of scenic countryside.

Tickets, fares and rail passes

Although you can just turn up at the station for short hops, **advance booking** is advisable for longer journeys between say, Seville and Granada or Almería and especially at weekends in summer or Spanish public holidays. Advance tickets can be bought at the stations between sixty days and five minutes before departure, but don't leave it to the last minute, as there are usually long queues (and often separate windows for the different types of train). Automatic **ticket machines** at main stations take some of the hassle out of queueing, or you can buy tickets at **travel agents** that display the RENFE sign – the cost is the same as at the station.

If your Spanish is up to it, you can call RENFE's 24-hour reservation service, or ask at local stations, but the best deals are always available **online** on the RENFE website, where "Web" and "Estrella" fares offer discounts of up to sixty percent on the full fares. Otherwise, **return fares** (*ida y vuelta*) are discounted by ten to twenty percent, depending on the service – you can buy a single, and so long as you show it

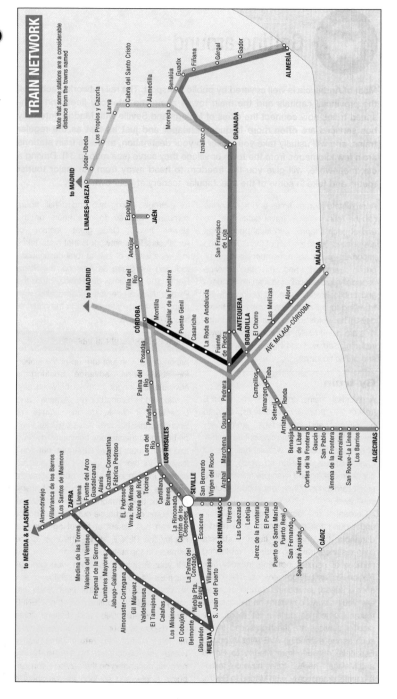

TRAIN NETWORK

Note that some stations are a considerable
distance from the towns named

when you buy the return, you'll still get the discount. There's also a whole range of other **discounted fares** of between 25 and 40 percent for those over 60 or under 26, the disabled, and children aged 4 to 11 years.

Actual fares vary wildly, but as an example, you'll pay around €17.50 one-way (10–20 percent discount for a return) on the regional service from Seville to Málaga (2hr 30min trip), while on the high-speed AVE service between Córdoba and Málaga (55min) you'll pay around €37 one way with no discount for a return.

The major pan-European **rail passes** (InterRail and Eurail) are only worth considering if you're visiting Spain as part of a wider European tour. Both schemes also have single-country rail passes available, which might be better value depending on your Spanish itinerary. The **InterRail Spain Pass** (ⓦwww.interrail.com) is only available to European residents and allows three, four, six or eight days' train travel within one month, with under 26, second- and first-class versions available. Again, these really only become cost-effective if you're combining your stay in Andalucía with journeys to other parts of Spain. For anyone else, **Eurail** (ⓦwww.eurail.com) has various Spain passes available, typically offering three days' travel in two months, again in various classes. You can check current prices on the websites, but bear in mind that it often works out cheaper to buy individual tickets in Spain as you need them, and it's certainly more convenient to be free to choose long-distance buses on some routes. All passes have to be bought before you leave home, and you'll still be liable for supplements and seat reservations on long-distance and high-speed trains.

By bus

Buses will probably meet most of your transport needs, especially if you're venturing away from the larger towns and cities. Many smaller villages and rural areas are only accessible by bus, almost always originating in the capital of their province. Services are pretty reliable, whether it's the two-buses-a-day school or market run or the regular services between major cities (the latter often far more conveniently

scheduled than the equivalent train services). **Fares** are very reasonable, too; Seville to Granada (3hr 40min) for example, costs around €20 or Málaga to Ronda (1hr 45min) €12. On inter-city runs, you'll usually be assigned a seat when you buy your ticket. Some destinations are served by more than one **bus company**, but main bus stations have posted timetables for all services or you can check timetables on the company websites (given in the Guide where appropriate); Alsa (ⓦwww.alsa.es) is one of the main companies with nationwide services, and has an English-language version of its website. Other bus companies and their contact details are given in the relevant chapters throughout the *Guide.*

There are only a few cities in Andalucía (Seville and Granada, for example) where you'll need to use the **local bus** network, and all the relevant details are given in the accounts. You'll also sometimes need to take a local bus out to a campsite or distant museum or monastery; fares are very cheap, rarely more than a euro.

By car

Andalucía's roads and highways are generally toll free but exceptions are the toll **autopista** (motorway) between Seville and Cádiz and the *Autopista del Sol* which passes all the major Costa del Sol resorts between Málaga and Estepona. The second-grade roads, **autovias**, often follow similar routes and in many respects resemble motorways, but their speed limits are lower. Locals tend to shy away from the toll routes, which are relatively expensive by local standards, but the lighter traffic encountered perhaps makes it a price worth paying for the visitor. You can usually pay with a credit card, although it would be wise to carry enough cash just in case. Toll roads are usually designated by an "AP" or "R" or the word "*peaje*".

The Spanish **drive on the right**, and **speed limits** are enforced throughout the country. On most *autopistas* it is 120kph, on the *autovia* 90kph, on minor roads 80kph or 90kph, and in towns and villages 50kph. Police have the power to fine drivers on the spot for speeding or any other transgressions (such as using a hand-held mobile

The Spanish driving experience

If it's your first time out on a Spanish road, especially in one of the bigger cities, you could be forgiven for thinking you've stumbled upon the local chapter of Mad Max devotees, out for a burn-up. In fact, those wild-eyed, dangerously speeding, non-signalling, bumper-hogging, mobile-talking, horn-sounding road warriors are normal law-abiding Spanish citizens on their way to work. **Traffic lights** and **pedestrian crossings** in particular present a difficult conceptual challenge – if you are going to stop at either, make sure you give plenty of warning to avoid another vehicle running into the back of you, and keep an eye out for cars crossing your path who have jumped the lights. **Signposting** is universally poor (yes, *that* was the turn you wanted), even on main roads and highways, while joining and exiting **autopistas/autovias** can be particularly dangerous, as it's almost a point of honour not to let anyone in or out. Many of the worst **accidents** are on the N roads, which have only a single carriageway in each direction, so take particular care on these. Major roads are generally in good **condition**, though some minor and mountain roads can be rather hairy and are little more than dirt tracks in the more remote regions. Sheep, goats and cattle are also regular hazards. Having said all this, things are (slowly) improving and drivers are a bit more careful these days because of increased use of radar and speed controls and the introduction of a points system for infractions which (if you accumulate too many) can lead to a driving ban. The police are also setting up more **drink-driving** controls than before, though you have to remember that this is a country where it's considered a good idea to have bars in motorways service stations.

phone while driving), and if you don't have any cash, they will escort you to the nearest cash machine and issue you with a receipt there and then. Failure to pay will result in your car being impounded until you do. You can pay by credit card (with proof of identity) at most petrol stations for **fuel** (*gasolina*), the main companies being Cepsa and Repsol. Unleaded petrol (*sin plomo*) comes in normal (95 octane) and super (98 octane) grades and diesel is referred to as *diesel* or *gasóleo*. Pumps are colour coded to avoid error: green for unleaded; red for leaded; yellow and black for diesel.

An EU **driver's licence** is sufficient to drive in Spain. US, Canadian, Australian and New Zealand licences should also be enough, though you may want to get an International Driver's Licence as well, just to be on the safe side. If you are bringing your own car, you will need your vehicle registration and insurance papers – and check with your insurers that you are covered to drive the car abroad. It's also compulsory to carry two hazard triangles, reflective jackets in case of accident or breakdown, an official first-aid kit and a set of spare bulbs. Rear seatbelts are also compulsory, as are child seats for infants.

Parking can be a major pain in the neck, especially in big cities and old-town areas. Finding on-street parking spaces is often impossible although if you can time your arrival with the start of the siesta (around 2pm, when everyone rushes home for lunch) you stand a better chance. Metered parking zones usually have stays limited to a couple of hours, though parking between 8pm and 8am, on Saturday afternoons and all day Sundays tends to be free. It's always worth double-checking street signs, or asking the locals, that you're allowed to park where you've just left your car, as any illegally parked vehicle will be promptly removed. If your car disappears off the street it is best to assume that it has been towed to the local pound, and enquiries in any hotel, government office or police station should produce the address. In cities it's probably best to pay extra for a hotel with parking or use a pay car park, for which you'll need to budget anything from €8 to €15 a day.

Car rental

The cheapest way to rent a car in Spain is to arrange it before you leave home. The major international chains (Avis, Budget,

Europcar, Hertz, Thrifty, for example) charge from around £100/$200 a week for a two-door Ford Ka or Ford Fiesta, more for larger vehicles and in peak holiday periods. Local Spanish companies (such as Pepecar; ⓦ www.pepecar.com) can sometimes offer better value for money, as can the online rental outfits easyCar (ⓦ www.easycar.com) and Skycars (ⓦ www.skycars.com), with high-season prices starting from around €20 per day for renting a small car in Andalucía. Reliable and competitive **Andalucía-based companies** include Málaga Car Hire (with pick-up and drop-off points throughout the region; ⓦ www .malagacarhire.com) and Aurigacrown Car Hire (ⓦ www.aurigacrown.com).

You'll need to be 21 or over (and have been driving for at least a year) to rent a car in Spain. It's essential to check that you have adequate **insurance cover** for your rental car, and that all visible damage on a car you're picking up is duly marked on the rental sheet. It's definitely worth considering paying the extra charge to reduce the "excess" payment levied for any damage, but these waiver charges (by the day) soon add up. However, you can avoid all **excess charges** in the event of damage by taking out an annual insurance policy with ⓦ insurance4carhire.com, which also covers windscreen and tyre damage.

Cycling

Cycling is a great way to see parts of the country that might otherwise pass you by, though bear in mind that peninsular Spain is one of the most mountainous countries in Europe and Andalucía contains its two highest peaks. Added to punishing climbs, there are often searing high-summer temperatures with which to contend. However, don't be put off, pacing yourself and using the cooler hours of the day (after dawn and before dusk) can make for a highly enjoyable trip.

For serious cycle touring, you'll need your own bike and to be properly equipped (see "Books", p.609, for information on this if you're a novice). **Bike rental** itself is not common, save in resort areas or in tourist-oriented cities such as Seville, Córdoba or Granada, where you can expect to pay up to €20 a day, or around €25 for a half-day bike tour. In Seville tourists can also use the excellent Sevici bike hire scheme run by the city government (see p.253). Although the Spanish themselves are keen sport cyclists, other facilities are practically nonexistent. Cycle paths, for example, are rare (again, Seville and Córdoba are exceptions), and cycling around most major Andalucian cities is a hair-raising, if not downright dangerous business.

Most airlines are happy to take bikes as ordinary **baggage**, though it's essential to check first, especially if you're flying with a budget airline, when extra charges may apply. Spanish bus drivers are reasonably amenable, and should let you throw your bicycle in with the baggage. Trains are more problematic, as there are specific trains, times and routes on which bikes are not allowed. As a rule, local trains are fine but high-speed trains are out, unless your bike is boxed up or you're travelling by overnight sleeper.

You should have no trouble finding bike shops in larger towns, and parts can often be found at auto repair shops or garages. On the road, cars tend to hoot before they pass, which can be alarming at first but is useful once you're used to it. On busier roads it's better not to ride two abreast as Spanish drivers (unused to cyclists) have frequently caused accidents when colliding with the cyclist on the outside. Finally, try not to leave your bike on the street overnight (especially in cities), even with a secure lock, as thieves view them as easy pickings.

Accommodation

There's a great variety of accommodation in Andalucía, ranging from humble family-run pensiones to five-star luxury hotels, often in dramatic historic buildings. The mainstay of the coastal resort is the typical beachfront holiday hotel, though renting an apartment or a villa gives you more freedom, while farm stays, village hostales rurales (guesthouses) and mountain inns are all increasingly popular possibilities.

Compared with other European countries, accommodation in Spain is still pretty good value. In almost any town, you'll be able to get a no-frills double room in a *pensión* or *hostal* (both terms used to describe small hotels) for around €40, sometimes even less, especially out in the sticks. As a rule, you can expect to pay upwards of €90 for a three-star city hotel in high season (less in small towns and country areas), around €120 for four-star and boutique places, and €150–200 for five-star hotels and historic paradores. However, the trend is bucked by Seville and Granada, in particular, and some coastal and resort areas, where hotel (but not *hostal*) rooms are often appreciably more expensive.

If you want to guarantee a room at a particular place, **advance reservations** are essential in major cities and resort areas at peak holiday, festival or convention times. Local festivals and annual events also tend to fill all available accommodation weeks in advance. That said, as a general rule, if you haven't booked, all you have to do is head for the cathedral or main square of any town, which is invariably surrounded by an old quarter full of pensions and hotels. Unlike most countries, you don't always pay more for a central location; indeed, the newer three- and four-star properties tend to be located more on the outskirts. **Families** will find that most places have rooms with three or even four beds at not a great deal more than the price for a double room; also extra beds for children can often be added to double rooms for little extra cost. However, **single travellers** often get a comparatively bad deal, and can end up paying sixty to eighty percent of the price of a double room. Accommodation prices are **seasonal**, but minimum and maximum rates should be displayed at reception. In high season (usually the month of Aug) on the coast, some hotels only take bookings for a minimum of a week, while others also require at least a half-board stay. We state in the *Guide* where this occurs. However, it's worth noting that high season isn't always summer, in the ski resort of the Sierra Nevada for

Accommodation price codes

All the establishments listed in this book have been coded according to price. They represent the price for the **cheapest available double/twin room in high season** (ie Christmas/New Year, Easter, July & Aug, and other local holidays), which means that at other times you'll often be able to stay for a lower price than that suggested. We've also used price codes for private rooms in youth hostels but have given the per-person euro rate for dorm beds. Note that **seven percent tax** (IVA) is added to all accommodation bills, which might not be specifically stated until it is time to pay, so always ask if you're uncertain.

❶ €30 and under
❷ €31–45
❸ €46–60
❹ €61–80
❺ €81–110
❻ €111–150
❼ €151–200
❽ €201–250
❾ €251 and over

example, while inland cities such as Seville, Córdoba and Granada tend to have cheaper prices in August, when everyone heads for the coast. You should also be aware that the Spanish love to build *puentes* (bridges) between a national or regional holiday that occurs on say, a Thursday or a Tuesday, and the weekend that follows or precedes it. The hotel trade treats this as "high-season" and not only are prices higher but accommodation in many places becomes tight.

Where possible, **website** bookings nearly always offer the best deals, especially with the larger hotel groups that have made big inroads into Spain – it's always worth checking NH Hoteles (Ⓦwww.nh-hotels .com), Accor/Ibis (Ⓦwww.accorhotels.com) and Sol Meliá (Ⓦwww.solmelia.com) for current deals. Many hotels also use specialist sites to fill their rooms, especially in low season, and often you can find some real bargains: two of the best, Ⓦwww.atrapalo .com and Ⓦwww.rumbo.es, are in Spanish only but fairly easy to use.

Rooms, pensiones, hostales and hotels

The cheapest beds are usually in **private rooms**, in someone's house or above a bar or restaurant. The signs to look for are *habitaciones* (rooms) or *camas* (beds), both becoming less obvious in Andalucía, or they might be touted at resort bus and train stations in summer as you arrive. The rooms should be clean, but might well be very simple and timeworn; you'll probably share a communal bathroom. Otherwise, official places to stay are classified as *pensiones*, *hostales* and hotels, though that's just the start of it, as several other names are used to describe accommodation throughout the region.

At the budget end of the scale are **pensiones** (marked P, classified by a two-star system), where straightforward rooms often have shared bathroom facilities (there's usually a washbasin in the room). Other variants are *fondas* (F), which traditionally had a restaurant or dining room attached, and *casas de huéspedes* (CH), literally an old-fashioned "guesthouse". In all such *pensiones*, facilities are likely to be minimal and comforts rationed; things like heating,

furniture (other than bed, chair and desk) and even external windows might be too much to hope for. On the other hand, some *pensiones* are lovingly cared for and very good value.

Next step up, and far more common, are **hostales** (Hs) and **hostal-residencias** (HsR), classified from one to three stars. These are not hostels, in any sense, but budget hotels, generally offering good, if functional, rooms, usually with private bathrooms, TV and – in the better places – probably heating and air-conditioning. Many also have cheaper rooms available without private bathrooms. Some *hostales* really are excellent, with good service and up-to-date furnishings and facilities, including wi-fi or internet access.

Fully-fledged **hotels** (H), meanwhile, are graded from one to five stars, with star-rating dependent on things like room size, staffing levels and whether or not there's a lift rather than any intrinsic attraction. There's often not much difference in price between a one-star hotel and a three-star *hostal*, for example, and the *hostal* might be nicer. At three and four stars, prices start to increase and you can expect soundproofing, a lift, an English-language channel on the TV and a buffet breakfast spread. At five stars, you're in the luxury class, with pools, gyms, jacuzzis, and prices to match.

You can pick up lists of local accommodation from any tourist office, and there are countless websites to look at, too, including the excellent Rusticae (Ⓦwww.rusticae.es), which highlights stylish rural and urban hotels across the country. The Asociación de Hoteles Rurales de Andalucía (Ⓦwww .ahra.es) has information on some of the region's most charming country hotels.

Paradores

Spain has over ninety superior hotels in a class of their own, called paradores (Ⓦwww .parador.es), often spectacular lodgings converted from castles, monasteries and other Spanish monuments (although some are purpose-built). They can be really special places to stay, sited in the most beautiful parts of the country, and in some of the most historic cities, and prices are very good when compared with the five-star hotels with which they often compete.

They are banded into five categories, depending on location and popularity, with rates starting at around €105 a night, though €150–170 is more typical. That said, a whole host of special offers and web deals (through the official website) offer rooms from as little as €60, and deals for the over 60s, the 20s to 30s or for multi-night stays. Three-night packages, where you stay in a different parador every night, start at around €150 per person (based on two sharing, car rental not included). All the details are on the website, or contact the official parador **agents**, Keytel in the UK (ⓦwww.keytel.co .uk) or Petrabax in the US (ⓦwww.petrabax .com). All Andalucía's paradores are covered in the *Guide*.

Villas, apartments and rural tourism

Most UK and European tour operators can find you a self-catering **villa** or **apartment**, usually (but not exclusively) on the coast or in one of the many sierras. They are rented by the week, and range from simple town-centre apartments to luxury coastal villas with private pools, and prices vary wildly. The best deals are often packages, including flights and car rental, with endless companies like First Choice (ⓦwww.firstchoice.co.uk /villas), Iglu Villas (ⓦwww.igluvillas.com) and Simpson Travel (ⓦwww.simpsontravel.com).

Casas rurales (rural houses) are where many Spanish holidaymakers stay if they have the choice. It's a wide-ranging concept, from cave dwellings to restored manor houses, many with pools and gardens, plus all mod cons. You can rent by the room, or by the property, either on a B&B basis or self-catering, depending on the accommodation. Many of the *casas* also come with opportunities to take part in outdoor activities such as horseriding, walking, fishing and cycling. They offer excellent value for money, starting at around €30 per person, even cheaper if you're in a group or staying for longer than a night or two.

ASETUR (ⓦwww.ecoturismorural.com), the association for rural tourism in Spain, has an excellent website where you can search thousands of properties by region, while many of Andalucía's tourist-office websites also carry information on *casas rurales*.

Holiday companies in your own country may also have Spanish rural properties available, or take a look at some websites: Top Rural (ⓦwww.toprural.com) has many properties in Andalucía, while Andalucía-based **agencies** such as the Red Andaluza de Alojamientos Rurales (ⓦwww.raar.es) or Rustic Blue (ⓦwww.rusticblue.com) are other possibilities.

Youth hostels

There are twenty official youth hostels (*albergues juveniles*) in Andalucía under the umbrella of the **Red Española de Albergues Juveniles** (REAJ; ⓦwww.reaj.com), the Spanish youth hostel association that is affiliated to the international organization, Hostelling International (HI; ⓦwww.hihostels .com). Partly funded by the Junta de Andalucía, the network in Andalucía is administered by **Inturjoven** (ⓦwww.inturjoven .com). There are full details of each hostel on the Inturjoven website (English-language version available), and we've included some of the best in the *Guide*. However, many hostels tend to be inconveniently located in some cities; they also generally have curfews (not so much of a problem in mountain areas) or can be block-booked by school/youth groups. You'll also need an HI membership card, though you can buy one at most hostels on your first night. Andalucía has some of the most modern youth hostels in the country (a stunning new one in Jaén has just opened), many with two or four-bed en-suite rooms. That said, it's the price that's the main stumbling block: at €16–20 per person a night in high season (less for under 26s, and out of season), they're no cheaper than a basic double room in a *hostal* or *pensión*. But hostels are also good places for cheap meals and meeting other travellers, and Andalucía has a handful in stunning rural locations.

Camping

There are literally hundreds of authorized campsites in Spain, mostly on the coast and in holiday areas. They work out at about €4.50 per person plus the same again for a tent, and a similar amount for each car or caravan. The best-located sites, or the ones with top-range facilities (restaurant, swimming pool, bar, supermarket), are significantly more expensive. If you plan to camp extensively, buy the annual *Guía de Campings*, which you can find in large bookshops, or visit ⓦwww .vayacamping.net.

In most cases, **camping outside campsites** is legal – but there are certain restrictions. You're not allowed to camp "in urban areas, areas prohibited for military or touristic reasons, or within 1km of an official campsite". What this means in practice is that you can't camp on the beach (though you can, discreetly, nearby). In national parks, camping is only allowed in officially designated areas. Aside from these restrictions, however, and with a little sensitivity, you can set up a tent for a short period almost anywhere in the countryside. Whenever possible, ask locally first.

Food and drink

The rich and varied cuisine of Andalucía is a reflection of its dramatic history. One of its signature dishes, gazpacho, was introduced by the Romans in the first millennium BC, and didn't reach its final version until peppers and tomatoes arrived in Spain following the voyages of Columbus. Another great influence came from the Moors who changed the face of southern Spain forever with the planting of orange, olive and almond trees. They also introduced spices such as cumin, cinnamon, nutmeg and saffron plus vegetables and fruits like aubergine, spinach, quince and pomegranate – all fundamental to the Andalucian cuisine of today.

The cooking of modern Andalucía falls into mountain and coastal food. Five of Andalucía's eight provinces have access to a coastline, and here fish and seafood is king. Inland, rich stews, *jamones* (cured hams) and game are preferred. In recent years there has been a revival of interest in developing the region's cuisine in a more creative direction, and a reflection of this is a number of very good restaurants with numerous chefs sporting one or even two Michelin stars. Of course, not every restaurant is a gourmet experience and not every dish is a classic of its kind. Tourist resorts – after all, where many people go – can be disappointing, especially those aimed at a foreign clientele, and a week on the Costa del Sol can just as easily convince you that the Spanish national diet is egg and chips, sangria, pizza and Guinness. However, even here you'll always find good restaurants and tapas bars where the locals eat, and few places in Europe are still as good value, especially if you have the *menú del día*, the bargain fixed-price lunch (and often dinner) that's a fixture across the region.

Each chapter of the *Guide* highlights the **regional specialities** you'll come across in various parts of Andalucía, while for a **menu reader** turn to pp.618–622.

Breakfast, snacks and sandwiches

The traditional *andaluz* **breakfast** (*desayuno*) is *chocolate con churros* – long, extruded tubular doughnuts served with thick drinking chocolate or coffee. Some places specialize in these but many city bars and cafés also serve cakes and pastries (*bollos* or *pasteles*), croissants (*cruasán*) and toast (*pan tostada*), or crusty sandwiches (*bocadillos*) with a choice of fillings (try one with omelette, *tortilla*). A "sandwich", incidentally, is usually a less appetizing ham or cheese sandwich in white processed bread. Other good places for snacks are **cake shops** (*pastelerías* or *confiterías*) or the local bakery (*panadería*),

41

where they might also have savoury pasties and turnovers.

Bars, tapas and raciónes

One of Spain's and Andalucía's glories is the phenomenon of **tapas** – the little portions of food that traditionally used to be served up free with a drink in a bar. The origins are disputed but the word is from *tapar*, "to cover", suggesting a cover for drinks' glasses, perhaps to keep the flies off in the baking sun. Tapas can be anything – a handful of olives, a slice or two of cured ham, a little dish of meatballs or *chorizo*, spicy fried potatoes or battered squid. They will often be laid out in a glass-fronted chill-cabinet on the counter, so you can see what's available, or there might be a black-board menu. Occasionally the *dueño* (boss) or barman carries the list around in his head to be verbally rattled off to each new customer – an exacting test of your Spanish comprehension. Most bars have a speciality; indeed, Spaniards will commonly move from bar to bar, having just the one dish that they consider each bar does well. Conversely, if you're in a bar with just some pre-fried potatoes and day-old Russian salad on display, and a prominent microwave, go somewhere else to eat.

Aside from a few olives or crisps sometimes handed out with a drink, you pay for tapas these days (the eastern end of Andalucía, particularly the city of Granada, is an honourable exception here), usually around €1–3 a portion. **Raciónes** (around €6–12) are simply bigger plates of tapas, perfect for sharing or enough for a meal – you're sometimes asked if you want a *tapa* or a *ración* of whatever it is you've chosen. And in the evenings many bars give up serving the cheaper tapas, and serve only the more profitable *raciones* when you'll be told "*solo hay raciones.*" Seville, as the city that claims to have invented tapas, is one of the best places to sample this culinary art, but in the *Guide* you'll find many other outstanding bars throughout Andalucía.

Most cafés and bars have some kind of tapas available, while you'll also find a decent display in **bodegas, tabernas, mesónes** (various kinds of taverns) and **cervecerías** (beer-houses). It's always cheapest to stand at the bar to eat; you'll pay more to sit at tables and more again to sit outside on a terrace.

Restaurants

The simplest kind of restaurant is the **comedor** (dining room), fast disappearing from the *andaluz* townscape. Often a room at the back of a bar or the dining room of a *hostal* or *pensión* it now survives only in rural areas. Traditionally, they are family-run places aimed at lunching workers, usually offering a straightforward set meal at budget prices.

Andalucía's top ten restaurants

Andalucía has some of the best restaurants in Spain and quite a few places where you could blow a pretty big hole in your credit card account. However, whilst many recommended in the *Guide* score higher points for cuisine alone, at any of the places below (ranked in no particular order) we feel the welcome, ambience, location and excellent food will all contribute to a memorable meal.

José Vicente Aracena (p.351)

Atxuri Cádiz (p.213)

El Chaleco Almuñécar (p.120)

Parador de Málaga-Gibralfaro Málaga (p.86)

El Almejero Garrucha (p.562)

El Bigote Sanlúcar de Barrameda (p.230)

Las Candelas Huelva (p.324)

El Faro de El Puerto El Puerto de Santa María (p.219)

Santiago Marbella (p.132)

Río Grande Seville (p.290)

The highway equivalent are known as **ventas**, or inns, dotted along the main roads between towns and cities. These have been serving Spanish wayfarers for centuries – some of them quite literally – and the best places are immediately picked out by the line of cars and trucks outside. Proper restaurants, **restaurantes**, come in a myriad of guises, from rustic village restaurants to stylish Michelin-starred eateries; **asadores** specialize in grilled meats, **marisquerías** in shellfish and seafood.

Almost every *venta* and *restaurante* serves a weekday, fixed-price lunchtime meal, the **menú del día**, generally three courses including a beer or glass of wine for €8–12, occasionally even cheaper, depending on where you are (you might also see the words *menú de la casa*). Many places (particularly roadside *ventas*) will often hang a sign outside advertising the price of their *menú* to attract custom. This is obviously a terrific deal; the *menú del dia* is only sporadically available at night, and in Andalucía it's generally not available at all at weekends, the time traditionally when families eat out together. The very cheapest places are unlikely to have a written menu, and the waiter will tell you what the day's dishes are. In smarter restaurants in bigger cities and resorts, there will still be a *menú del dia*, though it might be a shadow of the usual à la carte menu, and drinks may be excluded. Even so, it's a way of eating at a restaurant that might normally cost you three or four times as much. Top city restaurants often also feature an upmarket *menú* called a **menú de degustación** (tasting menu), which again can be excellent value, allowing you to try out some of the country's finest cooking for anything from €30 to €60 a head and some even throw in a bottle of decent wine.

Otherwise, in bars and so-called *cafeterías*, meals often come in the form of a **plato combinado** – literally a combined dish – which will be a one-plate meal of something like steak, egg and chips, or *calamares* and salad, occasionally with bread and a drink included. This will generally cost in the region of €5–9.

If you want a menu in a restaurant, ask for **la carta**; *menú* refers only to the fixed-price meal. In all but the most rock-bottom establishments it is customary to leave a small **tip** (*propina*), though five percent of the bill is considered sufficient and service is normally included in a *menú del día*. IVA, the seven-percent **tax**, is also charged, but it should say on the menu if this included in the price or not.

Spaniards generally eat very late and *andaluzes* eat later still, with **lunch** served from around 1pm (you'll generally be the first person there at this time) until 4pm, and **dinner** from 8.30pm or 9pm to midnight. Obviously, rural areas are slightly earlier to dine, but making a dinner reservation for 10.30pm or even later is considered perfectly normal in Andalucía and it's not uncommon to see a group of diners being ushered to a table with midnight approaching. Most restaurants **close one day a week**, usually Sunday or Monday or a combination of those evenings.

What to eat

If you like **fish and seafood** you'll be in heaven in Andalucía as this forms the basis of a vast variety of tapas and is fresh and excellent everywhere. It's not cheap, unfortunately, so rarely forms part of the lowest priced *menús* (though you may get the most common fish – cod, often salted, and hake – or squid) but you really should make the most of what's on offer. Fish stews (*zarzuelas*) and rice-based paellas (which also contain meat, usually rabbit or chicken) are often memorable in seafood restaurants. Paella comes originally from Valencia and is still best there, but you'll find *arroz marinero*, the Andalucian version, just as good. The coastal strip's obsession with seafood is detailed in the main body of the *Guide*, although Cádiz and the nearby "sherry triangle" of Sanlúcar, El Puerto de Santa María and Jerez deserve top spot for sheer volume and variety. Be aware when ordering fish in restaurants that often the price quoted is per kilo or per 100g, and an average white-fish portion will be around 200–300g (don't be afraid to ask the waiter for a price quote when ordering).

Meat is most often grilled and served with a few fried potatoes and a couple of salad leaves, or cured or dried and served as a starter or in sandwiches. *Jamón serrano* is superb, makes a wonderful starter and is consumed with a passion in Andalucía. The finest varieties, though, from Jabugo in the Sierra de Aracena (see p.362) and Trevélez in the Sierra Nevada (see p.525), are extremely expensive. If you're tempted, they are best appreciated with a glass of *fino* (see p.47). More meat is eaten in inland provinces than on the coast and Córdoba's *rabo de toro* (stewed bull's tail) is renowned. The Sierra de Aracena is also a good place for *setas* (mushrooms) and cooked pork dishes, with *solomillo de cerdo* (pork sirloin) usually outstanding. In country areas bordering the slopes of the Sierra Morena and in the province of Jaén, game is very much a speciality – venison, partridge, hare and wild boar all feature on menus in these parts, as well as fresh trout.

Vegetables rarely amount to more than a few fries or boiled potatoes with the main dish (but you can often order a side dish à la carte). The provinces of Córdoba and Jaén are again the exceptions, and the latter's *pipirrana jaenera* (salad with green peppers and hard-boiled eggs) is only one of a number of hearty vegetable-based dishes to be found in these parts. It's more usual, though, to start your meal with a simple salad or with Andalucía's most famous dish, chilled gazpacho. Made from puréed bread and garlic with added peppers, cucumbers and tomatoes, regional variations of gazpacho include Córdoba's *salmorejo*, Málaga's *ajo blanco* or Cádiz's *sopa de picadillo*.

Dessert (*postre*) in Andalucía tends to be sweet and sticky – another hangover from the region's long Moorish period. The cheaper places will usually offer little variety: nearly always fresh fruit or flan, the Spanish crème caramel, often replaced on Andalucian menus by the similar *tocino de cielo* ("heavenly lard") or *natillas* (custard). *Arroz con leche* (cold rice pudding), *crema catalana* (crème brûlée) and *helado* (ice cream) are other desserts often making an appearance in the more mundane places. Keep an eye out in upmarket restaurants for delicious regional specialities such as *peras al vino* (pears baked in wine with cinnamon) from Málaga, *piononos* (liqueur-soaked cakes) from Granada and *crema de Jerez* (sherry pudding) from Cádiz, as well as *brazo de gitano* (rolled pastry filled with cream), an Andalucía-wide dessert. In smarter places the desserts will always be made in house or by a reputable local artisan (or even convent) but in cheaper and out-of-the-way places they often cut corners by offering factory-produced desserts, anathema to most *andaluzes*; "*es casero*?" ("is it homemade?") is the question to ask.

Cheese (*queso*) is always eaten as a *tapa* rather than after a meal in Andalucía. The cheeses of the region don't usually travel beyond their immediate area of production, which offers you the chance to make some interesting discoveries, especially in areas such as Las Alpujarras. The best-known region-wide brand is Córdoba Province's sheep's-milk cheese from Pedroches, although the hard, salty *Manchego* from neighbouring La Mancha is also common. One cheese worth knowing about from the Sierra de Grazalema is cured goat's and sheep's-milk cheeses made by prizewinning cheesemaker Payoyo.

Vegetarians

Vegetarians generally have a fairly hard time of it in Andalucía, though there's an increasing number of veggie restaurants (and restaurants catering for vegetarians) in the bigger cities. In more rural areas, there's usually something to eat, but you may get weary of eggs and omelettes. Otherwise, superb fresh fruit and veg, and excellent cheese, is always available in the markets and shops.

In restaurants, you're faced with the extra problem that pieces of meat – especially ham, which the Spanish don't regard as real meat – and tuna are often added to vegetable dishes and salads to "spice them up". You'll also find chunks of *chorizo* and sausage turning up in otherwise veg-friendly soups or bean stews. The phrases to get to know are *Soy vegetariano/a. Como sólo verduras. Hay algo sin carne?* ("I'm a vegetarian. I only eat vegetables. Is there anything without meat?"); you may have to add *y sin marisco* ("and without seafood") and *y sin jamón* ("and without ham") to be really safe.

Some salads and vegetable dishes are strictly **vegan**, but they're few and far between. Fruit and nuts are widely available, nuts being sold by street vendors everywhere.

Coffee, tea and soft drinks

Café (coffee) is invariably an espresso (*café solo*); for a large cup of weaker, black coffee, ask for an *americano*. A *café cortado* is a *café solo* with a drop of milk; a *café con leche* is made with lots of hot milk. Coffee is also frequently mixed with brandy, cognac or whisky, all such concoctions being called *carajillo*. Iced coffee is *café con hielo* (you'll be served a coffee and a separate glass of ice cubes – you pour the former over the latter to make a great summer refresher). **Chocolate** (hot chocolate) is a popular breakfast drink, or for after a long night on the town, but it's usually incredibly thick and sweet. For a thinner, cocoa-style drink, ask for a brand name, like Cola Cao.

Spaniards usually drink **té** (tea) black, so if you want milk it's safest to ask for it afterwards, since ordering *té con leche* might well get you a glass of warm milk with a tea bag floating on top. Herbal teas (*infusions*) are widely available, like *manzanilla* (camomile), *poleo* (mint tea) and *hierba luisa* (lemon verbena).

Local soft drinks include **granizado** (slush) or **horchata** (a milky drink made from tiger nuts or almonds), available from summer street stalls, and from milk bars and ice-cream parlours (*heladerías*). Although you can drink the **water** almost everywhere, it tastes revolting in some cities and coastal areas – inexpensive *agua mineral* comes either sparkling (*con gas*) or still (*sin gas*).

Wine, beer and spirits

Wine (vino), either *tinto* (red), *blanco* (white) or *rosado/clarete* (rosé), is the invariable accompaniment to every meal and is, as a rule, extremely inexpensive. Andalucía's wine-making genius lies elsewhere (see p.47) and so most table wines are imported from outside the region (see box, p.46). One thing worth knowing about Spanish wine is the terms related to the **ageing process** which defines the best wines: *crianza* wines must have a minimum of two years ageing before sale; red *reserva* wines

at least two years (of which one must be in oak barrels); red *gran reserva* must have at least two years in oak and three in the bottle. *Vino de Mesa* and *Vino de la Tierra* are the equivalent of France's Vin de Table, and DO (Denominación de Origen) is Spain's version of the French Appellation Contrôlée regulating grape varieties and region of origin.

Dining out away from the larger towns and cities your choice of wine (especially in remoter *ventas*) will be severely limited. Busier *ventas* and restaurants with a healthy reputation, however, usually have well-stocked cellars and will only be too pleased to let you peruse their *carta de vinos*. In Andalucía you will often be asked in restaurants – especially at lunch times in summer – if you would like your wine "con Casera". This is a brand of lemonade (La Casera) which many *andaluzes* use to dilute the wine, turning it into a "spritzer". This combination is also a legitimate bar drink called *tinto de verano* where red wine is mixed with soda or lemonade and makes a great summer refresher. Equally refreshing, though often deceptively strong, is **sangría**, a wine-and-fruit punch which you'll come across at fiestas and in tourist bars.

In a bar, a small glass of wine will generally cost around €0.50–1.50 depending on location (rural bars are usually much cheaper than city places); in a restaurant, if wine is not included in the *menú*, prices start at around €6 a bottle in basic establishments but at anywhere with pretensions you're looking at paying at least €10–12 for a decent bottle and significantly more if you start fancying the vintage stuff. If wine is included, in a *menu del día* you'll usually get a whole bottle for two people, a *media botella* (a third to a half of a litre) for one. These days, in times of paring costs to the bone, many establishments are now tending to cut the "free" wine from their *menús*, or offering at best a single glass.

Beer (*cerveza*) is nearly always lager, though some Spanish breweries also now make stout-style brews, wheat beers and other types. It comes in 300ml bottles (*botellines*) or, for about the same price, on tap – a *caña* of draught beer is a small glass, a *caña doble* larger, and asking for *un tubo*

Wining and dining

One of the great pleasures of eating out in Andalucía is the chance to sample some of Spain's excellent wines. Restaurant **wine prices** compare very favourably with other parts of Europe and in most restaurants and *ventas* you'll often be able to find a decent bottle for under €12. Most establishments usually have an economical house wine too for around half this price or less, (ask for *caserío* or *vino de la casa*) and sometimes this will be served straight from the barrel in a half-litre or litre carafe (*jarra*). This can be great, it can be lousy, but at least it will be distinctively local.

The most common bottled red wine in Andalucía is **Valdepeñas**, a good standard wine from the central plains of New Castile (Los Llanos, Viña Albali and Señorío de Guadianeja are good labels). **Rioja**, from the area round Logroño in the north, is one of Spain's classic wines but a lot more expensive (Cune, Faustino I & V, Muga, Beronia, Marqués de Cáceres, Montecillo, Viña Ardanza, Marqués de Riscal and Izadi are some names to look out for). Another top-drawer, and currently fashionable, region is **Ribera del Duero** in Castilla-León which produces Spain's most expensive wine, Vega Sicilia, besides other outstanding whites (Belondrade y Lurtón) and reds (Pesquera, Viña Pedrosa, Protos and Señorío de Nava). There are also scores of other excellent wines to try from regions such as Catalunya (Bach, Raimat, Torres) which also produces the champagne-like Cava (Codorníu, Freixenet) and the new and pricey Priorat-zone reds which have taken the wine world by storm (Clos Mogador, Alvaro Palacios). Galicia, known for its fragrant whites (Fefiñanes, Fin de Siglo and San Trocado); Navarra (Gran Feudo, Señorío de Sarría, Ochoa); and Valencia (Murviedro, Gandía) are others, and even the once unpromising La Mancha (Santa Rita, Casa Gualda, Estola) is now making a name for itself as a producer of quality wines.

Andalucía's solitary table-wine area of any volume is the **Condado de Huelva**, which turns out reasonable dry whites, which go well with seafood. Red wines have also made some headway in a region long thought to be too hot to produce quality vintages: in 2007 US wine guru Robert Parker caused a sensation when he awarded 95 points (out of a hundred) to Arcos de la Frontera *bodega* Huerta de Albalá's Taberner no. 1, comparing it to "the best of the northern Rhones". There are also many local wines made in the country districts, with some, such as the **costa** wine of the western Alpujarras, and the **Laujar de Andarax** wines of the eastern Alpujarras, always worth trying.

(a tubular glass) gets you about half a pint. Mahou, Cruz Campo, San Miguel, Damm, Estrella de Galicia and Alhambra are all decent beers. A **shandy** is a *clara*, either with fizzy lemon (*con limón*) or lemonade (*con casera*).

In mid-afternoon – or, let's face it, even at breakfast – Spaniards take a *copa* of liqueur with their coffee, such as *anís* (similar to Pernod) or *coñac*, the local **brandy**, which has a distinct vanilla flavour. Most brandies are produced by the great sherry houses in Jerez and the best – such as Carlos 1 or Lepanto – compare favourably with any top Cognac. Other classy non-*jerezano* brands include the Armagnac-like Mascaró and Torres, both from Catalunya. Instead of

brandy, at the end of a meal many places serve **chupitos** – little shot glasses of flavoured schnapps or local fire water, such as *pacharán* (a sloes and anis combination).

You should order **spirits** by brand name, since there are generally less expensive Spanish equivalents for standard imports, or simply specify *nacional*. Larios gin from Málaga, for instance, is about half the price of Gordon's. Measures are staggeringly generous – bar staff generally pour from the bottle until you suggest they stop. Long drinks include the universal *Gin-Tónic* and the *Cuba Libre* (rum and Coke), and there are often Spanish Caribbean rums (*ron*) such as Cacique from Venezuela or Havana Club from Cuba.

Sherry

The classic Andalucian wine is **sherry** – *vino de jerez* or *fino* as it's popularly known – which is excellent, widely available and consumed with gusto by *andaluzes*. Served chilled or at *bodega* temperature – a perfect drink to wash down tapas – like everything Spanish, it comes in a perplexing variety of forms. The main distinctions are between *fino* or *jerez seco* (dry sherry), *amontillado* (medium), and *oloroso* (full-bodied) or *jerez dulce* (sweet), and these are the terms you should use to order. Similar in the way they are made – though not identical in flavour – are *Montilla* and *manzanilla*, which are not fortified with alcohol as is the case with other *finos*. The first of these dry, sherry-like wines comes from the province of Córdoba, and the latter from Sanlúcar de Barrameda, part of the "sherry triangle" along with Jerez and El Puerto de Santa María. More information about these wines is given in the *Guide* under each production centre.

The media

The ubiquitous Spanish newspaper kiosk is your first stop for regional and national newspapers and magazines, though hotels and bars nearly always have a few kicking around for customers. The bigger cities, tourist towns and resorts will also have foreign newspapers available (some of which are actually published in Spain), generally on the day of issue or perhaps a day late. Television is all-pervasive in bars, cafés and restaurants, and you're going to find yourself watching more bullfighting, basketball and Venezuelan soap operas than perhaps you'd bargained for; most pensión and hotel rooms have a TV, too, though only in the fancier places will you get any English-language programming, and then probably only BBC World, CNN or Eurosport satellite channels.

Newspapers and magazines

Andalucians, in line with the Spanish generally, are not great devourers of newsprint and none of the Spanish **national newspapers** has a circulation above 400,000. The best of these are the Madrid-based centre-left *El País* (ⓦ www.elpais.es) and the centre-right *El Mundo* (ⓦ www.elmundo.es), both of which have good arts and foreign news coverage, and include daily comprehensive Andalucía **regional supplements** with news and "what's on" listings. Other national papers include the solidly old-order *ABC* with a hard moral line against divorce and abortion, and Barcelona's centrist *La Vanguardia* (also available in Andalucía). Andalucía's **regional press** is generally run by local magnates and predominantly right of centre, but often provides an entertaining read; here the scandals and stories from around the parish pump can give the outsider fascinating (and often amusing) insights into the communities encountered besides providing handy information on festivals and entertainment. The best of Andalucía's regional dailies are Málaga's *Sur*, *Diario de Cádiz*, *Córdoba*, and Granada's *Ideal*; the website addresses for all Andalucía's daily papers can be found at ⓦ www.prensaescrita.com/andalucia.php. The paper with the highest circulation is *Marca* (ⓦ www.marca.com), the country's top **sports daily**, mainly football-dominated; there's also *As* (ⓦ www.as.com), *El Mundo Deportivo* (ⓦ www.elmundodeportivo.es) and *Sport* (ⓦ www.sport.es). The main cities such as Seville, Málaga and Granada are also awash with **free newspapers**, which are dished out at bus stops and train stations.

There's a bewildering variety of **magazines** specializing in celebrity gossip (known collectively as *la prensa rosa*), ranging from the more traditional *Hola* to the sensationalist *Que me Dices*. *El Jueves* is the Spanish equivalent to *Viz*, while the online daily *El Confidencial* (◉www .elconfidencial.com) gives the inside track on many serious economic and political stories. There are also various **English-language magazines** and papers produced by or for the huge expatriate community now resident in Andalucía. Málaga's *Sur* newspaper produces the free weekly *Sur in English* (◉www.surinenglish.com) which has a news digest and popular classified columns. Another decent production is the monthly online ◉www.andalucia.com, but the best of the bunch is the *Olive Press* (◉www.theolivepress.es) a fortnightly paper which often campaigns on local and regional issues.

Radio

There are hundreds of local radio channels (almost every major town in Andalucía has its local radio station), broadcasting alongside a handful of national ones. The state-run **RNE** (◉www.rtve.es/radio) network covers five stations: RNE 1, a general news and information channel; Radio Clásica, broadcasting mainly classical music and related programmes; the popular music channel

RNE 3; RNE 4, in Catalan; and the rolling news and sports channel RNE 5. Radio Exterior is RNE's international shortwave service. Other **popular channels** include Cadena Ser and Onda Cero (news, talk, sports and culture), the rightist Catholic church-run COPE, 40 Principales (for the latest hits, Spanish and otherwise) and Cadena 100 (music and cultural programming). Radio Marca (dedicated sports radio) is also very popular. Full listings, local stations and frequencies can be found in *El País*, and the local press, or bring a shortwave radio to tune in to the BBC World Service (◉www.bbc.co.uk/worldservice) or Voice of America (◉www.voa.gov).

Television

RTV (◉www.rtve.es/television) provides the main, state-run channels, namely TVE1, a general entertainment and news channel, and its sister La 2 (ie "Dos"), given over to sports and culture. As the state channels compete with the private stations for advertising they (particularly TVE 1) tend to go for audience share with a tedious mix of game and reality shows (such as the highly popular *Cambio Radical* where each week someone undergoes a radical cosmetic surgery "makeover"), sport, films and *telenovelas* (soaps). Private national stations are Antena 3, Cuatro (ie Four), Telecinco (Five) and La Sexta (Sixth) while Andalucía's Canal Sur has local programming. The main satellite channel is Canal+.

Festivals

The fiesta or feria is an absolutely crucial part of Spanish and Andalucían life. Even the smallest village or most modern city suburb devotes at least a couple of days a year to partying, and coinciding with such an event can be huge fun, propelling you right into the heart of Spanish culture. It's hard to beat the experience of arriving in some small village, expecting no more than a bed for the night, to discover the streets decked out with flags and streamers, spectacular fireworks lighting up the sky, a band playing in the plaza and the entire population out celebrating the local fiesta.

Everywhere in Andalucía, from the tiniest hamlet to the great cities, will take at least one day off a year to devote to partying. Usually it's the local saint's day, but there are celebrations, too, of harvests, of deliverance from the Moors, of safe return from the sea – any excuse will do.

Each festival has its own particular characteristics but there are facets common to them all. Horses, flamenco, fireworks and the guitar are essential parts of any celebration, usually accompanied by the downing of oceans of *fino* – which is probably why the sherry companies seem to provide most of the bunting. And along with the music there is always dancing, usually *sevillanas*, in traditional flamenco costume and an immense spirit of enjoyment. The main event of most fiestas is a parade, either behind a revered holy image, or a more celebratory affair with fancy costumes and *gigantones*, grotesque giant carnival figures which terrorize children.

Although these festivals take place throughout the year – and it is often the obscure and unexpected event that proves to be most fun – there are certain occasions that stand out. Easter Week (**Semana Santa**) and **Corpus Christi** (in early June) are celebrated throughout Andalucía with magnificent religious processions. Easter, particularly, is worth trying to coincide with – head for Seville, Málaga, Granada or Córdoba, where huge *pasos*, floats of wildly theatrical religious scenes, are carried down the streets, accompanied by weirdly hooded penitents atoning for the year's misdeeds. And just as moving in their own more intimate way are the countless small town and village observances of Semana Santa with smaller processions, traditional customs and sometimes a Passion play.

Among the biggest and best-known of Andalucía's **other popular festivals** are: the Cádiz Carnaval (mid-Feb); Seville's enormous April Feria (a week at the end of the month); Jerez's Feria del Caballo (Horse Fair, April/May); the Romería del Roció, an extraordinary pilgrimage to El Roció near Huelva (arriving there on Whit Sunday); and Málaga's boisterous and good-humoured Feria (mid-Aug).

The list is potentially endless, and although you'll find more major events detailed below, we can't pretend that this is exhaustive. The Junta de Andalucía publishes an annual **Ferias y Fiestas de Andalucía** guide, available from local tourist offices and the site Ⓦ www.fiestasdeandalucia.com also has information on hundreds of them. Outsiders are always welcome at these festivals, the one problem being that during any of the most popular (though usually not at the small town and village affairs) you'll find it difficult and expensive to find a bed. If you're planning to coincide with a major festival, try and book your accommodation well in advance.

Listed below are some of Andalucía's main fiestas, all worth trying to get to if you're going to be in the area around the time; more are listed under locations covered in the *Guide*. Note that saints' day festivals – indeed all Spanish celebrations – can vary in date, and are often observed over the weekend closest to the dates given.

January

1–2 Día de la Toma. Celebration of the 1492 entry of the Reyes Católicos into the city – at Granada.
5 Cabalgata de los Reyes Magos. Epiphany parade at Málaga.
6 Romería de la Virgen del Mar. Pilgrimage procession from Almería.
17 Romería del Ermita del Santo. Similar event at Guadix.

February

1 San Cecilio. Fiesta in Granada's traditionally gypsy quarter of Sacromonte.
Mid-month Carnaval. Extravagant week-long event (leading up to Lent) in all the Andalucian cities. Cádiz, above all, celebrates with fancy dress, flamenco, spectacular parades and street-singers' competitions.

March

5–15 El Puerto de Santa María (Cádiz) celebrates its *carnaval*.
Semana Santa (Holy Week) Following Palm Sunday, this has its most elaborate and dramatic celebrations in Andalucía. You'll find moving and memorable processions of floats and penitents at (in descending order of importance) Seville, Málaga, Granada and Córdoba, and to a lesser extent in smaller towns such as Jerez, Arcos, Baeza and Úbeda. All culminate with the full drama of the Passion on Good Friday, with Easter Day itself more of a family occasion. See also Semana Santa colour section.

April

Last week (2 weeks after Easter, usually in April, occasionally May; check with the tourist office). Week-long Feria de Abril at Seville: the largest fair in Spain, a little refined in the way of the city, but an extraordinary event nonetheless. A small April fair – featuring bull-running – is held in Vejer.
Last Sunday Romería de Nuestra Señora de la Cabeza at Andujar (Jaén). Three days of celebrations culminate in a huge procession to the sanctuary of the Virgin in the Sierra Morena.

May

1–2 Romería de Nuestra Señora de la Estrella at Navas de San Juan. Jaén Province's most important pilgrimage.
3 "Moors and Christians" carnival at Pampaneira (Alpujarras).
First two weeks Cruces de Mayo (Festival of the Patios) in Córdoba. Celebrates the Holy Cross and includes a competition for the prettiest patio and numerous events and concerts organized by the local city council.
Early May (usually the week after Seville's fair). Somewhat aristocratic Horse Fair at Jerez de la Frontera.
17 San Isidro Romería at Setenil (Cádiz).
Pentecost (7 weeks after Easter). Romería del Rocío – Spain's biggest: a million often inebriated pilgrims in horse-drawn carriages and processions converge on El Rocío (Huelva) from all over the south.
Corpus Christi (variable – Thurs after Trinity). Bullfights and festivities at Granada, Seville, Ronda, Vejer and Zahara de la Sierra. At Seville, Los Seises (Six Choirboys) perform a dance before the altar of the cathedral.
Third weekend Romería de Santa Eulalia at Almonaster La Real in the Sierra de Aracena. Pilgrimage, fireworks, parades and fandangos in honour of the village's patron saint.
Last week Feria de la Manzanilla, Sanlúcar de Barrameda. Prolonged binge to celebrate the town's major product which is used to wash down huge quantities of seafood whilst watching flamenco and sporting events from beachfront *casetas* (party tents).

June

Second week Feria de San Bernabé at Marbella. Often spectacular since this is the richest town in Andalucía.
13–14 Fiestas Patronales de San Antonio at Trevélez (Alpujarras). Includes mock battles between Moors and Christians.
23–24 Candelas de San Juan. Bonfires and effigies at Vejer and elsewhere.
23–26 Feria de Alhaurin de la Torre (Málaga). Processions, giants and an important flamenco competition.
30 Conil (Cádiz) feria.
End June/early July International Festival of Music and Dance. Major dance groups, chamber orchestras and flamenco artistes perform in Granada's Alhambra palace, Generalife and Carlos V palace.

July

Early July International Guitar Festival at Córdoba. Brings together top international acts from classical, flamenco and Latin American music.
9–14 Around feast of San Francisco Solano. Montilla (Córdoba) celebrates its annual feria.
End of July Almería's Virgen del Mar summer fiesta. Parades, horse-riding events and usually a handful of major jazz and rock concerts in its Plaza Vieja.

August

First week Berja (Almería) holds its annual fiesta in honour of the Virgin of Gádor.

3 Colombinas at Huelva celebrate Columbus's voyages of discovery with a fiesta.

5 Trevélez (Granadan Alpujarras) observes a midnight romería to Mulhacén.

13–21 Feria de Málaga. One of Andalucía's most enjoyable fiestas for visitors, who are heartily welcomed by the ebullient *malagueños*.

15 Ascension of the Virgin. Fair with *casetas* at Vejer and throughout Andalucía.

15 Noche del Vino at Competa (Málaga). A riotous wine festival with dancing, singing and endless drinking.

17–20 The first cycle of horse races along Sanlúcar de Barrameda's beach, with heavy official and unofficial betting; the second tournament takes place exactly a week later.

19–21 Vendimia. Grape harvest fiesta at Montilla (Córdoba).

Third week The Algeciras fair and fiesta.

Third weekend Fiesta de San Mamés at Aroche (Huelva) in the extremities of the Sierra de Aracena. Unpretentious and great fun, everything a village fiesta should be.

22–25 Feria de Grazalema (Cádiz).

23–25 Guadalquivir festival at Sanlúcar de Barrameda. Bullfights and an important flamenco competition.

25–30 Fiestas Patronales in honour of San Agustín at Mojácar (Almería).

September

6 El Cascamorras. Annual feria at Baza (Granada) where the Cascamorras or interloper from nearby Guadix attempts to make off with their Virgen and is doused in dirty oil for his pains.

7 Romería del Cristo de la Yedra at Baeza (Jaén). Singing and dancing in the streets.

7–14 Feria de la Moscatel/Feria de Nuestra Señora de Regla at Chipiona (Cádiz). Includes bull-running, flamenco tournaments and much wine-swilling to acclaim the sweet sherry grape grown hereabouts.

8 Romería de Nuestra Señora de los Ángeles at Alajar (Huelva). Lots of colour and horse races to the peak sanctuary of Arias Montano.

8–9 Fiesta de la Virgen de la Cabeza at Almuñecar (Granada).

First/second week Vendimia (celebration of the vintage) at Jerez. Starts with the blessing of the new grapes, after which everyone gets sozzled on the old.

6–13 Celebration of the Virgen de la Luz in Tarifa. Street processions and horseriding.

First two weeks Ronda bursts into life with a feria, flamenco contests and the Corrida Goyesca, bullfights in eighteenth-century dress.

24–25 Día del Señor (Lord's Day) at Orgiva (Granada). Celebrated with impressive fireworks and processions.

29 Úbeda's (Jaén) Fiesta de San Miguel with a fair and *casetas*.

October

1 Fiesta de San Miguel in Granada's Albaicín quarter and dozens of other towns, including Torremolinos.

6–12 Feria del Rosario. Fuengirola horse-riding events and flamenco.

15–23 Feria de San Lucas. Jaén's major fiesta, dating back to the fifteenth century.

November

1 Todos Los Santos (All Saints Day). Celebrated throughout Andalucía with church services and processions to graveyards.

December

28 Fiesta de los Verdiales/Santos Innocentes. Various towns and villages of Málaga's mountain districts celebrate Spain's equivalent of April Fool's Day with dances, pulsating Moorish-inspired music and outlandish headdress. Good places to see it include Comares, Almogía, Casabermeja in the Axarquía to the east of Málaga and the Venta de San Cayetano, Puerto de la Torre, slightly to the northwest.

Bullfights

Bullfights are an integral part of many Spanish festivals. In Andalucía especially, any village that can afford it will put on a corrida for an afternoon, while in big cities like Seville, the main festivals are accompanied by a week-long (or more) season of prestige fights attended by a veritable who's who of the great and the good. It is no coincidence that the fighting bull is the country's national symbol or that provinces like Cádiz – where many bulls are bred – is devoted to the whole culture of taurinismo and treats its matadores like gods.

Los Toros (or **La Lidia**), as Spaniards refer to bullfighting, is big business. Each year an estimated 24,000 bulls are killed before a live audience of over thirty million (with many more watching on television). It is said that 150,000 people are involved, in some way, in the industry, and the top performers, the *matadores*, are major earners, on a par with the country's biggest pop stars. There is some **opposition** to the activity from animal welfare groups but it is not widespread: if Spaniards tell you that bullfighting is controversial, they are likely to be referring to practices in the trade. That said, the city of Barcelona recently outlawed bullfighting as did the Canary Islands. In recent years, bullfighting critics (whom you will find on the arts pages of the newspapers) have been expressing their perennial outrage at the widespread but illegal shaving of bulls' horns prior to the *corrida*. Bulls' horns are as sensitive as fingernails, and shaving just a few millimetres deters the animal from charging; they affect the creature's balance, too, reducing the danger for the *matador* still further.

Notwithstanding such abuse (and there is plenty more), Los Toros maintains its loyal aficionados throughout the country. Indeed, in some areas they are on the rise, with the elaborate language of the *corrida* quite a cult among the young, as the days of Franco's patronage of bullfighting are forgotten, and TV stations pay big money for major events. To **aficionados** (a word that implies more knowledge and appreciation than "fan"), the bulls are a culture and a ritual – one in which the emphasis is on the way man and bull "perform" together – in which the *arte* (art) is at issue rather than the cruelty. If pressed on the issue of the slaughter of an animal, they generally fail to understand. Fighting bulls are, they will tell you, bred for the industry; compared to beasts bred for the abattoir they live a pampered and idyllic life before they are killed; and, if the bullfight went, so too would the bulls.

Whether you attend a *corrida*, obviously, is down to your own feelings and ethics. If you spend any time at all in Spain during the season (which runs from March to Oct), you will encounter Los Toros, at least on a bar TV, and that will as likely as not make up your mind. If you decide to go, try to see the biggest and most prestigious that is on, in a major city, where star performers are likely to dispatch the bulls with "*arte*" and a successful, "clean" kill. This happens much less frequently than many aficionados would have you believe and the beginners' fights, or *novilladas*, are often little more than a gruesome repetition of botched jobs. Even in the senior *corridas*, there are few sights worse than a *matador* making a prolonged and messy kill, while the audience whistles its disgust. Established and popular *matadores* include the current idol of the rings José Tomás, veteran Enrique Ponce, César Rincón, El Fandi, Finito de Córdoba, El Cid and Julian "El Juli" López who learned his trade in Mexico as an under-age teenager before he was legally able to fight in Spain. Since the eighteenth century women have also fought bulls and the recently retired Cristina Sánchez, became the first woman to have been carried shoulder high through the *puerta grande* of Las Ventas, the prestigious Madrid ring – a distinction awarded to few of her male peers. ⌐

Anti-bullfight organizations

If you want to know about **opposition to bullfighting**, contact the World Society for the Protection of Animals, 89 Albert Embankment, London SE1 2TP (℡020/7587 5000, ⓦwww.wspa.org.uk); their website has links to affiliates in Australia, Canada and the USA. Andalucía's anti-bullfighting pressure group is ASANDA (Asociación Andaluza para la Defensa de los Animales), c/Gracia Fernández Palacios 4, 41001 Seville (℡95 456 10 58, ⓦwww.asanda.org). Spain's national opposition to bullfighting is coordinated by ADDA (Asociación para la Defensa de los Derechos del Animal), c/Bailén 164, Local 2 interior, O8037 Barcelona (℡93 459 16 01, ⓦwww.addaong.org).

Perhaps the most exciting and skilful performances of all are by mounted *matadores*, or **rejoneadores** as they are known (from *rejón*, "lance"); this is the oldest form of *corrida*, developed at Ronda in the seventeenth century and the way these supremely skilful horsemen manoeuvre their steeds away from the bull's lethal horns to plant the *banderillas* and then make the kill – all the while mounted – can be breathtaking.

A complete **guide to bullfighting** with exhaustive links can be found at ⓦwww .mundo-taurino.org.

The corrida

The **corrida** begins with a procession, to the accompaniment of a *paso doble* by the band. Leading the procession are two *alguacilillos* or "constables", on horseback and in traditional costume, followed by the three *matadores*, who will each fight two bulls, and their *cuadrillas*, their personal "team", each comprising two mounted *picadores* and three *banderilleros*. At the back are the mule teams who will drag off the dead bulls. The ensuing *corrida* takes the form of a drama in three acts or stages (called **suertes**) presided over by a **presidente** who is there to see that a multitude of regulations are adhered to, and award trophies if a *matador*'s performance has merited them.

Once the ring is empty, at the president's signal the **alguacilillo** opens the *toril* (the bulls' enclosure) and the first bull (weighing 500–600kg) appears – a moment of great physical beauty – to be "tested" by the *matador* or his *banderilleros* using pink and gold capes. These preliminaries conducted (and they can be short, if the bull is ferocious), the **suerte de picar** ensues, in

which the **picadores** ride out and take up positions at opposite sides of the ring, while the bull is distracted by other *toreros*. Once they are in place, the bull is made to charge one of the horses, at which moment the *picador* drives his short-pointed lance into the bull's neck, while it tries to toss his padded and blindfolded (on the right eye) mount. The whole purpose here is to tire and weaken the bull's powerful neck and shoulder muscles, thus forcing him to lower his head – without which (as was discovered at the very outset of the *corrida*) it would be impossibly dangerous to fight and kill on foot. This is repeated up to three times, until the horn sounds for the *picadores* to leave. For most neutral spectators, it is the least acceptable and most squalid stage of the proceedings, and it is clearly not a pleasant experience for the horses, their ears stuffed with rags to shut out the noise of the bull and spectators, and their vocal cords cut to prevent any terrified cries from alarming the crowd.

The next stage, the **suerte de banderillas**, involves the placing of three sets of *banderillas* (barbed darts mounted on coloured shafts) into the bull's shoulders. Each of the three **banderilleros** delivers these in turn, attracting the bull's attention with the movement of his own body rather than a cape, and deftly placing the *banderillas* whilst both he and the bull are running towards each other. He then runs to safety out of the bull's vision, sometimes with the assistance of his colleagues, but occasionally a canny animal will set off in pursuit of his tormentor, often resulting in an undignified leap over the *barrera* to escape the charging horns.

Once the *banderillas* have been placed, the **suerte de matar** begins, and the **matador** enters the ring alone, having exchanged his pink and gold cape for the red *muleta*. He (or she) salutes the president and then dedicates the bull either to an individual, to whom he gives his hat, or to the audience, by placing his hat in the centre of the ring. It is in this part of the *corrida* that judgements are made and the performance is focused, as the *matador* displays his skills on the (by now exhausted) bull. He uses the movements of the cape to attract the bull, while his body remains still. If he does well, the band will start to play, while the crowd *olé* each pass. This stage lasts around ten minutes and ends with the kill. The *matador* attempts to get the bull into a position where he can drive a sword between its shoulders and through to the heart for a *coup de grâce*. In practice, they rarely succeed in this, instead taking a second sword, the *descabello*, crossed at the end, to cut the bull's spinal cord; this causes instant death. If things get really bad and he can't finish the job with this, then he will instruct one of his *cuadrilla* to end the business with a *puntilla*, a dagger stabbed into the base of the beast's skull. By this time the crowd will be whistling their derision whilst "the whole spectacle of theatre, courage and art is reduced to the level of a knacker's yard", as one commentator vividly described it.

Alternatively, if the audience are impressed by the *matador*'s performance, they will wave their handkerchiefs and shout for an award to be made by the president. He can award one or both ears, and a tail – the better the display, the more pieces the *matador* gets – while if he has excelled himself, he will be carried shoulder high out of the ring by the crowd, through the *puerta grande*, the main door, which is normally kept locked. The bull, too, may be applauded for its performance, as it is dragged out by the mule team.

Tickets for *corridas* in the major city *plazas de toros* start at around €20 for a *sol* seat (see below) rising to €100 and above for the prime seats at prestigious fights in rings such as Seville's Maestranza. The cheapest seats are *gradas*, the highest rows at the back, from where you can see everything that happens without too much of the detail; the front rows are known as the *barreras*. Seats are also divided into *sol* (sun), *sombra* (shade), and *sol y sombra* (shaded after a while), though these distinctions have become less relevant as more bullfights start later in the day, at 6 or 7pm, rather than the traditional 5pm. The *sombra* seats are more expensive – not so much for the spectators' personal comfort but because most of the action takes place in the shade. Tickets for *novilladas* (novice fights with young bulls) are much cheaper, costing €10–40, and are often given away free by bars or agents outside the bullring prior to the *corrida* if there hasn't been much demand (which often happens).

On the way in, you can rent cushions – two hours sitting on concrete is not much fun. They also count as something to toss in the ring when there's an especially awful performance – as frequently happens. Beer and soft drinks are sold inside.

Football

The nation threw a huge party when finally, at the 2008 European Championships, the Spanish national football team shook off decades of habitual underperformance and actually won something, beating Germany to become European champions in some style. It's been a good while coming, since although fútbol has long been the most popular sport in Spain, it's only recently that Spanish football has made much of an international splash, with the likes of coaches Juande Ramos and Rafa Benitez, and players of the calibre of Fernando Torres and Cesc Fabregas, now plying their trade in England's Premier League. Certainly, if you want the excitement of a genuinely Spanish event, watching a Sunday-evening game in La Liga (ⓦwww.lfp.es) usually produces as much passion as anything you'll find in the Plaza de Toros.

For many years, the country's two dominant teams have been Real Madrid and F.C. Barcelona, and these have shared the League and Cup honours more often than is healthy. Recently though, the big two have faced a bit more opposition than usual from clubs like Valencia (champions in 2002 and 2004), Villareal (league runners up in 2008) and Sevilla (UEFA Cup winners in 2006 and 2007).

Sevilla are the main team in Andalucía, followed in recent seasons by their fierce city rivals **Real Betis**. Other *andaluz* clubs in the top flight include yo-yo team **Málaga** who achieved promotion back to the First Division yet again in 2007–08 after a couple of seasons in Division Two, **Recreativo Huelva**, Spain's oldest club, and the remarkable **Almería** who reached the First Division less than twenty years after being founded in 1989. See the "Listings" sections of provincial capitals for details and grounds of the major teams.

With the exception of a few important games – such as when either of the big two plays Sevilla or the two Seville teams play their derbys – tickets are pretty easy to get; they start at around €25 for average First Division games but get close to double this when *Real* or *Barca* are in town. Trouble is very rare: English fans, in particular, will be amazed at the easy-going family atmosphere and mixed-sex crowds. And August is a surprisingly good time to catch games since there's a glut of warm-up matches for the new season, often involving top foreign clubs.

The league **season** runs from late August until mid-May or early June, and most games kick off at 5 or 7pm on Sundays, though live TV demands that one key game kicks off at 9 or 10pm on Saturday and Sunday. If you don't go to a game, the atmosphere can be pretty good watching on TV in a local bar, especially in a city whose team is playing away. Many bars advertise the matches they screen, which, if they have satellite connections, can include Sunday afternoon English League and Cup games. ⓦwww.soccer-spain.com is a very good website in English, where you'll find comprehensive news and articles.

Travelling with children

Spain is a good country to travel with children of any age; they will be well received everywhere, and babies and toddlers, in particular, will be the centre of attention. You will probably have to change your usual routine, since young children stay up late in Spain, especially in the summer. It's very common for them to be running around pavement cafés and public squares after 10 or 11pm, and yours will no doubt enjoy joining in. It's expected that families dine out with their children, too, so it's not unusual to see up to four generations of the same family eating tapas in a bar, for example.

Holidays and accommodation

Most tour operators can advise about **family-friendly resorts** in Andalucía, and many holiday hotels and self-contained club-style resorts offer things like kids' clubs, baby-sitting, sports and entertainment. The only caveat is that, of course, you're unlikely to see much of Spain on these family-oriented holidays. The region also has various theme parks and leisure activities specifically aimed at kids, most notably the **Isla Magica** in Seville (see p.283), **Tivoli World** near Benalmádena on the Costa del Sol (see p.125) and the Western film set of **Mini Hollywood** (Almería; see p.567).

Museums, galleries and sights throughout Andalucía either offer **discounts** or **free entry** for children (it's often free for the under 4s), and it's the same on trains, sightseeing tours, boat trips and all the other usual tourist attractions.

If you're travelling independently, finding **accommodation** shouldn't be a problem, as *hostales* and *pensiones* generally offer rooms with three or four beds. Bear in mind that much budget accommodation in towns and cities is located on the upper floors of buildings, often without lifts. It's also worth noting that some older-style *pensións* don't have heating systems – and it can get very cold in winter. If you want a cot provided, or baby-listening or **baby-sitting** services, you'll usually have to pay the price of staying in a more expensive hotel – and even then,

never assume that these facilities are provided, so always check in advance. **Self-catering accommodation** offers the most flexibility, and there's plenty of it throughout the region, from seaside apartments to country houses; even in major cities, it's easy to rent an apartment by the night or week and enjoy living like a local with your family.

Products, clothes and services

Baby food, **disposable nappies**, **formula milk** and other standard items are widely available in pharmacies and supermarkets, though not necessarily with the same range or brands that you will be used to at home. Organic baby food, for example, is hard to come by away from the big-city supermarkets and most Spanish non-organic baby foods contain small amounts of sugar or salt. Fresh milk, too, is not always available; UHT is more commonly drunk by small children. If you require anything specific for your baby or child, it's best to bring it with you or check with the manufacturer about equivalent brands.

Families might eat out a lot, but things like **high chairs and special childrens' menus** are rare, except in the resorts on the *costas* and islands. Most bars and cafés, though, will be happy to heat milk bottles for you. **Baby-changing areas** are also relatively rare, except in department stores and shopping centres, and even where they do exist they are not always up to scratch.

Travel essentials

Addresses

Addresses are written as: c/Picasso 2, 4° izda. – which means Picasso Street (*calle*) no. 2, fourth floor, left- (*izquierda*) hand flat or office; dcha. (*derecha*) is right; cto. (*centro*) centre; s/n (sin número) means the building has no number; bajo signifies ground floor.

Complaints

By law, all establishments (including hotels and restaurants) must keep a *libro de reclamaciones* (**complaints book**) and bring it out for regular inspection by the authorities. If you think you've been overcharged, or have any other problems, you can usually produce an immediate resolution by asking for the book. Most establishments prefer to keep them empty, thus attracting no unwelcome attention from officialdom, which, of course, works in your favour. If you do make an entry, English is acceptable but write clearly and simply; add your home address, too, as you are entitled to be informed of any action, including – but don't count on it – compensation. You can also take your complaint to any local turismo, which should attempt to resolve the matter while you wait.

Costs

Prices in Andalucía and Spain have increased considerably over the last ten years or so, but there are still few places in Europe where you'll get a better deal on the cost of simple meals and drinks, while public transport remains very good value. Big cities and tourist resorts are invariably more expensive than remoter areas. Prices are hiked, too, to take advantage of special events, so for example you'd be lucky to find a room in Seville during Semana Santa (Holy Week) or the Feria de Abril, at less than a third above the usual rate.

It's really difficult to come up with **a daily budget** for the region, as your sixty-cent glass of wine and €30 *pensión* room in rural Andalucía might be €1.50 and €50, respectively, in Seville or Granada. However, as a very rough guide, if you always share a room in the cheapest *pensiones* and hotels, use public transport and stick to local restaurants and bars, you could get by on between €40 and €70 a day. Stay somewhere a bit more stylish or comfortable, eat in fancier restaurants, and go out on the town, and you'll need more like €80–120 a day, though, of course, if you're holidaying in Spain's magnificent *paradores* or five-star hotels this figure will hardly cover your room. There's more detailed information about prices in the "Accommodation", "Getting around" and "Food and drink" sections.

Visiting museums, galleries, churches and monasteries soon adds up – if you visited every site we cover in Granada alone, for example, you'd be out of pocket by €40 or so. Accordingly, it pays to take along any **student/ youth or senior citizen cards** you may be entitled to, such as the International Student ID Card (ISIC; ⓦ www.isiccard.com), as most attractions offer discounts (and make sure you carry your passport or ID card, although most places will accept a reasonably clear photocopy of these). Some museums and attractions are **free** on a certain day of the week or month (though note that this is sometimes limited to EU citizens only; you'll need to show your passport). Any **entrance fees** noted in the *Guide* are for the full adult price; children (as well as seniors) usually get a discount, and the under 4s are often free.

Crime and personal safety

The police in Spain come in various guises. The **Guardia Civil**, in green uniforms, is a national police force, formerly a military organization, and have responsibility for national crime, as well as roads, borders and guarding public buildings. There's also the blue-uniformed **Policía Nacional**, mainly seen in cities, who deal with crime, drugs, crowd control, identity and immigrant matters, and the like. Locally, most policing is carried out by the **Policía Local** or

Emergency numbers

ⓣ **112** All emergency services
ⓣ **061** Ambulance
ⓣ **080** Fire service

ⓣ **062** Guardia Civil
ⓣ **091** Policía Nacional

Municipal, who wear blue-and-white uniforms, and these tend to be the most approachable in the first instance if you're reporting a crime. There's obviously a certain overlap between regional and municipal forces, and you may be passed from one to another, depending on what you're reporting.

In the unlikely event that you're mugged or otherwise robbed, go straight to the police, where you'll need to make an official statement known as a **denuncia**, not least because your insurance company will require a police report. Expect it to be a time-consuming and laborious business – you can do it by phone, or even online these days (details on ⓦ www.policia.es), but you'll still have to go into the station to sign it. If you have your passport stolen, contact your nearest embassy or consulate; to find this visit a site such as ⓦ projectvisa.com or ⓦ www.embassiesabroad.com who have complete lists with contact numbers. Alternatively, see the *Guide*'s Málaga and Seville "Listings" for consulates in Andalucía.

Avoiding trouble

Petty crime – pickpocketing and bag-snatching – is, unfortunately, a fact of life in Spanish cities and tourist resorts, though no more so than anywhere else in Europe. The usual sensible **precautions** include: carrying bags slung across your neck, not over your shoulder; not putting wallets in your back pocket; leaving passport and tickets in the hotel safe; and keeping a photocopy of your passport, plus notes of your credit card number helplines and so on. Take special care on public transport, and don't leave **bags** unattended anywhere, even if you're looking at rooms upstairs in a *hostal*; know where your belongings are at all times.

On the street, beware of people standing unusually close at street kiosks or attractions, or of those trying to distract you for any reason (pointing out "bird shit" – in reality, planted shaving cream – on your jacket, shoving a

card or paper to read right under your nose). Next thing you know, your purse has gone.

Drivers shouldn't leave anything in view in a **parked car** particularly in Málaga or Seville; if detachable take the radio/CD player with you. **On the road**, be cautious about accepting help from anyone other than a uniformed police officer – some roadside thieves pose as "good Samaritans" to persons experiencing car and tyre problems, some of which, such as slashed tyres, may have been inflicted at rest stops or service stations in advance. The thieves typically attempt to divert your attention by pointing out a problem and then steal items from the vehicle while you are looking elsewhere.

Incidentally, if you are stopped by a proper police officer for a **driving offence**, being foreign just won't wash as an excuse. They'll fine you on the spot, cash or card.

Sexual harassment

Spain's macho image has faded dramatically, and these days there are relatively few parts of the country where foreign **women travelling alone** are likely to feel intimidated or attract unwanted attention. There is little of the pestering that you have to contend with in, say, the larger Italian cities, and the outdoor culture of *terrazas* (terrace bars) and the tendency of Spaniards to move around in large, mixed crowds, help to make you feel less exposed. *Déjame en paz* ("leave me in peace") is a fairly standard rebuff and if you are in any doubt, take a taxi, always the safest way to travel late at night.

The major **resorts** of the *costas* have their own artificial holiday culture, where problems are more likely to be caused by other alcohol-fuelled holidaymakers. You are actually more vulnerable in isolated, **rural regions**, where you can walk for hours without coming across an inhabited farm or house, though it's rare that this poses a threat – help and hospitality are much more the norm. Many single women happily tramp the long-distance footpaths, from Galicia to the Sierra Nevada, though you are always best advised to stay in rooms and *pensiones* rather than camping wild.

Electricity

The current in most of Spain is 220 or 225 volts AC (just occasionally, it's still 110 or 125V); most European appliances should work as long as you have an adaptor for European-style two-pin plugs. North Americans will need this plus a transformer.

Entry requirements

EU citizens (and those of Norway, Iceland, Liechtenstein and Switzerland) need only a valid national-identity card or passport to enter Spain. Other Europeans, and citizens of the **United States**, **Canada**, **Australia**, **New Zealand and South Africa**, require a passport but no visa, and can stay as a tourist for up to ninety days. Other nationalities may need to get a visa from a Spanish embassy or consulate before departure. Visa requirements do change, and it's always advisable to check the current situation before leaving home.

Most EU citizens who want to stay in Spain for longer than three months, rather than just visit as a tourist, need to register at a provincial **Oficina de Extranjeros** (Foreigners' Office), where they'll be issued with a residence certificate; you'll find a list of offices (eventually) on the Ministry of Interior website (@www.mir.es). You don't need the certificate if you're an EU citizen living and working legally in Spain, or if you're legally self-employed or a student (on an exchange programme or otherwise). US citizens can apply for one ninety-day extension, showing proof of funds, but this must be done from outside Spain. Other nationalities wishing to extend their stay will need to get a special visa from a Spanish embassy or consulate before departure.

Gay and lesbian travellers

Gay and lesbian life in Spain has come a long way in the last three decades, and Spanish attitudes have changed dramatically. Same-sex marriages were made legal in 2005, giving same-sex couples the same rights as heterosexual couples, including the right to adopt, and the age of consent is sixteen – the same as for heterosexual couples.

Today, almost every town in Spain has its gay bars and associations, while gay magazines, newspapers and radio programmes are widespread. In 1995, Spain included a clause in its criminal code making it an offence to discriminate in housing and employment based on sexual orientation, and imposing tougher sentences on hate crimes against the gay community.

There's a thriving **gay scene** in most of Andalucía's main cities, most notably, of course, in Seville and Cádiz. The latter is long famous for its liberal traditions and its **Carnaval** is a wonderfully hedonistic time to visit while **Torremolinos** (voted best Spanish gay destination by one gay website) is another popular holiday location. The Spanish term for the gay scene is "*el ambiente*" ("the atmosphere"), while another useful expression is "*entiendo*", literally, "I understand", but meaning "I'm gay".

There are plenty of **websites** out there for further information, notably @www .fundacióntriangulo.es/andalucia, @www .andalucia.com/living/gay.htm and @www .gayinfospain.com, which give a good general view of the local scenes.

Health

The **European Health Insurance Card** (EHIC) gives EU citizens access to Spanish state public-health services under reciprocal agreements. While this will provide free or reduced-cost medical care in the event of minor injuries and emergencies, it won't cover every eventuality – and it only applies to EU citizens in possession of the card – so travel insurance (see p.60) is essential.

No **inoculations** are required for Spain, and the worst that's likely to happen to you is that you might fall victim to an upset stomach. To be safe, wash fruit and avoid tapas dishes that look as if they were prepared last week. Water at public fountains is fine, unless there's a sign saying "*agua no potable*", in which case don't drink it.

For minor complaints, go to a **farmacia** – they're easy to find, and pharmacists are highly trained, willing to give advice (often in English) and able to dispense many drugs that would be available only on prescription in other countries. They keep usual shop hours (Mon–Fri 9am–1.30pm & 5–8pm), but some open late and at weekends, while a rota system keeps at least one open 24 hours in every town. The rota is displayed in the window of every pharmacy, or you can check the list in the local newspaper.

If you have special medical or dietary requirements, it is advisable to carry a letter from your doctor, translated into Spanish, indicating the nature of your condition and necessary treatments. With luck, you'll get the address of an English-speaking **doctor** from the nearest *farmacia*, police station or tourist office – it's obviously more likely in resorts and big cities. Treatment at **hospitals** for EU citizens in possession of the EHIC card is free; otherwise, you'll be charged at private-hospital rates, which can be very expensive.

In **emergencies**, dial ☏112 for an ambulance.

Insurance

You should take out a comprehensive **insurance policy** before travelling to Spain, to cover against loss, theft, illness or injury. A typical policy will provide cover for loss of baggage, tickets and – up to a certain limit – cash or traveller's cheques, as well as cancellation or curtailment of your journey. When securing baggage cover, make sure that the per-article limit will cover your most valuable possession. Most policies exclude so-called **dangerous sports** unless an extra premium is paid: in Spain, this can mean most watersports are excluded (plus rafting, canyoning, etc), though probably not things like bike tours or hiking.

If you need to make a claim, you should keep receipts for medicines and medical treatment, and in the event you have anything stolen, you must obtain an official statement from the police – see p.58.

Internet

Internet access is widely available at cafés (often referred to as *cibercafés*), computer shops and phone offices (*locutorios*). You'll pay as little as €1 an hour in many places, though it can cost two or three times as much. Many backpacker hostels and small *pensións* provide cheap or free internet access for their guests, but hotel business centres or hotel bedrooms wired for access tend to be far more expensive than going out on the street to an internet place. **Wireless access** is increasingly widespread in bars, hotels and other public "hotspots", though if the networks are password-protected you'll have to check first with your host to get online. Many cities (such as Málaga) have set up free-access wi-fi zones in main squares and other locations and many of these are mentioned in the *Guide*. If you take your own laptop, make sure you've got insurance cover and all the relevant plugs and adaptors for recharging.

Laundry

You'll find a few coin-op self-service laundries (*lavanderías automáticas*) in most provincial capitals, but you normally have to leave your clothes for a service wash and dry at a *lavandería*. A dry cleaner is a *tintorería*. Note that by law you're not allowed to leave laundry hanging out of windows over a street, and many *pensiones* and *hostales* expressly forbid washing clothes in the sink. To avoid an international incident, ask first if there's somewhere you can wash your clothes.

Mail

Post offices (Correos; ⦿ www.correos.es) are normally open weekdays from 8am to

Rough Guides travel insurance

Rough Guides has teamed up with Columbus Direct to offer you tailor-made **travel insurance**. Products include a low-cost **backpacker** option for long stays; a **short break** option for city getaways; a typical **holiday package** option; and others. There are also annual **multi-trip** policies for those who travel regularly. Different sports and activities (trekking, skiing, etc) can usually be included.

See our website (⦿ www.roughguides.com/website/shop) for eligibility and purchasing options. Alternatively, UK residents can call ☏0870/033 9988; Australians ☏1300/669 999 and New Zealanders ☏0800/559 911. All other nationalities should call ☏+44 870/890 2843.

2pm and again from 5 to 7.30pm, though branches in bigger places may have longer hours, may not close at midday and may open on Saturday mornings. There's an office-finder on the website, which also gives exact opening hours and contact details for each post office in Spain. As you can also pay bills and buy phonecards in post offices, queues can be long – it's often easier to buy **stamps** at tobacconists (look for the brown and yellow *estance* sign).

Outbound mail is reasonably reliable, with letters or cards taking around three days to a week to the UK and the rest of Europe, a week to ten days to North America, New Zealand and Australia, although it can be more erratic in the summer. There's also a whole of host of express-mail services (ask for *urgente* or *exprés*).

Maps

In addition to the maps in this book, you'll probably want a reasonable **road map**. This can be bought online from traders like Amazon (@www.amazon.com) or in Spain from most bookshops (*librerías*), and at street kiosks or petrol stations. The best single map for Andalucía is the regularly updated *Michelin Andalucía* (1:400,000), which includes a plan to get you in and out of Seville, the region's only serious traffic headache. It's widely available from bookshops in Spain and abroad. This has recently been complemented by the equally excellent larger scale *Michelin Costa del Sol* (1:200,000) covering not only the coast between Algeciras and Almería but a considerable way inland too, taking in significant chunks of the provinces of Cádiz, Málaga, Granada and Almería. An alternative is the rip-proof/waterproof *Rough Guide Andalucía Map* (1:650,000/1:150,000).

You can buy **hiking/trekking maps** from specialist map/travel shops in Spain, including La Tienda Verde in Madrid (@www .latiendaverde.es), and Librería Quera (@www.llibreriaquera.com) or Altaïr (@www .altair.es) in Barcelona. These bookshops – plus a few overseas specialists such as Stanfords (@www.stanfords.co.uk) – stock the full range of **topographical maps** issued by two government agencies: the IGN (Instituto Geográfico Nacional; @www.ign.es) and the SGE (Servicio Geográfico del Ejército;

@www.ejercito.mde.es). They are available at scales of 1:200,000, 1:100,000, 1:50,000 and even occasionally 1:25,000. The various SGE series are considered to be more up to date, although neither agency is hugely reliable. Each of Andalucía's provincial capitals have a **CNIG** (National Geographical Information Centre, @www.cnig.es), which stocks the full range of **topographical maps** issued by the government agencies above; where appropriate, the addresses for these are given in the relevant city "Listings" sections. A Catalunya-based company, Editorial Alpina (@www.editorialalpina.com), produces useful 1:40,000 or 1:25,000 map/booklet sets for many of the **mountain and foothill hiking areas** in Andalucía, and these are also on sale in many bookshops; the relevant editions are noted in the *Guide* where appropriate.

Money

Spain's currency is the **euro** (€), with notes issued in denominations of 5, 10, 20, 50, 100, 200 and 500 euros, and coins in denominations of 1, 2, 5, 10, 20 and 50 cents, and 1 and 2 euros. Up-to-the-minute currency **exchange rates** are posted on @www.oanda.com.

By far the easiest way to get money is to use your bank debit card to withdraw cash from an **ATM**, found in villages, towns and cities all over Spain, as well as on arrival at the airports and major train stations. You can usually withdraw up to €300 a day, and instructions are offered in English once you insert your card. Make sure you have a personal identification number (PIN) that's designed to work overseas, and take a note of your bank's emergency contact number in case the machine swallows your card. Some European debit cards can also be used directly in shops to pay for purchases; you'll need to check first with your bank.

All major **credit cards** are accepted in hotels, restaurants and shops, and for tours, tickets and transport, though don't count on being able to use them in every small *pensión* or village café. You can also use your credit card in an ATM to withdraw cash, though remember that these advances will be treated as loans, with interest accruing daily from the date of withdrawal. If you use a foreign credit card in some shops, you may also be asked for photo ID, so be prepared to show a driving licence or passport. Make sure you make a note of the number for reporting lost or stolen cards to your credit card company.

Spanish **banco** (banks) and **cajas de ahorros** (savings banks) have branches in all but the smallest villages, and most of them are prepared to change traveller's cheques (albeit often with hefty commissions). **Banking hours** are usually Monday to Friday 8.30am–2pm, with some city branches open Saturday 8.30am–1pm (except June–Sept when all banks close on Sat), although times can vary from bank to bank. Outside these times, it's usually possible to change cash at larger hotels (generally with bad rates and low commission) or with travel agents – useful for small amounts in a hurry. One place that doesn't charge a hefty commission on exchange is the department store El Corte Inglés, with branches in all Andalucía's provincial capitals and many large towns.

In tourist areas, you'll also find specialist **casas de cambio**, with more convenient hours (though rates vary), while some major tourist offices, larger train stations and most branches of El Corte Inglés department store have exchange facilities open throughout business hours.

Opening hours

Almost everything in Andalucía – shops, museums, churches, tourist offices – closes for a **siesta** of at least three hours in the middle part of the day. There's a lot of variation, with many major supermarkets now tending to stay open all day, but you'll get far less aggravated if you accept that the early afternoon is best spent asleep, or in a bar, or both.

Basic **working hours** are Monday to Friday 9.30am–2pm and 5–8pm. Many **shops** open slightly later on a Saturday (at 10am) and close for the day at 2pm, though you'll still find plenty of places open in cities, and there are regional variations. Moreover, department and chain stores and shopping malls tend to open a straight Monday to Saturday 10am to 9 or 10pm.

Museums and galleries, with very few exceptions (Granada's Alhambra is one), also have a break between 1 or 2pm and 4pm.

On Sundays, most open mornings only, and on Mondays the majority close all day. Opening hours vary from year to year, though normally not by more than half an hour or so. Some are also seasonal, and usually in Andalucía, "summer" means from Easter until September, and "winter" from October until Easter. However, some museums and tourist offices regard summer as referring to the high summer months of July and August; we have detailed these exceptions where possible in the *Guide*.

The most important **cathedrals, churches and monasteries** operate in much the same way as museums, with regular visiting hours and admission charges. Other churches, though, are kept locked, opening only for worship in the early morning and/or the evening (between around 6 and 9pm), so you'll either have to try at these times, or find someone with a key. A sacristan or custodian almost always lives nearby, and most people will know where to direct you. It's usual to give a small tip, or donation.

Phones

Spanish **telephone numbers** have nine digits; mobile numbers begin with a "6", freephone numbers begin "900", while other "90-plus-digit" and "80-plus-digit" numbers are nationwide standard-rate or special-rate services. To **call Spain from abroad**, you dial your country's international access code + 34 (Spain's country code) + the nine-digit Spanish number.

Public telephones have instructions in English, and accept coins, credit cards and phonecards. **Phonecards** (*tarjetas*) with discounted rates for calls are available in tobacconists, newsagents and post offices, issued in various denominations either by Telefónica (the dominant operator) or one of its rivals. Credit cards are not recommended for local and national calls, since most have a minimum charge that is far more than a normal call is likely to cost. It's also best to avoid making calls from the phone in your hotel room, as even local calls will be slapped with a heavy surcharge.

You can make international calls from any public pay phone, but it's cheaper to go to one of the ubiquitous phone centres, or **locutorios**, which specialize in discounted overseas connections. **Calling home from Spain**, you dial ☎00 (Spain's international access code) + your country code + city/area code minus initial zero + number. For **reverse-charge calls,** dial the international operator (☎1008 Europe, ☎1005 rest of the world).

Most European **mobile phones** will work in Spain, though it's worth checking with your provider whether you need to get international access switched on and whether there are any extra charges involved. Even though prices are coming down, it's still expensive to use your own mobile extensively while abroad, and you will pay for receiving incoming calls, for example. You could always simply buy a local **SIM card** instead for your mobile, from operators such as Vodafone (☹www.vodafone.es) or Movistar (☹www.movistar.es). Or if you plan to spend some time in Spain, it's almost certainly better to buy a Spanish mobile, as the cheapest non-contract, **pay-as-you-go phones** cost from around €29. You can buy top-up cards, or have them recharged for you, in phone shops, *estancos* (tobacconists), newsstands, supermarkets and post offices, and from ATMs.

Public holidays

Alongside the Spanish **national public holidays** (see box below) there are scores of regional holidays and local fiestas (often marking the local saint's day), any of which will mean that everything except hotels, bars and restaurants locks its doors.

In addition, **August** is traditionally Spain's holiday month, when many of the big cities – especially Seville and Cordoba – are semi-deserted, with many of the shops and restaurants closed for the duration. In contrast, it can prove nearly impossible to find a room in the more popular coastal and mountain resorts at these times; similarly, seats on planes, trains and buses in August should if possible be booked in advance.

Shopping

Shopping in Andalucía can range from digging around in local **flea markets** to browsing the **designer boutiques** in Seville and Granada. In the larger towns and cities, most high streets will feature Spanish clothing favourites such as Mango and Zara, along with Camper, the country's most famous shoe brand. For food, **supermarkets** are easy to locate, while **street markets** (*mercados*) are held virtually everywhere, and are a great place to pick up fresh produce. The main department store found in most major towns and cities is El Corte Inglés, where you can buy almost anything.

The region is also well known for its local crafts. Leatherwork, such as belts, bags, purses and even saddles are best sought out in Córdoba or the medieval leather town of Ubrique (Cádiz), while Seville is where you'll be able to pick up the most authentic flamenco accessories such as dresses, fans, shawls and lace. Córdoba is also the place for stylish handmade hats, which are sold at bargain prices. Ceramics are widely available, but are especially good in Úbeda (where there's a thriving ancient pottery tradition), Níjar and Sorbas (both in Almería). Handwoven carpets and ponchos are to be found in Las Alpujarras and the Sierra de Grazalema, and the previously mentioned Níjar is also famed for its *jarapas* (carpets

---

Spanish and Andalucian public holidays

January 1 **Año Nuevo** New Year's Day
January 6 **Epifanía** Epiphany
February 28 **Día de Andalucía** Andalucía Day
Good Friday **Viernes Santo**
May 1 **Fiesta del Trabajo** May Day
August 15 **La Asunción** Assumption of the Virgin
October 12 **Día de la Hispanidad** National Day
November 1 **Todos los Santos** All Saints
December 6 **Día de la Constitución** Constitution Day
December 8 **Inmaculada Concepción**
December 25 **Navidad** Christmas Day

made from rags). Jerez is, of course the place for buying sherry, and nearby Sanlúcar de Barrameda's *manzanilla* variety shouldn't be overlooked either. Olive oil makes a great gift to take home and Andalucía has some of the finest producers in the world in places like Baena and Zuheros (Córdoba) and Segura de la Sierra (Jaén). Andalucía is, of course, the home of the guitar, of and some of the finest (and most beautiful) instruments are made by the craftsmen in Granada.

Taxes

Sales tax – **IVA** (pronounced "iba") – often comes as an unexpected surprise when you pay the bill for food or accommodation. It's not always specified, and is seven percent for hotels and restaurants and sixteen percent for other goods and services (though most other prices are quoted inclusive of IVA). **Non-EU residents** are able to claim back the sales tax on purchases that come to over €90. To do this, make sure the shop you're buying from fills out the correct paperwork, and present this to customs before you check in at the airport for your return flight.

Time

Spain is one hour ahead of the UK, six hours ahead of Eastern Standard Time, nine hours ahead of Pacific Standard Time, eight hours behind Australia, ten hours behind New Zealand, and the same time as South Africa. In Spain, the clocks go forward in the last week in March and back again in the last week in October. It's worth noting, if you're planning to cross the border, that Portugal is an hour behind Spain throughout the year.

Toilets

Public toilets are generally reasonably clean but don't always have any paper. They can very occasionally in rural locations still be squat-style. They are most commonly referred to and labelled *Los Servicios* (which is what you should ask for), though signs may point you to *baños* or *aseos*. *Damas* (Ladies) or *Señoras* (often signed with a "D" or "S") and *Caballeros* (Gentlemen, often marked simply "C") are the usual distinguishing signs for sex, though you may also see the potentially confusing combination of *Señoras* (Women) and *Señores* (Men).

Tourist information

The Spanish national tourist office, **Turespaña** (www.spain.info), is an excellent source of information when planning your trip. The website is full of ideas, information and searchable databases, and there are links to similar websites of Turespaña offices in your own country. In Andalucía, you'll find Junta de Andalucía (regional government) **Turismos** (tourist offices) in every provincial capital and many reasonably sized towns, typically open Monday to Friday 9am–2pm & 4–7pm, Saturday and Sunday 9am–2pm, but hours do vary from place to place. In major cities and coastal resorts the offices tend to remain open all day Saturday and on Sunday morning between April and September. In addition to the Junta's offices many towns and cities also provide their own **municipal tourist offices** which are frequently excellent and usually less busy than the Junta's outlets. We refer to these also throughout the *Guide*.

Travellers with disabilities

The classic tourist images of Andalucía – the medieval old towns, winding lanes, the castles and monasteries – don't exactly fill you full of confidence if you're in a wheelchair. However, Spain is changing and facilities are improving rapidly, especially in the more go-ahead, contemporary cities. There are accessible rooms and hotels in all major Spanish cities and resorts and, by law, all new public buildings (including revamped museums and galleries) are required to be fully accessible. Public transport is the main problem, since most local buses and trains are virtually impossible for wheelchairs, though again there are pockets of excellence throughout the region. The AVE high-speed train service, for example, is fully accessible, as is every city bus in Málaga. In many towns and cities, acoustic traffic-light signals and dropped kerbs are common.

Some organizations at home may be able to advise you further about travel to Spain, like the very useful UK-based **Tourism For All** (www.tourismforall.org.uk). Access Travel (www.access-travel.co.uk) can arrange flights, transfer and accommodation in Andalucía, and at the very least, local tourist offices in Spain should also be able to recommend a suitable hotel or taxi company.

Guide

Guide

Málaga and Cádiz

CHAPTER 1 # Highlights

✻ **Málaga** A vibrant city crammed with bars, cafés, museums and a fabulous Moorish fortress. See p.72

✻ **Museo Picasso** With over 180 artworks by Málaga's most famous son, this remarkable museum shouldn't be missed. See p.79

✻ **Costa del Sol** Despite a downmarket image, there are individual resorts – Nerja, Marbella and Estepona – with plenty of style. See p.122

✻ **Pueblos blancos** The White Towns are picturesque villages of whitewashed houses set amid spectacular scenery. See p.153

✻ **Ronda** Beautiful hill town set astride a yawning gorge with sensational views over the Serranía de Ronda. See p.156

✻ **Parques Naturales** Get away from it all in the natural parks of Sierra de Grazalema, Los Alcornocales and the Parque de El Torcal with its surreal limestone formations. See p.99, p.170 & p.176

✻ **Cádiz** A beguiling air of genteel decay pervades this old sea town, one of the great cities of the Spanish south. See p.201

✻ **Jerez** Visit a sherry *bodega* and sample the legendary *aperitivo* at one of the town's numerous tapas bars. See p.230

▲ Museo Picasso

Málaga and Cádiz

The Andalucian sun starts singing a fire song, and all creation trembles at the sound.

Federico García Lorca

The smallest of Andalucía's eight provinces, **Málaga** is also its most populous, swelling to bursting point with the sheer weight of visitors in high summer. Although primarily known as the gateway to the Costa del Sol and its unashamedly commercial resorts such as Torremolinos and Marbella, the province has much more to offer than just its coastline. To most incoming tourists the provincial capital **Málaga** is merely "the place by the airport", but it's also a vibrant city in its own right, with a population of half a million. In the west of Málaga's provincial heartland lies the **Serranía de Ronda**, a series of small mountain ranges sprinkled with gleaming, whitewashed **pueblos blancos** (White Towns), of which Ronda, located astride the stunningly beautiful El Tajo gorge, is justly the most famous.

To the north lies the appealing market town of **Antequera** with its remarkable prehistoric dolmens and sumptuous Baroque churches, and from here it's a quick hop south to the natural wonders of **El Torcal**, where vast limestone outcrops have been eroded into a landscape of weird natural sculptures. Another possible trip from Antequera is to the spectacular **El Chorro Gorge**, which, along with the Embalse de Guadalhorce, has become a major climbing and camping centre. Nearby, the saline **Laguna de Fuente de Piedra** is Europe's only inland breeding ground for the greater flamingo, whose flying flocks make a spectacular sight in summer.

The far eastern section of Málaga province is the largely unknown and little-visited **Axarquía** region, an area of rugged natural beauty and once the haunt of mountain bandits. Now the domain of the *cabra hispanica*, a distinctive Iberian long-horned goat, the area's magnificent scenery and earthy villages contrast starkly with the crowded **beaches** to the south.

With a two-hundred-kilometre coastline fronting both the Atlantic and the Mediterranean, **Cádiz** is the most southerly province of Andalucía. The sea has played a large part in the history of the province, and most of Cádiz's dozen or so major conurbations are within easy distance of a beach. Founded by the Phoenicians, the city of **Cádiz** itself makes up for in sheer elegance, atmosphere and sea-girthed location what it lacks in the way of irresistible sights.

After the tumult of the Costa del Sol, the bracing Atlantic winds and broad, white, dune-lined beaches of the **Costa de la Luz** – great stretches of which have so far survived the developers' attentions and are often deserted – can come as a welcome relief. Resorts such as **Conil, Chipiona** and **Sanlúcar de Barrameda** possess a low-key charm, while at the southern tip of the coast, **Tarifa** – also with miles of fine beaches – has become a major windsurfing centre. The entire thirty-kilometre stretch between Tarifa and **Algeciras** (Andalucía's main port for sailings to Morocco) has been designated a "potential military zone", placing strict controls on Spanish developments and preventing foreigners from buying up land. Across the Bay of Algeciras, the British colony of **Gibraltar** sits beneath its daunting mountain of rock, regarded uneasily by Spaniards and as a strange, hybrid curiosity to almost everyone else.

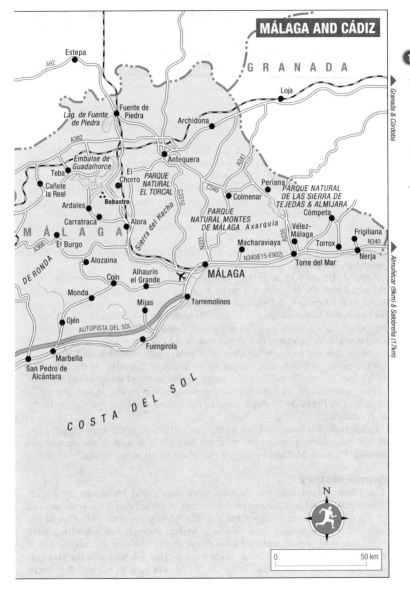

Inland, Cádiz offers a fascinating variety of landscapes and towns. The mountainous region in its northeastern corner, which it shares with Málaga, is dotted with hill-top White Towns such as **Zahara**, **Olvera** and **Arcos de la Frontera**, while the green oasis of **Grazalema**, the wettest point in Spain, is surrounded by its **natural park**, a paradise for walkers and naturalists. South of here sharp contours give way to rolling hills covered with clumps of walnut trees, pines and Spanish firs, and the ranches around **Medina Sidonia** where *toros bravos* – ominous black fighting bulls – graze in the shade of cork oaks. To the west, vines take over, covering thousands of acres of dazzling white chalk soil, and forming the famous **sherry triangle** between **Jerez**, a fine town in its own right, **Puerto de Santa María** and **Sanlúcar de Barrameda**, the oldest vineyards in Europe.

Málaga

First impressions of **MÁLAGA** are not encouraging. A large and bustling seaport with a population passing half a million, it's the second city of Andalucía (after Seville) and also one of the poorest, with unemployment numbers persistently among the highest in the region. Yet, though many visitors get no further than the train or bus stations, put off by the grim clusters of high-rises on the fringes, if you penetrate beyond these you will find yourself in one of the most atmospheric and historic cities in Spain. Lorca described Málaga as his favourite town and, given a chance, it can be a surprisingly attractive place, an impression boosted by the ebullient and big-hearted *malagueños*, among the friendliest people in Andalucía.

Around the traditional fishing villages of **El Palo** and **Pedregalejo**, now absorbed into the suburbs, is a series of small beaches and a *paseo* lined with some of the best fish and seafood cafés in the province. Overlooking the town and port, the Moorish citadels of the **Alcazaba** and **Gibralfaro** are excellent introductions to what you can expect at Córdoba and Granada, and while *sevillanos* loudly proclaim that there is only one Semana Santa worthy of the name, *malagueños* furiously disagree. The processions are celebrated here with great fervour and with much larger floats (*tronos* or "thrones" as they're called here) than those of Seville, carried by up to two hundred sober-suited males or robed penitents. In mid-August, at the peak of the tourist season, the town lets rip in its **Feria de Málaga** – one of the wildest and most spectacular fiestas in Andalucía.

Incidentally, **Picasso** was born in Málaga, and although the artist moved away in his early years, you can still visit his birthplace as well as the spectacular **Museo Picasso Málaga** housing a collection of his major works.

Some history

The **Phoenicians** founded the settlement they called Malaka in the eighth century BC, building a fortress on the summit of the hill that is today dominated by the Alcazaba. Later incorporated into the Roman province of Baetica in the wake of Rome's victory over Carthage, Málaga prospered as a **trading port** exporting iron, copper and lead from mines in the hills near Ronda, as well as olive oil, wine and *garum*, a relish made from pickled fish to which the Romans were particularly partial. After falling to the **Moors** early in the eighth century, Málaga was soon flourishing again as the main port for the city of Granada. Although in the fourteenth century the ruler Yusuf I constructed the Gibralfaro as defence, in 1487 Málaga was taken by Christian forces following a bitter siege, after which the large Moorish population was persecuted and its property confiscated on a grand scale; the city's main mosque was also transformed into a cathedral, and a further twenty into churches. Málaga then entered a period of decline only exacerbated by a revolt of the Moors in 1568 that resulted in their complete expulsion.

Málaga online

Online information about Málaga can be found at ⓦwww.malagaturismo.com, ⓦwww.ayto–malaga.es and ⓦwww.andalucía.org.

It was not until the nineteenth century that real prosperity returned – and then only briefly. Middle-class families arriving from the north invested in textile factories, sugar refineries and shipyards, and gave their names to city streets such as Larios and Heredia, while Málaga **dessert wine** became the favourite tipple of Victorian ladies. Then, in the early part of the twentieth century, the bottom fell out of the boom as the new industries succumbed to foreign competition and the phylloxera bug got to work wiping out the vines. A number of radical revolts leading up to the Civil War also brought the city an unhealthy reputation.

Given its volatile nature it was inevitable that Málaga would be staunchly Republican during the **Civil War**. In the turbulent years leading up to the war and during the conflict itself churches and convents were burned, while in 1937 Italian planes bombed the city, destroying much of its ancient central core, and mass executions of "reds and anarchists" by the conquering Franco forces left enduring emotional scars. This period is vividly described in a contemporaneous account, *Málaga Burning*, by Gamel Woolsey (see p.606).

The 1960s finally brought an economic lifeline in the form of **mass tourism** and the exploitation of the Costa del Sol, though the coastal night-mares, however, barely touch the heart of Málaga. The opening of the **AVE** high speed train line connecting Málaga with Madrid in two-and-a-half hours has also had an impact on raising the town's profile. In recent years the town has tried to muscle in on the Costa del Sol tourist boom by projecting itself as a beach resort as well as a cultural centre, and work has been carried out to landscape the beaches and promenades to the west of the harbour as far as El Palo. So far, however, all this seems to have had little adverse impact on the city's unique character.

Arrival

From the **airport** (☏95 204 88 04), the electric **train** (Ferrocarril) provides the easiest and cheapest way into town (every 30min 7am–11.45pm; €1.20). From the arrivals hall, go up one floor to the Salidas (departures hall), take any exit and follow the "Ferrocarril" signs, crossing the overpass (baggage trolleys allowed) to the unstaffed station. A kiosk, if open, sells tickets, or use the ticket machine close by; alternatively you can buy a ticket on the train. Make sure that you're on the Málaga platform (the one farthest away and reached by an underpass) and stay on the train right to the end of the line – the Centro-Alameda stop (a 12min ride). From here, you can cross the bridge over the Río Guadalmedina riverbed to the western end of the tree-lined Alameda, effectively the town centre. The #19 **bus** from the airport to the centre departs from a stop outside the arrivals hall (every 30min 7am–midnight; €1), and calls at the main train and bus stations en route. The same journey by taxi to and from the centre of town costs around €15 depending on traffic and time of day and takes roughly fifteen minutes.

RENFE, Malagá's gleaming new main **train station**-cum-shopping mall, is the stop before Centro-Alameda on the Ferrocarril; from here it is a slightly

Jardín Botánico La Concepción ▲

ACCOMMODATION

Albergue Juvenil Málaga	N
Hostal Derby	L
Hostal El Cenachero	S
Hostal La Hispanidad	T
Hostal La Palma	J
Hostal Victoria	I
Hotel Alameda	Q
Hotel Atarazanas	M
Hotel California	C
Hotel Don Curro	H
Hotel Ibis	E
Hotel Kris Tribuna	D
Hotel Larios	F
Hotel Lola	R
Hotel Málaga Palacio	G
Hotel Montevictoria	A
Hotel Sur	P
Hotel Venecia	O
Parador de Málaga–Gibralfaro	B
Pensión Juanita	K

Convento de la Trinidad

LA TRINIDAD

San Pablo

Museo de Artes y Tradiciones Populares **19**

Santo Domingo

Mercado central

El Corte Inglés

Ciber@lameda

Monumento a Pablo Picasso   Jardines de Picasso

San Pedro

Centro-Alameda Train Station

Delegación de la Junta de Andalucía

Centro de Arte Contemporaneo

EL PERCHEL

Nuestra Señora del Carmen

Bus Station

RENFE Train Station

◄ & Ronda

0   200 m

▼ Cádiz

74

RESTAURANTS AND CAFÉS

Adolfo	32	Bar Central	14	Café Lepanto	26	Casa Vicente	33
Al-Yamal	37	Bar Los Pueblos	33	Cañadu	2	Clandestino	6
Antonio	16	Bar-Restaurante Palacios	39	Casa Aranda	30	El Jardín	18
Antonio Martín	35	Café de Paris	31	Casa Mira	24	El Legado Celestial	38

MÁLAGA

N

MÁLAGA AND CÁDIZ

Antequera

PLAZA DE CAPUCHINOS

EL EGIDO

PLAZA DE LA RECONQUISTA

PUERTO PAREJO

Santuario de Nuestra
Señora de la Victoria

PLAZA SANTUARIO

PLAZA ALFONSO XIII

FÉLIX MESA

CHAVES
S. DUQUE
CIRCO

PLAZA
DE LA VICTORIA

FERRÁNDIZ

A. MENDOZA

ROSAL
PALAFOX
CAPUCHINOS
CARRERA CAPUCHINOS
TIZO

PLAZA
DE
EGIDO

DIEGO DE SILOÉ

C. VERDE

ALTOZANO

LA VICTORIA

CRUZ DEL
MOLINILLO

PARRAS

REFINO

LAGUNILLAS

Iglesia de
San Felipe
Neri

DOS ACERAS

FRAILES

Teatro
Cervantes

MARIBLANCA
PEÑA

Casa Natal
de Picasso

Meeting
Point

PLAZA
MERCED

PLAZA
M. GUERRERO

MUÑOZ NIEVO

Castillo de
Gibralfaro
(Parador)

Museo
Municipal

English
Cemetery

PASEO DE REDING

El Palo, Almería & Pedregalejo

CARRETERÍA

RODRÍGUEZ MENDOZA NÚÑEZ
COMEDIAS

ÁLAMOS

MADRE DE DIOS

BEATAS

Iglesia
de Santiago

GRANADA

ALCAZABILLA

Museo
Arqueológico

Museo
Picasso

Teatro
Romano

Alcazaba

Ayuntamiento

Fuente
de
Génova

Plaza
de Toros

MAESTRANZA

Santos
Mártires

A. PÉREZ

VÉLEZ

PLAZA
UNCIBAY

Santo
Cristo de
la Salud

SALLCA

CALDERERÍAS

Iglesia
del
Sagrario

PLAZA
CARBÓN

STA MARÍA

CISTER

Iglesia
del
Sagrario

STA AGUSTÍN

Catedral

Aduana

San Juan

Palacio
Episcopal

MOLINA LARIO

CORTINA DEL MUELLE

PLAZA
DE LA
MARINA

Retrato de
Cánovas
del Castillo

PASEO DE ESPAÑA

PASEO DE LOS CURAS

PASEO DEL PARQUE

AVDA. CERVANTES

GUILLÉN SOTELO

CÁNOVAS DEL CASTILLO

SAN NICOLÁS

REDING

PLAZA DE LA
MALAGUETA

LA MALAGUETA

CENTRO

ESPECERÍAS

FCO. RICA
FREIRE

MARQUÉS DE LARIOS
STRACHAN
BOLSA
DE LARA
LUJÁN
SALCEDO

LIBORIO GARCÍA

MARTÍNEZ

AVDA. MAR

ALAMEDA
PRINCIPAL

VENDEJA
CASAS

TRINIDAD GRUND

AVDA. TOMÁS HEREDIA

BARROSO

Trinitel

Cruceros
Málaga

Estación
Marítima
(ferry terminal)

Port

Monumento
a Manuel
Agustín Heredia

MUELLE DE HEREDIA

MUELLE DE RICARDO G. CORLETA

MUELLE DE ROMERO ROBLEDO

PASEO DE LA FAROLA

P. PICASSO

Playa La Malagueta

BARS AND TAPAS BARS

Antigua Casa Guardia	34
Antigua Reja	4
Bar Lo Güeno	25
Bar Orellana	17
Bodegas Quitapeñas	27
Cafetería Axarquía	36
Come y Caña	21
El Pimpi	8
La Dehesa de Santa María	20
La Quesería	13
Lizarran	12
Mesón Mariano	5
Mesón Las Garrafas	3

El Tintero	29	La Taberna del Obisbo	23	Refectorium	22
El Vegetariano de la Alcazabilla	10	La Tetería	11	Restaurante Tormes	9
El Viajero	7	Mesón Gibralfaro	15	Sal Gorda	28
Il Laboratorio	1	Parador de Málaga–Gibralfaro	B	Tetería Barraka	19

longer walk into the heart of town (bus #3 runs from here to the centre approximately every 10min).

All buses from and to destinations outside Málaga (run by a number of different companies) operate from the one **bus station** on Paseo de los Tilos (☎95 235 00 61), a little northwest of the RENFE station. Arriving in Málaga **by car** you face the serious problem of parking and you will have little choice but to use one of the many signed car parks around the centre or use a garage connected to your accommodation (for which you will still need to pay). **Theft** from cars is rampant in Málaga, so remember not to leave valuables inside especially when street parking.

Information

Slightly east of Plaza de la Constitución, the **Turismo**, Pasaje de Chinitas 4 (Mon–Fri 9am–8pm, Sat & Sun 10am–2pm; ☎95 221 34 45), can provide full accommodation lists and a large, detailed map of the city. and also has lots of information on the Costa del Sol. They stock the monthly *¿Que Hacer?* ("*What's On?*"), which covers events and entertainment throughout Andalucía, as well as the weekly *Sur in English*, published by Malaga's main daily, *Sur*, which has a useful listings section. An enthusiastic **Turismo Municipal** (Mon–Fri 9am–7.30pm, Sat 10am–7pm, Sun 10am–2pm; ☎95 212 20 20) is located in Plaza de la Marina, close to the ferry terminal; it also operates a kiosk (summer only) in Plaza de la Merced as well as other branches in the arrivals hall at the airport and at the bus station. The Plaza de la Marina office also offers self-guided free **iPod city tours** (credit card required for refundable payment of €150 to guarantee return of iPod) with five themed walks (Picasso's Málaga, Romantic Malagá, Historic Málaga etc).

One way to get to grips with the city is on an open-topped **bus tour.** This hop-on hop-off service is operated by Malagatour (☎902 10 10 81, ⓦwww .city-ss.com; €15, tickets valid 24hr), with services leaving the bus station every half-hour (first & last departures 9.15am & 7pm); its many stops include the cathedral, Alcazaba, Plaza de la Merced and the Alameda.

Accommodation

Málaga boasts scores of **hotels** together with plenty of **pensiones** and **hostales**, so budget rooms are rarely hard to come by except during Semana Santa and the August *feria* (when prices are also hiked). Málaga's high season is July and August and outside this period there are some real bargains to be had. Numerous possibilities are to be found in the grid of streets just north and south of the Alameda, which is probably the best place to start looking. The cheapest option is the **youth hostel** (*albergue juvenil*), though this isn't particularly convenient for the centre, as it lies out in the western suburbs. The town's central **hotels** are generally poorer value than the *hostales*, but for those who want a little more luxury, we've listed a handful of places slightly further out. Málaga has no **campsite**: the nearest facilities are at Torremolinos heading west (see p.123), and Torre del Mar (see p.103) to the east.

South of the Alameda

Hostal El Cenachero c/Barroso 5 ☎95 222 40 88. Clean, peaceful, third-floor *hostal* in a quiet street just off the seafront end of c/Córdoba. Friendly proprietors and most rooms en suite. ❸

Hotel Alameda c/Casas de Campos 3 ☎95 222 20 99, ⓦ www.hotelalamedamalaga.com. Pleasant small hotel in high-rise block which lessens traffic noise. Rooms with a/c and TV. ❹

Hotel Lola c/Casas de Campos 17 ☏ 95 257 93 00, ⓦ www.room-matehotels.com. New designer-chic boutique hotel where rooms come with flat-screen TV, free internet, DVD player, minibar and safe. Also has own bar-restaurant and garage. ❻

Hotel Sur c/Trinidad Grund 13 ☏ 95 222 48 03, ⓦ www.hotel-sur.com. Quiet, efficiently run hotel with garage; all rooms have a/c, bath and TV. ❹

Hotel Venecia Alameda Principal 9 ☏ 95 221 36 36. Central hotel with good facilities including a/c, balconies overlooking the Alameda and satellite TV. ❺

North of the Alameda

Hostal Derby c/San Juan de Dios 1 ☏ 95 222 13 01. Very friendly and excellent-value fourth-floor establishment, on a tiny street north of the Plaza de la Marina, with some rooms overlooking the harbour. Most rooms en suite. ❷

Hostal La Palma c/Martínez 7 ☏ 95 222 67 72. Pleasant central *hostal* run by a friendly couple. Rooms either en suite or sharing bath; discounts are sometimes available. ❷–❸

Hostal Victoria c/Sancha de Lara 3 ☏ 95 222 42 24. Smart, central *hostal* with good en-suite a/c doubles and singles with satellite TV. ❹

Hotel Atarazanas c/Atarazanas 19 ☏ 95 212 19 10, ⓦ www.balboahoteles.com. Central three-star hotel with reasonably priced and well-appointed rooms. Free wi-fi throughout hotel. ❺

Hotel Don Curro c/Sancha de Lara 7 ☏ 95 222 72 00, ⓦ www.hoteldoncurro.com. Central and comfortable, if rather featureless, hotel where a/c rooms come with satellite TV. Own car park. ❺

Hotel Ibis Paseo Guimbarda 5 ☏ 95 207 07 41, ⓦ www.ibishotel.com. On the west bank of the Guadalmedina, this is part of the international chain, offering functional rooms at attractive prices with frequent special offers. ❹

Hotel Kris Tribuna c/Carretería 6 ☏ 95 212 22 30, ⓦ www.krishoteles.com. Elegant hotel offering rooms with satellite TV, in-room safe and minibar. Two floors are reserved for non-smoking guests. There's a very pleasant cafetería, *La Barbacoa* (owned by the hotel), next door. ❺

Hotel Larios c/Marqués de Larios 2 ☏ 95 222 22 00, ⓦ www.hotel-larios.com. Modern, upmarket and central hotel inside the shell of an original Art Deco edifice; satellite TV, in-room safes and a panoramic rooftop bar are among the features. Frequent special offers. ❻ with breakfast.

Hotel Málaga Palacio Cortina del Muelle 1 ☏ 95 221 51 85, ⓦ www.ac-hotels.com. This central four-star with sea-view rooms pampers its guests with free minibar and bathrobes. Facilities include rooftop pool and gym. See website for special offers. ❻

Pensión Juanita c/Alarcón Luján 8 ☏ 95 221 35 86. Central and friendly *pensión* on the fourth floor (there's a lift), offering some en suites. Large, multi-bed family rooms also available. ❷

Out of the centre

Albergue Juvenil Málaga Plaza de Pío XII 6 ☏ 95 230 85 00. Pleasantly modern double rooms, complete with a shared sun-terrace. The #18 bus (heading west across the river) from the Alameda will drop you nearby on request. Under 25 €16, over 25 €20.

Hostal La Hispanidad Explanada de la Estación 5 ☏ 952 31 11 35. Facing the train station, this is a useful option if you've got an early train (or bus) to catch. The labyrinthine interior has refurbished en-suite rooms – with a/c and TV – named after different countries of the Americas, and there are plenty of eating places nearby. ❹

Hotel California Paseo de Sancha 17, 500m east of the bullring ☏ 95 221 51 64, ⓦ www .hotelcalifornianet.com. Charming small hotel near the beach with a flower-bedecked entrance. The well-appointed rooms come with a/c and safes, and the hotel has its own garage. Buses #11, #34 and #35 from the Alameda will drop you outside on request. ❺

Hotel Montevictoria c/Conde de Ureña 58 ☏ 95 265 65 25, ⓦ www .hotelmontevictoria.com. Sweet little hotel with friendly proprietors in an elegant villa in the hills above Málaga with great views over the city. Slightly pricier rooms 104 & 105 have their own terrace. Bus #36 from the Alameda (ask for the c/Conde de Ureña stop) stops almost outside. ❹

Parador de Málaga–Gibralfaro Monte de Gibralfaro ☏ 95 222 19 02, ⓦ www.parador.es. You won't get a better panoramic view of the coast than from this eagle's nest on top of the Gibralfaro hill. Rooms come with a/c and satellite TV and, although it's quite small for a parador, it does have a pool. Well worth calling in for a drink or a meal (see p.86). ❼

The Town

Málaga is bisected by the seasonal Guadalmedina river, which was unsuccessfully landscaped in the 1990s at colossal cost with dismal walkways and reluctant grass. All the major sights lie to the east of this and below the **Alcazaba**. From the **Alameda**, the city's main thoroughfare, the **cathedral**, **Museo Picasso** and a clutch of interesting **churches** all lie within a few-minutes' walk. The city has embarked upon a plan to revitalize the *casco antiguo* (old town) by pedestrianizing and refurbishing much of the monumental zone and laying with marble the whole of **c/Marqués de Larios** – a fashionable shopping street – and the focal **Plaza de la Constitución**. This regeneration programme is now well advanced and is set to transform central Málaga in the years ahead.

Alcazaba and Gibralfaro castle

Málaga's magnificent **Alcazaba** (Tues–Sun: April–Oct 9.30am–8pm; Oct–March 8.30am–5.45pm; €2 or combined ticket for Alcazaba and Gibralfaro €3.30) and Gibralfaro (see below) are an exuberant contrast to the dour fortresses of Castile. At the Alcazaba's entrance stands a **Teatro Romano**, unearthed in 1951 during building works. The theatre, constructed in the second century BC, is now used as an auditorium for various outdoor entertainment. From here a path winds upwards, lined by the cypresses and flower-encircled arbours so loved by the sybaritic Moors. The citadel too is Roman in origin, and interspersed among the Moorish brick of the double- and triple-arched gateways are recycled blocks and columns of classical marble.

Although the Moors began building on the hill in the 700s, the Alcazaba with its interior palace as we see it today dates from the early decades of the eleventh century and was substantially restored and rebuilt in 1930. It was the residence of the Arab emirs of Málaga, who carved out an independent kingdom for themselves upon the break-up of the Western Caliphate during the same period. Their independence lasted a mere thirty years, but for a while the kingdom grew to include Granada, Carmona and Jaén. Strolling among the restored patios and terraces lined with cypresses, aromatic plants and ornamental pools the impression is of a smaller-scale Alhambra (see p.477), and traces of stucco decoration surviving on the arches are similar to the artistry to be seen at Medina Azahara near Córdoba (see p.398).

The recently refurbished small **palace** houses displays of ceramics found during archeological excavations. To reach the Alcazaba without the climb, you can use a **lift** constructed inside the hill itself. With its entrance on c/Guillen Sotelo, directly behind the Ayuntamiento, it transports you effortlessly upwards to emerge in the heart of the palace.

Gibralfaro castle

Above the Alcazaba, and connected to it by a long double wall (the *coracha*), is the **Gibralfaro castle** (same hours and entry charges as Alcazaba). It's reached by climbing a twisting path that skirts the southern walls passing bougainvillea-draped ramparts and sentry-box-shaped Moorish wells. You can also approach from the town side, as the tourist coaches do, but this is a lengthy, rather unattractive walk and not one to be done alone after sundown.

Built by Yusuf I of Granada in the fourteenth century and last used in 1936 during the Civil War, the castle, with its formidable walls and turrets, has, like the Alcazaba, been wonderfully restored and now houses an interesting **museum** dealing with the Gibralfaro's history. Among a collection of military exhibits from all periods there is a splendid scale model letting you see how the city and Alcazaba complex would have looked in Moorish times. There's also a display of seventeenth-century playing cards that were made in the factory in nearby Macharaviaya (see p.102). A walk around the castle's **ramparts** affords terrific views over the city, the *coracha*, and the complex fortifications of the Alcazaba.

The Gibralfaro has its own **bar**, but while you're up here, a pleasant place for a **meal** or a **drink** is the nearby *Parador de Málaga–Gibralfaro*, with its terrace overlooking the city (see "Accommodation", p.77 and "Eating", p.86).It's reached by following the road leading out of the castle's car park for 100m and turning right into the parador's grounds. Next to the parador's entrance is a **mirador** with a stunning **view** over the harbour, city and Plaza de Toros. If you're feeling lazy, bus #35 from the Alameda Principal in the city centre will drop you by the castle entrance.

The Catedral

Dominating the views from the Gibralfaro is Málaga's peculiar, unfinished **Catedral** (Mon–Fri 10am–6pm, Sat 10am–5pm; €3.50). It lacks a tower on the west front, the result of a radical *malagueño* bishop having donated the earmarked money to the American War of Independence against the British. Despite this curiosity, which has resulted in the building's popular nickname La Manquita ("the one-armed lady"), the cathedral lacks much else of interest. The soaring interior is distinguished only by an intricately carved and natural-istic seventeenth-century *sillería* (choir stall) with outstanding sculptural work – in particular *St Francis* and *John the Baptist* – by Pedro de Mena. However, the **Iglesia del Sagrario** (same ticket and hours as cathedral; also open during services), on the cathedral's northern flank, is worth a look, if only for its fine Gothic **portal**, dating from an earlier, uncompleted Isabelline church. Inside, a restored and magnificent gilded **Plateresque retablo**, which is brilliantly illuminated during services, is the work of Juan Balmaseda.

The Museo Picasso

Located just round the corner from the cathedral on c/San Agustín, is the **Museo Picasso Málaga** (Tues–Sun 10am–8pm; permanent collection €6, temporary collection €4.50, combined ticket for both €8; ⓦ www.museopicassomalaga.org) housed in an impressive sixteenth-century mansion – the former residence of the counts of Buenavista – with an elegant patio.A source of enormous pride for the city, the museum was opened by the king and queen in 2003, one hundred and twelve years after Picasso left Málaga at the age of ten and to where he returned only once for an unhappy, fleeting visit in 1901. In later life he toyed with the idea of sending "two lorries full of paintings" to set up a museum in Málaga but vowed never to visit Spain while General Franco was still alive – Picasso died in 1973 and was outlived by the dictator by two years.

The museum's **permanent collection** consists of 204 works donated by Christine and Bernard Ruiz-Picasso, the artist's daughter-in-law and grandson, while the **temporary collection** comprises loaned works and special exhibitions (not necessarily connected with Picasso).Whilst not on a par with the Picasso museums in Paris and Barcelona, it does allow you to see some of the lesser-known works that Picasso kept for himself or gave away to his lovers, family and friends – rather harshly described as "the less saleable stuff" by one critic.

Among the highlights are, in Room 2, *Olga Koklova con Mantilla* (a portrait of his first wife, draped in a hotel tablecloth) and a moving portrait of his close-cropped son Paul, painted in 1923. Other rooms have canvases from the breadth of Picasso's career including his Blue, Pink and Cubist periods, as well as sculptures in wood, metal and stone and a few ceramics. Two other influential women who figured prominently in the artist's long and turbulent love life are also the subjects of powerful images: in Room 5 *Cabeza de Mujer 1939* is a portrait of the beguiling yet tragic Dora Maar,

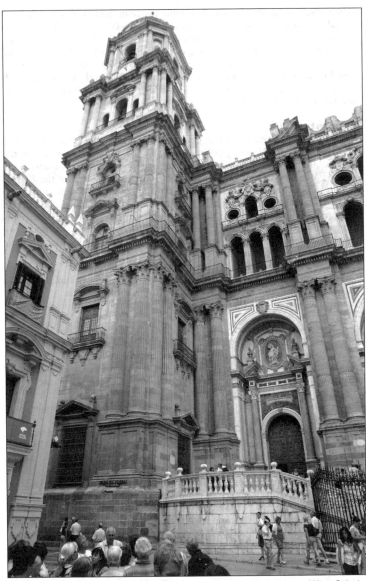

▲ Málaga Cathedral

and in Room 8, *Jacqueline Sentada* is a seated representation of his second wife, Jacqueline Roque.

The museum's basement has the unexpected surprise of **archeological remains** revealed during its construction. Substantial chunks of a Phoenician city wall and tower dating from the seventh century BC survive, while from later periods you can view the remains of a Roman *salazones* factory used to produce the famous *garum*, a fish-based sauce and Roman delicacy, and also the remains of the cellar of the sixteenth-century Palacio de Buenavista. A case nearby displays some of the finds unearthed in the excavations including Phoenician, Greek and Roman pottery fragments and a sixth-century BC Egyptian scarab.

The museum also has a good, if cramped, bookshop and an equally cramped *cafetería*, although this spills out onto a pleasant garden terrace in fine weather. The museum opens on certain Saturday evenings throughout the summer (€2; details from museum or website), with live music in the garden and other events.

The Picasso museum has taken over the building that previously housed the **Museo de las Bellas Artes** collection, which includes important works by Murillo and Zurbarán. There are plans afoot to relocate this collection in the Aduana (the old customs building on the Paseo del Parque) and either of the tourist offices should have the latest news on this, or check their websites.

Casa Natal de Picasso

Picasso's birthplace and family home during his early years, the **Casa Natal de Picasso**, Plaza de la Merced 15, is now the headquarters and museum of the Picasso Foundation (daily 10am–8pm; €1). It was during his formative years in Málaga that Picasso's prodigious talent for drawing was first noticed – "When I was a child I could draw like Raphael," he later wrote. "It took me all my life to learn to draw like a child." It was in the cafés around the square that the boy saw the first solid shape that he wanted to commit to paper: *churros*, those oil-steeped fritters that Spaniards dip into their breakfast chocolate.

The recently revamped exhibition space now displays lithographs, etchings and washes by Picasso – mainly with women as the subject matter – while on the stairs are displayed photos of the artist at various stages in his long life. The stairs lead to a reconstructed reception room, which has been furnished in the style of the late nineteenth century when Picasso was growing up here. Among the items on display is some embroidered bed linen by the artist's mother, a canvas by his art teacher father and the infant Picasso's christening robe, used in the ceremony at the nearby Iglesia de Santiago.

Pasaje de Chinitas and Museo Carmen Thyssen Bornemisza

Tucked behind the Plaza de la Constitución, and on the Turismo's doorstep, is one of Málaga's most evocative corners, the **Pasaje de Chinitas**. In the first half of the last century, when Málaga was a thriving industrial town, this narrow white-walled street was filled with *tascas*, or bars, where businessmen would meet to discuss deals over fine wines before slinking off to the *Café de Chinitas* to hear some of the best flamenco in town. In the 1920s and 1930s the fame of this flamenco shrine, now a mundane textile store, grew as it became a noted meeting place of artists and writers, bullfighters and singers. Lorca loved the place and composed a poem in its honour, part of which appears on a plaque fixed to the former café, at the junction with c/Sánchez Pastor:

In the Café de Chinitas
Said Paquiro to his brother:
"I'm more valiant than you,
more brave and more gitano."

Just off the west side of Plaza de la Constitución and housed in the refurbished sixteenth-century Palacio de Villalón is the **Museo Carmen Thyssen Bornemisza**, in c/Compañia. Scheduled to open at the end of 2009 (details from the Turismo) the core of the collection will be dedicated to Spanish art of the nineteenth century, but other periods will also be represented with works by artists such as Zurbarán and Juan Gris.

Museo de Artes y Tradiciones Populares and the Centro de Arte Contemporaneo

Just east of the Guadalmedina and housed in a seventeenth-century inn, the entertaining **Museo de Artes y Tradiciones Populares**, c/Pasillo Santa Isabel 10 (Mon–Fri 10am–1.30pm & 4–7pm, Sat 10am–1.30pm; €2), uses the former stables and stores on the lower floor as well as the lodging rooms above to mount displays of arts, crafts and furniture from previous eras. These include a collection of *barros malagueños* – typical painted clay figurines – as well as boats, carriages, farming and wine-making implements and rooms furnished in period style.

To the south of here, following the Río Guadalmedina, is the **Centro de Arte Contemporaneo** c/Alemania s/n (Sept–June Tues–Sun 10am–8pm; July & Aug 10am–2pm & 5–9pm; free), a modern art museum housed in a converted former market building. The permanent collection displays works by international artists Louis Bourgeois, Cindy Sherman and Damien Hirst while Spain is represented by Juan Muñoz, Miguel Barcelo and Juan Uslé among others. Check out the centre's website (Ⓦwww.cacmalaga.org) for information on frequent temporary exhibitions. The **cafetería** has a pleasant river-view terrace.

Jardines de Picasso

West of here across the Puente Tetuán and 200m or so beyond the El Corte Inglés department store stands a modern garden, the **Jardines de Picasso**. A memorial garden dedicated to the city's favourite son, it is the site of Spain's first monument to the artist, which was erected here in 1978 – a curiously restrained and abstract work by Ramón Calderón. Second thoughts, however, were in a much more monumental vein and Ortiz Berrocal was commissioned to produce something of the size required: a wonderfully intestinal bronze, flanked by two magnificent dragon trees that are fairly remarkable sculptures in their own right. Don't hang around here after dark, however, as the area has a dubious reputation.

Mercado Central

Lying at the heart of an area that bustles with life, the nineteenth-century wrought-iron, Mudéjar-style **Mercado Central** (officially the Mercado Central de Atarazanas), just north of the Alameda on c/Atarazanas, incorporates a little-known architectural gem, largely unnoticed by the daily shoppers. The remarkable fourteenth-century **Moorish arch** on its southern facade was built for Yusuf I of Granada – the ruler also responsible for that other great gateway, the Puerta de la Justicia in the Alhambra – when Málaga was part of the Nasrid kingdom. In those days it formed the entrance to the Moorish arsenal, and the original building's purpose is preserved in the market's present name: Atarazanas in Arabic translates as "the house that guards the arsenal". Note the two coats of arms in the upper corners inscribed in Arabic with the confident proclamation, "There is no Conqueror but Allah. All Praise to Him." Currently, the market is undergoing a refurbishment that should restore it to its former glory.

Paseo del Parque

An ideal place for a stroll, especially on summer evenings when the air has cooled, the **Paseo del Parque** is an elegant, palm-shaded avenue laid out at the turn of the twentieth century on land reclaimed from the sea. Along its length are a number of architectural delights as well as a remarkable **botanical garden** containing hundreds of exotic plants and flowers and many varieties of fig, bamboo, jacaranda and yucca trees. Discreet plaques placed at intervals along the esplanade identify the different species. Among the buildings of note are the Neoclassical **Aduana** (the former Customs house) started in 1788, with an austerely impressive patio and, further along, **El Correo**, or the old post office. Don't miss the paseo's star turn a little further on, the exuberant **Ayuntamiento**, a delightful cream and brown Art Nouveau pile, constructed to coincide with the opening of the esplanade. Almost opposite the Correo in the gardens stand the first two of Pimentel's trio of evocative bronzes which are among Málaga's best-loved sculptures: **El Jazminero** (*The Jasmine Seller*) celebrates the men who once sold trays of their blooms throughout the city while the nearby **El Verdialero** pays tribute to the colourful and frenetic Verdiales musicians from the mountains of Málaga to the northeast of the city. The third bronze, **El Cenachero** (*The Fish Seller*), commemorating men who, with their baskets of fish dangling from a yoke, used to be a common sight on the city's streets, is sited behind the municipal tourist office on Plaza de la Marina.

At the paseo's eastern end you'll come to the **Fuente de Genova**, or Genoa fountain, now encircled by traffic and difficult to appreciate. An Italian Renaissance work, it was captured by pirates during the reign of Carlos V while being transported to its Spanish buyer; when it was finally retrieved, the king awarded it to the city by royal edict.

The English Cemetery

Flanked by carved stone rampant lions, the **English Cemetery**, 150m northeast of Málaga's bullring (Mon–Fri 9am–5pm, Sat & Sun 10.30am–12.30pm; contributions welcome) dates from an era when gunboats flying Union Jacks held the world in awe. This did not, however, disturb the Spanish authorities from their post-*Reconquista* custom of denying Christian burial to all "infidels" unlucky enough to die on Iberian turf. British Protestants – who were included in this grouping – suffered the indignity after death of burial upright in the sand till their necks below the tide line. Málaga's expatriate population, which increased during the early nineteenth century, was, understandably, not amused when some of these "shore burials" were washed up on the beach or even seen bobbing on the waves. Thus in 1830 the British consul, William Mark, finally persuaded the authorities to let him found the English Cemetery. In the early days, and to get the place established, it seems that Mark pursued corpses with the zeal of a body-snatcher, hardly waiting for the deceased to expire before carting them off to the new graveyard. Traveller Richard Ford, whose wife's frailty was his original reason for coming to Spain, became alarmed when Mark began to make overtures. "Hearing of my wife's ill health, he tried all in his power to get me to Málaga to have a pretty female specimen in his sepulchral museum," he wrote to a friend.

The cemetery itself, once an isolated site overlooking the sea but now enveloped by urban sprawl, is still nevertheless a leafy and tranquil oasis. Follow the path from the Paseo de Reding up to the modest red stone **church of St George** where, just before it, stands the sepulchre of William Mark. Further up the hill you'll see the original **walled cemetery** containing the oldest graves, among them a number studded with seashells (an ancient symbol of immortality), marking the passing of child victims of fever and consumption, the scourge of that age.

Alongside the old cemetery's eastern wall the tombstone of Gamel Woolsey, poet and wife of **Gerald Brenan** and author of *Malaga Burning* (see p.606), is inscribed with a poignant message from Shakespeare's *Cymbeline*: "Fear no more the heat o' the sun." In 2001 the remains of her husband were finally placed in a grave alongside hers. The writer's epitaph is eloquently laconic: "RIP Gerald Brenan, Escritor Inglés, Amigo de España." Many of the other tombstones dotted around the cemetery with their dedications to wives, loyal servants and men of military zeal, most of them in English, make fascinating reading.

Due to funding problems in recent years the cemetery's future has been been thrown into doubt and burials are no longer allowed. A booklet *The English Cemetery at Malaga* by Marjorie Grice-Hutchinson (herself buried here in 2003) gives a detailed history and is on sale at the gatehouse, with proceeds going to the cemetery's upkeep.

Nuestra Señora de la Victoria and other churches

Sited on the spot where Fernando and Isabel pitched their tent during the 1487 siege of Málaga, **Nuestra Señora de la Victoria** (Mon–Fri 10am–noon & 5.30–7.30pm; €2), at the north end of c/de la Victoria, is, after the cathedral, Málaga's most prestigious church, where the city's Virgin patron is venerated. The fifteenth-century building was substantially rebuilt in the seventeenth century by the Count of Buenavista, whose remains, along with those of his descendants, lie in an eerie **crypt** decorated with symbolic stucco skeletons and skulls. Above, the main altar's centrepiece is an image of the Virgin in a *camerín* attributed to Pedro de Mena. Other interesting churches in the central zone incude the **Iglesia de Santiago** (where Picasso was christened), c/Granada, with an original fifteenth-century Mudéjar tower – note the intricate *sebka* brickwork reminiscent of the Giralda in Sevilla – and the **Iglesia de San Juan**, c/San Juan 3, founded in 1487, with the addition of a curious Baroque tower-portal.

Jardín Botánico La Concepción

A pleasant trip out of town if you want to escape the centre for a few hours is to the remarkable **Jardín Botánico La Concepción** (guided tours Tues–Sat: April–Sept 9.30am–8.30pm; Oct–March 9.30am–4pm; last visit 90min before closing; €4), the city's botanical garden 3km out of Málaga at La Concepción. Among the finest in Spain, the gardens were originally designed in the 1850s by Amalia Loring, granddaughter of the British consul, and only purchased in 1990 by Málaga city council, since when they have been converted into the present tropical gardens. Beneath the thirty species of soaring palms, waving pines and lofty eucalyptus, you'll find yellow-flowering acacia, violet-blooming jacaranda and all kinds of exotic blooms trying to steal the show. There are trees of all shapes and continents, such as the Australian banyan with its serpentine aerial roots, giant sequoias, and a variety of bamboos, all to be seen on any one of the five guided itineraries.

To get there by car, take the A45 north out of Málaga, turning off at Km166, and follow signs for the "Jardín Botánico". Departing from the north side of the Alameda, bus #61 will drop you at the gates on Saturday, Sunday and public holidays, but on weekdays it will drop you at its terminus, leaving a ten-minute walk. Another way of visiting the garden by bus is to use the Malagatour sightseeing bus (see p.76), which has a stop here. A taxi ride to La Concepción will cost about €8 one-way from the centre.

Eating

Málaga has a justified reputation for its splendid signature seafood platter, *fritura malagueña* (fried mixed fish). You'll find many fish restaurants grouped around the Alameda, and some of the town's big names cluster near the bullring and on La Malagueta seafront. Many of the more typically *malagueño* places are in the eastern seafront suburbs of Pedrogalejo and El Palo, served by bus #11 from the Paseo del Parque. On the seafront *paseo* at **Pedregalejo**, almost all of the cafés and restaurants serve terrific fish. Further on, **El Palo** is an even better place to eat, with a beach and fishing huts. Most of Málaga's non-seafood restaurants are hardly in the same league, but we've listed some places where the food is well above average for the price.

Plaza Merced and cathedral area

Antonio Fernando Lesseps 7. Popular small restaurant serving well prepared *malagueño* dishes such as *pepitorio de pollo* (chicken with almonds) with an outdoor terrace in an atmospheric cul-de-sac off the north end of c/Nueva; *menú* for around €12.

Cañadu Plaza de la Merced 21. A vegetarian option serving a good selection of salad and pasta-based dishes accompanied by organic wines and beers. There's a *menú* for €8.40.

Clandestino c/Niño de Guevara 3. Popular café-diner serving a variety of salads, pasta and other dishes with an Italian slant.

El Vegetariano de la Alcazabilla c/Pozo del Rey 5, off c/Alcazabilla. Good vegetarian restaurant serving soup, cheese, salads and pasta-based dishes in a cosy atmosphere. Main dishes €9–12; *menú* €9.

Il Laboratorio Plaza San Pedro de Alcántara, off c/Carretería. Great little Italian-style pizzeria-trattoria

serving (besides pizzas) salads and daily specials. Has small outdoor terrace under the trees in this charming plazuela.

La Taberna del Obispo Plaza del Obispo 1. Here the location upstages the food and drink – this little square is a delight on a summer's evening where the imposing cathedral frontage soars above terrace diners. Decent salads and snacks at economical prices.

Mesón Gibralfaro Pasaje Chinitas 6. Central and inexpensive restaurant serving *platos combinados*, salads and variety of *jamones* until after midnight.

Restaurante Tormes c/San Agustín 13. Decent meat and fish restaurant with terrace close to the Museo Picasso. They offer a tasty paella (for two) for €20 and also do a veggie version; main dishes €7–14.

Alameda Principal and Río Guadalmedina

Al-Yamal c/Blasco de Garay 3 ☎952 21 20 46. Good Moroccan restaurant serving up pricey but

---

Convento dulces

Many convents throughout Andalucía and Spain are in the business of supporting their orders by making **convent dulces**: cakes and pastries that they can sell to the community. Many recipes date back to the Arabs, who used rich combinations of eggs, almonds, sugar and honey to concoct their Moorish goodies. Each convent guards its recipes jealously, and many are so good that they supply local restaurants. The **sherry manufacturers** also had an influence on the development of *convent dulces*, for they traditionally used egg whites to clarify their wines and donated the leftover yolks to the nuns. This is the origin of many egg yolk-based creations such as *tocino de cielo* (Andalucía's richest flan) and *yemas* (sweet cakes), two of the region's most popular pastries.

In most convents you pay your money and are served with the sweets of your choice through a *torno* – a kind of revolving dumb waiter – which means you never see the nun who serves you. In Málaga the nuns at the Abadía (Abbey) of Santa Ana, c/Cister 11 (near the entrance to the Alcazaba), sell their *dulces* between 9am and 1pm. Specialities are coconut and quince cakes.

authentic meat in spicy sauces – *cordero* (lamb) *couscous* is a house special. Good selection of Moroccan wines. Main dishes €12–17. Closed Sun.

Bar Los Pueblos c/Atarazanas, opposite the *mercado*. Simple workers' place, serving satisfying food all day – bean soups and *estofados* are their speciality, while the gazpacho is served in half-pint glasses.

Casa Vicente c/Comisario. Lively *marisquería* in a narrow alley on the northern side of the Alameda. The similar *Bar El Puerto* next door is also good.

El Legado Celestial c/Peregrino 2 at the back of the *Correo*. Delightful vegetarian and vegan self-service restaurant with an Asian slant. The menu includes a large selection of salads and a dozen or so hot dishes as well as some tempting desserts; standard charge of €8. Drinks are squeezed juices (their lemon, orange, apple and carrot cocktail is recommended) and teas, but no alcohol.

Plaza de Toros and La Malagueta

Adolfo Paseo Marítimo 12 ☎ 95 260 19 14. One of the city's two Michelin-starred flagship restaurants, with a creative approach (the whole menu changes every four months) to cooking both meat and seafood dishes. There's a *menú de degustación* for around €45. Closed Sun.

Antonio Martín Paseo Marítimo 16 ☎ 95 222 73 98. One of Málaga's most celebrated fish restaurants, over a century old and the traditional haunt of *matadores* celebrating their successes in the nearby bullring. Expensive, but probably the best in town for *fritura malagueña*. Has a great sea-view terrace; main dishes €11–20.

Café de París c/Vélez Málaga 8 ☎ 95 222 50 43. One of Málaga's top restaurants for sampling *la cocina malagueña* at its creative very best, under the direction of Michelin-rosetted chef José Carlos García. Dining à la carte doesn't come cheap but there's a *menú de mercado* on

weekday lunch times for €40 and a *menú de degustación* for about €70. House specialities include *rodaballo salavaje con arroz negro* (turbot). Closed Sun & Mon.

Refectorium c/Cervantes 8, near the Plaza de Toros ☎ 95 221 89 90. Stylish, medium-priced, mainly fish restaurant where the *ajo blanco*, *fritura malagueña*, *urta* (sea bream) and *pez espada* (swordfish) are mouthwateringly tasty. A small bar also serves outstanding tapas. Main dishes €12–20.

Sal Gorda Avda. Canovas de Castillo 12. Excellent little *raciónes* (and *media raciónes*) bar-restaurant serving up a mouthwatering range of seafood and shellfish. Their *arroz marinero* at €26 (for two) is recommended. Also offers outstanding Asturian *sidra* (cider) on draught.

Out of the centre

Bar-Restaurante Palacios c/Eslava 4. Plain, honest food at bargain prices (*menú* €9) in a vibrant *comedor popular* with friendly waiters; specialities include *jamón iberico*, fish *surtido* and a mean paella.

El Tintero El Palo. Right at the far end of the seafront, just before the *Club Náutico* (stay on bus #11 and ask for "El Tintero"), this is a huge beach restaurant where the waiters charge around with plates of fish (all costing the same for a plate) and you shout for, or grab, anything you like. Haute cuisine it's not, but it's great fun and among the more worthy choices are *mero* (grouper) and *rosada* (rockfish).

Parador de Málaga–Gibralfaro Monte de Gibralfaro ☎ 95 222 19 02. Superior terrace dining with spectacular views over the coast and town, the parador's restaurant specializes in *malagueño* fish and meat dishes. Definitely worth a splurge, or try the *menú* (€31 dinner, €23.50 lunch) for excellent value. Book ahead if you want a table with a view. See also p.77.

Drinking

Málaga has a variety of places to **drink**, from bustling breakfast cafés for *churros* or fresh *cruasanes* (croissants) and coffee to atmospheric bars where you can while away an evening. The best of the breakfast places are clustered around the Atarazanas market, where the daily bustle starts at dawn. **Bars** for more serious drinking – usually with tapas thrown in – are concentrated north of the Alameda and around the cathedral. A number of traditional bars serve the sweet **Málaga wine**, made from muscatel grapes and dispensed from huge barrels; other options include the new, incredibly sweet wine, Pedriot, and the much more palatable Seco Añejo, which has matured for a year.

Cafés

Bar Central East side of Plaza de la Constitución. This venerable institution has been one of the city's favourite meeting places for generations and has the best terrace for people watching on this focal pedestrianized square. Serves tapas and also has an enticing cake counter. A recent refurb has (thankfully) preserved its unique character and there's a fascinating photo history on the walls inside.

Café Lepanto c/Larios 7. This smart central café with an outdoor terrace is the perfect place for afternoon tea or coffee and they cook up a magnificent array of tempting *pasteles* to accompany the beverages.

🏃 **Casa Aranda** c/Herrería del Rey, just east of the market. One of the best of the market cafés, renowned for its excellent *churros*, served at outside tables. There are actually two bars here, one each side of the alley, but owned by the same family and operating as one.

Casa Mira c/Larios 5. This is the place where *malagueños* flock on summer nights for the best ice creams in town.

El Jardín c/Canon s/n, directly behind the cathedral. Nice place for breakfast *café* and *pasteles*, with a fountain, garden and cathedral view fronting outdoor tables. Does *platos combinados* later in the day, and in the evening transforms into a piano bar with a vaguely Viennese ambience.

El Viajero c/Santiago 8, near the Iglesia de Santiago. Relaxed café with a travelling theme; mounts exhibitions on its walls by travel photographers.

La Tetería c/San Agustín 21. Cosy Moroccan tearoom almost opposite the Museo Picasso serving a wide range of herbal and Oriental teas.

Tetería Barraka c/Horno 10, close to the Museo de Artes y Tradiciones Populares. Another excellent Moroccan teahouse and confectioner's with an authentic *ambiente marroquí*. The *Tetería Zouk*, c/García Briz 3, slightly west of here, is a similar place with a wide selection of home-made confections.

Bars and tapas bars

🏃 **Antigua Casa Guardia** corner of c/Pastora, on the Alameda. Great old nineteenth-century spit-and-sawdust bar. Picasso was a devotee of their wines, and a photo on the wall shows him toting one of the bar's *jarras*. Try the house *mejillónes* (mussels) or *cola de langosto* (lobster's tail) with Málaga wine.

Antigua Reja (aka Casa Barcenas) Plaza de Uncibay. Lively bar at the northern end of this popular square with a wide tapas and *raciónes* range.

Bar Lo Güeno c/Marín García 9, off c/Larios. Excellent and atmospheric tapas place; *pincho* (spicy shrimp) and *habas* (broad beans with black sausage) are specials. They've recently opened a small restaurant sited immediately opposite.

🏃 **Bar Orellana** Moreno Monroy 5. Down a small side street off the east side of c/Marques de Larios close to Plaza Constitución, this is one of Málaga's very best and friendliest tapas bars. Tasty house specials include *atún mechada* (tuna) and *calamaritos* (squid in batter).

Bodegas Quitapeñas (aka La Manchega) c/Marín García 4. Another fine old drinking den with many tapas for under €1.50; *jibias guisadas* (stewed cuttlefish) is a speciality.

Cafetería Axarquía Alameda Principal 36. Businesslike bar near the Guadalmedina bridge with a decent tapas selection and a good value *menú* for €7. Also does breakfast *chocolate y churros*.

Come y Caña c/Cervantes 8. Popular and stylish tapas and *raciónes* bar which also does *sartenes* (fried dishes) and has a terrace fronting the bullring.

🏃 **El Pimpi** c/Granada 62. Cavernous and hugely popular bodega-style bar serving up tasty *vino dulce* by the glass or bottle. Do a bit of celebrity-spotting on their wall of photos (including a young Antonio Banderas) and don't miss a superb terrace (with Alcazaba view) out the back. A great place to start the evening.

La Dehesa de Santa María c/Cister 8. Located near the cathedral, this is a branch of a popular tapas bar chain; whilst not up to the standards of the better places in town, it certainly offers value for money, with every *tapa* costing around a euro.

La Quesería Sanchez Pastor 2, slightly west of Plaza de la Constitución. Some meat dishes are served but, as its name tells you, cheese is king here and a *tabla* (cheeseboard) for two costs €7. Try the prizewinning Payoyo cheese from the mountains of Cádiz.

Lizarran Sanchez Pastor 2, almost opposite *La Quesería* (see above). Part of a Basque chain of bars serving *pinxtos* – tapas on a stick. They claim to have more than 300 varieties to choose from and the bill is calculated by counting up the number of sticks (no cheating) on your plate.

Mesón Las Garrafas c/Mendez Núñez 5, off Plaza de Uncibay. Fine and atmospheric century-old bar-bodega with tiled walls, stacked barrels and good *fino*. Tasty fish and meat tapas and *raciónes*.

Mesón Mariano c/Granados s/n, off Plaza de Uncibay. Another excellent tapas stop with a tiny (mid-priced) restaurant serving a daily special (such as *cazuela de pescado*) for around €7.50. Try their *ensaladilla malagueño* with potatoes, oranges and cod.

Nightlife

You'll find most of Málaga's nightlife northeast of the cathedral around **Plaza de Uncibay** and **calles Granada** and **Beatas**, and **Plaza de la Merced** and **Plaza Uncibay**. In the summer months there's also a scene in **Malagueta**, south of the bullring. At weekends and holidays dozens of youth-oriented disco-bars fill the crowded streets in these areas, and over the summer – though it's dead out of season – the scene spreads out along the seafront to the suburb of **Pedregalejo**. Here the streets just behind the beach host most of the action, and dozens of discos and smaller music bars lie along and off the main street, Juan Sebastián Elcano. Málaga's daily paper, *Sur*, is good for local entertainment **listings** and there's a weekly English edition.

Anden Plaza de Uncibay. Music-bar that's open till very late and attracts a wild crowd; Fri & Sat only.

Asúcar Junction of c/Juan de Padilla & c/Lazcano west of Plaza de Uncibay. The place to come for salsa in Málaga.

Calle de Bruselas Plaza de la Merced 16. A laid-back, largely gay Belgian-style bar with lively terrace that stays open into the small hours.

Cervecería Brow Beer c/Ángel 3 off c/Granada. Bar specializing in a wide variety of world beers. Serious drinkers at midday, more youthful revellers at night. Also serves tapas.

Cosa Nostra c/Lazcano 5, slightly west of Plaza de Uncibay. Music bar with mafia-theme decor and regular live bands. Open Thurs–Sun 11pm–6am.

La Botellita adjacent to *Luna Rubia*, Pasaje Mitjana, off c/Lezcano slightly west of Plaza Uncibay. Wild place packed to the rafters with young local revellers dancing to the tunes of the Spanish top 40. Open till late.

Luna Rubia Pasaje Mitjana 4, slightly west of Plaza Uncibay and almost facing *Asúcar* (see above). Wide range of international sounds in a place that's open till dawn. At the end of this alley, the tiny Plaza Marqués Vado del Maestre is filled with drinking bars and plenty of night-time action.

Morrissey's Irish Pub Plaza del Siglo 3. Irish-style bar that occasionally stages live gigs; popular with a foreign crowd.

Picaro de la Habana c/Madre de Dios 11, off the north end of Plaza de la Merced. Drinking and dancing to salsa and other Latin sounds.

Puerta Oscura c/Molina Lario 5 near the cathedral. Slightly incongruous classical music bar – sometimes with live performers – which also mounts art exhibitions; serves cocktails, ices and baguettes, and opens until 3am. T-shirts are definitely a no-no here.

Siempre Así c/Convalecientes 5, north of Plaza Uncibay. Another late bar playing Spanish rock and techno.

White c/José Denis Belgrano 19. Slightly cheesy *ambiente*, this is one of the few options for midweek clubbing in the old town. Surprisingly good sounds are a mix of R'n'B and hip-hop.

Flamenco

Genuine **flamenco** is hard to come by and the few shows there are in Málaga aren't up to much. Many of the *peñas* where it is performed are private, but you could try the venues below for something approaching the real thing. Many flamenco events (generally free) happen in and around the town throughout the year and the Turismo Municipal (see p.76) is the best source of information on these. Two blocks south of the Plaza de Toros, the *bar-restaurante* **Doña Pepa**, c/Vélez-Málaga 6, has a flemenco show at weekends after 10pm. The flamenco centre *Kelipe*, c/Peña 11 (☎95 100 37 84; €10), puts on shows at 9pm on Thursdays, Fridays and Saturdays. There's a good atmosphere and the price includes a drink and a *tapa*.

Shopping

El Corte Inglés, Avda. de Andalucía 4, is a great **department store** and their supermarket has a terrific selection of wines and spirits. La Mallorquina, Plaza Felix Saenz (near the market), is also a good place to pick up *malagueño* cheeses, wines, almonds and dried fruit. The main **shopping area** for designer labels and shoes is c/Marqués de Larios together with its surrounding streets. For **books and music**, El Corte Inglés stocks most foreign newspapers and periodicals, though Librerías Prometeo y Proteo, c/Puerta Buenaventura 3, at the eastern end of c/Carretería, is the city's biggest bookshop with competition now being offered by the more central Libreria Luces, Alameda Principal 16 (north side). Málaga's best travel and outdoor bookshop is Mapas y Compañia, c/Compañia 33, west of Plaza de la Constitución. IGN **walking maps**, as well as 1:50,000 Mapas Cartografia Militar (military maps), are sold by Indice (Mon–Fri 8.30am–2pm, @www.ine.es), c/Panaderos 2 just north of the Alameda Principal, and at Mapas y Compañia (see above).

Listings

Airport Málaga's airport (☏ 95 204 88 38) is Andalucía's busiest and set to get busier once its new terminal is completed in 2010. See "Arrival" (p.73) for details on transport to and from the airport.

Banks and exchange Numerous places all over town have ATMs/cash machines, especially along c/Marqués de Larios and on the Plaza de la Constitución. El Corte Inglés (see above) will also change currency free of charge.

Consulates Ireland, Galería Santa Monica, Fuengirola ☏ 95 247 51 08; UK, Edificio Eurocom, c/Mauricio Moro Pareto 2 ☏ 95 235 23 00; USA, Avda. Juan Goméz 8, Fuengirola ☏ 95 247 48 91.

Ferries Daily sailings to the Spanish enclave of Melilla in Morocco (7hr). Tickets from Trasmediterranea, Estación Maritima in the harbour, south of Plaza de la Marina (☏ 902 45 46 45, @www .trasmediterranea.es).

Football After spending a few seasons in Division 2, in 2008 C.F. Málaga were promoted back into the top flight. Games are at La Rosaleda stadium, Paseo de Martiricos s/n, at the northern end of

the Río Guadalmedina. Tickets can be purchased from the stadium (☏ 95 261 42 10, @www .malagacf.es).

Hospital Hospital Carlos Haya, Avda. Carlos Haya, 2km west of the city centre ☏ 951 29 00 00. A handy 24hr pharmacy, Farmacia Caffarena is located on the Alameda at no. 2, near the junction with c/Marqués de Larios ☏ 95 221 28 58.

Internet Free wi-fi connection is available in the vicinity of the Teatro Cervantes and along the central c/Larios. Conventional cybercafés near the centre include Meeting Point, Plaza de la Merced 20 (daily 10am–11pm) and Cibercafé Teatro Romano, c/Alcazabilla s/n (10am–midnight).

Left luggage There are lockers and a *consigna* at the train station (daily 6.15am–00.45am), and lockers at the bus station (daily 6.30am–11pm).

Police The Policía Local are at Avda. de la Rosaleda 19 (☏ 95 12 65 00); in emergencies dial ☏ 092 (local police) or ☏ 091 (national).

Post office Avda. de Andalucía 1, on the left across the bridge at the end of the Alameda. Mon–Fri 8.30am–8pm, Sat 8.30am–2pm.

El Chorro Gorge and around

Some 50km north of Málaga, the **Garganta del Chorro** (El Chorro Gorge) is an amazing place. Located to the south of the Embalse del Guadalhorce (see p.91) it's impressive in itself – an immense cleft cut through a vast limestone massif by the Río Guadalhorce – with daunting walls of rock as high as 400m along its three-kilometre length. But the real attraction is a concrete catwalk, **El Camino del Rey**, which threads the length of the gorge hanging precipitously halfway up its side. Built in the 1920s as part of a burgeoning hydroelectric scheme and opened by King Alfonso XIII who walked its whole length and gave it its name, it used to figure in all the guidebooks as one of the wonders of Spain. Today it's largely fallen into disrepair and since 2000 has been officially closed. However, at present, despite a few wobbly – and decidedly dangerous – sections (one tourist fell to her death in 1998), with random holes in the concrete through which you can see the gorge hundreds of feet below, it's still possible to walk much of its length (see box below) although if you are not an experienced climber you are strongly advised to go with someone who is. You will, nevertheless, need a head for heights, and at least a full day starting from Málaga. If you've neither, it's possible to get a glimpse of both gorge and *camino* from any of the trains going north from Málaga – the line, slipping in and out of tunnels, follows the river for quite a distance along the gorge, before plunging into a last long tunnel just before its head.

If you want to explore the gorge, head for **EL CHORRO**, served by a single daily direct train from Málaga (currently running at 6.45pm) with two daily trains in the opposite direction (9am & 3pm). There are no bus services from Málaga but there is a **bus** from nearby Álora at 12.30pm (Mon & Fri only), which is served by ten daily **trains** from Málaga. A taxi from Álora to El Chorro costs about €20. The village is rapidly becoming a centre of outdoor activities for the gorge, particularly rock climbing, and there are a number of **accommodation** options. The village has an excellent shady **campsite** (☎95 249 52 44; ⓦwww.alberguecampingelchorro.com) with pool, bar and restaurant, reached by heading downhill to your right for 400m from the station entrance. The campsite also rents out wood cabins sleeping up to six (❸). *Bar-Restaurante Garganta del Chorro* (☎95 249 72 19, ⓦwww.lagarganta.com; ❹), at the southern end of the station platform, offers

---

Walking the Camino del Rey

Walking the **Camino del Rey** catwalk is a risky proposition whichever way you decide to do it, and it should not be attempted if you are of a nervous disposition or are without a very good head for heights. Due to the obvious dangers involved, the safest way (and the one we strongly recommend) to do the Camino is on an **organized trip** with expert climber Christine Hofer at *La Campana* (see p.91), who uses ropes to ensure maximum safety. Repeated accidents and even deaths led Endesa, the electricity company who are proprietors of the structure, to cut access to the catwalk from the El Chorro (southern) and Embalse (northern) ends. This was intended to prevent hikers from using it. The middle section, however, is still roughly intact – though in a terrible state of repair – and this can be accessed from the central part of the gorge, although you will have to return the way you came due to the demolition of each end of the catwalk mentioned above.

A safer way to view the Camino on your own – and easily accessed by car or a fine **walk** in itself – is to follow the road from El Chorro train station, signposted "Pantano de Guadalhorce", reached by crossing over the dam and turning right, then following the road north along the lake towards the hydroelectric plant. After 8km turn right at a junction to reach – after 2km – the bar-restaurant *El Mirador*, poised above a road tunnel and overlooking the various lakes and reservoirs of the Guadalhorce scheme. From the bar (where you should leave any transport), a dirt track on the right, just south of the tunnel entrance, heads towards the gorge. Follow this and take the first track on the right after about 700m. This climbs for some 2km to where it splits into two small trails. The trail to the left leads you to a magnificent viewpoint over the gorge from where you can see the Camino del Rey clinging to the rock face. The right-hand track climbs to an obvious peak, the Pico de Almochon, with more spectacular views, this time over the lakes of the Embalse del Guadalhorce. On both walks you'll need to return the way you came.

▲ The Camino del Rey

spacious and reasonably priced air-conditioned apartments inside a converted mill; there's also a pool and it has its own **restaurant**. At the opposite end of the station platform there's a grocery shop and a couple of bars, including *Bar Isabel*, which also has a few basic rooms (☎95 249 50 04; ❶). For a more tranquil option, follow the signs from the station along a track for 2km to the *Finca La Campana* (☎mobile 626963942, ⓦ www.el-chorro.com), a farmhouse set in rural surroundings, with an economical bunkhouse (€12 per person), en-suite cottages with kitchen and two or four beds (❷) and a campsite. The farm has a pool and a small shop where you can hire out climbing equipment and mountain bikes, and they offer climbing and caving courses as well as horseriding and guided tours along the Camino del Rey.

From the station it's about 12km to some attractive lakes and reservoirs, such as the **Embalse del Guadalhorce**. Recent years of prolonged drought have dramatically lowered the water levels, making this area a great deal less attractive than in the past, but the lakes are often swimmable. You can camp along the rocky shores; alternatively, the village of Ardales (see p.92), 4km beyond the lake, has shops, bars, a *hostal* and two daily buses to and from Ronda.

Bobastro

A few kilometres beyond El Chorro, amid some of the wildest scenery in the whole peninsula, lies **BOBASTRO**, the mountain-top remains of a Mozarabic fortified settlement. Famous as the isolated eyrie of colourful ninth-century rebel Ibn Hafsun (see box, p.92), the castle was said to be the most impregnable in all Andalucía, but only a ruined **church**, carved into an enormous boulder, remains of the once-great fortress. Situated outside the original fortified area, and below some cave dwellings of uncertain date, the church is typically Mozarabic in style, its nave and two aisles separated by horseshoe-arched arcades. The transept, and a deep apse chapel flanked by two side chapels, can clearly be seen, making the edifice one of the few identifiable traces of building from the period. Nearby and to the west is the **Cueva de Doña Trinidad** with

Ibn Hafsun

Born near Ronda around 860, **Ibn Hafsun** was a *muwallad* (of mixed Christian-Arab parentage) who, after killing a man, fell out with the Umayyad caliphate at Córdoba and resorted to a life of brigandage. Gathering around him a formidable army, he built his stronghold at Bobastro, and from 880–917 scored a number of spectacular victories over the many Umayyad forces sent to defeat him. At the height of his power Hafsun controlled an area between the straits of Gibraltar in the west and Jaén in the east. His defence of the poor against excessive Umayyad taxation and forced labour further served to increase the popularity of this Robin Hood-style figure, especially among his fellow *muwalladin* who believed they were getting a raw deal from their pure-blooded Arab rulers. After he converted to Christianity in 899, the church at Bobastro was constructed to receive his remains, which were duly interred there upon his death in 917. When Abd ar-Rahman III finally conquered Bobastro in 927, he exhumed the body of Hafsun and hung it on a gibbet outside the Alcázar in Córdoba as a "salutary warning to imitators and a pleasant spectacle to believers (true Muslims)".

paleolithic cave paintings; guided visits to see them are organized by the museum at Ardales (see below).

You can **get to Bobastro** from El Chorro by crossing the dam from the train station and turning right along the road to *El Mirador* (see box, p.90). After a couple of kilometres a signed turn-off for the site indicates a twisting 2km route to another sign (marked "Iglesia Mozárabe") pointing to a slope with steps on the left. Leave any transport here and follow the path for 400m through the pinewoods to the site. Back on the main road and continuing west to just beyond the *El Mirador* restaurant will allow you to view the impressive **dam** at the junction of the two great reservoirs, with the marble table and throne where Alfonso XIII signed the completion of the work on May 21, 1921. Across the dam and sited on the banks of the *embalse* is an attractive **hotel**, *La Posada del Conde*, Pantano del Chorro 16 (☎95 211 24 11, ⓦwww .hoteldelconde.com; ➍) where some rooms have a view over the "lake"; there's also a good **restaurant**.

Ardales

At the southern point of the third of the lakes that comprise the Guadalteba–Guadalhorce reservoir, the compact town of **ARDALES** tumbles down the hill below La Peña, a rocky outcrop topped by remains of the Iberian settlement of Turóbriga as well as a Roman fort and ruined Moorish *alcázar*. On the way up to the summit, look out for the fifteenth-century Mudéjar **Iglesia de la Virgen de los Remedios** with its distinctive, partly tiled, tower. When you reach the top, it becomes clear that the tower was the minaret of the former mosque. The interior also has Moorish arches dividing the nave and side aisles, the right of which has the mosque's original *mihrab* oriented towards Mecca. To see the interior – plus the remains of the Roman fort and Alcázar accessed via the church – call at c/Iglesia 48, slightly uphill from the church, for the key. The **Museo de la Historia y las Tradiciones** facing the bridge as you enter the village (June–Sept Tue–Sat 9am–2pm, Oct–May Tues–Sat 10am–2pm & 4–6pm; ☎95 245 80 46; €1) has Roman and Moorish archeological finds, sections dealing with local traditions and history, as well as copies of the rock paintings in the nearby paleolithic Cueva de Doña Trinidad (see p.91). The curator will also provide information on visits to see the cave (guided tours

Tues, Thurs, Sat & Sun 10.30am; 2hr; €5). Visits need to be booked and confirmed in advance with Señora Isabel Berrocal by phone (museum number) or email (€informacion@cuevadeardales.com). If the museum is closed (during the official hours) enquire at the **Ayuntamiento**, set on the wide and animated central Plaza San Isidro, around which most of the activity in Ardales revolves.

The same plaza is also where you'll find a lively **bar** scene – *Bar El Mellizo* is the meeting place for the locals and *Bar Millan*, across the square, does tapas. For something more substantial to **eat**, head for *La Alternativa*, a restaurant on the same plaza close to the Ayuntamiento, which offers *platos combinados* and *raciónes* and has a pleasant terrace on the square. Across the bridge at the bottom of the village *Hostal-Restaurante El Cruce* serves a good-value *menú* and has en-suite **rooms** (☎95 245 90 12; ❷). *Casa Marcos*, just along the tree-lined main street at c/San Isidro 31, is a *pastelería* renowned for its tasty *roscos de almendras* (almond cakes).

Six kilometres east of Ardales along the MA444 lies the village's scenic "lakeside" **campsite** (actually next to a reservoir), *Camping Parque Ardales* (☎95 211 24 01, ⓦwww.campingparqueardales.com), which also rents out apartments sleeping up to four (❹) and offers a variety of activities including canoeing on the lake. There's no bus to the campsite but a taxi from Ardales will cost about €12 (any of the bars should be able to arrange this for you).

Carratraca

Five kilometres south of Ardales, and reached via a turn-off from the A357 Málaga road, lies the village of **CARRATRACA**, once famous throughout Europe for its **sulphur spa**, now extensively refurbished as part of a five-star hotel (see below). Although the baths date back to the days of the Greeks and Romans, it wasn't until the nineteenth century that Carratraca became one of the foremost spas in Europe, and a gathering point for the continent's aristocracy. During its heyday the *balneario* (spa) attracted kings, princesses and literary bigwigs such as Lord Byron, Alexandre Dumas and Rainer Maria Rilke. The three *Casinos*, where these socialites used to while away their time between plunges in the stinking, sulphurous waters which gush from the rocks, are long gone. However, two wonderfully elegant, eighteenth-century open-air (now glassed-in) pools circled by classical Tuscan columns have survived intact, and now form the refurbished spa's centrepiece.

Carratraca's other sights include a Regency-style **Ayuntamiento**, on the edge of the village, formerly the residence of Doña Trinidad Grund, a local benefactor who donated funds for the excavation of the cave near Bobastro which bears her name. She also provided the backing for the curious **bullring** nearby, hacked out of solid rock and scene of the village Passion play during Semana Santa.

Practicalities

The royal palace built in Carratraca by the tyrannical King Fernando VII early in the nineteenth century to accommodate himself and his retinue while visiting the spa (although he probably never used it) has now been incorporated into the luxurious *Villa Padierna*, c/Antonio Rioboó 9 (☎95 248 95 42, ⓦwww.thermasdecarratraca.com; ❼), an opulent hotel and spa complex with its own dietary restaurant. You can still use the spa without staying at the hotel, however, and a basic fifteen-minute soak will set you back about €15 although other treatments (including various types of massage) are much pricier. Just along from the baths at the opposite end of the accommodation scale, *Casa Pepa* (☎95 245 80 49; ❷) also offers basic **rooms** with and without bath, plus meals for guests. Places **to eat and drink** include *Venta El Trillo*, on the main road as you enter from Ardales, with *Bar Venta Martillo* and *Venta El Punto* nearby, all of which offer decent *menús*.

Teba

About 15km north of Ardales, the village of **TEBA** spreads itself below a hill crowned by a striking ruined **Moorish castle** (open site) built on Roman foundations. There's a well-preserved dungeon in the castle, but you'll need a torch to find your way around. The castle battlements give wonderful **views** over the surrounding countryside – and you can also glimpse the tempting municipal **swimming pool** close by.

The plain below the castle was the site of a battle against the Moors that took place in 1331 when the forces of Alfonso XI recovered Teba for Christian Spain. In this battle fought Sir James Douglas, who had been commissioned by a dying **Robert Bruce** to carry the Scottish king's heart to the Holy Land "to be carried in battle against the enemies of Christ". Douglas took the long way round, via Spain, and ended up getting involved at the siege of Teba. He wore the royal heart in a silver case around his neck and – at a critical moment in the battle – to spur on his men he threw it into the fray and charged after it to his death. The well-travelled heart was then recovered and taken back to Scotland to be buried in Melrose Abbey, where it was rediscovered in 1996. Near the centre of the village, in the Plaza de España, a block of Scottish granite has been set up to mark Teba's illustrious connection with Robert Bruce and the exploits of Douglas; it was unveiled by one of Douglas's descendants in 1989.

Teba's other main sight is **Santa Cruz Real**, an eighteenth-century Baroque church at the western end of c/San Francisco, with quite a few surprises. The enormous triple-naved interior is divided by lofty Tuscan columns of red marble. Among the church's many treasures is a sixteenth-century **gold-plated cross** near the main altar that was given to the castle's church by Fernando and Isabel and is one of only two in the whole of Spain. When the castle was destroyed, the church's valuables were moved here. The **tesoro** (the church's treasure and valuables) contains some beautiful early sixteenth-century vestments embroidered in gold thread also donated (and probably partly made) by Isabel, who was an accomplished seamstress. To see the church, call (preferably 5–6pm) at the adjoining house of the *cura* who will open it up.

The town also has an interesting small **Museo Municipal** (Sat & Sun noon–2pm & 6–8pm; free) located inside the Ayuntamiento on Plaza de la Constitución. It displays artefacts from all periods of Teba's distinguished history including Iberian sculptures from the late first-millennium BC, a fine head of the emperor Tiberius and a superb carved pedestal from the Roman era as well as coins, ceramics and jewellery from the town's Visigothic and Moorish periods. On weekdays, if you call at the Ayuntamiento before 2pm they will open up the museum for you.

You'll find **places to stay** on and around the main thoroughfare c/San Francisco where, at no. 26, the *Hostal Sevillano* (☎95 274 80 11; ❷) has clean en-suite rooms above a **restaurant** with a good-value *menú*. The same street and the nearby Plaza de Andalucía have more places for eating and drinking. Some 3km south of Teba along the old Ronda road an elegant *cortijo* hotel is a step up in price and quality from anything else in Teba: the *Hotel Molino de las Pilas* (☎95 274 86 23, ⓦwww.molinodelaspilas.com; ❹) is housed in a nineteenth-century whitewalled farmhouse with stylish rooms and a restaurant located in the former olive oil mill, whose central feature is a gigantic 120-year-old wooden press.

About 3km to the east of the village lies the small but picturesque Garganta de Teba or **Teba Gorge**, where the oleander-fringed Río la Venta cuts through the limestone hills to join the reservoir. A haven for all kinds of butterflies, there's also plenty of birdlife along the riverbanks and the gorge is a nesting site for the Egyptian vulture and Bonelli's eagle, along with plenty of other varieties such as black kites and choughs. To reach the gorge, descend the unsigned track that leaves the roadside by the bridge over the Río la Venta on the edge of the reservoir.

Antequera and around

Sitting on two low hills in the valley of the Río Guadalhorce, **ANTEQUERA** is an attractive market town with some important ancient monuments and a clutch of fine churches. On the main train line to Granada and at the junction of roads heading inland to Córdoba, Granada and Seville, it's easy to get to, and makes a good day trip from Málaga, which lies 40km to the south. Travelling from Málaga, the bus takes you along the fast but largely uninteresting N331 *autovía*. If you're driving, it's far nicer to take the older, more picturesque road (MA424) that meanders through **Almogía**, a small hill town with tortuously narrow streets. It's a sleepy place, except on Friday – market day – when the

RESTAURANTS
El Angelote 5
Hospedería Coso San Francisco D
La Espuela 7
Plaza de Toros 1

TAPAS BARS
Bar-Cafetería A La Fuerza 3
Bar Chicón 6
Bar La Mandragora 4
Bar Numero Uno C
Café del Centro 2

ACCOMMODATION
Camas El Gallo I
Hospedería Coso San Francisco D
Hostal Reyes F
Hotel Casa del
  Conde de Pinofiel E
Hotel Colón G
Hotel Plaza San Sebastián H
Número Uno C
Parador de Antequera A
Pensión Toril B

ANTEQUERA

95

whole place spills over with shoppers: From Antequera itself a couple of enjoyable trips are to the vast **Parque Natural El Torcal** with its marvellous weathered limestone rock formations, and the important flamingo breeding grounds of **Fuente de Piedra**.

Arrival and information

Antequera's **RENFE station** (☎95 284 32 26) is 1km from the centre of town (no bus service) on Avda. Estacion. The bus from Málaga brings you closer in, disembarking at the **bus station** (☎95 284 19 57) near the bullring. From here the Alameda de Andalucía and its continuation the c/Infante Don Fernando – the effective centre of town – are within easy walking distance. For information on the town, or help with finding a room, head for the helpful **Turismo Municipal** (June–Sept Mon–Sat 11am–2pm & 5–8pm, Sun 11am–2pm; Oct–May Mon–Sat 10.30am–1.30pm & 4–7pm, Sun 11am–2pm ☎95 270 25 05, ⓦwww.turismoantequera.com) on Plaza San Sebastián alongside the church of the same name. They can also provide information on Torcal and details of houses to rent in the surrounding countryside. A private **tourist office** (Mon–Sat 9am–2pm, ☎95 270 00 05), which works closely with the above, is located nearby on Plaza Coso Viejo s/n, next door to the *El Angelote* restaurant. **Internet** access is available at Las Americas, c/Encarnación 15, northeast of the Plaza de San Sebastián (Mon–Sat 9.30am–2.30pm & 4.30–11pm).

Accommodation

You shouldn't have a problem finding a **place to stay**, as demand tends to be low and the generally good-value room prices reflect this. Most hotels have either their own garage (for which you usually pay extra) or can advise on street parking. The nearest **campsite** is at El Torcal (see p.100).

🏃 **Camas El Gallo** c/Nueva 2 ☎95 284 21 04. Very friendly place offering simple spotless rooms (with fans in summer) and equally pristine shared bathrooms. ❶

🏃 **Hospedería Coso San Francisco** c/Calzada 25 ☎95 284 00 14, ⓦwww .cososanfrancisco.com. Comfortable a/c en-suite rooms with TV plus a friendly welcome make this a winner. Also has a very good restaurant. ❷

Hostal Reyes c/Tercia 4 ☎95 284 10 28. Pleasant and central en-suite rooms with a/c and TV. ❶

Hotel Casa del Conde de Pinofiel c/ Tercia 10 ☎ 95 284 24 64, ⓦwww.hotelcondepinofiel.com. Antequera's newest hotel occupies a striking eighteenth-century *casa-palacio* with well-equipped a/c rooms situated around an elegant patio complete with Baroque chapel. ❹

Hotel Colón c/Infante Don Fernando 31 ☎95 284 00 10, ⓦwww.castelcolon.com. This welcoming central hotel is another reliable choice for rooms with a/c and satellite TV. ❷

Hotel Plaza San Sebastián Plaza San Sebastián 4 ☎95 284 42 39. Attractive two-star hotel facing the church of San Sebastián offering well-equipped a/c rooms with satellite TV. ❸

Número Uno c/Lucena 40 ☎95 284 31 34 ⓦwww.hotelnumerouno.com. A relatively new hotel with pleasant a/c en-suite rooms with TV, plus a roof terrace above a popular bar-restaurant. ❷

Parador de Antequera Paseo García del Olmo s/n ☎95 284 02 61, ⓦwww.parador.es. A recently refurbished modern parador, to the north of the *plaza de toros*, with well-appointed rooms plus pleasant gardens and pool. ❺

Pensión Toril c/Toril 3 ☎95 284 31 84. This tranquil and pleasant *pensión* has rooms with and without bath arranged around two patios. Free parking. ❷

The Town

A bustling agricultural centre where farmers from the surrounding *vega* come to stock up on everything from tractor tyres to seeding attachments, Antequera has a modern appearance that belies its history. In Roman times

Anticaria ("ancient city") seems to have had a substantial population; much later, in 1410, the town was the first in Andalucía to fall to the Christian forces in the *Reconquista*.

Antequera divides into two zones: a **monumental quarter** situated at the foot of the hill dominated by the Alcazaba, and the mainly nineteenth-century **commercial sector** concentrated around the Alameda de Andalucía. This end of town is where modern Antequera works and plays, and there's not much in the way of sights, though the nineteenth-century bullring is worth a look. Probably the most famous sights, however, are the prehistoric **dolmen caves**, on the northern edge of town.

Antequera's annual **feria** happens during the third week in August, a harvest fiesta (*recolección*) with *corridas*, dancing and parades.

The Museo Municipal and San José

At the heart of the monumental quarter, the **Museo Municipal**, c/Coso Viejo s/n (Tues–Fri 10am–1.30pm & 4.30–6.30pm, Sat 10am–1.30pm, Sun 11am–1.30pm; hourly guided tours; €1), is located in a striking eighteenth-century ducal palace. It's just as well that the palace is worth visiting for itself, because the exhibits do little justice to the setting. Largely a hotchpotch of church vestments, silver plate and indifferent paintings, the collection is, however, distinguished by two works of sculpture: a fine first-century AD **Roman bronze** of a youth known as the *Efebo de Antequera*, and an eerily lifelike carving in wood of **St Francis of Assisi** by the seventeenth-century *andaluz* sculptor Pedro de Mena. More fragments of ancient statuary and tombstones are dotted around the courtyard, and a room on the ground floor devotes itself to the artwork of a modern painter born in Antequera, Cristóbal Toral.

To the east of the museum, on the way to the Alcazaba, the eighteenth-century **Carmelite nunnery of San José** on Plaza de las Descalzas has a good selection of *dulces*. The entrance is behind the small fountain. Inside, asking for a *surtido* (sampler) gets you a bit of everything. You won't see the nun who serves you, but, in a sign of changing times, she may ask you to pay first.

Nuestra Señora del Carmen

The nearby Cuesta de los Rojas climbs steeply to the Postigo de la Estrella, an old postern gate. To the east of this – and not to be missed – lies the seventeenth-century Mudéjar church of **Nuestra Señora del Carmen** (Mon–Sat 10am–2pm & 4–7pm, Sun 10am–2pm; €2), whose plain facade little prepares you for the eighteenth-century interior, painstakingly restored to its former glory. The main altar's sensational thirteen-metre-high **retablo** – one of the finest in Andalucía – is a masterly late-Baroque extravaganza of carved wood by Antonio Primo and Diego Márquez, its centrepiece a Virgin in a *camarín* flanked by a bevy of polychromed saints and soaring angels.

The Alcazaba

Further up Cuesta de los Rojas lies the refurbished medieval **Alcazaba**, with its thirteenth-century Islamic fortification, the **Torre del Homenaje** (Tues–Fri 10.30am–2pm & 4.30–6.30pm, Sat & Sun 10.30am–2pm; free). The first fortress to fall to the Christians during the Reconquest of the kingdom of Granada, the ruined Alcazaba now encloses a municipal garden, giving fine views over the town towards the curiously anthropoid **Peña de los Enamorados** (Lovers' Rock) resembling the profiled head of a sleeping giant. The outcrop acquired its name from two lovers (a Christian girl and a Muslim youth) during the Moorish period, who are said to have thrown themselves from the top when their parents forbade their marriage.

Adjoining the Alcazaba, the sixteenth-century **Arco de los Gigantes** preserves stones and inscriptions embedded in its walls that were rescued by antiquaries from the destruction of the Roman town in the same period.

East of the castle, in the spacious Plaza Alta, the sixteenth-century collegiate church of **Santa María** (Tues–Fri 10.30am–1.30pm & 4.30–6.30pm, Sat & Sun 10.30am–1.30pm; free) boasts a great Plateresque facade inspired by a Roman triumphal arch. Inside the church – which now serves as a concert hall – you'll also see a superb Mudéjar coffered ceiling.

Antequera's other churches

Walking from the Alcazaba back into the centre you pass a number of churches. The seventeenth-century **San Sebastián** (daily 9.30am–1pm & 7.30pm for service), in the elegant plaza of the same name, possesses a striking brick steeple that dominates the town. Note the carved angels and the tower's weather vane, El Angelote, which has the remains of Antequera's patron saint, Santa Euphemia, in a reliquary hung around its neck. The interior contains some beautifully carved choir stalls, as does the nearby eighteenth-century **San Agustín**, at the start of c/Infante Fernando. At the western end of this street and close to the Palacio Consistorial – a stylish seventeenth-century mansion now functioning as the Ayuntamiento (access to view patio during working hours) – lies the Renaissance church of **San Juan de Dios** (Tues–Fri 7am–9pm, Sun noon), constructed (or so Richard Ford maintained) almost entirely with stone taken from the demolition of what was a perfectly preserved Roman theatre. Slightly further away up a steep climb at the southern end of the town, the Plaza del Portichuelo has the flamboyant Baroque-Mudéjar **Capilla de la Virgen del Socorro** with a double tier of triple arches built to house Antequera's most revered image, Nuestra Señora del Socorro (Our Lady of Succour). The nearby white-walled Baroque chapel of **Santa María de Jesús**, with storks' nests in its belfry, is also worth a look. From a *mirador* behind the churches there are great views towards the Alcazaba and the surrounding hills.

The Plaza de Toros

The western end of town has little in the way of sights, though the nineteenth-century **Plaza de Toros** (museum Tues–Sat 10am–2pm & 4–7pm; Sun 10am–2pm; free), on the Alameda de Andalucía, is well worth a look – access is usually available to the ring when the restaurant (see p.99) is open. This bullring staged its first *corrida* on August 20, 1848, and whatever your views on bullfighting, it's difficult not to pick up on the atmosphere that the old place generates, especially when you view the amphitheatre from the *matador*'s position in the centre of the arena.

The dolmen caves

On the town's northern outskirts – an easy one-kilometre walk along the Granada road – lies a group of **prehistoric dolmens** (Tues–Sat 9am–6pm, Sun 9.30am–2.30pm; free), which rank among the most important in Spain. Now enclosed in a futuristic "dolmen park" with visitor centre, car park and a Centro de Interpretación (opening 2010), the grandest of these megalithic monuments is the **Cueva de Menga**, its roof formed by massive stone slabs, among them a 180-ton monolith. Dating from around 2500 BC, the columned gallery leading to an oval burial chamber was probably the final resting place of an important chieftain. On the last stone slab of the left wall (nearest the entrance) you'll see some engraved – and probably symbolic – forms; the star, however, is a later addition. A recently discovered **well** in the rear of the chamber probably dates from the Roman period. If you stand just inside the entrance to the Menga dolmen you will be able to see the Lovers' Rock, precisely framed in the portal – something that cannot have been accidental and suggests that the rock may have had some religious or ritual significance. This is underlined by the fact that the sun rises behind the "head" of the rock at the summer solstice and penetrates the burial chamber.

The **Cueva de Viera**, dating from a century or two later, has better-cut stones, forming a long, narrow tunnel leading to a smaller burial chamber. To the west of here it's possible to make out the quarry on the peak of a nearby hill (topped by a rather incongruous school) from where the stone used to construct the dolmens was hewn before being hauled across the intervening valley.

The third dolmen, **El Romeral** (same hours), is a further 2km down the road on the left behind an old sugar factory (easily identified by its chimney). It is reached by following signs from a roundabout (direction Córdoba). Built more than half a millennium later than the other two dolmens and containing dual chambers roofed with splendid corbel vaulting, El Romeral has something of an eastern Mediterranean feel, and bears an uncanny resemblance to the tholos tombs constructed in Crete at around the same time.

Eating and drinking

Antequera, unlike its neighbours on the coast to the south, has little in the way of exciting **food** or entertainment options. You'll trail past a variety of fast-food outlets, bars and *heladerías* along the Alameda, but it's worth seeking out a few less obvious places for more interesting food. Good **tapas bars** include the excellent *Bar-Cafetería A La Fuerza*, c/Alameda de Andalucía 32, near the bullring (also a good stop for breakfast); the equally good *Bar Numero Uno*, attached to the hotel of the same name (see p.96) with delicious fish and a *menú* for €8; *Bar Chicón*, c/Infante Don Fernando 1 near the Plaza de San Sebastián; and *Bar La Mandragora*, Plaza Descalzas 1, an economical tapas bar with a penchant for modern art. A good breakfast bar is *Café del Centro* at c/Cantareros 3, slightly north of the main street, where the walls are decorated with photos from Antequera's past.

El Angelote, c/Encarnación, s/n ☎ 95 270 34 65. Probably the town's best restaurant, with a *menú* for €11.50 and a pleasant terrace.

Hospedería Coso San Francisco c/Calzada 25 On the central Plaza de San Francisco, this hospederia has a very good restaurant offering typical dishes of the region as well the adjoining bar-cafetería *La Bamboche* with a hearty and inexpensive *menú* for €8.

La Espuela, c/San Agustin 1, a small cul-de-sac off c/Infante Don Fernando. Another excellent mid-priced restaurant with a small terrace and a *menú* for €14.

Plaza de Toros Plaza de Toros. The bullring's very own restaurant, with a mid-priced *menú* for €20 as well as more expensive options.

Parque Natural El Torcal

EL TORCAL, 13km south of Antequera and 32km north of Málaga, is the most geologically arresting of Andalucía's natural parks. A massive high plateau of eroded grey limestone dating from the Jurassic period, tempered by a lush growth of hawthorn, ivy, wild rose and thirty species of orchid, it's quite easily explored using the **walking routes** that radiate from the centre of the park where the road ends. A **Centro de Recepción** here (daily

10am–5pm; ℡95 270 25 05 or 64 947 26 88) gives out maps and general information on the park and its walks, and has audiovisual presentations covering geology, flora and fauna. Try to leave your explorations until the more peaceful late afternoon, when the setting sun throws the natural sculptures into sharp relief.

The best-designed and most exciting **trails** are the yellow and red routes, the former climaxing with suitable drama on a cliff edge with magnificent views over a valley. The latter gives fantastic vantage points of the looming limestone outcrops, eroded into vast, surreal sculptures. Because of the need to protect flora and fauna the red route is in a restricted zone and can only be visited with a **guide** (information on this available from the Centro de Recepción). The **green** and **yellow routes** (waymarked) can be walked without a guide. The green route is the shortest at 1.5km (about 40min if you don't dawdle) while the yellow route takes about two hours. In early summer on the popular green route you may find yourself competing with gangs of schoolkids, who arrive en masse on vaguely educational trips, excitedly trying to spot La Copa (the wineglass), El Lagarto (the lizard) and La Loba (the she-wolf) as well as other celebrated rock sculptures. Keep an eye on the skies while you're here for Griffon vultures, frequent visitors whose huge wingspans make a spectacular sight as they glide overhead.

Park practicalities

No buses link El Torcal to Antequera, and it's an arduous 16km hike in high summer; the park is reached by following the C3310 road towards Villanueva de la Concepción and heading down the second signed turning on the right to El Torcal. Without your own transport you might consider a **taxi** (about €20 one-way for up to four). A better value deal is with the **taxi turistico**, which can be arranged through the Turismo at Antequera; for €32 (maximum four passengers) a taxi will drop you off at the Centro de Recepción and wait until you have completed the green route before returning you to Antequera.

Torcal has a **campsite**, *Camping Torcal* (℡95 211 16 08), just off the A3310, 6km south of Antequera, which also has a **restaurant**, supermarket and pool. Camping rough is not allowed inside the park. The Turismo at Antequera can provide information regarding some attractive **casas rurales** to rent in the area.

Laguna de Fuente de Piedra

About 20km northwest of Antequera lies **Laguna de Fuente de Piedra**, the largest natural lake in Andalucía and a celebrated site for observing birdlife. The shallow water-level and high saline content of the lake, and the crustaceans that these conditions encourage, attract a glorious flock of **greater flamingo** each spring, making this Europe's only inland breeding ground for the species. Unfortunately the droughts of recent years and the demands for more water by local farmers cashing in on an asparagus boom in the nearby Sierra de Yeguas have led to the lake almost drying up completely in the summer months, thus placing many of the young flamingo in peril. This resulted in rescue missions being mounted by teams from the Coto Doñana (see p.331) who transferred many young birds back to the wetlands of Huelva. Andalucía's environmental agency has put in place a system to prevent this happening again. However, even this has not been sufficient and the drought of 2005 resulted in low water levels surrounding the nesting sites and a reluctance by the birds to breed.

Besides supporting a variety of waders at all times of the year, in winter the lake is often a haven for **cranes**, and the surrounding marshes provide a habitat for numerous amphibians and reptiles. Remember that because this is a sanctuary, the beaches are strictly out of bounds (ruling out swimming) and because many sections are privately owned, limiting access, it's not possible to make a complete circuit of the lake. You're also at a distinct advantage with your own transport, as species such as flamingo often gather at the far end of the lake, up to 7km away, although **mountain bikes** can now be rented from the visitor centre (see below).

Practicalities

The village of Fuente de Piedra is easy to get to, being on the **train** route from Málaga to Córdoba, with the lake a ten-minute walk west of the station. There are four daily **buses** from Antequera or Málaga (changing at Antequera) or, with your own transport, take the N331 (direction Sevilla) north, to join the A92 *autovía*, and continue along this for 14km until the signed turn-off. Over the bridge beyond the train station the lakeside **Centro de Visitantes** (daily: April–Oct 10am–2pm & 6–8pm; Nov–March 10am–2pm & 4–6pm; ☎952 11 17 15) has displays of the flora and fauna of the lake, and rents out binoculars and mountain bikes (both €1.50 per hr).

For **rooms** the most attractive place to stay is the *Camping Fuente Piedra* (☎95 273 52 94, ⓦwww.camping-rural.com; ❸ with breakfast), close to the village and overlooking the lake. Accommodation here is in double rooms or fully equipped wood cabins (❺) sleeping four to six persons. The grounds are occupied by a **campsite** and there's also a swimming pool and a decent **restaurant** with an economical *menú*. The site also offers a variety of activities including guided walks, mountain biking, caving, canoeing and archery.

East from Málaga: the coast to Torre del Mar

The dreary eastern stretch of the **Costa del Sol** – the beaches within easy distance of Málaga – is a largely unbroken landscape of urbanization and unlovely holiday towns, packed to the gunnels in summer with day-tripping *malagueños*. There are enough places of interest, however, to warrant stopping off en route, before arriving at the unremarkable resort of **Torre del Mar**.

With your own transport it's possible to avoid the Málaga suburbs by using the N340 *circunvalación* (ring road) – picked up on the northern edge of town – which eventually becomes the *autovía* linking Málaga with Nerja. To follow the coastal route described below, leave the *autovía* at the Rincón de la Victoria exit (see p.102). Otherwise, the road heading out of Málaga along the Paseo de Reding (passing the north side of the bullring) traverses the suburbs of Pedragalejo and El Palo, where for most of the summer the beaches are covered with a forest of parasols, before arriving at the small resort of Cala de Moral.

Cueva del Tesoro and Rincón de la Victoria

Just beyond Cala del Moral, a signed road on the left indicates the **CUEVA DEL TESORO** (daily guided visits 10.45am–1pm & 4.45–7pm; €4.65; ⓦwww.cuevasturisticas.com), a spectacular network of underground marine caves less commercialized than those at Nerja (see p.114). A series of seven chambers leads to the eighth, the **sala de los lagos**, a Gaudí-esque rock cathedral with natural underground pools. Paleolithic cave paintings were discovered here in 1918 (presently not on view) as well as other prehistoric remains indicating almost continual human habitation. The cave's name (*tesoro* means treasure) derives from the legend that five fleeing Moorish kings took refuge in its depths and stashed a large quantity of gold here (now long gone).

Two kilometres further on, **RINCÓN DE LA VICTORIA** is a no-nonsense, scruffy sort of place, and a popular resort for *malagueño* families. It's a functional spot to swim if you have a day to fill before catching a plane home, but nothing more. A seafood speciality here is *coquinas*, tasty small clams.

Macharaviaya and around

To break the monotony along this strip of coast you could follow a small road north at the featureless suburb of Torre de Benagalbón that winds up into the hills and approaches the hamlet of **MACHARAVIAYA** (from the Moorish Machar Ibn Yahya or "lands of the son of Yahya"). Surrounded by slopes covered with olive and almond trees, the village was expanded in the eighteenth century by the Galvéz family, one of Andalucía's great imperial dynasties. Count Bernardo de Galvéz became governor general of Spanish North America and gave his name to Galveston in Texas after laying siege to the town in 1777. Today, even taking into account its impressive Baroque church (a Galvéz construction), it's hard to believe that this tiny, cobble-paved village was once known as "little Madrid". It was a wealthy place, benefiting from the extensive Galvéz family vineyards as well as a playing-card factory that had a monopoly for supplying cards to the Americas. This was all to end, however, when the phylloxera plague of the 1870s wiped out the vines, the card monopoly lapsed and the Galvéz line died out. The family title died with them, and the last visconte de Galveston is buried in the church crypt among the tombs and alabaster statues of his ancestors.

At the entrance to the village is a rather proprietorial whitewashed brick temple erected by the family in 1786 and, at its centre, the once crumbling exterior of the outsize church of **San Jacinto** (guided visits Sat & Sun 11am–3pm & service Sat 7pm), over-restored as part of the Expo '92 celebrations. Inside the single-nave church, altars dedicated to various Galvéz family members are decorated with fine marble, and inscriptions express the ultimately vain hope that Mass would be said on certain days for their souls *in perpetuum*. Don't miss the eerie crypt behind the church, where a remarkable collection of sombre **alabaster family busts** face each other around an alcove and seem about to start up a gloomy conversation. The great marble tomb of Don José Galvéz, marquis of Sonora and minister for the Indias during the eighteenth-century reign of Carlos III, stands nearby. Downhill from the *Taberna El Candil* (see below) lies the village **museum** (same hours as church) which consists mainly of artworks. Visits to the church can also be arranged outside official opening hours by calling the Ayuntamiento on ☎95 240 00 42 (English spoken).

Facing the church is the old playing-card factory, now converted into homes. For refreshment, continue uphill along c/Elvira, a short alleyway, to the simple and friendly *Taberna El Candil*, which serves **tapas** and **raciónes** and even full meals, if pushed.

Two kilometres north of Macharaviaya – and approached via a side road to the left at the entrance to the village – the village of **BENAQUE** has a Mudéjar church, **Nuestra Señora del Rosario**, whose tower conserves the minaret of the mosque it replaced. The building has recently been sensitively restored. Just before the church a house on the right was the birthplace of – and is now a **museum** (free, donations welcome) dedicated to – Benaque's most famous son, the modernist poet **Salvador Rueda** (1857–1933). Should you wish to view the disarmingly simple interior, which is more or less as it was when the poet lived here, the key is available from Señor José (Pepe) Cabrera, c/Salvador Rueda 19, just before the bus shelter to the left as you arrive.

Torre del Mar

Back on the main coast road, the chain of localities with "torre" in their names refers to the numerous *atalayas*, or watchtowers, which have been used to guard this coast since Roman and Moorish times, many strikingly visible on the headlands. There's little to detain you between Torre de Benagalbón and Almayate – though the latter has a reasonable **campsite**, *Almayate-Costa* (T 95 255 62 89) with limited shade – from where it's only a couple of kilometres to **TORRE DEL MAR**. A line of concrete tower blocks on a grey, pebble beach, this is Torremolinos without the money or bluster. Nevertheless, it's a fairly easy-going place and the central pedestrianized street, Paseo de Larios, which runs from the tram terminal down to the seafront provides a focus for numerous bars, **restaurants and cafés**. Adjacent to the Paseo de Larios is a small parade of **bars** with a rather tame nightlife scene, named El Copo. On the positive side, however, the resort has some of the best value **freidurías** and **marisquerías** on the Costa del Sol; among many places worth trying are *Bar-Marisquería Radar*, Paseo Marítimo 13, close to the *Hostal Don Juan* (see below) and *El Yate*, *Bar Fernando* and *Bar Toné* in a line with terraces along c/Saladero Viejo, 50m from the tourist office.

If you want to **stay**, the new and central *Hostal Don Juan*, c/Patrón Veneno 14 (T 95 254 58 70; ❸), lies just 30m from the beach and has en-suite a/c rooms with TV. A few doors away the *Hotel Miraya*, c/Patrón Veneno 6 (T 95 254 59 69, W www.hotelmiraya.com; ❹), offers a few more creature comforts. Like everywhere else around here, though, rooms are at a premium in high season, when your best hope will probably be the basic **campsite** *Torre del Mar* (T 95 254 02 24) on the Paseo Marítimo. Otherwise the central and helpful **Turismo**, Paseo de Larios s/n (Mon–Fri 9.30am–1.45pm & 4–6.30pm, Sat & Sun 11am–2pm & 6–9pm; T 95 254 11 04, W www.ayto -velezmalaga.es), may be able to advise; they can also supply a town map. **Internet** access is available at Cyber Costa del Sol, c/Blas Infante 4 (daily 9.30am to midnight) close to El Copo (see above). Walkers and readers may want to look up a useful **bookshop**, Pasa Tiempo, c/Infantes 30 (T 95 254 37 03), facing Plaza de la Paz, where a Yorkshire couple – both enthusiastic walkers – keep a wide range of maps.

The Axarquía

The Axarquía makes a refreshing change from the sun-bed culture of the Costa del Sol. Bounded by the coast, the Sierra de Alhama to the north and, on its eastern flank, the mountainous edge of the province of Granada, this rugged, ham-shaped wedge of territory offers excellent walking country and abundant wildlife, as well as a host of attractive mountain villages that make easy-going stopoffs. Long a breeding ground for *bandoleros* who preyed on traders carrying

THE AXARQUÍA REGION

produce from the coast to Granada, during the Civil War the Axarquía was also a notorious guerrilla encampment whose members fought on against Franco's Guardia Civil until the early 1950s: it is only in relatively recent times that the area has become safe for travellers.

The Axarquía is a great place to do some **hiking**: *Walk! the Axarquía* by Charles Davis is a book of hikes devoted to the region; alternatively, *Walking in Andalucía* by Guy Hunter-Watts has half a dozen hikes to follow in the western Axarquía (see "Books" on p.609).

Vélez-Málaga

Frequent buses – and now a new tram service – head the 4km inland from Torre del Mar to **VÉLEZ-MÁLAGA**, capital of the Axarquía and a bustling market town and supply centre for the region's farmers. In the fertile valley of the Río Vélez, Vélez-Málaga (often simply referred to as Vélez) was important in both Roman times – under the name of Menoba – and Moorish, when as

Ballix-Malaca ("Fortress of Málaga") it had an important role in subduing what has always been a turbulent zone. A number of Phoenician cemeteries and tombs discovered nearby testify to an older pedigree still. When Fernando conquered the town in 1487, the Christian flag was raised on the castle's battlements as the Moors were ejected. This victory, which drove a wedge through the kingdom of Granada, dividing it in two, paved the way for the fall of the Nasrid city five years later.

The town climbs up a slope from the main streets, Calle Canalejas and its continuation Calle Cristo – towards the **castillo**, as good a place as any to start a tour of the sights. What's left of it clings to a rocky outcrop, which from its dominant position above the white-walled *barrio* of San Sebastián gives good views out over the coast. The castle suffered badly during the War of the Spanish Succession, when the English lost to the French here after a bitter struggle in 1704. Visible from the castle is the sixteenth-century Mudéjar church of **Santa María de la Encarnación** whose beautiful sectioned tower still holds the minaret of the mosque that preceded it. Inside, Moorish arches separate a triple nave, and there's a fine Mudéjar ceiling. East of here, the late-Gothic **San Juan Bautista**, on Plaza Constitución, is also worth a look, featuring an elegant tower and, inside, a superbly naturalistic sculpture, *Cristo Crucificado* by Pedro de Mena.

The restored **Palacio del Marqués de Beniel**, Plaza Palacio 1, is an elegant sixteenth-century mansion – formerly the town hall – which now hosts the International Summer School of the Axarquía covering all aspects of culture, including poetry and theatre as well as flamenco and classical guitar. A prestigious annual **guitar competition** is held here every July, with free concerts taking place in the *palacio's* delightful patio. The Ayuntamiento (see below) has details of both of these and other cultural activities taking place throughout the summer.

Practicalities

Vélez-Málaga's **bus station** is on Avenida Vivar Téllez, the avenue leading out of town towards the sea. For **tourist information** the office in Torre del Mar (see p.103) now serves both communities but the Ayuntamiento (Mon–Fri 8.30am–2pm), located on the central Plaza de las Carmelitas, can supply a town map.

Finding **places to stay** isn't usually a problem and simple rooms are available at the *Casa Los Martínez*, c/Cristo 58 (T95 250 42 87; ●), on the main crossroad as you approach the centre from Avenida Vivar Téllez. Best of Velez's limited hotel accommodation is the newly arrived *Palacio Blanco*, c/Feliz Lomas 4 (T95 254 91 74, Wwww.palacioblanco.com; ●) a boutique hotel with elegant airy rooms and rooftop pool.

Many places to **eat and drink** at line the Avenida Vivar Tellez, including the medium-priced *Mesón Los Migueles* at no. 83, serving a variety of fish and meat dishes and a good-value *menú*. There's also a decent restaurant and tapas bar below *Casa Los Martínez*. Options nearer the centre of town include *Bar Niño Velez*, c/Joaquín Lobato 5, near the market, and *El Carmen* c/Albero 2, near the Ayuntamiento, both good for seafood.

North to Alfarnate

A number of good driving **routes** around the Axarquía begin at **Trapiche**, about 3km north of Vélez. One heads northwest along the MA145 towards **BENAMARGOSA**, a village surrounded by citrus orchards and avocado plantations. You could take a look at its sixteenth-century Gothic-style church of **La Encarnación** before moving on to La Zubía, where a winding road signed on the left climbs dizzily to **COMARES**, an impeccably tidy White Town (or village in this case) spectacularly clinging to the peak of its conical hill. At the highest point of all, beside an attractive cemetery, the ruined Moorish fort – built on Roman foundations – was one of the strongholds of rebel leader Ibn Hafsun (see p.92). In the village is yet another church of **Nuestra Señora de la Encarnación**, this time a sixteenth-century Mudéjar building with a picturesque hexagonal tower, the minaret of the mosque that preceded it. A **mirador** in the focal Plaza del Ayuntamiento gives fine views over the Axarquía. There's a **walking route** around the village's major sights taking in all the above plus an ancient Roman path down the mountain and various Moorish architectural remains; it's waymarked by ceramic footprints embedded in the pavement. En-suite **rooms** are to be had at the *Hotel Atalaya*, c/Encinilla s/n (T95 250 92 08; ❸), near the entrance to the village (where windows face the barracks of the Guardia Civil rather than the spectacular vista behind). The friendlier *Mirador de la Axarquía* (T95 250 92 09; ❷), slightly further up the hill as you enter the village, has more en-suite rooms above a restaurant. An altogether more luxurious alternative is *El Molino de los Abuelos* (T95 250 93 09, Wwww.hotelmolinodelosabuelos.com; ❷–❹ with breakfast), which offers rooms with and without bath plus suites in an enchantingly refurbished eighteenth-century former olive-oil mill on the Plaza del Ayuntamiento. For **eating and drinking** there are bars on the main square and *El Molino de los Abuelos* has its own good mid-priced restaurant (main dishes €9–15) located in the former oil pressing room with the ancient equipment still on view. The restaurants of both the *Mirador de la Axarquía* (with a pleasant terrace with stunning views) and *Hotel Atalaya* serve up regular *venta* food with good value *menús* for around €7. A welcome municipal **swimming pool** is sited between the latter restaurant and the *Hotel Atalaya*.

Continuing north out of La Zubía the road follows the course of the Río Cueva, finally ascending to **RIOGORDO**, a village with Phoenician and Roman origins that was a fortified stronghold during the Moorish period. After the *Reconquista* the Moors were replaced by settlers from Castile. The Semana Santa celebrated here is a particularly vivid affair, when local people – dressed for the part – act out the scenes from the Passion, often with bloodcurdling gusto. The village also boasts an attractive municipal swimming pool.

From Riogordo, you have a choice of routes: head east to Alfarnate (see p.108) or west, following a stiff climb, to **COLMENAR**, another brilliant-white hill town and the Axarquía's most westerly outpost. A centre of honey production thanks to the rich variety of flowering plants and shrubs growing in the surrounding hills, the village takes its name from *colmena*, Spanish for "beehive". Among a couple of places to stay here the welcoming *Hotel El Belén* (T95 273 05 78; ❷), near the Málaga road, is a good bet for en-suite a/c rooms with TV above a good restaurant with an economical *menú*. The route from here – via the Puerto del Léon – down to Málaga, twisting through forests of cork oaks and pines forming the **Parque Natural de los Montes de Málaga**, is wonderful, offering during its latter stages stunning **views** over the Costa del Sol. Sixteen kilometres before Málaga, close to a landmark roadside spring named La Fuente de la Reina, there's a delightfully rural **place to stay**, the ⚐ *Hotel Humaina* (T95 264 10 25, Wwww.hotelhumaina.es; ❹), a former hunting lodge tucked away in a wooded valley at the end of a five-kilometre-long track signed from the spring. Friendly staff, comfortable rooms, a small pool and its own good restaurant – together with a chance to spot copious birdlife and animals, such as the wild boar who are frequent visitors to the hotel's rubbish bins in search of nibbles – add up to a memorable hotel. The management can also provide maps and advise on exploring the waymarked rambling **paths** through the surrounding woods.

Alcaucín and Zália

Another route out of Vélez heads north from Trapiche and follows the old coach route from Málaga to Granada. At a second fork 8km beyond here, a fast new road – the A356 – skirts the western flank of the Embalse de Viñuela, speeding traffic north towards Casabermeja and the N331 Málaga-Sevilla *autovía*. Taking the right fork along the A335, however, passes a turn-off to **VIÑUELA**, 3km beyond this. Originally a *venta* stop for the traffic heading north and south between Málaga and Granada, the atmospheric old **inn** here, *La Viña*, dates from the eighteenth century and stands opposite the fountain in the narrow main street. A spit-and-sawdust place today, it's usually full on midsummer afternoons of old men arguing around the domino tables and farmhands sheltering from the burning sun. Just down the street, the simple sixteenth-century **Iglesia de San José** (get the key from the neighbour opposite) has a finely worked *Pietà*. For **rooms** on the shores of the nearby Embalse de Viñuela reservoir there's the luxurious *Hotel Viñuela* (T 95 251 91 93, W www.hotelvinuela.com; ❻ with breakfast), which also has its own **restaurant** and a garden **pool**.

Still following the old road, at the Puente de Don Manuel, a bridge 3km beyond Viñuela, a road cuts off on the right and ascends to the village of **ALCAUCÍN**. On the way up keep an eye to your left where, across a valley, you will be able to make out the ruins of the deserted medieval village of Zalía (see below) and, beyond, the Puerto de Zafarraya, a great U-shaped cleavage in the Sierra de Alhama through which the ancient route to Granada passes. Alcaucín itself, perched on the slopes of the Sierra de Tejeda, is a beautiful little village with wrought-iron balconies ablaze with flowering geraniums and a web of narrow white-walled streets reflecting its Moorish origins. As befits a mountain village, there are numerous spring-fed fountains, among which the five-spouted Fuente San Sebastián has been restored very much in the Moorish style, complete with *azulejos*.

Continuing north from the Puente de Don Manuel, the A335 heads on towards Granada, passing en route the dauntingly impressive **Zafarraya Pass**, where 30,000-year-old remains found in a nearby cave in 1983 have now been confirmed as the last-known site in Europe inhabited by Neanderthal man. On the way, the road passes the ruins of the fort and the deserted medieval village of **ZALÍA**. Local legend has it that the Moorish village was attacked by a plague of vipers after Patricio, a *malagueño* church minister, arrived in an attempt to convert the inhabitants to Christianity and they spurned him. The more likely explanation is that the population was put to the sword during the uprisings that followed the *Reconquista*. Throughout most of the Moorish period Zalía's fortress, together with those at Comares and Bentomiz (near Arenas to the south), formed a defensive triangle to control this central sector of the Axarquía region.

Alfarnatejo and Alfarnate

Taking the alternative C340 heading northwest from the junction just beyond Viñuela leads to **Periana**, a noted centre of peach-growing and *anís* production. Some 3km beyond here, heading into the Axarquía's more remote

▲ Ancient Venta de Alfarnate

extremities, you'll reach a fork; if you don't want to face a tortuous switch-back secondary road, ignore the sign labelled "Alfarnate 15km" and continue along the road signed to Riogordo and Colmenar. A further 4km will bring you to a right turn and an easier route to the village of **ALFARNATEJO** and, a little beyond this, the Axarquía's most northerly conurbation, **ALFARNATE**. Although they lie a mere couple of kilometres apart, it would be difficult to find two places in Andalucía with less in common. Alfarnatejo, the smaller of the two, is staunchly right-wing, while Alfarnate has always been on the left, and, unable to agree or cooperate on anything, they have built up a strong mutual animosity, which even discourages marriages between the two communities. In truth, neither village would win any beauty prizes, though Alfarnate, set on a plain covered with wheatfields, is worth a visit for its attractive church of **Santa Ana**, a sixteenth-century edifice with a graceful Mudéjar tower.

However, Alfarnate's real claim to fame is the thirteenth-century **Venta de Alfarnate** on the village's western edge, which maintains – with some justification – that it is the oldest **inn** in Andalucía. Situated in an isolated spot in the midst of brooding hills, it's not hard to see what attracted the various brigands and highwaymen to the place. Indeed, the interior, as well as being a bar-restaurant, is also a **museum** dedicated to keeping alive the memory of such outlaws as Luís Candelas who spent a night in the *venta's* well-preserved prison cell en route to justice in Málaga. By far the most terrifying *bandolero* of all, however, was El Tempranillo, who arrived unannounced one hot day in the 1820s, and, when there were no spoons for him to eat with, ordered the dining clients to eat their wooden ones at gunpoint, cracking their teeth in the process. The place is more civilized these days and its mid-priced restaurant serves a hearty mountain speciality, *huevos a la bestia* (fried eggs with local sausage, ham and black pudding). Keep your eyes peeled in this area for the amazingly agile **cabra hispanica**, the rare Spanish goat; the long-horned male is a spectacular sight as he effortlessly scales almost vertical cliff faces.

East from Torre del Mar: the coast to Nerja

The coast east from Torre del Mar is a nondescript stretch of faceless towns and the occasional concrete resort, dotted with more ancient *atalayas* (watchtowers). Inland lie more tempting villages in the **eastern Axarquía** but along the coast the first town of any real interest is **Nerja**, with some fine beaches and a relatively slow pace. Further east, **Almuñécar**, and even better **Salobreña**, are the city of Granada's Mediterranean playgrounds, flanked by numerous coves and inlets where for most of the year you can have a beach all to yourself.

Inland to Cómpeta

Beyond Torre del Mar the coast road climbs slightly to **Algarrobo-Costa**, an unappealing high-rise beach resort. With your own transport it's worth ignoring this – and the bleak stretch of coast that follows – to head inland for some delightful villages in the eastern Axarquía, finally rejoining the coastal road 10km east at Torrox Costa.

From Algarrobo-Costa the MA103 climbs inland for a stretch towards the village of Algarrobo proper. Look out for for some well-conserved **Phoenician tombs** (signposted on the right) dating from the eighth century BC. Originally these tombs formed part of an extensive cemetery, built of stone blocks and roofed in wood The older inland village of **ALGARROBO** 3km inland, which lent its name to the coastal settlement, is a pleasant enough place, though rapidly being enveloped by urban sprawl as the developers move inland from the coast.

Passing through Algarrobo, the road toils on upwards as the fruit orchards of the coastal strip give way to the olive groves and vineyards of the higher slopes. The road then passes **SAYALONGA** 5km further on, a pretty village nestling in the valley of the Río Algarrobo, and then ascends again, twisting and turning for a further 8km until it reaches **CÓMPETA**, a huddle of brilliant-white cubes tumbling down a hillside and surrounded by vineyards. A Moorish settlement in origin, and now discovered by migrants from northern Europe, Cómpeta retains a relaxed atmosphere, and the easy-going villagers don't seem too worried about being swamped by foreigners. The sweet – and potent – **wine** made from the area's muscatel grapes is renowned as the best in the whole province. You can try it for yourself at the *Museo del Vino* on Avenida de la Constitución close to the charming main square, Plaza de la Almijara (the *Jarel* brand is recommended). Each August 15 beneath the lofty bell tower (a later addition) of the sixteenth-century church of La Asunción, Cómpeta rolls out the barrels – scores of them – during its annual **fiesta**, the Noche del Vino. This is when the square fills with revellers determined to sink as much of the free *vino* as they can hold. Above the plaza to the left, c/San Antonio leads to a shrine with a superb **view** over the valley to the west and the sea beyond.

The road continues for a further 4km north of Cómpeta where it comes to a dead end at the village of **CANILLAS DE ALBAIDA**, something of a mini-Cómpeta, with a place to stay and a couple of decent restaurants (see p.110).

Practicalities

Cómpeta's **tourist office** (Wed–Sun 10am–3pm; ☏95 255 36 85, ⓦwww .competa.es) is located on the Plaza de la Constitución close to the where **buses** terminate. For a place **to stay**, the only budget possibilities are the unofficial rooms in places dotted around the village – the best way of contacting them is via the tourist office (or their website). The only other option is the central *Hotel Balcón de Cómpeta*, c/San Antonio s/n, southwest of the main square (☎95 255 35 35, ⓦwww.hotel-competa.com; ❹), with comfortable balcony rooms overlooking a pool. In neighbouring Canillas de Albaida, close to the main square, Posada La Plaza (☎95 255 48 07, ⓦwww.posada-laplaza .eu; ❸ with breakfast) is another option with en-suite balcony rooms with views and a roof terrace.

A good place **to eat** in Cómpeta is the economical *Bar-Restaurante Perico* on Plaza Almijara – their *pollo al vino de Cómpeta* (chicken cooked in the local wine) is recommended and there's also a *menú* for €7.50. Slightly southwest of the main square *El Pilón*, c/Laberinto s/n, offers more eclectic international cuisine with vegetarian options. *Restaurante María*, the restaurant of the *Hotel Balcón de Cómpeta* at the top of c/San Antonio, is another mid-priced possibility, while the restaurant of the *Museo del Vino* in Avenida La Constitución is also good for charcoal grilled meat and fish.

A friendly and informative English **bookshop**, Marco Polo, at c/José Antonio 3 (☎95 251 64 23), just off the main square, stocks walking books, maps and equipment. Copies of a local magazine, *Market Place*, are also stocked here which includes a useful map of Cómpeta (and many other towns and resorts along the coast to the south). **Internet** access is available at *Cómpeta Webs* (Mon–Sat 10am–2pm & 5–9pm) c/San Antonio 9, near the *Hotel Balcón de Cómpeta*.

Archez, Salares and Sedella

To penetrate further into the Axarquía from Cómpeta you'll need to double back for 2km to the turning north to **ARCHEZ**. Nestling in the foothills of the Sierra Almijara, it's an attractive village with strong Moorish roots. This influence is vividly in evidence at the church of **Nuestra Señora de La Encarnación** (open service times) whose remarkable fourteenth-century tower is the minaret of an earlier mosque. It is one of the best examples from this period, and the *sebka* brickwork and blind arches above are particularly fine. Archez's solitary **place to stay** is the charming and central *Posada-Mesón Mudéjar*, c/Alamo 6, (☎95 255 31 06, ⓦwww.posadamesonmudejar.com; ❸ with breakfast) with en-suite rooms and a restaurant.

The road climbs for another 5km to the brilliant white village of **SALARES**, a centre of olive oil and wine production and one of the most picturesque villages of the Axarquía. Its charms are enhanced by the banning of traffic from its narrow streets, where colourful potted geraniums line the walls and dogs lie prostrate in the afternoon heat. There's a car park at the top of the village; from here, head downhill to the friendly **Ayuntamiento** (Mon–Fri 9am–1pm), where you can pick up a small map. Next door, the church of **Santa Ana** should be your first stop. Just as the church at Archez, this one conserves a fine **minaret** of the mosque it replaced. Inside, a simple interior holds the image of Santa Ana, *patrona* of the village.

The road climbs on to **SEDELLA** 4km away, perched beneath a massive hill terraced with orchards and vegetable gardens. Looming up behind, the Sierra de Almijara is laced with numerous streams and springs that provide necessary irrigation. Apart from winding, narrow streets daubed with liberal amounts of whitewash, there are few sights, though the **Casa Torreón**, an ancient Ayuntamiento with a fine Mudéjar tower topped off by paired arches, is mildly interesting.

Nerja

Although **NERJA**, 20km along the coast from Torre del Mar, cannot claim to have been bypassed by the tidal wave of post-1960s tourist development, this attractive resort has, nevertheless, held out against Torremolinos-type tower blocks, and its mainly villa and *urbanizaciones* construction has been more in keeping with its origins. Its setting, too, is spectacular, nestling among the foothills of the Almijara range, with a striking seafront **belvedere** flanked by some attractive **beaches**.

Arrival and information

The **bus station** is at the north end of town. It's a five-minute walk south from here to the beach and old town along c/Pintada, at the end of which is the helpful **turismo**, c/Puerta del Mar 2 (July–Sept daily 10am–2pm & 6–10pm; Oct–June Mon–Fri 10am–2pm & 5–8pm, Sat 10am–1pm; ☏95 252 15 31, Ⓦwww.nerja.org). They can also provide details of the resort's **Festival de Flamenco** (Sept–Oct) in which many big names appear. Their *Guía del Ocio* free magazine also lists nightlife venues and upcoming special events.

If you'd like to do some **walking** in the area, the Turismo has its own leaflets (in English) and at the English bookshop W H Smiffs, a few doors along from the post office on c/Almirante Ferrandiz, you can buy individual leaflets detailing walks in the area by local resident and hiker Elma Thompson. Elma is

RESTAURANTS	
Ayo	16
Bar-Restaurante Los Trillizos	6
Casa Luque	13
El Pulguilla	10
El Refugio	9
El Viejo Sótano	5
La Marea	1
Marisquería La Marina	8
Mesón Pata Negra	7
Pizzería Gato Negro	11
Puerta del Mar	14
Restaurante Moreno	15

ACCOMMODATION	
Alhambra	H
Camping Nerja	A
Hostal Abril	C
Hostal Andalucía	G
Hostal Marissal	J
Hostal Mena	I
Hotel Nerja Princess	F
Hostal Nerjasol	E
Hotel Paraíso del Mar	L
Parador de Nerja	K
Pensión Montesol	B
Pepe Mesa Apartamentos	D

TAPAS BARS	
Bar Cavana	12
El Chispa	3
Las 4 Esquinas	4
Los Cuñaos	2

a chirpy Mancunian who also offers guided walks from November to May (℡95 253 07 82). Nerja also boasts one of the best second hand bookshops on the coast, The Book Centre, at c/Granada 30. **Internet** access is available at Locutorio Los Huertos, c/Huertos 45 (daily 10am–midnight).

Accommodation

There's usually no problem finding **rooms** in Nerja except in August, when you should book in advance. The lowest-priced possibilities are in the streets south of the bus station heading towards the sea. If everything's full, one solution is to stay inland at Frigiliana (see p.114), or try renting an apartment. The Turismo can help with information on apartments, and many of the *hostales* listed below have arrangements with *casas particulares* to soak up the overflow. There's a **campsite** *Camping Nerja* (℡95 252 97 14, ⓦwww .nerjacamping.com) with good shade, pool, bar and restaurant 4km east of the town close to Maro.

Alhambra c/Antonio Millón s/n ℡95 252 21 74, ⓦwww.hostalalhambra.es. Immaculate en-suite rooms, some with sea-facing balcony, in this pleasant *hostal* a little west of the centre. ❸

Hostal Abril c/Pintada 124 ℡95 252 61 67, ⓦwww.hostalabril.com. Sparkling *hostal* with excellent en-suite a/c rooms, lots of cool marble and a friendly proprietor. Also has apartments and studios (❹) sleeping up to four. Free internet access for guests. ❸

Hostal Andalucía c/Los Huertos 58 ℡95 252 10 58, ⓔhostalandalucia@hotmail.com. Charming *hostal* just east of the centre with spotless en-suite a/c rooms, marble throughout and rooftop *terraza/solarium*. ❸

Hostal Marissal Paseo Balcón de Europa 3 ℡95 252 01 99 ⓦwww.hostalmarissal.com. Bang in the centre of the action, this *hostal* offers a/c en-suite rooms, many (try for rooms 102–5 or 204–5) with sea view. Also rents apartments (❺) in same location. ❸

Hostal Mena c/El Barrio 15 ℡95 252 05 41, ⓔhostalmena@hotmail.com. Central rooms with bath, sea views, a/c or fans and a delightful garden at the rear. ❷

Hostal Nerjasol c/Arropieros 4 ℡95 252 21 21, ⓦwww.hostalnerjasol.com. On a quiet street, with spotless a/c en-suite rooms and a roof patio. They can direct you to a *casa particular* if full. ❸

Hotel Nerja Princess c/Los Huertos 46 ℡95 252 89 86, ⓦwww.hotelnp.com. Excellent small hotel

where well-equipped a/c balcony rooms come with satellite TV, minibar and safe. There's a terrace and pool at the rear and the best beaches are nearby. ❺ with breakfast.

Hotel Paraíso del Mar c/Prolongación de Carabeo 22, almost next door to the parador ℡95 252 16 21, ⓦwww.hotelparaisodelmar.es. Pleasant alternative to the *Parador de Nerja*, where all rooms come with jacuzzi and many have a sea-view balcony. There's also a pool, gardens, sauna dug out of the cliff face, and access to the beach. ❻ with breakfast.

Parador de Nerja c/Almuñécar 8 ℡95 252 00 50, ⓦwww.parador.es. Modern parador which, despite an exterior resembling an open prison, has comfortable rooms, a pleasant, plant-filled garden and patio, a small park with bar (worth a visit) overlooking the sea, plus an elevator down the cliff to Burriana, one of Nerja's most popular beaches. The restaurant serves a good-value *menú*. ❼ with breakfast.

Pensión Montesol c/Pintada 130 ℡95 252 00 14. Friendly *hostal* with en-suite rooms (fans provided) that is more impressive inside than its exterior suggests. ❷

Pepe Mesa Apartamentos c/Los Huertos 33 ℡95 252 41 38, ⓦwww.pepemesa.com. Good-value apartments and studios with kitchenette, satellite TV and rooftop pool. ❹

The Town

Nerja's **old town** fans out to the north of the **Balcón de Europa**, a natural palm-lined belvedere which offers magnificent views over the rocky coastline. The tangle of pretty, narrow streets is crowded with visitors all summer long, but the brash shops that service them have yet to suffocate the town's easy-going tranquillity. Nerja's obvious charm has attracted the inevitable colony of migrants – in this case the English – who make their presence felt in the numerous foreign-owned shops

▲ Nerja

and bars. Sights, as such, are few, and once you have strolled along the Balcón and taken a look at the nearby seventeenth-century whitewashed **El Salvador** church (open service times) – which has a fine *Dolorosa* – you should head for the beach or make a short excursion out of town. Nerja's best **beach** is Burriana, an easily walkable kilometre east of the centre. There's also a series of coves within walking distance if you want to escape the crowds.

An entertaining **market** takes place on Tuesday (main market) and Sunday (flea market) mornings and spreads along c/Antonio Ferrándiz (Chanquete), to the east of the centre.

Eating and Nightlife

Restaurant prices in the old town tend to be high and standards indifferent so you'll do better to head further out for good, reasonably priced places. On the western side of town, there are many authentic Spanish restaurants concentrated around Plaza Marina. For **tapas**, three of the best are: *Las 4 Esquinas*, on c/Pintada; *El Chispa*, c/San Pedro 12, which specializes in fried fish; and *Los Cuñaos*, c/Herrera Oria 19, northeast of the centre. For a lazy **breakfast** *Bar Cavana*, Plaza Cavana is one of Nerja's traditional old bars and has some tables on the square outside. **Nightlife** tends to happen in numerous music bars and clubs concentrated west of the centre around Plaza Tutti Frutti and along the nearby c/Antonio Millón.

Ayo Burriana beach. Very reasonably priced (for this location) with good seafood. Their giant open-air paella fry-up on Sunday lunch times (big plate for around €6) is a Burriana institution.

Bar-Restaurante Los Trillizos c/Los Huertos 38. Budget restaurant offering well-prepared standards with an attractive terrace at the back. Their €8.50 *menú* is probably the best value in town.

Casa Luque Plaza Cavana 2. Good but expensive nouvelle cuisine served up in stylish if rather pretentious surroundings, with a panoramic terrace at the rear. Main dishes €15–23.

El Pulguilla c/Almirante Ferrandiz 26. Long-established and outstanding seafood tapas and *raciónes* bar whose quality places it among the best venues in town to eat. Everything sold is straight from the sea and beyond the bar lies a superb terrace. On weekdays they offer a *menú del dia*.

El Refugio c/Diputación 12. Wide choice of fish, *mariscos* and regional dishes in a friendly rustic setting with a reasonable *menú* for around €9 and outdoor tables in the evening.

El Viejo Sótano c/Los Huertos 33. Good mid-priced restaurant with a range of meat and fish dishes as well as some vegetarian options including pastas and salads. Main dishes €8–18.

La Marea Plaza Cantarero s/n. Good and modestly priced fish restaurant with terrace, owned by the same proprietors as *La Marina*.

Marisquería La Marina Plaza la Marina s/n. *Marisquerías* don't come any better than this, which is why *La Marina* is so popular. Enjoy superb tapas at the bar or mouthwatering fresh fish (with some great wines) at their restaurant tables or outdoor terrace.

Mesón Pata Negra Plaza La Marina. Authentic regional dishes, and a little more expensive than the other restaurants on this square.

Pizzería Gato Negro c/Hernando de Carabeo 13. The town's best pizzeria, extremely popular with locals as well as visitors.

Puerta del Mar c/Puerta del Mar 2. Almost next door to the Turismo, this upmarket *marisquería* serves excellent fish and seafood but you pay for the stylish surroundings.

Restaurante Moreno Burriana beach. Nicest out of a cluster of economical eating places at the back of the beach; one of the chefs cooks barbecue-style (in an old boat) outside on the terrace. The fried *sardinas* and paella are excellent.

Around Nerja

A popular excursion from Nerja is the six-kilometre trip north to **FRIGIL-IANA**, a pretty Moorish hill village clinging to the lower slopes of Monte El Fuerte. After the *Reconquista*, Frigiliana became a Morisco settlement where only those Moors who had converted to Christianity were allowed to live. Although a little of the atmosphere of this period survives in the steep, narrow streets, the place is prettified today by the addition of geranium pots and historical plaques.

A **turismo**, Cuesta de Apero 10 (Mon–Fri 9am–8pm, Sat 10am–6pm, Sun 10am–3pm; ☎95 253 42 61, ⓦwww.frigiliana.es), 50m from the bus terminus, also houses a small **archeological museum** and can provide lists of apartments to rent around the village as well as a useful map. They also stock more of Elma Thompson's walks pamphlets (see p.111) for this area. In keeping with the village's status as a tourist draw, some of the restaurants and bars here tend to be somewhat overpriced, but the hospitable *Hotel Las Chinas*, Plaza Capitán Cortés 14 (☎95 253 30 73, ⓦwww.hotel-laschinas.com; ❷), is a good bet for balcony **rooms** with bath (ask for a room at the rear to avoid street noise). They also have a decent restaurant next door. Just along the street from here the new *Hospedería El Caravansar*, Callejón de la Ermita s/n (☎952 53 35 86, ⓦwww .hospederiaelcaravansar.es; ❸ with breakfast) has comfortable a/c en-suite rooms in a charming village house. The *Hotel Villa Frigiliana*, c/San Sebastian s/n (☎95 253 42 21, ⓦwww.ihmhotels.com; ❹–❺ with breakfast), is the luxury option and manages to squeeze in a small pool. Good **eating places** include the economical *La Bodeguilla*, c/Chorruelo s/n, near the focal Plaza de la Iglesia in the upper village, an excellent family-run restaurant, plus the nearby and pricier *Taberna del Sacristán*, (main dishes €13-17) with a terrace on the Plaza de la Iglesia itself fronting the church of San Antonio. At least six **buses** per day (Mon–Sat) leave for Frigiliana from the bus station in Nerja, the earliest of which gives you enough time to take a walk in the surrounding hills and catch the last bus back at 9pm.

Cynics might find the "accidental" discovery in 1957 of the **CUEVAS DE NERJA** (daily July–Aug 10am–7.30pm; rest of year 10am–2pm & 4–6.30pm; ⓦwww.cuevadenerja.es; €7) – neatly coinciding with the arrival of mass tourism – a little suspect. Immediately they were revealed, the series of enormous caverns, scattered with Paleolithic and Neolithic tools, pottery and cave paintings stretching back 30,000 years, became a local, then national, sensation. Nowadays, however, the fairy lights, piped muzak and cave theatre – which hosts various shows from rock to ballet and flamenco – can't help but detract from the appreciation of a spectacular natural wonder, and the cave paintings are currently not on public view (and possibly never will be). However, you might want to seek out the world's longest known **stalactite** – all 32m of it and verified by the *Guinness Book of Records* – while you're probing the depths. A new **Centro de Interpretación** (same hours as cave; free) located near the cave entrance uses dioramas to document the history of the cave and its geology and for more serious explorations (the tourist visit allows access to only one third of the cave's extent) there are fully equipped **speleological tours** in English and Spanish lasting seven hours (€90; ☎95 252 95 20 for details). The **restaurant** at the cave entrance serves a cheap buffet but can get very busy in high season; the restaurant of the *Hotel al Andalus*, down the hill, with economical *menú* and pleasant terrace is a good alternative. From Nerja the caves are an easy but not particularly pleasant three-kilometre walk east along the main coast road; taking a taxi (roughly €10 one-way) or a bus (running approximately hourly) from Nerja bus station is a better alternative.

Further east of Nerja, the coastal road zigzags around the foothills of the Sierra Almijara, climbing above a number of tiny coves. The first settlement, the coastal hamlet of **MARO**, is a sparkling cluster of white-walled houses set above an attractive cove beach. Lying close to the ancient Roman settlement of *Detunda*, the town was revitalized in the eighteenth century by the construction of a sugar factory, now a ruin behind the simple church of Nuestra Señora de las Maravillas, which dates from the same period. There are three **places to stay**. *Hotel Playa Maro* (☎95 252 95 82, ⓦwww.hotelplayamaro.com; ❹–❺ including breakfast) is a formal hotel at the entrance to the village, but *Casa Maro* (☎95 252 96 90, ⓦwww.hotel-casa-maro.com; ❸), a German-run apartment hotel

---

Walks around Frigiliana

One easy walk (roughly 3–4hr) is to follow the 15km dirt track through the foothills of the **Almijara range**, leading from Frigiliana, via the hamlet of Venta del Jaro, to the Axarquía village of Cómpeta (see p.109), which has good facilities and accommodation.

Another circular 8km walk covers the **hill country** to the northwest of Frigiliana. Follow the road north out of the village towards the pleasant refreshment stop of *Venta de Frigiliana* (summer daily 11am–4pm), which you'll reach after 3km. Turn left down the dirt track just beyond the entrance, which leads down the ridge, passing some old cottages and villas. Ten minutes or so further on you'll pass the gates of the Peñones and the Cortijo del Peñón farmhouses on the right. Continue down this track between pine woods and crags until you reach a crossroads, with a walled villa on the far side. Fork sharply left at this point, passing some more old cottages on the right. One of these has a single palm tree, the ancient Moorish sign of welcome. At the first fork, below a large villa, continue left, uphill. The road winds round the villa wall, swings right and crosses the lower Pedregal valley, from where it climbs up the hill to the col on the Loma de la Cruz. Just below the crest of the ridge, where a *carril* (track) comes up from the right, keep straight on up, passing a villa. In front of this villa, a water-cover stamped "SAT no. 7196 Monte Ariza" will confirm that you're on the right road. At the col, go straight across at the cross-tracks marked with red paint and follow the track down and round, keeping left of the fork on the next ridge. This will bring you down past the Casa del Valle, on the left. A little further on, round the bend, you'll see some tumbledown houses on the right; the first of these contains an old olive or wine press which is worth a look. The *carril* now passes through open country, then through *huertas*, rejoining the Torrox road at Casa Fernando. A right and then a left turn will take you to the upper car park on the edge of Frigiliana.

with sea-view balconies in most rooms, is much the more attractive option; they also have some apartments (**⑤**). Slightly cheaper sea-view balcony studios – sleeping up to four people – are on offer from *Balcón de Maro*, Plaza de las Maravillas (☎95 252 95 23, ⓦwww.balcondemaro.net; **❷**), near the church. There are numerous **places to eat** around the village and all three of the above hotels have restaurants and bars.

The Costa Tropical (west)

The **Costa Tropical** is the name given to Granada Province's 60km of coastline, much of it refreshingly tranquil after the concrete sprawls along the Costa del Sol; its western stretch, including the attractive towns of **Almuñécar** and **Salobreña**, is most conveniently reached from Nerja.

Beyond Nerja, the N340 passes tracks leading down to inviting coves with quiet **beaches**, a few of which have welcoming bars. Entering Granada Province, the N340 launches into one of the most panoramic stretches along the whole coast, climbing and twisting inland before running along sheer cliffs high above the jagged coast. Eventually it surfaces at **LA HERRADURA**, a fishing village-resort suburb of Almuñécar, and a good place to stop off and swim. There's also a **windsurf** centre here, Windsurf La Herradura (☎958 64 01 43, ⓦwww.windsurflaherradura.com) with an office on the seafront. The friendly *Hostal La Caleta*, Paseo Andrés Segovia 11 (☎958 82 70 07; **❸**), at the eastern end of the seafront, has en-suite a/c **rooms** with TV, and *Hostal Peña Parda*, Peña Parda Playa (☎958 64 00 66; **❸**), at the western end, where rooms lack a/c or TV, are the most reasonable budget options The new and comfortable *Hotel Almijara*, c/Acera del Pilar 6 (☎958 61 80 53, ⓦwww.hotelalmijara .com; **⑤**), slightly inland from the sea, is the three-star alternative but lacks a pool. There are also a couple of summer **campsites** with confusingly similar names, of which *Nuevo Camping La Herradura* (☎958 64 06 34) at the extreme western end of the beach is the best. For **food**, good tapas and *raciónes* are to be had in the bar of *Mesón El Tinao*, Paseo Maritimo s/n and set back slightly from the seafront, as well as full meals in its popular mid-priced restaurant filled with hanging *jamones*. The seafront *La Parilla*, Paseo Andrés Segovia 39, is another good place specializing in charcoal-grilled meat and fish (main dishes €13-21). *Restaurante El Rincón de Peña Parda* next door to the similarly named hostal (see above) is a good economical option with a *menú* for €12.50 plus tasty salads.

Almuñécar

ALMUÑÉCAR is Granada's flagship seaside resort and, although marred by a number of towering holiday apartments, has made admirable attempts to preserve its *andaluz* character. Founded early in the first millennium BC by the Phoenicians as the wonderfully named Sexi, it possesses ruins both from this and its later Roman and Moorish periods. The town's pebble beaches, it has to be said, are rather cramped and not improved by the greyish sand, but the esplanade, **Paseo Puerta del Mar** (aka Paseo del Altillo), behind them, with palm-roofed bars (many offering free tapas) and restaurants, is fun, and the *casco antiguo*, or old town, is attractive.

Arrival and information

The **bus station** – with frequent connections to Granada and Málaga – is at the junction of Avenida Juan Carlos I and Avenida Fenicia, northeast of the

ALMUÑÉCAR

2, **1** (300m), Roman Aqueduct (500m) ▲ & Ship House (800m)

N

Bus
Station

Aquarium
Almuñécar

PLAZA
NUEVA

Locutorio **A**
Africa Ciber @

PUERTA DE VELEZ

PLAZA DE LA
CONSTITUCIÓN
(AYUNTAMIENTO)

ORÓVIA

3 **B**

SAN JOSE

4

5

CARMEN

PL. ERAS DEL
CASTILLO

C
D

PL
DAMASCO

6

PL. KELIBIA

7

Museo
Arqueológico

@

Parqué
Botanico

E

Factoría
de Salazones

Laurie Lee
Monument

PASEO DEL ALTILLO

@

ACERA DEL MAR

8

PASEO PUERTA DE MAR

Turismo **i**

F

Castillo de
San Miguel

Playa Puerto del Mar

BIKINI

GRANEOS

Parque
Ornitológico

PASEO PRIETO MORENO

J

PLAZA
ABDERRAMAN

Playa
de la Caletilla

Penon del
Santo

Playa de San Cristobal

PASEO DE LAS FLORES

0   200 m

RESTAURANTS & BARS	
Bar-Taberna El Cortijillo	6
Bodega Francisco	5
Casa Morgan	2
El Chaleco	1
Horno de Candida	3
Jacquy Cotobro	9
La Última Ola	8
Manjar	7
Restaurante La Muralla	4

ACCOMMODATION	
Hostal Plaza Damasco	D
Hostal Rocamar	A
Hotel Almuñécar Playa	H
Hotel Casablanca	I
Hotel Goya	F
Hotel Helios	G
Hotel La Najarra	E
Hotel Palacio del Corregidor	B
Hotel Playa San Cristóbal	J
Hotel Victoria II	C

centre. Inconveniently, the **Turismo** (daily 10am–2pm & 5–8pm; Jul–Aug 6–9pm; ☎958 63 11 25, ⓦwww.almunecar.info) is at the opposite end of town (a good 10min walk away), near the sea on Avenida Europa. It is, however, located in a striking nineteenth-century neo-Moorish garden mansion and is well worth a look. The office should have information on Almuñécar's annual **jazz festival** – now one of the most important in Spain – held in July and often attracting big names. **Internet** access is available at Locutorio Africa-Ciber, Avda. de Andalucía 18 (daily 10am–2pm & 5pm–midnight), south of the bus station. Following Avda. de Andalucía from the bus station through the old town will take you close to many of the town's *hostales* and *fondas*.

Accommodation

The pressure on **accommodation** in Almuñécar is not quite as acute as at Nerja. There are more than enough hotels to cope with the summer crush, whilst good-value *hostales* encircle the central Plaza de la Rosa in the old town and there are more to be found just east of here, in the streets off the Avenida de Andalucía. Almuñécar's **campsite**, *Carambalo* (☎958 63 03 22), is some way inland off the N340 heading east; La Herradura (see p.116) is perhaps a better bet for camping.

Hostal Plaza Damasco c/Cerrajeros 8 ☎958 63
01 65. Cosy and recently renovated *hostal* just off
the plaza it's named after, offering en-suite rooms
with TV. ❸

Hotel Almuñécar Playa Paseo San Cristóbal s/n
☎958 63 94 50, ⓦwww.playasenator.com. The
glaring terracotta exterior of this 225-room monster
luxury hotel conceals a spectacular atrium lobby
with waterfall and plants dangling from the glass
roof. Not to everyone's taste, but you get all the
frills associated with a four-star hotel, including
internet access and a pool. ❻

Hotel Casablanca Plaza San Cristóbal 4 (aka
Plaza Abderramán) ☎958 63 55 75, ⓦwww
.almunecar.info/casablanca. Excellent family-run
establishment with flamboyant neo-Moorish facade
and interior, offering a/c en-suite rooms with
balcony and sea views. ❹

Hotel Goya Avda. Europa s/n ☎958 63 05 50.
Pleasant hotel with airy a/c rooms opposite the
Turismo and 50m from the Playa de San Cristóbal. ❹

Hotel Helios Paseo San Cristóbal s/n ☎958 63
44 59, ⓦwww.heliosalmunecar.com. Long
Almuñécar's leading hotel, the recently refurbished *Helios* offers tastefully furnished balcony
rooms with sea views, plus a pool and rooftop
solarium. ❻

Hotel La Najarra c/Guadix 12 ☎958 63 08 73,
ⓦwww.hotelnajarra.com. Well-equipped hotel with
a/c rooms plus garden pool, tennis courts and easy
parking a couple of minutes' walk from the Playa
de San Cristóbal. ❹

Hotel Playa San Cristóbal Plaza de San
Cristóbal 5 ☎958 63 36 12, ⓔjld00005@terra
.es. Old-worldy place with a bar full of characters
and a/c balcony rooms with TV above. The
eccentric proprietor, an ex-sea captain,
constructed the remarkable "ship house" in the
north of the town (see p.119). ❸

Hotel Victoria II Plaza de la Victoria 6, off Avda. de
Andalucía. Hotel ☎958 63 17 34. Decent one-star
hotel for rooms with a/c and TV. ❸

The Town

Almuñécar's impressive sixteenth-century **Castillo de San Miguel** (April–
Sept Tues–Sat 10.30am–1.30pm & 6.30–9pm, Sun 10am–12.30pm;
Oct–March Tues–Sat 10am–1.30pm & 5–7.30pm, Sun 10.30am–2pm; €2.30),
sitting atop a headland – the Peñon del Santo – which bisects the resort's two
bays, replaced the Moorish Alcazaba, itself built on top of an earlier Roman
fort, in the time of Carlos V. Distinctive for its massive tower known as La
Mazmorra ("the dungeon") this is where, in the Nasrid period, Granada's
rulers imprisoned out-of-favour ministers or overweening military commanders
whom they saw as a threat. During the *Reconquista* it was taken by Fernando
and Isabel in 1489, three years before the fall of Granada itself, and given the
name of Almuñécar's patron saint. Held by the French in the War of Independence, in 1808 it was bombarded by the British navy and largely ruined, after
which it served as the town's graveyard. This was recently dug up – bones,
coffins and all – and relocated to a new cemetery on the outskirts of town, and
the castle restored. The interior now houses the town's interesting **museum**
containing artefacts and information documenting Almuñécar's distinguished
three-thousand-year history.

Below the castle, to the west in the Parque Botanico El Majuelo, a remarkable
Factoría de Salazones or Roman fish-curing factory has been excavated. The
tanks in which the *garum* was prepared are well preserved, and the quality of the
famous fish sauce is recorded in the writings of Pliny the Elder. The surrounding
botanical garden is extremely peaceful with fine views towards the castillo and
walls (open site). Nearby to the south, the **Parque Ornitológico** (April–Sept
daily 11am–2pm & 6–9pm; Oct–March daily 11am–2pm & 5–7pm; €4, kids €2)
is an aviary filled with a squawking collection of 1500 birds representing 120
international species.

In town, it's well worth stopping off at the small **Museo Arqueológico**
(Tues–Sat 10.30am–1.30pm & 6.30–9pm, Sun 10.30am–2pm; €2.30 or same
ticket as castillo), located above and south of the elegant Plaza Ayuntamiento
(officially the Plaza de la Constitución, a name nobody uses) in the Cueva de
los Siete Palacios ("Cave of the Seven Palaces"), an ancient structure that may

Return to Castillo of the sugar canes

After being trapped in Spain during the Civil War, in the 1950s Laurie Lee revisited some of the places he knew well, one of which was Castillo (a pseudonym for Almuñécar). He describes the pain of this experience in *A Rose for Winter*:

Everything now was as it had been before – though perhaps a little more ignoble, more ground in dust. As I walked through the town time past hung heavy on my feet. The face of a generation had disappeared completely. A few old women recognized me, throwing up their hands with an exclamation, then came running towards me with lowered voices as though we shared a secret. But of the men I had known there was little news, and such as there was, confused. Most of them, it seemed, were either dead or fled. The old women peered up at me with red-rimmed, clouded eyes, and each tale they told was different. My ex-boss, the hotel keeper, who used to pray for Franco in his office, had been shot as a red spy; he had died of pneumonia in prison; he had escaped to France. Lalo, the hotel porter, had been killed on the barricades in Málaga; he ran a bar in Lyon; he was a barber in Jaén. Young Paco, the blond dynamiter of enemy tanks, was still a local fisherman – you could run into him at any time; no, he had blown himself up; he had married and gone to Mallorca. Luíz, the carpenter, had betrayed his comrades and been stoned to death; he lived in Vélez Málaga; he sold chickens in Granada ... In the end I gave up. There was no point in making any further inquiries. Nobody lied deliberately, but nobody wished to seem certain of the truth. For the truth, in itself, was unendurable.

In 1988 Almuñecar erected a monument to Laurie Lee in the seafront Paseo del Altillo.

well have been a water reservoir. The museum exhibits – mostly discovered locally – are from the Phoenician, Roman and Moorish periods, including an inscribed seventeenth-century BC **Egyptian vase** which carries not only the oldest piece of written text discovered on the Iberian peninsula, but also the only known reference to the early sixteenth-century BC pharaoh Apophis I, a ruler during Egypt's hazy Hyksos period when foreign usurpers grasped the throne. If archeology is your thing, the Turismo can provide directions to remains of a first-century two-level **Roman aqueduct** to the north of town.

The Turismo will also be able to provide information and opening hours for the **Aquarium Almuñecar** a sizeable marine aquarium almost ready to open at the time of writing.

One remarkable but little-known sight is the astonishing **ship house** built by an ex-merchant sea captain, José-María Pérez Ruiz, at Avda. El Mediterraneo 34, in the northeastern suburb of the town close to the N340 *autovía*. After captaining his ship for thirty years, upon retirement Señor Pérez Ruiz decided to re-create his vessel on dry land – in concrete. When you approach the house you see nothing less than a fifty-metre-long hull towering above the road complete with a bridge (now the captain's lounge and bedroom) sporting radar masts, radio antennae and all flags flying. The "deck" has all the paraphernalia of a real ship, and a swimming pool as well. It's not open to visitors but if you're a guest at señor Pérez Ruiz's hotel (see "Accommodation") you may just get a guided tour.

Eating, drinking and nightlife

There are countless **places to eat** lined along the Paseo Puerta del Mar, many of them offering cheap if unspectacular *menús*. The town's more interesting possibilities lie away from the seafront hurly-burly in the *casco antiguo* and beyond. The town has become something of a gastronomic hotspot in recent years and has a number of outstanding restaurants, two of which – *Jacquy Cotobro* and *El Chaleco* – are Belgian run; all the best places, barring the *Horno de Candida*, are located out of the centre but are well worth the effort.

Nightlife in Almuñecar centres around the bars circling the focal Plaza Kelibia and the revamped seafront Paseo del Altillo where a line of music **clubs** and **bars** – many with outdoor terraces – fill up on summer nights.

Bar-Taberna El Cortijillo Plaza Kelibia 4. Lively *freiduría* and *raciónes* bar popular with young locals, in an attractive square with a lively scene on summer nights.

Bodega Francisco c/Real 15, north of Plaza Rosa. Wonderful old bar with barrels stacked up to the ceiling and walls covered with ageing *corrida* posters and mounted boars' heads. The *fino* and *montilla* are both excellent, and the bar offers a wide range of tapas and *platos combinados*. A dining area has recently been added and impromptu flamenco sometimes adds to the fun.

Casa Morgan Urbanización El Montañes No 1 ☏ 958 63 57 75. Housed in the former mansion of a nineteenth-century Welsh hispanophile, this is the latest addition to the town's top-notch restaurants. The cooking has a creative slant (main dishes €12–19) which can also be tasted on a €14 *menú*. The views over the coast from the terrace are spectacular and there's also a bar for *aperitivos*. Reached via a signed turn-off about 2km west of town along the N340, give them a ring if you lose the way and they'll direct you.

El Chaleco Avda. Costa del Sol 37 ☏ 95 863 24 02. Slightly out of the way, this is an excellent Belgian-French restaurant with an outstanding kitchen. Among their signature dishes is *conejo a la cerveza con ciruelas* (rabbit with beer and prunes) and you can choose three courses off the menu for €19.95. Very reasonable wine prices. Closed Sun eve & Mon.

Horno de Candida c/Orovia 3 ☏ 958 88 32 84. The restaurant of Almuñécar's hotel school is located in an elegant mansion which itself incorporates a remarkable Moorish brick oven (*horno*), now a dining room. The food is excellent and there's a wonderful roof terrace as well. Main dishes €12–18 with a *menú de degustación* for €29. Closed Wed.

Jacquy Cotobro Playa Cotobro ☏ 958 63 18 02. Located on a delightful bay 1km west of the centre and easily reached on foot by following the Paseo San Cristóbal (Paseo de las Flores' western continuation) to its end, this makes a wonderful lunch or evening venue. Belgian chef (and ex-footballer with Standard Liège) Jacques Vanhoren has married the best of his native and Spanish cuisines and all dishes, both fish and meat, are cooked with panache. The à la carte doesn't come cheap, but the *menú de degustación* is excellent value at €30. Closed Mon.

La Última Ola Paseo Puerto del Mar 4. This excellent seafront fish restaurant also serves tapas and, pandering to carnivores, squeezes a few meat dishes onto its menu as well. One of its noted dishes is *dorada a la gaditana* (sea bream).

Manjar Avda. Europa 9, ☏ 958 63 51 12. Central new restaurant catering for vegetarians, with borrowings from around the Mediterranean fringe.

Restaurante La Muralla c/Ángel Gamay s/n. Excellent *bodega* serving a range of outstanding tapas and meals in their interior room or alfresco in a tiny alley. Main dishes €12–20.

Salobreña

The road east from Almuñécar crosses the Río Verde and slowly makes its way upwards, past slopes dotted with almond and custard apple trees until, 13km later, a spectacular vista opens up to reveal **SALOBREÑA**, a White Town tumbling down a hill topped by the shell of its Moorish castle and surrounded by a sea of sugar-cane fields. Comparatively undeveloped, the town is set back a two-kilometre hike from the sea (although there are hourly buses), and is thus less marketable for mass tourism, making it a far more relaxed destination than Almuñécar. Beginning life as a Phoenician city dedicated to Salambo (the Syrian goddess of love), the town retained some importance in Moorish times – as is evidenced by the much restored Alcázar – but then languished in poverty

Andalucian cuisine

The flavours of Andalucian cuisine reflect a dramatic history that has seen waves of traders and invaders attracted to the region's shores. It was the Phoenicians who introduced the olive to Andalucía – which today produces over twenty percent of the world's olive oil – the Greeks brought the vine, and the Moors introduced citrus fruits, almonds and spices. It only remained for Columbus (who sailed from Andalucía) to return from the New World with potatoes, tomatoes and green peppers and the main ingredients of modern Andalucía's cuisine had arrived.

Berenjenas fritas (aubergine) ▲

Bodegas Castañeda, Granada ▼

Pimientos salteados (sautéed peppers) ▼

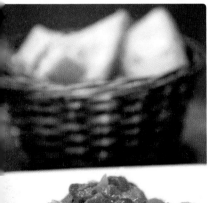

Tapas

Tapas, the small plates of delicious food served up by bars across Andalucía are arguably the world's greatest snacks. Dishes are surprisingly cheap, at around €1 to €3 for a standard plate, and for the vast majority of Andalucians, dining out means eating tapas.

Andaluzes are passionate about their tapas, which are normally eaten with a group of friends, and there's usually a lively debate as to the best place for, say, *pulpo gallego* (spicy boiled octopus) or *gambas con gabardinas* (prawns in batter "raincoats"). Normally they'll visit several establishments as part of a **tapeo** (bar tour), ordering just one or two rounds at each. This love of tapas cuts across the board; even King Juan Carlos once visited a particular *sevillano* bar, incognito, for its *papas aliñas* (marinated potatoes).

Andalucía's top ten tapas bars

The region has some of Spain's best tapas bars and here are a few of our particular favourites:

Bar Altamarino Marbella (see p.132)

Bar Coloniales II Seville (see p.292)

Bar Maestro Ronda (see p.164)

Bar Orellana Málaga (see p.87)

Bodega Sociedad Plateros Córdoba (see p.395)

Bodegas Castañeda Granada (see p.501)

Casa Balbino Sanlúcar de Barrameda (see p.230)

Casa Curro Osuna (see p.316)

Casa Puga Almería (see p.549)

El Pulguilla Nerja (see p.113)

Sherry and tapas: a perfect match

Sherry, or **fino** as it's popularly known, is Andalucía's great wine and the perfect partner for tapas. Jerez is the major producer although Córdoba province makes a similar wine called Montilla. Of the various *finos*, most popular is the dry, light and gloriously refreshing classic exemplified by the Tio Pepe and La Ina brands. Seaside Sanlúcar de Barrameda is also noted for Manzanilla, a dry and delicate *fino* with a salty tang. A celebrated *tapa* is **riñones al jerez**, veal kidneys in a sherry sauce.

▲ Tapa and Manzanilla

▼ Tapas bar, Jerez de la Frontera

Andalucía's favourite tapas

There are hundreds of tapas possibilities in the bars of Andalucía, many particular to different regions. Below are a few standards, justly popular and available everywhere.

▶▶ **Jamón Ibérico** Mountain-cured ham

▶▶ **Gambas al ajillo** Garlic-fried prawns

▶▶ **Atún escabechado** Marinated tuna

▶▶ **Espinacas con garbanzos** Spinach with chickpeas

▶▶ **Huevos relleños** Eggs stuffed with tuna

▶▶ **Boquerones en vinagre** Marinated anchovies

▶▶ **Tortilla de patatas** Potato omelette

▶▶ **Cazón en adobo** Marinated shark

▶▶ **Patatas bravas** Potatoes in a spicy sauce

▶▶ **Tortilla de Camarones** Shrimp fritters

Salmorejo gazpacho ▲

Carving jamón ▼

Gazpacho – the classic summer refresher

One of Andalucía's emblematic dishes is **gazpacho** soup, habitually served chilled in the heat of the day. It was the ancient Greeks who came up with the prototype gazpacho, in the form of a bread and salt soup. The Roman legions imported it into Spain, adding olive oil, while in the sixteenth century newly discovered tomatoes and green peppers went into the mix.

Pescaíto frito

A major passion along the coast is **pescaíto frito**, or quick-fried fish. Served at *chiringuitos* (beach restaurants) or as a take-away in a *cartucho* (paper cone) from a *freiduría* (fried-fish shop), it's invariably delicious. A famed dish available everywhere is a *fritura mixta* (fried white-fish selection) often including *cazón* (shark), *pescadilla* (whiting), *boquerones* (anchovies) and *chanquetes* (whitebait). If you buy from a *freiduría*, take your *cartucho* to a bar, order a chilled bottle of wine and you've got a feast made in heaven.

Jamón de Jabugo

Andalucía's most celebrated *aperitivo* is the crimson **jamón serrano**, salt-cured ham from small pigs fed on acorns. The very best *jamón* is the correspondingly expensive *pata negra* (named after the pigs' black hooves), and the most famous curing farms are to be found around the village of Jabugo in the Sierra de Aracena. Trevelez, a Sierra Nevada mountain village is another famous producer of these prized hams that send *andaluzes* into raptures.

until rescued by more recent prosperity, generated, in part, by its new trickles of tourism.

On the eastern side of town, the **Alcázar** (June–Oct daily 10.30am–1.30pm & 6–9pm; closes 8pm Nov–May; €3 including museum below) is worth a look, not least for the fine views from its crenellated towers. Below this, down at the foot of the hill, the sixteenth-century church of **Nuestra Señora del Rosario** (open service times) stands on the site previously occupied by a Moorish mosque. A stone's throw away, the old Ayuntamiento houses the town **museum** (same hours & ticket as the Alcázar), which displays artefacts from all periods of Salobreña's history. There's also an animated **market** each Tuesday and Friday morning in the central Plaza del Mercado, but that's about as far as sightseeing goes.

Practicalities

Buses arrive and leave from the Plaza de Goya, close to the **turismo**, Plaza de Goya s/n (Mon 9.30am–1.30pm, Tue–Sun 9.30am–1.30pm & 4.30–6.30pm; ☎958 61 03 14, ⓦwww.ayto-salobrena.org), whose town map will help you find your way around; a **kiosk** (same hours) opens in summer on the Paseo Marítimo near El Peñon, the seafront promontory. They also offer guided visits to the old town on Fridays at 6.30pm (July–Sept; €6). The Turismo also has its own bilingual (Spanish and English) book of coastal and hill **walks**, *Rutas y Senderos de Salobreña* (€6). **Internet** access is available at MAUI Informatica, c/Diego Ramirez 1 (Mon–Sat 10am–2pm & 5–9pm), 200m south of the Turismo.

There's usually no problem in finding **accommodation** in Salobreña, even in high season, and the lack of demand is reflected in the low prices. Most of the budget places are on the western side of town. Perhaps the best-value deal is the friendly French-run ⚓ *Hostal San Juan* (☎958 61 17 29, ⓦwww .hostalsanjuan.com; ❸) at c/Jardines 1, a couple of minutes walk from the Turismo; situated in a beautifully restored town house with elegant patio, the en-suite rooms come with a/c and TV. Close to Avenida García Lorca, the main avenue winding down from the town to the beach, worthy options for simple rooms include the *Pensión Castellmar*, c/Nueva 21 (☎958 61 02 27; ❶), which has terraces in some rooms and delightful sea views. Over the road, at no. 32, the similarly priced *Pensión Mari Carmen* (☎958 61 09 06; ❶–❷) is equally nice, with fans in the rooms and some en suites. To the south of here are two more en-suite options: the very pleasant and good-value *Hostal Miramar*, c/Arrabal Villa 37 (☎958 82 85 34; ❷), behind the bar of the same name; and the nearby *Hostal Mary Tere*, c/Fabrica Nueva 7 (☎958 61 01 26, ⓦwww.hostalmarytere.com; ❸), with balcony rooms. A pleasant new option in the upper town is *Hostal Jayma*, c/Cristo 24 (☎958 61 02 31, ⓦwww.hostaljayma.com; ❹) with sparkling en-suite rooms, roof terrace and wi-fi throughout.

Places to eat are limited, and the best-quality places in town are probably *Restaurante Pesetas*, c/Boveda s/n, near the Alcázar with terrace views, and *La Bodega* (main dishes €11–20), Plaza de Goya, near the Turismo. The latter offers a reasonably priced *menú del día* and serves tapas. *Mesón de la Villa*, Plaza F. Ramirez de Madrid, with a terrace on a palm-fringed plaza not far from the turismo, is another good place for tapas and *raciónes*. Perhaps the best of the economy places in town is *La Portería*, c/Fabrica Nueva 1, 50m from the turismo, who do decent and salads and have a *menú* for €8.50. Down on the seafront, your best bet is one of the many *chiringuitos* lining the shore, among which *El Peñon*, on the promontory from which it takes its name, is extremely popular, although it tends to exploit its location by charging higher prices. The nearby and more reasonably priced *La Bahía* is perhaps a better option. East of these two along the Paseo Marítimo, three more *chiringuitos*, *Tres Hermanos*, *Emilio* and *El Molino*, are also good.

The Costa del Sol

West of Málaga – or more correctly, west of Málaga airport – the real **Costa del Sol** gets going. If you've never seen this level of touristic development before, it can be quite a shock, not least when you see how grit-grey the sands are; you have to keep going, around the corner to Tarifa (see p.184), before you reach the golden sands of the tourist brochures. With their faceless 1960s' and 1970s' concrete tower blocks, these are certainly not the kind of resorts you find in Greece or even Portugal. Since the 1980s' boom in time-share apartments and leisure complexes, it's estimated that 300,000 foreigners live on the Costa del Sol, the majority of them retired and British. On the other hand, the cheap package-tour industry – largely responsible for the transformation of the string of poverty-stricken fishing villages that dotted this coast until the 1950s – no longer brings in the numbers it once did, placing the future of purpose-built resorts such as Torremolinos in peril.

Approached in the right kind of spirit, it *is* possible to have fun in **Torremolinos** and, at a price, in **Marbella**. The sea, at least, is reasonably clean around here, after a lot of work on the sewerage systems. But if you've come to Andalucía to discover the real Spain, keep going at least until you reach **Estepona**.

Torremolinos

The approach to **TORREMOLINOS** – easiest on the electric railway from Málaga or the airport – is a depressing trawl through a drab, soulless landscape of kitchenette apartments and half-finished developments. The town itself, rechristened "Torrie" by English package tourists, is certainly an experience: a vast, grotesque parody of a seaside resort with its own kitsch fascination. This bizarre place, lined with sweeping (but crowded) beaches and infinite shopping arcades, crammed with Irish pubs and estate agents, has a large permanent expat population of Britons, Germans and Scandinavians. It's a weird mix, which, in addition to thousands of retired people, has attracted – due to a previous lack of extradition arrangements between Britain and Spain – a notorious concentration of British crooks.

In recent years a dynamic town council has been moving heaven and earth to rid the resort of its "Terrible Torrie" image, and whilst they've stopped short of flattening the concrete monsters overlooking the beach they have made a few commendable improvements. The seafront promenade, which runs all the way to La Carihuela, can be quite scenic in parts and the maze of alleys in the old town – now largely cleared of their tawdry boutiques and tacky stalls – also have some charm.

Torremolinos will never be Marbella; its whole purpose is geared to giving people a roaring good time, and if that's what you're looking for, there are few places on the coast with as many bars and clubs. Throughout the summer the municipality puts on an infinite variety of free events, including festivals of music, dance and jazz, as well as beach volleyball and football competitions and children's theatre.

Arrival and information

The **train** from Málaga drops you right in the centre of the action, on Avenida Jesús Santos Rein (☎902 24 02 02), a couple of blocks west of the town's main artery, c/San Miguel. The **bus station** (☎95 238 24 19) is a five-minute walk away on c/Hoyo, to the east. The main **Turismo**, on Plaza de la Independencia (Mon–Fri 9.30am–1.30pm; ☎95 237 95 12, ⓦ www.ayto-torremolinos.org), is supported by a number of other sub offices (open April–Sept) which open longer hours; the most convenient are located on the seafront at Plaza de las Comunidades Autonomas (daily 10am–2pm & 6–8pm) southeast of the centre, and in the small fishing village of La Carihuela (1km west of the town centre) on the seafront just off Plaza del Remo (daily 10am–2pm & 6–8pm).

Accommodation

Outside August it's usually easy enough to find a **place to stay**, with plenty of economical *hostales* sandwiched between the high-rise horrors, and a couple of very pleasant places a little further out. You'll find a **campsite** (☎95 238 26 02) 3km east of the centre on the main Málaga–Cádiz highway, 500m from the sea. To get there, take the *cercanía* train (get off at Los Alamos) or go by bus (Línea B) from the central Plaza Costa del Sol. The campsite is near *Hotel Los Alamos*.

Central Torremolinos

Hostal Micaela c/Bajondillo 4 ☎95 238 33 10, ⓔ belen708@hotmail.com. Serviceable rooms with bath, close to the beach. ❷

Hotel Tarik Paseo Marítimo 49 ☎95 238 23 00, ⓦ www.hoteltarik.com. Attractive hotel facing the

beach with a garden pool and well-equipped a/c rooms with room safe; a stone's throw from the excellent *Yate El Córdobes* restaurant. ❺

Pensión Beatriz c/del Peligro 4, Playa Bajondillo ☎95 238 51 10 ⓔ hostalbeatriz@hotmail.com. Small and good, value *hostal* offering en-suite

123

rooms with a/c, TV and sea view, 20m from the beach. ❹

The Red Parrot Avda. Los Manantiales 4 ☏95 237 54 45, ⊛www.theredparrot.com. Bang in the centre with English proprietors, this recently refurbished *hostal* offers economically priced rooms with balcony, bath and fans, and the interior patio has a small pool. ❸

La Carihuela

Apartamentos Alegría c/Carmen 23, La Carihuela ☏95 238 02 73 ⊛www.lacarihuela.com. Charming, two-person seafront studios with kitchen and bath available for minimum stays of two days. ❹

Hostal Flor Blanco Pasaje de la Carihuela 4 ☏95 238 20 71, ⊜hostalflorblanco@hotmail.com. Friendly *hostal* with clean en-suite rooms, some

with partial sea views and terraces for the same price (ring ahead to reserve); 50m from the beach in La Carihuela. ❸

Hotel Miami c/Aladino 14, west of the centre in La Carihuela ☏95 238 52 55, ⊛www.residencia-miami.com. One of the most charming hotels on the whole Costa del Sol, this enchanting villa was built by a cousin of Picasso and contains many of the original designer furnishings. Behind its walls is a garden filled with palms and oleanders, and a swimming pool. ❸

Hotel Tiburón c/Los Nidos 7, La Carihuela ☏95 238 13 20 ⊛www.hoteltiburon.com. Attractive small hotel 50m from the beach with pool. All rooms have bath, TV, ceiling fans and sea views and there is internet access for guests, ❹ with breakfast.

The Town

To get the flavour of Torremolinos, take a stroll along **Calle San Miguel**, the main pedestrian mall east of the train station. Cutting through the old quarter (which even has a fourteenth-century Moorish tower), the street is lined with garish illuminated signs, tatty amusement arcades and boutiques, and even tattier restaurants serving steak and kidney pie and all its variations. One haven of tranquillity is Book Market, on the first floor at no. 28; an excellent source of used paperbacks.

Unlike the street itself, the maze of alleys around c/San Miguel give you a flavour of the old town prior to the tourist invasion and are dotted with bars used by locals. The seafront **promenade** is quite scenic in parts, and runs west all the way to the village of **La Carihuela**, the more elegant (and slightly saner) part of the resort, with a decent beach and a number of good fish restaurants on the seafront. Inland from the centre and close to the N340 *autovía*, **Aqualand Aquapark** (May–Sept 10am–6pm; €20.50, kids €14.50) is a water-based playground with chutes, slides and numerous variations on these.

Eating, drinking and nightlife

Hidden away among the many culinary disasters of Torremolinos are a surprising number of excellent **bars** and **restaurants** offering good value for money. At the cheaper end of the scale the sheer competition between outlets is so intense that if you're prepared to walk round, checking a few prices, you can have a decent night out for remarkably little money. For **afternoon tea** or an after-dinner coffee with scrumptious *pasteles* (cakes), head for *Pastelería Lepanto*, c/San Miguel 54, or the equally good *Goyesca* (on the same street at no. 42) whose *tartas de almendras* (almond cakes) are recommended.

Bodega La Guerola c/Las Mercedes 2, at junction with c/San Miguel. A real beehive of a place that's everything a tapas bar should be. It manages to squeeze in a few tables but serious *tapeadores* rest one elbow on the bar.

Bodega Quitapeñas c/San Miguel s/n. Delicious tapas and *raciónes* served in a bustling bar with a terrace by the steps at the beach end of c/San Miguel.

Casa Juan Plaza San Ginés, off the eastern end of c/Carmen, La Carihuela. Very good fish restaurant and *marisquería* now filling this plazuela on all sides as the empire grows. Closed Mon.

Frutos Avda. Riviera 80, Los Alamos. Mid-priced, high-quality fish and meat restaurant with a terrace. Closed Sun eve.

La Bodega c/San Miguel 40, near the northern end. Good central tapas bar with small *comedor*.

Specials include *boquerones en vinagre* (anchovies) and *ensalada de pulpo* (octopus).
Mesón Gallego Antoxo c/Hoyo 5 ☎95 238 45 33. Oozing class, this is an excellent mid-priced Galician restaurant offering dishes and wines from their northwestern homeland, including *merluza a la gallega* (hake) and *tarta de Santiago*. Main dishes €13-23. Closed Sun eve.
Restaurante Antonio Plaza del Remo 6, La Carihuela, near the *Hotel Tropicana* ☎95 238 52 10. One of Carihuela's more upmarket restaurants, *Antonio* specializes in superb seafood and fish dishes (*lenguado a la cava* is a speciality), but also serves meat. The legendary dessert trolley offers abundant temptations including the *malagueño* passion *peras al vino* (pears in red wine). Book at weekends. Main dishes €13-20. Closed Mon.
Restaurante El Roqueo c/Carmen 35, La Carihuela ☎95 238 49 46. Excellent and friendly mid-priced fish restaurant on the seafront, with sea view. Specialities include *fritura malagueña* and *dorada a la sal*. Superb tapas at the bar. Closed Tues.
Restaurante La Huerta c/Decano Higueras del Castillo 1, La Carihuela, near the *Hotel Miami*. Great little mid-priced restaurant festooned with plants and vines outside, serving up great fish and meat dishes and especially tasty desserts. Closed Wed.

Nightlife

When night falls, Torremolinos comes into its own, with a vibrant **nightlife** lifting off in high summer at about 10pm and continuing well beyond dawn, though it's not as wild as in recent years due to the competition of nearby Benalmádena's Puerto Deportivo nightlife zone. On the Plaza Sol y Mar in Benalmádena, *Kiu* is a massive club that pulls in the crowds from Torremolinos and Málaga, and manages to fill three dancefloors for most of the summer. Alternatively, **Atrevete**, Avda. Salvador Allende s/n, opposite the Hotel Pez Espada in La Carihuela, is a salsa venue with two dance floors and a real party atmosphere. Torrie does, however, maintain its thriving gay scene, with c/Casablanca, running west from c/San Miguel, the centre of **gay nightlife** with bars and clubs dotted along here and the streets off it. *Paladium*, Avda. Palma de Mallorca 36, has a swimming pool, balloons and foam, which makes this gay (mostly men) club one of the hottest in town (March–Oct only).

Benalmádena

Beyond Carihuela to the west of Torremolinos, the built-up coastline merges imperceptibly – after 4km – into the neighbouring resort of **BENALMÁDENA COSTA**, with its pseudo-Moorish harbour complex and a seafront lined with bars, restaurants and *chiringuitos*. Hardly an improvement on what has gone before, Benalmádena does have something that its sister resort lacks: a hilltop *pueblo*, the original Benalmádena, losing a battle to preserve its identity as it, too, is engulfed by the unremitting spread of coastal development. If you decide to make the 3km journey inland from its coastal namesake, **BENALMÁDENA PUEBLO** offers an interesting **Museo Arqueológico** on Avenida Peralta (Mon–Fri 10am–2pm & 4–6pm; free), displaying finds from around this area including a beautiful one-and-a-half-metre-high statue of Artemis retrieved from a Roman coastal wreck. There's also a section devoted to the Pre-Columbian peoples of South America.

A greater attraction by far for the majority of visitors to the Benalmádena resort, however, is **Tivoli World** (daily 1pm–midnight; July–Aug opens 6pm €4.50) the Costa del Sol's biggest amusement park, sited between the inland village and the coastal resort on the A368 and easily reached by train from Fuengirola or Torremolinos (Arroyo de Miel stop); the park has the usual cocktail of rides, restaurants and shows. Opposite the Tivoli World entrance the **Teleférico** (cable car; daily July–Aug 11am–4pm & 6pm–midnight, rest of year 10.30am–9pm; one-way €7.20, round trip €12.80) ascends to the peak of

Monte Calamorro, from where there are panoramic **views** over the Costa del Sol and – in summer – daily displays of falconry. If you choose the one-way fare you have the option of a **walk** back down the mountain along a signed path (a 60–90min trek). On the seafront and close to the Puerto Deportivo, **Sea-Life** (daily 10am–midnight, €11.95, kids €8.95) is the resort's well-presented and ethically slanted marine museum, with displays of the world's fish including a walk-through glass tunnel and a section devoted to sharks.

Fuengirola

FUENGIROLA, a thirty-minute train journey from Torremolinos, or a rapid 21km along the old N340 or the new toll *autopista*, is very slightly less developed and infinitely more staid, middle-aged and family-oriented than "Torrie".

Arrival and information

Fuengirola's helpful **Turismo** (Mon–Fri 9.30am–2pm & 5–7pm, Sat 10am–1pm; ☎95 246 74 57, ⊛www.fuengirola.org) can supply a town map and is located at Avda. Jesús S. Rein 6, close to the **train** (☎95 212 80 80) and **bus** (☎95 247 50 66) stations. The town has a number of **internet cafés**, and *Space Call*, c/Capitán 3 (daily 9am–10.30pm), off the focal Plaza Constitución, is one of the most central. Bookworld, Avda. Jesús Santos Rein s/n (opposite the train station) is a good English **bookshop** selling a wide range of titles.

Accommodation

Accommodation is only a problem in August when you'll struggle to find anything at all without a reservation. Rates fall sharply outside August (the rate we quote here).

Hostal Cuevas c/Capitan 7 ☎95 246 06 06. Pleasant, a/c rooms with bath. ❸
Hostal Italia c/de la Cruz 1 ☎95 247 41 93, ⊛www.hostal-italia.com. This friendy *hostal* is the nicest option around the Plaza de la Constitución for a/c en-suite rooms. ❹
Hostal Marbella c/Marbella 34 ☎95 247 58 02, ⊛www.hostalmarbella.info. Of the west side of

the Plaza Constitución, this is another possibility for en-suite rooms on a street with other *hostales*.
Hotel Las Piramides Paseo Marítimo s/n ☎95 258 32 97, ⊛www.hotellaspiramides.com. A luxury option at the western end of the seafront with its own pool and all the four-star frills. ❼

The Town

Fuengirola's main sights are easily located: on the road west out of town there's the restored but impressive **Castillo de Sohail** (daily Sept–June 10am–6.30pm; July–Aug 10am–9pm; €3), a tenth-century fortress built by Abd ar-Rahman III of Córdoba, as well as the scanty remains of a **Roman temple** at the eastern end of the Paseo Marítimo. A recently discovered and extensive Roman villa, **Finca El Secretario** (Mon–Fri 10am–2pm; free) is another Roman site at the eastern end of town close to the Los Boliches train station on the Fuengirola–Málaga line. Northwest of the centre, the recently opened **Museo de la Historia** in the Parque de España near the bullring (Mon–Fri 10am–2pm; €2) holds a mildly interesting museum documenting the town's development from Phoenician colony and Roman town to the present day.

Further in, the recently revamped Plaza de la Constitución is officially Fuengirola's centre, but most people are here for the **beach**; a huge, long strand divided into restaurant-beach strips, each renting out lounge chairs and pedalboats. A popular summer feature located along the N340 on the northwest edge of town is the **Parque Acuatico de Mijas** (daily May–Sept 10am–7pm,

€16, reductions for kids and family groups), a water park with all the usual water tubes and chutes. Taking its name from the nearby hill village of Mijas, it is in fact only a few-minutes ride from the Fuengirola bus station (frequent buses throughout the summer).

Eating

The streets to the south of the main square (Plaza Constitución) are lined with **restaurants** of a rather depressing similarity. One exception here is *Mesón Don Pé*, c/de la Cruz s/n, for mid-price meat dishes (main dishes €9-21; evening only). Plaza Constitución itself has the pleasant *La Plaza*, a good **breakfast**, tapas and late-night drinks bar with a terrace.

A quartet of Fuengirola's very best restaurants are slightly outside the normal tourist beat. The first, *Mesón del Mar*, Paseo Marítimo Rey de España, at the extreme western end of the seafront (100m from the landmark *Hotel Piramides*), is delightful, with one of the best seafront terraces in town; specialities include *filete de lenguado con espinacas* (sole with spinach). A little further east from here towards the centre *Old Swiss House*, c/Marina 28, is a small mid-priced restaurant where the Swiss-influenced cooking has a dash of panache (main dishes €9.50-19.50; closed Tue). Moving east again *Monopol*, c/Palangreros 7 is another good little restaurant with a *menú* for €19.80 (eves only; closed Sun). A couple of blocks to the north of the Turismo ⚔ *Restaurante Guy Massey*, Rotonda de la Luna (☎95 258 51 20; eve only), has rapidly become one of the town's top dining venues. The eponymous British chef (who has worked with Gordon Ramsey) turns out a varied menu – scallops wrapped in *jamón serrano* is a signature dish – and there's a recommended *menú de degustación* for €25. The less pricey *Bar La Paz Garrido* on the Avda. de Mijas just north of the Plaza de la Constitución serves some of the best-value seafood in town – the gazpacho and *cazón* (shark) are recommended.

Mijas

Often grouped with the more famous White Towns further north (see p.153), the once tranquil hill town of **MIJAS**, a winding eight-kilometre climb into the hills above Fuengirola is sited a little too close to the Costa del Sol for its own good, making it an obvious target for bus tours in search of the "typical" Andalucian village. However, despite a host of tacky gift shops and the numbered *burro* (donkey) taxis that transport visitors around the main square (Plaza Virgen de la Peña), the village retains some of its original character, and there are fine views towards the coast. Southeast of the main square the century old – and curiously rectangular – **Plaza de Toros** (daily 10am–7pm; €3) is worth a look, as is the nearby sixteenth-century **church** of the Inmaculada Concepción with a Mudéjar tower, the adjacent ruins of a Moorish fort and a **mirador** with a spectacular view over the coast far below. West of the main square, on Plaza de la Libertad, the **Casa Museo Etnográfico** (daily 10am–2pm & 3–7pm; free) holds a collection of artefacts from Mijas's past and a room that stages frequent art exhibitions by the village's amateur artists, of whom there are quite a number. Above the square, the ludicrous **Carromato de Max** (daily 10am–7pm; €3), a railway wagon full of junk, claims to house "the smallest curiosities in the world". If items such as Churchill's head sculpted from a stick of chalk, a copy of Leonardo's *Last Supper* painted on a grain of rice, or the shrunken head of a white man retrieved from South American Indians and "certified genuine by the FBI" grab you, then it's well worth the entry fee.

Practicalities

Frequent buses run between Fuengirola and Mijas. Information and a useful village **map** are available from a friendly **tourist office** (daily 9am–7pm, ℡95 258 90 34, Ⓦwww.mijas.es) on the east side of Plaza Virgen de la Peña, close to where the bus drops you and where there are also **car parks**. This office also gives out a free leaflet detailing a number of walks (2–3hr) in the surrounding hills and offers free **guided treks** on Wednesday & Saturday at 10am (3–5hrs). **Internet** access is available at Locutorio Mijas Pueblo (daily 10am–midnight), Pasaje Salvador Cantos Jiménez s/n just off the main square. Should you fancy **staying overnight**, the good value *Hostal La Posada*, c/Coín 47 (℡95 248 53 10; ❶–❸), has a range of room and apartment options. To get there, find your way to Plaza de la Constitución, a small square below the bullring, and ask for directions. Off Plaza de la Constitución, the village's second largest square, ⚹ *Casa El Escudo*, c/Trocha de los Pescadores 7 (℡95 259 11 00, Ⓦwww.el-escudo.com; ❹) is a delightful small hotel with charming a/c rooms equipped with TV, minibar and – in rooms 8, 9 and 10 – a terrace with fine views. The upmarket option is the pleasant *Hotel Mijas* (℡95 248 58 00, Ⓦwww.trhhoteles.com; ❻), signed to the left on the road into the village, with pool, garden, tennis court and gymnasium.

The village has plenty of **places to eat** and drink, some of them seriously overpriced. For tapas try *Bar González* on Plaza Virgen de la Peña, while decent *raciónes* along with *mariscos*, paellas and a *menú* for €7.25 are served at *Bar La Gamba*, c/San Sebastian 19, off Plaza de la Libertad. More elaborate meals are on offer at the good but pricey Basque restaurant *El Mirlo Blanco*, Plaza Constitución 13 (95 248 57 00), near the Plaza de Toros. The more modestly priced *El Castillo*, Pasaje los Pescadores 2, off the same square with terrace views is also worth a try. Finally, ⚹ *Bar-Restaurante Alarcón*, c/Lasta 1 (℡95 248 52 45; closed Sun), near the church of Santa Ana in the Barrio Santana in the older part of the village, is an excellent-value little place, worth seeking out for its superb traditional cooking (including tapas in the bar), friendly service and a pleasant roof terrace with fine views.

Marbella and around

Undisputedly the "quality resort" of the Costa del Sol, **MARBELLA** stands in considerable contrast to most of what's come before. Sheltered from the winds by the hills of the Sierra Blanca, it has a couple of excellent **beaches** which first brought it to the attention of the 1960s' smart set. However, don't strain your eyes for celebrities nowadays; the only time the mega-rich motor down from their villas in the hills is to attend a private club or put in an appearance at glitzy places like the *Puente Romano Hotel* on the way to San Pedro, where a beluga caviar starter in the restaurant will cost you the price of a good hotel room.

Marbella's image took a nose dive in the 1970s when British crooks and drug barons began setting up home here, bringing their feuds and rivalries with them. In the late 1980s the authorities became even more exercised by the arrival of Russian and Italian mafia bosses, who controlled their empires from luxury villas and yachts harboured in nearby Puerto Banus. Marbella's notoriety continued throughout the 1990s during the period of rule by the corrupt mayor Jesús Gil y Gil (who avoided a lengthy jail term by dying in 2004) and his GIL political party. A host of unsavoury characters and businesses moved into town and in 2005 Spanish police uncovered Europe's biggest ever money-laundering operation, channelling billions of euros from crime syndicates across Europe through Marbella companies into anonymous "trusts". In an ironic twist of history, there's also been a massive return of Arabs to the area, especially since the late King Fahd of Saudi Arabia built a White House lookalike, complete with adjacent mosque, on the town's western outskirts.

Arrival and information

The **bus** station is a twenty-minute walk north from the centre, at the end of c/Trapiche (℡902 143 144). Buses from Estepona and San Pedro de Alcántara (heading east) and Fuengirola (heading west) also make stops in the centre. Otherwise take buses #2 or #7 from the bus station, which will drop you near to the centre of the old town. Arriving **by car** will land you with the usual parking problem. There are signed pay car parks around the centre and all accommodations (if they don't have their own garage) will advise on possible on-street parking places. The **Turismo**, on the north side of Plaza de los Naranjos (Mon–Fri 9am–9pm, Sat 9.30am–2.30pm; ℡95 282 35 50), has detailed town maps and produces a leaflet, *Verano Cultural*, detailing the many

MARBELLA OLD TOWN

0 ──── 100 m

RESTAURANTS & CAFÉS

Atrium	14
Cafetería Marbella	11
Casanis	2
El Gallo	B
Gaspar	15
La Familia	3
Lepanto	16
Mamma Angela	13
Restaurante Buenaventura	6
Restaurante Semon	4
Santiago	18
Skina	1
Sociedad de Pesca Deportiva	17

TAPAS BARS

Bar Altamirano	7
Bar California	12
Cervecería Simon	10
El Estrecho	9
El Tonelito	8
Marisquería La Pesquera	5

ACCOMMODATION

Aubergue Juvenil	A	Hostal Paco	G
Gran Meliá Don Pepe	H	Hotel Don Alfredo	F
Hostal Berlin	J	Hotel El Fuerte	R
Hostal El Gallo	B	Hotel Finlandia	K
Hostal Guerra	P	Hotel La Morada	
Hostal Juan	L	Mas Hermosa	D
Hostal La Estrella	M	Hotel Lima	Q
Hostal La Luna	I	Hotel Linda Marbella	C
Hostal La Pilarica	N	Puerta de Aduares	E
		Refugio de Juanar	O

events held in the town throughout the summer, which often star big names. A second office (same hours) is sited on Glorieta Fontanilla, a roundabout at the eastern end of the seafront.

Internet access is available at Cibercafé, Travesía Carlos Mackintosh, on the south side of the Alameda (daily 9am–10pm) and the nearby *Locutorio Telekom*, Avda. Puerta del Mar 1, effectively the same square (daily 10am–midnight).

Accommodation

All Marbella's budget **accommodation** is in the old town, on or around c/Luna or, a couple of blocks west, along the pretty c/San Cristóbal, the street of a thousand plants carefully tended by its residents. In-town accommodation ranges between *hostal* and four-star luxury, with precious little in between. Pressure on rooms is tight in July and extremely so in August, when you should book ahead. There's also a very good **youth hostel** (*albergue juvenil*) at c/Trapiche 2 (☎95 277 14 91; under 26 €14, over 26 €19), with double rooms (some with bath), pool and plenty of activities.

Gran Meliá Don Pepe c/José Meliá s/n ☎95 277 03 00, ⊛www.solmelia.es. Five-star luxury hotel and part of the Meliá chain, with sea-view balcony rooms plus many facilities including extensive gardens, three pools (one indoor), gym, sauna, tennis courts and Michelin-starred restaurant. The cheapest high-season standard room (inland view) costs €315 per night and this doubles in Aug. ❾

Hostal Berlin c/San Ramón 21 ☎95 282 13 10, ⊛www.hostalberlin.com. Sparkling and very friendly *hostal*; all rooms come with bath, a/c and satellite TV, and free internet access is available to guests (also wi-fi throughout). Bargain rates outside July & Aug. ❹

Hostal El Gallo c/Lobatos 44 ☎95 282 79 98. Good value en-suite a/c rooms with TV above a great little restaurant. ❸

Hostal Guerra Llanos de San Ramón 2 ☎95 277 42 20. Clean, simple and economical rooms with bath, some with balcony, near the beach. ❷

Hostal Juan c/Luna 18 ☎95 277 94 7. A friendly proprietor and good value en-suite rooms with TV and fridge on a tranquil street. ❷

Hostal La Estrella c/San Cristóbal 36 ☎95 277 94 72. Nicely located option on a pleasant street, offering a/c rooms with bath, fridge, TV and some with balcony. ❺

Hostal La Luna c/Luna 7 ☎95 282 57 78. Delightful, spotless *pensión* with balconied rooms around a renovated old patio at the rear; all rooms have bath, fridge, fans and TV. ❸

Hostal La Pilarica c/San Cristóbal 31 ☎95 277 42 52. Pretty and good-value *hostal* in lovely location. En-suite rooms with TV and fridge. ❸

Hostal Paco c/Peral 16 ☎95 277 12 00, ⊛www.hostalpacomarbella.com. Central *hostal*; all rooms have bath, fans and TV. ❹

Hotel Don Alfredo c/Portada 11 ☎95 276 69 78, ⊛www.hoteldonalfredo.com. Very pleasant small two-star hotel facing the walls of the ruined castillo. All rooms exterior with a/c, satellite TV and balcony. ❹

Hotel El Fuerte Avda. Severo Ochoa 10 ☎95 286 15 00, ⊛www.hotel-elfuerte.es. The older and more charming of two four-star hotels with the same name fronting the Playa de Venus. Amenities include beach access, gardens, pool, gym, tennis courts and sauna. The standard high-season double price (inland view) is around €205 but you'll pay a supplement for a sea view. ❼

Hotel Finlandia c/Notario Luis Oliver 12 ☎95 277 07 00, ⊛www.hotelfinlandia.es. Welcoming and comfortable little one-star hotel on a quiet street. Rooms – some with balcony – come with TV. Fans are available on request and there's a wi-fi zone. ❹

Hotel La Morada Mas Hermosa c/Montenebros 16 ☎95 292 44 67, ⊛www.lamoradamashermosa.com. Taking its name from the first words of Columbus on sighting the New World ("beautiful place") this is an enchanting small hotel in a refurbished eighteenth-century town house with elegant, individually styled a/c rooms (most with terraces). ❺

Hotel Lima Avda. Antonio Belón 2 ☎95 277 05 00, ⊛www.hotellimamarbella.com. Efficient and central two-star hotel near the harbour where the higher a/c balcony rooms offer sea views. ❹

Hotel Linda Marbella c/Ancha 21 ☎95 285 71 71, ⊛www.hotel-lindamarbella.com. Attractive small hotel in a central position, with well-appointed rooms and a roof terrace. ❹

Puerta de Aduares c/Aduar 18 ☎95 282 13 12, ⊛www.puertadeaduares.com. Reasonably priced, stylishly decorated and fully serviced a/c apartments sleeping two or four. ❺

Refugio de Juanar 12km north of Marbella and signed off the A355 ☎95 288 10 00, ⓦwww .juanar.com. Tucked away in the pine forests of the Sierra Blanca, this former hunting lodge of the once-powerful *malagueño* Larios family (and where General de Gaulle holed up to write his memoirs) is now a luxurious, tranquil three-star hotel complete with attractive pool and restaurant. Make sure to do the 3km walk to the Mirador de Juanar with spectacular views over the coast. ⑤

The Town

Spared the worst excesses of concrete architecture that have been inflicted upon Torremolinos, Marbella is decidedly tasteful, retaining the greater part of its old town or **casco antiguo**. Slowly, this original quarter is being bought up and turned over to "quaint" clothes boutiques and restaurants, but you can still sit in an ordinary bar in a small old square and look up beyond the whitewashed alleyways to the mountains of Ronda. The resort has three main **beaches** stretching from the easternmost Playa de la Bajadilla and Playa de Venus, both located between its twin harbours and the Playa de la Fontanilla to the west, which gets progressively less crowded the further west you go.

The *casco antiguo*, partially walled, is set back from the sea and hidden from the main road. Here the main sights are clustered in the web of streets surrounding the picturesque **Plaza de los Naranjos**, whose delights are somewhat marred by the invasive terraces of the surrounding restaurants that use it as an open-air dining room. On the plaza (next to the Turismo) is the striking sixteenth-century **Ayuntamiento**, while in nearby Plaza de la Iglesia is the church of **Nuestra Señora de la Encarnación**. Built in the sixteenth century, it was later remodelled in the Baroque style and has a fine tower as well as a striking *retablo* inside. The **Museo Arqueológico** with Neolithic and Roman finds from the surrounding area – including the Roman villa at Río Verde (see p.135) – is currently closed while a new site is found for it; in the meantime a small display of finds from the Roman villa including a maquette and photos is housed in the Delegación de Cultura, (Mon–Fri 9am–2pm), Plaza Altamirano s/n, to the east of the Plaza de los Naranjos. The archeological museum's former home – a fine Renaissance hospital founded by Alonso Bazán, then mayor of

▲ Puerto Deportivo

Marbella – now hosts a mildly interesting **Museo del Grabado Contemporáneo**, c/Hospital Bazán s/n (Tues–Sat 10am–2pm & 6–9pm; €3), an engraving museum with works by Miró and Picasso. Northeast of the Plaza de los Naranjos you'll find Spain's one and only Bonsai tree museum, the **Museo Bonsai**, Arroyo de la Represa s/n (daily 10am–1.30pm & 5–8pm; €4), with 150 examples of this arboraceous curiosity.

Eating and drinking

When it comes to food and drink you're better off heading for Marbella's numerous and excellent **tapas bars**, rather than many of the touristy and overpriced **restaurants** around the Plaza de los Naranjos. There are, however, a fair number of good-value eating places within a five-minute walk of the square, and following the Avenida del Mar – lined with Dalí bronzes – towards the sea will lead you to the Puerto Deportivo and another zone filled with bars and restaurants.

Restaurants

Casanis c/Ancha 8 ☎95 290 04 50. Mid-priced bistro with a French/Belgian kitchen and plenty of ambience and style. *Confit de pato con lentejas* (duck with lentils) is a house special and main dishes cost €17–22. Closed Sun.

El Gallo c/Lobatas 44. Good and popular little neighbourhood restaurant serving up traditional *andaluz* dishes such as *langostino pil pil* (prawns with chilli) and *conejo al ajillo* (rabbit). There's a great value *menú* for €8.

Gaspar c/Notario Luis Oliver 19 ☎95 277 90 98. A gem of a restaurant run by a family from Rioja – which explains the comprehensive wine list. Besides their standard dishes (both fish and meat) you can also order a few plates of *raciónes* to share. If you have to wait for a table you can peruse the books in the restaurant's library, and impromptu flamenco sometimes happens when *cantantes* (singers) drop in for a meal.

La Familia c/Cruz 5, off the Plaza Puente de Ronda. Authentic mid-priced Italian cuisine served up in a pleasant atrium dining room. Main dishes €15–27.

Mamma Angela c/Virgen del Pilar 17 ☎95 277 68 99. Excellent mid-priced Italian restaurant which makes their own bread and pasta. Also do very good pizzas. Main dishes €9–18. Closed Tue.

Restaurante Buenaventura Plaza de la Iglesia 5 ☎95 285 80 69. High-class *andaluz* cuisine served on an elegant courtyard terrace. Prices have risen sharply here but there's a *menú de degustación* for €48 (excluding wine). Closed Nov.

Restaurante Semon c/Gregorio Marañón s/n ☎95 277 77 96. Top-notch mid-priced Catalan restaurant open lunch time until 10pm. The restaurant also has a delicatessen selling mouthwatering Catalan comestibles. Oct–Jun closed Sun.

Santiago Avda. Duque de Ahumada s/n, near the Puerto Deportivo ☎95 277 23 69. One of Marbella's swankiest and oldest restaurants founded in the 1950s, attracting many from the town's smart set to its seafront terrace. The food matches the hype, however, and as well as noted dishes such as *merluza a la sidra con perlas de tapioca* (hake with a cider sauce) there's a recommended *menú de degustación* for €48 (including wine). À la carte main courses €20–30. Also has an equally outstanding tapas bar. Closed Nov.

Skina c/Aduar 12 ☎95 276 52 77. Excellent small, if expensive, restaurant run by *vanguardista* chef Jacabo Vázquez who is making waves. *Cochinillo lechal con manzanas* (suckling pig) stands out on a short but creative meat and fish menu and there's a *menú de degustación* for €48. Has a small outdoor terrace. Closed Sun.

Sociedad de Pesca Deportiva Puerto Deportivo, Local 5. The Marbella fishermen's club should know a thing or two about seafood and they serve up delicious fish and *mariscos* at their restaurant with a terrace in the port. Closed Mon.

Tapas bars

Bar Altamirano Plaza de Altamirano 4, southeast of Plaza Naranjos. Great place for some of the freshest seafood tapas and *raciónes* in town; has terrace with tables spread across a small square.

Bar California Junction of c/Málaga & Avda. Severo Ochoa, east of the *casco antiguo*. Excellent *marisco* and *pescado frito* bar, where the *fino* (as proclaimed above the entrance) is as good as the seafood tapas and *raciónes*.

Cervecería Simon c/Pablo Casals 1, near the seafront at the western end. Fine tapas at low prices and a pleasant terrace on which to enjoy them. Specials include *chopitos fritas* (cuttlefish) and *rabo de toro*.

El Estrecho c/San Lázaro 12. Excellent and atmospheric little tapas bar with a wide range of possibilities. In the same alley, *Tierr Aranda* (opposite) and the nearby *Casa Bar Bartolo* are also worth a visit.

Marisquería La Pesquera Plaza de la Victoria s/n, west of Plaza de los Naranjos. More restaurant than *raciónes* bar these days, this remains a town favourite, with first-class *fino* too. House specials include *cigalitas cocidas* (Dublin Bay prawns) and *almejas marinera* (clams in wine).

Cafés and bars

Atrium c/Gregorio Marañón 11, west of the centre. One of several fashionable outdoor terrace bars in this area frequented by Marbella's well-heeled set.
Cafetería Marbella Alameda Gardens, Avda. Ramón y Cajal. Nice place for breakfast, in the gardens overlooking the main drag with two shady terraces.
El Tonelito c/Pantaleón 4. Popular *cervecería* with a "no music" policy, making it just the place to recover from the night before.
Lepanto Avda. Puerta del Mar s/n, southeast corner of the Alameda. Stylish café just south of the old quarter, which excels in chocolate confectionery creations.

Nightlife

Marbella has one of the liveliest **nightlife** scenes on the *costa*, with action centred around Plaza Puente de Ronda, c/Pantaleón and Plaza de Africa, all in the old town and Plaza de Olivos to the west of here. The once riotious Puerto Deportivo, the seafront yacht harbour, also has a scene, although this has cooled down in recent years due to complaints about noise and rowdiness by local residents. Nearby Puerto Banús is another nightlife hotspot.

Atrium Kopas c/Pantaleón 1. Popular late-night (till at least 4am) drinking hotspot playing an eclectic range of music (sometimes live) and with a courtyard to cool down outside.
Buddha Avda. del Mar 3. Retro *discoteca* rekindling the psychedelic days of "flower power" and "All You Need is Love."
Club Premiere Plaza de Olivos 2. Lively music venue often staging live gigs ranging from pop to electronica and acid-jazz. One of a clutch of clubs here which also includes *La Bastilla* and *Zimbabwe*.

Dreamer's Carretera de Cádiz 175, Río Verde. One of the bigger and better clubs on the outskirts of Puerto Banús playing a range of garage, house and techno sounds. Only hits its stride in the small hours.
Morrison's c/Ramón Gómez de la Serna 4, west of the centre. Popular Irish-style music bar playing loud chart hits.
Town House c/Alamo 1. Long-established *bar de copas* with rock/electronica sounds. Open all year, they light a roaring fire in winter.

Around Marbella: Ojén

Eight kilometres north of Marbella lies the charming hill village of **OJÉN**, which makes a pleasant and convenient alternative to the hurly burly of staying in Marbella itself. Although linked with Marbella by frequent buses, it's a much easier base with your own transport. From the picturesque main square, the Plaza de Andalucía with its sixteenth-century church of La Encarnación, the two options for **places to stay** are easily found. The most inviting is *La Posada del Angel*, c/Mesones 21 (☎95 288 18 08, ⓦwww.laposadadelangel.com; ❺), a charming small hotel in a restored town house with beautifully furnished rooms and a delightful patio. The enthusiastic proprietors can provide information on walks in the Sierra Blanca to the northwest of the village. The more economical accommodation option is the very welcoming *Hostería de Don Jose*, Paseo del Chifle s/n (☎952 88 11 47, ⓦwww.hosteriadedonjose.com; ❹ with breakfast), in the upper village, signed off the main road as you come in, with en-suite rooms, some with terraces and views.

The village hasn't got much in the way of sights although the **Museo del Vino de Málaga** (daily 11am–3pm & 4.30–8pm; free; ⓦwww.museovinomalaga .com), housed in Ojén's former *anis* distillery just below the main road at the eastern end of the village, is worth a look. Strictly speaking it's as much shop as museum but it does stock many of Málaga's great wines and – as they are out of fashion both in Spain and elsewhere today – provides a tasting opportunity to discover why they were so popular in the nineteenth and early twentieth centuries. Some of the dessert wines are particularly delicate and the *Jarel Moscatel* from a small *bodega* in Cómpeta is a stunner that could grace any dinner table.

For **eating and drinking** the village has many possibilities. There are bars around the main square and restaurants along the main road into the village. For excellent *jamón* and *queso* **tapas** make your way to the diminutive *Bodega de Fernando* down a narrow alley off c/Carreras. The nearby *El Caldero* is also good, but the village's best tapas and *raciónes* bar is *Al Norte*, with a lively terrace facing the church of La Encarnación.

San Pedro de Alcántara and around

The road west of Marbella (providing you don't take the toll-charged Autopista del Sol) soon passes – after 7km – the marina and casino complex of **PUERTO BANÚS**, where the jet set park up their yachts. An utterly modern resort devoid of any architectural charms, in summer the place presents a bizarre spectacle as crowds of Costa del Sol gawpers come to celebrity-spot, while the bronzed plutocrats attempt to steer their Bentleys and Ferraris through the crush to their vessels. If you're determined to see what the fuss is about – or fancy window-shopping at the numerous designer clothes and jewellery emporia – a useful tip coming in by car is to use the car park of the El Corte Inglés department store in the *centro comercial* (€0.50 per hr) and walk the five minutes to the gated harbour zone which only vehicles with permits may enter.

Six kilometres further, and about the only place on the Costa del Sol that isn't purely a holiday resort, is the small town of **SAN PEDRO DE ALCÁNTARA**, a none too inspiring place striving to go the way of its neighbour but hindered by the fact that its centre is set back over a kilometre from the sea. The seafront area behind a decent **beach** has been landscaped with the almost obligatory palm-lined promenade and some holiday *urbanizaciones* have been constructed, but this has done little to raise San Pedro's profile. In the town proper, what activity there is centres on the tranquil, palm-fringed Plaza de la Iglesia – at its most lively during the Thursday morning **flea market** – but there's not much else to disturb the calm.

There are three remarkable **ancient ruins** in the area (see p.135) that are definitely worth going out of your way to see; information regarding guided visits is available from the Marbella or San Pedro Turismos. The visits take place on Tues & Thurs at 12.30pm for which you will need your own transport. However, they must be **booked** at least one day in advance with Señora Conchita Cecilla on ☎952 77 14 42 (English spoken). When taking the booking she will inform you of the meeting point where you will rendezvous with the guide. The visit is free and lasts approximately two hours.

San Pedro practicalities

The San Pedro **turismo**, Avda. Marques del Duero 69 – the main street you turn in to when leaving the N340 (Mon–Fri 9am–9pm, Sat 10am–2pm; ☎95 278 52 52) – can supply a map of the town plus information on renting apartments for longer stays. A useful secondhand **bookshop**, Shakespeare, c/Lagasca 69, one street west from the Turismo, is a place to pick up some reading matter.

For a **place to stay**, the three-star *Hotel Doña Catalina* Avda. Oriental 14, southeast of the church (☎95 285 31 20, ⓦwww.hoteldonacatalina.com; ⑤) has a/c balcony rooms with satellite TV, while the central *Hostal Galea Centro*, Plaza de la Iglesia s/n (☎95 279 98 36, ⓦwww.hostalgalea.com; ❸), is a more economical option also offering a/c en-suite rooms. A budget possibility for more basic a/c ensuite rooms is *Hostal Acemar*, c/19 Octubre 17 (☎95 278 30 41; ❷) near the Turismo.

For **food** the place to head for is Avenida Andalucía to the west of the Turismo and just north of the N340. There are a number of restaurants here including a good Indian restaurant, *Sitar*. *Alfredos*, Avda. Andalucía 8, is generally regarded as the best for *cocina casera*. The nearest place to the seafront, an area dead at night, is *Restaurante Casa Fernando*, Avenida Mediterraneo s/n, about halfway down the avenue leading to the sea. It specializes in seafood and there's a leafy garden terrace to enjoy on summer nights (closed Sun).

Around San Pedro

Four kilometres back along the road east to Marbella are the remains of a **Roman villa** at Río Verde. To get there from San Pedro, pass the turn-off for Puerto Banús and, after crossing the river, take a right before the *Puente Romano Hotel* and follow the signs. Constructed in the late first or early second century, the rooms are decorated with an unusual series of black and white **mosaics** depicting not classical themes or intricate designs as elsewhere, but everyday kitchen equipment. The kitchen utensils are a delight, and the shoes portrayed by the door are evidence of the Roman custom of leaving one's footwear outside the *triclinium*, or dining room. One of the mosaic's Amphorae is so accurately portrayed that its style has helped to date the villa almost precisely. Note also the hanging fowl and fish, ready for the pot.

The sixth-century **Visigothic Christian basilica** of Vega del Mar lies close to the sea at the bottom of the Avenida del Mediterráneo, the main road from San Pedro towards the coast. Take the last road on the right before the beach and you'll come to the railed-off site in the midst of a stand of eucalyptus trees. It's one of the most important Visigothic monuments on the peninsula; the remains enable you to clearly make out a rectangular basilica with a double apse, unique in Spain. Large boulders cemented with lime-mortar were used in its construction along with still-visible brickwork at the corners. A wonderful **baptismal font** is especially well preserved and was deep enough for total immersion, the custom of the time. In and around the basilica is a cemetery of some two hundred tombs (which yielded a wealth of artefacts now in Marbella and Madrid museums), most with the head to the north, the orientation of the church. Note the graves lined with marble, evidence of social stratification even in death.

The third site, the **Roman bathhouse** of Las Bovedas, lies a little way west of here, almost on the beach. Leave any transport at the *chiringuito* and walk the fifty metres along the beach to the site. The substantial remains belong to an octagonal third-century Roman baths. Seven chambers, which would have served as a series of heated steam rooms, surround the well-preserved central bath (parts of the underfloor hypocaust system are visible). Above the central pool was a skylight surrounded by a roof terrace. Because the complex was constructed with a special lime – which, when mixed with sand and pebbles from the beach, set to a granite-like hardness – the building has defied the elements impressively.

Visiting the three sites is only possible through the turismo in San Pedro (and must be booked in advance; see p.134) but partial viewing of the Roman villa and Visigothic basilica can be had from behind their fences, whilst the Roman baths – which can be seen from the beach – now lie inside a new gated *urbanización* and are inaccessible without a guide.

Estepona

West of San Pedro the A7 toll *autopista* heads inland before turning west, while the coast road is littered with more depressing *urbanizaciones* bearing names such as Picasso or – taking irony to the limit – Paraíso (paradise), each served by its *centro comercial*. Should you feel the urge to stop, **ESTEPONA**, 17km beyond San Pedro, is about the only good bet, a more or less Spanish resort with much of its identity still intact. Lacking the enclosed hills that give Marbella character, it is at least developed on a human scale; the hotel and apartment blocks which sprawl along the front are restrained in size, and there's a pleasant EU blue-flagged beach in town, as well as the Costa del Sol's oldest nudist beach to the west. One feature of note is Estepona's four **museums**, all located in the modern Plaza de Toros to the east of the centre.

One of the best, and busiest, times to visit the town is during the first week of July, when the **Fiesta y Feria** brings out whole families of *esteponeros* in their flamenco-style finery and the town is transformed into a riot of colour.

Arrival and information

Estepona's **bus station**, on Avenida de España, lies west of the centre behind the seafront. Two hundred metres further west, a **Turismo**, Avenida San Lorenzo 1 (Mon–Fri 9.30am–2pm, Sat 10am–1.30pm; ☎95 280 20 02), will supply town maps and can help you find a room. **Internet** access is available at Sh@rk Net, Avda. de España 3 (daily 10am–10pm), on the seafront near the Correos (main post office). A **street market** is held in the Puerto Deportivo each Sunday morning.

Accommodation

Outside August you should have no problem finding a **place to stay** in Estepona. The nearest **campsite** is *Camping Parque Tropical* (☎95 279 36 18), 6km to the north on the N340 (km.162). Set back from the beach in a former tropical garden, it has a spectacular conservatory-pool and restaurant.

Hostal El Pilar Plaza Las Flores ☎95 280 00 18, ✉hostalpilar@telefonica.net Friendly *hostal* on a charming plaza offering en-suite balcony rooms with a/c and TV. ❸

Hotel Altamarina Avda. San Lorenzo 32, near the main Turismo ☎95 280 61 55, ⊛www .hotelaltamarina.com. Estepona's best in-town hotel with comfortable rooms but no sea views. It also imposes a silly rule during Aug forcing you to take lunch or dinner in the hotel restaurant (€12.50 per person added to room price). ❺ with breakfast.

Hotel Buenavista Paseo Marítimo 180 ☎95 280 01 37, ⊛www.buenavistaestepona.com. Reasonable-value hotel with en-suite sea-view balcony rooms with a/c and TV. ❹

Hotel Mediterráneo Avda. de España 68, on the seafront to the east of c/Terraza ☎95 279 33 93, ⊛www.mediterraneo-estepona.com. Functional but good-value seafront hotel, where rooms have bath, TV and (mostly) sea views. ❹

Pensión La Malagueña c/Castillo s/n ☎95 280 00 11, ⊛www.hlmestepona.com. Comfortable and reliable *pensión*, offering en-suite rooms with TV and fans. Parking for €6. ❷

Pensión San Miguel c/Terraza 16 ☎95 280 26 16. Friendly establishment with its own bar, a little west of Plaza Las Flores. All rooms are en suite and come with a/c and TV. ❷

The Town

Estepona is the last stop on the Costa del Sol and one of the most pleasant. The seafront is attractive, with a promenade studded with flowers and palms, and behind this, the older part of the town has some charming corners with cobbled alleyways and two delightful squares, the **Plaza Las Flores** and **Plaza Arce**. Calle Terraza bisects the centre and around this are most of the eating and drinking options, especially along pedestrianized **c/Real**. The **Puerto Deportivo**, to the west of town beyond the lighthouse and near the bullring, is a daintier version of Marbella's nightlife hotspot, with the few bars and clubs only becoming really animated at weekends.

From May onwards, the town's **bullfighting** season gets under way in the modern Plaza de Toros on the west side of town, reminiscent of a Henry Moore sculpture. The building is also home to four museums (Mon–Fri 9am–3pm, Sat 10am–2pm; free): the **Museo Etnográfico** (folk museum), **Museo Arqueológico**, **Museo Paleontológico** and the **Museo Taurino** (bullfighting). The folk museum has lots of artefacts from Estepona's agricultural and maritime past; the archeological museum has local finds from the Phoenician, Roman and Moorish periods; the paleontology museum, dedicated to serious research, has a collection of fossils and seashells millions of years old; while the Taurino museum – whatever your position on bullfighting – gives you some idea of the importance of *taurinismo* in Andalucian culture. There are the usual trophies and photos of past big names as well as (in the centre of the museum itself) the actual *toril* or bull-pen from where the raging bulls are released into the adjoining ring during *corridas*. To get there, take a taxi or walk west along the seafront to the Puerto Deportivo and then turn inland.

The **Selwo Adventure Park** (daily 10am–8pm; Ⓦwww.selwo.es; €23.50 adults, €16 kids) is a landscaped zoo 6km to the east of town where the two thousand-plus resident animals are allowed to roam in semi-liberty, and there are re-creations of African Zulu and Masai villages, where it's possible to stay overnight in an expensive "African-style" hut with all mod cons (details on website). To reach the park, there are signed exits indicated from N340 and the Autopista del Sol, plus regular buses from all the major Costa del Sol resorts.

Estepona's **nudist beach** and **naturist holiday village**, the Costa Natura (Ⓣ95 280 80 65, Ⓦwww.costanaturaresort.com), is located a short bus ride away, 4km west of town, and rents out apartments (Ⓖ) in a complex with bars, restaurant, pool and gardens.

Eating and drinking

Among Estepona's many **places to eat** is a bunch of excellent *freidurías* and *marisquerías*. Worth trying at the foot of c/Terraza is *La Gamba* at no. 25 and further up, at no. 57, *La Palma*. The central c/Real has *Aguilar* at no. 54 with a long list of *raciónes*, and to the west of the centre, *Simonito*, Avda. San Lorenzo 6, near the Turismo, is another good choice with an outdoor terrace. Of the town's **tapas bars**, *Mesón Genaro*, c/Lozano 15 (off c/Terraza) is a good choice, as is *Casa Típico Andaluz,* with a distinctly *andaluz* flavour at c/Caridad 55, to the east of c/Terraza; its speciality, called a *plaza de toros*, gets you a little of everything on one plate for around €8. For an after-dinner **ice cream**, *Heladería Vitín* in Plaza Las Flores has the edge, if only for location. For picnic supplies, there's a daily **market**; if you're self-catering, you could try the fish market.

La Casa de mi Abuela c/Caridad 54. This restaurant to the east of c/Terraza is worth trying for its grilled meats and Argentine steaks.

La Escollera Puerto Pesquero. Beneath the lighthouse in the fishing harbour, adjoining Puerto Deportivo, this is a vibrant, reasonably priced place for excellent fish and *mariscos*. In addition to a great tapas bar there's a wonderful sea-view terrace restaurant. Closed Mon.

La Rada Avda. España 4. At the extreme northen end of the seafront, this is a lively and excellent fish restaurant and *marisquería* that is popular with the locals.

Restaurante El Gavilán del Mar Plaza Arce. A decent place for seafood, specializing in paella, and with a decent terrace.

Nightlife

When it comes to **nightlife**, Estepona has a range of possibilities. There are the usual **flamenco** burlesques which are best avoided, but *Peña Flamenca* in c/Fuerzas Armadas in the north of town puts on the genuine stuff on Saturday nights at 10pm (the Turismo can provide more information). Nearer the centre, most night-time action takes place along and in the streets around **c/Real** where terrace bars, music places and clubs compete for the custom of a mainly local clientele. **Discotecas** and **music bars** proper are mostly grouped around the Puerto Deportivo, or in town there's the huge and glitzy *Plato 68*, Avda. Juan Carlos, 300m beyond the Turismo on the left, which attracts crowds from miles around.

Casares and around

The greyish coast west of Estepona is punctuated with watch towers used by peoples as diverse as Phoenicians, Romans and Arabs to protect themselves from pirate attacks. There's little reason to stop along here but one worthwhile detour is to head to **CASARES**, 18km inland from Estepona. One of the lesser known of Andalucía's White Towns, it's a beautiful place, clinging tenaciously – and spectacularly – to a steep hillside below a castle, and attracting its fair share of arty types and expatriates. The village is reputed to take its name from Julius Caesar, who is said to have used the still-functioning sulphurous springs at nearby Manilva (see below) to cure a liver complaint. More concrete historical evidence attributes the impressive Alcázar (built on Roman foundations) to the Moorish period, from the ruins of which there are spectacular **views** as far as Gibraltar on clearer days. There's little else in the way of sights, but it's satisfying enough simply to wander around, losing yourself in the twisting, narrow white-walled streets – another vestige of the Arab period. Flanked by an eighteenth-century church, the central plaza is a good place to sit and have a drink, cooled by breezes off the sierra. The surrounding hill country, richly wooded with cork oaks and pine as well as stands of *pinsapo*, the rare Spanish fir, offers a verdant contrast with the arid plains below and is fine **walking terrain** with plenty of dirt-tracks to follow winding through the folds of the Sierra Bermeja.

With your own vehicle you could return to the N340 and the coast by way of Manilva, reached by continuing through Casares to a junction and turning left (south) along the A377 towards Manilva. This route would allow you to see the remarkably well-preserved **Roman sulphur baths** (open access). To get there follow the signs 3km from Manilva, where the road passes beneath a spectacular viaduct carrying the latest extension of the Autopista del Sol. You'll need to park any vehicle and cross the Río de Manilva using the stepping stones, to follow a track heading inland. Pass the campsite beyond a ford on the right, and the *Bar Alamo* again on the right, and at the top of a rise, the small chapel of San Adolfo. The baths lie a little beyond this. Once at the baths – definitely Roman but now under a rather garish yellow concrete canopy – you'll need to plunge inside to see the original Roman stonework. One dubious souvenir you'll take away from the place is a sulphurous stench, which is guaranteed to cling to your swimwear for weeks. Alternatively, turning right at the junction above would allow you to make a 16km detour to Gaucín (see p.155).

Practicalities

Only two daily **buses** (Mon–Sat) leave for Casares from Estepona (currently at 1pm & 7pm; return 8am & 4pm; 45min), meaning, if you're without transport, a very brief visit or an overnight **stay**. Should you opt for the latter,

the upmarket choice is *Hotel Casares*, c/Copera 52 (T 95 289 52 11, W www
.hotelcasares.com; ❸), signed from the main square, Plaza de España, where
pleasant rooms come with balcony and views. On Plaza de España itself, the
budget-priced *Hostal Plaza* (T 95 289 40 30; ❶) has simple rooms with shared
bath above a bar.

Tourist information is available from a small office downhill from Plaza de
España at c/Carrera 51 (Mon–Fri 11am–2.30pm & 4–6.30pm; T 95 289 55
21) which can also provide information about activities such as walking and
horseriding, and has a list of *casas rurales* to rent for longer stays. Information is
also available from the delightful **Museo de Etnohistoria** (same hours as
tourist office; €2) at the top of c/Villa, to the south of Plaza de España, which
has much about Casares's illustrious past including a fascinating section on the
village's old cinema.

There are more bars than **places to eat**, but options do include *La Bodeguita
de en Medio*, a very good restaurant with a delightful roof terrace on Plaza de
España, *Mesón Los Claveles*, c/Arrabal 1 by the church, and *La Terraza*, a restaurant just outside the village on the Estepona road, which has great views.

On to Gibraltar

Beyond Estepona the scenery takes on a wilder and greener aspect as the Sierra
Bermeja yields to the Sierra Almenara. Once across the Río Guadiaro, the road
turns inland, offering, as it climbs, distant views of the Rock of Gibraltar, its
monumental silhouette often girdled with a halo of cloud. The views of the
urban sprawl and towers of the Bay of Algeciras's oil refineries signal that this is
also a major industrial zone.

San Roque and Los Barrios

SAN ROQUE, 35km south of Estepona in Cádiz Province, was founded in
1704 by the people of Gibraltar fleeing the British, who had captured the Rock
and looted their homes and churches. They expected to return within months,
since the troops had taken the garrison in the name of the Archduke Carlos of
Austria, whose rights Britain had been promoting in the War of the Spanish
Succession, but it was the British flag that was raised on the conquered territory
– and so it has remained. Today a rather undistinguished small industrial town,
the Ayuntamiento's council chamber, on the central Plaza de la Iglesia, has a
banner given to the earlier Spanish Gibraltar by Fernando and Isabel. On the
same square, the eighteenth-century church of **Santa María Coronada** – built
over the ancient hermitage of San Roque – has a fine image of the Virgin, also
rescued from the Rock in the flight from the British invaders.

San Roque's **campsite**, *Camping San Roque* (T 956 78 00 31), is on the N340
highway just east of the town. A far better place to stay is **LOS BARRIOS**,
10km to the west, a tidy and tranquil place away from the depressing nature of
this industrial zone. The elegant palm-lined main street leads to the first
accommodation option, the pleasant *Hotel Real*, Avda. Pablo Picasso 7 (T 956
62 00 24; ❸), with air-conditioned balcony rooms. Further along, and uphill
just beyond a central roundabout, there's a friendly *hostal*, *El Semáforo*,
c/Alhóndiga 5 (T 956 62 01 29; ❶), which has excellent value rooms sharing
bath above a restaurant. There are plenty of places for **eating and drinking**
including the *Hotel Real's* decent restaurant, with a *menú* for under €10, or that
at *El Semáforo*.

La Línea

Obscured by San Roque's huge oil refinery, the **Spanish–British frontier** is 8km south of San Roque at **LA LÍNEA** ("the line"). When Franco closed the frontier in 1969, it was La Línea that suffered most, as workers lost their jobs on the Rock overnight and the town's population dropped by 35 percent. After sixteen years of Spanish-imposed isolation, the gates were reopened in February 1985, and crossing between here and Gibraltar is now routine – except for the odd flare-up when petulant disputes impose long delays on those waiting to cross. La Línea remains in a largely depressed state, a fact that has pushed many of its people into assisting the Rock's smugglers by warehousing contraband tobacco prior to its distribution throughout Spain. There are no sights as such; it's just a fishing village that has exploded in size due to the employment opportunities in Gibraltar and the industrialized zone around the Bay of Algeciras.

Practicalities

The **bus station** and a friendly **Turismo** (Mon–Fri 9am–7.30pm, Sat 9am–3pm; ☏956 78 41 38) are both on Avda. 20 Abril, to the south of the main Plaza de la Constitución, a large modern square at the heart of La Línea. The Turismo's leaflet *Campo de Gibraltar* has street maps of both La Línea and Algeciras and they also give out a free *Ruta del Tapeo* (tapas route) leaflet. The closest mainline **train station** is San Roque–La Línea, 11km west of town from where you can pick up a train to Ronda and beyond.

Although La Línea's greater number of hotels make it a better overnight bet than Gibraltar, many of its **hostales** are depressingly grim and not cheap. Accommodation is concentrated around the Plaza de la Constitución. The friendly *La Campana*, c/Carboneras 3, (☏956 17 30 59, ⓦwww.hostalcampana .es; ❷) has good en-suite rooms with a/c and TV. Almost opposite, the slightly

Andalucía's Moroccan enclaves

Across the straits from Gibraltar on the north coast of Morocco lie the enclaves of **Ceuta** and **Melilla**, both Spanish territories and officially part of the autonomous region of Andalucía. When they celebrated in 1997 the quincentenary of their founding by the Catholic monarchs Fernando and Isabel, neither King Juan Carlos nor the prime minister José María Aznar saw fit to join in the deliberately low-key festivities – the Spanish establishment acceded to the wishes of Morocco, with which for economic reasons it desires good relations, for minimal observation of the event. This is because Morocco views the territories as China viewed Hong Kong – and as Spain views Gibraltar. Ceuta and Melilla are the remnants of a string of Spanish fortresses built along the coast of North Africa after Andalucía had been reconquered from the Moors. Intended to protect the peninsula from further incursions, they survived into modern times as an anachronism – the United Nations does not even list them as colonies because they were settled long before Morocco existed in its present shape. Their combined populations of 140,000 citizens have the same rights as those on Spain's mainland and vociferously oppose any plans to cede the territories to Morocco.

This opposition has complicated matters for Madrid who see the enclaves as burning up vast amounts of money in grants and subsidies as well as providing an easy entry point for illegal immigrants into Spain and the EU. In line with what is happening in the former Spanish Sahara, Ceuta and Melilla could eventually gain some form of autonomy within Morocco – but so far the inhabitants are unconvinced and the tug of war between Spain and its North African neighbour seems likely to continue for some time yet.

cheaper *Hostal-Restaurante Carlos*, c/Carboneras 6 (☎956 76 21 35, Ⓦwww
.hostalcarlos.es; ❷), is also good value for similar rooms with the same facilities.
The best upmarket option is *Hotel AC La Línea*, c/Caireles 2 (☎956 17 55 66,
Ⓦwww.ac-hotels.com; ❺), fronting the Bay of Algeciras with pool, gym and
garage and much better value than anything of the same standard in Gibraltar.

For **eating and drinking**, the *hostales Campana* and *Carlos* (see above) all
have good and economical restaurants. To eat in a more vibrant atmosphere,
however, make your way to Plaza Cruz de Herrera (undergoing a refurb at the
time of writing), through an arch off the east side of the Plaza de la
Constitución where various tapas bars and fast-food outlets congregate. The
nearby c/Real, the main pedestrianized shopping street, offers plenty of
reasonably priced bars and cafés – good for breakfast pastries – as well as
restaurants. *D'Antonio*, c/Dr Villar 19, just off the north side of the same street,
does decent tapas and *raciónes*. One of La Línea's best fish restaurants is
La Marina, Paseo Marítimo s/n, northeast of the centre and close to the sea; a
more central option, *La Pesquera*, Avda. José Meliá 2, the main drag leading
from La Línea towards the Gibraltar frontier and now flanked by a new
shopping arcade, serves decent fish and *mariscos* on a terrace with Rock views.
For picnic supplies, head for the market, north of c/Real.

Gibraltar

GIBRALTAR's interest is essentially its novelty: the genuine appeal of the
strange, looming physical presence of its rock, and the increasingly dubious one
of its preservation as one of Britain's last remaining colonies. This enormous
hunk of limestone, five kilometres long, two kilometres wide and 450 metres
high – a land area smaller than the city of Algeciras across the water – has fasci-
nated and attracted the people of the Mediterranean basin since Neanderthal
times, confirmed by the finds of skulls and artefacts in a number of the Rock's
many caves.

The Rock (as it is colloquially known) is a curious place to visit, not least to
witness the bizarre process of its opening to mass tourism from the Costa del
Sol. Ironically, this threatens both to destroy Gibraltar's highly individual
society and at the same time to make it much more British, after the fashion
of the expat communities and huge resorts up the coast. The frontier opening
has benefited most people: Gibraltarians can buy cheaper goods in Spain, a
place ironically where twenty percent of them now have second homes, while
expats living on the Costas can shop in familiar stores like Mothercare,
Morrisons and Marks & Spencer. Despite a healthy economy based on
tourism, offshore banking and its role as a major bunkering port, the colony
has reached yet another crossroads in its tortuous history, and the likely future
– whether its population agrees to this or not – is almost certain to involve
closer ties with Spain.

Some history

Recent discoveries in a cave on the southeast tip of the Rock suggest that
Gibraltar was one of the last habitats of Neanderthal man who may have lived
here some 24,000 years ago – much later than previously thought. Earlier finds
of flint tools and evidence of camp-fires and cooked meals are regarded as one
of the most important **prehistoric** finds in modern times. The cave appears to
have been inhabited by both Neanderthals and *Homo sapiens*, and it's hoped that

further excavations will provide vital evidence as to the extinction or amalgamation of our species with the earlier race.

The **Phoenicians** called the Rock "Calpe" and had a fortified naval base here, barring the way to jealously guarded Atlantic trading destinations such as Tartessus. In **Greek** mythology this was the northernmost of the two pillars erected by Heracles. Following the demise of the Roman Empire, the Rock became the bridgehead for a **Berber** assault on the Visigothic domains of southern Spain. In 711 Tariq ibn Ziryab, governor of Tangier, crossed the straits at the head of an army, defeated the Visigoths and named the Rock "Jabal Tariq" or the Mountain of Tariq, the name – albeit garbled – it still has today.

Gibraltar remained in Moorish hands until taken in 1309 by Guzmán el Bueno, but it was not long before it was recovered. The end finally came when another Guzmán, the duke of Medina Sidonia, claimed it for Spain in 1462. Apart from the raids of Barbarossa, which caused Carlos V to fortify the Rock, Spanish possession was undisturbed until the **War of the Spanish Succession**, when Britain sided with Spain against the French. The outcome of this was the seizure of the Rock in 1704 by the **British** forces whose admiral, Sir George Rooke, gave the inhabitants the choice of swearing allegiance to the Habsburg claimant to the throne – Archduke Charles of Austria – or getting out. Those that left to found San Roque (see p.139) thought their absence would be temporary, but in 1715 the British contrived to have Gibraltar ceded to them "in perpetuity" in the Treaty of Utrecht, no doubt having calculated the military advantages of such a strategic bastion. Despite military and diplomatic attempts by Spain to recover the Rock since, the British have maintained their grip, and Gibraltar played an important strategic role in both World Wars. General **Franco** mounted persistent campaigns to get it back and closed the access link with Spain in 1969, a period of enforced isolation that is indelibly etched into the Gibraltarian collective consciousness.

The Rock, it seems, is destined to be a recurring cause of friction between the two nations; in 1988 three **IRA suspects** were gunned down by British agents near the petrol station at the entrance to the town and close to the frontier. The British government – which went to enormous lengths to obscure the facts of the case – produced a version of events much at odds with that of the Spanish police and once more the issue of a "foreign power on Spanish soil" sparked a national debate.

One more curious twist in the colony's history occurred in the spring of 2004 when Gibraltar voted for the first time ever in **European Parliament elections** after being denied the vote by successive British governments wary of the political and diplomatic complexities involved. However, when the Gibraltarians won a victory in the European Court of Human Rights, the British government was forced into a U-turn and somewhat bizarrely Gibraltar's twenty thousand voters were appended to the southwest England constituency of Devon and Cornwall, almost one thousand miles away from the Rock – and to where the colony's ballot papers were airlifted once they had been counted. This success has fuelled demands for Gibraltar to have its own Westminster MP, another issue the British government would prefer not to think about. For more on the history of Gibraltar, see Contexts, p.580.

Arrival, orientation and information

If you have a car, don't attempt to bring it to Gibraltar – the queues at the border to get in (and out) are often atrocious, and parking on the Rock is limited, due to lack of space. Use the underground **car parks** in La Línea – there's one beneath the central Plaza de la Constitución – instead (it's worth paying for the extra security) and **walk** across. From the frontier, where passport checking is a formality, it's a short **bus ride** (#9, every 15min) or about a ten-minute walk across part of the airport's runway to **Main Street** (La Calle Real), which runs for most of the town's length a couple of blocks back from the port. Most of the shops – cheap, duty-free whisky and tobacco are major attractions with rock-bottom prices due to the non-application of excise duty – are clustered in and around Main Street, along with nearly all of the British-style pubs and hotels.

The main **tourist office** is housed in Casemates Square (Mon–Fri 9am–5.30pm, Sat & Sun 10am–3pm; ☏20074982, ⓦwww.gibraltar.gi/tourism) and there's a sub-branch in the customs and immigration building at the border (Mon–Fri 9am–4.30pm, Sat 10am–3pm; ☏20050762). **Internet** access is available at the public library in the John Mackintosh Hall (Mon–Fri 9.30am–10.30pm), at the south end of Main Street, which is also a cultural centre that mounts frequent exhibitions. Slightly east of here Callshop Gibraltar, 293a Main Street (daily 9am–9pm) is another possibility. The Gibraltar Bookshop, 300 Main St, is a good source for stocking up on holiday reading and has a good selection of books on the Rock's history. Much of Gibraltar, including restaurants and cafés but with the exception of the cheap booze shops, closes down on Saturday, but the tourist sights remain open, and this can often be a quiet time to visit. Virtually everything closes on Sunday.

The currency used here is the **Gibraltar pound** (the same value as the British pound, but different notes and coins although you'll often find British coins mixed in with your change); if you pay in euros (accepted without problems all over Gibraltar), you generally fork out about five percent more; ask for your change in euros if you are on a brief day trip. Gibraltar pounds can be hard to change in Spain or anywhere else. **Banks** with ATMs can be found along Main Street along with bureaux de change which stay open longer.

A word of warning **when leaving Gibraltar**: if approached by locals do not carry any packages for strangers across the border back into Spain. What may seem to be a simple carton of cigarettes could contain drugs and – if searched – you, and not they, will suffer the consequences.

Accommodation

Shortage of space on the Rock means that **accommodation** is at a premium, especially in summer, most of it is not overly inviting and (compared to Spain)

Phoning Gibraltar

From Spain dial 00+350 + number
From Europe and UK dial 00 + 350 + number
From North America dial 011 + 350 + number

expensive. It's really not worth your while searching out a good place to stay unless you have to: your best bet is to visit on day-trips from Algeciras (buses on the hour and half-hour; 30min) or La Línea. The cheapest deal is at the *Cannon Hotel*, 9 Cannon Lane, near the cathedral (T20051711, Wwww .cannonhotel.gi; £37.50 for a double sharing bath, £46 en suite, with breakfast). Otherwise, you're going to have to pay standard British **hotel** prices: the most economical are the *Queen's Hotel* on Boyd Street (T20074000, Wwww.queenshotel.gi), and the slightly pricier *Hotel Bristol* in Cathedral Square (T20076800, Wwww.bristolhotel.gi), each charging around £60–75 for their cheapest non-sea view double (supplement for sea view). The flagship *Rock Hotel*, 3 Europa Rd (T20073000, Wwww.rockhotelgibraltar.com; cheapest double £160), immediately below the Apes' Den, trades on its imperial connections (rooms are decorated in "colonial style" and come with ceiling fans and a trouser press). At Gibraltar's privately run *Emile Youth Hostel*, Montagu Bastion, Line Wall Rd (T20051106, Eemilehostal@yahoo.co.uk), expect to pay £15 a night for a dorm bed (with breakfast) or £35 for a double room sharing bathroom (with breakfast).

No **camping** is allowed on the peninsula, and if you're caught sleeping rough or inhabiting abandoned bunkers, you're likely to be arrested and fined.

Around the Rock

Be on your guard at the frontier for touting taxi drivers who offer "tours of the Rock" – they're generally overpriced (around £7 per person) and very rushed. Near the end of Main Street you can hop on the expensive **cable car** (daily 9.30am–6pm, last trip down 5.45pm; £8 return, £6.50 one way) which will carry you up to the summit – the **Top of the Rock** as it's logically known. A way to avoid paying the return fare is to walk back down (see p.147). Entry to the Top of the Rock area is 50p for pedestrians but the attractions cost extra (see below). The cable car ascends via the **Apes' Den** halfway up, a fairly reliable viewing point to see the tailless monkeys (Barbary apes) and hear the guides explain their legend. The story goes that the British will keep the rock only so long as the apes remain too; Winston Churchill was superstitious enough to augment their numbers during World War II when they started to decline. The Top of the Rock gives fantastic views over to the Atlas Mountains and the town far below, as well as an elaborate water catchment system cut into the side of the rock. This is also an ideal spot for observing bird migrations between Africa and the Spanish peninsula. From the Top of the Rock it's an easy walk south along St Michael's Road passing another of the apes' dens. Keep a tight grip on your belongings; the unruly primates are prone to stealing tourists' bags and sometimes their cameras – often tossing the items onto rocks a couple of hundred metres below.

Much of the area of the upper Rock has now been designated the **Upper Rock Nature Reserve** (daily 9.30am–7.15pm) which you can enter for the pedestrian fee but for which you will need to pay extra to view the attractions described below, plus the **Gibraltar: A City Under Siege** exhibition, housed in a former ammunition store on Willis's Road. An inclusive ticket (£8) allows entry to all of them.

From the Top of the Rock cable car station a leafy path leads to **Saint Michael's Cave** (daily 9.30am–7pm; inclusive ticket), an immense natural cavern that led ancient people to believe the rock was hollow and gave rise to its old name of Mons Calpe (Hollow Mountain). Used during World War II as a bomb-proof military hospital, the cave nowadays hosts occasional concerts.

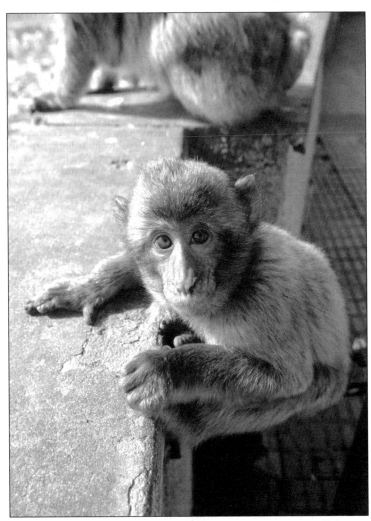

▲ Barbary apes

You can arrange at the tourist office for a guided visit to **Lower Saint Michael's Cave**, a series of chambers going deeper down and ending in an underground lake.

Although it is possible to be lazy and take the cable car both ways, you might instead continue up Queen's Road to visit the fourteenth-century **Tower of Homage** (daily 9.30am–7pm; inclusive ticket). This is the most visible survivor from the Moorish castle, today filled with wax dummies of British soldiers hacking at the stone and doing battle with the Spanish. Further up you'll find the **Upper Galleries** (aka the Great Siege Tunnels; daily 9.30am–7pm; inclusive ticket), blasted out of the rock during the Great Siege of 1779–1782 in order to point guns down at the Spanish lines.

To walk down from the Top of the Rock, you can take the **Mediterranean Steps** at the end of O'Hara's Road – but they're not very well signposted and you have to climb over **O'Hara's Battery**, a big gun emplacement with a very steep descent most of the way down the east side, turning the southern corner of the Rock. You'll pass through the Jews' Gate and into Engineer Road. From here, return to town through the Alameda Gardens and the evocative **Trafalgar Cemetery** (daily 9am–7pm; free) with graves of the Battle of Trafalgar dead and a good line in epitaphs.

The town and around

Back in town, incorporated into the **Gibraltar Museum** (Mon–Fri 10am–6pm, Sat 10am–2pm; £2), are two beautiful, well-preserved fourteenth-century **Moorish Baths**. Resembling the ancient Roman model, the baths had a cold room and hot rooms heated by a hypocaust. Note the star-shaped skylights, and the pillars used in the construction: one Roman, two Visigothic and four Moorish. Otherwise, the museum's collection is an odd assortment including an incongruous Egyptian mummy washed up in the bay, a natural history display of stuffed birds in glass cases, and a rather dreary military section documenting how the British came to rule the roost here. The museum's star exhibit should be a female skull, dating from around 100,000 years ago and unearthed in 1848 on the Rock's north face. Ironically, because the find was then stored away, it was the later discovery of a skull in Germany's Neander Valley that gave its name to the era we know as Neanderthal, which could just as easily have been termed "Gibraltarian". The museum now retains only a copy, the original having been removed to the research collection of the Natural History Museum in London. Not far away from the museum, and next door to the Governor's Residence, is the sixteenth-century **King's Chapel** (daily 9am–7pm; free) harking back to pre-colonial days. It's a fine old church – now rather marred by the military flags, regalia and wall plaques of Empire – and was formerly the chapel attached to the convent of Franciscan friars (now the Governor's Residence).

Other sites include **Nelson's Anchorage** (Mon–Sat 9.30am–5.15pm; £1 or free with inclusive Rock ticket) on Rosia Road, to the south of the harbour, where a monstrous **100-ton Victorian gun** marks the site where Nelson's body was brought ashore – preserved in a rum barrel – from HMS Victory after the Battle of Trafalgar in 1805. If you have the time to spare you can take a bus (#3 which runs along Line Wall Road and Europa Road – its continuation – with a stop at the Rock Hotel) south to the tip of the peninsula at **Europa point**; however, although on clear days you get fine views across the strait to Morocco and the sight of the odd leaping dolphin there's little else here but a lighthouse, souvenir shop, bus terminal and, interestingly, an impressive mosque donated in the 1990s by King Fahd of Saudi Arabia for the benefit of Muslim immigrants working in Gibraltar. A number of companies run rather pricey daily **dolphin-spotting** boat trips and trips around the bay. Most leave from either Marina Bay or the nearby Queensway Quay. Two established companies operating from Marina Bay are Dolphin Safari (☎20071914; £20, children £15) and Dolphin World (☎54481000; £20, children £10) but ring first to book a place or ask the Tourist Office (who have a complete list of all companies) to do it for you. Dolphin World offer a money-back guarantee should you not see dolphins.

The best **beach** is at the tiny fishing village of **Catalan Bay**, a characterless stretch of seafront reminiscent of a humdrum British holiday resort whose inhabitants like to think of themselves as distinct from the townies on the other side of the Rock. There's a bus service (#4 from Line Wall Rd; every 15min) to Catalan Bay and the other eastern beaches.

Gibraltar's sovereignty

Sovereignty over the Rock will doubtless eventually return to Spain, but at present neither side is in much of a hurry. For Britain it's a question of precedent – Gibraltar is in too similar a situation to the Falklands/Malvinas, a conflict that pushed the Spanish into postponing an initial frontier-opening date in 1982. For Spain, too, there are unsettling parallels with the *presidios* (Spanish enclaves) on the Moroccan coast at Ceuta and Melilla – both at present part of Andalucía (see box, p.140). Nonetheless, the British presence is in practice waning, and the British Foreign Office clearly wants to steer Gibraltar towards a new, harmonious relationship with Spain. To this end they are running down the significance of the military base, and now only a token force remains – most of these working in a top-secret hi-tech bunker buried deep inside the Rock from where the Royal Navy monitors the sea traffic through the straits (accounting for a quarter of the world movement of all shipping). In financial terms this has cut the British government's contribution to Gibraltar's GDP from 65 percent in the early 1980s to less than seven percent today, and the figure is still falling.

The majority of the 28,000 Gibraltarians see all these issues as irrelevant in light of their firmly stated opposition to a return to **Spanish control** over the Rock. In 1967, just before Franco closed the border in the hope of forcing a quick agreement, the colony voted on the issue – rejecting it by 12,138 votes to 44 (a poll not recognized, incidentally, by the UN). Most people would probably sympathize with that vote – against a Spain that was then still a dictatorship – but over forty years have gone by, Spanish democracy is now secure, and the arguments are becoming increasingly tenuous.

Gibraltar says "no"

May 1996 saw a change in the trend of internal politics with the **defeat of the Socialist government** of Joe Bossano (following two previous landslide victories) and the arrival in power of a **Social Democrat administration**, led by **Peter Caruana**. However, whilst Caruana had talked of opening up a more constructive dialogue with Spain during the election campaign, once in control he soon began to voice the traditional Gibraltarian paranoia and was re-elected with an increased majority in 2000, and has since repeated this feat with further victories in 2004 and 2007. His stance caused some dismay in Madrid and London, who were both behind Spain's offer in 1997 to give the colony the status of an autonomous region inside the Spanish state similar to that of the Basques or Catalans. The proposal was rejected out of hand by Caruana who made a speech at the UN castigating Spain's intransigence, and claiming the right of Gibraltar to exercise "self-determination."

In 2002, the then **Blair government** proposed that a **referendum** be held in Gibraltar on a new power-sharing agreement with Spain. When, in July of the same year the British government announced that they and their Spanish counterparts were in broad agreement regarding how Britain and Spain should share the sovereignty of Gibraltar, Caruana denounced this as an act of treachery. He then began a campaign to kill any idea of ever sharing sovereignty with Spain and announced that the Gibraltar administration would hold its own referendum on the issue. This duly took place on November 7, 2002 following a month-long campaign which resurrected the old slogan "Give Spain No Hope!" as its theme. The predictable result turned out to be a 99-percent vote against any sharing of sovereignty with Spain, in

Eating and drinking

Eating – with a few honourable exceptions – is a bit of a sad affair in Gibraltar: relatively expensive by Spanish standards, with pub grub or fish and chips as the norm and bottled wine prices to make your eyes water. Main Street is crowded with dismal touristy places and fast-food outlets, although the tiny *Smiths Fish & Chip Shop*, 295 Main St, is worth a try as is the nearby *G & P Cafetería* in the John an 88-percent turnout that sent shockwaves through the diplomatic corridors in London and Madrid.

An uncertain future
The **new Spanish administration** elected in 2004 and led by José Luis Rodríguez Zapatero has repeated the claims over Gibraltar voiced by all its predecessors and the political stalemate seems set to continue for as long as Britain uses the wishes of the Gibraltarians as a pretext for blocking any change in the colony's status – a policy that infuriates the Spanish government whose former foreign minister, Abel Matutes, stated that the wishes of the residents "did not apply in the case of Hong Kong".

Caruana has regularly been urged by Britain (under pressure from Spain) to crack down on the smuggling of contraband tobacco over the Spanish border and to curb the activities of the Rock's 75,000 "offshore" financial institutions which have mushroomed over the last decade. Many of these companies, Spain claims, are guilty of **drugs money laundering** besides providing a refuge for Russian mafia money, accusations given some credibilty by the EU's decision to start legal proceedings against a number of them in 1999. In 2005 Gibraltar finance companies were also implicated in the uncovering by Spanish police of a huge money-laundering operation based in Marbella (see p.126). Both governments hope that with the ending of Gibraltar's tax haven status in 2010 many of these issues will resolve themselves.

What most outsiders don't realize about the political situation is that the Gibraltarians feel very vulnerable, caught between the interests of two big states; they are well aware that both governments' concerns have nothing to do with their own personal wishes. Until very recently people were sent over from Britain to fill all the top civil service and Ministry of Defence jobs, a practice which, to a lesser degree, still continues – the present governor is Sir Robert Fulton, an old Etonian and former commanding officer in the Royal Marines. Large parts of the Rock are no-go areas for "natives", the South District in particular being taken up by military facilities. The withdrawal of British forces has somewhat improved the chronic housing shortage: there's a huge new development in the reclaimed land of the port, and much former army housing has been handed over to the local government.

Locals – particularly on the Spanish side of the border – also vigorously protest about the Royal Navy nuclear-powered and armed submarines that dock regularly at the naval base. Secrecy equally surrounds the issue of whether nuclear warheads and/or chemical and biological weapons are stored in the arsenal, probably deep inside the Rock itself which is honeycombed with 51km of tunnels.

Yet Gibraltarians stubbornly cling to British status, and all their institutions are modelled on British lines. Contrary to popular belief, however, they are of neither mainly Spanish nor British blood, but an ethnic mix descended from Genoese, Portuguese, Spanish, Menorcan, Jewish, Maltese and British forebears. **English** is the official language, but more commonly spoken is what sounds to an outsider like perfect Andalucian Spanish. It is, in fact, *llanito*, an Andalucian dialect with the odd borrowed English and foreign words reflecting its diverse origins – only a Spaniard from the south can tell a Gibraltarian from an Andalucian.

Mackintosh Centre serving sandwiches and salads plus tea and scones. Other budget choices are *Penny Farthing* at 9 King St, off Cathedral Square, a Lilliputian-sized restaurant with an English menu and, a couple of blocks north of here, *Jules Café*, 30 John Mackintosh Square, is a decent lunch stop with a *menú* for £12.50 (excluding wine) and a pleasant terrace. Off the east side of Main Street decent pasta in all its varieties is served up at *Buddies Pasta Casa*, 15 Cannon Lane, by the

Onward travel

One of the functional attractions of Gibraltar is its role as a port for **Morocco**. A catamaran service, the *Tanger Jet*, sails to Tangier on Fridays at 6pm, taking one hour. The return trip from Tangier is on Sundays at 8pm (local time). Tickets cost £25 one way and £45 return for a foot passenger, and £65 single and £117 return for a car. Tickets and updated timetables are available from the agent Turner, 65/67 Irish Town (℡20078305, ✉turner@gibtelecom.net).

Bland Travel, Cloister Building, Irish Town (℡20077012, enquiries: ✉elizabeth @bland.gi; ⊛www.blands.gi; closed Sat & Sun), is the leading travel agent in Gibraltar and runs twice weekly day **trips to Morocco** on Wed (Tangier; £45) and Fri (Tetouan & Tangier; £47) which include guided tour and lunch. They can also assist with booking easyJet (2 daily), British Airways (1 daily) and Monarch Airlines (1 daily) flights to London and the latter's (4 weekly) flights to **Manchester**. There are currently no flights between Gibraltar and Morocco.

cathedral. *Corks Wine Bar,* 79 Irish Town, is a tranquil venue for light meals, and nearby at no. 78 *The Clipper* serves pub grub in a varnished lounge. On the focal Casemates Square *Rock Fish & Chips,* a friendly Moroccan-run chip shop, makes an excellent job of the British national dish (eat-in or takeaway). On the same square at no. 11, the more serious *El Patio* is a Basque-run restaurant with well-prepared meat (and especially) fish dishes. An interesting option in the centre of town is the Morrocan *Marrakech Restaurant,* 9 Governor's Parade, with a pleasant terrace serving couscous, tagines and other Magrebí dishes with a set *menú* for under £10. *Saccarello's Coffee House* at 57 Irish Town is a local institution and a great place for tea and home-made confectionery. Just north of here *The Office Bistro* (open 8am–5pm), 30 Parliament Lane, is a good little lunch stop with lots of daily specials and a small terrace.

Further afield, at Marina Bay, try *Biancas,* for reasonably priced seafood as well as pizzas, burgers and salads, or the very good *Da Paolo,* which serves a selection of Italian-British-Spanish-style meat and fish dishes. At Catalan Bay the *Seawave Bar* does decent shellfish *raciónes* and good seafood, and the similar *Village Inn* next door is also worth a try. *La Mamela,* at the opposite end of the seafront is more restaurant-style and does fish dishes such as *John Dory a la roteña* for £9–15.

Gibraltarian **pubs** mimic traditional English styles (and prices), but are often rowdy, full of soldiers and visiting sailors. For pub food, the *Royal Calpe,* 176 Main St; *Gibraltar Arms,* 14 Main St; and *The Horseshoe,* 193 Main St, are among the best, all offering hearty meals. These pubs all have some outdoor seating – a rarity in Gibraltar. For a quieter drink try the *Cannon Bar* in Cannon Lane near the cathedral, or the *Piccadilly Garden Bar,* 3 Rosia Rd, just beyond the Referendum Gates (aka South Port).

Algeciras

ALGECIRAS occupies the far side of the bay from Gibraltar, spewing out smoke and pollution in its direction. The last town of the Spanish Mediterra-nean, it was once an elegant resort; today it's unabashedly a port and industrial centre, its suburbs sprawling out on all sides. When Franco closed the border with Gibraltar at La Línea it was Algeciras that he decided to develop to absorb the Spanish workers formerly employed in the British naval dockyards, thus breaking the area's dependence on the Rock.

Most travellers are scathing about the city's ugliness, and unless you're waiting for a bus or train, or heading for Morocco, there's admittedly little reason to stop. However, Algeciras has a real port atmosphere, and even if you're just passing through it's hard to resist the urge to get on a boat south. This is the main port for Moroccan migrant workers, who drive home every year during their holidays from the factories, farms and mines of Northern Europe. In summer, the port bustles with groups of Moroccans in transit, dressed in flowing *djelabas* and yellow slippers, and lugging unbelievable amounts of possessions. Half a million cross Spain each year, and at the major Islamic festival periods huge queues build up at the port as the ferries struggle to cope.

Arrival and information

The **bus station** is on c/San Bernardo, 250m or so behind the port, with services to and from Tarifa, Cádiz, Seville, Málaga, Granada and most other destinations: the bus to La Línea also goes every thirty minutes from here. Just beyond the bus station is the **train station**, from where the line heads to Ronda and the Bobadilla Junction, where there are connections with Seville, Málaga, Córdoba and Granada. The stunningly scenic route to Ronda is one of the best journeys in Andalucía; there are four departures a day.

If you need any information about the town, or want to pick up an accommodation list or map, make for the **Turismo**, c/Juan de la Cierva, on the south side of the train track (Mon–Fri 9am–7.30pm, Sat–Sun 9.30am–3pm; ☎956 57 26 36, ⓦwww.ayto-algeciras.es). **Internet** access is possible at *Locutorio Central*, c/Teniente Maroto 2 (Wed–Mon 10am–10pm), southwest of the market.

Accommodation

Algeciras has plenty of low-priced *hostales* and **hotels** in the grid of streets between the port and the train station, and lots of simple *casas de huéspedes* round the market. A good place to start is along c/Segismundo Moret facing the railway lines by the harbour. Here at no. 4 there's the reliable *Hotel Don Manuel* (☎956 63 46 06, ⓕ956 63 47 16; ❸) with air-conditioned rooms and in the grid of streets immediately north of here are several other possibilities. In c/José Santacana there's basic but clean *González* at no. 7 (☎956 65 28 43; ❶) where all rooms come en suite, or the diminutive but pleasant *Nuestra Señora del Carmen* (☎956 65 63 01; ❷) at no. 14, with similar facilities, adding a TV. On Plaza Palma, the market square, there's the surprisingly spruce *Hostal Nuestra Señora de la Palma* (☎956 63 24 81; ❷) for good a/c en-suite rooms with TV. A very pleasant hotel close to the waterfront is the *Marina Victoria*, Avda. de la Marina 7 (☎956 65 01 11, ⓦwww.hotelmarinavictoria.com; ❸), whose high, air-conditioned balcony rooms overlook the bay with great views towards Gibraltar. Lastly, there's the grand, historic *Hotel Reina Cristina* (see p.152; ☎956 60 26 22, ⓦwww.hotelesglobales.com; ❻ with breakfast) with all mod cons plus indoor and outdoor pools. Algeciras's luxurious **youth hostel**, Ctra. Nacional 340 (☎956 67 90 60, ⓕ956 67 90 17; under 26 €14, over 26 €19), with pool, tennis courts and en-suite double rooms, lies 8km west of town on the Tarifa road. Buses heading for Tarifa will drop you outside on request (ask for the "Albergue Juvenil").

The Town

Once you start to explore, you'll also discover that the old town has some very attractive corners that seem barely to have changed in fifty years, especially

On to Morocco

Morocco is easily visited from Algeciras: in summer there are hourly crossings to **Tangier** (daily; fast ferry 1hr, normal ferry 2hr 30min), and at least ten to the Spanish *presidio* of **Ceuta** (daily; fast ferry 35min), little more than a Spanish Gibraltar with a brisk business in duty-free goods, but a relatively painless way to enter Morocco. **Tickets** cost €38 (normal ferry) or €40 (fast) one-way to Tangier or Ceuta, and are sold at the scores of travel agents along the waterfront and on most approach roads; they all cost the same, though some places may give you a better rate of exchange than others if you want to pay in foreign currency. Viajes Transafric, Avda. Marina 4 (℡956 65 43 11, ⊛www.viajestransafric.com), near the port, is a reliable company and will provide up-to-date information on timetable changes. They also do a daily all-inclusive **day-trip** to Tangier by fast-ferry, which includes a guided tour, lunch, and time for shopping, for €48. Wait till Tangier – or Tetouan if you're going via Ceuta – before buying any Moroccan currency; rates in the embarkation building kiosks are very poor. Check the date and time on your ferry ticket, and beware the ticket sellers who congregate near the dock entrance wearing official Ceuta/Tangier badges: they add a whopping "commission" charge.

around the **Plaza Alta**. This leafy square, arguably the town's only sight of any note, lies a five-minute walk from the bus station/port area and if you're killing time provides a much more pleasant place to sit out than around the port. On the square, the eighteenth-century church of **Nuestra Señora de la Palma** and the Baroque chapel of **Nuestra Señora de Europa** – with a fine facade – are worth a look.

Nearer the port, where more impressive but now crumbling edifices echo faded glories, the romantic **Hotel Reina Cristina**, Paseo de la Conferencia s/n, south of the harbour, set in a park and built in the nineteenth century in British colonial style, is a wonderful throwback to the days of the Grand Tour and steam trains. Call in for a drink in their terrace bar and take a look at the plaques behind the reception desk bearing the signatures of famous guests, such as Sir Arthur Conan Doyle, W.B. Yeats, Cole Porter and Federico García Lorca.

Eating and drinking

The huge number of people passing through the town also guarantees virtually limitless possibilities for **food and drink**, especially around the port/harbour area but it's worth venturing a short distance away from here for a bit more quality. A little north of the bus station, the excellent ⚔ *Restaurante Montes*, c/Juan Morrison 27, is a traditional upmarket place where *asado de cabrito* (roast kid) is a signature dish; there's a great-value *menú* for €9.50. Nearby, they also have an equally excellent **tapas** bar lower down the hill on the same street, at the junction with c/Emilio Castelar. Close to their tapas bar, *Casa María*, c/Emilio Castelar 53, is another excellent little restaurant with a *menú* for €9.50. More tapas bars are to be found in the streets surrounding the Plaza Alta, where there are more bars, cafés and popular *heladerías*. The daily **markets** are useful places to buy food, as well as vibrant and fascinating to visit; the main one, on Plaza Palma down by the port, is a riot of colour on Saturday mornings.

Ronda and the White Towns

Though Andalucía boasts many pretty *pueblos blancos*, the best known are the group of **White Towns** – unfeasibly picturesque places, each with its own plaza, church and tavern – set in the roughly triangular area between Málaga, Algeciras and Seville. At their centre, in a region of wild mountainous beauty, is spectacular **Ronda**, very much the transportation hub and a great attraction in its own right. From Ronda, almost any route north or west is rewarding, taking you past a whole series of lovely little villages, among cherry orchards and vines, many of them fortified since the days of the Reconquest – hence the mass of "de la Frontera" suffixes. Of these, **Arcos de la Frontera**, a truly spectacular White Town perched on a high limestone spur, comes close to Ronda as the best place to spend a few days in the region.

To Ronda from the coast

Of several possible approaches to Ronda from the coast, the route up from Algeciras is the most rewarding – and worth going out of your way to experience. **From Málaga**, most of the buses to Ronda follow a rather bleak route, heading along the coast to San Pedro de Alcántara before turning into the mountains along the A376. The train ride up from Málaga is better, with three connecting services daily, the last currently running at 6.43pm.

From Algeciras – a route that goes via **Gaucín** – you can take either the bus or train, or, if you've time and energy, go on a four- or five-day walk. En route, you're always within reach of a river and there's a series of hill towns, each one visible from the next, to provide targets for the day.

Castellar de la Frontera

Heading north out of Algeciras along the A369, after 8km (and just beyond the turn-off for Castellar below) a turning on the left signed "Casa Convento" leads through expansive woodlands to the enchanting ⊁ *Convento La Almoraima* hotel (☎956 69 30 02, ⓦ www.la-almoraima.com; ⑤), which is located inside a rehabilitated seventeenth-century convent with a fine Florentine tower and a restaurant in the former cloister. There's a pool and tennis court and the hotel is surrounded by vast tracts of wooded walking country in the Parque Natural de los Alcornocales (see below), all making it hard to imagine a more serene stopover.

The next turning, about 2km further on, leads to **CASTELLAR DE LA FRONTERA**, a bizarre hill village within a thirteenth-century Moorish castle, whose population was moved downriver in 1971 to a "new" town on the edge of nearby La Almoraima. The relocation was subsequently dropped and a few villagers moved back to their old houses, but many of the vacated dwellings were taken over by retired hippies (mainly affluent Germans). Perhaps not surprisingly, the result wasn't totally successful, and the two groups didn't gel – reflecting this tension, the place today has a brooding, claustrophobic atmosphere. The solitary **accommodation** option lies within the castle walls: *Casas Rurales de Castellar*, c/Rosario 3 (☏956 23 66 20, Ⓦwww.tugasa.com; ❹), which has renovated a number of dwellings to rent as self-catering *casas rurales*. The same operation also runs the decent and adjacent *Restaurante Aljibe*, with a *menú* for around €18. The only other places for eating and drinking are a *venta* at the start of the road up to Castellar as well as a bar near the entrance to the castle.

Jimena de la Frontera

JIMENA DE LA FRONTERA, 20km further north along the A369, lacks the traumas of Castellar; again, it's a hill town but it's far larger and more open, rising to a grand if ruined thirteenth-century Moorish **castle** with a triple-gateway entrance and round keep. In recent years it has become home to a considerable contingent of British expats who probably feel the need to be within working and shopping distance of Gibraltar. Jimena is also a gateway to the **Parque Natural de los Alcornocales**, a vast expanse of verdant hill country stretching south to the sea and north to El Bosque and covered with cork oaks (*alcornocales*); a haven for large numbers of birds and insects, it's also a paradise for walkers. The tourist offices in this area should stock a *Junta de Andalucía* booklet in straightforward Spanish detailing eight **walks** of between 2km and 7km in various parts of the park, the first of which takes in the Tajo de las Figuras Neolithic cave paintings near Benalup de Sidonia (see p.177). *Walking in Andalucía* by Guy Hunter-Watts (see p.609) also describes half a dozen walks in the park, two starting in Jimena. Jimena holds an annual week-long international music **festival** in the second half of July which attracts a wide range of jazz, flamenco, folk and classical artistes, bands and orchestras from Spain and abroad.

In town the only place **to stay** is the charming *Hostal El Anon*, c/Consuelo 34 (☏956 64 01 13, Ⓦwww.hostalanon.com; ❹ with breakfast), a series of tastefully renovated houses and stables with patio, bar, restaurant and rooftop pool. They can also arrange horseriding in the scenic surrounding countryside. The only other option, *Hostal Los Arcos* (☏956 64 03 28; ❷), lies a little way out at the train station, and has decent rooms with bath. Jimena's **campsite**, *Camping Los Alcornocales* (☏956 64 00 60), occupies a superb location with great views on the north side of town (reached by following c/Sevilla to its end), rents out en-suite wood cabins (❸) and has its own restaurant. Other **places to eat** include *Bar Ventorrillero*, Plaza de la Constitución 2, at the foot of c/Sevilla with a lunch-time *menú* for around €8, and the equally good *Restaurante Bar Cuenca*, Avenida de los Deportes, on the way into town, which also serves tapas and has a pretty terrace patio at the rear.

Gaucín

Beyond Jimena the A369 climbs for 23km through woods of cork oak and olive groves to reach **GAUCÍN**, just beyond the Málaga border. Almost a mountain village and perched on a ridge below yet another Moorish fort, Gaucín commands tremendous views and makes a fine place to stay. The village has a prosperous air somewhat sustained by a long-standing international community comprised of British and other European emigrants.

The only attraction of any note is the **Castillo del Aguila** (daily 11am–1pm & 4–6pm; free), a Moorish castle reached by a track at the eastern end of the village. From the battlements there are great views across terrain studded with olive, oak and chestnut trees to Gibraltar and even the Moroccan coast beyond on a very clear day. Easter Sunday is always celebrated here with a fiesta and **encierro** (bull run) when beefy fighting bulls career through the streets looking for partying inebriates to get their horns into.

For **accommodation**, *Hostal Santa Isabel* is a good choice (☎95 215 13 24; ❷), with rooms above its restaurant next to the *gasolinera* (where you should enquire) as you come into the village from Jimena; get a room at the back for a view of the Serranía de Ronda – now somewhat obscured by a recent housing development. In the village proper a more upmarket option is the charming *Hotel Rural Fructuosa*, c/Covento 67 (☎95 215 10 72, ⓦwww .lafructuosa.com; ❺ with breakfast) owned by the restaurant of the same name (see below) where most of the lovely individually styled rooms enjoy spectacular views. They produce their own walks leaflets for guests and also rent out a couple of equally attractive houses in the village for longer stays (see website for details).

Places to eat include, as well as the *Hostal Santa Isabel's* economical terrace restaurant, the equally cheap *Venta Pilar*, down some steps over the road opposite, flanking the swimming pool. Near the centre of the village, the mid-priced *La Fructuosa* offers delicious traditional cooking with a Mediterranean slant (main dishes €10–18); the nearby also mid-priced *La Fuente*, on the main plaza, is also very good and has vegetarian options. *Venta Socorro*, on the main Ronda road, is another worthy choice and serves up a wide selection of tapas. Excellent tapas are also to be had at *Bar Paco-Pepe* on c/San Juan de Dios, near the centre of the village, which also serves meals.

You can reach Gaucín by **bus**, but perhaps more rewarding is the thirteen-kilometre walk from its **train station**, not served by buses. The station is actually at El Colmenar on the Algeciras–Ronda line, and should you need a fortifying snifter before the hike (getting on for 3hr, mostly uphill) opposite the station there's *Bar-Restaurante Las Flores*, who also offer a €10 menú. Across the tracks, the welcoming *Hotel Buitreras* (☎95 215 30 70, ⓦwww .ruralbuitreras.com; ❹) is a possible overnight stop. This is a walker-friendly place and can provide copious information about some great hiking in this zone. Besides rooms they also offer dormitory beds for €15. Moving upmarket, an inviting *hotel rural*, *Hacienda la Herriza* (☎95 106 82 00, ⓦwww .laherriza.com; ❺), lies halfway between El Colmenar and Gaucín and comprises a luxury chalet complex in woodland with a pool and restaurant. Horseriding is one of numerous activities on offer. There are several bars along El Colmenar's main street fronting the station and among them *Café-Bar España* is a decent place to eat with a *menú* for €7 and, behind *Bar Las Flores*, *Rincon del Cani*, c/Ruiz Zorrilla 2, is also good and popular with locals. *Bar Las Flores* can also arrange a taxi to Gaucín (about €20) should you chicken out of the hike.

Benarrabá and around

Five kilometres beyond Gaucín a turn-off the Ronda road leads to the village of **BENARRABÁ** sited amidst glorious wooded hill country. The very pleasant ⚹ *Hotel Rural Banu Rabbah* (☎95 215 02 88, ⓦwww.hbenarraba.es; ❸) here, adopting the village's original Moorish name, has comfortable balcony rooms with stunning views, pool and a good restaurant and bar. In the village proper, *Bar Barroso*, near the Ayuntamiento, is noted for its **tapas**. Guy Hunter-Watts's book *Walking in Andalucía* (see "Books", p.609) has an eleven-kilometre circular **walk** from the hotel which takes in the picturesque hill village of Genalguacil. If you are using this as a staging post on a hiking route to Ronda, there's a useful overnight possibility at La Jimera de Libar (see p.168), from where Ronda is in striking distance.

A couple of kilometres along the A369 beyond the Benarrabá turn-off, a turn on the left (the A373) leads to the village of **ALGATOCÍN** where the attractive *Hotel-Camping Salitre* (☎95 211 70 05, ⓦwww.turismosalitre.com; ❹ with breakfast) is a complex of hotel, cabins (❸) and campsite in wooded surroundings, and offering all kinds of outdoor activities as well as a full-blown observatory for use by guests. Next door, the *Venta Valdivia* is renowned for its *conejo asado* (grilled rabbit) and is a hugely popular Sunday lunch venue.

Twenty kilometres further along the A369 and then the MA536 the village of **JUBRIQUE** is another attractive hill village sited in the midst of more picturesque *serranía* walking country. The main street, c/Algatocín, ascending to its heart has a couple of bars and the inviting *Hotel Taha Baja* (☎95 215 23 76; ❷) with restaurant, which would also serve as a good base.

Ronda

Rising amid a ring of dark, angular mountains, the full natural drama of **RONDA** is best appreciated as you enter the town. Built on an isolated ridge of the sierra, it's split in half by a gaping river gorge (El Tajo, though the river itself is the Guadalévin) that drops sheer for 130m on three sides. Still more spectacular, the gorge is spanned by a stupendous eighteenth-century arched bridge, while tall whitewashed houses lean perilously from its precipitous edges.

Not surprisingly, this dramatic and dominant location attracted not only the early Celts, who named it Arunda, but Phoenicians and Greeks as well. Under Rome it became an important military bastion referred to by Pliny the Elder as Arunda Laus ("the glorious"). When the Moors later came to rule the roost here, Medina Runda was transformed and enlarged into the provincial capital of the Tarakuna district. Embellished with lavish mosques and palaces, the town ruled an independent and isolated **Moorish kingdom** until annexed by Seville in the mid-eleventh century. It then passed successively through the hands of the Almoravids, Almohads and Merinid Emirate of Morocco before ending up as a fief of Nasrid Granada in 1349. Only after a long and bitter struggle did the town finally fall to Fernando and Isabel in 1485.

Ronda is also notable for having been the birthplace of the **Maestranza**, an order of knights who laid down the rules for early bullfights performed on horseback. During the nineteenth century the town became an increasingly popular destination for Romantic travellers, and even today Ronda has sacrificed little of its enchanting character to the flow of day-trippers from the Costa del Sol, much of its attraction still lying in its extraordinary setting, or in simply walking down by the river, following one of the donkey tracks through the rich green valley. Birdwatchers should look out for the lesser kestrels, nesting in and launching themselves from the cliffs beneath the Alameda park, while, lower down, crag martins can be spotted.

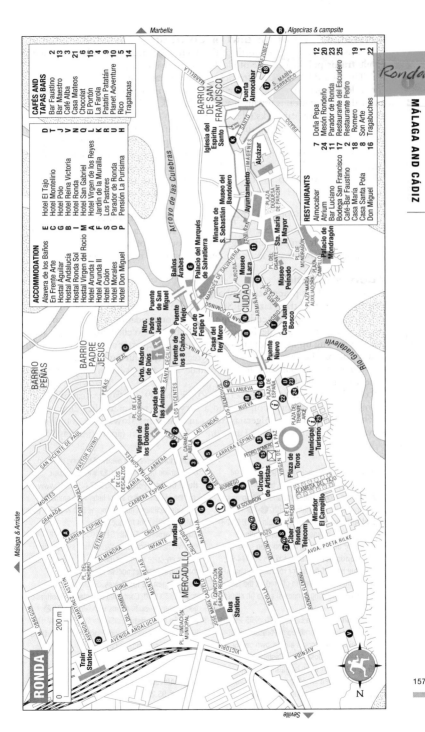

RONDA

▲ Marbella   ● R, Algeciras & campsite

▲ Málaga & Arriate

▲ Seville

200 m

ACCOMMODATION

Alavera de los Baños	E
En Frente Arte	C
Hostal Aguilar	G
Hostal Andalucia	B
Hostal Ronda Sol	I
Hotel Virgen del Rocio	M
Hotel Arunda I	A
Hotel Arunda II	F
Hotel Colón	S
Hotel Morales	O
Hotel Don Miguel	P
Hotel El Tajo	D
Hotel Montelirio	T
Hotel Polo	J
Hotel Reina Victoria	V
Hotel Ronda	Q
Hotel San Gabriel	N
Hotel Virgen de los Reyes	L
Jardin de la Muralla	K
La Farola	R
Los Pastores	U
Parador de Ronda	H
Pensión La Purísima	

CAFÉS AND TAPAS BARS

Bar Faustino	2
Bar Maestro	13
Café Alba	3
Casa Mateos	21
Chocolat	6
El Portón	15
La Farola	4
Patatin Patatán	9
Planet Adventure	10
Rico	5
Tragatapas	14

RESTAURANTS

Almocabar	12
Atrium	20
Bodega San Francisco	23
Café-Bar Faustino	25
Casa Maria	17
Casa Santa Pola	2
Don Miguel	19
Doña Pepa	7
Mesón Rondeño	24
Parador de Ronda	11
Restaurante del Escudero	17
Restaurante Pedro	18
Romero	8
Son Arte	16
Tragabuches	22

N

Arrival, information and orientation

The **bus station** is in the north of the Mercadillo quarter on Plaza Redondo, while **trains** pull in a couple of blocks east on Avenida Andalucía (℡95 287 16 73). There's a RENFE office for tickets and timetables at c/Infante 20, near the Plaza del Socorro. Arriving by **car**, your best bet is to park as far out as possible (near the train station is usually feasible) and walk to the centre, or head straight for one of the pay car parks (clearly signed).

At the northern end of the Plaza de España, Ronda's helpful **Turismo** (Mon–Fri 9am–7.30pm, Sat & Sun 9.30am–3pm; ℡95 287 12 72) has maps and walking information on the Serranía de Ronda (see p.167) plus details of organizations offering guided walks. There's an equally helpful **Turismo Municipal** (Mon–Fri 10am–7.15pm, Sat & Sun 10.15am–2pm & 3.30–6.30pm ℡95 218 71 19, Ⓦwww.turismoderonda.es) opposite the south side of the bullring.

Just north of the Plaza de España is the **Carrera Espinal**, Ronda's main pedestrianized thoroughfare (always referred to as "La Bola" by *rondeños*) and shopping area. It can be confusing walking around Ronda as many of the streets have **multiple names**: if in doubt, refer to as many maps as possible.

Accommodation

Many of the best **places to stay** are in the heart of the Mercadillo quarter, and to the east of the Plaza del Socorro off c/Borrego and its continuations, c/Cristo and then c/Almendra. Upmarket accommodation was once concentrated around the Plaza de Toros, but a number of excellent small hotels have recently sprung up in other parts of the Mercadillo quarter as well as La Ciudad quarter, across the Tajo bridge. Prices increase sharply during Semana Santa and the *corrida goyesca* bullfight festival (usually the first week in Sept) but are otherwise reasonable.

Ronda's **campsite**, *Camping El Sur* (℡95 287 59 39, Ⓦwww.campingelsur .com), with swimming pool, bar and a very good restaurant, lies 2km out of town along the road to Algeciras. You can rent **bungalows** here, too. It's not served by bus, so if you don't fancy the walk, take a taxi (approximately €9).

Budget

Hostal Águila c/Naranja 28 ℡95 287 19 94, Ⓔmturrillo@yahoo.es. Pleasant, friendly family-run *hostal* for a/c rooms with bath and TV. Also has some simpler rooms sharing bath. ❶–❷

Hostal Andalucía c/Martínez Astein 19 ℡95 287 54 50. Pleasant rooms in leafy surroundings opposite the train station, all rooms en suite. ❷

Hostal Ronda Sol c/Cristo 11 ℡95 287 44 97. Good-value budget *hostal* for rooms with shared bath, but check what you're offered as the two interior rooms (lacking windows) are a bit claustrophobic. ❶

Hotel Arunda I carrera Espinel 120 ℡95 219 01 02, Ⓦwww.hotelesarunda.com. Pleasant, good-value hotel with a/c rooms and its own garage. ❷

Hotel Arunda II c/José María Castelló Madrid 10 ℡95 287 25 19, Ⓦwww.hotelesarunda.com. Slightly more expensive offshoot of the above, this is equally good with a/c rooms with satellite TV near the train and bus stations. Computer with internet access for guests plus plenty of parking space in own garage beneath hotel. ❷ with breakfast.

Hotel Colón c/Pozo 1 ℡95 287 02 18, Ⓦwww .hcolon.es. Charming small hotel with sparkling en-suite facilities and – in rooms 301 & 302 – your own spacious roof terrace. ❷

Hotel Morales c/Sevilla 51 ℡95 287 15 38, Ⓦwww.hotelmorales.es. Welcoming small hotel where en-suite rooms come with TV and a/c and there's free internet access for clients. ❷

Hotel Virgen de los Reyes c/Borrego 13 ℡95 287 11 40. Congenial two-star hotel offering good-value en-suite rooms with a/c and TV. ❷

Pensión La Purísima c/Sevilla 10 ℡95 287 10 50. Family-run *pensión* with basic but comfortable rooms with and without bath. ❷

Moderate to expensive

Alavera de los Baños c/San Miguel s/n ℡95 287 91 43, Ⓦwww.alaveradelosbanos .com. Enchanting, small hotel with compact but elegant rooms, garden, pool and restaurant serving (Thurs & Fri eves; open to public) Morrocan dishes. ⑤ with breakfast.

En Frente Arte c/Real 40 ☎95 287 90 88, ⓦwww.enfrentearte.com. Stylish hotel inside a restored mansion with distinctive and elegant a/c rooms. Breakfast-brunch is included in the price as are self-service soft drinks and beer in the bar. Additional luxuries include a delightful garden pool and games room plus free sauna and Internet access. ④–⑤ with breakfast.

Hotel Don Miguel c/Villanueva 8 ☎95 287 77 22, ⓦwww.dmiguel.com. New hotel with comfortable rooms overlooking the Tajo, and a highly recommended restaurant (see p.164). Garage. ⑤ with breakfast.

Hotel El Tajo c/Cruz Verde 7 ☎95 287 40 40, ⓦwww.hoteleltajo.com. Pleasant traditional hotel with a/c rooms with satellite TV, its own economical restaurant, and a garage. ④

Hotel Montelirio c/Tenorio 8 ☎95 287 38 55, ⓦwww.hotelmontelirio.com. Spectacularly sited on the edge of the Tajo, this luxury four-star hotel occupies a tastefully renovated *casa palacio* where well-equipped rooms have stunning views. It also manages to squeeze in a small pool and a very good restaurant, the *Albacara*. ⑥

Hotel Polo c/Mariano Soubiron (c/Benitez on some maps) 8 ☎95 287 24 47, ℻95 287 24 49. This long-established hotel has stylishly renovated rooms with sparkling bathrooms and elegant fittings. Garage. ⑤

Hotel Ronda Ruedo Doña Elvira 12 ☎95 287 22 32, ⓦwww.hotelronda.net. Charming new flower-bedecked five-room hotel in a quiet street only minutes from the Tajo bridge. Light and airy exterior rooms with a/c and wi-fi. ⑤

Hotel Reina Victoria c/Jerez 25 ☎95 287 12 40, ⓦwww.husa.es. Nineteenth-century retreat for British military visitors from Gibraltar which, although refurbished (and now part of the Husa chain), has a lingering air of decaying grandeur. Ask for one of the corner rooms with a spectacular view over the Serranía de Ronda. Facilities include a pool, gardens and parking. Website special offers can make this a real bargain. ⑥

Hotel San Gabriel c/José Holgado 19 ☎95 219 03 92, ⓦwww.hotelsangabriel.com. Stunning restoration of an eighteenth-century mansion, with beautifully furnished a/c rooms, plus a five-seater cinema (for guests) with collection of classic films on DVD. Friendly proprietors. ⑤

Jardín de la Muralla c/Espiritu Santo 13 ☎95 287 27 64, ⓦwww.jardindelamuralla.com. New hotel in La Ciudad situated in a wonderful eighteenth-century *casa palacio* with classically furnished rooms, many overlooking a delightful leafy garden with pool. Ten percent discount for Rough Guide readers with this guide. ⑤

Los Pastores 4km outside town along the Algeciras road (A369), take right turn 400m after 4km sign ☎95 211 44 64, ⓦwww.lospastores.com. Very pleasant rural option in a remodelled former farmhouse surrounded by fine walking country and offering attractively furnished a/c apartment-rooms, many with terraces. All are provided with DVD & CD player and activities include horse riding lessons and hiking; breakfast available. ④

Parador de Ronda Plaza de España ☎95 287 75 00, ⓦwww.paradores.es. This imposing and relatively new parador teetering on the edge of the Tajo is Ronda's flagship hotel, a superb and tasteful building with luxurious accommodation, pool, terrace bar, restaurant and garage. ⑦

The Town

The town divides into three parts: on the northwest side of the gorge is the largely modern **Mercadillo** quarter, while across the bridge is the old, maze-like Moorish town, **La Ciudad**, and its **San Francisco** suburb. The late eighteenth-century **Puente Nuevo** bridge spans the gorge between them and allows you the chance to peer down the walls of limestone rock into the yawning Tajo and the Río Guadalvín, far below. The bridge has its own **Centro de Información** (April–Oct Mon–Fri 10am–9pm, Sat 10am–1.45pm & Sun 10am–3pm; €2), housed in a former prison above the central arch, with exhibits documenting the story of its construction and history. Hemingway, in *For Whom the Bell Tolls*, recorded how prisoners were thrown from the bridge to their deaths. Today the bridge and the gorge provide a habitat for a large flock of **chough** (members of the crow family) who glide around the rock cliffs seeking perches.

Casa Del Rey Moro to the Baños Árabes

Crossing the Puente Nuevo into La Ciudad brings you to the somewhat arbitrarily named **Casa del Rey Moro** (House of the Moorish King; daily

10am–7pm; €4), an early eighteenth-century mansion built on Moorish foundations, on c/Marqués de Parada (aka c/Santo Domingo). Local legend has it that this was the palace of the Moorish emir Badis, an Arabian Bluebeard, who was reputed to drink his wine from the skulls of the victims he beheaded. From the house a remarkable underground stairway (the Mina) descends to the river at the foot of the Tajo; these 365 steps, guaranteeing a water supply in times of siege, were cut by Christian slaves in the fourteenth century. There's a viewing balcony at the bottom where you can admire the towering walls of rock and the gorge's birdlife but the long climb back up will probably make you wonder if it was worth the stiff entry fee.

Further down the same street is the **Palacio del Marqués de Salvatierra**, a splendid Renaissance mansion with an oddly primitive, half-grotesque frieze of Adam and Eve on its portal together with the colonial images of four Peruvian Indians; the house is still used by the family. Just down the hill you reach the two old town bridges – the **Puente Viejo** of 1616 and the fourteenth-century single-span Moorish **Puente de San Miguel** and nearby, on the southeast bank of the river, are the distinctive hump-shaped cupolas and bizarre glass roof-windows of the refurbished **Baños Árabes** (Mon–Fri 10am–7pm, Sat 10am–1.45 & 4–7pm, Sun 10am–3pm; €3, Sun free). Dating from the thirteenth century and wonderfully preserved, these are truly remarkable structures, with star-shaped windows set in a barrel-vaulted ceiling and beautiful octagonal brick columns supporting horseshoe arches. An aqueduct carried water from the nearby river to the bathhouse complex which was formerly surrounded by plant-filled gardens. One room shows a film on the history of the baths every fifteen minutes.

Santa María La Mayor and around

At the centre of La Ciudad in Ronda's most picturesque square stands the cathedral church of **Santa María La Mayor** (daily 10am–7pm; €3), originally the Moorish town's Friday Mosque. Externally it's a graceful combination of Moorish, Gothic and Renaissance styles with the belfry built on top of the old minaret. Inside, the church itself is sombre and dull but you can see an arch covered with Arabic calligraphy, and, in front of the current street door, a part of the old Arab *mihrab*, or prayer niche. A little east of the church along the Callejón de los Tramposos stands the **Minarete de San Sebastián**, a tower that survives from a fourteenth-century mosque. Close by and to the rear of the cathedral on Plaza del Gigante, **Museo Joaquín Peinado** (Mon–Sat 10am–2pm & 5–7pm, Sun 10am–2pm; €3) displays the works – influenced by Cézanne and Picasso – of *rondeño* artist Joaquín Peinado. The museum is housed in the Palacio de Moctezuma, a former mansion with two fine patios.

A short distance west from Santa María La Mayor is the most important of Ronda's palaces, the fourteenth-century **Palacio de Mondragón** (Mon–Fri 10am–7pm, Sat & Sun 10am–3pm; €3) on the plaza of the same name. Probably the real palace of the Moorish kings, following the *Reconquista* it was much altered in order to accommodate Fernando and Isabel. Inside, three of the patios preserve original stuccowork and mosaics and there's a magnificent carved wood ceiling; the palace also houses a **museum** covering local archeology and aspects of Moorish Ronda, in particular burial practices relating to the recently discovered cemetery outside the walls (see p.161). From a restored Mudéjar courtyard there's a fine **view** over the Tajo towards the Serranía de Ronda.

Just north of here at **Casa Juan Bosco** (daily 9am–6pm; €1), c/Tenorio 20, you can visit a nineteenth-century mansion stuffed full of heavy mahogany furniture. The house itself is dull and oppressive, but the reconstructed

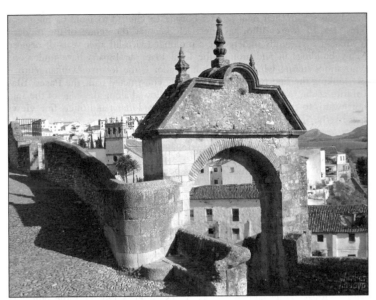

▲ Arch of Felipe V

Mudéjar gardens with fountain and mosaics are a delight, offering more great views over the Tajo.

Heading south on c/Armiñan, which bisects La Ciudad, on the left at no. 29 you'll find the **Museo Lara** (daily 11am–8pm; €4), containing the eclectic lifetime collection of *rondeño* Juan Antonio Lara, a member of the family who own and run the local bus company of the same name. An avid collector since childhood, Señor Lara has filled the extensive museum with a fascinating collection of antique clocks, pistols and armaments, musical instruments and archeological finds, as well as early cameras and cinematographic equipment. Further along at no. 65, the **Museo del Bandolero** (daily 10.45am–8pm; €3) is largely devoted to celebrating the Serranía's illustrious, mainly nineteenth-century bandits and includes displays of their weapons as well as tableaux and audiovisual presentations. Further along the same street, near the southern end of La Ciudad, are the ruins of the **Alcázar**, once impregnable until razed by the French in 1809 and now partially occupied by a school.

Continuing downhill along c/Armiñan you'll pass the sixteenth-century **Iglesia del Espíritu Santo** (Mon–Sat 10am–1.30pm and 3.30–6pm; €1) with a fine interior, en route to the town's principal Moorish gate, the magnificent **Puerta de Almocábar** leading into the Barrio San Francisco. Deriving from the Arabic *al maqabir* (cemetery) it would have led to the burial grounds which – following the Roman practice – were always located outside the walls. In 1485, the Christian conquerors, led by Fernando, passed through this gate to claim the town. The adjoining arch of **Puerta de Carlos V** was constructed during the reign of Fernando's successor, the Habsburg emperor.

El Mercadillo, the Plaza de Toros and Carrera Espinel

When Ronda was retaken from the Moors in 1485, the impoverished governors imposed such heavy taxes on all goods and foodstuffs entering it that the merchants set up their own quarter outside La Ciudad to avoid paying them. This area, **El Mercadillo**, has effectively become the centre of the modern town, and is currently undergoing a prolonged face-lift after years of neglect. Many buildings in and around the focal Plaza de España have undergone renovation, among which is a stylish parador – the former Ayuntamiento – overlooking the Tajo (see p.159). A recently constructed path, the **Paseo Blas Infante** at the rear of the parador, can be followed along the edge of the Tajo northwards to the Alameda and the *Hotel Reina Victoria* and offers fine **views** towards the Serranía de Ronda.

The *barrio*'s major monument has to be the **Plaza de Toros** (daily 10am–8pm; €6), to the north of the Plaza de España, the oldest, one of the largest and certainly the most venerated bullring in Spain. Opened in 1785, it became the stage upon which the father of the modern bullfight, Pedro Romero, laid down the rules of fighting bulls on foot (see box below). Once you've passed through the elaborate Baroque doorway, it's possible to wander around the arena with its unusual stone barriers and an elegant double tier of seats supported by stone columns. The **museum** gives an illuminating history of the *corrida* or bullfight; besides posters advertising the first *corrida* held here on May 19, 1785, and Pedro Romero's *traje de luces* ("suit of lights"), there are photos of Hemingway and Orson Welles, two regular visitors. Welles's last wish was to have his ashes buried in Ronda and they are now interred on the nearby estate of his friend and one of Spain's greatest *toreros*, the *rondeño* Antonio Ordóñez, whose bronze statue (alongside that of his father) stands near the bullring's Puerta Grande. The artist Goya made a number of paintings here of the *matadores* in action, and each September in a tribute to Goya and Romero the *corrida goyesca* is staged, with fighters garbed in eighteenth-century-style gear similar to those in the paintings.

A short distance along the pedestrianized **carrera Espinel**, the *barrio*'s main thoroughfare, the picturesque **Plaza del Socorro** opens to the left. Recently pedestrianized it has become a favourite spot with *rondeños*, especially on summer nights, when they gather to chat on the terraces of the numerous bars and restaurants. The northern end is overlooked by the **Circulo de Artistas**, a fine eighteenth-century *casa señorial* mansion and now superbly restored as the town's casino. The doorman will usually not object to you stepping inside to view the building's delightful patio.

Pedro Romero: father of the corrida

Born in Ronda in 1754, Pedro Romero is the father of the modern **bullfight**; previously bulls had been killed only on horseback with a *rejón* or spear, as a patrician pastime. However, Romero was not the first to fight bulls on foot: legend has it that this accolade goes to his grandfather Francisco Romero, who leapt into the ring when an aristocrat had been dismounted by a bull and began to distract it with his hat, delighting the crowd in the process. The hat was changed for the red *muleta*, or cape, and the bullfight was born. Once the *corrida* had been created, however, it was Pedro Romero who laid down the pattern for all future contests with his passes and moves, many still in use today, along with the invention of the almost mystical *arte* – the union of animal and man in a form of ballet. In the newly constructed Ronda ring, Romero killed over five thousand bulls and fought into his eighties, passing on to his students his soberly classical Ronda style, which is markedly different from the more flamboyant styles of Seville and Córdoba. A statue honouring Romero stands in the Alameda del Tajo.

To the north of the Plaza de Toros lies the **Alameda del Tajo**, a pleasant park completed in the early nineteenth century with views towards the Serranía de Ronda. The garden is said to have been laid out at no cost to the local council, the funds raised by fines on those using "obscene language in public, thereby causing a scandal". Continuing in the same direction will bring you to the Carmelite **Convento de la Merced** on Plaza de la Merced, its doors flanked by two great palms. Beyond a doorway at the end of the short street to the left of the church, the nuns sell their *dulces* (mornings and after 5pm): *pan rondeño* and *magdalenas* are two of their specialities.

From here, you can continue along Avenida Fleming (aka c/Jerez) to the **Hotel Reina Victoria**, built by an English company in the first decade of the last century to house British visitors, many of whom came from the military base at Gibraltar. The Austrian poet Rainer Maria Rilke put up here in 1913, and his room (no. 208) – complete with his fascinating framed hotel bill – has been preserved as a museum which the management will allow you to view on request. The hotel's bar has a terrace with stunning views down the Guadiaro river valley to the distant Serranía.

Finally, a couple minutes east from the Plaza de España lies the eighteenth-century **Virgen de los Dolores** in the street of the same name. This chapel has a curious porch projecting into the street. Carved on the porch's pillars are some weird, bird-like creatures, as well as others that are part beast, part human, with ropes fastened around their necks. The site of the church was formerly a gallows for condemned prisoners and this strange imagery may be a representation of these unfortunates.

Eating, drinking and nightlife

A great many of Ronda's best **eating and drinking** options are to be found on or around the pedestrianized Plaza del Socorro, the area to the of south Plaza de Toros and in the Barrio de San Francisco which has recently acquired some very good bars and restaurants. There are numerous good places for breakfast along carrera Espinel, and a couple of good restaurants in La Ciudad. For **tapas** aficionados there are plenty of quality places to try out. **Nightlife** tends to be provincial and low key, but with a little persistence and luck you may catch some memorable flamenco.

Restaurants

Almocabar c/Ruedo Alameda 27, Barrio San Francisco ☏ 95 287 59 77. Excellent tapas bar with an equally good restaurant behind. Creative variations on regional dishes are served in the restaurant and it's advisable to book. Main dishes €12–18. Closed Tues.

Atrium c/Blas Infante s/n. Pleasant all-day cafeteria 50m from the Plaza de Toros. Serves a range of interesting salads, pizzas and meat and fish dishes as well as a €20 paella (for two). Reasonable wine prices and there's an attractive terrace.

Bar Luciano c/Armiñán 42. Pleasant bar-restaurant with a good-value tapas and *platos combinados*, and an economical *menú*.

Bodega San Francisco c/Ruedo Alameda 32, close to the Puerta de Carlos V in the Barrio San Francisco (☏ 95 287 81 62). This highly popular tapas bar has now opened an equally good restaurant just opposite in this atmospheric *barrio*. The tapas are excellent and the restaurant specializes in *carnes a la brasa* (charcoal grilled meats). Main dishes €9–13.

Café-Bar Faustino c/Santa Cecilia 4. Excellent, economical and atmospheric tapas, *raciónes* and *platos combinados* bar that keeps serving till 1am.

Casa María c/Ruedo Alameda 27, Barrio San Francisco ☏ 95 287 62 12. Chef Elías Vega's little restaurant doesn't have a menu – he cooks whatever inspires him on the day. Excellent fish and meat dishes and and – as he's a wine aficionado – one of the best cellars in Ronda. Reckon on about €30–40 per person upwards. (Closed Wed.)

Casa Santa Pola c/Santo Domingo 3 ☏ 95 287 92 08. Impressive, expensive restaurant in a former *casa palacio* containing bits of the ninth-century house that preceded it. Spread over three floors, with views over the Tajo, it offers a wide range of local dishes – speciality is *carnes asados* (roasted meats). Main dishes €18–26.

Don Miguel *Hotel Don Miguel*, Plaza de España ☎95 287 77 22. One of the town's leading restaurants, with *rondeño* specialities such as *solomillo de venado* (venison) on the à la carte menu; their unimaginative *menú del dia* for €18 is less exciting. The main attraction, though, is the terrace, offering a marvellous view of the Tajo.

Doña Pepa Plaza del Socorro. Decent, family-run restaurant offering a variety of *menús del día* on a shaded terrace.

Mesón Rondeño c/Nueva 7. Good neighbourhood restaurant offering a wide-choice *menú* for €9, well prepared fish and meat dishes and a range of paellas with a vegetarian version priced at €14 (for two).

Parador de Ronda Plaza de España. The parador's restaurant has an excellent choice of local and regional dishes such as *cochinillo asado* (suckling pig), many of them appearing on a good value *menú gastronomico* for €31.

Restaurante del Escudero Paseo de Blas Infante 1 ☎95 287 13 67. Very good restaurant housed in an elegant mansion with Ronda's best garden terrace offering views towards the Serranía de Ronda. The same proprietors own the *Tragabuches* (see below) but prices here are a good deal more palatable and there's a *menú* for around €17. Main dishes €17–23.

Restaurante Pedro Romero c/Virgen de la Paz 18 ☎95 287 11 10. Excellent, mid-priced restaurant that's a favourite with locals. In winter dining is in the interior rooms surrounded by bullfighting memorabilia and *rabo de toro* is a signature dish; there's also a *menú* for around €17.

SonArte c/Santa Cecilia 1. Smart new restaurant serving Mediterranean meat and fish dishes, salads and fresh pasta as well as authentic pizzas. Main dishes €7.50–20.

Tragabuches c/José Aparicio 1 ☎95 219 02 91. Ronda's most stylish (and acclaimed) restaurant is named after a celebrated eighteenth-century *rondeño* bullfighter-turned-bandit, and, with an adventurous menu and minimalist decor, is worth a splurge. Current head chef Benito Gómez learned his trade at Ferran Adriá's *El Bulli* and a signature dish is *cordero lechal* (suckling lamb). However, the *menú de degustación* with a price tag of €75 is one of the most expensive in Andalucía. Booking advised. Closed Sun eve & Mon.

Tapas bars

Bar Maestro c/Espinel 7. Great hole-in-the-wall (and one of Ronda's oldest tapas venues) with a tempting menu recited verbally by proprietor Rafael Peña. It's also a bar *taurino* so the photos of past *torero* greats plus Ernest and Orson (all one-time customers) gaze down from the walls.

Casa Mateos c/Jerez 6, around the corner from the *Hotel Colón*. Efficient *marisquería* and tapas bar with plenty of seafood possibilities as well as good *jamón* and *queso*.

El Portón c/Pedro Romero 7, off the west side of Plaza del Socorro. Favourite haunt of bullfighting aficionados; does good *jamón* and *cazón* (shark) tapas and serves an inexpensive *menú*.

La Farola Plaza Carmen Abela 9. Tapas at the bar or *bocadillos* and *platos combinados* on a pleasant terrace.

Patatín Patatán c/Borrego 7, off the east side of Plaza del Socorro. Popular tapas bar with a wide range of specials. *La Viña*, next door at no. 9, is also good.

Tragatapas c/Nueva 4. Ronda's latest tapas bar is the offspring of its most famous restaurant, *Tragabuches*. Reflecting the decor of its progenitor, it is ultra modern and the reasonably priced tapas (and *pinchos*) have a creative slant. Try the *cordero ali-oli*.

Cafeterías, breakfast bars and heladerías

Café Alba carrera Espinel 44. Piping hot *churros* and delicious breakfast coffee. If this popular place is too packed, the nearby *Cafetería La Ibense* is a good alternative.

Chocolat c/Sevilla 16. This chocoholic's heaven has 32 different flavours of handmade chocolate in addition to serving one hundred different teas and seven kinds of coffee in its café. Delicious home-made cakes and tarts, too.

Planet Adventure c/Molino 6, just north of Plaza del Socorro. Good and friendly place for breakfast croissants and *platos combinados* later in the day. Also has an internet section.

Rico carrera Espinel 42, south side of the Plaza del Socorro. Nicest *heladería* (ice cream bar) in town – also good for afternoon tea and, in winter, steaming cups of hot chocolate.

Nightlife

El Grifo c/Virgen de los Remedios 4, near Plaza del Socorro. Stylish late-night drinking bar for cocktails and long drinks with the gimmick of table-top beer pumps, staying open into the small hours.

El Templo c/Jerez 6. Central and popular bar-*discoteca* with a jazz and rock playlist; shows music videos and occasionally stages live bands.

Flamenco Museo Lara, c/Armiñan 29 ☎95 287 12 63. This atmospheric small theatre in the basement of the museum stages performances (Thurs–Sat, April–Sept; 9.30pm) by the company of celebrated dancer Rocío Vázquez who has a flamenco school in Ronda. Tickets cost €23 which includes a drink. Performances in the Círculo de Artistas de Ronda, Plaza del Socorro (☎952 87 10 46), are also staged (Mon, Tues &

Wed) by Escuela de Danza Pilar Becerra for a similar price.

Kopas c/Rios Rosas 9, off Plaza Carmen Abela. Relaxed dancing and cocktails club for over 30s.
Pub Baco c/Molino, at the north corner of Plaza del Socorro. Lively music bar popular with a younger crowd.

Listings

Bus companies The following companies operate out of the Ronda bus station: Comes (☎95 287 19 92; Arcos de la Frontera, Jerez & Cádiz), Lara (☎95 287 22 60; Serranía de Ronda villages), Portillo (☎95 218 70 61; Málaga & Costa del Sol resorts), Sierra de las Nieves (☎95 287 54 35; Málaga & Setenil).
Internet access Ciber Ronda Telecom c/Jerez 4 (daily 11am–2pm & 4–11pm), Mundial, c/Cruz Verde 21 (Mon–Fri 11am–2pm, Sat 10am–10pm) Planet Adventure, c/Molino 6 (Mon–Sat 9am–10pm), and all of which are reasonably central.
Maps and equipment Hiking maps of the Serranía de Ronda and Grazalema are available from Librería Dumas, c/Jerez 8, near the Plaza de la Merced. Intersport, c/Molino 8 (opposite the

Hotel Polo), stocks a range of outdoor clothing and walking boots.
Outdoor activities Sierraventura Ronda, c/Sevilla 16 (☎679283521, ⓦwww.sierraventuraronda .com) offer all kinds of outdoor activities in and around Ronda including guided hiking, climbing, mountain biking, canoeing, canyoning and caving. Horseriding is available with Picadero La Granja, Camino de los Molinos del Tajo 27 (☎95 287 59 56), and prices start at €40 for a three-hour trek. Daily bird-spotting trips in the Serranía for beginners and experienced birders are offered by Ornironda (☎mobile 616891359, ⓦwww .spanishbirds.com).
Post office Virgen de la Paz 20, near the Plaza de Toros (Mon–Sat 9am–2pm).

Around Ronda

Ronda makes an excellent base for exploring the superb countryside in the immediate vicinity or for visiting more of the White Towns, one of the most unusual of which is **Setenil de las Bodegas**, 15km away, with curious cave-like streets. If you're attracted by ancient ruins and awesome caves don't miss Ronda's Roman predecessor **Ronda La Vieja** or the **Cueva de la Pileta** whose remarkable Stone Age cave paintings are unique on the peninsula. To the west are the temptingly scenic villages of **Benaoján** and **Montejaque**, ringed by rugged limestone heights that hold numerous underground caverns such as the Cueva del Gato, a magnet for cavers.

Ronda La Vieja

Some 12km northwest of Ronda are the ruins of **RONDA LA VIEJA**, the first-century Roman town of Acinipo, set in the midst of beautiful hill country. The **ruins** (Wed–Sun 10am–2pm) are reached by turning right (along the MA449) 6km down the main road to Arcos/Seville, and following the signs to a farmhouse, where the friendly farmer will present you with a plan (in Spanish) and record your nationality for statistical purposes. Entry to the site, which sprawls away up the hill to the west, is free.

Based on Neolithic foundations, and also an outpost of the Phoenicians, Acinipo reached its zenith in the first century AD as a Roman town. The piles of stones interspersed with small fragments of glittering marble strewn across the hillside once constituted the forum, baths, temples and other edifices of this prosperous agricultural centre, which also had access to iron ore, marble, good building stone and fine potters' clay in close proximity.

Today only an impressive **Roman theatre** – of which just the stage backdrop and some seating survives – alludes to the importance of Acinipo; inscriptions found here tell of crowds flocking to see the chariot races. Immediately west of the theatre, the ground falls away in a startlingly steep escarpment and from here there are fine **views** towards the hill village of Olvera to the north (see p.173). For reasons not entirely clear, Acinipo declined in the third century and, in the fourth, ceded its power in the area to nearby Arunda (modern Ronda). On your way out take a look at the foundations of some recently discovered prehistoric stone huts beside the farmhouse. From here a track leads off towards Setenil de las Bodegas (see below).

Setenil de las Bodegas

Six kilometres northeast of Ronda La Vieja as the crow flies, and slightly longer along the MA486, **SETENIL DE LAS BODEGAS** is the strangest of all the White Towns, its cave-like streets formed from the overhanging ledge of a gorge carved through the tufa rock by the Río Trejo. Many of the houses – sometimes two or three storeys high – have natural roofs in the rock that, in places, block out the sky completely. This was once a major wine-producing centre, since the caves made good wine cellars (*bodegas*); hence the latter part of the town's name. The phylloxera plague of the nineteenth century destroyed the vines, however, and brought economic ruin in its wake, from which Setenil has only in recent times recovered.

Other sights in Setenil are limited, but if you can get into the church of **La Encarnación** (ask the neighbours or contact the tourist office) – a sixteenth-century Gothic structure – you'll see a fine, twelve-panelled Flemish painting that survived Civil War devastation. The ruins of the nearby Moorish **castillo** are worth a look too, and below the church, the sixteenth-century **Ayuntamiento**, now serving as the **tourist office** (Tues–Sun 10am–2pm & 6–8pm; ☎956 13 42 61, ⓦwww.setenil.com) has a superb Mudéjar *artesonado* ceiling with an inscription dating from September 21, 1484 – the day Isabel and Fernando captured the town. They achieved this triumph only after seven previous attempts (*septem nihil* – seven times nothing) had failed, giving origin to the first half of Setenil's name today.

Good **places to eat** include *El Mirador*, through an arch and uphill from the tourist office with an economical *menú* and great views, *Bar-Restaurante Dominguez* on the focal Plaza de Andalucía with a pleasant terrace, and the welcoming *Bar-Restaurante Las Flores*, Avda. del Carmen 24, near the river at the opposite end of the town from the church, with more views. To stay, there's also a decent **hotel**, *El Almendral* (☎956 13 40 29, ⓦwww.tugasa.com; ❸), on the road just outside town, with an Olympic-size pool and a good restaurant downstairs.

Without your own car, the only **public transport** to Setenil is the infrequent bus service from Ronda (Setenil train station is 8km out of the village). Once here it's possible to **walk** the 6km to the ruins of Ronda La Vieja (see p.165) via the hamlets of Campiña and Venta de Leche.

Cueva de la Pileta

Probably the most interesting trip out from Ronda is to the prehistoric **Cueva de la Pileta** (daily 10am–1pm & 4–6pm; hourly guided tours; final tours leave at 1pm & 6pm or 5pm Nov–March; €8), set in a deep valley and surrounded by a spectacular wall of white rock. These fabulous caverns, with their remarkable **Paleolithic paintings**, were discovered by a local farmer in 1905 when hunting for guano fertilizer for his fields, and are still supervised by the same family, the Bullóns, one of whom will be your guide. After the usual jokes, as various "cauliflowers", "castles" and a "Venus de Milo" are pointed out among the stalactites and stalagmites en route, the paintings in the depths of the caves, when you reach them, are genuinely awe-inspiring, particularly those in the central chamber.

Etched in charcoal, and red and yellow ochres, they depict an abundance of wildlife including fish, the *cabra hispanica* and a pregnant mare, all painted on walls which bear the scorch marks of ancient fires. Other abstract signs and symbols have been interpreted as having some magical or ritual purpose. The occupation of the caves, and the earliest red paintings, dates from about 25,000 BC, thus predating the more famous caves at Altamira in northern Spain, down to the end of the Bronze Age. The section of the caves (and paintings) open to view is only a small part of a more massive subterranean labyrinth, and archeologists will be kept busy for many years to come documenting this Paleolithic art gallery.

Cave practicalities

To reach the caves **with your own transport**, take the A376 Arcos/Seville road northwest from Ronda, turning left after 14km along the MA505 to Montejaque; the caves are a further 12km from the turn-off, beyond Benaoján. By **public transport**, take an Algeciras-bound local train (4 daily; 20min) to the Estación Benaoján-Montejaque; or a bus, which drops you a little closer, in Benaoján. There's a bar at the train station where you can stock up on drink before the hour-and-a-half long (6km) **walk** to the caves. Follow the farm track from the right bank of the river until you reach the farmhouse (approximately 30min). From here a track goes straight uphill to the main road just before the signposted turning for the caves. Alternatively, you could take a taxi from Ronda for around €50 – get the Turismo to arrange the fare – though renting a car for

—

—

—

—

The Serranía de Ronda

Starkly beautiful and offering some of the best walking terrain in Andalucía, the **Serranía de Ronda** is a region of great natural diversity where wooded ravines, awesome crags and vast forests of cork oaks provide abundant habitats for a rich variety of flora and fauna. The remote hamlets are reachable by road, albeit often with difficulty, but the ideal way to travel this region is with a backpack and compass, from which perspective the landscape – with whitewashed villages set among cherry orchards and vines – becomes an enchanting adventure. Both the Ronda tourist offices (see p.158) should have details on the villages and the limited accommodation available.

The heart of the Serranía can be reached by a daily **bus** from Ronda operated by Autobuses Lara (currently Mon–Fri 2.30pm, returning early morning), passing the villages of Parauta, Cartajima, Juzcar (with the comfortable *Hotel del Arriero* ⊕952 18 36 60; ❷), Igualeja, Pujerra, Alpandeire (with the excellent *Hotel Casa Grande* ⊕95 218 04 00, ⓦwww.hotelcasagrande.es; ❸) and Farajan. There's also a very pleasant five-hour **walking route** from Ronda to Cartajima; again, the Ronda Turismo (see p.158) can provide details. The Centro de Iniciativas Turísticas de la Serranía de Ronda, c/Paseo Blas Infante, near the Plaza de Toros (Mon–Fri 10am–1pm; ⊕&ⓕ95 287 07 39, ⓦwww.serraniaronda.org), has a list of *casas rurales* to rent throughout the Serranía.

The Serranía villages have set up their own **website**, ⓦwww.serraniaronda.org which provides a comprehensive guide to the *pueblos* of the zone including places to eat, drink, sleep and camp. The best **maps** covering the Serranía are the 1:200,000 *IGN Mapa Provincial de Málaga*, complemented by the 1:50,000 IGN sheet, number 1065.

a day could work out cheaper. Upon arrival wait at the cave entrance; to protect the cave and its paintings a strict **maximum of 25 people** are allowed on each tour and groups larger than four should book ahead (⊕95 216 73 43; also useful for confirming opening times). Tours are in Spanish (though the guide may speak some English), and last one hour on average. No photography is allowed in the cave and if you leave your vehicle at the car park, make sure to remove any valuables not locked in a secure boot. And finally, remember to bring a sweater as it can get chilly in the subterranean caverns.

Benaoján, Montejaque and the Cueva del Gato

North of the Cueva de la Pileta the village of **BENAOJÁN** is worth a visit, with its sixteenth-century church of San Marcos built on the site of an earlier mosque (this was a Moorish stronghold well into Christian times). The only **place to stay** in the village is the upmarket *Molino del Santo*, Bda. Estación (⊕95 216 71 51, ⊛www.molinodelsanto.com; ❻ with breakfast), a British-run haven with gardens and pool near the train station, 300m below the village on the Ronda road. Mid-priced restaurant **food** is available at the *Molino del Santo*, and *Bar Tajillo*, c/Fuente 20, 100m from the church, has tasty tapas and *raciónes*. One place definitely worth seeking out is ⅔ *Restaurante El Muelle*, actually on the platform at the train station; dishes include *carnes al horno de lleña* (charcoal grilled meats).

    MONTEJAQUE, 3km northeast and cradled between two rocky crags, is also worth a stop, possessing a great, typically Spanish square – with its own sparkling white church – fringed with bars, any of which will rustle you up *raciónes* if asked; try the friendly *Bar El Rincón*. **Places to stay** include *Palacete*

A walk from Benoaján to Jimera de Libar

There's a fine, none too taxing **walk** from Benoaján to the attractive village of Jimera de Libar, 9km down the railway line linking the two communities. When you've reached Jimera you could take in a well-earned lunch at the *Restaurante Quercus* and return to Benoaján on the afternoon trains (currently leaving Jimera station at 5.03pm & 8.04pm; confirm current times with either of the Ronda tourist offices or the *Hotel Inz-Almaraz* – see below).

    The walk begins from the *Molino del Santo* hotel (see above). Turn left from the hotel and head downhill until you come to a stop sign at a level crossing. Turn left along the railway line, cross over a river, and at a second level crossing turn right and cross over the railway track. The road drops before crossing the Río Guadiaro and leads up to a sign marking the official start of the walk. The route from here is fairly straightforward except for a fork just beyond a ruined farm (after 3km), where you should veer left away from the river. At a second fork at a telegraph pole just before Jimera bear right (*not* towards Camino de Huertas Nuevas) to follow the path down to the station of Jimera de Libar. To reach the very good and mid-priced *Restaurante Quercus* (⊕952 18 00 41) you need to cross the railway tracks and turn right – the **restaurant** is housed in the former station building actually on the tracks. Overnight **accommodation** is possible in Jimera at the *Hotel Rural Inz-Almaraz*, c/Mártires de Igueriben 18 (⊕95 218 50 10, ⊛www.hotelruraljimera.com; ❸ with breakfast), which also has its own very good restaurant. The proprietor will pick up guests from and return them to the train station if you ring. Jimera also has a leafy **campsite** (⊕95 218 01 02, ⊛www.rural-jimera.com) close to the train station, which also rents out log cabins (❸) and has a pool. A map would be a useful tool to have on this walk (50:000 IGN sheets 1050 & 1064), or it is also well described with its own map in Guy Hunter-Watts' *Walking in Andalucía* (see "Books", p.609).

de Mañara, Plaza Constitución 2 (T 95 216 72 52, W www.palacete-de-manara .eu; ● with breakfast), a charming hotel in a converted *casa palacio* with **restaurant** and mini-pool; they can also arrange horseriding, walking and caving excursions. An alternative for longer stays is *Casitas de la Sierra* (T 95 216 73 92, W www.casitasdelasierra.com; ●) who rent out fully equipped village houses and will often agree to a couple of nights' stopover if there are places free. *Casas de Montejaque*, c/Manuel Ortega 16 (T 95 216 81 20, W www.casasdemontejaque.net) offers similar deals and prices.

Returning to Ronda along the direct road from Benaoján (MA555), after 2km you'll pass on the left the *Venta Cueva del Gato* (closed Sun) – famed for its superb *conejo casero* (grilled rabbit). A short distance beyond the *venta* a signed road on the left descends to the *Hotel Cueva del Gato* (T 95 216 72 96, W www.hotelcuevadelgato.com; ●) with comfortable rooms in a stone building and its own restaurant. From here a path leads down to a footbridge across the Río Guadiaro and tunnel beneath the rail line to arrive at the gaping mouth of the **Cueva del Gato**, a cave fronted by an oleander-fringed lagoon (a popular bathing spot). Continue ahead to a viewing platform overlooking a spectacular waterfall gushing out of the cave. Given the close proximity of the Cueva de la Pileta (see p.166) it seems likely that this cave, too, may well have been occupied by early humans, but no paintings have so far been discovered. The cave is open to all but to penetrate much further than 50m you'll need ropes, lights and some expertise, or, better still, contact climber Christine Hofer at El Chorro (see p.90) who leads fully equipped explorations of the cave and its dramatic subterranean lakes.

Grazalema, El Bosque and around

Looping through the rocky contours of the last foothills of the Cordillera Subbética mountain range, much of which is covered in pine forest, this route travels first west from Ronda through the verdantly spectacular **Parque Natural Sierra de Grazalema** before exploring yet more picturesque hill villages to the north and east of Ronda. Another great **walking** area, the books by John and Christine Oldfield (*Andalucía and the Costa del Sol*) and Guy Hunter-Watts (*Walking in Andalucía*) both describe a number of walks here (see "Books", p.609).

Grazalema

The A376 winds away from Ronda into the Sierra de Sanguijuela, and forking left after about 16km, along the A372, takes you across the provincial border into Cádiz. Another 17km from the turning, the road arrives at **GRAZALEMA**, the central point of the Sierra de Grazalema, now a protected **Parque Natural**. A pretty white village beneath the craggy peak of San Cristóbal, with lots of sloping narrow streets and window boxes full of blooms in summer, it makes an ideal base for delving into the park. This is also the spot with the country's highest rainfall – and there's quite a bit of snow in winter too – which explains the lush vegetation covering the surrounding area, home to a spectacular variety of flora and fauna. Quite apart from the attractions of the park, the village has its own charm. The simple main square, the Plaza de España with the eighteenth-century church of **Nuestra Señora de la Aurora**, is adorned with an emblematic *pinsapo* fir tree (see box, p.170). Various craft shops have sprung up in the village over the years and another interesting arrival is the Neilson Gallery of Contemporary Art, c/Mateos Gago 50 (Mon–Fri 6–8pm, Sat & Sun noon–2pm & 6–8pm; W www.neilsongallery.com; free) which mounts an eclectic range of exhibitions.

Parque Natural Sierra de Grazalema

Bounded by the towns of Grazalema, Ubrique, El Bosque and Zahara, the **Parque Natural Sierra de Grazalema** is an important mountain wilderness, unique to Andalucía. The limestone mass of the Sierra was formed in the Jurassic and Triassic periods and the close proximity of the range to the sea – which traps many of the clouds drifting in from the Atlantic – has produced a microclimate where numerous botanical species dating from before the Ice Age have survived. The most famous of these is the rare **pinsapo**, or Spanish fir, native only to this area of Europe, which grows at an altitude of between 1000m and 1700m. The high rainfall here, plus the wet, cool summers, are essential to its survival. The Sierra also supports a wealth of **birdlife**: eagles (Bonelli's, booted, and golden), vultures (griffon and Egyptian), as well as various owls and woodpeckers are all common. The streams and riverbanks are the domain of water voles and otters, the latter not popular with a number of fish farms in the area. On the Sierra's higher reaches the magnificent Spanish ibex has been reintroduced to a craggy habitat, and its numbers are increasing.

The best way to appreciate the park is by walking, but to protect wildlife and nesting birds access is restricted to different sections at certain times, and in July and August many routes are closed due to the high fire risk. The park's main **information office** is at El Bosque, c/Federico García Lorca s/n, next to the Plaza de Toros (Mon–Fri 10am–2pm & 5–7pm, Sat & Sun 9am–2pm; ☎956 72 70 29), and there are smaller branches in Grazalema and Zahara de la Sierra. The El Bosque office issues access *permisos* (permits; free) and will fax these free of charge to the tourist offices in Grazalema and Zahara de la Sierra. The office also stocks park maps with walking routes, and takes bookings for the Itinerario del Pinsapar, guided walks through the major stands of the *pinsapo* Spanish fir. In Grazalema, Horizon, c/Corrales Terceros 29 (☎956 13 23 63, ⓦ www.horizonaventura.com), organizes a broad range of outdoor **activities** in the park, including hiking (with English-speaking guides), horse-trekking, mountain bike tours, Land Rover trips and much more. They also conduct a variety of wildlife and bird-watching **excursions** and can even arrange **accommodation** for you.

Practicalities

Grazalema's **Turismo** on the main square, Plaza de España (Mon–Fri 10am–2pm & 5–9pm, Sat & Sun 10am–9pm; ☎956 13 20 73), sells good walking maps and can provide information about the park and activities such as horseriding.

The only budget **place to stay** is the hospitable *Casa de las Piedras*, c/Las Piedras 32 (☎956 13 20 14, ⓦ www.casadelaspiedras.org; ❸), above the main square, which has rooms with and without bath. Something of a walkers' refuge due to its use by organized groups, the proprietors can provide information on trekking in the area and arrange transport to the start of walks. One of the most attractive of the upmarket alternatives is *La Mejorana*, c/Santa Clara 6 (☎956 13 23 27, ⓦ www.lamejorana.net; ❸ with breakfast) housed in an elegant *casa señorial* and reached by following c/Mateos Gago 300m uphill from Plaza de España; it offers charming en-suite rooms (some with great views) plus a pool. Just off the main square, *Hotel Puerta de la Villa*, Plaza Pequeña 8 (☎956 13 23 76, ⓦ www.grazhotel.com; ❻), is a four-star option in a refurbished mansion with restaurant, jacuzzi, sauna, gym and even a tiny plunge pool. If the latter's opulence seems out of place in such a rustic enclave, the more reasonable *Hotel Peñon Grande*, Plaza Pequeña 7 (☎956 13 24 34, ⓦ www.hotelgrazalema.com; ❸), almost opposite, may be a better choice. Slightly out of the centre, the *Villa de Turística de Grazalema*, 500m along the Ronda road (☎956 13 21 36, ⓦ www.tugasa.com; ❸) has villa-style rooms, with restaurant, gardens and pool.

Grazalema's **campsite**, *Tajo Rodillo* (☎956 13 24 18), is located above the village at the end of c/Las Piedras; its office has literature on the park and will provide information about walks and horse-treks in the Sierra; they also rent out mountain bikes.

The **bars** and **restaurants** on the main square are reasonably priced for *raciónes* and *menús*; three places worth singling out are *Cádiz El Chico*, on Plaza de España, the excellent *Torreón*, c/Agua 44, just north of it, as well as the good-value *menú* at the *Casa de las Piedras* (see p.170). A new arrival, *Restaurante El Pinsapar*, c/Mateos Gago 22, has a good selection of local dishes and a *menú* for €10. For **tapas** and *raciónes*, *Bar Zulema* and *Bar Posadilla* on opposite sides of c/Agua – near the Plaza de España – are both popular and good value. The village's **nightlife** warms up in summer and centres around the *Disco de Verano* on Avenida Juan de la Rosa and the bars along c/Agua. If the weather's warm enough, try out the communal **swimming pool**, which is spectacularly sited on the Arcos/Benamahoma road at the village's eastern edge.

El Bosque

Located on the park's western flank, the village of **EL BOSQUE**, surrounded by slopes of planted pine, is easily reached from Grazalema via a delightfully wooded drive along the A372, which bisects the park. When travel writer Richard Ford passed through here in the 1830s he described it as a "robbers' lair" and counted "fifteen monumental crosses in the space of fifty yards" – victims of the ruthless bandits who preyed on travellers. He advised his readers to make sure they carried a watch to buy off these brigands, preferably one with a gaudy gilt chain, "the lack of which the bandit considered an unjustifiable attempt to defraud him of his right". Today it's a far more peaceful place, although the tranquillity is interrupted in August when nearby summer camps increase the two thousand-odd population threefold. El Bosque also has the natural park's main information office (see p.170), behind the Plaza de Toros. The **bus station** on the main road through has connections to all parts of the province and beyond.

El Bosque provides an alternative to Grazalema as a base for visiting the park: for **rooms** there's usually space at *Hotel Enrique Calvillo*, Avda. Diputación 5 (☎956 71 61 05; ❸), with a/c en-suite rooms, pool and free internet access. Close by, the aptly named and very comfortable *Hotel Las Truchas*, Avda. Diputacíon 1 (☎956 71 60 61, ⓦwww.tugasa.com; ❸), has a **restaurant** where fresh trout features strongly on the menu, often with a slice of *jamón serrano* tucked inside; El Bosque has the most southerly trout river in Europe, the nearby Río Majaceite. Tucked away in the woods behind, another possibility is the *Albergue El Bosque*, a **youth hostel** (☎956 71 62 12, ⓦwww.inturjoven .com; under 26 €14, over 26 €19 including breakfast), with double and triple en-suite rooms, restaurant and pool. To get there, follow the road that bends up behind the *Hotel Las Truchas*.

The village has **plenty of places to eat**, with trout much in evidence. For a great-value meal, head for the trout farm Piscifactoría Acuario, hidden in the woods just beyond the *Albergue El Bosque*; the *Mesón Majaceite* opposite the farm does the freshest trout you can get as part of a €8 *menú*. In the village proper the *Hotel-Hostal Enrique Calvillo* has a restaurant or there's *Venta Julian*, Avda. Diputacion 11, near the bus station, also with an economical *menú* plus a pleasant terrace that is popular on warmer evenings.

One scenic **walk** along the Río Majaceite is best started from Benamahoma, 4km east: the steep descent is easier this way. Starting from the *El Bujio* bar (a taxi will drop you there if you don't fancy the walk), make for some green gates at the end of the car park. Step through a small stand of eucalyptus to the right of the gates and keep ahead along the left bank of the river. As you follow the river back to El Bosque, there are plenty of opportunities for bird-spotting and picnicking. Benamahoma's **campsite** (T&F956 71 62 75) above the village has plenty of shade, a superb pool and some attractive wood cabin apartments for rent (❸).

Zahara de la Sierra

It's worth going back to Grazalema to take the spectacular CA531 road, which climbs to the Puerto de las Palomas (Pass of the Doves, at 1350m the second-highest pass in Andalucía). A little before the pass you'll see on the left an entrance to the forest of the *pinsapo* Spanish fir – this is the start of the Itinerario del Pinsapar walking route (see box, p.170). Once over the pass the road embarks on a dramatic descent to **ZAHARA DE LA SIERRA** (or de los Membrillos – "of the Quinces"), surrounded by olive groves. This is perhaps the most perfect of Andalucía's fortified hill *pueblos*, a landmark for miles around, its red-tiled houses huddled round a church beneath a ruined castle on a stark outcrop of rock. It was once an important Moorish town, and its capture by the Christians in 1483 opened the way for the conquest of Ronda – and ultimately Granada. The heart of the village, which was declared a national monument in 1983, is a cobbled main street which connects the church of **San Juan** and the eighteenth-century Baroque church of **Santa María de la Mesa**, which has a fine *retablo* with a sixteenth-century image of the Virgin. The surviving tower of the twelfth-century **Moorish castle** (free access) – constructed over a previous Roman one – looms over the village and incorporates the remains of an early church. The terrain near to the village has changed dramatically over recent years due to the creation of the Embalse de Zahara y El Gastor **reservoir**, the waters of which now lap the foot of its hill on the northern and eastern flanks.

At the eastern end of the main street, c/San Juan, a Parque Natural **information centre** (daily 9am–2pm & 4–7pm; T956 12 31 14) can provide information on the village and the natural park, and acts as a booking office for a number of local *casas rurales* and farmhouses. The village has a number of **places to stay**: on the main street, *Hotel Marqués de Zahara* (T956 12 30 61; ❸ with breakfast) has balcony rooms, a shady patio and a restaurant serving local specialities. Beyond here, on the road leading to the castle, the stylish, good-value *Hotel Arco de la Villa* (T956 12 32 30, Wwww.tugasa.com; ❸) has **rooms** with spectacular views over the nearby *embalse*. Towards the swimming pool on the eastern edge of the village, the *Hostal Los Tadeos*, Paseo de la Fuente s/n (T956 12 30 86; ❷), is another option for rooms with bath and views. Zahara's **campsite** is on the reservoir's shore: *Camping Entre Olivos* (T956 23 40 44, Wwww.entreolivos.net) is located 2km south of the village, reached by following the old Ronda road (C339) and turning off along a signed road to Arroyo Molinos, near the lake, where an artificial beach has been created for bathing and watersports. The campsite has its own restaurant.

For **tapas** and *raciónes* there are a cluster of bars around the church of Santa María, and for **meals**, *Mesón Los Estribos*, c/El Fuerte 3 (T956 12 31 45) near the *Hotel Arco de la Villa*, is a good bet with a weekday €8 *menú*. Both the latter hotel and the *Hotel Marqués de Zahara* have decent restaurants of their own. An interesting new arrival is the mid-priced *Al Lago*, c/Rodriguez de la Fuente 11, on the road in from Grazalema; they have the village's most attractive terrace and offer various Mediterranean influenced dishes, salads, paella and even have a curry night (main dishes €9–15).

Algodonales

Enclosed by the folds of the Sierra de Líjar, **ALGODONALES**, 6km north, is a pleasant enough place with a long, central plaza dominated by the lofty tower of the eighteenth-century Neoclassical church of **Santa Ana**. Although lying a couple of kilometres beyond the park boundary, the village is endeavouring to make itself an activity centre for the park and now has a private **tourist office** (Mon–Fri 10am–2pm & 5–8pm; ☎956 13 78 82, ⓦwww.al-qutun.com) at the entrance to the village as you come from Zahara. The proprietors also run a pleasant **youth hostel** with dormitory rooms (€13 per person) fifty metres away, down the road descending behind the tourist office; they also rent out *casas rurales* nearby, sleeping two (❷). Other places in the village offering rooms include the welcoming *Hostal Sierra de Líjar*, c/Ronda 5 (☎956 13 70 €lue.a ©hostalsierradelijar@hotmail.com; ❷ with breakfast), just below the main square, which also has a restaurant with a good-value *menú*. Similar rooms are on offer at the *Hostal Alameda* (☎956 13 72 29, ⓦwww.hostalalameda.net; ❷) on the same square below the church tower.

One place worth a visit in Algodonales is the workshop of renowned **guitar maker** Valeriano Bernal, whose beautiful instruments are sought after by many of the leading classical and flamenco guitarists in Spain. His modest workshop is located at c/Ubrique 8 (Mon–Fri 9am–2pm & 3–6pm, Sat 9am–2pm; ☎956 13 72 80, ⓦwww.valerianobernal.com), a two-minute walk from *Hostal Sierra de Líjar*, whose proprietor can provide directions. Should you want to take a guitar home, prices range from €500 for a student's model to €5000-plus for the virtuoso instrument.

The village's proximity to the main A382 *autovía* means that it has frequent daily **bus** connections with Seville, Jerez, Cádiz and Ronda as well as a bus to Zahara (Mon–Fri only) currently running at 7.45am and 1.45pm with the return to Algodonales at 9.15am and 3.15pm. Otherwise a taxi to Zahara will cost you about €20 one way.

Olvera

OLVERA, 18km beyond Algodonales in an area thick with olives (from which the town's name may derive), couldn't look more dramatic – a great splash of whitewashed houses tumbling down a hill below the twin towers of its church and a fine Moorish castle. You can ascend the hill along the town's long main street, c/Llana and its continuation, c/Calvario. The church, **La Encarnación**, is disappointing up close, as it's actually a nineteenth-century version of an earlier, fifteenth-century edifice. More interesting is the somewhat over-restored twelfth-century **Moorish castle** (Tues–Sun 10.30am–2pm & 4–6pm; donations), which formed part of Nasrid Granada's line of defence against the Christian lands; entry is gained through a gate to the side of no. 3 on the plaza (Plaza de la Iglesia) facing the church. There are great views from here over the town and to the surrounding hill villages. The same square also has a small **tourist office** (same hours as castle).

An imaginative development in Olvera is the transformation of the disused rail line – running 34km east to Puerto Serrano through rolling, wooded hill country – into a track for cyclists and walkers, known as the **Vía Verde** (ⓦwww.fundacionviaverdedelasierra.com), with stations along the route transformed into hotels and *ventas*. You can hire a mountain bike for around €12 per day from Olvera's dapper station-hotel, the *Hotel Estación Verde* (currently being expanded at the time of writing). They will give you a route map and ring ahead to book rooms at your next stop. If you don't want to do the return journey you can deposit the bike in Puerto Serrano. Alternatively you can rent a bike for up to four hours (around €9) to do part of the route.

Should you want to use the town as a base for exploring the region with its river, olive groves and stark backdrop of the Sierra de Líjar, there are a number of **places to stay**, including the above-mentioned *Hotel Estación Verde* (T mobile 661463207, ❷), which has its own restaurant. In the town proper at the foot of c/Calvario, *Pensión Medina*, c/Sepulveda 6 (T 956 13 01 73; ❷), has simple rooms, all en suite. The plusher *Hotel Sierra y Cal*, Avda. Nuestra Señora de los Remedios 2 (T 956 13 05 03, W www.tugasa.com; ❸), slightly out of the centre is also good with comfortable a/c rooms and a restaurant.

For **food**, *Bar Pepe Raya* on the small square below the La Encarnación church does good tapas in air-conditioned comfort, and you'll find decent tapas, *fino* and a budget *menú* at the friendly *Bar Manolo* in Plaza Andalucía about halfway up the hill. The restaurant of the *Sierra y Cal* hotel also offers a good-value *menú* for around €12.

From Ronda towards Cádiz

One truly spectacular White Town route is **from Ronda towards Cádiz** via the appealing villages of **Villaluenga** and **Benaocaz**, the remarkable site of Roman **Ocuris** and the larger settlements of **Alcalá de los Gazules** and **Medina Sidonia**. Following the A376 northwest out of Ronda and turning left along the A372, the route cuts across the Sierra de Grazalema and Los Alcornocales natural parks, winding through rocky hills, deep gorges and dense cork oak forests.

Villaluenga del Rosario

Some 18km beyond the turn-off on the A372 described above, and reached along on a winding secondary road, the tiny village of **VILLALUENGA DEL ROSARIO** is the highest in Cádiz Province. Tucked beneath a great crag, it's a simple place, with narrow streets, flower-filled balconies and pan-tiled roofs, frequently enveloped by mountain mists. In the twilight years of the Nasrid Emirate of Granada and after Ronda had fallen to the Christians in 1485, a now unprotected Villaluenga was conquered and repopulated with settlers from Arcos de la Frontera and Villamartín. Some ancient Moorish wells can be seen in the fields along the roadside to the left as you approach. The twentieth-century Civil War was also bitterly fought here when one of the village's two churches was torched: its gutted ruin, located at the top of the village, now serves as the cemetery. Villaluenga's curious **Plaza de Toros**, partly hacked out of the rock, is also worth a look and sees action once a year on October 7, when the feast of the Virgen Del Rosario is celebrated with a *corrida*. The village is famous for its goats' milk cheeses, which can be purchased at the multi-award-winning *Payoyo* cheesemaker's factory on the south side of the main road running through.

The village's only **place to stay**, the charming *Hotel La Posada*, c/Torre 1 (T 956 12 61 19, W www.tugasa.com; ❸), lies in the upper village near the ruined church; it's housed in a beautifully renovated stone-built house and has a **restaurant**. Villaluenga's best places to **eat and drink** however are *Bar Antonio* on the main square, Plaza Alameda, where they rustle up excellent tapas and *raciónes*, and *La Velada*, Avda. Los Arbolitos s/n, on the village's western edge who do a weekday *menú* for under €10.

Benaocaz

From Villaluenga the road continues through the spectacular Manga de Villaluenga Pass, an area that has yielded many prehistoric artefacts and dolmens, to the farming settlement of **BENAOCAZ**, another ancient village founded by the Moors in the eighth century. A series of wall plaques around the Barrio Nazari in the upper village provides information (in Spanish) on buildings and locations from this period. A pleasant place to stop over, the village's **Museo Historico** (Sat & Sun 11.30am–2pm & 5–8pm; free; when closed enquire at the Ayuntamiento), at c/Jabonería 7, has lots of historical background on life in the Sierra from prehistoric cave-dwellers to the nineteenth-century *bandoleros*, and its Baroque **church** of San Pedro is built over the former mosque, which used part of the minaret to make its tower. The elegant and recently renovated eighteenth-century Ayuntamiento on the main square, Plaza de la Libertades 1 (☏956 12 55 00), can provide **tourist information** on the village and the surrounding area.

If you want to stretch your legs, there's a fine 6km downhill walk from here to Ubrique along a superbly preserved **Roman road** complete with culverts to protect it from flooding. The start of the route (marked by an information board) is across the road from the bus stop on the main road below the village. If you time your arrival to coincide with the afternoon bus from Ubrique to Benaocaz (currently running at 3.30pm), this will save you the walk back up the hill.

You can get pleasant **rooms** – and apartments for a longer stay – at *Hostal San Antón*, Plaza de San Antón 5 (☏956 12 55 77; ❷), or at the nearby *El Parral* (☏956 12 55 65; ❷), which also squeezes in a small pool. Just outside the village on the Ubrique road *Los Chozos* (April–Sept; ☏956 23 41 63, ⓦwww .sierradecadiz.com/loschozos; ❹) rents out *chozos* (modern versions of traditional circular thatched-roofed dwellings) in a scenic location sleeping two or more. The Ayuntamiento can also provide a list of apartments to rent around the village.

For **food**, both *El Parral* and *Los Chozos* have restaurants. At the other end of the village and opposite the Ayuntamiento, *Bar Las Vegas* (closed eves) has a very good kitchen offering a weekday lunch-time *menú* for €7 and a more sophisticated one at weekends when the speciality is *jabalí al horno* (roast boar); it also serves a vital role as the vendor of daily newspapers for this corner of the Sierra.

Ocuris

Four kilometres west of Benaocaz, close to the junction with the A373, a small road on the right (signed "Consorcio Bahía de Cádiz") leads to the spectacularly situated Roman site of **Ocuris**. The road is easy to miss and if you reach the petrol station at the junction beyond it you will need to turn around. Leave any transport at the site **information centre** and **cafetería** opposite the entrance. At the time of writing the site is open weekends only (Sat & Sun 10am–2pm; free); however, the fence does not present a great obstacle. You should contact the Turismo in Ubrique (see p.176) to make a visit outside these times.

Once through the entry gate a paved path climbs into the woods for a good kilometre to the site, located on the crest of the hill above. Just before you arrive at the ruins, to the left stands a well-preserved (although partly restored) first-century AD **columbarium** tomb with wall niches for burial urns. This is followed by some impressive Cyclopean dry-stone **walls** that date from the site's origin as an Iberian *oppidum*, or tribal settlement, in the pre-Roman era, and the Romans would have had to overcome defences like these during the subjugation of the peninsula in the first and second centuries BC. Once through the walls, you enter the heart of the Roman settlement where the substantial remains of **dwellings**, **baths** and huge **cisterns**, with their mortar linings still intact, surround the ancient **forum**. Archeologists are still busy excavating here and it will be some time before the remains are entirely revealed and understood. On all sides of the site the hill falls sharply away and there are wonderful **views** over the Sierra and the town of Ubrique, far below. There's plenty of shade and lush grass up here and, if you've brought provisions, it's hard to imagine a better place for a picnic.

Ubrique

From Benaocaz the road corkscrews down from the mountainous sierra until the snow-white vista of **UBRIQUE** comes into view below, spreading along the valley of the Río Ubrique with the daunting knife-edged crag of the Cruz de Tajo rearing up behind. Despite this stunning first appearance, on closer contact it's a rather large and dull industrial centre, but the town's bustling prosperity ensures a good variety of places to eat and drink on and around Avenida Dr Solis Pascual, the tree-lined main artery.

A place that has always bred tenacious guerrilla fighters and which fought against the French in the War of Independence (actually defeating a contingent of the Imperial Guard near Gaucín), Ubrique is a natural mountain fortress which was one of the last Republican strongholds in the Civil War. Today, it's a relatively wealthy if unexciting town, surviving largely on its medieval guild craft of **leather manufacturing**, the products of which are sold in numerous shops lining the main street, where most of the bars and restaurants are also gathered. A **Turismo**, Avda. Dr Solis Pascual 19 (Mon–Sat 10am–6.30pm, Sun 11am–2.30pm; ☎956 92 29 75), where English is spoken, has information on the town and the area plus the Roman site of Ocuris (see p.175). For a **place to stay** you could try *Hotel Ocurris*, Avda. Dr Solis Pascual 49 (☎956 46 39 39; ④), close to the main junction and roundabout as you enter the town from the north, for en-suite rooms with TV, which also has a restaurant and serves good tapas and *raciónes* in its bar.

Alcalá de los Gazules

The A375 road from Ubrique towards Alcalá, 44km to the southwest, runs through the **Parque Natural de Los Alcornocales**, with magnificently rugged but sparsely populated mountain scenery. Close to the Sierra de Aljibe to the south, the road skirts the provincial border with Málaga before ascending to the Puerto de Galis pass, at the junction with the CA503. At the crossroads stands the isolated but excellent ♣ *Venta del Puerto de Galis*, a favourite lunch stop with local hunters which appropriately often has game on its menu. Beyond here the road joins the valley of the Río Barbate for the final descent into the White Town of **ALCALÁ DE LOS GAZULES**, the geographical centre of the province of Cádiz. When the Romans were conquering this area early in the second century BC, they tried to divide and rule the Iberian tribes by granting the status of *colonia* to selected settlements – a crucial first step on the way to full Roman citizenship and all the privileges such status could bestow. One such settlement so rewarded was the Iberian Turris Lascutana, as Alcalá then was, and this was an attempt by Rome to win its allegiance away from the Turditanian tribal capital at Hasta Regia near Jerez. A surviving bronze plaque (in the archeological museum in Madrid) records the decree of the Roman governor, Lucius Aemelius Paullus, in 189 BC, which granted Turris possession of the fields and town that they had formerly held as a fief of Hasta. Apart from the winding, narrow streets, little remains of the later Moorish settlement founded by the Berber family the Gazules, who gave their name to the town in the twelfth century when this was a *taifa* state of the kingdom of Granada.

A cascade of white dwellings gathered beneath its ruined Alcázar, Alcalá is a sleepy little place today. In the Plaza Alta in the upper town there's the fifteenth-century Gothic church of **San Jorge**, with an imposing tower, beautifully carved choir and an effigy attributed to Martínez Montañes, but not much else. In the lower town the **Plaza de Toros** has been turned into a *discoteca*, somewhat blasphemously given the surrounding bull-breeding country. Just over the road from the bullring-disco on the c/Paseo de la Playa is *Restaurante Pizarro*, a decent mid-priced **restaurant** with a good-value *menú*. A little further along the road, the same proprietors run the comfortable *Hostal Pizarro* (☎956 42 01 03; ②) with en-suite rooms; they also run the nearby and more expensive *Hotel San Jorge* (☎956 41 32 55; ③), where rooms come with a/c and a TV.

Tajo de las Figuras

From Alcalá the A381 *autovía* heads northwest to Medina Sidonia, but taking an alternative route 17km southwest to **Benalup de Sidonia** would enable a visit to the **Tajo de las Figuras** caves with important Neolithic **cave paintings.** Discovered in 1913, the vivid paintings depict a variety of birds, as well as deer and human figures, perhaps hunters. The caves (Wed–Sun 9am–3pm; free), 7km south of Benalup along the A5203, are signed on the left and the *abrigos*, or rock shelters, some half-a-kilometre distant, can be seen from the road. Park here and go through the gate towards the rock cliffs where you will eventually make out a steel ladder to the main cave above. If closed during this time, wait around and the site's guardian (who shelters among the rocks) will eventually emerge to open them up. He can also guide you to another cave nearby with more paintings of animals and human figures (one with a child) and, below this, to some remarkable anthropomorphic **sarcophagus tombs** – some for children – carved into the rocks. You may want to give the guardian a small consideration for his trouble, and it's worth checking current visiting arrangements with the Ayuntamiento in Benalup, c/Cantera s/n (☎956 42 40 09), or the Turismo in Medina Sidonia (see p.178), to save yourself a wasted journey.

Toros bravos

This part of Cádiz province is **bull country** and the roads around the towns of Álcala de los Gazules and Medina Sidonia are lined with the ranches of the breeders of fighting bulls destined for bullrings all over Spain. Behind warning signs posted on roadside fences it's often possible to catch a view of the mean, black *toros bravos*, or fighting bulls used in the *corridas*. These magnificent beasts weighing 500 to 600 kilos, the descendants of the *bos taurus ibericus* of ancient times, graze on pastures shaded by olives and holm oaks, and are tended by mounted vaqueros who guard them while noting their potential for valour. This is eventually tested in the *tienta* or trial ring, an important first step in deciding whether the bull will die in the *corrida* or the abattoir. The vaqueros are always on the lookout for the exceptional bull displaying outstanding bravery and physical construction and these are separated from the herd to be used exclusively at stud, to improve the breed. The bulls that leave these ranches to fight in the ring usually die there, although very occasionally bulls displaying exceptional bravery and spirit will receive the *indulto*, or pardon, to be returned to their ranch of origin for stud. If you'd like to visit a bull-breeding ranch A Campo Abierto (☎mobile 629565666) offers visits to the renowned Domecq ranch to the west of Medina Sidonia on Sun, Wed & Fri at 11am; €15. Get details from the Turismo in Medina or from their website: ⓦwww.acampoabierto.com.

Medina Sidonia

Heading from Alcalá to Medina Sidonia by the direct route along the A381 brings you, after 24km, to a junction with the A390 where you should turn left into the town. Incidentally, this crossroads has a great *venta*, the *Ventorillo de Carbón* serving up excellent **tapas** and an inexpensive *menú* and makes an ideal lunch stop.

Following its reconquest by Alfonso X in 1264, **MEDINA SIDONIA**, another ancient town, was to become one of Spain's most prestigious ducal seats; it supplied the admiral who led the Armada against England. The title of Duque de Medina Sidonia was bestowed upon the family of Guzmán El Bueno for his valiant role in battles against the Moors, a line which continues and was led by the firebrand socialist duchess of Medina Sidonia up to her death in 2008 (see p.229). Today Medina is an atmospheric hill town where tidy narrow cobbled streets lined with *reja*-fronted houses circle the lower slopes of a peak dominated by its striking church of Santa María.

Arrival and information

Buses to and from Cádiz and other locations throughout the province use the **bus station** on Avda. del Mar, a few-minutes walk northwest of the focal Plaza de España. Alcalá's **Turismo**, c/San Juan s/n off the west side of Plaza de España (daily: April–Sept 10am–2pm & 4–7pm, Oct–March 10am–2pm & 4–6pm; ☏956 41 24 04, ⓦwww.turismomedinasidonia.com), can provide a useful town map, plus information about visits to local bull-breeding ranches.

Accommodation

In recent years Medina has opened up to tourists and now has **rooms** to suit most pockets.

Casa La Loba c/La Loba 21 ☏956 41 20 51; ⓦwww.casalaloba.com. A charming small boutique hotel with airy, spacious rooms and a stunning roof terrace, east of Plaza de España. ❹ with breakfast.

Casa Napoleón c/San Juan 21 ☏956 41 01 83. The town's budget option is a spotless *pensión* with en-suite rooms, which often puts up *matadors* – their photos line the walls – who have come to train at the local bull-breeding ranches. ❷

Casa Rural Los Balcones c/La Loba 26 ☏956 42 30 33, ⓦwww.losbalcones.net.

Almost opposite *Casa La Loba*, this is a delightful apart-hotel inside an elegant nineteenth-century mansion where a/c roms come with kitchenette and fridge. ❹

Hotel Medina Sidonia Plaza Llanete de Herederos 1 ☏956 41 23 17, ⓦwww.tugasa.com. The best in-town conventional option, offering comfortable rooms in a restored *casa señorial*. ❹

La Tagarnina c/Moritos 10 ☏956 43 30 67, ⓦwww.latagarnina.com. This old mill and bakery has been converted into an intimate *casa rural* hotel with delightful patio. ❹ with breakfast.

The Town

A good place to begin a look around is the elegant **Plaza de España** dominated by the wonderful Renaissance facade of the seventeenth-century Ayuntamiento. To the rear of this edifice, at the top of a steeply climbing road (c/Arrieros), is the **Plaza Iglesia Mayor**, dominated by the tower and portal of **Santa María la Coronada** church (daily: April–Sept 10am–2pm & 4–8pm, Oct–March 10.30am–2pm & 4–7pm; €2.50), built over an earlier mosque. Inside, an enormous and exquisite **retablo** depicting scenes from the life of Christ is a stunning sixteenth-century work of craftsmanship in polychromed wood by the *sevillano* school. There's also an imposing sculpted image of *Cristo del Perdón* attributed to Luisa Roldán ("La Roldana") and a fine wood sculpture of *San Francisco de Asís* by Martínez Montañes. On the church's eastern aisle are two sixteenth-century benches used by the Inquisition. Medina's importance in

Roman times, when it was known as *Asido Caesarina*, is evidenced by some remarkable **Roman sewers** ("Cloacas Romanas"; entry at c/Ortega 10; April–Sept daily Tues–Sun 10am–2pm & 6–8pm, Oct–March Sun only 10am–2pm & 4–6pm; €3) buried beneath the town's eastern flank. Dating from the first century AD, the extensive stone-built sewers stand over two metres in height, and are a tribute to Roman engineering skills. The same ticket covers entry beneath another building nearby to see a remarkably preserved stretch of paved **Roman road** lying directly below the town's main street today, c/San Juan. Don't miss the child's game etched into one of the paving stones, which adds a wonderfully human touch. Medina Sidonia also boasts three **Moorish gates** of which the Arco de la Pastora, close to the Jerez road, is the best preserved.

Eating and drinking

For **food and drink** head for the Plaza de España where the excellent *Restaurante Cádiz* serves very good regional dishes, has a weekday *menú* for €14 and does tapas, too. Its neighbour, *Bar-Restaurante Ortega*, has fewer pretensions and a *menú* for €9, and the restaurant of the *Hotel Medina Sidonia* (see p.178) is also good. Medina was noted in Moorish times for its sweets and **pastries**, a tradition continued at Sobrina de las Trejas, Plaza España 7, whose *alfajores* (sugary tubes containing honey, almonds and dried fruit) are delicious.

Arcos de la Frontera

From whichever direction you approach it, your first view of **ARCOS DE LA FRONTERA** – the westernmost of the White Towns – will be fabulous. In full sun the town shimmers magnificently on its great double crag of limestone high above the Río Guadalete. This dramatic location, enhanced by low, white houses and fine sandstone churches, gives the town a similar feel and appearance to Ronda – except Arcos is rather poorer and, quite unjustifiably, far less visited.

Dating from Iberian times and known as Arco Briga to the Romans, Arcos came to prominence as a Moorish town within the Cordoban caliphate. When Córdoba's rule collapsed in the eleventh century, Arcos existed as a petty *taifa* state until its annexation by al-Mu'tamid of Sevilla in 1103. The seizure of Arcos by Christian forces under Alfonso El Sabio (the Wise) in 1264 – over two centuries before Zahara fell – was a real feat against what must have been a wretchedly impregnable fortress.

Each September 29, Arcos's narrow streets echo to the screams of hundreds of children when they run the bulls in the **Feria de San Miguel** honouring the town's patron saint. To see these girls and boys leap up to grab an overhanging balcony, to lift themselves clear of the horns of the rampaging *toro*, is a truly nail-biting sight, and remarkably few seem to get injured.

Arrival, information and orientation

Most of Arcos's monuments are located in the higher old town – where you'll be spending much of your time. The new town has spilled out to the west and east of here at the foot of the crag. The **bus station** is in the new town on c/Corregidores (☎956 70 49 77), served by the Comes and Amarillo companies, with regular buses to Cádiz and Jerez. **Parking** in the narrow streets of the old town is tricky (although all the hotels have their own arrangements) and you'd be much better off trying to find space on the Paseo de Andalucía or using a pay car park (there's one beneath the Paseo itself). A **Turismo** on the central Plaza del Cabildo (Mon–Sat 10am–2.30pm & 5–8pm, Sun 10.30am–1.30pm; ☎956 70 22 64, ⓦwww.ayuntamientoarcos.org)

▲ San Agustín

ARCOS DE LA FRONTERA (CASCO ANTIGUO)

0 — 200 m

Mirador

PIEDRA DE MOLINO

PEÑA VIEJA

CTA. DEL SOCORRO

ABADES

S. ANTÓN

CILLA

CADENAS

Casa Palacio de los Virues

Casa Palacio Marqués de Torresoto

Casa Palacio Juan de Cuenca

PLAZA DE BLASINAS

TABLADA

JUEGO PADILLA

CUNA

San Pedro

Misericordia

NÚÑEZ DE PRADO

Palacio del Mayorazgo

BÓVEDAS

MATEO GONZÁLEZ

ARENILLAS

Colegio de Las Nieves

Casa Palacio de Pedro Gamaza

Jesuitas

CALDEREROS

CUATRO ESQUINAS

MALDONADO

PLAZA M. MÁRMOL

PLAZA DE BOTICAS

Cvto. de las Mercedarias Descalzas

B

MAGDALENA AMAYA

M. DE TORRESOTO

ESCRIBANOS

F

G

E

H

PESAS DEL RELOJ

CRISTÓBAL COLÓN

Cvto. de la Encarnación

Balcón de Arcos

PLAZA DEL CABILDO

I

MONJAS

Ayuntamiento

Sta. María

Castillo

DEÁN ESPINOSA

NUEVA

Casa Palacio de D. Álvaro de Valdespino

LAS TORRES

Palacio Conde del Águila

MURETE

CRISTÓBAL COLÓN

AVENIDA DUQUE DE ARCOS

CUESTA DE BELÉN

ALHÓNDIGA

Hospital de S. Juan de Dios

PASEO DE LOS BOLICHES

Río Guadalete

▲ **A**

C **D** & Lago de Arcos

RESTAURANTS

Alcaraván	2
Bar-Restaurante Terraza	3
Café-Bar El Faro	4
Café Olé	5
Cafetería Albeniz	6
Mesón Los Murales	1
Taberna José Viuda	7

ACCOMMODATION

Casa Blues	A
Hacienda El Santiscal	D
Hostal-Bar San Marcos	F
Hostal Mesón de la Molinera	C
Hotel Arcotur	J
Hotel El Convento	H
Hotel Los Olivos	K
Hotel Marqués de Torresoto	G
La Casa Grande	E
Parador de Arcos de la Frontera	B
Pensión Callejón de las Monjas	I

New Town, Paseo de Andalucía, **J**, **K**, **3**, **4**, **5**, **6** & **7** ▼

can provide a detailed **map**, which you'll need to find your way around the new town. A summer **kiosko** (March–Oct Mon–Fri 10.30am–1.30pm) also operates in the Paseo de Andalucía, reached by following Paseo de los Boliches (left off our map). The Turismo does weekday **guided tours** of the monuments and patios of the old town, departing from their office at 11am (€7, including admission to churches).

Internet access is currently only available at Locutorio El Barrio, Plaza de las Aguas s/n in the new town (Mon–Sat 10am–2pm & 5–9pm). The Turismo also has a single computer for public use. A useful **minibus** service (Mon–Sat until 9.15pm; €0.80) runs back and forth between Plaza de España and the Paseo de Andalucía in the new town and Plaza del Cabildo in the *casco antiguo* – saving you a climb.

Accommodation

A number of **hostales** providing budget accommodation have recently opened up in the old town, formerly the exclusive preserve of a clutch of upmarket hotels. Lower down, the new town has many more options, including a renovated old *fonda* on the main street, c/Corredera. Staying a little out of town, at the **Lago de Arcos**, where there's a *hostal* and the *Lago de Arcos* **campsite** (☎956 70 83 33), is another possibility – though you'll need insect repellent in summer. There's a bus service to the lake (see p.183). It's worth noting that outside high season prices can fall by up to fifty percent.

Casa Blues c/Callejas 19 ☎956 70 06 15 ⓦwww.casablues.com. Friendly new *hostal* with light and airy en-suite rooms with TV & fans, all with stunning views. Also rents out a couple of adjoining apartments (❹). ❸

Hacienda El Santiscal 3km out of town on the lakeside, beyond the campsite ☎956 70 83 13, ⓦwww.santiscal.com. Small country hotel in a beautiful converted *hacienda* with very pleasant a/c rooms, restaurant and a pool in the grounds. Horseriding available. ❺

Hostal-Bar San Marcos c/Marqués de Torresoto 6 ☎956 70 07 21. Excellent *hostal* in the old town, offering pleasant rooms with bath. The friendly proprietors run a cosy bar-restaurant downstairs with a *menú* for €7. ❷

Hostal Mesón de la Molinera Lago de Arcos ☎956 70 80 02, ⓦwww.mesondelamolinera .com. Tranquil location on the waterfront with stunning views towards Arcos on its hill top. Chalet-style rooms with bath and terrace, great pool and easy parking. Also has its own bar and restaurant, and the restaurant at the nearby campsite is also good. ❺

Hotel Arcotur c/Alta 1, in the new town ☎956 70 45 25, ⓦwww.arcoturhotel.com. Welcoming small hotel offering good value a/c en-suite rooms with TV and balcony (some with great views); there's also a roof-terrace café for taking breakfast. ❸

Hotel El Convento c/Maldonado 2 ☎956 70 23 33, ⓦwww.hotelelconvento.es. Stunning hotel in a seventeenth-century former convent whose comfortable a/c rooms – 8 & 9 are recommended – have a spectacular view over the *vega*. Breakfasts are served in a charming courtyard. ❹–❺

Hotel Los Olivos c/San Miguel 2, in the new town ☎956 70 08 11, ⓦwww.hotelzaharadelosolivos .com. Charming and friendly little hotel near the Paseo de Andalucía gardens, in a superbly restored *casa antigua*. Some of the light a/c rooms have fine views, there's a plant-filled interior patio and there are more views from a rooftop terrace. Car park too. ❹

Hotel Marqués de Torresoto c/Marqués de Torresoto 4 ☎956 70 07 17, ⓦwww .hotelmarquesdetorresoto.com. Pleasant a/c rooms in a converted seventeenth-century mansion, the former seat of the marqueses de Torresoto. The delightful colonnaded patio – complete with Baroque chapel – now serves as their restaurant (open to the public) and their next door *cafetería* is also good and offers a *menú* for €6.50. ❹

La Casa Grande c/Maldonado 10 ☎956 70 39 30, ⓦwww.lacasagrande.net. Perched along the same cliff top as the parador, this elegant hotel has beautiful rooms inside a restored *casa señorial* with a columned inner patio and a sensational view from the terrace of their bar across the river valley. They also offer some more expensive suites. ❹

Parador de Arcos de la Frontera Plaza del Cabildo ☎956 70 05 00, ⓦwww .parador.es. Perched on a rock pedestal – with reassuringly reinforced foundations to prevent it from sliding over the cliff – this is one of the smaller paradores with elegant balcony rooms to enjoy the view. There's a delightful patio (open to the public for drinks and afternoon tea) and the "crow's nest" terrace has the best views in town. Also has a restaurant with a recommended *menú* for around €30. ⑥

Pensión Callejón de las Monjas c/Dean Espinosa 4 ⓣ&ⓕ 956 70 23 02. Decent if cramped *pensión* for en-suite rooms in the heart of the old town; some slightly pricier rooms come with a/c and terrace. ❷

The Town

By far the best thing to do in Arcos de la Frontera is take a stroll around the tangle of narrow streets, lined with a mix of Moorish and Renaissance buildings. At the heart of the **casco antiguo** or monumental quarter is the Plaza del Cabildo, easily reached by following the signs for the parador, which occupies one whole side of it. Flanking another two sides are (behind the Ayuntamiento) the **castle** walls and towers (the castle is privately owned and off limits) and the large fifteenth-century Gothic-Mudéjar church of **Santa María de la Asunción** (Mon–Fri 10am–1pm & 3.30–6.30pm, Sat 10am–2pm, Sun 8.30am for Mass; €1.50), built over an earlier mosque; one side is left open, offering spectacular plunging views to the river valley and the *vega*. Santa María's Plateresque south facade with later additions is a stunning work, although an unfinished bell tower unbalances the whole – the original was destroyed by the Lisbon earthquake of 1755 and the plan was to raise this new one to 58m, second in height only to Seville's Giralda. Three years later, however, the money ran out and the tower rested at a relatively feeble 37m. The tower can be visited (€3) and offers views over the town and surroundings. The church's gloomy interior has fine Gothic vaulting as well as a stunning *retablo*, exquisitely carved choir stalls by Pedro Roldán, and a treasury with all the usual collection of church silver and some dubiously attributed artworks.

East of here along c/Núñez de Prado, the Gothic church of **San Pedro** (Mon–Sat 10am–1pm & 4–7pm, Sun 10am–1.30pm; €1), perched precariously

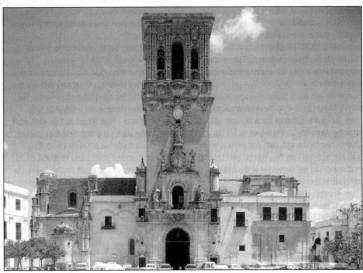

▲ Santa María de la Asunción

on the cliff edge, was rebuilt in the sixteenth century over an original Moorish fort. The later imposing Baroque exterior and tower are in strong contrast to the interior, where a fine sixteenth-century *retablo* documents the life of San Pedro and San Jerónimo and is the oldest in the province. To each side of this are paintings of *San Ignacio* and *La Dolorosa* by Pachecho, the tutor of Velásquez. There's also the rather grisly undecomposed body of San Victor (thankfully behind glass) and an image of the Virgin attributed to La Roldana, the sculptor daughter of Pedro Roldán. You can climb the tower, but you'll need a good head for heights, as there are few guardrails on the top to prevent a nasty fall.

Other monuments in this quarter include the **Palacio del Mayorazgo**, c/Maldonado, with a Renaissance facade and fine patios within (Mon–Sat 10am–2pm & 5–8pm, Sun 11am–2pm; free), and further east still, the convent of **San Agustín** (daily except Tues 10.30am–1pm & 3.30–6.30pm; free), on the narrow neck of the spur, whose church contains a fine seventeenth-century carved wood *retablo* and the town's most venerated image of Jesús Nazareno (Christ bearing the Cross). Nearby, in c/Cuna, there's **Casa Cuna**, formerly the synagogue of the old Jewish ghetto.

East of town, the A372 road to Ronda leads down to a couple of sandy **beaches** on the riverbank, and to the north of here the Lago de Arcos (actually a reservoir) is a good spot for swimming. The lake is served by nine daily buses in each direction (Sun service July & Aug only) leaving from the Plaza de España, below the old town.

Eating and drinking

There's little variety when it comes to **eating and drinking** in Arcos, but a couple of good places are worth seeking out. In addition to the list below, many of the hotels and *hostale* have restaurants of their own.

Alcaraván c/Nueva 1, close to the castle walls. Atmospheric cave restaurant serving tapas and *platos asados* (roasted meats).

Bar-Restaurante Terraza c/Múñoz Vásquez. Below the old town, in the gardens of the Paseo de Andalucía, this is a pleasant place to sit out and serves a wide variety of inexpensive *platos combinados* and a *menú* for €8.

Café-Bar El Faro c/Debajo del Corral 14, in the new town. Good tapas and *platos combinados*.

Café Olé Cerro de la Reina 8, off Plaza de España. Modern place serving drinks and decent *platos combinados* on a terrace in a revamped plaza.

Cafetería Albeniz c/Muñoz Vázquez 10, close to *Bar-Restaurante Terraza* (see p.181). Pleasant café-bar serving a variety of salads, fish and meat dishes as well as paella; has a small terrace.

Mesón Los Murales Plaza de Boticas 1. One of the best low-priced options in the old town, close to the church of San Pedro, and serving an economical *menú* for €9. Has a small street terrace. Main dishes €7.50–11.50.

Taberna José Viuda Plaza Rafael Pérez del Alamo 13 in the new town. Atmospheric and highly popular tapas and *raciónes* bar serving a wide range of tapas in an *ambiente flamenco* (flamenco venue).

Nightlife

Arcos locals tend to gravitate to the bars and restaurants for **nightlife**, however, in summer there are quite a few free outdoor events, such as flamenco (and even rock) concerts and it's worth checking with the Turismo, or perusing the local weekly paper, *Arcos Información,* to see what's coming up. On Thursdays at 10.30pm in July and August there are usually **flamenco** concerts in the Plaza del Cananeo, close to the Iglesia de San Pedro in the old town (details from the Turismo). The welcoming *Peña de Flamenco de Arcos* (☎956 70 12 51), Plaza de la Caridad 4, east of the old quarter, also stages regular – and authentic – flamenco, with *actuaciones* (shows) most weekends (not July & Aug), normally Saturdays after 10.30pm but ring first (Spanish only) to check. Alternatively,

Bora Bora is an open-air **discoteca** at the lakeside in summer, which gets going after 11pm, and in July and August there are tented **music-bars** ("Las Carpas") below the Paseo de Andalucía, to the west of the bus station.

The Costa de la Luz

The villages along the **Costa de la Luz** – the "Coast of Light" between Algeciras and Cádiz – are in a totally different class from the resorts along the Costa del Sol. West from Algeciras the road climbs almost immediately into the rolling green hills of the **Sierra del Cabrito**, a region lashed for much of the year by the ferocious *levante* (east) and *poniente* (west) winds which vie continuously, it seems, for the upper hand. Now cluttered by an inevitable wind farm, from these heights there are fantastic views down to Gibraltar and across the straits to the just-discernible white houses and tapering mosques of Moroccan villages. Beyond, the Rif Mountains hover in the background and on a clear day, as you approach **Tarifa**, you can distinguish Tangier on the edge of its crescent-shaped bay.

Tarifa

TARIFA, spilling out beyond its Moorish walls, was until the mid-1980s a quiet village, known in Spain, if at all, as the southernmost point on the European landmass and for its abnormally high suicide rate – attributed to the unremitting winds that blow across the town and its environs. Occupying the site of previous Carthaginian and Roman cities, Tarifa takes its name from Tarif Ibn Malik, leader of the first band of Moors to cross the straits in 710, a sortie that tested the waters for the following year's all-out assault on the peninsula. Today it's become a prosperous, popular and at times very crowded, resort, following its establishment as Europe's prime **windsurfing** and **kitesurfing** locale (see box, p.190). Indeed, according to windsurfing aficionados, Tarifa now

▲ Windsurfing in Tarifa

Andalucía's bird migrations

Whilst Andalucía's birdlife is fascinating throughout the year, the region also plays host to one of the remarkable spectacles of the natural world, the great **spring and autumn migrations**, attracting an audience of birdwatchers from far and wide. Many birds spend the winter in warmer African climes, a journey that involves a sea crossing – a major challenge for many large birds such as eagles, vultures and storks who rely on the warm air that rises from the earth to keep them aloft. With no thermals over the sea it's essential that they seek out the shortest possible crossing point: the Strait of Gibraltar.

The main "flight path" across the Strait hits land between Gibraltar and Tarifa. Gibraltar (there's an ornithological information centre on the Upper Rock) or the Punta del Carnero (south of Algeciras) are particularly worth a visit when the wind is in the west and anywhere along the main Algeciras–Tarifa road is good when there's an easterly breeze. The birds tend to cross in waves so there will inevitably be times when little is visible and few birds will attempt the crossing in gales or heavy rain. The variety you are likely to see varies from month to month but storks return from Africa in the first months of the New Year. Many black kites, short-toed eagles and other raptors cross the Strait in February and March, but April is the "rush hour" month when huge numbers of honey buzzards are often to be seen aloft and you may even be lucky enough to spot the rare and beautiful black stork.

ranks alongside Diamond Head in Hawaii and Fuerteventura in the Canaries as one of the top three windsurfing beaches in the world. Equipment rental shops line the main street, and in peak season crowds of windsurfers pack out every available bar and *hostal*. Even in winter, there are windsurfers to be seen, drawn by regular competitions held year-round. Development continues at a rapid rate as a result of this newfound popularity, but for the time being Tarifa remains an attractive place for a stopover.

Arrival and information

The **bus station** is in the north of town from where the main Algeciras–Cádiz road (c/Batalla del Salado) leads to the walled old town, a five- to ten-minute walk. Along this street also you'll find a supermarket, fried fish and *churro* stalls, windsurf equipment shops and many of the larger hotels. The friendly **Turismo** (April–Sept Mon–Fri 10am–2pm & 4–6pm, Sat & Sun 10am–2pm, Oct–March Mon–Fri 10am–2pm & 5–7pm, Sat & Sun 10am–2pm; ℡956 68 09 93, Ⓦwww.aytotarifa.com; the private Ⓦwww.tarifainfo.com and Ⓦwww.tarifaweb.com are also useful) is at the top of the Paseo Alameda, a tree-lined promenade flanking the old town's western wall. They can provide a useful town map – also available from many hotels and *hostales* – and a free tapas booklet to help you discover the best places for a snack and a *fino*.

Accommodation

Tarifa has plenty of **places to stay** although prices tend to be higher than other places along this coast. It's wise to book ahead throughout the year, and especially in August, or whenever there are windsurfing tournaments. As elsewhere, room prices fall sharply here outside July and August. The nearest **campsites**, *Río Jara* (℡956 68 05 70) and *Torre de la Peña* (℡956 68 49 03), lie 4km and 7km northwest of town on the Cádiz road respectively. Others nearby include *Tarifa* (℡956 68 47 78) and *Paloma* (℡956 68 42 03). Tarifa's campsites are served by a frequent **bus service** in July and August from Avenida Andalucía, just to the north of the Turismo.

TARIFA

N

Ⓐ, Ⓑ, Ⓒ, Ⓘ & Bus Station (400m)

ACCOMMODATION

Hostal Africa	G
Hostal Alameda	M
Hostal Facundo	C
Hostal La Calzada	H
Hostal Tarik	E
Hostal Villanueva	F
Hotel La Mirada	D
Hotel Misiana	I
Hurricane Hotel	B
La Casa Amarillo	K
Mesón de Sancho	A
Posada La Sacristía	L
Posada Vagamundos	J

RESTAURANTS & TAPAS BARS

Bar El Francés	12
Bar Morilla	6
Bar-Restaurante Voracera	2
Bodega Amarillo	9
Café Zumo	13
Casa Juan Luis	11
Casino	8
Geko	5
Mandragora	7
Mesón de Sancho	1
Restaurante Alameda	14
Restaurante Villanueva	4
Santa Fe	10
Tarifa Eco Center	3

JUAN XIII DEL SALADO

SAN JOSÉ

SAN SEBASTIAN

Beaches

D & E

Ⓐ Ⓑ

AVDA. DE ANDALUCÍA

Puerta de Jerez

SILOS

BATALLA DEL SALADO

PESO

SANTA BARBARA

JEREZ

MORENO DE MORA

SANTA ROSENDO

PARRAS

CALZADILLA DE TELLEZ

G. VIVES

M. A. TOLEDO

COLÓN

Market

NTRA. SRA. DE LA LUZ

PLAZA DE LA PAZ

CASTELAR

FLORINDA

JUSTINO P.

PLAZA DE OVIEDO

GEN. COPONS

INDEPENDENCIA

Ⓘ Turismo

PLAZA DE SAN MARTÍN

PLAZA DE SAN HISICIO

PEDRO CORTÉS

SANCHO IV EL BRAVO

San Mateo

AVENIDA DE LA CONSTITUCIÓN

PASEO ALAMEDA

PLAZA DEL ÁNGEL

SAN FRANCISCO

CERVANTES

SAN DONATO

Ciber Pandor@

CORONEL MOSCARDÓ

PADRE FÉLIX

SANTÍSIMA TRINIDAD

CARNICERÍA

SANCHO IV EL BRAVO

MENÉNDEZ ARANGO

MELO

GUZMÁN EL BUENO

ALMEDINA

AMOR DE DIOS

ALJARANDA

SANCHO IV EL BRAVO

GUZMÁN EL BUENO

Castillo de Guzmán el Bueno

PLAZA DE SANTA MARÍA

Museum

AMARGURA

PLAZA DEL VIENTO

Ayuntamiento

MIRADOR

Beaches

Ferry Port

Hostal Africa c/María Antonia Toledo 12 ☎956 68 02 20, ✉hostal_africa @hotmail.com. Charming small *hostal* with clean and simple rooms with and without bath and spectacular sea views from a communal terrace. Rooms 5 and 6, with individual balconies, are the ones to go for. ②–③

Hostal Alameda Paseo de la Alameda 4 ☎956 11 81, ⓦwww.hostalalameda.com. Pleasant *hostal-restaurante* on the Alameda with en-suite rooms with TV and sea views (from some). ⑤

Hostal Facundo c/Batalla del Salado 47 ☎956 68 42 98, ⓦwwwhostalfacundo.com. Reliable and friendly *hostal* for simple rooms sharing bath and a/c en-suite rooms with TV. There's a communal kitchen for guests, a storeroom for surfboards and free internet. ④–⑤.

Hostal La Calzada c/Justino Pertiñez 7 ☎956 68 03 66. Popular and friendly *hostal* in the centre of the old town, close by the church of San Mateo, offering a/c en-suite rooms with TV. ④

Hostal Tarik c/San Sebastián 32–36 ☎956 68 06 48, ⓦwww.hostaltarik.com. Outside the walls in the northern part of town and overlooking the coast, this *hostal* has helpful owners and decent balcony rooms with TV. ④ with breakfast.

Hostal Villanueva Avda. Andalucía 11 ☎956 68 41 49. Welcoming and good-value *hostal-restaurante* built into the north wall of the old quarter offering a/c en-suite rooms with TV. ④

Hotel La Mirada c/San Sebastian 41 ☎956 68 44 27, ⓦwww.hotel-lamirada.com. Comfortable hotel outside the walls, but only 3min from the beach.

On to Morocco

Tarifa offers the tempting opportunity of a quick approach to **Morocco** – Tangier is feasible as a **day-trip** on a daily catamaran ferry, normally leaving at 11am and 6pm (Fri 7pm), returning at 8.15am or 5.30pm (local time – which is 2hr behind Spanish time in summer, 1hr in winter); check current times with Viajes Marruecotur (see below) or the Turismo. The trip takes 35min, and tickets (around €55 round-trip) are available from the FRS office (Ferrys Rápido del Sur; ☎956 68 18 30, ⓦwww.frs.es) in the Estación Marítimo building in the harbour, Viajes Marruecotur, or travel agents along c/Batalla del Salado. If you're planning a day trip, book a few days in advance.

Catamaran-based one- or two-day **excursions** to Tangier are also available starting at €56 for the one-day package which includes a sightseeing tour, lunch and all transport. The two-day version (currently €93) adds a night in a four-star hotel. Details of these and all other ferry information are available from the helpful Viajes Marruecotur, Avda. Constitución 5, near the Turismo (☎956 68 18 21, ⓔmcotur1 @mcotur1.e.telefonica.net), where English is spoken.

Rooms come with balcony and sea view, satellite TV, a/c and safe. ⑤
Hotel Misiana c/Sancho IV El Bravo 18 ☎956 62 70 83, ⓦwww.misiana.com. Stylish hotel with arty decor and a mishmash of furnishings, some Moroccan. ⑥ with breakfast.
Hurricane Hotel Ctra. Cádiz s/n ☎956 68 49 19, ⓦwww.hotelhurricane.com. Set in dense gardens 7km west of Tarifa at the ocean's edge, this California-style hotel has tastefully decorated a/c rooms, fully equipped gym, two pools, stables, windsurfing school and its own restaurant. ⑥
La Casa Amarillo c/Sancho IV El Bravo 9. Elegant and reasonably priced rooms in a restored nineteenth-century town house with a/c and cable TV; also has serviced studios and apartments (⑤–⑥) sleeping two to four with own kitchen. ④
🏃 **Mesón de Sancho** Ctra. N340 Cádiz– Málaga, 8km east of town ☎956 68 49 00,

ⓦwww.mesondesancho.com. If you can bear being slightly out of the action then this country hotel is a real bargain compared to in-town rates. Leafy surroundings, elegant rooms, garden pool, and excellent restaurant – plus a couple of delightful en-suite log cabins (⑤) – make this pretty special. ④
Posada La Sacristia c/San Donato 8, off c/Sancho IV El Bravo. Stylish conversion of a seventeenth-century town house into a boutique hotel with rooms ranged around a central patio. Also has a decent restaurant with sushi and tempura often featuring on the menu. ⑥ with breakfast.
Posada Vagamundos c/San Francisco 8 ☎956 68 15 13, ⓦwww.posadavagamundos.com. Elegant new hotel filled with artistic features and furnishings in a restored eighteenth-century town house. All rooms exterior with a/c and TV, and there is a wi-fi zone. ⑤ with breakfast.

The Town

There's great appeal in wandering the crumbling ramparts of Tarifa's old walls, gazing out to sea or down into the network of lanes that surround the fifteenth-century church of **San Mateo** (daily 9am–1pm & 5.30–8.30pm; free). Don't be fooled by the crumbling Baroque exterior here, fine though it is; this was added in the eighteenth century and hides, inside, a beautiful late-Gothic church with elegant rib-vaulting in the nave and some interesting modern stained-glass windows. A very helpful leaflet in English will guide you around the church's many features, including a fine crucified Christ by the great eighteenth-century sculptor Pedro de Mena, situated along the right aisle. Nearby, a small seventh-century tombstone confirms that there was a Christian presence here before the Moorish invasion of 711. Further along, the *sagrario* is a stunning Baroque extravaganza in pink and violet, with an enchanting cupola. The church's stirring finale is at the top of the left aisle, where a copy of the original (and now lost) *retablo* contains the

Whales and dolphins

A popular innovation in Tarifa is **dolphin-** and **whale-spotting boat trips**, run by two non-profit-making organizations: Whale Watch, Avda. de la Constitución 6 (information ℡956 68 22 47, reservations ℡mobile 639476544, ⓦwww.whalewatchtarifa.net), and FIRMM (Foundation for Information and Research on Marine Mammals; ℡956 62 70 08, ⓦwww.firmm.org), c/Pedro Cortés 3, slightly west of the church of San Mateo. You need to **book in advance** (2 days' notice is preferable; €30 donation for each; children under 14 €20). The trips last about three hours and if you don't see any dolphins or whales you get a free trip on the next sailing. Whale Watch also runs longer trips to see Orca killer whales.

A more commercial operation, Turmares, Alcalde Nuñez 3, at an office on the beach road near the foot of the Paseo de la Alameda (℡956 68 07 41, ⓦwww.turmares .com), also runs whale-spotting trips with a glass-bottomed boat (€27, kids €18).

early seventeenth-century image of San Mateo by Martínez Montañés, Spain's greatest exponent of wood sculpture.

The restored **Castillo de Guzmán el Bueno** (Tues–Sun 11am–2pm & 5–7pm; €2) has great views from its towers and battlements, both over the town and across the water towards Morocco. In origin a tenth-century Moorish Alcázar constructed by the great Abd ar-Rahman III, ruler of Córdoba, on the ruins of a Roman fort, the building underwent many later alterations. It was also the site of many a struggle as a strategic foothold into Spain. Known today as El Castillo de Guzmán, the appendage refers to Guzmán El Bueno (the Good), Tarifa's infamous commander during the Moorish siege of 1292, who earned his tag for his role in a superlative piece of tragic drama. Guzmán's nine-year-old son had been taken hostage by a Spanish traitor – surrender of the garrison was demanded as the price of the boy's life. Choosing "honour without a son, to a son with dishonour", Guzmán threw down his own dagger for the execution. The story, a famous piece of heroic resistance in Spain, had echoes in the Civil War siege of the Alcázar at Toledo in 1936, when the Nationalist commander refused similar threats – an echo much exploited for propaganda purposes.

Also worth a look is the charming Plaza de Santa María, behind the castle, where you'll find the Ayuntamiento and a small **museum** (currently closed; check with the Turismo) containing an interesting display of artefacts from the Neolithic, Roman and Moorish periods through to modern times. A **mirador** to the east of the square offers more views of the African coast. The daily covered **market** (mornings) – close to the Puerta de Jerez and inside the walls – with Moorish-style arches is worth a visit; when in full swing the bars in the vicinity do a roaring trade. Incidentally, an alcove in the Puerta de Jerez arch itself now displays a large painting of *El Cristo de los Vientos* (Christ of the Winds) by Tarifa's most famous son, the renowned modern artist Guillermo Perez Villalta.

The beaches

The town **beaches**, separated by a causeway, are the small, popular and sheltered Playa Chica on the Mediterranean side and the Playa de los Lances (aka Playa Grande) facing the Atlantic. Heading northwest from Tarifa, towards the Punta Paloma, you find perhaps the loveliest beaches along the whole Costa de la Luz – wide stretches of yellow or silvery-white sand, washed by some magical rollers. The same winds that have created such perfect conditions for windsurfing

The straits of death

In Tarifa's cemetery above the town, lines of nameless headstones mark where the dead lie three deep, mostly the remains of unknown Africans washed up on the beach. In recent years the trickle of "wetbacks" eager for a share of European prosperity has turned into a flood, as gangs operating in Tangier offer to get **illegal immigrants** into Spain by evading the Spanish helicopters and coastal patrols. The usual method of transport is *pateras*, flimsy, easily capsized, flat-bottomed fishing boats designed to carry six people. Often packed with as many as thirty – who pay the equivalent of up to €1000 each – these fragile craft set out to cross one of the most treacherous stretches of water in the world. Crooked skippers often tip unfortunates into the water too far out from shore and many non-swimmers drown. More often though, the boats themselves don't make it and the toll of bodies washed up along Spanish beaches rose to alarming levels in the summer of 2008. Of those that do get safely across the straits, many are picked up by the authorities and held in the detention centre on Tarifa's harbourside, pending extradition. The few that wriggle through the police net face life as non-citizens without papers, drifting between illegal and low-paid jobs or street-selling. The high death toll seems to have no effect on the numbers willing to take their chances on the open seas and the temptation to migrate seems to be getting ever stronger. In the meantime, Tarifa's gravediggers are kept busy as increasing numbers of these desperate boat people perish en route to their promised El Dorado.

can, however, be a problem for more casual enjoyment, sandblasting those attempting to relax on towels or mats and whipping the water into whitecaps.

At **TARIFA BEACH**, a little bay 9km from town, there are restaurants, campsites and a *hostal* at the base of a tree-tufted bluff. There's a windsurfing school here, which acts as the local centre for the sport. Nearby *Hotel Dos Mares* (see p.191) is another windsurf centre that offers courses and rents out equipment. For more seclusion head for one of the numerous **beach-campsites** on either side (see p.185), signposted from the main road or accessible by walking along the coast.

Eating, drinking and nightlife

Tarifa has a wide range of **places to eat**, divided between the old town inside the walls and the new town beyond this. This is another place to try Cádiz's tasty *urta* (sea bream), available all over town.

There's little in the way of entertainment beyond style bars such as those attached to the hotels *Misiana* and *Posada La Sacristía* (see p.187) and *Bamboo*, Paseo de la Alameda 2, plus a couple of *discotecas*. Tarifa's main summer **nightlife** scene happens when the town council erects *carpas* (disco tents) on the Playa de los Lances beach at the eastern end of town. It's also worth finding out what's happening at the *Tarifa Eco Center* (Ⓦwww.tarifaecocenter.com; see p.191) as they stage frequent concerts and show films.

Bar El Francés Paseo c/Sancho IV El Bravo 21. A highly popular French tapas and *raciónes* bar adding a subtly Gallic touch to such staples as *calamares*, *rabo de toro* and *tortilla de camarones*. Has a small street terrace.

Bar Morilla c/Sancho IV El Bravo 2. Central bar where *tarifeños* gather to breakfast or munch early evening tapas while contemplating the ancient stones of nearby San Mateo. Later, cloths

are thrown over the tables as the restaurant hits its stride.

Bar-Restaurante Voracera c/San Sebastián 28. Great neighbourhood bar-restaurant with tasty tapas and good seafood; *besugo a la espalda* (red bream) is a house special and there's a *menú* (Mon–Fri) for €7.

Bodega Amarillo c/Sancho IV El Bravo 9. Lots of cool tiles and marble at this bodega serving up *raciónes* of *cerdo iberico jamón*, plus *calamares a la plancha* (fried squid) and in season *atun del almadraba* (the freshest tuna there is). Main dishes €13–18.

Café Zumo c/Sancho El Bravo IV 26b. Good breakfast bar with a selection of fruit and vegetable juices and a variety of breads and healthy snacks.

Casa Juan Luis c/San Francisco 15 ☏ 956 68 12 65. Despite its proximity to the sea this evening-only place is a shrine to meat, in particular pork in all its Iberian variations. The restaurant, housed in a *casa antigua*, also has a beautiful patio and outdoor terrace. The eponymous owner is a big *toros* fan and the restaurant closes when there's a *corrida*. *Menú* for about €25.

Casino c/Coronel Moscardó s/n, next the church of San Mateo. Opened in 1875, Tarifa's impressive multi-roomed, tiled and marble-floored *Casino* is open to all and is redolent of a bygone age. Its bar serves morning *café* and tasty tapas at lunchtimes and there's a library with all the papers and space to stretch out.

Geko Plaza de Oviedo 1. Fronting the church of San Mateo this is a pleasant little terrace bar serving a variety of economical salads,

tablas de queso (cheese boards) and pasta dishes, as well as *bocadillos* and plenty of vegetarian options. The similar *Delicatessen* next door is also good.

🏄 **Mandragora** c/Independencia 3 ☏ 956 68 12 91. One of a number of restaurants and tapas bars in town offering dishes from both sides of the straits: in addition to Moroccan couscous and *berenjenas bereber* (aubergine), it does excellent *raciónes*, including *boquerones rellenos* (stuffed anchovies). Main dishes €9–17. Closed Sun.

Mesón de Sancho ☏ 956 68 49 00. Attached to the hotel (see "Accommodation") of the same name, this is one of the best restaurants in this zone for both fish (*úrta a la roteña* is a house special) and meat dishes. Mid-priced, but there's a *menú* for around €18.

Restaurante Alameda Paseo Alameda 4. Popular restaurant outside the western wall, which does reasonable *platos combinados* and a tasty paella.

Restaurante Villanueva Avda. Andalucía 11. Fine restaurant of the *hostal* of the same name; their *urta* is prepared in five different ways and there's a good-value *menú* for €8.

Surfing on the Gulf of Cádiz

This stretch of Atlantic coast provides some of the best conditions in the world for **windsurfing** and the current rave watersport, **kitesurfing**. International competitions in both sports are held in Tarifa. Board surfing is currently less popular due to the often difficult conditions but on the right day you can still have some great rides. Courses in all watersports are available in Tarifa (see p.191) and equipment can be rented at numerous shops along c/Batalla del Salado (the Turismo can also supply information). Kitesurf novices are advised to get some instruction (especially regarding potential hazards) before striking out on their own. Below are some of the main beaches with a description of conditions. More information as well as details of courses and companies hiring out equipment is available on ⓦ www.tarifainfo.com /en/surfing.html.

Barbate Sheltered town beach protected by harbour wall. Good option when winds are strong and everywhere else is blown out.

Yerba Buena West-facing beach just beyond Barbate with 200m right-breaking wave off point. Generally needs 2m of swell. North/northeast winds are best. Experienced surfers only.

Caños de Meca South-facing bay approached via pine forest on road from Vejer de la Frontera. Right-breaking wave from point and left-breaking reef breaks. Works on northwest winds. Low tide. Experienced surfers only.

El Palmar West-facing beach with waves from both right and left. Best at mid-to-low tide when waves can reach heights of up to 3m (but is best on 1.5–2m swells).

Conil Good town beach but only works on pushing and dropping tide.

Cabo de Roche (northwest of Conil) Protection from strong east winds. Very fast hollow waves that have tendency to snap boards with no mercy.

La Barrosa (near Sancti Petri) Extensive beach breaks working on same conditions as El Palmar.

Santa Fe Paseo Alameda with entry also at c/Santísima Trinidad 19. Excellent mid-priced French-run bistro with a terrace on the Alameda. They serve up a range of fish and meat dishes accompanied by great (French) wines. Their crepes (served in afternoons with tea or coffee as well as to diners at other times) are mouthwateringly authentic.

Tarifa Eco Center c/San Sebastián 4, ☎956 62 72 20. This new complex has an organic vegetarian restaurant (pasta, pizzas, quiches, *taboulé* etc) out front, eco-shop at the rear and a chill-out zone serving herbal and other teas to the side. Off a courtyard terrace other rooms offer yoga and other courses.

Listings

Diving & Surfing courses The Turismo has an extensive list of companies. One company offering diving courses in English are Aventura Marina, Avda. Andalucía 1 ☎956 05 46 26, ⓦwww .aventuramarina.org. Surfing and kitesurfing courses (in English) are offered by X-trem, ☎956 68 18 14, ⓦwww.tarifaxtrem.com; Tarifa Max Sports ☎696 55 82 37, ⓦwww.tarifamax.net and Kite Surfing ☎956 68 16 68, ⓦwww.kitesurfingtarifa.com. Horseriding The area around Tarifa is good riding country and horses can be hired from

Hotel Dos Mares (☎956 23 66 32, ⓦwww .aventuraequestre.com & ⓦwww.hoteldosmares .com), on the N340, 9km northwest of town, which offers single or multiple-day excursions for around €30 per hr.
Internet El Navegante Ciber Pandor@, c/Sancho IV El Bravo 5, fronting the church of San Mateo.
Vehicle and bike rental Speedline, c/Batalla del Salado 10 ☎956 62 70 48. Tarifa Eco Center (see above) also rents out mountain bikes.

Baelo Claudia

Around the coast from the Punta Paloma to the west of Tarifa and almost on the beach at Bolonia Cove are the extensive ruins of the Roman town of **BAELO CLAUDIA** (June–Sept Tues–Sun 10am–8pm; March–May & Oct Tues–Sun 10am–7pm; Nov–Feb Tues–Sun 10am–6pm; free with EU passport, otherwise €1.50). The site is now entered via a new "concrete bunker" housing a small museum and video complex.

Established in the second century BC, the Roman town – rather like modern Zahara and Barbate nearby – became prosperous with the exploitation of tuna and mackerel to make the fish sauce **garum** of which the Romans were passionately fond. The town reached the peak of its prosperity during the first century AD when it was raised to the status of a *municipium* or self-governing township by Emperor Claudius, and the buildings you see today date from this period. Recently reorganized, there are now a series of information boards (in Spanish only) that guide you around the site concluding at the fish factory on the beach.

A tour of the site starts with a look at the bastions of an impressive entry gate in the town's eastern wall. The route then detours slightly southwest of here to take in what are probably the most interesting series of buildings, actually on the beach. Here has been revealed a **fish factory**, which produced the famous *garum* and you can still clearly make out the great stone vats used to make this concoction – always located as near to the sea and as far away from the town as possible because of the stench. The process involved removing the heads, entrails, eggs, soft roes and blood of the fish, layering these in the vats with salt and brine, and leaving them for weeks to "mature". The resulting mixture was then slopped into Amphorae and shipped all over the empire, particularly to Rome, where the poet Martial droolingly described it as "made of the first blood of a mackerel breathing still, an expensive gift". The mackerel sauce was the Roman equivalent of beluga and they paid the earth for small quantities of it; the tuna-based variety, however, was less of a luxury and much cheaper.

The route then takes in a well-preserved rectangular **forum**, best viewed from the platform at the northern end supporting a row of **three temples** to Jupiter, Juno and Minerva, the great gods of imperial Rome. Just west of here is a smaller temple dedicated to the Egyptian goddess, Isis, and directly ahead, occupying the whole south side of the forum, are the remains of the **basilica**, or law court. At the eastern end of this building stood a colossal white marble statue of the second-century emperor Trajan, the head of which is now preserved in the museum at Cádiz (see p.207). A replica of the statue now occupies the site. On the forum's eastern flank stood a line of *tabernae* or shops, which seem to have been superseded by the later *macellum* or **market** built to the west of the basilica. The newly restored **theatre**, built into the hillside to take advantage of the slope is also worth a look. The **main street**, the *decumanus maximus*, runs east–west behind the basilica and is crossed to the east of the forum by the *cardo maximus* which cuts through the centre on a north–south axis. You can also see the remains of the public **baths**, once supplied with water from the nearby Sierra de la Plata by three aqueducts.

Practicalities

To **get here** from the Tarifa–Cádiz road, turn off down a small side road (signed), on the left 15km beyond Tarifa, at a hotel-restaurant named *San José del Vallé* (which serves a good *menú*). You can also walk to Bolonia along the coast from either the Punta Paloma west of Tarifa, or coming from the opposite direction, Zahara de los Atunes (3–4hr), with a couple of natural obstacles en route.

There's a great beach fronting the site, with a scattering of **bars** and **eating places** open in summer. You'll also find a very pleasant **place to stay** at the eastern end of the village: ⚡ *Hostal La Hormiga Voladora,* c/El Lentiscal 15 (☎956 68 85 62; ❹), which has garden rooms and apartments close to the beach. Nearby *Hostal Lola*, c/El Lentiscal 26 (☎956 68 85 36, ⓦ www.hostallola.com; ❸), is another attractive possibility for rooms with and without bath and has a friendly proprietor. *Hostal Bellavista* (☎&ⓕ956 68 85 53; ❸), near the turn-off into the village, has decent en-suite rooms with TV. For **food** the restaurant at the latter isn't bad and has a *menú* for €10, but *Las Rejas*, near the *Hostal La Hormiga Voladora* above, is the best of the places here.

Zahara, Atlanterra and Barbate

Eight kilometres north as the crow flies (but a hefty 28km dog-leg by road along the N340), **ZAHARA DE LOS ATUNES** is an ancient fishing village long involved (as its name tells you) in the catching of tuna – now an industry in decline. Linked by an infrequent **bus** service with Barbate (see opposite), Zahara is now beginning to show signs of development, but outside of high summer it remains a slow-moving resort with good tapas bars, hospitable locals and a fabulous eight-kilometre-long **beach**.

The best of the budget **places to stay** is the friendly *Hostal Monte Mar*, c/Peñón 12 (☎956 43 90 47; ❹), bang on the shore and reached by turning right immediately after crossing the bridge into the village and following the road to the end; en-suite rooms come with balcony. Alternatives include an excellent seafront hotel, the *Gran Sol*, at Avda. de la Playa 20 (☎956 43 93 09, ⓦ www.gransolhotel.com; ❺ with breakfast), also with welcoming proprietors and an extension where rooms overlook a garden pool. Their restaurant is also good and has a daily *menú* for €18. Of the handful of other places (all of which are usually full in Aug), the newish *Hotel Doña Lola*, at Plaza Thomson 1, just over the bridge (☎956 43 90 09, ⓔ d.lola@teleline.es; ❻ with breakfast), is bright and swish with a garden pool, while close by, the pleasant

Hotel Almadraba & Almadrabeta, c/María Luisa 13 (☎956 43 92 74, ⓦwww
.hotelesalmadraba.es; ❹), with its own restaurant, is another possibility. Out on
the road to Atlanterra *Hotel Antonio*, c/Atlanterra km1 (☎956 43 91 35,
ⓦwww.antoniohoteles.com; ❻ with breakfast), has decent value rooms in its
two-star seafront hotel and more luxurious accommodation in the adjoining
extension. Zahara's **campsite** *Bahía de la Plata* (☎956 43 90 40) lies 1.5km
out of town on the road towards Atlanterra and also rents out bungalows and
studios (❻), both with cooking facilities.

Places to eat here include the central *Marisquería Porfirio*, Plaza Tamarón 5,
for seafood, and the nearby *Bar Ropiti*, c/María Luisa 6, for meat and fish *platos
combinados*. One of the best tapas bars on this stretch of coast is ⅍ *Casa Juanito*
at c/Sagasta 7, serving up deliciously fresh seafood; it has now added an equally
outstanding restaurant. Heading west from here *La Botica*, c/Real 13, is a very
good and fair-priced fish restaurant along a street with many other options. One
mid-priced place a cut above the rest is ⅍ *Antonio*, on the seafront 1km out of
town towards Atlanterra (☎956 43 95 42), where fish is king and *atún al horno*
and *dorada a la sal* are just two of the house specialities.

South from Zahara a road winds down for 4km to the settlement of
ATLANTERRA, another hamlet seized upon by developers and, a few
kilometres beyond this, to a wonderful **beach**, the Playa Camarinal. Atlanterra
itself is rapidly being transformed into a warren of holiday apartments ringed
around the bland *Hotel Melia*, part of the luxury hotel chain. Beyond here the
road continues for a further 4km passing a few secluded villas circled by lofty
palms before coming to a dead end at the **Playa Camarinal** and, a bit further
on, the Faro del Punta Camarinal lighthouse. It's a stunning beach, but there are
no facilities whatsoever.

BARBATE, next along the coast and linked by a frequent daily **bus** service
with Vejer de la Frontera, is an unkempt and rather featureless little town
dominated by its harbour and canning industry which processes the tuna

Andalucía and the bluefin tuna

The catch of the **bluefin tuna** is a ritual that has gone on along the Costa de la Luz
since ancient times and today still employs many of the age-old methods. The bluefin
is the largest of the tuna family, weighing in at around 200 kilos, and the season lasts
from April to June as the fish migrate towards the warmer waters of Mediterranean
(*el derecho*) to reproduce, and from early July to mid-August when they return to the
high seas (*el revés*). Fishing communities dotted along this stretch of Andalucian
coast have been taking advantage of this annual abundance of tuna since the
Phoenician period and probably long back into prehistory. The methods used to
catch the tuna are still referred to by the Moorish name *almadraba* ("place for
hitting"), which involved dragging the giant fish ashore in great nets and clubbing
them to death. Today the fish are caught at sea by herding and corralling them in a
huge net stretched between a circle of boats where they are gaffed – their blood
turning the sea crimson – before the weakened fish are then hauled aboard. The
biggest market is Japan, and Japanese factory ships can often be spotted waiting
offshore in season ready to buy up as much of the catch as they can. Once the tuna
are on board, the fish are rapidly gutted, washed, filleted and frozen ready to cross
another ocean to be eaten raw as sushi. In recent years tuna numbers have been
declining and the season shortening – probably the result of overfishing – much to
the concern of the people of Barbate, Conil de la Frontera and Zahara de los Atunes,
for whom the catch represents an important source of income for fishermen and a
provider of employment in the canning factories nearby.

caught along this stretch of coast. As the major fishing port in these parts Barbate has some excellent **tapas bars** and **fish restaurants** along its seafront, but that's about the limit of its appeal. There's a pleasant **walk** (about two and a half hours starting from the west side of the fishing harbour) from here to Los Caños de Meca, through a pine forest and passing the Torre de Tajo (a watchtower once used for spotting invading pirates) with great views, but take care at the cliff edges.

Los Caños de Meca and El Palmar

From Barbate a rolling scenic road winds its way through the verdant pinewoods of the **Parque Natural de Acantilado**. Although Barbate can hardly be recommended for a stopover the natural park does have a wonderful retreat at *El Palomar de la Breña* (☎956 43 50 03, Ⓦwww.palomardelabrena.com; ❺ with breakfast) a superb *hotel rural* with a remarkable eighteenth-century dovecote of immense proportions authenticated by the *Guinness Book of Records* as the largest in the world. No longer in use, the dovecote's eight thousand nesting places once produced birds for the Spanish Indies fleet who used them to communicate with Spain while out in the Atlantic. The hotel's proprietors have information on activities in the park including, hiking and mountain biking. The hotel is reached via a turn-off from the CA2143, 5km out of Barbate but ring or see their website to get precise details of its location.

A further 5km beyond the turn-off for the hotel the road descends into **LOS CAÑOS DE MECA** (served by sporadic **buses** from Barbate to Conil). A small village surrounded by pine groves and a favourite summer escape for *sevillanos*. Los Caños has a long, beautiful beach lined with rocky coves and freshwater springs, marred only by some unfortunate hotel developments on its southern flank. At the northen end of seafront a side road off Avda. Trafalgar (the road running behind the beach) road leads to a landmark lighthouse and the historically famous Cabo (or cape) de Trafalgar (see p.199). There used to be a hippy colony here and, although this crowd has now gone, some of the laid-back atmosphere lingers, especially among the groups of naturists who swim out to the more secluded coves along the coast.

Places to stay tend to be pricey, although rates drop dramatically out of high season, and among the hotels on Avda. Trafalgar you'll find the welcoming *Hotel Madreselva* at no. 102 (☎956 43 72 29, Ⓦwww.madreselvahotel.com; ❺ with breakfast), with charming rooms with terrace and a pool, and the slightly cheaper and friendly *Hotel Fortuna*, at no. 34 (☎956 43 70 75, Ⓦwww.hostalfortuna.com; ❺), where en-suite rooms come with balcony, sea view (most), room safe and TV. Another en-suite possibility is *Casa Karen* (☎956 43 70 67, Ⓦwww.casaskaren .com; ❹–❼), 500m east of the turning for the lighthouse and signed down a track for a further few hundred metres; various styles of rooms and apartments (including traditional *chozo* huts) enjoy a garden setting. Just west of village, towards Cape Trafalgar, is a **campsite**, the family oriented *Caños de Meca* (☎956 43 71 20), with plenty of shade. The central *Camping Camaleón* (☎956 43 71 54) on Avenida Trafalgar is less attractive and further from the beach.

The numerous **places to eat** close to the seafront include *El Caña* on c/Trafalgar, with a great balcony view of the beach. One place worth seeking out is *Venta Curro*, near the Caños de Meca campsite, where the food is excellent and there's a *menú* offering local specialities. Los Caños also has lots of **bars**, lively in season; *El Pirata* at Avda. de Trafalgar s/n sometimes features live music, including jazz. Next door, *La Jaima*, a tented disco, attracts quite a crowd in summer. In the lighthouse zone there are more bars where *Las Dunas* – a big log cabin with *copas* and music – is another popular place worth trying.

The coast road west from Los Caños (taking a left after 5km and continuing for a further 3km) brings you to **EL PALMAR**, a sleepy and isolated seafront settlement popular with surfers and about as peaceful a place as you could wish. Fronting an excellent, if narrow, beach you'll find a few seafood **restaurants** including *Hostal-Restaurant Francisco* (☎956 23 27 86, ⓦwww.casafranciscoeldesiempre.com; ⑤ with breakfast) with delightful balcony **rooms**. Slightly north of here *Hostal Francisco Alferez* (☎956 23 21 34; ❸) is a cheaper option for en-suite rooms above another fish restaurant. At the north end of the beach, the friendly *Hostal La Ilusión* (☎956 23 23 98; ❹ with breakfast) also has comfortable rooms and a good restaurant – with €12.50 *menú* – beyond an extensive garden. Set 1km back from the beach there's a very good **campsite**, *El Palmar* (☎956 23 21 61), with a great pool, plenty of shade, restaurant, bar and supermarket, and lots of activities on offer, including trekking, scuba diving, and horseriding.

Vejer de la Frontera

While you're on this stretch of the Costa de la Luz, be sure to take time to head inland and visit **VEJER DE LA FRONTERA**, a classically white, Moorish-looking hill town set in a cleft between great protective hills that rear high above the road from Tarifa to Cádiz. Until relatively recent times the women of Vejer wore long, dark cloaks that veiled their faces like nuns' habits; though still trotted out in many guidebooks, this custom is now virtually extinct outside fiestas.

Maintaining a brooding detachment from the world below for most of its history, Vejer has a remoteness and a Moorish feel as potent as anywhere in Spain. Almost certainly a prehistoric hilltop Iberian citadel, Vejer was utilized as a fortress during the **Phoenician** and **Carthaginian** epochs of the first millennium BC to protect coastal factories and fishing grounds from the warlike Iberians of the interior. Dubbed Besipo by the later **Romans**, it was as the **Moorish** town of Bekkeh that Vejer rose to prominence as an important agricultural centre on the western frontier of the kingdom of Granada. Taken by Fernando III in 1250, it was immediately handed over to Alonso Pérez de Guzmán, founder of the ducal house of Medina Sidonia and later hero of Tarifa.

Arrival and information

Arriving by **bus**, you're dropped at the Parque de Los Remedios just to the side of the turismo from where you'll need to ascend Avda. Los Remedios to reach La Plazuela, the effective centre of town. Coming in by **car**, you'd be advised park in the car park at the entrance to the town near the foot of Avda. Los Remedios as the old town's streets are narrow and convoluted. Sited next to the car park as you enter Vejer, the **Turismo**, Avda. Los Remedios 2 (April–Sept Mon–Fri 10am–2pm & 6–8pm, Sat 11am–1pm & 6–8pm, Sun 11am–1pm; Oct–March Mon–Fri 10am–2pm & 5–7pm, Sat 10am–2pm; ☎956 45 17 36, ⓦwww.turismovejer.com), gives out an excellent free **map** (also available from the *Hotel Convento* when the Turismo is closed). Bookend, c/Juan Relinque 45, is a good source of used **books** in English. Vejer's solitary **Internet** café *Vi@.PC*, Avda. San Miguel 18 (Mon–Fri 10am–2 & 5–8pm), is slightly out of the centre.

Accommodation

Vejer is a popular destination for most of the year and limited accommodation can often make finding a room hard work if you're here during Semana Santa or in July and August when it is worth ringing ahead. Vejer's **campsite** (☎956 45 00 98, ⓦwww.campingvejer.com) is located below the town on the main N340 road, close to the *La Barca de Vejer* restaurant.

Casa Los Cántaros c/San Filmo 14, close to La Plazuela ☎956 44 75 92. Very good and economical *pensión* with en-suite rooms; also has communal kitchen and roof terrace. ❶

Casa Rural Leonor c/Rosario 25, near the castillo ☎956 45 10 85, ⓦwww.casaleonor.com. This converted Moorish dwelling has comfortable en-suite rooms with TV, friendly proprietors, and fabulous views towards Morocco from a roof terrace. ❸

🏃 **El Cobijo de Vejer** c/ San Filmo 7 ☎956 45 50 23, ⓦwww.elcobijo.com. Excellent *hostal* inside a traditional house with delightful flower-filled patio and individual rooms on various levels. The higher priced *Zahara* and *Xauen* (the latter has two fabulous terraces) with own kitchens are the ones to go for. All rooms are a/c, internet-connected, and have fridges and satellite TV. ❺ with breakfast.

Hostal El Mirador c/Cañada de San Lázaro 39, near the bus stop at the entrance to the town ☎956 45 17 13, ⓔhostal_mirador@hotmail.com. Clean and tidy en-suite balcony rooms (with views) plus a/c and TV. ❸

Hostal La Janda Cerro Clarisas s/n, signposted up a side road on the way in ☎956 45 01 42. An excellent *hostal* with light and airy, en-suite rooms with a/c and TV. ❸

Hostal La Posada Avda. Los Remedios 2, near the top of the hill as you enter the town ☎956 45 02 58, ⓦwww.hostal-laposada.com. Good en-suite a/c rooms above a restaurant and most with fine views. Has some singles too, and rents out apartments (❺) sleeping up to four. ❸

Hotel Convento de San Francisco La Plazuela s/n ☎956 45 10 01, ⓦwww.tugasa.com. Housed in a converted seventeenth-century convent on the smaller of the town's two main squares, this very pleasant and surprisingly reasonable hotel has stylish a/c rooms with TV. Also has own restaurant and *cafetería* (see p.198). ❹

🎿 **La Casa del Califa** Plaza de España 16 Ⓣ956 44 77 30, Ⓦwww.lacasadelcalifa .com. Stunning hotel created inside a refurbished partly Moorish house, where individually styled rooms are decorated with Moroccan lamps and fittings. Guests have use of two patios, a terrace with views, library and there's also wi-fi and internet, and the price includes buffet breakfast. *Rough Guide* readers with this book are entitled to a ten-percent discount, which should be claimed at check-in. ❺

The Town

Vejer is best savoured by randomly exploring the brilliant-white, labyrinthine alleyways, wandering past iron-grilled windows, balconies and patios, and slipping into one of numerous bars. The **castillo** (daily 11am–2pm & 6–10pm; free), in the heart of the old quarter, is Moorish in origin but underwent substantial rebuilding in the fifteenth century when it was used by the dukes of Medina Sidonia as a summer retreat. The main things to see are a splendid horseshoe arch and some Moorish plasterwork, as well as great views from the terrace. A small **museum** displays ancient and more recent finds discovered in and around the town. To the northwest of the castle, at the end of c/Ramón y Cajal, the church of **Divino Salvador** (daily 11am–1.30pm & 6.30–8.30pm; free) is a sixteenth-century rebuild of an earlier mosque whose minaret now serves as its tower. The interior is a curious mix of mainly Gothic and Mudéjar styles. From here c/Castrillón descends to the **Plaza de España**, the lovely main square, overlooked by a white-walled Ayuntamiento, and centring on a delightful fountain decorated with nineteenth-century Triana tiles from Sevilla. North of here, the **Paseo de la Corredera** offers spectacular views over the countryside to the nearby hill towns of Medina Sidonia and Alcalá de los Gazules. The **Torre de la Corredera** halfway along here was a watchtower used for communicating with those towns.

One visit worth making outside Vejer is to the impressive new open-air **NMAC modern art museum** (April–Sept 10am–2pm & 5–8.30pm, Oct–March 10.30am–2.30pm & 4–60m; €5; Ⓦwww.fundacionnmac.org) located in the grounds of the Dehesa Montenmedio 5km southeast of the town along the N-340 (no bus service). Featuring major works by renowned international artists comprising installations (Fernandez Sánchez Castillo's work, *Fountain*, featuring a riot-control truck sunk in the middle of a pond is a showstopper), sculpture and photography, the route around the artworks passes through stunning parkland and forest replete with birdlife and (in season) nesting storks; there's also a luxury hotel and excellent mid-priced restaurant in the same complex (see website for details), although the more affordable *Café de Kurupay* with attractive shaded terrace makes a better lunch stop.

Eating, drinking and entertainment

Vejer has plenty of places for **eating** and **drinking**. In the old quarter, the *Hotel Convento de San Francisco*'s *cafetería* housed in the old convent's former chapel is one of the best places for **breakfast**. Nightlife is fairly tame, limited to a few bars around town that keep late hours. At the *Peña Flamenca Aguilar de Vejer*, c/Rosario (near the castle), you can sample *manzanilla* from the barrel and take in occasional weekend **flamenco** concerts; the Turismo keeps details of upcoming performances. *Bodegas Gallardo* (daily 10am–6pm), on the main Barbate road below the town, welcome visitors to sample and buy the wines and *finos* of the region.

Bar Peneque Plaza de España 27. Traditional local bar built into a cave with tables at the back for munching *raciónes* should you not feel like joining in the domino games favoured by regulars.

Café-Bar La Bodeguita c/Marqués de Tamarón 9, uphill from La Plazuela and near the church. Entertaining late-night *copas* bar with a street terrace and an often lively crowd; also does tapas among which *pimiento de piquillo* (peppers stuffed with cod) and *albondigas* (meatballs) are house specials.

Castillería Barrio de Santa Lucía s/n ☏ 956 45 14 97. Wonderful outdoor garden restaurant in this rural *barrio* below the town. Specializes in *carnes a la brasa* (charcoal grilled meats) and excellent salads. Open May–Sept.

El Jardín del Califa Plaza de España 16. The mid-priced restaurant attached to the hotel of the same name has a Moroccan chef and serves up a variety of Moroccan and Middle-Eastern inspired dishes on a tree-shaded courtyard terrace. Specialities include tagines and spicy Moroccan fish dishes. Has recently added a stylish new bar with stunning views from its roof terrace.

El Palenque c/San Francisco 1, in the market. Bistro-style diner with an outdoor terrace noted for its *guisos* (stews) and good fried fish.

El Refectorio La Plazuela. The upmarket restaurant of the *Hotel Convento de San Francisco* is a very good mid-priced place offering many local specialities and also has a *menú turístico* for €16.50.

La Posada c/Los Remedios 2. The tapas bar and restaurant of the *hostal* of the same name is a good place for economical *platos combinados* and simple meals.

La Vera Cruz c/Eduardo Shelly 1. Intimate French-run restaurant housed in a sixteenth-century former chapel offering a mix of dishes from both sides of the Pyrenees. *Conejo con ciruelas* (rabbit with prunes) and *dorada relleño al horno* (sea bream) are signature dishes. Main dishes €12–17. (Open May–Oct)

Mesón Pepe Julián c/Juan Relinque 7, just off La Plazuela. Popular local bar with *azulejo*-lined walls serving up decent tapas – specials include *chorizo iberico* and *calamares* (squid).

Restaurante Trafalgar Plaza España 31. One of Vejer's better restaurants with a pleasant terrace on the square for summer eating. Wide range of dishes including *revuelta con morcilla* (scrambled eggs with blood sausage) and *venado con cabrales* (venison with cheese sauce). *Menú* for €18. Main dishes €11–17.

Venta Pinto La Barca de Vejer. Down below the town at the road junction with the N340 this is an outstanding mid-priced restaurant with a great range of seafood, fish and game dishes. House specials include *solomillo* (pork loin) and *rape con azafran y langostinos* (monkfish with saffron and prawns) and there's a *menú* for around €20. Main dishes €9–20.

Conil

Back on the coast, a dozen or so kilometres further northwest of Vejer de la Frontera, is the increasingly popular resort of **CONIL**. Though this former fishing village appears entirely modern when viewed from the beach, plenty of older buildings survive, and its mainly domestic visitors create a fun, if family-oriented, atmosphere, and throughout the summer you can also indulge in some very lively nightlife. During the second week in June Conil celebrates the **Semana del Atun de Almedraba** (tuna catch week) when the first half of the tuna season reaches its peak (see box, p.193) and the town's restaurants participate in a *ruta gastronomica* offering different dishes prepared with the fish at discount prices (details from the Turismo).

Arrival and information

Most **buses** drop you off at the Transportes Comes station on c/Carretera; walk towards the sea and you'll soon pass Conil's helpful **Turismo** (May–Oct daily 8am–2pm & 5.30–8.30pm; Nov–April Mon–Sat 8am–2pm, Sun 8.30am–2pm; ☏ 956 44 05 01, ⓦ www.conil.org), at the junction of Carretera and c/Menéndez Pidal; a summer office is located in the Torre de Guzmán in the old town (June–Sept; same hours). Make sure to pick up their town map and useful booklet *Conil en su Bolsillo*, which details all the town's tapas bars, restaurants and much more. **Internet** access is available at the pleasant *Café de la Mar*, c/Carril de la Fuente, near the Torre de Guzmán, with plenty of screens, and also at *Café de la Habana*, Plaza de Santa Catalina s/n, with more limited facilities.

Accommodation

Conil has numerous **hotels and hostales** – August is the only time when you'll struggle to find a bed. This is when you may need to seek out one of a multitude of *casas particulares*, details of which are available from the Turismo. Nearby **campsites** include *Fuente del Gallo* (T 956 44 01 37; March–Sept) in the *urbanización* Fuente del Gallo, a three-kilometre walk (or taxi ride) to the north of the resort.

Hostal La Posada c/Quevedo s/n, just northeast of Plaza de España T 956 44 41 71, W www .laposadadeconil.com. Dapper *hostal* with clean and tidy en-suite a/c rooms with TV – many with sea views – above a good restaurant. ❹ with breakfast.

Hostal La Villa Plaza de España 6 T 956 44 10 53. Economical en-suite rooms above a bar-restaurant on a central square. ❷

Hostal Los Hermanos c/Virgen 2 T 956 44 01 96. A piece of Conil's history, this wonderful old *fonda* first opened its doors in 1900 but the house dates from the eighteenth century. As a plaque outside informs, the founder of Cádiz's *Carnaval* "Tío de la Tiza" was born here in 1833 (see p.202). Today the friendly owners offer en-suite rooms around a flower-bedecked central patio and also have some fully equipped apartments. ❸

Hostal Santa Catalina c/Carcel 2, off Plaza Santa Catalina T 956 44 15 83, W www.webconil.com /hostalsantcatalina. Pleasant small *hostal* with en-suite a/c rooms with TV. ❸

Hostal Sonrisa del Mar c/Huerto 3, close to the seafront Paseo del Atlántico T 956 44 27 18. Fronting the town beach (Playa de Los Bateles) this seafront *hostal* has a/c rooms with TV, balcony and sea views. ❹

Hostal Torre de Guzmán c/Hospital 5, southwest of Plaza de España T 956 44 30 61, W www.hostaltorredeguzman.com. Comfortable en-suite a/c rooms with TV in a relatively new place above a restaurant. ❹

Hotel Almadraba c/Señores Curas 4, south of Plaza de España T 956 45 60 37, W www .hotelalmadrabaconil.com. Taking its name from the annual tuna cull, this is a pleasant hotel with stylish well-equipped rooms ranged around a charming patio. It also has its own bar-*cafetería* and car park. ❺ with breakfast

Hotel Diufain Cañada del Rosal s/n, Fuente del Gallo T 956 44 25 51, W www.hoteldiufain.com. Good-value and comfortable balcony rooms in a three-star garden hotel with pool and restaurant a couple of hundred metres behind the beach. ❹

Hotel Flamenco Playa Fuente de Gallos T 956 44 07 11, W www.hipotels.com. Fronting the Fuente del Gallo beach this elegant and newly refurbished 100-roomer is one of the resort's older luxury places set in a tranquil location. Well-appointed rooms have balcony terraces and sea views and there's a bar-restaurant, two garden pools and steps down to a fine strand. ❼ with breakfast.

Hotel Oasis c/Carril de la Fuente 3 T 956 44 21 59, E hoteloasisconil@hotmail.com. Pleasant traditional small hotel fronting the town beach (Playa de Los Bateles) where a/c sea-view rooms come with minibar and balconies. ❺

The beaches

The **beaches** (the central Playa de Los Bateles and Playa de La Fontanilla to the north), Conil's *raison d'être*, appear as a wide bay of brilliant yellow stretching for miles to either side of town and lapped by an amazingly gentle Atlantic. The area immediately in front of town is the family beach: up to the northwest you can walk to some more sheltered coves; across the river to the southeast is a topless and nudist area. The beach here is virtually unbroken until it reaches the **Cabo Trafalgar**, off which Lord Nelson achieved victory but lost his life on October 21, 1805. If the winds are blowing, this is one of the most sheltered beaches in the area. You can get there by road, save for the last 400m across the sands to the rock.

Eating, drinking and nightlife

Conil has lots of good **seafood restaurants** and **tapas bars** along the seafront: *La Bahia*, Avenida de la Playa s/n, and *Casa Manolo* nearby are the town favourites where you should be able to try *ortiguillas* – deep fried sea anemones – a delicious regional speciality. Also worth a try are either of Conil's two outstanding seafood restaurants, *Francisco* (☎956 44 08 02) and *La Fontanilla* (☎956 44 07 79) side by side on the Playa de la Fontanilla. Beyond the *Hotel Diufain* (see p.199) another excellent fish restaurant worth making an effort to get to is ⅔ *Restaurante Mirador El Roqueo* (☎956 44 33 37; closed Mon), Urbanización Las Palmeras s/n, fronting the beach of El Roqueo. Two restaurants in one, the more formal dining room sits on the street behind the seafront *Mirador*, which has a great terrace overlooking the shore below.

Nightlife centres on the music and drinking **bars** to the north of the centre around calles Cádiz and Baluarte and Plaza Santa Catalina. **Las Carpas** is a remarkable all-summer long municipal disco and entertainment complex on the central Playa de Los Bateles, which caters for all ages and tastes from techno and house, to big band and flamenco. Best of all though, it's all completely free.

Sancti Petri and Chiclana

Heading north from Conil along the road (not marked on many maps) which hugs the coast brings you, after 18km, to the isolated fishing village of **Sancti Petri** surrounded by marshes and sand bars. The formerly wild stretch of coast that precedes it has been developed into a dismal chain of overspill *urbanizaciones* for the sealocked city of Cádiz.

When you reach it, the village of Sancti Petri (follow signs for the Puerto Deportivo) at the end of a causeway is a place under threat from the encroaching madness to the south and its future remains uncertain. The harbour now contains many more weekend yachts and launches than fishing vessels and, since the tuna-canning factory closed down, there are few jobs. The focal point of the tiny cluster of dwellings is the *Club Náutico de Sancti Petri* where the few fishermen that are left meet up. On Sunday mornings they sell their catch outside the club, offering some of the freshest oysters and *cañaillas* (murex sea snails) you've ever had for ridiculously low prices. They're best washed down with a beer from the *Náutico*'s bar (they'll also lend you a plate) at a table overlooking the harbour. The bar has recently added an inviting terrace restaurant.

There's a small but nice enough **beach** to the south, where a friendly water- sports centre, Novo Jet (☎956 49 20 26, ⓦwww.novojet.net), hires out windsurf boards, kayaks and catamarans and offers courses in scuba diving besides leading guided canoe expeditions around the *marismas* and watercourses of the Parque Natural de la Bahía de Cádiz to the north. Nearer to the *Club Náutico*, Escuela de Vela Zaida (☎956 49 64 45) offers sailing and windsurfing courses.

The nearby Cruceros Sancti Petri (☎mobile 617378894, ⓦwww.albarco .com) does tourist boat excursions to see dolphins and whales as well as trips (around €7) to the **Castillo de Sancti Petri**, a ruined thirteenth-century castle on an offshore island, where the Phoenicians built an important first millen-nium BC temple to their god Melkaart which the Romans later turned into a shrine to Hercules. Hannibal was a visitor to the former and Julius Caesar to the latter, and major archeological finds have been discovered which are now on display in the museum at Cádiz.

To reach Cádiz you'll need to head inland to the rather unexciting town of Chiclana de la Frontera to pick up the A48 *autovía*. Beyond Chiclana you emerge into a weird landscape of marshes, dotted with drying salt pyramids, in the midst of which lies the town of **San Fernando** – once an elegant place (and still so, at its centre) but quickly being swallowed up by industrial and commercial suburbs. These extend until you reach the long causeway that leads to Cádiz, an unromantic approach to what is one of the most extraordinarily sited and atmospheric towns of the south.

Cádiz

Cádiz, from a distance, was a city of sharp incandescence, a scribble of white on a sheet of blue glass, lying curved on the bay like a scimitar and sparkling with African light.

Laurie Lee, *As I Walked Out One Midsummer Morning*

Sited on a tongue of land enclosing a bay and a perfect natural harbour, with some fine beaches besides, **Cádiz** has – you would think – all the elements that make for an appealing place to visit. But despite an atmospheric old town and some fine museums, oddly enough the place seems unable to shake off a brooding lethargy when it comes to entertaining visitors, and the world of tourism has largely passed it by. Once you've got through the tedious modern suburbs on its eastern flank, inner Cádiz, built on a peninsula-island entered via the **Puertas de Tierra** (Land Gates) – a substantial remnant of the eighteenth-century walls – looks much as it must have done in the great days of the empire, with grand open squares, sailors' alleyways and high, turreted houses. Literally crumbling from the effect of the sea air on its soft limestone, it has a tremendous atmosphere – slightly seedy, definitely in decline, but still full of mystique. Above all, Cádiz is a city that knows how to enjoy itself. It has always been noted for its vibrant fiestas: the ancient Roman poet Martial was among the many who commented on the sensuous and swirling dances of the townswomen ("they click their Tartessian castanets with a deft hand"), implying a pre-Moorish origin for flamenco. Although settled after the *Reconquista* with immigrants from the northern city of Santander, Cádiz maintains its Roman reputation for joviality with an **annual carnival** in February, acknowledged to be the best – and wildest – in Spain.

Some history

Founded about 1100 BC by the Phoenicians as Gadir, a transit depot for minerals carried from the mining areas of the Río Tinto to the north, Cádiz has been one of Spain's principal ports ever since, and lays claim to being the oldest city in Europe.

Historically Cádiz served as an important base for the navies of Carthage, Rome and – following a long decline under the Moors – imperial Spain. Always prone to attack because of its strategic importance, the city's nose was bloodied on numerous occasions, especially by the English. Drake's "singeing of the king of Spain's beard" occurred here in 1587, not long after by Essex's ransacking of the port in 1596, and in 1797 Nelson's bombardment.

The city's greatest period, however, and the era from which much of **inner Cádiz** dates, was the eighteenth century. Then, with the silting up of the river to Seville, the port enjoyed a virtual monopoly on the Spanish-American trade in gold and silver: on its proceeds were built the **cathedral** – almost Oriental when seen from the sea – public halls and offices, broad streets and elegant squares, as well as a clutch of smaller churches. This wealth spawned Spain's first modern middle class which, from early on, was free-thinking and liberal, demanding such novelties as a free press and open debate. One historian has claimed that political dialogue in Spain originated along the Calle Ancha, Cádiz's elegant central thoroughfare where politicians met informally.

¡Carnaval!

Claiming to be saltier than the carnivals of Havana and Río de Janeiro rolled into one, each February Cádiz launches into its riotous **Carnaval**, the most important and wittiest in Spain. Largely a disorganized series of fiestas in origin, it was given its present shape in the late nineteeth century by Antonio Rodríguez Martínez, now known by his nickname El Tío de la Tiza ("Chalky" after the chalk or *tiza* he used in his job) who was improbably employed as a Customs official in the port. He organized the *murgas* or bands – a major feature of Carnaval – into four categories:

Coros These are (recently mixed) groups of about thirty who tour the city on flamboyantly decorated floats singing to the accompaniment of guitars, lutes and mandolins.

Comparsas Groups of around fifteen people who parade on foot with guitars and drums.

Chirigotas Arguably the most popular with *gaditanos*, these are groups of around ten people accompanied on a reed whistle or pito, who tour the bars singing hilarious satirical songs about people and events in the public eye.

Trios, **Cuartetos**, **Quintetos** These smaller groups not only sing, but also act out parodies and satirical sketches based upon current events as they tour the town in costume.

Illegales Given the city's innate anarchy these bands do not compete officially (see below), but take to the streets for the sheer hell of it with whatever instruments they can lay their hands on. They include whole families, groups of friends and even collections of drunks, staggering about as they attempt to make music.

The above groups provide only the focus, however, for the real Carnaval which takes place on the streets with everyone dressed up in costume and apparently drunk for ten whole days. The "legal" groups compete before judges in the Teatro Falla in between sessions on the streets and are symbolically awarded *un pelotazo* (good shot) for a bitingly witty composition and *un cajonazo* (a box drum) for a bomb. The various groups work at their repertoire for months before, road-testing their compositions during the two weekends prior to Carnaval (but not in costume, which is regarded as bad form) at the warm-up shindigs of the Erizada (hedgehog party) or the Ostionada (oyster party), great street fiestas which feature sea-urchin and oyster tasting.

Attending Carnaval

During Carnaval there are **no rooms** to be had in town at all unless you've made reservations well in advance. One way round this is to see it on **day trips from Seville**, catching an evening train (a couple of hours' journey) and returning with the first train the next day, around 5.30am. These trains are a riotous party in themselves and, packed as they are with costumed carnival-goers from Seville, you'd be well advised to get dressed up yourself if you don't want to stand out. The opening and final weekends are the high points of the whole show; for more information see Ⓦ www.carnavaldecadiz.com.

In the early nineteenth century the city made arguably its greatest contribution to the development of modern Spain, when a group of radicals set up the short-lived Spanish parliament or **Cortes** in 1812 during the Peninsular Wars. The Cortes drew up a Constitution that upheld the sovereignty of the people against the throne and set down a blueprint for a liberal Spain that would take a further century and a half to emerge. Loyal to its traditions, the city relentlessly opposed General Franco during the **Civil War**, even though this was one of the first towns to fall to his forces, and was the port through which the Nationalist armies launched their invasion. Later, when Franco often referred in power to the forces of "Anti Spain" he had in mind the sentiments expressed in the Cádiz Constitution of 1812, ramming home his disapproval by renaming the city's major plazas after himself and other members of the Falangist pantheon. Left-wing Cádiz merely bided its time and now, in the new democracy, these landmarks have regained their original designations. The city's tradition of liberalism and tolerance is epitomized by the way *gaditanos* (as the inhabitants of the city are known) have always breezily accepted a substantial **gay** community here, who are much in evidence at the city's brilliant Carnaval festivities.

Arrival and information

Arriving by train you'll find yourself on the periphery of the old town, close to the Plaza San Juan de Dios, busiest of the many squares. **By bus** you'll be a few blocks to the north, along the water – either at the Los Amarillos terminal, Avda. Ramón de Carranza 31 (serving Rota, Chipiona, Sanlúcar and resorts west of Cádiz), or a few blocks north again at the Autobuses Comes station, Plaza de la Hispanidad (serving Seville, Tarifa and other destinations toward Algeciras and the rest of Andalucía). Los Amarillos also runs a twice-daily service through Arcos to Ubrique, with a connection there to Ronda – by far the best route. Coming in **by car** you're best off taking accommodation with a garage (all the hotels will assist with parking) or heading for a car park. Two of the most central inside the city walls are by the train station and along Paseo de Canalejas near the waterfront. If you're coming in for a day-trip a useful tip is to park in the huge underground car park of the El Corte Inglés department store (just off the top right of our city map) which is free (but closes at 10pm) and take the bus from outside which goes to the centre.

Timetables as well as general information, a detailed street **map** and a useful *Ruta de Tapas* leaflet are available from the **Turismo**, Avda. Ramón de Carranza s/n (Mon–Fri 9am–7.30pm, Sat–Sun 9am–5pm; ☎956 20 31 91), just north of Plaza San Juan de Dios. At 11am on Saturdays they offer a free guided walk around the city. Seventy metres away there's also a useful **Turismo municipal** on the Paseo de Canalejas (Mon–Fri 8.30am–6pm & 4–8pm, Sat & Sun 10am–1.30pm & 4–7pm; ☎956 24 10 01), for maps and information and they produce their own *Ruta de Tapas* leaflet and self-guided themed walking-tour leaflets. Throughout the summer the city's theatres and concert venues stage a variety of performances from Beethoven to folk music, dance and flamenco and both tourist offices stock information on these.

City transport

City buses are a handy way of getting around and a route map is available from the Turismo. A ten-trip Bonobus travelcard (€6.20 from *estancos* – tobacconists, bus kiosks and many newspaper stands) gives you a healthy discount over buying single journey tickets. One way to get to grips with the city is to do an **open-top bus tour** – especially good if you're pressed for time; two competing

Cádiz online

Online information on Cádiz and its monuments and amenities can be found at ⓦwww.infocadiz.com, ⓦwww.cadizayto.es, ⓦwww.cadizturismo.com, ⓦwww.andalucia.org. Information on Cádiz province and its towns and villages is available from ⓦwww.cadiznet.com.

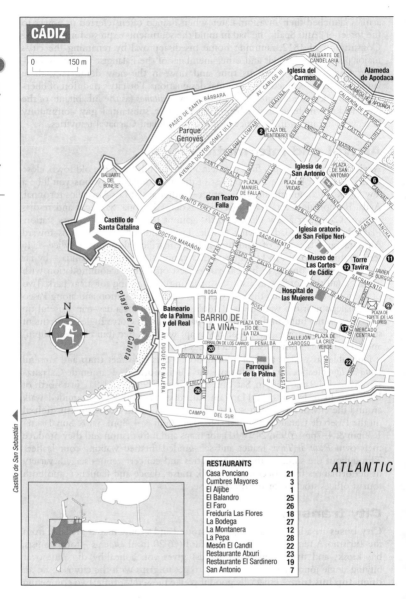

CÁDIZ

0   150 m

BALUARTE DE CANDELARIA

Iglesia del Carmen

Alameda de Apodaca

AV. CARLOS III

ALAMEDA DE APODACA

PASEO DE SANTA BÁRBARA

Parque Genovés

PLAZA DEL MENTIDERO

AVENIDA DOCTOR GÓMEZ ULLA

SANTA ROSALÍA

CALDERÓN DE LA BARCA

ENRIQUE DE LAS MARINAS

VEEDOR

Iglesia de San Antonio

PLAZA DE SAN ANTONIO

BALUARTE DEL BONETE

PLAZA MANUEL DE FALLA

PLAZA DE VILUDAS

Gran Teatro Falla

BENITO PÉREZ GALDÓS

CERVANTES

SAGASTA

ANCHA

Castillo de Santa Catalina

DOCTOR MARAÑÓN

Iglesia oratorio de San Felipe Neri

SACRAMENTO

SAN BASILIO

OBISPO CALVO Y VALERO

CONCEPCIÓN

Museo de Las Cortes de Cádiz

Torre Tavira

JAVIER DE BURGOS

SACRAMENTO

ROSA

Hospital de las Mujeres

HOSPITAL DE MUJERES

PLAZA DE TOPETE (DE LAS FLORES)

N

Playa de la Caleta

Balneario de la Palma y del Real

BARRIO DE LA VIÑA

PLAZA DEL TÍO DE LA TIZA

LIBERTAD

MERCADO CENTRAL

ROSA

AV. DUQUE DE NÁJERA

CORRALÓN DE LOS CARROS

PEÑALBA

CALLEJÓN CARDOSO

PLAZA DE LA CRUZ VERDE

VIROTÓN DE LA PALMA

Parroquia de la Palma

SAGASTA

CRUZ

SAN FÉLIX

PERICÓN DE CÁDIZ

CAMPO DEL SUR

Castillo de San Sebastián

ATLANTIC

RESTAURANTS

Casa Ponciano	21
Cumbres Mayores	3
El Aljibe	1
El Balandro	25
El Faro	26
Freiduría Las Flores	18
La Bodega	27
La Montanera	12
La Pepa	28
Mesón El Candil	22
Restaurante Atxuri	23
Restaurante El Sardinero	19
San Antonio	7

companies do the same hop-on, hop-off clockwise route around the peninsula. Tour por Cádiz (10am–11pm; €10) and Cádiz Tour (10am–9pm; €12 with a slightly longer route) both have stops at or near Plaza San Juan de Dios, the Cathedral, the Parque Genoves, the Playa de la Victoria and places in between and with the latter company your ticket is valid for 24 hours from the time you board (Tour por Cádiz tickets are valid only on the day of purchase).

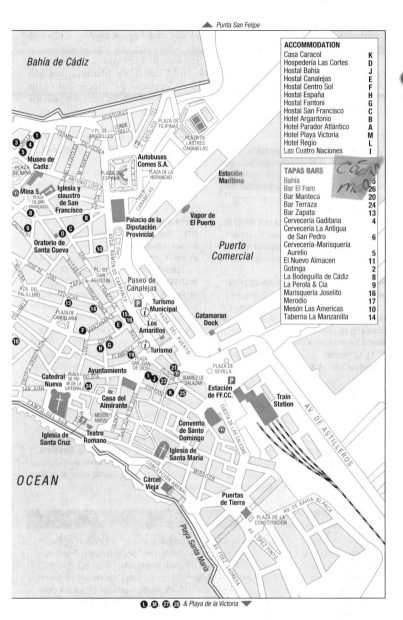

ACCOMMODATION

Casa Caracol	K
Hospedería Las Cortes	D
Hostal Bahía	J
Hostal Canalejas	E
Hostal Centro Sol	F
Hostal España	H
Hostal Fantoni	G
Hostal San Francisco	C
Hotel Argantonio	B
Hotel Parador Atlántico	A
Hotel Playa Victoria	M
Hotel Regio	L
Las Cuatro Naciones	I

TAPAS BARS

Bahía	5
Bar El Faro	26
Bar Manteca	20
Bar Terraza	24
Bar Zapata	13
Cervecería Gaditana	4
Cervecería La Antigua de San Pedro	6
Cervecería-Marisquería Aurelio	5
El Nuevo Almacen	11
Gotinga	2
La Bodeguilla de Cádiz	8
La Perola & Cia	9
Marisquería Joselito	16
Merodio	17
Mesón Las Americas	10
Taberna La Manzanilla	14

Accommodation

In tune with the city itself, much of Cádiz's budget **accommodation** has seen better days. Although things are slowly improving, there's still a shortage of good quality accommodation in all categories. However, many of the crumbling older places (and palaces, which many of them are, or were) are full of character, and efforts are now being made to retain this whilst upgrading the facilities. Except during the Carnaval, and July and August, finding a place to stay shouldn't be a problem.

A good place to start hunting is Plaza San Juan de Dios and the surrounding network of streets, crammed with *hostales* and *fondas*. Calle Marqués de Cádiz also has several budget options, as does the pedestrianized c/Plocia, east of the plaza. More good *pensiones* and *hostales* are a couple of blocks away, towards the cathedral or Plaza de Candelaria and beyond.

Budget

Casa Caracol c/Suárez de Salazar 4 ☎956 26 11 66, ⊛www.caracolcasa.com. Friendly backpackers' place with dorm beds (€16 per person) in a large house near Plaza San Juan de Dios. Price includes breakfast, free internet access and use of kitchen. ❷

Hostal España c/Marqués de Cádiz 9 ☎956 28 55 00, ⊛www.pensionespana.com. Rooms with and without bath in an elegant restored nineteenth-century *casa palacio*. En-suite rooms also have TV and fans. ❷–❸

Hostal Fantoni c/Flamenco 5 ☎956 28 27 04, ⊛www.hostalfantoni.es. Hostal occupying a charming, renovated eighteenth-century house filled with *azulejos* and cool marble. En-suite rooms come with a/c and TV. ❷–❹

Hostal San Francisco c/San Francisco 12 ☎956 22 18 42. Pleasant central hostal for rooms with and without bath, all a/c. Those en suite come with TV. ❷–❸

Las Cuatro Naciones c/Plocia 3 ☎956 25 55 39. Clean, unpretentious place with low-priced rooms sharing bath. ❷

Moderate to expensive

Hospedería Las Cortes c/San Francisco 9 ☎956 21 26 68, ⊛www.hotellascortes .com. Splendid hotel in a stylishly restored *casa señorial*. Elegant rooms have a/c, minibar and come internet-connected. Facilities include sauna and gym and there's a *cafetería* and restaurant. Can advise on parking. ❻

Hostal Bahía c/Plocia 5 ☎956 25 90 61, ⊜hostalbahia@hostalbahia.info. By far the nicest *hostal* in this area, offering rooms with bath, TV and a/c. ❹

Hostal Canalejas c/Cristóbal Colón 5 ☎956 26 41 13. Pleasant two-star hostal in completely restored town house. En-suite rooms come with a/c and TV and there's a pay car park nearby. Avoid the windowless interior rooms though. ❹

Hostal Centro Sol c/Manzanares 7 ☎956 28 31 03, ⊛www.hostalcentrosolcadiz.com. Slightly pricey for what you get, but the en-suite rooms are smart, come with a/c and TV and are arranged above a pleasant patio. Has its own café-bar. ❹

Hotel Argantonio c/Argantonio 3 ☎956 21 16 40, ⊛www.hotelargantonio.com. Very pleasant new hotel housed in an elegant nineteenth-century town house and decorated throughout with Moroccan furnishings and fittings (many of them for sale). All rooms come with plasma TV and minibar, and the top floor exterior rooms are the ones to go for. Wi-fi zone. ❺

Hotel Parador Atlántico Parque Genovés 9 ☎956 22 69 05, ⊛www.parador.es. Functional, modern parador, somewhat lacking in ambience, but with balcony rooms, Atlantic views, an outdoor pool and garage. ❻

Boats from Cádiz

Before the decline of passenger ships it was possible to sail to London or South America from Cádiz – today you can go only as far as the Canary Islands. Trasmediterranea, Estación Marítima (☎956 22 74 21, ⊛www.trasmediterranea.es), currently operates a weekly sailing to **Tenerife** (Sat 5pm; 36hr) and **Las Palmas** (48hr); return fares start at around €270 for a shared cabin. More locally – and for only €3/4 one-way/round trip – you can get a boat to **El Puerto de Santa María**, a forty-minute trip across the bay. Departures are from the Estación Marítima at 10.15am, 12.15pm, 2.15pm, 4.45pm, 6.45pm and (June–Sept) 8.45pm. The return from El Puerto is at 9.15am, 11.15am, 1.15pm, 3.45pm, 5.45pm and (June–Sept) 7.45pm. No service on Mondays from October to May. The service is run by Motonaves Adriano (☎mobile 629468014, ⊛www.vapordeelpuerto.com). A faster catamaran service running roughly hourly (☎902 45 05 50; ⊛www.cmtbc; 25min; €1.95 one way) goes from the Muelle Reina Victoria jetty near the train station.

Hotel Playa Victoria Glorieta Ingeniero La Cierva 4 ☎ 956 20 51 00, ⓦ www.palafoxhoteles.com. If you're seeking a beachfront location this giant four-star hotel fronting the Playa de la Victoria has good facilities including a pool, views (especially from rooms 609–11) and own garage. ❼

Hotel Regio Avda. Ana de Viya 11, ☎ 956 27 93 31, ⓦ www.hotelregiocadiz.com. Catering mainly to the corporate sector, this modern three-star is nevertheless a convenient and comfortable hotel for the city with parking nearby and a stop (for buses into the centre) almost outside. ❺

The Town

Unlike most ports of its size, Cádiz seems immediately relaxed, easy-going, and not at all threatening, even at night. Perhaps this is due to its reassuring compactness, the presence of the sea making it impossible to get lost for more than a few blocks. Although there are plenty of sights to aim for, including an excellent **museum**, a Baroque **cathedral** and some memorable church art, Cádiz is most interesting for its general ambience and for its **vernacular architecture** – elegant *mirador*-fronted facades painted in pastel shades, blind alleys and cafés, and ancient *barrio* backstreets imprisoned behind formidable fortifications.

Museo de Cádiz

The **Museo de Cadíz**, Plaza de Mina 5 (Tues 2.30–8.30pm, Wed–Sat 9am–8.30pm, Sun 9.30am–2.30pm; €1.50, free with EU passport), housed in an imaginatively restored Neoclassical mansion just across the square from the Turismo, is an ideal place to start a tour of the city. The ground-floor **archeological collection** (information in Spanish only) includes some fine Phoenician jewellery excavated in the city and bronze figurines from the shrine of the god Melkaart on the island of Sancti Petri (p.200). Etruscan artefacts found at the same site hint at sophisticated early trading links. Another Phoenician temple to Astarte/Venus on the site of the modern Bastion of Santa Catalina yielded incense burners (*quemaperfumes* – the only ones found in Spain) with Egyptian decoration and a terracotta head with striking negroid features. Two remarkable fifth-century BC **Phoenician carved sarcophagi** in white marble (one male, the other female) are also unique to the western Mediterranean. It's interesting to observe the fusion of influences here: Egyptian for the sarcophagus, Greek for the depiction of the sculpted images. In the same section there's a display of ancient glassware – some of it of a very high standard – from the Phoenician, Greek and Roman periods.

In the Roman section a **reconstructed boat wreck** displays various Amphorae exported from Cádiz to other parts of the empire; they contained *garum* (fish sauce), *salazones* (cured meat and fish), wine and olive oil, and the ship also carried minerals such as copper and lead – all demonstrating the great part played by Spain in making Rome rich. Two enormous anchors nearby, found off Cádiz, attest to the size of vessels that were used. Notable among the Roman statuary is a giant marble sculpture of the second-century emperor Trajan, which prior to excavation stood in the forum of Roman Baelo Claudia at Bolonia (see p.191) near Tarifa. A computer-measured duplicate was made in 2000 and now stands in the basilica at Baelo Claudia.

The second-floor **Museo de Bellas Artes** (fine art museum) is one of the best in Andalucía. The kernel of the collection is a group of 21 canvases by Zurbarán in Room 2, including a quite exceptional series of saints brought here from La Cartuja, the Carthusian monastery at Jerez, and one of only three such sets in the country preserved intact, or nearly so (the others are at Seville and Guadalupe). With their sharply defined shadows and intense, introspective air,

Zurbarán's saints are powerful and very Spanish, even the English figures such as Hugh of Lincoln, or the Carthusian John Houghton, martyred by Henry VIII, whom he refused to accept as head of the English Church. Perhaps this is not surprising for the artist spent much of his life travelling round the Carthusian monasteries of Spain and many of his saints are in fact portraits of the monks he met. Highlights of the many other works on display include, in Room 3, Murillo's *Ecce Homo* and *San Pedro y San Paulo*, as well as his final work, the *Mystic Marriage of Santa Catalina* – during the painting of which he fell from a scaffold to his death – and a *Sagrada Familia* by Rubens. The same room also contains *The Vision of San Félix Cantalicio*, a canvas displaying tenebrist influences by seventeenth-century sculptor, painter, architect and all-round genius, *sevillano* Alonso Cano.

The museum's third floor has an interesting **ethnological collection** divided into two rooms; the first has examples of traditional *artesanía* including ceramics, basketwork, leatherwork and textiles. The second room contains some wonderful **antique marionettes**, part of a section covering the long tradition of Tía Norica, or satirical marionette theatre, in Cádiz. This art form has often been used to pillory the city's rulers and dignitaries, through the "mouths" of its characters taken from the streets – travelling salesmen, waiters, sailors, fishermen, *toreros*, drunks – often in times when overt political activity was dangerous. The city still holds an annual marionette theatre festival. Fascinating though the puppets are behind glass, they need to be brought to life in a show – an idea that awaits an enterprising museum director.

Oratorio de Santa Cueva

A short walk from the museum, on c/Rosario, the eighteenth-century **Oratorio de Santa Cueva** (Tues–Fri 10am–1pm & 4.30–7.30pm, Sat & Sun 10am–1pm; €2.50) houses three fine Goya frescoes. The church is divided into two dramatically contrasting parts; in the elliptical **upper oratory** beneath an elegant dome are three frescoes representing the *Miracle of the Loaves and Fishes*, the *Bridal Feast* (either side of the main altar) and the *Last Supper* (above the entrance), an unexpected depiction of Christ and the disciples dining sprawled on the floor, Roman style. The other works here are depictions of biblical scenes by minor artists. In sharp contrast to the chapel above is the subterranean chapel containing a sculpture of the Crucifixion whose manifest pathos only adds to the gloom. An eighteenth-century work of the Genoa school, the image is said to have inspired visiting composer Joseph Haydn to write the score of his *Seven Last Words* (of Christ) oratorio. Each Good Friday a sermon on the theme of Christ's last words is preached in the chapel, following which Haydn's work is performed. Somewhat breaking with tradition, spotlights have been added recently to illuminate the lower chapel and a formerly blacked-out lunette has been cleaned, flooding it with light, both inevitably lessening the sculpture's dramatic impact. A small museum has been added between the two chapels giving background information – including a display of Haydn's score – on the building's history.

The Catedral Nueva

The huge **Catedral Nueva** (Mon–Fri 10am–6.30pm & 4.30–7pm, Sat 10am–4.30pm, Sun 1–6.30pm; €5 including museum; free entry Tues–Fri 7–8pm), so titled because it replaced the former cathedral, Santa Cruz, is one of the largest churches in Spain. Begun in 1722, it took 110 years to finish, and even then the towers – shortened when the money ran out – were completed only in 1853 in an unsympathetic white limestone whose patchwork effect jars with the original sandstone. The time lapse also led to a curious architectural potpourri, strikingly visible on the main facade, where the exuberance of the earlier Baroque below was topped off in a contrastingly sober Neoclassical style. What is more, on closer inspection you'll see that the distinctive "gilded" dome, which appears so impressive from afar, is in fact made from glazed yellow tiles. Sadly, in the latter half of the twentieth century the building fell into an advanced state of decay – caused by sea air calcifying the stone – as chunks of the ceiling started falling on the congregation below. A costly programme of restoration over the last few years has slowly restored the building to its former grandeur.

Even if you don't normally go for High Baroque, it's hard to resist the attraction of the austere interior, which has more of the architect Vincente Acero's original design. From inside, the soaring 52m-high dome is illuminated by a powdery violet light, the whole perfectly proportioned building decorated entirely in stone with no gold or white in sight. **Artworks** include a sculpture of *San Bruno* by Martínez Montañés in the chapel of San Sebastián and some other polychromed sculptures including an *Ecce Homo* attributed to Luisa Roldán ("La Roldana"), the daughter of Pedro Roldán. Also worth a look are the wonderful **choir stalls** dating from 1702 which were originally in the Cartuja of Seville and moved here upon the latter's Disentailment in 1835. In the crypt (same hours) is buried Manuel de Falla, the great gaditano composer of such Andalucía-inspired works as *Nights in the Gardens of Spain* and *El amor brujo*. The cathedral's museum holds some dubiously attributed paintings as well as a rather tedious collection of ecclesiastical silver enlivened only by a monstrance – an eighteenth-century bejewelled custodia nicknamed the *Millón* (million), a reference to the number of precious gems and pearls set into the work. For a magnificent view over the city you can also climb the **Torre de Poniente** (guided visits daily June–Sept 10am–8pm, Oct–May 10am–6pm; €4) one of the cathedral's twin towers.

Barrio del Populo and Plaza de las Flores

The best view of the cathedral is from the waterfront behind, where the golden dome is perfectly set off by the pastel-tinted facades of the adjacent houses along c/Campo del Sur. To the east of the Plaza de la Catedral fronting the cathedral lies the **Barrio del Pópulo**, a poor, run-down area of narrow alleyways and decaying tenements, a surviving remnant of the thirteenth-century medieval city. Many of its streets are graced by the odd crumbling palacio, formerly residences of merchants made wealthy by empire trade, and now split up into residential blocks. One of these, the **Casa del Almirante** on c/Posadilla, is a splendid Baroque pile with an ebullient facade featuring barley sugar and Tuscan columns in rose-tinted Italian marble. At the time of writing there are plans to turn this into a luxury hotel. An ancient, seventeenth-century inn, though recently restored as a community centre, the **Mesón del Pópulo**, c/Mesón Nuevo 11 – at the crook in the street – has the typical layout of these travellers' hostelries with stables below and living quarters above. Calles Sopranis and Santa María – where the Palacio Lasquetty (no. 11) and the church of Santa María are also worth a look – are other good places to sample the typical atmosphere of this quarter.

A couple of blocks to the west of the cathedral lies the **Plaza de las Flores** (aka Plaza Topete), one of the city's most emblematic squares. Fronted by the striking early twentieth-century Correos, the square is a riot of colour most days due to the many flower sellers that have their stalls here. There are a couple of elegant mansions, too: no. 1 with a portal decorated with pilasters in the Cádiz Baroque style dates from 1746 and, around the corner in c/Libertad, numbers 15 and 16 are a couple more eighteenth-century mansions with *torres-miradores* or lookout towers. Fronting these two, the whole of Plaza de la Libertad is taken up by the early nineteenth-century marketplace, the **Mercado Central** (currently undergoing a belated refurbishment) a beehive of activity on weekday mornings.

Iglesia de Santa Cruz and other churches

A little further east of the cathedral stands the "Old" Cathedral, the **Iglesia de Santa Cruz** (Tues–Sat 10am–2pm & 5–8pm, Sun 10am–2pm; free). Originally a thirteenth-century church built on top of a mosque, it was almost destroyed by the Earl of Essex during the English assault on Cádiz in 1596, and is effectively a seventeenth-century rebuild with only occasional vestiges such as the entrance arch surviving from the earlier Gothic structure. The sober grey stone interior contrasts with the magnificent seventeenth-century gilded *retablo*, a beautiful work with sculptures by Martínez Montañés, as is the Capilla de los Genoveses, its own stunning retablo of red, white and black Italian marble now wonderfully restored. Just behind the church is the **Teatro Romano** (Roman theatre; daily 10am–2.30pm; free) dating from the first century BC. Partly cut into by a corner of Santa Cruz and built over by a later Moorish Alcazaba, the remaining banks of seats have been restored. Across the square from the church the **Casa del Obispo**, Plaza Frey Félix 5 (June–Sept 10am–8pm, Oct–May 10am–6pm; €4), former residence of the bishops of Cádiz, contains beneath its recently excavated floor and basement evidence of a Phoenician burial site and wall paintings from the later Roman temple that superseded this.

Two other central churches noted for their paintings and sculptures are worth making an effort to visit. The first, to the northwest of the cathedral, is the chapel of the **Hospital de las Mujeres** (Mon–Fri 10am–1.30pm & 6–8pm, Sat 10am–1.30pm; €0.80) on the street of the same name. One of the most impressive Baroque buildings in the city, its church has a brilliant El Greco of *San Francisco in Ecstasy*. The second, the **Iglesia y claustro de San Francisco**, lies just east of Plaza de Mina on a tiny square of the same name; here in the church's *sacristia* are two sculptures of San Diego and San Francisco attributed to the *andaluz* master, Martínez Montañés.

Oratorio de San Felipe Neri and the Museo Histórico Municipal

The eighteenth-century oratory of **San Felipe Neri**, c/San José (Mon–Sat 10am–1.30pm; €2.50), to the northwest of Plaza de las Flores, is one of the most important historical buildings in Spain, evidenced by the number of commemorative plaques from countries as far apart as Chile and the Philippines attached to the exterior. It was here, on March 29, 1812, that a group of patriotic radicals defied the Napoleonic blockade and set up the Cortes, framing a liberal Constitution – the nation's first – which had a major impact on the development of European politics. The church itself, an elegant oval structure, has a double tier of balconies which would once have echoed with the roar of fierce debate, and above which eight *ventanillas* in the dome allow the brilliant light to illuminate the sky-blue decor and the central nave punctuated by seven chapels. The high altar's *retablo* is crowned by a fine *Immaculada* by Murillo.

Next door to the oratory in c/Santa Inés, the **Museo de las Cortes de Cádiz** (Tues–Fri 9am–1pm & 5–7pm, Sat & Sun 9am–1pm; free) was set up in 1912 to commemorate the first centenary of the 1812 Constitution. The highlights of the museum are a large Romantic-style mural depicting the events of 1812 together with a number of the original documents of the Cortes, and an enormous eighteenth-century scale model of the city – almost filling a room – made of mahogany and ivory at the behest of King Carlos III. Further north, the Plaza de España is dominated by a rather pompous monument to the Constitution, also set up in 1912 and now crowned with the rather appropriate addition of a crane's nest. *Gaditanos* like to claim that it's the only monument in the world honouring and topped by a book – a representation of the 1812 Constitution.

Just south of the Museo de las Cortes and off c/Sacramento, the **Torre Tavira**, c/Marqués del Real Tesoro 10 (daily 10am–8pm, closes 6pm Oct–May; €3.50), is an eighteenth-century mansion with the tallest tower in the old city, which you can climb to get a great view over the white roofs below and the sea beyond. Many houses had these towers added so that shipowners and merchants could see ships arriving in the port. The tower also holds a camera obscura, which gives equally dramatic views, and the rooms below contain historical displays covering Cádiz and its past. A couple of blocks north, the Calle Ancha – the historic thoroughfare that is today an attractive pedestrianized shopping street – makes a pleasant place for a stroll.

Barrio de la Viña

Squeezed between c/Campo del Sur and the Playa de la Caleta to the west of the cathedral lies the Barrio de la Viña, the old fishermen's quarter, typically *gaditano* and traditionally renowned for the spirited and sarcastic humour of its inhabitants. Its main street is the c/Virgen de la Palma, close to the eastern end of which lies the tiny Plaza Tío de la Tiza, a charming square (filled with terraces for seafood tapas and *raciónes* in summer) named after the man who, in the late nineteenth century gave the famous Carnaval the form it has today (see p.202).

The beaches

The western flank of the Barrio de la Viña faces the **Playa de la Caleta**, an over-popular – and often none too clean – beach in a small bay sandwiched between the most impressive of Cádiz's eighteenth-century sea fortifications, the **Castillo de Santa Catalina** and the **Castillo de San Sebastián**, the latter constructed on an islet and reached by a causeway. This is believed to be the site of the ancient Phoenician harbour where, tradition has it, there once stood an impressive temple to the Phoenician god Melkaart. A walk along the seafront here can be wonderfully bracing day or night (when cooling breezes blow in off the Atlantic and many of the monuments are floodlit), with the possibility of a stroll through the Parque Genovés, planted with palms and cypresses as far as the bastion of Candelaria, or onwards to the Alameda Apodaca, another waterfront garden, beyond. The town beach is the **Playa Santa María del Mar**, lying some five hundred metres east of the cathedral.

The city's main beach and the one with all the action – including restaurants and *chiringuitos* – is the **Playa de la Victoria**, 2km of excellent sand, cleaner and usually less crowded than those mentioned above. Getting there is an easy thirty-minute walk from the old town – just find the seafront on the south side of the peninsula and head east – or there's a bus (#7) which starts out from the Parque Genovés and follows the coast as far as the *Hotel Playa Victoria*. The **Playa Cortadura** begins where the Playa de la Victoria ends and it's an altogether less commercialized affair – in fact there are no bars or *chiringuitos* at all. To reach the Playa Cortadura by public transport you can take bus #7 (see above) and walk east from the Hotel Playa bus terminus or take the train from the main

▲ Castillo de San Sebastián

station; leaving every twenty minutes or so, there are stops at Segunda Aguada (for Playa de la Victoria) and Cortaduras, from where the Playa de la Cortadura is a short walk.

Eating and drinking

Cádiz's best **cafés**, **tapas bars** and **restaurants** tend to be clustered around its many grand squares, especially Plaza San Juan de Dios, dominated by the delightful wedding-cake facade of the late eighteenth-century Ayuntamiento (whose bells sound the hour with notes from de Falla's *El amor brujo*) and the pleasant Plaza de Mina. Across the old town there are more places to hunt down in and around the adjoining Plaza de las Flores and Plaza de la Libertad, the latter containing the **market**, and the atmospheric **c/Sagasta**, almost bisecting the peninsula north to south, is another place to find more typically earthy watering holes. The old seamen's quarter, the **Barrio de la Viña**, is where *gaditanos* make for on warmer nights to scoff *caballa a la gaditana* (mackerel) and shellfish at economical *marisquerías* in the narrow streets around Plaza Tío de la Tiza and along c/Virgen de la Palma. The city's summer playground, the **Paseo Marítimo** – the long boulevard fronting the Playa de la Victoria – is lively and fun all season, with tapas bars, restaurants and beach *chiringuitos* (*Marimba* and *Marea* are recommended) all doing a roaring trade.

A great **snack** at any time of the day are *empanadas gallegas* (fish or meat pies), obtained from the only Galician bakery in town, Casa Hidalgo, Plaza Catedral 8, fronting the cathedral.

Restaurants

Casa Ponciano c/Lazaro Dou. Lively and economical bar-restaurant for tapas, fish and meat dishes; there's also a three-course *menú* for €7.

Cumbres Mayores c/Zorilla 4. Excellent and atmospheric restaurant and tapas bar located in a century-old former brewery where *carne*

(particularly Huelva *jamón*) is king. The tapas bar has daily specials and in winter serves up a delicious *berza* – a chickpea and *morcilla* (blood sausage) based broth.

El Aljibe c/Plocia 25 ☎956 26 66 56. A very good restaurant serving up a range of traditional dishes on a menu that changes four times a year. Also serves very good tapas in its bar. *Menú de degustación* €32 including wine; main dishes €10–15. Closed Sun eve.

El Balandro c/Apodaca 22 ☎ 956 22 09 92. Highly popular venue with a view of the Bay of Cádiz. Wide range of excellent seafood tapas served at the bar or *raciónes* and fresh fish and meat dishes on a promenade terrace – a wonderful place to watch the sun set. Main dishes €10–20. Closed Sun eve.

El Escenario c/Honduras 4 ☎ 856 17 42 17. This wonderful café-restaurant opens for breakfast before moving on to tapas and lunches. Outstanding tapas (in the bar) include *úrta a la roteña* (sea bream in onion sauce) – a meal in itself – and in the comfortable restaurant *solomillo iberico al Pedro Ximénez* (pork fillet in wine sauce; €10.50) is a dream on a plate. Fair priced wines (and international beers) plus friendly service make this a winner.

El Faro c/San Félix 15 ☎ 956 21 10 68. In the heart of the Barrio de la Viña, this is one of the best fish restaurants in Andalucía. House specialities include *pulpo* (octopus), *merluza* (hake), *urta* (sea bream), and a delicious *arroz marinero* (Andalucian paella). There's a *menú de degustación* for €45 (excluding wine) and a *menú* for around €20 (Mon–Fri). Their tapas bar is also well worth a visit (see below).

Freiduría Las Flores Plaza de las Flores. One of the best *freidurías* in town. You can get a takeaway and eat it at the terrace tables of the nearby bar *La Marina* (facing the *correos*), who don't seem to mind – as long as you buy a drink. However, as they have now added their own café-restaurant you may wish to eat inside instead. Another good place is the nearby *Freiduría Europa*, c/Hospital de Mujeres 21 (at the junction with c/Sagasta).

La Bodega Paseo Marítimo 23, on the Playa de la Victoria seafront and close to Cádiz's football stadium, Estadio Ramón de Carranza ☎ 956 27 59 04. Excellent mid-priced restaurant and tapas bar with a wide range of meat and fish dishes.

La Montanera c/Sacramento 39. Good place for carnivores in this fish-crazy city. The lamb dishes, especially, are excellent, and check out the dish of the day.

La Pepa Paseo Maritimo 14, beyond the *Hotel Playa Victoria*. Terrace restaurant at the eastern end of the Paseo Marítimo serving excellent fish and rice dishes.

Mesón El Candil c/Abreu 7. Very pleasant restaurant whose popularity has led to it occupying premises on both sides of this small *plazuela* with a charming terrace between. The chef has been

fronting the *fogón* here for 38 years so he should know by now how to prepare the house special *pescado plancha a la Pepe*. Meat is also on offer and there's a *menú* for €8.

Restaurante Atxuri (former Achuri) c/Plocia 7 ☎ 956 25 36 13. This outstanding Basque fish restaurant has adopted the Basque form of its name and moved from its earthy diner to sparkling new premises down the street. The kitchen staff remains the same though, and it seems as popular as ever with *gaditanos*, making booking advisable. Excellent Basque- and *andaluz*-inspired fish dishes at reasonable prices. Also has an excellent tapas bar. Closed eves Sun–Wed.

Restaurante El Sardinero Plaza San Juan de Dios 4. Traditional *gaditano* fish restaurant offering good quality fish dishes served on a pleasant terrace.

San Antonio Plaza San Antonio 9 ☎ 956 21 22 39. Good mid-priced typically *gaditano* restaurant offering a variety of local meat and fish dishes. Mains €11–25.

Tapas bars

Bahía Avda. Ramón Carranza 29. Wonderful old harbourfront bar that does excellent *fino* and delicious *guisos* – tapas in sauce; there's no frying here. Try the *costillas de cerdo* (pork ribs) or *papas aliñas* (potatoes in sauce).

Bar El Faro c/San Félix 15. Tapas bar of the renowned restaurant (see above), and probably the best in town. A stand-up place where the *finos* are first rate, the service is slick and the seafood tapas are mouthwateringly delicious. House specials include *tortillitas de camarones* (shrimp in batter) and *tostaditas de pan con bacalao* (cod).

Bar Manteca Corralón de los Carros 66, near c/San Félix. Great old place in the Barrio de la Viña run by a retired *torero* and decorated with bullfighting memorabilia. Excellent *fino* and *oloroso*. House specials include *chicharrones* (pork crackling) and *lomo* (cured pork loin). Impromptu flamenco often takes place here too. *El Pescador*, opposite, is another good place.

Bar Terraza Plaza de la Catedral. Facing the cathedral and founded in 1952, this is a superb tapas bar and fair-priced fish restaurant with a very pleasant terrace. The nearby *Cervecería La Catedral* also does tasty fish tapas and *raciónes*.

Bar Zapata Plaza Candelaria, at the corner with c/Zapata. Atmospheric little bar with an excellent selection of *jamón* and chorizo tapas and wines.

Cervecería Gaditana c/Zorilla. Fine bar – the tasty *montaditos* (or titbits) are wonderful; try the salmon and Roquefort and their *bombita* (baby bomb), a ball of potato with onion and tuna fish.

Cervecería La Antigua de San Pedro c/San Pedro s/n. Great little *barrio* bar serving meat and fish tapas and *raciónes*.

Cervecería-Marisquería Aurelio c/Zorilla 1, near Plaza Mina. Vibrant and outstanding seafood tapas bar with excellent *manzanilla*. Founded by the legendary Aurelio, who sold shellfish outside the entrance for many years; specials include *merluza rebozada* (hake) and *ortiguillas* (fried sea anemones). They'll also serve you a great fish supper at tables in a side room.

El Nuevo Almacen c/Barrié 17, northeast of the Torre Tavira. Charming little shop/bar with tasty tapas selection. The *puntas de solomillo en salsa de vino* (pork loin in wine sauce) is a mini-meal in itself. Their delicatessen sells fine *jamones*, cheeses and wines of the region. Closed Sun.

Gotinga Plaza del Mentidero, 15. German bar with a wide tapas range, some vegetarian dishes and inviting terrace on one of Cadiz's most delightful (and little-known) squares dotted with jacaranda trees.

La Bodeguilla de Cádiz c/San Pedro 20. Fine little tapas and *raciónes* bar also serving up *platos combinados*.

La Perola & Cia c/Canovas del Castillo 34, southwest of the Santa Cueva chapel. Modern tapas and *raciónes* bar popular with a younger clientele and serving over seventy different tapas.

Marisquería Joselito c/San Francisco 38. Venerable old (recently modernized) haunt and one of a chain of tapas bars, but none the worse for that. There's a sister branch just around the corner (with a pleasant terrace), facing the port on Avda. Ramón Carranza. House specials include *salpicón de mariscos* (seafood cocktail) and *gambas al ajillo* (garlic prawns).

Merodio Plaza Libertad 4, fronting the market. One of the city's best-loved old bars, which gets riotous during Carnaval and really buzzes on Sunday lunch times. Specializes in *erizos de mar* (sea urchins) in season, as well as shellfish.

Mesón Las Americas c/Ramón y Cajal 1. Good tapas and *raciónes* bar near Plaza de España, specializing in Argentinian meat dishes. Closed Sun.

Taberna La Manzanilla c/Feduchy 18, north of Plaza Candelaria. Wonderful atmospheric eighteenth-century *bodega* serving the odd tapa in addition to excellent *manzanilla* served from huge butts. If you ask, the proprietor will show you his cellar with some classic vintages. The nearby *El Cañon* (junction of c/Feduchy & c/Rosario) is another good tapas place.

Nightlife

Outside carnival and fiesta times, **nightlife** in Cádiz centres on the areas around the Plaza de Miña and Plaza de España, while a new nightlife *copas* (drinks) zone has opened up in the Barrio del Populo with calles Mesón Nuevo and Silencio, and Plazuela San Martín as the focus. However, many places close during July and August and in summer much of the *marcha nocturna* (nightlife scene) migrates to the Paseo Marítimo, behind the beaches to the east of the centre (c/Muñoz Arenillas, behind the Hotel Playa Victoria is the focus), where you'll find most of the bars and clubs. In the winter revellers flock to the Punta de San Felipe (there's a less frenetic scene here in summer, too), known locally as La Punta, the peninsula beyond the harbour to the northeast of Plaza de España.

Flamenco is an irregular feature at private *peñas* or clubs, and isn't always that easy to find. We've listed a couple of places below, but check with the Turismo for more, as well as for details of special concerts and festivals at venues such as the Teatro Falla and the Diputación (regional government building) in Plaza de España.

Clubs and bars

Barabass c/Muñoz Arenillas, off Glorieta Ingeniero La Cierva and behind the Paseo Marítimo. In a street packed with clubs and bars which are full to bursting in high summer, this is a fairly big place with 60s decor and a great atmosphere when the dancing gets going.

Bhopal c/Manuel Rancés, just west of Plaza de España. Big disco-bar with dancefloor. There are quite a few other lively places in this street.

Café de Levante c/Rosario, near Plaza de San Agustín. Relaxed bar with an *ambiente cultural*; it often stages literary events, live music and even flamenco.

Cardenal c/Cardenal Zapata 7. Ultra-modern music and *copas* bar with cool lighting and equally cool *ambiente*.

El Hoyo c/Beato Diego de Cádiz 8, south of Plaza de España. A friendly late-night bar open until after 4am which gets packed out with a youngish crowd partying to the tunes of the 80s and 90s.

El Pay Pay c/Silencio 1, Barrio del Populo. Large café-bar with a long history as a former sailor's hangout. Now renamed and revamped, it stages live music, theatre and poetry readings and there are noticeboards with information on cultural events around the city. This is now a major *copas* zone and the adjoining c/Mesón Nuevo is filled with late night bars and clubs such as *La Favorita*, *El Malagueño* and *Mesón de la Posadilla*.

El Poniente c/R. Viesca, near Plaza de España. Busy and upbeat gay (but not exclusively so) scene bar with house music and frequent drag shows.

Flamenco Paseo Marítimo 14. Forget the name, this bar is home to aficionados of the alternative scene and those wanting to escape the more frenetic nightlife in nearby c/Muñoz Arenillas. A favourite for watching the sun go down.

Habana Café c/Rosario 21, near Plaza San Francisco. Stylish bar for late-night drinking.

La Guarida c/Virgen de las Angustias 6, in the Paseo Marítimo zone, slightly east of the *Hotel Playa Victoria*. Entertaining den of a club that manages to do a bit of everything: live concerts (including flamenco), theatre, the big football games on a large screen and free nightly salsa classes.

Malecon Punta de San Felipe. Good, popular salsa club – which only lifts off at 3am – with a view of the Bay of Cádiz on this frenetic street. A highly popular venue appealing to a lively young crowd and featuring showboating salsa dancers who command the floor. South of here a string of bars and clubs all add to the action.

Persígueme c/Tinte, near Plaza de Mina. Trendy music bar open Thurs–Sat in summer. It gets very lively at weekends and sometimes stages live bands.

San Francisco Uno Plaza San Francisco 1. This pleasant bar with a terrace on this delightful square is good for breakfast coffee and perfect for late-night liqueurs or even a wine from their extensive list.

Woodstock c/Canovas del Castillo at the corner with c/Sagasta and Paseo Marítimo 11. A duo of lively bars at each end of the town serving up eighty-plus of the worlds top beers to the accompaniment of rock, blues, jazz and the occasional blast of Celtic pipes. During winter the old town's branch is the most popular; in summer head for the one on Paseo Marítimo which has panoramic windows overlooking the beach.

Flamenco

Baluarte Candelaria On the northern tip of the peninsula. This sea bastion is the venue for some wonderfully authentic flamenco concerts by the Peña Flamenco Enrique Mellizo, staged every Thurs evening from mid-July to late Aug. Entry costs around €15, it gets going about 10.30pm and there's food and drink. It's also worth visiting the Peña Mellizo's very friendly bar (open daily) and flamenco theatre at Paseo de San Felipe s/n close to the Punto de San Felipe.

La Cava Taberna Flamenca c/Antonio Lopez 16, near the Plaza de la Mina ☎956 21 18 66, ⊛www.flamencolacava.com. Tourist-oriented place where the performers are reasonably serious. Shows Tues, Thurs and Sat at 9.30pm; €22 entry includes a drink.

Peña La Perla c/Carlos Ollera s/n ☎956 25 91 01. Down a tiny street behind the Cárcel Vieja (Old Prison), to the east of the cathedral, this wonderfully atmospheric old *peña* (where many "greats" have performed) is open to visitors and is somewhere that flamenco can happen spontaneously on any night of the week. Enquire in their bar, or alternatively, check with the Turismo.

Listings

Banks There are ATMs throughout the city centre with several banks around Plaza San Juan de Dios and Avda. Ramón de Carranza (facing the port).

Books and press Quorum, c/Ancha 27, is the city's best bookshop and stocks a decent selection of books in English. Librería Omega, Avda. Ramón de Carranza 31, fronting the port, is also worth a browse. *El Diario de Cádiz* (⊛www.diariodecadiz .es) is the city's daily paper – good for local information, upcoming flamenco concerts and entertainment details.

Cycle hire Cycles can be hired from Urban-bikeCádiz, c/Magistral Cabrera 7 off Plaza de la Catedral (☎664 08 13 81) costing approx. €2 per hr.

Football C.F. Cádiz, nicknamed *Submarino Amarillo* ("Yellow Submarine" – they play in canary shirts) is the town team, currently languishing in Division 2. Their ground is the Estadio Ramón Carranza, Plaza Madrid, behind the Playa de la Victoria (☎956 07 01 65, ⊛www.cadizcf.com). Tickets can be purchased at the ground.

Hospital For urgent medical treatment go to the Urgencias (emergency) department of the Residencia Sanitaria Hospital, Avda. Ana de Viya 21, near the Hotel Playa Victoria (☏956 00 21 00).

Internet Mina 5, Plaza de la Mina 5 (daily 10am–11pm); Ciber Columela, c/Columela 2 off Plaza de las Flores (daily 9am–10.30pm); Novap Computers, Cuesta de las Calesas 45, near the train station (daily 10am–11pm).

Police In emergencies dial ☏091 for the Policía Nacional (serious crimes) and ☏092 for the Policía Local (theft and petty crime). Both police forces have their headquarters in the Playa de la Victoria zone: the national police are located in Avenida de Andalucía s/n and the local police are in the Avda. José León de Carranza, next to the football stadium.

Post office Plaza de las Flores, near the market (Mon–Fri 8.30am–8.30pm; Sat 9am–2pm).

Shopping Cádiz's branch of the El Corte Inglés department store is at Avda. de las Cortes de Cádiz s/n (☏956 29 71 00), 1.5km east of the train station; buses #5 or #8 from a stop at the eastern end of Avenida del Puerto (close to the train station) will take you there. For the latest designer fashions head for c/Columela running between c/San Francisco and Plaza Flores where many famous-name shops have their outlets.

The Cádiz coast

For an alternative to Cádiz's often-crowded beaches, take a trip across the bay to the resorts of **El Puerto de Santa María**, **Rota**, **Chipiona** and **Sanlúcar de Barrameda**. All have fine and spacious beaches and are within day-tripping distance by bus, boat or train as well as being in striking distance for a visit to the inland sherry capital, **Jerez**.

El Puerto de Santa María

Just 10km across the bay, **EL PUERTO DE SANTA MARÍA** is the obvious choice for a day-trip from Cádiz, a traditional family resort for both *gaditanos* and *sevillanos* – many of whom have built villas and chalets along the fine **Playa Puntilla** which you'll pass as the boat comes in to dock at the Muelle del Vapor in the estuary of the Río Guadalete. The town itself, some distance from the beach, has an easy-going air and, despite some ugly modern development on its periphery, is surprisingly picturesque with many narrow, white-walled streets and plant-filled balconies, plus an impressive medieval castle, imposing *casas palacios*, some fine churches and Spain's third most prestigious bullring. On the cultural front, El Puerto will always be associated with one of the major Spanish poets of the twentieth-century, **Rafael Alberti**, who was born here in 1902 and died here in 1999; his birthplace at c/Santo Domingo 25 is now a museum (see p.219).

Today one of the three centres of **wine** production (along with Jerez and Sanlúcar) that make up the "sherry triangle", El Puerto de Santa María came to prominence in the eighteenth century as a botanical garden where plants brought from the New World were cultivated for seed. This and other trading enterprises increased prosperity, as demonstrated by the numerous mansions around the town, which was once known as the *ciudad de los cien palacios* (city of a hundred palaces).

Arrival and information

Whether you arrive by bus (the "station" is little more than a couple of bus stops next to the Plaza de Toros), train or *vapor* (see p.206), the helpful **Turismo** at c/Luna 22 (daily: May–Sept 10am–2pm & 6–8pm; Oct–April 10am–2pm; ☏956 54 24 13, @www.turismoelpuerto.com) is handily sited for picking up a free **street map** as well as a *Ruta del Tapeo* leaflet to find the best tapas bars. From here the heart of the town is within easy walking distance. Many of the main sights (including the Castillo San Marcos) are covered in a free guided

EL PUERTO DE SANTA MARÍA

ACCOMMODATION

Camping Playa Las Dunas	J
Casa de los Leones	D
Casa No. 6	F
Hostal Loreto	C
Hostal Sherry	H
Hotel Duques de Medinaceli	A
Hotel Los Cantaros	E
Hotel Santa María	I
Monasterio San Miguel	B
Pensión Santa María	G

RESTAURANTS & CAFÉS

Bodega Jerezana	
Café Central	12
Casa Flores	6
El Faro de El Puerto	1
La Solera	5
Las Capuchinas	B
Pasta Gansa	4
Romerijo	8

TAPAS BARS

Bar Tapia	2
Bar Vicente	3
El Laul	11
La Dorada	12
La Galera	10
Nuevo Portuense	7
Sol y Sombra	9

tour from the Turismo (Oct–June) on Tuesdays and Saturdays at 11am. **Internet** access is available at Ciber Bahía c/Micaela Aramburu 21 (daily 10am–1pm & 5–9pm) and Ciber Rapido, c/Ricardo Alcon 12 (Mon–Sat 10am–10pm, Sun 4–10pm). For **car hire**, Bahía Rent a Car, c/Misericordia 1 (☎956 87 76 97), is competitive and reliable. The town stages a cultural festival each summer (July–Aug) with concerts (mainly classical) taking place on Thursday evenings in the atmospheric Castillo San Marcos; details from the Turismo.

In July and August there are evening **boat trips** around the bay aboard the Vaporcito; the ninety-minute cruises sail on Tuesday, Thursday and Saturday evenings, leaving from the ferry quay near the Plaza del las Galeras at 9.45pm; tickets (sold on board) cost €5.

Accommodation

Many visitors come to El Puerto for the day, but should you be tempted to stay – and it makes a great break from Cádiz – there are plenty of **rooms** within easy walking distance of the ferry. Bear in mind that things get tight during August, when it's worth ringing ahead. If you have problems, ask at the Turismo for assistance; they also keep a list of **apartments** for longer stays.

El Puerto's **campsite**, *Camping Playa Las Dunas* (☎956 87 22 10), just behind the Playa Puntilla, has the advantage of plenty of shade. Take bus #2 from Plaza de Galeras, by the ferry dock.

Casa de los Leones La Placilla 2 ☎ 956 87 52 77, ⓦ www.casadelosleones.com. Stunning eighteenth-century *casa palacio* converted into an elegant apart-hotel where each a/c apartment comes with bedroom and salon plus kitchen equipped with washing machine, fridge and microwave. Higher apartments have more light. ⑥

Casa No. 6 c/San Bartoleme 14 ☎ 956 87 70 84, ⓦ www.casano6.com. Rooms in a delightful *casa-palacio* lovingly restored by an Anglo-Spanish couple; en-suite rooms above a gorgeous patio are well furnished and come with fans and there's a wi-fi zone. They also let two fully equipped rooftop apartments (⑥) with terraces. ④ with breakfast.

Hostal Loreto c/Ganado 17 ☎ 956 54 24 10. Pleasant hostal with an enchanting patio. Rooms come with or without bath; en suites have ceiling fans, fridge and TV. ②

Hostal Sherry c/Veneroni 1 ☎ 956 87 09 02. Housed in the crumbling but nonetheless impressive early nineteenth-century Aduana (customs building) this *hostal* offers en-suites and rooms sharing bath, all with TV and fans. ②

🏃 **Hotel Duques de Medinaceli** Plaza de los Jazmines 2 ☎ 956 86 07 77, ⓦ www.jale .com/dmedinaceli. A palatial hotel housed in the former mansion of the Irish sherry family Terry, this eighteenth-century edifice has been restored to its former glory with a stunning patio, opulent furnishings and rooms decorated with original artworks. There are all the trimmings of a five-star hotel including a pool, sauna and restaurant, plus a magnificent botanical garden in the hotel's grounds (open to the public daily 5–10pm). Double rooms in high season start at €280. ⑥

Hotel Los Cantaros c/Curva 6 ☎ 956 54 02 40, ⓦ www.hotelloscantaros.com Central hotel offering a/c rooms with TV and minibar. Light sleepers may be disturbed by nearby music bars. ⑥

Hotel Santa María Avda. Bajamar s/n ☎ 956 87 32 11, ⓦ www.hotelsantamaria.es. Good-value mid-range riverfront hotel in a converted eighteenth-century palacio with a/c rooms, restaurant, garage (or there's easy parking by the river) and rooftop pool. ⑥

Monasterio San Miguel c/Larga 27 ☎ 956 54 04 40, ⓦ www.hotelesjale.com. One of the best accommodation options in town, set in a sixteenth-century monastery converted into a luxurious four-star hotel complete with patios, pool and rooftop solarium. ⑦

🏃 **Pensión Santa María** c/Pedro Múñoz Seco 38 ☎ 956 85 36 31. Very welcoming family pensión, for clean rooms with and without bath (with a negligible difference in price) and run by an ebullient *dueña andaluza* (female proprietor). ①

The Town

Arriving by ferry, close to the landing quay, the Muelle del Vapor, you'll immediately spot the fine six-spouted eighteenth-century fountain, **El Fuente de las Galeras**, constructed, as the Latin inscription on it tells you, to provide galleys leaving for the Americas with water. West of here and a couple of blocks in is the **Castillo de San Marcos** on Plaza de Alfonso El Sabio (Tues–Sat visits 11.30am, 12.30pm, 1.30pm, 6.30pm & 8.30pm; €5, €2 kids), a thirteenth-century fort built by Alfonso X on the site of a Moorish watchtower and mosque. The towers of the castle bear the stirring proclamations of devotion to the Virgin, a symbol of the victory over the vanquished Moors. So besotted was the king with her that he sang the Virgin's praises in a surviving poetic work, *Las Cantigas*, and renamed El Puerto after her. Inside the fort – today owned by the Luis Caballero *bodega* – Alfonso also constructed a triple-naved Mudéjar church, in which the mosque's ancient *mihrab* can still be identified. The current proprietors have long used one of the castle's halls as a sherry *bodega*, stacked with butts. You can take a full tour of the castle, leaving via the *bodega* where they will invite you to taste (and buy) their *finos*. Slightly southwest of here the elegant eighteenth-century Antigua Lonja (aka el Resbaladero) on c/Micaela Aramburu served for two centuries as the town's fishmarket – note the piscatorial reliefs decorating its exterior.

Following the pedestrianized c/Luna west into town from the ferry quay will bring you El Puerto's **Plaza Mayor** (Plaza de España), fronted by the **Iglesia Mayor Prioral** (Mon–Fri 8.30am–12.45pm & 6–8.30pm, Sat 8.30am–12 noon & 6–8.30pm, Sun 8.30am–1.45pm & 6.30–8.30pm; free). A thirteenth-century Gothic edifice, it has suffered much rebuilding and the shell is now largely Baroque, but don't miss its superb Plateresque south entrance. Inside, a richly gilded *retablo* in the capilla de la Virgen de los Milagros holds *La Patrona*, a thirteenth-century image of the Virgin formerly housed in the castle of San Marcos and to which the town is devoted. Note also some fine choir stalls richly carved in walnut and cedar. Across the square from the church at c/Pagador 1, lies the **Museo Municipal** (Tues–Fri 10am–2pm, Sat & Sun 10.30am–2pm; free), housed in another mansion, the **Casa de la Marquesa de Candia**; it contains archeological finds from the surrounding area plus a selection of indifferent artworks.

Around the corner from here at c/Santo Domingo 25 lies the **Fundación Rafael Alberti** (Tues–Sun 11am–2.30pm; €3; ⓦwww.rafaelalberti.es), an excellent museum dedicated to El Puerto's great poet and artist who was born here. Many of his vibrant engravings decorate the walls and a fascinating photographic biography illustrates his life, contacts and friendships with many of Spain's twentieth-century literary and artistic giants including Lorca and Picasso.

A few blocks south of the Plaza Mayor the **Plaza de Toros** (Tues–Sun 11am–1.30pm & 5.30–7pm; free) is one of the largest in Spain (third only to Madrid and Seville) and among the most celebrated by aficionados. Opened in 1880 with a capacity of fifteen thousand, the bullring has hosted all the great names. A mosaic inside the entrance records the words of the legendary *sevillano* bullfighter Joselito, who fought here: "He who has not seen bulls in El Puerto does not know what bullfighting is." Scattered all over town are the **palacios** left behind by the great eighteenth-century families of El Puerto and decorated with their shield. The Turismo's town map marks them all, but three of the most outstanding are **Casa de Vizarrón** (aka as the Casa de las Cadenas) near the El Resbaldero market, with an elegant escutcheoned doorway; **Casa de los Leones** (now a hotel, see "Accommodation"), with a fine facade and patio; and **Palacio de Aranibar**, fronting the Castillo de San Marcos and now the law court.

The beaches

The closest beaches, **Playa La Puntilla** and **Playa Valdelgrana**, are some distance from the town (15min walk or local buses from the ferry dock; Plaza Las Galeras: #1 and #2 for La Puntilla or #3 for Valdelgrana) and are pleasant places to while away an afternoon with lots of lively *marisquerías* and beach bars. For fewer crowds you're better off on the **Playa Santa Catalina** to the west of the Playa La Puntilla; bus #3 (direction Fuenterrabía) from c/Micaela Aramburu near the ferry dock will take you there.

Eating and drinking

The best areas in town for **places to eat** are the Ribera del Marisco, a street upstream from the ferry dock lined with a variety of seafood restaurants and bars serving tapas and *raciónes*, and the nearby Plaza de la Herrería. You should also try the beaches of La Puntilla and Valdelgrana for a cluster of friendly bars.

Bars, cafés and restaurants

Bodega Jerezana Avda. de la Paz, Valdelgrana seafront. Briny tapas bar and restaurant with a wide range of well-prepared seafood dishes.

Café Central c/Luna 41, Relaxed café for tranquil breakfasts; their *desayuno especial* gets you fresh juice, *café* and *pan tostada* for €2.50.

Casa Flores Ribera del Río 9. Classic fish and *mariscos* restaurant. Main courses €12–25.

El Faro de El Puerto Half a kilometre out, along the Rota road ☎956 87 09 52. Outstanding seafood and meat dishes produced under the direction of top chef Fernando Córdoba in this stylish twin establishment of the restaurant of the same name in Cádiz. Widely regarded as having the best wine-cellar in the province, it also has a pleasant garden terrace and a *menú de degustación* for around €50. Main dishes €11–25. Closed Sun eve.

La Solera c/Ganado 17, next to the *Hostal Loreto* ☎956 54 35 62. Delightful if diminutive (booking advised) quality restaurant with fair-priced dishes such as *brocheta de rape con langostinos* (skewer-grilled monkfish). Offers *menú* for €7.50 (lunch) or €11.75 (eves); main dishes €8–15.

Las Capuchinas *Monasterio de San Miguel*, c/Larga 27. The *Monasterio* hotel's swish *cafetería* serves up good-value *platos combinados* and has a *menú* for €12.

Pasta Gansa c/Puerto Escondido 1, near the Ribera del Marisco. A stylish Italian restaurant where diners can enjoy pizzas and risottos at candlelit tables in an attractive patio.

Romerijo Ribera del Marisco. This enormous, economical and justifiably popular seafood bar dominates the strip. You can get a takeaway of *mariscos* in a *cartucho* (paper funnel) from their shop and eat it at outdoor tables where buckets are provided for debris and waiters serve beer; the *cóctel de mariscos* (seafood cocktail) or any of the six types of *langostinos* are delicious. The same firm's *freiduría* restaurant over the road is equally excellent, and a generous *frito variado* (assorted fried fish) easily serves two.

Tapas bars

Bar Tapia c/Mayorga 7. In a small street opposite the *Pasta Gansa* restaurant, this is an excellent and friendly small tapas and *raciónes*

bar with a charming summer patio. Specials include *arroz casero* and *mariscos*.

Bar Vicente c/Abastos 7. Wonderful old bar which first opened its doors well over a century ago and is part of El Puerto folklore. Show an interest and the latest Vincente (in a long line) will tell you its story. Also serves decent tapas and *raciónes*.

El Laul c/Avda. de la Bajamar s/n. Diminutive tapas bar facing the river 50m downstream from the Galeras fountain. Creative house specials include *tartar de pargo* (sea bream).

La Dorada Avda. Bajamar 26, 150m south of the ferry dock. Meal-sized and inexpensive *raciónes* where the *pescado frito* is superb. *Choco a la plancha* (cuttlefish) is a special. Has a terrace.

La Galera Plaza de las Galeras, close to the Muelle del Vapor. Good bar for beer and seafood tapas and *raciónes* if you're just off, or waiting for, the boat.

Nuevo Portuense c/Luna 31. Good, busy central bar with a wide range of seafood tapas and *raciónes* (*sardinas empanadas* are a special) and there's a *menú* for around €9.

Sol y Sombra Plaza de Ahuja, facing the bullring. Taking its name from the nearby bullring's seating arrangements, this is often a lively venue – especially on fight days – and prepares good and cheap tapas. House specials include *fideos con almejas* (vermicelli with clams) and paella. It's restaurant is also recommended and does a lunchtime *menú* for under €10.

The sherry bodegas of El Puerto de Santa María

The long, whitewashed warehouses flanking the streets and the banks of the Río Guadalete belong to the big **sherry bodegas**: Luís Caballero, Terry, Osborne and Duff Gordon, the last three founded in the eighteenth and nineteenth centuries by Irish and English families. Osborne (pronounced "Osbornay" in Spanish) and Duff Gordon are now co-owned after a takeover by Osborne, although separate production is maintained. Osborne is also the largest producer of Spanish brandy, and its black-bull logo – long used as a billboard perched on hills throughout Spain – has become a familiar part of the country's landscape.

In sherry circles, El Puerto is noted for a lighter, more aromatic *fino* with more *flor* aroma imparted due to its humid geographical location, close to the sea (see box, p.234 for details of sherry styles). It's easy enough to visit the *bodegas*; Osborne and Duff Gordon, c/Los Moros 7 (visits Mon–Fri: in English 10.30am; in Spanish 11am & midday; ☎956 86 91 00; €6); Fernando de Terry, c/Toneleros 1 (Mon–Thurs 10.30am–12.30pm; €8; Fri guided visit, including stables, at 11am; €15; ☎956 84 74), with a museum and situated in a beautiful, converted, seventeenth-century convent; Gutierrez Colosia, Avda. de Bajamar 40, near the Hotel Santa María (guided visits Fri 7.30pm & Sat 12.30 & 1.30pm; information ☎956 85 28 52). All welcome visitors for tours and tastings, although you'll need to **call in advance** to Osborne to book a place. Other *bodegas* also do visits and the Turismo can supply a full list with opening hours.

Nightlife

Nightlife in El Puerto means just that – in summer many places don't even open until around 11pm. The action centres on the bars around the eighteenth-century former fishmarket (El Resbaldero) and the focal Plaza Herrería, nearby c/Jesús de los Milagros and the river area. *Resbaldero* is a disco-bar actually inside the old fishmarket while music bars *Cohiba*, *El Niño Perdio* and *La Penultima Locura de Lola* are on the street behind, facing the castillo. Around Plaza de la Herrería, bars like *O'Donoghues* and *El Recuerdo* are in the middle of the action while just off the square along c/Curva *Rodeo* is a Wild-West themed bar with darts, pool and salsa that goes on till dawn. Just to the south along c/Jesús de los Milagros are *copas* bars *Barsito*, *Metropoli* and *Mahala* attracting plenty of late night (and early morning) revellers. On the river near the ferry dock the glass-walled *La Cristalera* – just to the north of the Galeras fountain – is a laid-back late night music bar; moored just upstream of here is *La Pontona*, a pontoon music bar with a popular roof terrace.

Rota

Much of the 15km between El Puerto and the town of **ROTA** is taken up by a massive tract of territory occupied by one of the three major **US military bases** in Spain. Installed in the 1950s as part of a deal in which Franco exchanged strips of Spanish sovereign territory for economic aid and international "respectability", the base is surrounded by a seemingly endless barbed-wire fence bristling with the technological gadgetry of war. Behind the wire it's possible to glimpse farms and whole villages linked by their own bus service along a road system where signs are in English. Huge Ford trucks trundle to and from Rota's harbour from where the base services and supplies the US Sixth Fleet – including nuclear submarines.

The US military population tends to keep to itself, however, and Rota exudes an affable character very much its own with an attractive *casco antiguo* and some excellent tapas bars. In season, the resort fairly bounces with life, its excellent **beach**, the Playa de la Costilla, being the main attraction for the crowds who flock here in August.

The town's sights can be seen in under an hour. Highlights in the old quarter include a thirteenth-century castle now housing the Ayuntamiento and Turismo – the frequently remodelled and much-restored **Castillo de Luna** (Sat & Sun 1pm–5pm; free) with a stunning patio. Also worth a look is the sixteenth-century Gothic church, **Nuestra Señora de la Expectación** (known locally as Nuestra Señora de la O; daily 9am–1pm and 6.30–9pm), which hides, behind a box-like exterior, a fine single-naved church with elegant vaulting, magnificent choir stalls depicting the twelve apostles by Diego Roldán and – in the chapel of Jesús Nazareno – a delightful eighteenth-century image of the Last Supper crafted in *azulejos* from Triana in Sevilla (the barely surviving image of Judas has received some rough treatment over the years). If churches are your thing you may also want to take in the **Capilla de San Juan Bautista** (aka Capilla de la Caridad; open service times only, try early evening 7–8pm), Plaza Andalucía, near the Turismo, with a spectacular Baroque *altar mayor* by Diego Roldán, one of the finest in the province.

Practicalities

Arriving by **car**, make your way to the seafront *Hotel Duque de Najera* (see p.222), where there is a public car park and from where all the sights and accommodation options are within a few-minutes' walk. The very helpful

Turismo – who can provide a useful town map – is located in the Castillo de Luna, c/Cuna 2 (daily: July–Sept 9.30am–1.30pm & 5.30–8.30pm; Oct–June 9.30am–1.30pm & 5–7.30pm; ☎956 84 63 45, Ⓦwww.turismorota.com), in the old quarter on the town's southern flank. The **bus station** lies off Plaza del Triunfo, which is a ten-minute walk or an easy bus ride to the centre along c/Calvario. Rota's big festival is the mid-August **Fiesta de la Urta**, when all the restaurants in town compete to win the prize for the best *urta*-based dish.

Accommodation
Places to stay include the excellent *Hostal Macavi*, c/Écija 11 (☎956 81 33 36; ❹), with en-suite a/c rooms off the main Avenida Sevilla, a mere 50m from the beach and which has added a decent restaurant. Perhaps the most interesting room option is ⚘ *Hostal El Torito*, c/Constitución 1, near the Plaza de España (☎956 81 33 69, Ⓦwww.eltoritoderota.com; ❹) a stunningly minimalist *hostal* which has to rank as one of Andalucía's most original. The a/c rooms (no. 5 with its own terrace is a gem) are ultra-stylish and there's wi-fi throughout. In the same price bracket the nearby *Hostal Sixto* (☎956 84 63 10, Ⓦwww.hostalsixto.com; ❹) is an enchanting small hotel with attractive rooms around a pretty patio or above their nearby restaurant. The town's sleek flagship hotel, the four-star *Duque de Najera*, c/Gravina 2 (☎956 84 60 20, Ⓦwww .hotelduquedenajera.com; ❺), is an elegant new hotel with pool overlooking the harbour. The nearest campsite is *Camping Playa Aguadulce* (☎956 84 70 78), 9km from Rota along the A491 to Chipiona.

Eating and drinking
The modern town fans out from the central Plaza Jesús Nazareno fronting the beach and it's here that you'll find most of the **bars**, **restaurants** and nightlife. Look out for the town's very own speciality, the outstandingly tasty *urta a la roteña* (sea bream in a caramelized onion and tomato sauce). Note also that the *urta* season lasts June–Sept, outside which many restaurants revert to *mero a la roteña* (grouper). Rota's tapas bars tend to be better value than the restaurants, many of which are overpriced and bland. Exceptions include *Mesón Alicantino*, Avda. Sevilla 39 (near the Hostal Macavi), for fish and seafood and *Bar–Restaurante La Costilla*, c/Higuereta 68, facing Plaza Jesús Nazareno, a great place to sample the town's signature dish. Another place to sample *urta* at its best is at the very good *Restaurante Sixto*, attached to the *hostal* of the same name (see above) with an inviting terrace. For tapas head down atmospheric c/La Mina, a little northwest of the Castillo de Luna, where a number of bars line the pedestrianized street, including the excellent *Emilio*, *Lari* and *La Mina*. One bar also worth a look is *Bar Torito*, c/Italia 2, a stone's throw from the chic *hostal* of the same name (see above); less stylistically cutting edge than it's namesake, it's nevertheless a cosy place with tapas, *raciónes* and some cool sounds.

Chipiona

From Rota the road north winds inland behind a coast lined with more golden sand beaches to **CHIPIONA**, 18km away, on a point at the edge of the estuary of the Guadalquivir.

Presenting itself as a modest, straightforward seaside resort crammed with family *pensiones* the town's a great place to spend a few days, except in August when its many charms are all but submerged beneath an onslaught of mainly Spanish visitors. Older tourists come here for the spa waters, channelled into a fountain at the fourteenth-century church of **Nuestra Señora de Regla** (daily 8am–12noon & 5–7.30), which incorporates a delightful Gothic cloister adorned with seventeenth-century Triana *azulejos*; often they don't open it so try and find a priest or churchwarden to do this for you. The town has a charming **old quarter** on its northern flank, cut through by sinuous, white-walled alleyways. The major thoroughfare here is the pedestrianized c/Isaac Peral (and its continuation c/Miguel Cervantes), lined with shops, bars and some elegant buildings and hotels. But for most it's the twelve kilometres of **beaches** that are the lure; stretching south of the town beyond Spain's tallest **lighthouse** (May–Sept 6–7.30pm, Oct–April 4–6pm; €3) is the long **Playa de Regla**, best avoided in August but where for much of the year it's possible to leave the crowds behind. Northeast, towards Sanlúcar, are sand bars and rocks with fine views towards the Marismas de Doñana and the Guadalquivir estuary.

Practicalities

Maps, **information** and help with accommodation plus a list of tapas bars can be picked up from the **Turismo**, Plaza Juan Carlos I s/n (Mon–Fri 10am–2pm & 5–7pm; ☎956 37 72 63, ⓦwww.turismochipiona.com), in the old quarter, close to the sea. **Buses** to and from Seville, Jerez, Cádiz and Sanlúcar arrive at the central bus station on Avenida de Andalucía.

Accommodation

Accommodation can be expensive in high summer and in August without an advance reservation you'll struggle to find anything at all; the Turismo may be able to help. The campsite and youth hostal, *Piñar de Chipiona* (☎956 37 23 21), lies 3km out of town towards Rota and has a cheap self-service restaurant and pool. Get the Rota-bound bus to drop you off.

Hostal Andalucía c/Larga 14, close to the seaward end of c/Isaac Peral ☎956 37 09 29. Welcoming central place with a/c en-suite rooms and rooftop solarium. ❸
Hostal Belén Avda. del Ejército 5 ☎956 37 26 80. Simple and economical rooms sharing bath, close to the central c/Miguel Cervantes. ❶
Hostal Gran Capitán c/Fray Baldomero González 3, close to the seaward end of c/Isaac Peral ☎956 37 09 29. Very attractive *hostal* housed in a venerable *casa antigua* – owned and run by one of the descendants of Spain's eponymous fifteenth-century military commander Gran Capitán Gonzalo de Córdoba – offering a/c en-suite rooms with wi-fi. ❸
Hostal San Miguel Avda. de la Regla 79 ☎956 37 29 76. Comfortable en-suite rooms in a charming

1930s mansion close to the church of Nuestra Señora de la Regla. ❸
Hotel Al Sur de Chipiona Avda. de Sevilla 101, facing the church of Nuestra Señora de la Regla ☎956 37 03 00, ⓦwww.hotelalsur.com. Comprising an older, elegant hotel with a new wing – complete with pool and gardens – tacked on, this is the best value of the more exclusive places with well-appointed rooms, all with terrace balcony. ❺
Hotel La Española c/Isaac Peral 4 ☎956 37 37 71, ⓦwww.hotellaespanola.com. Excellent-value and superbly renovated old hotel with many sea-view rooms and whose front door is a mere 20m from the Atlantic breakers; arriving by car here allows the luxury of taking the lift from the hotel's subterranean garage effortlessly to your room. ❸

Eating and drinking

Chipiona has a gratifying range of **restaurants**, all excelling in seafood. For a mid-priced *menú*, try the elegant *La Pañoleta* (the restaurant of the *Hotel La Española*; see above), which is very good. Equally tasty seafood is on offer at *Restaurante Peña*, Avda. Sevilla 14, near the lighthouse, in a beautiful white-washed building with a shaded terrace. Two superb seafront fish restaurants with shady terraces lie at each end of the tiny Playa de Las Canteras close to the lighthouse. Nearest is 🍴 *Las Canteras*, especially good for *urta* and *dorada*, as well as *mariscos* and they do pretty good chips, too; its neighbour to the north, *Los Corrales*, is also worth a try. North of here again and slightly inland *Bar-Restaurante Repostaero*, c/Dr Tolosa Latour 7, is a boisterous seafood *chiringuito* with a great atmosphere late at night when impromptu flamenco sometimes gets going.

For more tapas and drinking bars – some with music – take a stroll along the pedestrianized c/Isaac Peral, where, among many others, 🎵 *Bar Peña Betica* at the junction with c/Larga is highly popular. A little further along two more places worth a try are *Bar Paquito*, at the junction with Plaza Pío XII, and *Bar La Parra* at Isaac Peral 14.

Sanlúcar de Barrameda

Like El Puerto de Santa María, **SANLÚCAR DE BARRAMEDA**, 8km beyond Chipiona, is a major sherry town. A substantial place with an attractive old quarter set at the mouth of the Guadalquivir, it is the main depot for **manzanilla** wine – a pale dry *fino* variety with a salty tang – highly regarded by connoisseurs and much in evidence in the bars round here. Sanlúcar is also one of the best places in Andalucía for **seafood**, for which *manzanilla* is the perfect accompaniment.

Although there was a small settlement here in Roman times and the Moors built a fort to guard the vital Guadalquivir estuary from sea raiders, it was after

---

Sanlucar's Manzanilla bodegas

The delicate taste of Sanlúcar's distinctive **manzanilla** is created by the seaside environment where the wine is matured, and by not being fortified with alcohol (as happens in Jerez and El Puerto). The humid microclimate necessary for the growth of the dense *flor* (yeast) inside the wine butts is added to by the moist *poniente* wind that blows across the Coto de Doñana, imparting the characteristic saltiness to this driest of all sherries. Sanlúcar is less aggressive than Jerez in its public relations (despite *manzanilla* recently overtaking *fino* sales on the peninsula for the first time), and only a few of Sanlúcar's *bodegas* are open for **visits and tastings**. We have quoted the *bodega's* guided tours in English; visit their websites for other languages.

The town's major producer, **Antonio Barbadillo**, c/Sevilla 25, near the castle (visits Tues–Sat 11am; €3; ☎956 38 55 00, ⓦwww.barbadillo.com), which produces seventy percent of all *manzanilla*, also makes *manzanilla pasada*, an exceptional fifteen-year-old wine (as against the normal four for standard *fino*), besides one of Andalucía's best white table wines (Castillo de San Diego) from the same Palomino grape. The only other *bodegas* currently welcoming visitors are the central **Bodegas Hidalgo**, c/Banda Playa 24 (visits Thur, Fri & Sat noon; €5; ☎956 36 05 16, ⓦwww .lagitana.es), producers of the La Gitana brand, **Pedro Romero**, c/Trasbolsa 84, east of the Plaza del Cabildo (visits Mon–Sat noon & Tue–Fri 6pm; €6; ☎956 36 07 36, ⓦwww.pedroromero.es), **Bodegas Herederos de Argüeso** c/Mar 8 (Mon–Sat 10.30am & noon; €3, €6 if less than 10 people; ☎956 38 51 16, ⓦwww.argueso.es;) makers of the noted San León brand, and the tiny **Bodega de Velasco**, c/Truco s/n, near the market (Mon–Fri 8am–3pm), which is a friendly and intimate family-run place where they'll serve you their La Cigarrera brand *manzanilla* to try (and buy) straight from the butt. They are now part of the larger **Bodegas La Cigarrera**, Plaza Madre de Dios s/n (near the *Hotel Los Helechos*), who also do organized visits (Mon–Sat 10am–2pm; €2.80; ☎956 38 12 85, ⓦwww.bodegaslacigarrera.com). A *despacho de vinos* (wineseller), La Abuela Lola, c/Caballeros 21 near the *Posada de Palacio* (see p.227), stocks all the major brands and does tastings. The Bodegas Hidalgo shop is opposite the Turismo on the Calzada de Ejército.

Sanlúcar

SANLÚCAR DE BARRAMEDA

**Map labels:**

BARRIO ALTO

Bodegas Barbadillo

Castillo de Santiago

Iglesia N.Señora de la O

Palacio de Medina Sidonia

Palacio de Orleáns y Borbón

Bodegas Pérez Megía

Iglesia de la Trinidad

Convento de la Merced

Iglesia San Jorge

Museo del Mar Caracoles

Iglesia de San Nicolás

Iglesia de Santo Domingo

Iglesia de San Francisco

Bodegas Hidalgo

BARRIO BAJO

Bus Station

Centro de la Naturaleza

Río Guadalquivir

Bonanza & (5km)

& Bajo de Guía

Río Guadalquivir

0   100 m

Streets: JUAN GRANDE, MENALCRO, BORREQUEROS, SAN AGUSTÍN, POZO AMARGUILLO, PALMA, GITANOS, ALBACÍN, SANTIAGO, MISERICORDIA, MURO BAJO, SEBASTIÁN EL CANO, SEVILLA, QUARTEL, ESCUELAS, PLAZA DE LA PAZ, CASTILLO, EGUILAZ, PLAZA CONDES DE NIEBLA, CABALLEROS, CAVA DEL, CARMEN VIEJO, CHANCA, ALCOBA, DON CLAUDIO, FARINAS, REGINA, SAN JORGE, CERVANTES, BRETONES, C. TRUCO, BANOS, PLAZA DE LA SALLE, FERNANDO DE LEÓN NÚÑEZ, DE SANTO DOMINGO, CARRE DE SAN DIEGO, SANTA ANA, ANCHA, CRISTOBAL COLÓN, PLAZA DE SAN ROQUE, PLAZA DEL PABILLO, SAN JUAN, C. MAR, ARGUESO, BOLSA, CASTELAR, TARTANEROS, RUIZ DE SOMAVIA, PÉREZ GALDOS, BANDA DE LA PLAYA, TRASBOLSA, BANDA DE LA PLAYA, HERMANO FERMÍN, HERMANO FERMÍN, CORREO, AVDA INFANTA BEATRIZ, PESCADERÍA, CALZADA DE LA INFANTA, AVDA DE LA CIRCUNVALACIÓN, PADRE CUEVAS, FRANCISCO, JUAN XXIII, PICAZO, AVENIDA GUADALQUIVIR, AVENIDA CERRO FALÓN, PÍO XII, AVDA ESTACIÓN, CALZADA DE EJERCITO, TORRE DE ARENA, HORÓSCOPOS, ORFEÓN S. CECILIA, AVENIDA INFANTES DE ORLEANS, LEONOR DÁVALOS, PEDRO FERNÁNDEZ DE LUGO, ALONSO DE LUGO, FERNANDO DE MAGALLANES, ESTEBAN, MAYOR, VICT. PICON, RODRIGO TRIANA, MANUEL MASERO, M.M. HERMOSILLA, MIGUEL PÉREZ LEAL, AVENIDA DE BAJO DE GUÍA, PASEO MARITIMO

ACCOMMODATION

Algaida Alojamiento Rural	F
Hospedería Duques de Medina Sidonia	B
Hotel Barrameda	G
Hotel Guadalquivir	I
Hotel Los Helechos	D
Hotel Tartaneros	H
Pensión Blanca Paloma	E
Pensión Bohemia	C
Posada de Palacio	A

RESTAURANTS

Bar Central Station	5	Bar-Restaurante El Bigote	7
Bar El Cura	3	Casa Balbino	4
Bar Joselito Huerta	9	Casa Juan	6
Bar Juanito	2	Mirador de Doñana	8
Bar Parada "El Gallego"	1		

the recapture of the town in 1264 by Alfonso X that Sanlúcar grew to become one of sixteenth-century Spain's leading ports. **Columbus** sailed from here on his third voyage to the Americas and it was also from here in 1519 that Magellan set out to circumnavigate the globe. Decline in the eighteenth century, however, was exacerbated by the War of Independence and the town revived only in the mid-nineteenth century when the duke of Montpensier built a summer palace here. Since then Sanlúcar has grown into the popular resort it is today. During the last week of May the town stages a riotous **fiesta**, the Feria de la Manzanilla, to celebrate its great wine, which is copiously consumed throughout. In early and late August, the beach is the setting for some exciting **horse races**, a tradition dating from 1845, accompanied by riotous partying by revellers filling the bars and restaurants along the riverfront.

Arrival, orientation and information

Sanlúcar's **bus station** (with services to Chipiona, Cádiz, Seville and Jerez) is located between the river and the centre, to the west of the main avenue Calzada del Ejército. Coming in by **car** it's best to avoid the congested central zone and find a parking place along the Calzada del Ejército. Near the top of this avenue the **Turismo**, Calzada del Ejército s/n (Mon–Fri 10am–2pm & 6–8pm, Sat & Sun 10am–2pm; ☎956 36 61 10, ⓦwww.turismosanlucar.com) can provide a detailed street map and a tapas guide. They also offer a guided walking tour of the town in English and Spanish (Thurs 10.30am; €3) which includes a *bodega* visit. **Internet** access is available at Ciber Guadalquivir, c/Infanta Beatriz s/n (daily 10am–11pm), near the *Hotel Guadalquivir*.

Accommodation

There's a shortage of budget **accommodation** in Sanlúcar, and in August you'll be pushed to find anything at all. This is when a number of *casas particulares* open to mop up the overflow. Enquire at the Turismo for information about these, and for longer stays they have a list of **apartments** for rent (minimum three nights), plus *casas rurales* in and around the town.

Algaida Alojamiento Rural Calle 1, no. 4 Colonia Monte Algaida, 5km out of town beyond the village of Bonanza ☎956 38 73 72, ⓦwww.algaida.org. This friendly rural option offers rooms sharing bath in a large house in a village close to the Guadalquivir estuary. You'll need your own transport and when you ring them they will advise on how to get there. ②

🏃 **Hospedería Duques de Medina Sidonia** Plaza Condes de Niebla 1 ☎956 36 01 61, ⓦwww.ruralduquesmedinasidonia.com. The best address in town is the palace of the dukes of Medina Sidonia, one of Spain's most blue-blooded dynasties. Rooms are airy and tastefully decorated and the patio they surround has a tranquil *cafetería* (until 10pm). Rooms run from reasonably priced doubles to suites with private terrace. ④–⑥
Hotel Barrameda c/Ancha 10 ☎956 38 58 78, ⓦwww.hotelbarrameda.com. A new, central and welcome addition to the town's accommodation options offering light and airy a/c rooms with plasma TV, some with balcony. Also has a patio, solarium roof terrace and wi-fi throughout.

Hotel Guadalquivir Calzada del Ejército 20 ☎956 36 07 42, ⓦwww.hotelguadalquivir.com. Modern hotel towering over the thoroughfare leading to the river. Functional rooms are a/c, with vistas from the higher ones; some have balcony. ⑤
Hotel Los Helechos Plaza Madre de Dios 9 ☎956 36 13 49, ⓦwww.hotelloshelechos.com. Smart, very reasonably priced central hotel in converted former *bodega* with rooms around two charming patios and lots of traditional features. ④
Hotel Tartaneros c/Tartaneros 8 ☎956 36 20 44, ⓔhoteltartaneros@telefonica.net 93. Rather dull, old-fashioned hotel with a/c rooms and a dubious collection of dolls and effigies dotted around the staid interior. ⑤
Pensión Blanca Paloma Plaza de San Roque ☎956 36 36 44, ⓔhostalblancapaloma@msn .com. Good-value and friendly pensión with simple rooms sharing bath in a central position on this small plaza. ①
Pensión Bohemia c/Don Claudio 5 ☎956 36 95 99. Comfortable en-suite a/c rooms with TV – albeit slightly dark due to windows facing an internal

corridor – in a quiet street near the church of Santo Domingo. ❷

Posada de Palacio c/Caballeros 11 ☎956 36 48 40, ⓦwww.posadadepalacio.com. An elegant converted eighteenth-century *casa palacio* in the Barrio Alto with a delightful patio and tastefully furnished rooms with character. Rooftop terraces, bar and an intimate atmosphere together make this rather special. ❺

The Town

Sanlúcar is split into three distinct quarters, the older and formerly walled **Barrio Alto** on the hill, the **Barrio Bajo** below and the town's former port – the **Bajo de Guía** – 1km away on the river. Many of the monuments are in the higher town, where a good number of *bodegas* and their warehouses are also to be found, emitting a pleasant hint of sherry into the air.

Barrio Bajo

The **Plaza del Cabildo**, a charming, palm-fringed square ringed with bars and sporting a splendid fountain is a good place to start your explorations. Directly southwest of the square, Plaza de San Roque adjoins the **morning market**, one of the town's great shows when it's in full swing – Saturday mornings are best when burly *señoras* give no quarter in attempting to get their hands on the best fish. Just off this square, the interior of the fifteenth-century **Iglesia de la Trinidad** (Mon–Sat 10am–1.30pm; free) has a fine Mudéjar ceiling. West of here and parallel to c/Bretones at c/Truco 4 lies the curious **Museo del Mar Caracoles** (daily 10am–7pm; €2) exhibiting the bizarre lifetime collection of objects retrieved from the sea by eccentric proprietor Garrido García, who resembles a latter-day Long John Silver and conducts tours around his house/museum with a tame feral pigeon perched on one shoulder.

East of the Plaza del Cabildo, c/Ancha is the site of a colourful spectacle each August 15, the **fiesta of the Virgen de la Caridad**, when the street is laid with a carpet of colourful "flowers" – actually tinted sawdust – from end to end. A short way along here on the right, the short c/San Jorge contains the sixteenth-century **Iglesia de San Jorge** (Mon–Sat 10am–1pm; free),

▲ Museo del Mar Caracoles

The Coto de Doñana National Park

Access to the vast, marshy expanse of the **Coto de Doñana National Park** (see p.331), on the opposite shore from Sanlúcar, is strictly controlled to protect Europe's largest wildlife sanctuary and a vital wetland for a variety of migrating birds. However, a four-hour **boat cruise** aboard the Real Fernando allows visitors to access the park, giving a wonderful introduction to this remarkable area. The boat – which has a *cafetería* on board – leaves from the Bajo de Guía (March, April, May & Oct daily 10am & 4pm; June–Sept Mon–Sat 10am & 5pm; Nov–Feb daily 10am; €16.20, under 12 €8.10; booking essential on ☎956 36 38 13, ⓦwww.visitasdonana .com). The trips allow two short guided walks led by wildlife experts inside the park where you'll visit a village of *chozas* (traditional Doñana huts) and should see *jabalí* (wild boar), wild horses, flamingos and a profusion of birdlife including buzzards, herons, kites, cranes and eagles, as well as stunning wild flowers, depending on your luck and season. In summer it's best to book as early as you can, since the trips are limited to 94 passengers; binoculars (essential) can be hired on board.

Collect your tickets (at least 30min in advance of the sailing) from the Fábrica de Hielo, Bajo de Guía s/n (daily 9am–8pm), virtually opposite the Real Fernando's jetty. This extravagant exhibition centre in Sanlúcar's old ice factory was created by the National Park authority and contains stunningly unimaginative displays of the park's flora and fauna. The Centro Interpretación de la Naturaleza, almost next door on Avda. Bajo de Guía (Tues–Fri 10am–2pm, Sat–Sun 10am–2pm & 6–8pm), is the Junta de Andalucía's effort and has a slightly more interesting exhibition. Viajes Doñana, c/San Juan 20 (☎956 36 25 40), also do Land Rover-based trips into the park all year (Tues & Fri; booking essential; €39) starting from the Bajo de Guía at 8.30am and 4.30pm (Oct–April 8.30am & 2.30pm) and covering about 70km in four hours with an expert guide.

constructed by English sherry merchants with special permission from the duke of Medina Sidonia, who was keen to encourage their lucrative trade. Inside, a magnificent *retablo* by Juan González de Herrera is topped off by a mounted San Jorge (St George) slaying the dragon. Further east along c/Ancha, the sixteenth-century convent church of **Santo Domingo** (open for 30min viewing prior to service times: Mon–Sat 9.30am & 8pm, Sun 10.30am, 12noon and 8pm) is worth a look, especially for the tombs of a seventeenth-century duke and duchess of Medina Sidonia on either side of the main altar. At the end of the same street lies the church of **San Francisco** (open for services or ring ☎956 36 01 26 for appointment) with an elegant facade, built in the sixteenth century by Henry VIII of England – while he was married to Catherine of Aragón – as a hospital for British sailors.

Barrio Alto

The Barrio Alto is reached by following c/Bretones uphill from the Plaza San Roque. To the left, beyond the market the way soon bends right to pass the seventeenth-century **Convento de la Merced**. Continuing uphill eventually leads to the neo-Mudéjar **Palacio de Orleáns y Borbón**, a flamboyantly decorated nineteenth-century palace of the dukes of Montpensier, now occupied by the Ayuntamiento with the public library in the gardens. You are allowed to step inside the building's entrance to take a look. Taking a left at the top of this hill will bring you to – on the right – **Plaza de la Paz**, another delightful small square, and, almost opposite, the church of **Nuestra Señora de la O** (Tues–Sat 10am–1pm, Sun 10am–12 noon; also open for daily Mass at 8pm or can be visited on a Turismo tour), Sanlúcar's oldest church founded in the thirteenth century but much altered since and recently restored. The exterior has a fine Gothic-Mudéjar portal depicting lions bearing coats of arms and, inside, there's an impressive *artesonado* ceiling.

The church is connected to the *palacio* of the **duques de Medina Sidonia** (visits Sun 11am & noon; book in advance ☎956 36 01 61, ⓦwww .fcmedinasidonia.com; €3), whose sixteenth- to eighteenth-century interior, which also houses the family's important historical archive, offers wonderful views over the Coto de Doñana. Until her death in 2008 the duchess of Medina Sidonia – the last of the family line and inveterate opponent of the Franco regime – lived here. The palace and family estate is now in the care of the foundation she founded. The guided tour of the house and its beautiful gardens takes an hour and proceeds through impressive rooms stuffed with works by Spanish masters such as Roelas, Morales and Goya.

Heading along c/Eguilaz and its continuation c/Sevilla brings you to the recently restored fifteenth-century **Castillo de Santiago** (Tues–Sat visits on the hour 11am–1pm, €5, kids €3) where guided visits enable you to see the castle's barbicans, Plaza de Armas and towers with stunning views. It is still unclear at the time of writing what the new exhibition areas inside the castle will contain (details from the Turismo). A little further along the same street the sherry *bodega* of Barbadillo allows daily public visits (see box, p.224). A flight of steps beside the castle leads back down to the Barrio Bajo.

The Río Guadalquivir and Bonanza

A good kilometre walk from the centre (or a €3.50 taxi ride from Plaza del Cabildo or bus #3 or #4 from the Calzada del Ejército), Sanlúcar's shell-encrusted **river beach** – unfortunately marred by a lengthy and rather ugly concrete esplanade – is nevertheless a nice place to while away some time, and is usually quite deserted. The beach is also the setting for some exciting **horse races**, usually held at the beginning and end of August; the Turismo can supply the precise dates.

In summer, private motor boats from the Bajo de Guía, near the Real Fernando jetty, will ferry you to the opposite bank for about €6 (make sure to arrange a pick-up time with the boatman if you don't want to be stranded), where the **Coto de Doñana's** beaches, unfortunately not always the cleanest due to pollution from the Guadalquivir estuary currents, provide a change of scene and some bird-spotting possibilities. There are absolutely no facilities, so be sure to take along liquid refreshment and food. There are a number of companies who explore this area by **guided tours on horseback**: Club Equestre La Arboleda (☎mobile 630867672, ⓦwww.clubecuestrelaarboleda.com) is one, charging around €25 per hour. The Turismo can provide details of others.

Four kilometres upstream from Sanlúcar, the small port of **Bonanza** is where the town's sizeable fishing fleet is based, their catch sold at entertaining auctions on the harbourside Mon–Sat at 5pm. This is also the very spot from where Columbus and Magellan set sail on their epic voyages. Bonanza can be reached by taxi from the Plaza del Cabildo for €6 or by bus #1 from the top of the Calzada del Ejército.

Eating and drinking

Sanlúcar is renowned for the quality of its **seafood**, and the place to head for is the Bajo de Guía, the old fishing district upstream from where the Alameda meets the river. Numerous **bars** and **restaurants** lining the waterfront have terrace views towards the Coto de Doñana and serve excellent seafood, washed down with *manzanilla*. In the Barrio Bajo, the Plaza del Cabildo has a number of good tapas and breakfast bars, while higher up, Plaza de la Paz is a tranquil little square with various bars serving tapas. *El Rengue*, Avda.V Centenario s/n (at the end of c/San Juan off the right of our map), is a late night *rociero* bar with a great atmosphere that often stages impromptu flamenco. Nearby at c/San Miguel 5, *Bodegon "A Contratiempo"* also stages flamenco performances (Fri–Sat 11.30pm; €15 including drink; ☎673 07 10 99) in an atmospheric small theatre.

Bar Central Station c/Infanta Beatriz 1, by the side of the *Hotel Guadalquivir*. Highly original bar created by the train-mad owner of the hotel next door. Features include a steam engine and a full-size reconstruction of a wagon from the old Orient Express with sofa-style seats, lots of polished wood and a gleaming copper tea urn.

Bar El Cura c/Amargura 2, off Plaza del Cabildo. Relatively cheap and cheerful *platos combinados* at this pleasant bar/restaurant. They also do decent tapas.

Bar Joselito Huerta Bajo de Guía s/n, at the upstream end of the strip. Friendly seafood restaurant with a river terrace that is popular with locals. *Almejas* (clams), *cazón con tomate* (shark) and *acedias* (baby sole) are things to try. They also serve good tapas at the bar.

Bar Juanito Plaza San Roque 18. A popular tapas venue with locals, noted for its seafood. The nearby *Bar Clemente* on the same square is another good place.

Bar Parada "El Gallego" Plaza de la Paz 6. Galician bar that serves excellent *raciónes* at economical prices. *Bacalao con tomate* (cod) and *pulpo* (octopus) are good.

Bar-Restaurante El Bigote Bajo de Guía 10 ☎956 36 26 96. Celebrated establishment and one of the "big two" on the waterfront. You can eat outstanding tapas in their lively bar next door or more formally in the restaurant, where the fish and the house *arroz de marisco* (seafood paella) are outstanding. Don't miss the succulent local *langostinos* (prawns) too. An upstairs dining room offers panoramic views across the river towards the Doñana national park. Main dishes €8–20; reservation advised.

Casa Balbino Plaza del Cabildo 11. Behind an unassuming facade lies one of the best tapas bars in Andalucía. Long established, its walls are hung with faded photos and the obligatory bulls' heads, and the smoothly efficient bar staff will guide you through a daunting tapas menu. The *manzanillas* are outstanding and their *tortillita de camarones* (shrimp in batter) is justly famous. They have recently added a (self service) terrace.

Casa Juan Bajo de Guía 26. Another Bajo de Guía favourite where house specials include *arroz a la marinera* and *rape al cerco* (monkfish). Great terrace with river views.

Mirador de Doñana Bajo de Guía s/n ☎956 36 42 05. Outstanding restaurant with a summer terrace overlooking the river. Try their *mi barca Doñana*, white fish in a tomato sauce served in an edible "boat", or *sopa de Galeras*, a special *marisco* soup of which they're deservedly proud. When not busy, the waiters in the tapas bar will be happy to give you a master class in the thirty-plus brands of *manzanilla* on offer. Main dishes €9–20.

Jerez de la Frontera

Encircled by vines planted in the chalky, *albariza* soil, **JEREZ DE LA FRONTERA**, 22km inland from Sanlúcar and 35km from Cádiz, is the home and heartland of sherry (itself an English corruption of the town's Moorish name, Xerez) and also, less known but equally important, of Spanish brandy. Once you've penetrated some architecturally bleak suburbs, the town centre possesses a charming *casco antiguo* and a number of elegant, palm-fringed squares, as well as a handful of notable Renaissance and Baroque churches and palaces.

The **Barrio de Santiago**, a fascinating and authentic white-walled *gitano* (gypsy) quarter to the north of the cathedral, contrasts sharply with the great *bodegas* of the sherry houses located in the heart of the town. The sherry dynasties that own these companies (or used to own them, as many have been taken over by international conglomerates) are renowned as some of the biggest snobs in

JEREZ

ACCOMMODATION

Hostal Las Palomas	K
Hostal Sanvi	E
Hotel Al Andalus Jerez	G
Hotel Avila	I
Hotel Casa Grande	M
Hotel Chancillería	C
Hotel Doña Blanca	J
Hotel El Ancla	B
Hotel Nova Centro	H
Hotel Palacio Garvey	D
Hotel Nuevo	N
Hotel Royal Sherry Park	A
Hotel San Andrés	F
Hotel Serit	L

0   250 m

La Cartuja & ⑭

Train & Bus Station

Bodegas Harvey

Plaza de Toros

Jerez

Plaza de Canterbury

Convento de Sto. Domingo

Turismo ⓘ

Mercado

Palacio Domecq

Iglesia de San Dionisio & Plaza de la Asunción

Iglesia de San Miguel

El Alcázar

Catedral de San Salvador

Bodegas González Byass

Iglesia de San Juan

Centro Andaluz de Flamenco

Museo Arqueológico

Bodegas Domecq

Iglesia de Santiago

BARRIO DE SANTIAGO

Iglesia de San Mateo

City Wall

Royal Riding School, Bodegas Sandeman & Museo del Tiempo

Seville ▲ & ⑧ ▲

Sanlúcar de Barrameda ▲

Cádiz ▼

RESTAURANTS

Bodegon El Patio	9
Cafetería ONCE	4
Casa Pepa	14
La Carboná	10
La Parilla la Pampa	2
Mesa Redonda	1
Mesón Restaurante	11
Alcazaba	3
Restaurante Gaitán	3

BARS & MARISQUERÍAS

Bar El Poema	5
Bar Juanito	12
El Arriate	6
Freiduría Gallega	7
La Parra Vieja	13
La Reja	8

231

Spain, and take a haughty pride in apeing the traits and customs of the English upper-middle class – their strutting around on polo horses, wearing tweeds and speaking Spanish with an affected accent has earned them the nickname of *señoritos* or "toffs". Jerez's innate sobriety is thrown to the wind, however, during one of the two big **festivals** – the Feria Del Caballo or May Horse Fair (perhaps the most refined – or snooty depending on your viewpoint – of Andalucian *ferias*), and the celebration of the vintage towards the end of September.

Arrival, information and orientation

The **train** and **bus stations** are next door to each other, east of the Alcázar and the town's central square, the Plaza del Arenal. Line 10 urban buses, painted lurid lilac, stop close to the station entrance and will take you to the centre, a ten minute walk. Coming in by **car**, parking space is at a premium and you'd be advised to use the pay car parks signed in the centre or park further out and walk in. Buses (Mon–Fri roughly hourly 6.30am–9.45pm, Sat & Sun every 3hr) link Jerez with the **airport** (7km out of town on the NIV; ☎956 15 00 83). If you arrive outside these times you'll need to take a taxi (about €12–15) to the centre. The **Turismo** (June–Sept Mon–Fri 10am–3pm & 5–7pm, Sat & Sun 10am–2.30pm; Oct–May Mon–Fri 9.30am–3pm & 4.30–6.30pm, Sat & Sun 9.30am–2.30pm; ☎956 34 17 11, ⓦwww .turismojerez.com) is attached to the Convento de Santo Domingo and reached by following the pedestrianized main street, c/Larga north from the centre; it's well stocked with information about the town and can supply a detailed map. **Internet** access is available at Ciber Jerez, c/Santa María 3 (Mon–Sat 10am–10.30pm, Sun 5–10.30pm).

Accommodation

There's usually no problem finding **rooms** in Jerez except during April and May – the town's high season – when Semana Santa, the Festival de Jerez, the World Motorcycle Championship (held at the town's Formula 1 racing circuit) and the Fería del Caballo (May Horse Fair) come one after the other and fill the town to bursting point; make sure to ring ahead if you are planning to visit at this time. The high-season prices we quote below are for this April–May period, outside of which rates (especially for hotels) tend to fall by up to fifty percent. Most of the budget accommodation is conveniently located within a few-minutes' walk of the bus and train terminals. More possibilities are to be found in the streets surrounding the church of San Miguel. Jerez's modern *Albergue Juvenil*, Avda. Blas Infante 30 (☎856 81 40 01; under 26 €14, over 26 €18), has a fine pool but lies out in the suburbs; bus #9 from outside the bus station will take you there, with a stop closer to the centre on Plaza de las Angustias.

Budget

Hostal Las Palomas c/Higueras 17 ☎956 34 37 73, ⓦwww.hostal-las-palomas.com. In a quiet street, this *hostal* offers clean, simple rooms sharing bath plus some en suite; fans available. ❷
Hostal Sanvi c/Morenos 10 ☎956 34 56 24. Sparklingly clean *hostal* with lots of *azulejos* and friendly proprietors offering economical rooms with bath and TV. Garage parking available. ❸
Hotel Nova Centro c/Arcos 13 ☎956 33 21 38, ⓦwww.hotelnovacentro.com. Pleasant and central small hotel whose rooms are equipped with a/c, satellite TV and safe. Parking available. ❸
Hotel San Andrés c/Morenos 12 & 14 ☎956 34 09 83, ⓦwww.hotelsanandres .es. Great-value hotel and *hostal* side by side. Charming and friendly, there are en-suite rooms (with a/c and TV) and others sharing bath, plus a pleasant, plant-filled patio. They can advise on parking places nearby. ❷

Moderate to expensive

Hotel Al Andalus Jerez c/Arcos 29 ☎ 956 32 34 00, ⓦ www.alandalusjerez.com. Comfortable hotel with two pretty patios. Recently refurbished rooms – the better ones are off the inner patio – are equipped with a/c and TV, and there's a garage too. ❹

Hotel Avila c/Avila 3 ☎ 956 33 48 08, ⓦ www .hotelavila.com. Decent little two-star hotel with a/c rooms and own car park. ❹

Hotel Casa Grande Plaza de las Angustias 3, ☎ 956 34 50 70, ⓦ www.casagrande.com.es. Beautifully presented three-star hotel in a restored nineteenth-century *casa señorial*. The rooms are bright and comfortable, breakfast (extra) can be taken on a delightful roof terrace and there's free internet access. ❺

🔨 **Hotel Chancilleria** c/Chancilleria 21 ☎ 956 30 10 38, ⓦ www.hotelchancilleria .com. Welcoming new hotel in the Barrio Santiago with spacious a/c rooms with plasma TV. There's a wonderful roof terrace to take breakfast, rooms come with CD and DVD players (films may be borrowed from hotel library) and there's free internet access. Also has a very good restaurant. ❺ with breakfast.

Hotel Doña Blanca c/Bodegas 11 ☎ 956 34 87 61, ⓦ www.hoteldonablanca.com. One of the most central and intimate of the upper-range places with

well-equipped a/c balcony rooms with minibar and satellite TV, in a quiet street. Garage. ❹

Hotel El Ancla c/Mamelón 15 ☎ 956 32 12 97, ⓦ www.helancla.com. Dapper hotel with friendly proprietors. Rooms overlooking the noisy street (quieter at night) are compensated with views of square and fountains; all rooms a/c. ❹

Hotel Nuevo c/Caballeros 23 ☎ 956 33 16 00, ⓦ www.nuevohotel.com. Attractive and excellent-value hotel set in a lovely nineteenth-century *casa palacio*; rooms come with a/c and TV. ❹

Hotel Palacio Garvey c/Tornería 24 ☎ 956 32 67 00, ⓦ www.sferahoteles.net. Beautiful four-star hotel in the former mansion of the Garvey family, one of the great sherry dynasties in nineteenth-century Jerez. The elegant rooms have modern designer furnishings and come with free minibar, internet connection, CD player and satellite plasma TV. ❻

Hotel Royal Sherry Park Avda. Alvaro Domecq 11 ☎ 956 31 76 14, ⓦ www.hipotels.com. The nearest of the peripheral luxury hotels to the centre, this is a rather bland and modern affair despite an attractive pool, gardens and car park. ❻

Hotel Serit c/Higueras 7 ☎ 956 34 07 00, ⓦ www .hotelserit.com. Central and friendly hotel with bright, airy rooms equipped with a/c and satellite TV. Car park. ❹

The town and around

Quite apart from the **sherry bodegas** – indisputably Jerez's biggest draw – the town has many sights that warrant a look, not least the gypsy quarter, **Barrio de Santiago**, which is a fascinating place to stroll around. Conveniently, all the major sights and most of the *bodegas* are within just a few-minutes' walk of the central, elegant and palm-fringed **Plaza del Arenal**, dominated by a bronze statue of the 1920s dictator Primo de Rivera.

The Alcázar

The substantial **Alcázar** (May–Sept Mon–Sat 10am–8pm, Sun 10am–3pm; Oct–April daily 10am–6pm; €3 or €5.40 including camera obscura) lies just to the south of the Plaza del Arenal. To reach the entrance, take a right off the southern end of Plaza del Arenal into Plaza Monti, at the end of which you turn left into c/M. María González. The entrance lies uphill on the left. Constructed in the twelfth century by the Almohads, though much altered since, the Alcázar has been extensively excavated and restored in recent years. The **gardens** have received particular attention: the plants and arrangements have been modelled as closely as possible – using historical research – on the original. The interior contains a well-preserved mosque complete with *mihrab* from the original structure, now sensitively restored to its original state after having been used as a church for many centuries.

There's also a **bathhouse** modelled, by the Almohads, on those of the earlier Romans with cold and hot plunges, as well as impressive walls and towers on the site's outer perimeter. The eighteenth-century **Palacio de Villavicencio** constructed on the west side of the Alcázar's Patio de las Armas (parade ground) houses a **camera obscura** (same hours) offering views of the major landmarks of the town as well as the sherry vineyards and the sea beyond.

The Cathedral and Plaza de la Asunción

West of Plaza del Arenal, the eighteenth-century **Catedral de San Salvador** (Mon–Sat 11am–1pm & 6.30–8pm, Sun 11am–1.30pm; free) was rather harshly dismissed by Richard Ford as "vile Churrigueresque" because of its mixture of Gothic and Renaissance styles, but an elegant facade – largely the work of Vincente Acero – is not without merit. Inside, over-obvious pointing gives the building an unfinished, breeze-block aspect, while, in the sacristy, there's a fine, little-known painting by Zurbarán – *The Sleeping Girl*. The most exciting time

Sherry – Jerez's liquid gold

It's believed that the Phoenicians brought the vine to this area early in the first millennium BC. The Romans shipped wine from here to all parts of their empire, and the Roman settlement of Asido Caesaris may well be the town from which Jerez derives its name, later corrupted to **Xerez** (pronounced "Sherrish") by the Moors.

British merchants were attracted here in the fourteenth century and, following the expulsions of Moors and Jews in the wake of the *Reconquista*, they established firms that first traded, and later produced, Falstaff's "sack" (probably derived from the Spanish *sacar* – to draw out – referring to the *solera* system, see below). Some of the *bodegas*, or cellars, were founded by British Catholic refugees, barred from careers at home by the sixteenth-century Supremacy Act. The names of the great sherry firms today testify to the continuing love affair of the British with this wine: Britain, along with the Netherlands, still consumes up to seventy percent of all exports.

It's a particular combination of climate, soil and grape variety that gives **sherry wine** its distinctive style. The chalky, white *albariza* soil of the region is the natural habitat for the Palomino sherry grape, and though the resulting wine is fairly ordinary stuff, it's what happens inside the *bodegas* that transforms it into sherry. Here the wine is transferred to oak butts with loose stoppers to let in air. Then the *flor* – a puffy layer of scum (actually yeast) – magically appears on the surface of the wine not only preventing oxidization, but feeding on it too, in the process adding a special flavour and bouquet. It is the subtle nature of the *flor*, the ingredient that cannot be duplicated by competitors, that imparts a different flavour to the sherries of Jerez, El Puerto de Santa Maria and especially Sanlúcar, where it absorbs the salty breezes off the sea, producing the most delicate fino of all, *manzanilla*. The *bodegas* of Jerez, unlike in other wine-producing areas, are situated above ground in order to maintain the humid conditions necessary for the growth of this *flor* – helped by sprinkling the sand-covered floors with water.

The final stage in the creation of sherry – but not *manzanilla* – is the fortification of the wine with alcohol (up to fifteen percent in the case of *fino* sherry) before it enters the *solera* system. Because sherry is not a vintage, or yearly, wine it is always blended with older wines through the *soleras* and *criaderas*, as many as six rows of butts placed on top of each other from which the wine is gradually transferred from the topmost to the bottommost over a period of time. This process, mixing the new, younger, wine with the greater quantity of mature, older, wine, "educates" it to assume its character. The wine drawn off at the end for bottling has an even consistency year after year, conveniently with none of the problems of "good" and "bad" years. The classic sherry is the bone-dry *fino*, but variations on the theme include *amontillado* (where the *flor* is allowed to "die" in the butt, imparting a nutty flavour), *oloroso* (produced as *fino* but minus the *flor*) and *cream* – pronounced "cray-am" in Andalucía – a purely British concoction where sweet grapes are blended with *oloroso*.

to be here is September, when on the broad steps of the cathedral, below the free-standing bell tower – actually part of an earlier, fifteenth-century Mudéjar castle – the wine harvest celebrations begin with the crushing of grapes.

A little way northeast, along c/J. Luís Diez, lies the town's most charming square, the **Plaza de la Asunción** (known as Plaza San Dionisio to *jerezanos*), where a sixteenth-century former Ayuntamiento features ornamental statues of

▲ Plaza de la Asunción

Hercules and Julius Caesar on its facade. It's flanked by the fifteenth-century Mudéjar **Iglesía de San Dionisio** (undergoing restoration at the time of writing) with a graceful bell tower and an interior that underwent some later Baroque alterations.

Barrio de Santiago

Jerez's ancient *gitano* quarter, the Barrio de Santiago, stretches uphill from the cathedral in a maze of narrow lanes and alleys to the church of Santiago on its northern boundary. Part of the attraction of visiting the *barrio* is its many fascinating churches. The sixteenth-century Gothic **Iglesía de San Mateo**, with a fine *retablo* and superb vaulting over the chapels, is one of a quartet of churches dotted around the *barrio* dedicated to the four Evangelists (saints Marcos, Lucas and Juan, all to the east of San Mateo, are also worth seeking out; all four should be open for services 7–9am & 7–8pm).

Museo Arqueológico

Located inside a renovated eighteenth-century mansion, the **Museo Arqueológico**, in Plaza del Mercado (June–Aug Tues–Sun 10am–2.30pm; Sept–May Tues–Fri 10am–2pm & 4–7pm, Sat & Sun 10am–2.30pm; €3), is a delight to visit. A plant-filled patio leads to the early rooms dealing with prehistory; upstairs, Room 3 has some curious **Chalcolithic** (early second millennium BC) cylinder-shaped idols with starburst eyes from Cerro de las Vacas, 20km to the north of the town. Room 4 has a wonderfully preserved **Greek** military helmet dating from the seventh-century BC, and found on the banks of the nearby Río Guadalete. This was a time when the early Greeks were colonizing sites all around the Mediterranean, and they evidently expected to meet resistance from the Iberian tribes. Also in Room 4 are finds from the ancient town of **Hasta Regia**, as Pliny, Strabo and Ptolemy referred to Jerez in Roman times. A wide range of Amphorae, funerary stones and sculptures evidence Hasta's importance.

More Roman Amphorae – some stamped with the maker's name – appear in Room 5, once used for the shipping of *garum* (the fish sauce renowned for its quality in these parts; see p.191), olive oil and other products around the Mediterranean. Room 6 has items from the **Visigothic** period and in Room 7 there's an interesting chronological display of **coins** found around Jerez; a good image of the Roman emperor Tiberius (no. 44) is followed by dihrams of rulers Al-Hakam and Abd Ar-Rahman (no. 84) from the period of the Cordoban emirate. Upstairs again, you'll find a cafetería with roof terrace, and Rooms 8 and 9, both holding the Moorish and medieval collections, with some fine Moorish ceramics, especially a tenth-century Caliphal bottle vase with Kufic script, found near Jerez. Before leaving, take a look at the striking works placed around the ground-floor patio. Among them, there's a powerful third- to first-century BC Iberian sculpture of a lion mauling a ram, found nearby, and an intriguing seventh-century Visigothic sarcophagus from La Peñuela carved with curious vegetable, animal and human symbols.

The parroquia de Santiago and the Centro Andaluz de Flamenco

Just west of the museum, along c/Muro, is a bit of the original Moorish **city wall**, which you can follow north to another Gothic church, the fifteenth-century **Iglesia de Santiago**, with wonderfully florid Plateresque portals. Inside, a celebrated sixteenth-century sculpture of the *Prendimiento* – or arrest of Christ – attributed to La Roldana, is the centrepiece of Jerez's Semana Santa processions when it's carried through the streets. On the small square opposite the church stands a bronze bust dedicated to Fernando Terremoto, one of many legendary flamenco artists the *barrio* has produced. You'll come across others dotted around this quarter (there's one of Tío José de Paula behind the church), all testifying to the *barrio*'s great pride in its contribution to Andalucía's musical heritage.

Fronting the Plaza de San Juan, the **Centro Andaluz de Flamenco** (Mon–Fri 9am–2pm; ⓦwww.centroandaluzdeflamenco.es; free) is housed in an elegant eighteenth-century mansion, the Palacio de Pemartín. As one of the founding centres of flamenco song and dance, Jerez has created this library of *flamencología*, as well as a sound and vision archive, to preserve the works and performances of past greats in the art; on the top floor, a dance room is used to teach students from all over the world. The staff are welcoming and anyone is free to use the video archive to see performances by flamenco masters past and present – just give them a name and they'll do the rest. There's also a good audiovisual presentation in Spanish, *El Arte Flamenco* (hourly, on the half-hour), which – if you know little about flamenco – will give you a grasp of the basics and an understanding of why it is so important to Andalucians.

The Convento de Santo Domingo, Palacio Domecq and Iglesia de San Miguel

The northern end of the pedestrianized c/Larga – which passes, at the junction with c/Santa María, the old *Café Cena Cirullo*, a fine modernist building (now the *El Gallo Azul* café), which used to be the great meeting place of Jerez's salon society – is dominated by the august frontage of the **Convento de Santo Domingo** (open for services, generally 7–8pm). Although badly damaged by fire in the Civil War, it has been diligently restored and, in common with many of the town's other religious buildings, has a curious mixture of styles: in this case Mudéjar, Romanesque and Gothic. The church's seventeenth-century *retablo mayor* is an orgy of gilded wood, with the *Virgen de la Consolación* – the patron of the city, carved in Italian marble – as its centrepiece. Just to the north of here along the Alameda Cristina stands the eighteenth-century **Palacio Domecq**, a grand pile erected – and still owned – by the sherry family. Behind an entrance flanked by barley-sugar pillars, an exquisite marble-floored Baroque patio is occasionally open to view. One other church worth a visit is the fifteenth-century Gothic **Iglesia de San Miguel**, just to the south of the Plaza del Arenal. An ornate classical facade added in the eighteenth-century climbs dizzily to a pretty bell tower adorned with blue and white *azulejos*, whilst the interior (Mon–Fri 7–8pm; free) has a magnificent *retablo* by Martínez Montañés.

The Museo del Tiempo and the Riding School

At the northern end of town, the recently revamped and enlarged **Museo del Tiempo** (aka Museo de Relojes), c/Cervantes 3 (Tues–Sat 10am–2pm & 6–8pm, Sun 10am–3pm; €6), claims to have the largest collection of fully functioning antique clocks and watches in Europe, all chiming on the hour, while nearby, north of the Alameda Cristina, at the **Real Escuela Andaluz del Arte Ecuestre** (Royal Andalucian School of Equestrian Art), Avda. Duque de Abrantes s/n, you can see teams of horses performing to music (Tues & Thurs noon, plus July 15–Oct 15 Fri noon; seats €18–24; information & reservations ⓣ956 31 80 08, ⓦwww.realescuela.org). Watching training and rehearsals, and visits to the stables (Mon, Wed & Fri 10am–1pm) costs a more affordable €10.

La Cartuja

The remarkable Carthusian monastery of **LA CARTUJA** lies 4km along the road out of town towards Medina Sidonia (see p.178) in the midst of lush countryside and surrounded in summer by a sea of sunflowers. The monastery was founded in 1477 and, following great destruction by billeted French troops in 1810, was abolished in 1835 during the Liberal backlash against the church and male religious orders.

After serving as a military barracks for almost a century, La Cartuja was restored to the Carthusians in 1949, since when the handful of monks here have dedicated themselves to restoring and maintaining this beautiful building. The Baroque **facade** you see today – added in the 1660s – is one of the most spectacular in the whole of Spain. Unfortunately, access is restricted to the building's exterior (with a magnificent main doorway), gardens and cloister (daily 9.30am–6pm; free); currently the impressive church and its artworks may be seen only by those attending mass (Sat 8pm, Sun & Mon 5.30pm).

The bodegas

The tours of the sherry and brandy processes in Jerez can be a fascinating insight into the mysteries of **sherry production**, although sampling – nowadays restricted to a couple of tots at the end of a tour – is hardly as much fun as when Richard Ford was here in the nineteenth century and saw visitors emerging "stupefied by drink". There are a great many **bodegas** to choose from and, with the exception of August when all but a few firms close down, most welcome visitors throughout the year. Some companies insist that you **book at least a day in advance** and we state if this is the case. Below are a selection of *bodegas* offering tours throughout the whole or part of August; should you wish to visit some of the smaller establishments, get hold of a complete list from the Turismo. Details of many of these, together with visiting times, maps and contact details appear on ⓦwww.sherry.org or on the Turismo's site (see p.232). Visiting hours frequently change and it's worth confirming these in advance with the *bodega* or getting an updated list from the Turismo.

The most central *bodega* and one of the two giants of Jerez – whose establishments are almost small towns in their own right – is **González Byass**, c/Manuel González s/n, behind the Alcázar (daily except Sun afternoon 11.30am, 12.30pm, 1.30pm, 2pm, 3.30pm, 4.30pm, 5.30pm. €10 visit with wine tasting; ☎902 44 00 77, ⓦwww .bodegastiopepe.com), producers of Tío Pepe *fino* and Lepanto brandy. The González cellars are perhaps the oldest in Jerez and, though no longer used, preserve an old circular chamber, La Concha, designed by Eiffel (of Tower fame). The other major firm is **Domecq**, c/San Ildefonso 3, makers of La Ina sherry and Carlos I brandy (reservation required; Mon–Fri visits on the hour 10am–1pm; Tue & Thurs extra visit at 2pm; Sat noon & 2pm; €8; ☎956 15 15 00, ⓦwww.bodegasfundadorpedrodomecq.com), while others include **Sandeman**, c/Pizarro 10 (Mon, Wed & Fri visits at 11.30am, 12.30pm, 1.30pm, & 2.30pm; Tues & Thurs 10.30am 12.30pm & 2pm; €7; ☎956 31 29 95, ⓦwww.sandeman.eu), **Williams and Humbert**, Ctra. Nacional IV km641.75 (the Sevilla road; reservation required; Mon–Fri 10am, 12noon & 2pm; €7; ☎956 35 34 06, ⓦwww.bodegas-williams-humbert.com), and **Harveys** (now part of the Allied-Domecq group), c/Pintor Muñoz Cebrián s/n (reservation required; Mon–Sat 10am &12noon; €8; ☎956 34 60 00, ⓦwww.bodegasharveys.com).

Each *bodega* has its celebrity barrels signed by famous visitors – Martin Luther King, Orson Welles, Queen Victoria, Cole Porter and Franco (protected by a glass screen) are some of the big names in the González collection – while a transparent butt (most *bodegas* have one) allows you to see the action of the magical *flor* on the sherry. Nearly all *bodegas* have their own shop too where you can buy the house brands. In town, the Sherry Shop at c/Divina Pastora 1 (top centre of our city map; ☎956 33 51 84) is a friendly and informative place that stocks them all and where you can sample as well. Bodega San Rafael, c/Arcos 4, near the post office, is a similar place.

The Laguna de Medina
If you have transport, you could make another excursion from Jerez to the **LAGUNA DE MEDINA**, a small freshwater lake which – from late August on – attracts a great number of migrating birds returning from northern Europe to Africa. Under the care of ICONA (Instituto para Conservación de la Naturaleza), two paths skirt the lake from where, among a variety of waders, it's possible to spot white-headed duck, spoonbills and the greater flamingo in season. Fringed with reeds and tamarisk trees, the shallow lagoon is also home to numerous frogs, snakes and lizards. Because of its close proximity to the Coto Doñana across the Guadalquivir, many birds – particularly flamingos – use this as an alternative food source, especially if the Doñana's marismas are drier than normal towards the end of the summer.

To get there take the A381 out of Jerez for about 11km towards Medina Sidonia; the entrance to the lake area is signposted immediately opposite a cement factory, and there's a small car park.

Eating and drinking
Jerez's booming sherry trade ensures that the town's **restaurants** are kept busy, and a few of these are very good indeed. Befitting the capital of sherry production Jerez also has a range of great bars where *fino* – the perfect partner for tapas – can be sampled on its own turf. For tapas and snacks head for the atmospheric **Plaza Rafael Rivera** close to the Convento de Santo Domingo, where a number of bars around the square have pleasant terraces. For breakfast and afternoon tea, head for *Cafetería San Francisco*, Plaza Estebe 2, near the market, or its twin *Mesón Reina de León*, c/Latorre 8, slightly northeast of Plaza Arenal. For tapas and tasty *pasteles*, *jerezanos* visit *El Gallo Azul* at the junction of c/Larga and c/Santa María.

Restaurants
Bodegon El Patio c/San Francisco de Paula 2 ☎956 34 07 36. Housed in a former *bodega*, this mid-priced *ambiente jerezano* restaurant offers well prepared meat and fish dishes. *Cochinillo asado* (suckling pig) is a house special. Has a *menú* for €18. Main dishes €9–24.

Cafetería ONCE c/Gaitán 10. A napkin's throw from one of the best restaurants in town (the *Restaurante Gaitán*, the spotless, a/c *cafetería* of Spain's powerful charity for the blind has no such pretensions. Instead it serves up the cheapest three-course (including wine) *menú* in town for €6.50 – an excellent deal. During July & Aug and on Sat & Sun open lunch times only.

Casa Pepa Plaza Madre de Dios 14, near the train and bus stations. Good, inexpensive restaurant for meat and seafood dishes with a *menú del día* for around €8.

La Carboná c/San Francisco de Paula 2. Cavernous but wonderfully atmospheric mid-priced place inside an old *bodega*, specializing in charcoal-grilled fish and meat and – in season – fresh tuna.

La Parilla la Pampa c/Guadalete 24. Great Argentine restaurant with an excellent-value five-course meal of Argentine specialities (including steaks) – the meat is flown in from South America. Expect to pay around €40 for two.

Mesa Redonda c/Manuel de la Quintana 3, entered opposite the *Royal Sherry Park* hotel ☎956 34 00 69. One of the town's best places, this doesn't come cheap, but the food – fish and meat cooked under the direction of noted chef José Romero Valdespino – is truly memorable; as is their sherry trifle dessert. The *salteado de solomillo de añojo* (pork tenderloin) is a signature dish. Main dishes €10–20. Closed Sun.

Mesón Restaurante Alcazaba c/San Francisco de Paula 6. Excellent, economical and spacious restaurant where both meat and fish dishes are priced under €10 and there are *menús* for €8 and €11. Also opens for breakfast and does pretty good tapas, too.

Restaurante Gaitán c/Gaitán 3 ☎956 16 80 21. Small, attractive upmarket restaurant very popular with *jerezanos* specializing in Basque and *andaluz* dishes. Among a range of fish and meat dishes *cordero al brandy* (lamb) is a house special. Main dishes €12–16. Closed Sun eve.

Bars and marisquerías

Bar El Poema Plaza Rafael Rivero s/n. Great and friendly little tapas bar that has won prizes for its tapas: namely *chorizo al vino de jerez* and *el menudo* (cow, lamb and pig's tripe). Three other bars on the same square make this a *tapeadores* hot spot.

Bar Juanito c/Pescadería Vieja 4. In a small passage off the west side of Plaza del Arenal, this is the best tapas bar in town, with a menu as endless as the number of excellent *finos* on offer. Specials include *berza a jerezano* (chickpea stew). Closed Sun.

El Arriate c/Francos 43, in the Barrio de Santiago. Flamenco and jazz bar whose amiable proprietor is an aficionado of both traditions; live performances in winter. Also does tapas.

Freiduría Gallega c/Arcos 5, near the market. Popular bar serving up fried fish and *mariscos* prepared *a la gallega* by proprietors hailing from the northwestern Spanish province of Galicia; eat in or take away.

La Parra Vieja c/San Miguel 9. One of Jerez's oldest tapas bars (over a century in business), in an alleyway downhill from the Iglesia de San Miguel. Specials include *croquetas de jamón* and *mollejas de cordero* (sweetbreads). They've now added a small mid-priced restaurant too, with an economical *menú*. The nearby *La Marea* at no. 3 in the same street is also worth a call for its excellent fried-fish tapas. Closed Mon.

La Reja c/Mesones 2, near the market. Atmospheric tapas and *raciónes* haunt serving a wide range of dishes.

Nightlife

Much of Jerez's **nightlife** centres around the bars and discos near the bullring and the zone around the Avenida de Mexico to the northeast of here. One place which is very popular with younger *jerezanos* is Plaza de Canterbury, c/Nuño de Cañas s/n, a renovated plaza pulsing with numerous bars and discos where live music is frequently staged. The local paper *El Diario de Jerez* is a good place to find out about upcoming concerts and festivals.

Bar El Laga Plaza del Mercado, next to the Archeological Museum ☎ 956 33 83 34. Authentic (if somewhat tourist oriented) flamenco bar with recitals and dancing Mon to Sat starting around 10.30pm; tapas and *raciónes* are served. Tables can be reserved if you want to get a good view. €16 including a drink.

Bereber c/Cabezas 10, near the archeological museum. Spectacular transformation of a sixteenth-century *palacio* (with original wall paintings) into a multi-patio garden bar and flamenco club. The heart of the complex holds two (soundproofed) *discotecas*, one playing Sixties to Eighties sounds, the other more contemporary stuff.

Flamenco in Jerez

Given Jerez's great **flamenco** traditions, it's worth trying to hear some of the real thing at one of the many *peñas* (clubs) concentrated in the old *gitano* quarter of Santiago, north of the cathedral (though be careful in this area after dark). The following are some of the best; turning up at around 10pm at weekends (although they're open at other times, too) should provide an opportunity to hear some authentic performances. Otherwise consult the Turismo, who also publish a sheet listing all of Jerez's *peñas*; the Centro Andaluz de Flamenco, who also have details of the special flamenco festivals held in town over the summer; or El Diario de Jerez who have a special flamenco listings page on Fridays.

Centro Andaluz de Flamenco Plaza San Juan 1, Santiago ☎ 956 34 92 65.

Peña Los Cernicalos c/Sancho Vizcaíno 25, south of the church of San Miguel ☎ 956 34 30 84.

Peña Antonio Chacón c/Salas 12, Santiago ☎ 956 34 74 72.

Peña La Buena Gente Plaza San Lucas 9, Santiago ☎ 956 33 84 04.

Peña Tío José de Paula c/La Merced 11, Santiago ☎ 956 32 01 96.

La Habana c/Cádiz 181, near the riding school. Popular music bar; one of several along this street.
La Taberna Flamenca Angostillo de Santiago 3. Tucked down the west side of the Iglesia de Santiago. Slightly touristy flamenco Tues–Sat at midday, 4pm, 8pm and midnight. Serves lunch, dinner or tapas during performances.
Los Dos Deditos Plaza Vargas 1 off the end of c/Pescadería Vieja s/n, off Plaza del Arenal.

Relaxed *copas* (drinks and music) bar and one of the very few in the central zone; popular with over 25s. The nearby *Reino de León*, at c/Latorre 8, is similar.
O'Donoghues c/Nuño de Cañas 16, next door to the Plaza de Canterbury. Music bar that packs them in after midnight, especially at weekends.

Travel details

Trains

Algeciras to: Córdoba (2 daily; 3hr 15min); Granada (3 daily; 4hr 20min); Madrid (2 daily; 5hr 20min); Málaga (4 daily; change at Bobadilla; 4hr); Ronda (5 daily; 1hr 40min); Seville (1 daily; 3hr 20min).

Cádiz to: Córdoba (3 daily; 3hr); El Puerto de Santa María (13 daily; 30min); Granada (5 daily; change at Seville; 5hr); Jerez de la Frontera (14 daily; 35min); Seville (17 daily; 2hr).

Málaga to: Algeciras (2 daily; change at Bobadilla; 4hr 30min); Antequera (5 daily; 25min); Córdoba (1 daily; 2hr 20min; AVE 10 daily; 1hr); El Chorro (1 daily; 1hr); Fuengirola (every 30min); Granada (2 daily; change at Bobadilla, 3hr 30min); Ronda (6 daily; change at Bobadilla, 3hr); Seville (6 daily; 2hr 30min); Torremolinos (every 30min; 20min).

Buses

The bus times quoted are the fastest journey times, normally direct. There may be other buses to the same destination which make additional stops at towns and villages en route.

Algeciras to: Cádiz (16 daily; 2hr 15min); Jerez de la Frontera (11 daily; 1hr 30min); La Línea: (for Gibraltar; hourly, 30min); Madrid (4 daily; 8hr); Málaga (8 daily; 3hr); Seville (11 daily; 2hr 30min); Tarifa (10 daily; 30min).

Cádiz to: Alacalá de los Gazules (4 daily; 1hr 40min); Algeciras (10 daily; 2hr 15min); Arcos de la Frontera (5 daily; 1hr 30min); Córdoba (2 daily; 4hr); El Puerto de Santa María (23 daily; 35min); Granada (4 daily; 5hr); Jerez (20 daily; 45min); Los Caños de Meca (2 daily; 1hr 15min); Málaga (6 daily; 4hr); Ronda (3 daily; 3hr); Seville (12 daily; 1hr 45min); Tarifa (5 daily; 2hr); Vejer (8 daily; 1hr); Zahara de los Atunes (3 daily; 2hr).

Chipiona to: Cádiz (9 daily; 1 hr 30min); Conil (14 daily; 1hr); El Puerto de Santa María (9 daily; 45min); Granada (4 daily; 4hr 30min); Jerez de la Frontera (10 daily; 45min); Los Caños de Meca (2 daily; 1hr 15min); Ronda (3 daily; 2hr); Rota (3 daily; 30min); Sanlúcar de Barrameda (11 daily; 15min); Seville (12 daily; 2hr 30min).

Jerez to: Algeciras (11 daily; 1hr 30min); Arcos de la Frontera (17 daily; 35min); Cádiz (12 daily; 45min); Chipiona (10 daily; 40min); Córdoba (1 daily; 3hr 30min); El Puerto de Santa María (15 daily; 30min); Ronda (7 daily; 2hr 15min); Rota (7 daily; 30min); Sanlúcar de Barrameda (16 daily; 30min); Seville (10 daily; 1hr 30min); Vejer de la Frontera (2 daily; 1hr 30min).

Málaga to: Algeciras (15 daily; 3hr); Almería (8 daily; 3hr 30min); Antequera (11 daily; 1hr); Cádiz (7 daily; 3hr 45min); Conil (3 daily; 3–4hr); Córdoba (5 daily; 3hr 30min); Estepona (17 daily; 2hr); Fuengirola (8 daily; 45min); Granada (20 daily; 1hr 30min); Jerez (3 daily; 4hr 30min); La Línea (4 daily; 3hr); Marbella (25 daily; 45min); Motril-Lanjarón (8 daily; 2hr); Nerja (17 daily; 1hr 30min); Riogordo (7 daily; 1hr); Osuna (3 daily; 2hr); Ronda (18 daily; 1hr 45min); Seville (11 daily; 2hr 30min); Tarifa (3 daily; 3hr 30min); Torremolinos (14 daily; 35min); Vejer (3 daily, 4hr).

Ronda to: Arcos (6 daily; 2hr 30min); Cádiz (6 daily; 3hr 15min); Grazalema (2 daily; 35min); Jerez (6 daily; 2hr 30min); Málaga (6 daily; 1hr 45min); Marbella (2 daily; 1hr); Olvera (1 daily; 1hr 30min); San Pedro de Alcántara (2 daily; 45min); Setenil (1 daily; 1hr 15min); Seville (3 daily; 2hr 30min); Ubrique (2 daily; 1hr 30min); Zahara de la Sierra (1 daily; 55min).

Rota to: El Puerto de Santa María (9 daily; 20min); Cádiz (14 daily; 30min); Seville (8 daily; 1hr 45min); Chipiona (2 daily; 30min).

Sanlúcar de Barrameda to: Cádiz (9 daily; 1hr 15min); Chipiona (9 daily; 15min); El Puerto de Santa María (9 daily; 45min); Jerez (15 daily; 30 min); Seville (9 daily; 1hr 30min).

Ferries

Algeciras to: Ceuta (up to 24 daily; 35min); Tangier (up to 30 daily; 35min–1hr 30min); **Cádiz** to: Las Palmas (1 weekly; on Tues, 48hr); El Puerto de Santa María (El Vapor; 5 daily; 40min; Catamaran; 12–18 daily; 25min); Tenerife (1 weekly; on Tues; 48hr).

Gibraltar to: Tangier (1 weekly; on Fri; 48hr). **Málaga** to: Melilla (2 daily; 3hr 45min or 8hr). **Tarifa** to: Tangier (3–5 daily; 35min).

2

Seville and Huelva

CHAPTER 2

Highlights

✻ **La Giralda and the Catedral, Seville** The city's landmark building and the world's largest Gothic church whose soaring minaret – now the bell tower – is one of the most beautiful of all Moorish monuments. See p.257

✻ **Alcázar, Seville** A Moorish fortress-palace adorned with breathtakingly beautiful stuccowork, tiles and coffered ceilings within, and relaxing gardens without. See p.263

✻ **Tapas bars, Seville** The city that invented tapas has some of Spain's very best tapas bars – two not to miss are *Bar Giralda* and *El Rinconcillo*. See p.290

✻ **Semana Santa, Seville** The solemn pomp and pagan ecstasy of the Holy Week processions are the most impressive and moving in Spain. See p.296

✻ **Parque Nacional de Doñana** Europe's largest and most important wildlife sanctuary. See p.331

✻ **Costa de la Luz** Huelva's stretch of the Atlantic coast has a string of enjoyable resorts and some of the finest beaches in Andalucía. See p.338

✻ **Sierra de Aracena** A landscape of wooded hills, babbling streams and attractive villages which produce the best cured ham in Spain. See p.352

▲ Almonaster la Real, Sierra de Aracena

Seville and Huelva

With the major exception of the irresistible city of Seville, the central and western regions of Andalucía are not much visited – a great pity, as these areas, consisting of the city's province and the neighbouring province of Huelva, are capable of springing a variety of surprises, both scenic and cultural, on those visitors prepared to wander off the beaten track to find them.

Seville, Andalucía's capital, has many of the region's most beautiful monuments: the **Giralda** tower, a magnificent Gothic **Cathedral** and a rambling Mudéjar **Alcázar** with fabulous ornamentation are only the highlights of a marvellous architectural feast. Add to these a stunning **Museo de Bellas Artes**, the nearby Roman site of **Itálica** and a number of remarkable Renaissance mansions such as the **Casa de Pilatos**, and you're looking at a stay of at least two days. The most exciting parts of Seville, however, are its various **barrios**, each with its own strong character and traditions, and atmospheric places to explore.

East of Seville a clutch of smaller towns on the way to Córdoba include Moorish **Carmona**, which possesses a remarkable Roman cemetery, and Baroque **Écija**, with its striking churches and mansions. Also in Seville's **Campiña** – the name given to this broad and fertile agricultural plain watered by the Guadalquivir – are the towns of **Osuna** and **Estepa**, both with their own Renaissance architectural gems. To the north, the wooded hills of the **Sierra Morena** offer welcome respite from the intense summer heat, with charming small towns making excellent base-camps for hikes.

The **province of Huelva** stretches from Seville to the Portuguese border, and hardly deserves its tag as the least-visited province of Andalucía. The area boasts the huge nature reserve of the **Coto Doñana National Park**, spreading back from the Guadalquivir estuary in vast expanses of *marismas* – sand dunes, salt flats and marshes. The largest roadless area in western Europe, the park is vital to scores of migratory birds and to endangered mammals including the Iberian lynx, and is home to Andalucía's rumbustious Whitsuntide pilgrimage and fair, the **Romería del Rocío**.

Huelva, the provincial capital, although scarred by its industrial surrounds, tries its best to be welcoming and does have a number of things to see; it also makes a convenient base for trips to local sites associated with the **voyages of Columbus** which set out from here. It was at the nearby monastery of **La Rábida** that the explorer's 1492 expedition was planned and from the tiny port of **Palos de la Frontera** that he eventually set sail to discover a new route to the Indies. The province of Huelva was also the site of ancient **Tartessus**, a legendary kingdom rich in minerals that attracted the Minoans, Phoenicians

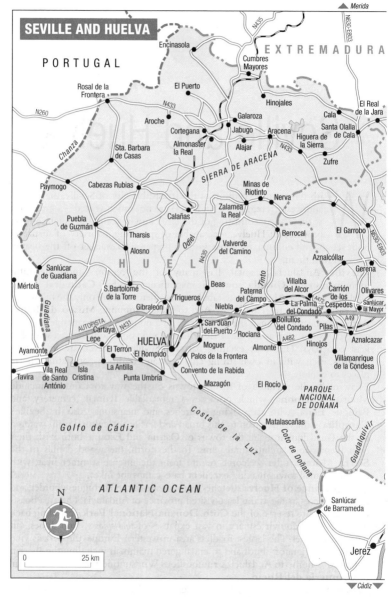

and Greeks in ancient times and is mentioned in the Bible. Minerals are still extracted from the hills to the north of the city – the awesome **Minas de Ríotinto** display evidence of the human quest for minerals stretching back over five thousand years.

Some of the most beautiful and neglected parts of this region are even further north, in the dark, ilex-covered hills and sturdy rural villages of the **Sierra de**

Aracena. Perfect walking country, with its network of streams and reservoirs between modest peaks, this is a botanist's dream, brilliant with a mass of spring flowers. You also find here some of the finest *jamón* in Spain, produced from acorn-eating *cerdos ibericos* (black pigs).

While the landlocked province of Seville takes its relaxation along the banks of the Guadalquivir, Huelva has a sea coast that harks back to pre-Costa del

Sol tranquillity. This section of the **Costa de la Luz** has some of the finest **beaches** in Andalucía, with long stretches of luminous white sand and little sign of development.

Seville (Sevilla)

"Seville," wrote Byron, "is a pleasant city, famous for oranges and women." And for its heat, he might have added, since summers here are intense and start in April, but the spirit of the quote, for all its nineteenth-century chauvinism, is about right. What is captivating about the city, as much as the monuments and works of art, is its essential romantic quality – the greatest city of the Spanish south, of Carmen, Don Juan and Figaro, and the archetype of Andalucian promise. *Sevillanos* are world leaders in the art of street theatre, too. During **Semana Santa**, for example, sandalled and helmeted Roman soldiers sombrely escort the *paso*, or effigy, of the condemned Christ through the crowded but silent streets, while a couple of weeks later the mood changes dramatically when the city launches into the wild exuberance of the **Feria de Abril** (which also inaugurates the start of the bullfighting season – second only to Madrid's in importance – another *sevillano* passion).

Despite its considerable charm, and its wealth – based on food processing, aircraft production, shipbuilding, construction and a thriving tourist industry – the city lies at the centre of a depressed agricultural area and has an unemployment rate of over twenty percent. The refurbishment of the infrastructure for the 1992 Expo – held to celebrate the 500th anniversary of Columbus's "discovery" of the New World – was intended to regenerate the city's (and the region's) economic fortunes but was not the catalyst for growth and prosperity promised at the time.

Some history

Seville began when ancient Iberian tribes settled on the banks of the Guadalquivir perhaps early in the first millennium BC. The settlement grew into the town now known as **El Carambolo**, whose great wealth derived from the minerals mined in the mountains to the north. The demand for copper, silver and gold lured in the Greeks and Phoenicians, who traded their own ceramics, jewellery and ivory goods. It was the same Phoenicians, or perhaps their successors the Carthaginians, who attacked and then conquered the settlement around 500 BC, subsequently renaming it **Hispalis**, meaning "flat land".

When the **Romans** finally wrested Spain from Carthage the Roman general Scipio founded **Itálica** in 206 on a hill overlooking the river. The final conquest of the peninsula cost the Romans a further two hundred years of dogged campaigning against the ferocious Iberian tribes, and in the latter stages of this struggle, during the Roman civil war, **Julius Caesar** captured Hispalis in 45 BC and renamed it Julia Romula ("Little Rome"). As a leading centre of the Roman province of Baetica (roughly corresponding to modern Andalucía) the city flourished and nearby Itálica provided Rome with two of its greatest second-century emperors, **Trajan** and **Hadrian**. The city later fell to the Visigoths, whose Christian archbishop **San Isidro** made sixth-century Seville into a European centre of learning.

Conquered by the **Moors** in 712, Seville briefly became **the capital of al-Andalus**. The Moors left an indelible imprint on the city, not only in its

Semana Santa

Nothing can prepare you for the overwhelming spectacle and passion of Semana Santa (Holy Week) in Andalucía. The most important celebration in the Christian calendar, it is at its most dramatic and intense here. Every town and village celebrates the feast in its own way, and a simple candlelit procession with floats of Christ and the Virgin passing through darkened streets in a hill village can be just as moving as the big city affairs. It's not all about piety either, as this is southern Spain, home of the fiesta, and between processions the bar scene is in full swing day and night.

Semana Santa in Seville

Seville, the vibrant, quintessential city of Andalucía, stages the most spectacular Semana Santa celebrations in the world. Its old quarter, the white walled Barrio Santa Cruz, provides the backdrop to a week of processions when the whole tragedy of the Passion is replayed with moving ceremony.

Seville's Gothic cathedral is the focus for the 57 **brotherhoods** (*hermandades*) who carry floats (*pasos*) bearing large and elaborately sculpted scenes from the Passion through streets lined with thousands of onlookers. As each *paso* represents a stage in the drama leading up to the Crucifixion (Palm Sunday, Betrayal by Judas, Judgment by Pilate), they normally process on the same day in Holy Week each year.

Several hundred members of each brotherhood accompany the *pasos* dressed as hooded penitents or **nazarenos**, wearing Ku Klux Klan-like capes and tall pointed caps leaving only narrow slits for the eyes. Many of these *hermandades* have impressive histories and some, such as **El Silencio**, date back to the thirteenth century. Each of the *hermandades* spends months preparing for their big day and their images of Christ and the Virgin are meticulously readied in their home church. Finally, the Virgin is draped in beautiful robes and adorned with valuable jewels. Then the whole glittering *paso* is decorated with a dazzling array of flowers.

Paso of La Piedad (the Pietà) ▲

Paso detail, Seville ▼

The role of the costaleros

La salida, the moment when the *paso* emerges from the church, is an occasion of great emotion and attracts huge crowds. This is when the skills of the **costaleros** – the men underneath the *paso* who are carrying it and remain concealed behind a curtain – are put to the test. Manoeuvring these delicate yet heavy floats (up to two tons in weight) is a hazardous operation, especially if church steps need to be negotiated. Its weight also means that it can only be carried for a short distance – usually 50m or so – before the *costaleros* have to rest. In fact, each *paso* has two teams of up to forty men, and even though one team rests while the other works, progress is still very slow.

▲ Paso crossing Puente de Triana, Seville

▼ Nazareno in procession, Seville

La Macarena

The climax of Semana Santa takes place during the early hours of **Good Friday**, when candlelit floats depicting the Crucifixion leave their churches at midnight and move through darkened

Local variations

Although processions through the streets to the cathedral or main church are common to all celebrations of Semana Santa, each town and village has its own customs and traditions. On Palm Sunday, the Alpujarras village of **Carataunas** starts its Passion week by tossing an image of Judas Iscariot onto a huge bonfire. **Málaga** has the largest *pasos* in Andalucía – many over 20m long carried by two hundred *costaleros* – and is where a prisoner is freed from the jail on the Wednesday of Holy Week and joins the parade. The hill village of **Carratraca** stages a daily Passion play in its bullring, with the villagers – dressed in costume – playing the part of the crowd. At **Baena**, in Córdoba province, streets resonate to the cacophony of two thousand drums as the processions move around the town.

streets, watched by sombre crowds and followed by a band playing traditional dirges. In Seville, the image of the crucified Christ is accompanied by the most important of the city's Virgins, **La Macarena**, a stirring seventeenth-century work by Luisa Roldán. As she nears the cathedral, where the air is thick with a pungent cocktail of fragrant orange blossom, incense and burning candle wax, an individual will often step out in front of the *paso* to sing an impromptu **lament** in flamenco style (a *saeta*), listened to by the silent crowd. When it's over, there's a ripple of applause and the *paso* moves on.

Paso of Christ being lowered from the cross, Seville ▲

La Macarena ▼

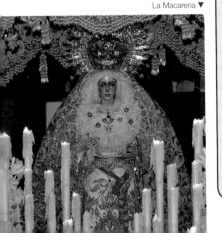

Traditions and customs

▶▶ **Depicting the Virgin** Semana Santa Virgins are portrayed in the trauma of the Passion and their tears are in fact priceless diamonds.

▶▶ **Dressing the statue** Even though a male sculptor will have carved it, no other man is allowed to see the Virgin unclothed, and dressing is carried out exclusively by female members of the brotherhoods.

▶▶ **Procession etiquette** When two processions cross each other's paths – inevitable in the major cities – the pasos of the Virgin and Christ salute each other in beautifully choreographed movements executed by both teams of *costaleros*. A poignant Semana Santa moment, this is always applauded by the crowd.

▶▶ **Bollos de cera** Processions in major cities deposit tons of candlewax onto the streets. Children pester the candle-toting penintents along the route for drops of wax which they "snowball" into a *bollo* – a Holy Week souvenir.

NO 8 DO

On every manhole cover, bus and public building in Seville you will see the curious cipher **NO 8 DO**. What looks like a figure 8 is actually the symbol of a twisted skein of wool (*madeja* in Spanish). During the eleventh-century *Reconquista*, Alfonso the Wise, king of Castile, tired of the endless war, made a truce with the Moors. This so angered his excitable son Sancho, that he rebelled against his father and launched a civil war. When the people of Seville stayed loyal to Alfonso, the king lauded them with the royal testimonial **"No me ha dejado"** ("You have not deserted me"). In medieval Spanish this came out as "*no ma dejado*" from which the *sevillanos* – long aficionados of word riddles – came up with NO MADEJA DO, soon encrypted as NO 8 DO and swiftly adopted as the city's crest.

architecture, but also in the Arabic-influenced local dialect, renaming the River Baetis Wadi El Kabir ("great river"), a title it still retains as the Guadalquivir. The **Almohad** dynasty of the twelfth and thirteenth centuries brought great prosperity, and when Seville was captured during the *Reconquista* by **Fernando III** in 1248 the city became a favoured residence of the Spanish monarchy, in particular Pedro the Cruel, who was responsible for the construction of the outstanding Mudéjar Alcázar. Religious intolerance racked the city in the wake of the Reconquest, however, and in 1391 the Jewish quarter in the Barrio Santa Cruz was sacked – a harbinger of the banishment of all Jews from Spain, to be proclaimed by Fernando and Isabel a century later.

The fifteenth century also saw, as well as the construction of the **Cathedral**, an event that would catapult the city to the forefront of Spanish affairs – the **discovery of the New World**. Seville's navigable river, with access to the Atlantic, made it a natural choice for the main port of commerce with the Americas. In the 1500s, as fabulous wealth poured in from the empire, Seville was transformed into one of the great cities of Europe and, with a population of over 150,000, one of the largest.

The **silting up of the Guadalquivir** in the 1680s deprived Seville of its port and with it the monopoly of trade with the Americas. The merchant fleet was transferred to Cádiz and the city went into a decline exacerbated by the great **earthquake** of 1755 which, although centred on Lisbon, caused much destruction. The city was further ravaged by the **Napoleonic occupation** of 1810–12 and was largely bypassed by the industrial revolution which permeated slowly from the north. It was only in the later nineteenth century that Seville was rediscovered by travellers such as Richard Ford, who declared it to be "the marvel of Andalucía".

Arrival

Seville's **airport** (☏95 467 65 49) is 12km northeast of town along the A4 (NIV) *autovía* towards Córdoba. From here the Amarillos airport bus (every 30min; 30min; €2.10) runs to the Avda. del Cid (also the departure point), close to the Fábrica de Tobacos, stopping at the train station en route. At the time of writing, the regulated taxi fare was €20 (plus €1 per bag) with a modest surcharge after 10pm and on Sunday. Check with the driver before setting off and if he does not agree to a fare similar to this, take another taxi. The city's **train station**, Santa Justa (☏902 24 02 02), is some way northeast of the centre, on Avenida Kansas City. A central point for train information and tickets is the RENFE office (Mon–Fri 9am–1.30pm & 4–7pm; ☏902 24 02 02), off Plaza Nueva at c/Zaragoza 29.

SEVILLE

Airport

Jardines
del Valle

San
Román

S. M. del
Socorro

Sta. Catalina

Convento
Sta. Paula

Convento de
Capuchinos

San
Hermenegildo

Convento
Sta. Isabel

S. Marcos

Jardín de
Capuchinos

Iglesia de
Sta. Marina

Palacio de
las Dueñas

S. Pedro

City
Walls

Hospital de
las Cinco
Llagas

Puerta
de la
Macarena

San Gil

LA MACARENA

Iglesia de
San Luis

Iglesia del la
Anunciación

Basílica de
la Macarena

Omnium
Sanctorum

CENTRO

Ciberducke @

Alameda de Hércules

S. Lorenzo y
Jesús del
Gran Poder

Monast.º de
Sta. Clara

Monasterio de
S. Clemente

S. Vicente

Meandro de San Jerónimo
(Río Guadalquivir)

0   250 m

Parque
Jardín del
Guadalquivir

La Cartuja

Centro
Andaluz
de Arte
Contemporáneo

ACCOMMODATION

Albergue Juvenil Sevilla	20
Hostal Alameda	33
Hostal Arias	17
Hostal Atenas	13
Hostal Doña Feli	35
Hostal Goya	15
Hostal La Gloria	38
Hostal La Muralla	18
Hostal Naranjo	39
Hostal Paco's	41

Hostal Pérez Montilla	3	Hostal Santa María		Hostal Unión	29	Hotel Amadeus	11
Hostal Puerta Carmona	1	de la Blanca	5	Hostería del Laurel	12	Hotel Casona de	
Hostal Redes	43	Hostal Sierpes	19	Hotel Adriano	34	San Andrés	27
Hostal Romero	44	Hostal Toledo	8	Hotel Alcántara	7	Hotel Casa Sacristía	
Hostal Santa María	21	Hostal Trajano	31	Hotel Alfonso XIII	16	Santa Ana	32

Main Bus Station

Prado de San Sebastián

Plaza de España

Internetia

Parque de María Luisa

MENÉNDEZ PELAYO

Jardines de Murillo

Casa de Pilatos

PLAZA DE STA. CRUZ

Jardines de los Reales Alcázares

Fábrica de Tabacos

SANTA CRUZ

Iglesia de Sta. Cruz

PLAZA DE LOS VENERABLES

Casino-Teatro Lope de Vega

San Leandro

Alcázar

San Ildefonso

Hotel Alfonso XIII

Palacio de San Telme

Museo del Baile Flamenco

Palacio Arzobispal

PL. DEL TRIUNFO

PL. VIRGEN DE LOS REYES

PUERTA DE JEREZ

El Salvador

Catedral

PLAZA DEL SALVADOR

Casa de la C. de Lebrija

Hospital de la Casidad

Torre del Oro

Ayuntamiento

PLAZA DE SAN FRANCISCO

Capillata de San José

PLAZA NUEVA

EL ARENAL

Teatro de la Maestranza

S. Buenaventura

Plaza de Toros de la Maestranza

Igl. de la Magdalena

See 'Seville: The Old City' map for detail

Santa Ana

Capilla de los Marineros

TRIANA

Museo de Bellas Artes

San Jacinto

Mercado del Barranco

Mercado de Triana

Plaza de Armas Bus Station

Nuestra Señora de la 'O'

Canal de Alfonso XIII

Puerta Triana

PLAZA PATROCINIO

PUERTO FLUVIAL

Bus #32 will get you from the train station to the central Plaza de la Encarnación, while bus lines #28 or C1 take you to the main Prado de San Sebastián (℡95 441 71 11) **bus station** on the eastern edge of the Barrio Santa Cruz. Most **buses** operate from here; however, services from and to northern Seville (including Itálica), Extremadura (provinces of Cáceres and Badajoz), Huelva province, Madrid and international destinations arrive and depart from the station at Plaza de Armas (℡95 490 80 40) by the Puente del Cachorro, on the river; from here, bus C3 will get you to the Prado de San Sebastián bus station.

Driving in Seville is an ordeal, especially in the narow streets of *barrios* such as Santa Cruz. Your best bet for parking is to find a pay car park (see the city map, p.250), or to choose a hotel with a garage (see p.253).

Information

Seville's **Turismo**, just south of the cathedral at Avda. de la Constitución 21 (Mon–Fri 9am–7.30pm, Sat 10am–3.30pm; ℡95 478 75 78), can provide good city maps and an excellent free monthly listings guide, *El Giraldillo* (ⓦwww .elgiraldillo.es), but is often overwhelmed in high season. There's a quieter and very helpful **municipal tourist office** (Mon–Fri 9am–7.30pm, Sat & Sun 10am–2pm; ℡954 22 17 14, ⓦwww.turismo.sevilla.org) at c/Arjona 28, next to the Puente de Triana (aka Isabell II) bridge on the east bank of the river, which gives information on the province as well as Seville itself. A smaller municipal office located in the Ayuntamiento building on Plaza de San Francisco (same hours; ℡95 459 01 88) is another possibility. Almost next door to the main Turismo, the Iconos tourist shop, Avda. Constitución 21, is the official sales point for the **SevilleCard** which gives you access to all the major monuments and (depending on which version you choose) can include free public transport and tour buses. If your time is limited and you plan to see as much as possible the card could save you money. The cheapest one-day version costs €28. The *Guía Verde Callejero* **street guide**, available from kioskos and bookshops, is an invaluable aid to finding your way around the city's more convoluted corners.

City transport

One of the best ways to see Seville is from a cycle saddle (see box, p.253). If you're planning on getting around a lot by **bus**, invest in a *bonobus* ticket which gives you ten rides for €6 and allows you to change lines on the same journey for up to an hour; otherwise all bus journeys throughout the city have a flat fare of €1.10. The *bonobus* is available from Tussam (Seville's bus company) street kiosks (there are central ones in Plaza Nueva and Plaza Encarnación), news stands or *estancos* (tobacconists). A Tussam route map is available from the same kiosks or tourist offices, or on their website ⓦwww.tussam.es. Useful buses are the C1, C3 (clockwise), C2 and C4 (anti clockwise) lines, which go roughly circularly around the city centre. The main central **taxi ranks** are in Plaza Nueva, the Alameda de Hércules and the Plaza de Armas and Prado de San

Seville online

A wide range of **online information** about Seville, its monuments, amenities and the province is available on ⓦwww.turismo.sevilla.org, ⓦwww.discoversevilla.com and ⓦwww.exploreseville.com.

Seville by bike

An enjoyable way to get around Seville is by **bike**: a wonderfully innovative new scheme by the Seville's local council is Sevici (ⓦwww.sevici.es; currently in Spanish only), a bike rental system with 250 pick-up/drop-off stations throughout the city. You pick up a bike, ride it to your destination and drop it off at the nearest station to your destination or (using the bike's lock) secure it to a stationery object. You are charged for the time the cycle is away from its station (ie on the road) – the first thirty minutes of each journey is free, after which it is €1 per hour or fraction of, €2 for the second hour and so on. When the bike is returned to one of the pick-up/drop-off stations and secured, the charging stops. At the end of the rental period your total hire bill will be deducted from the credit card which you use to register. The cycles are elegant new machines with gears and a luggage basket. You can pick up a seven-day hire card (the minimum subscription period) by registering with a credit card at machines located at each pick-up/drop-off station. Registering costs €5 and €150 will be deducted as security (refunded when your rental expires); the machine will also issue you with a subscriber card and a personal pin number. Allied to the scheme a network of cycle lanes has been constructed across the city making cycling in Seville not only pleasurable but also safe.

Sebastián bus stations. The basic charge for a short journey is around €4. Reliable taxi services include Radio Taxi, ☏95 458 00 00 and TeleTaxi ☏954 62 22 22.

One way to get to grips with the city is on one of the **open-top bus tours** operated by two companies – Sevirama (☏95 456 06 93) and Seville Tour (☏mobile 901101081). The buses leave half-hourly from the Torre del Oro, stopping at or near the main sites (€15).

Seville's new **tram** system (tickets €1.10) presently runs only from Plaza Nueva to the Prado de San Sebastian bus station but will be expanding in the years to come. A new **metro system** will eventually crisscross the city, the first sections of which – linking the southern suburbs to the Puerto de Jerez and Triana – should be opening in 2009.

Accommodation

Rooms in Seville are relatively expensive and during the big festivals you can find yourself paying ridiculous amounts for what is little more than a cell. Out of high season (early summer, Semana Santa and Feria de Abril), however, prices can drop dramatically, and with owners competing for trade, it's worth checking websites for special offers. For Semana Santa and the April *feria*, book as far ahead as possible. As most hotels and *hostales* regard high season as the two weeks covering Holy Week and the Feria de Abril (sometimes referred to as *temporada extra*) we have quoted the *temporada media* (mid-season) rate below, which applies to the rest of the year, barring January and February when prices are at their lowest.

By far the most attractive (and priciest) area to stay is the **Barrio Santa Cruz**. You'll find lower-priced options around its periphery (especially immediately north, and southeast towards the bus station). Central and more reasonably priced options are around the churches of **Santa Catalina** and **San Pedro**, and along as well as south of the newly revamped and tree-lined **Alameda de Hércules**. Also promising is the area north of the **Plaza Nueva** and the **Maestranza bullring**, especially the streets beyond c/Reyes Católicos towards the Museo de Bellas Artes. Further out still, but walkable from the centre, the solidly working-class *barrio* of **La Macarena** is a wonderful introduction to the real Seville.

Seville's **youth hostel** is out in the university district to the south of the centre, and the nearest **campsite** (see p.256) lies some 6km outside the city.

Barrio Santa Cruz and Cathedral area

Hostal Arias c/Mariana de Pineda 9 ☏ 95 421 83 89, ⓦ www.hostalarias.com. Cosy *hostal* with smart if simple rooms – all en suite with a/c and TV – in a quiet pedestrian street. ❸

Hostal Atenas c/Caballerizas 1 ☏ 95 421 80 47, ⓔ atenas@jet.es. A pretty, plant-festooned passage leads to a charming *pensión* decorated with *azulejos*; all rooms with bath and a/c. ❹

Hostal Pérez Montilla Plaza Curtidores 13 ☏ 95 442 18 54, ⓔ perezmontilla@hotmail.com. Spotless *hostal* on a tranquil square. Cheaper rooms come without bath and those with have a/c. Quoted prices can drop dramatically when business is slack. ❷

Hostal Puerta Carmona Plaza de San Agustín 5 ☏ 95 498 83 10, ⓦ www.hostalpuertacarmona.es. Very pleasant *hostal* owned by the proprietors of *Hotel Maestre* in Córdoba (see p.381). Good value modern en-suite rooms with a/c and TV; they will advise on where to park nearby. ❸

Hostal Santa María c/Hernando Colón 19 ☏ 95 422 85 05. Small, simple and friendly place on a busy street in the Giralda's shadow. All rooms en-suite, with a/c and TV. ❷

Hostal Santa María de la Blanca c/Santa María La Blanca ☏ 95 442 11 74. Friendly small *hostal* above a shop, through which you gain entry; has some en-suite a/c rooms plus cheaper ones sharing bath. ❷

Hostal Sierpes Corral del Rey 22, northeast of the cathedral ☏ 95 422 49 48, ⓦ www.hsierpes.com. Welcoming *hostal* with light and airy en-suite a/c rooms (104 & 306 are particularly spacious) arranged around a central patio. Has own restaurant and garage. ❹

Hostal Toledo c/Santa Teresa 15 ☏ 95 421 53 35. Atmospheric and recently refurbished *pensión* in the heart of the *barrio*. All rooms with bath, heating and a/c. ❹

Hostería del Laurel Plaza de los Venerables 5 ☏ 95 422 02 95, ⓦ www.hosteriadellaurel.com. Comfortable en-suite rooms above a very good restaurant and tapas bar. Superb location which can get a bit overrun with visitors in high season. ❺

Hotel Adriano c/Adriano 12, ☏ 95 429 38 00, ⓦ www.adrianohotel.com. Close to the bullring, this is a stylish two-star hotel where elegantly furnished a/c rooms come with satellite TV; there's also a roof terrace. ❻

Hotel Alcántara c/Ximénez de Enciso 28 ☏ 95 45 00 95, ⓦ www.hotelalcantara.net. Smart, compact two-star hotel close to Plaza Santa Cruz, with tastefully furnished a/c rooms. ❹–❺

Hotel Alfonso XIII c/San Fernando 2 ☏ 95 491 70 00, ⓦ www.hotel-alfonsoxiii.com. A monument in its own right (see p.269), this has a fair claim to being Seville's number-one hotel; the public rooms and patio are stunning but unless you're into pompous decor, a visit to the bar or restaurant might be a better suggestion than overnighting here. The cheapest double room currently costs €440. ❾ with breakfast.

🏃 **Hotel Amadeus** c/Farnesio 6, near the Iglesia de Santa Cruz ☏ 95 450 14 43, ⓦ www.hotelamadeussevilla.com. Welcoming hotel – housed in an eighteenth-century *casa señorial* – owned by an *aficionada* of the great composer. There's a grand piano for use by guests (other instruments can be borrowed), and the sound-proofed and stylish rooms come with a/c, satellite TV and wi-fi. The house is topped off with a stunning roof terrace for breakfast, where there's also a telescope for night-time astronomical contemplations. Public car park nearby. ❺

Hotel Doña Manuela Paseo de Catalina de Ribera 2 ☏ 95 454 64 00, ⓦ www.hoteldonamanuela.com. With views over the Jardines de Murillo from rooms on the west side this is a good value 2-star hotel with great location. Rooms are a/c, have satellite TV and there's a roof terrace with sun loungers. Own car park. ❺

Hotel El Rey Moro c/Lope de Rueda 14 ☏ 95 456 34 68, ⓦ www.elreymoro.com. Attractive new and reasonably priced hotel with elegantly furnished rooms and bathrooms – equipped with wi-fi and plasma TV – overlooking two patios. Ask for a room (any of nos. 10–25) on the "interior" (ie quieter) patio – the other gets noise from the hotel's restaurant. ❺

Hotel Goya c/Mateos Gago 31 ☏ 95 421 11 70, ⓦ www.hostalgoyasevilla.com. Small hotel with good range of attractive a/c en-suite rooms with satellite TV and wi-fi, in the heart of Santa Cruz. ❺

Hotel La Rábida c/Castelar 24 ☏ 95 422 09 60, ⓦ www.vinccihoteles.com. Recently refurbished traditional hotel with a nice patio, lots of marble and good facilities. Rooms in the older part have more character. Special offers (see website) can reduce rates considerably. ❻

🏃 **Hotel Las Casas de la Judería** c/Callejón de Dos Hermanas 7 ☏ 95 441 51 50, ⓦ www.casasypalacios.com. Stunningly beautiful old aristocratic mansion transformed into a delight-fully serene hotel with pastel-tinted rooms, exquisite patios and a restaurant. Good value for this category. Parking available. **7**

Hotel Las Casas de los Mercaderes c/Álvarez Quintero 12 ☎ 95 422 58 58, ⊛ www .casasypalacios.com. Luxurious hotel in converted former *bodega* with delightful patio, roof terrace and great views from some rooms (especially nos. 201–206). Good value for this category with own garage. **7**

Hotel Murillo c/Lope de Rueda 7 ☎ 95 421 60 95, ⊛ www.hotelmurillo.com. Traditional hotel in restored mansion with all facilities including wi-fi zone, plus amusingly kitsch features such as suits of armour, and paint-palette key rings. Also rents some attractive and full-equipped studios and apartments nearby (sleeping 1–5) for not much more than the room price (details on website). Public parking nearby. **5**

Hotel Simón c/García de Vinuesa 19 ☎ 95 422 66 60, ⊛ www.hotelsimonsevilla.com. Eighteenth-century mansion with elegant patio and excellent position near the cathedral. Pleasant a/c individu-ally styled rooms. **5**

🏃 **Las Casas del Rey de Baeza** Plaza Jesús de la Redención 2 ☎ 95 456 14 96, ⊛ www .hospes.es. Wonderful hotel with rooms arranged around an eighteenth-century *corral sevillano*. The plant-bedecked interior patio is charming and the stylishly furnished rooms come with traditional exterior *esparto* blinds, a neat finishing touch – and there's a rooftop pool to cool off. **7**

Pensión Doña Trinidad c/Archeros 7 ☎ 95 454 19 06, ⊛ www.donatrinidad.com. Sparkling new *hostal* with tastefully decorated en-suite rooms (some single) around a central patio. **3**

Plaza Nueva, Reyes Católicos and Museo de Bellas Artes

Hostal La Gloria c/San Eloy 58 ☎ 95 422 26 73, ⊛ www.hostallagloria.com. Very good value rooms, some en suite, in an exuberantly painted building – with pleasant roof terrace – above the *Café Zafiro*. **2**

Hostal Naranjo c/San Roque 11 ☎ 95 422 58 40, ⊛ www.bbsevilla.com. Welcoming and competi-tively priced *hostal* offering a/c en-suite rooms with TV; also has internet access and wi-fi. **3**

Hostal Paco's c/Pedro del Toro 7, off c/Gravina ☎ 95 421 71 83, ⊛ www.sol.com/hostales-sp. Friendly place with clean and economical en-suite rooms. The same proprietor has a number of similar *hostales* nearby (some sharing bath are even cheaper). **2**

Hostal Redes c/Redes 28 ☎ 95 490 19 46, ⊛ www.pensionredes.es. Clean and tidy *hostal*

where all rooms are en suite and fans are provided in summer. Extra charge for a/c. Internet access. **3**

Hostal Romero c/Gravina 21 ☎ 95 421 13 53. Basic but efficient *hostal* with another plant-bedecked patio. Rooms sharing bath and en suite (the latter come with TV and fans). **2**

Hotel Europa c/Jimios 5 ☎ 95 421 43 05, ⊛ www.hoteleuropasevilla.com. Elegant, traditional and friendly hotel in an eighteenth-century mansion that has comfortable rooms with safes and satellite TV. Garage available. **6**

Hotel Madrid c/San Pedro Mártir 22 ☎ 95 421 43 06, ⊛ www.hotelmadridsevilla. Pleasant family-run hotel offering functional a/c balcony rooms with TV. Internet access. **3**

Hotel Petit Palace c/Canalejas 2 ☎ 95 421 07 73, ⊛ www.hthoteles.com. The former *Hotel Plaza-Sevilla* has changed its name but a stunning Neoclassical facade – the work of Aníbal González, architect of the Plaza de España – remains the same. Rather small but well-equipped rooms come with PC and exercise cycle. **6**

Hotel Zaida c/San Roque 26 ☎ 95 421 11 38, ⊛ www.hotelzaida.com. Charming and intimate hotel with a fine exterior and an interior replete with Moorish-inspired decor. All rooms with bath, TV and a/c. Some of the single rooms lack light. **4**

Santa Catalina, San Pedro, Alameda de Hércules

Hostal Alameda Alameda de Hércules 31 ☎ 95 490 01 91, ⊛ www.hostalalameda.es. Modern, pleasant and very friendly *hostal* overlooking the tree-lined Alameda. En-suite rooms come with a/c and TV. **3**

🏃 **Hostal Doña Feli** Jesus del Gran Poder 130 ☎ 95 490 10 48, ⊛ www.hostaldfeli.com. At the northern end of the atmospheric Alameda de Hércules this is a very pleasant (and economically priced) small *hostal* with cosy en-suite rooms equipped with a/c and TV. Own garage with low rates. **2**

Hostal Trajano c/Trajano 3 ☎ &☎ 95 438 24 21. This friendly *hostal* has decent value en-suite rooms with TV. Can provide fans. **3**

Hostal Unión c/Tarifa 4 ☎ 95 422 92 94. One of this zone's best-value *hostales* where en-suite rooms come with a/c and TV. **2**

🏃 **Hotel Casa Sacristía Santa Ana** Alameda de Hercules 22 ☎ 95 491 57 22, ⊛ www .sacristiadesantaana.com. Beautiful new hotel with delightful rooms – the preferable external ones have Alameda views – inside a seventeenth-century *casa señorial* with many original features. The hotel has wi-fi and DVD players can be rented. **5**

Hotel Casona de San Andrés c/Daoiz 7 ☎95 491 52 53, ⓦ www.casonadesanandres.com. Former nineteenth-century *casa palacio* that's been transformed into a pleasant new hotel. Well-equipped balcony rooms face a pedestrianized square or two interior patios. ❺

Hotel Sevilla c/Daóiz 5, fronting the church of San Andrés ☎95 438 41 61, ⓦ www.hotel-sevilla.org. Revamped and refurbished pleasant old hotel with a nice patio, en-suite rooms with a/c and TV plus views (from front rooms) onto a pleasant *plazuela* near the church of San Andrés. ❹

🏃 Patio de la Alameda Alameda de Hércules 56 ☎95 490 49 99, ⓦ www .patiodelaalameda.com. Partly sixteenth-century *casa palacio* revamped into an elegant and fair-priced apart-hotel with light and airy balcony rooms (with kitchenette) plus three patios and own garage. ❺

🏃 Patio de la Cartuja c/Lumbreras 8 ☎95 490 02 00, ⓦ www.patiosdesevilla.com. Unique, stylish and excellent-value apart-hotel created from an old *corral sevillano*, with balconies around a tiled patio. All rooms have kitchen and *salon* and there's a garage. ❺

La Macarena

Hostal La Muralla c/Macarena 52 ☎95 437 10 49, ⓦ www.terra.es/personal8/hmuralla. Pleasant and good-value *hostal* facing the medieval walls. All rooms are en suite and come with bath, a/c and TV. Own car park. ❷

Hotel San Gil c/Parras 28 ☎95 490 68 11, ⓦ www.fp-hoteles.com. Luxurious hotel in a beautifully restored early 1900s *palacio*. Rooms are bright and spacious, there's a garden with palms and cypresses, plus rooftop pool, garage, and an interior decorated with mosaics and *azulejos*. ❼ with breakfast.

Youth hostel and campsites

Albergue Juvenil Sevilla c/Isaac Peral 2 ☎95 461 31 50, ⓦ www.inturjoven.com. Seville's leafy if sometimes crowded youth hostel has basic en-suite double and triple rooms. It's also some way out: take bus #34 from Puerta de Jerez by the Turismo or from Plaza Nueva. Note that they tend not to answer the phone. Under 26 €16, over 26 €20.

Camping Villsom 10km out of town on the main Cádiz road ☎&ⓕ95 472 08 28. Recently overhauled campsite with a pool. Half-hourly buses from c/La Rabida (near the Fábrica de Tabacos) take 20min. Make sure to take the bus M-132 signed "Dos Hermanas por Barriadas", which will drop you outside the campsite.

Club de Campo 12km south of the centre in Dos Hermanas ☎95 472 02 50, ⓕ95 472 63 08. Pleasant, shady site with pool which has the edge on the nearby *Villsom*. Follow the directions for *Camping Villsom* (above) but take bus M-132 signed "Dos Hermanas Directo" (direct route), a 20min trip.

The City

The **old city**, where you'll spend most of your time, takes up the east bank of the Guadalquivir. At its heart, side by side, stand the three great monuments: the **Giralda tower**, the **Cathedral** and the **Alcázar**, with the cramped alleyways of the **Barrio Santa Cruz**, the medieval Jewish quarter and now the heart of tourist life, extending east of them. North and west of the *barrio* is the main shopping and commercial district, its most obvious landmarks the **Plaza Nueva** and **Plaza Duque de la Victoria**, and the smart pedestrian-ized **Calle Sierpes** which runs between them. To the north of the area enclosed by the medieval walls lies the gritty **Macarena quarter**, from whose church the *paso* of the bejewelled Virgin of Macarena – the most revered in Seville – sails forth on the Maundy Thursday of Semana Santa to enormous popular acclaim. Just beyond the walls here in the converted sixteenth-century Hospital de las Cinco Llagas ("Five Wounds of Christ") is the permanent seat of the **Andalucian parliament**.

Across the river is the earthier, traditionally working-class district of **Triana**, flanked to the south by **Los Remedios**, the former business zone and now an upmarket residential quarter. Adjoining this to the south lie the grounds where Seville's Feria de Abril is held, and also on this bank, to the north of Triana, lie the remains of the Expo 92 exhibition ground, at Isla de la Cartuja.

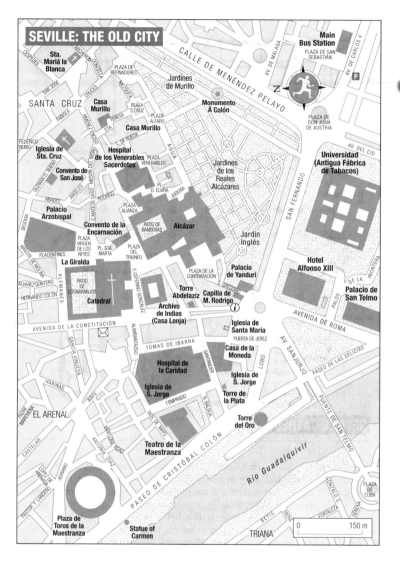

The Cathedral and the Giralda

After the Reconquest of Seville by Fernando III (1248), the Almohad mosque was consecrated to the Virgin Mary and kept in use as the Christian cathedral. As such it survived until 1402, when the cathedral chapter dreamed up plans for a new and unrivalled monument to Christian glory: "a building on so magnificent a scale that posterity will believe we were mad". To this end the Almohad mosque (see box, p.262) was almost entirely demolished, and the largest Gothic church in the world, Seville's **Cathedral** (July–Aug Mon–Sat 9.30am–4pm, Sun 2.30–6pm; Sept–June Mon–Sat 11am–5pm, Sun 2.30–6pm; ticket valid for

Puerta del Perdón
(Exit)

C. ALEMANES

C. ALEMANES

N

Parroquia
del Sagrario

Biblioteca
Colombina

Patio de los Naranjos

Capilla de
San Antonio

Puerta de
la Concepción

Puerta del Lagarto

GIRALDA

PLAZA
VIRGEN
DE LOS
REYES

Puerta del
Baptisterio

Capilla de
San Pedro

Puerta
Principal

Tomb of
Hernando
Colón

Coro

Capilla
Mayor

AVENIDA DE LA CONSTITUCION

Capilla
Real

Puerta del
Nacimiento
(de San Miguel)

Tomb of
C. Colón

Puerta de las
Campanillas

Monument to
Cristóbal Colón

Capilla de
San Andrés

Bookshop

Puerta de
S. Cristóbal

PLAZA DEL
TRIUNFO

Sala
Capitular

Visitor's
Entrance

Sacristía
de los Cálices

Sacristía Mayor

SEVILLE CATHEDRAL

Cathedral and Giralda tower; €7.50, under-16s free; Ⓦ www.catedraldesevilla.es),
was completed, extraordinarily, in just over a century (1402–1506). As Norman
Lewis said, "it expresses conquest and domination in architectural terms of sheer
mass". Built upon the huge, rectangular base-plan of the old mosque whose
minaret, the Giralda, now served as the bell tower, it was given the extra
dimension of height by the Christian architects, probably under the direction of
the French master architect of Rouen Cathedral. It was previously reckoned to
be the third-largest church in the world – after St Paul's in London and St Peter's
in Rome – but new calculations based on cubic measurements have now placed
it in the number one position, a claim upheld by the *Guinness Book of Records*, a
copy of whose certificate is proudly displayed in the church.

Entry to the cathedral is through the **Puerta de San Cristóbal,** on the
building's south side where, beyond a reception area displaying minor artworks
by Murillo and Zurbarán among others, you enter the church to the west of
the portal itself. If you're interested in studying the abundant artworks dotted
around the various chapels en route, visit the bookshop at the entrance to
obtain a copy of the official *Guide to the Cathedral of Seville*, which deals with
them in detail.

Turn right once inside to head east, where you are soon confronted by an enormous late nineteenth-century **Cristobal Colón** (**Monument to Christopher Columbus**), by *sevillano* sculptor Arturo Mélida, which may or may not be the navigator's tomb. It was originally intended to be erected in the Cuban cathedral of Havana, then a Spanish colony, where it would become a sepulchre for Columbus's remains, but the Spanish-American War – and Cuba's subsequent independence – intervened. As a result the plans were changed and the work was placed here in Seville's cathedral. The mariner's coffin is held aloft by four huge allegorical figures, representing the kingdoms of León, Castile, Aragón and Navarra; the lance of Castile should be piercing a pomegranate (now inexplicably missing), the symbol of Granada (and the word for the fruit in Spanish), the last Moorish kingdom to be reconquered.

Moving into the **nave**, first impressions are of the sheer size and grandeur of the place, but as you grow accustomed to the gloom, two other qualities stand out with equal force: the rhythmic balance and interplay between the parts, and an impressive overall simplicity and restraint in decoration. Successive ages have left monuments of their own, but these have been limited to the two rows of side chapels. In the main body of the cathedral only the great box-like structure of the **coro** (choir) stands out, filling the central portion of the nave.

The *coro* extends and opens onto the **Capilla Mayor**, dominated by a vast and fabulous **Gothic retablo** composed of 45 carved scenes from the life of Christ. Begun in 1482 and the lifetime's work of a single craftsman, Fleming Pieter Dancart, this is the supreme masterpiece of the cathedral – the largest and richest altarpiece in the world and one of the finest examples of Gothic woodcarving. Above the central tabernacle, the **Virgen de la Sede** (Virgin of the Chair) is a stunning thirteenth-century Gothic figure of silver-plated cedar. Just to the right, a panel depicts an **image of the Giralda** as it appeared prior to any Renaissance additions.

Before proceeding around the edge of the nave in a clockwise direction it's best to backtrack to the church's southeast corner to take in the **Sacristía de los Cálices** where many of the cathedral's main art treasures are displayed. Among some outstanding works are a masterly *Santas Justa y Rufina* by Goya, depicting Seville's patron saints who were put to death in 287 during the Roman emperor Diocletian's persecution of the Christians. Behind the **Capilla de San Andres**, which has an exceptional polychromed image of the crucified Christ by Martinez Montañés, lies the grandiose sixteenth-century **Sacristía Mayor** designed in 1528 by Diego de Riaño. It's a prime example of the rich Plateresque style, and Riaño was one of the foremost exponents of this predominantly decorative architecture of the late Spanish Renaissance. Forming a veritable church-within-a-church it induced Philip II to remark to the members of the chapter: "Your sacristy is finer than my Chapel Royal". The sacristy houses more paintings, including a poignant *Santa Teresa* by Zurbarán, and the treasury, a dull collection of silver reliquaries and monstrances. Also here are the **keys** presented to Fernando by the Jewish and Moorish communities on the surrender of the city; sculpted into the Moor's key in stylized Arabic script are the words "May Allah render eternal the dominion of Islam in this city". Nearby is a polychromed image of Fernando III by Pedro Roldán, one of Andalucía's great eighteenth-century sculptors.

Through a small antechamber here – and beyond the diminutive Patio del Cabildo – you enter the remarkable oval-shaped **Sala Capitular** (Chapter House), whose elaborate domed ceiling is mirrored in the outstanding geometric marble decoration of the floor. The stone benches provide seats for the members of the chapter. It contains a number of paintings by Murillo, a native of Seville, the finest of which, a flowing *Concepción Inmaculada*, occupies a place of honour high above the bishop's throne.

The route continues by proceeding to the southwest corner and the **Puerta del Nacimiento**, the door through which pass all the *pasos* and penitents who take part in the Semana Santa processions, and then turning right (north) along the west wall, passing the **Puerta Principal**. In the northwest corner the **Capilla de San Antonio** contains the *Vision of St Anthony*, a magnificent work by Murillo, depicting the saint in ecstatic pose before an infant Christ emerging from a luminous golden cloud. Try and spot where the restorers joined San Antonio back into place after he had been crudely hacked out of the picture by thieves in the nineteenth century. He was eventually discovered in New York – where art dealers recognized the work they were being asked to buy – and returned to the cathedral. The *Baptism of Jesus* above this is another fine work by the same artist. The nave's north side leads to the **Puerta de la Concepción**, where an altar on the left side has a fine portrayal of the *Virgen de Belén* painted in 1635 by *granadino* artist Alonso Cano. Before exiting here, head for the northeast corner to view the domed Renaissance **Capilla Real** (normally open for daily services at 8.30am, noon and 5pm), built on the site of the original royal burial chapel and containing the body of Fernando III (El Santo) in a suitably rich, Baroque silver sepulchre before the altar. The large tombs on either side of the chapel are those of Fernando's

Where lies Christopher Columbus?

The dispute about **Christopher Columbus**'s birthplace – claimed by both Italy and Spain – is matched by the labyrinthine controversy surrounding the whereabouts of his **remains**.

After his death in **Valladolid** in 1506, Columbus was originally buried there, but three years later his remains were removed to **Seville** and interred at the monastery of Santa María de las Cuevas, across the river on La Cartuja island, to be joined shortly afterwards by those of his son Diego. But Diego's widow was determined to have both bodies interred in Hispaniola (modern Haiti and the Dominican Republic), the site of Columbus's first landfall in 1492, the capital of Spanish America and where Diego had served as governor. Following an intervention by the emperor Carlos V supporting her wishes, in 1544 the remains of both bodies were packed into lead coffins and shipped to the island, where they were placed in the cathedral. The remains of Columbus's grandson, Luís, were interred in the same cathedral in 1783.

Later, during repairs to the cathedral in Hispaniola, it seems that the coffins were mislaid, then opened, and the names mixed up. It did not take the authorities long to resolve the dilemma of which was which, by having all three sets of remains placed in one coffin. Shortly after 1795, when Spain was forced to cede Santo Domingo to the French, the remains were moved to Cuba and the cathedral in **Havana**, still Spanish territory. When Cuba was lost in 1898 the remains were transported back across the Atlantic and placed in the tomb in Seville. The lingering uncertainty lies in the accidental discovery in 1879 of another lead coffin in the cathedral in **Santo Domingo** bearing a silver plate inscribed with Columbus's name. This box of remains then disappeared, and despite the government of the Dominican Republic's claim to have recovered them (now enshrined in a national monument), numerous coffins of bones claiming to be the same have made frequent appearances at auction houses ever since.

Were the correct remains dispatched from Santo Domingo to Havana in 1795? Was the discovery of 1879 a fraud? Are the remains in the tomb today really those of Christopher, Diego and Luís? The only certainty in the story is that one member of wife, Beatrice of Swabia, and his son, Alfonso the Wise. To the left of here, the **Capilla de San Pedro** has a fine seventeenth-century *retablo* by Diego López Bueno with nine Zurbarán scenes depicting the life of St Peter (except for the image of God, which is a later replacement). Also here is the Puerta del Lagarto (Door of the Alligator), so named in commemoration of a stuffed reptile given to Alfonso X by the sultan of Egypt in 1260. A wooden replica now hangs in place of the perished original.

The Giralda and the Patio de los Naranjos

The entrance to the **Giralda** (same ticket as the cathedral) lies to the left of the Capilla Real. Unquestionably the most beautiful building in Seville, the Giralda, named after the sixteenth-century *giraldillo* or weather vane on its summit, dominates the skyline and, with its perfect synthesis of form and decoration, is one of the most important examples of Islamic architecture in the world.

The **minaret** – said to be built on a foundation of destroyed Roman statuary – was the culmination of Almohad architecture, and served as a model for those at the imperial capitals of Rabat and Marrakesh. It was designed by the architect of the original mosque, Ahmed ibn Baso, and was used by the Moors both for calling the faithful to prayer and as an observatory. They so worshipped the building that they planned to destroy it before the Christian conquest of Seville, but were prevented from doing so by the threat of Alfonso (later King Alfonso X)

the Columbus family, at least, was buried in Seville's cathedral and has stayed here – Christopher's bookish son Hernando, who wrote a biography of his father and donated his large library to what became the cathedral's **Biblioteca Colombina**. His tombstone lies in the centre of the pavement towards the main west door, the Puerta Principal, flanked by smaller slabs portraying sailing vessels.

In 2002, science was called on to try to resolve the mystery and a plan was drawn up to subject all the known remains of Columbus family members to DNA testing in the hope that a common genetic code could be established. Initial reports on samples taken from the Seville tomb by scientists at Granada university were inconclusive due to the poor condition of the remains, although the tests did indicate that there were matches with other members of the family. A request was then made to test the remains in Santo Domingo which – if this proved negative – would go some way to confirming the authenticity of those in Seville. After initially agreeing to this request the government of the Dominican Republic had second thoughts. An announcement by scientists that the Santo Domingo remains are not those of Columbus would be hugely embarrassing for a country where the navigator is a national hero. Thus in early 2005 the republic's government stated that it didn't have sufficient confidence in the reliability of DNA testing to allow the research to go ahead. When the Spanish ambassador announced that Spain would not make an issue of the matter the outcome of this tortuously tangled tale was, for the time being, put on hold, leaving the location of Columbus's remains a mystery for at least a few more years yet.

Some experts are convinced that Columbus's remains may lie in both the Dominican Republic and Seville as the remains found in the cathedral tomb do not make up a complete skeleton. When the Dominican Republic eventually allows access to their remains it could well be proven that the navigator's bones lie on both sides of the Atlantic: a messy but probably apt ending to the story. Experts are now using the DNA samples to try to unravel the other prickly problem – where he was born.

that "if they removed a single stone, they would all be put to the sword". Instead the Giralda went on to become the bell tower of the Christian cathedral. The Patio de los Naranjos (see below), the old entrance to the mosque, also survives intact.

From inside the cathedral you can ascend to the **bell chamber** for a remarkable view of the city – and, equally remarkable, a glimpse of the Gothic details of the cathedral's buttresses and statuary. Keep an eye out, too, for the colony of kestrels which has long nested in the tower – the descendants no doubt of the "twittering, careering hawks" seen by Ford when he climbed up here in the 1830s. Most impressive is the tower's inner construction, a series of 35 gently inclined ramps wide enough for two mounted guards to pass. The Moorish structure took twelve years to build (1184–96) and derives its firm, simple beauty from the shadows formed by blocks of brick trelliswork or *ajaracas*, different on each side, and relieved by a succession of arched niches and windows. The original harmony has been somewhat blemished by the Renaissance-era addition of balconies and, to a still greater extent, by the four diminishing storeys of the belfry – added, along with the Italian-sculpted bronze figure of Faith which surmounts them, in 1560–68, following the demolition by an earthquake of the original copper spheres. The fact that a weathervane blown by the four winds should epitomize the ideal of constant faith, or that this female figure should possess a masculine name ("Giraldillo"), has never seemed to trouble whimsical *sevillanos*.

To reach the cathedral's **exit**, retrace your steps to the Puerta de la Concepción and pass through here to enter the **Patio de los Naranjos**, taking its name from the orange trees that now shade the former mosque's entrance courtyard where ritual ablutions were performed prior to worship. In the centre of the

---

Moorish Seville

Seville was one of the earliest **Moorish conquests** (in 712) and, as part of the caliphate of Córdoba, became the second city of al-Andalus. When the caliphate broke up in the early eleventh century it was by far the most powerful of the independent states (or *taifas*) to emerge, extending its power over the Algarve and eventually over Jaén, Murcia and Córdoba itself. This period, under a series of three Arabic rulers from the Abbadid dynasty (1023–91), was something of a golden age. The city's court was unrivalled in wealth, luxury and sophistication, developing a strong chivalric element and a flair for poetry – one of the most skilled exponents was the last ruler, al Mu'tamid, the "poet-king". But with sophistication came decadence, and in 1091 Abbadid rule was usurped by a new force, the **Almoravids**, a tribe of fanatical Berber Muslims from North Africa, to whom the Andalucians had appealed for help against the threat from the northern Christian kingdoms.

Despite initial military successes, the Almoravids failed to consolidate their gains in al-Andalus and attempted to rule through military governors from Marrakesh. In the middle of the twelfth century they were in turn supplanted by a new Berber incursion, the **Almohads**, who by about 1170 had recaptured virtually all the former territories. Seville accepted Almohad rule in 1147 and became the capital of this last real empire of the Moors in Spain. Almohad power was sustained until their disastrous defeat in 1212 by the combined Christian armies of the north, at Las Navas de Tolosa in Jaén. Within this brief and precarious period Seville underwent a renaissance of public building, characterized by a new vigour and fluidity of style. The Almohads rebuilt the Alcázar, enlarged the principal **mosque** and erected a new and brilliant minaret, a tower over 100m tall, topped with four copper spheres that could be seen from miles around: the Giralda.

patio a **Moorish fountain** incorporates a sixth-century carved marble font, a surviving remnant of the earlier Visigothic cathedral which was itself levelled to make way for the mosque. Cross to the patio's northern side and the **Puerta del Perdón**, the mosque's original entrance. Although sadly marred by Renaissance embellishments, there remains some exquisite Almohad plasterwork and the original great doors made from larchwood faced with bronze. Minute Kufic script inside the lozenges proclaims that "the empire is Allah's". The pierced bronze door-knockers are copies of the beautiful hand-crafted twelfth-century originals now preserved inside the church (not currently on view).

The Archivo de las Indias and the Ayuntamiento

Should you have been inspired by the Columbus saga after seeing his monument in the cathedral, visit the **Casa Lonja**, opposite the cathedral. Built in the severe and uncompromising style of El Escorial near Madrid, and designed by the same architect, Juan de Herrera, it was the former merchants' commodity exchange (*lonja*), adapted in the eighteenth century to house the remarkable **Archivo de las Indias** (Mon–Sat 9am–4pm, Sun 10am–2pm; free), a monumental storehouse of the archives of the Spanish empire. Following the building's three-year restoration programme the archive (holding 38,000 documents and files covering four centuries of Spanish rule) has been moved around the corner to the Cilla Cabildo in c/Tormes. This now enables you to appreciate Herrera's masterpiece in all its splendour. The exterior is defined by four identical facades, while corner pyramids supporting weathervanes are the main decorative feature. Inside, the sumptuous marble floors, bookcases in Cuban wood, arcaded central patio and grand staircase in pink and black marble are a visual feast. The upper floor houses temporary exhibitions of interesting documents from the archive; these frequently include items such as Columbus's log and a letter from Cervantes (pre-*Don Quijote*) petitioning the king for a position in the Americas – fortunately for world literature, he was turned down.

Another building worth a visit and sited to the north of the cathedral is the sixteenth-century **Ayuntamiento** at the top of Avenida de la Constitución, with a richly ornamented Plateresque facade by Diego de Riaño, one of the finest in Spain. Substantially enlarged early in the nineteenth century, the building's western exterior facing Plaza Nueva dates entirely from this time and forgoes the exuberant decoration of the original. The interior – decorated with numerous artworks including canvases by Zurbarán and Murillo – is open for guided visits allowing Riaño's star-vaulted **vestíbulo** (entrance hall), the elaborately ornate **Sala de Consistorio** (council chamber) and an **upper Sala de Consistorio** above it, with a ravishing gilded coffered ceiling dating from the time of Philip II, to be seen (Tues, Wed, Thurs at 5.30pm; closed Aug; free). During the Semana Santa processions Plaza de San Francisco in front of the Ayuntamiento is part of the official route leading to the cathedral, and huge temporary grandstands fill the square providing prime vantage points for the city's dignitaries and their families and friends. The pointed *capirote* hoods worn by the penitent brotherhoods are eerily identical to those worn by the inquisitors of the Spanish Inquisition who, between the fifteenth and eighteenth centuries, sentenced an untold number of "heretics" to death by burning in public *autos da fé*, or trials, held in this same square.

The Alcázar

Rulers of Seville occupied the site of the **Alcázar** (April–Sept Tues–Sat 9.30am–7pm, Sun 9.30am–5pm; Oct–March Tues–Sat 9.30am–5pm,

Sun 9.30am–1.30pm; €7; Ⓦ www.patronato-alcazarsevilla.es) from the time of the Romans. The fortified palace was probably founded in the eighth century on the ruins of a Roman barracks, with the surrounding walls being added in the ninth.

In the eleventh century it was expanded to become the great court of the Abbadid dynasty, who turned the wealth gained from the production of olive oil, sugar cane and dyes into a palace worthy of their hubris. This regime reached a peak of sophistication and decadence under the ruthless al Mu'tamid, a ruler who further enlarged the Alcázar in order to house a harem of eight hundred women, and decorated the terraces with flowers planted in the skulls of his decapitated enemies. Later, in the twelfth and thirteenth centuries under the **Almohads**, the complex was turned into a citadel, forming the heart of the town's fortifications. Its extent was enormous, stretching to the Torre del Oro on the bank of the Guadalquivir. Parts of the Almohad walls survive, but the present structure dates almost entirely from the Christian period following the fall of the city in 1248.

Seville was a favoured residence of the Spanish kings for some four centuries after the Reconquest – most particularly of **Pedro the Cruel** (Pedro I, 1350–69) who, with his mistress María de Padilla, lived in and ruled from the Alcázar. Pedro embarked upon a complete rebuilding of the palace, utilizing fragments of earlier

Visiting the Alcázar

The pressure of visitors to the **Alcázar** has resulted in the introduction of a flow-control system whereby 750 people are allowed in every 20–30min. It's still advisable, however, to visit early morning or late afternoon to savour the experience in relative calm. An official guidebook to the complex on sale at the entrance has detailed maps of the palaces and information on the gardens beyond.

Moorish buildings in Seville, Córdoba and Valencia. Pedro's works form the nucleus of the Alcázar as it is today and, despite numerous restorations necessitated by fires and earth tremors, offer some of the best surviving examples of **Mudéjar architecture** – the style developed by Moors working under Christian rule. Later monarchs have also left many traces and additions. In the fifteenth century Isabel built a new wing in which to organize expeditions to the Americas and control the new territories; in the sixteenth century Carlos V married a Portuguese princess in the palace, adding huge apartments for the occasion; and under Felipe IV (c.1624) extensive renovations were carried out to the existing rooms. On a more mundane level, kitchens were installed to provide for General Franco, who stayed in the royal apartments whenever he visited Seville.

The Patio del León and Patio de la Montería

The Alcázar is entered from the Plaza del Triunfo, adjacent to the cathedral, through the **Puerta del León**, which bears a heraldic image of a lion in fourteenth-century glazed tiles above the lintel. The gateway, flanked by original Almohad walls, opens onto a courtyard – the Patio del León – where Pedro (who was known as "the Just" as well as "the Cruel", depending on one's fortunes) used to give judgement; to the left is the **Sala de Justicia** built by Alfonso XI in the 1340s with exquisite *yesería* (plasterwork) in the Grenadine style and a beautiful *artesonado* ceiling. Beyond, the restored **Patio del Yeso** has more fine plasterwork and the whole patio is the only visible surviving remnant of the Almohads' Alcázar. The main facade of Pedro's palace stands at the end of an inner court, the **Patio de la Montería**, or "hunting patio", where the royal hunt gathered; on either side are galleried buildings erected by Isabel. This principal facade is pure fourteenth-century Mudéjar and, with its delicate, marble-columned windows, stalactite frieze and overhanging roof, is one of the finest features of the whole Alcázar. The castles, lions and other heraldic devices were intended to emphasize the king's power over both Christians and Muslims, but Kufic lettering still proclaims that "There is no God but Allah".

The Salón del Almirante

It's a good idea to look round the **Salón del Almirante** (or Casa de la Contración de Indias), the sixteenth-century building on the right, before entering the main palace. Founded by Isabel in 1503 as an office where personnel could be hired to man expeditions to the New World, this gives you a standard against which to assess the Moorish forms. Many of the early voyages were planned in the first room, the **Cuarto del Almirante**, a name that commemorates Columbus's appointment as Gran Almirante (Senior Admiral), although he probably never used it. Balboa, discoverer of the Pacific, Vincente Pinzón, discoverer of the Amazon, and many other *conquistadores* all spread their maps across tables here and planned the plunder of the Americas. Most of the rooms seem too heavy, their decoration ceasing to be an integral part of the design, and much of the time many of them are closed to public view – as is the whole of the upper floor (except for periodic visits, see below), which provides the residence of the royal family when staying in Seville. The only notable exception, architecturally speaking, is the **Sala de Audiencias** (or Capilla de los Navigantes), with its magnificent *artesonado* ceiling inlaid with golden rosettes. Within is a fine early sixteenth-century *retablo* by Alejo Fernández depicting the *Virgin of the Navigators* spreading her protective mantle over the *conquistadores* and their ships – which are so well portrayed that they have been of great assistance to naval historians. Columbus (dressed in gold) is flanked by the Pinzón brothers who sailed with him on his first voyage to the New World, while Carlos V (in a red cloak) shelters beneath the Virgin. In the rear to the left are the kneeling figures of the Indians to whom the dubious blessings of Christianity had been brought by the Spanish conquest. The painting synthesizes the sense of a divine mission – given to Spain by God – prevalent at the time. Beside the altarpiece stands a model of the *Santa María*, Columbus's first flagship. Slightly further along the patio to the right lies the entrance to the **Sala de los Azulejos** containing a display of relatively modern tilework and, beyond, a couple of delightfully serene patios.

The royal apartments, known as the **Palacio Real Alto**, have now been opened for visits when not in use and shouldn't be missed. A temporary desk located in front of the Salón del Almirante sells tickets (an additional €4) for a guided tour lasting about thirty minutes. This takes in the royal chapel, with an exquisite early sixteenth-century **retablo** consisting of painted *azulejos* (tiles) by Nicola Pisano, the so-called bedroom of Pedro I, with fine early Mudéjar plasterwork and *artesonado* ceiling, and the equally splendid **Sala de Audiencias** – with more stunning plaster and tile decoration – which is still used by the royal family when receiving visitors in Seville.

The Palace of Pedro I

Entering the main **Palace of Pedro I**, the "domestic" nature of Moorish and Mudéjar architecture is immediately striking. This involves no loss of grandeur but simply a shift in scale: the apartments are remarkably small, shaped to human needs, and take their beauty from the exuberance of the decoration and the imaginative use of space and light. There is, too, a deliberate disorientation in the layout of the rooms, which makes the palace seem infinitely larger and more open than it really is. From the entrance court a narrow passage leads beyond the **Vestibulo**, where visitors removed their outer clothing, straight into the central courtyard, the **Patio de las Doncellas** (Patio of the Maidens), its name recalling the Christians' tribute of one hundred virgins presented annually to the Moorish kings. The heart of the patio has been restored to its fourteenth-century original state after being buried under a tiled pavement for four centuries. Archeologists have replanted the six orange trees that once grew in sunken gardens to either side of a central pool, filled with goldfish – as it was in the time of Pedro I – a medieval method of eliminating mosquitoes in summer. The court's plaster frieze and dado composed of polychrome *azulejos* and doors are all of the highest Granada craftsmanship, and are the finest in the palace. Interestingly, it's also the one location where Renaissance restorations are successfully fused – the double columns and upper storey were added by Carlos V, whose *Plus Ultra* ("Yet still further") motto recurs in the decorations here and elsewhere.

Past the **Salón de Carlos V**, distinguished by a truly magnificent *artesonado* ceiling, are three rooms from the original fourteenth-century design built for María de Padilla (who was popularly thought to use magic in order to maintain her hold over Pedro – and perhaps over other gallants at court, too, who used to drink her bath water). These open onto the **Salón de Embajadores** (Salon of the Ambassadors), the most brilliant room of the Alcázar, with a stupendous

ALCÁZAR (PALACE OF PEDRO I)

Salon de Carlos V

Habitaciones de Maria de Padilla

Palacio de Carlos V

Capilla

Patio de Las Doncellas

Salon de Embajadores

Comedor

Dormitorio de Felipe II

Dormitorio de los Reyes Moros

Patio de las Muñecas

Dormitorio de Isabel la Católica

Alhamia

Vestibulo

Cuarto del Principe

N

Main Entrance

wooden dome of red, green and gold cells, and horseshoe arcades inspired by the great palace of Medina Azahara outside Córdoba. An inscription in Arabic states that it was constructed by craftsmen from Toledo and completed in 1366. Although restored, for the worse, by Carlos V – who added balconies and an incongruous frieze of royal portraits to commemorate his marriage to Isabel of Portugal here – the salon stands comparison with the great rooms of Granada's Alhambra. Note also the original **Mudéjar tiles**, with their Moorish geometric patterns expressing artistically the fundamental Islamic tenet of the harmony of creation. Adjoining are a long dining hall (*comedor*) and a small apartment installed in the late sixteenth century for Felipe II.

Beyond is the last great room of the palace, the **Patio de las Muñecas** (Patio of the Dolls), which takes its curious name from two tiny faces decorating the inner and outer surfaces of one of the smaller arches. The elegant columns in the tenth-century Caliphate style are believed to have come from the ruins of Medina Azahara near Córdoba. Thought to be the site of the harem in the original palace, it was here that Pedro is reputed to have murdered his brother Don Fadrique in 1358; another of his royal guests, Abu Said of Granada, was murdered here for his jewels, one of which, an immense ruby which Pedro later gave to Edward, England's "Black Prince", now figures in the British Crown Jewels. The upper storey of the court is a much later, nineteenth-century restoration. On the other sides of the patio are the **bedrooms** of Isabel and of her son Don Juan, and the arbitrarily named Dormitorio del los Reyes Moros (Bedroom of the Moorish Kings).

Palacio de Carlos V and the Alcázar gardens

To the northeast of the main palace (and reached via a stairway out of the southeast corner of the Patio de las Doncellas) loom the large and soulless apart-ments of the **Palacio de Carlos V**. With its many tapestries (eighteenth-century

▲ The Estanque del Mercurio and the Alcázar gardens

copies of the sixteenth-century originals now in Madrid) and pink-orange or yellow paintwork, the apartments' classical style asserts a different and inferior mood to the main palace. It's best to hurry through to the beautiful and relaxing **Alcázar gardens**, the rambling but enticing product of several eras. Here are the vaulted baths in which María de Padilla was supposed to have bathed (actually an auxiliary water supply for the palace), and the **Estanque del Mercurio**, a pool with a bronze figure of the messenger of the gods at its centre, specially built for Felipe V (1733), who whiled away two solitary years at the Alcázar fishing here and preparing himself for death through religious flagellation. In the gardens proper – and close to an unusual **maze** of myrtle bushes – lies the **pavilion** (*pabellón*) **of Carlos V**, the only survivor of several he built in the gardens. This one, designed by Juan Hernández, was completed in 1543 and has the king's motto *Plus Ultra* displayed on the tiles of the steps leading to the pavilion's entrance.

The gardens are a spacious and tranquil haven to escape the crowds – particularly the Jardín Inglés on the southwest side – and make an ideal place for a picnic. A **cafetería** can be reached via the Puerta de Marchena, to the left of the Estanque del Mercurio, which has a pleasant terrace overlooking the gardens. The way out is via the **Apeadero**, a large coach hall built for Philip V in the eighteenth century, which housed not only the coaches used by the royals, but also legions of servants who slept on the floor. Beyond lies the impressive **Patio de las Banderas** (Patio of the Flags) edged with orange trees and until fairly recently the parade ground of the military barracks surrounding it, now luxury apartments. The flags of the various regiments were assembled here and reviewed by the king prior to battle. Exit from this square to the street, where you emerge on the edge of the Barrio Santa Cruz.

The Barrio Santa Cruz

The **Barrio Santa Cruz** is very much in character with Seville's romantic image, its streets narrow and tortuous to keep out the sun, the houses brilliantly whitewashed and festooned with flowering plants. Many of the windows are barricaded with *rejas* (iron grilles) behind which girls once kept chaste evening rendezvous with their *novios* who were forced to *comer hierro* ("eat iron") as passion mounted. Almost all of the houses have patios, often surprisingly large, and in summer these become the principal family living room. Most of the time they can be admired from the street beyond the wrought-iron screen inside the doorway, something the residents don't appear to mind. One of the most beautiful is within the Baroque **Hospital de los Venerables Sacerdotes** (guided tours daily 10am–2pm & 4–8pm; €4.75), near the centre in a plaza of the same name. Built around the patio and originally a home for infirm clerics, the hospice and church now form a gallery of outstanding artworks. These include **sculptures** by Martínez Montañés, Pedro and Luisa Roldán, a painting of the *Last Supper* by Lucás Valdés, plus some wonderfully restored **frescoes** by the same artist and his son Valdés Leal, as well as a recently acquired work, *Santa Rufina*, by **Velázquez**.

Hotel Alfonso XIII to the Museo Arqueológico

South of the cathedral stand a number of buildings of note: the **Hotel Alfonso XIII**, the **Palacio de San Telmo** and the **Fábrica de Tabacos**, the city's old tobacco factory that was also the setting for Bizet's *Carmen*. Further south, but still just ten minutes from the Giralda, lies the **Plaza de España** and adjoining **Parque de María Luisa** (María Luisa park) – laid out in 1929 for a gargantuan "Fair of the Americas" they are among the most impressive public spaces in Spain. Within the park the **Museo Arqueológico** houses Andalucía's most important archeological collection.

Hotel Alfonso XIII and Palacio de San Telmo

The **Hotel Alfonso XIII**, Seville's grandest, is worth a look inside – no one minds as long as you aren't dressed too outrageously. Named after the ill-starred monarch Alfonso XIII who was forced to abdicate soon afterwards, it was built

▲ Hotel Alfonso XIII

A walk around the Barrio Santa Cruz

The Barrio Santa Cruz is a great place for a stroll with no set route to follow. The following **walk** highlights just a few of the *barrio*'s many features.

Starting out from Plaza Virgen de los Reyes, behind the cathedral, the **Palacio Arzobispal** (free access to its patio if open) conceals, behind a Baroque facade, a remarkable staircase made entirely of jasper. Along c/Mateos Gago, *Bar Giralda*, at no. 2, incorporates part of a Moorish *hammam* or steam baths. Along up a bit, at no. 20, is one of Seville's institutions, the hole-in-the-wall **bodega of Juan García Aviles**, with its prized gleaming bar counter of Spanish mahogany, well over a century old and one of the few remaining in the city. Juan García passed away in 1996, and the bar has been retitled *Bar Alvaro Peregil*, but otherwise it remains as its original owner left it and locals have fixed a plaque to the exterior honouring Juan García's memory and his service to the community. When you've downed a *manzanilla*, continue east and turn right into c/Mesón del Moro where the slightly incongruous *San Marco Pizzeria*, at no. 4, is another establishment operating inside a splendid **Moorish bathhouse**. Further up c/Mateos Gago, a left turn will bring you into c/Guzmán El Bueno where, at no. 10, the charming sisters at the **Convento de San José** will allow you to view (outside siesta period) some remarkable Mudéjar plaster decoration (its ornate appearance is on a par with the Alcázar) in what was the salon, and is now the chapel, of this former fourteenth-century palace. This street is an especially good one for patio hunting – no. 4, with its plants, *azulejos*, wall-mounted bulls' heads and Roman statuary, is particularly beautiful.

Retracing your steps and following c/Mesón del Moro will bring you – via c/Ximénez de Enciso (a left and then a right) – to c/Santa Teresa where, at no. 8, you'll find the **Casa Murillo** (currently closed for refurbishment). Located in the artist's seventeenth-century home, this house-museum is furnished with contemporaneous artworks, craftsmanship and furniture, but, somewhat disappointingly, none of Murillo's original paintings.

Continuing along this street – note the old grindstones sunk into the wall on the left – will bring you to the delightful **Plaza Santa Cruz** where, until the French burned it down in 1810, stood the church which gave the square (and the *barrio*) its name and

to house important guests attending the 1929 exhibition, and an elegant neo-Baroque facade conceals one of the city's most beautiful patios, best enjoyed over a beer or afternoon tea.

Slightly west of here, the **Palacio de San Telmo** (currently undergoing refurbishment), built as a marine training academy for the Indies fleet and completed in 1734, is another expression of Seville's full-tilt Baroque period. During the mid-nineteenth century, it was purchased by the dukes of Montpensier, a member of whose family – the dowager duchess María Luisa – in 1893 presented part of the palace's vast grounds to the city, which became the park now named after her. The palace's main facade overlooks Avenida de Roma and has a marvellous Churrigueresque entrance arch topped – in a central niche – by San Telmo (of St Elmo's fire fame), patron saint of navigators.

Nearby, on the northeast side of the Puerta de Jerez traffic junction – a name referring to its former importance as one of the twenty gates in the city's ancient walls – on the corner of c/San Gregorio, lies the small former mosque and now chapel of **Santa María de Jesús**. Converted into a Christian church in 1248, it was frequently visited by Columbus on his trips to the city.

in which Murillo was buried. The French consulate appears to see no irony in occupying a building directly overlooking the scene of Napoleonic devastation. The attractive seventeenth-century cross, circled by rose bushes, marks the centre of the original church and was placed here when the plaza was created in 1918. Of three possible directions from here a route east (along calles Mezquita and Doncellas) would bring you to the ancient Gothic-Baroque church of **Santa María La Blanca**, on the street of the same name, which has, built into its south wall in c/de los Archeros, the entrance to the original synagogue, the only surviving architectural remnant of the Jewish quarter. The church's main portal is flanked by Visigothic columns probably from a church pre dating both the synagogue and the Moorish period, while the interior has lots of *azulejos* from Triana as well as an extravagant filigree stucco ceiling and two artistic gems: a moving *Piedad* (pietà) by the sixteenth-century artist Luís de Vargas, and a fine *Last Supper* by Murillo, the latter a rare tenebrist work. In the next street along from the church on the right heading north, the tiny c/Dos Hermanas has, at no. 7, the *Casas de la Judería* hotel – a restored *casa señorial* formerly the residence of the dukes of Bejar – whose beautiful patio is worth a look, perhaps over a drink from the bar.

Directly south from Plaza de Santa Cruz are the **Jardines de Murillo**, another peaceful oasis and a place to get your breath back in the midst of shady arbours decorated with Triana tiles. Alternatively, the Callejón del Agua will take you west and back towards the town centre where, at no. 6, the **Corral del Agua** restaurant has yet another fine patio quickly followed by the charming, plant-bedecked c/Pimienta (Pepper St), thought to take its name from a Jewish spice merchant who once lived here. Turn right along here, at the end turning right again to reach the Plaza de los Venerables where, if you didn't want see the artworks inside the Hospital de los Venerables (see p.269), you could visit the celebrated tapas bars on the plaza, the *Hostería del Laurel* and the *Casa Román*. Otherwise, heading north and then west along c/Jamerdana and the Pasaje Vila returns you to the c/Mateos Gago, just before which (on the tiny c/Rodrigo Caro) there's the *Bodega Santa Cruz*, another – and cheaper – Seville tapas institution.

Antigua Fábrica de Tabacos

The **Old Tobacco Factory**, just behind the *Hotel Alfonso XIII* along Avenida San Fernando, was where Carmen – in the nineteenth-century story by Mérimée made into an opera by Bizet – worked as a cigar maker. A beautiful and sensual *gitana* (gypsy), she falls in love with Don José, a corporal, who deserts his regiment to join her band of smugglers. When Carmen tires of him and transfers her affections to the toreador Escamillo, an insanely jealous Don José stabs her to death outside the bullring where a statue of "Carmen" now stands. Legions of foreign travellers later made pilgrimages to Seville in search of their own Carmen. The disillusion of the 1930s Irish traveller Walter Starkie was typical: he said that he had never seen "an uglier collection of women in my life", and was then hounded out of the workshops with a chorus of obscene abuse.

Now part of the university and only open during term time, this massive structure – 250m long by 180m wide – was built in the 1750s and still retains its position as the largest building in Spain after El Escorial in Madrid. Above the main entrance – facing c/San Fernando – perches a marble angel, a trumpet to its lips, which malicious popular legend has it would only sound when a virgin entered the factory for the first time. The entrance arch below aptly incorporates medallion busts of Columbus (discoverer of the tobacco lands) and Cortés (reputedly Europe's first smoker) – in effect the factory's founding fathers.

The building was divided into residential quarters below with the work areas on the upper – and lighter – level. The entrance leads through a vestibule into the Clock Patio (with fountain) off which is a **cafeteria**. At its peak in the nineteenth century the factory was also the country's largest single employer, with a workforce of some ten thousand women *cigarreras* (cigarette makers) – "a class in themselves" according to Richard Ford, and forced to undergo "an ingeniously minute search on leaving their work, for they sometimes carry off the filthy weed in a manner her most Catholic majesty never dreamt of". Production of cigars, cigarettes and snuff – originally ground by two hundred donkey-driven rolling mills – continued here until 1965 when its operations were moved to a new factory across the river close to the Puente de Los Remedios.

The Plaza de España and Parque de María Luisa

The **Plaza de España** lies beyond the Avenida del Cid – the latter, incidentally, the site of the Inquisition's *quemadero*, or burning platform, where for three hundred years convicted heretics were put to death; the last witch was burned here in 1781. The vast semicircular complex was designed as the centrepiece of the Spanish Americas Fair, which was somewhat scuppered by the Wall Street Crash abroad and political upheavals at home. Designed by Anibal González with theatrical towers, sprinkling fountains, majestic stairways and masses of brick and tile work, its flamboyance would seem strange in most Spanish cities but here it looks entirely natural, carrying on the great tradition of civic display. At the fair, the Plaza de España was used for the Spanish exhibit of industry and crafts, and around the crescent are *azulejo* scenes and maps of each of the provinces: an interesting record of the country at the tail-end of a monied era.

Locals and tourists alike come out to the plaza – crumbling for years but finally undergoing refurbishment – to potter about in the little boats rented out on its tiny strip of canal (currently lacking water), or to hide from the sun and crowds amid the ornamental pools and tree-shaded avenues and walkways of the **Parque de María Luisa**. The park is designed, like the plaza, in a mix of 1920s Art Deco and mock-Mudéjar. Scattered about, and round its edge, are more buildings from the fair, some of them amazingly opulent, built in the last months before the Wall Street Crash undercut the scheme's impetus.

The Museo Arqueológico and Museo de Costumbres Populares

Towards the southern end of the park, the grandest mansions from the fair have been adapted into museums, of which the **Museo Arqueológico** (Tues 2.30–8.30pm, Wed–Sat 9am–8.30pm, Sun 9am–2.30pm; €1.50, free with EU passport) is the most important of its kind in Andalucía. The collection's wide remit, divided among 27 rooms on two floors, spans the period from prehistory to the end of the Moorish age.

Starting in the basement with the prehistoric sections, Room 4 displays a collection of funerary stelae from the Iberian period, while Room 6 has a unique eighth-century BC bronze **statuette of Astarte–Tanit**, the Phoenician fertility goddess once worshipped throughout the Mediterranean. This room also contains the stunning **Carambolo Treasures** discovered in the Seville suburb of Camas in 1958. This remarkable hoard of gold jewellery further fuelled the debate surrounding the whereabouts and existence of the ancient land of Tartessus, known to the Greeks and mentioned in the Bible as

Tarshish. The legendary mineral wealth of Tartessus probably indicates a location in the area between Seville and the mineral-rich hills of Huelva, but despite investigations by archeologists for most of the last hundred or so years it has never been found.

Rooms 11 to 24 on the ground floor contain the substance of the **Roman** collection with an interesting display of kitchen equipment in Room 13, including what appears to be a modern-looking fork, contradicting the theory that the implement was a medieval invention. The same room also has a fine third-century mosaic from Écija (see p.308), depicting the god Bacchus being transported on a chariot drawn by tigers. In Room 17 there's a sensitive, second-century **sculpture of Venus** from Itálica, which was imported from Greece. There's yet more statuary in rooms 19 and 20, as well as portrait busts of the emperors Augustus and Nero and local boys Trajan and Hadrian, the latter particularly striking. In a small room off Room 19 you'll find a number of remarkable **bronze plaques** inscribed with the "Lex Irnitana", a rare set of laws illustrating how the Romans – the inventors of jurisprudence – went about ruling their empire. The laws make a fascinating read but are sadly translated only into Spanish. Rubric 72 of the code deals with the freeing of public slaves whilst number 82 relates to the upkeep of roads, tracks, irrigation channels, drains and sewers, all vital to the Roman way of life. The laws are sanctioned by the despotic emperor Domitian, whose name appears at the end of the document dated April 10, 91 AD. A portrait bust of Domitian is displayed in Room 20. Finally, rooms 26 and 27 display post-Roman finds including early Christian tombstones and Mudéjar ceramic works, among which a fifteenth-century green-glazed **baptismal font** stands out.

Opposite is the fabulous-looking **Museo de Costumbres Populares** (Popular Arts Museum; Tues 2.30–8.30pm, Wed–Sat 9am–8.30pm, Sun 9am–2.30pm; €1.50, free with EU passport) with, inside, an equally fine patio, which despite displays of costumes, implements, furniture, photos and posters describing life in eighteenth- and nineteenth-century Andalucía, feels a bit lifeless. The basement ceramics displays are the highlight, illustrating the regional developments of this craft inherited from the Moors. In spring there are also special exhibitions devoted to Semana Santa and the April *feria*.

Along the river to the Museo de Bellas Artes

Down by the **Río Guadalquivir** the main riverside landmark is the twelve-sided **Torre del Oro** (Tower of Gold), built by the Almohads in 1220 as part of the Alcázar fortifications. It was connected to another small fort across the

---

Boat trips on the Río Guadalquivir

A great way to get a different view of Seville is to take a **boat trip on the Guadalquivir**. Cruceros Turísticos (☏95 456 16 92, @www.crucerostorredeloro.com) have a quayside office below the Torre del Oro and run an hour-long cruise (daily every 30min 11am–9pm; €16) which takes in all the major riverside sights, including a view of the Expo 92 site. On Saturdays (May–Oct) they also run a scenic downriver cruise to **Sanlúcar de Barrameda** (see p.224), leaving the Torre del Oro at 8.30am (€33 round-trip). The cruise docks at 1pm at Sanlúcar's Bajo de Guía with its outstanding fish restaurants. A bus departing at 5.30pm returns you to Seville, arriving around 7pm.

To do the river under your own steam, **pedalos** (pedal boats; €10 per hr) can be hired from Acuaterraza (daily noon until sunset; ☏mobile 679194045) on the east bank of the river near the Puente de Isabel II. They also hire out rowing boats, canoes and motor boats.

river by a chain which had to be broken by the Castilian fleet before their conquest of the city in 1248. The tower later saw use as a repository for the gold brought back to Seville from the Americas; hence its name. It now houses a small, mildly interesting **naval museum** (Tues–Fri 10am–2pm, Sat & Sun 11am–2pm; €1, free with EU passport), which exhibits charts and engravings of the port in its prime.

The Hospital de la Caridad

One block east of the Torre del Oro is the **Hospital de la Caridad** c/Temprado 3 (Mon–Sat 9am–1.30pm & 3.30–7.30pm, Sun 9am–1pm; €5, ⓦ www.santa-caridad.org), founded in 1674 by Don Miguel de Mañara, who may well have been the inspiration for Byron's *Don Juan*. According to the testimony of one of Don Miguel's friends, "there was no folly which he did not commit, no youthful indulgence into which he did not plunge … (until) what occurred to him in the street of the coffin". What occurred was that Don Miguel, returning from a wild orgy, had a vision in which he was confronted by a funeral procession carrying his own corpse. He repented his past life, joined the Brotherhood of Charity (whose task was to bury the bodies of vagrants and criminals), and later set up this hospital for the relief of the dying and destitute, for which it is still used. Touchingly, whenever a patient dies here, the chapel is closed on the day of the funeral.

Between 1670 and 1674 Don Miguel commissioned a series of eleven paintings by **Murillo** for the chapel, seven of which remain after Marshal Soult looted four of them during the Napoleonic occupation. Murillo always created pictures "made to measure" for the available light, and it's a real treat to see the pictures in the place they were originally intended to hang. Among the surviving works are a colossal *Loaves and Fishes* depicting Christ feeding the Five Thousand, and "a *San Juan de Dios* equal to Rembrandt" as Richard Ford, a fervent Murillo fan, described it. Mañara himself posed as the model for the saint. Alongside them hang two *Triumph of Death* pictures by Valdés Leal. One, portraying the fleeting nature of life, features a skeletal image of Death pointing to the message *in ictu oculi* ("in the blink of an eye"), while the other depicts a decomposing bishop being eaten by worms (beneath the scales of justice labelled *Ni más, Ni menos* – "No More, No Less"). Murillo found this so repulsive that he declared "you have to hold your nose to look at it". The mood of both works may owe a lot to the vivid memory of the 1649 plague that killed almost half the population of the city. The main altar's **retablo** features a super-lative *Burial of Christ* carved by Pedro Roldán, and the steps to the left of this descend to a crypt where Mañara is buried.

As you're leaving the Caridad, look out for the **Torre de Plata** (Tower of Silver), a castellated Moorish watchtower, at c/Santander 13. Now visible from just inside a car park, it probably got its name to correspond with the nearby Torre del Oro, although there is no evidence to suggest that it was once coated with silver tiles or was ever a silver store, as local legends have it.

Plaza de Toros de la Maestranza and around

The **Plaza de Toros de la Maestranza** (Maestranza bullring; daily 9.30am–7pm, fight days 9.30am–3pm; €5) is the most famous and, for aficio-nados, the most beautiful bullring in the world. It was completed in the latter half of the eighteenth century to provide a home for the Real Maestranza de Caballería (Royal Equestrian Society). Subsequently altered, it is still one of the finest in Spain and has featured in numerous novels, poems and films

Murillo in all his glory

Born in Seville in 1618 and orphaned ten years later, **Bartolomé Estebán Murillo** grew up in the home of his brother-in-law. After enrolling as a student under Juan de Castillo he came to the attention of another *sevillano*, Velázquez, who was by then established in Madrid. Murillo studied with Velázquez for three not very happy years in the capital, where he found the social scene oppressive, but was apparently much impressed by the works of the Flemish and Italian schools he saw in the royal collections there.

Once back in his native city Murillo started work in earnest, often using poor *sevillanos* from districts such as La Macarena as his models. In 1682, still at the height of his artistic powers he was painting an altarpiece for the Capuchin church in Cádiz when he fell from the scaffold, suffering serious injury. He was brought back to Seville where he died in the Convent of San José near to his home in the Barrio Santa Cruz.

Downgraded by critics in the nineteenth century for his sentimentalism – a view largely based on the genre paintings of rosy-faced urchins that had found their way across Europe – Murillo's reputation has since been restored. A greater familiarity with the powerful works that remained in Seville, such as those in the Caridad, substantiates Ford's proclamation: "At Sevilla Murillo is to be seen in all his glory … a giant on his native soil."

– most enduringly in *Carmen*, the opera by Bizet. Once inside the arena, you will see a metal frame in the roof holding a furled canvas. On fight days this is unfurled – not to give spectators more shade but to temper the wind, which often whips up over the river causing the capes of the *matadores* to behave in unpredictable and possibly dangerous ways. The Maestranza's **museum** has the usual posters, prints, photographs and memorabilia. A monument to "Carmen" (see p.271) stands opposite the entrance to the bullring, across the road near the river.

Three blocks downriver – with a dome that's hard to miss – is the new **Teatro de la Maestranza** concert hall and opera house. Built as part of the *Expo 92* improvements, it incorporates the remains of the Artillería ammunition works that previously occupied the site. The rather dominating and uninspired design caused much controversy when it was unveiled because of its detrimental effect on the magnificent view of the city from across the river.

The Museo de Bellas Artes

To the north of c/Reyes Católicos on the Plaza del Museo and fronted by a formidable bronze statue of Murillo, the **Museo de Bellas Artes** (Tues 2.30–8.30pm, Wed–Sat 9am–8.30pm, Sun 9am–2.30pm; €1.50, free with EU passport), housed in recently modernized galleries in a startlingly beautiful former convent, the Convento de la Merced, ranks second in Spain only to the Prado in Madrid. Founded in the thirteenth century by Fernando III after Seville had been taken from the Moors, the building was subsequently remodelled and reached its present form in the eighteenth century. The convent lost most of its own commissioned paintings during the nineteenth-century Disentailment when it was secularized, and it opened as a museum in 1838. You should be aware that the museum has a policy of rotating its collection and not all the works mentioned here may be exhibited. A Sunday morning **art market** (9am–3pm) takes place in the plaza fronting the museum where local artists and craftworkers sell their work.

The downstairs galleries

Among the highlights of an outstanding collection is a wonderful late fifteenth-century painted terracotta sculpture in Room 1, *Lamentation over the Dead Christ*, by the *andaluz* **Pedro Millán**, founding father of the Seville school of sculpture. A marriage of Gothic and expressive naturalism, this style was the starting point for the outstanding seventeenth-century period of religious iconography in Seville – a later example, in Room 2, is a magnificent *San Jerónimo* by the Italian **Pietro Torrigiano**, who spent the latter years of his life in Seville. Ever his own man, Torrigiano once broke the nose of his contemporary Michelangelo in a quarrel and eventually died at the hands of the Inquisition in Seville, condemned for impiety after he had smashed his own sculpture of a Virgin when the duke of Arcos refused to pay the price asked. His *Virgen de Belén* here is another powerful work. This room also has **El Greco**'s portrait of his son, *Jorge Manuel Theotokopoulos*.

Room 3 has a *retablo* of the Redemption, c.1562, with fine woodcarving by Juan Giralte. Originally made for the Convento de Santa Catalina in Aracena, tableaux 6 (the crowning with thorns) and 10 (Mark writing his gospel) are especially fine. There's also a **Velázquez** work here, a portrait of *Don Cristóbal Suarez de Ribera* produced in his teens, betraying sure signs of the master's touch as well as an unparalleled ability to illuminate his figures from within.

A monumental *Last Supper* by **Alonso Vásquez** painted for the monastery of La Cartuja covers an end wall of Room 4, while the grisly terracotta sculpture of the severed head of *John the Baptist* by **Núñez Delgado** may not be something you want to see too soon after lunch. Dated 1591, this work is a prototype of the Baroque images later carried on the *pasos* during Semana Santa. This room also has works by **Pachecho**, one of the protagonists of the Mannerist school and the father-in-law and tutor of Velázquez. His series of canvases for the Convento de la Merced (this building) is represented here by images of *San Pedro* and *San Ramón Nonato*.

Beyond a serene patio and cloister, Room 5 is located in the monastery's former church. The restored **paintings on the vault and dome** by the eighteenth-century *sevillano*, Domingo Martínez, are spectacular. Here also is the nucleus of the collection: **Zurbarán's** *Apotheosis of St Thomas Aquinas* as well as a clutch of **Murillos** in the apse crowned by the great *Immaculate Conception* – known as "*la colosal*" to distinguish it from the other work here with the same name. In an alcove nearby you'll see the same artist's *Virgin and Child*. Popularly known as **La Servilleta** because it was said to have been painted on a dinner napkin, the work is one of Murillo's greatest. In the same room are more Murillos and also works by the early seventeenth-century *sevillano* **Roelas**, including a magnificent *Martirio de San Andrés*.

The upstairs galleries

Room 6 (quadrated around the patio) displays works from the Baroque period, among which a moving *Santa Teresa* by **Ribera** – Spain's master of *tenebrismo* (darkness penetrated by light) – and a stark *Crucifixión* by **Zurbarán** stand out. Room 7 is devoted to Murillo and his school and has a superb *San Agustín y la Trinidad* by the master. In Room 8, eighteenth-century *sevillano* **Valdés Leal** symbolizes the city's enduring fascination with agony and mortality: his depiction of *Fray Juan de Ledesma* wrestling with the devil disguised as a serpent has the brooding intensity of much of his work. Room 9 contains works from the **European Baroque**, among which there's an outstanding *La Adoración de los Pastores* (Adoration of the Shepherds) by the Flemish painter Pieter Van Lint and an *Adoración de los Reyes* (Adoration of the

Kings) by his compatriot Cornelis de Vos, both connected with the school of Rubens. There's more sculpture in Room 10, this time by the sixteenth-century genius **Martínez Montañés**, whose early *Saint Dominic in Penitence* and *San Bruno* from his mature period display mastery of technique. Also here are imposing canvases by **Zurbarán**: San Hugo visiting the Carthusian monks at supper (*San Hugo in the Refectory*), *The Visit of San Bruno* to Pope Urban II and the *Virgen de los Cartujos* were all painted for the monastery of La Cartuja across the river. There's also another almost sculptural *Crucifixión* to compare with his earlier one in Room 6.

The collection ends with works from the Romantic and Modern eras where an austere late work by **Goya**, in Room 11, of the octogenarian *Don José Duaso* compensates for some not terribly inspiring works accompanying it. There's also a portrait of the incompetent and indolent ruler *Alfonso XIII* painted in 1929 by Gonzalo Bilbao, which tells you all you need to know about this monarchical disaster. The same artist has more works in Room 12 – his *Las Cigarreras* is a vivid portrayal of the wretched life of women in the tobacco factory during the early years of the last century. Room 13 has an evocative image of *Sevilla en Fiestas* dated 1915 by Gustavo Bacarisas and the monumental canvas by José Villegas Cordero, *La Muerte del Maestro*, depicting the death of a *torero*. Finally, in Room 14 there's *Juan Centeño y su cuadrilla* by Huelvan artist Daniel Vásquez Díaz who worked in Paris and was a friend of Picasso. This stirring image of the *torero* and his team provides an appropriately *andaluz* conclusion to a memorable museum.

El Centro

El Centro, or central zone, lies north of the cathedral at the geographical heart of the city. It contains the main shopping areas, including **Calle Sierpes**, the city's most fashionable street, as well as a new **museum of flamenco dance**. Here, too, you'll find many of Seville's finest churches, displaying a fascinating variety of architectural styles. Several are converted mosques with belfries built over their minarets, others range through Mudéjar and Gothic (sometimes in combination), Renaissance and Baroque. Most are kept locked except early in the morning, or in the evenings from about 7 until 10pm – a promising time for a church crawl, especially as they're regularly interspersed with tapas bars.

The Casa de Pilatos and Museo del Baile Flamenco

Of Seville's numerous mansions, by far the finest is the **Casa de Pilatos** (daily 9am–7pm, Oct–Feb closes 5.30pm; €5 ground floor only, both floors €8, Tues 1–5pm free) in the Plaza de Pilatos, on the northwestern edge of Santa Cruz. Built by the marqués de Tarifa of the Ribera family on his return from a pilgrimage to Jerusalem in 1519, the house was popularly – and erroneously – thought to have been an imitation of the house of Pontius Pilate, supposedly seen by the duke on his travels. In fact it's a harmonious mixture of Mudéjar, Gothic and Renaissance styles, featuring brilliant *azulejos*, a tremendous sixteenth-century stairway and the best domestic patios in the city. After the Civil War the dukes of Medinaceli returned to live here and inaugurated a programme of restoration which has gradually brought the house back to its original splendour.

Entering by the Apeadero (refer to the plan on the back of your ticket), where the old carriages were boarded, and which for most of the year is a riot of magenta bougainvillea, brings you to a gateway leading into the wonderful **Patio Principal**. Here, Muslim elements such as the irregular arches, plaster work and glazed tiles combine with Gothic tracery on the upper balustrades and an Italian Renaissance fountain and columns below. The imposing statues in each corner of the patio are classical originals, of which the **Athene** (bearing a spear) is attributed to the fifth-century BC school of the Greek master, Phidias; the others are Roman. Antique Italian busts of Roman emperors and men of letters such as Trajan, Hadrian and Cicero occupy niches in the arcades.

The **Salón Pretorio** is notable for its coffered ceiling, incorporating the Ribera family's coat of arms. The Roman sculptures – collected in Italy by the sixteenth-century duke of Alcalá – in the nearby Zaquizamí corridor are extremely fine, especially the slumbering Venus and a marble relief fragment, depicting weapons, above. Passing the Jardín Chico (Small Garden), the Chapel of the Flagellation (its central column is supposed to represent the one at which Christ was scourged) and Pilate's "study", you reach the **Jardín Grande**, a verdant oasis with palms, pavilions and a bower, not to mention a wonderful abundance of orange trees. A tradition associated with this garden relates that the first duke of Alcalá obtained from Pope Pius V the ashes of the emperor Trajan, which were then displayed in a vase in the library. Later, a servant is supposed to have dumped them in the garden thinking the urn to be full of dust. The legend grew that an orange tree sprouted up wherever the ashes had fallen.

The **upper floors** (still partly inhabited by the Medinaceli family) are reached from the Patio Principal via the fine, tiled staircase with a gilded, sixteenth-century semicircular dome, but can be seen only by guided tour. The rooms are decorated with various frescoes, canvases by Goya (a tiny bullfighting scene), Ribera and Jordáns, and *objets d'art* collected by the family. Outstanding here is the **Salón de Pachecho** with the *Apotheosis of Hercules* painted on the ceiling in 1603 by the *sevillano* artist after whom the room is named. As you leave the house, note a rather curious bust of Julius Caesar at the entrance to the toilets. It's a fine portrait and, given the wealth of artefacts the family have hauled back from classical parts, is probably a two-thousand-year-old original deserving a more seemly location.

A few-minutes' walk to the east of the Casa de Pilatos lies the new **Museo del Baile Flamenco**, c/Manuel Rojas Marcos 3 (daily 9am–7pm; €10; ☎954 34 03 11, ⓦ www.museoflamenco.com) an innovative and entertaining museum dedicated to the history and evolution of this emblematic *andaluz* art form. Set up in collaboration with celebrated flamenco dancer Cristina Hoyos, the museum is interactive (and multilingual) employing the latest sound and image technology to enable the visitor to become familiar with origins of flamenco and the range of dance styles or "*palos*" which can all be seen at the touch of a button. The final section of the museum displays photos of, as well as costumes used by, some of the flamenco great names. There is also a **shop** selling books and CDs, a school of dance (sampler classes possible) and frequent live performances are staged in the museum's theatre (see website for details).

Churches, convents and monuments in El Centro

Leaving the Casa de Pilatos, a circuit of the churches in the area will take you first via c/Caballerizas to **San Ildefonso**, a fourteenth-century church later rebuilt in the classical style. Inside, behind the altar on the north aisle, there's a **fresco of the Virgin** dating from the original building. The church also has some seventeenth-century wood sculptures by Roldán and a bas-relief, *The Trinity*, by Martínez Montañés dated 1609.

Not far away, and still heading in a more or less westerly direction, c/Boteros will bring you to **Plaza Alfalfa**, the forum of Roman Hispalis and a good place for tapas bars. A couple of blocks south of here, along c/Candilejos and c/Muñoz y Pavón, in c/Marmoles are the remains – three enormous columns known as **Los Monolitos Romanos** – once belonging to what must have been a gigantic Roman temple. Continuing north from Plaza Alfalfa, however, along calles Sales y Ferrer and Padre Llop you'll reach the Plaza del Buen Suceso on which lies the **convent** of the same name. Inside, there's a marvellous sculpture of St Anne with the Virgin by Martínez Montañés. North again, c/Velilla leads to the Gothic **San Pedro**, with a Mudéjar tower modelled on the Giralda, and where a marble tablet records Velázquez's baptism. Just behind the church on c/Dueñas, the splendid **Palacio de los Dueñas** was the birthplace (marked by a plaque) of another *andaluz* genius, the poet Antonio Machado.

A stroll west from San Pedro along c/Imagen passes the Renaissance Iglesia de la **Anunciación** on c/Larana, leading to c/Cuna on the left where, at no. 8, stands the eighteenth-century **Palacio Lebrija** (May–Sept Mon–Fri 10.30am–1.30pm & 5–8pm, Sat 10am–2pm; Oct–April Mon–Fri 10.30am–6.30pm, Sat 10am–2pm; €4 one floor, €8 both floors, Ⓦwww.palaciodelebrija.com) which has a collection of Iberian and Roman antiquities and some fine Roman mosaics from Itálica built into its three ground-floor patios. A route directly north from here brings you to the tree-lined **Alameda de Hércules**, once a swamp and converted in the sixteenth century into a promenade. The southern end has two pillars taken from a Roman temple to Hercules, which give the promenade its name. Once fashionable, in the latter part of the last century this area went to seed and became the city's red-light district. However, in recent years a costly makeover has transformed it, attracting numerous new bars and hotels and the Alameda is re-emerging as a vibrant centre of *sevillano* life.

West of the Alameda, on Plaza de San Lorenzo, lies the church of San Lorenzo and, next to it, the modern church of **Jesús del Gran Poder** (daily 8am–1.30pm & 6–9pm; free). In the latter's **retablo** is displayed the much venerated figure of *Jesús del Gran Poder* (Christ bearing his cross) by Juan de Mesa, carved in 1620. This image is borne in procession in the small hours of Good Friday morning.

Plaza de San Francisco and Calle Sierpes

Because of the Muslim origin of its vernacular architecture – which was designed primarily to keep out the sun – Seville had no great squares on the European model until relatively recently. Most of the plazas it does possess are the result of palaces and convents being torn down: some, such as the uninspiring Plaza del Duque de la Victoria, site of the *palacio* of the Guzmán family, were created as recently as the 1960s.

In the shadow of the Giralda, the **Plaza de San Francisco**, slightly north of the cathedral, takes its name from the great monastery that once covered much of this and the Plaza Nueva to the west. To the north of here you'll find the true heart of Seville, **Calle Sierpes**, where, according to Cervantes – who spent some time in prison here serving a sentence for his tax debts – "all the social classes of the city come together". This narrow pedestrianized street, today lined with souvenir stores, private clubs and smart *pastelerías* (cake shops), is a wonderful place to stroll. It's particularly dramatic – though quite uncharacteristic – during Semana Santa, when the brotherhood of El Silencio passes through in total silence in the early hours of Good Friday, watched by an equally hushed crowd lining the route. Look out for Seville's most famous *pastelería*, La Campana, at no. 1 (the northern end). At no. 65 a wall plaque indicates the site of the Cárcel Real, or royal prison, where Cervantes was incarcerated. A short way down on the left, in c/Jovellanos, lies the small **Capillata de San José**, one of the best examples of full-blown Baroque in the city with a beautiful gilded *retablo*. Otherwise, just behind c/Sierpes in the parallel c/Tetuan, a detour will lead you to a wonderful old tiled billboard advertising a 1924 Studebaker car. It's opposite the C&A department store.

Nearby, and to the east of c/Sierpes, the Plaza del Salvador contains the collegiate church of **El Salvador** (Mon–Sat 8.45–10am & 6.30–9pm; free), built on the site of a ninth-century – and the city's first – Friday mosque. Most of what you see today dates from the seventeenth century, with remnants of the mosque preserved in its tower, formerly the minaret, and its patio, originally the ablutions courtyard. Inside, there's a magnificent Churrigueresque **retablo** as well as a number of sculptures, among them the renowned *Jesús del Pasión* by the great master of wood sculpture, Juan Martínez Montañés, who also embellished the church's exterior and whose bronze monument stands in the plaza outside.

The Barrio Triana

Over the river is the **Triana** *barrio*, an endearingly scruffy, lively and not at all touristy neighbourhood, generally believed to have taken its name from the Roman emperor **Trajan** who was born at nearby Itálica. This was once the

---

A walk around the Barrio Triana

There are any number of ways to explore Triana, taking time to stop off in some of the wonderful tapas bars on the way (for details see p.292). This particular walk starts out from the Plaza de Cuba, reached by crossing the Puente de San Telmo to the river's western bank. From here head down c/Genova to the Plaza de la Virgen de la Milagrosa. In the centre of this square is a modern statue to **Rodrigo de Triana**, a sailor on Columbus's initial voyage who was the first to set eyes on the New World. In spite of his name, however, more recent research suggests that he hailed not from Triana, but Lepe, in the neighbouring province of Huelva. Determined not to be put off by this academic meddling with their history, the *barrio* erected the sculpture anyway with the laconic "Tierra" ("Land") inscribed on its base, the word an unidentified Rodrigo is presumably yelling as he clings to the mast.

Turning right along c/Troya to c/Betis, which fronts the river, leads you into the **old docklands area** of Triana, smartened up in the earlier part of the last century and planted with trees. To the right, in c/Gonzalo Segovia, was the site of the former gunpowder factory that supplied the vessels of the Indies fleet. An enormous explosion here in 1579 not only destroyed half of Triana but also blew the stained-glass windows out of the cathedral across the river. In Roman times, clay was collected from this riverbank to make the Amphorae used to transport cereals, wine, oil and pickled fish to the imperial capital – much of the broken pottery piled up in ancient Rome's towering rubbish dump at Monte Testaccio has now been identified as coming from Triana. The same clay also made the bricks for the Giralda and many more of the city's houses and monuments.

Further along, a left turn at c/Duarte brings you to Triana's main church of **Santa Ana**, the oldest parish church in Seville. Built for Alfonso X in the thirteenth century, it includes many later additions: note, for example, the Mudéjar tower with blocked lobed windows topped by a Renaissance belfry. Should you be able to gain entry – early evening is your best bet – look out for the fine sixteenth-century **retablo** of the *Virgen de la Rosa* and the church's baptismal font – **Pila de los Gitanos** – from which, according to tradition, the gifts of flamenco singing and dancing are bestowed on the newborn infants of the *barrio*. Take c/Pureza (at the church's eastern end) heart of the city's gypsy community and, more specifically, home of the great flamenco dynasties of Seville. The gypsies lived in extended families in tiny, immaculate communal houses called *corrales* around courtyards glutted with flowers; today only a handful remain intact. Triana is still, however, the starting point for the annual pilgrimage to El Rocío (at the end of May), when myriad painted wagons leave town, drawn by elephantine oxen. And one of the great moments of Semana Santa occurs here in the early hours of Good Friday when the candlelit *paso* of the Virgin *Esperanza de Triana* is carried back over the Puente de Triana (Isabel II) to be given a rapturous welcome home by the whole *barrio* assembled on the other side. Triana has long been a centre of **glazed-tile production**, and you'll see plenty of examples of this fine ceramic work as you stroll around the streets.

La Cartuja and the Expo 92 site

Across the river and reached by the Pasarela de la Cartuja (or by buses C1 or C2 from the Prado de San Sebastián bus station or the Puente de los Remedios), a pedestrian bridge constructed for Expo 92, is the fourteenth-century **La Cartuja** (April–Sept Tues–Fri 10am–9pm, Sat 11am–9pm, Sun 10am–3pm; Oct–March Mon–Fri 10am–8pm, Sat 11am–8pm, Sun 10am–3pm; €3, free on Tues with EU passport), a former Carthusian monastery.

north to no. 53, the **Capilla de los Marineros**, an eighteenth-century chapel that is now seat of the *Cofradía de Jesús de las Tres Caídas y Nuestra Señora de la Esperanza* (Brotherhood of Jesus of the Three Falls and Our Lady of Hope), one of the major brotherhoods who march in the Semana Santa processions. The chapel's Baroque *retablo* incorporates the figure of the Virgin known as the **Esperanza de Triana** to which the *barrio* is devoted.

Continue north, turning left along calles Rocío and Flota and then right along c/Rodrigo, crossing c/San Jacinto into c/Alfarería, where there are traditional *corrales*. A left turn a short way along here into c/Antillano Campos brings you to *Bar Anselma* (fronting c/Pages), a great old tiled place with occasional impromptu flamenco. Still heading north along c/Alfarería, take a right along c/Procurador and right again to the sixteenth-century church of **Nuestra Señora de la "O"** at c/Castilla 30, with its splendid tiled tower. The interior, as well as holding more ceramics, contains a seventeenth-century sculpture of Jesús Nazareno by Pedro Roldán.

Heading south, with the river on your left, a small alley bears the name Callejón de la Inquisición. This was the site of the former **Castillo de Triana** (Triana Castle), the original residence of the Inquisition until it was forced out by a flood in 1626 or, as Ford colourfully puts it, until "the Guadalquivir, which blushed at the fires and curdled with the bloodshed, almost swept it away as if indignant at the crimes committed on its bank". Almost opposite, *Cervecería Casa Cuesta* is a welcoming bar with tiled interior serving good tapas. Continuing around the corner you'll come to the spectacular tiled facade of **Cerámica Santa Ana** at Plaza Callao 12. The city's oldest working ceramics factory, over a century old, this is a good place to buy hand-painted Triana pots and tiles. Continuing south brings you to **Plaza Altozano** where there are monuments to the great 1920s flamenco singer Pastora Pavón and Triana's famous *torero*, Juan Belmonte. The latter sculpture by Venancio Blanco nestles against the Puente de Triana – designed by Gustave Eiffel of "tower" fame. Before crossing the bridge back to the centre, take a look at the new Mercado de Triana (market) which has been cunningly constructed over **excavations** of the same Castillo de Triana. The exposed remains can be viewed beneath a reinforced glass cover with the market now on top.

Founded in 1399 on the site where there had been an apparition of the Virgin in some pottery workshops (*cuevas*) installed here during the Almohad era, the monastery of **Santa María de las Cuevas** was expanded by the Carthusians in the fifteenth and sixteenth centuries with donations from Seville's leading families. This was where Columbus lodged on his visits to Seville, where he planned his second voyage to the New World, and where he was buried for a few years. The core of the monastery suffered eighteenth-century Baroque additions and was made the headquarters of the notorious Marshal Soult's garrison during the Napoleonic occupation of 1810–12, when the monks were driven out and fled to Portugal. A final indignity was visited on the place when, after Disentailment in 1836, it was purchased by a Liverpudlian, Charles Pickman, and turned into a ceramics factory, which it remained until 1982. The whole complex – including the towering brick kilns and chimney that can be glimpsed from outside the site, and which are now regarded as industrial history – was restored for Expo 92 at enormous cost.

The visit begins at the **Capilla de Afuera** where the chapel's gilded Baroque *retablo* has lost its central effigy of the *Virgen de las Cuevas*, a carved work in cedar and once the monastery's most venerated image. In the chapels of **Santa Catalina** and **San Bruno** (the founder of the Carthusian order) there are fine Triana tiles, and Felipe II used the latter chapel as his oratory when he visited Seville in 1570. Apart from a few surviving architectural fragments, the monastery's church is now bare, but maintains a serene dignity after its use as a workshop in the ceramics factory. Off it, the chapel of Santa Ana contains the **tomb of Christopher Columbus** where the navigator's bones rested for 27 years prior to beginning their travels (see p.260). Also here in wall niches are the remains of some fine polychrome tile panels depicting San Juan Evangelista and San Mateo.

Also off the church are the elegant **Mudéjar cloister**, the centre of Carthusian community life and where there is more tile work, and the **Capítulo de Monjes** (Chapter House) with the sixteenth-century tombs of the Ribeira family and finely sculpted *retablos* made in Italy. Finally, the **refectory**, with more partially tiled walls and a tiled pulpit, retains a beautiful *artesonado* ceiling which was used by the French for target practice. The visit ends with a chance to view Pickman's enormous bottle-shaped kilns close up en route to the *huerta* (market garden) of the former monastery, which has been transformed once again into a tranquil oasis as the recently planted trees mature. Along the garden's northwest wall you can see the pumps which once drew water from the river to irrigate the garden, and from a *mirador* in the reconstructed **Casilla de Santa Justa y Rufina** there is a great **view** over the whole complex to the west, the river and city to the east and, to the north, the rather forlorn and weed-festooned site of Expo 92.

A separate building within the same complex now houses the **Centro Andaluz de Arte Contemporáneo** (same hours and ticket as La Cartuja; Ⓦ www.caac.es), one gallery of which displays rotating selections from a large and interesting collection of contemporary work by *andaluz* artists, including canvases by Antonio Rodríguez de Luna, Joaquin Peinado, Guillermo Pérez Villalta, José Guerrero and Daniel Vásquez Díaz. Two other galleries stage temporary exhibitions by international artists and photographers (see website for details).

Expo 92

The staging of **Expo 92** secured a year of publicity and prosperity for Seville during which the sybaritic *sevillanos* started to believe their own hype, billing it as the "event of the century". After the fuss died down and the visitors departed, the city was left with a staggering debt of sixty billion pesetas (€360 million), financial scandals, endless recriminations, and a dilapidated site which no one knew what to do with. Plans to turn it into a science park came to nothing and the western side of the complex has now been split between the University of Seville and a technological/industrial park. Expo's artificial lake on the east side of the site has been revamped as the focus of the **Isla Mágica** amusement and theme park (April–Nov daily 11am–7pm, closes later in summer; €27, children €19; *Tarde* or evening-only tickets €19, children €14; ⓦ www.islamagica.es) with rides and attractions (included in ticket price) based on the theme of the sixteenth-century Spanish empire.

The remains of the Expo site lying beyond this and to the south of La Cartuja are mostly a hotchpotch of desolate and weed-festooned buildings, including the Navigation Pavilion celebrating Columbus's voyages, the soaring but now rusting Torre Mirador plus gimmicks such as the Omnimax giant cine screen. All have been closed to the public for some years.

Should you decide to walk back to the city via the Pasarela de la Cartuja footbridge across the river, look out upstream for the spectacular **Puente de la Barqueta**, another hugely extravagant Expo innovation connecting the city to La Cartuja. Designed by renowned architect Santiago Calatrava, its taut suspension cables resemble the strings of an elongated lyre.

The Barrio Macarena

"The **Macarena**, now as it always was, is the abode of ragged poverty, which never could or can for a certainty reckon on one or any meal a day." Things have changed considerably for the better since Ford was here in the middle of the nineteenth century, and since Murillo used the *barrio*'s beggars and urchins as models for his paintings. Northwest of the Centro and enclosed by the best surviving stretch of the city's ancient walls, Macarena's very unfashionability, along with its solid working-class traditions, have helped prevent its wholesale dismemberment at the hands of speculators and builders. The result today is an

▲ The Macarena Church

A good place to start a tour around **La Macarena** is the **Plaza de los Terceros**, slightly to the northwest of the Casa de Pilatos. Here you'll find the fourteenth-century Mudéjar church of **Santa Catalina** with a tower modelled on the Giralda and topped off with Renaissance embellishments. The interior (access is difficult but try 6.30–7.30pm) has some interesting Mudéjar features including an elegant panelled ceiling as well as – in the Cristo de la Exaltación chapel (the most easterly on the south side) – a fine sculpture of Christ by Roldán. Within spitting distance of the church (on the corner of c/Gerona) lies another of Seville's great institutions, the bar **El Rinconcillo** (see p.293), founded in 1670 and believed to be the oldest in the city.

Follow c/Sol out of the Plaza Terceros to Plaza San Román where another fourteenth-century Gothic-Mudéjar church, **San Román** has a fine coffered ceiling. Taking c/Enladrillada along the north side of the church will bring you to the fifteenth-century **Convento de Santa Paula** (Tues–Sun: April–Sept 10am–1pm, Oct–May 10am–1pm & 4.30–6.30pm; €3), renowned for its beautiful belfry and church. The church is entered through an imposing fifteenth-century **Gothic doorway** built with Mudéjar brickwork and decorated with Renaissance *azulejos* by Pedro Millán, with ceramic decoration by Niculoso Pisano. Inside there's a sumptuously gilded *San Juan Evangelista retablo* by Alonso Cano with a magnificent central figure of St John by Martínez Montañés dated 1637. The convent **museum**, crammed with treasures, is entered through a small patio to the left of the church entrance. Guided tours (in Spanish) are led by one of the convent's 48 nuns who has been given a special dispensation to break the order's vow of silence. The first room has a painting of *San Jerónimo* by Ribera, and, almost as beautiful, a view out onto a seventeenth-century patio cloister. In Room 2 there's a fascinating **maquette** made by Torrigiano before starting on his full-size masterpiece of *San Jerónimo Penitente*, which is now in the Museo de Bellas Artes (see p.276). Room 3 holds two outstanding, though damaged, painted **sculptures by Pedro de Mena**, a *Virgin* and an *Ecce Homo*. Immediately before the exit there is also a *Crucifixión* by **Zurbarán**. The hard-working sisters are famous for their *dulces* and *mermaladas* (including a tomato jam), which you can buy from their small shop. Facing the convent's entrance, a wall plaque marks a house described in *La Española Inglesa* by Cervantes.

From Santa Paula, head north along Pasaje Mallol to **San Julián**, yet another fourteenth-century church, with a Gothic-Mudéjar portal. Calle Madre Dolores Márquez will then take you the short distance to the **Puerta de Córdoba** (Córdoba Gate) with its horseshoe arch and the best surviving section of the **city wall**. The Almoravids constructed the wall in the early twelfth century, possibly on Roman foundations, and it was further strengthened by the later Almohads as wars against the Christians intensified. This stretch of the fortification – which once spanned twelve gates and 166 towers – owes its survival to the poverty of the *barrio* during the nineteenth century when, elsewhere in the city, it was pulled down to allow expansion.

Follow the wall west until you reach the **Puerta de la Macarena**, the only one of the city's gates to retain its pre-Christian name and reconstructed in the eighteenth century. Just beyond it stands the **Basilica de la Macarena** (daily 9.30am–2pm & 5–8pm; museum €3) which, despite an apparently Baroque facade, dates from the 1940s. The basilica's importance, however, derives from the revered image of the *Virgen de la Esperanza Macarena* it was constructed to house. Inside the church, to the left, is the solid silver *paso* used to carry the image around the city during the Semana Santa processions. To the right is a second *paso* (the brotherhoods normally carry them in pairs), *Jesús de la Sentencia*, depicting Pilate washing his hands with a fine, but now modestly cloaked, Christ by the seventeenth-century sculptor, Felipe Morales. The *retablo* of the main altar is dominated by a seventeenth-century image of La Macarena, as the Virgin is popularly called by this city of fanatical devotees. Depicted in the trauma of the Passion when her son has been condemned, the work is attributed to La Roldana – largely based on the *sevillano* sentiment that only a woman could have portrayed the suffering of a mother with such intensity. La Macarena's elaborate costume is often decorated with five diamond and emerald brooches bestowed on her by Joselito el Gallo, a famous *gitano torero* of the early part of the last century, and on which he spent a considerable fortune. She didn't return the favours though – he died in the ring in 1920. Despite this mishap, the Virgin is still regarded as the patron of the profession and all *matadores* offer prayers to her before stepping out to do business in the Maestranza. The basilica's treasury **museum** features a rather gaudy display of the Virgin's other jewels and regalia.

Over the road and beyond a small garden lies the sixteenth-century **Hospital de las Cinco Llagas** (aptly, of the Five Wounds Of Christ), one of the first true hospitals of its time and the largest in Europe. Sited outside the walls because hospitals then were places of pestilence and contagion, the restored building is now the seat of Andalucía's autonomous **government** (and many *sevillano* wags drily comment that nothing's changed). The enormous edifice, once capable of holding a thousand beds, is noted for a fine Mannerist facade with a Baroque central doorway of white marble. The interior – including the hospital's impressive former church, now the debating chamber – is open infrequently for public view when the parliament is not sitting (guided tours Oct–May twice weekly; must be booked in advance ℡95 459 21 00; free).

Crossing back to the Puerta de la Macarena, follow c/San Luís to the church of **San Gil** just behind the Macarena Basilica. Badly damaged in the Civil War, the church nevertheless still has a Mudéjar tower and, inside, a timber Mudéjar ceiling. Continuing south along the same street you'll come to the Gothic-Mudéjar church of **Santa Marina**, set back from the road in a plazuela. Founded in the thirteenth century, the oldest feature here must be the doorway, dating from around 1300, which has Gothic archivolts, or arch mouldings, with Mudéjar star decoration on the outer band. Another church badly damaged in the Civil War, Santa Marina was in ruins for decades, only spruced up for Expo 92 when the interior was entirely restored. It is now home to the Cofradía del Resucitado (Brotherhood of the Resurrection – see box, p.286).

Back on c/San Luis, the eponymous church of **San Luís** (Tues–Sat 9am–2pm, plus Fri–Sat 5–8pm; closed Aug; free) is a glorious eighteenth-century structure, preserved in 1995 from the demolition hammer after the city government had said they couldn't afford to save it. Public outcry forced a change of heart and the riot of a Churrigueresque facade, topped by glazed-tile domes, has now been restored along with the interior, which features a fine fresco by Lucas Valdés on the central dome. The church is also floodlit at night to spectacular effect.

Further along you'll come to the fourteenth-century **San Marcos** in the plaza of the same name. Another fine Macarena church built on the site of an earlier mosque, it has a Mudéjar tower – note the Giralda-style *sebka* brickwork – and a superb Gothic-Mudéjar entrance. Although gutted by fire during the Civil War and since restored, its interior uniquely preserves the original Mudéjar horseshoe arches dividing nave and aisles. At the head of the north aisle there's a seventeenth-century sculpture in painted wood of *San Marcos*, by Juan de Mesa. Cervantes used to climb San Marcos's tower to view the plant-filled and peaceful patio of the convent of **Santa Isabel** just behind the church. You can see why.

area full of character, with many attractive cobbled streets, and quite a few jewels to show off in the way of **churches** and **convents**. The Macarena's pride was further enhanced when it was decided that the *barrio* would become the home of the newly autonomous **Andalucian parliament** in the converted Renaissance hospital of the Cinco Llagas.

Restaurants

Seville is tremendously atmospheric in the evening, packed with lively and enjoyable bars and clubs. That the city has never been particularly noted for its **restaurants** may have a lot to do with its strong tapas tradition (see p.290). Great though this is, even the most enthusiastic *tapeadores* eventually tire of "plate-pecking" to seek out a place to sit down for a more conventional meal.

Barrio Santa Cruz and Cathedral area

To eat well without breaking the bank, you generally have to steer clear of the restaurants around the major sights and in the **Barrio Santa Cruz**. However, there are some reasonable options to be found: the streets around the *barrio*'s northern edge (framed by calles Menéndez Pelayo and Santa María la Blanca), make for a good hunting ground.

Bar Modesto c/Cano y Cueto 5. More a touristy terrace restaurant these days than purely a bar, it is still renowned for its tapas which (unless trade is slow) you'll need to eat at the bar. The kitchen is pretty good at straightforward meals, too, and there's a *menú* for around €20.

Café Rayuela c/Miguel de Mañara 9. Pleasant lunchtime venue serving economically priced tapas, *raciónes*, *montaditos* (*tapa* on bread) and

salads at outdoor tables in a pedestrianized street behind the Turismo.

Carmela c/Santa María la Blanca 4. Candlelit outdoor tables at this pleasant restaurant/tapas bar; tasty dishes include quiche, *patatas con crema de queso*, and quite a few vegetarian options.

Corral del Agua Callejón del Agua 6 ☎95 422 07 14. Very good restaurant where you can eat *cocina andaluza* in a lovely, plant-filled patio. Pricey, but

The forgotten brotherhood

The Macarena church of Santa Marina is home to the **Cofradía del Resucitado** (Brotherhood of the Resurrection), the newest of all the brotherhoods who march in the Semana Santa processions. Founded in 1969, it has never been taken to its heart by a citizenry whose apparent lack of interest in this celebration of the Redeemer's return is in marked contrast with the grisly enthusiasm they evidence for each act in the Passion leading up to his death. However, this apathy is the visitor's opportunity, for when El Resucitado leaves Santa Marina at four-thirty in the early dawn of Easter Sunday you'll get a perfect view of the intricate manoeuvres performed by the *costaleros* (porters) to negotiate the two *pasos* – the Risen Christ and the aptly titled Vírgen de la Aurora (Virgin of the Dawn) – through the church's doors, which are normally obscured by vast crowds elsewhere. And as there are no seats lining the atmospheric c/Sierpes, which is almost impossible to get near during the other processions, you will be able to accompany the *pasos*, the band and the masked, candle-bearing *nazarenos* (penitents) in their all-white tunics along here as the dawn breaks – calling in at nearby bars for a *café* and maybe a *churro* or two.

The procession then passes through a sombre Plaza de San Francisco where the normally packed grandstands are eerily empty. Security is also lax at the cathedral, and with a bit of nimble footwork you should be able to follow the *pasos* through the church and past the enormous monstrance inside to emerge in a sunlit Plaza Vírgen de los Reyes beneath the Giralda tower, where a few *sevillanos* have usually gathered to pay their respects. If you wanted to follow El Resucitado back to Santa Marina it's a great (if slow) meander until they arrive home at about two in the afternoon.

well worth it. There's a *menú* for around €22.
Closed Sun.

Doña Francisquita c/Álvarez Quintero 58.
Authentic pizzas near the cathedral.

El Cabildo Plaza del Cabildo s/n ☎95 422 79 70,
near the cathedral. Elegant and reasonably priced
traditional restaurant serving well-prepared
standards. Has a daily €18 *menú* which you may
need to ask for.

Kaede Hotel Alfonso XIII c/San Fernando 2. In
the gardens of the town's swishest hotel this is an
authentic Japanese restaurant. Sushi and sashimi
are included on a good-value *menú* for €18, but if
you go for the Sapporo beer rather than the *té
japonés* (which comes free with the *menú*) you'll
substantially increase the bill.

La Albahaca Plaza Santa Cruz 9 ☎95 422 07
14. Charming and excellent traditional restaurant
housed in a converted mansion where three
intimate period rooms hung with paintings provide
the ambience. Fairly expensive, but there's a
menú for around €30. Main dishes €15–25.
Closed Sun.

La Judería c/Cano y Cueto 13 ☎95 441 20 52.
Popular and pleasant mid-priced restaurant with a
daily *menú* for €20. *Revueltos* (scrambled egg
dishes) are a speciality here. Main dishes €9–17.

Mesón del Pulpo c/Tomás Ibarra 10. Excellent
little Galician bar-restaurant popular with locals.
Specializes (as its name implies) in *pulpo a la
gallega* (octopus) and there's a good-value *menú*
for €12.

The Río Guadalquivir and Triana

Across the river, **Triana** offers some excellent restaurants. Near the Puente San
Telmo, a number of restaurants along c/Salado cater for workers from the Los
Remedios business quarter, and along c/Betis close to the water's edge are a
number of restaurants with terraces looking out over the city. Around c/García
Vinuesa to the west of the cathedral there's an abundance of reasonable *bocadillo*
bars and delis for picnic food.

As-Sawïrah c/Galera 5. Superb Moroccan restaurant offering a variety of North African dishes
including a delicate couscous and their house
special *tajin de cordero con membrillos* (lamb with
quinces). Lunch *menú* €12. Closed Sat eve & Sun.

Casablanca c/Adolfo Rodriguez Jurado 12, facing
the Turismo. Smart mid-price restaurant noted for
its excellent fish dishes – including *mero con
frambuesa* (grouper with raspberries) – but also
does meat. Has a small tapas bar which, they
insist, King Juan Carlos once visited incognito to
sample their *papas aliñás* (marinated potatoes).

El Manijero c/Trastamara 15 (corner with
c/Albuera). Excellent and economical neighbourhood bar-restaurant with a tapas and *raciónes*
bar beyond the entrance and a dining room off
this. Fried fish and *solomillo* (pork tenderloin) are
their specialities.

Horacio c/Antonia Díaz 9. Moderately priced fish
and meat dishes at this very pleasant small restaurant near the bullring. *Magret de pato en salsa de
uvas* (duck) is a house special and there is a
seasonally changing *menú* for around €30
including wine.

La Primera del Puente c/Betis 66. One of the
city's best options for economical yet generous
raciónes of fish, meat and *mariscos*; sweet talk a
waiter to get a frontline table for the spectacular
river view from their terrace.

La Sopa Boba c/Torneo 85 ☎95437 97 84. Mid-
priced, modern and attractive place with a creative

approach; specials include *manzana con bacalao y
cabrales* (cod with apples and goat's cheese) and
magret de pato en salsa de peras (duck with pear
sauce); also does good salads, some vegetarian
dishes and a range of teas. Main dishes €10–19.
Closed Sun eve & Mon.

Mamma Terra corner of Paseo Colón & Avda.
Cristina. Organic cafeteria with large selection of
vegetarian food ranging from grilled vegetable pitas
to tofu burgers. There's a *menú* for €10.

Mesón Serranito c/Antonia Díaz 11, south side
of the Plaza de Toros. Twin restaurant of the one
near El Corte Inglés and with similar dishes and
platos combinados and – due to the location – a
line of bulls' heads gazing down from the walls.
Menú for €9.

Poncio c/Charles Darwin 4, west of La Cartuja
☎95 446 07 17. This excellent mid-priced Triana
restaurant has moved to stylish new premises with
minimalist decor. But the creative *andaluz* cuisine
continues, guided by owner-chef Willy Moya.
There's a *menú de degustación* for €45 (ex wine).
The restaurant is easily reached by crossing the
Pasarela de Cartuja footbridge and turning right
and then left. Closed Sun.

Restaurante Enrique Becerra c/Gamazo 2,
east of the bullring ☎95 421 30 49. Mid-priced
restaurant with a solid reputation for well-prepared
andaluz dishes such as *cola de toro* (bull's tail) and
pez espada al amontillado (swordfish). Main dishes
€10–23. Closed Sun and Aug.

SEVILLE RESTAURANTS AND TAPAS BARS

Map labels:

PLAZA DE S. AGUSTÍN
CALLE MARÍA AUXILIADORA
RECAREDO
Jardines del Valle
PLAZA GIRALDILLO
AVENIDA DE LA CRUZ ROJA
Jardín de Capuchinos
Casa de Pilatos
PLAZA DE PILATOS
San Leandro
Puerta de Córdoba
ENLADRILLADA
Convento Sta. Paula
PASAJE MALLOL
S. M. del Socorro
PLAZA JERÓNIMO DE CÓRDOBA
PLAZA DE PONCE DE LEÓN
Sta. Catalina
San Hermenegildo
Convento Sta. Isabel
S. Marcos
PL. SAN MARCOS
PL. DE LOS TERCEROS
PL. C. BURGOS
Iglesia de Sta. Marina
DOÑA MARÍA CORONEL
S. Pedro
PLAZA ALFALFA
City Walls
Palacio de las Dueñas
SOR ÁNGELA DE LA CRUZ
El Salvador
SAN LUIS
Iglesia de San Luis
PLAZA DE LA ENCARNACIÓN
Iglesia de la Anunciación
LA MACARENA
San Gil
Casa de la C. de Lebrija
Omnium Sanctorum
Basílica de la Macarena
CENTRO
FERIA
CERVANTES
AMOR DE DIOS
Alameda de Hércules
Ciberducke @
TRAJANO
PERAL
JESÚS DEL GRAN PODER
PLAZA DE GAVIDIA
BLANQUILLO CALATRAVA
S. Lorenzo y Jesús del Gran Poder
Monast.º de Sta. Clara
PZA. DE S. LORENZO
Monasterio de S. Clemente
SANTA CLARA
TEODOSIO
S. Vicente
SAN VICENTE
NUEVA TORNEO
PUENTE DE BARQUETA
TELECABINA
TORNEO
(Río
La Cartuja
Centro Andaluz de Arte Contemporáneo

TAPAS BARS

Bar Alicantina	39	Bodega Siglo XVIII	74	La Albariza	80
Bar Anselma	87	Bodeguita Santa Justa	40	La Alcena	21
Bar Antonio Romero	61	Café Universal	37	La Giganta	20
Bar Bistec	70	Casa Los Caracoles	31	La Ilustre Victima	59
Bar Dos de Mayo	76	Casa Morales	42	La Moneda	38
Bar El Tito	43	Casa Robles	35	La Sopa Boba Tapas	60
Bar Enrique Becerra	56	Casa Román	11	Las Golondrinas	88
Bar Eslava	78	Cervecería		Las Teresas	13
Bar Europa	33	Internacional	53	Lizarrán	66
Bar Giralda	26	El Bacalao	17	Mama Terra	34
Bar Hermanos Gómez	5	El Cabildo	45	Mariscos Emilio	57
Bar Santa Ana	75	El Faro de Triana	84	Mesón Serranito	72
Bar Sol y Sombra	90	El Rincón Gallego	49	Patio San Eloy	69
Bar Quita Pesares	16	El Rinconcillo	19	Puerta de la Carne	2
Bodega Belmonte	18	Entrecárceles	47	Puerta Grande	64
Bodega de Juan		Freiduría La Isla	46	Sopa de Ganso	29
García Aviles	23	Hostaría del Laurel	12	Taberna Coloniales	25
Bodega Santa Cruz	15	Kiosko de las Flores	55	Taberna Coloniales II	48

RESTAURANTS

As-Sawîrah	77	Café Rayuela	27	El Ajo Blanco	22	La Albahaca	10	Lar Gallego
Bar Dueñas	28	Carmela	7	El Manijero	82	La Judería	3	Mesón del Pulpo
Bar Modesto	4	Casablanca	36	Habanita	30	La Primera del Puente	62	Mesón Serranito
Bar-Restaurante Casa Manolo	85	Corral del Agua	14	Horacio	63	La Sopa Boba	86	Pando
		Doña Francisquita	32	Kaede	24	La Yerbagüena	44	Poncio

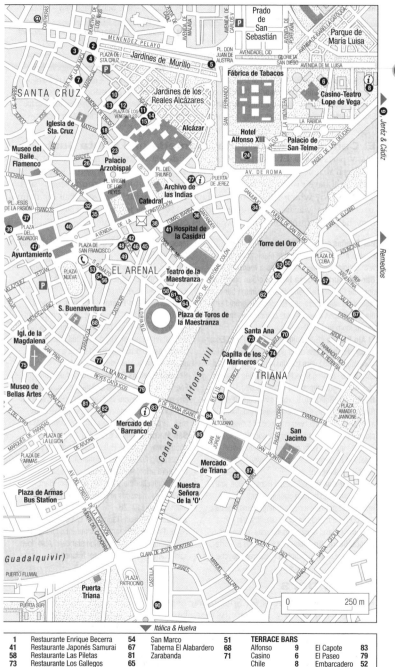

▼ Itálica & Huelva

1	Restaurante Enrique Becerra	54	San Marco	51	**TERRACE BARS**			
41	Restaurante Japonés Samurai	67	Taberna El Alabardero	68	Alfonso	9	El Capote	83
58	Restaurante Las Piletas	81	Zarabanda	71	Casino	6	El Paseo	79
73	Restaurante Los Gallegos	65			Chile	8	Embarcadero	52
89	Río Grande	50						

Restaurante Japonés Samurai c/Salado 6. Interesting little Japanese restaurant with versions of Oriental dishes slanted towards Spanish palates; has an economical *menú* for €6.50.

Río Grande c/Betis 70 ☎ 95 427 39 56. One of the best places for a lunch-time feast of traditional meat and fish dishes. Whether you're seated behind the panoramic windows or on the terrace, the view across the river to the Torre del Oro and Giralda, illuminated at night, is stunning. Their next door tapas bar – also with terrace view – is worth a visit too. Main dishes €12–20.

🏃 Taberna El Alabardero c/Zaragoza 20, just west of Plaza Nueva ☎ 95 450 27 21. Elegant nineteenth-century *casa-palacio sevillana* with attractive decor and an upmarket clientele. Pricey – and outstanding – restaurant upstairs where the *menú de degustación* costs €60; however, the daily €17.50 lunch-time *menú* in the patio bar below comes from the same kitchen.

El Centro, La Macarena, Alameda and Santa Justa

Many parts of the **El Centro** zone still possess a seedy charm, especially in its southern reaches and the remoter bits of **La Macarena**. This is the real Seville and you'll have no trouble finding low-priced *comidas* in and around streets such as c/San Eloy which runs into Plaza Duque de la Victoria, as well as all the main arteries of La Macarena. The **Alameda de Hércules** is a formerly dubious area now heading upmarket with new places opening all the time.

Bar Dueñas c/Dueñas 1, on corner of three streets. Ancient and attractive place to have lunch with delicious home cooking and a *menú* for €8.

Bar-Restaurante Casa Manolo c/San Jorge 16, near the Puente de Triana. Buzzing Triana bar-restaurant with tapas and *raciónes* (or breakfast) in the bar or economical *platos combinados* in a dining room just off it.

El Ajo Blanco c/Alhóndiga 19, east of Plaza Encarnación. Friendly little diner serving up Mexican *enchiladas* (filled corn tortillas) and a pretty good *ajo blanco* (white gazpacho with floating grapes). Also does South American tapas. Closed Aug.

Habanita c/Golfo s/n, a small street off c/Pérez Galdos. Meat, fish and some vegetarian dishes with a Caribbean slant served on wooden tables in a pleasant diner or on an atmospheric terrace. Specials include *yuca con salsa mojito* (sweet potato in a spicy sauce) and *berenjenas Habanita* (sautéed aubergine).

🏃 Lar Gallego c/Gonzalo Bilbao, close to the Santa Justa train station. Excellent little mid-priced bar-restaurant serving *platos típicós gallegos* – fish and *mariscos* (shellfish) in the restaurant – and equally good tapas at the bar.

Mesón Serranito Alfonso XII 9, behind El Corte Inglés. Cosy little economical restaurant beyond the tapas bar out front, with good fish and meat dishes. *Menú* for €9.

Pando c/San Eloy 47. Lively, stylish and economical tapas and *raciónes* restaurant which also does salads. An ideal lunch stop.

Restaurante Las Piletas c/Marqués de Paradas 28 ☎ 95 422 04 04. Diminutive, atmospheric and typically *sevillano* mid-priced restaurant with tapas bar (listing 50 possibilities) attached. Specialities include fish and *mariscos* and it has a small outdoor terrace. Main dishes €10–15.

Restaurante Los Gallegos c/Capataz Franco. Friendly and inexpensive Galician restaurant in a tiny alley off c/Martín Villa, serving *gallego* specialities and a wide range of *platos combinados* (try their *tarta de Santiago* dessert). *Menú* for €14.

San Marco c/Cuna 6 ☎ 95 421 24 40. A few doors away from the Palacio de Lebrija, in an elegant eighteenth-century mansion, this is one of the more affordable of Seville's upmarket restaurants, with (like the wine list) an Italian slant. *Raviolis de mariscos al pesto* is a house special. Main dishes €12–20.

Zarabanda c/Padre Tarín 6, off c/Jesus del Gran Poder. Friendly little family restaurant cooking pizzas and traditional dishes to a high standard. Also does salads and is just the place for a lunch stop.

Tapas bars

A popular saying here is *En Sevilla no se come sino que se tapea* ("In Seville you don't eat but *tapear*"). As the city that claims to have invented **tapas**, Seville knocks spots off the competition. There is simply nowhere else in Andalucía – or even Spain – with such a variety of places to indulge this culinary art. *El tapeo* means eating "on the go" and *sevillanos* do it on their feet, moving from bar to bar where they stand with a *manzanilla* or beer – leaving the seats to tourists – whilst wolfing back fistfuls of whatever tapas take their fancy. Locals tend to drink the cold, dry *fino* with their tapas, especially *gambas* (prawns), but sometimes beer. Another popular tapas partner is a *tinto de verano* – the local version of *sangría* – consisting of wine mixed with lemonade and ice. Finally, don't think that because the servings are small they are always low-priced. Some seafood tapas can be pricey, as can the cured *jamón*, and the plates have a tendency to mount up. Making your way to some of the bars listed below will lead you into areas where tapas outlets tend to congregate, enabling you to make discoveries of your own – an essential part of becoming a *tapeador*.

Barrio Santa Cruz and the Cathedral area

The ancient heart of Seville is filled with tapas possibilities and has a few of the very best places in town.

Bar Enrique Becerra c/Gamazo 2. Outstanding bar and restaurant. House specials include *bocadito de mejillones* (mussels) and *ajo blanco*. Closed Sun.

Bar Europa Junction of c/Alcaicería de Loza and c/Siete Revueltas. Fine old watering hole with lots of cool tiled walls plus excellent *manzanilla* and a variety of tapas served on marble-topped tables.

Bar Giralda c/Mateos Gago 1. One of the city's leading bars, in a Moorish bathhouse with arched doorways and lots of *azulejos*, and serving a wide selection of tapas. House specials include *calabacín al horno* (baked courgette) and *cazuela Tío Pepe* (meat stewed with *fino*).

Bar Hermanos Gómez Jardines de Murillo. One of a chain of similar places offering excellent value for money; economical tapas and *raciónes* served on a big garden terrace. *Habas con jamón* (broad beans) is particularly recommended and there's a low-priced *menú* for €6.50.

Bodega Belmonte c/Mateos Gago 24. A classic place with vibrant ambience and superb *raciónes* (and *media raciónes*) – try their tasty *queso de cabra horneado* (baked goat's cheese).

Bodega de Juan García Aviles c/Mateos Gago 20. Also known as *Bar Alvaro Peregil*, this ancient and renowned bathroom-sized spit-and-sawdust place serves top-notch *manzanilla* while tapas are limited to *jamón* and olives.

Bodega Santa Cruz c/Rodrigo Caro 1. Close to the Hospital de Venerables, serving up generous tapas portions. House specials include *tortilla de bacalao* (cod omelette).

Bodeguita Santa Justa c/Hernando Colón 1. Prize-winning tapas and *raciónes* outlet with a long list of mouthwatering possibilities including *pinchito de lomo con dátiles y miel* (pork with dates and honey). Also has an economical *menú del dia* for €9.90.

Casa Morales c/García de Vinuesa 11. Pleasant old bar, founded in 1850, which once served

barrelled Valdepeñas wine from great butts (now empty) behind the counter. Today a few simple tapas are served on *tablas* (wooden boards).

Casa Robles c/Álvarez Quintero 58. Fronting the cathedral, this first-rate tapas venue has an equally fine restaurant. House specials are paella and *pez espada al ajillo* (swordfish with garlic).

Casa Román Plaza de los Venerables 1. Ancient and renowned tapas haunt specializing in *jamón*, eaten at the bar or at the tables outside. Closed Sun eve.

Cervecería Internacional c/Gamazo 3. High ceilinged beer bar serving up 15 world beers on draft and many more in bottle. Also offers tapas such as *garbanzos con bacalao* (cod with chick-peas) to go with them.

El Rincón Gallego c/Harinas 21. Tiny outpost of Galicia serving only tapas (which change daily) from this northwest province. House specials include *pulpo a la feira* (octopus with paprika) and *empanada* (Galician pie).

Entrecárceles c/Manuel Cortina s/n. Tiny, century-old bar, on the site of the prison that once housed Cervantes, serving a magnificent, rare (and pricey at around €18) *Fino Imperial* sherry by the glass. Specials include *anchoas con queso* (anchovies with cheese) and *melva con pimientos* (tuna with peppers).

Freiduría La Isla c/García de Vinuesa 13. Great little *freiduría* serving up a wide variety of mouthwatering fried fish and tucked away in the back streets off the south side of Plaza Nueva. The nearby *freiduría El Arenal* on c/Arfe is another excellent place and you should be able to take your *cartucho* of fish into the *El Arenal* bar almost next door (providing you buy a drink).

Hostaria del Laurel Plaza de los Venerables 5. Historic and popular bar whose superb decor with Triana tiles is complemented by hanging *jamónes* and mouthwatering tapas. House specials are *riñones al jerez* (kidneys in *fino*) and *zarzuelita de mariscos* (shellfish cocktail).

La Alcena c/Aguilas 6. New style tapas bar with shop attached selling high-class *andaluz* products like *jamón* and cheese. Good tapas range includes *bacalao en aceite* (cod); they also do desserts should you want to make a meal of it.

La Moneda c/Almirantazgo 4. Lively haunt serving up tapas and excellent *manzanilla*. Specials include *langostinos* (king prawns) and *calamares rellenos* (stuffed squid). Also has its own attractive little restaurant.

Las Teresas c/Santa Teresa. Atmospheric, traditional L-shaped bar with cured hams hanging above tiled walls lined with photos of *toreros* and bottles of vintage sherry. Also a nice place to relax over breakfast. Specials include

queso viejo (mature cheese), *calamares a la riojana* (squid) and a tasty *arroz dominical* ("Sunday rice") served only on the sabbath.

Puerta de la Carne c/Santa María La Blanca 36. Not strictly a tapas bar but a *freiduría* where you can buy a *cartucho* (bag) of delicious fried fish and – with a beer from the bar – eat it out of the paper on a very pleasant terrace.

Taberna Coloniales II c/Fernandez y González 36 (at the junction with c/Jimios). Newly opened twin establishment to the original bar in Plaza Cristo de Burgos (see p.294), this is up to the same high standard. Tapas are served at the bar but cornering a table will allow you to feast on a range of wide tapas including *solomillo al whisky* (pork loin); and they also let you round it off with *café* and desserts *de la casa*.

The Río Guadalquivir and Triana

The streets near the **river** surrounding the Maestranza bullring have always been a prime spot for tapas bars, no doubt to serve the gargantuan appetites of fight fans. Owing perhaps to its *gitano* traditions, **Triana** is another excellent hunting ground for tapas, both on the riverfront along c/Betis, and further into the *barrio*.

Bar Anselma c/Pagés del Corro 49. Fine old place with neo-Moorish facade owned by a *dueña* (female proprietor) with many Rocio connections (every night at midnight the lights are dimmed and the Rocío hymn is sung). If you're lucky you may just catch some of the best impromptu flamenco in town. House specials include *caldereta* (lamb stewed in *fino*), and *pisto* (stewed vegetables). Doesn't open till 11pm. Closed Sun.

Bar Antonio Romero c/Antonia Díaz 19. A real *tapeador*'s bar that is much visited by the Maestranza crowd before and after *corridas*. Specials include *muslo de pato* (duck) and *salmón ahumado con alcaparras* (smoked salmon with capers). They have another bar slightly east of here at c/Gamazo 16.

Bar Bistec c/Pelay y Correa 34. Ancient and hearty Triana hostelry opposite the church of Santa Ana, with outdoor tables in summer. Specials include *cabrillas* (spicy snails), *codorniz en salsa* (quail) and *pan de mi pueblo* (cod *gazpacho*). Closed Wed.

Bar Santa Ana c/Pureza 82. Lively *barrio* bar fronting the church of Santa Ana. Wide tapas and *raciónes* range plus outdoor tables. House special is *tortillitas de camarón* (shrimps in batter).

Bar Sol y Sombra c/Castilla 151. At the northern end of Triana, this is another favourite with bullfight fans as well as an atmospheric bar in its own right. House specials include *cola de toro* (oxtail), *almejas* (clams) and *cazuela Tío Pepe* (stew with *fino*). Daily 1–3.30pm & 8.30pm–midnight.

Bodega Siglo XVIII c/Pelay y Correa 32. Close to *Bar Bistec*, this solid Triana establishment has pretty tiles, plenty of *corrida* posters and good tapas.

El Faro de Triana Puente de Triana. Sitting atop the western end of the Puente de Triana (aka Puente de Isabel II), the dining room and roof terrace here give amazing river views. Tapas at the bar and *raciónes* at the tables consist of fish, meat and *mariscos*.

Kiosko de las Flores c/Betis s/n, on the river. A Seville institution, this *freiduría* has a prime riverside location with fine views. In season you can eat *raciónes* at outdoor tables. Specials include *coquinas* (clams).

La Albariza c/Betis 6. Triana bar fitted out like a Jerez *bodega* with butts used as tables. House specials include *tortilla de camarones* (shrimps in batter) and *caña de lomo* (cured pork).

Las Golondrinas Antillano Campos 26. Charming bar on two floors filled with Triana *azulejos* and serving quality tapas. Specials include *punta de solomillo* (sirloin steak) and *alcachofas aliñados* (artichokes). Closed Wed.

Mariscos Emilio (aka Cervecería La Mar) c/Génova 1. Excellent bar specializing in self-service seafood tapas. House specials include *almejas* (clams), *ostras* (oysters) and *cañaíllas* (murex shellfish). Equally good Triana offshoots of the same bar are to be found at c/López de Gomara 18 (with a terrace) and c/San Jacinto 39 (corner with c/San Romero).

Puerta Grande c/Antonia Díaz 33. This popular bar-restaurant takes its name from the gate through which successful *matadores* get carried shoulder high. Serves up tasty *raciónes* in the bar and there's also a stylish restaurant decked out with bullfighting regalia and a decent-value *menú* for around €20.

Centro, Alameda de Hércules and La Macarena

The **Centro** is the bustling heart of Seville in a culinary as well as geographical sense. The areas surrounding four of the *barrio*'s focal landmarks – the Museo de las Bellas Artes, the vibrant artery c/Sierpes, Plaza Alfalfa and the Iglesia de Santa Catalina – provide rewarding hunting grounds for the *tapeador*. The **Alameda de Hércules** used to be the town's red-light district but all that has gone, and it's now become a new focus for tapas bars and nightlife.

Bar Alicantina Plaza del Salvador 2. Famous bar with outdoor tables on a pleasant pedestrianized square, offering excellent, pricey seafood tapas and a celebrated *ensalada rusa*. House specials include *gambas rebozadas* (prawns fried in breadcrumbs).

Bar Dos de Mayo Plaza de la Gavidia s/n. A popular bar with a good tapas range. Specials include *tortilla relleña* (*marisco*- or tuna-stuffed omelette) and *tostaditas de bacalao* (cod on toast).

Bar El Tito c/Macarena 8. Close to the Basilica Macarena this is a busy little bar with a good fish and meat tapas range.

Bar Eslava c/Eslava 3, facing the Iglesia de San Lorenzo. Excellent and popular tapas place with low prices and great atmosphere. House specials include *cordero con miel* (lamb with honey), *boquerones rellenos* (stuffed anchovies) and *pasteles de verduras* (vegetable pies). Has added a very good restaurant next door.

Café Universal c/Blanca de los Rios 3, off the east side of Plaza del Salvador. Quality tapas in pleasant surroundings with a small terrace; house special is *patatones* (potatoes with various dips). Also does *platos combinados*.

Casa Los Caracoles c/Pérez Galdós, just off Plaza Alfalfa. Long-established and friendly bar with lively outdoor terrace serving most tapas. House specials include *caracoles* (snails) and *espinacas con garbanzos* (spinach with chickpeas).

El Bacalao Plaza Ponce de León 15. This venue is devoted to *bacalao* (cod) in all its manifestations, but they do have other dishes, too. Specials to try are their *tortillas*, *croquetas* and *taquitos* (all cod). Closed Sun.

El Rinconcillo c/Gerona 32. Seville's oldest bar (founded in 1670), just off Plaza Los Terceros, and full of atmosphere. A meeting place for the city's literati, excellent tapas are often washed down with a *coronel* (colonel), an ample glass of Valdepeñas red wine. Renowned for its *jamón* and cheese tapas, other specials include *espinacas con garbanzos* (spinach with chickpeas) and *bacalao con tomate* (cod). Closed Wed.

La Giganta c/Alhóndiga 6 (actually facing church of Santa Catalina). Taking its name ("The Big Lady") from the city's nickname for the figure of Faith atop the Giralda tower, there are numerous images of her throughout. House special is tablas (boards of cheese or meat) and it has a wide tapas range including *costillas* (ribs) and *lomo a la cerveza* (beef stewed in beer).

La Ilustre Victima c/Dr Letamendi 35. Great tapas and drinking bar with original decor, laid-back music and house specials such as couscous and *shoarmas* (kebabs). Opens till late.

La Sopa Boba Tapas c/Joaquín Costa 10. Offshoot of the diner of the same name (see p.287), this modern tapas bar has a range of economical tapas including *carpacho de magret de pato* (duck).

Lizarrán c/Javier Lasso de la Vega 14, corner with c/Trajano. Cheap, cheerful and busy bar serving Basque-style *pintxos* (snacks on sticks). There's a wide variety to choose from (around €1 each) and when you want to pay, the barman/woman counts up the number of sticks on your plate (no cheating).

Mesón Serranito Alfonso XII 9, behind El Corte Inglés. The bar adjoined to the restaurant of the same name (see p.290) is also worth a mention for great-value tapas. The house special, *serranito* (*bocadillo* with pork loin and *jamón*) uses the diminutive ironically – it's a meal in itself.

Patio San Eloy c/San Eloy 9. Youthful bustling and economical bar on a busy pedestrianized street with a giant tiled "staircase" at the back where everyone sits to eat their *bocadillos*; other options include *salmón ahumado* (smoked salmon) and *montaditos* (titbits on bread).

Sopa de Ganso ("Duck Soup") c/Pérez Galdós 8, close to Plaza Alfalfa. Young, lively bar in one of the city's main nightlife zones. On offer are *tagarninas* (a pastie) and *pudín de verduras* (vegetable bake).

Sweet-tooth Seville

Many of Seville's **conventos de clausura**, or enclosed orders of nuns, earn money to support themselves by turning out **dulces** (confectionery). So skilled have they become in this trade that today they supply many of the city's leading restaurants with their desserts. Among convents only too willing to lead you into temptation are the Convento de San Leandro, Plaza Ildefonso 1, renowned for its *yemas*, a sugar, syrup and egg-yolk concoction, or the Convento de Santa Inés, c/Doña María Coronel 5, near the church of San Pedro, whose speciality is *bollitos* (sweet buns) and *tortas almendradas* (almond cakes). In the heart of Macarena, Santa Paula – more famous for its nineteen varieties of jams and marmalades – also gets into the *dulces* business with Andalucía's signature dessert, the egg-yolk confection *tocino de cielo* (translated, very inadequately, as "heavenly lard").

For the best **cakes** and **pastries** in town, head for the *pastelerías* along c/Sierpes. *La Campana*, at no. 1, is the most celebrated, although many of the others, such as *Ochoa* at no. 45, are just as good. 🏃 *Horno de San Buenaventura*, at c/García de Vinuesa 10, on the cathedral's doorstep, has two floors where *sevillanos* love to indulge themselves with creamy pastries and *andaluz* classics such as *tocino de cielo*. To cool down in Seville's intense summer heat the city's favourite **ice cream** maker, Heladería Rayas, c/Almirante Apodaca 1 (near the church of San Pedro), has the best selection and there's a terrace, too.

🏃 **Taberna Coloniales** Plaza Cristo de Burgos 19. Typical ancient *sevillano* tavern decorated with photos of the town's bygone days serving up outstanding, generous and fair-priced tapas. House specials include *salmorejo* plus a variety of *ensaladas*. Has a very pleasant terrace that you'll need to queue for in summer.

Nightlife

Seville has plenty to offer in the way of **nightlife**, from expensive, touristy flamenco shows to atmospheric, tucked-out-of-the-way drinking holes. On summer evenings bar terraces by the river (see p.299) often put on live musical entertainment. Major **concerts** take place in one of the football stadiums (see "Listings", p.300) or in the Auditorio de La Cartuja across the river. La Teatral, c/Velázquez 12, near Plaza Duque de la Victoria (☏95 422 82 29), are the official ticket agents for many concerts. Throughout the summer the Alcázar, the Prado de San Sebastián gardens and other squares host occasional **free concerts**. Information on these and most of the above should be available from the Turismo, the local press and the *El Giraldillo* listings magazine.

Flamenco

Flamenco music and dance are on offer at dozens of places around the city, some of them extremely tacky and over priced. Finding *flamenco puro*, the real thing, isn't easy, possibly because – like good blues or improvised jazz with which flamenco shares an affinity – its spontaneous nature is almost impossible to timetable. Visitor demand for this romantic Spanish art form has resulted in a form of "theatre flamenco", where you can pay to see two shows a night – a far cry from the time when the *gitanos* sang in their *juergas* (shindigs) for as long and as often as the mood took them.

Various **festivals** such as the Bienal de Flamenco, A Palo Seco (Cante Jondo), Un Verano de Flamenco, as well as concerts staged by the various *barrios*, take place throughout the summer months and are worth keeping an eye out for as your chances of hearing something special are high. They are widely advertised and the Turismo and local press should have details. One place where you are guaranteed to hear some authentic flamenco is in the Triana *barrio*'s annual festival **Velá de Santa Ana** held during the final week in July. There are flamenco performances (free) every night starting around 10 or 11pm in the Plaza del Altozano and along the waterfront c/Betis. Performances by top artistes are also staged at the **Museo del Baile Flamenco** (see p.278).

▲ Feria de Abril, Seville

Seville boasts two of the largest festival celebrations in Spain. The first, **Semana Santa** (Holy Week), always spectacular in Andalucía, is here at its peak with extraordinary processions of masked penitents and lavish floats. The second, the **Feria de Abril**, is unique to the city – a one-time market festival, now a week-long party of drink, food and flamenco. The *feria* follows hard on the heels of Semana Santa so if you have the energy, experience both.

Semana Santa

Semana Santa may be a religious festival, but for most of the week solemnity isn't the keynote – there's lots of carousing and frivolity, and bars are full day and night. In essence, it involves the marching in procession of brotherhoods of the church (*cofradías*) and penitents, followed by *pasos*, elaborate platforms or floats on which sit seventeenth-century images of the Virgin or of Christ. For weeks beforehand, the city's fifty-plus *cofradías* painstakingly adorn the hundred or so *pasos* (each brotherhood normally carries two; Christ and a Virgin), spending as much as €350,000 on flowers, costumes, candles, bands and precious stones. The bearers (*costaleros*, from the padded *costal* or bag protecting their shoulders) walk in time to traditional dirges and drumbeats from the bands, which are often punctuated by impromptu street-corner *saetas* – short, fervent, flamenco-style hymns about the Passion and the Virgin's sorrows.

Each procession leaves its district of the city on a different day and time during Holy Week and finally ends up joining the official route at La Campana (off Plaza Duque de la Victoria) to proceed along c/Sierpes, through the cathedral and around the Giralda and the Bishop's Palace. **Good Friday** morning is the climax, when the *pasos* leave the churches at midnight and move through the town for much of the night. The highlights then are the procession of El Silencio – the oldest *cofradía* of all, established in 1340 – in total silence, and the arrival at the cathedral of **La Esperanza Macarena**, an image of the patron Virgin of bullfighters, and by extension of Seville itself.

On **Maundy Thursday** women dress in black and it's considered respectful for tourists not to dress in shorts or T-shirts. Triana is a good place to be on this day when, in the early afternoon, **Las Cigarreras** (the *cofradía* attached to the chapel of the new tobacco factory) starts out for the cathedral with much *gitano* enthusiasm.

To see the climax of all the processions, save that of the Cofradía del Resucitado (Resurrection) on **Easter Sunday**, there's always a crush of spectators outside the cathedral and along c/Sierpes. However, without a seat (the best of which are

---

Bar Quita Pesares Plaza Jerónimo de Córdoba, near the church of Santa Catalina. A tapas bar by day run by the flamenco singer Peregil, after dark it metamorphoses into a frequently chaotic flamenco venue where there's often spontaneous music, especially at weekends. Things get lively around midnight and, more importantly, when the owner is on song. If he isn't, he'll sell you a CD of an occasion when he was.

Casa Anselma c/Pages del Corro 49, in Triana. Live flamenco most nights starting around 10.30pm; free.

Casa de la Memoria de Al Andalus c/Ximénez de Enciso 28, in the Barrio Santa Cruz ☎ 95 456

06 70. Cultural centre with fine patio mounting excellent and reasonably priced concerts of flamenco throughout the year. The programme changes monthly so you'll need to ring or pick up a leaflet. Tickets (which need to be booked in advance) €14.

El Arenal c/Rodo 7, one block south of the Plaza de Toros ☎ 95 421 64 92. Most palatable of the pricey tourist flamenco spots, and run by a former dancer who sees to it that the spectacle doesn't veer too far into burlesque. Tickets for shows at 9pm and 11pm cost a steep €36 (including one drink) or, including dinner, €70. If they're not too busy after the first show you can stay to see the second for free.

rented by the hour and booked up weeks in advance; contact the Turismo for details) or an invitation to share someone's balcony, viewing spots near the cathedral are almost impossible to find. A good place to stand is beneath the Giralda, where the processions exit into Plaza de la Virgen de los Reyes, but even here it gets chaotic. The best way of all to see the processions is to pick them up on the way from and to their *barrios*, which is where you'll see the true *teatro de la calle* – the theatre of the streets.

During Semana Santa the pattern of events changes every day, and while newsstands stock the official programme – *Programa de la Semana Santa* – they quickly sell out. A daily detailed **timetable** is issued with local papers (*El Correo* and *Diario de Sevilla* both do coloured route maps) and is essential if you want to know which processions are where. The ultra-Catholic *ABC* paper has the best background information, and the Turismo's *El Giraldillo* listings magazine prints a brief programme, whilst the banks and bigger hotels tend to produce their own guides. The national *El País* and *El Mundo* newspapers also carry excellent daily supplements with all the routes and *cofradías* tunics listed in colour. A dedicated **website**, ⓦ www.lapasion .net, also has lots of background information and links.

The Feria de Abril

The nonstop, week-long **Feria de Abril** takes place in the second half of the month when a vast area on the west bank of the river, the Real de la Feria, is taken over by rows of *casetas*, canvas pavilions and tents of varying sizes. Some of these belong to eminent *sevillano* families, some to groups of friends, others to clubs, trade associations or political parties. Each one resounds with flamenco singing and dancing from around 9pm until perhaps 6am or 7am the following morning. Many of the men and virtually all the women wear traditional costume, the latter in an astonishing array of brilliantly coloured, flounced gypsy dresses.

The sheer size of this spectacle makes it extraordinary, and the dancing, with its intense and knowing sexuality, is a revelation. But most infectious of all is the universal spontaneity of enjoyment; after wandering around staring, you wind up a part of it, drinking and dancing in one of the "open" *casetas* which have commercial bars. Earlier in the day, from 1pm until 5pm, *sevillana* society **parades** around the fairground in carriages or on horseback in an incredible extravaganza of display and voyeurism with subtle but distinct gradations of dress and style. Each day, too, there are **bullfights** (at around 5.30pm; very expensive tickets in advance from the ring), generally reckoned to be the best of the season.

El Tamboril Plaza de Santa Cruz s/n. Tucked into the northeast corner of the plaza, this is another place with a great *ambiente flamenco* where singers often drop in, guitars are strummed, hands start to clap and the magic takes over.
La Carbonería c/Leviés 18. Excellent bar that often has spontaneous flamenco – Thurs is the best night, but not before 10pm. Once a coal merchant's building (hence the name), this is a large, welcoming place, run by flamenco expert Paco Lira, with its own patio at the back. They also do tapas and *raciónes*. Tricky to find, but well worth the effort.

Los Gallos Plaza de Santa Cruz ☎ 95 421 69 81. Reputable flamenco show using a professional group of singers and dancers who sometimes get close to the real thing, although a nagging feeling persists that the performers are just going through the motions. Performances at 8 & 10.30pm; entry is €30 and includes one drink.
Teatro Central Isla de Cartuja ☎ 95 446 06 00. Worth checking on this venue in the local press or with the Turismo, as they often stage festivals featuring up-and-coming flamenco talents as well as established performers.

Discotecas and live music

Earlier on in the evening, Seville's **discotecas** attract a very young crowd; the serious action starts after midnight and often lasts till well beyond dawn. For **live music** the bars around Plaza Alfalfa and Alameda de Hércules have the best of the action. In summer as the town heats up, much of the *movida* (action) switches to the **terrace bars** along the river to the north of the Puente de Triana (aka Puente de Isabel II as far as the Puente de la Barqueta.

Abril c/Luis Montoto 118. The ultimate in chic, trendy *sevillano* nightlife and known for hosting well-known international DJs. If you're in the mood to dance, this is the place.

Antique Avda. Matemáticos Rey Pastor y Castro s/n, near southern edge of Isla Magica theme park. Popular with Seville's *pijo* (yuppie) crowd, this place comes with a transparent dancefloor and music that goes from Latin pop to heavier stuff. Open Thurs, Fri & Sat from midnight. It also has a summer *terraza* named *Aqua*.

Bestiario Plaza Nueva end of c/Zaragoza. All-day (and night) disco-bar throbbing with manic techno sounds. Sun is the big day of the week here.

Boss c/Betis 67. Cavernous disco which takes off after midnight; has a penchant for house.

Buddha del Mar Plaza Legión 8 inside the Plaza de Armas shopping mall. Three storey Asian-fusion resto-lounge-*discoteca* where you can follow a meal by smoking a hookah on terrace loungers or take a drink in the *discoteca*.

Café Central Alameda de Hercules s/n. As it's always the last bar to close on the Alameda this bar draws in an eclectic, international crowd. The atmosphere is laid-back and conversational – just the place to chill out.

Catedral c/Cuesta del Rosario, near the Iglesia del Salvador. Upmarket but attractive smaller club playing techno, funk and soul and hip-hop. Sometimes has live bands.

Fun Club Alameda de Hércules 86. Popular weekends-only music and dance bar with live bands. Open Thurs–Sat from 11.30pm.

Copas and music bars

Copas bars (drinking bars) are scattered all over the centre and many play music. Clusters of good ones are to be found in the Alameda de Hércules and Plaza Alfalfa zones in El Centro, with more gathered to the north of the Maestranza bullring – where there's also a **gay** scene – and along c/Betis in Triana.

Antigüedades c/Argote de Molina 10, near the cathedral. Arty music bar with paintings and sculptures hanging from the ceiling, many the work of the owner.

Azúcar de Cuba Paseo de las Delicias 3 (next door to McDonalds), at the junction with Avda. San Jurjo and near the Puerta de Jerez. A corner of Cuba in Seville where the proprietors (from Havana) play salsa sounds accompanied by authentic nibbles. Open daily and till 3am at weekends.

Bar Garlochí c/Boteros 4, one block northeast of Plaza Alfafa. Claims the title as the city's most eccentric bar, a wonderfully kitsch "religious shrine" complete with incense, candles and flying angels. Their sacrilegious Sangre de Cristo crimson cocktail is a must.

Bauhaus c/Marqués de Paradas 53, north of the bullring. Bar with resident and guest DJs, techno and electronic music, and light shows.

Bulebar Alameda de Hércules 83. Late-opening bar with a plant-filled terrace facing the Alameda.

Often stages theatre, music or other events and serves tapas and *pasteles* (cakes).

Café Moderniste c/Dos de Mayo 28, near the Maestranza theatre. Pleasant, relaxing bar that fills up on opera and concert nights, often with musicians and performers themselves. Noted for its mojitos.

Elefunk c/Adriano 10, near the bullring. Modish *copas* bar with funky *latino* sounds, frequent live bands, and late hours.

Trinity Irish Pub c/Madrid s/n, just off Plaza Nueva. For those with a fondness for Guinness this is Seville's nearest approximation to a Dublin hostelry. *Flahertys*, c/Alemanes 7, next to the Cathedral is an earthier Celtic venue with big sports screens and pub grub.

Urbano Comix c/Matahacas 5, near the Convento de Santa Paula in Macarena. Popular student bar with zany urban decor for rock, punk and R&B sounds plus live bands, staying open till dawn.

Summer terrace bars

On sultry summer nights it's worth doing what *sevillanos* do and making a beeline for these riverside oases which are the only place to stay really cool in July and August (and often in June & Sept too). Note that many of these bars stay open only for a season and open up the next under different names and owners.

Alfonso Avda. de la Palmera, at the junction of Paseo de las Delicias and Plaza America in the Parque de María Luisa. Popular terrace bar in the park for cooling off over a long drink. Open from mid-evening to 5am. The neighbouring *Bilindo* and *Libano* opposite are similar relaxing places.

Casino Avda. María Luisa s/n, in the gardens of the Lope de Vega theatre. The Lope de Vega theatre provides a scenic backdrop to this tropical-themed terrace. The crowd is always dressed to impress, but far from stuffy.

Chile Paseo de las Delicias, near the Parque de María Luisa. Housed in the old Chile pavilion of the 1929 Fair of the Americas, this a colourful bar with a pleasant terrace sometimes featuring live music.

El Capote Next to the Puente de Triana (aka Isabel II). Highly popular riverside bar with outdoor terrace which often stages live bands in summer.

El Paseo c/Paseo de Colón 2, just opposite the Puente de Triana. Small gay bar playing 1970–90s music.

Embarcadero c/Betis 69. Down a narrow passage to the side of the Río Grande restaurant, this is a great little *copas* bar with a riverside terrace and a stunning view towards the Torre del Oro and cathedral across the river. Open 5pm until late.

Ritual c/José de Gálvez s/n, in La Cartuja. This Indian inspired terrace is decorated with Hindu art and whimsical swings. You can cosy up in one of many secluded corners or do your moves to techno music on the dancefloor. A surprise here is the miniature model of Andalucía rescued from Expo 92.

Shopping

Seville is a great place to **shop**, offering everything from regional crafts and ceramics to chic designer fashions and accessories. Shops – except for the larger department stores such as El Corte Inglés – generally close during the afternoon siesta (roughly 1.30–5.30pm) and stay open until 8 or 9pm.

For typically Andalucian souvenirs, Ceramica Santa Ana, c/San Jorge 31, near the Puente de Triana, has a wide selection of Triana **pots** and **tiles**. Nearby, at Ceramica Rocio-Triana, c/Antillano Campos 8, Rafael Muñiz is a creative potter with a more modern slant who will also create a customized painted tile image (any size) to take home or have sent.

Flamenco dresses to sport during the *fería* or take home are available from Duende, c/San Eloy 29, the nearby Doña Ana, c/San Eloy 14, and Angeles Berral, c/Francos 16, while El Corte Inglés, Plaza Duque de la Victoria, also stocks a wide range leading up to the *fería*; prices start at around €180 but you can sometimes pick up a bargain for half this. Molina, c/Sierpes 11, is another good place to try. Casa Damas, c/Sierpes 61, has a wide range of **flamenco CDs** and books and Compás Sur, Cuesta del Rosario 7, just east of the Iglesia de El Salvador, is another well-stocked little flamenco place.

Cutting-edge women's **designer fashions** are sold by Purificación García, c/Rioja 13 (off c/Sierpes), while Daniela, c/San Eloy 25 and Cuqui Castellanos, c/Rosario 8, both do imaginative women's shoes. Attractive modern porcelain can be seen at Sargadelos, c/Albareda 17 (off Plaza Nueva), and glassware and candles at Mercedes Marquez, c/Méndez Núñez 7, nearby.

A wide range of **books** in English (and other languages) is stocked by Casa del Libro, c/Velázquez 8, just east of c/Sierpes. Vértice, c/San Fernando 33, near the Alcázar, is also good and the Beta chain also has guides and maps: central branches include Avda. Constitución 20, Plaza de Gavidia 7 and c/Sagasta 5, just west of Plaza El Salvador. El Corte Inglés, Plaza Duque de la Victoria, stocks English titles and international press. A more comprehensive range of international **newspapers** is offered by Esteban, c/Alemanes 15, right next to the cathedral.

Listings

Airport information ☎95 444 90 00 for flight information.

Banks and currency exchange Numerous places around the centre, specifically on the Avda. de la Constitución and around Plaza Duque de la Victoria, have ATMs. Bureaux de change can be found on Plaza Nueva but banks are a cheaper option.

Bike rental See "City transport", p.253.

Bullfights The main *corridas* are staged during the April *feria*. Tickets from the Plaza de Toros (☎902 22 35 06) or (with commission) the nearby Impresa Pagés ticket office at c/Adriano 37.

Consulates Australia, c/Federico Rubio 14 ☎95 422 09 71; for Britain contact Málaga consulate ☎95 235 23 00; Ireland, c/Conde Galvez 7 ☎954 62 92 05; USA, Plaza Nueva 8 ☎95 421 87 51.

Football Seville has two major teams playing in Division One. Sevilla FC play at the Sánchez Pizjuan stadium, Avda. Eduardo Dato s/n (☎902 51 00 11, ⓦ www.sevillafc.es), on the east side of town. Their fierce rivals Real Betis play at Estadio Benito Villamarín, Avda. Heliópolis s/n (☎902 19 19 07, ⓦ www.realbetisbalompie.es), in the southern suburbs. Pick up schedules from local or national press; you can usually buy tickets at the ground and also at the main Turismo at Avda. de la Constitución 21.

Hospital English-speaking doctors are available at Hospital Universitario Virgen Macarena, c/Dr Marañon s/n (☎95 00 80 00), behind the Andalucía parliament building to the north of the centre. For emergencies, dial ☎061.

Internet There are numerous internet cafés all around the centre of town and several hotels now have pay-as-you-go computers or wi-fi for internet access. Two central internet cafés are Seville Internet Center, c/Almirantazgo 2, almost opposite the cathedral's main entrance (first floor; daily 9am–10pm) and Ciberducke, c/Trajano 8 (daily 10am–11pm) near the El Corte Inglés department store.

Laundry Tintorería Vera, c/Arjona 3, close to the Plaza de Armas bus station (Mon–Fri 9.30am–1.30pm & 5–8pm, Sat 10am–1.30pm); Lavandería Roma, c/Castelar 4, east of the bullring (Mon–Fri 9.30am–1pm & 5–8.30pm, Sat 10am–2pm).

Left luggage There are coin-operated lockers (ask for the *consigna*) at the Santa Justa train station. The Prado de San Sebastián bus station has a left-luggage office (daily 7am–10pm), and there is

another *consigna* at the Plaza de Armas bus station (9am–1.30pm & 3.30–7pm); note that it's not inside the bus station but around the right side of the building by the taxis.

Lost property Oficina de Objetos Perdidos, c/Manuel V. Sagastizabál 3, next to the Prado de San Sebastián bus station (Mon–Fri 9.30am–1.30pm; ☎95 442 04 03).

Maps and hiking For made-to-measure maps in 1:50,000, 1:100,000 and 1:200,000 scales for a defined area, ring Francisco Marquez, c/Las Cruzadas 7, immediately behind the Plaza de España (☎95 442 30 63). The excellent LTC, Avda. Menéndez Pelayo 42 in Santa Cruz (☎95 442 59 64), and Risko, Avda. Kansas City 26, close to Santa Justa train station (☎95 457 08 49), also stocks maps, and has a wide range of outdoor equipment.

Markets Entertaining Sunday markets (*mercadillos*; roughly 10am–2pm depending on weather) take place on the Plaza del Cabildo opposite the Cathedral (stamps, coins, pins, ancient artefacts) and the Plaza del Museo fronting the Museo de las Bellas Artes (various art, tiles and woodcarvings). Calle Feria's long-standing El Jueves Thursday market near the Alameda de Hércules, with secondhand articles and antiques, is another good one. An excellent *artesanía* market, El Postigo, c/Arfe s/n, just west of the cathedral, displays a range of fans, glassware, ceramics, silverware and jewellery with innovative designs made by local craftspeople.

Newspapers Seville's best all-round daily paper is currently *El Diario de Sevilla*, although the older *El Correo* also sells well; both are good for enter-tainment listings and local news.

Police For emergencies dial ☎092 (local police; less serious matters) or ☎091 (national; violent crime and so on). Central local police stations are at c/Arenal 1 (☎95 459 05 58) and c/Credito 11 (☎95 437 84 96), off the north end of the Alameda de Hércules. Petty crime in the city is a notorious problem, but violent crime is rare; avoid leaving anything at all in a car parked on the street overnight; the guarded underground car parks are a possible alternative.

Post office Avda. de la Constitución 32, by the cathedral; also for poste restante (*Lista de Correos*). Mon–Fri 8.30am–8.30pm, Sat 9.30am–2pm.

Taxis See "City transport", p.252.

North of Seville: Itálica and around

The Roman ruins and remarkable mosaics of **Itálica** and the exceptional Gothic monastery of **San Isidoro del Campo** lie some 9km to the north of Seville, just outside the village of **Santiponce**, and both are easily reached by bus from the Plaza de Armas bus station in Seville (Bay 34; Mon–Sat every 30min, Sun every hr), a journey of about twenty minutes. The bus passes the monastery (see p.302) on its way to the terminus outside the archeological site entrance.

Itálica and Santiponce

Once inside the entrance to **Itálica** (April–Sept Tues–Sat 8.30am–8.30pm, Sun 10am–3pm; Oct–March Tues–Sat 9am–5.30pm, Sun 10am–4pm; €1.50, free with EU passport) a free site map from the ticket office will enable identification of the main features. As you survey the dusty, featureless landscape of the site today it's hard to believe that this was once the third largest city of the Roman world, surpassed only by Alexandria and Rome itself. Itálica was the birthplace of two emperors (Trajan and Hadrian) and was one of the earliest Roman settlements in Spain. Founded in 206 BC by Scipio Africanus after his decisive victory over the Carthaginians at nearby Alcalá del Río, it became a settlement for many of his veterans, who called the place "Italica" to remind them of home. With a thriving port – now beneath Santiponce – the city rose to considerable military importance in the second and third centuries AD, when it was richly endowed during the reign of Hadrian (117–138). Grand buildings dripped with fine marble brought from Italy, Greece, Turkey and Egypt, and the population swelled to half a million. Itálica declined as an urban centre only under the Visigoths, who preferred Seville, then known as Hispalis. Eventually the city was deserted by the Moors after the river changed its course, disrupting the surrounding terrain.

In the Middle Ages the ruins were used as a source of stone for Seville, and, from the eighteenth century onwards, lack of any regulation allowed enthusiastic amateurs to indulge their treasure-hunting whims and carry away or sell whatever they found. The Duke of Wellington spent some time "excavating" here during the Peninsular Wars and later the Countess of Lebrija conducted her own "digs" to fill her palace in Seville with mosaics and artefacts (p.279). Somehow, however, the shell of its enormous **amphitheatre** – the third largest in the Roman world and originally standing outside the city walls – has survived. It is crumbling perilously, but you can clearly detect the rows of seats for an audience of 25,000, the access corridors and the dens for wild beasts.

Beyond, within a rambling and unkempt grid of streets and villas, about twenty **mosaics** have been uncovered in what was originally the northern, richer sector of the city. Look for the outstanding Neptune mosaic in the house of the same name, as well as the colourful bird mosaic in the Casa de los Pájaros depicting 33 different species. Towards the baths, in the Casa del Planetario, there's a fascinating representation of the Roman planetary divinities who, in the Roman calendar, gave their names to the days of the week. Finally, the Hadrianic **baths** – named the Termes Mayores to distinguish them from a smaller baths discovered in the village of Santiponce – on the site's western edge are divided into those for men to the centre and right, and those for women to the left.

Itálica today is at the leading edge of archeological technology: advanced X-ray techniques, ground-penetrating radar and infrared aerial photography are being used to gauge the scope of the subterranean remains in those parts of the site not yet excavated. So far a large stretch of fourth-century wall, a necropolis, a monumental arch, another baths complex and numerous dwellings (possibly containing mosaics) have been identified along with what is believed to have been a great religious complex constructed by Hadrian and dedicated to the worship of his adoptive father Trajan. Recently unearthed and now named the **Traianeum**, this lies on the site's southern edge to the rear of the still-functioning walled cemetery of Santiponce which was here long before excavations began. Outside the site, in the village of **Santiponce** itself – beneath which lies another sizeable chunk of unexcavated Itálica – there's also a well-preserved **Roman theatre** (Tues–Thurs 8am–3pm, Fri–Sat 8am–3pm & 4–7pm, Sun 10–3pm; free) and baths (the Termes Menores), both a five-minute walk away from the site entrance and signposted from the main road.

On the way there you'll pass Santiponce's very helpful **tourist office** at c/La Feria s/n (Tues–Fri 8am–2.30pm, Sat–Sun 10am–2.30pm; ☎955 99 80 28). For a meal before or after your visit, the *Ventorrillo Canario* **restaurant** almost opposite the Itálica site entrance does good *platos combinados* and is famous for its charcoal-grilled steaks served with *papas arrugadas* – small baked potatoes in *mojo* spicy sauce. Fifty metres away down a side street behind this, ✸ *La Caseta de Antonio*, c/Rocío Vega 10 (☎955 99 63 06) is even better, and undisputedly the place to go for fish or an outstanding paella. Comfortable **rooms** are also available at the *Hotel Anfiteatro Romano* (☎955 99 67 00; ❸) attached to the *Ventorrillo Canario* restaurant (see above).

Monasterio Isidoro del Campo

A little over 1km to the south of Santiponce on the road back to Seville lies the former Cistercian **Monasterio Isidoro del Campo** (Wed & Thurs 10am–2pm, Fri & Sat 10am–2pm & 5.30–8.30pm, Sun 10am–3pm; €2, Wed free). Closed for many years, it has now been painstakingly and gloriously restored by the Junta de Andalucía and shouldn't be missed.

Founded by the thirteenth-century monarch Guzmán El Bueno of Tarifa fame (see p.188), the monastery is a masterpiece of Gothic architecture which, prior to its confiscation during the nineteenth century Disentailment, was occupied by a number of religious orders. Among these were the *ermitaños jerónimos* (Hieronymites) who, in the fifteenth century, decorated the central cloister and the Patio de los Evangelistas with a remarkable series of **mural paintings** depicting images of the saints – including scenes from the life of San Jerónimo – as well as astonishingly beautiful floral and Mudéjar-influenced geometric designs. In the sixteenth century the monastery was renowned for its library and in 1569 Casiodoro de Reina made the first translation of the Bible into Castilian Spanish (a copy is on display). But when de Reina and others began to display an over-zealous interest in the Protestant ideas of Martin Luther the community fell foul of the Inquisition and was dissolved, with some monks being executed and others escaping abroad.

The monastery was then assigned to the non-hermitic main order of San Jerónimo which employed the seventeenth-century sculptor Juan Martínez Montañés to create the magnificent **retablo mayor** in the larger of the complex's twin churches. Depicting scenes from the *Nativity*, the *Adoration of the Kings* and San Jerónimo himself, this is one of the greatest works by this *andaluz* master of wood sculpture. In wall niches alongside the *retablo* – and positioned above their tombs – are images of Guzmán El Bueno and his spouse, also by Montañés. Other highlights of this remarkable building include the **Sala Capitular** (chapter house) with more wall paintings and **Refectorio** (refectory) with a fine mural of the *Sagrada Cena* (Last Supper) occupying an end wall and displaying more geometric designs worked into the table linen.

To **get here** without your own transport the easiest way to see both monuments is to ask the bus to drop you at the monastery stop ("Parada Monasterio") on the outward journey. When you've seen the monastery you can then cover the 1.5km (a 15min walk or take a later bus) through the village of Santiponce to the Itálica site entrance, from where buses return to the city.

East from Seville

The direct route east by train or car along the valley of the Guadalquivir heading towards Córdoba is a flat and largely unexciting journey. The more interesting route follows the A4-E5 route just to the south of this (the one used by most buses), via **Carmona** and **Écija**, both ancient towns with plenty to see. To the south of Écija lies the ducal town of **Osuna** and its neighbour **Estepa**, both with compelling architectural delights. A short distance from the latter lies the time-warp communist village of **Marinaleda**, run along Utopian lines. With good bus connections to Seville (and trains running from Osuna), these towns are all easily reached on a day trip – Carmona in particular is an easy 30km journey.

Leaving Seville the A4-E5 crosses **La Campiña**, a rich and undulating lowland framed between the Guadalquivir to the north and the hills of Penibetic Cordillera to the south. It's a sparsely populated area, its towns thinly spread and far apart – a legacy of post-*Reconquista* days when large landed estates were doled out to the nobility by the crown. The feudal nature of this system of *latifundia* (great estates where the nobles owned not only the towns but also the inhabitants and the serfs on the land) wrought much bitterness in Andalucía, vividly described in Ronald Fraser's book, *Pueblo*.

Carmona

Sited on a low hill overlooking a fertile plain planted with fields of barley, wheat and sunflowers, **CARMONA** is a small, picturesque town that has burst beyond its ancient walls. Founded by the Carthaginians in the third century BC probably on the site of a Turditani Iberian settlement, they named it Kar-Hammon (City of Baal-Hammon) after their great deity – the origin, via the Roman "Carmo", of its present name. A major Roman town (from which era it preserves a fascinating subterranean necropolis), it was also an important *taifa* state in Moorish times. Following the *Reconquista*, Pedro the Cruel built a palace within its walls, which he used as a "provincial" royal residence – it's now the modern parador.

Arrival and information

The **bus from Seville** will drop you on the Paseo del Estatuto in sight of the Moorish Puerta de Sevilla, a grand and ancient fortified gateway to the old town. Located inside the gateway is an efficient **Turismo** (Mon–Sat 10am–6pm, Sun 10am–3pm; ☏95 419 09 55, ⓦwww.turismo.carmona.org). Arriving by **car**, the subterranean **car park** beneath the Paseo de Estatuto (on the left of our map) is central and convenient. Parking places also become free along

ACCOMMODATION

Alcázar de la Reina	A
Casa de Carmona	B
Hacienda del Triguero	G
Hospedería Palacio Marques de las Torres	C
Hostal Comercio	F
Hotel San Pedro	E
Parador Nacional	H
Posada San Fernando	D

RESTAURANTS

La Almazara	1
Molino de la Romera	9
Parador Nacional	G
Restaurante El Ancla	8
Restaurante San Fernando	3
Taberna el Zahori	7

TAPAS BARS

Bar Goya	2
Bar Plaza	5
El Tapeo	6
Mingalario	4

Lora del Río

CARMONA

El Arahal Marchena Córdoba & Madrid

the main c/San Pedro during the siesta period and after 7pm. The Paseo de Estatuto is also the halt for **buses from Córdoba and Éjica**.

Accommodation

Carmona has a shortage of **places to stay**, especially in the budget category; particularly in spring and high summer, it's worth ringing ahead. The cheaper places lie outside the walls, whilst a clutch of more upmarket options all occupy scenic locations in the old town and have their own restaurants and garages. Prices below reflect the *temporada media* (shoulder season), which covers the months of May, September and October. All other periods are low season when (particularly hotel) prices will be significantly cheaper.

Alcázar de la Reina Plaza de Lasso 2 ☎ 95 419 62 00, ⊛ www.alcazardelareina.com. Rather bland addition to Carmona's luxury hotel list. Fully equipped rooms have internet access and there's a pool. ⑥

Casa de Carmona Plaza de Lasso 1 ☎ 95 419 10 00, ⊛ www.casadecarmona.com. Stylish transformation of a seventeenth-century *casa palacio* into a serene hotel where individually styled rooms are decorated with genuine antiques and artworks. ⑦ with breakfast.

🏃 **Hacienda El Triguero** 4km southwest of town along the A398, direction El Viso ☎ 595 36 26, ⊛ www.eltriguero.com. With your own transport this elegant *cortijo* with cosy en-suite

rooms becomes an inviting rural possibility; an evening meal is available in its restaurant (€18) and there's also a fine garden pool and some great walks nearby. Ring ahead before turning up. ③ with breakfast.

🏃 **Hospedería Palacio Marqués de las Torres** c/Fermín Molpeceres 2 ☎ 95 419 62 48, ⊛ www.hospederiamarquesdelastorres.com. A delightful eighteenth-century palace converted into a welcoming option in the old town. In addition to comfortable double rooms there are intriguing dormitories divided into two-bed and four-bed partitioned cubicles (€23 per person) sharing bath. Offers internet access and wi-fi for guests. Rates include breakfast. ③–④

Hostal Comercio c/Torre del Oro 56 ☎95 414 00 18. Built into the Puerta de Sevilla gateway, this is a charming small *hostal* with compact a/c en-suite rooms (without TV) around a pretty patio. ❸

Hotel San Pedro c/San Pedro 3 ☎95 419 00 87. This is a central and pleasant budget option for a/c en-suite rooms with TV. ❸

Parador Nacional Alcázar Rey Don Pedro ☎95 414 10 10, ⓦwww.parador.es. Despite more recent competition at this end of the market, a superb location, patios and swimming pool ensure that this is still the nicest – and best value – of the luxury places in town. Pay a few euros extra for a room with a balcony. It's worth calling in for a drink at the bar, to enjoy the fabulous views from the terrace. ❼

Posada San Fernando Plaza San Fernando 8 ☎954 14 14 08, ⓦwww.posadasanfernando.com. New and attractive small hotel on this focal square with individually styled rooms with a/c, minibar and plasma TV. ❹

The Town

The majority of Carmona's monuments and churches lie inside the ancient walls. The only site involving a bit of effort to get to is the remarkable **Necrópolis Romana** (Roman cemetery) on the west side of town, a ten-minute walk from the old quarter.

San Pedro and the Puerta de Sevilla

The fifteenth-century church of **San Pedro** (Thurs–Mon 11am–2pm plus Wed–Mon service at 8.30pm; €1.20), near the main bus stop, is a good place to start exploring Carmona. With its soaring tower built in imitation of the Giralda and added a century later, San Pedro evokes a feeling of Seville – entirely appropriate since the two towns share a similar history, and under the Moors Carmona was often governed by a brother of the Sevillian ruler. Inside, the church has a superb Baroque **sagrario chapel** by Figueroa. Just behind the church at the top of Avda. de Portugal lies a famous fifteen-spouted **fountain**, which has figured in many flamenco songs and poems about the town.

The **old town** – circled by 4km of ancient walls containing substantial Carthaginian, Roman and Moorish elements – is entered by the **Puerta de Sevilla**, an impressive double gateway (tours organized by the Turismo Mon–Sat 10am–6pm, Sun 10am–3pm; €2, Mon free). Although most of what you see now is of Roman origin there has been a gate of some form here since Iberian times: remains dating back to the late second millennium BC have been found in recent excavations. Through this gate passed the great Vía Augusta on its way from Hispalis (Seville) to Corduba (Córdoba). During the Moorish period a fortified *alcázar* was added creating the great bastion that still dominates the town's western flank today.

Inside the walls, narrow streets wind upwards past Mudéjar churches and Renaissance mansions. Follow c/Prim uphill to the **Plaza San Fernando** (or Plaza Mayor), modest in size but overlooked by splendid Moorish-style buildings, including the **Casa del Cabildo** (the old Ayuntamiento). A striking Renaissance facade fronts the town's present **Ayuntamiento** (Mon–Fri 8am–3pm) in the square's southeast corner, which is worth a visit to view in its patio a striking geometric-patterned Roman mosaic with a head of Medusa. Behind the plaza (reached by taking c/Sacramento and turning right along c/Dominguez de Aposanto) there's a bustling fruit and vegetable **market** in an elegant porticoed square.

Santa María La Mayor and the Museo de la Ciudad

Moving east from the Ayuntamiento – along c/El Salvador, then left into c/Barrera and right along c/Ildefonso – you'll reach **Santa María la Mayor**

(Mon–Fri 10am–2pm & 5.30–7.30pm, Sat 10am–2pm, closed second half Aug & first half Sept; €3), a fine fifteenth-century Gothic church built over the former Almohad Friday (main) mosque, whose elegant patio it retains, complete with orange trees and horseshoe arches. Like many of Carmona's churches it's capped by a Mudéjar tower, possibly utilizing part of the old minaret. One of the patio's pillars is inscribed with a Visigothic liturgical calendar, said to be the oldest in Spain. The church's high altar has a splendid Renaissance *retablo* and, in the third chapel to the right, a fifteenth-century triptych by Alejandro Fernández. Off the patio is a museum containing artworks by Zurbarán, Roldan and Bocanegro.

Slightly east of here and housed in the elegant eighteenth-century Casa del Marqués de las Torres is the **Museo de la Ciudad** (Mon 11am–2pm, Tues–Sun 11am–7pm; €2, Tues free), documenting the history of the town with mildly interesting displays of artefacts from the prehistoric, Iberian, Carthaginian, Roman, Moorish and Christian epochs. The most entertaining feature is a series of interactive screens in a section dedicated to the role of flamenco in Andalucian culture – enabling you to call up a flamenco style of your choice and fill the museum with the sound. There's little in the way of bars in this area so the museum's **cafetería** provides a useful refreshment stop.

The Alcázar and around

Looming above the town's southeastern ridge are the massive ruins of Pedro's **Alcázar**, an Almohad fortress transformed into a lavish residence by the fourteenth-century king – employing the same Mudéjar craftsmen who worked on the Alcázar at Seville – but which was destroyed by an earthquake in 1504. It received further architectural attentions from Fernando (after Isabel's death) but later fell into ruin, until it was more recently renovated to become a remarkably tasteful parador, entered through an imposing Moorish gate.

To the northeast, beyond and below Pedro's palace, the town comes to an abrupt and romantic halt at the Roman **Puerta de Córdoba**, a second-century gateway with later Moorish and Renaissance additions, from where the old Córdoba road (now a dirt track) drops down to a vast and fertile plain. Following this ancient route for a few kilometres will lead you to a five-arched **Roman bridge** just visible on the plain below. Near to the gate, the church of **Santiago**, at the end of c/Calatrava, is another impressive fourteenth-century Mudéjar building with an elegant brick tower decorated with *azulejos*. Following c/Dolores Quintanilla (and its continuation, c/López) from the Puerta de Córdoba back to the centre, you'll pass by more *palacios* and churches, among them the fifteenth-century **Convento de Santa Clara** (Sat & Sun 10am–1pm), with a *mirador* tower on the left and paintings by Valdés Leal in its church, and beyond the eighteenth-century **Convento de las Descalzas**, the Baroque **Palacio de los Águilar** on the right with a fine facade.

The Necropolis Romana (Roman cemetery)

Lying on a low hill outside the walls, as was the Roman custom, Carmona's remarkable **Necrópolis Romana** (guided tours only, English spoken: Tues–Fri 9am–6pm, Sat & Sun 9.30am–2.30pm; €2, free with EU passport) is one of the most important in Spain. To get there, walk out of town from San Pedro along Paseo del Estatuto and its continuation c/Enmedio, parallel to the main Seville road, for about 450m. Here, amid the cypress trees, more than nine hundred family tombs dating from the second century BC to the fourth century AD were excavated between 1881 and 1915. Enclosed in subterranean *columbaria* – chambers hewn from the rock – the tombs are often frescoed in the Pompeian style with images of garlands, birds and fruit, and contain a series of niches in which many of the funeral urns remain intact.

Some of the larger tombs, such as the **Tumba del Elefante** (complete with a stone elephant, perhaps symbolic of long life) are enormously elaborate, in preparation for the ceremonies that went with burial and after, when the tomb became a focus for family ritual centred on the dead. Alongside its burial chamber, a bath, pantry and kitchen with chimney as well as stone benches and tables for funeral banquets are wonderfully preserved. Most spectacular is the **Tumba de Servilia**, a huge colonnaded temple with vaulted side chambers and separate *columbaria* for the servants of the family. The tours lead you in gratifying detail round this extraordinary site, pointing out the various types of tombs, together with the **cremation pits** where the corpse would have been burned while members of the family (and hired mourners if they were rich) threw clothes and food into the flames for use in the afterlife. The paths between the tombs were also used in Roman times, and it doesn't take a lot of imagination to visualize a slow procession of grieving relatives and mourners preceded by flute players or trumpeters making their way to the family vault.

The site also has a small **museum**, whose finds from the tombs include gravestones, mosaics and vases. Opposite is a partly excavated second-century **amphitheatre**.

Eating and drinking

There are plenty of places to eat both in the old and new town and you don't need to spend a fortune to eat well. However, a step up in price will allow you to sample some of the best food in the province. In addition to the places below, all the upmarket hotels have their own **restaurants**, often with a reasonably priced *menú*. Carmona has its fair share of **tapas bars** too, and the Turismo have made it easy to do a *tapeadores* tour by producing a free tapas guide and map, called *Des Tapa Carmona*. In the old town it's worth seeking out *Mingalario*, Plaza Cristo del Rey 1, facing the church of El Salvador, which is a fine old bar with excellent tapas. *Bar Goya* c/Prim 42, off the west side of Plaza de San Fernando has a nice terrace, *El Tapeo*, almost opposite (which also does a very good-value *menú* for €10), and *Bar Plaza*, on the square itself, are also well worth a try.

La Almazara c/Santa Ana 33 ☎954 19 00 76. Slightly out of the centre, this excellent, stylish restaurant and tapas bar in a refurbished old oil mill (*almazara*) offers a *menú* for €21, and is definitely worth the walk. *Cabrito* (roasted kid), *cochinilla* (suckling pig) and game dishes are among its specialities.

Molino de la Romera c/Pedro s/n, close to the Alcázar ☎954 14 20 00. With a great terrace view across the *Campiña* and housed in a former Moorish oil mill, this pleasant restaurant serves up the dishes of the region, has a good value *menú* for around €18 (including wine) and its *dulces* are prepared by the nuns of the nearby Convento de Santa Clara.

Parador Nacional Alcázar Rey Don Pedro ☎95 414 10 10. The restaurant of the parador is a model of baronial splendour which can be experienced on a *menú del día* for €34 which includes

many local dishes; they also offer vegetarian and diabetic *menús*, a laudable initiative. Main dishes €18–23.

Restaurante El Ancla c/Bonifacio IV, about 500m along the Alcala road ☎954 14 38 04. Out of the centre but well worth the effort, this is a great fish restaurant; there's also an outstanding tapas bar with a tempting *menú* for under €10.

Restaurante San Fernando c/Sacramento 3 ☎954 14 35 56. Carmona's top restaurant is situated in an ancient *casa señorial* and serves fish (especially *bacalao*), game and meat dishes to a high standard; *menú de degustación* for €30. Main dishes €12–18. Closed Sun eve & Mon.

Taberna El Zahorí Costanilla del Pozo Nuevo s/n. Atmospheric *taberna* housed in refurbished former stables of a nearby *casa señorial*. Has a good tapas range in its bar while more elaborate meat, fish and game dishes are served in the restaurant.

Écija

One of the most distinctive and individual towns of Andalucía, **ÉCIJA** lies almost midway between Seville and Córdoba, in a basin of low sandy hills. The town is known, with no hint of exaggeration, as *la sartenilla de Andalucía* (the frying-pan of Andalucía) and once registered an alarming 52°C on the thermometer. In mid-August the only way to avoid this heat is to slink from one tiny shaded plaza to another, putting off sightseeing until late in the day. It's worth the effort, since Écija has eleven superb, decaying **church towers**, each glistening with brilliantly coloured tiles. The town also has a unique domestic architecture – a flamboyant style of twisted or florid forms, displayed in a number of fine mansions close to the centre.

The Romans knew Écija as Astigi (the modern inhabitants are known as *astigitanos*), probably the name of an earlier Iberian settlement. It was an important and prosperous olive-growing town, trading the prized Baetican oil all over the empire during the first and second centuries. In the early Christian era Écija became a bishopric, but in Moorish times (now named *Estadja*) sank into relative obscurity as part of the caliphate of Córdoba. Conquered by Fernando III in 1240, it was only in the seventeenth and eighteenth centuries that it staged a recovery, when the prosperity brought by the new *latifundia* – harking back to the great slave-worked Roman estates – encouraged the nobility to build impressive mansions in the town. Following the devastation wrought by the Lisbon earthquake of 1755, Écija's ruined churches were restored at great cost; hence the magnificent collection of the late **Baroque towers** that are the glory of the place today.

Arrival, information and accommodation

Frequent daily **buses** to and from Seville and Córdoba stop at the station on Avenida Andalucía. The main **turismo** is located inside the Ayuntamiento on the Plaza Mayor (Plaza de España) (Mon–Fri 9.30am–3pm, Sat & Sun 10am–2pm; ☎95 590 29 33, ⓦwww.turismoecija.com). It also offers guided visits to the town's major monuments departing from the tourist office (Wed–Sun 11am; free). The Biblioteca Municipal (public library; Mon–Sat 9.30am–1.30pm & 4–8.30pm) off the western end of the Plaza Mayor in an elegant mansion has free **internet** access.

Limited **accommodation** options include, off the east of the Plaza Mayor, the comfortable *Hotel Platería*, c/Garcilópez 1 (☎955 90 27 54, ⓦwww .hotelplateria.net; ❹), with modern air-conditioned rooms and its own restaurant. East of here again, *Hotel Palacio de los Granados*, c/Emilio Castelar 42 (☎95 590 53 44, ⓦwww.palaciogranados.com; ❻ with breakfast) is a beautifully restored eighteenth-century mansion with delightful patios, small pool and rooms decorated with original contemporary artworks. Another option is *Hotel Sol Pirula*, c/Miguel de Cervantes 50 (☎95 483 03 00, ⓦwww.hotelsolpirula.com; ❹), south of the centre, which also has decent air-conditioned rooms above its own restaurant.

The Town

Écija's most important churches and palaces are all within a few-minutes' stroll of the once delightful arcaded and palm-shaded **Plaza de España** (known locally as the Plaza Mayor). A building site for seven years during the construction of a subterranean car park, the revamped square has been turned into a rather desolate and controversial modern architectural eyesore jarring with the Baroque splendours surrounding it. A Roman bath discovered in the course of these works – only one of many archeological discoveries (see p.311) – can now be viewed from a walkway in the plaza's southeast corner.

At the western end of the plaza the **Ayuntamiento** has a tourist office (see above) and also contains – in the imposing council chamber – a fine second-century Roman mosaic depicting the mythological Dirce being dragged by a bull as a punishment meted out by the two sons of Antiope, Zethus and Amphion – whose mother she had mistreated. Ask in the tourist office for permission to view. An additional feature here is a **camera obscura** (same hours as tourist office; €2.50) providing an effortless way to appreciate Écija's marvellous collection of church towers.

To the west of Plaza Mayor and just behind the Ayuntamiento, the lyrically beautiful tower of **Santa María** (Mon–Sat 10am–1pm & 5.30–8pm, Sun 10am–1pm) – one of the eighteenth-century rebuilds – overlooks the square. Inside, a cloister displays archeological finds from the surrounding area. Behind this church, on c/Castillo, the magnificent eighteenth-century **Palacio de Benamejí**, with a fine portal in contrasting tints of marble, has been relieved

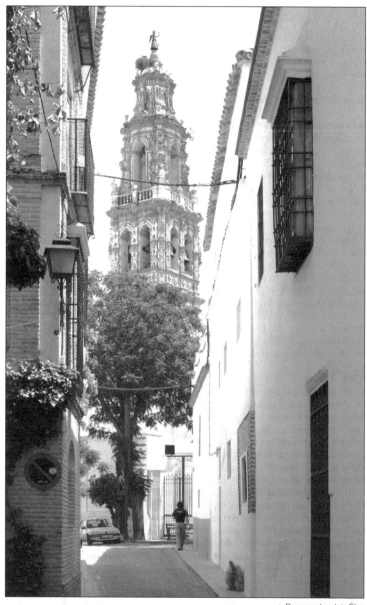

▲ Baroque church in Éjica

of its former role as an army barracks in order to house the **Museo Historico Municipal** (June–Sept Tues–Sun 10am–2.30pm, Oct–May Tues–Sat 10am–1.30pm & 4.30–6.30pm, Sun 10am–2pm; free). A visit to the museum also provides an opportunity to view this magnificent mansion and its patio, now declared a national monument. The museum's collection of artefacts illustrates the town's history, stretching from Neolithic hunters and gatherers, through the Romans – there's a particularly good section on Astigi's role in the olive-oil trade – to the Moorish and medieval epochs. In 2002 the excavations in the Plaza Mayor unearthed the remarkable **Amazona de Écija** a stunning, over two-metre high first-century AD Roman statue depicting an Amazon resting against a pillar. Of the highest craftsmanship and still bearing traces of ochre paint, the image has become the museum's dramatic focal exhibit and the town's civic icon.

South of here the fifteenth-century church of **Santiago** (Mon–Fri 7–9pm) has a Mudéjar side facade and, inside, a fine *retablo* and stunning *Cristo de la Expiration* (Crucifixion sculpture) by Roldán.

To the north of the Plaza Mayor, at the end the street of the same name, lies the church of **Santa Cruz** (Mon–Sat 9am–1pm & 5–9pm, Sun 10am–1pm & 6–8pm; free), whose brick tower was once a minaret and carries tenth-century Arabic inscriptions recording the setting up of public fountains. Inside, there are more superb *retablos* and an early Christian sarcophagus, all beneath a lofty cupola. The charming plazuela fronting the church has two fine old iron crosses on a plinth, backed in summer by a wonderful avalanche of crimson bougainvillea down the wall behind.

Heading along a narrow street out of the Plaza Mayor's northeast corner, you'll soon spot the ornate belfry of **San Juan Bautista**, perhaps the best of all Écija's Baroque towers. In its churchyard are the substantial ruins of the earlier church destroyed in the eighteenth-century earthquake. Continuing east leads you to the sixteenth-century **Palacio de Valdehermoso**, with a Plateresque facade incorporating Roman pillars and, almost opposite and running along c/Castellar, the enormous eighteenth-century **Palacio de Peñaflor** (currently closed; enquire at the Turismo), where a magnificent painted curved frontage is complemented by a full-blown Baroque portal topped with twisted barley-sugar columns. Formerly the residence of the marquises of Peñaflor until the line became heirless in 1958, the edifice was sold to the town council for the nominal sum of 50,000ptas (€300). Unable to support the cost of restoration and maintainence it is now rumoured that the palace will again be sold, to be converted into a luxury hotel. The interior has a fine staircase with intricate stuccowork and cupola off a twin-tiered arched central patio. Nearby on c/San Antonio the Gothic-Mudéjar church of **San Gil** (Mon–Sat 10am–1pm; free) is famed for its pencil-slim tower, and has a recently restored interior with an elegant *retablo* in its *sagrario*. Just beyond San Gil more archeological **excavations** are in progress and have so far revealed the foundations of enormous Roman buildings, plus some extremely fine mosaics on view under canopies. The progress of the excavations can be viewed through the surrounding fence.

Finally, Écija's **bullring**, laid over a Roman amphitheatre on the western edge of town, much impressed a visiting Laurie Lee: "Big, empty, harsh and haunted, for two thousand years this saucer of stone and sand has been dedicated to one purpose, and even in this naked daylight it still exuded a sharp mystery of blood."

Eating and drinking

The number of places to eat are limited in Ecija, but there is enough choice to suit most budgets. For **tapas** and **raciónes** try *Casa Emilio* on the south side of the Plaza Mayor or, better, *Bar La Reja* at c/Garcilopez 1, which has a wider choice. For more substantial **meals** the restaurant of the neighbouring

The nuevas poblaciones of Carlos III

A modern **monument** 20km northwest of Écija, just off the A4-E5 at La Carlota, commemorates one of the more curious episodes in Andalucía's history, when thousands of settlers were attracted from Germany, France, Switzerland and the Low Countries to resettle this corner of Andalucía after disastrous **depopulation** due to the eviction of the Jews and Moors and a plague around 1600. The government also believed that increasing the population would reduce banditry in an area through which passed the *camino real* (royal road), transporting the wealth and bullion of the empire from the port of Cádiz to Seville and Madrid. However, when **Carlos III** – urged on by a radical administrator named **Pablo de Olavide** – added a Utopian wish that these colonies should be egalitarian settlements untrammelled by "rank, privilege or parasitic religious orders", he ran into opposition from the landed class of *señoritos*, who were utterly opposed to parting with even the smallest plots of land.

The scheme was eventually set in train nevertheless, and twelve **colonies** were founded, stretching from La Carolina in Jaén to La Luisiana, 160km away near Écija. The foreigners – an application received from Casanova was turned down – soon came, attracted by grants of free land and cattle. But the scheme ran into trouble when many of the Germans were found to be Protestants; this greatly disturbed the Inquisition, who had them expelled. Others, unable to settle in one of the hottest areas of Europe, packed up and left of their own accord. Within two generations most of the foreign colonists had either been assimilated into Spanish stock or had died out. All that remains of this early attempt at social engineering today are place-names on the map, the geometrical layouts of their streets, and the odd German, French or Flemish name listed in the phone books – and now the monument depicting the king and de Olavide bestowing the document of settlement on another colony.

The village of **La Carlota**, as its name indicates, was one of twelve colonies set up by Carlos III in the 1760s. It's a tidy, anonymous place today, but its eighteenth-century **Ayuntamiento** on the main road is worth a look, as is the **coaching inn**, the *Real Casa de las Postas*, opposite, dating from the same period.

Hotel Platería (see p.309) has a bargain weekday *menú* for €7 while *Cafetería Pasareli*, Pasaje Virgen del Rocío, off c/Emilio Castelar, offers another budget *menú* for €10 and has a terrace. Alternatively the *Bodegón del Gallego, c/A. Aparicio 3*, near the Palacio de Peñaflor, is a step up in price but serves fish, shellfish and meat dishes to a high standard and is noted for its *arroz marinero* (seafood paella). Another inviting option and highly popular with locals is the mid-priced *Casa Machin*, c/Galindo 4, housed in an elegant *casa señorial* where *dorada a la sal* is a house special. Owned by the same proprietors, the nearby and also mid-priced *Las Ninfas* is situated inside the Palacio de Benamejí (see p.309), with a terrace in the palace's courtyard, and *arroz con perdiz* is one of its signature dishes.

Osuna

Some 34km south of Écija along the A351 **OSUNA** is one of those small Andalucian towns which are great to explore in the early evening: slow and quietly enjoyable, with elegant streets of tiled, whitewashed houses and some of the finest **Renaissance mansions** in Spain.

Another settlement of obscure Iberian origin, Osuna first came to prominence as the Roman town of Urso, and ten bronze tablets from this period recording the town's statutes are preserved in Madrid's Archeological Museum.

OSUNA

ACCOMMODATION
Hostal Caballo Blanco — B
Hostal Granadino — D
Hotel Esmeralda — E
Hotel Palacio Marqués
de la Gomera — C
La Casona de Calderón — A

RESTAURANTS
Bar San Agustín — 5
Casa Curro — 4
Doña Guadalupe — 2
Hostal Caballo Blanco — B
La Casa del Marqués — C
Mesón del Duque — 3
Taberna Raspao — 1

Bus station (300m)

In Moorish times the town was of little note and it was during the post-*Reconquista* period, when it became the seat of the dukes of Osuna with enormous territories, that it was embellished with most of the outstanding buildings that make it so attractive today.

Arrival and information

Osuna lies on the Seville–Granada line and is served by three daily trains from the provincial capital, which arrive at the **train station**, Avenida de la Estacion s/n (☎95 481 03 08), on the western edge of town. The **bus station**, Avda. de la Constitución s/n (☎95 481 01 46), with frequent buses to Seville and less frequent services to Málaga and Granada, lies to the southeast of the centre, and is almost as far out. Osuna's **Turismo** lies 300m to the northwest of the Plaza Mayor at c/Carrera 83 (Tues–Sat 9.30am–1.30pm & 4–6pm, Sun 9.30am–1.30pm; ☎95 481 57 32, ⓦwww.ayto-osuna.es), can provide a detailed town map and information on the zone.

Accommodation

Accommodation in Osuna is not plentiful, but outside of national holiday periods and the local *fería* (third or fourth week in May) there's usually no great problem finding a place to stay. All the same, it's worth ringing ahead.

Hostal Caballo Blanco c/Granada 1 ☎95 481 01 84. Welcoming and comfortable *hostal* with en-suite a/c rooms with TV in a remodelled old coaching inn. It has an equally good restaurant and large car park at the back. ❸

Hostal Granadino Plaza Salitre 1 ☎95 481 00 00. Slightly further away from the centre and southwest of the Plaza Mayor, this is a friendly place offering a/c en-suite rooms above a restaurant. ❷

Hotel Esmeralda c/Tesorero 7 ☎95 582 10 73, ⓦwww.hotelesmeralda.es. A recently refurbished former *hostal* offering pleasant a/c en-suite rooms with minibar, TV, safe and wi-fi. Own parking. ❸

🏃 **Hotel Palacio Marqués de la Gomera** c/San Pedro 20, ☎95 481 22 23, ⓦwww .hotelpalaciodelmarques.com. The town's four-star

option, set inside one of the most beautiful *casa palacios* in the country, is a dream. A monument in its own right, this eighteenth-century mansion has a breathtakingly beautiful patio with a Baroque chapel just off it and all rooms are tastefully and individually furnished. Room 7 was used by Franco Zeffirelli when here making a film about the life of María Callas and has a spectacular exterior balcony, while the irresistibly romantic Room 10 is situated in the palace's tower. ❺ with breakfast.

La Casona de Calderón Plaza de Cervantes 16 ☎95 481 50 37, ⓦwww.casonacalderon.com. Charming new hotel in a restored eighteenth-century *casa palacio* with regally furnished and well-equipped rooms, wet-room style bathrooms, elegant patio, small pool and its own restaurant. ❺ with breakfast.

The Town

Osuna's major sights are its collection of stunning **Renaissance mansions** within easy walking distance of the Plaza Mayor and, on the hill to the east of the centre, the old university, Collegiata church and the convent of La Encarnación.

Plaza Mayor and the palacios

Before leaving the elegant **Plaza Mayor** in the heart of the town, take a look at the eighteenth-century **Ayuntamiento** here and, on the west side of the square, the sixteenth-century **Convento de la Concepción** (open service times) with a fine eighteenth-century *retablo*.

The best of the mansions (many of which have an information board outside) erected by the aristocrats and wealthy landowners are off c/Carrera, running north from the Plaza Mayor, particularly c/San Pedro. Here the **Cilla del Cabildo** (at no. 16) has a superb geometric relief round a carving of the Giralda. Further along, the eighteenth-century **Palacio de los Marqueses de Gomera** is another Baroque extravaganza with undulating ornamentation, balcony and solomonic columns beneath the family crest; it has now been converted into an upmarket restaurant and hotel (see above). Calle de la Huerta, off the Plaza Mayor, has more interesting buildings, including the **Palacio de los Cepadas** (now the palace of justice) with an elegant patio and staircase, and nearby slightly north, on c/Sevilla, the **Palacio de Puente Hermoso**. On the same street are more fine *palacios* with the outstanding – but tragically crumbling – **Palacio de Govantes y Herdara** in urgent need of salvation. More *casa palacios* are to be found in calles Gordillo and Compañia (a street off the latter) to the west of the Plaza Mayor.

Old University and Colegiata

Two huge stone buildings stand on the hilltop overlooking the town. The first is the **old university**, now part of the Universidad de Sevilla (patio open term-time Mon–Fri 10am–7pm; closed July–Aug) with an elegant arcaded Renaissance patio. Founded in 1548 by one of the predecessors of the dukes of Osuna, it was later suppressed by the reactionary Fernando VII in 1820 and only recently recovered its academic status. The other edifice is the lavish sixteenth-century **Colegiata** (guided tours only, English spoken, Mon–Sat 10am–1.30pm & 4–7pm, Sun 10am–1.30pm plus Sept–June 3.30–6.30pm; €2.50), which should be visited first. This latter is a fine Renaissance building with a damaged Plateresque west doorway caused, so the story goes, by French soldiers in the War of Independence who used it for target practice. Inside, a guide will point out a sumptuous gilded *retablo* and the remarkable seventeenth-century *Expiración de Cristo* (Crucifixion) by Ribera – one of the artist's greatest works. Also in the church some exquisite sculptures include a superb *Crucified Christ* by Juan de Mesa, from the same period. More Riberas are to be seen in the **sacristía**, which now holds the church's impressive art collection. His *San Jerónimo*, *San Pedro* and a moving *Martirio de San Bartolomé* are all of the highest quality. The high-point of any visit is the descent to the subterranean depths to view the gloomy **pantheon and chapel of the dukes of Osuna**, where these descendants of the kings of León and once "Lords of Andalucía" are buried in niches in the walls. Some of the Renaissance ornamentation is extremely fine, especially the polychromed wooden *Santo Entierro* (burial of Christ), as well as panels from the Flemish school and a fine relief of *San Jerónimo*. The tour ends with the guide pointing out an antique portable **sixteenth-century organ** – one of few to survive from the period.

La Encarnación, Museo Arqueológico and churches

Downhill, opposite the entrance of the Colegiata, is the Baroque convent of **La Encarnación** (same hours as the Colegiata; €2), founded in the seventeenth century by a duchess of Osuna. The highlight of the nun-led guided tour is a fine plinth of eighteenth-century Sevillian *azulejos* (from Triana) round its cloister and gallery, depicting curiously secular scenes. After filling up on the tasty convent *dulces* sold here, you could take a walk north, passing the **Torre de la Merced**, the tower of the former convent church of the same name with its stupendously carved late Baroque tower and portal by Alonso Ruiz Florindo, and the ruins of Las Canteras, once a hermitage, on c/Camino de las Cuevas. Further along here you'll find the **excavations** of Roman Urso, including a necropolis with tombs quarried from the sandstone, as well as the vague remains of a theatre, fort and a gigantic quarry where the Romans obtained their stone to build the city. Otherwise, the more direct descent to the town takes you past the Torre del Agua, a twelfth-century Almohad tower which houses a small **Museo Arqueológico** (Mon–Sat 10am–1.30pm & 4–7pm, Sun 10am–1.30pm; €2) containing finds – and unfortunately many copies of the best items, the originals of which are in Madrid – discovered hereabouts.

Other churches around the town worth seeking out (Mon–Sat from 7pm is the best time to find them open) are the sixteenth-century **Santo Domingo**, at the northern end of c/Carrera, a fine Renaissance church with a couple of superb Mudéjar chapels; nearby, **Nuestra Señora de la Victoria** has an impressive Baroque *retablo* by José Mora. To the west of the Plaza Mayor, the **Convento del Carmen**, on the street of the same name, has another stunning sixteenth-century *retablo* in carved wood and, to the south of the Plaza Mayor, the recently refurbished sixteenth-century **San Agustín** has a beautiful single-naved interior and more fine *retablos*.

Eating and drinking

There are food and drink possibilities all over town and many of the accommodation options also have restaurants of their own. One place not to miss is the wonderful **Casino** on the east side of the Plaza Mayor; with 1920s Mudéjar-style decor and a grandly bizarre ceiling it's open to all visitors and makes an excellent place for a drink (or breakfast) while lounging in armchairs overlooking the square.

Bar San Agustín c/San Agustín 15. Good little neighbourhood bar-restaurant offering economical *platos combinados*. Closed Thurs.

Casa Curro Plaza Salitre 5. The town's best (and liveliest) tapas and *raciónes* bar cooks up a tasty range of seafood and meat dishes. There's a superb restaurant in the back, too.

Doña Guadalupe Plaza Guadalupe 6 ☎ 95 481 05 58. The town's top mid–priced restaurant specializes in *cocina andaluza* and has a terrace on this pleasant square. *Lomo ibérico en salsa de almendras* (pork loin) is a signature dish and there's a *menú* for around €17. Main dishes €12–18. Closed Tue.

Hostal Caballo Blanco c/Granada 1. The *hostal's* restaurant is very good for *comida casera* serving up dishes such as *redondillo guisado* (beef stew)

and *gachas de osuna* (local gruel) as well as the usual standards.

La Casa del Marqués c/San Pedro 20. The very good restaurant of the *Hotel Marqués de la Gomera* is on the high side of mid-priced, and with a rather formal dining room you may well prefer their slightly cheaper courtyard brasserie, the *Asador del Marqués* (June–Sept) on sultrier nights. Main dishes €12–26.

Mesón del Duque Plaza de la Duquesa 2. Excellent little mid-priced restaurant, with the best terrace in town. Wide range of meat and fish dishes including *lomo a la almendra* (pork loin with almonds) and a weekday *menú* for around €10.

Taberna Raspao Plaza de la Merced 7. A very good neighbourhood restaurant for fish and meat tapas and *raciónes* with a pleasant terrace on this square.

Estepa

Another delightful Baroque town, **ESTEPA**, 24km east of Osuna, resembles a miniature version of its larger neighbour. Originally a Carthaginian settlement, it took the side of the North African state during the Punic Wars with Rome, and when the victorious Romans finally took the city in 208 BC they found that the citizens had burned their possessions and killed themselves rather than surrender. Repopulated, it eventually became the Roman Ostipo and, later, the Moorish Istabba.

The Town

Close by the central Plaza del Carmen, the eighteenth-century **Iglesia del Carmen** (7–9pm; free) has an exuberant Baroque facade in black and white stone and a stunningly ornate interior, recently restored. Above, in the *ciudad alta*, the **Iglesia de Santa Clara** (7–9pm; €0.50) is another impressive church, dating from the sixteenth century, with a fine gilded *retablo*. Nearby, the fifteenth-century **Iglesia de la Santa María de la Asunción** (same hours as Turismo, below; €3), built on the remains of a tenth-century *mezquita*, is one of Estepa's oldest churches, and currently undergoing a gradual restoration. The Gothic interior, entered via the tourist office (see p.317) – as well as a new **museum** – has various treasures, many rescued from other churches and monasteries. Look out for a fine sculpture of *San Juan Evangelista* by Juan de Mesa. Immediately to the west of the church lie the ruins of the Moorish **alcazaba**, also undergoing restoration. Lower down in the *ciudad baja*, you'll notice the elegant **Torre de la Victoria** – all that remains of the convent of the same name. Taking c/Mesones (and its continuation, c/Castillejos) from the Plaza del Carmen back through the town, you pass another fine church, the **Iglesia de la Asunción**, known locally as Estepa's Sistine Chapel due to a splendid painted ceiling depicting scenes from the life of the Virgin. The church was originally the chapel of one of Estepa's best mansions, the **Palacio de los Marqueses de Cerverales** (Mon–Fri 9am–1pm; €4 including church) next door, a superb eighteenth-century palace with barley-sugar columns supporting its balcony and delightful patio within. One block south, c/Nueva has some of the town's oldest mansions; among them nos. 12 and 14 are good examples.

Practicalities

To reach Estepa's **Turismo** (daily 9.30am–2pm & 4.30–7pm; ☎ 95 591 47 04), you'll need to climb the hill to the church of Santa María (see p.316) – the office is located in a new annexe which also allows admission to the church. **Rooms** in Estepa are not plentiful but what there is you'll find along the main Avenida de Andalucía. The best deal is *Hostal Balcón de Andalucía* at no. 23 (☎ 95 591 26 80, ⊛ www.balcondeandalucia.com; ❸), where comfortable a/c rooms come with TV, and there's an excellent **pool** at the back. **Places to eat** are also along the Avenida de Andalucía, where the *Hostal Balcón de Andalucía* and *Hostal Rico* at no. 98 both serve decent meals and *menús*. Close to the latter, *Bar-Restaurante Cala D'Or*, c/La Senda 2, is another good option for tasty tapas and *raciónes* or more formal dishes in its restaurant.

Marinaleda

Sited 14km north of Estepa, the unassuming agricultural village of **MARINA-LEDA** seems to have inherited the do-or-die qualities of the early inhabitants of Estepa who resisted the might of Rome. Along with El Arahal to the east, "Red" Marinaleda has become the standard-bearer in the struggle of the *braceros*, or day labourers, against their exploitation by the great landowners. The leader in this struggle is Marinaleda's mayor of over 30 years standing, Sánchez Gordillo, the village schoolteacher and – like the rest of the village almost to a man and woman – a committed communist. He came to prominence as the organizer of a "hunger strike against hunger", but since then has moved on to taking over large estates in the area, by force if necessary. A few years back he occupied a nearby estate belonging to one of Andalucía's major landowners, the duke of Infantado.

The romantic *cortijos* to be seen dotted across the Andalucian landscape – brilliant white pantiled farm buildings surrounded by walls and often shaded by a cluster of elegant palms – have for generations been the focus of the misery of the landless poor, for these are the homes of the landowners, or more often their overseers on whom the day labourers are dependent for what little seasonal work they can get. From the Casa de Cultura at Marinaleda – in reality a workers' club, on the main Plaza de la Libertad – the Sindicato de Obreros del Campo, led by Gordillo, continues to fight for change. Despite the ever-present blight of chronic unemployment Marinaleda marches on and has constructed an impressive new Casa de Cultura (incorporating a full-size theatre) and Ayuntamiento complex at the east end of the village complete with low-power TV station, communally owned crèche and a secondary school.

One of the village's most established and successful customs is **Domingos Rojos** (Red Sundays), a number of days throughout the year when the council requests that the population – young and old – turn out to do voluntary work (street cleaning, painting, gardening, and the like) in public places. Crime is so low that the village has only one police officer for its 2500 population in comparison with the norm of five or six. And, despite an ambivalent attitude towards Marinaleda by previous and current socialist governments in Madrid, and complete indifference from the rightist Partido Popular administrations, significant tracts of land have been transferred into the ownership of the village cooperative which now controls over a thousand acres. Banners hanging from house balconies proclaim opposition to nuclear testing and landowner exploitation, and each street sign bears the legend "A Utopia building peace". In harmony with these sentiments, in the old Casa de Cultura's lively **bar** on the main square you'll be served up the cheapest tapas, beer and *fino* in the whole of Andalucía. The nearest **accommodation** is in Estepa (see p.316), some 14km away.

West from Seville

With your own transport, the fastest – but dullest – way from Seville west to Huelva is via the A49 *autovía*. More tranquil and interesting is the A472 which cuts through the area to the west of the city called El Aljarafe by the Moors (the "high lands," actually rather flat), planted with olives, vines and orange trees, passing a string of farming villages until it arrives, after 12km, at **Sanlúcar la Mayor** where celebrated Catalán chef Ferran Adrià has located the *andaluz* outpost of his culinary empire (see box below).

Some 35km further along the A472, in the province of Huelva, the wine-producing town of **LA PALMA DEL CONDADO** lies off the road to the left. It's highly probable that this terrain, an area first planted with vines by the Greeks, produced the local wine taken on the voyage to the New World by Columbus when he sailed from nearby Palos. The wine produced here today is the Condado de Huelva, which hardly ranks with Spain's top-drawer vintages, but the dry whites are an excellent partner for seafood. With its impressive eighteenth-century Baroque church of **San Juan Bautista** towering over a palm-fringed central plaza, this slow-moving, white-walled country town makes a good stopping point for a drink of the local brew at one of the central bars. If you're tempted to **stay**, the *Hostal Garle* (☏959 40 07 50; ②), on the junction of the A472, has a/c en-suite rooms over a decent **venta**. A new and stylish **restaurant**, ✷ *La Agencia*, c/Real 19, lies a few minutes walk away in the town proper and serves excellent and reasonably-priced dishes in the main room or tasty tapas in its bar.

Heading south from La Palma for 6km, **BOLLULLOS DEL CONDADO** is a busy little town filled with **bodegas** and **ventas** (called *bodegones* here) which are big, high-ceilinged places capable of seating over a hundred diner-imbibers at long trestle tables. A number of them line the main street – *Abuelo Curro*, *Tío Paco* and *El Postigo* are all worth a try.

The A483 continues south from Bollullos to El Rocío (see p.334) and the Coto de Doñana.

El Bulli In Andalucía

The *Hacienda Benazuza* (☏955 70 33 44, ⊛ www.elbullihotel.com; cheapest double room €350; ◉) is the latest venture into the world of hostelería by Spain's internationally renowned chef, Ferran Adrià. Created inside a restored and partly Moorish *hacienda* (from which it takes its name) this hotel and restaurant complex is the last word in luxury and pampered living. Bougainvillea-draped courtyards with tinkling fountains, evocative belfries, aromatic herb and jasmine-scented gardens with palms and orange trees surround the extravagant and individually styled bedrooms and salons. Three on-site restaurants cater to the sybaritic fancies and fantasies of the hotel's clientele (and visitors) with the Michelin double-rosetted *La Alquería* (*menú de degustación* €124) under cordon bleu chef Rafael Morales serving up a changing selection of Adrià's greatest "*cocina experimental*" hits from twenty years of his famous *El Bulli* restaurant in Catalunya. To reach the complex, follow the signs on entering the village.

Niebla and around

Twelve kilometres west from La Palma along the A472, the salmon-pink ancient walls and towers of **NIEBLA** make a spectacular sight. The approach is wonderful, almost a medieval fairy tale come true, for this is a real walled town and looks the part. The Roman **bridge** you cross to reach it – probably built in the second century during the reign of Trajan – is remarkably well preserved and carried traffic for two thousand years until it was blown up during the Civil War. It has since been meticulously restored.

Little is known about a Phoenician settlement here or the possible Iberian village of the Turditanian tribe which may have preceded it. However, coins found dating from the Roman period gave the town's name as Ilipla, which is probably derived from the Iberian name. Described by the Roman writer Pliny as a fortified city of strategic importance, it was a crucial link in the massive Roman mining operations carried out upriver at the Río Tinto mines. The metals – mostly silver – were moved down the river by barge and then transferred to galleys here for the voyage to Rome and other parts of the empire. A bishopric under the Visigoths, after the Moorish conquest it became successively part of the Almoravid and then Almohad domains until, as an independent *taifa* state, it experienced its greatest period of prosperity during the twelfth century, trading in saffron and raisins. After falling to the Christian forces under Alfonso X in 1262, Niebla was passed around as a fief of various rulers, until in 1369 it came into the hands of the Guzmán dynasty, following which it entered a long period of decline.

The Town

Once inside the two-kilometre-long encirclement of the walls, Niebla's tidy streets of whitewashed houses and small squares are a delight to explore. The Puerta del Socorro leads from the Seville–Huelva road to the Plaza Santa María in the heart of the town, dominated by the church of **Santa María de Granada**. The key is available from the custodian of the Casa de Cultura (itself the former fifteenth-century Hospital de Nuestra Señora de los

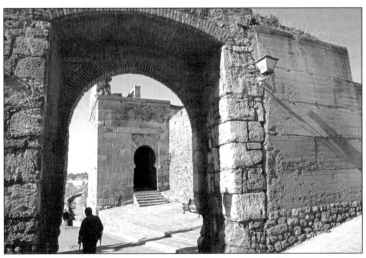

▲ The walled town of Niebla

Ángeles) almost facing the church. Entered through a splendid Mozarabic eleven-lobed portal, the original tenth-century church is believed to have been constructed over a Visigothic cathedral, and was used by Christians during the Almoravid period. It was converted into a mosque by the Almohads in the thirteenth century: the *mihrab* now to be seen in the side wall, as well as the elegant tower – its minaret – date from this period. The pillars in the second-floor windows of the tower, incidentally, are believed to have come from the original Visigothic church. Among the artefacts dotted around the austere and much restored Mudéjar-Gothic interior are a couple of Roman altars and the remarkable, stone-carved **Silla Episcopal**, the throne of the Visigothic bishops. Outside the entrance, a **patio** is dotted with remnants of the building's chequered history – various Visigothic, Christian and Moorish stones and pillars.

Of the ruined church of **San Martín** near the town's main gate and sliced through by a plazuela, only the apse, bell tower and a chapel survive. It was built in the fifteenth century on the site of a former synagogue donated in more tolerant times by Alfonso X as a concession to the Jews of Niebla, and before the Inquisition began its grisly work. The locked chapel contains a fifteenth-century sculpture of Christ being scourged.

The town's **four gates** are also worth seeking out, each with its Moorish horseshoe arch and features, as is the **Castillo de Guzmán** (daily 10am–6pm; €4) with views from its towers. In origin the Moorish Alcázar, but much added to by Enrique de Guzmán in the fifteenth century, it later fell into decay and was ruined after Marshal Soult used it as a barracks for French troops during the War of Independence. Today it stages concerts and theatrical productions over the summer months as part of Niebla's annual festival of theatre and dance.

Practicalities

You can pick up a map and visitor information at the town's **Turismo** (daily 10am–6pm; ☎959 36 22 70, ⓦwww.castillodeniebla.com) located inside the Castillo. Niebla's **train station**, on the Seville–Huelva line, is served by two trains daily in each direction. The station lies at the end of c/Walabonso, heading downhill between the Casa de Cultura and the church of Santa María. There's a **hostal**, the clean and friendly *Pensión Los Hidalgos*, c/Moro 3 (☎959 36 20 80; ❶), with some en-suite rooms, outside the walls near the Seville–Huelva **bus stop**. For **food** you'll need to look on the main road outside the walls, where the *Brasería Las Almenas* at c/Padre Marchena 2 (with a daily *menú* for €10) is a decent place, and *Bar Parada* on the road leading out to Huelva is also worth a try.

Seven kilometres further towards Huelva a turn-off on the left leads to Moguer, one town on the Columbus trail (see p.329).

Huelva and around

Large, sprawling and industrialized, the city of **HUELVA** struggles to present an attractive face to visitors. Still, once you've got past the messy suburbs with their fish canneries, cement factories and petrochemical refineries, the tidy city centre – perched on a peninsula between the confluence of the Odiel and Tinto river estuaries – comes as a pleasant surprise. Huelva's populace escapes the city in summer to enjoy the Atlantic beaches and sea breezes at the resorts of **Punta Umbría** and **El Rompido** across the Río Odiel estuary to the south and southwest.

Huelva was born as Onuba, a trading settlement founded by the Phoenicians early in the first millennium BC (modern inhabitants still call themselves *onubenses*). These early merchant traders were attracted by the minerals in the mountainous areas to the north, and by the time the Carthaginians came to dominate the area in the third century BC Onuba was an established port, conveying these minerals throughout the Mediterranean world. When Spain fell into Roman hands the mining operations at Río Tinto were dramatically expanded to satisfy the empire's insatiable demand for metals such as silver and copper and the city prospered even more. Following Rome's demise the Visigoths and Moors displayed little interest in mineral extraction; the latter concentrated on dominating the seaborne trade with North Africa.

Huelva's maritime prowess gained for the city its crowning glory when **Columbus** set out from across the Río Tinto to find a new sea passage to India in ships manned by hardy Huelvan sailors. The city enjoyed a boom when the Extremadurans to the north of Huelva – the men who conquered the Americas – used the port as a base for their trade with the new territories overseas, but eventually Seville, and later Cádiz, came to dominate the silver and gold routes from the Americas and Huelva was squeezed out. Largely flattened by the Lisbon earthquake of 1755, it is only in the last century that the place has begun to regenerate itself: first as the base for mineral exports from Río Tinto in the early 1900s, when the British Río Tinto Mining Company largely ruled the roost here, and later when Franco established a petrochemical industry in the 1950s.

Arrival and information

Huelva's **bus station** is at Avda. Dr Rubio s/n (☎959 25 69 00). The Autobuses Damas (ⓦwww.damas-sa.es) timetable lists all services throughout the province – handy if you're going to be using the town as a base. Frequent trains to Seville and at least three through-trains a day to Madrid leave from the splendid neo-Moorish **train station** (☎902 24 56 14), a short distance southeast of the centre on Avenida Italia. Completed in 1880 at the behest of the Río Tinto Mining Company, the station is a perfect expression of the burgeoning self-confidence of that period, and is well worth stopping by for a look even if you're not travelling by train. Coming in **by car**, finding a parking place can often verge on the impossible. The easiest solution is to use a pay car park (see our map): one of the most convenient is sited immediately to the north of the bus station.

The **Turismo**, Plaza Coto Mora 2, is located opposite the Gran Teatro (Mon–Fri 9am–7.30pm, Sat & Sun 9am–2pm; ☎959 25 74 03).

Accommodation

Finding a **place to stay** is usually not a problem this far off the tourist trail, although options for the budget traveller are severely limited. Huelva's **youth hostel** (☎959 65 00 10; under 26 €16, over 26 €20) is at Avda. Marchena Colombo 14, in the northern suburbs (bus #6 from the bus station, or #4 from Plaza de las Monjas), and has en-suite rooms. The town's nearest **campsite** is in Punta Umbría, a fifteen-minute bus ride away (see p.324).

Hostal Calvo c/Rascon 35 ☎959 24 90 16. Uninspiring, if clean, central place for rooms sharing bath. ❶

Hotel Costa de la Luz José María Amo 8 ☎959 25 32 14, ⓦwww.hotelcostaluzhuelva.com. A good mid-price option near the market; the higher rooms have balcony terraces. ❸

Hotel Los Condes Alameda Sundheim 14 ☎959 28 24 00, ⓦwww.hotelfamiliaconde.com. Comfortable hotel near the museum, with a/c rooms. Garage available. ❹ with breakfast.

Hotel Tartessus Avda. Martín Alonso Pinzón 13 ☎959 28 27 11, ⓦwww.eurostarshotels.com. Refurbished upmarket hotel on the main street, with soberly furnished a/c rooms, gym and wi-fi internet connection, plus a conveniently located public garage around the corner. ❺

Pensión La Vega Avda. Aleman 96 ☎959 24 45 44. Pleasant new *hostal* near the cathedral offering clean and tidy en-suite rooms with TV. ❷

The City

Many of Huelva's key sights are a short walk from **Plaza de las Monjas**, the city's palm-lined main square including the city's combined archeological and Bellas Artes (fine arts) museums. Other sights worth a look are couple of interesting churches and a curious British-built quarter and hotel, in addition to a couple of notable buildings – the impressive Neoclassical **Gran Teatro**, on c/Vásquez López, and the Art Nouveau **Clínica Sanz de Frutos** (now the Conservatorio de Música), c/Rico 26, both just a short walk from the Plaza de las Monjas.

The Museo Provincial and Casa Colón

The best place to start a tour of the city – especially if you're pressed for time – is at Huelva's **Museo Provincial**, Alameda Sundheim 17 (April–Sept Tues 2.30–8.30pm, Wed–Sat 9am–8pm, Sun 9am–2pm; Oct–March Tues–Sat 9.30am–2pm & 4.30–7pm; free), where the interesting **archeological collection** has exhibits of equipment, tools and oil lamps used by slave miners at Río Tinto in the Roman period as well as information about early mining in the north of the province. The museum's star exhibit (located in a huge glass case next to the entrance) is a magnificent **Roman water wheel** – used to drain water from the mineworkings at Río Tinto. On the second floor, the **Museo de Bellas Artes** is a fairly humdrum collection of works alleviated by a few canvases by Huelvan artist and friend of Picasso, Daniel Vásquez Díaz.

Just to the south of the Museo Provincial lies the elegant pink and white **Casa Colón**, Huelva's first luxury hotel which played a large part in the story of "Huelva británica" housing many of the Río Tinto Mining Company's visitors, and providing a venue for important functions. Built in the final years of the nineteenth century in a variety of styles around a central courtyard with palms and a fountain, when it got into financial difficulties the hotel was purchased by the mining company who used it to house guests and families of mining employees. Today, owned by the city council, it functions as a conference centre and holds the municipal archive. You are free to take a look at the public areas and view the central court.

The Barrio Reina Victoria and Río Tinto pier

One of Huelva's more bizarre features is a whole quarter designed by English architects. The **Barrio Reina Victoria** (or Queen Victoria housing estate), east of the museum alongside the Avenida de Guatemala, was constructed by the Río Tinto Mining Company in the early years of the twentieth century to house its British workers. It's a truly weird experience to stroll along the tree-lined avenues flanked by bungalows with rose gardens and semis with dormer windows and mock-Tudor gables – more resembling Acacia Avenue, Essex, than an Andalucian town. Even the street names have a colonial symmetry about them: Calle A, Calle B and so on. Given the drab uniformity it's little wonder that the present native occupants have attempted to relieve these humdrum northern exteriors with a few primary colours.

Another legacy of the British era is the **Río Tinto pier** (Muelle Río Tinto), on the east side of the harbour, a huge nineteenth-century ironwork structure formerly used to ship out the minerals which arrived by train from the mines to the north. Designed by the British engineer George Barclay Bruce and finished in 1874, the redundant pier's decaying ironwork curves gracefully out into the estuary, and today serves as a boardwalk for loungers and courting couples.

The British workers employed in the mines were also responsible for the importation of **football** into Spain, helping set up Huelva's league club Recreativo in 1889, which is the oldest in the country. It's a pedigree hardly matched by the club's record, however, which has been to languish for over a hundred years in the lower leagues. However, in recent seasons they have managed to hold down a place among the elite of the Spanish first division.

Huelva's churches

The **Catedral de la Merced** (open for services at 7.30pm), just to the north of Plaza de las Monjas off Paseo de Buenos Aires, was one of the few buildings to survive the eighteenth-century earthquake, resulting in its upgrading to cathedral status which – apart from a brilliant-white Baroque interior and an interesting salmon-pink colonial facade with elegant belfries – it hardly merits. It's worth looking inside at the image of the Virgen de la Cinta (the city's patron) attributed to Martínez Montañés.

A more interesting church and one with Columbus connections lies 3km further north along Avenida Manuel Suirot. This is the restored fifteenth-century **Virgen de la Cinta** (daily 9am–1pm & 5–8pm; free), a simple white-walled sanctuary set on a low hill overlooking the sea where Columbus is said to have prayed before setting out on his voyage. Inside, beneath the Mudéjar roof, you can see a medieval fresco of the Virgin, a fine altar grille, and a series of 1920s faïence tiles by the painter Daniel Zuloaga depicting scenes from the explorer's life. To get there, take the #6 bus from Plaza de las Monjas, and ask for the "Parada de Santa Marta" stop.

Eating and drinking

Most **bars** and **restaurants** are to be found in the streets around the Plaza de las Monjas. For **tapas**, east of Plaza de las Monjas, *Bar Agmanir*, c/Carasa 9, is a great local bar with outdoor tables and a wide tapas range. Nearby, the atmospheric *Taberna El Condado*, at c/Sor Angela de la Cruz 3, specializes in Huelva's celebrated *jamón serrano*.

Azabache c/Vásquez López 22. Excellent tapas bar and mid-priced restaurant near the Gran Teatro with a stylish tiled interior. Offers fish, meat and *jamón* based dishes (*cerdo ibérico al vino* is a house special) with a *menú* for €38.

El Portichuelo c/Vázquez López 15, opposite the Turismo. Pricey but good restaurant offering a variety of fish and meat dishes. *Raciónes* served on a pleasant terrace. Main dishes €10–15.

Las Candelas 7km from town at the Aljaraque crossroads on the road to Punta Umbría ☎959 31 83 01. An old *venta* (roadside inn), and one of Huelva's best seafood venues, this place is worth making the effort to get to; the outstanding food is complemented by impeccable service. Without your own transport you'll need to take the Punta Umbría bus or take a taxi. Main dishes €12–19. Closed Sun.

Las Meigas Avda. de Guatemala 48 ☎959 27 19 58. Traditional upmarket restaurant offering Basque, Galician and *andaluz* dishes (especially seafood). There's a *menú* for about €20. Closed Sun.

Pizzeria Don Camillo e Peppone c/Isaac Peral s/n. Authentic and delicious Italian pizzas, served up east of the Plaza de las Monjas. Closed Wed.

Restaurante Jeromo Plaza de la Merced 6. Attractive and economical little bar-restaurant near the cathedral that offers a lunch-time *menú* for €8.20 in its bar or more elaborate fare in a pleasant dining room.

Punta Umbría

PUNTA UMBRÍA, 20km away (hourly buses from the bus station) and sitting astride a finger of land between the Atlantic and the Tinto-Odiel river estuary, is Huelva's nearest – and biggest – seaside resort. English managerial staff from the Río Tinto Mining Company (see p.344) initiated the resort in the 1880s when seeking a place to sojourn by the sea. They constructed the first dwellings here in the British colonial style, quite a few of which survived until the 1970s; these buildings have now gone and the only vestige from this era is the *barrio*'s name, Los Ingleses. The tourist resort has paid a belated tribute to its British founders by reconstructing one of these curious stilted dwellings and this now houses the **Casa Museo de los Ingleses**, Avda. Ciudad de Huelva s/n, close to the Turismo (Tues–Fri 10.30am–1.30pm & 7–9pm, Oct–Mar 5.30–7.30pm, Sat 11.30am–1.30pm; free) decorated with typical period furnishings and a photo history.

Punta Umbría's later growth into a seaside town has produced a tidy if uninspiring resort which does, however, have magnificent blue-flag **beaches** flanking the north and south sides of its *punta* (point). It makes a reasonable place to stop over if you don't want to stay in the city; be warned, though, that for the latter part of July and most of August every room will be taken.

Practicalities

The long and sandy beach – lined with some tasteless private villas – leads down to the *punta* where, following the road into town from Huelva (Avenida de Huelva), you'll come to a helpful **Turismo**, located at the junction of Avenida de Andalucía and Avda. Ciudad de Huelva (April–Sept Mon–Sat 10am–2pm & 6–9pm, Sun 10am–1pm; Oct–March Mon–Fri 9am–2pm & 5–8pm, Sat 10am–1pm; ☎959 49 51 60), which stocks copious amounts of information and a useful town **map**. You can't miss the place as it lies just beyond one of the most peculiar Ayuntamientos in Spain – a bizarre glass and wood structure perched on an artificial mudbank, floating in a bath of green water and fronted by a clock tower resembling an oil rig. Turismar (☎959 31 55 26) runs **boat trips** around the estuary and nature reserve of Marismas del Odiel from the Muelle Viajeros quay near the fishing harbour. **Internet** access is available at Znet (daily 5.30–10.30pm) c/Delfin 2, near the fishing harbour on the north side of the point.

Most **places to stay** are located within walking distance of the Turismo on the east and west sides of the point. Near the harbour on the *punta*'s river flank, there's the friendly *Hostal Manuela*, c/Carmen 8 (☎959 31 07 60; ❸) with en-suite rooms, while the nearby *Hotel Emilio*, c/Ancha 21 (☎959 31 18 00, ⓦwww.hotelemilio.com; ❺) is a slightly more upmarket possibility. On the opposite side of the point, places with an Atlantic sea view include, at Avda. del Océano 95, the recently refurbished *Hostal Playa* (☎959 31 01 12; ❸) with en-suite rooms 50m from the strand, and the beachfront *Hotel Barcelo*, Avda. del Oceano s/n (☎959 49 54 00, ⓦwww.barcelopuntaumbria.com; ❼) one of the resort's top-end addresses. High-season pressure on rooms could mean that the very pleasant **youth hostel**, Avda. del Océano 13 (☎959 52 41 29; under 26 €14, over 26 €19; ❷), with a seafront location and some double en-suite rooms, is the only alternative. The nearest **campsite**, *Camping La Bota* (☎959 31 45 37), lies 6km west, near the hamlet of La Bota. They also rent *cabañas* (cabins) sleeping up to four persons (❸).

For **food** and **drink**, *chiringuitos* – open-air bars on the seafront serving snacks – are popular, and the resort is full of the usual *freidurías* and *marisquerías*. On the river side of the point *Juanito Coronel*, opposite the fishing harbour, is good for inexpensive fried fish, while the similar *Antonio*, c/Combes Ponzones 10, around the corner is also popular. On the seaward side, Plaza de la Atlantico, off Avenida del Océano, has the *Restaurante Tiburón*, which is a good choice for seafood, and, just west of here next to the *Hotel Barcelo*, *Camarón* is a popular beachfront *chiringuito*. Close to the youth hostel,

Miramar, c/Miramar 3, is a welcoming place for *platos combinados* and *fritados variados* with a seafront terrace.

The Columbus Trail

Huelva's greatest source of pride lies with the momentous expeditions of **Christopher Columbus** to the New World, the first of which sailed from Palos de la Frontera (or simply Palos), across the Tinto estuary from the city. When he was unable to get backing for his voyages, Columbus cooled his heels for many years in and around Huelva and the La Rábida monastery until he finally managed to obtain a commission from the king and queen in the spring of 1492. The main sites connected with Columbus – **La Rábida**, **Palos** and **Moguer** – are all within a 30km round-trip from Huelva. Buses running between Huelva and Moguer call at all three locations.

La Rábida

The monastery of **LA RÁBIDA**, 8km from Huelva, can be reached by bus (roughly hourly from Huelva) or, with your own transport, by taking the Mazagón road southeast across the Río Tinto road bridge. At the Punta del Sebo – the tip of land where the Tinto and Odiel rivers meet – there's a **monument** to Columbus that was donated by the USA. A monster Cubist-inspired statue, sculpted by Gertrude Vanderbilt Whitney in 1929, it has the navigator looking a bit like a cowled boxer on his way to the ring.

Situated amid a forest of umbrella pines (which serve to mask the petrochemical refineries across the polluted river estuary), the small whitewashed Franciscan **monastery** is a surprisingly pleasant oasis once you reach it. Lying at the end of the Avenida de la América, a road linking it with Palos and lined with ceramic pavement tiles marking all the countries of the New World, the monastery may be visited only by guided tour (hourly: Tues–Sat 10am–1pm & 4–7pm, Sun 10.45am–1pm & 4–7pm; ⓦwww.monasteriodelarabida.com; €3). Dating from the fourteenth century, the buildings suffered structural damage during the Lisbon earthquake of 1755 and have been extensively restored.

The tour begins with the room containing stylized modern frescoes of the explorer's life by distinguished Huelvan artist Daniel Vásquez Díaz. At the building's heart is a tranquil fifteenth-century Mudéjar cloister, opening off the monks' refectory where Columbus would have dined during his many stays here. You will also see the cell where the abbot, Juan Pérez, and Columbus discussed the explorer's ideas. Beyond the cloister, a fourteenth-century **church** contains an alabaster statue of the Virgin and Child to which the mariner and his men prayed before setting sail. Upstairs, above the refectory, lies the **Sala Capitular** (Chapter House) an impressive beamed room with heavy period furniture where Fray Pérez, Columbus and the Pinzón brothers discussed the final plans before the first voyage set sail. On August 3, 1992, the king and the whole Spanish government gathered in this room to mark the 500th anniversary of the event. In other rooms on the same floor you can see models of the three caravels, as well as navigation charts, cases containing various artefacts brought back from the expedition and "team pictures" of the crew. Don't miss the curious **Sala de Banderas**, or Flag Room, where, beneath flags of the various South American nations of the New World, is a casket of earth donated by each. If some of these caskets look a bit roughed-up it's probably due to visiting South Americans who, after reverentially handling the soil of their fatherland, often treat the caskets of their neighbours with some disrespect.

The recently constructed **Muelle de la Carabelas** (Harbour of the Caravels; June–Sept Tues–Fri 10am–2pm & 5–9pm, Sat & Sun 11am–8pm; Oct–May Tue–Sun 10am–7pm; €3.40), on the nearby Río Tinto estuary, has impressive full-size replicas of the three caravels that made the epic voyage to the New World. Realistic displays on board reconstruct the grim realities of life at sea, while the surrounding quays are lined with re-creations of fifteenth-century quayside bars and market stalls. In the adjoining **museum** are displays illustrating Columbus's life (including facsimiles of some of his geographical books annotated in a suprisingly delicate hand), video presentations on a giant screen and a *cafetería*.

The monastery's gardens contain an **information office** as well as a pleasant **bar-restaurant** with terrace tables. In summer a tourist **road train** links La Rábida with Palos de la Frontera.

Palos de la Frontera

Four kilometres north along the Río Tinto estuary lies **PALOS DE LA FRONTERA**, a rather featureless village but an important site in the Columbus story. It was from the silted-up bay below the church of San Jorge – then a major harbour and sea port – that the three caravels, the *Niña*, the *Pinta* and the *Santa María,* set out to reach Asia by crossing the western ocean.

O Palos, no one can equal your glory.
Not Memphis, nor Thebes nor eternal Rome.
Not Athens nor London.
No city can dispute your historical fame!

This modern poem fixed to the exterior wall of the fifteenth-century parish church of **San Jorge** leaves you in no doubt of how Palos views its role in world history. It was here that Columbus and his crewmen attended Mass before taking on water for their voyage from the nearby **La Fontanilla**, a medieval well tarted up in 1992 as the centrepiece of a dismal park to mark the quincentenary. The harbour lay to the west of the fountain in an area now marshland, and it was due to the river's silting up that the decline of Palos set in. The church (Mon–Fri 10am–noon & 6–7.30pm) has a simple, bare-brick interior containing some mural fragments as well as a distinctive wrought-iron pulpit – from which the edict was read ordering an initially reluctant Palos to provide ships, crew and provisions for the voyage – and some thirteenth- and sixteenth-century alabaster sculptures of *Santa Ana* and the *Crucifixion*.

On that August morning in 1492 Columbus is supposed to have left the church through its southern Mudéjar **portal** flanked by his captains Martín Alonzo Pinzón and his younger brother Vicente, both from Palos. And it is these native sons that Palos today celebrates, even more than its Columbus connection, claiming that their contribution to the epic voyage has been eclipsed. Indeed, at the time the Pinzón family insisted that Martín – a mariner of great local repute – had planned such a voyage long before Columbus. South of San Jorge on the main street, the house of Martín Alonzo Pinzón at c/Colón 24 survives, and has been converted into a **museum** (Mon–Fri daily 10am–2pm & 5–9pm; free) with reconstructions of daily life, fashions and food from the sixteenth century.

The road north from Palos to Moguer runs through **strawberry fields** (see box, p.329) owned by one of the largest cooperatives in Europe, which

The voyages of Columbus

Probably born in Genoa around 1451 to the son of a weaving merchant, **Christopher Columbus** (in Spanish, Cristóbal Colón) went to sea in his early teens. After years of sailing around the Mediterranean, in 1476 he was shipwrecked off the coast of Portugal and it was in Lisbon – then the world leader in navigation – that Columbus learned the skills of map-making. In 1479 he married into a high-ranking Portuguese family and spent the following years on trading voyages to the British Isles and elsewhere, including in 1482 a journey down the coast of West Africa to **Ghana**, a major source of spices, ivory and slaves. During this time the idea germinated in his mind of attempting to sail west to reach the **Indies** and the Far East, thus shortening the route that Portugal was then exploring around the coast of Africa. He built up an enormous library of ancient and contemporary geographical writings now preserved in Seville, all heavily annotated in his own hand. By some optimistic interpretations of these works and a misreading of an Arab geographer, Alfraganus, Columbus seriously undercalculated the earth's circumference, believing that Marco Polo's fabulous island of **Cipangu** (Japan) lay a mere 2400 miles west of the Canaries instead of an actual 10,600.

Trying to find backers, when the Portuguese monarch, still more interested in the African route, demurred, Columbus turned to Spain. In 1486 at Córdoba he presented his plan to reach the gold-rich Orient to Fernando and Isabel, still involved in the protracted and costly war of *Reconquista* against the Moors. Desirous of the gold to boost their fortunes but wary, after consultations with advisers, of Columbus's calculations, they both refused support. Now desperate, Columbus turned to France and then to Henry VII of England, with no success. During his earlier journey from Portugal to Córdoba, Columbus had stayed at **La Rábida** Franciscan monastery. It was to here that he returned frustrated and depressed in the autumn of 1491. The explorer's luck turned when Juan Pérez, the abbot of La Rábida and a former confessor to Isabel, was moved to write to the queen on Columbus's behalf. It was a timely moment. In January of 1492 Granada had fallen, the treasury was empty, and the promise of gold and glory for a resurgent Spain now attracted the monarchs.

Columbus set out from Palos on August 3, 1492, with three small vessels, the *Santa María*, the *Niña* and the *Pinta*, carrying a total of 120 men recruited from Palos and Moguer by the Pinzón brothers. Columbus's discovery of the Atlantic wind patterns ranks alongside his other feats; he sailed via the Canaries to take advantage of the trade winds, but the incredible voyage almost ended in mutiny by crews who believed that they would never find a wind to bring them home. This was avoided when, on October 12, Columbus made landfall on Watling Island (aka San Salvador) in the **Bahamas**. Watched by naked and silent natives he took the island in the name of Spain and gave thanks to God. After leaving a colony of men on **Hispaniola** (modern Haiti) he returned to Palos on March 15, 1493, to enormous acclaim.

Successful as a mariner, Columbus was disastrous as a colonizer, epitomized by his forcing of the native population of Hispaniola into the gold mines in a brutal process that reduced their numbers from a quarter of a million in 1492 to 60,000 fifteen years later. In 1500, Columbus was removed from office as governor and sent back to Spain in chains and disgrace. He was eventually released and made his final voyage in 1502 – a last desperate attempt to find a strait leading to India – but ended up stranded in Jamaica for a whole year after losing his ships to sea worms. Columbus died at Valladolid in 1506, still believing that he had reached the East Indies.

has brought welcome prosperity to the area. By playing the market, which entails close scrutiny of weather forecasts for northern European customers such as Germany and Britain – sunshine there means high strawberry profits – they decide when is the best moment for picking. Then, loaded with

10,000 kilos of *fresones* apiece, the great refrigerated trucks roll north through the night.

Practicalities

The Ayuntamiento (Mon–Fri 9am–3pm; ⊤959 350 100), facing the Plaza Mayor on c/Rábida 3, the main street, can provide tourist **information** and a town map, as well as assistance in viewing the church and museum if these are closed. You'll find **places to stay and eat** close by: *Pensión Rábida*, c/Rábida 9 (⊤959 35 01 63; ❷), is a good bet for recently refurbished en-suite rooms; nearby there's the pleasant and pricier *Hotel La Pinta*, c/Rábida 75 (⊤959 35 05 11, ⊛www.hotellapinta.com; ❸). The best place to eat is a little further along the same street from the *Pinta* at *Restaurant El Paraiso*, Avda. America 15, offering a wide range of dishes and a great-value *menú* for about €10.

Moguer

The compact and beautiful whitewashed town of **MOGUER**, 8km north of Palos, also takes pride in its Columbus connection: many of the crew members were recruited here. Quite apart from this, it's a place with plenty to see, and achieved worldwide fame in 1956 as the birthplace of the Nobel prize-winning poet Juan Ramón Jiménez.

Starting from the **Plaza del Cabildo** in the centre – where there's a bronze statue of Jiménez – it's easy to find your way around. First take a look at the elegant eighteenth-century **Ayuntamiento** (free access to patio in mornings when open) on the same square, a quintessentially Andalucian edifice in cream and brown paint described by one art historian as "the finest Neoclassical building in the whole of Huelva Province".

Strawberry Fields

Between February and May, the strawberry fields surrounding Palos de la Frontera are a frenzy of activity, providing ninety percent of the strawberries eaten in the whole of Europe. To supply this market tens of thousands of workers are required to do the picking and the packing. Formerly many of these workers came from the Maghreb, but as the government has clamped down on North African *indocumentados* (illegal workers without papers), the strawberry farms are now recruiting from Eastern Europe.

Most of the new hands come from Poland and Romania and almost all are women under thirty on short-term contracts that specify the period of work from February to June, after which they must return to their own country or lose the opportunity to work legally in Spain again. In 2005, twelve thousand such work permits were issued with the women earning an average of €30 per day. This annual eastern invasion into an area of rural Andalucía has had some dramatic repercussions. Coming from a vastly different cultural background and speaking little or no Spanish, the women are housed in communal cabins/bunkhouses alongside the strawberry orchards. Once work is over they put on their finery and head for the limited nightlife in Palos or, at weekends, the coastal resorts of Mazagón and Punta Umbría. Understandably, this female flood upsets the delicate social balance and local *españolas* are not amused at the prospect of potential *novios* and husbands being enticed from their grasp by glossy northern blondes looking for a good time. The increasing number of weddings between the migrants and local men as well as the rising number of divorces caused (local women say) by men dazzled by Polish charms has led to calls for the invasion to be stopped.

Close to here in c/Monjas lies the Gothic-Mudéjar **Convento de Santa Clara**. Founded in the fourteenth century, this housed nuns from the order of St Clare until 1898, but is now a **museum** (hourly guided tours Tues–Sat 11am–7pm; €2). Inside, a Mudéjar cloister leads into the nuns' former quarters, which include kitchen and refectory and a large sixteenth-century dormitory. The church possesses a fine *retablo* and some notable alabaster **tombs** of the Portocarrero family, the convent's founders, as well as – at the entry to the choir – a seventeenth-century **diptych** of the Sienese school portraying the Immaculate Conception. Look out for an inscription in the right aisle, which tells of Columbus's visit to offer thanksgiving for his safe return. He is reputed to have spent the whole night in prayer here upon returning from his first voyage in March 1493, in fulfilment of a vow he made in the middle of a terrifying storm. Other parts of the tour take in sculptures by La Roldana, Martínez Montañés and many other beautiful if anonymous works from the fourteenth, fifteenth and sixteenth centuries.

Additional sights in town include the fifteenth-century monastery of **San Francisco**, behind Santa Clara (cloister open daily, church only at service times; free), with its stunning ochre-tinted Mudéjar brick church and from where legions of missionaries were sent out to the New World; its elegant Mannerist patio/cloister can be viewed by entering through the archival museum next door. To the east of the centre **Nuestra Señora de la Granada** (open at service times, try 7.30pm) boasts a scaled-down, whiter version of Seville's Giralda tower "which from close up looks like Seville's from far away", wrote Jiménez. The house where Jiménez was born, c/Jiménez 5, has been restored as an interesting **museum** (Tues–Sat hourly visits 10.15am–1.15pm & 5.15–7.15pm, Sun 10am–1pm; €3) displaying various mementoes from the poet's life. On Avenida Hermanos Niño, the road leading towards the Seville–Huelva highway, the **cemetery** has the grave of the poet and his wife, Zenobia. His body was returned to the town he loved for burial in 1958 after twenty years spent in exile in Puerto Rico, to where he had emigrated after Franco came to power. The work that most Andalucians remember him for today is *Platero y yo* ("Platero and I"), the story of a little donkey who is a "friend of the poet and children" based on his own donkey, Platero, in whose company he often toured Moguer's streets. Glazed plaques on walls around town mark streets or buildings that occur in the story.

Practicalities

Moguer's **Turismo** (Mon–Fri 10am–2pm & 4.30–7pm, Sun 10am–3pm; ☎959 37 18 98, ⊕www.aytomoguer.es) lies just off the main square, inside the former castle at c/Castillo s/n, and can provide a basic map and information. **Buses** drop off and leave from c/Coronación to the north of Plaza Cabildo. If you're tempted to **stay**, close to the Convento de Santa Clara at the end of c/Monjas there's the excellent-value *Hostal Pedro Alonso Niño*, c/Pedro Alonso Niño 13 (☎959 37 23 92; ❶), where all rooms come with a/c, shower and TV; get a room overlooking the pleasant patio at the back. Around the corner, the slightly more expensive *Hostal Platero*, c/Aceña 4 (☎959 37 21 59; ❶), has similar en-suite rooms.

For **food**, *Mesón Restaurante Paralla*, Plaza de las Monjas 22, opposite the entrance to Santa Clara, is the best restaurant in town, and serves up excellent regional fish and meat dishes, does tapas and has an inexpensive *menú*. Moguer has some interesting night-time places to eat and drink, including one of the most bizarre bar/restaurants in Andalucía. This is *Mesón El Lobito* on c/La Rábida 31, which includes among its eccentric decor vast numbers of unidentified objects hanging from the ceiling, chickens in cages in a patio and walls completely covered in graffiti (which you're welcome to add to). There's usually a good atmosphere if you turn up after 10pm.

Music bars are located along c/San Rafael, three blocks south of Plaza del Cabildo. Moguer holds an annual **Festival de Flamenco** at the beginning of September.

Coto de Doñana National Park

Sited at the estuary of the Guadalquivir, the vast roadless area of the **COTO DE DOÑANA** is Spain's largest wildlife reserve, a world-class wetland site for migrating birds and one of Europe's greatest areas of wilderness. The seasonal pattern of its delta waters, which flood in winter and then drop in the spring, leaving rich deposits of silt, raised sandbanks and islands, give the Coto de Doñana its special interest. Conditions are perfect in winter for ducks and geese, but spring is most exciting: the exposed mud draws hundreds of flocks of breeding birds. In the marshes and amid the cork oak forests behind you've a good chance of seeing squacco heron, black-winged stilt, whiskered tern, pratincole and sand grouse, as well as flamingos, egrets and vultures. There are, too, occasional sightings of the Spanish imperial eagle, now reduced to a score of breeding pairs. In late summer and early autumn, the swamps – or *marismas* – dry out and then support far less birdlife. The park is also home to an estimated 25 pairs of the pardel or Spanish lynx, now in severe peril of extinction.

Inevitably, it seems, the park is under threat from development and several lynx have been killed by traffic on the road to the beach resort at **Matalascañas**. Even at current levels the drain on the water supply is severe, and made worse by pollution of the Guadalquivir by farming pesticides, Seville's industry and Huelva's mines. The seemingly inevitable disaster finally occurred in April 1998, when an upriver mining dam used for storing toxic waste burst, unleashing millions of litres of pollutants into the Guadiamar river which flows through the park. The noxious tide was stopped just 2km from the park's boundary, but catastrophic damage was done to the surrounding farmland, with nesting birds decimated and fish poisoned. What is even more worrying is that the mining dams have not been removed (the mines are a major local employer) but merely repaired. The proposals for a huge new tourist centre – to be known as the Costa Doñana – on the fringes of the park have now been shelved, but the pressure for development remains. Bitter demonstrations organized by locals who saw the prospect of much-needed jobs in the Costa Doñana development – accompanied by mysterious outbreaks of vandalism against park property – have abated into an uneasy truce. Some experts have proposed that "green tourism", allowing a greater but controlled public access to the park, and thereby providing an income for the local community, is the only way to bring both sides together.

Some history

This area was known to the **Romans** as Ligur, and in the 1990s archeologists were surprised to discover a Roman quayside three kilometres into the *marismas*, showing just how much the area has expanded in the ensuing two millennia. It was Alfonso X, however, who claimed the territory of Las Rocinas as a hunting reserve for the Spanish crown in 1262 during the *Reconquista*. In

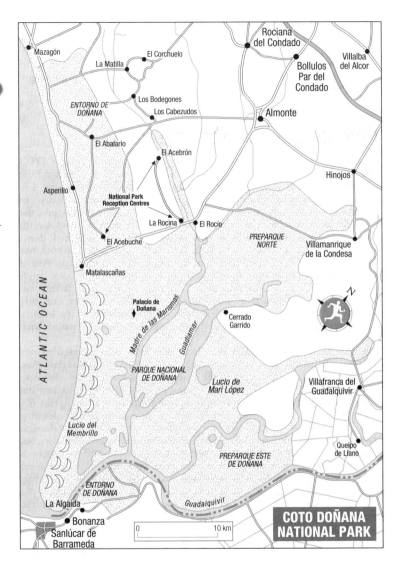

1294 his heir, Sancho IV (the Brave), rewarded the "hero" of the siege of Tarifa, Guzmán El Bueno, with the territories of Doñana. The area, still a hunting reserve, remained part of the lands of the dukes of Medina Sidonia – as the Guzmán line became – for the next five centuries, and the park's hunting lodge was named the palace of Doña Aña in honour of the wife of the seventh duke in 1595. The reserve hit a bad patch when it was sold by the Medina Sidonias in 1897 to sherry baron William Garvey, whose company is still operating in Jerez. Garvey turned it into a hunting club and sold off much of the woodland for profit, but saner times followed upon his death in 1909, when people began to realize the unique importance of the area.

In 1957 scientific interest in the park began in earnest and, as a result of concern expressed about proposals to carve a highway across the zone and build tourist developments along its coastline, the **World Wildlife Fund** was set up in 1964. Five years later the Fund persuaded the Spanish government to set up the national park. Since then the Coto de Doñana, now under the management of the National Institute for the Conservation of Nature (ICONA), has expanded to 190,000 acres. The park's administrators then enlisted divine assistance in safeguarding its future when they diplomatically petitioned the brotherhoods to allow the Virgin of Rocío (see p.336) to become the National Park's patron. The brotherhoods graciously acceded to this request and the park's future now seems assured.

Doñana practicalities

Visiting the Coto de Doñana still involves – understandably – a certain amount of frustration. At present the heart of the reserve is still open only to brief, organized bus **tours** (see box below), though you can also take a boat cruise into the park from Sanlúcar de Barrameda (see p.228).

Day visitors are currently restricted to the **hides** at three access and information centres open to the public. The first of these (moving north from Matalascañas) is the **Centro Recepción del Acebuche** (daily April–Sept 8am–9pm, Oct–March 8am–7pm), where there's also an information office (which can supply a useful free map), bookshop, natural history exhibition, a rather tedious audiovisual presentation and a **cafeteria** with an economical *menú*. The five hides adjacent to the Centro overlook a lagoon where marbled teal, purple gallinule, various grebes and – around the trees – azure-winged magpies have all been spotted and where, with luck, you may even glimpse the extremely rare Audouin's gull. You'll need to bring your own binoculars or they can be hired from the centre (€1.50 per hr).

Touring the Coto de Doñana

The starting point for **tours of the park** in all-terrain 24-seater buses, and the place to book them, is at the Centro de Recepción del Acebuche, 4km north of Matalascañas towards El Rocío and Almonte, then 1.5km up a signed road on the left. For details of the tours (run by the Cooperativa Marismas del Rocío), which need to be booked in advance (April–Sept daily 8.30am & 5pm; Oct–March Tues–Sun 8.30am & 3pm; €25), call in at the centre or phone ahead (daily 9am–8pm; ☎959 43 96 27 English spoken, ⓦwww.parquenacionaldonana.com). Although the Centro has some **binoculars** available for rent (€2.50 per trip), you'd be well advised to bring your own as they are essential. Outside July, August and holiday periods you should be able to get on to the next day's trip, otherwise you'll need to book at least a week in advance. Tours consist of an eighty-kilometre, four-hour trip sampling the park's various ecosystems: dunes, beach, *marismas* and woodland, with the guide pointing out only spectacular species such as flamingo, imperial eagle, deer and wild boar.

If you're a serious ornithologist or naturalist, the tour isn't for you and you should consider a **group booking**, which costs a little more than the daily excursion and lets you create your own itinerary (details from the Centro). Other organizations offering **tours** into the park (details from their websites) are: Discovering Doñana (☎959 44 24 66, ⓦwww.discoveringdonana.com), Doñana Bird Tours (☎95 575 53 99, ⓦwww.donanabirdtours.com) and Doñana Nature (☎959 44 21 60, ⓦwww.donana-nature.com).

The best **map** for the national park is the IGN *Parque Nacional de Doñana* (1:50,000) sold at the Acebuche centre.

Nine kilometres north, **La Rocina** (daily 9am–3pm & 4–8pm), close to the El Rocío bridge, has a car park, information centre (with more free maps) and a small open-air **museum** with historical reconstructions of life in the *marismas*. Beyond here a 2km route called the "Charco de la Boca" leads to five well-concealed hides in marshland, pine woods and along the riverbank where you might see Cetti's warbler, the spectacular hoopoe, red-crested pochard and herons as well as – in summer – flamingos and a plethora of singing nightingales. A minor road leads 5km west from here to **El Palacio de Acebrón** (same hours) – an impressive former hunting lodge – where there is another car park and information centre housing an ethnographic exhibition dealing with the zone's history and development. A 1.5km marked route threads from the centre, circling a lake mainly through woodland, and offering possibilities to sight the rare hawfinch. This would also make an ideal location for a **picnic** if you've come prepared. It's worth noting that during the Pentecost *romería* (the seventh week after Easter) all three visitor centres are closed.

Back on the main road, the **El Rocío bridge** on the village's southern edge has been described by one naturalist as "the best free bird-watching site in Europe". From this spot, red kite – a common sight here – soaring flocks of whiskered terns, disturbed by the ominous approach of a majestic booted eagle, and migrating greenshank, ruff and sandpiper are all to be seen in season. In high summer, though, the marshes dry out and are grazed by horses while the birdlife is restricted to coot and avocets breeding by the river. The **view** across the marshes towards the village and church of El Rocío from here is superb.

El Rocío

Set on the northwestern tip of the marshes, **EL ROCÍO** – a tiny cluster of white cottages, sandy streets and an imposing church where the most famous pilgrimage-fair of the south occurs annually at Pentecost – is one of the most atmospheric places in Andalucía. As the cowboy-hatted farmers nonchalantly ride horses along the wide sandy streets and tie up at Wild West-style hitching

▲ Horseriders in El Rocío

rails in front of their timber cabins, you half expect Clint Eastwood to emerge from a nearby saloon chewing on a cheroot. And this frontier-like feeling isn't altogether accidental, as it was from this area that many of the colonizers of the New World set out, exporting their vernacular architectural preferences with them. In the evening the street lights do little to undermine the time-warp quality of an area unchanged for centuries.

Centre of the town's Pentecost celebrations, the church of **Nuestra Señora del Rocío** (8.30am–7.30pm; free) was, despite its Baroque appearance, built in the 1960s on the site of a church which collapsed in the eighteenth-century Lisbon earthquake. It holds the venerated image of the **Virgen del Rocío**, a thirteenth-century work in carved wood. Beyond the village's core, ghostly streets of dwellings belonging to the brotherhoods – all with hitching rails and verandahs – stand empty most of the year waiting to be put to service each May or June in the *romería* when the ninety or so brotherhoods use them to house their members.

In the spring, El Rocío is probably the best **bird-watching** base in the area. The *marismas* and pine woods adjacent to the town itself are teeming with birds, and following tracks east and southeast along the edge of the reserve you'll see many species from white stork, herons and egrets to masked great grey shrike and honking wild geese. The Boca del Lobo ("wolf-breath") sewage treatment plant near to the *Hotel Toruño* (see p.336) is an unlikely-sounding bird-spotting location, but vultures and storks are frequent patrons here.

With your own transport another great bird-watching location is the **Cerrado Garrido** (aka Centro José Antonio Valverde; 10am–7.30pm) on the park's northern fringes. To get there from El Rocío follow the signs from the centre of the village, a 30km trip via Villamanrique de la Condesa. Approaching the centre the route traverses the Preparque along unmade tracks and is quite feasible in summer; after heavy rains access may not be possible and you should check with the El Acebuche visitors' centre (see box, p.333). Cerrado's visitors' centre has a **cafetería-bar**, as well as telescopes and hides. You'll have plenty of other birdwatching and wildlife-spotting opportunities en route – keep an eye out for purple gallinules in the ditches between the paddy fields. The sunrises and sunsets over the *marismas* at Cerrado Garrido are quite spectacular, too.

Practicalities

A **tourist office** kiosk (Mon–Fri 9.30am–2.30pm; ☎959 44 26 84) is located on the square fronting the church of Nuestra Señora del Rocío, and can supply a village **map** and lots of information about the national park including a 5km scenic **walk** along the Raya Real to the Palacio del Rey, northeast of the village where deer, wild boar and the Spanish lynx have all been spotted. The village now has a number of **cash machines** and a bank (sited alongside the *Hotel Rocío Doñana*). There are at least three **buses** a day to and from Seville en route to Matalascañas, enabling a stop to be made at the La Rocina or El Acebuche National Park visitor centres (see p.333; make sure to let the driver know you want to be dropped there). Getting to or from Huelva is rather more compli-cated, requiring a change at Almonte.

On the opposite side of the main A483 road to the village Doñana Ecuestre (☎959 44 24 74, ⓦ www.donanaecuestre.com) is another organization offering jeep tours into the national and natural parks of Doñana. They also do **horse-riding** excursions in and around the park lasting from one day to a week.

El Rocío makes a nice **place to stay** – except during the *romería* when rooms (costing a whopping €200–500 per night) are booked up months, even years, in advance. Economical options for en-suite rooms include *Hostal Cristina*,

The Romería del Rocío

The **Romería del Rocío**, a Whitsun pilgrimage to the sanctuary of the Virgen del Rocío, is one of the most extraordinary spectacles in Europe, with whole village communities and some ninety local "brotherhoods" from Huelva, Seville, Málaga and even one from Gibraltar, converging on the village on horseback and in lavishly decorated ox-carts. The event is part pilgrimage and part jamboree as the intense emotions awakened by the two- to four-day journey (not to mention the drinking) often spill over uncontrollably.

The brotherhoods coming from **Sanlúcar de Barrameda** have a special dispensation to follow their ancient route across the heart of the Parque de Doñana which takes them three nights and four days with all the attendant fire risks en route. The army is employed to get them and their carts over the Guadalquivir safely, and the park's rangers set up campsites for them and provide firewood for their great feasts in the woods. Sadly, the rubbish left behind by these large crowds is the cause of many wildlife fatalities as species such as boar choke on the plastic containers they attempt to devour. Throughout the *romería*, which climaxes on the Saturday evening, everyone parties in fiesta costume, while by the time the carts arrive at El Rocío they've been joined by hundreds of busloads of pilgrims.

What they have all come for – apart from the spectacle itself – is the commemoration of the miracle of **Nuestra Señora del Rocío** (Our Lady of the Dew). This is a statue believed to have been found on this spot by a shepherd in the thirteenth century – conveniently after the eviction of the Moors – which, so it is said, resisted all attempts to move it elsewhere. A shrine was built, miraculous healings and events were reported, and El Rocío was suddenly on the map. In the early hours of Pentecost Sunday when many of the revellers either are gripped by religious frenzy or lie prostrate in an alcoholic stupor, the image of the Virgin, credited with all kinds of magic and fertility powers, is paraded before the faithful as she visits each one of the brotherhoods' houses (which lie empty for the rest of the year).

In recent years the sheer size of the Romería has begun to worry the authorities as it has exploded from a few thousand pilgrims in the 1970s to an incredible half a million in the early years of the new century. Despite the whole affair having become a spectacular TV event with arc lamps, amplified music and fireworks, popular enthusiasm is undiminished. The brotherhoods wrestle with each other to carry the Blanca Paloma ("the White Dove" as the Virgin is fondly known) one more time in procession before she's returned to her shrine for another year, and the weary homeward trek begins.

Accompanying one of the brotherhoods on their pilgrimage to El Rocío is a memorable and exhilarating experience. Anyone is entitled to be a pilgrim: just turn up when the processions leave the major villages in the provinces of Seville and Huelva in the days leading up to Pentecost, taking with you a sleeping bag and some food and water. The walking is easy with plenty of stops for dancing and liquid refreshment, and the nightly encampments, when folk songs are sung around campfires, are magical.

---

c/Real 58, behind the church (☎959 44 24 13; ❷) and *Hostal Isidro*, Avda. Los Ansares 59 (☎959 44 22 42; ❸), on the village's east side is another place for a/c rooms with bath. Upmarket options include the elegant and enormous *Hotel Rocío de Doñana*, Avda. Canaliega 1 (☎959 44 25 75, ⓦwww.rociodonana.com; ❹), for a/c rooms with TV access. The best of the more expensive places is ⚜ *Hotel Toruño*, Plaza Acebuchal 22 (☎959 44 23 23, ⓦwww.toruno.es; ❹ with breakfast), with comfortable rooms overlooking the *marismas*. The best view is from Room 225 but some of the ground floor rooms (109, 111 & 115) also allow you to spot flamingos, herons, avocets and lots more whilst lying in bed.

A couple of hundred metres southeast of the Toruño lies the new ⚓ *Hotel La Malvasia*, c/Sanlúcar 38 (☎959 44 38 70, ⓦwww.lamalvasiahotel.com; ❺) housed in a former *casa señorial* with stylish rooms around a patio and sensational view over the *marismas* from its suite (Room 13) as well as a rooftop *mirador*. El Rocío's pricey **campsite** *La Aldea* (☎959 44 26 77, ⓦwww.campinglaaldea.com; €6.50 per tent) lies on the village's northern edge along the Almonte road (A483).

For **eating and drinking** all the hotels and *hostales* above have restaurants – both the *Cristina* and *Isidro* offer economical *menús* – but the more upmarket *Hotel Toruño's* restaurant located opposite the hotel itself is worth the extra, serves fish and organic beef raised in the national park and has a *menú* for around €15. Other in-town possibilities include the *Hotel La Malvasia*'s stylish restaurant with a pleasant terrace or *Aires de Doñana*, Avda. de la Canaliega 1, near the church, with a panoramic vista over the *marismas* and where – in spring – flamingos, spoonbills and herons entertain diners. All El Rocío's eating places tend to close earlier than is normal in Andalucía and start shutting down around 10.30–11pm. Tapas and *raciónes* are served at many other restaurants and bars on and around the village's main street – but to eat out on their terraces after sundown in summer you'll need plenty of mosquito protection.

Matalascañas

Birds and other wildlife apart, **MATALASCAÑAS**, a fast-growing beach resort just outside the reserve, is unlikely to excite; with five large hotel complexes, a grim concrete shopping centre and tasteless beachfront developments along a featureless promenade, it looks as if it's just been thrown together (as indeed it has), and it would be difficult to imagine a more complete lack of character. The **beach**, it must be said though, is attractive and you're allowed to use the strand inside the national park, too. You enter by a gate at the eastern end of the village and can walk along the sand (but not into the park proper) with plenty of opportunities for birdwatching; no vehicles or camping are allowed. The least disagreeable part of the resort is reached by continuing straight on at the roundabout on the edge of the town (ignoring signs to Matalascañas centre) along the Avenida de las Adelfas to an area known as **Torre de la Higuera** where, beyond another roundabout, parking area (where the **bus** will drop you) and kiosk, a line of *marisquerías* front the excellent golden-sand beach which also has a few *chiringuitos* (beach restaurants), too. An area of sand dunes here has been transformed into the **Parque Dunar** which you can explore on foot. There are maps of the park at the various entry points near the beach or on the roundabout at the entry to the town. The Parque Dunar Centro de Información also serves as a **tourist office** (Mon–Fri 9am–6.30pm; ☎959 43 00 86). Matalascañas's **campsite** is the sprawling *Camping Rocío Playa* (☎959 43 02 40), 1.5km down the A494 towards Huelva. This site lacks shade and is a little inconvenient without your own transport if you're planning to take regular trips into the fringes of the national park; if you just want a beach, though, it's not a bad option. The Playa de Doñana and its continuation Playa de Mazagón – with two more campsites, *Fontanilla Playa* (☎959 53 62 37; just beyond the parador, see p.338), and the vast, densely wooded *Doñana Playa* (☎959 53 63 13; also has bungalows, ❹) – stretch the whole distance to Huelva, with fine beaches backed by dunes and hardly another visitor in sight. With your own transport there are a number of access points (with car parks) to tranquil **beaches** such as the signed Playa Questa Maneli between the two campsites. This route is covered at present by three daily **buses** in both directions in summer with a less frequent service the rest of the year.

Mazagón

The small resort of **MAZAGÓN**, 23km west of Matalascañas, makes a preferable stopover with another fine sandy beach and ample restaurants and bars. The village is well served by **buses** from Huelva, Palos and Moguer, and from the centre – where the bus drops you – it's just a short walk to the beach. Outside August, **rooms** are easy to come by; the pleasant *Hostal Álvarez Quintero*, c/Hernández de Soto 174 (℡959 37 61 69; ❷), just off the beach road, is an excellent-value place to try first where en-suite rooms come with air-conditioning. In the town proper other choices include the pricier *Hostal Hilaria*, c/Hilaria 20 s/n (℡959 37 62 06; ❸), which has a/c terrace rooms with bath above a bar, and the nearby and similarly equipped *Hostal Acuario*, Avda. Fuentepiña 29 (℡959 37 72 86; ❸–❹), on a busy central avenue lined with bars and places to eat. The central three-star *Hotel Carabela Santa María*, Avda. de los Conquistadores s/n (℡959 53 60 18, ⓦwww.hotelcarabelasantamaria.com; ❸), is a step upmarket with good-value well-equipped rooms. For five-star comfort, head for the modern *Parador Cristóbal Colón* (℡959 53 63 00, ⓦwww.parador .es; ❼), 6km east of Mazagón and set among pine woods; with its own decent restaurant, this is a modern addition to the upmarket chain with functional rooms offset by attractive gardens (with pool) leading down to a fabulous beach. Mazagón's **campsite**, *Camping Playa de Mazagón*, Cuesta de la Barca (℡959 37 62 08), lies at the eastern end of the resort above the beach. There are plenty of places for **eating** and **drinking** around the central zone and the beach; in the centre the Avenida Fuentepiña has an economical restaurant, *El Choco*, next to the *Hostal Aquario* (see above), and the nearby *Bar Torre del Loro* is also good for tapas. Two restaurants that are a cut above the rest are *El Remo*, Avda. de los Conquistadores 123, specializing in seafood at the eastern end of the seafront with a terrace, and *Las Dunas*, Avda. de los Conquistadores 178, at the western end near the yacht harbour.

Along the coast to Portugal

The stretch of coast between the Guadiana – which marks the border with Portugal – and Tinto rivers is lined with some of the finest **beaches** in Andalucía and a scattering of low-key resorts that rarely see a foreign tourist. There's no train service, but plenty of buses run along this main route to the frontier, easily crossed by a spectacular road bridge over the Guadiana estuary.

From Huelva the **coast road to Portugal** loops around the Marisma de San Miguel, passing through the dull towns of Cartaya and **Lepe**. Geoffry Chaucer (whose father was a vintner), in the *Pardoner's Tale*, wrote that the potent white wine of Lepe "creepeth subtilly … that whan a man hath dronken draughtes three, and weneth he be at hoom in Chepe, He is in Spaigne, right at the toune of Lepe" – an out-of-body experience no doubt familiar to many modern inebriates. Lepe's main claim to fame today, however, is as the butt of hundreds of "did you hear about the man from Lepe …?" jokes, in which the town's supposedly gormless inhabitants are pilloried by the rest of the nation.

Some 5km south of Lepe on the *marismas* of the Río Piedras, the tiny fishing port of **EL TERRÓN** boasts one of the best **fish restaurants** in this area. Located on the harbour, *El Ancla* (℡959 38 04 52), which specializes in mouthwatering fried fish and marinated prawns, doesn't come cheap but there's an affordable *menú*. Cheaper options are provided by a couple of tapas and *mariscos* bars on the quayside. If you want to know a bit more about what you've just scoffed the nearby Aula Marina **aquarium** (daily: July–Aug 5.30–9.30pm, Sept–June noon–2pm & 4.30–7.30pm; €4) has examples of most species to be found in the Mediterranean and Atlantic waters. About 2km down the road from here a **campsite**, *La Antilla* (☏959 48 08 29), may be your best bet if rooms are tight.

The road hits the coast at the **PLAYA DE LA ANTILLA**, a low-key beach resort invitingly peaceful outside high season. There's an excellent blue-flag **beach**, plus a scattering of *marisquerías* and **restaurants** to choose from. Many of these line the main street, Avenida de Castilla, a couple of blocks in from the sea. Locals pack the popular *Cervecería Estoril* about halfway down on the right but more formal dining takes place at *Bar-Restaurante Lino*, Avda. de Castilla 2 and *Casa Rodri* (c/Adelfa s/n, just off the same street) with an astonishingly good-value *menú* for €6.50. *Bar-Restaurante Feria*, Avda. Castilla 16, at the far end, is another excellent place for fish and also serves tapas. For **breakfast** snacks, with a sea view, and evening *platos combinados*, *Café-Restaurante Coral Playa* lies on the seafront close to the *hostales* below.

You won't find a room here in August without pre-booking. **Places to stay** cluster around the junction of Avenida Castilla and c/La Parada, which is also where the bus drops you. The nearest to the sea of a line of *hostales* is the dapper *Hostal Azul*, La Parada 9 (☏959 48 07 00, ⓦwww.hostalazul.com; ❹), where balcony en-suite rooms have sea views and there's an attractive roof terrace with loungers. Slightly further along *Hostal La Parada*, Plaza La Parada s/n (☏959 48 14 62; ❸), has newly refurbished a/c en-suite rooms. Around the corner from here, the pleasant *Hostal El Álamo*, Avda. Castilla 82 (☏959 48 10 18, ⓦwww .elalamoplaya.com; ❸–❹) has distinctively decorated rooms with bath and a decent restaurant, too. Otherwise there's a **campsite**, *Luz* (☏959 48 64 54), with a pool, 5km west towards Isla Cristina.

Isla Cristina

The road passes some pretty awful beach development on the western edge of La Antilla as well as, a couple of kilometres further, the newly created coastal nightmare of **La Islantilla,** where a clutch of fairly tasteless upmarket hotels and *urbanizaciones* are flanked to the right of the road by a sprawling 25-hole golf course. A misguided joint venture by Lepe and Isla Cristina to attract well-heeled visitors, the complex has a conveniently located **Turismo** (daily 10am–2pm & March–Oct 5–7pm; ☏959 64 60 13), on the left of the through road, with stacks of information on the whole Costa de la Luz. Beyond the **campsites** *Luz* (see above) and *Taray* (☏959 34 11 02), the vista clears to provide a pleasant few kilometres of pine woods and, behind the dunes, more good beaches.

ISLA CRISTINA, 8km further on, was, as its name implies, once an island but infilling has transformed it into a pleasant resort surrounded by *marismas* and tidal estuaries. For most of the year the town's prevailing atmosphere is one of nonchalant tranquillity, punctuated only in August by the annual invasion of *sevillanos*, who fill its holiday apartment blocks and beaches to bursting point. The commercial centre is concentrated around the **port** which is the second most important in the province and from where shellfish and wet fish are trans-ported overnight on ice to the markets, bars and restaurants of Seville, Córdoba and Madrid. At the end of Carretera de la Playa, an avenue shaded by giant eucalyptus trees, the town's fine sandy **beach** somewhat makes up for a drab seafront. Back in town, life revolves around the central **Plaza de las Flores**. The beach is an easy ten-minute walk from here or there's a half-hourly bus (except during the siesta) from the same square. The big event in Isla Cristina is its annual **Carnaval** held in February.

Practicalities

Slightly northwest of of Plaza de las Flores is the **Turismo** c/San Francisco 12, (Mon–Fri: March–Oct 10am–2pm & 5.30–7.30pm; Nov–April 10am–2pm; ☎959 33 26 94) which can provide a town map. The **bus station** lies on Avenida de Huelva, a couple of blocks east of Plaza de las Flores, and is served by frequent daily buses from Huelva and Seville and buses (May–Sept) to the beach. **Internet** access is available at Soft Tony, Paseo de los Reyes 2, east of Plaza de las Flores (Mon–Sat 10.30am–2pm & 5–9.30pm).

Due to the severe shortage of **accommodation**, if you want to stay – in August especially – you'll have to book ahead. The most central possibility is the pleasant *Hotel Brisamar*, c/Baja 187 (☎959 33 11 30; ❹) to the southeast of the central zone. Seafront options – all near the Playa Central beach at the eastern end of the town – include the friendly *Hotel Sol y Mar* (☎959 33 20 50, ⓦ www.hotelsolymar.org; ❺) right on the beach with its own economical restaurant, and, slightly inland, the *Hotel Paraíso Playa*, Carretera de la Playa s/n (☎959 33 18 73, ⓦ www.hotelparaisoplaya.com; ❻), which also has a pool. The nearest **campsite**, *La Giralda* (☎959 34 33 18), lies 2km out of town on the La Antilla road, and offers canoeing and sailing.

For **eating** *Restaurante Reyes* on Plaza de las Flores is noted for its fish and *mariscos* while, northwest of here, ⚑ *Hermanos Moreno*, Avda. Padre Miravent 39, is sited close to the harbour; their upstairs fish restaurant is excellent and everything served in the tapas bar beneath is as fresh from the sea as you can get. Along Carretera de la Playa, the avenue leading to the beach, you'll find ⚑ *Casa Rufino* (☎959 33 08 10), an outstanding fish restaurant which does a great *arroz negro de marisco* (rice with squid), a good-value *menú* for about €20 and a house special called a *tonteo* featuring eight different kinds of fish.

For **music bars** – which is about as near to nightlife as Isla Cristina gets – you need to head for the northwest point of the town's peninsula between Plaza de las Flores and the harbour. Here along the narrow, white-walled and cobbled streets of the old fishing quarter is where most of the bars are congregated; you could try *Pipirigaña*, c/Diego Pérez Pascual 198, with inside and outdoor patios. There's often **flamenco** staged at *Bar Gonzalo*, c/Romeu 18, a fine old drinking den with a flamenco room at the back close to Plaza de las Flores. A little further away *Peña Flamenco La Higuerita*, Nuestra Señora de los Angeles s/n, around the corner from the *Hotel Brisamar*, is another great flamenco venue; their bar is open daily but check with the Turismo about upcoming performances.

Ayamonte and around

Although the sprawling, slightly down-at-heel border town of **AYAMONTE** lies only 8km from Isla Cristina, the road has to dogleg 16km around the *marismas* to get there. With **Portugal** only a few hundred metres away on the opposite bank of the Río Guadiana – and easily visitable – there's a pronounced Portuguese feel to the town, and in the *horario comercial* the streets hum with the conversations of cross-border visitors who come over to do their shopping.

The warren of narrow streets behind the main square, Paseo de la Ribera (and its continuation Plaza de la Coronación) overlooking the harbour, leads up to the old town, with a couple of churches to see. The mildly interesting fourteenth-century **Iglesia de San Francisco** (open service times, try 7–9pm), with a beautiful Mudéjar *artesonado* ceiling, comes first, and, following the same street, c/San Francisco, even further north will bring you to the fifteenth-century **Iglesia de San Salvador** (Mon–Sat 5–8pm; free) with a striking tower which you can climb, when open, for fine views across the river to Portugal. The town's EU blue-flagged **beach** at Isla Canela, 7km to the south, can be reached by half-hourly **bus** (April–Sept) from Paseo de la Ribera.

The beaches

Ayamonte's beaches, the **Playa Isla Canela** and its eastward continuation, the **Playa Punta del Moral**, are excellent places for a bit of basking in the sun, although what was once an attractively wild stretch of coast has undergone a mammoth building programme turning the Punta del Moral into a complex of high-rise holiday apartments and hotels with the gargantuan and tasteless *Hotel Ríu* as its centrepiece.

The picturesque old fishing village of **PUNTA DEL MORAL** sits on an inlet slightly north of here warily eyeing the concrete monsters dominating the skyline to the south. It's worth seeking out this tiny place for a line of excellent **tapas bars** along its only recently asphalted main street: *Bar Nuevo Simón*, *Chiringuito III* and *El Contrabando* are all good for fresh fish, *raciónes* and a wide range of tapas.

Practicalities

Frequent daily buses from Huelva and Seville arrive at the **bus station** on Avenida de Andalucía north of the centre. Ayamonte's **Turismo** (Mon–Fri 10am–1.30pm & 5.30–8.30pm; ☎959 32 07 37, ⦿www.ayto-ayamonte.es), c/Huelva 17, slightly northwest of the Paseo de la Ribera, can provide a town map and information. The **internet** café Todoapc, Avda. Villa Real de Santo Antonio 5 (daily 10am–9pm), is located on the waterfront facing the fishing harbour.

Places to stay are limited and rooms can be hard to find, especially in summer; if things become really tight one option may be to cross the Guadiana to the Portuguese side and the town of Vila Real de Santo Antonio on the opposite bank (see p.342). As you enter Ayamonte from Isla Cristina, opposite the petrol station are two of the best-value options in town: the *Hostal Las Robles*, Avda. Andalucía 121 (☎959 47 09 59; ❷) and, next door, the new and plusher *Hotel Luz del Guadiana* (☎959 32 20 02; ❹). Both offer pleasant en-suite rooms and those at the latter come with a/c and TV. To the east of the harbour along the beach road, *Hotel Don Diego*, Avda. Ramón y Cajal 2 (☎959 47 02 50, ⦿www.hoteldondiegoayamonte.com; ❺ with breakfast), is a step up in price and quality while the town's *Parador Costa de la Luz* at El Castillita overlooking the Río Guadiana (☎959 32 07 00, ⦿www.parador.es; ❻) is modern and rather bland.

Ayamonte scores well in terms of **eating and drinking**, with many options clustered around the central Paseo (or Plaza) de la Ribera. Slightly west of here the very pleasant *La Casona*, at c/Lusitania 2, offers an inexpensive *menú*, and has a small terrace. On the main square *Cafetería Restaurante Barberi*, Paseo de la Ribera 13, is also worth a try and its café next door has an inexpensive *menú del día* for around €9. On the west side of the same square *Mesón Juan Macias*, Paseo de la Ribera 2, is another good place with plenty of chorizo- and *jamón*-based dishes. For a pricey feast, the town's best place – especially for fish – is the mid-priced *Casa Luciano*, c/Palma 2, on the east side of the harbour (☎959 47 01 71).

Nightlife is mainly confined to the summer months when the tourist invasion fills a number of music bars in and around c/Médico Rey García, one block in from the harbour: current hot spots are *Nox*, *Sacapuntas*, *Hangar* and *Paraguayo*.

On to Portugal

For a change of scene you can cross over the expansive Río Guadiana to **Portugal** by boat or over the impressive new road bridge. A **ferry** (July–Sept 9.30am–9pm every 30min; Oct–June 9.30am–9pm hourly; €1.45 one way) plies across the estuary and frontier to the busy and pleasant border town of **VILA REAL DE SANTO ANTONIO**, with a riverside promenade and streets behind lined with popular bars and economical restaurants. The ferry leaves from the Muelle de Portugal dock in Ayamonte – easily reached by taking the main pedestrianized thoroughfare, c/Lusitania, from the west side of Paseo de la Ribera. **By car** you simply head north out of town along c/Galdames following signs for Portugal and fairly soon you'll be flying effortlessly – and without any border checks whatsoever – high above the river via the magnificent Puente del Guadiana.

Should you want to **spend the night in Portugal** there are quite a few decent room possibilities within a couple of minutes walk of the Vila Real de Santo Antonio ferry quay. The waterfront *Hotel Guadiana*, Avda. da República 94 (from Spain ☎00 351 281 511 482, ⓦwww.hotelguadiana.com.pt; ❹), is an elegant, refurbished and reasonably priced upmarket choice, whilst the nearby *Residencia Villa Marquez*, Rua José Barão, 61 (from Spain ☎00 351 281 530 420; ❸) is a sparkling *hostal* offering a/c en-suite rooms with TV.

Inland to Río Tinto

Of the potential routes to the mountainous north of the province, the westernmost, from near Ayamonte, is the least interesting. Here the road ploughs on endlessly through a dreary landscape dominated by stands of voracious and alien eucalyptus which have sucked the lifeblood from the soil. Far more attractive is the N435 route heading northeast from Huelva city towards Extremadura which offers – with your own transport – an interesting detour to the **mines of Río Tinto** (see box, p.344). The **bus** uses the same route to reach Aracena or you could take a **train,** which will drop you at Almonaster La Real at the Sierra de Aracena's western end. For visits to the mining area without your own

vehicle there are at least three daily **buses** from Huelva to Minas de Ríotinto and Nerva from where there are not-so-frequent daily connections to Aracena and Seville. Once clear of Huelva the N435 climbs steadily towards **Trigueros**, a pleasant agricultural village, followed by the market town of **Valverde del Camino**, 24km north and now by-passed by the arterial road, noted more for its leather footwear factories than its charms.

A further 10km on, a turn on the right towards the hamlet of **El Pozuelo** allows you to see three **dolmens** from the third millennium BC. Following this minor road for about 2km brings you to a signed road just before a cemetery on the outskirts of the village. Follow this on foot or by car as it loops around the village for a further 2km to reach a rest area and **information board**. Leave any transport here and follow the track on the right which ascends the hill through trees for about 100m to the first dolmen, from where the other two can be seen on hills nearby. The first is the most impressive and has three burial chambers, two with their capstones still in place. The second has four burial chambers, and the last is in ruins. A further six dolmens displayed on the information board are not so easy to spot.

The N435 soon begins to wind into the wooded hill country of the Sierra Morena until – just beyond Zalamea La Real – a right turn along the A461 leads you into the area of the Río Tinto mines.

Minas de Riotinto and around

Set in an area dramatically scarred by open-cast mineworkings, where the exposed faces of mineral-rich rock are streaked with glinting rivulets of ochre, rust and cadmium, the village of **MINAS DE RIOTINTO**, 6km east of the N435, was created by the Río Tinto mining company in the early twentieth century after they had dynamited its predecessor – complete with Baroque church – which had stood in the way of mining operations.

As you approach it from the west, watch out on the left for the **Barrio de Bella Vista**, or what the locals refer to as the "English colony". This estate of Victorian villas, complete with mock-Gothic Presbyterian church and village

Año De Los Tiros

In 1888 the village of Río Tinto was the setting for possibly the first **ecological protest** in modern times. The Río Tinto Mining Company was using a copper processing method (banned many years before in Britain) that polluted the village and surrounding agricultural zone with a "*manta*" (blanket) of toxic fumes. Unable to convince the company or the Spanish governmental authorities (who were very much in awe of the company) to end a practice which was grievously affecting the health of the miners' families and children, the whole community staged a protest demonstration on February 4, 1888 culminating in a march to the Ayuntamiento where miners' representatives had requested a meeting with the mayor, company officials and the provincial governor. The latter had brought with him a regiment of Spanish troops to ensure that order was maintained. While the meeting was taking place within, the troops outside received an order (it is unclear who gave it) to open fire on the peaceful demonstrators. In what is now infamously known as the Año de los Tiros (Year of the Shootings) up to two hundred men, women and children lost their lives. In an attempt to obscure the scale of the tragedy many corpses were disposed of in disused mine shafts which is why the precise death toll was never known.

Noted Spanish writer **Juan Cobos Wilkins**, a native of Río Tinto and the descendant of an English Río Tinto employee who married a Spaniard, recently produced a novel, *Corazon de la Tierra* (Heart of the Earth), centred upon these events. In 2007 the novel was made into a film of the same title with an English–Spanish cast portraying the protagonists on both sides of the struggle. Cobos Wilkins has also written extensively about growing up in Río Tinto at the tail end of the Río Tinto Mining Company's great days, and before the mines were sold to Spanish proprietors. His work in Spanish, *La Huelva Británica* (published in 2007) is a fascinating history of the British in Huelva and particularly in the village of Bella Vista.

green, was constructed to house the largely British management and engineering staff when the mines passed into Anglo-German hands in the nineteenth century. The attitude of this elite to the surrounding village – where the mineworkers lived – is indicated by the estate's high perimeter wall and once-guarded entry gates intended rigorously to exclude "the natives", as they were disdainfully described. In a company policy with racist overtones these "colonialists" were forbidden from living in Bella Vista if they dared to marry a Spanish woman, thus deterring any dangerous interbreeding.

The estate now houses local people and no one minds if you wander in for a look around. The former "Social Club", membership of which was exclusively male (women were allowed only as guests), is now a **bar** named *Club Inglés* with a terrace overlooking the former village green/cricket pitch with a recently added **pool** (open to patrons of the bar). The mining museum (see p.345) recently acquired a house in Bella Vista which has been wonderfully restored in the style of the late nineteenth century when the British were here. Known as **Casa No. 21** (same ticket and hours as the mining museum) it uses period furnishings, clothing, domestic appliances, and fascinating photos of the

The mines of Río Tinto

The **Río Tinto** (Red River) takes its name from the oxidized iron minerals that flow down from the fissured crags of this strange, forbidding landscape, turning the river blood-red. Evidence of mineral exploitation here goes back at least five millennia – popular tradition asserts that these were the legendary mines of King Solomon, as seen in place names such as Cerro (or hill) de Saloman and Zalamea La Real. More secure historical evidence shows it was the **Phoenicians** (giving the name Ur-yero – "river of fire" – to the Río Tinto) who encouraged exploitation here early in the first millennium BC, during the age of the fabled kingdom of Tartessus from where they acquired the copper to smelt with the tin of Cornwall to make bronze. It was not copper but silver, however, which attracted the **Romans** in the second century BC. Production was dramatically stepped up during the late republic and early empire using remarkable – if brutal – systems to combat flooding, the perennial hazard in deep mining. This they overcame by means of slave-operated *norias*, or water wheels; in some workings as many as eight pairs of these wheels were used in relays to raise water from depths of 100m and more. For the shackled slave miners working with primitive tools by the light of small clay lamps in warrens of cramped, dark galleries (now vividly reconstructed in the Río Tinto mining museum), life must have been wretched. The scale of the Roman operations can be judged from the fifty million tons of visible slag left behind.

After the Romans had gone, the **Visigoths** worked out the Roman shafts but the mines were then run down during the Moorish period – although Niebla built part of its prosperity on its rights of ownership by granting permits. The *conquista* brought further decline in its wake as cheap mineral wealth flooded into Spain from the New World. Loss of empire and hard times induced efforts to restart the industry which, in 1873, resulted in the Spanish government selling the mines to a consortium of British and German bankers. Out of this the **Río Tinto Mining Company** was born, bringing numerous northern Europeans to work here. In 1954 control of the company returned into Spanish hands but falling world mineral prices led to it being sold on to a succession of multinational companies before, in 1995, it was purchased by its 523 employees for the symbolic price of one peseta. The worker-owned company also ran into difficulties and went bankrupt. After lying dormant for over a decade, the soaring price of copper on world markets has led another multinational, Emed Mining, to put in a bid for the mines with a view to returning them to full production.

village and its social life at the turn of the twentieth century to re-create a bygone age.

To continue to the village proper head east along the A461 and turn right following "*centro urbano*" signs. The road leads to a roundabout with palms on its central island, with the former Río Tinto Mining Company's offices (now the Ayuntamiento) to the left. The village's centre lies to the left or east from here while the mining museum is reached by taking a right uphill from the roundabout. **On foot**, from the west side of the same roundabout you can follow a path which ascends through the pine and eucalyptus woods to emerge at the museum.

The mining museum

At the village's western edge on a hill above the Río Tinto company's former offices lies the Río Tinto Foundation's remarkable **mining museum**, Plaza del Museo s/n (daily 10.30am–3pm & 4–7pm; €4). Housed in the company's former hospital, the museum presents an interesting panorama of mining in the area from prehistoric to modern times. The **Roman period** is the best represented, with exhibits illustrating their mining methods, daily life and burial practices in addition to a variety of coins and statuary. A recently opened section here has a walk-through reconstruction of a **Roman mineworking gallery** discovered in the nearby mining area. The actual site cannot be visited as it lies within the zone of the modern mineworkings and is thus dangerous, but the museum has done an excellent job in re-creating it. The section includes a functioning reconstruction of a *noria*, or **water wheel**, which were worked by slaves and used to drain the mines of flood water. Modern mining is also covered, as well as the geology, flora and fauna of the area. Don't miss the luxurious **wagon of the maharaja**, built in 1892 by the Birmingham Railway Carriage and Wagon Company to be used by Queen Victoria on her proposed visit to India. When this didn't happen it was sold to the Río Tinto company and used for the visit of King Alfonso XIII to the mines. The museum can also provide information on visits to old underground mine workings at Peña de Hierro, the source of the Río Tinto river and the site where NASA and Spanish academics are carrying out their research for the Mars project (see box, p.346). A **cafetería** serves snacks and drinks and its adjoining **shop** sells a wide variety of souvenirs.

In addition, the Río Tinto Foundation also runs **train trips** (tickets from the museum), lasting a couple of hours, through the mining area aboard century-old restored rolling stock – on the first Sunday of each month they use a 120-year-old steam locomotive (daily: March–May 1pm; June–July 15 1.30pm; July 16–Sept 1.30pm & 5.30pm; ring ☎959 59 00 25 or consult website for winter timetable; ⊛parquemineroderiotinto.com; €10).

Practicalities

There are a number of places to **stay** here; just around the corner from the museum there's *Hostal Galán*, Avda. de la Esquila 10 (☎959 59 08 40; ❷), with en-suite rooms and a good bar-restaurant below. A stone's throw away at the top of the hill descending to the village, *Hostal-Restaurante Atalaya*, Avda. de Esquila 13, (☎959 59 28 54, ⊛www.hostalrestauranteatalaya.com; ❷) is a pleasant new establishment offering comfortable en-suite rooms with TV. On a hilltop at the village's eastern end – and a bit of a hike without transport – the *Hotel Santa Barbara* (☎959 59 04 30, ⊛www.hotelsantabarbaragolf.com; ❸) with outstanding views and its own pool is an attractive upmarket option.

With your own transport the 🏕 *Cortijo Zalamea* (☎959 56 10 27, ⊛www .cortijozalamea.com; ❻–❼), 8km west and off the main N435 close to the

The Río Tinto and outer space

The almost Martian landscape of much of this zone has attracted scientists from Madrid University's Centro de Astrobiologia and the Astrobiological Institute of NASA, who have begun joint research into the remarkable microbial life that has developed here in some of the most inhospitable conditions on the planet. The enormous diversity of eukaryotic life forms (organisms with genetic cells) able to prosper in the poisonous and highly acidic waters of the Río Tinto mining zone initially astonished experts, who went on to discover here a variety of previously unknown life forms. Now formally known as the **MARTE Project** (Mars Astrobiology Research and Technology Experiment; @marte.arc.nasa.gov) researchers hope that the thousands of species of micro-organisms that have evolved here over millennia in the toxic depths of the Red River will provide clues as to how life may have developed and evolved in other parts of the universe, including Mars.

village of Zalamea La Real, is a delightful oasis with accommodation in self-contained cottages; there's also pool and horseriding, mountain biking and walking are some activities on offer. In Río Tinto, **eating** options are provided by the *hostales Galan* and *Atalaya* (the latter with a weekday *menú*) plus, heading 150m west downhill from these two, *Restaurante Epoca*, Paseo de los Caracoles 6, offers well-cooked *platos combinados* and its own *menú*. The *Hotel Santa Barbara* also has its own decent restaurant.

La Dehesa and Nerva

Two kilometres northeast of the village, and reached by following the A461 as it heads north towards Aracena, you pass two spectacular open-cast mines: the **Corta Atalaya**; and, with 5000 years of exploitation, the **Cerro Colorado**, set in an awesome landscape of rock cliffs glittering with iron pyrites, copper, silver and gold. From a **viewing platform** by the roadside you can see into the giant elliptical basin of the Corta Atalaya, which at 1200m long and 330m deep is one of the biggest open-cast mines in the world – far below, enormous trucks are dwarfed by the immense walls of rock. Another 2km further on, at **LA DEHESA**, the Río Tinto Company headquarters are backed by a **Roman graveyard** discovered in the 1990s featuring a number of interesting tombstones. Alarmingly close to the present mining operations which rumble on in the background, the graveyard (signed "Necropolis Romana") can currently only be viewed behind a fence, set slightly back from the road.

NERVA, 4km east of Minas de Riotinto, is a pleasant little place, its pedestrianized main street fringed with orange trees and overlooked by a splendid redbrick Ayuntamiento with a wonderful minaret-inspired octagonal tower. Opposite there's an extravagant new **Centro de Arte Contemporáneo** (Tues–Sat 11am–2pm & 5–8pm, Sun–Mon 10am–2.30pm; free) honouring Daniel Vásquez Díaz (a Paris contemporary of Picasso), who was born here. In addition to a handful of canvases by Díaz, the museum also displays an indifferent collection of works by other *nerveuses*, plus temporary exhibitions to fill the rather cavernous interior.

A **bus** runs from Nerva to Aracena at 5.45am from Monday to Saturday. The friendly, family-run *Hostal El Goro*, c/Reina Victoria s/n (T&F 959 58 04 37; ●), close to the centre, is a pleasant **place to stay**, with well-equipped en-suite rooms. *Hotel Vásquez Díaz*, c/Cañadilla 51 (T 959 58 09 27; ●), is a slightly more upmarket option reached by turning first left into the town coming from Minas de Riotinto. Good places for **eating and drinking** include *Cervezería Robles*,

Avda. de Andalucía 9, almost opposite the Ayuntamiento and, further along (facing the fountain), *El Circulo Comercial* (aka Mercantil) whose spacious interior is a great place to sample their excellent tapas and *raciónes*. The *Hotel Vásquez Díaz* (see p.346) also has its own restaurant with a daily *menú* for €12.

Leaving the mining area by the A461, beyond Campofrío the landscape softens as the road progresses through verdant forests of cork and holm oaks, chestnut and walnut trees towards Aracena.

The Sierra Morena

The longest of Spain's mountain ranges, the **Sierra Morena** extends almost the whole way across Andalucía from Rosal on the Portuguese frontier to the dramatic pass of Despeñaperros, north of Linares. Its hill towns once marked the northern boundary of the old Moorish caliphate of Córdoba and in many ways the region still signals a break today, with a shift from the climate and mentality of the south to the bleak plains and villages of Extremadura and New Castile. The range is not widely known – with its highest point a mere 1110m, it is not a dramatic sierra – and even Andalucians can have trouble placing it. All of which, of course, is to your advantage if you like to be alone.

Visiting the Sierra Morena

The Morena's **climate** is mild – sunny in spring, hot but fresh in summer – but it can get very cold in the evenings and mornings. A good time to visit is between March and June, when the flowers, perhaps the most varied in the country, are at their best. You may get caught in the odd thunderstorm but it's usually bright and hot enough to swim in the reservoirs or splash in the springs and streams, most of which are good to drink from. This is an area rich in **wildlife** – including frogs, turtles, lizards, dragonflies, bees, hares and foxes – while bird fanciers should keep an eye out for imperial and booted eagles, as well as goshawks, peregrine falcons and the rare black vulture. In villages such as Cortegana, Zufre and Santa Olalla del Cala the black stork nests on the church towers. The Sierra de Aracena sector of the sierra has been designated as a ZEPA (Zona de Especial Protección a las Aves) in recognition of its importance as a bird sanctuary. The sierra is also home to one of two surviving populations of Spanish lynx on the peninsula, although, with only thirty or so pairs eking out an existence as their forest habitat is gnawed away, you're unlikely to spot one. Locals maintain that while the last bears disappeared only a short time ago, there are still a few wolves in remoter parts.

East–west **transport** in the Sierra (see p.370) is limited but with a little planning most places mentioned below can be reached on public transport. For the zone east of Aracena, specifically the terrain beyond the main N630-E803 in Seville Province, bus services are radial and north–south, with Seville as the hub. Tracks are still more common in these hills than roads, and rural tourism, which the government of Andalucía is keen to encourage, has so far led to little more than a handful of signs pointing out areas of special interest. The wealth of good **walking country** invites organizing your routes around hikes if you want to spend any amount of time here. **Cycling**, too, is an option, though you'll need a sturdy bike with plenty of gears, especially on the winding and muscle-taxing hill roads. **Places to stay** are plentiful and most villages run to at least a decent *hostal* and a few now have hotels, too. Rural tourism accommodation has really taken off in recent years and there are also a great number of **villas** and **farmhouses** to rent in lovely settings; the best way to find one is through RAAR (Red Andaluza de Alojamientos Rurales; ☎902 44 22 33, English spoken, ⓦwww.raar.es).

Aracena

Clustered beneath its hilltop medieval castle, the attractive town of **ARACENA** is the highest conurbation in the Sierra Morena as well as the gateway to its own **Sierra de Aracena** to the south and west. Sheltered by this offshoot of the larger Morena range, Aracena is blessed by remarkably sharp, clear air – all the more noticeable, and gratifying, if you've arrived from the heat of Seville.

Although traces of Paleolithic occupation of this area have been found, it was only in the Middle Ages that more concrete historical events happened here, namely the passing of this territory into the kingdom of Castile by a treaty of 1267 following a long struggle with Portugal. Once inside the domains of Castile, Alfonso X ceded the zone around Aracena to the Knights Templars to maintain and protect the Sierra. They constructed the castle, one of many erected in this frontier zone, and ruled the roost here until 1312 (see box below). Today, the town's main role is as a centre of agriculture and cattle breeding, assisted by the tourist magnet of the **Gruta de las Maravillas** (Cave of Wonders).

Arrival and information

Aracena's **bus station**, Avda. de Sevilla s/n, lies on the southeast side of town close to the Parque Municipal. For information and a town map, the **Turismo** lies beneath the Gruta de las Maravillas ticket office (daily 10am–1.30pm & 3.30–6pm; ☎959 12 82 06, ⓦwww.sierradearacena.net). Information on the surrounding Parque Natural Sierra de Aracena y Picos de Aroche is obtainable from an **information centre** in the Cabildo Viejo, Plaza Alta 5 (Tues–Sun: July–Aug 10am–2pm & 6–8pm; Sept–June 10am–2pm & 4–6pm). They can also supply information on the town, including a useful town map. The town's two **internet** cafés are Servicio Informatica at Calle Constitución s/n near the main square (Mon–Fri 10.30am–2pm & 5.30–9pm, Sat 11am–2pm) and the

---

The Knights Templars

A military religious order founded in the twelfth century to protect pilgrims bound for the Holy Land, the **Knights Templars** derived their name from the Temple of Solomon, in Jerusalem. An army of fighting monks in reality, their *raison d'être* became a permanent crusade against the Saracen infidel from their "commanderies" in the Holy Land and western Europe.

For over a century the Templars fought the Muslims for control of Jerusalem and its surrounding territories. A series of defeats culminated in the loss of Acre in 1291, their last Latin outpost in Palestine, and heralded the order's demise. They were also mistrusted by the European monarchs, especially Philip IV of France, who saw the order as a threat to their power. Long accused of being involved in witchcraft due to their interest in the occult, magic and the supernatural as paths to ultimate knowledge, the Templars were persecuted, condemned and executed for heresy by an alliance of monarchs and clerics across Europe. The order was finally dissolved by a bull of Pope Clement V in 1312. In the light of the above it's rather ironic that Aracena's Templar outpost was built on top of one of the most magical and mysterious places in Spain: the Gruta de las Maravillas, of which they must have been completely unaware.

RESTAURANTS

Café-Bar Manzano	1
Casas	4
La Serrana	5
Mesón del Pedro	2
Restaurante José Vicente	3

ARACENA

ACCOMMODATION

Casa Manolo	E
Hospedería Reina de Los Angeles	G
Hostal Molino del Bombo	B
Hotel Aracena Park	A
Hotel de los Castaños	F
Hotel Finca Valbono	C
Hotel Sierra de Aracena	D

0   500 m

publicly funded Centro Guadalinfo, Plaza de Doña Elvira (Mon–Fri 5–7pm; free), to the west of the centre.

Accommodation

Aracena has plenty of places **to stay** and there's usually no problem finding a room at any time of the year. The nearest **campsite**, *Camping Aracena Sierra* (⊕959 50 10 05), which has a pool, lies 3km along the Seville road, then left for 500m towards Corteconcepción.

Casa Manolo c/Barberos 6 ⊕959 12 80 14. The budget option, this is a simple and friendly place but outside summer make sure to get an exterior room as the inside ones (which get no sun) can be freezing. ❶

Finca Valbono Carretera Carboneras, Km1 ⊕959 12 77 11, ⓦwww.fincavalbono.com. A rural hotel set in thirty acres of scenic woodland, 1km north of town on the road to Carboneras. Rustic-style self-contained *casas rurales* (+5) come equipped with chimeneas (wood burning stoves) or there are conventional rooms with mini bar, satellite TV, heating and a/c.

Facilities include bar, restaurant and pool and hiking and horseriding excursions are on offer. ❹

Hospedería Reina de los Angeles Avda. Reina de los Angeles s/n ⊕959 12 83 67, ⓦwww .hospederiareinadelosangeles.com. Located close to the Gruta de las Maravillas, this rather institutional hotel betrays its origins as a former student hostel. Redecorated and refitted, its ninety en-suite and rather Spartan rooms are nevertheless clean, bright and good value. ❷

Hostal Molino del Bombo c/Ancha 4, close to the bullring in the upper town ⊕959 12 84 78,

Ⓦ www.molinodelbombo.com. Very pleasant new *hostal rural* in a refurbished town house offering bright, comfortable en-suite rooms with the option of breakfast. ❷

Hotel Aracena Park Carretera Sevilla-Lisboa Km88 Ⓣ 959 12 79 59, Ⓦ www.aracenapark.es. New luxury hotel at the north end of the town on the main N-433 road coming from Seville. Spacious rooms (many with views) are well-equipped with mini bar, internet access and satellite TV and the public areas include three bars, two restaurants, pool and spa. ❺

Hotel de los Castaños Avda. de Huelva 5 Ⓣ 959 12 63 00, Ⓦ www.loscastanoshotel.com. This hotel offers decent if formally furnished rooms (aimed at the business traveller) with heating, a/c and TV. Facilities include a restaurant and garage. ❸

Hotel Sierra de Aracena Gran Via 21 Ⓣ 959 12 61 75, Ⓦ www.sierradearacena.es. Recently refurbished traditional hotel with pleasant, decent sized rooms (including ten singles), all with heating and a/c, some with views. Public areas include a bar-cafetería. ❸

The Town

Aracena is a modest but pretty Sierra town, its southern flank rambling up the side of a hill topped by the **Iglesia del Castillo** – or, more correctly, Nuestra Señora de los Dolores – a fine thirteenth-century Gothic-Mudéjar church built by the Knights Templar around the remains of a Moorish castle. The track up to the church begins from the **Plaza Alta**, where there's the unfinished church of **Nuestra Señora de la Asunción** with remnants of Renaissance craftsmanship, flanked by a sixteenth-century *cabildo* or **Ayuntamiento**, the oldest in the province which now houses the Natural Park information centre. The building's imposing main portal is by Hernán Ruíz II and dates to 1563. Slightly northeast of here, the interior of the **Convento de Santa Catalina**, with its fine fifteenth-century gothic panels, is also worth a look. It was for this convent that the stunning carved wood *retablo* by Juan Giralte, now in Seville's Museo de Bellas Artes, was made. The climb to the castle offers good views over the town from an imposing sixteenth-century brick gate complete with belfry, which allows access to the castle area. The church's elegant **Mudéjar tower** was formerly the minaret of the twelfth-century Almohad mosque prior to its destruction by the Templars, and its *sebka* brickwork ornamentation echoes the Giralda tower in Seville. Inside there's an unusual and finely made glazed clay tomb of the sixteenth-century prior, Pedro Vásquez de Miguel.

▲ Gateway to castle, Aracena

Aracena's principal attraction is the **Gruta de las Maravillas** (daily 10.30am–1.30pm & 3.30–6pm; guided hourly visits, half-hourly at weekends €7.70, seniors and kids €5.50), the largest and arguably the most impressive cave in Spain, discovered, so they say, by a local boy in search of a lost pig. The Gruta lies at the western end of c/Rosal which you can pick up just south of the Plaza Mayor (Plaza Marqués de Aracena): due to the cave being damaged by the overwhelming number of visitors, a maximum of 35 visitors per tour is now in force. The best **time to visit** is before noon; if you are planning an afternoon visit (the time favoured by coach tours) ring ☎959 12 83 55 and they will advise whether you will be able to gain entry. It can be chilly inside (the visit lasts 50min) so bring a sweater.

A guide takes you round the cave and the "marvels" are explained in Spanish only (leaflet in English). Although the garish coloured lighting is more Santa's Grotto than geological wonder, the cave is still astonishingly beautiful, and entertaining too – the last chamber of the tour is known simply as the Sala de los Culos (Room of the Buttocks), its walls and ceiling an outrageous, naturally sculpted exhibition, tinged in a pinkish orange light. You might care to ponder why this section of the caves did not appear in the film *Journey to the Centre of the Earth*, much of which was shot here.

In the plaza outside there's a permanent **outdoor museum of contemporary sculpture** with donated works by many noted artists including *Reconocimiento del Vacío* by the famous Basque sculptor Eduardo Chillida, a graceful cube-like structure, and Carmen Perujo's work *Paloma*, sited near the cave entrance

A recent new attraction in the town is the **Museo del Jamón**, Gran Via s/n (daily; guided tours, some in English, every 40min between 11.10am–1.50pm & 2.30–17.10pm; €3) dedicated to explaining the story of the Sierra de Aracena's famous *jamón ibérico* hams: how they're made and the importance of the *dehesa* (evergreen parklands with sparse plantations of holm and cork oaks) where the pigs are pastured. The traditional and modern methods of slaughter and subsequent curing of the *jamones* is informatively explained and a separate (and free) section of the museum deals with the sierra's *setas* (wild mushrooms) – almost seven hundred species have been identified in the sierra. During the season (Sept–Dec) it's possible to examine the latter at close quarters on **setas field trips** run by Doñana Aracena Aventura (☎959 12 70 45, ⊛www.donana-aracena-aventura.com); expert-guided hikes cost €8 in groups of twenty or €15 in groups of ten. As their office is some way from the centre contact them by phone (or book tours on their website).

Eating, drinking and nightlife

As Aracena is at the heart of a prestigious *jamón*-producing area, anything with **pork** is highly recommended – you should also try the delicious wild asparagus (spring to autumn), mushrooms (Sept onwards) and local **snails** (June–Aug). Aracena has plenty of places to eat and some are excellent. On the Plaza del Marqués de Aracena, *Café-Bar Manzano* serves good tapas and *raciónes* and has a terrace. For a memorable splurge, head for ⚘ *Restaurante José Vicente*, Avda. Andalucía 51 (☎959 12 84 55; closed Tues), where patrons gather to savour the five grades of Jabugo *jamón ibérico* (black-pig ham) under the approving gaze of owner/chef Vicente Sousa. The €20 *menú*, which often includes a mouthwatering *solomillo* (pork loin), is recommended, as is the tapas bar next door, *Despensa de José Vicente*, which also sells natural products from the sierra. Vicente is an expert on the sierra's *setas* (mushrooms), many remarkable examples of which he keeps in his freezer for use in the kitchen. At lunch time (that is, until 4pm), decent alternatives are provided by two restaurants near the entrance to the Gruta de las Maravillas: the excellent *Casas*, Pozo La Nieve 39, and the nearby *La Serrana*, both slightly extravagant with a *menú* at the latter for around €18. Close to the *Hotel Sierra de Aracena*, *Mesón del Pedro*, Gran Via 23, has an economical bar serving decent *platos combinados* as well as a more expensive restaurant which tends to close in the evening. Many of the hotels also have their own restaurants. Just up from the restaurants near the cave *Conservas Jabugo S.L.*, c/Pozo de la Nieve s/n, sells the famous *jamones* (hams) and many other products of the Sierra.

For **breakfast** or **evening drinks**, sit with the locals at the outdoor tables of the *Casino* bar (the building is the work of noted architect Anibal Gonzalez who also designed the Plaza de España in Seville) above the main square, from where you get a wonderful view towards the castle. Finally, for superb *dulces*, the 125-year-old Confitería Casa Rufino, off the main square at c/Constitución 3, is a must; their *tocino de cielo*, *vitorías* (liqueur-soaked, iced cakes) and *sultanas* (filled coconut cakes) are truly memorable – in the afternoon do what everyone else does, and take your cakes to *Café-Bar Manzano*'s terrace.

Nightlife is low-key, but turning left at the end of Gran Vía along c/Juan del Cid will bring you to a few **bars** and a **disco** –*Malh'aman* – frequented by Aracena's younger set. *D'Acuña*, at Gran Vía 20 is another popular *copas* bar while one block south on c/Rosal, *Pub Moncloa* and the nearby (at the junction with c/Santa Teresa) *La Reserva*, *Flick Flack* and *Rin-Ran* are other good late-night music bars with a lively atmosphere.

The Sierra de Aracena

With a few days to spare, the rugged villages perched on the hills to the **west of Aracena** make a fine walking tour. Along the route you'll find a number of good places to stay and plenty of tracks to follow through this rich landscape of orange and lemon orchards and forests of cork oaks, chestnut and gum trees. In spring the profusion of flowers is extraordinary: rosemary, French lavender,

A good **hiking guide**, *Sierra de Aracena* by David & Ros Brawn (see p.609) details 27 clearly described walks in the sierra ranging between four and fourteen kilometres. An accompanying map for the book is sold separately and all walks also have GPS waypoints identifying key locations en route. *Walking in Andalucía* by Guy Hunter-Watts (see p.609) also has half a dozen clearly described walks in the Sierra de Aracena. Alternatively, the Aracena and Huelva Turismos give out the free *Senderos de la Sierra de Aracena y Picos de Aroche* map listing twenty-three waymarked routes or there is a more detailed *Mapa Guía de la Sierra de Aracena y Picos de Aroche* on sale at the Aracena Turismo. It's also worth enquiring at all the Ayuntamientos along your route, as many of them are now producing their own walking guides, literature and lots of useful local information.

peonies and Spanish irises are most common, and you may also be lucky enough to see the rare brown bluebell and members of the orchid family. You probably won't glimpse the Spanish lynx in one of its last native habitats (outside the Coto de Doñana), but the skies are the place for sightings of black vultures on patrol, and even the occasional imperial eagle, a stirring image as they glide regally above their domain. Black vultures have been reintroduced into the park along with peregrine falcons and on the church towers of Cortegana and Zufre you may be lucky enough to sight the rare black storks that are known to nest there.

If you're coming to the Sierra for a few days and need a base there are lots of **houses to rent** in scenic locations (see p.348). The **bus service** between Aracena and the villages of Alájar, Almonaster, Cortegana and Aroche currently runs twice daily from Monday to Saturday at 1pm and 5.45pm, the latter terminating at Cortegana. There are also five daily buses from Monday to Saturday between Aracena and Galaroza, Jabugo, Cortegana and Aroche at 7.10am, 10.30am (also Sun), 1.15pm (terminating at Cortegana) and two at 5.30pm (buses with one calling at Linares, Alájar and Cortegana, the other passing all the rest along the main N432. Similar services return in the reverse direction. All leave from Aracena's bus station on Avenida de Sevilla s/n near the Parque Municipal.

Linares de la Sierra and Alájar

Leaving Aracena by the minor A470, after about 7km a turn-off left leads to the tiny village of **LINARES DE LA SIERRA**, a fairly simple and impoverished place huddled around its eighteenth-century Baroque church, a typical example of the sierra style, and curious unpaved bullring plaza. The sandy surface and *barreras* of the latter, behind which the *toreros* dodge the fearsome fighting bulls, seem a somewhat eccentric aberration considering that the ring is put to use only a couple of times a year in the village's fiestas. There's no accommodation, but *Bar Riandero* in the bullring/plaza serves tapas and sometimes meals when they're in the mood. There's also an excellent mid-priced **restaurant** here, *Mesón Arrieros*, c/Arrieros 2 (☎959 46 37 17; closed Mon;), below the church and off a street to the right, which has arguably the sierra's most creative chef, Luis Miguel López. Its main room has a homely, rustic whitewalled interior and any of the *cerdo iberico* dishes are recommended; *setas* (wild mushrooms) also feature in season. During July and August it is only open for dinner and offers a *menú de degustación* for around €30.

A further 4km along the A470, lined with chestnut orchards and great clumps of oregano, a turning on the left descends to **ALÁJAR**, a delightful, cobble-streeted hamlet at the foot of the Peña de Arias Montano. There's another eighteenth-century Baroque church here – dedicated to San Marcos – with the typical spire, besides plenty of places to eat or have a beer, all clustered around the main square. Each September 7 and 8, the village holds a pilgrimage to the hermitage of the **Virgen de los Ángeles** on the Peña de Arias Montano hill, 1km above the village. This involves the young men of the village in the *polleo*, a rite of passage in which they race horses along the narrow streets and then up the steep slope to the shrine. The horses are spurred mercilessly and arrive foaming and bleeding at the top of the climb.

For overnight **accommodation** there's the pleasant *Hotel La Posada*, c/Emilio González 2, off the west side of Plaza Constitución (℡959 12 57 12, Ⓦwww.laposadadealajar.com; ❸ with breakfast), which has rooms with bath and heating and also serves food. The proprietors can provide information and maps for walking and mountain biking, and horse trekking is also on offer. One kilometre out of the village in the direction of Santa Ana La Real, *Molino Río Alájar* (℡959 50 12 82; Ⓦwww.molinorioalajar.com; ❺–❻, minimum stay two nights) comprises six superbly equipped cottages sleeping between two and six persons. There's also a pool, donkey riding and the Dutch proprietor has produced a pamphlet of half-a-dozen walks all starting and ending at the *Molino*'s estate.

For **places to eat** in the village, on the Plaza itself *Bar-Restaurante El Corcho* serves up hearty sierra dishes and has, beyond a shop and an artistically cobbled floor, a dining room where all the fittings (and even the "glasses") are made

A Walk From Alájar To Linares De La Sierra

A fine **walk** (6km) from Alájar to Linares de la Sierra takes in the delightful isolated hamlet of **Los Madroñeros**, whose grassy streets can only otherwise be reached by tractors and off-road vehicles. To find the start of the walk take the street left along the north side of Alájar's church to a plazuela (small square) and follow the street downhill to an open area. The path follows the old road, climbing beyond an indicator board (detailing the walk) on the far side. Should you lose the way, ask for the *camino antiguo a Los Madroñeros*. Once on the track it soon leads away from the village running between dry stone walls behind which are cork oaks sheltering *pata negra* black pigs, soon to be turned into the region's prized *jamón*. The settlement of Los Madroñeros is a tranquil haven: a huddle of traditional white-walled dwellings topped by distinctive chimney-pots with green grass all around. You'll be lucky to see any inhabitants as they seem to keep a low profile, unlike their numerous cats who will eye you curiously as they sun themselves on rooftops or any convenient flat stone.

The *camino* (with frequent yellow and white *PR – Pequeño Recorrido* – waymarks to guide you) leads on eastwards away from the village, gently climbing and falling with only one place which may confuse. Just after crossing a stream, about half way between Los Madroñeros and Linares, you'll come to a deserted semi-ruined farmhouse; the path here isn't immediately clear but you need to go through the gateway of the farmhouse to pick up the track on the other side. Soon after this, you reach **Linares**. To return to Alájar you can retrace your route or follow the road back (the A470). In David and Ros Brawn's book (see box, p.353) they describe an alternative route back to Alájar with one steep climb. Alternatively you could time your arrival to meet up with Alájar-bound buses (see above) passing through about 1.30pm or 6pm. Going in the other direction the Aracena bus currently passes through at 4.15pm.

from cork. An excellent place for more elaborate meals is the *Mesón El Molino*, in a converted old mill with all its original features just up from the main square at c/Alta 9. Follow the street uphill from the main square for 50m, turning left into a narrow alley; the restaurant lies at the end of here. Further in, to the rear of the church, *Casa Padrino*, c/Miguel Moya 2, is another decent restaurant with a pleasant terrace. There's also a first-rate restaurant at the *Peña de Arias Montano* (see below).

Peña de Arias Montano

On quieter days the **Peña De Arias Montano**, the rock cliff that towers above the village, is a beautiful leafy spot set among woods of cork oaks, with cold springs surrounding its **shrine**. The Sierra Morena is liberally dotted with these buildings, almost always in isolated spots and dedicated to the Virgin. The site has been hallowed since prehistoric times, and Iberian shamans or priests are reputed to have gained their "second sight" from the hallucinogenic *amanita muscaria* mushroom which grows in the woods here – don't experiment yourself though as some species found in these hills can kill in thirty minutes. The sixteenth-century *ermita* (hermitage) of the **Virgen de los Ángeles**, filled with ex-votos from pilgrims and distinguished more by the beauty of its setting than for any architectural qualities, is the former retreat of the humanist Benito Arias Montano, confessor and librarian to Philip II, who was born nearby in 1527 and gave his name to the site. The belfry to the side of the church dates from the same period and offers glorious **views** over Alájar beneath, and the Sierra beyond. A **cavern** below the car park is said to be where magical and religious ceremonies were carried out in ancient times and where Philip II is supposed to have meditated during a visit here – giving it the name Sillita del Rey (The King's Chair), a reference to the huge boulder at the cave's mouth.

The true peace of the place is best appreciated by leaving the visitors' area – and its stalls selling honey, garish pots and religious tack – and heading along the track into the woods of cork oaks where there are plenty of likely picnic spots, and more fine views over the Sierra. Continuing along the track for a couple of kilometres will bring you to a ferociously steep climb leading to the "true" *peña* or peak where Arias Montano is said to have done much of his meditating; at the summit there's a *mirador* with fine **views** to be had should you attempt it. Opposite the *ermita* is a very good **place to eat**, *La Peña* (℡959 50 13 40), serving tapas in its bar and a variety of dishes made with the products of the sierra in its restaurant (*menú de degustación* €20).

Santa Ana La Real and Almonaster La Real

Six kilometres west of Alájar the modest but pretty white-walled village of **SANTA ANA LA REAL** – with another crumbling eighteenth-century church at its heart – is worth a detour. *Bar Garrafa* is a handy place for refreshment, and a couple of kilometres beyond the village is a convenient and good value **place to stay**, at the junction of the A470 and the N435 – the modern and flower-bedecked *Hostal El Cruce* (℡959 12 23 33; ❷), set in fine scenery with a lively tapas bar and popular restaurant.

Continuing west for another 6km brings you to the main village of this corner of the Sierra, the picturesque **ALMONASTER LA REAL** huddled in a river valley below the peak of the same name, which at 912m is the sierra's highest summit. A solid and picturesque agricultural centre today, Almonaster has an impressive Moorish past and an important tenth-century **mosque** (daily 9am–7pm; free) on a hill to the south of the town. The mosque may have Roman and Visigothic antecedents, and after it became Christianized in the thirteenth century was little altered, thus preserving its square minaret, the *mihrab* (said to be the oldest in Spain) and beautiful interior of five naves with brick horseshoe arches supported by what are probably recycled Roman columns. It should be open, but if not, ask at the Ayuntamiento, Plaza de la Constitución, for the key. Tacked on to the mosque/church is the village **bullring** where each August a *corrida* is staged during Almonaster's annual fiesta (see box above). The mosque's tower is a favourite with the kids of the village at this time, as it provides a free (if dangerously precarious due to a lack of barriers) view of the ring.

A popular event here in early summer is the **Cruz de Mayo** – a religious and flamenco festival held over the first weekend in May – at which the celebrated *fandangos* of Almonaster are sung and the local women parade in the magnificent costume of the *Serrana* (highlands): colourful flounced dresses and tasselled shoes and shawls, complemented by bouquets of wild flowers. The whole affair provides the participants with an excuse to soak up prodigious quantities of the local *aguardiente* firewater, which is misleadingly described as brandy. If you can't make this one, similar festivals take place in the surrounding villages all through May. In October the village puts on a series of **Jornadas Islamicas** when a *Zoco* (Arab-style market) is set up around the main square and there are lots of cultural activities with an Islamic theme.

Country Corridas

Like many country rings, the **bullring** at Almonaster does not see much action. In fact, the prohibitive cost of mounting a **corrida** with six bulls, three *matadores* and their retinues often restricts a small village to one *corrida* each year, usually in the middle of its annual fiesta. To see a bullfight at places like Almonaster, however, is to get a fascinating insight into many of the secrets of the *corrida* as, with the ring barely big enough to contain the crowd, bulls and *matadores*, many of the preparations have to take place outside.

First of all, while the arena is doused from a water tanker, the *picadores* select their eight-foot-long lances from a couple of dozen leaning against the wall of the ring. When they've chosen, a blacksmith attaches one of three lethal-looking steel points, again selected by the *picador*. Meanwhile, below the walls of the mosque, the grooms prepare the horses – whose vocal chords are severed so as not to alarm the crowd with their terrified shrieks – by fastening on the *peto* or heavy padding, protection against the bull's ferocious horns. Next the horses' ears are stuffed with oil-soaked rags and securely tied to block out the sound of the crowd and the bull. Finally, they are blindfolded over the right eye, the side from which the bull will attack.

Fifteen minutes before the *corrida* is due to start the village band marches up the hill playing a lively tune before disappearing into the arena. Once inside, they strike up a *paso doble* for the pre-fight parade before the grotesque figure of the helmeted and armoured *picador* is pushed through the small doorway into the ring and a great cheer goes up from the crowd inside. They are soon yelling *"fuera!"* (away), however, because they don't want the bull too weakened by the lance to be able to put up a decent fight. A few minutes later the trumpets sound and the door opens to allow the *picador* to exit from the arena. With fresh blood dripping from his lance, the image of this warrior is almost medieval. Big-name *toreros* appear in these village *corridas* because the pay is good, but equally the risks are high. The primitive nature of rings such as the one at Almonaster means a long journey to reach a hospital with adequate facilities should the *matador* be seriously gored, a factor that has, in the past, proved fatal.

▲ View of the bullring in Almonaster la Real

Almonaster's **train** station – with infrequent services to Huelva – lies 3km north of the village and is, in fact, nearer to Cortegana. Outside the festival period, finding a **place to stay** is usually no problem. At the entrance to the village *Hotel Casa García* (☏959 14 31 09; ⓦwww.hotelcasagarcia.com; ❸) is comfortable, and the rooms on the front have great views; it also has a decent restaurant downstairs. Further in, the village's other possibility for en-suite rooms, *Hostal La Cruz*, Plaza El Llano 8 (☏959 14 31 35; ❷), is less expensive, nicely located on a tranquil square, and also has its own restaurant and tapas bar. Modern, heated apartments are also available from *Las Palmeras* (☏959 14 32 40, ⓦwww.laspalmerasrural.com; ❸, minimum 2 nights) and are located opposite the restaurant of the same name (see below).

Perhaps the most entertaining place of all for **food** is the plant-bedecked ✲ *Las Palmeras* on the road into the village before *Casa García*. Voluble proprietor Alejandro produces everything on the economical (and ecological) *menú* himself, from the tasty *caña de lomo* (cured ham from his own pigs) to the salads (which shouldn't be missed) from his *huerta* (vegetable garden). Nearby, *El Rincón de Curro*, on the Cortegana road a short distance beyond *Casa García*, is a small family restaurant serving up *platos de la sierra*: *solomillo de cerdo iberico* is a house special.

Cortegana

Roughly 2km out of Almonaster the road forks left to **CORTEGANA**, a pleasant and populous *pueblo* spreading along the valley of the Río Carabaña below a heavily restored castle. Built in the thirteenth century during the frontier disputes with the Portuguese, the heavily restored **Castillo** (officially Tues–Sun 11am–2pm & 5–7pm; otherwise enquire at the Ayuntamiento, c/Maura 1, just off the Plaza de la Constitución; €1.50) provided a necessary observation post and today gives fine **views** from its battlements. It is flanked by the fourteenth to fifteenth century **ermita** of Santa María del Castillo whose chapel has been recently refurbished with the addition of some rather tedious modern frescoes. To reach the castle take the Almonaster road – signed

SEVILLE AND HUELVA | The Sierra Morena

Walks Around Almonaster

There are some superb **walks around Almonaster**, following the old cobbled mule paths and village tracks (*senderos*). The paths are well preserved, on the whole – though at times you are forced on to the tarmac road – and are waymarked with paint-splashes on trees and rocks. You need sharp eyes to spot the beginning of the paths, below the road, and if you can, you should try to get hold of the *Senderos de la Sierra de Aracena y Picos de Aroche* walks pamphlet which the Ayuntamientos in Almonaster, Cortegana or Jabugo should stock. This is easy to follow with minimal Spanish and has route descriptions and an excellent fold-out survey map. Cortegana also produces its own leaflet, *Senderos de Pequeño Recorrido en el Entorno de Cortegana*, with a good map and covering much of the same ground, which is usually available from the Ayuntamiento (if they haven't run out). You'd be advised to take along as well a decent 1:100,000 or 1:50,000 map (CNIG sheets 895 & 916 for the latter), just in case you lose the way.

One of the most enjoyable walks, starting from Almonaster, is the **PRA-5** which leads off to the left of the Cortegana road, around 1km out of Almonaster. This takes you through woodland peppered with streams to the hamlets of **Arroyo** and **Veredas** (2hr), where there are bars with food, and on to Cortegana (3hr). Alternatively, if it's just a brief country ramble you're after, follow the sign to Acebuches along the **PRA-5-2** path, under an hour from Almonaster, and again endowed with a small bar.

Another fine walk from Almonaster is to head straight up the hillside northeast of the village along the **PRA-5-1**. This is actually a paved Roman track, presumably built for some kind of quarrying. It takes a couple of hours' strenuous walking to get up to the summit, and if you're making a day of it, you could continue on to Cortegana or Jabugo.

from the N433 on the village's eastern edge. After 100m you come to a junction where a drivable road on the left climbs to the castle.

Two churches here are also worth visiting. The **Iglesia del Divino Salvador** (open service times, try 7–9pm) was started in the late sixteenth century but has elements added from much later, such as its bell tower, when the original collapsed in the earthquake of 1755. The interior has a finely worked Baroque pulpit. Built in Gothic Mudéjar style, the church of **San Sebastián** (open service times, try 7–9pm) nearby has interesting Renaissance doors.

Cortegana's big annual knees-up is the Jornadas Medievales **fería** held in the first or second week in August with archery contests, falconry, various tournaments and re-enactments of the storming of the castle walls – accompanied by much music, drinking and dancing. Its other main *fería*, Fiestas Patronales, occurs in early September with *corridas*, processions and concerts.

Practicalities

If you want to **stay** in Cortegana, you could try the excellent *Pensión Cervantes*, c/Cervantes 27, just off the focal Plaza Constitución (℡959 13 15 92, ⓦwww.pensioncervantes2000.com; ❷), which has clean and comfortable heated en-suite rooms with a/c and TV; try for a room overlooking a peaceful garden at the rear. Another tempting option for a longer stay is ⚘ *Los Gallos* (℡959 50 11 67, ℡mobile 687365754, ⓦwww.alojamientolosgallos.com; ❹), a leafy and tranquil oasis where you can rent cottages and apartments in and around a restored farmhouse set in spectacular countryside, with gardens and a pool. It lies on the Almonaster road, a couple of kilometres to the southeast, and close to the delightfully rustic Almonaster train station. Although trains still stop here (two daily in both directions) the former station has now been converted into a charming *casa rural*, *Antigua Estacion* (☎mobile 655527801, Ⓦwww.casasantiguaestacion.com; ❸) with train-inspired decor throughout its three apartments. At the start of the road out towards Almonaster and 200m east of the bullring (at no. 61 – with a *Casa Rural* sign) the friendly ⚑ *Villa Cinta* (☎959 13 15 22, Ⓦwww.casaruralvillacinta.com; ❷ with breakfast) is another very pleasant possibility where rooms (or more expensive suites ❸) are en suite and have stunning views. Another out-of-town possibility is *La Posada de Cortegana* (see box above), which can be reached with transport

A Walk From Cortegana To La Posada

A scenic **walk** (10km) north from Cortegana follows the densely wooded valleys of the Arroyo Carabaña and Río Caliente to *La Posada de Cortegana*, a unique rural hotel and restaurant serving an excellent lunch. If you happen to be staying at *La Posada* (see below) you can follow the second part of this walk to reach Cortegana and the first part to return to the hotel. Look out along the route for trees and stones daubed with the yellow and white GR (Gran Recorrido) markings which will confirm you are on the correct route. The walk leaves Cortegana by c/Sevilla, located behind the church of Divino Salvador on the southeast side of the village, becoming Callejón Carabaña – a rough track which descends to an *arroyo* or stream. When you meet the main N433 road cross this and follow a track (asphalted in its begin) to the left heading downhill. Cross a stream (the Arroyo Carabaña) in the valley and follow the path as it heads north along the right bank soon passing a *finca* (house) to the left named Los Molinos (the windmills). Not far beyond this you'll reach a house at a ford over the stream with a log-built verandah.

The path continues north along the river's left bank before narrowing to cross a stone barrage protecting a water pipe. Shortly beyond this, cross the river to the opposite bank by the use of stepping stones and continue north on the opposite bank. GR markings confirm the new route. The path continues north climbing above the river and passing two ruins – the first substantial – visible on the opposite bank. After the second ruin the path passes a barrage and continues north along the right bank through dense bracken and ferns. This is the most uncomfortable part of the route, and a machete or secateurs would be helpful here, but are by no means essential. After a hundred metres or so of this the path rejoins the river at a wire fence. Cross the fence and a GR marker will guide you to the now reasonable path heading north. When you reach a fallen tree (which may bear GR markers) lying prostrate across the river you should cross to the left bank and ascend to a wire gate ahead (not the green one off to the right). The track beyond this leads to the path to *La Posada* (☎959 50 33 01, Ⓦwww.posadadecortegana.es; ❺ with breakfast) some 70m distant. A wonderful *hotel rural* comprising log cabins set in woodland, its restaurant with a riverside terrace makes it the high point of the hike. Any of the pork dishes are recommended.

To return to Cortegana from *La Posada* follow the same track back that brought you to the hotel and follow it as it heads uphill through woodland. The track eventually fords a stream (the Arroyo Carabaña) where you should keep ahead (resisting the temptation to follow the path as it swings left uphill) along a rough stony track. The route continues to ascend until you reach a junction (marked by a pole carrying a power cable) with one path climbing to the left (with GR markers) while the other heads along more level ground. The second path will eventually bring you to the H2211 minor road where you turn left to head into Cortegana. The first-mentioned GR route climbs along an old Roman cobbled way, finally cresting near Cortegana's rubbish tip. Veer left along the tip to reach a path which ascends steeply through various shanties to reach the edge of Cortegana, and following a left turn, the main N433 road. Crossing this will bring you into the centre of the town.

by following a badly potholed minor road north (signed for the hotel) just east of the village of El Repilado for about 4km.

For **eating and drinking** a number of bars around the centre serve **tapas**: the *Casino*, a turn-of-the-twentieth century institution on the focal Plaza Constitución, is one that also makes a pleasant **breakfast** and morning-coffee stop as it has all the newspapers. *Bar España* on the same square does decent tapas and *raciónes*. The town isn't over-endowed with eating places and for more substantial fare you should head for the reasonably priced *El Aceiton*, Avda. de Portugal 5, where *solomillo de cerdo con castañas* (pork loin with chestnut sauce) is a house special. The nearby *comedor*, *Los Peroles*, Calle Eritos 32, located in an old *bodega* is also good, lies off the end of the same street and offers a good variety of *platos combinados*. Both places are sited close to the Guardia Civil barracks on the main N-433. To reach them from the from the central Plaza Constitución (a five-minute walk) follow c/Talero (and its continuation) from here to the end and turn right into the Avenida de Portugal.

Aroche

Heading west for 14km along the N433 brings you to **AROCHE**, in sight of the border with Portugal. Perched on a hill dominated by its castle with a fertile plain below, it's a neat little place, with white-walled, cobbled streets where – because it gets so few visitors – you can be sure of a hearty reception. Aroche was originally the Roman town of Arruci Vetus, but many more ancient vestiges of habitation have been discovered here, including giant prehistoric single standing stones, or **menhirs** erected in the Megalithic period. Arriving with your own transport take the first – and fully asphalted – entry on the left into the town coming from Aracena; using the other entry road to the east leads up into a warren of steep cobbled backstreets which are difficult to negotiate.

Once you have made it up the hill to the village, the obvious place to aim for is the Castillo. Constructed by the Almoravids in the twelfth century, the fort was remodelled after the *Reconquista*, but the most bizarre alteration of all was to make the interior into a full-scale **bullring**. A curiosity here are the sallyports – narrow openings in the arena's stone wall – used by the *toreros* to dodge the bull, instead of the normal *barrera* or fence. Note that for **access to all the town's sights**, including the Castillo, you'll need to call at the **Centro de Visitantes** (May–Sept Fri–Sun & public holidays 10am–2pm & 4–6.30pm, Oct–Apr Sat & Sun 10.30am–1.30pm & 3.30–5.30pm; ☎959 14 02 82) up a stepped street to the right of the Ayuntamiento on the main square, Plaza de Juan Carlos I. They also sell copies of *Guía de la Sierra de Aracena y Picos de Aroche*, a useful book with information about all the villages of the sierra. When this is closed the Ayuntamiento can usually help out with information.

In the same building as the Centro de Visitantes, the splendid seventeenth-century former convent of La Cilla incorporating an olive-oil pressing room from the original edifice, is housed the town's **archeological museum** (open same hours as Centro de Visitantes). An interesting collection has numerous finds from the Roman and Moorish periods as well as ceramics and other artefacts from Turóbriga, a first-millenium BC Iberian settlement discovered 3km north of the town (see p.361).

Just below the castle, the parish church of **Nuestra Señora de la Asunción** was started in 1483 but added a mixture of Mudéjar, Gothic and Renaissance styles before its completion 150 years later. Behind a dour, buttressed exterior, the triple-naved church has a trio of *retablos*: the image of Christ lowered from the cross at the top of the right hand (or south) nave is by La Roldana; the representation of Christ *nazareno*, bearing his cross, in

A walk from El Repilado to Los Romeros

Returning to Aracena from Aroche by the N433 takes you through the village of **El Repilado** from where you could make a picturesque five-kilometre **walk** south along the Río Caliente to the charming village of Los Romeros. Leave Repilado by the N433 road towards Cortegana and after crossing the bridge over the river, turn left along the HV-111 going to Los Romeros. Where the road traverses to the east bank of the river, follow the track along the west bank which leads through woods of chestnut and black poplar, and where in spring you'll see a profusion of wild flowers. When the road recrosses the river, use the bridge to gain access to the tiny and picturesque village of **Los Romeros**, a place devoted to *jamón* production (it takes its name from a major ham family). For **accommodation** you could try *Finca La Silladilla*, a *cortijo* with several refurbished farmhouses and facilities such bar, restaurant and a pool (T959 50 13 50; ⑤). In the village proper the Hermanos Marquez supermarket (T959 12 44 50; ④) also lets out houses in and around Los Romeros (minimum two nights, sleeping two to four people). For **food** and **drink** *Bodegón Los Romeros* in Plaza del Valle Florido (by the church) does good tapas and *raciónes* and has a terrace, while *La Albardería*, a hundred metres up a signed road beyond the church, is a more elaborate but still economical place with a good selection of the sierra's *platos tipicos*.

the *retablo* at the end of the left aisle is a seventeenth-century work by Alonso Cano. Along the north wall nearby, another *retablo* has – below and to the left of Nuestra Señora de Los Remedios, the town's patron – a small and sensitively worked image of the Virgin perched on an inverted half-moon and coiled serpent, another seventeenth-century work by La Roldana. The church's other treasures (only viewable when the *cura* or priest is available due to their value) include the fifteenth-century crucifix of Cardenal Mendoza of Seville, the supporter of Isabel, as well as a seventeenth-century Russian icon from St Petersburg.

There are some pretty strange museums in Andalucía, but Aroche's **Museo del Santo Rosario** (Museum of the Holy Rosary), c/Ordoñez Valdes s/n, has to be one of the most eccentric. Located a little downhill to the east of the Ayuntamiento and near the *correo*, the exhibits consist of well over a thousand rosaries donated by such leading religious luminaries as Pope John XXIII and Mother Teresa, in addition to others from *toreros* and soccer players and one each from John F. Kennedy and King Juan Carlos. Those sent in by Richard Nixon and General Franco betray suspiciously little sign of wear.

A pleasant **walk** out of the village starts on the opposite (north) side of the main N433 to the 12–14th century Gothic–Mudéjar **Ermita de San Mames**. The (drivable) track leading to it is signed between the two entry roads to the town. Following this for 2km leads to the *ermita* (Wed–Fri 8am–3pm, Sat & Sun 10am–2pm & 4–7pm; free) a triple-naved church with wall-painting fragments. Next to the church are the extensive and recently revealed remains of the Roman town of **Turóbriga**. Substantial buildings surrounding what appears to be a forum have been unearthed, while further excavations – now revealing a substantial ancient conurbation – are continuing in the surrounding fields where a bathhouse has been discovered.

Practicalities

Unfortunately, due to recent closures there is currently no accommodation in Aroche. As regards **eating and drinking** there are a number of good **tapas bars** including the central *Centro Cultural Las Peñas*, c/Real 8, near the church, which has a relaxing bar serving up a great selection – try the *chocos* (cuttlefish).

Other possibilities are the popular *Cafetería Las Peñas* – specializing in seafood tapas – on the square near the Ayuntamiento, and the smaller *Cafetería Lalo* above this with its entrance on c/Cilla. More elaborate fare is on offer at *Mesón San Mames*, c/Del Postigo 2, downhill from the main square along c/Dolores Rosada and left after fifty metres. Below the church, along c/Bellido, *Mesón Los Arcos* is another popular tapas haunt.

Jabugo and around

The mere mention of the name of **JABUGO** is enough to make any Spaniard's mouth water, and once you have tasted what all the fuss is about it's easy to understand why. As roadside billboards depicting smiling pigs proclaim, *jamón* is king in Jabugo. To get stuck into ham sampling, when you approach the village from the N433, ignore the sign directing you to the *centro urbano* and continue straight on. You'll pass half a dozen **bars** and **restaurants** all eager to sell you a *bocadillo* stuffed with *jamón de Jabugo* – or even a whole ham shank should you feel like splashing out. *Bodega Restaurante Jabugo* and *Mesón Cinco Jotas* are probably the best. There are tapas, too, but keep an eye on the prices as the *pata negra* doesn't come cheap.

Ham apart, the village of Jabugo is a sleepy place gathered around a charming square, the Plaza de Jamón, with a central fountain overlooked by the *Casino* – a relaxing place for a beer – and the restored, Baroque **Iglesia de San Miguel**. The nearby Casa Irene is another good source for the pork products of the region.

The villages **around Jabugo** – Aguafría, Castaño del Robledo and Fuenteheridos (for the latter two see below and p.364) – all make rewarding destinations for walks amid splendid wooded hills, though all are equally ill-served by public transport and you may well find yourself in for a walk both ways.

There is currently no accommodation in the village itself. For full **meals**, *El Molino de Jabugo*, Plaza de la Constitución 8 (reached by following c/de la Fuente for 200m from Plaza de Jamón), is a charming restaurant housed in an old oil mill; any pork dishes are recommended.

Castaño del Robledo

Four kilometres southeast of Jabugo, but a few kilometres more by road, lies the isolated village of **CASTAÑO DEL ROBLEDO**, which has not one but two outsized churches for its meagre population. Both named Santiago, they attest to a time in the seventeenth and eighteenth centuries when the population here was growing so rapidly that the church of Santiago la Mayor, then under construction, had to be enlarged. However, the population declined as quickly as it had grown and the crumbling, cavernous and now little-used church was left unfinished, while the congregation remained in the older and smaller of the two churches built in the sixteenth century. The larger Neoclassical hulk – containing a rare and recently restored eighteenth-century organ – today looks down grimly on the surrounding pantiled roofs. Other remnants from more illustrious days are a number of decaying mansions along the village's narrow, cobbled streets.

On the main square, Plaza del Álamo, just above the smaller church, *Bar La Bodeguita* is a pleasant old place serving decent **tapas**. Across the same square, the mid-priced **restaurant** *El Dornillo* (usually open weekends but not always in the week), is a surprisingly swish place, specializing in *platos tipicos* of the region. Castaño now has a decent **place to stay**, the *Posada del Castaño*, c/José Sánchez Calvo 33, close to the Plaza del Alamo (⊤959 46 55 02, ⓦwww .posadadelcastano.com; ❸ with breakfast). Run by an expat Scottish couple

The king of hams

Surrounding Jabugo is a scattering of attractive but economically depressed villages mainly dependent on the **jamón industry** and its curing factory, which is the major local employer. Things were little different when Richard Ford passed through here a century and a half ago, describing these mountain villages as "coalitions of pigsties", adding that it was the duty of every good pig to "get fat as soon as he can and then to die for the good of his country".

Sought out by classical writers such as Strabo for its distinctive flavour, and produced since long before by the peoples of the Iberian peninsula, *jamón serrano* (mountain ham from white pigs) is a *bocadillo* standard throughout Spain – the English words "ham" and "gammon" are both derived from the Spanish. Some of the best ham of all, **jamón ibérico** or **pata negra** (both acorn-fed ham), comes from the Sierra Morena, where herds of sleek pigs grazing beneath the trees are a constant feature. In October the acorns drop or are beaten down by their keepers and the pigs, waiting patiently below, gorge themselves, become fat and are promptly whisked off to the factory to be slaughtered and then cured in the dry mountain air. The meat of these black pigs is exceptionally fatty when eaten as pork but the same fat that marbles the meat adds to the tenderness during the curing process. This entails first of all covering the hams in coarse rock or sea salt to "sweat", after which they are removed to cool cellars to mature for up to two years. *Jamón serrano* from mass-produced white pigs is matured for only a few weeks, hence the incomparable difference in taste. At Jabugo the best of the best is then further graded from one to five *jotas* (the letter "J" for Jabugo) depending on its quality – a whole leg of **cinco jotas jamón** will set you back anything from €250 to €350.

The king of hams also demands an etiquette all of its own: in bars and restaurants everywhere it has its own apparatus (*la jamonera*) to hold it steady, and carving is performed religiously with a long, thin-bladed knife. The slices must not be wafer-thin nor bacon rashers and once on the plate *jamón ibérico* becomes the classic partner for a glass of *fino*.

who are enthusiastic hikers, they can advise on walking in this zone as well as places to eat in or near the village if they are not offering supper themselves.

Galaroza and Valdelarco

The N433 east from Jabugo rolls along through country filled with dense oak woods surrounded by dry stone walls, where you may catch a fleeting glimpse of a herd of *cerdos ibéricos*, the celebrated black pigs of the Sierra. The enlongated village of **GALAROZA**, encircled by chestnut and fruit orchards, seems awash with water which for much of the year splashes and bubbles in its fountains and along the culverts lining the narrow streets. This may explain its annual Fiesta de los Jarritos during which everyone – including visitors – gets soaked with water when the town goes *agua* mad. A **water sculpture** in the focal Plaza los Alamos celebrates the village's water obsession and September 6 is the date to avoid if you want to stay dry. The village also has a striking **Baroque church**, La Purisima Concepción, which contains a unique seventeenth-century image of a pregnant Virgin by the sculptress La Roldana.

Good **places to stay** include the excellent *Hostal Toribio*, c/Primo de Rivera 2 (☎959 12 30 73, ⓦwww.hostaltoribio.com; ❸), with en-suite rooms (and its own small restaurant) behind the church. More opulent lodgings are to be had at the *Hotel Galaroza Sierra* (☎959 12 32 37, ⓦwww.hotelgalaroza.com; ❸), an attractive country hotel with pool in its own grounds just outside the village on the Jabugo road. They also rent out fully equipped bungalows sleeping up to four (⑤). For **eating and drinking** the decent restaurant *El Encinar*, at the *Hotel Galaroza Sierra* (which also does breakfasts) is worth a try, and on Plaza Ayuntamiento, near *Hostal Toribio*, *Casa Castulo* is a new mid-priced restaurant serving dishes from the Sierra and further afield (try the *tempura de berenjenas con miel*) with a recommended *menú de degustación* for €34. *Bar-Restaurante Las Salinas*, Tío Máximo 3, further into the village is another option with an attractive courtyard terrace; you may need to ask for directions. For bars with **tapas** *Bar La Fuente*, Plaza Alcalde Luis Navarro, the square fronting the entry to the village at its western end, is a humble place with an eccentric proprietor and good economical tapas – try the *jamón con tomate*. The earthy *Bar Alonso* on the square on the right as you come in from Aracena (eastern entry) also has a decent tapas selection.

A long and winding but very pretty 6km road leads north from just beyond Galaroza to the village of **VALDELARCO**. Set amongst cork oaks, chestnut and almond trees it's an attractive place with a charming main square, Plaza Domínguez, off which lies the eighteenth-century **church** of El Divino Salvador. It also has an attractive **restaurant** with courtyard terrace, *La Majá*, c/Dr Rodiño 27, on the right as you enter (☎959 12 49 15; closed Mon–Thurs in low season); venison and *solomillo de cerdo* are specialities. The proprietor here intends to open a **hotel** in the village in the near future offering opportunities for walking and mountain biking in this zone; in the meantime there are some attractive fully equipped **houses** for rent (☎959 12 49 16 for information or enquire at *La Majá*; ⑤). It is also possible to **walk** here from Galaroza along the GR42.1 footpath.

Horseriding is available at Finca La Suerte (☎959 12 30 10, ⓦwww .fincalasuerte.com), located between the two villages. Contact them in advance regarding guided excursions for one or more days. They also rent out a couple of charming *casas rurales* (see website for details).

Fuenteheridos

About 5km further east from Galaroza, a right turn brings you almost immediately to **FUENTEHERIDOS**, one of the most picturesque of the Sierra *pueblos* – a huddle of whitewashed dwellings with contrasting red pantiled roofs. The typical tiled Sierra spire of its fine eighteenth-century Neoclassical **Iglesia del Espíritu Santo** hovers above the rooftops.

Accommodation is on offer at the welcoming *Hostal Carballo*, c/La Fuente 16 (☎959 12 51 08, ⓦwww.hostalcarballo.com; ②), where the various rooms come with and without bath. About 100m up from the main square *El Barrio*, c/Esperanza Bermúdez s/n (☎959 12 50 33; ②), is another possibility with air-conditioned en-suite rooms with TV above a decent restaurant. The *Bar-Restaurante Biarritz* (☎959 12 50 88, ⓦwww.biarritzrural.com; ③–④) also lets a number of charming and well-equipped cottages and apartments in and around the village. A good **campsite**, *El Madroñal* (☎959 50 12 01), lies half a kilometre out of the village towards Castaño Robledo and has plenty of shade.

Fuenteheridos also has plenty of possibilities for **food**. On the main road at the edge of the village, the pleasant *Restaurante La Capellanía* serves up a succulent *solomillo de cerdo ibérico* (pork loin) and has a *menú*. Nearer the centre ⚡ *Bar-Restaurante Biarritz*, c/Virgen de la Fuente s/n, just off the main square, is a very good restaurant with a weekday *menú* for €6.50 (which you may need to ask for) and tasty tapas. An economical *menú* (€7) is also available at *El Barrio's* restaurant (see above) while *Casa Andres* is perhaps the best of the bars on the main square and a good place for **tapas** and breakfasting on its shady terrace.

Los Marines

Beyond the turn-off for Fuenteheridos and 8km east of Galaroza, **LOS MARINES** is the last village before Aracena, and its prosperity depends on the dense chestnut orchards that encircle it. These woods now harbour a pleasant new **rural retreat**, the *Finca La Media Legua* (☏669490648, 🖥www .fincalaemedialegua.es; ❹–❺) with stylishly decorated two- to six-person apartments with kitchenette and there's also a pool. Mountain bikes can be hired and the complex has its own bar and restaurant. The entry to the property lies about a kilometre to the east of the Los Marines turn-off on the main N-433.

Zufre and east towards Cazalla

East of Aracena there's more good hiking country – if slightly less wooded – along the northern frontier of Seville Province, which traverses the **Parque Natural de Sierra Norte**, a wildlife and nature zone stretching across the north of Seville province to the border with Córdoba. The park's comprehensive **website** (🖥www.sierranortedesevilla.com) has information on most of the towns and villages in the sierra, including accommodation, in addition to flora and fauna and lots of useful links. See p.369 for the natural park information centre.

From Aracena one bus a day (Mon–Sat; 5.30pm), connecting with the bus from Seville, covers the 25km southeast to Zufre. If you miss it, you'll have to walk, which takes the best part of a day but can be good in itself. From Aracena you need to pick up the waymarked PRA-44 *sendero* which heads roughly north for 8km to meet the waymarked GR-41. Turn east along this and you'll soon come upon the **Embalse de Aracena**, one of the huge reservoirs that supply Seville, dammed by a massive construction across the southern end of the valley. From here a lovely but circuitous seventeen-kilometre route (still following the GR-41) will take you down towards Zufre along the **Rivera de Huelva**. The free **map** (available from the Turismo in Aracena), *Senderos de la Sierra de Aracena y Picos de Aroche*, details the above routes plus others should you want to work out a shorter alternative.

Zufre

ZUFRE, about 25km southeast of Aracena, must be one of the most spectacular villages in Spain, hanging like a miniature Ronda on a high palisade at the edge of a ridge. Below the crumbling Moorish walls, the cliff falls away hundreds of feet, terraced into deep green gardens of orange trees and vegetables. In town, and sharing a charming and leafy plazuela, the arcaded **Ayuntamiento** and parish **church** of Purísima Concepción – built of brick and pink stone – are both interesting sixteenth-century examples of the Mudéjar style, the latter built on the foundations of a mosque. In the basement of the Ayuntamiento, too, is a gloomy line of stone seats, said to have been used by the Inquisition. Enquire at the Ayuntamiento during working hours (see p.366) for the key to the basement. Zufre's real centre, however, is the **Paseo**, a little park with rose gardens, balcony and a bar at one end and a *Casino* at the other, with spectacular **views** over the sierra from its open southern flank. The villagers gather round here for much of the day – there's little work either in Zufre or the surrounding countryside, and even the local **bullring**, cleverly squeezed on to a rock ledge above the Paseo, only sees use twice a year: at the beginning of the season in March, and at the town's September *feria*.

The Ayuntamiento, Plaza de la Iglesia (Mon–Fri 8am–3pm; ☎959 19 80 09), can provide **information**. There is also a friendly and central **hostal**, *La Posá*, c/Cibarranco 5 (☎959 19 81 10, ☎mobile 658972705; ❷), with tidy en-suite rooms close to the bars *Aleman* and *Benito* (see below). The rooms have fine views and, as the proprietors don't live on site, you may need to use their mobile number.

Finding **food and drink** in Zufre shouldn't be a problem, as plenty of bars in the warren of Moorish streets above the park serve tapas – seek out *Aleman* and *Benito* on the focal Plaza La Quebrada. Just off this square, *Casa Pepa* is a pleasant little country restaurant run by the family who own *Bar Benito*.

Santa Olalla del Cala and El Real de la Jara

There's no bus link between Zufre and busy small town of **SANTA OLALLA DEL CALA**, 16km to the northeast, but it's not hard to arrange a lift with one of the many locals (try asking in the local bars) who drive the route daily on the way to school and work. If you do choose **to walk**, there's the road or the slightly longer, but infinitely preferable, country route via the waymarked *senderos* PRA-42 and GR-48; pick up the PRA-42 at Calleja del Cementerio, on the edge of Zufre. The latter hike is a memorable experience: a mostly flat route through open country, with pigs and fields of wheat and barley and then a sudden view of the Santa Olalla's impressive **castillo** – a thirteenth-century Christian construction but incorporating Moorish features – above the town. Below the walls, the fifteenth-century parish **church** has a fine Baroque interior and an image of the *Virgen de los Dolores* by Juan de Mesa.

It's a surprise to find several *hostales* in Santa Olalla, but the town is actually on the main Seville–Badajoz road and sees a fair amount of traffic (which somewhat dents its charm), including regular buses between both cities. Now its lifeline, the town is ribboned along the N630 with the castle at the northern end. At the south end, **buses** to and from Seville stop outside the basic *Bar Primitivo*, at c/Marina 3, as this stretch of the main thoroughfare is named. Nearby there's the friendly *Casa Carmelo*, c/Marina 23 (☎959 19 01 69; ❶), which has en-suite **rooms** with TV. Both places serve **food** and offer economical *menús del día*, with the latter specializing in the region's excellent *jamones* and *salchichas* (sausages) from the numerous pig farms hereabouts.

Still heading east you enter the **Parque Natural de la Sierra Norte**, a wildlife and nature zone extending across the north of Seville province to the border with Córdoba. **El Real de la Jara**, the next village you reach, has two ruined but impressive Moorish **castillos**. A friendly guesthouse, *Casa Molina* at c/Real 70 (☎954 73 30 53; ❶) has **rooms**, plus there are **places to eat** and a welcome public swimming pool in summer, but no buses. Beyond El Real, the route traverses more hill country for 25km, where it crosses the scenic Embalse del Pintado reservoir. On the banks of the reservoir the remote hamlet of **El Pintado** is a curious settlement with a modern church, a couple of swanky houses surrounded by woodland and a **bar** that sees few customers.

Cazalla and the Central Sierra

The next place of any size, **CAZALLA DE LA SIERRA**, is some 20km further east along a mountainous and lonely route, stunning to look at if you're driving, but a real test on foot. When you finally reach it, Cazalla de la Sierra feels like a veritable metropolis and makes an ideal base for exploring the surrounding Sierra Norte natural park. A charming country

❷

Walks around Cazalla

There are some fine spots within easy wandering distance of Cazalla and some of these are listed in a useful booklet (in Spanish) available from the tourist office titled *La Sierra Morena de Sevilla*. A walk of just 5km, for example, will take you southeast to the **Ermita del Monte**, a little eighteenth-century church on a wooded hill above the Ribera del Huéznar.

If you're heading southwards for the village of **El Pedroso**, however, you might as well walk from the Cazalla train station, a lovely five-hour route along the banks of the Huéznar, flowing through woods of alder, elm and ash with the occasional weeping willow and a fabulous variety of valley flora and fauna. It's an excellent trout river and a wonderful place to swim, and it can get very crowded with locals during holidays and summer weekends. **To start the trail** from Cazalla station, take the road heading east towards Constantina, crossing the rail line. Just after this you'll come to a forest track on the right signed for the "Molino de Corcho", an old water mill. A short way downstream, cross the first bridge, and carry on along the prettier east bank of the river. Cross back at the third bridge and continue past the *Molino del Corcho* itself and on to the Fábrica de Pedroso (an old factory which also has a train station). From here you can follow the road to El Pedroso, or continuing along the river, at a bridge 4km on you should climb up to the road, and follow the A432 from where the village lies 3km east. With planning you could take a northbound train back to Cazalla from El Pedroso (currently running at 4.43pm & 9.09pm).

town with a number of sights, it's also one of the few places in the Sierra with regular **buses** (daily between here and Seville). The town is also served by **trains** (on the Seville–Mérida line) but as the station lies 7km east and buses are infrequent, you'll need to take a taxi (☎954 88 40 94) if you don't fancy the to walk.

An ancient Iberian settlement, Cazalla became the Roman *Callentum* and later the Moorish Kazalla ("fortified city") from which the modern name derives. Its importance in post-*Reconquista* days was as a staging post along the route to Extremadura and the north. The place was noted in Roman times for its vines and wines, a tradition which survives today in the production of *aguardiente* and *anis* (aniseed liqueur), sold in *bodegas* around the town. The Turismo can advise on where to find them if you're interested.

Cazalla's main attraction is the huge fortress-like church of **Nuestra Señora de la Consolación** (open service times: 11am–12noon and 7–8pm) at the southern end of town, an outstanding example of *andaluz* mix-and-match architecture begun in the fourteenth century in Gothic-Mudéjar style, with some later Renaissance touches, and finally completed in the eighteenth century. The interior has a fine sixteenth-century *retablo* and an image of San Bruno by Juan Hernández. Fronting the church's northern door, c/Virgen del Monte – lined with some elegant **casas señoriales** – leads to the market area, a colourful and bustling place on weekdays.

A little out of town, Cazalla's fifteenth-century **Cartuja**, or Carthusian monastery (daily 9am–2pm & 4–8pm; ⓦwww.cartujadecazalla.com; €3), was until recently a near ruin; it's now being gradually and privately restored as an upmarket hotel and arts centre. What remains, particularly a beautiful portal and a cupola of the church with Mudéjar frescoes, is set in picturesque surroundings. The proprietors have now added an art gallery and there are frequent artistic and musical events held here. To reach it, take the A455 for 3km towards Constantina, turning off along a signposted side road.

Practicalities

You'll find the town's **Turismo** in the Plaza Mayor, next to the church of Nuestra Señora de la Consolación (Tues–Fri 10am–2pm, plus Thurs & Fri 6–8pm, Sat 10am–2pm & 6–9pm, Sun 11am–2pm; ☎95 488 35 62, ⓦwww .cazalladelasierra.es), which can provide information on the area and a useful **map** of the town.

Accommodation.

For **accommodation** there is a wide range of options all of which would make an excellent base for exploring the Sierra Norte.

Casa Palacio c/Llana 2 ☎95 421 96 69, ⓦwww .casapalacio.es. A slightly upmarket place on the main street, with four charming, reasonably priced and fully equipped apartments in a sixteenth-century *casa palacio*. ❸–❹

El Palacio San Benito ☎95 488 33 36, ⓦwww .palaciodesanbenito.com. Housed in a magnificent fifteenth-century former hospice of the knights of the Order of Calatrava which gave shelter to pilgrims travelling the Via de la Plata to Santiago de Compostela, all rooms are sumptuously decorated with period furniture and artworks. There's a glittering Mudéjar chapel as well as a bar, library and pool. ❻ with breakfast.

🏃 **Hospedería** ☎95 488 45 16, ⓦwww .cartujadecazalla.com. Out of town and surrounded by rolling hill country, the enchanting La Cartuja monastery (see p.367) has its own atmospheric inn with pool and eight elegantly rooms in what was formerly the monastery's gatehouse. It also has its own restaurant and *cafetería*. ❺

Hostal Castro Martínez c/Virgen Monte 36 ☎95 488 40 39. Near the main street, this is the best budget choice; some a/c en-suite rooms come with terraces and views. ❷

🏃 **Las Navezuelas** ☎&ⓕ95 488 47 64, ⓦwww.lasnavezuelas.com. An inviting option, offering delightful rooms and studios (❺) in a white-walled sixteenth-century *cortijo* and olive mill set among woods and olive groves; it also has a pool and its own reasonably priced restaurant and the owners can arrange horse-riding excursions and advise on trekking routes. The farm is signed on the left, 3km out of town along the A432 road to El Pedroso. ❹ with breakfast.

Posada del Moro c/Paseo del Moro s/n ☎95 488 48 58, ⓦwww.laposadadelmoro.com. A 5min walk southeast from the turismo, this hotel offers comfortable tile floored rooms overlooking a patio garden and pool. ❹

Eating and drinking

For **eating and drinking** there are numerous bars dotted around the town where tapas are on offer. The central *Bar Torero*, c/Virgen del Monte, near the former Convento de San Francisco, serves up substantial *raciónes* and the friendly *Bar Gonzalo*, c/Virgen del Monte 3, in the centre, is an atmospheric place also serving *raciónes* and a good *menú*. Nearby, *Los Mellis* – which also has a decent restaurant – and the town *Casino* next door to each other on the pedestrianized La Plazuela are more good places for a drink and a *tapa*. More formal dining takes place at the *Restaurante del Moro*, the excellent mid-priced restaurant of the hotel of the same name (see above) which has a good-value *menú* for around €18. *Cafetería-Restaurante Manolo* at Paseo del Moro s/n at the end of the same street offers a cheaper selection of game and meat dishes of the region. Off the top end of the Paseo del Moro in the Plaza del Consejo, *La Agustina* is a new and stylish little restaurant serving tapas (try the *queso de cabra con miel*) in the bar below and full meals in a restaurant above.

Constantina

Eighteen kilometres southeast of Cazalla lies **CONSTANTINA**, an important and beautiful mountain town and the main administrative centre for Seville's section of the Sierra Morena. For hikers this is as good a place as any to cut back to Seville if you're not counting on continuing across the provincial border into Córdoba. Founded in the fourth century by the Romans during the reign of the emperor Constantine, and named after his son, this was an important centre of wine-production which sent a vintage named *cocolubis* to the imperial capital. The town is a delightful place to wander around, particularly the old quarter, which is dotted with a number of notable eighteenth-century mansions. Topping the hill flanking the western edge of town and high above the streets below, the **Castillo de la Armada** is an impressive medieval fortress surrounded by shady gardens descending in terraces to the old quarter. At the base you'll find the sixteenth-century parish church of **La Encarnación** (open 7–8pm), once again with a Mudéjar tower – Moorish influence having died hard in these parts – and a splendid, if crumbling, Plateresque portal by Hernán Ruíz, the architect of the cathedral inside the Mezquita at Córdoba and the belfry added to the Giralda in Seville. The church's *altar mayor*, a magnificent gilded work by Juan de Oviedo, is also worth a look. Constantina has a public **pool** sited below the castle, very welcome to beat the intense summer heat. With transport you can make a trip to **La Pantalla** – a lake for swimming and fishing – east along the A452 road to El Pedroso. Constantina's **feria**, a rumbustious Sierra affair with horse riding contests plus drinking, dancing and singing galore, takes place during the last week in August.

Practicalities

There's a **Turismo** cabin (Tues–Thurs 9–1pm, Sat & Sun 9am–2pm; ☏95 588 12 97, ⓦwww.constantina.org) on Avenida Andalucía, near the entry to the town from El Pedroso, who can provide a useful town **map**. When closed, you can also pick up the map from the Ayuntamiento, c/Eduardo Dato 7, near the Encarnación church. Two kilometres out of the town on the El Pedroso road, the El Robledo Centro de Visitantes (Tues–Thurs 10am–2pm, Fri 6–8pm, Sat & Sun 10am–2pm & 6–8pm; ☏95 558 15 97) is an **information centre** for the Sierra Norte natural park and has lots of maps, guidebooks and information on activities (such as horseriding and hiking) in the park. There's also a **botanical garden** (same hours; free) displaying a wide variety of the park's flora.

The cheapest of the **places to stay** is the modern *Albergue Juvenil*, c/Cuesta Blanca s/n, which lies slightly out of the centre, uphill behind a petrol station at the southern end of the town (☏95 588 95 00; under 26 €14, over 26 €18) with double rooms and shared showers; they also have some fully equipped apartments (❸). Otherwise, the only *hostal* is the central *La Casa Mari Pepa* at c/José de la Bastida 25 (☏95 588 02 82; ❸), where a *casa señorial* has been lovingly transformed into a delightful series of distinctively decorated en-suite rooms. There's also a three-star hotel, *San Blas*, c/Miraflores 4 (☏95 588 00 77, ⓦwww.fp-hoteles.com; ❹), with an elevated location at the northern end of town and a pool.

There are numerous good **tapas bars** along and around c/Mesones, the pedestrianized main street, including *Casino de Labradores* at no. 36 and *Bar Bullhy* nearby at no. 30. Others worth seeking out are *La Bodeguita*, Alférez Cabrera 1, the nearby *Bar Gregorio*, at no. 11 on the same street, which lies behind the Encarnación church and *Marisquería El León*, c/Mesones next to the church. Two of Constantina's best places to eat lie near to the Plaza de Toros, at the town's northern end. The first, the atmospheric and friendly *El Mesón de la Abuela*, Paseo de la Alameda 39, is good for *carnes a la brasa* (charcoal grilled meats). Slightly further north and arguably the town's best restaurant is ⚑ *Cambio de Tercio*, c/Virgen del Robledo 53 (☏95 588 10 80). Taking its name from the stages in a *corrida* and continuing the theme with an amusing entrance imitating a *plaza de toros*, this is also where King Juan Carlos gets his victuals during sessions gunning down the local wildlife (in one of his favourite hunting zones) – they deliver elaborate picnics to him in the field as a photo on one wall demonstrates. There's a lively bar for tapas – with its own economical *menú* for €8 – in the front and a pleasant room at the back for more formal dining. All is reasonably priced and the *solomillo de cerdo* (pork loin) is excellent.

Travel details

Trains

Huelva to: Almonaster (1 daily; 2hr 20min); Jabugo (2 daily; 2hr); Seville (3 daily; 1hr 30min); Zafra (1 daily 5hr).

Seville to: Algeciras (5 daily; change at Bobadilla, 5hr); Almería (4 daily; 5hr 20min); Cádiz (10 daily; 2hr); Córdoba (14 daily; 45min); Granada (5 daily; 3hr); Jaén (3 daily; 3hr 15min); Huelva (3 daily; 1hr 35min); Málaga (10 daily; 2hr 30min); Osuna (9 daily; 1hr).

Buses

Bus times are quoted for the fastest journey times, normally direct. There may be other buses to the same destination which make additional stops at towns and villages en route.

Aracena to: Alájar (2 daily; 30min); Aroche (4 daily; 1hr); Cortegana/Almonaster (2 daily; 50min); Huelva (2 daily; 2hr); Jabugo (2 daily; 35min); Nerva/Rio Tinto; (2 daily; 1hr; 15min); Seville (2 daily; 1hr 45min); Zufre (1 daily; 45min).

Huelva to: Aracena (2 daily; 2hr); Ayamonte/ Portuguese border (6 daily; 1hr); Granada (1 daily;

4hr); Isla Christina (14 daily; 1hr); La Antilla (7 daily; 45min); Málaga (1 daily; 4hr); Matalas-cañas (2 daily; 50min); Mazagon (13 daily; 35min); Moguer (15 daily; 40min); Palos de la Frontera (15 daily; 30min); Punta Umbría (17 daily; 30min); Seville (20 daily; 1hr 15min).

Osuna to: Antequera (3 daily; 1hr 15min); Granada (1 daily; 3hr 15min); Málaga (2 daily; 2hr); Seville (9 daily; 1hr).

Seville to: Algeciras (3 daily; 3hr 30min); Almería (3 daily; 5hr 45min); Aracena (2 daily; 1hr 20min); Arcos de la Frontera (2 daily; 2hr); Ayamonte (access to Portugal's Algarve; 3 daily; 2hr); Cádiz (10 daily; 1hr 45min); Carmona (10 daily; 30min); Constantina: (3/5 daily; 1hr 40min); Córdoba (13 daily; 1hr 45min); Écija (7 daily; 1hr 15min); El Rocío (4 daily; 1hr 30min); Granada (8 daily; 3hr); Huelva (24 daily; 1hr 15min); Jaén (3 daily; 4hr); Jerez de la Frontera (8 daily; 1hr 15min); Málaga (9 daily; 2hr 30min); Madrid: (8 daily; 6hr); Marbella (2 daily; 2hr 30min); Matalascañas (3 daily; 2hr); Osuna (9 daily; 1hr 25min); Ronda (6 daily; 2hr); Sanlúcar de Barrameda (7 daily; 1hr 30min.

Córdoba and Jaén

CHAPTER 3 # Highlights

* **Córdoba** The city of Córdoba is a feast of museums and palaces, with an old Jewish quarter and some excellent tapas bars and restaurants. See p.376

* **Mezquita, Córdoba** This twelve-hundred-year-old mosque is one of the world's Moorish architectural masterpieces. See p.382

* **Medina Azahara** The ruins of this sumptuous tenth-century Moorish palace evoke the dazzling grandeur of the Córdoba caliphate. See p.398

* **Zuheros** A delightful white village perched on a ridge in the midst of some stunningly picturesque walking country. See p.412

* **Priego de Córdoba** The Baroque showpiece of Córdoba province, this charming town is crammed with fine churches and monuments. See p.414

* **Baños Arabes, Jaén** One of the largest and best-preserved Moorish bath complexes in Spain. See p.431

* **Baeza and Úbeda** The twin Renaissance jewels of Jaén province are filled with a wealth of magnificent monuments in honey-tinted stone. See p.435 & p.441

▲ Zuheros village

Córdoba and Jaén

ndalucía's most northerly province, **Córdoba** is horizontally bisected by the Río Guadalquivir. Sited on the river's northern bank, the provincial capital is a handsome city whose outstanding attraction is its twelve-hundred-year-old Moorish **Mezquita**, one of the world's great buildings. In the tangled lanes of the Judería, the old Jewish quarter, that partially surrounds it, the sense of Córdoba's history as the centre of a vast and powerful empire is overwhelming. After the brilliance of the Mezquita the rest of the city, particularly the northern sector of modern Córdoba, can seem like an anticlimax; but persist and you'll discover a host of striking post-*Reconquista* **churches** in addition to a number of elegant **convents and mansions**. Despite a reputation for aloofness and sobriety among its neighbours, Córdoba has some of the most distinctive old **bars** in Andalucía, where taking a drink and a *tapa* is a particularly unique experience. A few kilometres away there's more lingering Moorish splendour at the ruins of **Medina Azahara**, a once-fabulous palace of the caliphs which is being painstakingly restored.

To the south of the river lies Córdoba's **Campiña**, a rolling landscape of grainfields, olive groves and vineyards, where Montilla, the province's rival to the wines of Jerez, is made. Little visited, the more elevated southern reaches of this area are particularly delightful, with a number of towns and villages such as **Baena**, **Cabra** and **Zuheros** ringed by excellent hiking country. The equally unsung town of **Priego de Córdoba**, further south still, has a clutch of spectacular Baroque churches that are worth a trip in themselves. To the north of the capital, the hardy mining towns in the foothills of the **Sierra Morena** attract even fewer visitors, but there's a rich variety of birdlife here, and the higher slopes are home to deer and wild boar zealously stalked by the hunting fraternity in winter.

The **province of Jaén** has been regarded since Moorish times as Andalucía's gateway – through the **Despeñaperros Pass** – to Castile and the cities of Toledo and Madrid to the north. Although often used as this gateway's doormat and something of a forgotten entity, the region's poorest province has some surprisingly worthy sights. The **city of Jaén** has a fine **Renaissance cathedral** as well as impressive **Moorish baths** but is more often used as a stop on the way to the magnificent twin Renaissance towns of **Baeza** and **Úbeda**. Sharing a similar history, the nobilities of these two conurbations competed in using their sixteenth-century wealth to employ some of the best architects and builders around. These craftsmen, such as the great architect **Andrés de Vandelvira** – whose imprint is everywhere – have left behind a monumental treasure in golden sandstone, one of the marvels not only of Andalucía, but of

Spain and Europe as well. The province's mountainous eastern flank now forms the heart of the **Cazorla Natural Park** and cradles the source of the Guadalquivir. Extending northeast from the town of **Cazorla**, the park's vast expanse of dense woodlands, lakes and spectacular crags crowned by eagles' and vultures' nests and patrolled by the agile ibex is a paradise for naturalists and walkers. Its northerly reaches are guarded by many ruined Moorish castles, the most spectacular of which sits on the hill above the village of **Segura de la Sierra**. The rest is mainly **olive groves**, which cover a vast area of Jaén, and whose exclusive cultivation is the cause of much seasonal unemployment. But there is a beauty in the orderly files of trees, stretching across the red and creamy white hills to the horizon, which seem "to open and close like a fan," as Lorca poetically put it, as you pass.

Córdoba

CÓRDOBA stands upstream from Seville beside a loop of the Guadalquivir, which was once navigable as far as here. It is today a minor provincial capital, prosperous in a modest sort of way, but a mere shadow of its past greatness. The city's name – a possible corruption of the Syrian *coteba* or "oil press" – is believed to be of Phoenician origin dating from the time when merchant venturers sailed up the river to carry away the region's much-prized olive oil.

Córdoba is now principally famous for a single building, the **Mezquita** – the grandest and most beautiful mosque ever constructed by the Moors. It stands right in the centre of the city, surrounded by the Judería, the old Jewish and Moorish quarters, and is a building of extraordinary mystical and aesthetic power. Head for it on arrival and keep returning as long as you stay in the city; its beauty and power increase with each visit.

The Mezquita apart, Córdoba is a city of considerable charm. It has few grand squares or mansions, tending instead to introverted architecture, calling your attention to the tremendous and often wildly extravagant **patios**, yet another Moorish legacy. Filled with pot plants, decorative tiles, tinkling fountains and a profusion of flowers in summer, these shady oases can usually be glimpsed beyond a forged iron *verja* (gate), and are indisputably the best to be seen in Andalucía. They are also actively encouraged and often maintained by the city council, which runs a "Festival of the Patios", usually held during the first half of May. Besides the city's Moorish treasures, there is another Córdoba, to the **north of the old quarter**, an area rarely touched upon by visitors, but with its own rewarding churches and palaces, not to mention bars. In addition to the Patios festival above, the **Cruces de Mayo** celebrations – immediately preceding it – fill the town with lavishly decorated crosses whilst the **Feria de Mayo** during the final week in May is the major fiesta.

Some history

Although archeological finds document an antiquity stretching back to Neolithic times, Córdoba's verifiable history begins with a Bronze Age **Iberian** settlement at the end of the second millennium BC trading on the mineral wealth – silver and copper – brought down from the Sierra Morena to the north. Apparently of little importance during the next millennium, and largely bypassed by the Carthaginian expansion into Spain, Córdoba rose to prominence under **Rome** in the years following the crushing victories against her North African enemy at the end of the third century BC.

Founded as the Roman city of **Corduba** in 152 BC, Córdoba flourished as the capital of Hispania Ulterior and, foreshadowing its later brilliance, became famous for its poetry as well as its olive oil. Cicero once cracked that Cordoban poetry sounded as if it had got mixed up with the oil due to its guttural style of delivery. Later, after Córdoba had backed the wrong horse in the wars between Caesar and Pompey at the end of the Republic, Caesar sacked the city and an estimated thirty thousand died. When Augustus reorganized Spain in 27 BC, Córdoba's fortunes improved as the capital city of the new province of Baetica, roughly corresponding to modern Andalucía. A brilliant period followed during which the city produced the poets **Lucan** and **Seneca** whilst prosperity – based on oil, wool and minerals – increased. Córdoba's importance continued for another three centuries as evidenced by recent excavations opposite the city's new train and bus station complex where the remains of a huge fourth-century **palace** constructed by the emperor Maximian have been unearthed.

As Roman power waned in the fifth century the area was overrun first by **Vandals** and then by **Visigoths** before falling to the **Moors** early in the eighth century. In 756 Córdoba became the capital of Moorish Spain and the succeeding three centuries – when the city formed the heart of the Western Islamic Empire – were Córdoba's golden age, as it grew to rival Cairo and Baghdad as a centre of Muslim art and learning. Though later its political power declined, Córdoba remained a centre of culture and scholarship and was the birthplace of the twelfth-century thinkers **Averroës**, the great Muslim commentator on Aristotle, and **Maimónides**, the Jewish philosopher.

After conquest by **Fernando III** in 1236, Córdoba's glory vanished as the city sank into a long and steady decline. Such aspects of civilized life as the elaborate Moorish systems of water supply and sewage disposal fell into ruin and the mosques were turned into churches. Little of the wealth of imperial Spain found its way here, although the city's leatherworkers, silversmiths and *parfumeurs* (all continuing Moorish traditions) achieved some renown in the sixteenth century. Plagues in the next century decimated the population and when Ford arrived in the 1830s he found "a poor and servile city". Córdoba suffered terrible repression in the wars against the **French** as it was to do again in the twentieth century when, during the Civil War, it was captured by the **Nationalists** who carried out brutal atrocities.

Local voters took belated revenge for this in the first post-Franco elections of 1979 when it elected a **communist** council – the only major city in Spain to do so. Befitting its past, Córdoba is now a city of learning once again (the university was re-established in 1971) and its latest faculty is a centre devoted to the study of Muslim history and culture. The town today boasts a progressive air, and has built up a modestly successful economy based upon its agricultural wealth, light industry and tourism.

Arrival and orientation

Córdoba's impressive **train station** (☎902 24 02 02) and **bus station** (☎957 40 40 40) complex is located on Plaza de las Tres Culturas, off the Avenida de America to the northwest of the old town. In the adjacent bus station each bus company has its own *ventanilla* (sales window) and beneath the central concourse (and in the subterranean car park) impressive Roman and Moorish excavated remains from the city's distinguished past have been imaginatively incorporated into the new edifice. To reach the centre from the station, pick up the Avenida de los Mozarabes, then veer east onto the broad Avenida del Gran Capitán which will lead you to the old town and the Mezquita, fifteen minutes to the south. Bus #3 from outside the bus station will take you to the focal Plaza Tendillas, and calle de San Fernando on the old quarter's eastern flank, if you can't face the hike.

Arriving **by car** can be a pain, especially during rush hour in the narrow streets around the Mezquita. Parking is also a major headache, so the best solution is to park your vehicle (stripped of any valuables) for the duration of your stay – the Avenida de la República Argentina on the western edge of the old quarter and across the river in the streets either side of the new *Hotel Hespería* (see p.382) are possible places – and get around the city on foot which is both easy and enjoyable.

Information

The city's main **Turismo** (Mon–Fri 9am–7.30pm, Sat & Sun 9.30am–3pm; ☎957 35 51 79) is at the Palacio de Congresos y Exposiciones at c/Torrijos 10

CÓRDOBA

Train & Bus Station (200m)

Jardines de la Agricultura

El Corté Inglés ❷

Colegiata de San Hipólito

Iglesia de San Miguel ❺ ❻

Ciudad Jardín

Jardines de la Victoria

Iglesia de San Nicolás de la Villa

PLAZA TENDILLAS ℹ️ ❾

San Juan

PUERTA DE ALMODÓBAR

Museo Arqueológico ⓘ

Sinagoga ✡ LA JUDERÍA ⑭ ⑮

Museo Taurino

Convento de la Encarnación

CALLEJA DE LAS FLORES

Iglesia de San Francisco

Hospital de San Sebastián

Mezquita

Museo Diocesano 🛈 Turismo

Triunfo de San Rafael

Puerta del Puente

Alcázar de los Reyes Cristianos

Albolafia Water Wheel

Puente Romano

Río Guadalquivir

Jardín Botánico, Seville & Granada ▼ *Torre de la Calahorra & ㉞*

ACCOMMODATION

AC Córdoba Palacio	**D**	Fonda Agustina	**X**	Hostal Almanzor	**Z**	Hostal La Fuente	**N**
Albergue Juvenil	**L**	Hospedería de Churrasco	**H**	Hostal Cruz del Rastro	**bb**	Hostal La Milagrosa	**M**
Casa de los Azulejos	**E**	Hostal & Hotel Maestre	**V**	Hostal El Portillo	**S**	Hostal Lineros 38	**Y**
Casa de los Naranjos	**B**	Hostal Alcázar	**W**	Hostal El Triunfo	**cc**	Hostal Luís de Góngora	**C**

& Campamento Municipal

Torre de la Malmuerta

Convento de la Merced

Iglesia del Cristo de los Faroles

Hospital de San Juan y San Jacinto

Convento de Santa Isabel

Iglesia de Santa Marina

Palacio del Marqués de Viana

Iglesia de San Agustín

Círculo de la Amistad

Convento-Hospital de Jesús Nazareno

Templo Romano

Iglesia de San Pablo

Iglesia de San Andrés

Iglesia de San Rafael

Iglesia de San Lorenzo

Plaza de la Corredera

Museo de Bellas Artes and Museo Julio Romero de Torres

SANTA MARINA

SAN LORENZO

AVENIDA DE LAS OLLERÍAS

RESTAURANTS

Albergue Juvenil	L
Almudaina	28
Amaltea	33
Bar-Restaurante Federación de Peñas	19
Barril	4
Café Gloria	9
Círculo Taurino	3
El Caballo Rojo	26
El Choto	16
El Churrasco	17
El Rincón del Carmen	24
Los Mochuelos	31
Marisquería El Faro	15
Salón de Té	14
San Basilio	32

TAPAS BARS

Bar Gaudí	2
Bar La Cavea	22
Bar-Mesón Rafaé	21
Bar Miguelito	34
Bar Regina	23
Bodega Guzmán	13
Bodega Sociedad Plateros	27
Bodegas Campos	29
Casa El Juramento	20
Casa La Paloma	18
Casa Paco Acedo	1
Casa Rubio	11
Casa Salinas	10
El Gallo	8
El Olivo	25
Sociedad Plateros	7
Taberna El Potro	30
Taberna Gongora	5
Taberna Salinas	12
Taberna San Miguel	6

Peñarroya & Badajoz

Jaén & Madrid

Hostal Osio	P	Hotel Albucasis	F	Hotel Los Omeyas	Q	Hotel Plateros	I
Hostal Plaza Corredera	G	Hotel Amistad Córdoba	K	Hotel Marisa	O	Parador Nacional Arruzafa	A
Hostal Santa Ana	aa	Hotel González	R	Hotel Mezquita	T	Pensión Los Arcos	U
Hostal Séneca	J	Hotel Hespería Córdoba	dd				

Córdoba online

Online information about Córdoba and its monuments and amenities can be found at Ⓦwww.ayuncordoba.es, Ⓦwww.turismodecordoba.org, Ⓦwww.infocordoba.com and Ⓦwww.turiscordoba.es.

alongside the Mezquita, and has a detailed town plan. Córdoba's municipal tourist office (Turismo Consorcio, ☏957 20 17 74, Ⓦwww.turismodecordoba .org) has joined forces with a private company to provide tourist information from three **kioskos**; one is in the Plaza Campo de los Martires almost facing the Alcázar (daily 9.30am–2pm & 4.30–7.30pm); there's another in the Plaza de las Tendillas in the centre of the modern town (daily 10am–1.30pm & 6–9.30pm); and the third is on the main concourse of the train station (daily 9.30am–2pm & 4.30–7.30pm). The same company also offers guided **walks** around the old city (Paseos por Córdoba; English spoken; €15); the walks start from the Plaza de las Tendillas office at 9.30pm, lasts two hours and ends up at a typical *cordobés* taverna. You should be aware that Córdoba changes its **monument opening hours** more than any other town in Andalucía and these ought to be confirmed with any tourist office. All keep copies of the monthly *Welcome y Olé*, a free bilingual listings magazine detailing the main events. During the May patios festival they also hand out a free guide-map to enable viewing the entries in the competition for best patio.

Accommodation

Places to stay can be found all over Córdoba, but the majority are concentrated in the narrow maze of streets around the Mezquita, and if you can resist the urge to lodge on the Mezquita's doorstep, a five-minute walk in any direction leads to some real bargains. Finding a room at any time of the year – except during Semana Santa and the May festivals (the city's high season) – isn't usually a problem and it's worth bearing in mind also that July and August are the hotel trade's low-season months when upmarket places often drop their prices considerably; also its always worth checking their websites for frequent special offers. Where listings below have a garage, unless otherwise stated you will be charged a daily rate for parking (around €10–15).

Budget

Fonda Agustina c/Zapatería Vieja 5 ☏957 47 08 72. Charming and spotlessly clean little *fonda*, with basic rooms in a tranquil location. ❷

Hostal Alcázar c/San Basilio 2 ☏957 20 25 61, Ⓦwww.hostalalcazar.com. Comfortable and welcoming, family-run *hostal* with a nice patio and range of a/c rooms (most en suite) with TV. Also has some good-value fully equipped apartments opposite (sleeping up to four) for around €75 per night (minimum stay of two nights). Own garage nearby (€6). ❷ with breakfast.

Hostal Almanzor c/Corregidor Luís de la Cerda (aka Cardenal González) 10 ☏957 48 54 00, Ⓦwww .hostal-almanzor.es. Attractive and recently refurbished central *hostal* where en-suite rooms come with TV and a/c. Free use of their car park. ❷–❸

Hostal Cruz del Rastro c/Cruz Rastro 3 ☏957 48 25 82, Ⓦwww.paseoribera.com. Pleasant riverside *hostal* above a bar-restaurant. The en-suite rooms have a/c and TV, and many have river views. ❷

Hostal El Portillo c/Cabezas 2 ☏&Ⓕ957 47 20 91, Ⓦwww.hostalelportillo.com. Beautiful old *hostal* with an elegant patio and friendly management. Refurbished rooms – many with balconies – come with showers and include a few singles. ❷

Hostal La Fuente c/San Fernando 51 ☏957 48 14 78, Ⓦwww.hostallafuente.com. Welcoming *hostal* in a refurbished town house with a delightful patio and pristine en-suite rooms with TV and a/c. Also rents out some nearby apartments (❺). Parking nearby. ❷

Hostal La Milagrosa c/Rey Heredia 12 ☏957 47 33 17, Ⓦwww.lamilagrosahostal.com. Pleasant and welcoming *hostal* with a beautiful patio and lots of plants, plus clean and attractive en-suite a/c rooms. ❷

Hostal Luís de Góngora c/Horno de la Trinidad 7 ☏ 957 29 53 99. En-suite rooms with fans in a friendly *hostal* in pleasant location on the northern edge of the Judería. ❸

Hostal & Hotel Maestre c/Romero Barros 4 & 16 ☏ 957 47 53 95 for the *hostal*, ☏ 957 47 24 10 for the hotel, ⓦ www .hotelmaestre.com. Friendly *hostal* with fine patio and attractive en-suite rooms (room 22 has its own terrace); rooms both here and at the nearby hotel (which are slightly larger) have a/c and TV. They also let a number of nearby apartments (❸). *Rough Guide* readers with this guide get free underground parking (except April–May). ❷–❸

Hostal Plaza Corredera c/Rodríguez Marín 15, ☏ 957 47 05 81, ⓦ www.hostallacorredera.com. On the Plaza Corredera (but entry is on c/Rodríguez Marín), this refurbished *pensión* on the wonderful old square has spacious beamed rooms sharing bath and some with great views over the plaza. There are some single rooms, plus a roof terrace above and a bar below for breakfast. Easy parking nearby. ❷

Hostal Santa Ana c/Corregidor Luís de la Cerda (aka Cardenal González) 25 ☏ 957 48 58 37, ⓦ www.hostalsantaana.com. Good upmarket *hostal* with a nice roof terrace and a/c en-suite rooms with TV. Own garage. ❹

Hostal Séneca c/Conde y Luque 7 ☏ & ℻ 957 47 32 34, ⓔ hostalseneca @eresmas.com. Delightful *hostal* in ancient house with a stunning patio complete with original Moorish pavement. Rooms with and without bath, and some singles. In summer you'll need to book ahead. ❸ with breakfast.

Pensión Los Arcos c/Romero Barros 14 ☏ 957 48 56 43, ⓦ www.pensionlosarcos.com. Simple rooms (some en suite) with fans in a quiet street behind the Plaza del Potro; charming place with a great plant-filled patio. ❷

Moderate and expensive

AC Córdoba Palacio Jardines de la Victoria s/n ☏ 957 29 80 66, ⓦ www.ac-hotels.com. A controversial "rusting skin" facade has been applied to Cordoba's oldest luxury hotel (now part of the AC chain) and an internal refurb has furnished rooms with plenty of four-star frills. There's a pool, restaurant, wi-fi throughout and you're a 1min walk from the Judería. Garage. ❼–❽

Casa de los Azulejos c/Fernando Colón 5 ☏ 957 47 00 00, ⓦ www.casadelosazulejos.com. Stylish

small hotel with distinctively furnished rooms, featuring iron bedsteads and artworks, arranged around a leafy patio, itself used for art shows. ❺

Casa de los Naranjos c/Isabel Losa, 8 ☏ 957 47 05 87, ⓦ www.casadelosnaranjos.com. In the north of the town near the Plaza de Colón, this is a small two-star hotel with lots of charm and rooms overlooking a leafy patio. Garage. ❺ with breakfast.

Hospedería de Churrasco c/Romero 38, ☏ 957 29 48 08, ⓦ www.elchurrasco.com. Elegant new nine-room hotel in the Judería belonging to the restaurant of the same name. Entry is through a double patio and rooms are classically furnished with chintz drapes and bedcovers, and some have sit-out terraces. Facilities include minibar, computer with internet access in all rooms (free) and rooftop terrace/solarium. ❻ with breakfast.

Hostal El Triunfo c/Corregidor Luís de la Cerda (aka Cardenal González) 79 ☏ 957 49 84 84, ⓦ www.hostaltriunfo.com. Traditional hotel-style *hostal* on the Mezquita's east face. Some of the pleasant rooms (on the front) have a Mezquita view, while attic rooms share a rooftop terrace with stunning views over the river and Mezquita. Rooms come with safe and there's a decent bar and restaurant below. Garage. ❺

Hostal Lineros 38 c/Lineros 38 ☏ 957 48 25 17, ⓦ www.hostallineros38.com. This Moorish extravaganza of a *hostal* has been lovingly created by its friendly proprietors inside an ancient Mudéjar mansion; the furnishings and fittings are all Moorish-inspired, there are arabesques and horseshoe arches everywhere. Some single rooms. ❸

Hostal Osio c/Osio 6 ☏ 957 48 51 65, ⓦ www .hostalosio.com. Charming *hostal* in a refurbished mansion with two fine patios (one a listed monument) and attractive a/c en-suite rooms. The friendly proprietors speak English. ❸

Hotel Albucasis c/Buen Pastor 11 ☏ & ℻ 957 47 86 25, ⓦ www.hotelalbucasis.com. Charming small hotel with ivy-clad courtyard, spotless en-suite bedrooms with a/c and TV plus breakfast bar. Garage. ❺

Hotel Amistad Córdoba Plaza de Maimónides 3 ☏ 957 42 03 35, ⓦ www.nh-hoteles.com. Four-star hotel (now part of the NH chain) incorporating two eighteenth-century mansions with Mudéjar patio and staircase. Internet access and car park available. ❽

Hotel González c/Manríquez 3 ☏ 957 47 98 19, ⓔ hotelgonzalez@wanadoo.es. Converted sixteenth-century *casa palacio* in the heart of La Judería with comfortable rooms overlooking a brilliant white-walled, geranium-filled patio. ❹

Hotel Hespería Córdoba Avda. de la Confederación s/n ☎957 42 10 42, ⓦwww .hoteles-hesperia.es. Luxurious four-star hotel with great views across the river towards the Mezquita and city from rooms on the front. Features include restaurant, *cafetería*, pool and rooftop bar (with the same view) and easy access to the town across the pedestrianized Puente Romano. Does frequent special offers. ❼

Hotel Los Omeyas c/Encarnación 17 ☎957 49 22 67, ⓦwww.hotel-losomeyas.com. Pleasant and airy hotel built around a nice patio but with a severe kitsch problem throughout; rooms come with a/c, TV and wall safe. Garage. ❹

Hotel Marisa c/Cardenal Herrero 6 ☎957 47 31 42, ⓦwww.hotelmarisacordoba.com. You won't get closer to the Mezquita than this. Rather plain hotel where rooms come with a/c (but not TV). Garage. ❹

🏃 Hotel Plateros Plaza Seneca 4 ☎957 49 67 85, ⓦwww.hotelplateros.com. Small and friendly hotel belonging to the *Plateros* (see p.395) chain of tapas bars and housed in an elegant refurbished old mansion on a charming plazuela. Pleasant a/c rooms have internet access and there's a *Plateros* tapas bar below incorporating the ancient house's *bodega* (where the proprietor still makes his own wine) whose walls were once part of the ancient Roman theatre. The hotel encourages cycle travellers and can store bikes. ❹

Hotel Mezquita Plaza Santa Catalina 1 ☎957 47 55 85, ⓦwww.hotelmezquita.com. Atmospheric and central hotel in a converted sixteenth-century mansion facing the Mezquita's eastern wall. Attractive rooms equipped with satellite TV. ❹

Parador Nacional Arruzafa Avda. de la Arruzafa s/n, 5km north of town in El Brillante suburb ☎957 27 59 00, ⓦwww.parador.es. Attractive, modern parador with pool, tennis courts, shooting range and views over the city. Worth a trip out for a drink in its gardens or a good value meal (lunch *menú* €23.50, dinner €30) in its terrace restaurant. ❻

Youth hostel and campsites

🏃 Albergue Juvenil Plaza Judá Leví s/n ☎957 35 50 40, centralized bookings ☎902 51 00 00, ⓦwww.inturjoven.com. 81 double, triple and four-person rooms with en-suite bath/shower at this modern, relaxed and superbly located hostel make it a prime destination for budget travellers, so you'll need to book ahead at busy periods. Wi-fi throughout. Under-26 €16, over 26 €20.

Campamento Municipal El Brillante Avda. Brillante s/n, 2km north on the road to Villaviciosa ☎957 40 38 36. Good site with pool, reached by taking bus #10 or #11 from the bus station. Open all year.

Camping Los Villares ☎957 33 01 45. With your own transport, this site is a better option than the *Campamento Municipal*, set in woodland with nature trails and a restaurant. It lies 7km north of the city along a minor road (CP45), just beyond a turn-off for the village of Santo Domingo. Open all year.

The City

The outstanding highlight of any visit to Córdoba and where you'll want to begin your wanderings is the astonishing **Mezquita** in the heart of the old Jewish quarter, **La Judería**. However, just a few streets away from here in any direction the city offers a wealth of fine buildings, churches, monuments and museums, all well worth seeing.

The Mezquita

As in Moorish times, the **Mezquita** (April–Sept Mon–Sat 10am–7pm, Sun 2–7pm; Oct–March Mon–Sat 10am–5pm, Sun 2–5pm; €8, kids €4) is approached through the **Patio de los Naranjos**, a classic Islamic ablutions court with fountains for ritual purification before prayer, which still preserves its orange trees. None of the original ablutions fountains survives, the present ones being purely decorative later additions. Originally, when in use for the Friday prayers, all nineteen naves of the mosque were open to this court, allowing the rows of interior columns to appear as an extension of the trees. Today, with all but one of the entrance gates locked and sealed, the image is still there, though subdued and stifled by the loss of those brilliant shafts of sunlight filtering through. The mood of the building has been distorted a little, from the open and vigorous simplicity of the mosque, to the mysterious half-light of a cathedral.

Nonetheless, a first glimpse inside the Mezquita is immensely exciting. "So near the desert in its tentlike forest of supporting pillars," Jan Morris found it, "so faithful to Mahomet's tenets of cleanliness, abstinence and regularity." The mass of supporting pillars was, in fact, an early and sophisticated improvisation to gain height.

The original architect, Sidi ben Ayub, working under the instruction of Abd ar-Rahman I, had at his disposal columns in marble, porphyry and jasper from

MEZQUITA

CALLE CORREGIDOR LUIS DE LA CERDA

Tesoro

Capilla del Sagrario

Sacristia

Capilla del Cardenal

Mihrab

3

Puerta del Sagrario

Capilla de Villaviciosa

Puerta de Palacio

Capilla Real

Location of Visigothic Cathedral

Puerta de San Miguel

CALLE GONZÁLEZ FRANCÉS

4

Trasaltar

Capilla Mayor

Crucero

Coro

Trascoro

2

CALLE DE TORRIJOS

Puerta de San Esteban

1

Puerta de Santa Catalina

Puerta de Las Palmas

Puerta de Los Deanes

Patio de los Naranjos

Fuente de Santa Maria

Torre del Alminar

Puerta del Caño Gordo

CALLE HERRERO

Puerta del Perdón

Puerta de la Leche

| 1 | Original Mezquita of Abd ar-Rahman I | 2 | Enlargement of Abd ar-Rahman II | 3 | Enlargement of al-Hakam II | 4 | Enlargement of al-Mansur |

Córdoba's domination of **Moorish Spain** began thirty years after the conquest – in 756, when the city was placed under the control of **Abd ar-Rahman I**, the sole survivor of the Umayyad dynasty which had been bloodily expelled from the eastern caliphate of Damascus. He commenced the building of the **Great Mosque** (**La Mezquita**), purchasing the site of the former Visigothic Cathedral of Saint Vincent from the Christians. This building which, divided by a partition wall, had previously served both communities had itself been constructed on top of an earlier Roman temple dedicated to the god Janus. Incidentally, some sixth- and seventh-century fragments from the Visigothic church are on display in the cases on the west side of the mosque. Demolishing the church as they built, Abd ar-Rahman's architects, for reasons of speed and economy, incorporated one of the cathedral's original walls – that facing west – into the new structure and this is the reason why the *mihrab*'s prayer wall is not precisely aligned towards Mecca. This original mosque was completed by his son **Hisham** in 786 and comprises about one-fifth of the present building, the first dozen aisles adjacent to the Patio de los Naranjos.

Abd ar-Rahman II

The Cordoban emirate soon began to rival Damascus both in power and in the brilliance of its civilization. **Abd ar-Rahman II** (822–52) initiated sophisticated irrigation programmes, minted his own coinage and received embassies from Byzantium. He in turn substantially enlarged the mosque. A focal point within the culture of al-Andalus, this was by now being consciously directed and enriched as an alternative to Mecca; it possessed an original script of the Koran and a bone from the arm of Muhammad, and, for the Spanish Muslim who could not go to Mecca, it became the most sacred place of **pilgrimage**. In the broader Islamic world it ranked fourth in sanctity after the Kaaba of Mecca, the city of Medina in Saudi Arabia, and the Al Aksa mosque of Jerusalem.

Abd ar-Rahman III

In the tenth century Córdoba reached its zenith under **Abd ar-Rahman III** (912–61), one of the great rulers of Islamic history. He assumed power at the age of 23 after his grandfather had killed his father during a period of internal strife. During his reign, according to a contemporary historian, he "subdued rebels, built palaces, gave impetus to agriculture, immortalized ancient deeds and monuments, and inflicted great damage on infidels to a point where no opponent or contender remained in al-Andalus. People obeyed en masse and wished to live with him in peace." In 929, with Muslim Spain and a substantial part of North Africa firmly under his control, Abd ar-Rahman III adopted the title of "caliph", or successor of the Prophet. It was a supremely confident gesture and was reflected in the growing splendour of Córdoba itself which, with a population approaching (if we take the not always reliable Moorish historians at face value) 500,000, had become the largest, most prosperous city of Europe, and outshone both Byzantium and Baghdad (the new capital of the eastern caliphate) in science, culture and scholarship. At the turn of the tenth century it could boast some 27 schools, 50 hospitals (with the first separate clinics for the leprous and insane), 600 public baths, 60,300 noble mansions, 213,077 houses and 80,455 shops. One of Córdoba's most magnificent buildings during this and later periods would have been the Umayyad palace of the caliphs, of which little except a bath complex remains (see p.388). Extending to the west of the Mezquita from c/Torrijos to the city walls and southwards to the river, the palace was connected to the Mezquita by a secret passage. Built in the ninth century to allow the caliph privileged access to the mosque at all times, traces of this tunnel (not on view) have been found in the building's southwest corner. The construction of a glorious new palace at **Medina Azahara** in the 930s as well as further **development** of the Great Mosque paralleled these new heights of confidence and splendour. Abd ar-Rahman III provided the Mezquita with a new minaret 80m high, topped by three pomegranate-shaped spheres, two of silver and one of gold and each weighing a ton. The minaret was badly damaged in a storm in 1589 and was later used as the core of the sixteenth century Torre del Alminar which replaced it.

Al-Hakam II

The caliph's successor **al-Hakam II** (961–76) was a man from another mould than that of his warrior father, best epitomized by his advice to his own son:

Do not make wars unnecessarily. Keep the peace, for your own wellbeing and that of your people. Never unsheathe your sword except against those who commit injustice. What pleasure is there in invading and destroying nations, in taking pillage and destruction to the ends of the earth? Do not let yourself be dazzled by vanity; let your justice always be like a tranquil lake.

In tune with these sentiments, al-Hakam was a poet, historian and the builder of one of the great libraries of the Middle Ages. This cultured ruler was also responsible for the mosque's most brilliant **expansion**, virtually doubling its extent. After demolishing the south wall to add fourteen extra rows of columns, he employed Byzantine craftsmen to construct a new **mihrab** or prayer niche. This has survived due to having been bricked up following the Christian Reconquest. Only rediscovered in the nineteenth century, it remains complete and is perhaps the most beautiful example of all Moorish religious architecture.

Al-Mansur

Under the vizier-usurper **al-Mansur** (977–1002), who used his position as regent to push al-Hakam's child successor, Hisham II, into the background, repeated attacks were carried out on the Christians in the north, including the daring expedition to Santiago de Compostela in 997, when the pilgrimage cathedral's bells were seized. This **military might** was built on the incorporation of thousands of Berbers from North Africa into al-Mansur's army – a policy that was to have devastating implications for the future when the same Berbers turned on their paymasters and sacked and plundered the city, destroying al-Hakam's treasured library in the process. Within less than thirty years the brilliant caliphate of Córdoba had collapsed in a bloody turmoil as short-lived puppet caliphs attempted to stave off the inevitable.

When he was not away on his military campaigns, al-Mansur gave his attention to further embellishing the Great Mosque. As al-Hakam had extended the building as far to the south as was possible, he completed the final enlargement by adding seven rows of columns to the whole east side. This spoiled the symmetry of the mosque, depriving the *mihrab* of its central position, but Arab historians observed that it meant there were now "as many bays as there are days of the year". They also delighted in describing the rich interior, with its 1293 marble columns, 280 chandeliers and 1445 lamps. Hanging inverted among the lamps were the bells of the cathedral of Santiago de Compostela. Al-Mansur had made his Christian captives carry them on their shoulders from Galicia – a process which was to be observed in reverse after Córdoba was captured by Fernando el Santo (the Saint) in 1236.

the old Visigothic cathedral and from numerous Roman buildings, as well as many more shipped in from all parts of the former Roman Empire. This ready-made building material could bear great weight, but the architect was faced with the problem of the pillars' varying sizes: many were much too tall but the vast majority would not be tall enough, even when arched, to reach the intended height of the ceiling. The long pillars he sank in the floor, whilst his solution for the short pillars (which may have been inspired by Roman aqueduct designs) was to place a second row of square columns on the apex, serving as a base for the semicircular arches that support the roof. For extra strength and stability (and perhaps also deliberately to echo the shape of a date palm, much revered by the early Spanish Arabs), he introduced another, horseshoe-shaped arch above the lower pillars. A second and purely aesthetic innovation was to alternate brick and stone in the arches, creating the red-and-white striped pattern that gives a unity and distinctive character to the whole design. This architectural *tour de force* was unprecedented in the Arab world and set the tone for all future enlargements – excepting the Christian cathedral – of the building. Most impressively, it was completed within a year of its commencement in 785.

The Mihrab

The mosque's overall uniformity was broken only by the culminating point of al-Hakam II's tenth-century extension – the domed cluster of pillars surrounding the mosque's great jewel, the sacred **Mihrab**. Even here, although he lengthened the prayer hall by a third, al-Hakam carefully aligned the new *mihrab* at the end of the same central aisle which had led to the previous two. The *mihrab* had two functions in Islamic worship: it indicated the direction of Mecca (and hence of prayer) and it amplified the words of the *imam*, or prayer leader. As Titus Burckhardt wrote, in *Moorish Art in Spain*:

> The design of the prayer niche in Córdoba was used as a model for countless prayer niches in Spain and North Africa. The niche is crowned by a horseshoe-shaped arch, enclosed by a rectangular frame. The arch derives a peculiar strength from the fact that its central point shifts up from below. The wedge-shaped arch stones or voussoirs fan outwards from a point at the foot of the arch and centres of the inner and outer circumferences of the arch lie one above the other. The entire arch seems to radiate, like the sun or the moon gradually rising over the edge of the horizon. It is not rigid; it breathes as if expanding with a surfeit of inner beatitude, while the rectangular frame enclosing it acts as a counterbalance. The radiating energy and the perfect stillness form an unsurpassable equilibrium. Herein lies the basic formula of Moorish architecture.

The paired pillars that flank the *mihrab* and support its arch were taken from the earlier *mihrab* of Abd ar-Rahman I, their prominent position no doubt a mark of respect by al-Hakam to his great predecessor. The inner vestibule of the niche (which is frustratingly fenced off) is quite simple in comparison, with a shell-shaped ceiling carved from a single block of marble. The chambers to either side, as well as the dome above the *mihrab*, are decorated with exquisite **mosaics** of gold, rust-red, turquoise and green, the work of Byzantine craftsmen supplied by the emperor Nicephorus II at al-Hakam's request. These constitute the *maksura*, where the caliph and his retinue would pray, a fitting monument to this scholarly and sensitive ruler.

The Cathedral and other additions

Originally the whole design of the mosque would have directed worshippers naturally towards the *mihrab*. Today, though, you almost stumble upon it, as in the centre of the mosque squats a Renaissance **cathedral coro**. This was built in 1523, nearly three centuries of enlightened restraint after the Christian conquest, and in spite of fierce opposition from the town council. The erection of a *coro* and *capilla mayor*, however, had long been the "Christianizing" dream of the cathedral chapter and at last they had found a monarch, predictably Carlos V, who was willing to sanction the work. Carlos, to his credit, realized the mistake (though it did not stop him from destroying parts of the Alhambra and Seville's Alcázar); on seeing the work completed he told the chapter, "You have built what you or others might have built anywhere, but you have destroyed something that was unique in the world." Some details are worth noting, though, particularly the beautifully carved Churrigueresque **choir stalls** by Pedro Duque Cornejo, created with mahogany brought from the New World. To the left of the *coro* stands an earlier and happier Christian addition, the Mudéjar **Capilla de Villaviciosa**, built by Moorish craftsmen in 1371 (and now partly sealed up). Beside it are the dome and pillars of the **earlier mihrab**, constructed under Abd ar-Rahman II. The mosque's original and finely decorated timber-coffered ceiling was replaced in the eighteenth century by the present Baroque cupolas. Further post-Reconquest additions include the **Capilla Real**, installed by Alfonso X in the thirteenth century, with *azulejo* panels and lobed niches in Mudéjar style, and the early eighteenth-century **Capilla del Cardinal** (Chapterhouse), the *tesoro* (treasury) and *sacristía*, none of which detracts from the building's imposing majesty.

The evocative belfry, the **Torre del Alminar** (currently closed to visitors) at the corner of the Patio de los Naranjos, is built on the site of the original minaret and contemporary with the cathedral addition. The belfry was designed by Hernán Ruíz, who used the earlier tower as a core to support two additional sections more than doubling its height. The climb to the top is a dizzying experience and the **views** over the town and Mezquita itself tremendous. Close by, the **Puerta del Perdón**, the main entrance to the patio, was rebuilt in Moorish style in 1377. It's worth making a tour of the Mezquita's **outer walls** before leaving; parts of the original "caliphal" decoration (in particular some exquisite latticework) surrounding the portals are stunning. The west wall along c/Torrijos is the most striking where the **Puerta de San Esteban** was an important side entrance into the original mosque and is the oldest of the doorways, dated by an inscription above it to 855. The **Puerta de San Miguel** is sited in the oldest stretch of wall, and dates from the earlier Visigothic cathedral.

Museo Diocesano

Opposite the Mezquita's west wall on the site of the former Moorish *alcázar* lies the **Museo Diocesano** (July & Aug Mon–Sat 9.30am–3pm, Sept–June 9.30am–1.30 & 4–6pm; €1.50, free with Mezquita ticket). This elegant seventeenth-century building with a fine patio and fountain is now a mildly interesting **museum of religious art**, mainly sculpture. The highlights are in the early rooms where there are some outstanding examples of medieval wood sculpture – a great Spanish tradition. The anonymous thirteenth-century *Virgen de las Huertas* in Room 1 is finely worked, as is a striking fifteenth-century *Calvario Villaviciosá* or Crucifixion. In Room 3, an anonymous early sixteenth-century *pietà* has the agonized expressions of the onlookers beautifully portrayed. The remainder of the museum comprises more wood sculpture from later periods, including an image of *Santo Tomás* by José de Mora as well as tapestries and furniture. Room VI finishes the tour with a vibrant eighteenth-century image of San Miguel Arcángel attributed to La Roldana, the daughter sculptor of Pedro Roldán. On the ground floor, there's a beautiful Baroque **chapel** dedicated to the Virgin (which may be closed).

The Alcázar and the Jardín Botanico

Dating from the time of the *Reconquista*, the **Alcázar de Los Reyes Cristianos** (July & Aug Tues–Sun 10am–2pm; Sept–June Tues–Sat 10am–2pm & 5.30–7.30pm, Sun 9.30am–2.30pm; gardens only Tues–Sun 8pm–midnight; €4, evening gardens visit €2; free on Fri), a palace fortress, was completed in the fourteenth century and now houses a small municipal museum. The original Moorish *alcázar* stood beside the Mezquita, on the site presently occupied by the Palacio Episcopal. After the Christian conquest it was rebuilt a little to the west and used by monarchs – including Fernando and Isabel who were visited here by Columbus in 1486 – when staying in the city, hence its name. That the buildings retain little of their original opulence today is due to their use as the residence of the **Inquisition** for three centuries prior to 1821, and later as a prison until as recently as 1951. The palace underwent extensive Mudéjar rebuilding during the fifteenth century, when the attractive **Moorish-style gardens** were added. One of the glories of Córdoba today with lots of arbours and shady corners, the gardens are dotted with hefty chunks of Roman columns and other masonry all testifying to the city's importance in the Roman era. From the tower's belvedere there are great **views** over the town and river, while the **interior** of the Alcázar has some mildly interesting fifteenth-century royal baths and some fine **Roman mosaics** discovered in the city. The second-century depiction of *Polyphemus and Galatea* is outstanding and the monochrome mosaic beside it is one of the largest complete mosaics in existence. A fine third-century carved sarcophagus – thought to have been made in Rome and sent for the burial of a distinguished person – is also worth a look; a half-ajar portal on the sarcophagus's side indicates that access is open to the person within.

In the gardens across the plaza to the north of the Alcázar are the impressive remains of a tenth-century Moorish *hammam*, or bathhouse, the **Baños Califales**, Campo Santo de Los Mártires s/n (same hours and ticket as Alcázar), constructed in the reign of al-Hakam II. As their name implies, the baths were possibly attached to the Ummayad palace which once covered most of this area. Inside you can see the various bathing rooms, which would have had gradated temperatures, lit by star-shaped windows set in barrel-vaulted ceilings. The baths' western rooms date from the post-calital Taifa, Almoravid and Almohad periods. Travellers to Moorish Córdoba record between three and six hundred bathhouses similar to these throughout the city which would probably not be excessive for a population of half a million inhabitants. The baths – a focal feature of Muslim life – would originally have been surrounded by plant-filled gardens and arbours where bathers could relax and chat. In the afternoon the baths normally passed into feminine hands when a towel would be hung outside to warn absent-minded males of the change of use. See p.390 for details on visiting a modern reconstruction of the Moorish bathing experience.

Three hundred metres downriver from the Alcázar lies the **Jardín Botánico**, Avda. de Linneo s/n (April–June Tues–Sun 10am–9pm; July&Aug Tues–Sat 10pm–3pm & 7–12pm, Sun 10am–3pm; Sept–March Tues–Sat 10am–7.30pm, Sun 10am–3pm; €2, ⓦwww.jardinbotanicodecordoba.com). The gardens are extensive and there are hothouses with exotic species of succulents, ferns and prickly plants, as well as a rose garden. At the garden's northern end a paleobotanical museum – housed inside a medieval water mill – displays 150,000 specimens of fossil plant life. The nearby arboretum exhibits trees and shrubs from all over the world including in one section samples of Andalucía's own arboreal rarity, the **pinsapo** Spanish fir, transplanted from its only European habitat in the Sierra de Grazalema. Other features include a garden for the visually impaired with a collection of plants recognizable by their aroma and texture and a **cafetería**.

The Puente Romano and around

The pedestrianized **Puente Romano** is an impressive 250-metre-long bridge across the Río Guadalquivir probably built during the first or second centuries AD. Inscriptions record repairs to it carried out in Moorish times by the *wali* or governor Al-Samh in the eighth century, and by Al-Hakam II in the tenth, but the structure still retains much Roman stonework. A controversial refurbishment of the bridge in 2007, which replaced its former cobblestones with a redstone pavement, added ultra modern lighting and remodelled the support walls, has outraged many architectural experts and archeologists.

Guarding the southeastern end of the Puente Romano is the **Torre de la Calahorra** (daily: May–Sept 10am–2pm & 4.30–8.30pm; Oct–April 10am–6pm; €4.50), a medieval tower that now houses a museum full of hi-tech gimmicks including weird tableaux, a lit-up Alhambra, a model of the Mezquita prior to its Christian alterations and, improbably, a multimedia presentation on the history of man. From the tower you get a wonderful panoramic **view** towards the Mezquita and city beyond.

Sited just west of the bridge at its northern end is one of the ancient **Moorish water wheels**, the Albolafia. This is the reconstructed sole survivor of a number of mills which crossed the river here and which, besides grinding flour, pumped water to the Alcázar's gardens. So noisy were this wheel's rumblings that Queen Isabel – resident at the Alcázar during a royal visit – had it dismantled when it disturbed her sleep.

The Judería and synagogue

Between the Mezquita and the beginning of the Avenida del Gran Capitán lies the **Judería**, Córdoba's old Jewish quarter. A fascinating network of lanes, it's just as atmospheric as Seville's Barrio Santa Cruz (see p.268), although here too tasteless souvenir shops are beginning to gain ground. Near the heart of the quarter, at c/Maimónides 18, is the **Sinagoga** (synagogue) (Tues–Sat 9.30am–2pm & 3.30–5.30pm, Sun 9.30am–1.30pm; €0.30, free with EU passport), one of only three in Spain – the other two are in Toledo – that survived the Jewish expulsion of 1492. This one, built in 1315, is minute, particularly in comparison

▲ View of the Alcazar from its gardens

to the great Santa María in Toledo, but it has some fine stuccowork elaborating on a Solomon's-seal motif together with Hebrew texts in the Mudéjar style, and it also retains its women's gallery. Just south of the synagogue in the plazuela named after him is a statue of Maimónides, the Jewish philospher, physician and Talmudic jurist born in Córdoba in 1135.

On the same square the small **Museo Taurino** (Bullfighting Museum; Tues–Sat 10am–2pm & 5.30–7.30pm, Sun 9.30am–2.30pm; €3, free on Fri) warrants a look, if only for the kitschy nature of its exhibits: among a number of mounted bulls' heads (some dating from the nineteenth century), two of them were given this "honour" for having killed matadors. Beside a copy of the tomb of Manolete, most famous of the city's fighters, is exhibited the hide of his taurine nemesis, Islero. In addition to Manolete's bloodstained vest from his ill-fated bullfight in 1947, other items on display include eighteenth-century bullfight posters and a series of photos from 1914 depicting a bullfighter being gored and killed.

Finally, close to the Mezquita's northeast corner, you shouldn't miss Córdoba's most famous street, the **Callejón de las Flores**. This is a white-walled alley from whose balconies and hanging pots cascades a riot of geraniums in summer and which, when viewed from its northern end, neatly frames the Mezquita's belfry – the picture that decorates every postcard rack in town.

Plaza del Potro

A short walk east from the Mezquita along c/Corregidor Luís de la Cerda and its continuation, c/Lucano, is the **Plaza del Potro**, one of Córdoba's more historic landmarks. This fine old square is named after the colt (*potro*) that adorns its sixteenth-century fountain. Originally a livestock market dealing in horses and mules, the area once had a villainous reputation, as did the remarkable inn opposite, the **Posada del Potro**, which Cervantes mentions in *Don Quijote*, and where he almost certainly stayed. Sensitively restored, the building, with an atmospheric cattle yard, is currently being transformed into a centre for the study of the art flamenco (details from the Turismo).

Slightly southwest of the plaza, back towards the Mezquita, a glimpse of how Córdoba may have lived in its Moorish heyday is obtainable at the **Hammam Baños Arabes**, c/Corregidor Luis de la Cerda 51 (☎957 48 47 46, ⓦwww .hammamspain.com), a full-scale Moorish bath complex which re-creates the architecture and atmosphere of a medieval *hammam*. It is open daily but reservations (by phone is fine) must be made in advance and sessions (lasting 2hr) are available from 10am to midnight; prices start at €24 for a simple soak and you'll need a bathing suit.

Museo de Bellas Artes and Museo Julio Romero de Torres

On the eastern side of Plaza del Potro, the former Hospital de la Caridad, founded in the sixteenth century, now contains the **Museo de Bellas Artes** (Tues 2.30–8.30pm, Wed–Sat 9am–8.30pm, Sun 9am–2.30pm; €1.50, free with EU passport). Among a fairly unremarkable collection is an *Immaculate Conception* by Murillo as well as works by Valdés Leal and some dubious Zurbaráns. A couple of interesting drawings by the Victorian British artist David Roberts (not always displayed) depict the Mezquita's Patio de los Naranjos and the Puerta del Puente as they were at the end of the nineteenth century. The ground floor has a small archeological collection, as well as a collection of rather humdrum modern sculpture and paintings.

Across the courtyard is a small museum (May–Sept Tues–Sat 10am–2pm & 5.30–7.30pm, Sun 9.30am–2.30pm; Oct–April Tues–Sat 8.30am–2.30pm, Sun

9.30am–2.30pm; €4, free on Fri) devoted to the Cordoban artist **Julio Romero de Torres** (1885–1930), painter of some sublimely dreadful canvases, most of which depict reclining female nudes with furtive male guitar players. Attacked by feminists and dubbed "the king of kitsch" by critics, the *cordobeses*, however, won't have a word said against him. If you wish to decide for yourself, the nightmarish *Cante Jondo* or the raunchy *Naranjas y Limones* (Oranges and Lemons) should be enough to give you the measure of Romero's oeuvre; alternatively, just flick through a catalogue in the foyer.

Probably more rewarding would be a visit to *Bodegas Campos*, just east of here at c/Lineros 32, a wonderful rambling old place where they will allow you to see the cellars – stacked with giant oak *botas* (barrels) – in which the company matures its wine through the *solera* system of blending. You can sample the finished article – plus tapas – in their **bar**, and a very good Montilla it is, too.

Plaza de la Corredera

To the north of Plaza del Potro, in an area which was once the *plateros* or silversmiths' quarter, you'll find **Plaza de la Corredera**, a once ramshackle but now wonderfully refurbished colonnaded square, much resembling Madrid's or Salamanca's Plaza Mayor. Unique in Andalucía, the square's complete enclosure occurred in the seventeenth century and presented the city with a suitable space for all kinds of spectacles. These have included burnings by the Inquisition as well as bullfights, from which event the tiny Callejón Toril (Bull Pen) on the square's eastern side takes its name. After decades of delay the city has finally rescued this remarkable construction and now bars and restaurants have opened and their terraces have become popular places to sit out on summer evenings.

Museo Arqueológico

To the northeast of the Mezquita, on Plaza de Jerónimo Páez, lies the excellent **Museo Arqueológico** (Tues 2.30–8.30pm, Wed–Sat 9am–8.30pm, Sun 9am–2.30pm; €1.50, free with EU passport), essential to gaining an understanding of Córdoba's importance as a Roman city in particular, as so little from this period survives above ground today. During the original conversion of the Casa Páez, this small sixteenth-century Renaissance mansion was revealed as the unlikely site of a genuine Roman patio. As a result, it is one of the most imaginative and enjoyable small museums in the country, with good local collections from the Iberian, Roman and Moorish periods.

Following the **prehistoric section**, which displays some Iberian sculptures from various sites in the province, the visit continues in **Room 3** where you can see evidence of the original Roman building. Highlights here include a large number of finds from the excavation of Córdoba's western necropolis, among which are a number of inscribed first-century gladiatorial tombstones (including the moving exhibit no. 10.681, translated into Spanish). **Room 4** has a fine maquette of the Roman villa of El Ruedo at Almedinilla (see p.420) in the south of the province, incorporating a unique cascade feature in its *triclinium* (dining room). **Room 5** has more exhibits and statuary from the Roman period including a superb bronze hermaphrodite from the villa at El Ruedo, and a fascinating carved stone relief depicting the olive harvest. The stairs leading to Room 7 are flanked by fine mosaics including an outstanding one depicting a *quadriga* (four-horse chariot) in action. The intricate wooden Mudéjar ceiling here is worth a look too and predates the mansion, which was built to incorporate it.

Room 7 contains exhibits from the Moorish period among which is a fine inlaid tenth-century bronze stag – a gift of the Byzantine emperor Constantine VII to Abd ar-Rahman III – and found at the Moorish palace of Medina Azahara (see p.398) where it was used as the spout of a fountain. Also here are a number of fine polychromed ceramic pieces from Medina Azahara. On the **balcony** a collection of wells attests to the Moorish attraction to water – a tradition continued by fountains throughout Andalucía today.

The museum's beautiful double **patio** contains miscellaneous Roman statuary, mosaics and a superb fourth-century Christian marble sarcophagus. Also here is a fine second-century **sculpture of Mithras** slaying the bull from a mithraeum excavated at Cabra in the south of the province. This conventional image, which was placed in the *retablo* position in the small mithraic cult temples, shows Mithras plunging his dagger into the bull whose blood, initiates believed, gave birth to all living things, hence the dog and the snake trying to get their share. The ever-present problem of evil is portrayed by the symbolic scorpion attacking the bull's vitals.

The rest of the city

Many visitors to Córdoba make a stopover at the Mezquita and then leave without ever discovering the other Córdoba, to the north of the monumental quarter and the Judería, where the city's everyday life is carried on. Here, interspersed among the modern streets – many still built on the ancient grid – are **Gothic churches**, **convents** and **Renaissance palaces** that are little visited but well worth an hour or two. Note that churches are usually locked outside service times: early mornings or evenings (about 7–9pm) are the most promising times to catch them open, perhaps visiting a few tapas bars en route.

Plaza Tendillas and around

Plaza Tendillas is the vibrant centre of modern Córdoba, as it was in Roman times. Dominated by the bronze equestrian statue of El Gran Capitán, a Cordoban general whose Italian campaigns in the late fifteenth century helped to project post-*Reconquista* Spain onto the world stage. The square's recent makeover installed new fountains – spurting water two metres into the air from outlets in the pedestrianized pavement – which are a big hit with tourists, children and dogs.

Off the east side of the plaza, along c/Claudio Marcelo, lies the **Templo Romano**, the tortuously reconstructed remains (mostly pillars) of a first-century Roman temple thought to have been of a similar form to the Maison Carrée at Nîmes. Turning left along c/Capitulares from here brings you to the **Iglesia de San Pablo** fronting the street of the same name. A fine Romanesque-Gothic church, dating from the period following the *Reconquista*, it has undergone numerous later modifications including a Baroque facade. Its interior retains a fine Mudéjar dome and coffered ceiling as well as a seventeenth-century sculpture of the Virgin, *Nuestra Señora de las Angustias* (*Our Lady of the Sorrows*), a masterpiece by Juan de Mesa, himself a native of Córdoba.

Northwest from here, at no. 14 c/Alfonso XIII, is the striking **Circulo de la Amistad**, a *Casino* founded in 1842 and set inside a former convent. Ask the porter to let you see the marvellous Renaissance **patio**, originally the convent's cloister. Continuing east again, beyond San Pablo lies **San Andrés**, another post-*Reconquista* church and, further on, at the end of c/Santa María de la Gracia, is the Gothic **San Lorenzo**, whose converted Moorish minaret tower, outstanding rose window and triple-arched portico combine to make it the best-looking church in the city. Inside, the apse has some fine fifteenth-century frescoes depicting scenes from the Passion.

Turning north along c/Roelas, passing the nineteeth-century Neoclassical Iglesia de San Rafael, you'll come to another *Reconquista* church, **San Agustín**, in the plaza of the same name. Originally a Gothic church, it was substantially altered in the sixteenth century; inside it has frescoes and another sculpture of the Virgin by Juan de Mesa.

Palacio del Marqués de Viana

Slightly west of San Agustín in Plaza de Gome you'll find the **Palacio del Marqués de Viana** (guided tours Mon–Fri 10am–1pm & 4–6pm, Sat 10am–1pm; €6, patios only €3), one of Córdoba's finest palaces and seat of the marquises of Viana until the family sold up to a bank in 1981, after which it was opened – apparently just as the family left it – to the public. Started in the fourteenth century, the building has had numerous later additions tacked on, including most of the **twelve outstanding patios**, filled with flowers, the main attraction for many visitors today.

The compulsory forty-five minute guided tour shunts you around a bewildering number of drawing rooms, gaudy bedrooms (one with a telling Franco portrait), kitchens and galleries, linked by creaking staircases, whilst a commentary delivered in Spanish (foreign-language room descriptions available) points out a wealth of furniture, paintings, weapons and top-drawer junk the family amassed over the centuries, giving you little time to take anything in.

More churches, convents and tabernas

North of the Palacio de Viana, the fortress-like **Iglesia de Santa Marina** dates from the thirteenth century (with Baroque modifications) and shares the charming plaza of the same name with a monument to the celebrated Cordoban *torero* **Manolete**, who was born in the Santa Marina *barrio* and died in the ring in 1947. At the square's western end, strictly speaking the Plaza del Conde Priego, the fifteenth-century Franciscan **Convento de Santa Isabel** has a delightful patio with an imposing cypress. The *capilla mayor* inside the convent's church has sculptures by Pedro Roldán. In the convent's shop (usually Mon–Sat 9.15am–12.45pm & 5–7.30pm, Sun 9.30am–1pm) the nuns also sell their home-made *dulces* – one nun is given a special dispensation from the order's rule of silence to serve you.

Calle Conde de Priego leads west to the Puerta del Rincón. By turning right off this after a short distance you enter the simple white-walled Plaza de Capuchinos, the site of **Cristo de los Faroles** (Christ of the Lanterns), an eighteenth-century sculpture of the Crucifixion which is the centre of much religious fervour. At night, when the lanterns flanking the cross are illuminated, the place has an unearthly, mystical ambience.

North from here are two features – on either side of the Plaza de Colón – worthy of a detour. Close to the northeast corner of this garden-square, the **Torre de la Malmuerta** (Tower of Bad Death) is an early fifteenth-century battlemented tower, once part of the city walls. It takes its name from a crime of passion when a guard posted here is supposed to have killed his adulterous spouse. At the foot of the tower is one of the city's best loved *tabernas*, the *Casa de Paco Acedo* (see p.396), housed in part of a former barracks. The west side of the Plaza de Colón is dominated by the lavishly ornate facade of the eighteenth-century former **Convento de la Merced**, (entry to patio daily 9am–2pm & 5–9pm; free) now the seat of the provincial government, and the biggest and best example of full-blown Baroque in town. Inside is an exquisite Renaissance patio with paired columns, elegant staircases and a central fountain.

Picking up the route south towards the centre, follow c/del Osario until, just before Plaza Tendillas, a left turn brings you into Plaza San Miguel and its charming **Iglesia de San Miguel**, yet another *Reconquista* church founded in the thirteenth century by Fernando III, with a magnificent rose window above the early Gothic entrance. Tucked behind the church lies one of Córdoba's most atmospheric taverns, the **Taberna San Miguel** (see p.396).

Eating, drinking and nightlife

Coming from Seville or the coast, the nightlife in Córdoba will seem rather tame by comparison. Places start closing at around 11pm, and by midnight the empty streets around the Mezquita, lit by lanterns, have a melancholy air. When they are open, however, many of the city's **bars and restaurants** are among the best in Andalucía and well worth seeking out.

Restaurants

Córdoba's **restaurants** are on the whole reasonably priced – and quite a few of the upmarket establishments are really excellent. While here be sure to try Córdoba's two most celebrated **dishes**, *rabo de toro* (slow-stewed bull's tail) and *salmorejo* (a chunky gazpacho with bits of ham and egg), available all over town.

Albergue Juvenil Plaza Judá Levi s/n. The youth hostel's *cafetería* (open to all) has some of the cheapest food in town with three-course lunch (2–3pm) and dinner (8.30–9.30pm) *menús* for a bargain €7.

Almudaina Plaza Campo Santo de los Martires 1 ☏ 957 47 43 42. Top-notch restaurant with four stylish rooms in an atmospheric sixteenth-century mansion facing the walls of the Alcázar. Among many fine dishes *rabo de toro a la cordabesa* is a house special. Expensive (main dishes €15–21), but there's a *menú* for about €25. Closed Sun eve.

Amaltea c/Ronda de Isasa 10 ☏957 49 19 68. Excellent organic restaurant with lots of veggie options where specialities of the house include couscous, *carpaccio de cecina* (described as cured ham made with beef) and *calabacín con cabrales* (courgettes with strong blue cheese). There are plenty of organic wines and a few special beers too – try the Alhambra 1925 – along with occasional art exhibitions on the walls. Closed Mon. Main dishes €8–12.

Bar-Restaurante Federación de Peñas c/Conde y Luque 8. Moorish-style patio dining room offering a variety of economical *menús*.

Café Gloria c/Claudio Marcelo 15. Attractive café-diner done out in Art Deco style with big windows onto the street; offers economical *platos combinados* and a variety of *menús* starting at around €7.

Círculo Taurino c/Manuel María de Arjona 1. An excellent, mid-priced, family establishment offering a wide range of local dishes, this is a place where *cordobéses* come to eat. Elegant dining room at the rear and a tapas and *raciónes* bar out front.

El Barril c/Concepción 16. Efficient tapas and breakfast bar with a small terrace and all-day *platos combinados*. Some vegetarian dishes.

El Caballo Rojo c/Cardenal Herrero 28 ☏957 47 53 75. Beneath the Mezquita's belfry, this is one of Córdoba's choicest restaurants, although the café-style interior lacks intimacy. It prides itself on a Moorish-influenced menu offering such specialities as *cordero a la miel* (lamb in honey) and tasty desserts like *canutillo de almendra* (almond pastry). Expensive (main dishes €13–22) but offers a *menú de degustación* for around €36.

El Choto c/Almanzor 10 ☏ 957 76 01 15. Attractive, small restaurant offering a range of well-prepared fish and meat dishes including its signature dish *choto asado* (roast kid). Comfort-able – if slightly formal – dining room plus a small terrace at the entrance (which you will need to book for). There's a four course *menú de degustación* (Tues–Fri) for €35 including wine and a *menú de la casa* for around €18. Closed Sun eve & Mon.

El Churrasco c/Romero 16 (*not* c/Romero Barros) ☏957 29 08 19. Probably the best of Córdoba's top restaurants, with sumptuously decorated dining rooms and patio, and a long-standing reputation for its *churrasco* (a kind of grilled pork dish, served with pepper sauces). Prices match its reputation (main dishes €14–23), although there's an interesting set *menú* at €29. Closed Aug.

El Rincón del Carmen c/Romero 4. Small, pleasant café-restaurant, with a charming patio terrace below and restaurant upstairs, serving inexpensive *raciónes* and *media raciónes*.

Los Mochuelos c/Agustín Moreno 51. Traditional tapas and *raciónes* restaurant with large variety of dishes including *mochuelitos* (spicy meat); plenty of atmosphere, stacked butts, bullfight posters and a pleasant patio.

Marisquería El Faro c/Ricardo de Montís 1, off c/Blanco Belmonte. Small upmarket restaurant with good seafood *raciónes* and a *menú* for €12 (Mon–Fri); also does a decent paella (€20 for two).

Salón de Té c/Buen Pastor 13. To the northwest of the Mezquita's belfry is this very pleasant small Moroccan tea salon with a charming patio offering over fifty varieties, including a special *hierba buena* (mint tea), as well as snacks.

San Basilio c/San Basilio 19. Great little neighbourhood restaurant with a pleasant patio, friendly service and a weekday *menú* for €12. House specials include *presa iberica* (pork) and *berenjenas fritas* (aubergine).

Tabernas and tapas bars

The *cordobeses* are proud of their **tabernas** – and with good reason, for few places anywhere can match them for sheer character and variety, not to mention **tapas**. Remember, too, when ordering *fino* that the equivalent brew here is Montilla and the best way to get up a barman's nose is to ask for any of the wines of Jerez, the product of the upstart province downriver. If you're new to Montilla-Moriles to give it its full title, or have been unimpressed with the insipid concoctions sold abroad under the *Montilla* name, prepare for a pleasant surprise. Montilla, which vaguely resembles a mellow, dry sherry, is a giant on its native soil, and is considered a healthier tipple by the *cordobeses*; whereas Jerez sherry is fortified with alcohol, here the process is totally natural, leading (they insist) to fewer hangovers.

Around the Mezquita and Judería

Bar Caballo Rojo c/Cardenal Herrero 28, facing the Mezquita. The smoothly efficient – and slightly pricey – bar of the famous restaurant has excellent tapas and *raciónes* including *boquerones en vinagre* (anchovies in vinegar).

Bar La Cavea Plaza Jerónimo Páez, near the archeological museum. Pleasant little bar with nice terrace where you can knock back a *jarrón* of beer with meat and fish tapas and *raciónes*. Also serves *platos combinados*.

Bar Miguelito Acera Pintada 8, across the river near the Torre de la Calahorra. *Barrio* bar slightly off the tourist beat which is locally reputed for its tapas range and its *gambas* house special. Entertaining *terraza* filled in the evenings with babies in prams and nattering clientele.

Bar-Mesón Rafaé c/Deanes 2. North of the Mezquita in the Judería, this pleasant old bar offers a broad tapas range, well-kept Montilla and a reasonably priced *menú*.

Bodega Guzmán c/Judíos 7, close to the synagogue. Cavernous old bar frequented by bullfight aficionados, with a small *taurino* "museum" in its inner sanctum and outstanding *amargoso* Montilla served from a butt behind the bar.

Casa Rubio Puerta de Almodóvar 5, in the city wall. Atmospheric and popular local bar with Mezquita-inspired decor, a tempting tapas range – try *berenjenas con miel* (aubergine with honey) and excellent Montilla. Restaurant upstairs. *Casa Bravo*, a few steps away and serving equally good tapas, is also worth a visit.

Casa Salinas Puerta de Almodóvar s/n. Stacked with butts holding its celebrated Montillas, this bar has long-standing flamenco traditions – well-known practitioners often meet up here and impromptu *juergas* (music sessions) can result.

El Olivo Avda. Dr Fleming 25, close to the Plaza Maimonides. Inviting little bar-restaurant with a very pleasant evening terrace which is just the place for enjoying a few tapas or *raciónes* (*jamón* is a speciality).

Around the Plaza del Potro

Bodegas Campos c/Lineros 32. Large *bodega* with great oak barrels (many signed by celebrities including former British premier Tony Blair) stacked up in the *sacristía* cellar at the rear. The bar at the entrance sells their own excellent Montilla, where there are also pricey tapas on offer, plus there's an expensive, highly rated – and rather snooty – restaurant behind.

Bodega Sociedad Plateros c/San Francisco 6. Headquarters of the *Plateros* chain, and in a converted former convent. What started in 1868 as a mutual benefit society for the workers in Córdoba's silversmith trade eventually branched out into the *bodega* business, presently owning three excellent bars around the city. This bar – now over a century old and serving a wide range of tapas – is light and airy with a glass-covered patio complemented by hanging plants and *azulejos*.

Taberna El Potro c/Lineros 2, near the Plaza del Potro. Somewhat over-adorned with reproductions of Julio Romero de Torres's "art works" but serving tasty tapas, *platos combinados* and a *menú*.

Around and north of Plaza Tendillas

Bar Gaudí Avda. Gran Capitán 22, near El Corte Inglés. Named after the great architect and aptly decorated in Art Nouveau style, this place serves excellent tapas (try their *bonito en escabeche* – marinated tuna) and a range of European beers.

Casa Paco Acedo Beneath the Torre de Malmuerta. Fine old bar serving up a superb range of tapas, including *salmorejo* and all kinds of fried fish. The house speciality is a memorable *rabo de toro*, the perfect complement to the house Montilla, and best eaten at the tables outside.

Taberna Góngora c/Torres Cabrera 4, near Plaza San Miguel. Welcoming modern bar carrying on the tapas tradition and much favoured by *tapeadores*. Specials include *carne de monte* (cured meats) and *boquerones al limón* (anchovies with lemon).

Taberna San Miguel Plaza San Miguel 1, behind the church. Known to all as *El Pisto* (the barrel) and virtually unchanged for over a century, this is one of the city's legendary bars and not to be missed. Wonderful Montilla and tapas; *rabo de toro* and *callos en salsa picante* (tripe in a spicy sauce) are big favourites. Closed Aug.

Taberna Seneca Plaza Seneca 4. Sharing the same building as the *Hotel Plateros* (see p.382) this is another bar in the *Plateros* chain with the same great tapas and Montilla.

Around Plaza Corredera and beyond

Bar Regina Plaza de Regina, slightly northeast of Plaza Corredera. Century-old bar with plenty of bullfight memorabilia, a nice patio and good tapas, including their noted *patatas bravas*.

Casa El Juramento c/Juramento 6, on east side of Plaza Corredera (go north along c/Toril and turn left). Atmospheric old bar with a charming patio and a good tapas selection. House specials include *pimientos rellenos* (stuffed peppers) the favourite tapa of artist Julio Romero de Torres (see p.390) who was a regular here. Closed Tues.

Casa La Paloma Plaza Corredera 5. A good and economical bar on this atmospheric enclosed square serving vegetarian dishes, *raciónes* and *media raciónes*, soups and fish.

El Gallo c/María Cristina 6, close to the Roman temple. Fine old *cordobés* drinking hole which has changed little since it opened at the turn of the twentieth century. Good tapas selection includes *calamares*, *bacalao* (cod), *croquetas* and *gambas rebozadas* (fried prawns). The outstanding *amargoso* Montilla comes from their own *bodega* and is also sold by the bottle.

Sociedad Plateros c/María Auxiliadora 25, close to the old city wall on the northeast side of town. Aficionados of the *Plateros* chain will enjoy this cavernous old mini-Mezquita serving up excellent *raciónes* and *medias* (half *raciónes*). Some way from the centre, it's definitely worth the walk, with a couple of nice churches to see along the way.

Taberna Salinas c/Tundidores 3. Century-old *taberna* with dining rooms around a charming patio and an outstanding range of *raciónes*; try their delicious *bacalao con naranja* (cod with orange and olive oil) or *setas en salsa* (mushrooms).

▲ Taberna San Miguel

Flamenco, nightlife and discotecas

Outside Semana Santa and the annual fiesta at the end of May, the city's nightlife centres around bars and restaurants. The only **late-night drinking** you are likely to find is in the north of the city, where the bars in the El Brillante district and around Avenida Tejares, Avenida Gran Capitán and those near the provincial government building in c/Reyes Católicos tend to stay open after midnight. Córdoba's best non-membership **flamenco** *tablao* is *Tablao Cardenal*, c/Torrijos 10 (Mon–Sat 10.30pm; €25, includes first drink; ☏957 48 33 20, ⓦwww.tablaocardenal.com), next door to the Turismo, where you can catch performances by established artists in a pleasant open-air patio, and reserve a table in advance. Also good is *La Bulería*, c/Pedro López 3, near Plaza de la Corredera, open from 10pm every night (performance starts 10.30pm; €12.00, includes first drink; they also serve food). The singer El Calli and his family are the core of the show, and get near enough to the real thing, although corners are sometimes cut when trade is slack. Free flamenco performances are also mounted by the local council in summer and various other concerts are staged at the Gran Teatro, Avda. Gran Capitan 3, and in the Alcázar gardens (details from the Turismos).

Córdoba's nightlife scene centres on the Ciudad Jardín zone between c/Albeniz (top left of our map) and the bullring a few blocks further west and the streets to the south of c/Antonio Maura, in a quarter with plenty of music and drinking bars favoured by the city's student set. Popular long-standing bars here include *Galía* at c/Alcalde de la Cruz Ceballos 3, and the Lilliputian but lively *La Quadra* at c/de los Alderetes 25. Conventional **discotecas** are in the centre of town around c/Cruz Conde, north of Plaza Tendillas. *Gongora*, c/Góngora 10, is an all day *copas* (drinks) café playing blues and other sounds which transmutes nightly into an all-night dance venue, often staging live gigs. Nearby, *Underground*, c/Conde de Robledo 1 (open Thurs–Sun), plays Latin and rock until the early hours. The ♪ *Jazz Café*, c/Espartería s/n (50m from the Roman temple), is a great and atmospheric jazz and blues bar that stays open till the early hours, regularly stages live bands and is famous for its Jam Sessions. Slightly north from here *Soul*, c/Alfonso XIII 3, is also good, with a wide variety of sounds.

Shopping

Córdoba is known for silver **jewellery** and embossed **leather** goods, both on offer at many workshops in the streets around the Mezquita; for the former – particularly filigree silver jewellery – try the **Zoco** (market) in c/de los Judios close the synagogue, while Meryan in the tiny Calleja de las Flores has a wide selection of leather goods.

A remarkable century-old **hat** shop, Sombrería Rusi (founded 1903), c/Conde de Cardenas 1, near the Roman temple, is still making hats by hand on site and stocks a wide range of headwear including the flat-topped *cordobés* style worn by men at fiesta times. Almacen Rafael, c/Dr Marañon s/n, to the northeast of the Alcázar, is a well-stocked *bodega* selling most of Córdoba's wines. Stylish silver jewellery is on sale at Espaliu, c/Corregidor Luis de la Cerda 3, near the Mezquita, who fabricate their own designs. Córdoba's branch of the El Corte Inglés department store is on Avenida del Gran Capitán, at the junction with Avenida Ronda de los Tejares.

The twice-weekly **market** sells a wide variety of clothes, food and hardware, and takes place in the El Jardín *barrio*, along Avenida Gran Vía Parque west of the old quarter, on Tuesday and Friday mornings.

Listings

Banks Numerous banks with ATMs are located along Ronda de los Tejares and Avda. del Gran Capitán. In the Judería there are ATMs in c/Magistral González Francés near the Mezquita and along c/Judería, off its northwest corner.

Buses and trains Contact Alsina Graells, Estación de Autobuses, Plaza de las Tres Culturas (℡957 27 81 00), for buses to Seville, Granada, Málaga, Almería, Cádiz, Jaén and the Costa del Sol. Get details of services to all other destinations from the bus station information desk (℡957 40 40 40). Train information is available from RENFE, Plaza de las Tres Culturas (℡902 40 02 02, ⓦwww.renfe.com).

Hospital Hospital Reina Sofía, Avda. Menendez Pidal s/n (℡957 01 00 00) to the southwest of the centre. Cruz Roja, Avda. del Dr Fleming s/n (℡957 29 34 11); for emergencies dial ℡061.

Hiking maps 1:50,000, 1:100,000 and 1:200,000 maps are available from CNIG branch office (National Geographic Service; ℡957 98 92 68), Plaza de la Constitución 1, west of the Judería. Librería Luque (see "Press and books") is another option.

Internet Numerous hotels and *hostales* now have their own wi-fi connection or have computers for guests' use. A couple of central internet cafés are Ch@t (Mon–Sat 10am–2pm & 5–9.30pm) c/Claudio Marcelo 15, near Plaza Tendillas, and *Hostal El Pilar del Potro* (daily 10am–1pm & 5–10pm) c/Lucano 12.

Laundry Seco y Agua, c/Dr Marañon 3, slightly northwest of the Alcazár (Mon–Fri 9.30am–1.30pm & 5.30–8.30pm, Sat 9.30am–1.30pm), is an efficient *tintorería* who will wash, dry and fold 5kg of clothes the same day for around €17.

Police A local police station is located in Plaza Judá Levi, near the Mezquita (℡957 29 07 60). For emergencies dial ℡092 (local police), ℡091 (national).

Post office The main office is at c/Cruz Conde 15 (just north of Plaza Tendillas). Mon–Fri 8.30am–8.30pm; Sat 9am–2pm.

Press and books Córdoba's daily paper, *El Diario Córdoba* (ⓦwww.diariocordoba.com), is good for local and provincial news, events and entertainment. For a good selection of books and walking maps try Librería Luque, c/José Cruz Conde 19 (near Plaza Tendillas). One of the town's biggest and best bookstores is Beta, c/Córdoba de Veracruz 2, near the El Corte Inglés store.

West of Córdoba

Just a few kilometres from the city is the historic site of **Medina Azahara**, a must for those on the Moorish trail, and with a fascinating eighteenth-century hermitage nearby. Continuing west, along the southern fringes of the Sierra Morena, following the Río Guadalquivir, there's a remarkable castle at **Almodóvar del Río**, a string of charming rural towns and Cordoba province's largest natural park, the **Parque Natural de la Sierra de Hornachuelos**.

Medina Azahara

Some 7km to the west of Córdoba lie the vast and rambling ruins of **Medina Azahara**, a palace and administrative complex built on a dream scale by **Caliph Abd ar-Rahman III**. Naming it after a favourite wife, az-Zahra (the Radiant), he spent one-third of the annual state budget on its construction each year from 936 until his death in 961. Since the first archeological excavations were carried out in 1911, work has been going on more or less continuously to piece together the fragments of this once fabulous creation, which is the reason it is currently only possible to visit a fraction of the excavated site.

The site

The **site** (April–Sept Tues–Sat 10am–8.30pm, Sun 10am–2pm; Oct–March Tues–Sat 10am–2pm & 5–6.30pm, Sun 10am–1.30pm; check winter hours with site; ℡957 35 55 06; €1.50, free with EU passport) is entered by the **Puerta Norte**, the typically Moorish "twisted gate" which forced would-be invaders to double back on themselves, thus making them easy targets. Behind you at this point lies the Dar al-Mulk or royal palace (currently not open to visitors) which is thought to have been the residence of Abd ar-Rahman III. The signed route leads to **Dar al-Wuzara** (House of the Viziers, aka Edificio Basilical), believed to have been the bureaucratic heart of the complex with administrative rooms, archives and a grand salon (with reconstructed horseshoe arches), originally fronted by a patio, now a garden. To the east of here, the route leads to the elegant arched **portico** and the **Plaza de Armas** – formerly a grand parade ground – beyond, still awaiting excavation. The portico is thought to have supported a balcony terrace from where the caliph reviewed his troops. Turning south, you can see the **great mosque** below, one of the first buildings to be constructed on the site, oriented towards the southeast and Mecca. Its ground plan allows you to make out the main entrance, flanked by the base of a minaret (*alminar*), with patio, prayer hall – the floor of which was covered with esparto mats found in the excavations – and *mihrab*. The route now veers west passing the princely baths to the right, presently being painstakingly restored by archeologists repairing washing fountains and marble surfaces, beyond which lay the royal apartments.

For centuries, the site was looted for building materials; parts, for instance, were used in the Seville Alcázar and much of the surrounding town served as a quarry for the fifteenth-century construction of the monastery of San Jerónimo (now privately owned) at the end of the track which climbs above the ruins. In 1944, however, excavations unearthed the buried materials from a crucial part of the palace, the **Royal House**, where guests were received and meetings of ministers held. This has been meticulously reconstructed and, though still fragmentary, its main hall, the **Salón Rico de Abd al-Rahman III**, decorated with exquisite marble carvings, must rank among the greatest of all Moorish rooms. Modelled on the Roman basilica, it has a different kind of artistic representation from that found in the palaces at Granada or Seville – closer to natural and animal forms in its intricate Syrian Hom (Tree of Life) motifs. Unlike the later Spanish Arab dynasties, the Berber Almoravids and the Almohads of Seville, the caliphal Andalucians

The rise and fall of Medina Azahara

Ten thousand workers and 1500 mules and camels were employed in the construction of **Medina Azahara** in the early tenth century, and the site, almost 2000m long by 900m wide, stretched over three descending terraces above the Guadalquivir valley. Roman masonry was taken from sites throughout Andalucía and reused, while vast quantities of marble were shipped in from North Africa. In addition to the palace buildings, the complex contained a zoo, an aviary, four huge fish ponds, three hundred baths, four hundred houses, weapons factories, two barracks for the royal guard as well as numerous baths, markets, workshops and mosques. Visitors, so the chronicles record, were stunned by its wealth and brilliance: one conference room contained a pile of pure crystals, creating a rainbow when lit by the sun; another was built round a huge shallow bowl of mercury which, when the sun's rays fell on it, would be rocked by a slave, sending sunbeams reflected from its surface flashing and whizzing around the room, apparently alarming guests but greatly amusing the caliph.

Medina Azahara was a perfect symbol of the western caliphate's dominance and greatness, but it was to last for less than a century. **Al-Hakam II**, who succeeded Abd ar-Rahman, lived in the palace, continued to endow it, and enjoyed a stable reign. However, distanced from the city, he delegated more and more authority, particularly to his vizier Ibn Abi Amir, later known as **al-Mansur** (the Victor). In 976 al-Hakam was succeeded by his eleven-year-old son Hisham II but after a series of sharp moves al-Mansur assumed the full powers of government, keeping Hisham virtually imprisoned at Medina Azahara, to the extent of blocking up connecting passageways between the palace buildings.

Al-Mansur was equally skilful and manipulative in his wider dealings as a dictator, and Córdoba rose to new heights of prosperity, retaking large tracts of central Spain and raiding as far afield as Galicia and Catalunya. But with his death in 1002 came swift decline as his role and function were assumed in turn by his two sons. The first died in 1008; the second, Sanchol, showed open disrespect for the caliphate by forcing Hisham to appoint him as his successor. At this a popular revolt broke out and the caliphate disintegrated into civil war and a series of feudal kingdoms. Medina Azahara was looted by a mob at the outset and in 1010 was plundered and burned by retreating Berber mercenaries – splashes of molten metal from this conflagration are still to be seen in the Salon Rico. The ruins slowly disappeared under the earth until archeologists arrived at the site in the early twentieth century. But it was never secure and as late as the 1930s a visiting Gerald Brenan saw stones being carted off to service other buildings. In the 1960s academic study, excavation and reconstruction of the complex began in earnest, and this is set to continue for many decades to come.

were little worried by Islamic strictures on the portrayal of nature, animals or even men – the beautiful stag in the Córdoba museum is a good example (see p.391) – and it may well have been this aspect of the palace's artistic decor that led to such zealous destruction during the civil war. The reconstructed palace gives a scale and focus to the site, while elsewhere work continues in restoring and rebuilding more ruined structures. Beyond these there are little more than foundations, gardens and the odd horseshoe arch to fuel your imaginings, amid an awesome area of ruins, hidden beneath bougainvillea and rustling with cicadas.

Over a decade ago biologists from Córdoba University carried out a study of soil samples from the site to gain an understanding of exactly which plants and flowers the Moors had cultivated in the extensive gardens. When the study was completed, planting began in an attempt to reconstruct the gardens of Medina Azahara as accurately as possible. The planted trees, shrubs, plants and herbs are now maturing into a delightful and aromatic garden the caliphs would recognize.

Practicalities

To reach Medina Azahara, follow the Avenida de Medina Azahara out of Córdoba and on to the road to Villarubia and Posadas. After about 4km, make a right turn, after which it's another 3km to the site. Alternatively, the #01 city **bus** from a stop at the northern end of the Avda. de la Republica Argentina will drop you off at the intersection for the final three-kilometre walk. Ask the driver for "El Cruce de Medina Azahara". A **dedicated bus service** also links the city with the site (April–Sept Tues–Fri 11am & 6pm, Sat, Sun & hols 10am & 11am; Oct–March Tues–Fri 4pm; €6.50 return). The bus departs from a signed stop on the Avendia del Alcázar directly below the Alcázar but tickets must be purchased in advance from any municipal tourist office (there's one in the Plaza Campo de Los Martires fronting the Alcázar).

An alternative way to make a visit without your own transport is with the **bus tour** organized by the municipal tourist authority. Buses to the site (April–Sept Tue–Fri 11am & 6pm, Sat 10am, 11am & 6pm, Sun 10am & 11am; Oct–March Tue–Fri 11am & 4.30pm, Sat 10am, 11am & 4.30pm, Sun 10am & 11am; €6.50) leave from a stop at the northern end of Paseo de la Victoria (just above Plaza A. Grillo on our map) and return to the city two hours later. Tickets must be booked in advance from any of the three municipal tourist office kioskos (see p.380). The trip includes a free map-guide to the site and your return bus ticket is valid only for the bus you arrived with, so ensure that you don't miss it. Córdoba Vision also runs **guided trips** to the site (English spoken; Tues–Sun 11am; ☏957 29 97 77; €18); buses leave from the same stop on the Avenida del Alcázar as the dedicated bus service (see above) A **taxi** will cost you about €25 one-way or there's a special round-trip fare of €40, which includes a one-hour wait at the site (details from tourist offices). With your own transport, an atmospheric **place to eat** near the site is *Bar-Restaurante El Cruce* – with a leafy terrace and often serving *jabalí* (wild boar) – a 3km climb from the signed junction on the way to the entrance.

Las Ermitas

A scenic signed road climbs for 4km beyond the *Bar-Restaurante El Cruce* to **Las Ermitas** (Tues–Sun 10am–1.30pm & 4.30–8pm; Oct–March closes 6.30pm; €1.50), a beautiful jasmine-scented hermitage filled with cypresses, olives and cacti. Here you can see twelve cells dating from the eighteenth century – spaced out around a central shrine – where hermit monks once flagellated themselves in splendid isolation. These hills were inhabited by hermits from the earliest days of Christianity through the Visigothic and Muslim periods and solitaries occupied the hermitage until as recently as 1957. There are dramatic **views** over the valley of the Guadalquivir from the *mirador* of the giant cross, La Cruz del Humilladero.

Almodóvar del Río and around

If you have your own transport, it's possible to continue a further 17km west along the A431 to **ALMODÓVAR DEL RÍO**, where an impressive multi-turreted **castle** (Mon–Fri 11am–2.30pm & 4–8pm, Sat & Sun 11am–8pm; Oct–March closes 7pm; €5) sits on a hill high above the town dominating the landscape. Dating originally from the eighth century, and significantly expanded by Abd al-Rahman II in the ninth, the fortress underwent many later additions and restorations, most of them following its fall to the Christian army of Fernando III in 1240. Today the castle is privately owned by the Marqués de Motilla. It's easy to find your way up to the castle from the town – a pleasant walk – or, with transport, follow signs and park by the castle walls. There's little to see in the over-restored interior – now filled with rather tedious "historical" tableaux – but there are fine **views** from the battlements over the valley of the Guadalquivir; watch your step as there are few handrails. Almodóvar is served by at least five daily **buses** from Córdoba.

Some twenty kilometres further west along the A431, a turn on the right (the A2212) leads after 8km to **HORNACHUELOS**, the gateway village to the extensive **Parque Natural de la Sierra de Hornachuelos**, a heavily wooded area on the lower slopes of the Sierra Morena. The park is home to a wide variety of wildlife including the threatened Iberian lynx, as well as deer, wild boar and, in the river valleys, otters. A zone rich in birdlife, Andalucía's second largest colony of black vultures also resides here. On the way through the village a **Turismo** (Mon–Fri 8am–3pm, Sat & Sun 10am–2pm; ☎957 64 07 86) is signed on the right and can provide information on the park as well as a map. Heading into the park along the A2212, two kilometres beyond Hornachuelos and signed on the left, the **Centro de Visitantes Huerta del Rey** (Mon–Fri 10am–2pm & 4–7pm, Sat 10am–7pm; ☎957 64 11 40) is the park's main information centre. It lies in woods beyond the car park, a couple of hundred metres distant. The centre has informative displays on the park's flora and fauna and can provide maps and information on numerous waymarked walking routes. A good-value **place to stay** in Hornachuelos is *Bar-Casa Alejandro* (☎957 64 00 98; ❶), Avda. del Guadalquivir 4, on the village's southern edge; it offers en-suite rooms above an inexpensive bar-restaurant with a daily *menú*. If you find this too rustic, continue up the road beyond the Turismo to *El Alamo*, Ctra. Comarcal 141 (☎957 64 04 76, ⓦ www.hornaocio.com; ❸) where a/c en-suite motel-style rooms come with parking space and there's a restaurant.

South of Córdoba – the Campiña

To the south of Córdoba, and stretching to the mountains of the province's southern border, lies the **Campiña Cordobesa**. A fertile, undulating region of wheatfields, olive groves and productive vineyards, it has been renowned since Roman times when the eminent Roman writers Pliny and Martial praised its artichokes, fruit, wool and the excellence of its olive oil. The town of **Baena** keeps up the tradition with an oil so good that it carries an official *denominación de origen* label. Each of the villages of the Campiña has its own interesting castle, church, palace or Roman villa and sometimes a *bodega* – and there are towns such as **Priego de Córdoba**, a Baroque architectural feast and well off the tourist trail, that are undiscovered jewels. The two itineraries described here roughly follow the **bus routes** from Córdoba to Málaga and Granada respectively, making it easy to stop off along the way, as even the smallest villages usually have a *hostal* or hotel to provide a **bed** for the night. This opens up the possibility of **walks** exploring some of the Campiña's delightful countryside including – in its lower reaches – the **Parque Natural de las Sierras Subbéticas**, replete with wooded hills and river valleys. Obviously, your own transport – and a little zigzagging and backtracking – would allow you to combine both routes. Many of the tourist offices in this zone stock a free bilingual booklet, *La Subbética Senderismo Guide*, which details fourteen walks in the park.

The Ruta del Vino

This itinerary leaves Córdoba by the A4–E5 (or more directly via the new A45) and, after 14km, forks left along the N331 towards Fernán Núñez, a pleasant hill village a further 14km down the road. Among a number of interesting places along this route are **Montilla**, the centre of Córdoba's wine production, and **Rute**, where *anís*, a far stronger brew, is concocted. The itinerary ends at the beautiful lakeside village of **Iznájar** in the midst of some good trekking country.

Montemayor

Just beyond the village of Fernán Núñez is **MONTEMAYOR**, a charming and typical *campiña* village with a fourteenth-century **castle**. In the centre of its neat little plaza, there's an amusing copy of the Alhambra's fountain of the lions in Granada. More interesting is the sixteenth-century church of **Nuestra Señora de la Asunción** with a beautifully painted stucco *sagrario* and a sixteenth-century carved baptismal font, still used to initiate the newborn of the parish. You'll need to find the priest, Padre Pablo Moyano, to open the church and he may well be in the *Casino*, a fine old institution across the square. If you ask, he will also let you see his personal **archeological collection** (daily 9–10.30am & 6.30–8pm; free), kept in a vault beneath the church and for which he is famous for miles around. This enormous accumulation of artefacts includes coins, agricultural implements, grindstones, jewellery and sculpture – most of it from Ulia, as Montemayor was in Roman times – and has been collected on his walks over the years in the surrounding fields. Close to the village on the N331, there are **rooms** at *Hotel Castillo de Montemayor*, Carretera Córdoba–Málaga s/n (℡957 38 42 53; ❸), which is friendly, efficient and has a good-value **restaurant**.

Montilla

The N331 (now the A45) presses on into the Sierra de Montilla and endless rows of vines begin to creep across the landscape as you enter Córdoba's **wine-producing region**. The tough Pedro-Ximénez vines planted here have to withstand searing summer temperatures, and send their roots deep down into

Montilla–Moriles: no hangover guaranteed

The Romans and later the Moors (in spite of the Prophet's prohibition) developed the Campiña as a **wine region**. The great wine of Córdoba, **Montilla** (often called Montilla-Moriles, the latter village being its partner in production to the south) has suffered over the years from comparison with the wines of Jerez, with which it shares similar characteristics. The reasons for this are largely historical as, prior to the 1940s, much of Córdoba's vintage was sold to the great *fino* houses of Jerez and eventually marketed as sherry. In 1944 this was made illegal, since when Montilla was granted its own *denominación*, but the notion that the wines of this region are merely a less expensive alternative to sherry has been a tag that the industry here has found hard to shake off.

The most visual difference in the production of Montilla is the great **tinajas** – huge, earthenware urns in which the wine undergoes its fermentation. These Ali-Baba jars, the direct descendants of the Roman *dolium*, have pointed ends which are buried in the earth inside the *bodegas* and are believed to impart a unique character to the wine. As in Jerez, the wine in these great vats also develops a *flor* (a thick layer of yeast) which covers the narrow neck of the urns. Later, the *solera* system (see p.234), during which the wine is aged and blended in oak butts for two years, is used to finish the process. The response you get around these parts should you bring up the subject of comparisons with the *finos* of Jerez is the assertion that Montilla is a natural product, whilst the wines of Jerez need to have their alcohol added. The Pedro-Ximénez grape used for Montilla is baked in the furnace heat of the Campiña sun and produces wines of sixteen percent proof which, the *bodegas* here like to claim – unlike that synthetic *jerezano* – never give you a hangover.

the whitish-grey *albariza* soil searching for moisture. Eleven kilometres beyond Montemayor, **MONTILLA**, the capital of Córdoba's wine country, comes into view. Hardly the region's prettiest town, you may want to call in, however, to visit one of the leading **bodegas**, Alvear SA, Avda. María Auxiliadora 1 (visits and tastings daily at 12.30pm; €3.50 weekdays, €4.70 Sat & Sun; shop open Mon–Sat 10am–2pm; ☏957 66 40 14, ⓦ www.alvear.es), a picturesque place founded in the eighteenth century.

For **food**, a good in-town restaurant is the popular *Don Quijote*, c/Ballén 4, in the heart of the town with a *menú* for €9.50. The medium-priced *Restaurante Camachas* (☏957 65 06 58; main dishes €10–15), on the main road at the entrance to the town, is also recommended and there's a good-value weekday *menú* for around €10. A/c en-suite **rooms** are available at the welcoming and good value *Hostal Bellido* c/Enfermería 57 (☏957 65 19 15, ⓦ www.hostalbellido.com; ❷), housed in an elegantly refurbished mansion a stone's throw from *the Don Quijote* restaurant (see above).

Aguilar and the Laguna de Zóñar

AGUILAR, 7km further south, perched on top of a hill, is worth a visit to see its wonderful eighteenth-century octagonal plaza of **San José**, probably inspired by the better-maintained one at Archidona in Málaga. The rest of the town is equally charming, its sloping streets lined with white-walled houses, their windows protected by *rejas*, or iron grilles. From the **Torre del Reloj**, a Baroque clock tower and local landmark, there are excellent views over the Campiña. At the top of the Cuesta de Jesús, the sixteenth-century **Santa María del Soterraño** (open service times 7–9pm), with an *artesonado* Mudéjar ceiling, Plateresque doorway and an impressive *sagrario* with a sculpture of Christ in a *camarín* by Donaire Trexo, is Aguilar's best church.

At the foot of this hill, the **Turismo**, Cuesta de Jesús 2 (daily 10am–2pm; ☏957 66 15 67) can provide information on the town and the Sierra Subetica. If you're looking for **accommodation**, the central *Hostal-Restaurante Queen*, c/Pescadería 6 (☏957 66 02 22; ❷), just off the Plaza de San José, has decent a/c en-suite rooms with TV. Aguilar's best **place to eat** is *La Casona*, on the edge of town along the Puente Genil road, with large helpings, reasonable prices and a *menú* for around €8.

Some 4km southwest of Aguilar along the A309 and easily walkable, the **Laguna de Zóñar** is the largest of a group of little-known inland salt lakes. Visited in winter by large numbers of **migrating waterfowl**, this time of year is best for spotting white-headed duck, a species that once almost disappeared but is now on the increase. Other species that can be seen here include red-crested pochard, mallard, great-crested grebe, tufted duck and marsh harrier. In summer there's less to see, although sometimes flamingos fly in from the Fuente de Piedra in nearby Málaga, for a change of scene. There are observation **hides** as well as an **information centre** (April–Sept Tues–Sun 9am–2pm & 6–8pm, Oct–March Tues–Sun 9am–2pm & 4–6pm; ☏957 33 52 52). You can gain access to routes around the lake and the hides when the centre is closed. Other lakes in this group include the Laguna del Rincón, north of Moriles, and the Laguna de Tiscar, north of Puente Genil, both of which, unlike this one, tend to dry up in summer.

Cabra

At Monturque, 9km south of Aguilar, there's a turn-off to Moriles, the other great *Montilla* name but in truth a dull village, and only to be sought out if you're a wine aficionado. Much more rewarding is the A342 road which heads

The decline of the railway in this part of Andalucía has had a beneficial knock-on effect for walkers and cyclists. The old line of the *Tren de Aceite* (olive oil train) which was closed in the 1980s has now been transformed into a rambling and biking route linking the towns and villages of Puente Genil, Lucena, Cabra, Doña Mencía, Zuheros and Luque with a further extension planned to the east. Some of the stations along the route have been transformed into bars, restaurants and information centres. There are two outdoor activity centres and at its eastern end the route passes La Laguna del Conde (aka Laguna Salobral), the largest lagoon in the Subbética with a wealth of birdlife and its own information centre. The Centro de Interpretación for the whole project is located in Cabra (see below). For more information see ⓦ www.viasverdes.com.

12km east from Monturque to **CABRA**, another pleasant Campiña town. Possessing an old quarter with steep, winding streets lined with *rejas* – many holding pots sprouting colourful geraniums in summer – and a number of Baroque mansions, it's a lovely place to wander for an hour or so, or even stop over. At the end of the town, near the castle, the Baroque **Iglesia de la Asuncíon** (open service times, try 7–9pm), built over a mosque, is surrounded by palms and cypresses. It has a fine portal with twisted marble Solomonic pillars, and inside, an altar of red and black jasper together with fine choir stalls. The church of **San Juan Bautista** (open service times, try 7–9pm) in the old quarter – Visigothic in origin but much altered since – is reckoned to be one of Spain's oldest, with Moorish and Baroque features added. The Casa de Cultura, c/Martín Belda 27, holds a modest **archeological museum** with local finds from the prehistoric, Visigothic, Roman and Moorish periods. Just to the north of the central Parque Alcántara Romero the town's ancient **Plaza de Toros**, built in 1857, is also worth a look (its gate is usually left open and you're free to look around).

On the road leading east out of town towards Priego de Córdoba, there's a wooded picnic and swimming area, **La Fuente del Río**, centred around a natural spring which is the source of the Río Cabra. Seven kilometres beyond this, a road on the left climbs 6km to the **Ermita de la Virgen de la Sierra**, a hermitage sited at an altitude of over 1200m from where there are stupendous **views** west towards the valley of the Guadalquivir, and east to the mountains of the Sierra Nevada. This is also the starting point for a hike to Zuheros (see box, p.413) At the start of the road to the Ermita the outstanding ⚜ *Venta Los Pelaos* is a great place for a **meal**, and has economically priced dishes and a terrace, though you'll struggle to get a table on Sunday lunch times.

Near the Fuente del Rio, Cabra's former railway station, signed on the left along the Avendia de Gongóra 500m before the Fuente itself, has been transformed into a **Centro de Interpretación** (Mon–Fri 10am–4pm, Sat & Sun ring ⓣ 957 52 31 56) for the Vía Verde (see above) and has information on walking and cycling (mountain bikes can be hired) along the route; the building also houses a *cafetería* and **museum** – complete with an original steam engine from the *Tren de Aceite* (oil train) – documenting the history of the line.

Practicalities

Cabra's **Turismo** is at c/Mayor s/n, close to the Asunción church (Mon–Fri 10am–1.30pm & 5–7.30pm, Sat & Sun 10am–2pm; ⓣ 957 52 34 93, ⓦ www .turismodecabra.es) and can supply a town map. Opposite the Casa de Cultura (see above), Ciberia, c/Santa Rosalía 5 (daily 11am–2pm & 6–8pm) has **internet** access. **Places to stay** in Cabra are usually easy to come by; you could try the very friendly *Pensión Guerrero*, c/Pepita Jiménez 7 (℡957 52 05 07; ❸; ten percent discount for *Rough Guide* readers with this guide), with en-suite rooms with TV, close to the Parque Alcántara Romero (a tree-lined garden in the centre). Slightly more upmarket and west of the Turismo, the *Hospedería Horno Grande*, c/Muñiz Terrones 17 (℡957 52 44 77, ⓦwww.hospederiahornogrande.com; ❹), offers attractive a/c en-suite rooms in an elegant town house and there's a rooftop pool. Alternatively, on the outskirts along the A318 heading towards Baena, the *Hotel Fuente Las Piedras* (℡957 52 97 40, ⓦwww.mshoteles.com; ❹ with breakfast) is a pleasant hotel with its own restaurant and tempting garden pool.

There are numerous bars and **places to eat** around the town; one of the best is *Mesón El Vizconde*, c/Martín Belda 16, near the tourist office (℡957 52 17 02; main dishes €9–25) where there's also a less expensive weekday *menú* for around €10. The popular *Mesón San Martín*, with a terrace on the focal Plaza de España, faces the Ayuntamiento and serves up a range of economical *raciónes*. Facing the bullring the *Rincón Gallego*, Avda. de Andalucía 1 (Tues–Sun), is a great little Galician restaurant with a very good weekday *menú* for €9.50 and tapas at the bar. One of the most remarkable places to visit is Cabra's extraordinary ❧ *Cervecería Botinero*, Avda. Fernando Pallares 3, off the south end of Parque Alcantara Romero, which stocks an amazing five hundred beers from around the world, more than two hundred whiskies, a bewildering number of brandies and over three hundred wines, boasting impressive *reserva* and *gran reserva* vintages dating back to 1927.

Lucena

Surrounded by hills covered with vines and olives, **LUCENA**, 11km down the N331 from Monturque, is a large industrial town that makes its money from furniture production and the manufacture of the great *tinajas*, or earthenware urns, used in the making of Montilla. However, once you've penetrated the rather drab outskirts, Lucena's revamped town centre is not without charm and there are a handful of sights well worth a look. A centre of learning in Moorish times, Lucena fell into Christian hands in 1240 when it was besieged by the armies of Fernando III El Santo, following which event most of its churches and other monuments were erected.

A good place to make for first is the focal **Plaza del Coso** (aka Plaza de España) overlooked by the **Castillo del Moral** whose tower, the Torre del Moral, is the surviving remnant of an earlier castle where Boabdil, the last sultan of Granada, was briefly imprisoned by Isabel la Católica in 1483. The castle now houses the tourist office and an interesting **archeological museum** (entered through the Turismo; Tues–Fri 9am–2pm & 6–8pm, Sat & Sun 11am–2pm & 6–8pm; free) which focuses on Lucena's role in Roman times as a centre of *alfarería* (pottery). The town's other major monument is the nearby church of **San Mateo** (daily 7.30am–1.15pm & 7–9.30pm; free) on the Plaza Nueva, a short walk northwest of the castle, housing one of the Baroque glories of the province. The church was started in the fifteenth century over a former mosque and has a superb Mannerist *retablo* and a beautiful eighteenth-century Baroque *sagrario*, with painted stucco cherubs and a feast of decorative detail topped off by a remarkable cupola, all the work of local artist Antonio de Castro.

At the town's southern end of town, a road climbs to the **Sanctuario de Nuestra Señora de Araceli** (daily 8am–9.30pm; free), Lucena's much-venerated 900-metre-high hill-top shrine to the Virgin. The six-kilometre trip is only really worth doing if you've got your own transport, though note that at weekends and in fine weather the car park and small café at the summit are often full to bursting point. The eighteenth-century Baroque shrine has plenty of over-the-top polychrome decor and an image of the Virgin in a *camarín*. Perhaps the best reason for a trip here is the stunning **views** which, weather permitting, allow you to look out over five of Andalucía's eight provinces.

Practicalities

The Castillo del Moral houses a helpful **Turismo** (Tues–Fri 9am–2pm & 6–8pm, Sat & Sun 11am–2pm & 6–8pm; ☎957 51 32 82, ⓦwww.turlucena.com) who can provide a town map. For a **place to stay**, the former eighteenth-century Convento de Nuestra Señora de la Victoria, the central *Hotel Santo Domingo*, c/Juan Jiménez Cuenca 16 (☎957 51 11 00, ⓦwww.mshoteles.com; ❹), must rank as one of the most beautiful hotels in Andalucía. The convent's former cloister has been transformed into a stunning patio lounge (where non-guests can enjoy a drink). A cheaper and good-value alternative is the friendly *Hotel Veracruz*, c/Veracruz 1 (☎957 50 03 00, ⓔhotelveracruz@infonegocio.com; ❸), a couple of blocks north of the Turismo, with a/c rooms, while the best budget deal is at the welcoming *Hostal Sara*, c/Cabrillana 49 (☎957 51 61 51; ❷), a couple of blocks west of *Hotel Santo Domingo*, which offers a/c en-suite rooms with TV.

Lucena's size and high turnover of business travellers means that there's plenty of choice when it comes **eating and drinking** plus a bevy of good **tapas bars**. A full list of these can be obtained from the Turismo but a couple of decent central ones are *Gambrinus*, c/Montenegro 14, with plenty of *ambiente* and the nearby *Olympo*, c/El Peso 35, for *media raciónes* and which also has a restaurant. For a more formal meal the *Hotel Santo Domingo* has its own stylish restaurant with a *menú* for around €15. A more atmospheric choice is *Golem*, Condesa Carmen Pizarro 8, a hundred metres south of the Castillo de Moral, a stylish new bar-restaurant partly housed inside a former eleventh-century synagogue; the food is *andaluz* with a modern slant and it also mounts art shows and cultural events. *El Valle*, c/Federico García Lorca 14, (reached by following c/El Peso eastwards from Plaza Nueva) is another excellent restaurant and tapas bar with a weekday *menú* for €11, plus it has a terrace.

Rute

The scenic N331 Málaga road continues south from Lucena to **Benamejí**, 20km away, a pleasant agricultural village with a couple of *fondas*, close to the provincial border. However, the more interesting route lies along the road (CP167) which turns off left 8km out of Lucena, heading towards the small town of **RUTE**. Twelve kilometres from the turning, the whitewashed town, sited picturesquely on a hill overlooked by the hazy Sierra de Rute behind, comes into view. Beyond a ruined Moorish castle and a Baroque church, it has few monuments to attract visitors and Rute's fame throughout Andalucía is based on a far more potent allure: the manufacture of a lethal **anís** (aniseed), the local eau de vie, with springwater from the Sierra. It comes in varying strengths and the variations on the *anís* theme can be tasted at the twenty or so small *bodegas* scattered around the town; *Bodega Machaquita*, Paseo del Fresno 7, is regarded as one of the best.

A guided tour at the **Museo del Anís** (Mon–Sat 9am–2pm & 4–7pm; ⓦwww.museodelanis.com; €1) on the Paseo del Fresno square will tell you all you need to know about the making of *anís* and its history, with a chance to taste and buy at the end. There's a **tourist office** in the Parque Nuestra Señora del Carmen (Mon–Fri 8am–3pm; ☎957 53 29 29), close to the landmark Anís monument (complete with copper still) on the road through, who can provide a town map.

3

Save the donkey

One of Rute's more surprising features is a **sanctuary** for ill-treated donkeys. Founded by local draper Pasqual Rovira in 1989, ADEBO (Association for the Defence of the Donkey) is Spain's first-ever donkey refuge, and well worth a visit. Spain's donkey population has shrunk dramatically from over one million fifty years ago to a current 100,000 – most of which are crossbreeds. Only a few hundred remain of the five breeds of pure Spanish *burro* that have existed on the peninsula since pre-Roman times. One of these, the *raza córdobes*, was so renowned in the eighteenth century for its strength that George Washington asked the Spanish king, Carlos III, to send him some for his farm.

Used for centuries as beasts of burden, the **donkeys** often receive brutal treatment at the hands of uncaring owners. Working with scarce resources, and using the meagre profits from the family drapery business, Pasqual and his wife Quika have devoted their lives to ending this cruelty and saving the Spanish breeds – including the *cordobés* – from extinction. They were greatly helped in this when Queen Sofía rang Pasqual in 1999 after reading about his work and offered her support, expressing a wish to visit the sanctuary. This changed everything, and previously sceptical politicians in Córdoba and Madrid became suddenly enthusiastic.

The work of the sanctuary continues with the aid of voluntary contributions, and both the queen (who visited the sanctuary again in 2008) and her husband King Juan Carlos have sponsored donkeys, as have the late writer Camilo José Cela, Bill Clinton (remarking that the donkey is the mascot of the Democratic Party) and Fidel Castro. Tenor Placido Domingo also donated royalties from his recorded version of the popular Christmas carol *Arre, Borriquito* ("Gee up, donkey") to the centre.

A charming and voluble *cordobés*, Pasqual has a fund of horror stories concerning the animals he's rescued: one poor beast spent five years locked up in a small shed (after arriving at the sanctuary he was christened Mandela) whilst another, a jenny named Alondra, was found abandoned halfway down a ravine with a washing machine tied around her neck. The sanctuary is normally open daily from 9am until noon. To get there, continue uphill from the Museo de Anís in the Paseo del Fresno, following the road for the campsite. The sanctuary (℡957 53 20 32, ✆mobile 610841720) will provide directions, or enquire at the Turismo (℡957 53 29 29) who can supply a map.

Rute's only **accommodation** options are two hotels sited close to each other at the southern end of the town. The first is the comfortable *Hotel María Luisa*, Ctra. Lucena–Loja 22 (℡957 53 80 96, Ⓦwww.hotelmarialuisa.es; ❸ with breakfast), on the A331, with an excellent garden pool. A couple of hundred metres west of here down the A344, the pleasant *Hotel El Mirador* (℡957 53 94 04, Ⓦwww.miradorderute.com; ❸) offers rooms with views over the sierra and also has a pool. Both hotels have their own decent **restaurants** serving economical *menús*. Other good places in the town include *Restaurante Casa Paco*, c/Blas Infante s/n, near the Anís monument on the main road through, and the nearby *Casa Hernández*, both serving inexpensive *menús del día*.

Iznájar

Reached by following the scenic A331 road for 13km from Rute, **IZNÁJAR** is a picturesque, whitewashed farming village, with a spectacular location overlooking a reservoir. Despite the beauty, this is a place of long-standing poverty; it was here in 1861 that peasants, or *braceros*, revolted against the injustices of the landowning class – an uprising that was viciously suppressed.

Of Moorish origin (from the Arabic *hizn*, fort, and *achar*, refuge), Iznájar's ruined **Alcazaba** was constructed in the eighth century, and the church of **Santiago** was added to its interior in the sixteenth. In the arch leading to the church is a small **tourist office** (Mon–Fri 9.30am–1.30pm & 4.30–7.30pm, Sat & Sun 10am–2pm; ℡mobile 649218783, ⓦwww.iznajar.net). From the plaza next to the church there are stunning **views** over the *embalse* and village below. Currently the only **place to stay** is the *Cortijo La Haza*, (℡957 33 40 51, ⓦwww.cortizolahaza.com; ❹) a pretty farmhouse sited 7km out of the village with comfortable rooms, a pool and its own restaurant (with vegetarian options); ring for directions. **Camping** for the odd night is allowed on the nearby Valdearenas beach fronting the *embalse*. For **food** you could try *Restaurante Rosi* on the road towards Loja; alternatives are *El Montecillo* on the Salinas road near the *gasolinera*, or *El Charcon*, a good bar-restaurant 2km along the Rute road on the left. In summer *Mesón Valdearenas*, a "beach" *chiringuito* on the shores of the *embalse* is also popular.

Twenty kilometres south of Iznájar close to the junction with the A92 *autovía*, a signed entrance on the left indicates a long drive, at the end of which lies the grandiose *Finca La Bobadilla* (℡902 10 10 01, ⓦwww.barcelolabobadilla.com; ❾), one of the most exclusive hotels in Spain. Surrounded by acres of woodland and built on the model of a "typical" Andalucian village, it has appealed to guests as diverse as Tom Cruise, King Juan Carlos and many Japanese tourists, for whom this is a favourite place to get married. To stay at this Iberian Xanadu will cost you a king's ransom too (currently around €350 per night for the cheapest high-season room, but serious guests take suites), and dinner at the à la carte restaurant – supplied by its own farm on the estate – doesn't come cheap either. Call in for a drink at the bar if you're curious.

The Ruta del Aceite

This itinerary towards Priego de Córdoba, known as the **Ruta del Aceite** (Oil Route), follows the N432 southeast out of Córdoba. It takes in the olive-oil producing region centred on **Baena** before visiting some of the province's most picturesque villages, including Luque and Zuheros.

Espejo and Castro del Río

At **ESPEJO**, 31km to the south of Córdoba, an impressive Moorish castle looms above the white-walled village, vineyards and olive groves spread out below. The fourteenth-century Gothic-Mudéjar **castillo** is the property of the dukes of Osuna, the great ruling family based in Osuna to the southwest (see p.312), which once owned an enormous tract of Andalucía. The nearby and recently restored Gothic-Renaissance church of **San Bartolomé** dating from the fifteenth and sixteenth centuries, is also worth seeking out for its fine *retablo mayor* by Pedro Romana and its *artesonado* ceiling.

Sited on a low hill on the north bank of the Río Guadajoz, **CASTRO DEL RÍO**, 9km on from Espejo, has a Roman **bridge** spanning the river and a ruined Moorish **castle** built on the foundations of a Roman fort. The village also claims a footnote in Roman history as this is believed to be the place where Pompey's troops rested up prior to their showdown battle with Caesar in 45 BC at nearby Montilla (Munda) which ended the civil war and, briefly, gave Caesar control of the whole Roman world. The **Iglesia de la Asunción**, founded in the thirteenth century with later additions, has a fine if somewhat eroded Plateresque portal, and the **Ayuntamiento** preserves the prison in which Cervantes was locked up for a week in 1568 when, then working as a tax collector, he was falsely accused of fiddling the books. A modern sculpture of Don Quijote, honouring the great writer's literary creation, now adorns the exterior.

Baena

The road continues south into the area geographically known as the Sierra Subbética Cordobesa, a rugged, rambling spur of the Cordillera Betica range in the province's southeastern corner, and now officially designated the **Parque Natural de las Sierras Subbéticas** (@www.subbetica.es). Beyond Castro del Río the N432 climbs gently through hills covered with olive groves until it reaches Andalucía's most celebrated oil production centre, **BAENA**. Famous for centuries for the high quality of its olive oil, the huge metal tanks for storing the oil can be seen on the outskirts of town. Baena was an important and populous place in the Moorish period, but the town shrunk as a result of emigration in the twentieth century. However, in recent years it has made a comeback based upon its oil and agricultural wealth and today exudes a busy and prosperous air.

Arrival, information and accommodation

On arrival, you should aim for the **Turismo**, c/Virrey del Pino 5 (Tues–Sat 10am–2pm & 6–8pm, ☏957 67 17 57), slightly east of the focal Plaza de España, which can supply a useful town map. Finding **places to stay** outside the Semana Santa period is not a problem and all budgets are catered for. The central and friendly *Hostal Rincón*, c/Llano del Rincón 13, off Plaza de España (☏957 67 02 23; ❷), has en-suite a/c rooms with TV. Nearby, the good-value *Hotel Iponuba*, c/Nicolas Alcalá 9 (☏957 67 00 75, ✉iponuba@interbook.es; ❸),

---

Baena's oil for connoisseurs

Spain produces, and probably consumes, more **olive oil** than any other country in the world. However, this wasn't always so, and when the Greeks introduced the olive to the peninsula in the first millennium BC, it was regarded with suspicion by the native Iberians who went on using their traditional lard. Only with the arrival of the Roman legions did they begin to acquire a taste for it, and under Roman supervision Hispanic oil became the finest and most expensive in the empire. Later, sophisticated Moorish invaders taught the Iberians better cultivation techniques, as well as culinary and medicinal possibilities. The Moorish, and now Spanish, names for oil and the olive, *aceite* and *aceituna*, are a legacy of this time.

Today, Spaniards are great connoisseurs of quality oil and **Baena** has its own official **denominación de origen**, backed by an official regulatory body, the *Consejo Regulador*, guaranteeing the standards attained by strict methods of production. Baena's finest oil stands comparison with the best in Europe, and *almazaras* (oil mills), such as that operated for several generations by the Núñez de Prado family in the town, take a great amount of care at every stage in the production process. The olives cultivated on the estate are all harvested by hand prior to being ground to a paste on ancient granite stone mills. The "free run" oil – with no further pressure applied – that results from this process is regarded as the *grand cru* of the oil trade and it takes eleven kilos of olives to yield just one litre of such oil. With a markedly low acid content and an unfatty, concentrated flavour, this oil is far too good (and expensive) for cooking and is sparingly used to flavour gazpacho – in Córdoba province, *salmorejo* – or tasted on a morsel of bread as a *tapa*.

The Núñez de Prado mill, Avda. de Cervantes 15 (June–Sept Mon–Sat 8am–3pm, Oct–May Mon–Fri 9am–2pm & 4–6.30pm, Sat 9am–1pm; ☏957 67 01 41), with parts dating from the eighteenth century, is close to Plaza de España and can be visited, although most of the action takes place between November and February when the harvested olives are pressed. Their shop sells a range of oils including the celebrated *flor de aceite* at bargain prices.

is more upmarket with a garage. Near the Turismo, the elegant, aptly named *Casa Grande*, Avda. Cervantes 35 (☏957 67 19 05, ⓦwww.lacasagrande.es; ❺) is a very comfortable – if a tad overpriced – three-star hotel inside a converted mansion. Perhaps the most attractive budget option is the Ayuntamiento's *Albergue Ruta del Califato*, c/Coro 7 (☏656 25 27 17, ⓦwww.baenarural.com; ❷ with breakfast), a **youth hostel** close to the church of Santa María in the upper town. Most rooms are doubles (sharing bathrooms) and there are dorms charging €15 per person per bed. Add in spectacular views, a bar-restaurant for breakfast and meals with a €7.50 *menú*, and it all adds up to a praiseworthy piece of municipal enterprise.

The Town

Most of Baena's sights lie in the upper town, reached by following c/Juan Rabadan from Plaza de España to the **Plaza de la Constitución**. The eighteenth-century arcaded **almacén** (warehouse) is now a cultural centre and another part of the same building houses *Mesón Casa del Monte*, a good tapas bar and restaurant (see p.412).

From the same square, c/Henares leads uphill again to the eighteenth-century **Casa de la Tercia** (Tues–Sat 11am–2pm & 6–8pm, Sun 11am–2pm; free), an elegant *casa señorial* that contains an interesting **archeological museum** (with much about ancient olive oil production) and the **Museo de Semana Santa**, which covers the history of Baena's Holy Week and its drums. Continuing along c/Henares and veering left brings you to the early sixteenth-century Gothic church of **Santa María** (service times only, try 7–8pm) with a fine portal and a Moorish tower, probably the minaret of a former mosque. The church is a sad testament to the ferocity of the Civil War, during which this beautiful edifice was put to the torch. Ruined and roofless for many years, it has now undergone a substantial restoration which features a magnificent vaulted roof in wood.

▲ Olive oil factory

The fine iron *reja* (altar screen) also survives as a reminder of former days. An image of what was lost, including a precious *retablo*, is preserved in a faded photograph hanging in the sacristy (the Turismo also displays a copy in its entry lobby). Behind the church is the sixteenth-century Mudéjar convent of **Madre de Dios** (open service times 7–8pm), with a fine late Gothic porch, and equally fine *retablo*, *coro* and *artesonados* in its church. A little way northwest of the Plaza de España, the **Museo del Olivar**, c/Cañada 7 (Tues–Sun 11am–2pm & 6–8pm, Sun 11am–2pm; ℡957 69 16 41; free) pays tribute to the history and development of olive oil production in the area with displays explaining history and production methods plus a chance to sample and buy Baena's famed oils. One section also deals with the modern uses of oil and its by-products – Baena now has a power station fuelled by olive waste.

Besides oil, Baena is also famous for its Semana Santa rituals, which include a **drum-rolling contest** when the streets are filled with the deafening sound of up to two thousand drums being struck simultaneously. From Wednesday to Friday during Holy Week is the time to avoid, unless you have ear plugs.

Eating and drinking

There are plenty of places for **eating and drinking** around the centre; the *Hostal Rincón* (see p.410) has a very good restaurant with a *menú* for €9 and, next door, *Primero de la Mañana* is a good place for **breakfast**. One restaurant a cut above the rest is *Mesón Casa del Monte*, in the upper town on Plaza de la Constitución, facing the Ayuntamiento with an economical *menú*. Another excellent place to eat is the *Mesón de los Arcos*, on the eastern side of the Parque Ramón Santaella near to the *Hotel Casa Grande* (see p.411); besides tapas and *raciónes* it also offers an excellent value *menú* for €8.50 and has a terrace.

Luque

Seven kilometres beyond Baena, a right turn leads to the attractive village of **LUQUE**, spread out below a daunting rocky outcrop topped by the almost obligatory castle. Dating from the thirteenth century, the ruins of the **Moorish castillo** are worth a look, and beside them is the golden limestone facade of the Gothic-Renaissance church of **La Asunción** with a *retablo* whose central image of San Juan is attributed to Martínez Montañés. There is no accommodation, but for **food** the *Bar-Restaurante La Plancha*, across from the church, is a lively local meeting place, serving up tapas and *raciónes* as well as *platos combinados*.

Zuheros

Nestling in a gorge backed by steep rock cliffs some 5km west of Luque, **ZUHEROS** is another stunningly beautiful Subbética village. A cluster of white houses tumbles down the hill below a romantic Moorish **castle** built on and into the rock (see below for visiting details). Later Christian additions were made after it fell to Fernando III (El Santo) in 1240 and became a frontier bastion against the kingdom of Granada.

The nearby early seventeenth-century **Iglesia de los Remedios** (open service times 7–9pm) has a fine *retablo* as well as a tower built on the remains of a minaret from an earlier mosque, while on the neighbouring small square a **mirador** gives a great view over the surrounding countryside. On the edge of this square and facing *Bar-Mesón de los Palancos* is the village's **archeological museum** (guided visits Sat, Sun & hols on the hour: April–Sept 10am–2pm & 5–7pm; Oct–March 10am–2pm & 4–6pm; outside these times enquire at the *Hotel Zuhayra* or ring ℡957 69 45 45; €1.90 including guided castle visit), displaying fascinating finds from the Cueva de los Murciélagos (see p.413) as well as exhibits from the Roman and Moorish periods. A well-presented **Museum of Customs and Popular Arts** (Tues–Sun 10.30am–2pm & 5.30–8.30pm; €2) displaying implements, furniture and decor from bygone days can be found at c/Santo s/n near the *Mesón Atalaya* (see p.414).

In the hills above the village, reached by a paved, four-kilometre road, the **Cueva de los Murciélagos** (guided visits April–Sept Sat, Sun & hols 11am, 12.30pm, 2pm, 5pm & 6.30pm; €5.40; ring ☎957 69 45 45 or *Hotel Zuhayra* for winter hours and to see the cave outside these times) is spectacular and well worth a visit. First explored in 1938, its name means "cave of the bats" and the hour-long tour (bring a sweater) takes in impressive stalagmites, stalactites and awesome rock formations while the guide relates the fascinating story (revealed by recent excavations) of the remarkable **Neolithic cave paintings** and human remains found here.

Practicalities

A small **tourist office** (Tues–Sun 10am–2pm; ☎957 69 46 92), is located just below the village on the Baena road and has **information** about renting *casas rurales* in the area. Downhill from the castle there's a charming **place to stay**, the ⚘ *Hotel Zuhayra*, c/Mirador 10 (☎957 69 46 93, 🅦www.zercahoteles.com; ❸ with breakfast; ten percent discount for *Rough Guide* readers with this guide), which uses the village's ancient Moorish name and makes a perfect base to

Walks around Zuheros

With the aid of a good map (1:50,000 CNIG sheet 967, or the 1:50,000 *Parque Natural Sierras Subbéticas* published by the Junta de Andalucía), you can follow the Bailón river valley south from Zuheros to the Ermita de Nuestra Virgen de la Sierra near Cabra, a splendid **walk** through rugged hill country. The distance is about 14km, with a stiff climb at the end to the Ermita. From here, you could continue 13km to Cabra, taking a taxi back to Zuheros (about €20) if you don't want to stay overnight in Cabra itself. An alternative way of doing this walk (and conveniently avoiding the steep climb to the Ermita) is to do it in reverse, taking a taxi from Zuheros to the Ermita, then following the valley of the Bailón back to Zuheros. For taxis from and to Zuheros ask at the tourist office or the *Hotel Zuhayra* (see above).

A shorter and circular variation on this walk starts in the same way by descending into the Bailón Gorge where you should take a zigzag track following the river. Cross the river five times before meeting the junction of the Arroyo (watercourse) de Moreno and Zareilla (just after some concrete manholes) where you should bear left and follow the stream up a verdant valley, keeping the stream on your right. When you reach some white buildings on the left cross the stream and bear left ascending, keeping an eye out for a ruined *cortijo* on the right. Continue up and to the right, passing another manhole and zigzag through woods to emerge onto a wide, open plain. Continue east past a white *cortijo* on the right until you come to two springs: this is Fuenfría. Here turn right to pick up a well-established goat track which is now waymarked in red and green. Pass below the ruined Cortijo de Fuenfría which is a splendid picnic **lunch stop**. Follow the waymarked path until you reach a clearing and a junction. Fork left here and quit the waymarked path and soon fork left again into the woods to emerge at the Bailón Gorge. Follow the track down to a junction. Here you can return to Zuheros by the way you came.

Zuheros's tourist office (or the *Hotel Zuhayra*) also sells a guide book *Walking in the Subbética Natural Park* detailing a number **walks** in this zone by local resident and walking guide Clive Jarman. Any queries regarding the above walks can be directed to the manager of the *Hotel Zuhayra*, Juan Carlos Ábalos, who speaks English, or to Clive Jarman, who can be contacted on ☎957 69 47 96.

explore the surrounding natural park; guests get free use of the village swimming pool. They also stock copies of local resident and walking guide Clive Jarman's book *Walking in the Subbética Natural Park* which details a number of excellent hikes; the hotel can also arrange canoeing, mountain biking and bird-watching excursions in the surrounding natural park. Fully equipped studios and apartments are available to rent from the *Señorio de Zuheros* restaurant c/Hornos 3 (☎957 69 55 27; ❸–❹) near the castle.

The *Zuhayra* has a very good **restaurant** with a *menú*, and there are a couple of lively bars for **tapas** and **raciónes** – *Bar-Mesón Los Palancos*, facing the castle with its own restaurant, and *Mesón Atalaya*, c/Santo 58, at the eastern end of the village, next to the turn-off to the Cueva de los Murciélagos.

Doña Mencía

Not quite as pretty as some of its neighbours, **DOÑA MENCÍA**, 5km to the west of Zuheros, is a sizeable oil and wine centre lying at the foot of a slope covered with silver-leaved olives, interrupted by the occasional vineyard. On the town's western flank there are the walls and bastions of a fifteenth-century **castle** next to which there's an elegant carved stone **portal**, all that remains of an eighteenth-century Dominican monastery destroyed in the Civil War and now incorporated into a new municipal open-air theatre. Off the main square (Plaza Andalucía) at the end of c/Juan Valera is a small **town museum** (Tues–Sat 5–7.30pm; ☎957 67 60 20), c/Juan Ramón Jiménez 8, on the site of the house of the nineteenth-century novelist Juan Valera, whose best-known work, *Pepita Jiménez*, was set in nearby Cabra.

An excellent and welcoming small *hostal*, just off Plaza Andalucía, ⚞ *Casa Morejón*, c/Obispo Cubero 3 (☎957 67 61 69; ❶) offers remarkably economical en-suite rooms around a charming tiled interior patio; it also serves a bargain *menú* for €8 in its restaurant. There are a surprising number of wine *bodegas* here, and a clutch of **places to eat** around the pleasant and palm-fringed Plaza Andalucía. Another good place for a meal is the *Mesón la Cantina*, a lively *venta* housed in the town's disused railway station which uses the former platform as its terrace now looking out on to the Via Verde cycling and hiking route (see box, p.405); there's also a good value *menú*. It lies at the junction with the A318 – near the turn off to Zuheros – on the southern edge of town.

Priego de Córdoba and around

PRIEGO DE CÓRDOBA, 20km southeast of Luque and capital of the Subbética, is one of Andalucía's little-known Baroque wonders offering visitors a feast of superb churches and a remarkable fountain, making it an inviting place to stop over. Situated beneath the province's highest mountain, the 1600m La Tiñosa, the northern approach to the town presents a dramatic view of the whitewashed buildings of its old quarter, laid out along the edge of a pictur-esque escarpment known as the Adarve.

Despite evidence of long prehistoric habitation in nearby caves and a later Roman settlement, it was under the Moors that Medina Bahiga, as Priego was then known, flourished as part of the kingdom of Granada. Following a tug of war between the Moors and Christians during the fourteenth century, in which the town changed hands three times, it finally fell to the Christians in 1341. Recovery from the aftermath of this turbulent era came only in the eighteenth century when, in 1711, Priego became a dependency of the dukes of Medinaceli. An economic resurgence based on the production of silk and textiles poured great wealth into the town and it was during this time that most of the **Baroque churches**, Priego's outstanding attraction today, were constructed or remodelled.

In the nineteenth century, though, the industry found it hard to compete with cheap cotton textiles produced in Catalunya and Britain, and a slow decline set in. The Europe-wide slump in textiles in the 1950s and 1960s caused by imports from Asia accelerated the problems and, as factories closed, many people emigrated to seek work elsewhere. Today the remnants of the textile industry, along with farming, are the town's main employers.

The towns and villages surrounding Priego generally lack anything compelling in the way of sights, but two outstanding exceptions are the village of **Almedinilla**, where a remarkable Roman villa has recently been discovered, and, a little further afield, the picturesque town of **Montefrío** and its nearby prehistoric site to the southeast, also well worth a visit.

Arrival, information and accommodation

Buses arriving in Priego will drop you in the central Plaza de la Constitución although the actual bus station is a five-minute walk to the west of the centre on c/Nuestra Señora de los Remedios. There are easy connections with Córdoba, Granada and Málaga.

The town's helpful **turismo**, c/Carrera de las Monjas 1 (Tues–Sat 10am–2pm & 4.30–7pm, Sun 10am–2pm; ☎957 70 84 20, ⓦwww.turismodepriego.com), effectively on the central Plaza Constitución, can provide a detailed **map** and has information (also on their website) on *casas rurales* to rent in the surrounding area. Internet access is available at the central Locutorio Priego, c/Antonio de la Barrera 4 (daily 10.30am–2.30pm & 5–10pm).

PRIEGO DE CÓRDOBA

RIBERA MOLINOS · Carnicerías Reales · ADARVE · CABALLOS · Iglesia San Pedro · Castillo · BARRIO DE LA VILLA · BAJONDILLO · SAN PEDRO ALCANTARA · AVDA DE AMERICA · RAMON Y CAJAL · LUIS BRAILLE · SENECA · CONDE SUPERUNDA · CAVA · Ayuntamiento · Iglesia de San Juan · PL. SAN PEDRO · PLAZA DE ABAD PALOMINO · Iglesia de la Asunción · REAL · STA. ANA · ARGENTINA · RIBERA · ALVAREZ · PASEO DE COLOMBIA · PUERTA SOL · VELERO · Museo Histórico · CARRERA DE LAS MONJAS · Locutorio @ Priego · Turismo ⓘ · PL. CONSTITUCION · PL. ANDALUCIA · SOLANA · MESONES · RAMIREZ · Iglesia de la Aurora · Iglesia de las Angustias · Iglesia del Mercedes · PL. PALENQUE · AZAHAR · MORALES · RIO · TORREJON · ALTA · PUERTAS NUEVAS · F. FCO · DEAN PADILLO · PASILLO · LAVADERO · POLO · ENMEDIO PALENQUE · TUCUMAN · PEREZ MUÑOZ · Museo Niceto Alcalá Zamora · MONTENEGRO · NUEVA · STA. TERESA · BUEN SUCESO · Iglesia de San Francisco · OBISPO PEREZ MUÑOZ · CANA · USCALDO CALVO · CALLEJON DE LA JOYA · CANO DE FRAILES · Iglesia del Carmen · MALAGA · S. ESTEBAN · Fuente del Rey · Fuente de la Salud

Zagrilla, ⓓ & ⓑ
Bus Station
Ermita del Calvario

0 · 100 m

TAPAS BARS
Bar Río 4
Mesón el Telar 5

RESTAURANTS
Balcón del Adarve 3
El Aljibe 1
El Virrey 2

ACCOMMODATION
Hostal Rafi F
Hotel Huerta de las Palomas D
Hotel Zahori B
La Posada Real C
Río Piscina A
Villa Turística E

The number of **places to stay** in Priego has increased in recent years, prices are reasonable, and there are quite a few very pleasant options. Outside the first week in September when the town celebrates its annual *Feria Real* there's usually no great demand for rooms.

Hostal Rafi c/Isabel la Católica 4 ☎957 54 72 69, ⓦwww.hostalrafi.net. In a tiny street near the main square, this welcoming hostal housed in a refurbished mansion is an excellent deal. Comfortable a/c en-suite rooms come with satellite TV; own car park and restaurant. ❷

Hotel Huerta de las Palomas Ctra. Priego-Zagrilla km 3 ☎957 72 03 05, ⓦwww.zercahoteles.com. Four kilometres northwest of town along the CO230 (direction Zagrilla), this is a stylish four-star hotel with gym, pool and restaurant in rolling Subbética countryside. It offers lots of activities including mountain biking, tennis and hiking. Ten percent discount for *Rough Guide* readers with this guide. ❺ with breakfast.

Hotel Zahori c/Real 2 ☎957 54 72 92, ⓦwww.hotelzahori.es. In the picturesque Barrio de la Villa, this is a charming recent arrival offering excellent a/c en-suite rooms in a refurbished town house. ❸

La Posada Real c/Real 14 ☎957 54 19 10, ⓦwww.laposadareal.com. Another possibility in the Barrio de la Villa, this is an attractive, flower-bedecked little place with cosy, a/c en-suite balcony rooms. Also rents some apartments (❹) nearby. ❷

Río Piscina ☎957 70 01 86, ⓦwww.hotelriopiscina.com. Newly refurbished hotel on the eastern edge of town for spacious a/c terrace rooms overlooking garden pool. Other features include restaurant, tennis court, gardens and a car park. ❸

Villa Turística Aldea de Zagrilla s/n, three kilometres beyond the *Huerta de las Palomas* hotel (see above) along the CO230 leading to Zagrilla ☎957 70 35 03, ⓦwww.villadepriego.com. Built on traditional lines with lots of Moorish-inspired decor, this country hotel has 52 apartment/chalets sited in gardens where water features set the mood. Offers a range of outdoor activities including horseriding and mountain biking. ❹

The Town

The centre of this tranquil town is the Plaza de la Constitución, an elegant square fronted by the **Ayuntamiento**, from where all the monuments are within easy walking distance. By studying the **opening times** (available in list form from the Turismo or downloadable from their web page), it should be possible to see most of Priego's main **churches** (all with free entry) on the same day; though note that some churches close on Sunday and Monday. The Turismo also offers free guided tours of the town.

From the Plaza de la Constitución, head northeast towards the **Barrio de la Villa**, the old quarter, which contains most of Priego's principal monuments. A good place to begin is with the austere Moorish **Castillo** (Mon 11.30am–1.30pm, Tues–Sat 11.30am–1.30pm & 4.30–6.30pm, Sun 11.30am–1.30pm; €2) whose impressive keep dominates the small Plaza de Abad Palomino. Altered in the thirteenth and fourteenth centuries, the interior is now privately owned but can be visited.

Iglesia de la Asunción

In the square's southeast corner lies the first of the Baroque churches, the **Iglesia de la Asunción** (Mon 8.15–9pm, Tues, Thurs, Fri & Sat 11.30am–1.30pm & 8.15–9pm, Wed & Sun 11.30am–1.30pm), its modest whitewashed exterior dating from the sixteenth century. The original Gothic building was remodelled in the Baroque style in the eighteenth century by Jerónimo Sánchez de Rueda, an architect who did a similar job on many of Priego's other churches.

It is inside, however, that the surprises begin: an ornate white stucco Baroque interior leads towards a stunningly beautiful carved Mannerist **retablo** with images attributed to Juan Bautista Vázquez. The greatest surprise of all, though, lies through a portal on the left aisle where you enter the breathtaking **sagrario**, one of the masterpieces of Spanish Baroque. Here, a dazzling symphony of wedding-cake white stuccowork and statuary, punctuated by scrolls and cornices, climbs upwards beyond a balcony into a fabulous cupola illuminated by eight windows. The frothy depth of the stucco plaster was achieved by the use of esparto grass to lend it additional strength – a material which has played a remarkable part in the craft history of Andalucía, even found in hats, baskets and sandals discovered in the Neolithic caves of Granada. This recently restored octagonal chapel is the work of Francisco Javier Pedrajas, a native of Priego and one of a number of leading sculptors, carvers and gilders working in the town at this time. The *altar mayor* and the *sagrario* have been declared national monuments.

Barrio de la Villa and Paseo del Adarve

Before taking in more Baroque mastery, the nearby and delightful **Barrio de la Villa** provides a welcome opportunity for a stroll. The ancient Moorish part of the town, a maze of sinuous whitewashed alleys with balconies and walls loaded with pot plants, leads to a number of typical plazuelas. You should eventually stumble on one of the most charming, the **Plazuela de San Antonio**, replete with palms and wrought-iron *rejas*. Behind the Iglesia de la Asunción, c/Bajondillo leads to the **Paseo de Adarve**, a superb, and originally Moorish, promenade with a spectacular **view** over the valley of the Río Salado and undulating groves of olives stretching to the distant hills.

San Pedro and San Juan de Dios

Just to the west of the castillo, the **Iglesia de San Pedro** (Mon–Sat 10.30am–1.30pm & 8.15–9pm, Sun 11.15am–noon) is another Baroque treat with more stucco and a wonderful **altar mayor** in painted wood and stucco with a delightful domed *camarín* (shrine) behind, which holds a stirring image of the *Inmaculada*. The side chapel of the **Virgen de la Soledad**, with another *camarín*, has an image of the Virgin at the centre of its *retablo* by Pablo de Rojas. To the rear of San Pedro, on c/San Pedro de Alcantara, the **Carnicerías Reales** (Tues–Sat 11.30am–1.30pm & 5–7pm, Sun & Mon 11.30am–1.30pm; €2) is a sixteenth-century abattoir and meat market with a fine cobbled patio. A short distance west of San Pedro the church of **San Juan de Dios** (daily 10am–1pm), with a finely crafted cupola, is an early example of Priego Baroque, completed in 1717.

La Aurora and San Francisco

Moving south along c/Argentina and its continuation c/Álvarez will lead you to the church of **La Aurora**, (Tues–Sat 10am–1pm, Sun 11am–1pm) yet another Baroque gem remodelled from a former *ermita*, whose exuberant facade, with Corinthian and Solomonic pillars topped by a Virgin and flanked by exquisite stone and marble decoration, is only a prelude to the interior. This, now restored to its full glory, is a single-naved Baroque explosion in painted wood and stucco descending from the grey and white cornices, with polychromed figures on its ceiling, dome and walls, to an animated and sumptuously theatrical **retablo**. This *retablo* is a glittering amalgam of *vegetal* and geometrical forms, and the crowning achievement of Juan de Dios Santaella, another native Priego talent, born here in 1716. The church is also home to the **Cofradía de la Aurora**, a brotherhood whose sixteenth-century articles of foundation stipulate that they must proceed through the streets in musical procession every Saturday at midnight. Thus, whatever the weather, this band of men, hatted and cloaked, gather behind their banner and a huge lantern to proceed through the streets singing hymns to *La Aurora* (Our Lady of the Dawn) accompanied by guitars, accordions and tambourines.

▲ Church of La Aurora

Just south of here, along c/Buen Suceso, the **Iglesia de San Francisco** (Mon–Sat 10am–1pm & 7–9pm, Sun 9am–12.30pm) on an elegant old square, is another late-Gothic church that Santaella had a hand in remodelling and which has recently been restored to its former splendour. Once you've admired the facade and portal (both by Santaella), employing contrasting tones of marble, look inside: the *retablo mayor* is a splendid gilded work by Santaella again. The **chapel of Jesús Nazareno** has a sumptuous gilded and polychromed wood and stucco *retablo* by Pedrajas, the creator of the *sagrario* in the Asunción, and is topped off by another extravagant cupola by Santaella. The altarpiece's central image of *Jesús Nazareno* (Christ bearing the Cross) is a fine work, attributed to Pedro de Mena.

The Fuente del Rey and around

At the southwestern end of the town, and easily reached by following c/Río – a street dotted with many fine Baroque portals – to its end, lies the **Fuente del Rey**, a spectacular sixteenth-century 180-jet fountain (with many later additions) which pours water into a number of basins. The highest of these has a sculpture of a lion struggling with a serpent, whilst the second contains a larger late eighteenth-century depiction of Neptune and Amphitrite, the king and queen of the sea. Amphitrite is clutching the dolphin that returned her to Neptune after her attempted escape, incidentally emphasizing the power of the king, the work's intended ideological message, given that over the border in France, monarchs were losing their heads. There are in fact two fountains here, the second being the **Fuente de la Salud**, to the rear of the plaza, a sixteenth-century Italianate work built on the spot, according to legend, where the conquering Alfonso XI pitched his camp in 1341. One of the most tranquil squares in Andalucía, this leafy area is a wonderful place to relax and get away from it all, which is why there are so many seats.

From just beyond the square you can **walk** to the Ermita del Calvario from where there are fine **views** over the town. Take the steps to the left of the Fuente de la Salud.

Another historic building on c/Río at no. 46 is the birthplace of, and now **museum** (Tues–Sat 10am–1.30pm & 4.30–7pm, Sun 10am–1.30; free) dedicated to, Niceto Alcalá Zamora, first president of the ill-fated Spanish republic from 1931 to 1936. Much of the furniture of this middle-class nineteenth-century family mansion survives intact, and you are free to look around.

The rest of the churches and museums

When you've seen the main churches, there are many more almost as good. Just off the Plaza de la Constitución at the start of c/Río, the **Iglesia de las Angustias** (Sat 11am–1pm) is a charming small church and another work by Santaella. The interior has a fine cupola with more typically exuberant polychromed stucco decoration. Further along c/Río, the **Iglesia del Carmen** (Mon–Tues & Thurs–Sun 7.30–8pm plus Sun 11am–1pm) has a *retablo* by Santaella, probably an early work. Finally, to the west on Carrera de las Monjas, the **Iglesia del Mercedes** (Wed 7.30–8pm, Thurs & Fri 10am–1pm) was an ancient hermitage prior to its remodelling in the latter part of the eighteenth century when it was decorated in Rococo style by Pedrajas, highlighted by the four winged archangels at the scalloped corners. Another stunningly ornate snow-white cupola (which is almost Pedrajas's trademark), is balanced by an elegant *retablo* below. The exterior is an incomplete later addition.

Almost opposite the Iglesia de Mercedes, Priego's **Museo Histórico Municipal** (Tues–Sat 10am–1.30pm & 6–8.30pm, Sun 10am–1.30pm; free), c/Monjas 9, is housed in an elegant *señorial* mansion with a fine patio. The interesting collection displays finds from the surrounding area dating from the Paleolithic down to the Roman and Moorish periods.

Eating and drinking

The bars around the main square are good for **breakfast** and **tapas**, and the restaurant attached to the *Hostal Rafi* is especially good with a *menú* for €9. The *Hotel Zahori's* mid-priced restaurant (see p.416) in the Barrio de la Villa is also worth a try. Other tapas and *raciónes* bars include the highly popular *Bar Río* at the start of c/Río and the equally good *Mesón El Telar*, c/Buen Suceso 2, close to the Iglesia de San Francisco. **Restaurants** are few, but *El Aljibe*, c/Abad Palomino 7, opposite the Iglesia de la Asuncion, is built over a Moorish bathhouse (which you can glimpse through a glass floor in the lower dining room) and has some aptly Moorish inspired dishes and a lunch *menú* for €10; there's also an attractive outdoor terrace. Another good place is *El Virrey*, c/Solana 16, off Plaza San Pedro, preparing a wide range of local dishes and again with another €10 *menú* which you may need to ask for. Priego's most celebrated restaurant is the *Balcón del Adarve*, Paseo de Colombia 36 (☎957 54 70 75; main dishes €10–18), close to the promenade it's named after and part of which it uses as a pleasant terrace; specialities include *rabo de toro* (oxtail) and other dishes of the area.

Carcabuey

Seven kilometres west of Priego and reachable by bus, **CARCABUEY** is a charming place laid out on a hill topped by a ruined castle. The Gothic-Renaissance church of **La Asunción** lower down has a good portal flanked with Solomonic marble pillars, and inside a superb **retablo** with the central figure of Christ attributed to Pedro de Mena and Alonso Cano. It is usually locked, so you'll need to enquire at the nearby houses for the key. For **rooms**, on the nearby main highway 3km towards Cabra, the *Hostal La Zamora*, Ctra. Cabra-Priego, A340 km-62 (☎957 70 42 08, ⓦwww.hostal-lazamora.com; ➋), is a comfortable roadside motel with en-suite a/c rooms above a bar-restaurant with an economical *menú*.

Amedinilla

ALMEDINILLA, 9km east of Priego on the Jaén border, is another character-istic Subbética village squatting along the valley of the Río Caicena. Hardly worth a second glance until recently, it has catapulted itself onto the visitor itinerary with the discovery of a remarkable **Roman villa** with unique features as well as a fine **museum**.

Villa Romana de El Ruedo

The villa, officially known as the **Villa Romana de El Ruedo** (March–Sept Wed–Sun 10.30am–2pm, Sat 5.30–7pm, Oct–Feb Wed–Sun 10.30am–2pm, Sat 4.15–6pm; ☎957 70 33 17, ⓦwww.almedinillaturismo.es; €2.20), is located at the edge of the village close to the main A340 highway. Once inside the entrance you will pass to the left the remains of an ancient **pottery kiln**. This would have provided the numerous ceramic containers necessary for the substantial oil and grain farming centred on the villa. Beyond this and beneath a canopy lies the villa proper, constructed and inhabited between the first and fifth centuries AD. Laid out around a central patio or **atrium**, with remains of walls well over a metre high, the bedrooms and living rooms – many bearing vestiges of frescoes and laid with mosaic floors – are adjoined by a bath and kitchen as well as *bodegas* for storing wine, the ruins of an oil mill and warehouses for holding grain. But it is on the north side of the patio in the dining room, or **triclinium**, where the most sensational finds were discovered. In the centre of this room is a well-preserved **podium** upon which diners would have reclined whilst eating. Behind this and set into the wall are the remains of a spectacular artificial **cascade** fed by a diverted nearby stream, unique in Spain and added when the villa was substan-tially remodelled in the third century AD, providing an aural backdrop to the diners' meals. Also unearthed here were a number of outstanding sculptures; the major work, a bronze figure of Hypnos, in Greek mythology the god of sleep, is now displayed in the Museo Historico (see below).

To the north and east of the villa lie the remains of a **necropolis** that would have served the Roman settlement here, as well as the remnants of numerous other Roman dwellings. In the coming years it is planned to excavate these too, eventually transforming the whole area into an archeological park. At the moment a **museum–information centre** (same hours), with reconstructions and exhibits discovered during the excavations, is sited opposite the entrance to the villa.

Museo Historico

Almedenilla's **Museo Historico** (April–Sept Wed–Sun 10am–1.30pm plus Sat 6–8pm; ring ☎957 70 33 17 for winter hours; €2.20) lies on the east side of the village and is housed in a former oil and flour mill, El Molino de Fuente Ribera, whose grindstones were powered by the adjacent Río Caicena. The exhibits are distributed on three floors with the ground floor displaying the mill's grind-stones, once used for making olive oil. Taking its theme from this machinery, the rest of the room charts the development of olive oil production from Iberian and Roman times to the present day – not losing an opportunity to remind visitors that the oil produced here today is as highly prized as it was in Roman times, carrying its own *denominación de origen*. The second floor is devoted to the **Iberian period**, particularly finds from Cerro de la Cruz, a hill settlement discovered on the crag behind the village by archeologists early in the last century. The remains displayed – pottery, burial goods, weapons and tools – detail a well-planned urban development existing between the fourth century BC and the first century AD. The museum can provide information about guided visits to the Cerro de la Cruz site.

The third floor houses the **Roman collection** with the finds from the Roman villa. Pride of place goes to the sculptures, particularly the fine and superbly restored bronze of the Greek god of sleep **Hypnos**, discovered in the villa's dining room, and a work of exceptional quality. For the Greeks (and the Romans who knew him as Somnus) Hypnos was the personification of sleep and his mission was to lead the soul to a peaceful death, as in a dream. Made from individual casts of bronze later welded together, in his left hand he would have held an opium poppy to induce sleep, and in his right a horn from which he cast the night as he flew across the sky with the aid of wings protruding from his temples. Almost as fine is a bronze **hermaphrodite** depicting the dancing figure staring into a mirror held in its right hand (now lost) which would have reflected the feminine parts thus exciting the masculine side of its androgynous nature. This ancient fascination with dualism – as in life and death, darkness and light, male and female – is undoubtedly the work's underlying message. Other sculptures in stone include a genius of the house, perhaps depicting spring, a partially damaged image of Perseus and Andromeda, and a head of Dionysos. A **maquette** of the Roman villa gives you an idea how it would have looked when in use.

Practicalities

Should you have any problems gaining access to the Roman villa or museum, call at the Ayuntamiento, Plaza de España s/n (☎957 70 30 85, ⓦwww .almedinillaturismo.org), who should be able to help. Excellent en-suite **rooms** are available in the heart of the village at *Mesón Rural La Era*, Plaza La Era 1 (☎957 70 32 01; ❸) a cunningly re-created copy of an ancient town house which, despite appearances, is completely new. It also has its own bar and restaurant. *Bar-Restaurante La Bodega*, Plaza de España, in front of the Ayuntamiento serves **meals** at midday with a *menú* for €8, and tapas should be available at other times.

Alcalá La Real and Alcaudete

ALCALÁ LA REAL, 27km east of Priego, is a pleasant country town at the foot of a hill dominated by one of the most impressive Moorish forts in eastern Andalucía. Later reconstructed as the **Castillo de la Mota** (daily: July–Sept 10.30am–1.30pm & 5–8pm; Oct–June 10.30am–1.30pm & 3.30–6.30pm; €5), it preserves among its earlier gates the Moorish **Puerta de la Imagen**. After the fort had been taken during the *Reconquista*, Alfonso XI built – and this became the custom – the Renaissance church of **Santa María la Mayor** inside the walls. Designed by the leading architect of the sixteenth century, Diego de Siloé, and now magnificently restored, its interior floor conserves scores of Visigothic burial niches from an earlier building on the site. Displays in the church's small museum evidence activity on this hill going back to prehistoric times, over five thousand years ago. The fort's imposing **Torre de la Homenaje** also has an interesting small **museum** with great views from the top of the tower. The castle's ticket office doubles as the **Turismo** (same hours; ☎mobile 639647796) which can provide information on the town's many other monuments and museums. For a **place to stay**, *Hotel Torrepalma*, c/Conde de Torrepalma 2 (☎953 58 18 00, ⓦwww.hoteltorrepalma.com; ❸), off the town's main street, Avenida de Andalucía, has comfortable a/c rooms.

Montefrío and the Peña de los Gitanos

One of the more spectacularly sited towns in this part of the country is **MONTEFRÍO**, 24km southeast of Priego (or 32km by road), and just over the Granada border. Cradled between two rocky outcrops, each topped by a church which can be visited, the town has the even bigger Neoclassical **Iglesia de la Encarnación** (daily 10am–2pm & 8–9pm; free) at its heart, with an enormous dome and bizarre acoustics. The most interesting of the hill-top churches is the sixteenth-century **Iglesia de la Villa** (daily 12–2pm; €2.50), a superb building designed by Diego de Siloé, and now converted into a themed museum based on the reconquest of this part of Andalucía from the Moors. The interior has some exquisite **vaulting** and is surrounded by the ruins of the Moorish *alcazaba*; there are fine **views** over the town and beyond from its tower. The church is reached by a bracing climb along the road which ascends beyond the Turismo (see below).

Nearby, 8km east along the NO26 towards Illora and signposted, is the remarkable Neolithic site of **Las Peñas de los Gitanos**. Six kilometres long and demarcated by limestone outcrops, the site was occupied by Stone-Age people in the third millennium BC. The overhanging rocks and caves were used as shelters by bulls, goats, sheep and other ancient beasts and this food source attracted early humans who would have hunted these animals in groups. These ancient hunters left behind paintings inside the caves (currently not on view), various **stone tombs** – some with carvings of animals and horns – and the remains of later stone and clay dwellings when they became Chalcolithic (copper-age) village dwellers. A detailed leaflet (in Spanish) is available from the Turismo in Montefrío.

To visit the site, which is on private land, you will need to organize a visit through the company now responsible for these, Las Peñas de Los Gitantos S.L. (℡628 305 337; English spoken). Visits lasting about two hours (two daily, morning and late afternoon; €5–9 per person depending on group size) must be booked at least 24 hours in advance through the guide responsible for visits, Paqui Sanchez. She will inform you of the time of the visits, the price and the meeting point, which is normally at the site entrance, meaning that you will need your own transport.

Although the site is on private land, access to it is open, but as many of the dolmens and other remains are hard to find a guided visit is recommended. Once at the site (see directions from Montefrio, above) park your car at the signed entry road (with locked gate barring vehicles) on the left. Follow the asphalt road for 100m beyond this to a *Prohibido El Paso* sign where you should veer right onto a dirt track, soon crossing large stones. Two hundred metres further, upon reaching a stone quarry, you need to veer left. A further 200m brings you to an open area of grassland with trees in the centre. Continue straight ahead for 300m – passing a ruined dolmen – to a low mound beyond which you will see more dolmens and an information board. Off to the right, Dolmen 23 has another information board and is the best preserved, with a finely worked entrance still intact.

Practicalities

Montefrío's **Turismo** (Mon–Fri 10am–2pm; ℡958 33 60 04, ⓦwww .montefrio.org) lies just uphill on the left from the Encarnación church and can supply a town map and information. Montefrío's **accommodation** options are severely limited but easily the best is the two-star ⚐ *Hotel La Enrea*, Paraje de la Enrea s/n (℡958 33 66 62, ⓦwww.zercahoteles.com; ❸ with breakfast; ten percent discount for *Rough Guide* readers with this guide), reached by following the Granada road out of the centre. It's an easy five- to ten-minute walk from the centre and the hotel – a converted nineteenth-century water mill – lies in a picturesque river gorge with comfortable a/c rooms. A number of **casas rurales** are available for rent in and around the town – one is sited on the outcrop just below La Villa church; information is available from the Turismo or by ringing ℡958 31 01 24 (English spoken).

When it comes to **eating and drinking**, Montefrío is acclaimed for its *morcilla* (black pudding) and chorizo both excellent at the *Bar Pregonero*, next door to the Turismo. Another good place to try these delicacies is *Bar Uno Más* ("*One More*") facing the Encarnación church. More elaborate meals are to be had at the *Hotel La Enrea*'s good restaurant (see p.422; main dishes €7.50–12) where the local *chachinería* (charcuterie) and *embutidos* (sausages) are a speciality.

Northeast of Córdoba

The A4-E5 highway which heads northeast out of Córdoba along the valley of the Guadalquivir is the main road to Madrid and one of the great historical highways of Andalucía. Not only was this the bullion route between Madrid and its imperial seaports of Seville and Cádiz, but over a millennium and a half earlier, as the Vía Augusta, it formed the vital overland link joining Roman Spain with Gaul, Italy and Rome itself. This route has a number of delightful stop overs including the handsome small town of **Montoro**, an outstanding Moorish castle at **Baños de Encina** and the historic **Despeñaperros Pass**. Transport is easy and **buses** link Córdoba with most places on the route. Montoro, Andújar and Bailén are also served by **trains** on the Córdoba–Linares–Madrid line.

Montoro

MONTORO lies 43km from Córdoba, past the villages of El Carpio and Pedro Abad, and just off the A4-E5. Dramatically sited on an escarpment above a horseshoe bend in the Guadalquivir, the town is a centre of olive-oil production obtained from extensive groves planted in the foothills of the Sierra Morena to the north. A labyrinth of narrow, white-walled streets surrounds the main square, the Plaza de España, dominated by the lofty tower of its Gothic-Mudéjar church, **San Bartolomé**. The interior, behind the red sandstone facade, has a fine *artesonado* ceiling inlaid with mother-of-pearl, recently recovered from under layers of whitewash. On the same square is the sixteenth-century **Ayuntamiento**, an old ducal mansion with a fine Plateresque frontage, and a historic inn – now closed – at no. 19 whose kindly owner will let you in for a look around (avoid siesta time). A narrow street uphill out of the north side of the square leads into an atmospheric old quarter whose main feature is the thirteenth-century church of **Santa María de la Mota**, with some interesting Romanesque capitals, now converted into a small **archeological museum** (Sat, Sun & hols 11am–1pm, outside these times contact the Turismo; free). One other curiosity that also shouldn't be missed is the **Casa de las Conchas** in nearby c/Grajas 17 (and signed from the plaza) – the exterior and interior are covered with thousands of seashells; the proprietor or his wife will proudly show you around and relate the story behind their 25-year-old obsession.

The narrow main street connects Plaza de España with **Plaza del Charco** (aka Plaza Caridad), which contains the town's main **bars** and two *Casinos*, the larger Casino de los Ricos (Rich) and the Casino de los Pobres (Poor), reflecting the bitter class divisions that once existed here and to some extent persist. Both places welcome visitors, and *Bar Yepez* also on the square is another possibility for a drink and a *tapa*. Slightly uphill from the square lies the eighteenth-century Capilla de San Jacinto, now converted into the **Museo Antonio Rodríguez de Luna** (Sun & hols 11am–1pm, or contact the Turismo; free) housing some powerful abstract works by the Montoro-born artist who spent part of his life in Paris and Mexico and died in 1985.

Montoro's other notable monument is the elegant sixteenth-century bridge of **Las Donadas** over the Guadalquivir, paid for by local women who, tradition holds, sold their jewellery to place the town on a more direct, and lucrative, route to the north. Across the bridge, the Cardeña road leading up into the hills offers superb **views** back over the town.

Practicalities

The small **tourist office** (Mon–Fri 9.30am–3pm, Sat 10am–1pm, Sun 10am–2pm; ☎957 16 00 89) at Plaza España 8, near the church of San Bartolomé, can provide basic information. An excellent **place to stay** is the new hotel *Mirador de Montoro*, Cerro de la Muela s/n (☎957 16 51 05, ⓦwww.zercahoteles .com; ◐), located at the south end of the town with a pool, its own restaurant and great views over the river valley.

Andújar

Flanked by the mountains of the Sierra Morena, which are visible on the northern horizon, the A4-E5 continues to Villa del Río and enters the province of Jaén. Lying some 32km beyond Montoro, **ANDÚJAR** is a sizeable if simple country town which claims to be the world's biggest centre of sunflower-oil bottling. There's also a thriving commercial ceramics industry, as well as a couple of churches worth a visit for their artworks.

The road into the town crosses a fifteen-arched Roman **bridge** spanning the Guadalquivir, which has been considerably restored from Moorish times onwards. The central Plaza de España, a baking furnace in the heat of high summer, contains the impressive Gothic church of **San Miguel** (Mon–Sat 7.30–9pm; free) with a fine stone tower and Plateresque features, flanked by an equally striking late-Baroque **Ayuntamiento** – recently restored to its full glory – with elegant portals. But the most interesting church is the **Iglesia de Santa María** (Tues–Sun 11.30am–1.30pm & 5.30–8pm; free) on the plaza of the same name, reached by following c/Feria between the two squares. Built on the site of a former mosque, the free-standing bell tower probably replaced the mosque's minaret and now houses a small tourist office (see below). Inside, a chapel on the left has a fine *Christ in the Garden of Olives* by **El Greco**, a startling surprise in a nondescript country church. The superb **reja** which stands before the El Greco is the work of Master Bartolomé of Jaén, who also created the more famous one in the Capilla Real at Granada. The town's **archeological museum** (Tues–Sat 10am–2pm; free) is housed in the striking seventeenth-century Palacio Don Gome, c/Don Gome, to the southeast of Plaza de España, decorated with moustached figures of feathered Indians inspired by the burgeoning Spanish American empire. The collection consists of mainly Roman ceramic exhibits testifying to the town's importance in this field. There are a number of other elegant **Renaissance palaces** within walking distance of the centre and, should you have the time and inclination, the tourist office can provide a map detailing their locations.

Practicalities

The Ayuntamiento on the Plaza Mayor (Plaza de España) and the **tourist office** (Mon–Sat 9am–2pm & 5.30–7pm; ☎953 50 49 59) next to the Iglesia de Santa María can provide information and a **town map**, which is also stocked by most of the hotels. The more attractive options for **accommodation** in the area are in the *Parque Natural* (see p.425) but the central *Hotel Logasasanti*, c/Dr Fleming s/n (☎953 50 05 00, ⓦwww.logasasanti.com; ◑) has comfortable a/c rooms and its own restaurant.

Plenty of **bars** in town offer tapas – *Bar El Pozuelo* on Plaza de España and *Cafetería Los Naranjos*, c/Guadalupe 4, slightly north of here are both good and the latter has a €10 *menú* in its restaurant. Other places to eat include the very pleasant *Mesón El Churrasco*, Corredera de Capuchinos 24, to the east of Plaza de España, a very good restaurant that also serves excellent tapas and *raciónes*. Nearby, and another place worth seeking out is the mid-priced family-run *Restaurante Madrid-Sevilla*, Plaza del Sol 4, a little to the east of Plaza de España specializing in *perdiz* (partridge) and other game dishes.

Parque Natural Sierra de Andújar

A wonderful thirty-kilometre drive into the **Parque Natural Sierra de Andújar** to the north of Andújar along the A1208 leads to the thirteenth-century hermitage of **Nuestra Virgen de la Cabeza**, one of the most revered of Andalucía's shrines. To break the journey, on the way up there are three decent **ventas** – *El Tropezón, El Toledillo* and *Los Pinos* – all with weekday *menús del día*. At the 13km point you will come to a **Centro de Visitantes** (April–Sept Fri–Sun 10am–2pm & 6–8pm; ☎953 54 90 30) with displays of the natural park's flora and fauna including the threatened *lince ibérico* (pardel lynx); they can also provide a **map** of the park and have leaflets detailing **hiking** routes.

Once you arrive at the shrine, there's not much left of the ancient building, which was destroyed in the Civil War when two hundred Guardia Civil officers seized it, declaring their support for Franco's rebellion. Bombarded for eight months by Republican forces, the sanctuary was eventually set alight and the guards captured on May 1, 1937. (Pre-democracy Spanish guidebooks felt obligated to append an emphatic exclamation mark to the eight months the siege lasted and the more sycophantic compared it to Numancia and Sagunto, two of the great Spanish sieges of Roman times – thus turning the episode into a symbol of fascist heroism.) The distasteful rebuild flanked by equally bleak Guardia Civil monuments was carried out during the Franco period, but the famous *romería* – in which brotherhoods and pilgrims converge on the shrine from all over Andalucía and Spain on the last Sunday in April – carries on undaunted. In a crypt to the side of the church is a display of hundreds of crutches, Zimmer frames and all kinds of surgical supports and braces left behind by "healed" pilgrims – a bizarre testament to the Virgin's curative powers.

There are a number of attractive **places to stay** in the park. Near to the Centro de Visitantes (see above), the tourist complex *Los Pinos* (☎953 54 90 23, Ⓦwww.lospinos.es; ❷) has rooms, and *apartamentos rurales* and cottages (both ❺) in a pleasant woodland setting with a pool and restaurant. Three kilometres down a track heading east from here (signed "La Jandula") *Villa Matilde* (☎953 54 91 27, Ⓦwww.villamatilde.org; ❷) is another pleasant rural retreat offering (mostly) en-suite rooms in a converted villa with a pool and a restaurant that caters for vegetarians. Six kilometres down a road heading west (direction Alcaparrosa) from near the Centro, *Sierra Luna* (☎mobile 653805129, Ⓦwww.sierra-luna.com; ❺) is another rural option with accommodation in fully-equipped wood cabins sleeping up to four. Close to the shrine itself, *La Mirada* (☎953 54 91 11; ❸) is a pleasant hotel-bar-restaurant with a/c rooms above and there's an adjoining small mini-market for buying picnic items.

Baños de la Encina

Just beyond Andújar the A4-E5 turns away from the Guadalquivir valley to head northeast to **Bailén**, a dull farming town where Napoleon's troops suffered a crushing defeat in 1808. From here it pushes on for another 45km to Andalucía's border with La Mancha at the Despeñaperros Pass (see p.428) and Madrid.

Other **possible routes** from this junction lead south to the city of Jaén, or east to Baeza and Úbeda via Linares.

Some 6km after Bailén a left turn leads to the sizeable village of **BAÑOS DE LA ENCINA**, which has one of the most impressive Moorish castles in Andalucía. Crowning a low hill above the village, the tenth-century **Alcázar** is a magnificent sight with its fourteen square towers and enormous keep spaced out along a crenellated curtain wall. Built by al-Hakam II of Córdoba, the fort was completed in 967, no doubt to control the rugged and mountainous territory to the north, the domain of various unruly Iberian clans. Entered through a double-horseshoe arch, where a plaque in Arabic script dates the edifice to year 357 of the *hegira* (967 AD), the fort has an oval ground plan and from the battlements there are **fine views** over the village and towards the Sierra de Cazorla to the east and the less impressive reservoir behind.

At the time of writing archeological investigations inside the Alcázar are restricting visits to weekends only (Sat 6.30–7.30pm; Sun 10.30am–12.30pm; €1). However, it is intended that the monument will again be open on a regular basis and it's worthwhile ringing the helpful **tourist office**, Callejón del Castillo 1 (July–Aug Tues–Sun 10am–1.30pm, Sept–June Tues–Sun 10am–1.30pm & 5–7.30pm, ☎953 61 32 29, ⊛www.bdelaencina.com), just off the main square, for the latest information. The tourist office also does a ninety-minute guided tour of the castle and monuments below (Tues–Sun: May–Aug 11am & 6pm; Sept–June 11am & 5pm; €5).

On the main square, Plaza de la Constitución, the splendid red stone Gothic-Renaissance church of **San Mateo**, with an elegant octagonal tower, is also worth a look inside to view an exquisite *sagrario* (sanctuary) constructed in ebony and adorned with silver, marble and tortoiseshell, as are the village's narrow, whitewashed streets dotted with a clutch of *señorial* mansions. The **Ermita de Cristo del Llano**, an eighteenth-century hermitage in the upper village and a ten-minute walk from the tourist office, is worth the trek to see this remarkable church attached to a convent. If you call at the convent (preferably outside siesta time) the nuns will allow you to gain entry to view the church and its startlingly beautiful (and recently restored) **Baroque camarín** with stellar decoration and stucco polychromed angels and saints climbing to the roof.

For a **place to stay**, the pleasant *Hotel-Restaurante Baños*, Cerro de la Llaná s/n (☎953 61 40 68, ⊛www.hotelbanos.com; ❹), occupying a hill behind the castle, has good-value balcony rooms, many with stunning castle views (Room 101 has the best). For **food** you can get **tapas** and *raciónes* at **bars** on the main square and at the *Bar-Restaurante Mirasierra*, c/Bailén s/n, near the tourist office, which also does full meals. Behind the castle, *Restaurante La Encina*, c/Consultorio 3, serves hearty Sierra dishes and a good-value *menú* and the restaurant of the *Hotel Baños* is another tempting possibility with an economical weekday *menú*.

La Carolina

LA CAROLINA, 20km further to the northeast, is the most important of the new towns set up by Carlos III in the eighteenth century (see p.312) to protect the bullion route from Cádiz to Madrid. As with the other settlements it was named after a member of the royal family – in this case the king himself – settled with foreign immigrants and laid out on a regular grid-pattern street plan that still survives today. The town's central square, the Plaza del Ayuntamiento, has the imposing, honey-coloured sandstone **Palacio de Pablo de Olavide**, built for Carlos III's radical minister, the force behind the Nuevas Poblaciones idea. De Olavide did not long enjoy the fruits of his labours, however, for the clergy, who were denied access to these new towns, wreaked their vengeance by denouncing him to the Inquisition. Arrested in 1776, he was divested of his property and confined to a convent in La Mancha subject to whatever penances the monks thought appropriate. He subsequently escaped to France. Flanking the *palacio*, the parish church of **La Concepción** contains a fine Baroque image of the *Virgen de las Angustias* in alabaster. The square is linked by a thoroughfare to an impressive tree-lined avenue entered via a gateway bearing images of Carlos III, at the far end of which lies the municipal **swimming pool**.

There are a couple of **places to stay**: the friendly *Los Jardineros*, c/Sanjurjo 1 (T953 66 16 13; ●), a few blocks north of the focal Plaza de España, has en-suite rooms with TV and next door the **restaurant** *El Retorno* is also good. Moving upmarket, there's also the luxurious *La Perdiz* (T953 66 03 00, Wwww .nh-hoteles.es; ●) – not be confused with the uninviting *Orellana Perdiz* nearby – on the main A4-E5 highway (km-268) at the edge of town.

The Despeñaperros Pass

Two kilometres beyond La Carolina, slightly before the village of Navas de Tolosa, a huge roadside **monument** marks the site of the important battle that took place in 1212 between the Christian armies under Alfonso VIII and the Almohad forces.

The Moors suffered a crippling defeat, opening the way for the Reconquest of Andalucía. The monument depicts the Christian monarchs as well as the

> ## Don Quijote and the Despeñaperros Pass
>
> **Cervantes** would have been familiar with the route through the **Despeñaperros Pass**, connecting La Mancha with Seville and Córdoba, where he lived both as a child and in later life. The brooding and threatening nature of the pass – probably greater before it was blasted to make room for road widening and the railway line – appealed to him, for he used it in two of the most memorable scenes in the adventures of **Don Quijote** and Sancho Panza. The centre of the pass is where Don Quijote ran mad and played "the desperate, the raving, the furious lover", in order that Sancho could convey news of this penance to his fantasized Lady Dulcinea del Toboso, in reality a slatternly country lass named Alonza Lorenzo:
>
> "Observe the landmarks, and I will try to remain near this spot," said Don Quijote. "And I will even take the precaution of climbing the highest of these crags to look out for you on your return. But your surest way of not missing me, and not getting lost yourself, will be for you to scatter some of the broom that is so plentiful around here. Scatter it at intervals as you go till you get out to open country. The sprigs will serve as landmarks and signs for you to find me by when you come back, just like the thread in Theseus's labyrinth."
>
> This botanical link with the world of Quijote is still strong when, in early summer, the clumps of brilliant yellow flowers are everywhere. About 1km further on, the **Venta de Cardenas** was the inn that the deluded knight errant imagined to be a castle. When the morning after a night's hospitality the innkeeper demanded payment, Quijote refused with the explanation that knights never paid for their accommodation and made his exit. Sancho, however, was not so lucky and was given a violent tossing in a blanket to teach him a lesson. The old *venta* apparently survived until the nineteenth century, when it was seen by Borrow. However, it was subsequently demolished and a characterless hotel now stands on the site. But it's still a stopover on this major transportation route and the lines of articulated lorries parked outside belong to the truck drivers who use this inn today, the successors of the muleteers, drovers and carriers of Cervantes's time.

shepherd, an apparition of St Isidore in disguise, who, according to Christian belief, guided them through the well-defended Sierra Morena, thus enabling a surprise attack on the Moorish army who fled after defeat through the Despeñaperros Pass. This event, in fact, gave the pass its name – meaning the "overthrow of the dogs" (or Moors).

The **Despeñaperros Pass**, 14km further on, is the dramatic gateway between Andalucía and La Mancha and the only natural breach in the 500km length of the Sierra Morena. This narrow defile, flanked by daunting crags and slopes covered with dense pine woods, was for centuries the main point of entry into Andalucía from the north and many travellers have left vivid accounts of arriving in the lush promised land of the south after traversing the dry and arid plains of La Mancha (from the Moorish *manxa*, or parched earth). George Borrow, however, also related the sense of foreboding due to the pass's evil reputation "on account of the robberies which are continually being perpetrated in its recesses". Ford, when going the other way, described the land beyond the pass as where "commences the *paño pardo*, the brown cloth, and the *alpargata*, or the hempen sandal of the poverty-stricken Manchegos".

The whole area surrounding the Despeñaperros pass is now a *Parque Natural* and just off the A4-E5 at Santa Elena there is a **Centro de Visitantes** (Tue–Sun 9am–2pm & 4–7pm; ☎953 66 43 07) with exhibitions of flora and fauna and lots of information on activities and accommodation in the park.

Jaén

Surrounded by olive groves and huddled beneath the fortress of Santa Catalina on the heights above, **JAÉN**, the provincial capital and by far the largest town in the eponymous province, is an uneventful sort of place. Derived from the Arabic *Geen*, meaning a stop on the caravan route, the modern town is more northerly than Andalucian in its appearance and character, doubtless stemming from its resettlement with emigrants from the north following the *Reconquista,* and the subsequent long centuries spent as the front line bulwark of Christian Spain against Moorish Granada. At the centre of an area impoverished by lack of economic development and chronic unemployment, while you would hardly want to go out of your way to get here, the city makes an easy place to stop over en route to destinations such as Baeza, Úbeda and Cazorla to the northeast. And, given a chance, it has a surprising number of worthwhile sights, including a fine cathedral, the largest Moorish baths in Spain, some elegant old churches and mansions and an important museum. To the northeast of Jaén along the Baeza road lies the **La Laguna** complex (see p.440) with a comprehensive museum dedicated to explaining the history and development of olive oil production.

Some history

Although the area around the city is liberally dotted with Iberian settlements, it was probably as the Roman settlement of *Auringis* that Jaén was born. A centre noted for its **silver mines** and settled by the Moors shortly after the conquest of 711, judging by the number of mosques it must have been a thriving place. The Moors also made use of the **hot springs** that had been known to the Romans and utilized them in the construction of several baths. Fernando III's Christian forces captured the city – then part of the newly founded Nasrid kingdom of Granada – in 1246 and made its ruler Ibn al-Ahmar (aka Muhammad ibn Yusuf ibn Nasr) into a vassal, obliged to pay annual tribute. It was from Jaén,

3

CÓRDOBA AND JAÉN

Córdoba ▶

Iglesia De La Magdalena ▶

Palacio de Los Uribes (250m) ▶

Train Station (700m) & Museo Provincial (250m) ▶

Granada & Madrid ▶

◀ & Jabalcuz

ACCOMMODATION

Albergue Inturjoven	B
Hostal Estación RENFE	D
Hotel Europa	E
Hotel Xuen	C
Parador Castillo de Santa Catalina	A

RESTAURANTS & TAPAS BARS

Bar 82	3
Bar del Posito	7
Bar El Gorrión	1
Casa Antonio	8
El Mirador	6
Gamba de Oro	11
La Catedral	4
La Viña	2
Mesón Nuyra	10
Mesón Río Chico	9
Parador Castillo de Santa Catalina	A
Tasca los Amigos	5

Castillo de Santa Catalina & Centro de Interpretación

Ancient Walls

Ancient Walls

JAÉN

0   200 m

▼ Granada, Úbeda & La Guardia

two and a half centuries later, that the final assault on Boabdil's Granada was launched. The city then entered into a slow decline which gathered pace in the seventeenth and eighteenth centuries and led many of its citizens to emigrate to the imperial colonies, evidenced by towns with the same name in countries as far apart as Peru and the Philippines. Although Jaén's strategic importance played a part in the War of Independence, the economic disruption caused brought further decline in its wake, from which the city never really recovered. In various surveys carried out by the Junta de Andalucía the province and city continually register the lowest income levels in the region, with well over fifty percent of the population describing themselves as living in poverty.

Arrival and information

Jaén's **bus station** (☎953 25 01 06, ⓦwww.epassa.es has details of all Jaén's provincial services) is on Plaza Coca de la Pinera, just off the Paseo de la Estación. There are frequent daily services to and from Úbeda and Baeza and, less often, Cazorla. The **train station** (☎953 27 02 02) is a bit further out, at the end of Paseo de la Estación, and a good ten-minute walk (or an easier ride on bus #19) from the centre. There are train connections to Córdoba and Madrid. Arriving **by car** either use the signed pay car parks around the centre or consult where you're staying; even if they don't have a garage they should be able to advise. The **Turismo**, c/Ramon y Cajal s/n (Mon–Fri 9am–7.30pm, Sat–Sun 9.30am–3pm; ☎953 19 04 55), to the rear of the cathedral, has lots of information on the town, while inside the striking nineteenth-century Diputación Provincial building fronting Plaza de San Francisco the **provincial tourist office** (Mon–Fri 8am–3pm; ☎953 24 80 00) has information on the province. **Internet** access is available at the central Almadena Telecom, c/Hurtado 18 (daily 11am–3pm & 5–11pm).

It's worth noting (and applauding) that **admission** to all Jaén's monuments – barring the audiovisual attraction in the Castillo de Santa Catalina – is free.

Accommodation

Places to stay in town are limited and – with the exception of a sparkling new youth hostel – relatively expensive. There's usually no problem in finding accommodation at any time of the year and there are no seasonal rate changes. Mosquitoes can be a real problem in the town during the high summer season when places with air-conditioning come into their own.

Albergue Inturjoven c/Borja s/n ☎953 31 35 40, ⓦwww.inturjoven.com. Behind the imposing facade of a former eighteenth-century hospital lies the new youth hostel's excellent modern, if minimalist in style, en-suite a/c rooms and "apartments" (which add a *salon* but no kitchen). There's also a pool. Somewhat incongruously the *albergue* also houses a full-blown spa with a variety of detox and *anti-edad* (ageing) cures costing much more than the rooms. Doubles ❷, apartments ❸

Hostal Estación RENFE Estación de Tren ☎953 27 46 14, ⓦwww.hostalrenfejaen.cjb.net. The RENFE's own *hostal* at the front of the station is a rather swish affair with comfortable a/c rooms with TV, wi-fi throughout and a car park. ❸

Hotel Europa Plaza de Belén 1 ☎953 22 27 00, ⓦwww.gremiodehospedaje.com. Perhaps the best of the more upmarket places in the centre, where attractive a/c rooms come with safe and satellite TV. Garage. ❹ with breakfast.

Hotel Xauen Plaza Deán Mazas 3 ☎953 24 07 89, ⓦwww.hotelxauenjaen.com. Off the west side of the Plaza de la Constitución, this is a reasonable option with decent a/c rooms. ❺

Parador Castillo de Santa Catalina Castillo, sited on a hill 3km from town ☎953 23 00 00, ⓦwww.parador.es. For a truly memorable experience you could stay at this most spectacularly sited of hotels in Spain. The comfortable rooms have fine balcony views with a sheer drop to the valley below, facilities include a pool, restaurant, bar and ample parking. ❻

The Town

Most of Jaén's sights lie within a few minutes' walk of the rather characterless main thoroughfare, the **Paseo de la Estación**. This cuts through the heart of the city from north to south linking the train station with the Plaza de la Constitución, the major hub of activity. The *paseo* is interrupted only by the Plaza de las Batalles, a square dominated by a grotesque sculpture commemorating the battles of Nava de Tolosa (against the Moors) and Bailén (against the French).

The Catedral

Jaén's massive and magnificent **Catedral** (Mon–Sat 8.30am–1pm & 5–8pm, Sun 9am–1.30pm & 5–7pm; museum daily 10.30am–1pm & 5–8pm; church free, museum €3), lying to the west of the Plaza de la Constitución, dwarfs the city. Begun in 1492 after the demolition of the great mosque that had previously occupied the site, the cathedral was not completed until 1802. A number of architects turned their hand to the project during this period, including the great Andrés de Vandelvira, whose work had the most influence over the building as it looks today. The spectacular **west facade**, flanked by twin sixty-metre-high towers framing Corinthian pillars and statuary by the seventeenth-century master, Pedro Roldán, is one of the masterpieces of Andalucian Renaissance architecture. Inside, the overall mood of the building is more sombre, with bundles of great Corinthian columns surging towards the roof of the nave. Fine sixteenth-century **choir stalls** have richly carved images from the Old Testament as well as a number of grisly martyrdoms. The dim side chapels also have some interesting artworks, among them an eighteenth-century *Virgen de las Angustias* (Our Lady of the Sorrows) by José de Mora in the fifth side chapel to the right. The church fills up on Fridays (11.30am–1pm) when the **lienzo del Santo Rostro** is ritually removed from its coffer behind the high altar. This Byzantine cloth icon bearing a likeness of Christ is believed locally to be the napkin with which St Veronica wiped his face en route to Calvary. Long queues form to kiss the icon (preserved behind glass) and the attending priest wipes it with a handkerchief after each devotee.

The sacristy **museum** displays works by artists of the region as well as the Tenebrario, a fifteen-armed candlestick by Master Bartolomé de Jaén who also made the magnificent *reja* in the Capilla Real at Granada. Two fine seventeenth-century sculptures by Martinéz Montañés, *San Lorenzo* and *Cristo Nazareno*, are also on display.

The Baños Árabes

The main cluster of the city's other sights lies to the north of the cathedral, along c/Martínez Molina in what was formerly the old Moorish quarter. The most interesting of these is the **Baños Árabes** (Tues–Sat 8.45am–9.30pm, Sun 9.30am–2.45pm; free), a remarkable Moorish *hammam* or baths, and the largest to survive in Spain. Originally part of an eleventh-century Moorish palace, the baths fell into disuse after the *Reconquista* and were used as a tannery. In the sixteenth century the Palacio de Villadompardo, now the **Museo de Artes y Costumbres Populares** (arts and crafts museum; same hours; free) was built over them. They were rediscovered early last century and in the 1980s were painstakingly restored. Recent modifications now lead you into the baths over a glass floor allowing views of the Roman and Moorish remains which surround the complex. The various rooms (cold, tepid and hot) have wonderful brickwork ceilings with typical star-shaped windows, and pillars supporting elegant horseshoe arches. An underground passage (now closed) connected the baths with the centre of the Moorish palace, on top of which was built the

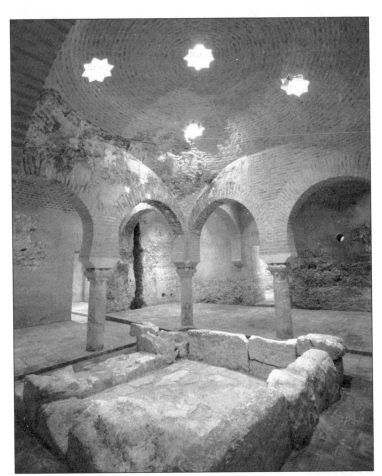

▲ The Baños Arabes

Monastery of Santo Domingo (see p.433). The **museum of arts and crafts** contains a fascinating and well-presented folk history of the province on three floors using artefacts, clothing, toys, ceramics, photos and audiovisual aids. A recent addition here is the **Museo Internacional de Arte Naïf** (same hours; free) with works by (mainly) Spanish and some international artists.

The baths are flanked by the **Palacio de los Uribes**, a sixteenth-century mansion, on the northern side, whilst the church of **San Andrés** (daily 10am–12.30pm or ring ☎953 23 74 22 to view), which contains a fabulous altar screen depicting the *Holy Family* and the *Tree of Jesse* by Maestro Bartolomé of Jaén, here working on his home patch, lies just to the south. Slightly west of here, the ancient post-*Reconquista* church of **San Juan** (Mon–Thurs 8am–2pm & 5–8pm, Fri 8am–2pm; free) in the Plaza de San Juan, has an elegant Romanesque tower and, inside, a fine sixteenth-century sculpture of the Crucifixion by Sebastián de Solís. A couple of streets north, c/Santísima Trinidad leads to a **path** which climbs, ruggedly in parts, to the castle of Santa Catalina, a much shorter route than the three-kilometre-plus road. The path starts from the *Bar Sobrino Bigotes*.

Santo Domingo, La Magdalena and around

Standing on c/Santo Domingo, north of San Juan, the **Monastery of Santo Domingo** (patio can be viewed Mon–Fri 8.30am–2pm; free), erected over a Moorish palace, was originally a fourteenth-century Dominican monastery and later became Jaén's university; later still it was a seat of the Inquisition, before being transformed in more recent times into the office of the provincial historical archive (Archivo Historico). From its earlier incarnations a fine sixteenth-century **portal** by Vandelvira and a beautiful **patio** with elegant twinned Tuscan columns survive.

A little further north still, the **Iglesia de La Magdalena** (Tues–Sat 5–8pm, Sun 9am–1.30pm; free), the oldest in Jaén, was built over a mosque, the minaret of which is now its bell tower, and a patio at the rear preserves a pool used in Moorish times for ritual ablutions. In the cloister you can still see a few Roman tombstones used in the construction of the original Moorish building; this quarter was also the centre of the ancient Roman town. Inside, the church has a superb **retablo** by Jacobo Florentino depicting scenes from the Passion.

Two more interesting churches can be seen on the way back to the cathedral zone. The first, on c/Huérfanos to the southeast of the Palacio de Villadompardo, is the **Convento de Santa Clara** (open service times, try 7–9pm), with a fine choir and sixteenth-century Ecuadorian sculpture of *Cristo debambú*. South of here on the Plaza de San Bartolomé, the sixteenth-century **San Bartolomé** (Mon 10–11am, Tues–Sat 10am–7pm, Sun 10am–12.30pm; entry through the sacristy), has a fine Mudéjar *artesonado* ceiling, Gothic ceramic font and an outstanding *Expiration of Christ* by José de Medina.

The Museo Provincial

Five-minutes' walk northeast of the centre, the **Museo Provincial** at Paseo de la Estación 27 (Tues 2.30–8.30pm, Wed–Sat 9am–8.30pm, Sun 9am–2.30pm; free) is worth a visit for its remarkable collection of Iberian stone **sculptures**, among the most important in Spain. Recently housed in a separate building to the side of the museum (ask at the admission desk for directions) these remarkable objects were found near the town of Porcuna, close to the province's western border, and date from the fifth century BC. One is of a magnificent bull, whilst another is a strange fragment – titled *grifomaquia* – depicting a struggle between a man and a griffon. All the works betray the artistic influence of the classical Greek world on the fertile Iberian imagination. The strange fact revealed by the archeological excavations when these works came to light is that they had been deliberately broken a short time after their execution and then laid in a long trench. No satisfactory explanation for this has yet been put forward. More sculptures are being put on show each year as they are uncovered by archeologists, and it's intended that this will eventually become the major museum for Iberian art in Spain.

Items on display in the main building include Phoenician jewellery and ointment phials, Greek vases, as well as Roman mosaics and sculpture, including an outstanding fourth-century **sarcophagus** found near Martós depicting seven miracles of Christ including the transformation of water into wine. A new addition here is a complete full-scale walk-in reconstruction of the remarkable fourth-century BC Iberian necropolis **tomb** at Toya near Cazorla (see p.449). Room 7 deals with Jaén's significant **Moorish period** and has lamps and stoneware as well as a whole jugful of money – dirhams and califalas – that someone buried and never came back to collect. This room also has some fine **ceramics** that verify the Moorish origin of the green glazed plates and vases, still the hallmark of the pottery of Jaén province. A Visigothic section has examples of jewellery, vases and metalwork from this hazy period in Spanish history.

Upstairs, the **Museo de Bellas Artes** starts out with some interesting medieval wood sculpture before quickly degenerating into a hotchpotch of fairly awful stuff from the nineteenth and twentieth centuries, although there are a few laughs, not to mention a large number of steamy nudes. The tedium is somewhat relieved by a recently acquired work by Huelvan artist Daniel Vasquéz Díaz, an engraving by Picasso and some interesting drawings and paintings by Manuel Angeles Ortiz, a native of Jaén who was a great friend of both Picasso and García Lorca.

Castillo de Santa Catalina

The **Castillo de Santa Catalina**, dominating the crag that rises behind the city, was in origin a Moorish fortress constructed in the thirteenth century by Ibn al-Ahmar. After the Reconquest, the castle was much altered and today part of it has been stylishly converted into a modern parador, and little of the Moorish edifice now survives. What does remain has been reconstructed as a **Centro de Interpretación** (daily: April–Sept 10am–2pm & 5–9pm; Oct–March 10am–2pm & 3.30–7.30pm; €3.50), housing in the fort's five towers a series of hi-tech interactive audiovisual gadgets explaining the building's history. A number of secret passageways connected the Moorish fortress with the town below and a few of these have been discovered.

A path from the parador car park leads to the older and ruined part of the edifice at the castle's southern tip where a *mirador* beneath a huge, whitewashed cross gives a **spectacular view** of the city laid out below your feet and dominated by the massive cathedral. Beyond, Jaén's wealth and misery, the endless lines of olive groves, disappear over the hills into the haze. Nonresidents are welcome to use the parador's bar and restaurant. If you don't fancy the three-kilometre, near-vertical hike to reach the castle, you can take a taxi (about €6 one way) from Plaza Coca de la Piñera by the bus station. Alternatively, there's a much shorter path up from c/Santísima Trinidad, to the east of Santo Domingo (see p.433).

Eating, drinking and nightlife

Jaén tends to shut down after dark and in the absence of much nightlife you'll probably compensate by **eating and drinking**. In the centre, the best place to find food is on the east side of Plaza de la Constitución. Here, the tiny c/Nueva has a whole crowd of **tapas** bars and places to eat; *Mesón Río Chico* and *La Gamba de Oro* are both good. Above the west side of the Plaza de la Constitución, you'll find *Bar del Posito*, a popular tapas, *raciónes* and *copas* venue on Plaza del Posito with outdoor tables. More bars for tapas around the centre include the cosy *Tasca Los Amigos*, c/Bernardo López, where there's good *jamón* and *morcilla* (blood pudding); the nearby *Bar 82* and *El Gorrión* on c/Arcos del Consuelo (this street is a tapas hot spot) are also worth a visit. Nearby, *La Catedral* c/F. M. Mora 6, is popular with a younger crowd.

Restaurants

Casa Antonio c/Fermin Palma 3, north of the bus station ☎953 27 02 62. Top culinary choice in town, this upmarket place offers innovative *jiennense* and Basque-inspired dishes and there's a *menú de degustación* for about €50. Closed Mon & Aug.

El Mirador Ctra. de Jabalcuz km-7.9 ☎953 24 36 58. A popular haunt with *jiennenses* – especially on Sun – this great family-run restaurant offers excellent local dishes, an economical *menú* and fine views from its terraces (closed Mon).

La Viña c/Maestra 8. Stylish new *cervecería*, restaurant and *raciónes* bar close to the cathedral with a pleasant terrace on this pedestrianized street.

Mesón Nuyra Pasaje Nuyra s/n, off c/Nueva. Quality mid-priced restaurant serving the predominantly game dishes of the region as well as Mediterranean oriented fare. Main dishes €12–21.

Parador Castillo de Santa Catalina To feast in baronial splendour you'll need to climb – or take a taxi – to this spectacularly located restaurant inside the parador. Dining is in a re-created medieval banqueting room, the cooking is excellent and many local specialities – such as *morcilla* (blood sausage) and *pipirrana* (*jamón* and vegetable salad) – are offered on a good-value *menú*, costing around €30.

CÓRDOBA AND JAÉN | Baeza and around

Baeza and around

Campo de Baeza, soñaré contigo cuando no te vea.
Fields of Baeza, I will dream of you when I can no longer see you.

Antonio Machado (1875–1939)

Fifty kilometres from Jaén along the winding A316, **BAEZA** is a tiny, compact and provincial country town with a perpetual Sunday air about it. Sited on the escarpment of the Loma de Úbeda, both Baeza and the neighbouring town of Úbeda have an extraordinary density of exuberant **Renaissance palaces**, richly endowed churches and magnificent public squares which are among the finest in Spain.

Important in Roman times as Beatia, Baeza was later a Visigothic bishopric and then a prosperous commercial and agricultural centre under the Moors. After a prolonged and bitter struggle the town fell to the Christian forces in 1227, and *hidalgos* or nobles were granted estates in the surrounding countryside with orders to defend this frontier zone. The power of these noble houses was so untrammelled that they were soon warring among themselves for control of the town (a favoured place of battle being Baeza's Alcázar – until Isabel had it demolished). It was later, in the sixteenth century, however, that Baeza embarked on its most prosperous period. The nobility, made rich by farming and textile production, endowed the town with numerous striking Renaissance buildings as the population expanded.

Arrival and information

The nearest **train station** to Baeza is **Linares-Baeza**, 14km away and served by frequent trains from Seville, Córdoba and Granada (buses connect with most trains, or it's a €20 taxi ride), where you'll find fronting the station a good *hostal* and restaurant, *Las Palmeras* (☎953 69 89 79; ❷). Otherwise, you're dependent on buses; all services (around fourteen daily) between Jaén and Úbeda, 9km further east, call in at Baeza. The **bus station** (☎953 74 04 68), officially at Paseo de Elorza Garat 1, is actually at the end of c/San Pablo and along the Paseo Arca del Agua. Baeza's **Turismo** (Mon–Fri 9am–7.30pm, Sat & Sun 9.30am–3pm; ☎953 77 99 82) in the sixteenth-century former **Audiencia** (appeal court) on the Plaza del Populo can supply maps and information as well as a *Ruta del Tapeo* booklet and details of daily **guided tours** of the town. **Internet** access is available at the central Micro Ware (Mon–Thurs 10.30am–2pm & 5–9.30pm, Fri–Sun 11am–2pm & 5–10pm), c/Portales Tundidores 13, facing the Paseo de la Constitución.

Baeza's lively annual **feria** takes place during the second and third weeks in August and is a wonderfully rural affair with processions of *gigantones* (carnival giants), fireworks and an enormous funfair on the edge of town. There's occasional **flamenco** at the *Peña Flamenca*, c/Romanones 6; ask the Turismo for details of performances.

435

▲ Ⓐ, Ⓑ, Úbeda & Train Station (14km)

BAEZA

0   200 m

RESTAURANTS & TAPAS BARS
Arcediano 4
Bar Cafetería
  Mercantil 5
Bar Diego 3
Bar Pedrito 2
Casa Juanito B
Bar Mibel 1
El Pasaje 7
El Sarmiento 6
El Señorío de Baeza F
Restaurante Andrés
  de Vandelvira 8
Restaurante El Sali 9

PASEO DE LA PRIEGA
COCA DE LA PRIEGA
ACERA DE SAN ANTONIO
AVENIDA DEL BALDIONEDO (PASEO)
Bus Station
SAN ILDEFONSO
Parque de Obras Públicas
CARMEN
JULIO BURELL
LA MERCED
C.Cabrera
San Pablo
C.Acuña
Pal.Cerón
C.Elorza
Pal.Garciez
LAS MINAS
Puerta de Úbeda Ⓔ
Santa Cruz
Torre de los Aliatares
PL.STA.CRUZ
CONCEPCIÓN
PLAZA DE ESPAÑA
Pósito
Pal. de Jabalquinto
Casas Consistoriales Altas
Catedral
Purísima Concepción Ⓕ
Alhóndiga
PASEO CONSTITUCIÓN
PL.STA. MARÍA
PZA. DEL ARCEDIANO
San Francisco Ⓖ
Microware @
Machado's House
Antigua Universidad
Antigua Carnicería
Ayuntamiento
S.Felipe Neri Ⓗ
S. CATALINA
IMAGEN
LOS MOLINOS
Casa Consistorial
Audiencia ⓘ
PINTADA BAJA
Fuente de los Leones
Arco de Villalar
Pta. de Jaén
PLATERÍAS
PLAZA DE LOS LEONES
CAPILLA
SAN ANDRÉS
Sta. María del Alcázar y San Andrés
Cvto. de la Encarnación
El Salvador
CAMPANARIO
AGUA
SANTA MARÍA DE GRACIA
Palacio de los Mejorada
PLAZA DE MIGUEL DE CERVANTES

ACCOMMODATION
Hotel Baeza F
Hotel Baeza Monumental C
Hotel El Alcázar A
Hotel Fuentenueva D
Hotel Juanito B
Hotel Puerto H
Hotel Santa Ana G
La Casona del Arco E

▼ Jaén

Accommodation

The town has a decent range of **places to stay**, some of which are architectural gems. There's usually no problem finding rooms in Baeza except during the summer *feria* in mid-August and even then you should have no trouble if you ring ahead. It's worth noting that many hotels have a weekend surcharge policy so if you can avoid a Friday to Saturday stay prices often fall considerably.

Hotel Baeza c/Concepción 3 ☎953 74 81 30, ⓦwww.trhhoteles.com. Well-equipped a/c rooms partly housed in a stylishly converted Renaissance monastery with a glassed-in patio. They do frequent cut-price deals so it's worth giving them a ring or checking the website. ❺ with breakfast.
Hotel Baeza Monumental c/Cuesta de Prieto 6, ☎953 73 72 82, ⓦwww.hotelbaezamonumental .com. Very pleasant small hotel with attractive rooms equipped with plasma satellite TV, minibar, strongbox and there's internet access plus a car park. Higher rates (❺) apply Fri–Sat. Reduced

rates for longer stays. ❸ with breakfast.
Hotel El Alcázar Paseo Arca del Agua s/n ☎953 74 00 28. Decent if unadorned rooms (there's no TV) with bath above a restaurant. ❷
Hotel Fuentenueva c/del Carmen ☎953 74 31 00, ⓦwww.fuentenueva.com. Delightful and friendly small hotel housed in a stylishly refurbished nineteenth-century town house with *cafetería* and garden plunge pool. Ultra-modern rooms come with minibar, safe, satellite TV, internet connection and power shower or jacuzzi. Also has some equally stylish apartments (❺)

nearby in a refurbished eighteenth-century mansion. *Rough Guide* readers with this guide can claim a ten percent discount. ❹

Hotel Juanito Paseo Arca del Agua s/n ☎ 953 74 00 40, ⓦ www.juanitobaeza.com. Very reasonably priced hotel for rooms with a/c and TV above the top-notch restaurant of the same name. Insist on a west-facing room at the back or a high room on the front (both with views) to avoid the smell of the *gasolinera* next door. ❷

🏃 **Hotel Puerta de la Luna** c/Pintada Alta s/n ☎ 953 74 70 19, ⓦ www.hotelpuertadelaluna .com. Beautiful four-star hotel situated in a refurbished seventeenth-century *casa palacio*. Facilities include two delightful patios, restaurant, gym,

library, spa and a small pool. The comfortably furnished tiled-floor rooms are airy and well equipped, and it has its own car park. Prices rise slightly Fri–Sat. ❹

Hotel Santa Ana c/Santa Ana Vieja 9 ☎ 953 74 07 65, ⓦ www.palacetesantana.com. Charming hotel with stylish a/c rooms in a striking stone-built sixteenth-century *casa señorial*. ❸

La Casona del Arco c/Sacramento 3 ☎ 953 74 72 08, ⓦ www.lacasonadelarco.com. Comfortable, classically furnished rooms in yet another wonderfully restored eighteenth-century *casa palacio*. Also squeezes in a small pool. Prices rise by forty percent Fri–Sat. ❹

The Town

Most of Baeza's main attractions lie within a few minutes' walk of the pleasant central joined squares of **Plaza de España** and the larger **Paseo de la Constitución**. There are no charges to enter any of the monuments but you may offer the guardian a small *propina* (tip).

Paseo de la Constitución

On the eastern side of the bar-lined *paseo* is **La Alhóndiga**, an elegant porticoed sixteenth-century corn exchange and, almost opposite across the gardens, the arcaded eighteenth-century **Casa Consistorial**, or old town hall, which once fronted the old market square. At the southern end of the *paseo*, you'll find the **Plaza de los Leones** (also called the Plaza del Populo), a delightful cobbled square enclosed by Renaissance buildings. A central fountain incorporates Roman lions and a statue – which locals believe is Imilce, the Iberian wife of the Carthaginian general, Hannibal. The fountain is overlooked by some remarkable buildings including the **Antigua Carnicería** (old slaughterhouse), bearing the arms of Carlos V, and beside the arch at the far end, the Audiencia housing the Turismo (see p.435). Also here, on a rounded balcony flanking the double arch of the Arco de Villalar and the Puerta de Jaén, the first Mass of the Reconquest is reputed to have been celebrated. The Puerta de Jaén was a memento (or rebuke) left by Carlos V to the town that had opposed him,

Walks around Baeza

There are some nice **wandering routes** in town: heading up through the Puerta de Jaén on the Plaza de los Leones and along the Paseo de las Murallas Paseo Antonio Machado takes you round the edge of Baeza and gives good views over the surrounding plains. **El Abuelo**, a house on the Paseo de Don Antonio Machado, is noteworthy for its garden sculpture and towering wrought-iron work. It's the first house past the modern bronze bust of the poet Antonio Machado – who was a frequent walker here – looking out over the olive groves. You can cut back to the Plaza de España via the network of narrow, stone-walled alleys – with the occasional arch – that lies behind the cathedral.

Going further afield, near El Abuelo, some tracks lead down to the plain. Take the right-hand fork and after about 45 minutes you'll come to the route of a former rail line now used as a road for farm vehicles. This offers scope for easy walks across country.

and commemorated the Germanic ruler's procession through here in 1526 en route to marry Isabel of Portugal.

Palacio de Jabalquinto and the Antigua Universidad

The stepped street behind the Plaza de los Leones ascends (via c/Romanones and c/Juan de Ávila) to another cluster of monuments including the finest of Baeza's palaces, the **Palacio de Jabalquinto** (patio Mon–Fri 9am–2pm), now a seminary, with an elaborate "Isabelline" front (showing marked Moorish influence in its stalactite decoration). Built in the fifteenth century by the Benavides family, the tranquil interior patio has a double tier of arcades around a central fountain and a superb Baroque **staircase** with fine carving. Next to this palace, the **Antigua Universidad** (old university; patio daily 10am–2pm & 5–9pm) was founded in 1538 and, after functioning for nearly three centuries as a centre of study and debate, its charter was revoked in 1824 during the tyrannical reign of Fernando VII. From 1875 the buildings were used as a school until, in 1979, the building once again became a centre of higher learning albeit as a summer school for the University of Granada. The interior has an elegant patio and, next to a sixteenth-century lecture hall, the preserved **classroom** used by the great *sevillano* poet and writer Antonio Machado when he served as a teacher here from 1912 to 1919. This experience must have provided much of the material for his most famous prose work, *Juan de Mairena*, the observations on life and culture of a fictional schoolmaster.

A little to the north of here in Plaza Santa Cruz, the remarkable church of **Santa Cruz** (Mon–Sat 11am–1pm & 5–7pm, Sun 11am–1pm; free) is Baeza's oldest, built shortly after the Reconquest in the thirteenth century, although later much restored. Converted from an earlier mosque, the church betrays a combination of late Romanesque and early Gothic architectural styles. The austere, white-walled interior has slender stone columns as well as some fourteenth- and fifteenth-century frescoes, and (east aisle) the preserved arch of the *mihrab*.

At c/Arcos de las Escuelas 2, near the north end of c/Romanones, stands one of Baeza's more eccentric attractions – a shop (Mon–Sat 8.30am–10pm) ostensibly selling local ceramics. Once you've penetrated the shelves of pots and a bottling plant for mineral water behind, you'll enter a studio that has a series of remarkable **marble replicas** of Baeza's famous buildings, including the Ayuntamiento and the Palacio Jabalquinto. Created in eye-straining detail by the shop's self-taught owner, the replicas are well worth a look.

The Cathedral

To the east of Santa Cruz along the Cuesta de San Felipe, the **Plaza de Santa María** is another of Baeza's glorious squares, with a few welcome, shade-providing trees, fronted by a nucleus of fine Renaissance buildings. The rather squat sixteenth-century **Catedral de Santa María** (daily 10.30am–1pm & 5–7pm; church free, museum €2) dominates the square and inside has a fine nave by Andrés de Vandelvira which is, in many ways, a scaled-down version of his cathedral at Jaén. Like several of Baeza's and Úbeda's churches, the cathedral also has painted *rejas* by Maestro Bartolomé, a local craftsman who was responsible for some of the finest examples of this uniquely Spanish contribution to Renaissance art. His work enclosing the choir, with its depictions of a Virgin and Child accompanied by angels and cherubs, is stunning. In the Gothic **cloister**, part of the old mosque – which the church replaced – has been uncovered, but the cathedral's real novelty is a huge silver *custodia* cunningly hidden behind a painting of St Peter which whirls aside on the insertion of a coin. To the east of the cathedral, and beyond Plaza de Arcediano, a narrow street leads to a *mirador* with a fine **view** over the olive groves in the valley of the Guadalquivir towards the distant Cazorla mountain range beyond.

Adjoining the cathedral on the north side is the old Renaissance **Casas Consistoriales Altas** (town hall) with Plateresque features, formerly the palace of the Cabrera family who have another mansion in the town. In the centre of the **Plaza de Santa María** is a sixteenth-century fountain erected by the same family, with pilasters and crude caryatids supporting the arms of Felipe II. Beyond this are the graffiti-covered walls of the sixteenth-century seminary of **San Felipe Neri** where students record their names and dates in bull's blood – a traditional way of celebrating graduation. The building now houses the International University of Andalucía.

The Ayuntamiento and more churches

West of the Paseo de la Constitución, in c/Benavides, the magnificent **Ayuntamiento** was originally the Palace of Justice and prison. Completed in 1559, its richly ornamented facade is exuberantly Plateresque with elegant balconies, coats of arms and, above, a phalanx of gargoyles decorating the cornice. Inside, the main hall upstairs (viewing Mon–Fri 9am–2pm) has a fine coffered ceiling. At the end of the street and facing the same edifice is the charming (privately owned) little **house of Antonio Machado**, marked with a plaque, where the poet lived for most of his time in Baeza.

The nearby c/San Francisco passes the exterior of the **Hospital of the Purísima Concepción** with an elegant Renaissance facade. Adjoining it is the ruined convent of **San Francisco**, designed by Vandelvira and badly damaged during the War of Independence. Sections of both buildings have now been converted into a hotel, banqueting hall and restaurant. At the end of this street and then right along c/San Andrés – lined with ancient *casas señoriales* – lies the early sixteenth-century church of **San Andrés** (open service times, 7–9pm) with an elegant Plateresque facade and *sagrario* off the left aisle by Vandelvira.

Renaissance palaces

Heading north from the Plaza de España, pedestrianized c/San Pablo has a number of interesting Renaissance palaces, many with impressive facades, dating from the sixteenth century. You'll pass the Gothic **Palacio Garcíez** (or Salcedo), with a fine patio and now an upmarket hotel, followed by the **Palacio Cerón**, long Baeza's *Casino* and a place that's played an important role in the cultural life of the town; ask to be shown the wonderfully evocative *salon* upstairs with elegant mirrors and velvet curtains where former member Antonio Machado gave poetry readings and which preserves the piano once played by a visiting García Lorca. Next in line is the **Casa Acuña**, but the best of all is the **Casa Cabrera**, with an elegant Plateresque facade incorporating a double window and frieze over the entrance. In a street to the west of here, the fifteenth-century Gothic church of **San Pablo** (open service times, 7–9pm) has an image of **Christ** by Roldán, and in c/Biedma, behind the church, you'll find the **Palacio de los Elorza**, which is also worth a look.

Eating and drinking

Baeza has a range of restaurants with prices to suit all pockets. For **tapas** and **raciónes** there are plenty of places in and around Paseo de la Constitución and the adjacent Plaza de España. The atmospheric *Bar Cafetería Mercantil* overlooking the latter is the town's most popular haunt, well over a century old and once patronized by Antonio Machado; the terrace is a great place for breakfast and eavesdropping on local gossip – in winter there's a dining room upstairs. Other good tapas bars to seek out are *Arcediano*, c/Barbacana s/n, off the east side of Plaza de España, and *Pedrito* and *Mibel*, neighbours at c/San Pablo 42 & 44, to the north of Plaza de España with adjoining terraces.

For picnickers, the Alacena de la Loma, c/San Pablo 33 (actually a passage on the left off it), serves good **takeaway** roast chicken. Alternatively, all kinds of local provisions are on offer at Alimentación Cantos, c/San Pablo 10, just off Plaza de España; delicacies include local *jamón*, *ciervo* (cured venison), *jabalito* (wild boar) as well as Jaén's top olive oils. Teatime treats are to be had nearby at *Pastelería Martínez*, c/San Pablo, next to the Palacio Cabrera, a pleasant **café** serving delicious pastries made on the premises

Restaurants

Bar Diego c/San Pablo 33. Down a passage off the upper end of c/San Pablo this pleasant little place has a nice terrace, does economical *platos combinados* and offers the town's cheapest *menú* (€8, lunch and dinner).

Casa Juanito Paseo Arca del Agua s/n ☎953 74 00 40. Attached to the hotel of the same name, Baeza's most celebrated restaurant has walls covered with photos of the great and the good who have dined here. The restaurant is famed for its traditional approach with dishes such as *paté de perdiz*, *bacalao con tomate* (cod) and *cabrito al horno* (roast kid) often featured. Main dishes €13–21. Closed Sun & Mon eves.

El Pasaje c/Benavides 3. A reliable place with a pleasant terrace offering a variety of fish and meat dishes – *ensalada de perdiz* (partridge) and *pierna de choto* (kid) are specials – with a *menú* for around €11. Closed Mon.

El Sarmiento c/Plaza del Ardeciano 10. Excellent new restaurant with a terrace on this attractive square behind the cathedral. Specializes in roasted meat dishes and has a Tues–Fri *menú* for €17. Main dishes €10–20. Closed Sun eve & Mon.

El Señorío de Baeza c/Concepción 3. The restaurant of the *Hotel Baeza* is popular with *baezanos* and offers a good-value *menú* incorporating local dishes such as *pipirrana* (*jamón* and vegetable salad) for around €15 (or €11.50 Mon–Fri).

Restaurante Andrés de Vandelvira c/San Francisco 14 ☎953 74 81 72. Baeza's other noteworthy restaurant is installed in the restored ruin of Vandelvira's once-magnificent sixteenth-century convent, which is worth a look, even if you don't intend dining; the convent's former patio/cloister has been fitted with a temporary roof to create a banqueting hall, and the restaurant lies beyond this. The rather narrow dining room is pleasant and signature dishes include *arroz con conejo* (rabbit) and *trucha* and *atun escabechada* (marinated trout or tuna). Main dishes €15–20 and there's a *menú de degustación* for €32. Closed Sun eve & Mon.

Restaurante El Sali c/Cardenal Benavides 15. Opposite the Ayuntamiento, the very good *Restaurante Sali* has a weekday *menú* for around €11 and tables outside so you can feast your eyes on this beautiful building. *Rabo de toro* (bull's tail) and *cochinillo ibérico* (suckling pig) are two specialities. Main dishes €8–20. Closed Wed.

La Laguna

Some 9km southwest of Baeza lies **La Laguna**, a former *hacienda* or olive-oil estate and mill. Purchased in 1992 by the Junta de Andalucía, the complex now houses the impressive **Museo de la Cultura del Olivo** (daily: April–June 10.30am–1.30pm & 4.30–7pm, July–Aug 10.30am–1.30pm & 5.30–8pm, Sept–March 10.30am–1.30pm & 4–6.30pm; ☎953 76 51 42, ⓦwww .museodelaculturadelolivo.com; €3), dedicated to the history and development of Jaén's great wealth earner, describing the history of the olive and production methods used since Roman times. The patio garden has examples of olive species from all over the world. La Laguna also possesses its own farm and lake (*laguna*) while another part of the complex houses the province's hotel and catering school. The school's mid-priced **restaurant** (open weekdays Oct–June), where the trainee chefs serve up their creations, is the *hacienda's* former chapel, with a stunning domed ceiling. Their *menú de degustacíon* for around

€38 is recommended. The adjoining **hotel**, *La Laguna* (☎953 77 10 05, Ⓦwww.ehlaguna.com/hotel; ④), has a pool and pleasant air-conditioned rooms with TV and their mini-suites add in a jacuzzi. A separate restaurant attached to the hotel is open all year. *La Laguna* is aptly located in a sea of olive groves 2km down a signed right turn off the A316 just after the village of Puente del Obispo, 8km out of Baeza.

Úbeda

Little is known of **ÚBEDA**'s previous incarnation as the Roman town of Betula, and it was only in the Moorish period that Obdah, as it became, grew into a prosperous and important centre endowed with walls and a castle. Following the Christian victory over the Moors at Navas de Tolosa in 1212, the Moors from Baeza moved into the city, feeling it provided a more secure refuge against the Christian forces. Despite this, Úbeda was taken a week later and, although an interlude of further freedom for the Muslim occupants was purchased from the Christian armies with massive donations, the town fell conclusively to Fernando El Santo in 1234. As happened in Baeza, numerous noble families were then established by the king and built their mansions in the town. These haughty "lions of Úbeda", as they styled themselves, were soon warring amongst each other, the Arandas fighting the Traperas, and the Molinas against the Cuevas. The fighting got so bad at one point that in 1503 Fernando and Isabel ordered the destruction of the town's walls and towers, to enable the unruly aristocrats to be kept in check. Twelve of these noble families are represented by the twelve lions on the town's coat of arms.

In common with Baeza, it was in the sixteenth century, as a producer of textiles traded across Europe, that Úbeda's fortunes reached their zenith and members of the same noble families came to hold prominent positions in the imperial Spanish court. This was the age of the houses of **Cobos** and **Molinos**, two families who, linked by marriage, dominated the town's affairs. They were also responsible for employing **Andrés de Vandelvira** as their principal architect, whose buildings are the glory of Úbeda today. This prosperity, however, was short-lived and the town declined in the seventeenth century as sharply as it had flourished in the sixteenth, which explains its architectural unity and lack of any significant Baroque edifices. Úbeda is a moderately prosperous provincial town today, its main source of income coming from tourism, the manufacture of farm machinery and sodium sulphates, as well as the more traditional olives and ceramics, and carpets and baskets made from esparto grass.

Arrival and information

The main **bus station**, c/San José s/n, lies to the west of the centre beyond the Hospital de Santiago; there are currently fourteen buses a day from Jaén (all stopping en route at Baeza). **Linares-Baeza** is the nearest **train station**, about 15km from Úbeda (connecting buses for most trains, Mon–Sat; a taxi costs around €20). A central **car park** lies beneath the focal Plaza Andalucía.

Úbeda's **Turismo** (Mon–Fri 8.30am–7.30pm, Sat–Sun 9.30am–3pm; ☎953 72 92 04) is located in the elegant Palacio del Marqués del Contadero, c/Baja del Marqués s/n. They can provide a detailed map and, if you are visiting in the between May and June, a leaflet on Úbeda's annual International Festival of Music and Dance, which attracts big names from the fields of flamenco, rock, opera, jazz, blues and ballet. They also have details of daily **guided tours**

ÚBEDA

Potters' Quarter

RESTAURANTS
& TAPAS BAR

El Gallo Rojo	3
El Seco	5
Mesón Gabino	1
Mesón Navarro	4
Bar la Paloma	7
Pintor Orbaneja	2
Restaurante Marqués	6

ACCOMMODATION

Hostal Miguel	B
Hostal Victoria	J
Hotel Alvar Fáñez	F
Hotel Dos Hermanas	A
Hotel La Paz	B
Hotel María de Molina	G
Hotel Ordóñez Sandoval	H
Las Casas del Consul	J
Palacio de la Rambla	I
Parador Condestable Dávalos	E
Rosaleda de Don Pedro	D

Madrid

A & B (1km)

Linares & Bailén

Baeza & Jaén

Granada

Hospital de
los Honrados
Viejos del
Salvador

Capilla del
Salvador

Palacio de
D. Francisco
de los Cobos

Oratorio de
San Juan

Puerta
del Losal

San Pablo

Casa de
Los Salvajes

Casa de
Los Manueles

Palacio del
Condestable
Dávalos

Palacio de Mancera

Sta. María de los
Reales Alcázares

Antiguo
Pósito

Palacio de
las Cadenas

Museo Arte
Andalusí

Puerta
de Granada

Iglesia de
San Lorenzo

Ayuntamiento
Viejo

Casa
Montiel

Casa
Mudéjar

Palacio de
los Cobos

Santa
Clara

Casa de
las Torres

Pal.
Guadiana

San Pedro

El Marqués

Torre del
Reloj

Palacio Rambla

Iglesia de
la Trinidad

San Nicolás

Casa del
Caballerico
Ortega

Palacio
de los
Bussianos

Hospital de
Santiago

Parque de
Vandelvira

Bus
Station

Plaza de
Toros

of the town. **Internet** access is available at Cibernetworld, c/Niño 22 (daily 11am–2pm & 4.30–10pm), close to the Parque de Vandelvira to the west of the old quarter.

The **flamenco** *tablao* El Marqués, c/Santo Domingo s/n near the *Palacio de la Rambla* hotel, mounts flamenco performances each Saturday (10pm; €18) and entry includes tapas and the first drink. Flamenco performances are often staged in the Hospital de Santiago throughout the summer and the Turismo should have details. Úbeda's big **fiesta** is the *Día de San Miguel* on September 29, when carnival giants, fireworks and a flamenco festival honour the town's patron saint.

Accommodation

You'll find the only budget **places to stay** within walking distance of the bus station, in the modern part of town. The *casco antiguo* (old quarter) now has a great choice of more upmarket places, some in stunning ancient palaces and mansions. Úbeda's high season is in April and May and thus hotel (but not *hostal*) rooms tend to be significantly cheaper in July and August. As in Baeza, many hotels apply a Friday to Saturday surcharge.

Hostal Miguel Avda. Libertad 69 ☏ 953 75 20 49. Úbeda's cheapest *hostal* is a 10min walk away from the centre in the north of town, offering decent en-suite rooms with a good and inexpensive restaurant below. Just around the corner the friendly *Hotel Dos Hermanas*, c/Risquillo Bajo 1 (☏ 953 75 21 24; ❸) is also good. ❷

Hostal Victoria c/Alaminos 5 ☏ 953 79 17 18. Comfortable, welcoming and *hostal* offering pleasant, a/c en-suite rooms with TV. Own car park, too. ❷

Hotel Alvar Fáñez c/Juan Pasquau 5 ☏ 953 79 60 43, ⓦ www.alvarfanez.com. Hotel situated in a reconstituted Renaissance *casa palacio* arranged around an elegant patio. The slightly sombre rooms are nevertheless comfortable and there's a restaurant and good tapas bar. Slightly higher rates Fri & Sat. ❺ with breakfast.

Hotel La Paz c/Andalucía 1 ☏ 953 75 08 48, ⓦ www.hotel-lapaz.com. This decent mid-range hotel has a/c balcony rooms with TV. ❸

Hotel María de Molina Plaza del Ayuntamiento s/n ☏ 953 79 53 56, ⓦ www.hotel-maria -de-molina.com. In the heart of the old quarter, this hotel is housed in a magnificent sixteenth-century *casa palacio* with a superb patio. Rooms come with a/c, strongbox and satellite TV, and some have balconies. Very good value for this category; rates rise slightly Fri–Sat. They also let a number of attractive apartments (❺). ❸

Hotel Ordóñez Sandoval c/Antonio Medina 1 ☏ 953 79 51 87, ⓦ www.hotelordonezsandoval .com. Following the example of the Marquesa de la Rambla (see below), proprietor Amalia Perez Ordóñez has opened part of her family's

nineteenth-century mansion as a hotel. There's a cloistered central patio and the three en-suite guest rooms are tastefully furnished in grand style. Free parking. ❺ with breakfast.

Las Casas del Consul Plaza del Marqués 5 ☏ 953 79 54 30, ⓦ www.lascasasdelconsul .com. Very comfortable new hotel with elegant, well-equipped rooms plus fine patio and garden pool in a refurbished eighteenth-century *casa palacio*. ❻

Palacio de la Rambla Plaza del Marqués 1 ☏ 953 75 01 96, ⓦ www.palaciodelarambla.com. In the old quarter, this upmarket *casa palacio* is owned by the Marquesa de la Rambla. The lavish interior – with eight palatial rooms set around a stunning Renaissance patio designed by Vandelvira – contains valuable furnishings and artworks, which is why you have to use an entryphone to get in. Price includes breakfast – brought to your room if you wish. Closed mid-July to mid-Aug. ❻ with breakfast.

Parador Condestable Dávalos Plaza de Vázquez de Molina 1 ☏ 953 75 03 45, ⓦ www.parador.es. On arguably the most beautiful plaza in Andalucía, Úbeda's parador is housed in a fabulous sixteenth-century Renaissance mansion, with some of the well-appointed rooms overlooking the square. Call in for a drink if you're not staying. ❼ with breakfast.

Rosaleda de Don Pedro c/Obispo Toral 2 ☏ 953 79 51 47, ⓦ www.rosaledadedonpedro .com. Efficient three-star hotel offering well-equipped rooms with satellite TV and a small pool in their terrace garden at the rear. Has own restaurant, library and garage. Rates double Fri–Sat. ❸

The Town

Some 9km east of Baeza and built on the same escarpment overlooking the valley of the Guadalquivir, Úbeda looks less promising when you reach it. Don't be put off, though, for hidden away in the old quarter is one of the finest Renaissance architectural jewels in the whole of Spain, and perhaps even in Europe.

The Plaza de Vázquez de Molina

Follow the signs for the "Zona Monumental" and you'll eventually reach the **Plaza Vázquez de Molina**, a magnificent Renaissance square at the heart of the old town. Most of the buildings around this square are the late sixteenth-century work of Andrés de Vandelvira, the architect of Baeza's cathedral and of numerous churches in both towns. At the western end he built the **Palacio de las Cadenas** (or "chains", which once decorated the facade) for the secretary of Felipe II, Juan Vázquez de Molina, whose family arms crown the doorway of a beautiful classical facade. The interior, these days occupied by the Ayuntamiento, features a superb double-tier arcaded patio. To see this you'll need to go to the back of the building and the Ayuntamiento entrance where the security guard will allow you a peep.

Back on the Plaza Vázquez de Molina, opposite the Palacio de las Cadenas, and between the lions marking the edge of the mansion's domain, lies the church of **Santa María de los Reales Alcázares**, built on the site of a former mosque. Behind the facade, topped by a double belfry, an elegant Gothic cloister encloses what was once the ablutions patio of the mosque. The church contains another fine *reja* by Maestro Bartolomé of Jaén depicting the Tree of Jesse. At the side of the church, as you move east, is the entrance to the sixteenth-century **Cárcel del Obispo** or bishop's prison, which was formerly a convent and is now used as the courthouse. Opposite this is the **Palacio de Marqués de Mancera**, another stately Renaissance edifice with an elegant tower. Adjoining this building and fronting the plaza is the **Antiguo Pósito** or old granary, which later served as a prison and now houses the police station. Close by is a **statue** honouring Vandelvira, the architectural genius who made it all possible. Across the square again, the **Palacio del Condestable Dávalos**, which Vandelvira had a hand in designing, is the former dwelling of the chaplain of the church of El Salvador. This elegant building now houses what must be the most impressive parador in Andalucía (see p.443). Above the door two stone angels support the arms of the first chaplain, Déan Fernando Ortega Salido, who was also responsible for its construction. A stunning arcaded interior patio now serves as the hotel's bar, and is best contemplated over a cool drink.

Chapel of El Salvador

At the eastern end of the Plaza Vázquez de Molina, Vandelvira erected the **Capilla del Salvador** (Mon–Sat 10am–2pm & 4–6.30pm, Sun 11.15am–2pm & 4–7pm; €3), Úbeda's finest church and one of the masterpieces of Spanish Renaissance architecture. Although executed by Vandelvira, he was in fact working to a design created in 1536 by Diego de Siloé (architect of Málaga's and Granada's cathedrals) but typically added his own flourishes. The church was originally the chapel of the mansion – which later burned down – of Francisco de Cobos y Molina, secretary of state to Carlos V and one of the most powerful men of his time. This remarkable building is almost unique in Spain for being built within a very short period (1540–1556) with hardly any later alterations. It also preserves many of its interior furnishings. The exterior **facade** has a carving of the Transfiguration of Christ flanked by statues of San Pedro and San Andrés with a wealth of Plateresque detail. Above the north door around the corner, Vandelvira has placed an image in the tympanum which is almost his trademark – Santiago the Moor slayer, used in Baeza and on the hospital of Santiago in the north of the town.

Entry to the church is via the doorway on the south side. The single naved interior with a beautiful cupola has a brilliantly animated *retablo* on the high altar representing the Transfiguration with a sensitively rendered image of Christ by Alonso de Berruguete who studied under Michelangelo; this is the only part of the altarpiece that completely survived the Civil War. The **reja** fronting the altar is yet another fine work by Maestro Bartolomé de Jaén. In the **sacristy** (all Vandelvira's work) there's a photograph of a statue by Michelangelo given to Francisco de Cobos by the state of Venice, which alas was another Civil War casualty.

Behind El Salvador, and beyond the sixteenth-century **Hospital de los Honorados Viejos del Salvador** (another Vandelvira work), Úbeda comes to a sudden halt at a **mirador** with fine views over a sea of olive groves backed by the Sierra de Cazorla.

The Casa de las Torres and Palacio Vela de los Cobos

To the west of the Plaza Vázquez de Molina along calles Orbaneja and Luna y Sol lies the **Casa de las Torres** (Mon–Fri 8am–2.15pm, Tues 4–6pm), a sombre building with two enormous keeps, framing an ornate Plateresque facade. Now an art school, when it is open you can view the building's elegant double-tiered patio.

Just behind Plaza Vázquez de Molina, the Plaza del Ayuntamiento has the **Palacio Vela de los Cobos**, another impressive building by Vandelvira dating from the middle of the sixteenth century, with an interesting corner balcony and an elegant facade topped off by a delightful arcaded gallery. This is one of the few palaces that can be visited but prior application must be made to the Turismo. Incidentally on the west side of this square, Plaza del Ayuntamiento, Juan Martínez Tito, one of the famous Tito brothers, a noted group of Úbeda potters (see p.446), has his workshop, which is well worth a look.

Oratorio de San Juan de la Cruz and San Pablo

To the north of Plaza Vázquez de Molina (easily reached along c/Francisco de los Cobos), the **Oratorio de San Juan de La Cruz** is where San Juan (St John of the Cross), an accomplished poet and mystic, died of gangrene in 1591. The original monastery was damaged in the Civil War and little of it survives, although a small **museum** (Tues–Sun 11am–1pm & 5–7pm; €1.50) preserves memorabilia from the saint's lifetime as well as his writing desk and the cell in which he died. At the end of c/San Juan de la Cruz facing the monastery, the **Plaza del Primero de Mayo** (formerly the Plaza del Mercado) is a charming acacia-lined square with a bandstand at its centre marking the site of the fires of the *autos-da-fé* that were once carried out here on the orders of the Inquisition. The Town Council presided over these grisly events from the superb arcaded sixteenth-century **Ayuntamiento Viejo** on the square's western side. Dominating its northern flank is the idiosyncratic **Iglesia de San Pablo** (Mon–Wed 11am–noon, Thurs–Sat 11am–1pm, Sun 11am–1.30pm, plus Mon & Sat 7–8pm; free), incorporating various Romanesque, Gothic and Renaissance additions and crowned by a Plateresque tower. It boasts a thirteenth-century balcony (a popular feature in Úbeda), and a superb portal. The interior has a fine capilla by Vandelvira (chapel of Camarero Vago) as well some intricate carving in the Capilla de la Mercedes and more superb *rejas*.

Around Plaza del Primero de Mayo

Calle Horno Contado, which leaves Plaza del Primero de Mayo at the southeast corner, has two more palaces you might want to see: a short way down on the right, the **Casa de los Manueles** has a fine facade and, a little further down on the left, the fifteenth-century **Casa de los Salvajes** (savages) is named after the two figures clothed in animal skins supporting the arms of its founder, Francisco de Vago. In reality they are probably natives of the imperial colonies, from whose exploitation much of this conspicuous wealth was derived. Off the north side of the square in c/Cervantes the **Casa Mudéjar** at no. 6 is a fine fourteenth-century building whose elegant Mudéjar **patio** has pointed horseshoe arches. It houses a small **archeological museum** (Tues 2.30–8pm, Wed–Sat 9am–8.30pm, Sun 9am–3pm; free).

Calle Melchor Almagro, leaving the square on the north side of San Pablo, has another mansion, the wonderful Plateresque **Casa Montiel**, and, further along, a sixteenth-century Carmelite convent.

The Potters' Quarter

Leaving the Plaza del Primero de Mayo by the c/Losal in its northeast corner leads to the **Puerta del Losal**, a magnificent thirteenth-century Mudéjar gate with a double-horseshoe arch which was formerly one of the main entrances to the old walled town. Through the arch you enter c/de la Merced, soon arriving at Plaza Olleros (Potters' Square), marked by an enormous pot on a plinth. Leading off this square, c/Valencia is the old **potters' street** where the workshops of Úbeda's main ceramic craftsmen are located. Alfarería y Museo Tito, c/Valencia 22 (Ⓦwww .pacotito.com), is one of the friendliest, where renowned ceramic artist Paco Tito has his workshop and museum and will usually will give you a demonstration on the potter's wheel. Nearby in the yard is the kiln, where the system used to fire the pots – many glazed and tinted with Úbeda's traditional deep green – is one inherited from the Moors; once the wood is burning, olive stones are introduced into the fire which creates smoke and soaks up oxygen producing a more even heat with superior results in both colour and glaze. There are only six of these traditional kilns left in the whole of Spain and three are in this street. The museum/ gallery upstairs is devoted to Paco's more ambitious works including statuary, huge Amphorae and a completely ceramic (and fully functioning) bathroom. He is famous also for his sculptural work and has sculpted many eminent Spaniards including King Juan Carlos who sat for him during the making of a statue for Baeza's national Guardia Civil training college. Nearby are the workshops of other potters – including Juan and Antonio Almarza, and Góngora – all famous throughout Spain. Paco Tito's equally well-known brother, Juan, also has a workshop on the Plaza del Ayuntamiento, near the Turismo (see p.445).

Plaza San Pedro and Calle Real

Starting out from the Plaza San Pedro (to the west of the Plaza del Ayuntamiento) there are a number of other important sights to see in the northwest of the town. On the Plaza San Pedro itself, the thirteenth-century **Convento de Santa Clara** contains a patio with a fine Gothic-Mudéjar multi-lobed portal. The convent also sells its home-made *dulces* – tasty cakes, biscuits and pastries. Just south from here along c/Narvaez at no. 11 the privately owned **Museo Arte Andalusi** (Mon–Sat 11am–2pm & 6–9pm; €1.50) is housed in a sixteenth-century mansion filled with period artefacts from other houses around the town. Heading west from Plaza San Pedro you come to another mansion, the **Palacio de la Rambla**, sited at the end of c/Medina. The facade is another graceful work by Vandelvira, and the interior is now an upmarket hotel (see p.443). Otherwise, across the square, the church of **San Pedro** with a noteworthy portal leads into c/Pascua where, on the junction with c/Real, stands the impressive tower of the **Palacio del Conde de Guadiana**, one of the most striking of all Úbeda's palaces. The tower is, in fact, a seventeenth-century work and the richly ornamented balconies are a delight.

Turning into **Calle Real** brings you to the heart of the old town's commercial centre and its former main shopping street. Many establishments are now deserting this area for new premises in the modern town but a few of the more traditional traders are still here. Pedro Blanco at no. 47 is still making and selling goods made from traditional esparto grass, a versatile material used in the area since ancient times. Heading north along here brings you eventually to the **Plaza de Andalucía**, an unremarkable square overlooked by the **Torre del Reloj**, a remnant of the thirteenth-century ramparts, crowned with a later sixteenth-century temple. Interestingly, a monument to General Saro, a Civil War officer with Fascist affiliations, has returned to the square after a five-year absence; the general's bullet-hole-riddled metal skull evidences how local disapproval of his ideas was expressed.

Hospital de Santiago

Five minutes west of the Plaza de Andalucía along c/Obispo Cobos, and worth every bead of sweat getting there, is Vandelvira's huge **Hospital de Santiago** (Mon–Fri 8am–2.30pm & 5–10pm, Sat–Sun 11am–3pm; free). Perhaps the scale put him off, for the exterior decoration is untypically restrained, and its austere dignity has led to the building being described as "Andalucía's Escorial". Commissioned by Bishop Cobos y Molina and begun in 1562, the flight of steps at the entrance is flanked by more "lions of Úbeda", beyond which Vandelvira has inserted his trademark – Santiago the Moor slayer – above the arch. The equally restrained interior has a patio with columns of Genoa marble and a staircase with stunning vaulting, in addition to a striking chapel – all further evidence of Vandelvira's mastery.

Eating and drinking

Most reasonably priced **restaurants** are in the modern part of town, along the Avenida Ramón y Cajal. *Bar La Paloma*, at the junction of calles Rastro and Cava, is a good tapas haunt. A number of restaurants attached to hotels are also worth considering: the mid-priced *Rosaleda de Don Pedro* (€18) and *Alvar Fáñez* (€12) both offer *menús del día*.

El Gallo Rojo c/Torrenueva 3. Set back from the road, this is one of the town's better restaurants, offering local specialities, a *menú* for €15 and outdoor tables in the evening.

El Seco c/Corazón de Jesús 8. Close to the Plaza del Ayuntamiento, this mid-priced restaurant is a cut above the norm; it is noted for its tasty *potaje carmelitano* (chickpea, leek and cod soup) but also does excellent meat and game dishes and there's a weekday *menú* (main dishes €11–18).

Mesón Gabino c/Fuente Seca. On the northern edge of the old quarter, near the Puerto del Losal, this is a good place for *raciónes*, in a converted old cellar. Its mid-priced restaurant also does decent fish dishes and a house special is a tasty *solomillo* (pork loin); there's a *menú* for €20.

Mesón Navarro Plaza del Ayuntamiento. In the old quarter, behind the Palacio de las Cadenas, this popular place is one of only a handful of restaurants in the area; it also has a lively tapas and *raciónes* bar.

Parador Condestable Dávalos Plaza de Vázquez de Molina 1. If you want to dine in style in the old quarter, the parador's expensive restaurant serves superbly prepared regional dishes that are available on a tasting *menú* (€38); there are also equally good-value lunch-time (€23.50) and evening (€31) *menús*.

Pintor Orbaneja c/Virgen de Guadalupe 5. Just north of El Gallo Rojo, this place serves up pretty good tapas and fish and meat dishes in its restaurant.

Restaurante Marqués Plaza Marqués de la Rambla 2. Serving a good-value *menú* often featuring *merluza con almejas y esparragos* (hake with clams and asparagus), and with a terrace on the square that allows you to contemplate the *Palacio de la Rambla's* elegant exterior.

Towards Cazorla

From Úbeda, the next destination for most travellers is spectacular **Cazorla Natural Park** (officially titled the Parque Natural de Cazorla, Segura y Las Villas), a wilderness area filled with deep ravines and wooded valleys and which, in its mountains, gives birth to the mighty Río Guadalquivir. The park's towering rock cliffs are the preserve of the acrobatic ibex, whilst the valleys and gorges swarm with birdlife and are home to unique pre-Ice Age plants. From Úbeda there are two **routes into the park**. The more conventional one, taken by the bus, is via the small town of Cazorla, located on the park's southern edge and the main gateway to it. Another route, however, skirts the park's western flank and allows visits to a number of interesting sights – including the picturesque hill villages of **Sabiote**, with a castle and Renaissance mansions, and **Iznatoraf**, with its distinctive Moorish feel – before turning into the park close to the small town of Villanueva.

Into the Park via Sabiote, Villacarillo and Iznatoraf

Leaving Úbeda by the N322 brings you first to Torreperogil, 8km east and – unusually for Jaén province – a centre of wine rather then olive production. A turning here leads to the pretty hill village of **SABIOTE**, 4km distant, a cobble-streeted place still girdled by much of its medieval walls and with a pedigree dating back to Roman times. At its heart, the sixteenth-century church of **San Pedro Apostól** has a fine, if worn, Plateresque facade. At the foot of c/Castillo, which has a couple of striking Renaissance mansions (one is now a hotel, see below), the ruined **Castillo** dates back to Roman times, although the Moors made subsequent alterations. More modifications were added during the Renaissance period by Francisco Cobos of the noble house based at Úbeda, and it's thought that he drafted in his architect Andrés de Vandelvira to carry them out. The elegant cloister of the sixteenth-century Carmelite convent (open service times, try 7–8pm) is also worth a look. All these monuments can be seen on a free **guided tour** organized by the Ayuntamiento (Sat & Sun all year; 11am); the tour meets at and departs from the Ayuntamiento at the northern end of the village near the Puerta de la Villa. Sabiote has an excellent **place to stay**: the *Palacio de Manillas*, c/Castillo 1 (℡953 77 43 46, ⓦwww.palaciolasmanillas .com; ❹) is a wonderful sixteenth-century palace sensitively transformed into a very comfortable hotel with bar and good-value **restaurant**. Even if you're not a guest, the friendly proprietor, Manolo Cabrera, will give you a map of the village and is a fount of information on its monuments and history.

Villacarillo and Iznatoraf

VILLACARILLO, 20km further along the N322, is a fairly featureless town surrounded by olive groves but with an impressive Renaissance **Church of the Asunción** by Vandelvira (July–Sept daily 10.30am–1.30pm & 7.30–9pm, Oct–June 7.30–9pm; free), whose major interior features are some spectacular **domes** with sixteenth-century paintings. About 6km after this, a road on the left snakes dizzily upwards to the spectacularly sited hill-top village of

IZNATORAF. The village is clustered around a pleasant Plaza Mayor with a Renaissance arch and the great stone church of **Santo Cristo** dominating its eastern end. After you've wandered around the narrow Moorish streets, many decorated with colourful geraniums in summer, and had a look over the ruins of its walls and castle, don't miss the spectacular **views** over the valley of the Río Guadalimar towards the bordering province of Albacete from the *mirador* perched above the cliff at the village's northern edge.

Not quite 2km beyond the turn-off for Iznatoraf and before Villanueva del Arzobispo, a road leaves the N322 on the right for Tranco and the Cazorla Natural Park. Take note of the signs warning you that there is limited petrol to be had in the park – a full tank would be a wise precaution. Some 7km from the turn-off the road joins the densely wooded valley of the newly born Guadalquivir, a mere stream compared to the mighty torrent which flows through Seville over 200km downstream. After a further 14km the road arrives at Tranco on the banks of the Embalse del Tranco (reservoir) which is described in the main account of the park on p.459.

Into the Park via Peal de Becerro and Cazorla

The bus route to Cazorla heads southeast from Úbeda, passing through olive country and crossing the Guadalquivir before turning off the main road to the village of **PEAL DE BECERRO**. The village spreads over a low hill beneath the crumbling towers of its medieval fort. With your own transport, you can take a minor road out of the village 4km southwest to **Toya**, where there's an important Iberian underground tomb. Should you want to **stay**, two accommodation options lie within a hundred metres of the Ayuntamiento (see below). *Hostal-Restaurante Juanito* (T 953 73 07 16; ❷), Avda. Constitución 32, has tidy en-suite rooms, and the nearby *Hotel Al-Andalus* (T 953 71 64 80, W www.halandalus.com; ❸), Carrera Santo Tomé 5, which is the slightly plusher option. Both places have decent restaurants. Continuing the loop around to Cazorla would enable you to take in a remarkable **Roman villa** near to Quesada which has superb mosaic pavements.

Toya's necropolis and Bruñel's Roman villa

In 1909 a large rectangular underground stone tomb was discovered by a farmer near the hamlet of **Toya**, the former Iberian settlement of *Tugia*. Unfortunately, the family cleared the tomb – used from the fifth to the second century BC – of a whole treasure house of artefacts, which they then sold. Some fine Greek vases were later recovered, and testified to this remote tribe's sophistication and trading contacts with the Mediterranean world. The totally intact stone-built **necropolis** is impressive and the largest of its kind in Spain. The tomb is located a few kilometres outside Toya, but first you'll need to visit the *Policia Local* station (T 653 661 810; Spanish only) inside the Ayuntamiento at the centre of the town to get the key (in return for the deposit of a passport); they will also clarify directions. From the Ayuntamiento you should head west along the Hornos de Peal road, forking left at a signed road for Toya just outside the town. Three hundred metres before the village of Toya a signed lane on the right leads to the site. A full-scale walk-in replica of the tomb has recently been constructed inside the Museo Provincial in Jaén (see p.433)

To reach the **Roman villa** at **Bruñel**, set off south from Peal along the A315 in the direction of Quesada. A couple of kilometres before the village (which you will see on its hill in the distance) a minor road on the left is signed for the Roman villa. However, you will need to visit the *Policia Local* station

(☎696 653 905; Spanish only) inside the Ayuntmiento in the centre of Quesada to collect the keys (same procedure as for Toya on p.449). Once on the minor road (see p.449), keep going for 3km until you reach a signed track on the left. A short distance up the track, again to the left, you will pass a gated house named Villa Josefina. Beyond here, continue up the track for about a kilometre until, at the top of a rise by a ruined building to the left, you will see the site entrance opposite. The keys unlock the outer and inner fence gates. At the time of writing the outer fence was left unlocked and the inner fence had a large hole in it rendering the keys uneccessary.

Once inside the site you can appreciate why it was decided to locate the villa here as it enjoys fine views towards the mountains of the Sierra de Cazorla. The villa – possibly the country seat of an important official or farming family – was a substantial affair based around a large atrium with another atrium to the side. The **mosaics** are delightful, all the more so because you will most likely have them all to yourself. The images of animals, particularly a wonderful mosaic featuring ducks, are of the highest quality, as is a powerful image of what is thought to be the sea goddess Tethys, wife of Oceanus. Coin evidence has dated the original building here to the mid-fourth century AD and this was substantially enlarged in even grander style later in the same century with the addition of a new peristyled courtyard surrounded by a series of spacious rooms. In the final phase of its existence the villa appears to have been abandoned following a fire and in the middle of the sixth century a double-apsed early Christian basilica was constructed on top of the remains, the walls of which dominate the site today. Fortunately many of the mosaics survived both events, although, and rather surprisingly, they are not protected from the elements in any way.

After you've re-locked the site and returned the keys, continuing along the same minor road from the Villa Josefina will let you follow the A322 to Cazorla, some 7km distant.

Cazorla

The small town of **CAZORLA**, 15km beyond Peal at an elevation of 900m, huddles towards the top of a valley that runs from the rugged limestone cliffs of the Peña de los Halcones. This rocky bluff, with its wheeling buzzards and occasional eagle, marks the southwestern edge of a vast, protected area, the **Parque Natural de Cazorla**, containing the sierras of Cazorla and Segura and the headwaters of the Río Guadalquivir.

As the gateway town for visitors to the natural park, little about the attractive town today would lead you to believe that Cazorla had been around for over two thousand years. However, not only were there significant Iberian and Roman settlements here, this was also the see of one of the first bishoprics of early Christian Spain. Under the Moors it was a strategic stronghold and one of dozens of fortresses and watchtowers guarding the Sierra. Taken after a bitter struggle in 1235, during the *Reconquista*, the town then acted as an outpost for Christian troops. Nowadays, the two castles that dominate the village testify to its turbulent past; both were originally Moorish but later altered and restored by their Christian conquerors.

Arrival and information

The main road climbs between concrete blocks of flats, disgorging you into the busy Plaza de la Constitución. Arriving **by car**, you should take a right here

CAZORLA

Iglesia de Santa María

Frondosa Naturaleza

PLAZA DE SANTA MARÍA

Castillo la Yedra

SAN JUAN

CARMEN

CARMEN

Iglesia de San José

Ayuntamiento

Turisnat

PLAZA DE LA CONSTITUCIÓN

DR. MUÑOZ

PLAZA DE LA CORREDERA

Market

Iglesia de San Francisco

CRUZ DE OREA

Río Cerezuelo

PUENTE DE LA VILLA

Camping Cortijo

RESTAURANTS & TAPAS BARS

Bar Niño	3
Bar Julian	1
Bar La Montería	6
Bar Las Vegas	5
Bar Rincón Serrano	2
Bar Rojas	7
Bar Sola	4
Caracoles	9
Juan Carlos	10
La Sarga	11
Mesón Don Chema	8
Mesón La Cueva de San Pedro	B

ACCOMMODATION

Apartmentos San Pedro	C
Albergue Juvenil	F
Hostal Betis	H
Hotel Ciudad de Cazorla	G
Hotel de Montana Riogazas	D
Hotel Sierra de Cazorla	E
Hotel Guadalquivir	I
Mesón la Cueva de don Pedro	B
Molino La Farraga	A
Villla Turística de Cazorla	J

0   100 m

C D E & La Iruela

Turismo & Parque Natural

Jaén & Úbeda

downhill to the **car park**, as trying to find a place to park anywhere else can be futile, especially in high summer. Up to five **buses** a day (currently Mon–Fri at 7am, 8am, noon, 3.45pm & 5.30pm) go from Úbeda to Cazorla. The same buses leave Baeza half an hour earlier and there are also buses from Jaén and Granada. Alsina Graells (Ⓦwww.alsa.es), the main bus operator, has a ticket office at the bus stand in c/Hilario Marco, where the bus drops you, 300m downhill from Plaza de la Constitución.

In the Plaza de la Constitución, La Despensa del Parque (daily 10am–2pm & 5–8pm; ☏953 72 01 15) is a privately run **tourist office**, also acting as an agent for Turisnat (daily 10am–1pm & 5.30–8pm; ☏953 72 13 51, Ⓦwww.turisnat.es) one of the major providors of activities in the park. The staff are friendly but the office exists to promote Land Rover excursions, photo safaris and the like, though they do sell the Alpina map series covering the Cazorla park (see p.456). The town's official **Turismo** (April–Sept Wed–Sun 10am–2pm; ☏953 71 01 02, Ⓦwww.cazorla.es) on Paseo del Santo Cristo 19, 100m north of Plaza de la Constitución, can provide a useful town map. Both can also provide details on all aspects of the park and activities. **Internet** access is available at Parra Multi-store, Plaza de la Constitución 12 (daily 10.30am–2pm & 4.30–10pm). On May 15, Cazorla honours its patron, San Isicio, with a vibrant **romería** preceded the night before by **La Hoguera** (bonfires). In mid-September there's the **fiesta de Cristo del Consuelo**, with fairgrounds, fireworks and religious processions.

Accommodation

Outside August, finding a **place to stay** is usually no problem, as most visitors are either en route to, or leaving, the park. Cazorla's **campsite**, *Camping Cortijo*

(T953 72 12 80), is located beyond the Castillo de la Yedra, 1km from the centre; to get there, follow the Camino San Isicio from the Plaza de Santa María. It's worth noting that outside the high summer months it can get quite chilly here in the evenings and whilst all the hotel rooms have heating, not all the *hostales* do, so enquire if you think this may be a problem.

Albergue Juvenil Plaza Mauricio Martínez 6 T953 71 13 01, Wwww.inturjoven.com. Cazorla's tidy youth hostel, housed in a former convent, has some double rooms and a pool, and is reached by following c/Juan Domingo (reached via steps) from Plaza de la Constitución. Under 26 €14, over 26 €19 inc. breakfast.

Apartamentos San Pedro Carretera de la Sierra s/n, La Iruela, 2km out of Cazorla heading into the park T953 72 00 15, Wwww.hotelsierradecazorla .com. Pleasant apartments sleeping from two to six. All come with kitchen, TV, washing machine and heating, and there's a small pool too. You are also permitted to use the facilities at the nearby *Hotel Sierra de Cazorla*. Surcharge in Aug. **4**

Hostal Betis Plaza Corredera 19 T953 72 05 40. Friendly proprietor and good-value accommodation for rooms sharing bath; rooms at the rear (nos. 101–104) have great views. **1**

Hotel Ciudad de Cazorla Plaza de la Corredera 8 T953 72 17 00, Wwww.rlhoteles.com. Cazorla's newest hotel caused a ruckus when it was unveiled (see below), but inside a/c rooms come with minibar and safe, some have terraces and there's a circular pool at the back. Wi-fi throughout. Surcharge Fri–Sat & Aug. **4** with breakfast.

Hotel de Montaña Riogazas 7km south of Cazorla along the road to El Chorro and the Nacimiento del Río Guadalquivir T953 12 40 35, Wwww.riogazas.com. An appealing country option in the Sierra de Cazorla with rooms inside a handsome *casa forestal* with pool and restaurant. They offer a wide range of park-based activities from guided hikes to wildlife photography courses and 4x4 excursions. **3**

Hotel Guadalquivir c/Nueva 6 T&F953 72 02 68, Wwww.hguadalquivir.com. Charming and friendly small hotel in a central location offering en-suite a/c rooms with fridge and TV. **3**

Hotel Sierra de Cazorla 2km outside Cazorla, in the village of La Iruela T953 72 00 15, Wwww .hotelsierradecazorla.com. Modern complex comprising three- and four-star hotels plus a spa. The three-star option is particularly good-value with balcony rooms and scenic surroundings; there's also a restaurant, bar and great pool. Produces its own walks guide for guests. Surcharge in Aug. **4–5**

Mesón La Cueva de Juan Pedro Plaza Santa María T953 72 12 25, Wwww.turismoencazorla .com/juanpedro.html. Rustic and friendly restaurant that also offers en-suite rooms with bath and excellent studio apartments nearby with kitchen, TV and terrace. **2**

Molino La Farraga Camino de la Hoz s/n, 5min from Plaza Santa María T953 72 12 49, Wwww.molinolafarraga.com. An enchanting *casa rural* in a densely wooded garden location above the valley of the Río Cerezuelo with cosy en-suite rooms, pool and friendly proprietors. **4** with breakfast.

Parador El Adelantado 25km away in the park T953 72 70 75, Wwww.parador.es. Somewhat featureless modern building made attractive by its wonderful setting and a swimming pool. Make sure to get a room with a view. Also has its own bar and restaurant. See map, p.455. **6**

Pensión Taxi Travesía de San Antón 7 T953 72 05 25. Up steps opposite the bus stop in Plaza de la Constitución, this is a friendly budget option with a good-value *comedor* (dining room). En-suite rooms have a/c, heating and TV. **2**

Villa Turística de Cazorla Ladera de San Isicio s/n, reached by crossing the bridge over the river below Plaza de la Constitución T953 71 01 00, Wwww.villacazorla.com. One of the most attractive of the upmarket in-town places and set in leafy surroundings, it comprises a series of self-contained, a/c chalets with terraces plus communal pool and restaurant. Own car park. **4**

The town and around

A few-minutes' walk south from the Plaza de la Constitución along the main c/Dr Muñoz leads to the **Plaza de la Corredera** (or *del Huevo*, "of the Egg", because of its shape). This is the traditional meeting place for the *señoritos*, the class of landowners and their descendants who, through influence and privilege, still lay claim to the most important jobs and mould local destiny. The Ayuntamiento is here too – a fine Moorish-style palace off the far end of the plaza. The arrival of the *Hotel Ciudad de Cazorla* on the square's east side caused a controversy in the town because of its jarring architectural style.

▲ Cazorla town

Beyond Plaza de la Corredera, c/Gómez Calderón (passing the Ayuntamiento) is one of a labyrinth of narrow, twisting streets descending to Cazorla's liveliest square, the **Plaza de Santa María**. This takes its name from the sixteenth-century cathedral church of **Santa María**, designed by Andrés de Vandelvira, which was damaged by floods in the seventeenth century and later torched by Napoleonic troops. Its impressive ruins, now preserved, and the fine open square with a Renaissance fountain form a natural amphitheatre for concerts and local events as well as being a popular meeting place. Just behind the church lies the **Frondosa Naturaleza** (Tues–Sat 10am–2pm & 5–8pm; free), a *Centro de Visitantes* for the Parque Natural with information and displays on the park's flora and fauna.

Wild and relatively unspoiled country, with grand panoramas west over the olive plains of Jaén, begins at the edge of Cazorla, and if you choose to base yourself here, you can make a number of good **day trips**.

Just over an hour's walk away (head up behind the fountain on Plaza Santa María, then pick up the mule track which skirts the hill topped by the ruined upper castle of Cinco Esquinas) is the intriguing sixteenth-century **Monasterio de Monte Sion**. One of the brothers who worked on its reconstruction remains there (summer only), and will proudly show you round his isolated domain, particularly the monastery's chapel with restored frescoes. Be prepared to step back into the Middle Ages – as exemplified by the scourges hanging over the beds in the cells used for retreat. Another hour's walk beyond the cloister to the south will bring you to the base of **Gilillo**, highest point in the southwest of the park, with a yawning gorge to the right.

You can follow the main path over a pass from here to a dilapidated *casa forestal* and then down to **Cañada de las Fuentes**, source of the Guadalquivir, within another two hours. Alternatively – and a more feasible day-walk – you might bear left at the saddle onto a trail descending towards Cazorla town through the canyon of **Riogazas**. This path ends in a jumble of tractor tracks after an hour, after which you must pick your way down through the various water courses for another hour and a half. This five-hour walking day allows ample time for dawdling, but unfortunately many of the pools in the stream on the descent are either difficult to get to or on private property. A good **map** such as the *Alpina Sierra de Cazorla* map (available from La Despensa del Parque – see p.451) would be a useful aid to staying on the right track on all the above hikes.

A popular trip **by car** is to the source of the Guadalquivir river, in the mountains to the south of Cazorla. When you reach the source you'll find the infant river innocently bubbling from beneath a rock as it begins its seven-hundred-kilometre journey to the Atlantic. To get there, take the road out to La Iruela and then follow the signs for La Cañada de las Fuentes, around a 25km journey.

The square itself is dominated by **La Yedra**, the austere, reconstructed tower of the lower of two Moorish castles. It also houses the **Museo de Artes y Costumbres** (Tues 2.30–8pm, Wed–Sat 9am–8pm, Sun 9am–2pm; free), a notable folklore museum. There's a fine **view** from just above the plaza of the castle perched on its rock.

Some 2km up the road heading into the park from Cazorla, the village of **LA IRUELA** has the other ruined Moorish **fortress**, perched on a daunting but picturesque rock peak which must have been a wretched struggle for the Christian troops to subdue. It was later rebuilt by the Templars. There's also another ruined church here, Santo Domingo, attributed to Vandelvira. The village has a number of upmarket hotels (see p.452).

Eating, drinking and nightlife

You'll find several bars serving up good **tapas** around the Plaza Santa María, where for more substantial **eating** there's also the rustic *Mesón La Cueva de Juan Pedro* (see p.452) which has been in the Muñoz family for over a century and offers authentic local food – the *conejo* (rabbit) is recommended – cooked on a wood-fired range, plus a *menú* for €9. Nearby in the tiny c/Nueva, *Caracoles* at no. 9 is a new small restaurant with a *menú* for €10. On Plaza de la Corredera, *Bar Las Vegas* does good sit-down tapas and *raciónes* including tasty *revueltos*. Between here and Plaza de la Constitución left off c/Muñoz – and down some steps – *Mesón Don Chema* is a good choice for *platos combinados*, offering many local specialities. Continuing down the same steps to the market square leads to

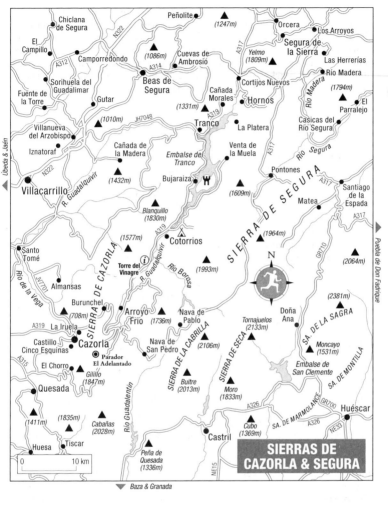

SIERRAS DE CAZORLA & SEGURA

0   10 km

Baza & Granada

the rather swish *La Sarga*, (☎953 72 15 07) Cazorla's top – and very good – restaurant preparing regional dishes with flair; *lomo de jabali en salsa de castañas* (wild boar with chestnut sauce) is one of a number of game options prepared here, and there's also a *menú de degustación* for around €28. At the southern end of the same square, *Juan Carlos* (☎953 72 12 01) is similar but slightly cheaper, serving up delicious trout and game dishes with a *menú* for around €12. Two restaurants attached to accommodation (see p.452) are also worth considering: *Pensión Taxi* has a good-value all-in *menú* for €10 and, moving upmarket, the *Hotel Cuidad de Cazorla* has its own popular *menú* (including wine) for around €15.

A few of Cazorla's excellent **tapas bars** provide the route for an entertaining bar crawl between the town's three squares. On Plaza de la Constitución you'll find what many locals believe to be the best in town, *Bar Sola*, and the nearby *Bar Rojas*. Plaza Corredera has the popular *Bar La Montería* (try its famous *plato olimpico* for €5 which gets you a selection of all their tapas) and the earthier *Bar Niño* offering fresh seafood. On the same square and near the Ayuntamiento, the justly popular *Bar Rincón Serrano* has a pleasant terrace by the ancient fountain, and provides a free *tapa* with every drink. Plaza de Santa María has *Bar Julián* where the delicious *callos* (tripe) and *caracoles* (snails) are only a couple of the many dishes popular with locals who fill its lively terrace all summer. The **market** (Mon–Sat until 2.30pm) in Plaza del Mercado (below c/Dr Muñoz) is a good place to gather ingredients for picnics in the park.

The Cazorla Natural Park

The **Cazorla Natural Park** – or Parque Natural de Cazorla, Segura y Las Villas to give its official name – is not as lofty as the Sierra Nevada (the highest peaks are 2000m), but outdoes it for beauty, slashed as it is by river gorges and largely covered in forest. The best **times to visit** are late spring and early autumn. The winters can be uncomfortably wet and cold, and roads are often closed due to snow. In high summer, although walking is pleasant before noon, the climate tends to be hot and dry.

Inside the park, **public transport** is scarce and currently there are just two daily buses running between Cazorla and Coto Ríos, 39km into the park. Distances between points are enormous, so to explore it well you'll need a car or be prepared for long hikes; otherwise day-trips to the outskirts of the park are possible. However, a number of **campsites** – both *camping libre* (free camping) and official sites – dotted around the park make walking tours possible. The **Turismo** at Cazorla (see p.451) will provide a complete list and map of campsites within the park.

Places to stay – hotels, apartments, villas and wood cabins – are to be found throughout the park, many of them very attractive indeed if getting away from it all is what you're after. Be aware, however, that while for most of the year you should be able to find accommodation with ease, they all tend to fill up in August, when ringing ahead is strongly advised. The high season price quoted for accommodation in the park applies only to August.

Judging from the number of *cabra hispanica* (Spanish mountain goat), deer, *jabalí* (wild pig), birds and butterflies that even the casual visitor is likely to spot, the Cazorla reserve is fulfilling its role handsomely. Ironically, though, much of the best wildlife viewing will be at the periphery, or even outside the park, since the wildlife is most successfully stalked on foot and walking opportunities within the park itself are somewhat limited. There are, in fact, only three **signposted tracks**, all pitifully short. One leads from the Empalme de Valle to the Puente de las Herrerías via the Fuente del Oso (2km one way); another of about 1.7km curls round the Cerrada (Narrows) del Utrero near Vadillo-Castril village; the best-marked segment, through the lower Borosa gorge (see p.458), is also a mere 1.7km long. Good **hiking guides** for the park include Guy Hunter-Watts' *Walking in Andalucía*, which details five walks of between five and nineteen kilometres (see p.609); also it's advisable to take a reliable map (see below) when doing any serious walking here. Before heading into the park, it's worth stopping at the private **tourist office**, La Despensa del Parque, in Cazorla (see p.451). Both they and the Torre del Vinagre Centro de Interpretación (see p.457) should have copies of the 1:40,000 **map and guide packs** titled *Mapa y Guía Excursionista* (Editorial Alpina). This series splits the park in two parts: *Sierra de Cazorla* (covering the southern zone) and *Sierra de Segura* (the central and northern sectors). These are now the most accurate maps available on the park and detail *senderos* (footpaths), mountain bike routes, refuges, campsites and hotels. The accompanying booklet (in Spanish or English versions) has useful background information on the park's flora and fauna as well as villages, and includes half a dozen described walks.

Arroyo Frio, Torre del Vinagre and Coto Ríos

Two **buses** (April–Sept, Mon–Fri only) link Cazorla town with **Coto Ríos** – where there's a campsite and accommodation – near the middle of the park via Torre del Vinagre: one currently running at 7.15am, the other at 2.30pm. Return buses from Coto leave at 9am and 4.15pm (confirm these plus winter timetable with bus company, Carcesa: ☎953 72 11 42). Taking the early departure allows you to do the classic **walk along the Río Borosa** as a day-trek (see box, p.458; confirm all the above times in Cazorla to avoid being stranded). The road into the park passes Burunchel and climbs over the Puerto de las Palomas with spectacular views before descending into the valley of the Guadalquivir. A little further on there's a turning for the scenically sited **parador** which, with your own transport, would allow you to stop off for a drink; they also offer a good-value set *menú* for lunch and dinner which sometimes includes the excellent local river trout served *a la cazuleña* (with *jamón serrano* and almonds).

Arroyo Frio

The road into the park soon passes the hamlet of **Arroyo Frio** where the *Hotel Cazorla Valle* (☎953 72 71 00, ⓦwww.cazorlavalle.com; ❸ with breakfast) rents out rooms and apartments, has a restaurant and pool and offers numerous outdoor activities. Further along the tourist complex of *Los Enebros* (☎953 72 71 10, ⓦwww.lfhoteles.com; ❺) has a campsite, hotel and restaurant and rents out freestanding wood cabins; there's a wide variety of activities on offer here too, such as mountain biking, canoeing and guided walks. **Horseriding** is available from a ranch, Bujarkay (☎953 72 11 11, ⓦwww.guiasnativos.com), next door to the *Los Enebros* complex. In the centre of the village the *Hotel Montaña* (☎953 72 70 11, ⓦwww.hmontana.com; ❹) is a straightforward affair with restaurant, bar and pool. At the village's northern end (down a signed side road) more horseriding is available at the *Picadero El Cortijillo* riding school (☎690697850), which provides tuition and hires out **horses** for guided half- and full-day treks. Some 4km out of Arroyo the *Monte Piedra Aparthotel* (☎&⒡953 71 31 45, ⓦwww.turismoencazorla.com/montepiedra.html; ❸) has great views, pool, restaurant and good-value rooms, as well as apartments sleeping up to six (❹) that are available for day-lets outside high summer, when you're looking at one week minimum.

Torre del Vinagre

The Río Borosa walk (see box, p.458) begins at **TORRE DEL VINAGRE**, 9km from Arroyo and 34km from Cazorla, where there is a visitors' centre, the **Centro de Interpretación Torre del Vinagre** (Tues–Sun: April–Sept 10am–2pm & 5–8pm; Oct–March 10am–2pm & 4–6pm; ☎953 71 30 40). Packed with motoring tourists in high summer, the centre has recently been transformed from a dull museum into a series of interactive sections dealing with the park's flora and fauna, and has a shop and **café**. Next to the centre a **botanical garden** (daily 11am–2pm & 5–7pm) has living specimens of the park's flora. Following the road downhill from opposite the Torre del Vinagre building leads to yet another *centro*, **Rio Borosa** (July & Aug daily 10am–2pm & 5–9pm; Sept–June Wed–Sun 10am–2pm & 5–9pm), with information and displays

The Río Borosa walk

The Río Borosa walk is one of the most popular walks inside the park and follows the Río Borosa upstream. From the visitors' centre at Torre del Vinagre, cross the road and take the path to the side of the Jardín Botánico. When you reach an electricity pylon turn left onto a downhill track. After passing a campsite and sportsfield on the left cross a footbridge over the river and turn right, aiming for a white building peeping above the trees. Soon you'll pass a small campsite (with an open-air bar in summer) and about a kilometre from the footbridge you'll come to a car park at a *piscifactoría* (trout hatchery).

From here follow the path as it crosses back and forth over the Borosa, swift and cold even in summer. After some 6km a signposted footpath diverges to the right; this also marks the beginning of the Cerrada de Elías **gorge**. Two or three wooden bridges now take the path back and forth across the river, which is increasingly confined by sheer rock walls. At the narrowest points the path is routed along planked catwalks secured to the limestone cliff. The walk from Torre del Vinagre to the end of the narrows takes about two hours.

Here the footpath rejoins the track; after another half-hour's walk you'll see a turbine and a long metal pipe bringing water from two **lakes** – one natural, one with a small dam – up the mountain. The road crosses one last bridge over the Borosa and stops at the turbine house. When you get to the gate, beyond which there's a steeply rising gully, count on another full hour up to the lakes. Cross a footbridge and start the steep climb up a narrow track over the rocks below the cliff (at one point the path passes close to the base of the palisade – beware falling stones). At the top of the path is a cavernous amphitheatre, with a waterfall in winter. The path ends about halfway up the cliff, where an artificial tunnel has been bored through the rock; walk through it to get to the lake.

Allow three and a half hours' walking time from Torre del Vinagre for the whole route, slightly less going down. It's a full day's excursion but you should have plenty of time to catch the afternoon bus back, which currently passes the visitors' centre at around 4.30pm, but it would be a good idea to confirm this before starting out. This walk is clearly detailed on the Editorial Alpina **map** (see p.456).

relating the park's fluvial wildlife living in and along the bank's of the Guadalquivir and its tributaries.

For **accommmodation**, a couple of kilometres before Torre del Vinagre, *Hotel Noguera de la Sierpe* (☎953 71 30 21; ⓦwww.lfhoteles.com; ❺ with breakfast) is one of a string of relatively upmarket hotels close to the road and is partly housed in a converted *cortijo* with views over a lake and the Guadalquivir valley. Frequented in winter by the hunting fraternity, the *patrón* is a hunting fanatic and images of his exploits plus trophies (including a stuffed lion) litter the foyer and public rooms. They also rent out some self-catering *casas rurales* overlooking the lake (❻), and there's a pool and horse stables. More economical accommodation is available at Coto Ríos (see below).

Coto Ríos

Some 5km on from Torre del Vinagre, **COTO RÍOS** is a pleasant village with a river beach on the Guadalquivir. There's a **campsite** here, the shady *Camping Chopera de Coto-Ríos* (☎953 71 30 74), plus two others – *Llanos de Arance* (on the opposite bank; ☎953 71 31 39) and *Fuente de Pascala* (☎953 71 30 28), 1km and 2km to the north respectively. A couple of kilometres back towards Torre del Vinagre you'll find good-value **accommodation** at the ⚹ *Hotel La Hortizuela* (☎&Ⓕ953 71 31 50; ⓦwww.lahortizuela.com; ❸), a delightfully serene hideaway down a signed track on the left with garden pool and restaurant. Slightly closer to Coto Ríos, the marginally cheaper and welcoming

Hotel Mirasierra (℡953 71 30 44, Ⓦwww.turismoencazorla.com/mirasierra
.html; ❸), is comfortable with air-conditioned rooms and serves excellent *ciervo*
(deer) and trout in its restaurant. Some 7km further along the Tranco road from
Coto Ríos, *El Hoyazo* (℡953 12 41 10, Ⓦwww.turismoencazorla.com/hoyazo
.html; ❸) has well-equipped apartments and bungalows sleeping up to four, with
a fine pool. Nearby, and slightly before the Parque Cinegético (see below), the
lakeside *Hotel Paraiso de Bujaraiza* (℡953 12 41 14, Ⓦwww.paraisodebujaraiza
.com; ❹ with breakfast) is a small, friendly and good-value hotel with comfortable rooms, pool, restaurant and plenty of greenery. It's worth noting that there
are no further campsites or places to stay until Tranco.

Eight kilometres beyond Coto Ríos, keeping to the river's west bank, at the
southern end of the Embalse del Tranco reservoir, is the **Parque Cinegético**,
a wildlife park which eventually hopes to include specimens of all the park's
fauna including ibex and mouflon, although at present you'll be lucky to see
some rather bewildered deer and the odd wild boar from the viewing balcony.
To reach the viewing areas, park at the entrance and walk a good kilometre
through the woods to get to the first viewing hide. Early morning and evening
are the best times to see the animals not struck down by midday torpor.

Tranco and the north of the park

The road continues along the west bank of the river, passing more picnic spots
and *ventas* along the way, en route to **TRANCO**, 21km north, where the
Guadalquivir is dammed to create a reservoir, the Embalse de Tranco. The island
in the centre of the lake contains the ruined castle of **Bujaraiza**, all that remains
of the village of the same name which disappeared beneath the waters when the
dam was created. Apart from a few holiday villas, a lakeside bar, and a **campsite**
at *Montillana* (℡953 12 61 94), 4km north of the village, Tranco has little to
detain you. A couple of places **to stay** beyond here are, after 3km down a turning
on the right, the attractive, friendly and excellent value lakeside ⚐ *Hotel Los
Parrales* (℡953 12 61 70, ☏mobile 699834049; ❷) with en-suite rooms and a
pool and, 4km further, *Hotel Losam* (℡&Ⓕ953 49 50 88, Ⓔhotel-losam@terra
.es; ❷), a functional and modern roadside place with a decent restaurant serving
a weekday *menú* for €8.50.

Hornos

From Tranco, the road heads north and circles around the northern end of the
reservoir before turning into the valley of the Río Hornos from where you can
glimpse the village of **HORNOS**, perched on a daunting rock pinnacle beneath
the tower of its Moorish castle. When you reach it, the village has an isolated air
with plenty of Moorish atmosphere. Its narrow, white-walled streets are perfect
for meandering, and the castle is worth a look, although once you've got up close
there isn't much to it apart from the tower. The pleasant Plaza Mayor is
overlooked by a solid sixteenth-century church, the **Iglesia de la Asunción**,
with an early, if worn, Plateresque portal. Close by and reached through a small
arch off the square lies a *mirador* with wonderful **views** over the reservoir, flanked
by the heights of the Sierra de Segura. The waters, which lapped the foot of the
outcrop below, have receded dramatically in recent years – a symptom of
Andalucía's chronic and continuing drought. A stretch of the village's ancient
walls is still intact, complete with a horseshoe-arched Moorish gateway.

A pleasant **walk** can be made from Hornos along the reservoir's eastern banks
to the hamlet of **La Platera** and the hill of Montero, with views along the
reservoir, 4km beyond. Close by, ⚐ *El Mesoncillo* (two nights minimum; ℡953
49 62 86, ☏mobile 636810252, Ⓦwww.mesoncillo.com; ❸–❹) has some

The magnificent **Lammergeier** or bearded vulture was once a frequently spotted resident of the Sierras of Segura and Cazorla as it soared and glided around the crags in search of prey. Then in the Sixties and Seventies the species declined dramatically, largely due to the drying up of the supply of carrion that these scavengers rely on to survive. The last sighting of the bird here occurred in the early Eighties. However, in the spring of 2008 four young birds were liberated in the park as part of a programme to reintroduce the species to Cazorla. Two of the juveniles were bred in a rearing centre in the park while the others came from the mountains of the Pyrenees and Austria. All the birds have been fitted with radio transmitters enabling the park's naturalists to monitor their adaptation to their new environment. Sadly, one of the birds released in 2007 as part of the same programme was recently found dead as a result of being (illegally) shot by hunters, but it is hoped that this was an isolated incident. The vultures are known as *quebrantahuesos* (bone-breakers) in Spanish, after their practice of hoisting the leg bones of victims high into the air and dropping them onto a rock below – nearly always the same one – splitting them open to allow the birds to extract the marrow.

delightful cottages to rent for longer stays. The rock faces above the pine-covered slopes are home to a variety of plants, including yellow-flowered flax and throatwart. Common bird species in this area include azure-winged magpies, kestrels and sparrowhawks, but you will be extremely lucky to see the **Lammergeier** or bearded vulture in this, its only habitat in Spain outside the Pyrenees (see box above).

Places to stay in Hornos include the welcoming *Hostal El Cruce* (☎953 49 50 35; ❷), where a/c en-suite rooms come with TV and whose garden terrace **restaurant** is hard to miss as you enter the village. They also rent **apartments** in the village (❸) and have free mountain bikes for guests. More rooms with bath are available at *Hostal El Mirador* (☎953 49 50 19; ❷) towards the centre, with fine balcony **views** over the Embalse de Tranco; the proprietor also rents out apartments for longer stays. *Raisa Apartments* (☎953 49 50 23, ⓦwww.apartamentosraisa.es), on the right as you enter from Cazorla, is another place for en-suite a/c rooms (❷) and apartments (❹) with a restaurant below. The best **place to eat** is probably on the *Hostal El Cruce's* leafy terrace (with a weekday *menú* for €9), although for a change of scene the central *Restaurante Raisa*, at c/Enmedio 5, about 30m from the church, is also pretty good for Sierra dishes.

Río Madera

If you are seeking a dreamy end-of-the-world location to hole up for a couple of days, few places could better fit the bill than **RÍO MADERA**, a hamlet at the end of a densely wooded road some 20km to the east of Hornos. Surrounded by woods of beech, oak, pine and poplar, intermingled with clumps of sweet-scented wild thyme and lavender, the river valley is located in the midst of some magnificent hiking country. What makes the place even more attractive, however, is a welcoming **place to stay**, the ⚐ *Hospedería Río Madera* (☎953 12 62 04; ❷), a small country bar-restaurant and hotel that has some good rooms with heating and TV and some well-equipped apartments (❸). There's also a good **bar-restaurant** offering many dishes from the Sierra with a weekday *menú* for €10.

To get there, follow the (signed) Río Madera road from Hornos. There's only one tricky bit where you reach an unsigned junction: here you need to turn right (along the A317) and then left after 100m along a road that *is* signed (direction Siles). This route is clearly shown on the *Sierra de Segura* map (see p.456) and the same map has many tracks and footpaths marked in this zone, enabling you to create your own hiking routes. Give the *Hospedería* a ring if you get lost and they will endeavour to set you right.

Segura de la Sierra

Scenic though Hornos is, it is overshadowed in every sense by the Cazorla park's most spectacularly sited village, **SEGURA DE LA SIERRA**, 20km to the northeast. With a romantic castle crowning an almost conical 1100-metre-high hill top, beneath which the tiered village streets seem in danger of collapsing into the olive groves far below, it's a landmark for miles around. Segura's top-notch **olive oil** (including an organic variety) is famed throughout Spain, for which it has a coveted *denominación de origen* label (one of only twenty in the whole country); not always easy to get hold of in the village itself, the *almacen* near the church should have a few bottles, or enquire at the tourist office (see below) who now have their own small shop selling products of the Sierra.

Once you've managed to climb the road that snakes up to it and passed through the medieval gate, Segura is a warren of narrow streets left behind by its former Moorish occupants. But its history goes back much further, perhaps as far as the Phoenicians who, local historians claim, called it Tavara. Greeks, Carthaginians, Romans and Visigoths came in their wake, until the last of these were prised out of this mountain eyrie by the invading Moors who constructed the castle they called Saqura. When it fell to the Christian forces under Alfonso VIII during the thirteenth century, the fort became a strategic outpost on the frontiers of the kingdom of Granada, whose borders were framed by the Guadalquivir and Segura river valleys.

The **castle** – now somewhat over-restored after being torched by French troops during the War of Independence – is open to visitors (April–Sept Tues–Sun 11am–2pm & 5–8pm, Oct–March Wed–Sun 11am–2pm & 5–8pm; €3). On your way up to it you can take in views over the country for miles around, including an amusingly primitive rectangular **bullring** below. Once inside the walls, climb the tower for more magnificent **views**. The village's other major monument is the **Baños Arabes** (same hours as castle), a splendid Moorish bathhouse off the central Plaza Mayor. Inside, three well-preserved chambers are illuminated by overhead light vents and contain elegant horseshoe arches. To reach the baths follow a descending street to the right-hand side of the parish church of Nuestra Señora Collado which brings you to a superb Moorish double arch in a preserved tower of the ancient walls. The baths are facing this. Near the church there's also a fine Renaissance **fountain** which bears the arms of Carlos V. Incidentally a waymarked footpath, the GR147, leaves the double arch for Río Madera, a downhill none-too-challenging fifteen-kilometre hike.

Practicalities

There are no bus services to Segura. The village's **tourist office** (daily 10.30am–2pm & 6.30–8.30pm; ☎953 48 02 80, ⓦwww.seguradelasierra.com) lies to the right 50m before the arch at the top of the street (c/San Vicente) leading into the village. The nearest **campsite** is *Camping El Robledo* (☎953 12 64 69), 4km east of Cortijos Nuevos, passed on the road from Hornos. If you need to cool down, there's a pleasant **swimming pool** on the road leading to the castle.

A number of places to stay have recently opened in the village. The most attractive choice is the welcoming ⚘ *Los Huertos de Segura*, c/Castillo 11, in the upper village (☎953 48 04 02, ⓦwww.loshuertosdesegura.com; ❸–❹) where the comfortable studios and apartments come with kitchenettes and terrace or balcony and fine views. The proprietor has produced a set of walking leaflets for guests and can provide maps and advice. The other two possibilities are located in the tiny c/Postigo, above the church. One, *La Mesa Segureña* (☎953 48 21 01, ⓦwww.lamesadesegura.com; ❸) rents well-equipped studios and apartments, while *El Mirador Messia de Leiva* (☎953 48 08 06, ⓦwww.messiadeleiva .com; ❹) has similar places. Among Segura's **places to eat** are the restaurants attached to *La Mesa Segureña* and the *El Mirador Messía de Leiva* accommodation options (see above) in c/Postigo. Both prepare dishes from the Sierra and the *Mesa Segureña* probably has the edge for quality, with a daily *menú* for €10. At the entrance to the village, *Restaurante Peñalta* (with a weekday *menú* for €10) is another possibility with a great view from its terrace.

Moving on from the park

With your own transport, you can avoid backtracking to Cazorla and take an alternative and attractive route out of the park heading south from Hornos along the A317 through the **Sierra de Segura** to **Pontones** and **Santiago de Espada**, on the border with Granada. There are plenty more campsites signed along this route and Santiago – try the *Hotel San Francisco* (☎953 43 80 72; ❸) – has hotels and *hostales*. The same road continues to Puebla de Don Fadrique where there is another decent hotel-restaurant, *Puerta de Andalucía* (☎958 72 13 40; ❷), on the main road through. From here you have a choice between the routes to Granada and Almería. The Granada route via the cattle town of Huéscar, following the A330, takes in the interesting towns of Baza and Guadix and provides an opportunity en route to see the remarkable prehistoric discoveries at Orce (see p.565); otherwise the A317 heads across the deserted but picturesque wheatfields of Granada province's eastern panhandle towards Vélez Blanco (see p.564) with its prehistoric caves, and eventually hits the coast near the Almerian resort of Mojácar (see p.559).

Travel details

Trains

Córdoba to: Algeciras (2 daily; 3hr 30min); Granada (2 daily; 2hr 45min); Jaén (4 daily; 1hr 30min); Málaga (6 daily; 1hr; Ronda (2 daily; 2hr); Seville (12 daily; 45min).
Jaén to: Andújar (4 daily; 40min); Córdoba (4 daily; 1hr 30min); Seville (3 daily; 3hr).

Buses

Bus times quoted are for the fastest journey times, normally direct. There may be other buses to the same destination which make additional stops at town and villages en route.
Baeza to: Cazorla (2 daily; 1hr 30min); Granada (11 daily; 2hr 20min); Jaén (16 daily; 1hr); Úbeda (14 daily; 15min).

Cazorla to: Granada (5 daily; 2hr 45min); Jaén (4 daily; 2hr 30min); Úbeda (4 daily; 1hr).
Córdoba to: Algeciras (2 daily; 6hr); Almería (1 daily; 5hr 30min); Cádiz (2 daily; 4hr); Écija (5 daily; 55min); Granada (9 daily; 4hr); Jaén (4 daily; 1hr 45min); Málaga (7 daily; 2hr); Seville (7 daily; 2hr).
Jaén to: Almería (2 daily; 4hr); Almuñecar (2 daily; 3hr); Baeza/Úbeda (14 daily; 1hr 25min); Cazorla (3 daily; 2hr 30min); Córdoba (4 daily; 1hr 45min); Granada (11 daily; 1hr 10min); La Guardia (8 daily; 20min); Málaga (4 daily; 3hr 15min); Seville (1 daily; 4hr).
Úbeda to: Baeza (14 daily; 15min); Cazorla (4 daily; 1hr); Córdoba (24 daily; 50min); Granada (8 daily; all calling at Baeza; 2 direct); Jaén (10 daily; 1hr 15min); Seville (3 daily; 5hr).

Granada and Almería

CHAPTER 4 # Highlights

* **The Alhambra** One of the world's great monuments and the pinnacle of Moorish architectural splendour in Spain. See p.477

* **The Albaicín** Granada's ancient, atmospheric Moorish quarter. See p.488

* **Capilla Real** Stunning Gothic chapel built to house the remains of Isabel and Fernando, conquerors of Moorish Granada. See p.492

* **Las Alpujarras** A wildly picturesque mountain region dotted with traditional villages and many other vestiges of a Moorish past. See p.511

* **Los Millares** This third millennium BC settlement with a remarkable necropolis is one of the most important

prehistoric sites in Europe. See p.532

* **Alcazaba, Almería** One of Andalucía's finest Moorish forts dominates the provincial capital. See p.543

* **Parque Natural de Cabo de Gata** Desert plants and volcanic hills are the features of this natural park edged with coastal resorts where the beaches are often deserted. See p.554

* **Mojácar** Attractive "sugar cube" village on a rocky hill with a lively beach resort below. See p.559

* **Mini Hollywood** The Almería deserts have provided the backdrop for many Westerns and some of the movie sets can still be visited. See p.569

▲ Generalife gardens, Alhambra

Granada and Almería

Here is no more convincing proof of the diversity of Andalucía than its eastern provinces: **Granada**, dominated by the Spanish peninsula's highest mountains, the snowcapped Mulhacén and Veleta peaks of the Sierra Nevada; and **Almería**, a waterless and, in part, semi-desert landscape. For most visitors, the city of **Granada** is not only the highlight of its province but one of the great destinations of Spain, as the home of Andalucía's most precious monument, the exquisite Moorish **Alhambra** palace and gardens. The city preserves, too, the old Moorish quarter of Albaicín and gypsy *barrio* of Sacromonte – places filled with the lingering atmosphere of this last outpost of Muslim Spain – as well as a host of Christian monuments, including the beautiful Capilla Real, with the tombs of Fernando and Isabel, Los Reyes Católicos, who finally wrested the kingdom from Moorish rule. Granada is also an atmospheric place to be during **Semana Santa** (the Easter week of floats and processions, see *Semana Santa* colour section), and a place of literary pilgrimage through its associations with Spain's greatest modern poet, Federico García Lorca.

South of Granada rear the peaks of the **Sierra Nevada** and its lower slopes, **Las Alpujarras**, a series of wooded valleys sprinkled with attractive whitewashed villages. This is wonderful country for walks and wildlife, with ancient cobbled paths connecting many of the villages, among them **Yegen**, one-time base of author Gerald Brenan, and **Trevélez**, Spain's highest village, famed for its snow-cured *jamón serrano*. The province makes the boast that you can ski in the Sierra Nevada's snowcapped peaks in the morning and swim on the coast in the afternoon. And so you could, if you really wanted to: the resorts of **Almuñecar**, **Salobreña** and **Castell de Ferro**, along the **Costa Tropical**, all have fine beaches and less development than the Costa del Sol.

There's less of interest west and east of Granada. To the west, **Alhama de Granada** is a delightful spa on a scenic back road to Málaga. To the east, amid a landscape of dusty hills covered with clumps of esparto grass, lies **Guadix**, famous for its cave dwellings hacked out of the soft tufa rock, and the red stone Renaissance castle of **La Calahorra**. Beyond here, Granada's panhandle extends past the ancient country town of **Baza** to a lonely landscape of rolling *sierras* where small farms and isolated villages watch over fields of wheat, fruit orchards and pasture.

The **province of Almería** is a strange corner of Spain. Inland it has an almost lunar landscape of desert, sandstone cones and dried-up riverbeds; on the coast, with a few exceptions, it's relatively unspoilt, with development thwarted by sparse water supplies. As Spain's hottest province, the beach resorts are worth considering during what would be "off-season" elsewhere, since Almería's

GRANADA & ALMERÍA

summers start well before Easter and last into November. In midsummer it's incredibly hot – frequently touching 35°C in the shade – while all year round there's an intense, almost luminous, sunlight.

The provincial capital and port, **Almería**, enjoyed a brief period of prosperity under the Moors but has been a bit of a backwater ever since, overlooked by the largest castle the Moors built in Andalucía, the **Alcazaba**, below whose walls is a cave quarter, still populated by gypsies.

Almería's best **beaches and resorts**, the least developed of the Spanish Mediterranean, lie to the east of the capital. One of the nicest, the small resort of **San José**, lies inside the **Cabo de Gata Natural Park**, a wildlife and wetland area that is home to some interesting desert plants as well as a breeding ground for enormous flocks of **flamingos** in summer. Heading north, **Los Escullos**, **Las Negras** and **Agua Amarga** are all attractively low-key places fronting a crystal-clear blue sea where there are sandy strands that see few

467

visitors. North again, things liven up at **Mojácar**, Almería's most fashionable resort, an ancient hill-top village that has spawned an enjoyable seafront quarter. To the west of Almería city a dismal sea of plastic tents – *invernaderos* – covers the **plain of Dalías** from the hills to the coast: a bonanza of drip-irrigation agriculture where exotic vegetables are force-grown to supply northern European markets all year round.

Inland, to the northeast of Almería, begins the most remarkable **desert landscape** in Europe: badlands of twisted gulches, dry riverbeds and eroded hills that have long attracted film producers. Much of *Lawrence of Arabia* was shot here, along with scores of spaghetti westerns, whose sets have been preserved at **Mini Hollywood**, near Tabernas: a fun visit, especially if you have kids to entertain. This weird scenery also shelters some interesting villages such as **Níjar**, a long-established ceramics centre, and the cliff-top **Sorbas**.

The province of Almería also maintains relics of a rich prehistoric past, when the rains were regular and the landscape verdant. In the northeast, near the village of **Vélez Rubio**, is the **Cueva de los Letreros**, whose prehistoric cave paintings are among the most important in Spain, while north of the provincial capital, in the Almerian reaches of Las Alpujarras, is the exceptional archeological site of **Los Millares**.

Granada

Los dos ríos de Granada
Bajan de la nieve al trigo . . .

Granada's twin rivers
Tumble down from the snow to the wheat . . .

Federico García Lorca

The city of **GRANADA** has one of the most dramatic locations in Spain, poised below a magnificent backdrop of the snowcapped peaks of the Sierra Nevada. It's the perfect setting for a near-perfect edifice, the extraordinary **Alhambra** – the most exciting, sensual and romantic of all European monuments. It was the palace-fortress of the Nasrid kings, rulers of the last Spanish Muslim realm, and in its construction Moorish art reached a spectacular yet serene climax. The building, however, seems to go further than this, revealing something of the whole brilliance and spirit of Moorish life and culture. It should on no account be missed – and neither should the city, with its network of Moorish streets, panoply of Christian monuments and atmospheric gypsy quarter.

Some history

Before the arrival of the Moors, Granada's mark on history was slight. An early Iberian settlement here, Elibyrge, was adapted by the **Romans** as Illiberis, but although its fertility was prized, it was greatly overshadowed by the empire's provincial capital at Córdoba. Later, after the region had come under **Visigothic** control in the sixth century, the old Roman town, centred on the modern-day Albaicín, grew a **Jewish suburb**, Garnatha, on the south slope of the Alhambra hill. Popular tradition has it that friction between this Jewish settlement and the Christian town led to the Jews assisting the **Moors** to take the city shortly after the invasion of 711.

The Moors adapted the name to Karnattah, and for three centuries it was an important city under the control of the Cordoban caliphate and, when this fell in 1031, under the Almoravid and Almohad Berber dynasties of Seville. When, however, Almohad power crumbled in the thirteenth century as the Christian *Reconquista* gathered momentum, an astute Arab prince of the **Nasrid** tribe, which had been driven south from Zaragoza, saw his opportunity to create an independent state. The kingdom, established in the 1240s by **Ibn al-Ahmar** (aka Muhammad ibn Yusuf ibn Nasr), was to outlast the vanished al-Andalus by a further two and a half centuries.

Nasrid Granada was always a precarious state. Ibn al-Ahmar proved a just and capable ruler but all over Spain the Christian kingdoms were in the ascendant. The Moors of Granada survived only through paying tribute and allegiance to Fernando III of Castile – whom they were forced to assist in the conquest of Muslim Seville – and by the time of Ibn al-Ahmar's death in 1273 Granada was the only surviving Spanish Muslim kingdom. It had, however, consolidated its territory, which stretched from just north of the city down to a coastal strip between Tarifa and Almería, and, stimulated by Muslim refugees, developed a flourishing commerce, industry and culture. Over the next two centuries, Granada maintained its autonomy by a series of shrewd manoeuvres, its rulers turning for protection, as it suited them, to the Christian kingdoms of Aragón and Castile and the Merinid sultans of Morocco. The city-state enjoyed its most confident and prosperous period under **Yusuf I** (1334–54) and **Muhammad V** (1354–91), the rulers responsible for much of the existing Alhambra palace. But by the mid-fifteenth century a pattern of coups and internal strife became established and a rapid succession of rulers did little to stem Christian inroads.

In 1479 the kingdoms of Aragón and Castile were united by the marriage of Fernando and Isabel and within ten years had conquered Ronda, Málaga and Almería. The city of Granada now stood completely alone, tragically preoccupied in a **civil war** between supporters of the sultan's two favourite wives. The Reyes Católicos made escalating and finally untenable demands upon it, and in 1490 war broke out. **Boabdil**, the last Moorish king, appealed in vain for help from his fellow Muslims in Morocco, Egypt and Ottoman Turkey, and in the following year Fernando and Isabel marched on Granada with an army said to total 150,000 troops. For seven months, through the winter of 1491, they laid siege to the city. On January 2, 1492, Boabdil formally surrendered its keys. The Christian Reconquest of Spain was complete.

There followed a century of repression for Granada, during which Jews and then Muslims were treated harshly and finally expelled by the Christian state and Church, both of which grew rich on the confiscated property. The loss of Muslim and Jewish artisans and traders led to gradual economic decline, which was reversed only temporarily in the seventeenth century, the period when the city's Baroque monuments – La Cartuja monastery and San Juan de Dios hospital – were built. The city suffered heavily under **Napoleonic occupation**, when even the Alhambra was used as a barracks, causing much damage, and, although the nineteenth-century Romantic movement saw to it that the Alhambra suffered few more such violations, the sober *granadino* middle class have been accused repeatedly since of caring little for the rest of their city's artistic legacy. Over the last century and a half, they have covered over the River Darro – which now flows beneath the town centre – and demolished an untold number of historic buildings to build avenues through the centre of the city. Things have hardly changed and in recent years the Andalucian parliament has had to block a preposterous plan by the city council to cover much of the Alhambra hill with a luxury housing estate – the bulldozers had actually begun digging.

Lorca described the *granadinos* as "the worst bourgeoisie in Spain", and they are regarded by many other Andalucians as conservative, arrogant and cool, like a colony somehow transplanted from northern Spain. A strong small-shopkeeper

Guadix & Murcia
La Cartuja
Jaén & Madrid
Bus Station
Train Station

ACCOMMODATION

Albergue Juevnil	oo
Apartamentos Trillo	F
Casa del Aljarife	L
Casa del Capitel Nazari	O
Casa Federico	gg
Casa Morisca	D
Cuevas el Abanico	A
El Ladrón de Agua	M
El Numero 8	I
Hostal Arteaga	Z
Hostal Britz	V
Hostal Costa Azul	bb
Hostal La Ninfa	P
Hostal Landázuri	T
Hostal Lisboa	ff
Hostal Márquez	jj
Hostal Meridiano	ll
Hostal Moni Albayzín	E
Hostal Navarro Ramos	S
Hostal Salvador	ii
Hostal San Joaquin	ee
Hostal Santa Ana	Q
Hostal Suecia	K
Hostal Viena	R
Hotel Zurita	kk
Hotel Albero	G
Hotel Alhambra Palace	H
Hotel Guadalupe	C
Hotel Hesperia	cc
Hotel Inglaterra	Y
Hotel Los Angeles	aa
Hotel Los Tilos	hh
Hotel Macía Plaza	X
Hotel Molinos	U

Hotel Navas	dd
Hotel Palacio Santa Inés	J
Hotel Reina Cristina	mm
Hotel Santa Isabel La Real	N
Pensión Gomérez	W
Pensiones La Milagrosa y Matilde	nn
Posada Doña Lupe	B

RESTAURANTS

Bar Ferroviaria	32	Café-Bar Oliver	29	Centro	20	La Esquinita	10
Bar La Mancha Chica	8	Café-Bar 380	16	El Ladrillo II	6	La Ninfa	13
Bar-Restaurante Sevilla	24	Carmen de Aben Humeya	5	El Trillo del Reca	7	Lago de Como	9
Café au Lait	27	Casa Cepillo	28	El Yunque	12	Las Cuevas	15
				Juanillo	1	Mesón Andaluz	21

Mesón La Alegría	31	Restaurante Las		Restaurante-Marisquería		Taberna La Higuera	3
Mirador de Morayma	2	Tinajas	33	Cunini	30	Tetería Kasbah	19
Nueva Bodega	22	Restaurante León	18	Samarcanda	17		
Pilar de Toro	11	Restaurante Nuevo	25	Seis Peniques	23		
Restaurante Chikito	26	Restaurante-Bar Tomasas	4	Taberna de Baco	14		

economy – which discouraged industrial development – and a society where military and clerics were dominant inhibited innovation and liberal ideas through the early part of the twentieth century. This introverted outlook perhaps contributed also to the events of the **Civil War**, one of the greatest stains on the city's name. In 1936, following Franco's coup, a fascist bloodbath was unleashed during which an estimated seven thousand of the city's liberals and Republicans were assassinated, among them poet and playwright **Federico García Lorca**. The poet deserved better from his native city, of which he had written, "The hours are longer and sweeter here than in any other Spanish town … Granada has any amount of good ideas but is incapable of acting on them. Only in such a town, with its inertia and tranquillity, can there exist those exquisite contemplators of water, temperatures and sunsets."

Arrival and orientation

The **train station** (☎902 43 23 43) lies a kilometre or so out on the Avenida de Andaluces, off Avenida de la Constitución; to get into town take bus #11 which runs a circular route: inbound on the Gran Vía de Colón and back out via the Puerta Real and Camino de Ronda. Buses #3, #4, #6, and #9 also run between the station and Gran Vía.

The city's **main bus station**, Carretera de Jaén s/n (☎958 18 54 80), is some way out of the centre in the northern suburbs, and handles all services, including those to the Sierra Nevada but not to Viznar. The bus station is served by the #3 bus which leaves from outside and will drop you in the centre on Gran Vía Colón near the cathedral (a 15min journey). If you're heading for the *Albergue Juvenil* (youth hostel) you should take bus #10 from the bus station.

Central Granada is often choked with more traffic than its streets are able to bear, and finding on-street parking can be close to impossible. If you do arrive **by car**, you're best off leaving it in a car park or garage for the duration of your stay. Public Underground car parks (*parking subterráneo*) are located at Puerta Real (down the right-hand side of the post office), La Caleta near the train station, and on c/San Agustín beneath the municipal market off the west side of Gran Vía near the cathedral. Long-term free street parking places are often to be found along Carrera del Genil and the Paseo del Salón slightly southwest of the centre, but you should strip your car of any contents.

Flights into Granada's **airport**, 17km to the west of the city on the A92 *autovía*, are served by fourteen daily buses into town (30min; €3); buses also run out to the airport from a stop on the east side of Gran Vía opposite the cathedral. Check with the bus operator, Gonzalez S.L. (☎958 490 164), for the latest timetable. Alternatively, a taxi will cost about €20–25, depending on time of day and destination.

Practically everything of interest in Granada, including the hills of **Alhambra** (to the east) and the **Albaicín** and **Sacromonte** (to the northeast), is within easy walking distance of the centre. The only times you'll need a local bus or taxi are if you're arriving or leaving on public transport, since both the bus and train stations are some way out. **Gran Vía (de Colón)** is the city's main street, cutting its way through the centre along a roughly north–south axis between the Jardines del Triunfo and **Plaza Isabel la Católica**. It forms a T-junction at its southern end with **c/Reyes Católicos**, which runs east to the **Plaza Nueva** and west to the **Puerta Real**, Granada's two focal squares.

Information and tours

The city's **Turismo** c/Santa Ana 2 (Mon–Fri 9am–7.30pm, Sat 9.30am–3pm & 4–7pm, Sun 9.30am–3pm; ☎958 57 52 02) is located up steps to the right

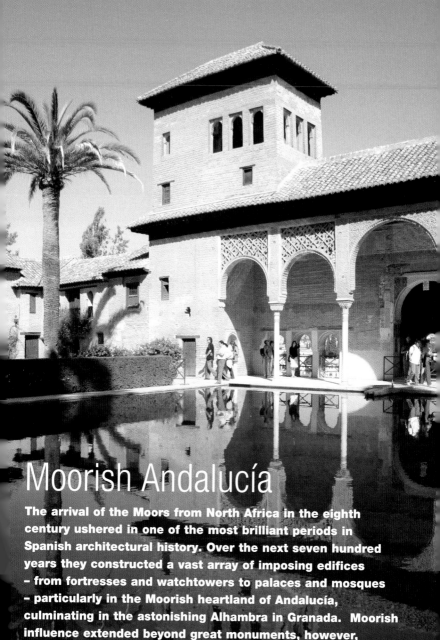

Moorish Andalucía

The arrival of the Moors from North Africa in the eighth century ushered in one of the most brilliant periods in Spanish architectural history. Over the next seven hundred years they constructed a vast array of imposing edifices – from fortresses and watchtowers to palaces and mosques – particularly in the Moorish heartland of Andalucía, culminating in the astonishing Alhambra in Granada. Moorish influence extended beyond great monuments, however, into other areas of local life, from irrigation to domestic architecture. Andalucía today would be a very different place

Mihrab, Mezquita, Córdoba ▲
Salon Rico, Medina Azahara ▼

Andalucía's Moorish monuments

The Mezquita

The **Mezquita** (see p.382), or Great Mosque of Córdoba, is the architectural apex of the Cordoban caliphate and one of the great buildings of the Middle Ages. From its commencement in 784, it grew in magnitude and magnificence over the succeeding centuries, becoming the third largest mosque ever built, and reflecting the growth of the city itself. Employing many astonishing architectural innovations, the caliphs Abd ar-Rahman I, II and III drove the project forward climaxing in the tenth century with the addition of a spectacularly ornate **mihrab** (prayer niche) by the caliph al-Hakam II. This architectural tour de force encapsulates the splendours of Moorish Córdoba, with its shell-shaped dome carved from a single block of marble, and exquisite mosaic, arabesque and filigree decoration.

Medina Azahara

The Cordoban caliphate's other remarkable architectural legacy is the palace-fortress of **Medina Azahara** (see p.398), sited on a low hill to the west of the city and with outstanding views over the valley of the Guadalquivir. Built in the tenth century by the cultured ruler Abd ar-Rahman III and named after his favourite wife, this edifice epitomized the confidence, power and splendour of the Cordoban court. In 1944 excavators revealed the remains of a royal palace and in its main room – the **Sálon**

Rico de Abd al-Rahman III – they found exquisite carvings in marble depicting the Syrian Hom (Tree of Life). Painstakingly reconstructed in the years since, this magnificent room finally gives some credence to the descriptions of gaping wonder recorded by medieval visitors to the caliph's palace.

The Giralda

In the eleventh-century, Andalucía fragmented into rival kingdoms, allowing successive waves of Moorish invaders to move into the power vacuum. One of these, the ultra-fundamentalist **Almohads**, left behind a number of remarkable buildings of which the foremost is the magnificent **Giralda** tower in Seville (see p.257), the surviving minaret of the Friday mosque demolished to construct the cathedral. At 100m high with elaborate *sebka* brickwork panels adorning its exterior walls, it was started in 1184 under the architect Ahmed ibn Baso and completed twelve years later.

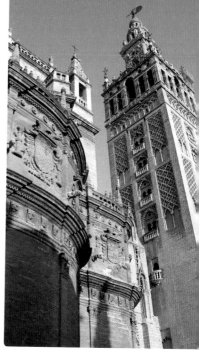

▲ Giralda tower, Seville

▼ Title decoration, Alhambra

The Alhambra

The pinnacle of Moorish architectural splendour in Spain was achieved in the sunset years of Nasrid-ruled Granada. Dominating the city from its hilltop location, the **Alhambra** (see p.477) is the finest example of a medieval Islamic palace. Constructed between 1230 and 1354, it is a treasure house of craftsmanship where subtle use of space, light and water add lustre to the complex's architectural brilliance. From marble, pillared arcades to magnificent domes with stalactite and honeycomb decoration to exquisite stuccowork, the genius of the design is breathtaking.

Patio de los Leones ▲

Baños Árabes, Ronda ▼

The Moorish legacy

Grand monuments may be the Moors' most obvious legacy, but they also had a profound effect on other aspects life. From domestic architecture and advances in irrigation to the introduction of new crops including almonds, rice, saffron, oranges and lemons, the changes they made are today seen as quintessentially Andalucian.

For the Moors it was the plentiful rivers that were the most wondrous aspect of their new domain and irrigation was extended and upgraded with hundreds of **water wheels** (*nurias*) mounted on all major rivers. Mountainous districts such as Las Alpujarras and Almería were criss-crossed with **water channels** (*acequias*) bringing irrigation to inaccessible areas and even deserts. Water was also employed as a decorative, inspiring and contemplative feature in their houses, palaces and public squares. Often it was pumped from a source far below, as happened with the **Patio de los Leones** fountain in the Alhambra.

The Moors' influence on domestic architecture was also fundamental. They developed the Roman atrium or **patio** into a sanctuary away from the hustle and bustle of the streets outside. The *carmen*, meanwhile, is a **walled garden** version of the patio that was added to urban villas. Into the mountainous Las Alpujarras south of Granada, the Moors imported another form of architecture: clay-roofed dwellings with a *tinao* or bridge enabling access from one building to another and a *terrao* or **roof terrace**.

Central to the Moorish way of life were public *hammams* or **bathhouses**, based on the Roman model with gradated temperatures and a hypocaust (under-floor heating).

The Bono Turístico

The **Bono Turístico** (City Pass) gives you access to eight of the city's monuments including the Alhambra, Capilla Real, Catedral and La Cartuja for €30. Valid for five days it's a plastic card that you swipe through the gates at any of the monuments listed. You may enter once only and when purchasing (or booking online) can choose a time for visiting the Alhambra's Palacios Nazaríes (subject to availability). It also includes nine bus journeys, a ride on the Granada sightseeing bus, and small discounts in some restaurants. The Bono can be purchased from the Audioguías: This is Granada kiosk in Plaza Nueva (commission free) or (during business hours) the Caja Granada bank at Plaza Isabel La Católica 6, and also online (ⓦwww.granadatur.com or ⓦwww.cajagranada.es) in which case you will need to collect it (see website for collection points) on arrival in Granada. They can also be ordered by phone (ⓣ902 10 00 95). Note that bank, internet and phone purchases incur a €2.50 commission charge. The card does not save you a great deal unless you intend to visit all the monuments included but one bonus of getting it is **entry to the Alhambra**, which each card includes. Even when the Alhambra is sold out this scheme has a guaranteed 250 places per day.

of the church of Santa Ana, off Plaza Nueva. They also have a branch in the Alhambra's ticket office (open same hours as the monument). There's a good and less frenetic **Turismo Municipal** at Plaza Mariana Pineda 10 (Mon–Fri 9am–8pm, Sat 10am–7pm, Sun 10am–3pm; ⓣ958 24 71 28), east of Puerta Real, which also stocks information on the province of Granada. From April to September **kiosks** on Plaza Nueva and Plaza Bib-Rambla also give out maps and information. An **information office** (Mon–Fri 10am–2pm & 4.30–8pm) inside the Ayuntamiento on Plaza del Carmen is another source of city maps and transport information. A detailed city **map** (€1.20) can be obtained from a machine in the central Plaza Isabel La Católica, near the cathedral.

If you're pressed for time, a way to get around the city is by hop-on hop-off **open-top bus tour**; City Sightseeing Granada (ⓣ902 10 10 81) buses and microbuses make a roughly circular tour around the city with stops at the Cathedral (starting point), Alhambra, La Cartuja, Museo García Lorca and Plaza Nueva among others. Tickets (€18) are valid for 48 hours from the time of purchase.

An officially approved **guided walking tour** taking in the city's major sights (not the Alhambra) is operated by Cicerone Granada (ⓣmobile 600412051, ⓦwww.ciceronegranada.com; €12, under-14s free; booking recommended in high season). The walks take place in all weather, last around two hours and leave from the northeast corner of the Plaza de Bib-Ranb daily at 10.30am (11am Nov–Feb; English & Spanish).

Accommodation

Finding **a place to stay** in Granada usually isn't a problem, except during Semana Santa (Easter week) and very occasionally during August. However, if you want to be certain of finding rooms at some of the more popular options – and the city has some of the most beautiful hotels in Spain – it's wise to ring or book ahead. Lower down the scale there are plenty of *pensiones* and *hostales*, a frequent turnaround of visitors, and prices are extremely competitive. It is also worth bearing in mind that spring and early autumn are the high season months here. Where hotels have a garage expect to pay around €10–15 per vehicle per day.

Most visitors want to be as close to the Alhambra as possible, and there are a couple of pricey options up inside the walls. Unless you book these ahead, however, you'll have to content yourself with streets such as the Cuesta de

Granada online

Information on Granada, its monuments and amenities can be found at ⓦwww
.granadatur.com, ⓦwww.turismodegranada.org, ⓦwww.granadainfo.com, ⓦwww
.andalucia.org and ⓦwww.albaicin-granada.com.

Gomérez, which ascends towards the Alhambra from the Plaza Nueva, itself a focus for many hotels. The zone surrounding the cathedral is also a good hunting ground for rooms and other attractive options are to be found in the streets between the picturesque Plaza de Bib-Rambla and Plaza de la Trinidad in the university area.

The atmospheric **Albaicín** quarter also makes a wonderful place to stay and while most of its addresses are upmarket, a few recent arrivals also cater for the budget traveller. **Self-catering accommodation** (minimum stay two nights) is also an option: we've listed a couple below but for a wider choice visit ⓦwww.granadahotel.com. With your own transport, staying in one of the pleasant **rural villages** to the south of the city is also an option and we've included a couple of attractive possibilities in and around the villages of La Zubia and Monachil.

Around Plaza Nueva and towards the Alhambra

Hostal Britz Cuesta de Gomérez 1 ☏958 22 36 52, ⓦwww.lisboaweb.com. Small, welcoming, very comfortable and well-placed *hostal* near the Plaza Nueva. Some rooms en suite and a couple of singles. ❷

Hostal Landázuri Cuesta de Gomérez 24 ☏958 22 14 06, ⓦwww.hostallandazuri.com. Pleasant, good-value rooms, some en suite, plus its own restaurant, bar and a roof terrace with a view of the Alhambra. Some single rooms. Garage available. ❷

Hostal Navarro Ramos Cuesta de Gomérez 21 ☏958 25 05 55. Very pleasant small *hostal* en route to the Alhambra; neat and tidy rooms with and without bath and some singles. ❶–❷

Hostal Santa Ana c/Hospital de Sta. Ana 8 ☏958 22 58 20. Elegant *hostal* inside a restored 200-year-old mansion. Attractive en-suite rooms come with a/c and TV. ❸ with breakfast.

Hostal Viena c/Hospital de Sta. Ana 2 ☏958 22 70 75, ⓦwww.hostalviena.com. Efficient, friendly, Austrian-run *hostal* in a quiet street. The a/c rooms come with and without bath, and it has its own car park. If this place is full, try their nearby *Hostal Austria* (same phone number). Own garage. ❷–❸

Hotel Macía Plaza Plaza Nueva 4 ☏958 22 75 36, ⓦwww.maciahoteles.com. Centrally located hotel, offering comfortable, a/c rooms, most overlooking the square, with internet connection. *Rough Guide* readers with this guide can claim a ten percent discount. ❺

Pensión Gomérez Cuesta de Gomérez 10, ☏958 22 44 37. Friendly, simple and convenient guesthouse with clean and basic rooms, some single, sharing bath. ❶

Cathedral area

🏃 **Casa Federico** c/Horno de Marina 13 ☏958 20 85 34, ⓦwww.casadefederico .com. Enchanting boutique hotel in a refurbished traditional town house with individually styled and well equipped wood-beamed a/c rooms. The roof terrace – for breakfasting and drinks – has spectacular views. ❺

Hostal Arteaga c/Arteaga 3 ☏958 20 88 41, ⓔhostalarteaga@hotmail.com. Central and economical *hostal* offering en-suite a/c rooms with TV in a quiet street. ❸

🏃 **Hostal Costa Azul** c/Rosario 5 ☏958 22 22 98, ⓦwww.hostalcostaazul.com. Friendly, central, refurbished small *hostal* for pleasant en-suite rooms with heating and a/c. Has own restaurant and free internet. It also rents out some luxurious apartments (❺) nearby. *Rough Guide* readers with this guide can claim a fifteen-percent discount on apartments. ❸

Hostal Lisboa Plaza del Carmen 27 ☏958 22 14 14, ⓦwww.lisboaweb.com. Modern, clean and comfortable *hostal* bang in the centre. Many rooms are en suite and it provides fans in summer. Wi-fi and internet access. ❷–❸

Hostal Salvador c/Duende 6 ☏958 26 19 55, ⓦwww.casasalvador.net. Small and comfortable *hostal* in a quiet pedestrianized street. All rooms are en suite with a/c and TV, and rooms 303 &

304 come with terrace. There's a decent restaurant too. ❷

Hotel Hesperia Plaza Gamboa s/n ☎958 01 84 00, ⊛www.hesperia-granada.com. Stylish new luxury hotel in a beautiful old mansion with delightful patio. The rather staid rooms are less inviting, but an interesting tariff structure has frequent special offers which can reduce rates by up to sixty percent; ring or check website for details. Own car park. ❻

Hotel Inglaterra c/Cetti Meriem 4 ☎958 22 15 59, ⊛www.nh-hoteles.com. Three-star hotel with comfortable, a/c rooms with satellite TV, internet and minibar in a stylishly modernized building. Car park available. ❼

Hotel Los Tilos Plaza de Bib-Rambla 4 ☎958 26 67 12, ⊛www.hotellostilos.com. Pleasant, two-star hotel on this atmospheric square. Decent rooms have TV, but make sure to request one on the exterior as the interior rooms are gloomy. Higher rooms 401 & 402 or 301 & 302 with Alhambra views are the ones to go for. Car park nearby. ❹

Hotel Navas c/Las Navas 24 ☎958 22 59 59, ⊛www.hotelesporcel.com. Elegant and central small hotel on a quiet street with a/c rooms, which have safe, minibar and satellite TV. Own garage. ❻

Plaza de la Trinidad and around the university

Hostal Márquez c/Fábrica Vieja 8 ☎958 27 50 13, ⓔhosatl-marquez@ozu.es. Recently refurbished *hostal* with some rooms en suite, a few singles and all with a/c. The lobby is dominated by a snarling boar's head bagged by the *patrón*. Parking spaces. ❷–❸

🏃 **Hostal Meridiano** c/Angulo 9 ☎&ⓕ958 25 05 44, ⓔhostalmeridiano@telefonica .net. Friendly and efficient *hostal* offering bright a/c rooms with and without bath. There's free internet access available to guests, and they can assist with parking. ❷

Hostal San Joaquin c/Mano de Hierro 14 ☎958 28 28 79, ⊛www.pensionsanjoaquin.com. A great, rambling old place with simple and en-suite rooms (some with a/c and TV) and charming patios. ❷

Hostal Zurita Plaza de la Trinidad 7 ☎958 27 50 20, ⊛www.pensionzurita.com. Welcoming *hostal* where immaculate balcony rooms come with and without bath, and all have TV and a/c. Garage. ❷

Hotel Reina Cristina c/Tablas 4, close to Plaza de la Trinidad ☎958 25 32 11, ⊛www .hotelreinacristina.com. Modern and welcoming hotel inside an older building – with fine patio – where Lorca spent his last days before being seized by the fascists. Twin-bedded rooms tend to be larger and also has its own good

restaurant and garage. Forty percent cheaper in July & Aug. ❻

Pensiones La Milagrosa y Matilde c/Puentezuelas 46, slightly southwest of Plaza de la Trinidad ☎958 26 34 29. Two serviceable *pensiones* under the same ownership; their cheaper rooms (which you need to ask for) are good value. Some rooms en suite. ❷

Albaicín, Sacromonte and north of the centre

🏃 **Apartamentos Trillo** c/Aljibe de Trillo 26 ☎958 22 78 43, ⓔrainey.fuimus@mac .com. Five 2–4 person apartments in a refurbished and traditional *casa andaluza* with well-equipped balcony rooms, charming patio, garden and Alhambra views. ❹

🏃 **Casa del Aljarife** Placeta de la Cruz Verde 2 ☎&ⓕ958 22 24 25, ⊛www .casadelaljarife.com. Charming small upmarket *hostal* in a restored sixteenth-century house, near the heart of the Albaicín; three beautiful en-suite rooms (two with Alhambra views) and patio, plus free use of internet. ❺

🏃 **Casa del Capitel Nazari** Cuesta de Aceituneros 6 ☎958 21 52 60, ⊛www .hotelcasacapitel.com. Beautiful sixteenth-century *palacio* transformed into an enchanting small hotel with attractively furnished wood-ceilinged rooms overlooking a triple-tiered patio; room 22 has an Alhambra view. Own restaurant too. Special offers in Jan, Feb, July & Aug can cut prices significantly. Parking nearby. ❺

🏃 **Casa Morisca** Cuesta de la Victoria 9 ☎958 22 11 00, ⊛www.hotelcasamorisca .com. Stunningly romantic small hotel inside an immaculately renovated (for which it won an award) fifteenth-century Moorish mansion with exquisite patio below the walls of the Alhambra in the Albaicín; there are re-created Moorish furnishings throughout (though the splendid Mudéjar wooden ceilings are original), and room 15 (❼) with Alhambra views, is the one to go for. Exterior rooms cost more. ❻

Cuevas el Abanico Verea de Enmedio 89, near the Casa del Chapiz ☎&ⓕ958 22 61 99, ⊛www.el-abanico.com. Fully equipped and stylishly renovated en-suite cave-dwellings with kitchen, available for a minimum stay of two nights. ❹

El Ladrón de Agua Carrera del Darro 13 ☎958 21 50 40 ⊛www.ladrondeagua.com. Beautiful hotel inside a restored sixteenth-century Mudéjar *palacio* with lots of exposed brick, cool marble, understated furnishings and a charming patio. Some rooms have Alhambra views. ❺

El Numero 8 c/Virgen Carmen s/n ☎958 22 06 82, ⓦwww.elnumero8.com. Charming and good value self-catering apartments and studios in a small street in the Albaicín. All are tastefully furnished and come with radio/CD player and there's a rooftop terrace with Alhambra views. Owner lives off-site so you'll need to make contact before turning up. ❸

🏃 **Hostal Moni Albayzín** Plaza San Bartolomé 5 ☎958 28 52 84, Ⓔhostalalbayzin @hotmail.com. The Albaicín's first budget *hostal* and it's a cracker. The proprietors provide a hearty welcome and the en-suite rooms – with TV and a/c – are spotless. The roof terrace has views of the Alhambra and Sierra Nevada and guests have use of fridge and washing machine. Also rents some good-value (❸) fully equipped apartments nearby. ❷

🏃 **Hotel Palacio Santa Inés** Cuesta de Santa Inés 9 ☎958 22 23 62, ⓦwww .lugaresdivinos.com. Sumptuous eleven-room hotel in a beautiful, restored sixteenth-century Mudéjar mansion on the south side of the Albaicín with Alhambra views – especially from rooms 31–34. The nearby, slightly cheaper and equally delightful *Carmen de Santa Inés*, Placeta de Porras 7, off c/San Juan de los Reyes (same number; ❺), is owned by the same proprietors and occupies an equally attractive restored Moorish *carmen*. ❻

Hotel Santa Isabel la Real c/Santa Isabel la Real 19, ☎958 29 46 58. ⓦwww.hotelsantaisabellareal .com. Enchanting new small hotel housed in a wonderfully restored sixteenth-century Albaicín mansion close to the church of San Nicolas. Elegantly furnished rooms (some with Alhambra views) are equipped with minibar and wi-fi and there's a car park. ❺ with breakfast.

Inside and around the Alhambra

Hostal La Ninfa Campo del Principe s/n ☎958 22 79 85, ⓦwww.hostallaninfa.net. On one of the nicest squares in town, this place – with an exterior studded with multicoloured stucco flowers – is easy to find. The interior offers pleasing white-walled, en-suite rooms with individual furnishings, a/c and TV. The rooms with *cama de matrimonio* (double bed) are significantly cheaper (❸) than those with two beds. ❹

Hostal Suecia Huerta de los Ángeles 8 ☎958 22 77 81, Ⓕ958 22 50 44. Charming, good-value small *hostal* – with some rooms en suite – in a quiet, leafy area below the Alhambra with garden terrace to eat breakfast. Rooms have heating but no TV. Relatively easy parking. ❸

Hotel Albero Avda. Santa María de La Alhambra 6 ☎958 22 67 25, ⓦwww.hotelalbero.com. This

excellent-value, attractive and friendly small hotel lies on the access road to the Alhambra to the south of the centre. Sparkling a/c balcony rooms come with TV and there's easy parking. Ring if you have problems finding them and they will advise (English spoken). ❶

Hotel Alhambra Palace Peña Partida 2–4 ☎958 22 14 68, ⓦwww.h-alhambrapalace.es. On the Alhambra hill and a 5min walk from the palace entrance, this opulent four-star *belle époque* hotel in neo-Moorish style offers every service you would expect for the price, except a pool. The bar's terrace (open to the public) has dramatic views over the city. Car park. ❼

Hotel América Real de la Alhambra 53 ☎958 22 74 71, ⓦwww.hotelamericagranada.com. Charming small hotel in the Alhambra grounds, bang opposite the parador, so you can get an early march on the queues and take a siesta midday. You pay for the location rather than creature comforts (a/c rooms but no TV) and prices have risen steeply (and unjustifiably) here. ❻

Hotel Guadalupe Paseo de la Sabica ☎958 22 34 23, ⓦwww.hotelguadalupe.es. Smart three-star hotel a stone's throw from the Alhambra's entrance. Some of the well-equipped a/c rooms have partial Alhambra views. In July & Aug rates drop by thirty percent. Clients get reduced-rate parking in Alhambra car park, or the Alhambra bus from Plaza Nueva drops you nearby. ❺

Hotel Los Angeles Cuesta Escoriaza 17 ☎958 22 14 23, ⓦwww.hotellosangeles.net. Attractive three-star hotel on a leafy, quiet avenue in walking distance of the Alhambra. Elegant, individually styled rooms come with minibar, satellite TV and terrace balcony and there's a pool. Own car park. ❹

Hotel Molinos c/Molinos 12 ☎958 22 73 67, ⓦwww.hotelmolinos.es. Little over 4m wide, this place is listed in the *Guinness Book of Records* as the narrowest hotel in the world. Pleasant a/c en-suite rooms (some with balcony), and friendly proprietors. ❸

🏃 **Parador de San Francisco** Real de la Alhambra ☎958 22 14 40, ⓦwww .parador.es. Without doubt the best hotel in Granada – a converted fifteenth-century monastery (itself created from a Nasrid palace) in the Alhambra grounds. Alas, this top-of-the-range parador is also the most expensive in the city with the cheapest rooms costing around €310; rooms to go for are nos. 209–216, with views of the Alhambra and Generalife. Booking is advised at least four months ahead in summer or over Easter. Non-guests can call in for a drink on the terrace bar. Own car park. ❾

Posada Doña Lupe Avda. Generalife-Alhambra s/n ☎958 22 14 73, ☏958 22 14 74. Rambling and potentially inviting place on the Alhambra hill blighted by a student hostel atmosphere (toilet paper and towels are doled out at check-in); there are numerous permutations of prices, some exceptionally cheap. Many rooms are en suite and there's a *cafetería* and small swimming pool. Easily reached by the Alhambrabus from Plaza Nueva. ❶–❷

Out of town: La Zubia & Monachil

For all three of the places listed below ring or check their websites for detailed directions on how to reach them.

Balcón de Cumbres Verdes Cerro del Caballo, La Zubia, 8km south of Granada ☎958 89 10 58, ⓦwww.hotelcumbresverdes.com. Fifteen minutes from the city centre, this is a pleasant rural hotel in rolling countryside beyond the village of La Zubia. Rooms come with kitchenette and there's a pool. ❸

Hotel El Balcón de las Nieves C/Alayos 174, in the village of Cumbres Verdes beyond La Zubia ☎958 89 20 62, ⓦwww.elbalcondelasnieves.es. This is another charming place in the foothills of the Sierra Nevada but within easy striking distance of the city. Comfortably furnished rooms have satellite TV and there's a pool plus a decent restaurant (*La Gitarra*) over the road. ❹

El Molino de Rosa María Serrano Avda. del Río 23, Monachil, 11km southwest of the city ☎958 30 19 14, ⓦwww.molino-rosa-maria-serrano.com.

Very pleasant and good value rural hotel in this pretty village a mere 10min from the city centre with attractive rooms and its own restaurant. ❷

Youth hostel and campsites

Albergue Juvenil Avda. Ramón y Cajal 2, off the Camino de Ronda ☎958 00 29 00, ⓦwww .inturjoven.com. If you arrive late, this is handy for the train station: from there, turn left onto Avda. de la Constitución and left again onto the Camino de Ronda – it's the large white building by a sports stadium (Estadio de la Juventud); from the bus station take bus #3 to the cathedral and then bus #11, which will drop you outside. Recently renovated with lots of facilities, all rooms are en-suite doubles, the staff are friendly but the food is institutional. An excellent alternative is the hostel at Viznar, in the hills above the city (see p.498). ❷

Camping Reina Isabel 4km along the Zubia road to the southwest of the city ☎958 59 00 41. With a pool, less noise and more shade than the site below, this makes a pleasant rural alternative and – with your own transport – the city is within easy reach.

Camping Sierra Nevada Avda. de Madrid 107, northwest of the centre and 200m south of the bus station ☎958 15 00 62. Easiest reached from the centre on bus #3, this is the most convenient city site, and – with a pleasant pool – probably the best too.

The Alhambra

The Sabika hill sits like a garland on Granada's brow,
In which the stars would be entwined
And the Alhambra (Allah preserve it)
Is the ruby set above that garland.

Ibn Zamrak, vizier to Muhammad V (1362–91)

One of the most sensual architectural creations in the world and the greatest treasure of Moorish Spain, the **Alhambra** sits on a hill overlooking the city it has captivated for seven centuries. There are three distinct groups of buildings on the Alhambra hill (known as Sabika to the Moors): the **Casa Real** (Royal Palace or Palacios Nazaríes), the palace gardens of the **Generalife**, and the **Alcazaba**. This last, the fortress of the eleventh-century Ziridian rulers, was all that existed when the Nasrids made Granada their capital, but from its reddish walls the hill top had already taken its name: Al Qal'a al-Hamra in Arabic means literally "the red fort".

The first Nasrid king, Ibn al-Ahmar, rebuilt the Alcazaba and added to it the huge circuit of walls and towers which forms your first view of the castle. Within the walls he began a palace, which was supplied with running water by diverting the Río Darro nearly 8km to the foot of the hill; water is an integral part of the Alhambra and this engineering feat was Ibn al-Ahmar's greatest contribution. The Casa Real was essentially the product of his fourteenth-century successors,

▲ View of the Alhambra from Mirador De San Nicolás

particularly **Muhammad V**, who built and decorated many of its rooms in celebration of his accession to the throne (in 1354) and conquest of Algeciras (in 1369). Also within the citadel stood a complete "government city" of mansions, smaller houses, baths, schools, mosques, barracks and gardens.

After their conquest of Granada, **Fernando and Isabel** lived for a while in the Alhambra. They restored some rooms and converted the mosque but left the palace structure unaltered. As at Córdoba and Seville, it was their grandson **Emperor Carlos V** who wreaked the most insensitive destruction. He demolished a whole wing of rooms in order to build yet another grandiose Renaissance palace. This and the Alhambra itself were simply ignored by his successors and by the eighteenth century the Royal Palace was in use as a prison. In 1812 it was taken and occupied by **Napoleon's forces**, who looted and damaged whole sections of the building, and on their retreat from the city tried to blow up the entire complex. Their attempt was thwarted only by the action of a crippled soldier (José García) who remained behind and removed the fuses; a plaque honouring his valour has been placed in the Plaza de los Aljibes.

Two decades later the Alhambra's "rediscovery" began, given impetus by the American writer **Washington Irving**, who set up his study in the empty palace rooms and began to write his marvellously romantic *Tales of the Alhambra* (on sale all over Granada – and good reading amid the gardens and courts). Shortly after its publication the Spaniards made the Alhambra a **national monument** and set aside funds for its restoration. This continues to the present day and is now a highly sophisticated project, scientifically removing the accretions of later ages in order to expose and restore meticulously the Moorish creations.

Approaches to the Alhambra

The standard approach to the Alhambra is along the Cuesta de Gomérez, a narrow, semi-pedestrianized road that climbs uphill from Plaza Nueva. The only vehicles allowed to use this road are taxis and the **Alhambrabus** (line #30), a dedicated minibus service (daily 7am–10pm, every 10min; €1.10) linking the Plaza Nueva with the Alhambra palace. To approach the Alhambra

Tickets and admission to the Alhambra

To protect the **Alhambra** (daily: April–Oct 8.30am–8pm; Nov–March 8.30am–6pm; last admission 1hr before closing time; €12; ⊛www.alhambra-patronato.es), only 8100 daily **admissions** are allowed. If you are buying your tickets in person you have two options: they can be purchased at the entrance (ticket office opens at 8am), but queues can be long and there is no guarantee of getting in (see below). It may be possible to avoid the queues by paying with a credit card. Signed off the car park near the entrance with a board in English and Spanish stating "Credit Cards/Tarjetas de Credito" is a small building with ServiCaixa ticket machines operated by the La Caixa bank. You insert a credit card into the machine and request a day and time (morning or afternoon: see below); if there are tickets available for the day and time requested the machine will issue tickets and debit your card. You should be be aware that for technical reasons not all credit cards will work on these machines. It is also important to remember that the tickets put on sale in the manner above are only what remain after the ticket sales below have taken priority. This could well mean in high season that **no tickets** are on sale at the entrance. All tickets purchased will state whether they are for (morning) 8.30am–2pm or (afternoon) 2–8pm (Oct–March 2–6pm) sessions and you must enter between the stated times (once inside you may stay as long as you wish).

Alternatively, and this is the method strongly recommended by the Alhambra to guarantee entry on a specific day, you can **book in advance** on one of two websites: ⊛www.alhambra-tickets.es and ⊛www.servicaixa.com. Internet reservations carry a booking fee of €1 levied on each ticket. Booking is also possible by **phone** on (from Spain) ☎902 888 001 or (from abroad) ☎934 923 750 (24hr; English spoken). When using either of the above methods you will be allocated a time slot for visiting the Palacios Nazaríes (see p.482) that you will need to remember. The tickets should then be collected from the Alhambra's ticket office (reservation counter not main queue) at least one hour before this time. You will need your reservation number (issued with all internet and phone transactions), the same credit card with which you made the booking plus your passport for identification.

The tickets have **sections** for each part of the complex – Alcazaba, Palacios Nazaríes (royal palace), Generalife (gardens) – which must be used on the same day. Note that you will not be allowed to enter the complex (even with pre-booked tickets) less than an hour before closing time. To alleviate overcrowding, tickets are stamped with a half-hour **time slot** during which you must enter the Palacios Nazaríes. You will not be allowed to enter before or after this time, but once inside the palace you can stay as long as you like. Note also that the Museo de la Alhambra (see p.485) and the Museo de las Bellas Artes (see p.486), both in the palace of Carlos V, have different hours and admission fees to those of the Alhambra. It's worth pointing out too that only the palaces, museums and Generalife require a ticket to gain entry – the rest you are allowed to wander around freely.

The Alhambra is also open for floodlit **night visits** (limited to the Palacios Nazaríes; €12) from Tuesday to Saturday from March to October (10–11.30pm) and on Friday and Saturday nights from November to February (8–9.30pm). Note that for evening visits the **ticket offices** are open only 15min before and 15min after each opening time and availability of tickets (which can be pre-booked) is subject to the same terms as for daytime visits. Themed **guided visits** (in Spanish; Sept–June; €5) also allow visitors to view parts of the complex (many in the process of restoration) not normally open to the public. A leaflet, *Programa de Visitas Guiadas*, is available from the Alhambra ticket office, but they need to be booked at an office in the Corral de Carbón, slightly south of the cathedral.

THE ALHAMBRA

1	Torre de la Vela	11	Baños Reales
2	Torre del Homenaje	12	Cripta del Palacio de Carlos V
3	Torre Quebrada	13	Sala de los Abencerrajes
4	Patio de Machuca	14	Puerta de la Rawda
5	Mexuar	15	Sala de los Reyes
6	Patio del Cuarto Dorado	16	Patio de los Leones
7	Cuarto Dorado	17	Sala de las Dos Hermanas
8	Salón de Embajadores	18	Patio de la Lindaraja
9	Sala de la Barca	19	Patio de la Azequia
10	Patio de los Arrayanes	20	Patio de la Sultana

Alhambra Palace Hotel ▼

by car use the signed route heading from Puerta Real along the Paseo del Salón and the Paseo de la Bomba to the Alhambra's car park on the eastern edge of the complex.

Should you decide to walk up the hill (a pleasant 20min stroll from Plaza Nueva), after a few hundred metres you reach the **Puerta de las Granadas**, a massive Renaissance gateway topped by three pomegranates which became the city's symbol (*granada* is the fruit's Spanish name). Beyond the gate the path on the right climbs up towards a group of fortified towers, the **Torres Bermejas**, parts of which may date from as early as the eighth century (see p.487 for other sights on this route). The left-hand path heads through woods of closely planted elms and past a huge terrace-fountain (courtesy of Carlos V), eventually reaching the main gateway of the Alhambra in Moorish times, the **Puerta de la Justicia**. A magnificent tower that forced three changes of direction, making intruders hopelessly vulnerable, it was built by Yusuf I in 1348 and preserves above its inner arch the Koranic symbol of a key (for Allah, the opener of the gates of Paradise) and, over the outer arch, an outstretched hand whose five fingers represent the five Islamic precepts: prayer, fasting, alms-giving, pilgrimage to Mecca and the oneness of God. A Moorish legend stated that the gate would never be breached by the Christians until the hand reached down to grasp the key. To reach the ticket office continue uphill for 400m.

Leaving the Alhambra, a lovely alternative route down to the city is the Cuesta de los Chinos, and its continuation the Cuesta del Rey Chico, which descends beneath two arches to the right of the *La Mimbre* restaurant near the Alhambra's ticket office. It winds gradually down, passing beneath the Alhambra's northern walls, to the Río Darro and a terrace of riverside cafés.

Starting your visit

The ticket office entrance (p.479) to the Alhambra brings you into the complex at the eastern end, near to the Generalife gardens. However, your time slot for entering the Palacios Nazaríes (usually up to an hour ahead) means that it makes sense to **start your visit** with the Alcazaba, the oldest part of the complex, at the Alhambra's opposite (western) end. To get there from the entrance, walk up the short avenue lined with cypresses to a three-way fork, taking the signed path to the Alhambra. Cross the bridge over the "moat" following signs to the Alcazaba and Palacios Nazaríes. You will eventually pass the gates of the *Parador de San Francisco* (right) and the *Hotel América* to enter the Calle Real. Continue alongside the palace of Carlos V to reach the Puerto del Vino where our account begins (see below).

The Alcazaba

Having made your way from the ticket office (see box, p.479), go through the **Puerta del Vino** – named from its use in the sixteenth century as a wine cellar – and across the Plaza de los Aljibes you are confronted by the walls of the **Alcazaba**, the earliest, though most ruined, part of the fortress. Quite apart from filling in time before your ticket admits you to the Palacios Nazaríes, this is an interesting part of the complex and one where you can get a grip on the whole site.

Once inside, thread your way through remnants of the barracks to the Alcazaba's summit, the **Torre de la Vela**, named after a huge bell on its turret which until recent years was rung to mark the irrigation hours for workers on the *vega*, Granada's vast and fertile plain. The views from here are spectacular: west over the plunging ravine of the Darro with the city and the *vega* beyond, and north towards the Albaicín and Sacromonte hills, with the Alhambra itself behind and the snowcapped peaks of the Sierra Nevada forming a backdrop. It was on this same parapet at 3pm on January 2, 1492, that the Cross was first displayed above the city, alongside the royal standards of Aragón and Castile and the banner of St James. Boabdil, leaving Granada for exile in the Alpujarras, turned and wept at the sight, earning from his mother Aisha the famous rebuke: "Do not weep like a woman for what you could not defend like a man." The visit route continues via the **Jardín de los Ardaves**, a delightful seventeenth-century garden laid out along the fort's southern parapets with creepers, fountains and sweet-scented bushes.

To gain access to the palace you need to recross the **Plaza de los Aljibes** (where there's a very welcome drinks kiosk). In Nasrid times this area was a ravine dividing the hill between the Royal Palace on one side, and the Alcazaba on the other. Following the *Reconquista* the ravine was filled in to hold two rainwater cisterns (*aljibes*) and the surface above laid out with fortifications. During the construction of Carlos V's palace in the sixteenth century, the area was cleared of these structures to create a parade ground, the rather desolate form it retains today. The underground **cisterns** can now be seen only as part of a guided visit (see box, p.479). Follow the arrows indicating the Palacios Nazaríes (Nasrid Palaces) to reach the royal palace. Fronting the entrance to the palace a **Sala de Presentación** has a small exhibition – with some informative maquettes – detailing the development of the Alhambra.

The Palacios Nazaríes

It is amazing that the **Palacios Nazaríes** has survived, for it stands in utter contrast to the strength of the Alcazaba and the encircling walls and towers. It was built lightly and often crudely from wood, brick and adobe, and was designed not to last but to be renewed and redecorated by succeeding rulers. Its buildings show a superb use of light and space but they are principally a vehicle for ornamental stucco decoration. This, as Titus Burckhardt explains in *Moorish Culture in Spain*, was both an intricate science and a philosophy of abstract art in direct contrast to pictorial representation:

With its rhythmic repetition, [it] does not seek to capture the eye to lead it into an imagined world, but, on the contrary, liberates it from all pre-occupations of the mind. It does not transmit any specific ideas, but a state of being, which is at once repose and inner rhythm.

Burckhardt adds that the way in which patterns are woven from a single band, or radiate from many identical centres, served as a pure simile for Islamic belief in the oneness of God, manifested at the centre of every form and being.

Arabic inscriptions feature prominently in the ornamentation. Some are poetic eulogies of the buildings and builders, others of various sultans – notably Muhammad V. Most, however, are taken from the Koran, and among them the phrase "Wa-la ghaliba illa-Llah" (There is no Conqueror but God) is tirelessly repeated. It's said that this became the battle cry of the Nasrids upon Ibn al-Ahmar's return from aiding the Castilian war against Muslim Seville; it was his reply to the customary, though bitterly ironic, greetings of *Mansur* (Victor).

The palace is structured in three parts, each arrayed round an interior court and with a specific function. The sultans used the **Mexuar**, the first series of rooms, for business and judicial purposes. In the **Serallo**, beyond, they would receive embassies and distinguished guests. The last section, the **Harem**, formed their private living quarters and would have been entered by no one but their family and servants.

The Mexuar

The council chamber, the main reception hall of the **Mexuar**, is the first room you enter. It was completed in 1365 and hailed (perhaps obsequiously) by the court poet and vizier Ibn Zamrak as a "haven of counsel, mercy and favour". Here the sultan heard the pleas and petitions of the people and held meetings with his ministers. At the room's far end is a small **oratory**, one of a number of prayer niches scattered round the palace and immediately identifiable by their angular alignment to face Mecca.

This "public" section of the palace, beyond which few would have penetrated, is completed by the Mudéjar **Cuarto Dorado** (Golden Room), redecorated under Carlos V, whose Plus Ultra motif appears throughout the palace, and the **Patio del Cuarto Dorado**. This latter has perhaps the grandest facade of the whole palace, for it admits you to the formal splendour of the Serallo.

The Serallo

The **Serallo** was built largely to the design of Yusuf I (1333–54), a romantic and enlightened sultan who was stabbed to death by a madman while worshipping in the Alhambra mosque. Its rooms open out from delicate marble-columned arcades at each end of the long **Patio de los Arrayanes** (Myrtles) with its serene fountain and pool flanked by clipped myrtle bushes. At the court's northern end

Wa-la ghailiba illa-Liah
"There is no Conqueror but God"

(stylized inscription from the Alhambra)

is the **Sala de la Barca**, with a fine copy of its original cedar ceiling (destroyed by fire in the nineteenth century), and beyond this the fortified **Torre de Comares**, two floors of which are occupied by the royal throne room.

This room, known as the **Salón de Embajadores** (Hall of the Ambassadors), is the palace's largest and most majestic chamber. It was where the delicate diplomacy with the Christian emissaries would have been transacted – the means by which the Nasrid dynasty preserved itself – and as the sultan could only be approached indirectly it stands at an angle to the entrance from the Mexuar. It is perfectly square, with a stunning wooden dome, a superb example of *lacería*, the rigidly geometric "carpentry of knots" domed roof, and with a complex symbolism representing the seven heavens of the Muslim cosmos. The walls are completely covered in tile and stucco decoration and inscriptions, one of which states simply "I am the Heart of the Palace". It was here, symbolically, that Boabdil signed the terms of his city's surrender to the Reyes Católicos, whose motifs (the arms of Aragón and Castile) were later worked into the dome. Here, too, so it is said, Fernando met with Columbus to discuss his planned voyage to find a new sea route to India – the trip which led to the discovery of the Americas.

Carlos V tore down the rooms at the southern end of the Patio de los Arrayanes. From the arcade there is access (frequently closed) to the gloomy **chapel crypt** (*cripta*) of his palace; it has a curious "whispering gallery" effect, whereby words whispered on one side of the crypt can be heard quite clearly on the opposite side.

The Harem

The visit route continues to the **Patio de los Leones** (Court of the Lions), which has become the archetypal image of Granada, and constitutes the heart of the harem section of the palace. It was this area that moved Washington Irving to write in his *Tales of the Alhambra*:

> It is impossible to contemplate this scene, so perfectly Oriental, without feeling the early associations of Arabian romance, and almost expecting to see the white arm of some mysterious princess beckoning from the gallery, or some dark eye sparkling through the lattice. The abode of beauty is here as if it had been inhabited but yesterday.

The recently restored stylized and archaic-looking lions beneath its fountain probably date, like the court itself, from the reign of Muhammad V, Yusuf's successor; a poem inscribed on the bowl tells how much fiercer the beasts would look if they weren't so restrained by respect for the sultan. The court was designed as an interior garden and planted with shrubs and aromatic herbs; it opens onto three of the finest rooms in the palace, each of which looks directly onto the fountain.

The most sophisticated rooms in this part of the complex, apparently designed to give a sense of the rotary movement of the stars, are the two facing each other across the court. The largest of these, the **Sala de los Abencerrajes**, has the most fabulous ceiling in the whole Alhambra complex: sixteen-sided, supported by niches of astonishing stalactite vaulting and lit by windows in the dome. Based on Pythagoras's theorem, the whole stupendous design – with a final and deft artistic flourish – is reflected in a fountain on the floor. Its light and airy quality stands at odds with its name and history, for it was here that Abu al-Hassan, Boabdil's father, murdered sixteen princes of the Abencerraj family, whose chief had fallen in love with his favourite, Zoraya. The stains in the fountain are popularly supposed to be indelible traces of blood from the severed heads thrown into it – but are more likely to be from rust.

At the far end of the court is the **Sala de los Reyes** (Hall of the Kings), whose dormitory alcoves preserve a series of unique paintings on leather. These, in defiance of Koranic law, represent human scenes. They were probably painted by a Christian artist in the last decades of Moorish rule and were once thought to portray images of the Nasrid rulers – hence the room's name.

The second of the two facing chambers on the court's north side, the **Sala de las Dos Hermanas** (Hall of the Two Sisters), is more mundanely named – from two huge slabs of white marble in its floor – but just as spectacularly decorated, with a dome of over five thousand honeycomb cells. It was the principal room of the sultan's favourite, opening onto an inner apartment and balcony (with surviving fragments of Moorish tinted glass in the dome), the **Mirador de la Daraxa** (Eyes of the Sultana); the romantic garden patio below was added after the Reconquest.

Beyond, you are directed along a circuitous route through **apartments** redecorated by Carlos V (as at Seville, the northern-reared emperor installed fireplaces) and later used by Washington Irving. Eventually you emerge at the **Peinador de la Reina** (Queen's Pavilion), which served as an oratory for the sultanas and as a dressing room for the wife of Carlos V; perfumes were burned beneath its floor and wafted up through a marble slab in one corner.

From there, passing the **Patio de la Lindaraja** added in the sixteenth century (though the basin of its marble fountain was taken from outside the Mexuar), you come to the **Baños Reales** (Royal Baths), wonderfully decorated in rich tile mosaics and lit by pierced stars and rosettes once covered by coloured glass. The central chamber was used for reclining and retains the balconies where singers and musicians – reputedly blind to keep the royal women from being seen – would entertain the bathers. At present, entry is not permitted to the baths, though you can make out most of the features through the doorways.

The visit route exits via the exquisite **Portico del Partal** with a tower and elegant portico overlooking a serene pool. What appears no more than a garden pavilion today is in fact the surviving remnant of the early fourteenth-century Palace of the Partal, a four-winged structure originally surrounding the pool, the Alhambra's largest expanse of water. The **Jardines del Partal** lie beyond this and the nearby gate brings you out close to the entrance to the Palace of Carlos V.

The Palacio de Carlos V

Entering the **Palacio de Carlos V** strikes a totally different mood to what has gone before. The architecture of the palace with its rigid symmetries and dour exterior could not be more different than that of the Nasrid palaces. The building is dominated by its interior circular courtyard, where bullfights were once held. The palace itself was begun in 1526 but never finished – the coffered ceilings of the colonnade were added only in the 1960s before which the Ionic columns had projected into open sky – as shortly after commissioning it, Carlos V left Granada never to return, his plan to turn the city into the seat of the Spanish monarchy forgotten. Despite seeming totally out of place, however, the edifice is a distinguished piece of Renaissance design in its own right – the only surviving work of Pedro Machuca, a former pupil of Michelangelo. Lorca once referred to the stylistic clash between the two palaces as symbolic of "the fatal duel that throbs in the heart of each of Granada's citizens".

The palace's lower floor houses the **Museo de la Alhambra** (Tues–Sat 9am–2.30pm; €1.50, free with EU passport), a wonderful collection of artefacts that visitors are often too jaded to take in after the marvels of the Moorish palace outside. As well as fragments of sculptured plaster arabesques saved from the Alhambra and a splendid ceramic collection, look out for some outstanding fourteenth- and fifteenth-century Nasrid paintings and equally stunning carved wood panels and screens. The rare and beautiful fifteenth-century **Alhambra Vase** (Jarrón de las Gacelas) is the museum's centrepiece. Almost a metre and a half in height, and made for the Nasrid palace from local red clay enamelled in blue and gold with leaping *gacelas* (gazelles), it is the ceramic equal of the artistic splendours in the palace.

On the upper floors of the palace is the **Museo de Bellas Artes** (Tues 2.30–8pm, Wed–Sat 9am–8pm, Sun 9am–2.30pm; Nov–Feb closes 6pm; €1.50, free with EU passport), a cavernous gallery whose paintings and sculpture might command more attention elsewhere. In Room 1 there's a fine sixteenth-century woodcarving of the *Virgin and Child* by Diego de Siloé. Room 2 is dedicated to the works of Alonso Cano, the seventeenth-century *granadino* painter and sculptor. His powerful portrayals of *San Diego de Alcalá* and *San Antonio* stand out, as does a head of *San Juan de Dios*, the latter made with some assistance from Granada's other great sculptor, Pedro de Mena. Room 3 has more examples of the Andalucian sculptural tradition, incuding an *Ecce Homo* by José de Mora and a *Dolorosa* by his less famous brother Diego. Room 4 displays some minor Flemish works from the Golden Age, while the later rooms, devoted to paintings from the nineteenth and twentieth centuries, are fairly forgettable. Exceptions here are a typical work by Mariano Fortuny of Granada's *Ayuntamiento Viejo* and two vibrantly coloured abstract works by Granada-born José Guerrero (see p.492).

On the Palace's lower floor is one of the three official Alhambra **bookshops** (Librería de la Alhambra) with a wide variety of texts and postcards relating to the monument; the others are next to the ticket office at the entrance and along the Calle Real.

The Baño de la Mezquita and Convento de San Francisco

Behind Carlos V's palace are the remnants of the town (with a population of forty thousand during the Nasrid period) which once existed within the Alhambra's walls. The main street, c/Real, today lined with tedious tourist shops, guides you east towards the Generalife, and on the way it's worth looking into the well-preserved **Baño de la Mezquita** (entry with Alhambra ticket) where ablutions were performed prior to entering the Alhambra's main mosque which was demolished to make way for the undistinguished sixteenth-century church of Santa María de la Alhambra. At the southern end of c/Real the fifteenth-century **Convento de San Francisco** is also worth a visit. Built by Fernando and Isabel on the site of another Moorish palace, this is now a parador whose marvellous plant-filled patio, dominated by a soaring cypress projecting above the roof, preserves part of the chapel where the Catholic monarchs were buried – commemorated by a marble slab – before being removed to the cathedral. It's tricky to find, and you'll need to ask for directions at the hotel's reception. At the rear of the parador, there's a restaurant and a very pleasant terrace bar, both open to nonresidents.

The Generalife

Paradise is described in the Koran as a shaded, leafy garden refreshed by running water where the "fortunate ones" may take their rest under tall canopies. It is an image that perfectly describes the **Generalife**, the gardens and summer palace of the Nasrid rulers. Its name means literally "garden of the architect" and the grounds consist of a luxuriantly imaginative series of patios, enclosed gardens and walkways.

By chance, an account of the gardens during Moorish times, written rather fancifully by fourteenth-century Moorish historian, poet and palace vizier Ibn Zamrak, survives. The descriptions that he gives aren't all entirely believable but they are a wonderful basis for musing as you lounge around by the patios and fountains. There were, he wrote, celebrations with horses darting about in the dusk at speeds that made the spectators rub their eyes (a form of festival still indulged in at Moroccan *fantasías*); rockets shot into the air to be attacked by the stars for their audacity; tightrope walkers flying through the air like birds; men bowled along in a great wooden hoop, shaped like an astronomical sphere.

Today, even devoid of such amusements, the gardens remain deeply evocative, above all, perhaps, the **Patio de la Sultana** (aka Patio de los Cipreses), a dark and secretive walled garden of sculpted junipers where the sultana Zoraya was suspected of meeting her lover Hamet, chief of the unfortunate Abencerrajes. The trunk of the seven-hundred-year-old **cypress tree** (marked by a plaque) is where legend says their trysts took place and where the grisly fate of the Abencerraj clan was sealed. Nearby is the inspired flight of fantasy of the **Escalera del Agua** (aka Camino de las Cascadas), a staircase with water flowing down its stone balustrades. At its base is a wonderful little **Summer Palace**, with various decorated belvederes.

If you're looking for a lunch time **place to eat** or a refreshing drink between palaces and museums, the shady terrace of *Restaurante La Mimbre* is one of the best-value places on the hill (see p.500).

Other sights on the Alhambra hill

From the Puerta de las Granadas, taking the right-hand path uphill leads, in its higher reaches, to the **Casa Museo Manuel de Falla**, c/Antequerela s/n (Tues–Sun 10am–2pm; guided visits, last visit 1.30pm; €3), the former home of the great Cádiz composer. The tiny house has been re-created to appear just as he left it in 1939 – with piano, domestic clutter, medicine bottles by his bed (he was a life-long hypochondriac), and stacks of books – before quitting fascist Spain for an exile spent in Argentina where he died in 1946. The walls and surfaces are dotted with mementoes and gifts from friends – including a series of sketches by Picasso – and the pleasant garden with its bench and vista is where the composer relaxed ("I have the most beautiful panoramic view in the world," he wrote to friend). A summer café (April–Sept) here serving *pasteles* (cakes) and drinks opens from 8.30pm to 1am. Occasional concerts of de Falla's works are performed in the nearby **Auditorio de Manuel de Falla**, Paseo de los Mártires s/n, on Saturday evenings and Sunday mornings throughout the year (details from the Turismo). Beyond here at the end of the same avenue is the **Carmen de los Mártires** (March–Oct Mon–Fri 10am–2pm & 6–8pm, Sat & Sun 10am–8pm, Nov–Feb Mon-Fri 10am–2pm & 4–6pm, Sat & Sun 10am–6pm; free), a turn-of-the-twentieth-century house set in a delightfully tranquil garden filled with grottoes, statues, and follies as well as peacocks and black swans. Part of the grounds is currently being transformed into a botanical garden.

Just opposite the de Falla Museum, the terrace of the exclusive neo-Moorish **Hotel Alhambra Palace** (open to the public providing you're decently dressed) with fine **views** over the city is a great place for a drink. Ask at the reception desk to see the hotel's charming **theatre**, also in pseudo-Moorish style and where on June 7, 1922, an evening of poetry and song launched the career of a youthful Federico García Lorca (the guitarist Segovia appeared on the same bill). Just to the north of here on the Paseo del Generalife, the nineteenth-century **Hotel Washington Irving** is another of Granada's hotels with many historical associations. The hotel – run down and in serious need of attention – closed its doors in 2001 but it is to be hoped that such an important part of Granada's modern history will at some point be rehabilitated. In 1928, *New York Times* journalist Mildred Adams met Federico García Lorca here for the first time and fell under his spell. The poet sat down at the hotel's battered, out-of-tune piano in the lobby and sang her a ballad about the arrest and death of a local flamenco singer. "In gesture, tone of voice, expression of face and body, Lorca himself was the ballad," she wrote later.

The rest of the city

If you're spending just a couple of days in Granada it's hard to resist spending both of them in the Alhambra. There are, however, a handful of minor Moorish sites in and around the run-down medieval streets of the **Albaicín**, the largest and most characteristic such quarter to survive in Spain. After the delights of Moorish Granada it takes a distinct readjustment and effort of will to appreciate the city's later Christian monuments – although the **Capilla Real**, at least, demands a visit, and Baroque enthusiasts are in for a treat at the **Cartuja**.

The Albaicín

Declared a World Heritage Site by UNESCO in 1994, the **Albaicín** stretches across a fist-shaped area bordered by the Río Darro, Sacromonte hill, the old town walls and the winding Calle de Elvira (which runs parallel to the Gran Vía). From the centre, the best approach is from the Plaza Nueva and along the Carrera del Darro, beside the river. Coming from the Alhambra, you can make your way down the Cuesta de los Chinos – a beautiful path and a short cut. Following the walking route into the Albaicín described below is pleasant and takes in many of the most notable sights. To save your legs, **buses** #31 and #32 from Plaza Nueva can take you to Plaza del Salvador in the heart of the *barrio*, and Plaza San Nicolás, near the famous *mirador*. Roughly one bus per hour (#34) deviates from this route to take in the adjoining *barrio* of Sacromonte.

Plaza Nueva and Cuesta De Gomérez

Before starting out from the **Plaza Nueva**, take a look at the square itself. It was constructed just after the *Reconquista* as a new focus for the city, and soon served as the site of an act of stunning Christian barbarity: a bonfire of eighty thousand books from the former Muslim university. The square's elegant

---

Personal security in the Albaicín

There has been an increasing number of **thefts** from tourists in the Albaicín in recent years, often by drug addicts to fund their addiction. The preferred method is bag snatching, and is rarely accompanied by violence. However, don't let the threat put you off visiting one of the city's most atmospheric quarters; applying a few common-sense measures should ensure that you come to no harm.

Firstly, do not take any valuables (including airline tickets and passports) or large amounts of cash with you when visiting the Albaicín and keep what you have on your person, not in a bag. If your bag is snatched don't offer resistance – the thief will be concerned only with making a speedy getaway. Finally, try not to look like an obvious tourist (map/guidebook in hand is a dead giveaway) or flaunt expensive-looking photographic equipment and keep to streets where there are other people around, especially at night.

sixteenth-century fountain, the **Pilar del Toro**, is the last known work by the eminent Renaissance architect Diego de Siloé.

Flanking the plaza's north side is the austerely impressive **Real Chancillería** (Royal Chancery), built at the same time as the square, and now the law courts. Beyond its monumental entrance lies an elegant two-storeyed **patio** designed by Diego de Siloé with marble Doric columns and a staircase with stalactite ceiling.

On the opposite side of the square, the **Cuesta de Gomérez** leads up to the Alhambra. It's here that many of Granada's renowned guitar manufacturers are gathered. Behind the windows of these places – Casa Morales at no. 9 is one of the most famous – you may catch sight of a major concert or flamenco musician trying out a new instrument; they are not averse to giving the shop's customers a free concerto or two.

Santa Ana and the Baños Árabes

Perched over the Río Darro at the Plaza Nueva's eastern end is the sixteenth-century church of **Santa Ana** (open service times, 6–7.30pm) whose elegant bell tower is the converted minaret of the mosque it replaced. The church's interior has flamboyantly decorated Baroque side chapels and a fine *artesonado* ceiling. Following the river's northern bank along the **Carrera del Darro**, glance back to where the river disappears from sight under the city and "moans as it loses itself in the absurd tunnel" as the young Lorca put it.

A little way up at no. 31 are the remains of the **Baños Árabes** (Tues–Fri 10am–2pm; €1.50, free with EU passport), a marvellous and little-visited Moorish public bath complex. Built in the eleventh century, the sensitively restored building consists of a series of brick-vaulted rooms with typical star-shaped skylights (originally glazed) and columns incorporating Roman and Visigothic capitals. When Richard Ford was here in the 1830s he found it being used as a wash house by the local women because "one of the first laws after the conquest of the Catholic sovereigns was to prohibit bathing by fine and punishment". To get an idea of what a **Moorish bathhouse** was like when functioning, one has been re-created just behind the church of Santa Ana. At *Hammam*, c/Santa Ana 16 (reservation required ℡958 22 99 78; bath €17), you can wallow in the graded temperatures (cold, tepid and hot) of the traditional bath surrounded by marble pavements, mosaic wall decor and plaster arabesques. There's also a pleasant *tetería* (tearoom) upstairs too.

Casa de Castril: the Museo Arqueológico

At Carrera del Darro no. 43 is the **Casa de Castril**, a Renaissance mansion with a fine Plateresque facade and doorway, which houses the city's **Museo Arqueológico** (Tues 2.30–8.30pm, Wed–Sat 9.30am–8.30pm, Sun 9.30am–2.30pm; €1.50, free with EU passport), with its interesting exhibits of finds from throughout the province. Rooms 1 and 2 cover the Paleolithic and Neolithic periods, among which are some remarkable artefacts from the **Cueva de los Murciélagos** near Albuñol. In this fourth-millennium BC Neolithic cave, alongside a dozen cadavers arranged in a semicircle around that of a woman, were found some modern-looking esparto grass sandals and baskets, as well as a **golden diadem**. Room 3 has some interesting reconstructions of social life and culture in the Bronze Age and one exhibit shows how copper weapons and tools were manufactured using primitive moulds. Room 4 contains the Iberian and pre-Roman collection with some fine examples of early lapidary work, including a hefty carved stone bull, stone vases and outstanding alabaster vessels. The finds from the necropolis at **Punté Noye** near Almuñecar (the Phoenician Sexi) suggest a large colony here trading as far afield as Egypt and Greece from where the vases (some bearing pharaonic titles) were imported. The Roman section in Room 5 has a striking third-century bronze statue of a man in a toga as well as some interesting **early Christian lamps** from the fourth century.

Pride of place in the **Moorish section** (Room 7) is a fourteenth-century **bronze astrolabe**, demonstrating the superior scientific competence of the Arabic world at this time. The instrument was adopted by the Arabs from ancient Greece and used for charting the position of the stars in astrology, precisely orienting the *mihrab* of the mosques towards Mecca, determining geographical coordinates as well as trigonometry and converting Muslim dates into Christian ones. Its transmission from the Arab to the Christian world made possible the voyages of discovery to both east and west. More Moorish symmetry is evident in the designs on the vases, wooden chests and Amphorae also displayed here.

Further along the Darro and the Casa del Chapiz

Alongside the Casa de Castril, c/Zafra has a Moorish house, the **Casa Zafra**, with a pleasant patio and pool, whilst close by again is the convent of **Santa Catalina de Zafra**, housed in a sixteenth-century Mudéjar palace. The nuns here are renowned for their convent *dulces* and will gladly supply you (through a *turno*) with their speciality, *glorias* (almond cakes); they're open daily except in August. At the top of the same street, **San Juan de los Reyes** is another church – the first established in Granada after the *Reconquista* – built around the courtyard of a former mosque whose minaret, with characteristically Moorish *sebka* decoration, now serves as a belfry.

Continuing along the Río Darro you'll eventually come to **Paseo de los Tristes** (aka Paseo del Padre Manjón), a delightful esplanade beside the river overlooked by the battlements of the Alhambra high on the hill above, a great spot for a drink and especially so at night when the Alhambra is floodlit. There are several terrace bars fronting the river.

Two streets off here also contain **Moorish houses**: c/del Horno de Oro (no. 14) and, two streets further along, Cuesta de la Victoria (no. 9). The street

---

Sacromonte: Granada's gitano quarter

Granada has an ancient and still considerable **gitano** (gypsy) population, from whose clans many of Spain's best flamenco guitarists, dancers and singers have emerged. Traditionally the gypsies inhabited cave homes on **Sacromonte hill**, and many still do, giving lively displays of dancing and music in their *zambras* (shindigs). These were once spontaneous but are now blatantly contrived for tourists, and are often shameless rip-offs: you're hauled into a cave, leered at if you're female, and systematically extorted of all the money you've brought along (for dance, the music, the castanets, the watered-down sherry …). Which is not to say that you shouldn't visit – just take only as much money as you want to part with. Turn up mid-evening; the lines of caves begin off the Camino de Sacromonte, just above the Casa del Chapiz (centre top on our city map). When the university is in session, the cave dwellings are turned into **discotecas** and are packed with students at weekends.

For revelations of a different kind, wander up to Sacromonte a little earlier in the day and take a look at the old **caves** on the far side of the old Moorish wall – most of them deserted in 1962 after severe floods. There are fantastic views from the top. Sacromonte now has its own museum, the **Centro Interpretación del Sacromonte**, Barranco de los Negros s/n (March–Oct Tues–Sun 10am–2pm & 5–9pm; Nov–Feb Tues–Sun 10am–2pm & 4–7pm; €5), depicting the life and times of the *barrio*. In this area and Sacromonte generally it would also be wise to heed the warnings on personal security mentioned in the box on p.488.

after this, the **Cuesta del Chapiz**, climbs left into the heart of the Albaicín, passing first, on the right, the **Casa del Chapiz**, in origin a Moorish mansion – with a charming patio – and today reclaimed as a school of Arabic studies. The **Camino del Sacromonte**, just beyond it, heads east towards this *barrio*'s celebrated caves where, after sundown, the *gitanos* (gypsies) will attempt to entice you in for some raucous but often dubious flamenco (see box, p.490).

The Cuesta del Chapiz eventually loops around to the Plaza del Salvador where the church of **San Salvador** (daily 10.30am–1pm & 4.30–7.30pm; €1) is built on the site of a mosque of which the **courtyard** – with whitewashed arches and Moorish cisterns – is beautifully preserved. Diego de Siloé, the architect of the sixteenth-century church, which was badly damaged in the Civil War, converted the mosque's original **minaret** into its tower.

Plaza Larga and the Mirador De San Nicolás

From San Salvador, c/Panaderos leads into **Plaza Larga**, the busy heart of the Albaicín, with a concentration of restaurants and bars. The nearby c/Agua has more **Moorish dwellings**: take a look at nos. 1, 37, 28 and 19. A busy little **market** is held in Plaza Larga on Saturday mornings selling the usual fruit and vegetables as well as potted plants and bootleg DVDs.

From here the obvious route is to the **Mirador de San Nicolás** with its justly famous panoramic **view** of the Sierra Nevada, the Alhambra and Granada spread out below. To get there from Plaza Larga, go through the Arco de las Pesas, an old arch in the west corner, and turn sharply left up Callejón de San Cecilio. When you reach it, the fifteenth-century church of San Nicolás is of little note but the nearby **aljibe** (fountain) is a Moorish original, one of many in the Albaicín to survive from the time when every mosque – there were more than thirty of them – had its own.

Below the *mirador*, c/Nuevo de San Nicolás descends into c/Santa Isabel la Real, passing, on the right, the early sixteenth-century convent of **Santa Isabel la Real** (Tues, Thurs & Fri guided visits 10am & 11.30am; free) with a superb patio. The **convent church** has a superb Plateresque doorway and, inside, a fine Mudéjar ceiling, and holds sculptures by Pedro de Mena and José Mora. The convent was partly constructed within a fifteenth-century Nasrid palace – part of which was the adjoining **La Daralhorra** (Tues & Thurs 10am–2pm; free) of which only the patios and some arches survive. This was the residence of Aisha, the mother of the last king of Granada, Boabdil.

Plaza de San Miguel Bajo and San José

Calle Santa Isabel drops into one of the Albaicín's most delightful squares, **Plaza de San Miguel Bajo**, lined with acacia and chestnut trees. The church of **San Miguel** on its eastern side is another sixteenth-century work by Diego de Siloé, built over yet another mosque, and preserves its original thirteenth-century *aljibe* (fountain) where the ritual ablutions would have been performed before entering. The square also has a clutch of good bars, whose terraces are extremely popular at night; *Bar Lara* serves the potent barrelled *costa* wine brewed in the Alpujarras. The opposite end of the plaza leads to the **Mirador del Carril de la Lona** with its views over the western side of the city. You could also detour north from here – climbing uphill beyond the walls – to the church of **San Cristóbal**, which has another fine **view** of the Alhambra from its own *mirador*.

A pleasant walk back to the centre from Plaza San Miguel is to head roughly south along calles San Miguel and San José, eventually meeting up with calles Calderería Nueva and Calderería Vieja which have been transformed into a vibrant and delightful "Little Morocco" with food shops, restaurants and excellent teahouses serving a wide variety of refreshing teas, infusions and pastries (see box, p.502).

Other Moorish remains

A further group of Moorish buildings are located just outside the Albaicín. The most interesting of them, and oddly one of the least known, is the so-called **Palacio de la Madraza** (Mon–Fri 8am–10pm; closed Aug; free), a vividly painted building opposite the Capilla Real. Built in the early fourteenth century at the behest of Yusuf I – though much altered since – this is a former Islamic college (*medressa* in Arabic) and retains part of its old prayer hall, including a magnificently decorated **mihrab**. Note that the hours change here when it is used for exhibitions.

Slightly south of here lies the **Corral del Carbón**, a fourteenth-century *caravan-serai* (an inn where merchants would lodge and, on the upper floors, store their goods) which is unique in Spain. A wonderful horseshoe arch leads into a courtyard with a marble water trough. Remarkably, the building survived intact through a stint as a sixteenth-century theatre – with the spectators watching from the upper galleries – and later as a charcoal burners' factory, the origin of its present name. The building is a little tricky to find: it lies down an alleyway off the c/de los Reyes Católicos, opposite the **Alcaicería**, the old Arab silk bazaar, burned down in the nineteenth century and poorly restored as an arcade of souvenir shops.

East of here, an impressive Mudéjar mansion, the **Casa de los Tiros**, stands on c/Pavaneras, just behind Plaza de Isabel Católica. This was built just after the *Reconquista* ended and has a curious facade adorned with various Greek deities and heroes as well as a number of *tiros* (muskets) projecting from the upper windows. Above the door is a representation of the sword of Boabdil that the family who lived here claimed they held in custody. The interior – which is worth a look – now houses the mildly interesting **Museo Casa de los Tiros** (Tues 2.30–8.30pm, Wed–Sat 9am–8.30pm, Sun 9am–2.30pm; free) exhibiting documents, furniture, engravings and photos from the city's past.

Capilla Real and Centro José Guerrero

The **Capilla Real** (Royal Chapel; April–Sept Mon–Sat 10.30am–12.45pm & 4–7pm, Sun 11am–12.45pm & 4–7pm; Oct–March Mon–Sat 10.30am–12.45pm & 3.30–6.15pm, Sun 11am–12.45pm & 3.30–6.15pm; €3.50) is Granada's most impressive Christian building, flamboyant late Gothic in style and built ad hoc in the first decades of Christian rule as a mausoleum for Los Reyes Católicos, the city's "liberators". Before entering, note the stone frieze above the entrance which romantically alternates the initials of the two monarchs. Isabel, in accordance with her will, was originally buried on the Alhambra hill (in the church of the San Francisco convent, now part of the parador) but her wealth and power proved no safeguard of her wishes; both her remains and those of her spouse Fernando, who died eleven years later in 1516, were placed here in 1522. Isabel's final indignity occurred in the 1980s, when the candle that she asked should perpetually illuminate her tomb was replaced by an electric bulb – after many protests the candle was restored. But, as with Columbus's tomb in Seville, there is considerable doubt as to whether any of the remains in these lead coffins – so reverentially regarded by visiting Spaniards – are those of the monarchs at all. The chapel and tombs were desecrated by Napoleon's troops in 1812 and the coffins opened and defiled.

The monarchs' **tombs** in a plain underground crypt below are as simple as could be imagined: Fernando and Isabel, flanked by their daughter Juana ("the Mad") and her husband Felipe ("the Handsome"), rest in lead coffins placed in a plain crypt (a not easily spotted "F" marking that of the king on the left of the central pair). The smaller coffin to the right is that of the infant Príncipe de Asturias who died before reaching the age of two. Above them, however, is an elaborate Renaissance monument, with sculpted effigies of all four monarchs – the response of their grandson Carlos V to what he found "too small a room for so great a glory". The figures of Fernando and Isabel are easily identified by the rather puny-looking lion and lioness at their feet. Popular legend has it that Isabel's head sinks deeper into the pillow due to the weight of her intelligence compared with that of her husband; this is not without some truth as Fernando was never much more than a consort. Carved in Carrera marble by the Florentine Domenico Fancelli in 1517, the tomb's **side panels** depict the Apostles and scenes from the life of Christ and are especially fine. The Latin inscription at the monarchs' feet is brutally triumphalist in tone: "Overthrowers of the Mahometan sect and repressors of heretical stubbornness." The tomb of Joana and Felipe, a much inferior work, is by Ordóñez.

In front, dating from the same period, is an equally magnificent **reja**, or gilded grille, the work of Maestro Bartolomé of Jaén, and considered one of the finest in Spain. Its outstanding upper tier has scenes from the life of Christ and the Crucifixion. The altar's striking **retablo** is by Felipe Vigarny dated 1522, depicting in one scene San Juan being boiled in oil; beneath the kneeling figures of Fernando and Isabel – sculptures possibly by Diego de Siloé – are images depicting events close to both their hearts, Boabdil surrendering the keys of Granada for him, the enforced baptism of the defeated Moors for her.

In the capilla's **Sacristy** are displayed the **sword of Fernando**, the **crown of Isabel**, and the banners used at the conquest of Granada. Also here is Isabel's outstanding personal collection of **medieval Flemish paintings** – including a magnificent **El Descendimiento** (Descent from the Cross) triptych by Dirk Bouts. Here too, are important works by Memling, Bouts and van der Weyden – as well as various Italian and Spanish paintings, including panels by Botticelli, Perugino and Pedro Berruguete.

South of the chapel, along c/Oficios, stands the **Centro José Guerrero** (Tues–Sat 11am–2pm & 5–9pm, Sun 11am–2pm, Ⓦwww.centroguerrero.org; €1, free Wed), a museum dedicated to the city's most famous modern artist and brilliant colourist José Guerrero (1914–91). Influenced early on by Cubism and later by Miró, in 1950 Guerrero moved to New York where he became a leading exponent of American Expressionism, before returning to Spain in 1965. The museum displays arresting works from all his major periods of artistic development.

The Catedral

For all its stark Renaissance bulk, Granada's **Catedral** (April–Sept Mon–Sat 10.45am–1.30pm & 4–8pm, Sun 4–8pm; Oct–March Mon–Sat 10.45am–1.30pm & 4–7pm, Sun 4–7pm; €3.50), adjoining the Capilla Real and entered from a door on Gran Vía, is a disappointment. It was raised on the site of the Great Mosque, with work commencing in 1521 – just as the royal chapel was finished – but it was then left uncompleted until well into the eighteenth century. However, the main west facade by Diego de Siloé and Alonso Cano is worth a look. It still carries a provocative inscription honouring Primo de Rivera, founder of the fascist Falange Party, added in the Franco period, and, significantly for Granada today, never removed.

Inside, the church is pleasantly light and airy due to its painted stonework and twenty giant pillars which push the central dome to a height of over thirty metres. The Capilla Mayor has figures by Pedro de Mena of Fernando and Isabel at prayer, with, above them, oversized busts of Adam and Eve by *granadino* Alonso Cano, who also left quite a bit of work in the other chapels and is buried in the crypt – a marble and bronze plaque next to the main door honours him.

In the eighteenth-century **sagrario** there are more works by Cano as well as a fine *Crucifixión* by Martínez Montañés. In the side chapels are a triumphant sculpture of *Santiago* (St James) in the saddle, by Pedro de Mena (Capilla de Santiago) and an **El Greco** *St Francis* (Capilla de Jesús Nazareno).

The University Quarter: San Juan and San Jerónimo

North of the cathedral, and ten minutes' walk along c/San Jerónimo, the Renaissance **Hospital de San Juan de Dios** is well worth a visit. It was founded in 1552 by Juan de Robles (Juan de Dios) as a hospital for the sick and a refuge for foundlings, and its elaborate facade has a statue by José de Mora depicting the saint on his knees holding a cross, which popular legend says is how he died. The hospital itself still functions and you'll have to pass the entrance hall to reach two marvellous **patios**. The outer and larger one is a beautiful double-tiered Renaissance work with a palm at each of its four corners and a fountain in the centre; the inner patio – with orange trees in the corners here – has delightful but deteriorating frescoes depicting the saint's miracles. Next door, the impressive church, a Baroque addition, has a Churrigueresque *retablo* – a glittering, gold extravaganza by Guerrero.

Close by lies a little-known jewel: the sixteenth-century **Convento de San Jerónimo** (daily 10am–2.30pm & 4–7.30pm, Nov–March closes 6.30pm; €3), founded by the Catholic monarchs, though built after their death. This has a further exquisite pair of Renaissance **patios** (or cloisters in this context), the largest an elegant work by Diego de Siloé with two tiers of 36 arches. The **church**, also by Siloé, has been wonderfully restored after use as cavalry barracks and has fabulous eighteenth-century frescoes, another monumental carved and painted *retablo*, and, on either side of the altar, monuments to "El Gran Capitán" Gonzalo de Córdoba and his wife Doña María. The remains of this general, responsible for many of the Catholic monarchs' victories, may lie in the vault beneath, but the Napoleonic French were here too and, as Ford noted not much later, had "insulted the dead lion's ashes before whom, when alive, their ancestors had always fled". The church is little visited, and in late afternoon you may hear the nuns singing their offices in the railed-off choir loft above. A small shop at the entrance sells the convent's marmalade and *dulces*.

A few blocks to the north east of the Hospital de San Juan de Dios, reached by following c/San Juan de Dios and Avda. Hospicio, the **Hospital Real** (Mon–Fri 9am–1pm) is a magnificent Renaissance building designed by Enrique Egas. Formerly known as the Hospital de los Locos, it was founded by the Catholic monarchs and finished by Carlos V. As its former name implies, it was one of the first lunatic asylums in Europe, though it now houses the main library of the University of Granada. Inside, a beautiful arcaded patio and some fine *artesonado* ceilings are worth a look.

La Cartuja

Granada's **Cartuja** (daily 10am–1pm & 4–8pm; Nov–March closes 6pm; €3.50), on the northern outskirts of town, is the grandest and most outrageously decorated of all the country's lavish Carthusian monasteries. It's a ten- to fifteen-minute walk beyond the Hospital Real; alternatively, bus line #8, going north along Gran Vía, passes by.

The monastery was founded in 1516 on land provided by "El Gran Capitán", Gonzalo de Córdoba (see above), though the building is noted today for its

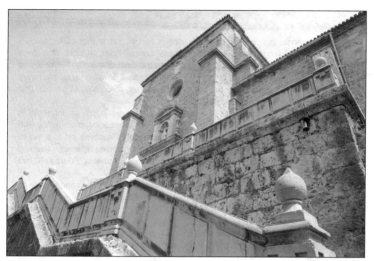

▲ La Cartuja

heights of Churrigueresque-inspired Baroque extravagance – added, some say, to rival the Alhambra. The **church** is of staggering wealth, surmounted by an altar of twisted and coloured marble described by one Spanish writer as "a motionless architectural earthquake". There are Bocanegra paintings and a seventeenth-century sculpture of the *Assumption* by José de Mora.

The **sagrario** drips with more marble, jasper and porphyry and has a breathtakingly beautiful gilded and frescoed **cupola** by Antonio Palomino, while the **sacristía** pulls out yet more stops with another stunning painted cupola and fascinating sculptural features influenced by the art of the Aztec and Maya civilizations encountered in the New World. Here also are fine sculptures of *San Bruno* by José de Mora in a side niche, and an *Inmaculada* by Alonso Cano.

Eating, drinking and nightlife

Granada is quite a sedate place, at least compared to Seville or Málaga, and if it weren't for the university, you sense the city would go unnaturally early to bed. However, on a brief stay, there's more than enough to entertain you, with some decent restaurants and plenty of animated bars, especially in the zone between **Plaza Nueva** and **Grand Vía**, the plazas of the **Albaicín** quarter, whose streets make for enjoyable (if confusing) evening wanderings, around the **Campo del Príncipe**, a spacious square with outdoor eating and drinking, at the foot of the west slopes of the Alhambra hill, and along the **Carrera del Darro**. Granada's *discotecas* – mostly dismal teenage hangouts – are mainly concentrated along **c/Pedro Antonio de Alarcón** to the west of the centre, which turns into one big disco at weekends. For serious drinking into the early hours head out to the bars along the same street as well as calles Gran Capitán and San Juan de Dios, both in the university area.

The monthly *Pocketguía de Granada* (available from newspaper kioskos; €1) has **listings** for most of what's happening on the cultural and entertainment front though it tends to be less up to date than the city's rather staid daily paper, *Ideal*, which has a more reliable entertainment guide, particularly in its weekend editions.

One of the ghosts that walks Granada's streets and plazas is that of Andalucía's greatest poet and dramatist **Federico García Lorca**. Born in 1898 at Fuente Vaqueros, a village in the *vega*, the fertile plain to the west of the city, he moved to Granada eleven years later. But it was his childhood spent growing up on the family farm, where he soaked up both the countryside and the folklore of its people, that was to have an enduring influence on his work.

Lorca published his first book of essays and poems while still at university in Granada, in 1918. It was in 1928, however, that he came to national prominence with *El Romancero Gitano*, an anthology of gypsy ballads. This success led to a trip to New York in 1929 where he spent a year at Columbia University ostensibly learning English, but actually gathering material for the collection of poems, *Poeta in Nueva York*, published after his death.

He returned to Spain in 1931 at the advent of the Spanish Republic and was given a government grant to run a travelling theatre group, La Barraca (the cabin). From this period the poet's major works for the stage – *Bodas de Sangre* (Blood Wedding) and *Yerma* – emerged.

In July 1936, on the eve of the Civil War, Lorca went back to Granada for the summer. This visit coincided with Franco's coup and control of the city was wrested by the Falangists, who initiated a reign of terror. Lorca, as a Republican sympathizer and declared homosexual, was hunted down by fascist thugs at the house of a friend (now the *Hotel Reina Cristina*, see p.475). Two days later he was murdered in an olive grove near the village of Viznar. His body was never found.

It has taken the city a long time to accord Lorca the recognition he deserves, partly because of his sexual inclinations, and mainly through guilt concerning the way he died. If you have an interest in tracing the locations of his life, the most important are detailed below. More avid followers should get hold of the excellent *Lorca's Granada* by Ian Gibson, his biographer.

Huerta de San Vicente

West of the centre is the **Huerta de San Vicente** (July–Aug Tues–Sun 10am–2.30pm; Sept–June Tues–Sun 10am–12.30pm & 4–6.30pm; €3, Wed free; guided tours every 45min; ⊛www.huertadesanvicente.com), an orchard where the poet's family used to spend the summer months. It spreads back from c/de la Virgen Blanca, behind *Los Jardines Neptuno Flamenco* nightclub; to get there take the southbound bus #4 from Gran Vía or Plaza del Carmen (direction Palacio de Deportes), or a taxi.

The **house** – now restored and opened as a museum – is set in the centre of what is now the largest rose garden in Europe, the **Parque Federico García Lorca**, the city's belated tribute. When the Lorcas had it, the five-acre holding was planted with vegetables and fruit trees. Then a tranquil rural plot on the city's edge, it has since been enveloped by ugly urban sprawl and it's hard to square the scene today with the poet's description of a "paradise of trees and water and so much jasmine and nightshade in the garden that we all wake up with lyrical headaches". The light and airy rooms contain some of their original furniture including, in Lorca's bedroom, his work desk, bed, a poster of the Barraca theatre company and the balcony (from outside, the furthest left of the three) looking towards the Sierra Nevada, which inspired one of his best-known poems, *Despedida* (Farewell):

Si muero, dejad el balcón abierto.
El niño come naranjas. (Desde mi balcón lo veo.)
El segador siega el trigo. (Desde mi balcón lo siento.)
Si muero, dejad el balcón abierto!
If I die, leave the balcony open.
The child eats oranges. (From my balcony I see him.)

The harvester scythes the corn. (From my balcony I hear him.)
If I die leave the balcony open!

In a *hornacina* or wall niche outside is the tiny image of San Vicente placed there
by Lorca's father – and where it has remained ever since – when he bought the house
in 1925 and changed its name to that of the saint.

Fuente Vaqueros and Valderrubio

In this village I dreamt my first ambitious dreams. In this village one day I will
merge with the earth and flowers ...

Lorca's birthplace in the tranquil farming village of **Fuente Vaqueros**, 17km west
of Granada, is the site of the **Lorca Museum** (July & Aug Tues–Sun 10am–2pm;
April–June & Sept Tues–Sat 10am–2pm & 5–6pm, Sun 10am–1pm; Oct–March
Tues–Sat 10am–1pm & 4–5pm, Sun 10am–1pm; guided visits on the hour; ☎958 51
64 53, ⓦwww.museogarcialorca.org; €1.80) The house lies just off the village's main
square on c/Poeta García Lorca. Now a charming shrine to Lorca's memory and
watched over by the amiable director Juan de Loxa (a poet himself), the museum is
stuffed with Lorca memorabilia, manuscripts and personal effects. It also has a
fleeting video fragment of Lorca on tour with the Teatro Barraca – the only piece of
cinema film to capture the poet and his engaging smile. An impressive new theatre,
the Teatro Lorca, has been constructed opposite the house.

After you've seen the house, pay a visit to the parish church (open service times,
7–9pm) at the end of the street opposite, where Lorca's mother took him regularly as
a child. Although the church has been heavily reconstructed since, the old stone font
can still be seen where Lorca – or "Federico" as he is known to all the world here –
was baptized.

From Granada, **buses** operated by Ureña (hourly from 9am; last bus returns to
Granada at 8pm; 20min) leave from Granada's Avenida de Andaluces, fronting the
train station. The village makes a pleasant overnight stop and **accommodation** is
available at Hostal-Restaurante Moli-Lorc, c/Ancha Escuelas 11 (☎958 516 532; ❷),
next to the church. There's a decent place **to eat**, *Restaurante Genil*, 2km out of the
village on the Chauchina road with a good-value *menú* and on Saturday mornings a
lively **market** fills the street fronting the church.

The Lorca family also had a house 4km to the northwest in the pleasant village of
Valderrubio. Each year the Lorcas moved here at harvest time (Lorca's father was a
wealthy landowner) and the infant Lorca spent many summers playing in surrounding
fields. The house at c/Iglesia 20 (which remained in the Lorca family until 1986) has
been opened to the public as a **museum** (Wed–Sun 10am–1.30pm; €1) and is signed
from the main road into the village.

Viznar

The village of **Viznar**, 10km northeast of Granada, will always be linked with the assassination of Lorca in August 1936. After his arrest in Granada, he was held for two days
at a farmhouse called La Colonia before being taken to a bleak gully (*barranco*) nearby
and shot. A poem of Lorca's seemed eerily prescient about his own end:

I realized I had been murdered.
They searched cafés and cemeteries and churches,
they opened barrels and cupboards,
they plundered three skeletons to remove their gold teeth.
They did not find me.

Contd...2

They never found me?
No. They never found me.

From the centre of the village the road towards La Fuente Grande passes the site of **La Colonia** (later demolished), near to a white-walled cottage. From here, the road curves around the valley to the **Parque Federico García Lorca**, a sombre monumental garden marking the *barranco* and honouring all the Civil War dead. Climb the steps to the garden and veer left up more steps: the site of Lorca's murder was here, beneath a solitary olive tree. After the killing – he was shot with three others – a young gravedigger threw the bodies into a narrow trench. The supposed site is marked by a granite memorial.

Viznar is served by **buses** run by Fernandez de la Torre (☎958 40 54 13) which leave from Granada's Arco de Elvira terminal on the Plaza del Triunfo at the northern end of Gran Vía. Services from Granada leave hourly Monday to Friday from 8.30am until 9.30pm with a reduced service on Saturday and Sunday. Returning from Viznar, buses depart hourly Monday to Friday from 8.50am until 8.50pm with a reduced service Saturday and Sunday (25min). The village also has a superb **youth hostel** (☎958 89 35 24 54; under 26 €14, over 26 €18), complete with a swimming pool open to all.

Restaurants

Granada is not noted for the quality of its **restaurants**, and service and standards even at the best places often leave a lot to be desired. That said, good-value food is to be found all over town, and there are a number of places worth paying a bit more for, too. Beware, of course, the inevitable tourist traps, particularly around the Plaza Nueva and on the Alhambra hill. It's worth remembering that you can also get substantial meals at many of the bars listed in the following section.

Granada's two classic **ice-cream parlours** *Los Italianos* (opposite the cathedral at Gran Via 4) and *La Perla* (Plaza Nueva 16) now have a serious competitor in *Tiggiani* whose exciting new flavours have *granadinos* in raptures. If you want to taste what the fuss is about they have *heladerías* on c/Reyes Catolicos at the junction with c/Cuchilleros off the south side of Plaza Nueva, and another at Plaza Bib Rambla 11.

Plaza Nueva and cathedral area

Bar-Restaurante Sevilla c/Oficios 12 ☎958 22 12 23. One of the few surviving pre war restaurants, this place is steeped in literary history and Lorca spent many happy hours here. The cooking is good, there's a *menú* for €36 and, in the evenings, tables outside give a view of the Capilla Real. Main dishes €10–18. Closed Mon.

Café au Lait Callejón de los Franceses 31, near the cathedral. Laid-back French-style café-bar with pleasant palm-shaded terrace; serves a good-value breakfast complete with domestic or foreign newspapers and later does economical pizzas, tapas and crepes.

Café-Bar 380 c/Imprenta 3, off Plaza Nueva. Stylish small diner serving breakfast snacks, and later in the day tapas, *raciónes* and crepes to finish. Free *tapa* with every drink and there are plenty of veggie options.

Centro c/Cetti Meriem 6. New and highly popular open-kitchen Italian restaurant (with Italian chef) offering all kinds of pizza and home-made pasta (try the pumpkin-stuffed ravioli) dishes for around €9.

Las Cuevas c/Calderería Nueva. Crepes, couscous, *dulces arabes*, tagines and pizzas cooked in a wood-burning oven make this a popular place with locals. There's a small terrace facing San Gregorio church.

Mesón Andaluz c/Cetti Meriem 10 ☎958 22 73 57. Pleasant, reliable restaurant with a renowned *fritura mixta* (fried fish platter) and *menú* for €11.

Nueva Bodega c/Cetti Meriem 9. Good-value local *bodega* that serves up basic tapas, *bocadillos* and *platos combinados* with a *menú* for €9.60; open till midnight.

Pilar de Toro c/Hospital de Santa Ana 12 ☎958 22 38 47. Stylish, medium-priced bar-restaurant inside a former seventeenth-century *casa señorial* with exterior *terraza*, elegant patio bar (serving tapas) and, upstairs, a mid-priced restaurant with its own leafy and secluded patio. Main dishes €12–20.

Restaurante León c/Pan 3 (occupying premises on both sides of the street). Long-established economical *cordobés* restaurant serving many *carne de monte* (game) dishes and *migas* (fried breadcrumbs); offers an economical *menú* for €10.

Samarcanda c/Calderería Vieja 3. Excellent Lebanese restaurant (with quite a few vegetarian options) and the best of the few places in "Little Morocco" where it's worth having a full meal.

Tetería Kasbah c/Calderería Nueva 4. Styled as a "tea-house" serving delicious *pasteles árabes* (cakes) and crepes, this little Morrocan place also serves up more elaborate dishes including couscous and tagines and offers a vegetarian *menú* for €8.50.

Albaicín

Bar La Mancha Chica c/Nueva de San Nicolás 1. Simple place with an outdoor terrace serving *platos combinados*. and some Moroccan dishes.

Carmen de Aben Humeya c/Cuesta de las Tomasas 12. Superb Alhambra views from the terrace of this *bar–cafetería* serving tea and *pasteles* in the afternoon, and salads, meat and fish dishes in the evenings. Main dishes €8–15.

El Ladrillo II Plazoleta de Fatima. This place specializes in *barcos* (boats) of fried fish, served at economical prices on tables beneath the stars – all of which make the climb here worthwhile.

🏃 **El Trillo del Reca** Callejón del Aljibe del Trillo 3 ☎958 22 51 82. Enchanting little mid-priced restaurant in an Albaicín *carmen* (villa and garden) offering Basque-influenced cuisine: *bacalao al pil-pil* (salted cod with garlic) is a signature dish. It has outdoor tables on a delightful garden patio shaded by pear and quince trees. Main dishes €9–15.

El Yunque Plaza San Miguel Bajo 3. Probably the best of this square's bar-diners, owned and run by a noted *flamenco cantaor*, Antonio, and his wife – who was a well-known dancer in her time. House specials include *pollo en salsa de almendras* (chicken in almond sauce) and they have inside seating on the adjacent corner if it's chilly or wet.

Juanillo Camino del Monte 81. Well-known low-priced restaurant in Sacromonte serving typical no-nonsense but well-prepared *raciónes*, paella and other rice dishes with great views of the Alhambra. Take the bus from Plaza Nueva if you can't face the hike.

Mirador de Morayma c/Pianista García Carrillo 2 ☎958 22 82 90. Situated in a gorgeous Albaicín *carmen* with a fine view of the Alhambra, the cooking is here is traditional offering many *granadino* specialities; the desserts are made by the sisters at the Convento de Santa Catalina. Insist on a terrace table (fine weather) or ground floor or first floor table (but refuse the cellar). Main dishes €10–20; *menú* for around €35. Closed Sun eve.

🏃 **Restaurante-Bar Tomasas** Carril de San Agustín 4, just below the Mirador de San Nicolás ☎958 22 41 08. Mid-priced summer restaurant serving *cocina andaluz* in a huge and beautiful *carmen* with a stunning terrace view of the Alhambra. *Ajo blanco* (white gazpacho) is a speciality. You can also nurse a drink here if you don't want to eat. Closed Sun and (July–Aug) midday. *El Agua*, nearby to the south at c/Aljibe del Trillos 7, is a similar place – with more Alhambra views – specializing in fondues.

Taberna La Higuera Horno de Hoyo 6. Economical and highly popular place with a broad terrace under a huge fig tree (*higuera*). There's a wide range of dishes and a *menú* for €7.50.

Plazas Bib-Rambla and Trinidad

Bar Ferroviaria c/Lavadero Tablas 1, off c/Tablas. This is in fact a pensioners' club for former railway workers but don't let that put you off. Behind the anonymous exterior you'll find an amazingly cheap *menú* (currently €4.50) that attracts workers and students for miles around; if the paella is on, it's your lucky day. Open daily 1.30–8pm (lunch 1.30–4.30pm). Closed Aug.

Café-Bar Oliver Plaza Pescadería 12, slightly northwest of the Plaza de la Trinidad. Good *raciónes* bar featuring a popular (with the *granadino* smart set) outdoor terrace.

Casa Cepillo Plaza Pescadería 8 – a marketplace linking Plazas Bib-Rambla and Trinidad. Cheap *comedor* with an excellent-value *menú* for €9.50; the soups are especially good here.

Restaurante Las Tinajas c/Martínez Campos 17, to the southwest of the centre ☎958 25 43 93. One of Granada's top-notch restaurants offering a range of *granadino* dishes as well as some northern Spanish specialities. Typical dishes include *solomillo de ciervo mozárabe con frutos secos* (deer Moorish style with dried fruits) and *berenjenas rellenas de setas* (aubergine stuffed with wild mushrooms). There's also a *menú de degustación* for €37. Closed mid-July to mid-Aug.

🏃 **Restaurante-Marisquería Cunini** Plaza Pescadería 14 ☎958 25 07 77. A gleaming, marble-topped bar serves standing customers with high-quality fish tapas and *raciónes* and there's a pricier and equally excellent small seafood restaurant behind (for which reservation is advised).

Plaza Mariana Pineda and the south central area

Mesón La Alegría c/Moras 4, east of Puerta Real. This economical *mesón* is a favourite of *granadinos* working nearby and specializes in *carnes a la brasa* (charcoal grilled meats).

Restaurante Chikito Plaza del Campillo 9 ☎958 22 33 64. Fronted by four towering plane trees, and formerly the *Café Alameda* where Lorca, Falla and the *Rinconcillo* group met. Literary lights from abroad such as Kipling and H.G. Wells all visited the bar's corner table (*rincón*). Today's restaurant – with outdoor terrace – is one of Granada's better ones for à la carte, but the medium-priced *menú* is unexciting. Decent tapas (free with each drink) in its bar. Main dishes €10–20. Closed Wed.

Restaurante Nuevo c/Navas 25. Good budget restaurant with economical *platos combinados* and *menús* and terrace tables.

Seis Peniques Plaza de Padre Suárez. Quite a good little bar-restaurant with a small terrace facing the Casa de los Tiros; serves a decent *menú* for €8.50.

Alhambra and Campo Del Príncipe

El Carmen de San Miguel Plaza Torres Bermejas 3 ☎958 22 67 23. One of Granada's top places to eat with a fabulous terrace looking out over the city. An innovative approach (occasionally overdone) to *andaluz* cuisine is illustrated by a signature dish, *conejo relleno de langostinos escabechados con ostras y limón* (rabbit with prawns and oysters). Main dishes €16–25, *menú de degustación* for around €50. Closed Sun.

La Esquinita Campo del Príncipe s/n. The plaza's best place for reasonably priced *cocina andaluz* is renowned for its fried fish with a €10 *menú*.

Lago de Como Campo de Príncipe 8. Slightly pricier than *La Ninfa* (below), this two-storeyed Italian restaurant is more routine but is also more likely to have a table.

La Mimbre Paseo del Generalife s/n, near the Alhambra's entrance. With a delightful terrace shaded by willows (*mimbres*) this is one of the best restaurants on the Alhambra hill. The food is good but they are sometimes overwhelmed in high season. Decent *menú* for around €17.50, which you may need to ask for. Main dishes €10–25.

La Ninfa Campo del Príncipe. Popular Italian restaurant for pizza, pasta and salads that puts out tables on this pleasant plaza, and is often full to bursting at weekends.

Parador de San Francisco Alhambra ☎958 22 14 40. The parador's restaurant is one of the best in an upmarket chain often noted for its blandness. It boasts fine views and offers a varied and not-too-bank-breaking *menú* for around €32.

Taberna de Baco Campo de Principe 22. Economical Peruvian-run diner famous for its *pastela* (Peruvian corn, beef and tomato pie). They also do great tapas: try the *surtido* (selection) that includes stuffed mushrooms, honey ribs and fillets with mango sauce. Their lamb's lettuce, goat cheese and raisin salad with balsamic vinaigrette is also a winner.

Out of the centre

Ruta del Veleta Carretera de Sierra Nevada 136 (Cenes de la Vega) ☎958 48 61 34. Three kilometres out of town along the Sierra Nevada road, this is currently Granada's top restaurant. The cooking is outstanding, as is the wine list. Try their *caldaretas de arroz con bogavante* (lobster) or *cordero segureño* (lamb with rosemary). If you're going to be up in the Solynieve ski resort (see p.510) they have an offshoot there, too. Main dishes €11–30; *menú de degustación* €60. Closed Sun eve.

Tapas and drinking bars

Granada's proximity to the Sierra Nevada brings a coolness to the city that carries over into its imbibing and its nightlife. In the **bars** here you're just as likely to find locals ordering a glass of *rioja* as soon as the beloved *fino* of the rest of Andalucía. One local wine which the *granadinos* do cherish, though (and which you shouldn't miss), is *vino de la costa* (coast wine – ironically made in the mountains of the Alpujarras); amber in colour, fairly potent, but relatively easy on hangovers, it's the ideal partner for a *tapa*.

The **bars** recommended below are mainly for drinking, though most serve tapas and *raciónes* and you could happily fill up and forget about going to a restaurant. The city has quite a reputation for its **tapas**, which are more elaborate than is usual in Andalucía and in most bars one comes free with each drink – a laudable trait in a city generally regarded as penny-pinching by most *andaluzes*.

Plaza Nueva and cathedral area

Al Pie de la Torre c/Pie de la Torre s/n. Close to the foot of the cathedral's tower this is an atmospheric little bar for tasty tapas out front with an intimate – and very good – small restaurant behind for fish and meat dishes (main dishes €12–15).

Bar Reca Plaza de la Trinidad, corner with c/ Infantes. Lively tapas venue on a leafy square which fairly hums at lunch time and in the early evening.

Bar Sabanilla c/San Sebastián 14. Not easy to find, just off the northeast corner of Plaza Bib-Rambla, down a passageway behind an unmarked door, this bar claims to be the oldest in Granada (it certainly looks it) and stays open till late. It's a basic, poky place, run by two friendly women who offer a free *tapa* with every drink. The barrelled *costa* wine here (from the Alpujarra village of Albondón) is recommended.

🏃 **Bodegas Castañeda** c/Almireceros 1, at the corner of c/Elvira, across Gran Vía from the cathedral. A *granadino* institution and one of the city's oldest bars, though much refurbished and prettified; it's still an attractive first stop of an evening. Good tapas include generous paté and cheese boards (*tablas*), *montaditos* (small open sandwiches), baked potatoes and gazpacho.

Bodegas La Mancha c/Joaquín Costa 10, around the corner from *Bodegas Castañeda*. Monumental spit-and-sawdust establishment (slightly more refined after refurbishment) hung with hams, and with great wine vats stationed behind the bar like rockets on a launch pad. Tasty tapas on offer include *jamón serrano*; they also sell excellent hot and cold *bocadillos* to eat in or take away.

Casa Enrique Acera de Darro 8, near the Puerta Real. This hole-in-the-wall has been open for almost 150 years and is a popular daytime or early-evening haunt with an extensive – but no freebies here – tapas selection. Specializes in *jamón iberico* and chorizo from Salamanca. Wide-ranging wine list.

Casa Julio c/Hermosa, off Plaza Nueva. A pocket-sized boozers' bar lined with fine old *azulejos* that nonetheless turns out some excellent fried seafood tapas. Treat yourself to the fried *berenjenas* (aubergine) or a refreshing gazpacho (served in a glass) which – the bar's clientele will assure you – is the best in town.

El Rinconcillo Plaza Nueva, next to *Pilar de Toro* restaurant. Friendly compact bar with lively *terraza* serving good tapas and *raciónes*.

🏃 **Hannigan and Sons** c/Cetti Merriem s/n. Independent Irish house whose owner *is* named Hannigan. The usual range of beers and stouts are on offer and the place has an airy feel to it with a snug, decorative stained glass and the only wooden floor in town. If you throw your cigarette ends on it Tony Hannigan will chuck you out; confusingly for locals, every other bar in town encourages you to do just that.

La Bodeguilla de al Lado c/Tendillas de Sta. Paula 4, just north of the cathedral. Pricey but authentic tapas (from ancient family recipes) in a cosy bar where the charming female proprietor is an authority on Spanish wines. Closed July & Aug.

La Trastienda c/Cuchilleros 11, on a small plaza just off c/Reyes Católicos. Plush little drinking den hidden behind a shop selling wine, cheese and ham. Once you've negotiated your way around the counter it's surprisingly cosy in the back.

Taberna Salinas c/Elvira 13, slightly west of Plaza Nueva. Elegant brick and wood drinking taverna serving up *tablas* (boards) of cheese and *ahumados* (smoked fish and meat); also has international beers on draught. No smoking.

Albaicín

Al Sur de Granada c/Elvira 150, near to the Moorish Puerta de Elvira arch. Great modern little bar-shop serving delicious cheese, ham and *salchichón* tapas. Each drink comes with a generous free *tapa* of its own and they often stage exhibitions of work by local artists. No smoking.

Bar Aixa Plaza Larga. Welcoming bar with terrace tables serving up well-prepared tapas and *raciónes*. Try their *migas* (breadcrumbs) stir-fried with crispy pork fat and green peppers or fresh anchovies.

Bar Caracoles Plaza Aliatar, slightly northeast of the Iglesia del Salvador. Popular and atmospheric tapas place on this pleasant square, famous for its *caracoles* (snails).

Bar Lara Plaza San Miguel Bajo. A fine bar which puts out tables on this picturesque Albaicín square, and serves tapas, *platos combinados* and an excellent *costa* wine.

Paprika Cuesta de Abarqueros 5, close to *Al Sur de Granada* (above). Very popular place with a younger international crowd serving Asian-inspired tapas and informal snacks accompanied by laid-back sounds including jazz. Has a pleasant summer terrace.

Rincón del Aurora Plaza San Miguel Bajo 7. Another good bar with outdoor tables on this square. Try the *fritura* (fried fish) or *carne al la Rondeña*.

Campo del Príncipe and Carrera del Darro

Ajoblanco c/Palacios 17, close to the church of Santo Domingo. Charming, cosy bar with artistic cheese and pomegranate tapas.

Bar Candela c/Sta. Escolástica 1. A mixture of students and neighbourhood artists fill this Basque

Time for tea

In the "Little Morocco" district in and around the calles Calderería Nueva and Calderería Vieja a large number of **teterías** or **teahouses** have sprung up to become a colourful part of the city's social scene and are definitely worth a visit. The friendly, Moroccan-run *As-Sirat* ("bridge between earth and paradise"), c/Calderería Nueva 5, is one of the oldest and offers eighty-plus teas in its Moorish-inspired interior while at no. 7 **Al-Faguara** serving teas (try their "*té Pakistani*"), juices and crepes is another classic. Nearby at no. 11 *Dar Ziryab* is another option which often stages live concerts of Middle-Eastern and North African music; its cultural centre offers classes in guitar and Maghrebi music. At the top of the hill, the multistoreyed *Pervane*, Calderería Nueva 24, is popular with a younger crowd. Also worth a try is *Tetería Tuareg*, c/Corpus Cristi 5, just off the foot of c/Calderería Vieja, where a cave-like interior recesses into a candlelit gloom where teas are sipped with crepes in summer and *pasteles* in winter. At Calderería Vieja 4, Tetería Al-Andalus is another popular place and in the same street at no. 12 *Repostería Morisca*, is a bakery selling Moroccan cakes, pastries and pies – try their *pastela*, a delicious spicy chicken-and egg-filled filo pastry.

bar every night. Serves *jamón*, cheese and chorizo tapas.

Bar Casa 1899 Paseo de los Tristes 3. Another decent tapas place on this atmospheric square with an old *bodega* inside and terrace seats – with Alhambra view – for summer evenings.

Rabo de Nube Paseo de los Tristes 1 (aka Paseo del Padre Manjón). One of many terrace bars on this plaza – at the far end of the Carrera del Darro – and a wonderful place to sit out at night with a drink whilst gazing up at the Alhambra's illuminated battlements. This place serves *tablas* (paté and cheese boards) and pizza. The city council often puts on concerts in this plaza during the summer.

University zone

Bar Lax c/Veronica de la Magdalena 31, a couple of blocks west of Plaza de la Trinidad. Pleasant Swedish bar serving – amongst others – salmon tapas and smorgasbord and with a small terrace on which to enjoy them.

Bodega 3M c/Santa Barbara 12, near the Hospital de San Juan de Dios. Classic old-style, spacious *bodega* serving great tapas – try the *salazones* (smoked fish) – and whose Portuguese proprietor is known to cook up plates of *bacalao* on Sundays; it often hosts exhibitions by local artists.

Discobares and discotecas

Conventional **discotecas** aren't too popular with the restrained *granadinos*, though the university guarantees a bit of action during term time and particularly at weekends; **c/Pedro Antonio de Alarcón**, to the west of the centre, is where the action is and the stretch between Plaza Albert Einstein and Obispo Hurtado is the main focus. There are, as everywhere in Spain, a fair scattering of **discobares** – drinking bars with loud sound systems, trendy decor and a fashion-conscious clientele. Granada has a lively **gay scene** and visiting any of the gay and lesbian places mentioned below is a good introduction to this.

Angel Azul c/Lavadero de Tablas 15, west of Plaza Trinidad. Along with the nearby *Tic Tac* (c/Horno de Haza 19) this is the most gay of Granada's gay bars with lots of action at weekends (Spanish language skills not required).

Babylon c/Silleria (between Plaza Nueva and Gran Vía). Reggae club – and popular pick-up venue – much favoured by US students.

Camborio Camino del Sacromonte s/n, Sacromonte. Fashionable *discobar* housed in a cave which is especially lively at weekends from about

4am. Other similar late-night venues run along the same street and are lots of fun in the early hours.

Chupitería c/Pedro Antonio Alarcon 69. Popular music and shots bar that has a hundred selections listed on a board. If you can't choose one they'll make up your own poison. A dubious bonus here is that each shot purchased gets you a token that can be exchanged for prizes: 20 tokens gets you a T-shirt and 25 some underwear, but by then you'll be too smashed to know.

Eshavira c/Postigo de la Cuna 2, a tiny alley off c/Azacayas which is off the east side of Gran Vía. Jazz/flamenco bar which gets quite lively. Wed, Thurs and Sun nights only.

Fondo Reservado c/Santa Ines 4, northeast of Plaza Nueva. Funky gay and straight bar with a hilarious drag show every weekend.

Granada 10 c/Carcél Baja 10, off Gran Vía near the cathedral. Small and popular central *discoteca* inside a beautifully restored retro cinema.

La Estrella c/Cuchilleros near Plaza Nueva. Congested, smoky *discobar* with great sounds.

La Sal c/Santa Paula 11, off the west side of Gran Vía. Originally a lipstick lesbian dance bar, but now attracting gay males too.

Peatón Pub c/Socrates 25, off c/Pedro Antonio de Alarcón. Rock bar popular with a student crowd. Other lively places nearby include *Babel*, *Van Gogh* and *Genesis*.

Planta Baja Horno de Abad, off Carril del Picón and slightly northwest of Plaza de la Trinidad.

Long-established *discobar* – garage is big here – now in a new home.

Potemkin Plaza Hospicio Viejo s/n, southwest of Plaza Nueva. Great new pint-sized *copas* bar with cool sounds run by Richard Dudanski, former drummer with Johnny Rotten in London's punk era. He's calmed down a bit since, and has discovered a great Japanese chef, Hide, whose mouthwatering tapas (one comes free with every drink) are the icing on the cake of a night out here.

Quilombo c/Carril de San Cecilio 21, uphill from the Campo del Principe. With a pool table and big dancefloor that get busy from around 3am. Sometimes stages live music.

Son c/Joaquín Costas 3, slightly west of Plaza Nueva. Ultra-cool two-level bar with older salsa scene upstairs and younger heavy-metal scene in the smoky (not tobacco smoke) downstairs.

Live music, theatre and dance

Like many cities of Andalucía, Granada lays claim to the roots of **flamenco**, though you'd hardly believe it from the travesties dished up these days in the gypsy quarter of Sacromonte (see box, p.490). The bus-'em-in "flamenco shows" on offer in the city aren't much better, either, being geared firmly to the tourist trade. However, up in the Albaicín there is one genuine *peña* (club; see below), with consistently good artists and an audience of aficionados, and we also list a number of other places that are reasonably authentic. Generally more rewarding are the **festivals** held throughout the year, such as the city's Theatre Festival at the end of May, or the International Music and Dance Festival at the end of June (Ⓦwww.granadafestival.org), during which you may just be lucky enough to see a performance under the stars in the Alhambra. Information on these events is available from any tourist office and tickets are sold at a kiosko on Acero del Casino, close to the post office on Puerta Real. It's also worth watching out for street posters, as well as checking listings in the local daily paper *Ideal* or the monthly listings mags *Guía del Ocio* (Ⓦwww.guiadelocio.com) and *Pocketguía de Granada* (Ⓦwww.pocketguia.es) on sale at kioskos. There's also an annual **jazz festival** in October or November – the Turismo will have details.

Flamenco

Bar-Restaurante La Zeta c/Pages 10, Albaicín, a couple of blocks northwest of Plaza Larga (☎958 29 48 60). Stages frequent flamenco shows.

El Niño de los Almendras c/Muladar de Doña Sancha, at the junction with c/La Tiña southeast of Plaza San Miguel Bajo, Albaicín. This tiny, unsigned bar – done up inside to resemble a cave – is owned by the flamenco singer of the same name. Only open Fri nights (starts around midnight), but there's unforgettable flamenco when it happens.

Los Faroles Sacromonte. Almost at the very end of the line of "caves" – ask anyone for directions as it's well known – this is a good place for a lunch-time or evening drink, with a view of the Alhambra from its terrace. The genial owner is a fount of information on flamenco and the impromptu real thing often happens here after dark.

Peña Platería Plazoleta de Toqueros 7, Albaicín ☎958 21 06 50, Ⓦwww.laplateria.org.es. Private club devoted to the celebration of Andalucía's great folk art. There are frequent flamenco performances (Thurs or Sat are your best chances; entry €8), and visitors are generally welcomed so long as they show a genuine interest and aren't in too large a group. You'll need to speak some Spanish and use a bit of charm. Closed Aug.

Sala Vimaambi Cuesta de San Gregorio 30, Albaicín ☏958 22 73 34, ⊛www.vimaambi.com. A cultural and craft centre with frequent presentations of flamenco and *raíces* (roots) music from North Africa and South America. Concerts usually take place on Fri & Sat at 9pm & 10.30pm (€15 including a drink) but ring or check their website for the current programme.

Shopping

Artesanía El Suspiro, at Cuesta de Gómerez 45, on the way up to the Alhambra, has an interesting range of *granadino* **ceramics**, tiles and marquetry as well as *andaluz* foodstuffs and books on Granada-related themes. Castellano, meanwhile, c/Almireceros 6, between c/Elvira and Gran Vía, also caters to **food** and **drink** shoppers by being the best place to buy *jamón serrano* and also stocks regional wines and brandies. La Casa de Los Tés, c/Calderería Vieja s/n, sells herbs and spices, incenses and exotic teas and La Alcena de Salinas, c/Almireceros 5 (near Castellano above), sells a wide range of wines and local deli products. La Oliva, c/Rosario 9, close to Plaza Mariana Pineda, is a wonderful shop specializing in the *gastronomía* of Andalucía (olive oil, wines, cheeses, honey) and you can sample before you buy. La Alcena, c/San Jerónimo 3, on the cathedral's north side, is a similar place specializing in the region's olive oil, wines and cheeses (try the *queso de almendras* made with almonds). Granada's branch of the **El Corte Inglés** department store is on the Acera del Darro, to the south of Puerta Real and has a great basement **supermarket** with a wide range of Spanish and international food and wines.

The main – and ultramodern – **market** is in Plaza San Agustín, just north of the cathedral (Mon–Fri early until 1.30pm). For a wide range of Moroccan/ traditional Spanish fruits and groceries try c/Calderería Nueva and neighbouring c/Calderería Vieja. Encarni II is a recommended general store in the latter and La Tienda is an excellent health food store (at no. 8) in the former. Metro, c/Gracia 31, off c/Alhóndiga, to the southwest of Plaza de la Trinidad, is the best international **bookshop** with a wide selection of titles on Granada and Lorca, plus it has walking maps. Librería Atlantida, Gran Vía 9, has a wide selection of books, including a good array on aspects of Granada. **Foreign press** is sold by the kioskos in Plaza Nueva and Puerta Real.

Listings

Airport Granada airport (☏958 24 52 00) handles domestic flights to Madrid and Barcelona as well as international and budget flights. See p.472 for information on buses to and from the airport.

Banks Numerous banks and ATMs are available along c/Reyes Católicos and Gran Vía.

Bus departures See p.472 for details of the bus terminal. For information on bus services and current timetables check with the companies, which are all – except for the service to Viznar – based at the bus station. Alsina Graells (☏958 18 54 80, ⊛www.alsa.es) for Almería, Alpujarras (high and low), Córdoba, Jaén, Málaga, Motril, Úbeda, Seville and the coast. Empresa Autedia (☏902 42 22 42, ⊛www.maestra-autedia.com) for Baza and Guadix. Autocares Bonal (☏958 46 50 22) for Veleta and the north side of Sierra Nevada.

Camping and hiking equipment Deportes de Aire Libre, c/Paz 20, just southeast of Plaza de la Trinidad (☏958 52 33 61), is a good outdoor pursuits shop selling climbing, camping and trekking gear. Armería, c/Mesones 53 (off the same plaza) is similar.

Hiking maps Maps of the Sierra Nevada and Las Alpujarras can be obtained from the Turismo, though for a more specialist selection try Carto-grafica del Sur, c/Valle Inclán 2, southwest of the train station in the university zone (☏&⊕958 20 49 01, ⊛www.cartograficadelsur.com), which sells a wide range, including military maps. The CNIG (National Geographic Institute), c/Divina Pastora 7, by the Jardines del Triunfo (☏958 90 93 20), also sells 1:50,000 and 1:25,000 maps. See also the Metro bookshop.

Hospital Cruz Roja (Red Cross), c/Escoriaza 8 ☏958 222 222, or Hospital Clinico San Cecilio, Avda. del Doctor Olóriz, near the Plaza de Toros ☏958 023 000. For advice on emergency treatment phone ☏061.

Internet Two of the most central internet locations are Uninet Plaza del la Encarnación 2 (Mon–Sat daily 9.30–10pm, Sun 4.30–10pm) to the east of the cathedral, and Locutorio Azahara c/Colcha s/n (daily 9am–12midnight), southwest of Plaza Nueva.

Laundry Lavandería Duquesa, c/Duquesa 24, near the church of San Jerónimo (Mon–Fri 9.30am–2pm & 4.30–9pm, Sat 9.30am–2pm; ☎958 28 06 85), is very efficient and will wash, dry and fold 4kg the same day for €15. Lavandería La Paz, c/La Paz 19, just west of Plaza de la Trinidad, has similar hours and prices.

Left luggage There are lockers at both train and bus stations as well as a *consigna* (left luggage office) at the latter.

Police For emergencies dial ☎091 (national) or 092 (local). The Policía Local station is at Plaza de Campos 3 ☎958 80 85 02. There is also a property lost-and-found section in the Ayuntamiento building on Plaza del Carmen (☎958 24 81 03).

Post office Puerta Real: Mon–Fri 9am–8pm, Sat 9am–2pm.

West towards Málaga: Alhama de Granada

Travelling from Granada to Málaga by bus will take you along the fast but dull A92 *autovía*, which crosses the *vega* to the west of the city. With your own transport and time to spare, a more interesting and scenic route passes through the delightful but little-visited town of **Alhama de Granada** and traverses the spectacular **Zaffaraya Pass**, descending into Málaga by way of the ruggedly beautiful **Axarquía** region.

Leave Granada by the route for Motril and the coast, along the N323 – but avoid the *autovía*. At Armilla, 4km southwest of the city, follow the A338 which branches right, towards the village of **La Malá** (which has a fine roadside *venta*), and, 10km beyond, **Ventas de Huelma** where *Luciano* is another excellent *venta* stop. From here the road twists and climbs into the Sierra de la Pera and, after descending to the lakeside village of **Poblado del Embalse** – where there's a good **campsite**, *Los Bermejales* (☎958 35 91 90), with pool and restaurant – continues through a rich landscape of bubbling streams and rocky gulches overlooked by hills planted with olives, to Alhama de Granada, 14km further.

Alhama de Granada

Scenically sited along a ledge overlooking a broad gorge or *tajo* created by the Río Alhama, the spa town of **ALHAMA DE GRANADA** is one of the unsung gems of Granada province and makes a wonderful overnight stop. It has a couple of striking churches in a well-preserved old quarter, and its baths, dating back to Roman and Moorish times (Al Hamma in Arabic means "hot springs"), still draw in numerous visitors to take the waters. They were greatly treasured during Moorish times, and the Spanish expression of regret "¡Ay de mi Alhama!" was the cry of sorrow attributed to Abu al-Hacen (the Mulhacen after whom the Sierra Nevada peak is named) when he lost the town in a crucial battle here against the Christian forces in 1482. It was this loss that severed the vital link between Granada and Málaga (and hence North Africa), foreshadowing the end of eight centuries of Moorish rule. Settlement started here much earlier, however, and the ancient Iberian town on the site was referred to by the Romans as Artigi.

Information and accommodation

The **Turismo**, at Paseo Montes Jovellar s/n (Mon–Fri 9.30am–3pm; ☎958 36 06 86, ⓦwww.turismodealhama.org), below the Plaza de la Constitución can provide maps and information on walking in the area. The office also does free **guided tours** of the town and its monuments (Tues, Thurs & Sat; free), which leave from in front of the Turismo at noon. Alhama has a **swimming pool** with shade just out of town along the Málaga road.

On the **accommodation** front things have improved immeasurably since Ford was here (see box, p.507) and the dreaded *La Grande* is no more. If you want to stay, outside August there's usually no problem fixing up a room at 🎋 *La Seguiriya*, c/Las Peñas 12 (☎958 36 08 01, Ⓦwww.laseguiriya.com; ❸ with breakfast; reductions for longer stays), a charming *hospedería rural* and restaurant 50m uphill off the main road. Housed in an eighteenth-century house with fine views over the Tajo, the friendly proprietor is a retired flamenco *cantante*, and the en-suite rooms are appropriately named after flamenco styles. They also offer various outdoor activities including hiking, canoeing and mountain biking. Just up from the main square and housed in a refurbished old *casa palacio*, *Casa de la Sonrisa*, c/Alta de Mesones 17 (☎958 36 07 88, Ⓦwww.casadelasonrisa.nl; ❸ with breakfast), is a possible alternative. A cheaper option is *Hostal San José*, Plaza de la Constitución 27 (☎958 35 01 56; ❶), right on the main square, with clean en-suite rooms and some singles. On the square in the lower town, the friendly and sparkling *Hostal Ana*, Ctra. de Granada 8 (☎958 36 01 08; ❷) has a/c en-suite rooms with TV. An attractive rural alternative is the *Hotel El Ventorro* (☎958 35 04 38; ❸ with breakfast), 3km out of town on the Málaga road (take the turn-off for Játar), fronting a lake with a decent restaurant. A more upmarket option is the spa hotel *Balneario de Granada* (☎958 35 00 11, Ⓦwww.balnearioalhamadegranada .com; ❹), at the baths 1km off the road into town from Granada, which, although situated in dense pine woods, has the ambience of a sanatorium.

The Town

Most of Alhama's sights are within a short walk of Plaza de la Constitución, the main square fronted by bars and restaurants. To see the interior of some of them, however, you will need to go on a **guided tour** organized by the Turismo (see p.505). At the square's northern end there's a ruined and now

▲ Alhama de Granada

Very few books have been written about Spain that do not draw on **Richard Ford** and his 1845 *Murray's Handbook for Spain* – arguably the best, the funniest and the most encyclopedic guidebook ever written on any country.

Born in 1796 into a family of means, Ford studied law but never practised and in 1824 married Harriet Capel, the attractive daughter of the Earl of Essex. When she received medical advice to seek a warmer climate for her health, Ford – inspired by Irving's recent publication of the *Conquest of Granada* – took his family off to Spain where they lived for three years, wintering in Seville and spending the summers living in part of the Alhambra in Granada.

Ford spent most of his time traversing the length and breadth of the country – but particularly Andalucía – on horseback, making notes and sketches. It's hard to believe that all this was not meant for some literary purpose, but it was only back in England – and six years after his return – when publisher John Murray asked him to recommend someone to write a Spanish travel guide, that Ford suggested himself.

His marriage now broken, he settled in a Devon village in a house to which he added many Spanish features (including some souvenirs from the Alhambra) to work solidly for nearly five years on what became the *Handbook for Spain* (see p.601). When Murray and others took exception to the final manuscript's often caustic invective, he was advised to tone it down and a revised – but still gloriously outspoken – edition finally appeared in 1845 to great acclaim. Curiously, although he became *the* resident expert on Spain, he never returned to the country that had put him on the literary map.

Ford's blind spots, such as British prejudice against Baroque architecture (the more extravagant styles of which he dismissed as "vile Churrigueresque"), are often irritating, and the High Tory attitudes sometimes verging on jingoism, added to a splenetic francophobia, often threaten to tip over into the worst kind of churlishness. However, the author's enduring fascination with Spain and all things Spanish – he personally introduced *amontillado* sherry and Extremaduran *jamón serrano* into England – allied to a crisp writing style and a dry wit, invariably save him, and some of his passages are still hilariously funny and related with a wry irony. His description of the hostelry at Alhama is typical:

The posada at Alhama, albeit called La Grande, is truly iniquitous; diminutive indeed are the accommodations, colossal the inconveniences; but this is a common misnomer, en las cosas de España. Thus Philip IV was called El Grande, under whose fatal rule Spain crumbled into nothing; like a ditch he became greater in proportion as more land was taken away. All who are wise will bring from Málaga a good hamper of eatables, a bota of wine, and some cigars, for however devoid of creature comforts this grand hotel, there is a grand supply of creeping creatures, and the traveller runs risk of bidding adieu to sleep, and passing the night exclaiming, Ay! de mi, Alhama.

privately owned **Moorish castle** with the unfortunate addition of nineteenth-century crenellated battlements. Heading east alongside the castle, the sixteenth-to-eighteenth-century **Iglesia del Carmen** (8am–9.30pm) is Alhama's prettiest church, overlooking the **Tajo** and fronted by an old fountain where the farmers water their donkeys on sultry summer evenings. Just off to the right here, with its back to the Tajo, is Artesanía Los Tajos, c/Peñas 34, selling local ceramics as well as some remarkable traditional clay water-whistles called *canarios*. Once used by local shepherds and goatherds, they make an ear-splitting racket, as the proprietor will eagerly demonstrate.

To reach the other monuments, backtrack slightly to c/Baja Iglesia which leads up to Plaza los Presos, passing en route (up a ramp to the left) the **Casa de la Inquisición**, which may have nothing to do with the Inquisition at all but is noted for a fine Plateresque facade. The town's main church, **La Encarnación** (Turismo guided tour), dominates the Plaza de los Presos, a pleasant little square with a central fountain. Donated by Fernando and Isabel after the conquest of the town from the Moors, the church was completed in the first half of the sixteenth century by some of the major architects of the time – among them Enrique Egas and Diego de Siloé, the designers of the Capilla Real and cathedral at Granada. Siloé was responsible for the striking and massive Renaissance belfry that towers above the town. The restrained interior has an impressive *artesonado* ceiling and the *sacristía* has fifteenth-century vestments with embroidery attributed to Isabel herself.

Opposite the church, on the same square, is an ancient **posito** (granary) dating from the thirteenth century but incorporating parts of an earlier synagogue. Just downhill from here the sixteenth-century **Hospital de la Reina**, c/Vendederas s/n (Turismo guided tour), was the first building of this kind to be built in the kingdom of Granada. Leaving the square to the right of the church along c/Alta Iglesia takes you past the misleadingly named **Casa Romana** on the right, an eighteenth-century mansion believed to have been constructed on the site of a Roman villa. The same street returns to the Plaza Mayor.

Alhama's only other site of note is a well-preserved first-century BC Roman **bridge** at the edge of the town, close to the A338 to Granada, a short distance along the road to the *balneario* (baths). Beyond here, a (signed) twisting road leads 1km to the **baths** that give the town its name. Although little remains of the Roman baths seen by Ford in the nineteenth century, elements of the Moorish *hammam* survive and can be seen by enquiring at the *Balneario de Granada* (guided visits daily 2–4pm; €1) whose staff will conduct you into the depths to see some astonishing Moorish arches and the odd stone inscribed in Latin.

Eating and drinking

The main square, Plaza de la Constitución, has plenty of **places to eat** with terraces – *Mesón Diego* is worth a try for the usual standards and across the square *El Sibanco* does **tapas** and **raciónes**. However, the town's best restaurant is that at *La Seguiriya* (see p.506) where specials include *lomo con ciruelas pasas* (pork with prunes) and *atún a la roteña* (tuna). *Bar Ochoa* (off the main square and slightly uphill from *Hostal San José*) serves up tasty **tapas**.

Towards the Zaffaraya Pass

South of Alhama, the A335 climbs towards Ventas de Zaffaraya passing, 10km out, a great value *venta*, 🍴 *Los Caños de Alcaicería*, with an economical weekday *menú*. The road then toils on, cutting through a rich agricultural area where tomatoes, cereals and other vegetables are grown. The spectacular **Zaffaraya Pass**, which slips through a cleft in the Sierra de Tejeda and was part of the old coach route, provides a dramatic entrance into the Axarquía region of Málaga Province, with superb **views** to the distant Mediterranean. Roughly 6km beyond the pass lies the deserted medieval village of **Zalía**, after which the road continues to **Vélez-Málaga** and the coast.

The Sierra Nevada National Park

Southeast from Granada rise the mountains of the **SIERRA NEVADA**, designated Andalucía's second **national park** in 1999, a startling backdrop to the city, snowcapped for most of the year and offering skiing from November until late May. The ski slopes are at **Solynieve**, an unimaginative, developed resort just 28km away (40min by bus). Here, the direct car route across the range stops, but from this point walkers can make the relatively easy two- to three-hour trek up to **Veleta** (3394m), the second highest peak of the range and the second-highest summit on the Spanish peninsula.

Before the road was constructed in the 1920s few *granadinos* ever came up to the sierra, but one group who had worn out a trail since the times of the Moors were the *neveros* or icemen, who used mules to bring down blocks of ice from the mountains, which they then sold in the streets. Their route to Veleta can still be followed beyond **Monachil**, to the southeast of the city, a pleasant village on the Río Monachil, which is well worth a visit. There's a nice place to stay (see p.477) and Ride Sierra Nevada (☎958 50 16 20, ⓦ www.ridesierranevada.com), in the centre of the village, organize all kinds of outdoor pursuits in the area including mountain biking, horseriding, climbing and hiking in the spectacular Los Cahorros gorge; they can also provide information on renting *casas rurales* and cave dwellings for longer stays. The village is connected by frequent buses to Granada running from the terminal at the Paseo del Salón. The main A395 road, though, has been a mixed blessing for the delicate ecosystem of the Sierra, and the expanding horrors of the Solynieve ski centre, which was chosen to hold the 1995 World Ski Championships (subsequently cancelled due to lack of snow and then held in 1996), has only made things worse.

The best general **map** of the Sierra Nevada and of the lower slopes of the Alpujarras is the one co-produced by the Instituto Geográfico Nacional and the Federación Española de Montañismo (1:50,000). Not far behind is the Editorial Alpina's *Sierra Nevada y La Alpujarra* (1:40,000) map which has the bonus of a booklet (with an English edition) describing fourteen hikes in the Sierra as well as useful background information on the zone. The CNIG's 1:25,000 sheets are more detailed for trekking purposes, and all three can be obtained in Granada (see p.504).

Inside the park, to report any **emergencies** such as forest fires, stranded hikers or personal injuries there's a coordinated emergency service contactable on ☎112; the park's Guardia Civil unit can be reached on ☎062.

Solynieve and the Veleta/Mulhacén ascent

Throughout the year Autocares Bonal runs a **daily bus** from Granada to the Solynieve resort and, just above this, to the *Albergue Universitario* (see p.510). It leaves Granada bus station at 9am, returning from the *Albergue Universitario* at 5pm (and passing Solynieve 10min later). For the winter service (Oct–March) ring the bus company (see p.504) or check with any Turismo. Tickets to Solynieve (€8 round trip) should be bought in advance at the bus station, although you can pay on board if the bus is not full.

The route leaves Granada via the Paseo del Salón (with a bus stop should you wish to pick it up here) where two wagons stand as a memory to the tram service which, from the 1920s until 1970, used to ascend as far as Güejar Sierra. Beyond Pinos de Genil the road begins to climb seriously and, after 28km, the ski resort of **Solynieve** appears.

With **your own transport** take the Acera del Darro south from the Puerta Real and follow the signs for the Sierra Nevada. Once on the ascent to the mountains the road is dotted with alpine-style **eating places** which do good business in season. Some 16km out, a signed turn on the right leads – after 3km – to *Camping Ruta del Purche* (☎958 34 04 07) the only **campsite** in these parts, with a restaurant and pool and which also rents out en-suite log cabins (❸). After some 17km you could make a stop at the **Balcón de Canales** with fine views over the Río Genil and its dam. At the 22km mark and signposted just off the

---

The Sierra Nevada's flora and fauna

The Sierra Nevada is particularly rich in **wild flowers**. Some fifty varieties are unique to these mountains, among them five gentians, including *Gentiana bory*, the pansy *Viola nevadensis*, a shrubby mallow *Lavatera oblongifolia*, and a spectacular honey-suckle, the seven- to ten-metre-high *Lonicera arborea*.

Wildlife, too, abounds away from the roads. One of the most exciting sights is the *Cabra hispanica*, a wild horned goat which you'll see standing on pinnacles, silhou-etted against the sky. They roam the mountains in flocks and jump up the steepest slopes with amazing agility when they catch the scent of the walker on the wind. The higher slopes are also home to a rich assortment of **butterflies**, among them the rare Nevada Blue as well as varieties of Fritillary. **Birdwatching** is also superb, with the colourful hoopoe – a bird with a stark, haunting cry – a common sight.

---

road is the **"El Dornajo" Sierra Nevada National Park Visitors' Centre** (daily 10am–2pm & 4–6pm; ☎958 34 06 25) which sells guidebooks, maps and hats (sun protection is vital; see below), has a permanent exhibition on the park's flora and fauna, provides hiking information (English spoken), and rents out horses and mountain bikes. The centre also has a pleasant **cafetería** with a stunning terrace **view** beyond the ancient tram parked in a garden behind.

Solynieve

SOLYNIEVE ("Sun and Snow") is a hideous-looking ski resort and regarded by serious alpine skiers as something of a joke. But with snow lingering so late in the year (Granada's Turismo should be able to advise on the state of this, or contact Sierra Nevada Club on ☎902 70 80 90 or visit �www.sierranevadaski .com) it has obvious attractions for *granadinos* and others determined to ski in southern Spain. From the middle of the resort a lift takes you straight up to the main ski lifts, which provide access to most of the higher **slopes**, and when the snow is right you can ski a few kilometres back down to the *zona hotelera* (the lifts run only when there's skiing). There are plenty of places to rent gear. If you intend to ski (or walk) here be sure to double your **skin protection** as this is the most southerly ski centre in Europe with intense sun at high altitudes. Visiting Solynieve in high summer is a surreal experience as it's almost a ghost town with only the odd shop or bar open and a vast, central plaza – teeming with crowds sporting multicoloured ski-suits in winter – eerily empty.

The Turismo at Granada can advise on **places to stay** at the resort (many hotels open only during the ski season) or contact the Sierra Nevada Club (see above). The cheapest accommodation is the modern and comfortable *Albergue Juvenil*, c/Peñones 22 (☎958 57 51 16, �www.inturjoven.com; under 26 €10/25, over 26 €14/30; open all year), on the edge of the ski resort, where you can get good-value double (April–Oct; ❶) and four-bed studios and apartments, all en suite. They also rent out skis and equipment in season when room prices increase significantly. Other places in the resort proper are incredibly **expensive** in season, with even the cheapest doubles priced at the top end of our ❹ price band. Heading higher, 3km away in isolated Peñones de San Francisco is another attractive option: the *Albergue Universitario* (☎958 48 01 22, �www .nevadensis.com; ❷ with breakfast; ❸ in ski season), just off the main road where the bus drops you, has bunk rooms, doubles and a restaurant. It's a stunning location for exploring the national park but without transport extremely isolated, which may, of course, be just what you're looking for. The bus (which only runs beyond the ski resort in summer) turns around at the *Albergue* and this marks the start of the Veleta ascent.

> ### Ruta Integral de los Tres Mil
>
> The classic **Ruta Integral de los Tres Mil**, a complete traverse of all the Sierra's peaks over 3000m high, starts in Jeres del Marquesado on the north side of the Sierra Nevada (due south of Guadix) and finishes in Lanjarón, in the Alpujarras. It's an exhausting three- to four-day itinerary described in detail in Andy Walmsley's book *Walking in the Sierra Nevada* (see p.610). For any serious exploration of the Sierra Nevada, essential equipment includes a tent, proper gear and ample food. It's a serious mountain where lives have been lost so come prepared for the eventuality of not being able to reach (or find) the refuge huts, or the weather turning nasty.

The Capileira road, Veleta and Mulhacén

The ascent of **Veleta** is a none-too-challenging hike rather than a climb but should only be attempted between May and September – unless you're properly geared up – but even then you'll need warm and waterproof clothing. From the *Albergue Universitario*, the **Capileira-bound road** – now permanently closed to traffic to protect the Sierra's delicate environment – actually runs past the peak of Veleta. Recently asphalted – somewhat removing the sense of adventure from the trek – it is perfectly, and tediously, walkable (bikes are allowed but it's a fierce climb). However, most hikers follow the well-worn shortcuts between the hairpins the road is forced to make. With your own transport it's possible to shave a couple of kilometres off the total by ignoring the no-entry signs at the car park near to the *Albergue Universitario* and continuing on to a second car park further up the mountain from which point the road is then barred. Although the peak of the mountain looks deceptively close from here you should allow two to three hours to reach the summit and one and a half hours down. Make sure to bring **food and water** along as there's neither en route and a picnic at the summit is one of the best meals to be had in Spain, weather permitting.

With a great deal of energy you could conceivably walk to Capileira, though it's a good 30km, there's nothing along the way and temperatures drop pretty low by late afternoon. En route, an hour beyond Veleta, you pass just under **Mulhacén** – the tallest peak on the Iberian peninsula at 3483m. The climb is two hours of exposed and windy ridge-crawling from the road, and with a sudden, sheer drop on its northwest face. There is a gentler slope down to the Siete Lagunas valley to the east.

Las Alpujarras

The N323 road south from Granada to Motril crosses the fertile *vega* after leaving the city and then climbs steeply until, at 850m above sea level, it reaches the **Puerto del Suspiro del Moro** – the Pass of the Sigh of the Moor. Boabdil, last Moorish king of Granada, came this way, having just handed over the keys of his city to the Reyes Católicos in exchange for a fiefdom over the Alpujarras. From the pass you catch your last glimpse of the city and the Alhambra. The road then descends and beyond Padul crosses the valley of Lecrín planted with groves of orange, lemon and almond trees, the latter a riot of pink and white blossom in late winter. To the east, through a narrow defile close to Béznar, lie the great valleys of **Las Alpujarras** – "the Switzerland of Spain" as Ford described them – first settled in the twelfth century by Berber refugees from Seville, and later the Moors' last stronghold.

LAS ALPUJARRAS

▲ Láujar de Andarax

Bayárcal

Laroles
GR431

Mairena

Mecina
Alfahar

C 331

Cherín

Lucainena

Hirmes

Emb. de Beninar

Turón

Valor

Ugíjar

Vegen

Yátor

Múrtas

Cojáyar

A348

Jorairátor

Cádiar

Arroyo de Valor

Alto de San Juan
(2781m) ▲

Vátor

Mecina-
Bombarón

N

Bérchules

Las
Angosturas

Juviles

Trévelez

Castaras

GR421

SIERRA DE LA CONTRAVIESA

A345

Torvizcón

A348

Cerro
Vacares
(3149m) ▲

Mulhacén
(3483m) ▲

Siete
Lagunas ▲

Prado
Llano
(2579m) ▲

Busquístar

Ferreirola

Mecina
Fondales

Almegíjar

Pórtugos

Pico
Veleta
(3394m) ▲

High road to Granada
permanently
closed to vehicles

Capileira

Pitres

PARQUE NATIONAL

Bubión

Pampaneira

Caratáunas

Soportújar

Los
Tablones

Solynieve

Caballo
(3013m) ▲

DE SIERRA NEVADA

Cañar

Órgiva

Guadalfeo

L451

Monachil

Lanjarón

A346

Pico de
la Carne
(1886m) ▲

(2079m) ▲

Cumbres
Verdes

La Zubia

Monachil

Nigüelas

N323

Vélez Benaudalla & Motril

▲ Granada

Dilar

(1524m) ▲

Suspiro
del Moro
(660m)

Padul

Dúrcal

Lecrín

Restábal

Saleres

Albuñuelas

Pinos del
Valle

Guájar
Alto

Guájar
Faragüit

Abondón Albuñol

Abondón Albuñol

10 km

0

512

Walkers' guides to the Alpujarras are now beginning to mushroom and useful publications include Charles Davis's *34 Alpujarras Walks*, Jeremy Rabjohns' *Holiday Walks in the Alpujarras* and *GR142: Senda de la Alpujarra* (in Spanish) by Francisco Jiménez Richarte; there are also half a dozen Alpujarras treks in *Andalucía and the Costa del Sol* by John and Christine Oldfield and an equal number in Guy Hunter-Watts' *Walking in Andalucía* (see p.609 for details of all these publications). See p.517 for details on maps to this area.

Some history

The valleys are bounded to the north by the Sierra Nevada, and to the south by the lesser *sierras* of Lujar, La Contraviesa and Gador. The eternal snows of the high *sierras* keep the valleys and their seventy or so villages well watered all summer long. Rivers have cut deep gorges in the soft mica and shale of the upper mountains, and over the centuries have deposited silt and fertile soil on the lower hills and in the valleys; here the villages have grown, for the soil is rich and easily worked. The intricate terracing that today preserves these deposits was begun perhaps as long as two thousand years ago by **Visigoths** or **Ibero-Celts**, whose remains have been found at Capileira.

The **Moors** carried on the tradition, and modified the terracing and irrigation in their inimitable way. They transformed the Alpujarras into an earthly paradise, and there they retired to bewail the loss of their beloved lands in al-Andalus. After the fall of Granada, many of the city's Muslim population settled in the villages, and there resisted a series of royal edicts demanding their forced conversion to **Christianity**. In 1568 they rose up in a final, short-lived revolt, which led to the expulsion of all Spanish Moors. Even then, however, two Moorish families were required to stay in each village to show the new Christian peasants, who had been marched down from Galicia and Asturias to repopulate the valleys, how to operate the intricate irrigation systems.

Through the following centuries, the villages fell into poverty, with the land owned by a few wealthy families, and worked by peasants. It was one of the most remote parts of Spain in the **1920s**, when the author Gerald Brenan settled in one of the eastern villages, Yegen, and described the life in his book *South from Granada*, and things changed little over the next forty-odd years. During the **Civil War**, the occasional truckload of Nationalist youth trundled in from Granada, rounded up a few bewildered locals, and shot them for "crimes" of which they were wholly ignorant; Republican youths came up in their trucks from Almería and did the same thing. In the aftermath, under Franco, there was real hardship and suffering, and in the **1980s** the region had one of the lowest per capita incomes in Spain, with – as an official report put it – "a level of literacy bordering on that of the Third World, alarming problems of desertification, poor communications and high under-employment".

Ironically, the land itself is still very fertile – oranges, chestnuts, bananas, apples and avocados grow here, while the southern villages produce a well-known dry rosé wine, *costa*. However, it is largely the recent influx of **tourism** and foreign purchase of houses and farms that has turned the area's fortunes around, bringing pockets of wealth and an influx of new life to the region.

The so-called **High Alpujarras** – the villages of **Pampaneira**, **Bubión** and **Capileira** – have all been scrubbed and whitewashed and are now firmly on the tourist circuit, as popular with Spanish as foreign visitors. Lower down, in the **Órgiva area**, are the main concentration of expatriates – mainly British, Dutch and Germans, seeking new Mediterranean lives. Most seem to have moved here permanently, rather than establishing second homes (though there are houses for rent in abundance), and there's a vaguely alternative aspect to the new community, which sets it apart from the coastal expats. In addition to property owners, the area has also attracted groups of New Age travellers. The locals, to their credit, seem remarkably tolerant of the whole scene.

Approaches to the Alpujarras

From Granada, the most straightforward **approach to the Alpujarras** is to take the Lanjarón turning – the A348 – off the Motril road. Coming from the south, you can bear right from the road at Vélez de Benaudalla and continue straight along the A346 to Órgiva, the market town of the western Alpujarras. There are several **buses** a day from both Granada and Motril, and one a day from Almería, to Lanjarón and Órgiva. One operated by Alsina Graells (☏902 42 22 42) direct to the High Alpujarras, via Trevélez as far as Bérchules, leaves the main Granada bus station at noon and 5pm daily: in the other direction it leaves Bérchules at 5.35am or 5.05pm, passing Trevélez half an hour later, to arrive in Granada at 8.45am or 8.45pm respectively. There's also a service from Granada to Ugíjar in the Low Alpujarras, via Lanjarón, Órgiva, Torvizcón, Cádiar, Yegen and Valor, currently departing at 8.30am and 5.30pm; this takes a little over four hours to the end of the line. The return journey from Ugíjar currently runs at 6.15am and 3pm. There are also frequent daily buses between Granada and Órgiva (three via Lanjarón) and vice versa, and three daily buses link with Pampaneira, Bubión, Capileira and Pitres.

Lanjarón

LANJARÓN has known tourism and the influence of the outside world for longer than anywhere else in the Alpujarras due to the curative powers of its **spa waters**. These gush from seven natural springs and are sold in bottled form as mineral water throughout Spain. Between March and December, when the spa baths are open, the town fills with the aged and infirm and the streets are lined with racks of herbal remedies, all of which imparts a rather melancholy air. This might seem good reason for passing straight on to the higher villages, though to do so would be to miss out on some beautiful local walks, and a town centre that, now a new bypass has removed much of the traffic, grows on you. Should you wish to try a cure at the **Balneario** (☏958 770 137, ⒲www .balneariodelanjaron.com) a basic soak will cost about €13.50 with add-ons for massage, mud baths, pressure showers and all kinds of other alarming-sounding treatments such as *drenajes linfáticos* and *pulverizaciones faríngeas*.

Like so many spa towns, Lanjarón is Roman in origin, though today the place is largely modern, with a ribbon of buildings flanking its pleasant, tree-lined main thoroughfare, split into three sections running west to east: Avenida de Andalucía, Avenida de La Alpujarra and c/Real. Below this, and beyond the town's new bypass, marking Lanjarón's medieval status as gateway to the

Walks from Lanjarón

The countryside and mountains around Lanjarón are spectacularly beautiful. Wander up through the backstreets behind the town and you'll come across a track that takes you steeply up to the vast spaces bordering on the Reserva Nacional de la Sierra Nevada.

For a somewhat easier day's **walk** go to the bridge over the river just east of town and take the sharply climbing, cobbled track which parallels the river. After two to two and a half hours' walk through small farms, with magnificent views and scenery, a downturn to a small stone bridge lets you return to Lanjarón on the opposite bank. Allow a minimum of six hours for a leisurely expedition.

Alpujarras, is a **Moorish castle**, newly refurbished and due to open for visits in 2009 (details from the turismo). It was here on March 8, 1500, that the Moorish population made its final heroic stand against the Christian troops under the command of Fernando. Pounded by artillery, hundreds died as the town was taken. A ten-minute stroll reveals its dramatic setting – follow the signs downhill from the main street and out onto the terraces and meadows below the town.

Lanjarón puts on a stirring **Semana Santa** – one of the best in the province, and worth going out of your way to see if you're in the area. It's other great shindig is the **water festival** on the eve of San Juan (June 24) when the unaware get drenched by cascades falling from balconies and "water bombs" are thrown around with abandon.

Practicalities

Opposite the Balneario at the village's western end is Lanjarón's **municipal tourist office**, Avda. Andalucía s/n (Mon–Sat 10am–2pm & 6.30–8.30pm, Sun 10–2pm; ☎958 77 04 62), which can provide basic information. Midway along the main street is the Alsina Graells **bus terminal** (☎958 77 00 03). **Internet** access is available at Cyberplay Lanjaron (daily except Wed 6pm–midnight), Avda. de Andalucía 30, near the La Caixa bank.

Accommodation

Due to the Balneario, there's no shortage of **places to stay** in town, most along the main road. In high summer it's essential to book ahead, while in winter many places close in January and February.

Hotel Alcadima c/Francisco Tarrega 3, down a signed turn-off from the main street ☎958 77 08 09, ⓦwww.alcadima.com. An excellent-value hotel with the best pool and prettiest restaurant terrace in town. Many of the comfortable rooms have stunning balcony views towards the castle and guests may use the small gym. They also have a number of two-bedroomed family suites. Free internet access for guests. **④**
Hotel El Sol Avda. de La Alpujarra 30 ☎&ⓕ958 77 01 30, ⓦwww.hotelelsol.net. Good-value choice if you're here in winter or early spring as there is reliable heating in their en-suite rooms. Guests also have use of sauna and jacuzzi. **③** with breakfast.
Hotel España Avda. de La Alpujarra 42 ☎&ⓕ958 77 01 87, ⓦwww.lanjaron.biz. Grand-looking, good-value hotel near the Balneario which has played host to such luminaries as García Lorca (Room 107) and Manuel de Falla in its time. Friendly staff, comfortable rooms, own bar and restaurant plus a pool. **③**

Hotel Miramar Avda. de Andalucía 10 ☎&ⓕ958 77 01 61. For a step up in price you can enjoy the relative luxury of the town's top hotel where a/c rooms come with strongbox and (some) a balcony. It also has a bar, restaurant, pool, garden and garage. **⑤**
Hotel Nuevo Palas Avda. de La Alpujarra 24 ☎958 77 01 11, ⓦwww.hotelnuevopalas.com. Pleasant hotel with a/c rooms, rooftop pool, gym and – in the bar – pool tables. **③**
Hotel Paris Avda. de La Alpujarra 23 ☎958 77 00 56, ⓕ958 77 03 74. A charming and very good-value recent arrival to the main street; rooms come with TV and there's a good-value restaurant and large pool. **②**
Venta El Buñuelo 1km from the centre along the Órgiva road ☎958 77 04 61. Refurbished and revitalized roadside *hostal-restaurante* where en-suite a/c rooms come with great views and there's easy parking. **①**

Eating and drinking

Plenty of **bars and restaurants** line the Avenida de Andalucía and many of the hotels and *hostales* have good-value meals and tapas, too – especially the hotels *España* and *El Sol*. Best choice for dining out, however, has to be the terrace restaurant of the *Hotel Castillo Alcadima* which is a pretty well perfect place to while away a summer evening with a superb terrace view of the castle and a *menú* for €15. At the eastern end of the main street, *Bar Galvez*, c/Real 95, is a good choice if you're on a tighter budget with *platos combinados* and an €11 *menú*. Further east still, and beyond the Ayuntamiento, *Café-Bar Health*, c/Señor la Expiración s/n, serves breakfasts and full meals with many vegetarian options and often has live music in the evenings. Continuing out of town brings you to *Venta El Buñuelo* (see p.515), another place for good low-priced *alpujarreño* cooking with a weekday *menú* for €8. For seafood, try *Los Mariscos*, Avda. de Andalucía 6, close to the "main square" (see below). Nearby, the justly popular *Jamones Gustavo Rubio*, Avda. de Andalucía 38, is worth a visit for its excellent tapas bar behind a shop selling the wines, cheeses, *jamones* and other local products.

On the Avenida de Andalucía's "main square", midway between the Balneario and the church, lies Lanjarón's celebrated *churrería*, claimed by some to sell the best home-made potato crisps in Andalucía, opposite which are a couple of good ice-cream parlours. Almost next door to the *churrería*, *Noche Azul* is a popular **nightclub**.

Órgiva (Órjiva)

Heading east out of Lanjarón brings you after 7km to a turn-off for Las Barreras, notable for a **campsite**, *Puerta de la Alpujarra* (☏958 78 44 50, ⓦwww .campingpuertadelaalpujarra.com) with its own shop, bar and restaurant and panoramic views; it also rents out wood-cabin bungalows (❸) sleeping up to four. Three kilometres further lies **ÓRGIVA**, the market centre of the western Alpujarras. It's a lively little town, with a number of good bars and hotels, and an animated and entertaining **Thursday market**. The contrast between the timeworn *campesinos* and their pack-mules, and some of the foreign New Age travellers who seek their indulgence and charity, is as bizarre as anything this side of Madrid. Many of the New Agers here inhabit a **tepee village**, *El Beneficio*, above the town where a polyglot community of mainly northern Europeans and their offspring endure freezing winters under canvas. Another local resident is writer and farmer **Chris Stewart** who moved with his wife to an isolated *cortijo* (farmhouse) on the outskirts of Órgiva over twenty years ago. His trilogy of books (see p.600) wittily describing life among the peasants, shepherds, New Age travellers and expats of the western Alpujarras proved highly popular and helped to place this area of Andalucía on the map.

Orgiva's other sights line the main street: the sixteenth-century Baroque **church** of Nuestra Señora de la Expectación, whose towers add a touch of fancy to the townscape, and a once crumbling but now over-restored Moorish **palace** that today houses the Ayuntamiento.

Órgiva comes to life with its **annual fiesta** on the days each side of September 29, the feast day of San Miguel, when the population doubles as prodigal sons and daughters all return to join in the fun. A more eccentric festival is the **Dia del Señor** on the second Friday before Easter. Opening with a terrifying salvo of rockets on the Thursday before, the town's womenfolk attack the church until they are able to make off with the effigies of El Señor (Christ) and the Virgin. The fiesta went disastrously wrong a few years back when the bank's windows were blown in by errant fireworks. On the Friday evening both Christ and his mother are paraded around town before re-entering the church in the early hours accompanied by great displays of emotion – not to mention more deafening rocketry.

Practicalities

Daily **buses** from the Alsina Graells stop on Avenida González Robles, serve the Low Alpujarras to Ugíjar (currently passing Orgiva at 10.15am and 7.15pm), as well as the High Alpujarran villages (passing at 11.30am, 1.30pm & 6.30pm).

Internet access is available at Ananda's Mundo, c/Cristo de la Expiración 4 (daily 10am–2pm & 6–10pm), behind the church and there's a useful notice-board for locals and visitors in the wholefood shop Herbolario La Alacena, downhill from the Ayuntamiento.

Órgiva has a fair choice of **accommodation**. Just beyond the traffic lights at the town's main intersection, the pretty, economical and friendly *Pensión Alma Alpujarreña* (T958 78 40 85; ❷) has en-suite rooms (some single), plus a restaurant beneath a vine trellis. Good a/c en-suite rooms are also available at *Hotel-Hostal Mirasol*, c/González Robles 3 (T958 78 51 59, W www.hotelmirasol .es; ❶–❷), on the way in from Lanjarón where their hotel rooms come with TV and wi-fi. Near the main junction, the charming ⚡ *Casa Rural El Molino*, c/González Robles 12 (Tmobile 646616628, W www.casaruralelmolino .com; ❸ with breakfast), is the most attractive in-town option offering excellent a/c rooms in a refurbished old olive mill, with pleasant patio and pool. Almost next door, *Hostal-Bar Semaforo* (T958 78 43 09, W www.elsemaforo.es; ❸), is another option for a/c en-suite rooms with TV. An inviting place to stay with your own transport is the rural *Hotel Taray* just over a kilometre along the A348 south of the town (T958 78 45 25, W www.hoteltaray.com; ❹); it's surrounded by lovely gardens with a superb pool, has a decent restaurant and does frequent special offers. The town's **campsite**, *Camping Órgiva* (T958 78 43 07) 2km south of the centre beyond the *Hotel Taray*, has a pool and also rents out cabins (❷), bungalows (❸), *casas rurales* (sleeping up to six; ❺) and a tree house; it has its own restaurant and pool and can advise on walking routes and renting horses in the nearby Sierra de Lújar.

Places for **meals** include the *Pensión Alma Alpujarreña* (see above) which has a decent kitchen and serves a good-value *menú* for €8.50. The *Hostal Mirasol* (see above) also does tapas and offers a restaurant *menú* for €8 inside or on their terrace, and the restaurant of the *Hotel Taray* (see above) with a *menú* for €10.50 is also good. *La Almazara*, almost next door to the *Pensión Alma Alpujarreña*, does excellent freshly made pizzas as well as more elaborate fare and has a garden terrace. Almost opposite the church, *Bar Santiago*, in c/García Moreno, has a wide selection of beers and wines plus you get to choose your own (free) *tapa* with each drink – a bonus for vegetarians. *El Limonero* in c/Yanez (off the main road close to the *Almazara*), which has music on Wednesday nights, and *Café Libertad* in c/Libertad at the top of the main street behind the church are more good places to try. A place worth seeking out near the market is the economical *Baraka*, c/Estación 12, a pleasant small Moroccan café and *tetería* offering felafel, couscous, tagines and a variety of teas.

The High Alpujarras: Órgiva to Capileira

From Órgiva, you can reach the High Alpujarran villages by car or bus, or you could walk – the best way to experience the region. There is a network of paths in this area, though to avoid getting lost it's wise to equip yourself with a compass and the *Instituto Geográfico Nacional/Federación Española de Montañismo* 1:50,000 **map**, which covers all the territory from Órgiva up to Berja. A reasonable knowledge of Spanish is also invaluable.

At their best, Alpujarran **footpaths** are remnants of the old Camino Real, the mule routes that crossed Spain, and are engineered with cobblestones, and beautifully contoured, alongside mountain streams, through woods of oak, chestnut and poplar, or across flower-spangled meadows. In their bad moments they deteriorate to incredibly dusty firebreaks, forestry roads or tractor tracks, or (worse) dead-end in impenetrable thickets of bramble and nettle. Progress is slow, gradients are sharp and the heat (between mid-June and Sept) is taxing. Over the

High Alpujarras hikes: the highlights

Rewarding **hikes** in the High Alpujarras include:

Pitres to Mecina Fondales: Twenty minutes' hike to Mecina Fondales, and then a good hour-plus from neighbouring Ferreirola to Busquístar.

Busquístar toward Trevélez: One hour's hike, and then two-plus hours of road walking.

Pórtugos toward Trevélez: Two hours, meeting the tarmac a little beyond the end of the Busquístar route.

Trevélez to Bérchules: Four hours, with the middle two hours on a dirt track.

Trevélez to Juviles: Three hours, including some sections of firebreak.

past few years part of the path network through the High Alpujarras has been upgraded as the final section of the **European long-distance footpath** that begins in Athens and ends in Algeciras. Designated as footpaths E4 or GR7 in Spain, the full route is now waymarked (in theory – you'll still need a good map where the posts are missing or misplaced) with red and white ringed posts.

Cañar, Soportújar and Carataunas

Following the high road from Órgiva, the first settlements you reach, almost directly above the town, are the isolated but pretty **CAÑAR** – at the end of a sinuous 5km drive off the main road – and **SOPORTÚJAR**, a maze of picturesque white-walled alleys bridged by numerous *tinaos* (see box, p.519). Like many of the High Alpujarran villages, they congregate on the neatly terraced mountainside, planted with poplars and laced with irrigation channels. Both have **bars** where you can get a meal, and Soportújar can provide good-value **rooms** (with and without bath) for the night; ask at the friendly *Bar Correíllo* (☎958 78 75 78; 2) on c/Real (behind the church); they will also do *platos combinados* on request. Perched precariously on the steep hillside, both villages share a rather sombre view of Órgiva in the valley below, and on a clear day the mountains of North Africa over the ranges to the south. Each village has a sixteenth-century church, both of which fell into a terrible state of disrepair at the end of the last century, and both of which, thankfully, have now been refurbished and saved.

Just below the two villages, the tiny hamlet of **CARATAUNAS** is particularly attractive, and puts on a lively start to its Semana Santa on Palm Sunday, when an effigy of Judas is tossed on a bonfire.

The Poqueira Gorge

Shortly beyond Carataunas the road swings to the north after passing the turn-off to the Buddhist monastery of Osel Ling (see p.519), and you have your first view of the **Gorge of the Poqueira**, a huge gash into the heights of the Sierra Nevada. Trickling deep in the cleft is the Río Poqueira, which has its source near the peak of Mulhacén. The steep walls of the gorge are terraced and wooded from top to bottom, and dotted with little stone farmhouses. Much of the surrounding country looks barren from a distance, but close up you'll find that it's rich with flowers, woods, springs and streams. A trio of spectacular villages – Pampaneira, Bubión and Capileira – teeter on the steep edge of the gorge among their terraces. They are, justifiably, the most touristy villages in the region and a bit over-prettified, with craft shops and the like, but nonetheless well worth it, as is some walking on the local mule paths. A number of fine **walking routes** are detailed with maps in *Landscapes of Andalucía and the Costa del Sol* (see p.609).

Alpujarran architecture

Alpujarran **village houses** are unlike any others in Spain – though they are almost identical to Berber houses across the straits in the Rif mountains of Morocco, where many of the Moorish refugees settled. They are built of grey stone, flat-roofed and low; traditionally they are unpainted, though these days *cal* (whitewash) – a luxury until recent times – is increasingly common. The coarse walls are about 75cm thick, for summer coolness and protection from winter storms. Stout beams of chestnut, or ash in the lower valleys, are laid from wall to wall; on top of these is a mat of canes, ilex or split chestnut; upon this flat stones are piled, and on the stones is spread a layer of **launa**, the crumbly grey mica clay found throughout the area, which is made waterproof when pressed down.

The *launa* must – and this maxim is still observed today – be laid during the waning of the moon (though not, of course, on a Fri) in order for it to settle properly and thus keep rain out. Gerald Brenan wrote in *South from Granada* of a particularly ferocious storm: "As I peered through the darkness of the stormy night, I could make out a dark figure on every roof in the village, dimly lit by an esparto torch, stamping clay into the holes in the roof."

Another feature peculiar to the Alpujarras are the **tinaos**, a kind of portico or bridge that enables access from a dwelling in one row to another in an upper or lower row. In summer, time is passed on the roof terrace or *terrao*, especially once the sun has cooled in early evening. Bubión, Capileira and Pitres all have good examples of the traditional architectural style.

Pampaneira and the Tibetan monastery

PAMPANEIRA, the first of the Poqueira villages, is a neat, prosperous place, and a bit less developed and spoilt than its neighbours. Around its main square are a number of bars, restaurants, *hostales* and craft shops, one of which, just down the hill, is a weaving workshop that specializes in traditional Alpujarreño designs. For **rooms**, near to the **bus stop** there's *Hostal Pampaneira*, c/José Antonio 1 (℡958 76 30 02; ❷ incl. breakfast), with some en-suite rooms or, continuing up the road for a couple of hundred metres, at the plush new *Hotel Estrella de las Nieves* (℡958 76 33 22, ⓦwww.estrelladelasnieves.com; ❸).

For **food**, the *Hostal Pampaneira* has its own decent restaurant, and another good bet worth considering is *Casa Julio*, up some steps nearby offering solid mountain fare with an €8 *menú*. On the main square, the leafy Plaza de la Libertad, *Bar Belezmín* is one of the village's best places to eat, offering a menu filled with hearty *alpujarreña* dishes; the nearby *Casa Diego* is another possibility, with a terrace and *menú* for €9.

Also on Plaza de la Libertad you'll find Nevadensis (Tues–Sat 11am–2pm & 4–6pm, Sun & Mon 10am–3pm; ℡958 76 31 27, ⓦwww.nevadensis.com; English spoken), a private, efficiently run **information centre** for the National Park of the Sierra Nevada. As well as providing information, they sell large-scale topographical maps of the area, walking guidebooks and outdoor clothing. They also organize themed guided walks in all seasons and offer organized activities and excursions including mountain biking, climbing, canyoning, hiking, and cross-country skiing. If you're thinking of a longer stay, this is also where you can pick up a list of hostels, village houses, and farmhouses for rent throughout the Alpujarras.

Above Pampaneira, on the very peak of the western flank of the Poqueira gorge in a stunning location, is the small Tibetan Buddhist **Monastery of Osel Ling** (Place of Clear Light) founded in 1982 by a Tibetan monk on land donated by the communities of Pampaneira and Bubión. The simple stone-built monastery complete with stupas and stunning **views** across the Alpujarras welcomes visitors between 3 and 6pm daily; lectures and courses on Buddhism are held regularly and facilities exist for those who want to visit for periods of retreat in simple cabins dotted around the site (☎958 34 31 34 for details). The monastery is reached by a track on the left – signed "camino forestal" – 1km east of the turning to Soportujar. Should you encounter difficulty locating it, enquire at Nevadensis (see p.519) or Rustic Blue (see below) who will set you right.

Bubión

BUBIÓN is next up the hill, backed for much of the year by snowcapped peaks. Lacking the focus of a proper main square, it's probably the least attractive of these high villages but – perhaps because of this – it certainly seems the most peaceful. The tranquillity may not last long, though, if the property developers have their way, and already there is quite a bit of building taking place on the lower slopes. There are no sights as such but a municipal **museum**, the Casa Alpujarreña (daily 11am–2pm, Sat & Sun also 5–7pm; €2), just off Plaza de la Iglesia near the church, displays aspects of the folklore, daily life and architecture of the Alpujarras in a traditional house. Towards the end of August, Bubión celebrates its **Fiestas Patronales** with music, dance, fireworks and copious imbibing.

For **places to stay**, there's a comfortable *pensión*, *Las Terrazas* (☎958 763 034, ⓦwww.terrazasalpujarra.com; ➊–➋), which has en-suite rooms and apartments with views. *Los Tinaos*, downhill from here at c/Parras s/n (☎958 763 217, ⓦwww.lostinaos.com; ➋), offers more excellent apartments which come with garden terrace, kitchen, satellite TV and fine views. Just behind the museum the friendly *La Locana*, c/Real s/n (☎958 76 30 95, Ⓔlurdes.lalocana@gmail .com; ➋–➌), is a pleasant small *pensión* with en-suite rooms plus a charming fully equipped studio with kitchenette. Rustic Blue (see below) can also direct you to rooms in private houses plus apartments for longer lets.

A very good **restaurant** on the main road, *La Artesa*, at c/Carretera 2, turns out *alpujarreño* specialities with a *menú* for €8.50. *Teide*, just over the road, is another decent place for solid mountain cooking and has a pleasant leafy terrace. Also of note, in the lower village, are the pleasant *Bodega La Casilla*, Plaza de la Iglesia, serving tasty tapas and *raciónes*, plus *Estacion 4*, using its address as its name, for *cocina mediterránea*, vegetarian dishes, salads and a variety of teas.

A private **information office**, Rustic Blue (Mon–Fri 10am–2pm & 5–7pm, Sat 11am–2pm, ☎958 76 33 81, ⓦwww.rusticblue.com; English spoken), at the entrance to the village on the right, is a useful source of local knowledge and stocks walking guides to the area as well as organizing week-long guided treks and horse-riding tours. It can also provide information on renting apartments and houses throughout the Alpujarras. For **horse-riding trips** of one to five days, the friendly *Rancho Rafael Belmonte* (☎958 76 31 35, ⓦwww.ridingandalucia.com), at the bottom of the village near Rustic Blue, or Dallas Love (☎958 76 30 38, Ⓔdallaslove@arrakis.es) are the places to contact.

Capileira

CAPILEIRA is the highest of the three villages and the terminus of Europe's highest road across the heart of the Sierra Nevada from Granada. This is now closed to traffic except for a summer bus service (see box, p.521). A picturesque and tranquil place, except in high summer when it is deluged with visitors and coach tours, Capileira makes a fine walking base from which to explore the Poqueira Gorge, or you could even strike out for Trevélez about five hours to the northeast.

Scaling Mulhacén – the easy way

In summer (June–Oct depending on weather) the Parque Nacional authorities run a daily minibus service along the closed road from Capileira to the **Mirador de Trevélez** (with spectacular **views** on clearer days) and on to the **Alto del Chorrillo**, some 20km above the village. The 75-minute trip (with on-board guide) is great to do in itself but why not add in the conquest of the peninsula's highest peak as well?

From the Alto del Chorillo bus stop it's a roughly four hour hike to make the ascent and descent of Mulhacén (clearly described in Charles Davis's 34 *Alpujarras Walks* – see p.609). The kiosko (see below) can provide a simple map, but you'd be wise to take the *Editorial Alpina* map along, too (see p.50). Outward-bound morning buses currently leave from Capileira at 8.30am and 11am and return from Alto del Chorillo at 4.15pm and 6.15pm (confirm the timetable at the kiosko). Seats on the bus (€8 return) should be booked **in advance** at the kiosko from where the buses depart. As you'll be in the high mountains you should be prepared for any sudden changes in weather conditions and equip yourself accordingly.

Just downhill from the kiosko (see below) lies the village's **museum** (Tues–Sun 11.30am–2.30pm; €1), containing displays of regional dress and handicrafts as well as various bits and pieces belonging to, or produced by, Pedro Alarcón, the nineteenth-century Spanish writer, born in Guadix, who made a trip through the Alpujarras and wrote a (not very good) book about it. On the Sunday prior to August 5, Capileira embarks on its annual **romería** to the summit of Mulhacén and the *ermita* of the Virgen de las Nieves.

Practicalities

There are daily **buses** to Capileira from Granada (see p.514). Buses out of Capileira to Órgiva and Granada currently leave at 6.35am, 4.45pm and 6.15pm. The national park information **kiosko** (daily 9am–2pm & 5–8pm) at the centre of the village, near where the bus drops you, sells newspapers, large-scale walking maps, hands out a free village **map** and acts as an **information** office.

Among several **places to stay**, on the way into the village on the right *Hostal Atalaya* (℡958 76 30 25; ❶–❷ with breakfast) has pleasant en-suite rooms with great views. Near the bus stop, the friendly *Mesón-Hostal Poqueira* (℡958 763 048, ⓦwww.hotelpoqueira.com; ❷), offers en-suite heated rooms, some with terraces and views and has a pool and good restaurant with a substantial *menú* for around €10. It also offers some attractive apartments sleeping up to four (❹) for longer stays. The new *El Cascapeñas* (℡958 76 30 11; ⓦwww.elcascapenas .com; ❷), also near the bus halt, has good value en-suite rooms with TV. Continuing uphill, you come to the more luxurious *Finca Los Llanos* (℡958 763 071, ⓦwww.hotelfincalosllanos.com; ❹ with breakfast), offering apartment-style rooms with kitchenettes and terraces, a pool and a decent restaurant. *Ruta de Las Nieves* (℡958 76 31 06; ❷) higher up the same road has rooms with bath and heating and a few good-value apartments. Some 500m beyond this (and signed up a track on the left), another delightful hideaway, *Cortijo Catifalarga* (℡958 34 33 57, ⓦwww.catifalarga.com; ❹–❺), has charming rooms inside a traditional *alpujarreño cortijo*, along with fabulous views and a pool. Should you desire even more solitude, continue along the mountain road for a further 3km, turning right along a signed track to *Cortijo Prado Toro* (℡958 34 32 40, ⓦwww .pradotoro.es; ❹) where, at an altitude of 1500m, accommodation is in attractive apartments and studios with terraces enjoying spectacular views.

In addition to the **restaurants** mentioned above, other places worth seeking out are *Mesón Rural Panjuila*, a little way uphill from the bus halt to the right serving *alpujarreña* specialities with a €9 *menú* and, further uphill near the *Finca Los Llanos* hotel, *La Casa de Paco y Pilar*, Ctra. Sierra Nevada 16, offers well-prepared mountain fare (with some vegetarian options) on a pleasant garden terrace with a €10 *menú*. *Restaurante El Tilo*, on the focal Plaza Calvario in the lower village, is a decent place for *platos combinados* or watching-the-world-go-by drinks on its tranquil terrace shaded by a lime tree. Downhill from here *Bodega La Alacena*, Callejon de las Campanas s/n, is a popular option for ham and cheese tapas and its shop also sells local products. Near the museum (see p.521) the tangerine-tinted dining room of *Casa Ibero*, c/Parra 1 (open evenings only), is another good place for vegetarian dishes such as very tasty couscous, Indian and other adventurous concoctions.

The Poqueira Gorge

Capileira is a handy base for easy day walks in the **Poqueira Gorge**. For a not-too-strenuous ramble, take the northernmost of the three paths below the village, each of which spans bridges across the river. This one sets off from alongside the Pueblo Alpujarreño villa complex and winds through the huts and terraced fields of the river valley above Capileira, ending after about an hour and a half at a dirt track within sight of a power plant at the head of the valley. From here, you can either retrace your steps or cross the stream over a bridge to follow a dirt track back to the village. In May and June, the fields are labori-ously tended by hand, as the steep slopes dictate.

A number of reasonably clear paths or tracks also lead to **Pampaneira** (2–3hr; follow the lower path to the bridge below Capileira), continuing to **Carataunas** (a further 1hr, mostly road) and **Órgiva** (another 45min on an easy path) from where – if you time it right – you can get a bus back.

In the other direction, taking the Sierra Nevada road and then the first major track to the right, by a ruined stone house, you can reach **Pitres** (2hr), **Pórtugos** (30min more) and **Busquístar** (45min more). Going in the same direction but taking the second decent-sized track (by a sign encouraging you to "conserve and respect nature"), **Trevélez** is some five hours away. Rather than doing Mulhacén the "easy way" (see box, p.521), more skilled, equipped and ambitious climbers may wish to attempt the whole circuit, starting from Capilieira. The summit of **Mulhacén**, the peninsula's highest peak at 3483m, is achievable in a day from here, but is perhaps more sensibly done over two days with an overnight stop at the *Refugio Poqueira* (☎958 34 33 49; open all year but book in advance) at the head of the Poqueira valley and marked on the *Editorial Alpina* map (see p.509).

Further along the High Route to Trevélez and Cádiar

The High Route continues east from Pampaneira through **Pitres** and **Pórtugos** before making a great loop to Trevélez, Spain's highest permanent settlement. From there, the road drops down to a junction, with a crossing to **Torvizcón**, on the south side of the Alpujarras, and east to the valley and village of **Cádiar**.

Pitres

PITRES is far less picturesque and less developed than the trio of high villages to its west and, like its equally unpolished neighbour, Pórtugos, offers more chance of a room during high season. All around, too, spreads some of the best Alpujarran walking country.

Currently the only en-suite room option in the village proper is the *Hotel San Roque*, c/Cruz 1, on the east side (℡958 85 75 28; ❸ with breakfast), offering pleasant rooms with (on the south side) views. Nearby and down a track on the opposite side of the road, the *Refugio Los Albergues* (℡958 34 31 76; ❶) is an old Civil War hostel rustically refurbished to provide dormitory beds (€10), one double room (❶), kitchen facilities, but outdoor toilets. It's signposted from the main road, but if you get lost ask for Casa Barbara (Hauck), the name of the friendly German who runs it. Pitres's **campsite**, the *Balcón de Pitres* (℡958 76 61 11; March–Oct), lies in a stunning position just out of town to the west, with a swimming pool, restaurant and great views. Perhaps Pitres's most tempting overnight option is *Hotel Maravedi* (℡958 76 62 92, ⓦwww.hotelmaravedi.com; ❹) which lies 2km above the village on a (signed) minor road to the hamlet of Capilerilla. It's housed in a traditional *launa*-roofed *cortijo*, rooms are comfortable and well-equipped, and there's a restaurant and bar plus stunning views.

For **food** in Pitres, you have a choice between the bars on the village's main square, Plaza de la Alpujarra, and the campsite or the *Hotel San Roque* (see above) which also has its own restaurant.

Pórtugos, Mecina Fondales, Ferreirola and Busquistar

PÓRTUGOS is equally rustic and its centre has a couple of **places to stay**, including the pleasant *Hostal Mirador* (℡958 76 60 14; ❷), on the main square with bargain-priced en-suite rooms and its own decent **restaurant** with a €10 *menú*.

Down below the main road are a trio of villages – **MECINA FONDALES**, **FERREIROLA** and **BUSQUÍSTAR** – which along with Pitres and Pórtugos and a couple of smaller settlements formed a league of seven villages known as the **Tahá** (from the Arabic "Tá" meaning obedience) under the Moors. These are among the most unspoilt of the Alpujarra *pueblos* where you can find plenty of examples of typical regional architecture (see box, p.519). Ferreirola and Busquístar – the latter a huddle of grey *launa* roofs – are especially attractive, as is the path between the two, clinging to the north side of the valley of the Río Trevélez. You're out of tourist country here and the villages display their genuine characteristics to better effect.

For **accommodation**, Mecina Fondales has the very pleasant upmarket *Hotel Albergue de Mecina* (℡958 76 62 41, ⓦwww.hoteldemecina.com; ❹), a delightful hideaway with an excellent garden pool – and passed on the Tahá walk (see box, p.524) – where you can also hire horses and mountain bikes. The hotel has its own restaurant, but the best place for **food** here is at the French-run ⚔ *L'Atelier* (℡&℻958 85 75 01, ⓔmecinilla@yahoo.com), a restaurant specializing in vegetarian/vegan cuisine, located in the old village bakery at c/Alberca s/n. Booking is advised at weekends. It also lets a few rooms (❷ incl. breakfast) and acts as agent for some delightful *apartamentos rurales* (❸) most with views, gardens and pool (two night minimum); ring or send them an email for details.

Nearby Ferreirola has the wonderful Scandinavian-run ⚔ *Sierra y Mar*, c/Albaycin 3 (℡958 76 61 71, ⓦwww.sierraymar.com; ❸ with breakfast), with fine views and where the owners – enthusiastic walkers – will advise on routes in the area; guests also have use of a kitchen to prepare their own food. To get there, take the road to the right of the fountain out of the main plaza. There's also a pleasant *tetería* (Arabic tearoom), *FaRe*, c/Soledad s/n, at the bottom of the village. Neighbouring Busquistar also has a charming place to stay: in the

A circuit of the Tahá villages – with many fine stopping places for a picnic – is a good introduction to the Alpujarras, offering opportunities to appreciate both typical architecture and landscape within a compact area. The following walk around the **Southern Tahá** is an easy two-hour hike, although you'll probably want to take the diversion down to the picturesque Trevélez Gorge which adds another half-hour or so; allow three hours for the full circuit. There's little shade on parts of the route, so avoid the afternoon sun in summer. Remember that the second (uphill) part of the walk is the most strenuous.

The route starts in **Pitres**. Follow the narrow path, which begins as a concrete driveway curving behind *Restaurante La Carretera* (on the main road to the right as you enter the village) and descends southwards – veering left – to **Mecinilla**, which is soon visible below; you should be aiming for the left of the church tower. Ignoring turnings, after fifteen minutes or so you emerge in the upper part of the village (Mecilla). Cross the main Pitres–Ferreirola road into the lower village (Mecinilla), following the road past the *Hotel Albergue de Mecina* (with a decent tapas bar and restaurant) and the church on the left. Just after the *Bar El Aljibe* (on the left), go through a gap and take an immediate right. After a drinking fountain (marked "1964"), turn left; continue downwards through the narrow streets, eventually leaving the village beneath a *tinao* (see box p.519). Initially following the edge of a ravine, the path continues downwards through orchards (crossing the road once but continuing clearly a little to the right) until reaching the maze of narrow, white streets that make up **Mecina–Fondales** – this should take another half-hour or so. Take your time here, partly as it's one of the most peaceful and least spoilt villages, but also as the maze of streets makes it easy to get lost and the vociferous dogs zealously guarding their patches can be off-putting; ask for directions if you can.

From here, for the **shorter route**, take the Camino Real towards Ferreirola, a well-maintained mule track leaving the centre of the village heading east. For the **longer route**, head to the wash area known as "La Fuente" in the village's southeast corner – veer downhill to the left from the road to pass beneath an elaborate *tinao* topped by a vine trellis – to reach the five-basined wash place. From here take the track descending towards the river, bearing left where there's any confusion. After a while the gushing waters become audible below, and the path emerges high above the gorge with the Trevélez bridge visible ahead. Immediately before the bridge, turn left up a small path which crosses the Río Bermejo, before climbing steeply over rocks (ignore the right-hand fork) and continuing uphill to **Ferreirola**.

In Ferreirola, head for the church square; close by is another wash place. Take the path rising north alongside it, which, after another steepish climb, leads to **Atalbéitar**. The path actually emerges on the road below the village from where you turn left to continue the walk, but first you should visit Atalbéitar, another unspoilt hamlet, well off the usual tourist trail. Leaving the village, passing a lifeless oak tree and rubbish container on the right, turn left as the road bends to the right and follow this track in the direction of Pitres (now visible above) past a few houses. The path twice briefly joins the "road" (more of a dirt track); each time, take the path to the left where the road bends right. Leaving the track the second time, just before it joins the "main road", the path first skirts the Bermejo Gorge but then drops sharply to cross the river – some welcome greenery here hides the bridge until you're close to it. Across the river, the path climbs to an *acequia* (irrigation channel); turn right here and continue along the wooded path, past the *Albergue*, till emerging on the main road slightly to the east of **Pitres**.

heart of the village near the church the newly arrived *Casa Sonia*, c/San Francisco 5 (☎958 857 503, ⓦwww.casasonia.eu; ❸) has elegant en-suite a/c rooms, some with great views. A good option for **tapas** and *raciónes* is Bar Paco, just below the main road as you pass through the village.

Trevélez

The cut into the mountain made by the Río Trevélez is similar to the Poqueira, but grander and more austere. **TREVÉLEZ** village stands on a flank at the end of the ravine and its altitude – this is Spain's highest conurbation – makes it a cool place even in high summer when many of the inhabitants continue to don sweaters and coats. It's built in traditional Alpujarran style, with a lower and two upper *barrios* overlooking a grassy, poplar-lined valley where the river starts its long descent. The upper *barrios* (*alto* and *medio*) are probably the most pleasant places to stay as the lower (*barrio bajo*) is more touristy and filled with stalls and shops selling *jamones*, crystals, earrings and herbal remedies all attracting streams of visitors, especially at weekends. There are fine walks in the valley and you can swim, too, in a makeshift pool by the bridge.

Trevélez is traditionally the jump-off point for the high **Sierra Nevada** peaks (to which there is a bona fide path) and for treks across the range (on a lower, more conspicuous track). The latter begins down by the bridge on the eastern side of the village. After skirting the bleak Horcajo de Trevélez (3182m), and negotiating the Puerto de Trevélez (2800m), up to which it's a very distinct route, it drops down along the north flank of the Sierra Nevada to Jerez del Marquesado.

Practicalities

The village is well provided with **places to stay**, in both the lower and upper squares; if you are susceptible to low temperatures, outside July and August you may want a place with efficient heating. In the *barrio medio* the pleasant and welcoming *Hostal Fernando*, c/Pista del Barrio Medio s/n (☎958 85 85 65; with heating; ❶), offers rooms with bath and great terrace views (from some rooms); it also lets out some excellent-value apartments with kitchen and terrace (❷). Beside the Ayuntamiento in the *barrio alto*, the 🏠 *Hotel La Fragua*, c/San Antonio 4 (☎958 85 86 26, ⊛www.hotellafragua.com; ❷–❸), is probably the most luxurious of the village places with pine-furnished, en-suite, heated rooms with more fine views; there's also an excellent and good-value restaurant and the proprietors can give information on walking in the area. As it's a popular place with walking groups, it may be worth ringing ahead. In the *barrio bajo*, *Hostal*

On horseback to Las Siete Lagunas

In late spring and summer (when the mountain snows have retreated) you might want to try a trip on horseback to **Las Siete Lagunas**, a spectacular collection of mountain lakes in a valley on the upper slopes of the mighty Monte Mulhacén. It's a five-hour journey each way and you spend a night on the mountain at an altitude of 3000m; you'll need your own sleeping bag and it's possible to pitch a tent at Siete Lagunas, although this is not essential. The highpoint of the trip is the sun rising above the Sierra de Gador in the east. The trips are organized by Rutas de Caballo Virgen de Las Nieves, c/Puente s/n, in the *barrio alto* (☎958 85 86 01, ☎mobile 619031821; Spanish only) and cost around €210 per person (meals included) for two people (marginally cheaper for larger groups). This is to ride both ways; if you decided to walk down the price would be €105. The same company also do shorter trips (a couple of hours or a half-day; €15 per hr). Note that a little Spanish would help (although this is not a major problem) and that no insurance cover is provided, so check your policy. The route can also be done **on foot** and although the ascent is signed ("Siete Lagunas") in its early stages you'd be much better off following the trekking route clearly described in Jeremy Rabjohn's book *Holiday Walks in the Alpujarras* (see p.609). If you don't plan to sleep out at the lakes you should allow at least ten hours walking time to get up and down the same day.

Regina, Plaza Francisco Abellán 12 (☎958 85 85 64, ✉hostalregina@wanadoo .es; ❷), has heated rooms, some with bath and views. Also in the lower *barrio, Hostal Mulhacén*, Ctra. Ugíjar s/n (☎ 958 85 85 87; with heating; ❷), 100m along the Juviles road from Plaza Francisco Abellán, is another pleasant possibility for rooms with and without bath, and offers more great views down the valley. One of the most attractive places to stay in this area is out of town at the *Alcazaba de Busquístar* (☎958 85 86 87, ⓦwww.alcazabadebusquistar.com; ❺), a tranquil hideaway some 5km south along the GR421 road which descends along the east side of the ravine to meet the A348. This apart-hotel has traditional-style Alpujarran dwellings (no. 411 is recommended) with *launa* roofs and fine views, plus a restaurant and pool; horseriding, mountain biking, trekking and fishing are some of the activities on offer. Heating comes from a *chimenea* (wood burning stove) that you feed yourself. Trevélez's **campsite** (☎958 85 87 35) lies 1km out along the Órgiva road and is officially open all year, although you can expect arctic conditions in midwinter. It also rents out some heated cabins (❷).

Among **places to eat**, besides the excellent and reasonably priced *Hotel La Fragua* (see p.525), are *Casa Julio*, Plaza de la Iglesia, also in the *barrio medio*, and the *Río Grande*, off the east side of Plaza Francisco Abellán in the *barrio bajo*, both serving up *alpujarreño* dishes. The great-value *Mesón Haraicel*, in c/Real just above the same square in the *barrio bajo*, offers tasty tapas and *raciónes* in its bar. A little way out along the Ugíjar road, *Piedra Ventana* is another popular eating place. A couple of good **tapas bars** worth seeking out are *Bar Rosales* (near *Hostal Fernando*) and *Bar Cerezo*, both in the *barrio medio*.

Trevélez's celebrated **jamón serrano** is justifiably a local passion and can be tried, along with many other specialities, at the bars above and also at *Mesón del Jamón*, which has an attractive terrace above the Plaza de la Iglesia in the *barrio medio*. Another *jamón* specialist is *Mesón Joaquín*, at the entrance to the village in the *barrio bajo*, where beneath a ceiling hung with hams, regional specialities are served including *habas con jamón* (beans with ham), *plato alpujarreño* (mixed fry-up with blood pudding, *jamón* and egg) and *trucha* (river trout) with *jamón*; there's also a €7 *menú*. These famous *jamones dulces* sent Richard Ford into raptures when he passed through Trevélez on horseback in the 1830s: "No gastronome should neglect these sweet hams. Very little salt is used; the ham is

---

Birdwatching in the High Alpujarras

This corner of the Alpujarras is an excellent place for **birdwatching**, particularly in late spring. Quiet roads, an abundance of footpaths and dirt tracks make access easy. At this time of the year, most of the species associated with the upland areas of southern Spain can be found in the Poqueira Gorge (p.522) and the Trevélez River Valley. Above the village of Capileira, a walk from the end of the metalled road in areas clear of pine woods can turn up sightings of southern grey shrike, rock thrush, black-eared wheatear and the striking black-eyed race of northern wheatear as well as Ortolan bunting. Higher up, in autumn, honey buzzards can occasionally be seen heading for the Straits of Gibraltar and winter quarters in Africa. Higher still, the alpine accentor is to be spotted around mountain huts.

The more wooded parts of the Trevélez Valley have booted eagle, buzzard, raven and the short-toed treecreeper, whilst lower down, near Pitres, Scops owl and red-necked nightjar can be heard at dusk, and in late summer bee eaters congregate for their migration south. Throughout these areas golden eagle, crag martin, black redstart and rock bunting are also to be seen and, with a little more persistence and patience, the members of the warbler family – Dartford, spectacled, selodius and Bonelli's – can be turned up in suitable habitats.

placed eight days in a weak pickle, and then hung up in the snow." A good place to buy and try *jamón* is at Jamones Jiménez, 50m before the bridge.

East to Juviles, Bérchules and Cádiar

Heading east from Trevélez, either by vehicle or on foot, you come to **JUVILES**, a great centre of silk production in Moorish times, and today an attractive village straddling the road. At its centre is an unwhitewashed, peanut-brittle-finish church with a clock that's slightly slow (like most things round here). The villagers don't appear to have taken to their renovated plaza with its jarring ornamental fountains, lamp-standards and trees in brick boxes, and in the evening people still promenade in the road, knowing that there will be no traffic. Juviles also takes its share of the **jamón** business and a large attractive building on the main road as you exit towards Ugíjar houses Jamones de Juviles S.A. (Ⓦwww.jamonesdejuviles.com), a curing factory for this *alpujarreño* delicacy. Ring the doorbell indicated at the entrance and you will be invited inside to taste their fine hams, which can be bought whole or in smaller cuts. The atmospheric *Bar Fernández* on the main street does inexpensive **meals** and for **rooms** *Pensión Tino* (Ⓣ958 76 91 74; ❷), on the same road at the western end of the village, has en-suites above a bar, views and a pretty, flower-filled terrace.

BÉRCHULES, a high village of grassy streams and chestnut woods, lies just 6km beyond Juviles, but a greater contrast can hardly be imagined. It is a large, abruptly demarcated settlement, three streets wide, on a sharp slope overlooking yet another canyon. For **accommodation** *Alojamiento Rural La Tahoma*, c/Baja de la Iglesia s/n, which (as the street name tells you) is just below the church (Ⓣ958 76 90 51, Ⓣmobile 628281882; ❷), offers excellent-value apartments with kitchen, *salon* and TV, and one-night stays are possible. In the upper village, fully equipped apartments (sleeping up to four) are also on offer at *El Mirador de Berchules*, Plaza de Zapata 1 (Ⓣ958 76 76 90, Ⓦwww.miradorbeberchules .com; ❹), with terraces and views and it also has its own good restaurant, tapas bar and pool. On the main road into the village from Juviles, the more upmarket *Hotel Bérchules* (Ⓣ958 85 25 30, Ⓦwww.hotelberchules.com; ❸) has comfortable rooms above its own restaurant and there's also a pool. For **food**, in addition to the places mentioned above, *Bar Vaqueras*, on the focal Plaza Victoria, does decent tapas and *raciónes*.

CÁDIAR, just below Bérchules and the central town – or "navel" as Gerald Brenan termed it – of the Alpujarras, is in fact a fairly humdrum market town whose life centres on its main square, fronted by a sixteenth-century stone church, where a colourful produce **market** takes place on the 3rd and 18th of every month, sometimes including livestock. Otherwise there's not much else to detain you here, but for **accommodation** if you're looking for something a little more special, the upmarket apart-hotel ⚲ *Alquería de Morayma* (Ⓣ958 34 33 03, Ⓦwww.alqueriamorayma.com; ❹), is a converted Alpujarran *cortijo* sited in 86 acres of farmland; there are charmingly rustic rooms and apartments (almost same price) many with terraces, and it has its own good restaurant (open to visitors) and offers guests mountain biking and horseriding while there are also plenty of hiking trails. The *Morayma*'s own organic farm and vineyard on the estate, the *bodega* of which is open to visitors, also supplies the restaurant and provides its virgin olive oil and bottled wine.

The eastern and southern Alpujarras

Cádiar and Bérchules mark the end of the western Alpujarras, and a striking change in the landscape; the dramatic, severe, but relatively green terrain of the Guadalfeo and Cádiar valleys gives way to open, rolling and much more arid land. The villages of the **eastern Alpujarras** display many of the characteristics of those to the west but as a rule they are poorer and less visited by tourists. There are attractive places nonetheless, among them **Yegen**, which Brenan wrote about, the market centre of **Ugíjar**, plus a remarkable museum at **Jorairátar**.

Yegen and Mecina Bombarón

YEGEN, some 7km northeast of Cádiar, is where **Gerald Brenan** lived during his ten or so years of Alpujarran residence (see box below). Brenan connections aside, Yegen is one of the most characteristic of this zone's villages, with its two distinct quarters, cobbled paths and cold-water springs. It has a couple of **places to stay**, one of which, *Bar La Fuente*, opposite the fountain in the square (T958 85 10 67, Wwww.pensionlafuente.com; ①) has en-suite rooms and apartments to let (③) and serves **tapas** and **raciónes** in a bar dotted with Brenan memorabilia and photos. The proprietor can provide a leaflet of walks (in Spanish; one route is named after Brenan) around the village. There are more bright and airy en-suite rooms at *El Tinao* (T958 85 12 12, Eloranne123@hotmail.com; ①) on the main road through which also lets apartments (④) and serves meals.

Heading east out of the village, the more luxurious *El Rincón de Yegen* (T958 85 12 70, Eelrincondeyegen@telefonica.net; ③) has heated rooms with TV, as well as apartments (④) sleeping up to four for longer stays, a pool and a good mid-priced **restaurant** with a weekday €10 *menú*. Slightly before this, *Alojamientos Las Eras* (T&F958 85 11 91, Wwww.alojamientoslaseras.com; ④) rents out fully equipped apartments with TV and terrace. One **bar** worth finding your way to in Yegen's *barrio bajo* (lower quarter) is *Bar Muñoz*, on c/Iglesia, where on cooler nights locals gather around the fireplace to enjoy *jamón serrano* cured on the premises by the proprietor; if someone decides to unhook one of the guitars from the wall, sessions of singing can continue late into the night.

From Yegen there's an easy 4km **walk** up to the hamlet of **Mecina Bombarón**, along one of the old cobbled mule paths. This starts out from the old bridge across the gorge and is easy to follow from there, with Mecina clearly

---

South from Granada

Gerald Brenan's autobiography of his years in the Alpujarras, **South from Granada**, is the best account of rural life in Spain between the wars, and also describes the visits made here by Bloomsburyites Virginia Woolf, Bertrand Russell and the arch-complainer Lytton Strachey who attributed his Iberian ailments to "crude olive oil, greasy tortillas and a surfeit of *bacalao*" and proclaimed when he got home that "Spain is absolute death". Disillusioned with the strictures of middle-class life in England after World War I, Brenan rented a house in Yegen and shipped out a library of two thousand books, from which he was to spend the next eight years educating himself. Since only a handful of the inhabitants of Yegen were literate, the reserved, lanky stranger was regarded as an exotic curiosity by the villagers. With glazed windows in only two dwellings, no doctor, electricity or telephone and no road to the outside world, Yegen's rustic isolation together with its characters, traditions, superstitions and celebrations provided the raw material for his great work. Towards the end of his stay he became involved in a number of scandals and, after getting a young teenage girl pregnant, moved to the hills of Churriana behind Torremolinos, with his wife, US writer and poet Gamel Woolsey. Here he died in 1987, a writer better known and respected in Spain (he made an important study of St John of the Cross) than in his native England. The contribution he made to informing the world about the Alpujarras, its history and culture, is recorded on a plaque fixed to his former home, now the **Casa de Brenan**, just along from the fountain in Yegen's main square.

visible on the hill above. In the village (also reachable by road) the *Casas Blancas* rural **hotel** (T&F 958 85 11 51, W www.casasblancas.org; ❸) is a pleasant place to stay, where studio rooms come with TV, kitchen and sun balcony. The new *Apartamentos Altas Vistas* next door is owned by a branch of the same family with similar prices and is also good. For **food** there's *Casa Joaquín*, just below the church, with an economical weekday *menú del día*.

Válor, Ugíjar and Jorairátar

Six kilometres beyond Yegen, and sited between deep ravines, **VÁLOR** is a charming and sleepy hamlet, a fact which belies its history as a centre of stubborn resistance in the sixteenth-century revolt by the Moors against the "insults and outrages" of the Christian ascendancy. These events are "celebrated" in the annual **Fiestas Patronales** in mid-September when the whole story – including battles between Moors and Christians – is colourfully re-enacted in the main square. En-suite **rooms** are available at the comfortable *Hostal Las Perdices* on the road through (T 958 85 18 21; ❷) with – as its name implies – a good **restaurant** noted for its partridge dishes. On the main road on the village's eastern edge the *Balcón de Válor* (T 958 85 18 21, W www.balcondevalor.com; ❹) has attractive fully equipped apartments, with terraces and sharing a pool. The tranquillity here doesn't seem to have been disturbed by the arrival of the *Aben Humeya* disco-pub (down a street almost opposite the *Hostal Las Perdices*) which, in daytime transmutes into a tranquil bar serving up good **tapas** and *platos combinados*, with a €9 *menú*.

UGÍJAR, 6km on from Válor, is the largest community of this eastern sector, and an unassuming, quiet market town. There are easy and enjoyable walks to the nearest villages – up the valley to Mecina-al-Fahar, for example – and plenty of **places to stay**. Try the comfortable *Hostal Pedro*, c/Fábrica de Sedes s/n (T 958 76 71 49; ❷), which has en-suite heated rooms with TV, or the nearby *Hostal-Restaurante Vidaña* (T&F 958 76 70 10; ❶) on the Almería road which has good-value en-suite rooms above a **restaurant** with outdoor terrace and a good-value *menú* for €8.50. The town's best place to eat, however, is *Pepe Aguado*, Trasera de la Iglesia 8, behind the church, specializing in *carnes a la brasa* (charcoal grilled meats). Two **tapas bars** to seek out are *Bar La Peña* on the corner of the main road by the church, serving a bargain *menú* for €8 (their *sopa de picadillo* is delicious) and where a huge *tapa* comes with every drink, and *Bar Progreso*, just a few metres away up a side street. About 150m beyond the church in the direction of Lanjarón, *Info-Ugíjar* (T 958 76 70 72) is a small **internet** café. **Buses**, which stop in the central plaza, run onwards to Almería (3hr). Slightly west of Ugíjar a road heads north to Laroles to join the A337, which climbs over Puerto de la Ragua pass (see p.539), descending beyond to the spectacular castle of La Calahorra (see p.538) on the northern slopes of the Sierra Nevada.

With your own transport you may wish to detour 10km to **JORAIRÁTAR** to take in the remarkable **Museo Historico de las Alpujarras** (daily 1–8pm; free; T 958 85 31 14, Spanish only). Occupying two floors of an enormous building, the museum is a labour of love devoted to the disappearing traditions and way of life of the people of the Alpujarras. Spread over numerous rooms, highlights include a reconstructed kitchen kitted-out as it would have been a hundred years ago and a school room complete with period desks, in addition to firewater stills, musical instruments, books and maps, plus a host of other fascinating paraphernalia. When you arrive in the village, a charming place in itself, make for the *barrio alto* (upper village) and ask for the house of the museum's guardian, Señora Angelita Martínez, and her husband Juan Soría who will give you an enthusiastic tour (a little Spanish would be an advantage). A contribution to the museum's upkeep is likely to be much appreciated.

To get to Jorairátar from Ugíjar, take the A348 in the direction of Cádiar, turning off (after some five kilometres) along the SE29 to reach the village.

The Almerian Alpujarras

From Ugíjar the A348 toils eastwards and, once across the Río de Alcolea, enters the province of Almería where the starker – but no less impressive terrain – gradually takes on the harsh and desiccated character of the deserts that lie ahead. There are still the odd oases to be found, however, in **Láujar de Andarax** and the spa of **Alhama de Almería** and, just beyond the latter, a remarkable prehistoric site, **Los Millares**.

Laroles and Bayárcal

If you're in no hurry to reach Láujar, a scenic detour along the A337 and AL612 through the hamlets of Laroles and Bayárcal offers a chance to see some of the National Park's magnificent upland terrain, and the possibility of overnighting at two attractive bases for exploring an area rich in trekking possibilities and on the route of the E4 (marked GR7 on Spanish maps) pan-European footpath. At **LAROLES**, 12km from Ugíjar, the *Refugio de Nevada*, c/Mairenas s/n (T 958 76 03 20, W www.refugiodenevada.com; ❷–❸), has comfortable en-suite heated rooms with TV and stunning views, and they also rent out some slightly more expensive fully equipped studios; **food** is available at their own good restaurant or at the nearby village bars, and the attractive village swimming pool is sited at the rear of the building. On the village's western edge there's a decent **campsite**, *Puerto de las Espinas* (T 958 76 02 31), with a good pool. Five kilometres further (via a short cut just outside Laroles) in **BAYÁRCAL**, the *Posada de los Arrieros* (T 950 52 40 01, W www.posadadelosarrieros.com; ❸ with breakfast) is a wonderful stone-built mountain hotel, and well equipped to withstand the winter snows that engulf it until well into spring. There are comfortable heated en-suite rooms and Swiss-style chalets nearby sleeping up to four persons. Use of their **bunkhouse** is also possible (own sleeping bag required; ❶). The hotel's **restaurant** – serving hearty *alpujarreño* specialities – is recommended and has a good-value *menú*. Built on the site of an old muleteers' inn on this important commercial route between the Alpujarras and Almería, there are spectacular **walks** to be made from the hotel including one to the Puerta de la Ragua, which at 2000m is Andalucía's highest pass. Information on this and other walks in the area is available from the hotel's friendly English-speaking staff, and horseriding, mountain biking and archery are also on offer. The cool temperatures at this altitude (even in Aug) make walking in this area pleasant all summer, although you still need to protect yourself from the sun.

Láujar de Andarax

It was at **LÁUJAR DE ANDARAX**, 16km east of Ugíjar, at the source of the Río Andarax, that Boabdil, the deposed Moorish king of Granada, settled in 1492 and from where he intended to rule the Alpujarras fiefdom granted to him by the Catholic monarchs. But Christian paranoia about a Moorish resurgence led them to tear up the treaty and within a year Boabdil had been shipped off to Africa, an event which set in train a series of uprisings by the Alpujarran Moors, ending in their suppression and eventual deportation, to be replaced by Christian settlers from the north.

The **Río Andarax's source** is at the town's eastern edge – signposted (*nacimiento*) – and is a pleasant and shady spot, with a restaurant, the *Mesón El*

Nacimiento, serving hearty *platos combinados* at lunch time, beside the falls. If you're here on a Sunday you'll find the falls a hive of activity as families pour in to make barbecues at a line of purpose-built "barbies" under the trees. In Láujar's centre the **Plaza Mayor** has a seventeenth-century four-spouted fountain – one of many dotted around the town – and an elegant late eighteenth-century **Ayuntamiento**, where you can pick up a street map. This will enable you to find four crumbling seventeenth-century **palacios** as well as an impressive Mudéjar-style seventeenth-century church of **La Encarnación**, which contains a sculpture of the Virgin by Alonso Cano. The eastern panhandle of the Sierra Nevada National Park lies 15km to the north of Láujar and a National Park **information office**, the Centro de Visitantes (Thurs–Sun 10.30am–2.30pm & 5–7pm,) is located on the edge of the town as you come in from Ugíjar.

Láujar is the centre of a burgeoning **wine industry**, and although smoother and slightly less potent than the *costa* wines further west, the brew is just as palatable. The Cooperativo Valle de Láujar, on the main road 2km west of town, was founded in 1992 and is beginning to commercialize these wines both within Spain and abroad. At their small shop (Mon–Sat 8.30am–noon & 3.30–7.30pm) you can taste and buy their four good reds as well as whites and a rosé, and their *digestif* made from grape juice, coffee and *anís*, plus cheeses and other local produce.

Láujar offers two **accommodation** possibilities: the budget option, *Hostal Nuevo Andarax*, c/Canalejas 27 (T950 51 31 13; ❷), lies west of the centre along the main street, with en-suite rooms above a bar-restaurant. Alternatively, the good-value *Hotel Almirez*, on the main road at the extreme western edge of town (T&F950 51 35 14, Wwww.hotelalmirez.es; ❷), has en-suite balcony rooms with TV, plus its own restaurant.

East to Alhama de Almería

The road east of Láujar de Andarax passes a series of unremarkable villages, surrounded by slopes covered with vine trellises, little changed since Moorish times and little visited today. Among them is **FONDÓN**, with a **campsite** (T950 51 42 90) and whose church tower was the minaret of the former mosque, and **PADULES**, 11km beyond Láujar, where the municipal swimming pool might prove a greater lure in the baking heat of high summer. The prettier village of **CANJÁYAR**, 4km further on, also has a swimming pool, and becomes a centre of frenetic activity during the autumn *vendimia*, when the grapes are gathered in.

The road then trails the course of the Andarax river valley through an arid and eroded landscape, skirting the Sierra de Gádor before climbing slightly to **ALHAMA DE ALMERÍA**, 16km further on. This is a pleasant spa town, dating back to Moorish times, and most of its visitors are here to take the waters – hence the rather incongruous three-star *Hotel San Nicolás*, c/Baños s/n (T951 64 13 61, Wwww.balneariosannicolas.es; ❹), sited on the location of the original baths. If you want a cheaper **place to stay** – and Los Millares (see p.532) is a reason why you might – the unsigned *Pensión Chiquito*, c/Pablo Picasso 5, near the church (T950 64 02 31, Tmobile 625379850; ❷), has very pleasant a/c en-suite rooms with TV. The only **places to eat** are a couple of *raciónes* bars along the main street or at the restaurant of the *Hotel San Nicolás*. Alhama also has a delightful municipal **swimming pool** with plenty of shade, close to a magnificent **cascade** tumbling down rocks at the western end of the town. Information on the limited transport to Los Millares is available from a new and central Turismo, c/Médicos 13 (Mon–Fri 10am–2pm & 6–8pm, Sat 9am–1pm; T950 64 04 69) It's worth noting that there is **no public transport** from here or the provincial capital to the Los Millares site, although the 5km distance is walkable at a push or you could take a taxi (about €7 one-way).

Los Millares: the Chalcolithic settlement

Leaving Alhama by the Almería road, after 5km the road passes a signed turn-off leading to the remarkable pre-Bronze Age settlement of **LOS MILLARES**, one of the most important of its kind in Europe. Situated on a low triangular spur between two dried-up riverbeds, it was exposed in 1891 during the construction of the Almería-to-Linares railway line that passes below the site today. Two Belgian mining engineers, Henri and Louis Siret, who were also enthusiastic amateur archeologists, took on the excavations at the turn of the twentieth century, funding them from their modest salaries. What they revealed is a Chalcolithic or Copper Age (the period between the Neolithic and the Bronze Age) **fortified settlement**. It dates from c.2700 BC and was occupied until c.1800 BC, when both stone and copper but not bronze were used for weapons and tools. Whilst it is not entirely clear who the occupants were – possibly emigrants from the eastern Mediterranean or perhaps an indigenous group – the settlement they left behind is exceptional. Spread over twelve acres it consists of four sets of defensive walls, with a number of advanced fortlets beyond these, as well as an extraordinary cemetery with over one hundred **tombs** which are without equal in Europe.

Looking over the barren landscape that surrounds the site today, it's hard to believe that five thousand years ago this was a fertile area of pine and ilex forests, inhabited by deer and wild boar. The nearby Río Andarax was then navigable and the inhabitants used it to bring copper down from mines in the Sierra de Gádor to the west. The population – perhaps as many as two thousand – not only hunted for their food but bred sheep, goats and pigs, grew vegetables and cereals, made cheese and were highly skilled in the manufacture of pottery, basketwork and jewellery, as is evidenced by the finds now in museums in Almería (see p.547) and Madrid.

Excavations are continuing at the site and information boards (in English and Spanish) have been set up at various points; a map on the wall of the entrance office shows **walking routes** outside the site which take in dolmens and ten forts related to the Los Millares settlement discovered in the surrounding hills.

The most impressive of the forts (with fine **views** over the Los Millares site), *Fortín Uno* (Fort One), lies up a track on the opposite side of the road from the site entrance and the site guardians will advise how to reach it.

The site

A tour of the **site** (Wed–Sun 10am–2pm; free; ring to confirm opening hours ☎950 01 11 31 or mobile 677903404; the Almería Turismos can also advise) begins with the outermost of four exterior **walls** which were constructed successively further west as the settlement expanded across the escarpment in the latter part of the third millennium BC. An impressive structure, 4m high when built, the fourth (and last) wall was lined with outward-facing bastions or towers, and at 310m is the longest wall known in Europe from this period. Its layout bears a striking similarity to a wall of the same epoch at the early Cycladic site of Halandriani on the island of Síros in Greece, suggesting a possible link with the Aegean. The **main gate**, towards the centre, is flanked by watchtowers, beyond which a walled passage gave access to the settlement.

A little way north of here are the remains of a primitive **aqueduct** which cut through the wall to carry water from a spring near to the village of Alhama into the populated area. Fifty metres east of the main gate remains can be seen from the third wall. Close to here also are the remains of a number of circular **huts** – one of which has been partially reconstructed – in which the inhabitants of the site lived. Six to seven metres in diameter with pounded earth floors, they consisted of cavity stone walls filled with mud and pebbles, with a roof probably made from straw. Inside the huts the excavators found remains of hearths as well as grindstones, pottery and a variety of utensils.

Moving east again, beyond the second wall lies a primitive **foundry** where the copper ore was crudely smelted by means of fire and bellows before being hammered into the required form. Moulds arrived only in the later Bronze Age. Further north, on the line of the wall, lies a **silo** used for storing grain. Behind this wall are the foundations of a **rectangular edifice**, 32m in length, whose function is as yet unknown. The settlement at first appeared to lack a hierarchical social structure due to the overall similarity of the huts, but after the discovery of this building – much larger than the rest – some have speculated that it could have served as a form of council chamber or even a royal palace.

The remains of the first wall, enclosing what may have been the citadel, lie further back still and excavations here recovered many of the patterned, bell-shaped vases to be seen in the museum at Almería.

The necropolis

Retracing your steps to the outer (or fourth) wall will bring you to one of the reconstructed tombs, part of the ancient **necropolis**. This "beehive" tomb, originally sited outside the third wall, was encompassed by the later fourth wall. It is one of more than a hundred tombs (the rest lie west of this wall), and the typical structure of a low corridor punctuated by perforated slate slabs leading to a domed burial chamber bears a striking resemblance to tholos tombs of a similar date from the Aegean, particularly southern Crete. It has been suggested that early Cretans (for whom the bull was religiously significant) may have found their way here and that the importance of bulls and bullfighting on the Iberian peninsula may owe something to this link. Present academic thinking, however, tends towards the idea that the civilization here was of local origin.

More tombs, most in a collapsed state, in which clan members were buried together with their possessions such as arms, tools and what appear to be ceramic idols (suggesting the existence of a cult), lie beyond the outer wall.

Originally, and again as in the Aegean, the tombs were covered with an earth mound or tumulus. Try to resist climbing over them as many are in a fragile condition and the importance of this site for posterity is hard to overstate.

Guadix, Baza and La Calahorra

An alternative route from Granada to Almería – via the N342 and A92 and covered by Empresa Autodía buses from the main bus station – goes via **Guadix**, a crumbling old Moorish town with a vast and extraordinary cave district. For those with transport, the route also offers the opportunity for a detour to the impressive Renaissance castle of **La Calahorra**.

To the northeast, the A92N *autovía* speeds traffic from Guadix towards Lorca and Murcia, and there is a possible stop at the pleasant market town of **Baza** beyond which the road pushes on through a sparsely populated landscape for the 70km between here and the towns of Vélez Rubio (p.563) and Vélez Blanco (p.564).

Guadix

Sited on the banks of the Río Guadix, in the midst of a fertile plain, **GUADIX** is a ramshackle, windblown sort of town, often coated in the red dust which gusts in from the surrounding hills. It's not a particularly attractive place and if it were not for its remarkable cave district there would be little reason to stop.

An ancient settlement dating back to Paleolithic times, it became the Roman town of Julia Gemella Acci in 45 BC, established by Julius Caesar as a base for exploiting seams of silver in the surrounding hills. Following a period of decline during the Visigothic era, the conquering Moors revived its fortunes, renaming the town Guadh-Haix ("River of Life"), and it rapidly grew in size, soon becoming a rival for Granada. It was renowned for its poetry, and bards such as Ibn Tofayl sang the praises of Guadix's beauty and its valley. It was also during the Moorish period that the town developed an important silk industry, whose mulberry trees can still be seen along the river. More recently, industrial development was based upon the production of esparto grass products and cutlery. Guadix endured terrifying atrocities during the Civil War, which Gerald Brenan vividly described in *South from Granada*.

Arrival and information

Guadix is not a large place and, if you arrive at the **bus** station (frequent services to and from Granada and Almería), to the southeast of the centre off Avenida Medina Olmos, it's easy enough to set your sights on the walls and cathedral – around five-minutes' walk. The **train station** (4 services daily to and from Granada and Almería) is on the northeast side of town, 1.5km out along Avda. de Buenos Aires (the Murcia road). A small and helpful **Turismo** (Mon–Fri 9am–1.30pm & 4–6pm; ☎958 69 95 74) along the Avda. Mariana Pineda (aka Ctra. de Granada), not far from the cathedral, will provide a useful town **map**, or many of the kioskos around the centre will sell you a small fold-out version. **Internet** access is available at Habana Café Internet, Plaza de la Constitución 4, near the cathedral.

Accommodation

Should you want a **place to stay** overnight, the *Hotel Mulhacén*, Avda. Buenos Aires 41 (☎958 66 07 50, ⊕958 66 06 61; ❸), is near the centre and functional.

The slightly higher priced *Hotel Comercio*, c/Mira de Amezcua 3 (☎958 66 05 00, ⓦwww.hotelcomercio.com;❹),an elegant and refurbished turn-of-the-twentieth-century hotel, is easily the best place in town. Rooms here come with a/c, minibar, room safe and TV and guests get a free sampler of their spa and sauna.

If you're taken with the idea of cave life there's a chance to experience it for a night in the cave district at the spotless cave *Hostal Chez Jean & Julia*, c/Ermita Nueva 67 (☎958 66 91 91, ⓦwww.altipla.com/jj; ❷ with breakfast), where you have a choice of a double "cave room" sharing bath or your own en-suite cave apartment (sleeping up to four; ❹) with salon, kitchen and washing machine. It's near the cave museum (see p.536) and to find it make your way there and give the proprietors a ring for directions (English spoken). Another possibility is the cave hotel *Pedro Antonio Alarcón* (☎958 66 49 86, ⓦwww.cuevaspedroantonio .com; ❹), on the other side of town beyond the train station; this is a more luxurious complex of nineteen caves with pool, gardens and restaurant; it lies a couple of kilometres from the centre along Avenida de Buenos Aires.

The Town

Guadix's old quarter is still largely walled, and the circuit includes an imposing Moorish gateway, the Puerta San Turcuato. Within, it's dominated by the red sandstone towers of its sixteenth-century **Catedral** (Mon–Sat 10.30am–1pm plus April–Sept 5–7pm, Oct–March 4–6pm; €3) – circled on Saturdays by a lively **market** – built on the site of a former mosque. This has been much hacked around and embellished over the years and the exterior is eighteenth-century Corinthian, the work of Vincente Acero. The sombre, late-Gothic interior was designed by Diego de Siloé, based on that of the cathedral at Málaga. Its best feature is the superb Churrigueresque choir stalls by Ruíz del Peral. Civil War reminders from both sides of the conflict include the defaced and destroyed heads of the saints on the carved marble pulpit and, near to the entrance, two plaques recording the names of local priests "killed by Marxism".

Just across from the cathedral entrance, beneath an arch, stands the elegant **Plaza Mayor** (aka Plaza de la Constitución), an arcaded Renaissance square which was reconstructed after severe damage in the Civil War. A right turn in the stepped street (c/Santisteban) at the far end of the square leads up to the Renaissance **Palacio de Peñaflor**. Nearby in the Placeta de Santiago the whitewashed church of **Santiago** (daily 6.15–7pm; free), another work by de Siloé, has an imposing Plateresque entrance and, inside, a beautiful *artesonado* ceiling.

Next to the Peñaflor mansion, a former theological seminary alongside the sixteenth-century church of **San Agustín** gives access to the conclusively

Fiesta de los Cascamorros

Guadix and Baza are linked by old rivalries that are kept alive in the annual **Fiesta de los Cascamorros** from September 6–9. At the outset of this festival, a man dressed as a jester and carrying a sceptre walks from Guadix to Baza in an attempt to retrieve an ancient image of the Virgin, over which the two towns have disputed ownership since the sixteenth century. However, to retrieve the sacred image from the church, he must remain unblemished and so, as he nears Baza, a huge reception committee awaits him armed with drums of used engine oil at the ready.

Needless to say, he is coated from head to toe in the stuff within seconds of crossing the city limits – as are a whole crowd of the Virgin's protectors – and the oily mass then squelches its way to the Plaza Mayor where, amidst the tolling of church bells, the mayor (from the safety of a balcony) proclaims that Guadix has blown it yet again, after which the town lets rip on a three-day binge of celebration.

ruined ninth-century Moorish **Alcazaba**. At the time of writing the town council has purchased both the disused seminary and the Alcazaba and a major programme of rebuilding and restoration has begun. This programme of work has been delayed by ongoing archeological investigations and, once these are complete, the Turismo will be able to advise on the new visiting times. From the Alcazaba's battlements there are **views** over the cave district of Santiago (see below) and beyond towards the Sierra Nevada.

The cave district

South of the Alcazaba and sited in a weird landscape of pyramidal red hills, the **Barrio de las Cuevas** or cave district still houses some ten thousand people (most of whom, and contrary to popular belief, are not *gitanos* or gypsies), and to take a look round it is the main reason for most visitors stopping off.

The quarter extends over a square mile or so in area, and the lower caves, on the outskirts, are really proper cottages sprouting television aerials, with upper storeys, electricity and running water. But as you walk deeper into the suburb, the design quickly becomes simpler – just a whitewashed front, a door, a tiny window and a chimney – and the experience increasingly voyeuristic. Penetrating right to the back you'll come upon a few caves which are no longer used: too squalid, too unhealthy to live in, their whitewash faded to a dull brown. Yet right next door there may be a similar, occupied hovel, with a family sitting outside, and other figures following dirt tracks still deeper into the hills.

Be aware that offers to show you around the interior of a cave will often be followed by a demand for substantial sums of money when you emerge. A **Cueva Museo**, Plaza Padre Poveda (Cave Museum; Mon–Fri 10am–2pm & 4–6pm, Sat 10am–2pm; €2.50), opposite the church of San Miguel (aka Iglesia de las Cuevas) – and signed along c/San Miguel heading south from the centre – is the easiest way to get an understanding of cave culture. Sited in a series of rehabilitated cave dwellings, it documents the history and reality of cave living with audiovisual aids and reconstructed rooms.

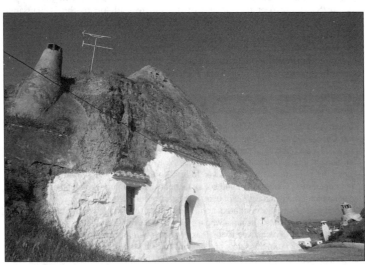

▲ Cave dwelling in Guadix

Eating, drinking and nightlife

The **restaurant** of the ⚒ *Hotel Comercio* is the best in town – the *perdiz* (partridge) dishes are recommended – with a good-value *menú* for €12. Another decent option, *Boabdil*, c/Manuel de Falla 3, with great salads, is to be found halfway between the cathedral and the Turismo, turning right off Avda. Mariana Pineda. To the northeast of the cathedral, *La Bodeguilla*, c/Doctor Pulido 4, is another good option for tapas and *raciónes* in a splendid old *bodega*. For even cheaper meals head for the Plaza de Naranjos, a stone's throw east of the cathedral. Here, among a bunch of popular eating places, *Cafetería Cart Luis* does **tapas**, **raciónes**, hamburgers and a cheap *menú*.

Baza

BAZA, 44km northeast of Guadix along the A92N, is another old Moorish town, well worth a detour if you have time and transport. Approached through an ochre landscape dotted with weird conical hillocks covered with esparto grass, the town is slightly smaller than Guadix, with a web of streets encircling its ancient central plaza. As with many towns in these parts, it has a history dating back well into prehistoric times. A prosperous Iberian settlement here named *Basti* produced the remarkable *Dama de Baza* sculpture (see p.538) and the town remained a considerable centre under the Romans, and later, like Guadix, a focus of silk production under the Moors; it was especially renowned for its silk prayer mats. Taken by Christian forces in 1489 after a long siege, the town has had a less-than-glorious past few centuries, in part due to trouble from earthquakes, which have crumbled away most of the old Moorish Alcazaba. Like Guadix, Baza also has a **cave quarter**, albeit less touristic, on the northern side of town, close to the bullring.

Heading on from Baza, possible destinations include the Cazorla Natural Park, to the north, or the Almería coast via the A92N *autovía* with the option of a detour to Orce, the site of sensational finds concerning early humans in Spain, and the prehistoric cave paintings at Vélez Rubio.

Arrival, information and accommodation

The **bus station** (with frequent connections to Guadix) is located on Avenida Reyes Católicos to the west of the centre, and an easy five-minute walk to the Plaza Mayor. In the Plaza Mayor's Museo Arqueológico (see p.538), a **tourist office** (April–Sept Mon 10am–2pm, Tues–Fri 10am–2pm & 5.30–7pm, Sat & Sun 11am–2pm; Oct–March Mon–Fri 4.30–6.30pm, Sat & Sun 11am–2pm; ☏958 86 13 25) will provide you with a good town map. When this office is closed, maps are also available from the reception of the Ayuntamiento on the opposite side of the Plaza Mayor.

There are limited **places to stay** in Baza, but demand is usually low outside festival periods. The only central option is the very comfortable *Hotel Anabel* (☏958 86 09 98; ❸), about four blocks east of the Plaza Mayor at c/María de Luna s/n, with its own restaurant. A ten-minute walk south of the centre, *Hostal Casa Grande*, Ctra. de Ronda 28 (☏958 70 27 32; ❷), has excellent-value, immaculate non-smoking en-suite rooms with a/c, heating and TV. It also has its own very good restaurant with a €7 *menú* next door.

The Town

The impressive Renaissance collegiate church of **Santa María** – and its eighteenth-century brick tower – leads you to the pedestrianized Plaza Mayor. Built over an earlier mosque, the church's elegant **Plateresque main door** – attributed to Diego de Siloé – is worth a look and inside there's an interesting marble pulpit and elegant vaulting. On the opposite side of the Plaza Mayor, a small **Museo Arqueológico** (Mon–Fri 9am–2pm, Sat 11am–2pm; free) preserves finds from the town's ancient past, including a copy of the *Dama de Baza*, a magnificent life-size fourth-century BC Iberian painted sculpture unearthed in 1971 in a necropolis on the outskirts of the town. The original is now in Madrid, where it is exhibited alongside the century-later *Dama de Elche*, another iconic work of Spain's early artistic tradition.

A few-minutes' walk to the east of Plaza Mayor, following c/Cabeza then turning left along c/del Agua, are the **Baños Árabes**, an impressive tenth-century Moorish bath complex – one of the oldest surviving in Spain. At the time of writing the Junta de Andalucía had purchased the baths from the private owner and – following a programme of restoration – they will soon be reopened to the public. Consult the tourist office for the opening times. Close to the baths the **Iglesia de Santiago** (service times only, try 7–8pm), Plaza de Santiago, is a fine sixteenth-century church built over a former mosque and inside has a magnificent Mudéjar *artesonado* coffered ceiling in nave and apse.

Eating and drinking

There are plenty of places for **eating** and **drinking** in Baza, including the excellent *La Curva*, c/Corredera 3 (☎958 70 00 02), a few blocks northeast of the Plaza Mayor, a mid-priced restaurant renowned for its ham and seafood. *Mesón Siglo XX*, c/Solares 5, slightly southeast of here, is the kind of splendid local restaurant that Andalucía excels in; an all-female kitchen cooks up a range of local delicacies including great soups, stews and a tasty paella, and the *menú* is a gift at €9. *Mesón los Moriscos*, c/Cava Alta 3, 100m north of the church of Santa María, lives up to its name and dishes up fine tapas and *platos combinados* in a mini-Alhambra inspired dining room. A cluster of pleasant **tapas bars** – some with terraces – lie slightly west of the Plaza Mayor at the end of c/Serrano, with *Bar Perdiz* and *La Solana* good possibilities. Just south of here, *Bar Los Canteros*, in Plaza Arcipreste Juan Hernández, is another good place for seafood and meat *raciónes* with a pleasant terrace. The terrace of the *Casino* on the west side of the Plaza Mayor is a great place for a leisurely **breakfast** and they also serve up tapas later in the day.

La Calahorra

Continuing southeast of Guadix along the A92 to Almería, the spectacular domed Renaissance castle of **La Calahorra** heaves into view at the 16km point. A turn-off to the right takes you the 4km to the village of the same name, where, on a hill above it, this brooding red stone monster was constructed in 1509–12. Its architect was Italian and its owner, one Rodrigo de Mendoza, was the bastard son of the powerful Cardinal Mendoza, who did much to establish Isabel on the throne. Rodrigo, created marquis of Zenete by Isabel, acquired a taste for the Renaissance during an Italian sojourn, and ordered the castle as a wedding gift for his wife, María de Fonseca. The bleak situation proved unattractive both to them and to their descendants, however, and it was rarely used.

The privately owned castle is open to the public on Wednesdays only (10am–1pm & 4–6pm; €3); outside these times access is possible by visiting c/de los Claveles 2 in the village (☎958 67 70 98; avoid siesta time), home of the guardian, Antonino Tribáldoz who was born in the castle. Once inside you'll be able to view an exquisite Renaissance **patio** – the last thing you'd expect behind such a dour exterior. The doorways, arches and stairway of this two-storey courtyard are beautifully carved from Carrara marble. Some of the palace's rooms have finely crafted *artesonado* ceilings and there's also a curious women's prison. Leave your vehicle at the bottom of the boulder-strewn track leading up to the castle and walk up to avoid severe damage to the underside of your hire car.

Rooms are available at the comfortable *Hospedería del Zenete*, Ctra. La Ragua 1 (T&F 958 67 71 92, W www.hospederiadelzenete.com; **5**), the road leading into the village, a four-star hotel with great views of the castle from most rooms (make sure to request this). One plus point about staying here is that if you ring at least 24 hours ahead they will arrange a visit to the castle for you. The hotel's **bar–restaurant** is good for tapas and formal meals and has an economical *menú*. Further along the same road, *Hostal-Restaurante La Bella*, Crta. de Aldeire 1 (T 958 67 70 00, W www.hostallabella.com; **2**), in the village proper, is the budget option and offers good a/c rooms with TV above a restaurant with a decent weekday €9 *menú*.

From La Calahorra, a lonely but scenic mountain road – the A337 – toils south to the **Puerto de la Ragua**, at 1993m Andalucía's highest all-weather pass. The hairpin climb offers spectacular views back over the plain of the Hoya de Guadix and the rose-tinted La Calahorra castle. When you reach the pass – where it can be chilly even in high summer – you'll find a pleasant **refuge** with comfortable bunk accommodation and a restaurant. To be certain of a bed, ring ahead (T 958 34 51 62, English spoken; **1**). Antonio Mesa, the friendly warden, can provide details of fine **walks** in the vicinity, plus horseriding and (in winter) cross-country skiing, both available at the refuge. There's also **an information centre** here (Thurs–Sun 10am–2.30pm plus Sat 5–7pm; T 950 52 40 20) with maps of the area. Beyond the pass the road forks, offering alternative descents to the Alpujarras villages of Válor or Ugíjar to the west, and Láujar de Andarax in the east. Forking left towards Láujar would bring you to Bayárcal and the superb mountain hotel *Posada de los Arrieros* (see p.530).

Towards Almería

East beyond La Calahorra, the A92 crosses the border into Almería and passes by **FIÑANA**, with another **castle**, this time Moorish and in a more ruinous state, and a well-preserved Moorish **mezquita**. Some 25km further on there's a turn-off for **GÉRGAL**, with another well-preserved fortress and, on the highest summit of the Sierra de los Filabres behind, an observatory housing one of the largest telescopes in Europe, sited here by a German–Spanish venture to take advantage of the almost constantly clear skies (see p.567). The A92 gradually descends into the valley of the Río Andarax – where you could detour to the prehistoric site of Los Millares (see p.532) – which it follows for the final 15km to Almería.

Almería

Cuando Almería era Almería
Granada era su alquería

When Almería was Almería
Granada was but its farm.

Traditional Almerian couplet

ALMERÍA is a pleasant and largely modern city, spread at the foot of a stark grey hill dominated by a magnificent Moorish fort. Founded by the Phoenicians and developed by the Romans, who named it Portus Magnus, it was as a

RESTAURANTS & TAPAS BARS

Añorga	12
Bar Bahía de la Palma	15
Bodega El Ajoli	11
Bodega Aranda	5
Bodega Las Botas	6
Bodega Montenegro	17
Bodega Ortega	4
Casa Joaquín	18
Casa Puga	14
El Quinto Toro	7
El Quinto Toro II	10
La Encina	13
La Espartería	2
Los Sobrinos	21
Marisquería Veracruz	19
Pavía	20
Peña Taurina Almeriense	3
Restaurante Alfareros	1
Restaurante Torreluz Mediterraneo	9
Restaurante Valentin	8
Tetería-Restaurante Almedína	16

ACCOMMODATION

Hostal Estación	D
Hostal Nixar	C
Hotel Costasol	F
Hotel La Perla	B
Hotel Sevilla	A
Hotel Torreluz	E

▼ Motril, Málaga & 21

Moorish city – renamed al-Mariyat (The Mirror of the Sea) – that Almería grew to prominence. The sultan Abd ar-Rahman I began the building programme soon after the conquest, in 713, with an arsenal beside the port, and the great **Alcazaba**, still the town's dominant feature, was added in the tenth century by Abd ar-Rahman III when the city formed part of the Cordoban caliphate.

The splendours created here by the Moors – most of which have been lost – inspired the popular rhyme at the beginning of this section, contrasting this early prosperity with the much later glories of Nasrid Granada. After the collapse of Moorish Córdoba, Almería's prosperity was hardly affected and, as a principality or *taifa* state, it became the country's major port, famed for its exports of silk, as well as a pirates' nest feared around the adjacent coasts. This period ended when the city fell to the forces of Fernando in 1490 and the Moors were expelled. Their possessions and lands were doled out to the officers of the conquering army, forming the basis for the *señoritismo* which has plagued

Almería and Andalucía throughout modern times. Predictably, there followed a prolonged decline over the next three hundred years, reversed only by the introduction of the railway and the building of a new harbour in the nineteenth century, as well as the opening up to exploitation of the province's vast mineral wealth, particularly iron, lead and gold.

The Civil War interrupted this progress. The city's communist dockworkers gave staunch backing to the Republic, at one point in 1937 causing Hitler to order that the city be subjected to aerial bombardment and shelled from offshore by the German fleet (see p.547). It was one of the last cities to fall to Franco's forces in 1939, after which many suicides took place to avoid the fate planned for the most bitter enemies of the new order.

Although still the centre of one of the poorest areas in Europe, Almería today is seeking a more prosperous future based upon intensive vegetable production in the surrounding *vega*, in tandem with gaining a greater share of Spain's tourist economy. Whilst even its most devoted admirers wouldn't describe it as a beautiful place, the provincial capital deserves more visitors than it gets. Enjoying something of a recent renaissance, the city has sunk enormous funds into smartening up the town centre which has areas with considerable charm. Add to this a handful of fascinating sights and a friendly welcome in some great bars and restaurants, and you may be induced to give it a bit longer than the customary one-night transit.

Arrival, orientation and information

Almería's **bus station** (☎950 26 20 98) and **train station** (☎902 24 02 02) have recently been combined into a striking Estación Intermodal, Carretera de Ronda s/n, a couple of blocks east of the Avenida de Federico García Lorca, with the bus terminals and train platforms side by side. The splendid old stone, brick and steel nineteenth-century **train station** at Plaza de la Estación s/n, beside the new edifice, is worth a look, and is possibly going to be revamped as a cultural centre. Almería's **airport** (☎950 21 37 00), 8km east from the city along the coast, handles scheduled budget services from the UK and other parts of Europe. For airport buses and details of onward travel, see p.550 and "Travel details", p.570.

The **Avenida de Federico García Lorca**, formerly an unsightly dry river-bed but now dramatically transformed into a stately avenue with palms, fountains and newsstands, bisects the city from north to south. Most of the action takes place to the west of this artery, where you'll find the **old town** and, to the north, the **Puerta de Purchena**, a busy traffic junction where six thoroughfares meet, effectively marking the centre of the modern city.

The **Turismo** (June–Sept Mon–Fri 9am–7.30pm, Sat & Sun 9.30am–3pm; Oct–May Mon–Thurs 8.30am–3pm, Fri–Sun 8.30am–2pm & 5–7.30pm; ☎950 17 52 20), at Parque Nicolás Salmarón s/n (junction with c/Martínez Campos) and fronting the harbour, has a good city map (€0.60). The friendly **Oficina Turistica Municipal**, Avda. Federico García Lorca s/n (Mon–Fri 8.30am–2pm & 5–7.30pm; Sat–Sun 8.30am–2pm; ☎950 28 07 48), has lots of information on the town and province, including a good map and a free

Almería online

Online information on Almería, its monuments and amenities and the province in general can be found at ⓦwww.almeria-turismo.org, ⓦwww.almeriacultura.com, ⓦwww.indalia.es and ⓦwww.andalucia.org.

tapas-bar guide. They also offer a guided tour of the town (Fri, Sat & Sun 10.30am; €1.50) departing from the Puerta Purchena.

Accommodation

Rooms are generally easy to come by at any time of the year and there are concentrations of *hostales* and hotels around the focal Puerta de Purchena. Note that *hostal* rates here tend to be higher than elsewhere in the province. Almería's nearest **campsite**, *La Garrofa* (☎950 23 57 70), lies 5km west, on the coast at La Garrofa, and is easily reached by the buses to Aguadulce and Roquetas de Mar (where there's another, giant site).

Albergue Juvenil Almería c/Isla de Fuerteventura s/n ☎950 17 51 36, Ⓦwww.inturjoven.com. Almería's swish and friendly youth hostel has 150 double rooms and some singles, all en suite. It lies on the east side of town next to the Estadio Juventud sports arena; take bus #1 from the junction of Rambla del Obispo Orberá and Avda. F. García Lorca (top right corner of our map). Under 26 €16, over 26 €20, ❷.

Hostal Estación c/Calzada de Castro 37 ☎950 26 72 39. Sited close to the train and bus stations with decently furnished en-suite rooms and garage parking. ❷

Hostal Nixar c/Antonio Vico 24 ☎&Ⓕ 950 23 72 55. Decent-value en-suite rooms with a/c and TV in a quiet street; ask for the higher floors, which are airier. ❷–❸

Hotel Costasol Paseo de Almería 58 ☎950 23 40 11, Ⓦwww.hotelcostasol.com. Central and

comfortable hotel with spacious rooms; some on the front have terrace balcony. ❺

Hotel La Perla Plaza del Carmen 7 ☎950 23 88 77, Ⓦwww.githoteles.com. The city's oldest hotel has pleasant a/c rooms with satellite TV; some at the rear can be rather cramped, so check what you're offered. ❹

Hotel Sevilla c/Granada 25 ☎950 23 00 09. Welcoming, modern, small hotel with en-suite rooms equipped with a/c and TV. ❸

Hotel Torreluz Plaza Flores 2 ☎950 23 43 99, Ⓦwww.torreluz.es. The town's leading hotel contains good-value two-star and four-star options in the same complex. Aimed at the corporate sector, the rather staidly furnished rooms underline this. Weekend deals (in the four-star hotel) cut rates by 25 percent. ❸–❹

The Town

Almería's most impressive monument, the formidable **Alcazaba**, is probably the best surviving example of a Moorish military fortification. It can be reached by following any of the narrow streets which climb the hill west of the cathedral, aiming for the entrance below the walls in the Plaza Joaquín Santisteban, at the end of c/Almanzor. The city's other sights pale by comparison, though it is worth taking time to look over the **cathedral** and, nearby, Andalucía's regional **photographic museum**. More sights surround the focal **Puerta de Purchena** where some remarkable **air-raid shelters** from the Civil War have been opened up for visits while to the east lies the city's striking new **archeological museum** which should not be missed.

The city **beach**, southeast of the centre beyond the railway lines, is long but crammed for most of the summer. For a day-trip, the best options are Cabo de Gata or San José, both easily accessible by bus.

The Alcazaba

The **Alcazaba** (Tues–Sun 9am–8.30pm, closes 6.30pm Nov–March; €1.50, free with EU passport) was begun by Abd ar-Rahman III of Córdoba in 955 and was just one part of a massive building programme that included a great mosque and city walls. During the eleventh century when the city enjoyed a period of prosperous independence, between the fall of the Cordoban caliphate and its capture by the Almoravids, the medina (walled city) here contained immense

▲ Almería port with the Alcazaba behind

gardens and palaces and housed some twenty thousand people. It was adapted after the *Reconquista* by the Catholic monarchs but severely damaged during a great earthquake in 1522. A programme of restoration in recent years has begun to reverse the centuries of crumbling decay.

Through the **Puerta Exterior**, a zigzagged entrance ramp – a traditional Moorish architectural feature to make attack precarious – leads to the **Puerta de la Justicia**, the gateway to the first of the Alcazaba's three great compounds

Halfway up the ramp to the right is the **Tower of Mirrors**, a fifteenth-century addition, where mirrors were employed to communicate with ships approaching the port below.

The first compound

The first compound is the largest of the three. Now filled with delightful gardens and aromatic plants, it was originally designed as a military camp and an area in which the populace could seek protection when under siege. A **well** in the centre of this area raised water from a depth of 70m to supply the site. At the eastern end of the enclosure, the **Saliente Bastión** was a lookout point over the town below, and the sea beyond.

Below the north side of the compound, the **eleventh-century wall** (Muralla de San Cristóbal) descends the hill; it originally formed part of a great complex of walls, not only surrounding the city but also dividing it internally. Above the wall, which divides the first and second compounds, is the **Campana de Vela**, a bell erected during the eighteenth century to announce ships sighted nearing the port, or to summon soldiers to their battle stations.

The second compound

The second compound accommodated the Moorish kings, when resident in the city, and at other times served as the governor's quarters. In the eleventh century, when Almería was the wealthiest, most commercially active city of Spain, the buildings here were of unparalleled brilliance. Their grandeur was even reputed to rival the later court of Granada, but the ruins that remain today make a valid comparison impossible.

What you can see, however, are the remains of **cisterns**, the old **mosque** – converted into a chapel by the Reyes Católicos – and once palatial dwellings, but sadly no sign of the magnificent stuccowork said to equal that of the Alhambra, the last remnants of which were sold off by the locals in the eighteenth century. The **Ventana de Odalisca**, a *mirador* window in the compound's northern wall, is a poignant reminder of lost glory. A legend attached to this concerns an eleventh-century Moorish slave-girl, Galiana, the king's favourite, who fell in love with a prisoner and arranged to help him to escape. But the guards discovered them in the attempt and the prisoner threw himself from this window into the valley below, whilst Galiana died of a broken heart a few days later. Recent archeological excavations here have uncovered Moorish bath houses and other structures.

The third compound

The third and highest compound demonstrates the starkly contrasting style of the conquering Christians. When they took the city, the Catholic monarchs found the fortress substantially damaged due to an earthquake a couple of years before. They therefore built walls much stronger than the original Moorish structure, to cope with both potential future earthquakes and the recent innovation of artillery. Triangular in form, this upper fort is guarded by three semicircular towers built of ashlar masonry, both features at odds with the earlier Moorish design.

To the right, the **Torre del Homenaje** (Tower of Homage) bears the crumbling escutcheon of the Catholic monarchs and looks out over the **Patio de Armas** (Courtyard of Arms) where the guard would be assembled. From the **Torre de Pólvora** (Gunpowder Tower) and the battlements (take care as there are few handrails) fine views are to be had of the coast and of Almería's *gitano* cave quarter – the Barrio La Chanca – on a low hill to the west.

The Catedral

Located in the heart of the old quarter, the **Catedral** (Mon–Fri 10am–2pr
& 4–5.30pm, Sat 10am–2pm; €2) is another building with a fortress loo
about it. Begun in 1524 on the site of the great mosque – convenient!
destroyed by the 1522 earthquake – it was designed in the late-Gothic styl
by Diego de Siloé, the architect of the cathedral at Granada. Because of th
danger of attack in this period from Barbarossa and other Turkish and Nort
African pirate forces, the corner towers once held cannons. The threat was re
and not long after its construction the cathedral chapter is recorded purchasin
guns, muskets and gunpowder.

Like many of Andalucía's cathedrals, it was never completely finished and
may be that the city's inhabitants had no great affection for this austere gian
preferring instead their more intimate parish churches. The **exterior** is of littl
interest apart from a curious, pagan-looking relief of a garlanded radiant sun o
the eastern wall – that is, facing the rising sun. Echoing the Roman Sol Invictu
or unconquerable sun, its appearance on the church has been put down to
sixteenth-century bishop with masonic leanings, but its true significance wi
probably never be known. Appropriately, as the province with the highest sun
hours statistic in Spain, Almería now uses the image as its official logo.

The cathedral is entered through the Puerta Principal, an elegant Renaissanc
doorway flanked by buttresses. Within, the sober Gothic **interior** is distin
guished by some superb sixteenth-century choir stalls carved in walnut by Jua
de Orea. Just behind this, the **retrochoir** is a stunning eighteenth-century alta
in contrasting red and black jasper. Behind the Capilla Mayor (or high altar
with some elegant and sinuous vaulting, the Capilla de la Piedad has a paintin
of the *Annunciation* by Alonso Cano and *Immaculate Conception* by Murillo
whilst the Capilla de Santo Cristo – next door to the right – contains th
sixteenth-century sculptured tomb of Bishop Villalán, the cathedral's founde
complete with faithful hound at his feet. Further along again, a door (ofte
closed) leads to the sacristy and a rather uninspiring Renaissance cloister
relieved by a small garden with palms and orange trees. The church also contain
a number of fine **pasos** of the Passion carried in the Semana Santa processio
at Easter; among these, *El Prendimiento* (the Arrest of Christ) is outstanding.

Around the old town

West of the cathedral stands the seventeenth-century church of **San Juan** (ope
service times, daily 6.30–7.30pm; free), built over a tenth-century mosqu
Inside, the church's southern wall preserves the *mihrab* (or prayer niche) of th
original building. Next to this, there's another niche that would have containe
the wooden pulpit used for readings from the Koran.

Further west lies the **Barrio de Chanca**, an area of grinding povert
occupied by *gitanos* and hard-pressed fisherfolk which has hardly changed sinc
Brenan vividly described it in his *South from Granada*; there are some occupie
cave dwellings here, too, but it's not a place to visit alone at night. East toward
the port, on c/Hospital, the eighteenth-century **Hospital Real** has an elegan
Neoclassical facade and, inside, a beautiful marble-tiled patio usually containin
a few prostrate patients on hospital trolleys. Like many others in Spain, this is
still fully functioning infirmary two and a half centuries after it was built.

A couple of blocks south of the cathedral, and housed in a converte
nineteenth-century theatre, the **Centro Andaluz de la Fotografía** c/Pinto
Diaz Molina (daily 11am–2pm & 5.30–9.30pm; free), is Andalucía's first phot
museum, often staging interesting exhibitions of work by *andaluz* and interna
tional photographers. To the north of the cathedral the **Plaza Vieja** (officiall

Plaza de la Constitución) is a wonderful pedestrian square which – because of its restricted entrance – you would hardly know was there. It contains the **Ayuntamiento**, a flamboyant early twentieth-century building with a brown and cream facade, and a monument to citizens put to the firing squad in 1824 for opposing the tyrannical reign of Fernando VII. This square has bags of potential and elsewhere would probably be full of restaurants and nightlife; at present, though, it's a rather melancholy place after dark. However, all this may be about to change as work has started on a complete refurbishment of its buildings and monuments.

Around the Puerta de Purchena

Further sights are located within a couple of minutes' walk of the **Puerta de Purchena**, which takes its name from a Moorish gate – long gone – where al-Zagal, the city's last Moorish ruler, surrendered to the Catholic monarchs in 1490. On the west side of the junction, at the end of c/Tenor Iribarne at c/de los Aljibes 20, are some well-preserved eleventh-century Moorish water cisterns – known as **Los Aljibes Arabes** (Mon–Fri 9am–2pm; free).

Off the southwest side of the Puerta de Purchena is the remarkable **Los Refugios**, Plaza Manuel Pérez García s/n (guided visits Tues–Sun 9.30am–1pm & Tues–Fri 5.30pm & 6pm; ☎950 26 86 96; €2), a series of underground air-raid shelters used by the city's population during the Civil War bombardments by Nazi and Italian aircraft and naval forces. Between February 1937 and the spring of 1938 city engineers (using experience gained in the province's mining industry) constructed no less than 4.5km of tunnels beneath the city with 67 access points to shelter 35,000 citizens. Much of the rest of the then fifty thousand population took cover in the caves of the La Chanca district, now inhabited by the city's *gitano* community. Open to the public for the first time as a museum, the tunnels are superbly constructed with ventilation pipes and shields to prevent fifth columnists throwing in hand-grenades, and there is also an operating theatre. Places on the tours should be **booked in advance** by phone to guarantee entry.

Just south of here, **Calle de las Tiendas** (the continuation of c/de los Aljibes) – the oldest street in the city – was formerly called Calle Lencerías (drapers' st) and in the nineteenth century was Almería's most fashionable shopping thoroughfare. Some of the street lamps survive from this period, although the place has now become rather seedy.

A little further down you'll arrive at the **Iglesia de Santiago**, dating from the same period as the cathedral, and built with stone from the same quarry. A fine Plateresque portal incorporates a statue of Santiago slaying the Moors as well as the coat of arms of the all-powerful Bishop Villalán, the cathedral's founder.

Finally, across the Paseo de Almería, the main street that leaves the Puerta de Purchena from its southern side, the colourful daily **market** (7am–2pm) at the end of c/Aguilar de Campo is also worth a look.

Museo Arqueológico and Centro de Arte

Almería's **Museo Arqueológico** (Tues 2.30–8.30pm, Wed–Sat 9am–8.30pm, Sun 9am–2.30pm; €1.50, free with EU passport) is an impressive new hi-tech museum to the east of the city centre and well worth a visit. The main attraction for most visitors is the first floor display of finds from the remarkable Chalcolithic site at **Los Millares** (see p.532) which are superbly displayed. There is also an informative maquette depicting how the site would have looked at its zenith in the third millennium BC. The second floor displays more finds from Los Millares plus other prehistoric sites in the province, and has sections dealing with funerary rites and burial customs. The third floor is devoted to Almería province's Roman and Moorish past, with some particularly outstanding ceramics displayed in the latter.

Near to the train-bus station an impressive **Centro de Arte**, Plaza de la Estación s/n (Mon 6–9pm, Tue–Sat 11am–2pm & 6–9pm, Sun 11am–2pm; free), often stages interesting art exhibitions with Spanish and international themes (details from either tourist office).

❹ Eating, drinking and entertainment

Almería has a surprising number of interesting and good-value places to eat **and drink**. Most of the best eating options are to be found around the Puerta de Purchena and in the web of narrow streets lying between the Paseo de Almería and the cathedral.

In August the city holds its annual music and arts **festival**, the Fiesta de los Pueblos Ibéricos y del Mediterráneo, with concerts and dance events, many of them free, taking place in the squares and various other locations throughout the city (details from either tourist office). Tacked on to the end of this is the **Festival de Flamenco** with big-name artists performing on a stage set up in the atmospheric Plaza de la Constitución. During the last week of the month, the city's main annual fiesta, the **Romería de Augusto**, also takes place with lots of street parties and spectacular processions with carnival giants. Details of the exact dates for all these again are available from the tourist office.

Restaurants and tapas bars

The best place for early-evening **tapas** is around the Puerta de Purchena, where – especially at weekends – the whole town turns out during the evening *paseo* to see and be seen. Places around the cathedral and old town are more lively at lunch time. For **afternoon tea** or coffee with delicious pastries head for *La Dulce Alianza*, Paseo de Almería 8, near the Puerta de Purchena, a century-old *pastelería* with a terrace.

Around Puerta de Purchena

Bodega Aranda Rambla del Obispo Orbera 8, near the Puerta de Purchena. Great tapas bar which fairly hums at lunch times when local professionals come to grab a bite. In former days this was the "sordid" *pensión* where a penurious Gerald Brenan put up in 1921 (sleeping 6 to a room) while waiting for a letter with money from England – which never came.

Bodega Las Botas c/Fructuoso Pérez 3, just south of the Puerta de Purchena. Great tapas place with hanging *jamón serrano* shanks and upturned sherry butt tables; the excellent *fino* and *manzanilla* (served with a free *tapa*) goes well with the house special, *merluza en escabeche* (marinated hake).

Bodega Ortega c/Obispo Orbera 5, almost opposite the *Aranda* (see above). Great old rambling tapas bar decorated with bullfight posters where a friendly proprietor serves up seafood tapas made with fish fresh from the nearby market.

🏃 **El Quinto Toro** c/Reyes Católicos 6. Top-notch atmospheric tapas bar taking its name from the fifth bull in the *corrida* (reputed to

always be the best). Friendly service and mouthwatering *patatas a lo pobre* (potatoes baked with garlic; lunch times only). The same proprietor also runs *El Quinto Toro II* slightly southeast of here at the junction of c/Javier Sanz with c/Padre Santaella which is also worth a visit.

🏃 **La Encina** c/Marín 16 ☎950 27 34 29. Excellent little mid-priced restaurant with rising female chef Francisca Pérez fronting the *fogón* (stove). Serves outstanding tapas in its bar at the front and creative and innovative fish and meat dishes in a cosy restaurant at the rear (where a feature is a Moorish well found during the restaurant's refurbishment; *menú de degustación* for €37.

La Espartería c/Granada 8. New and stylish diner-style restaurant with some interesting takes on *andaluz* favourites with a few Japanese inspired flourishes, too. Offers dishes of the day, with a reasonably priced wine list and a *menú de degustación* for €40.

Peña Taurina Almeriense c/Regocijos 23, north of the Puerta de Purchena. Great old bar where *corrida* aficionados gather to talk about fights past, present and to come, looked down on by historical photos and paraphernalia.

Restaurante Alfareros c/Marcos 6, slightly northeast of the Puerta de Purchena. Wonderful cheap place to eat, packed at lunch time with people in town for the market, with an excellent-value *menú* for €10.

Restaurante Torreluz Mediterraneo Plaza Flores 1 ☏ 950 28 14 25. Close to the hotel of the same name, this is a very good mid-priced restaurant with a creative bent. Try their outstanding *presa de paleta ibérica escabechada* (marinated pork shoulder). There's a *menú de degustación* for €35.

Restaurante Valentin c/Tenor Iribarne 19 ☏ 950 26 44 75. Owned by the same people as *Bodega Las Botas*, this is a stylish mid-priced restaurant and tapas bar noted for its seafood; it has a *menú de degustación* for around €35. Closed Mon.

Tetería-Restaurante Almedina c/Paz 2. Very friendly little Moroccan-run *tetería* which serves full meals later in the day including couscous and chicken and lamb tagines. Often stages live concerts of flamenco and north African music at weekends.

Around the cathedral

Añorga c/Padre Alfonso, slightly south of the Iglesia de San Pedro. Basque tapas bar with a range of *pinxtos* (tapas on sticks) and *raciónes*. Has a small terrace on this pedestrianized street.

Bar Bahía de la Palma Plaza Administración Vieja 1, next to Plaza Vieja. Great old bar and a good lunch-time tapas stop; they also serve *platos combinados*. Recorded flamenco music is the accompaniment to the drinking here and some evenings they even put on live sessions.

Bodega El Ajoli c/Padre Alfonso s/n. Opposite *Añorga* (above), this tapas and *raciónes* bar also has outdoor tables. Specializes in pork dishes – ordering their *surtido* gets you a bit of everything.

Bodega Montenegro Plaza Granero, just west of the cathedral. Delightful neighbourhood bar, stacked with barrels. Once they've got over the initial novelty of seeing a foreigner walk through the door, they serve up great local wines and seafood tapas.

Casa Joaquín c/Real 111, near the port. Fine and popular tapas bar which buzzes with contented drinkers most evenings. All tapas and *raciónes* are excellent, especially the seafood.

Casa Puga Corner of c/Lope de Vega and c/Jovellanos. With hams hanging from the ceiling, marble-topped tables and walls covered with *azulejos*, this is another outstanding tapas bar – founded in 1870 – with a great atmosphere and loyal clientele; try the *atún en escabeche* (marinated tuna) or *boquerones en vinagre* (fresh anchovies in vinegar). Also has one of the best wine-cellars in Andalucía.

Nightlife and flamenco

For drinking and music **bars**, try the streets around Plaza Masnou, off the southern end of the Alameda, and c/Trajano slightly northeast of here, both areas bouncing with action especially at weekends. To move the night-time *marcha* (scene) away from the residential area in summer, the city council erects a line of **discoteca marquees** at the start of the Paseo Marítimo, near the beach – around 3am these places start to get quite wild. On the Paseo de Almería at no. 56, *Molly Malone* is a popular bar housed in the elegant old *Casino* with a theatre behind; their outdoor terrace is a great place for a drink on summer nights.

For **flamenco**, the only genuine establishment is *Peña El Taranto*, taking its name from the *taranto*, Almería's dramatic and clamorous contribution to the flamenco canon. Based in the Moorish Baths, near the Puerta de Purchena, this club holds regular concerts (except in Aug) and details are available from either tourist office.

Getting to Morocco

There is a **daily boat to Melilla** on the Moroccan coast throughout the summer (less often out of season), a six-hour journey, but one that cuts out the haul to Málaga or the usual port for Morocco, Algeciras. In summer (June–Sept) a high-speed vessel does the trip in four hours. For information and tickets contact the Compañía Tras-mediterránea (☏ 950 23 69 56, ◉ www.trasmediterranea.es), Parque Nicolás Salmerón 19, near the port. The daily six-hour route to Nador (south of Melilla) is operated by Ferrimaroc (☏ 950 27 48 00, ◉ www.ferrimaroc.com) who have an office in the port.

Listings

Airport Local buses make the journey from the centre every 30min between 7am and 9pm; take line #20 labelled "El Alquián" from the junction of the Avda. Federico García Lorca and c/Gregorio Marañón (one block above the top right corner of our map).

Banks The major banks, most with ATMs, are along the Paseo de Almería and close at 2pm; there is also an ATM at the airport.

Football Almería supports two teams, both founded in the 1980s. U.D. Almería (☏ 950 25 44 26, ⓦ www.udalmeriasad.com), reached the dizzy heights of the first division just 18 years after their foundation where they are currently holding their own; rivals Polideportivo Almería (☏ 950 24 56 42) are meanwhile toiling in the lower leagues. U.D. Almería play at the Estadio Juegos Mediterráneos, east of the train and bus stations, while "Poli" play matches at the Estadio Municipal, Avda. Torre-cardenas s/n, in the northern suburbs.

Hiking maps Librería Cajal, c/Navarro Rodrigo 14, just south of the market, stocks walking guides and maps. Nearby Picasso, c/Reyes Católicos 16 is a similar place.

Hospital The main infirmary is Hospital Torrecárdenas (☏ 950 01 60 00) in the north-eastern suburbs.

Internet Locutorio del Puerto c/Alvarez de Castro 24 (daily 10am–10pm), fifty metres from the Turismo, is a handy place for internet access.

Left luggage There are coin-operated lockers at the Estación Intermodal (train-bus) station.

Police Contact the Policia Municipal c/Santos Zárate 11, off the north end of the Avda. Federico García Lorca, to report thefts or lost property (☏ 950 62 12 05). In case of emergency dial ☏ 092 (local police) or ☏ 091 (national).

Post office Plaza Cassinello 1 (Mon–Fri 9am–8pm, Sat 9am–1.30pm), near Plaza del Ecuador, off Paseo de Almería.

Train tickets Train tickets are available at the train station and the RENFE office at c/Alcalde Muñoz 7, behind the church of San Sebastián near the Puerta de Purchena.

West of Almería: the Costa Tropical

Almería's best beach resorts lie on its eastern coast, the Costa de Almería, between the city and Mojácar. On the so-called **Costa Tropical**, west of the city, the nearest beaches such as **Aguadulce**, **Roquetas de Mar** and **Almerimar** are overdeveloped and the landscape is dismal, backed by an ever-expanding plastic sea of *invernaderos*, hothouses for cultivation of fruit and vegetables for the export market (see box, p.551). Beyond Adra things improve slightly, but not much, and there's little to detain you until you reach the smaller resorts of **Castell de Ferro** and **Calahonda**, both tolerable places to stop.

Castell de Ferro and beyond

CASTELL DE FERRO, 22km over the Granada provincial border, is by far the best of the resorts along this stretch of coast and even preserves remnants of its former existence as a fishing village. Dominated by a hill-top *atalaya* (watch-tower), it's quite sheltered and has a couple of wide, if pebbly, **beaches** to the west and especially east, although the town beach fronting the small assemblage of bars, restaurants and *hostales* is less inviting. Among the **places to stay** (all on the seafront Plaza de España), the friendly *Hostal Bahia* (☏ 958 65 60 60; ❶) is good value and has sea-view rooms with terrace, with the *Costa Sol* (☏ 958 65 60 54; ❷), offering rooms above a decent restaurant, a good second choice. Of Castell's four **campsites**, *Camping Las Palmeras* (☏ 958 65 61 30), the westernmost of the bunch, is the one to go for, with shade, plenty of space and access to the beach. For **meals**, *Restaurante La Brisa* does **raciónes** plus a good and inexpensive *menú*, as do most of the places along the seafront.

The coast road east again from here skirts the foothills of the Sierra de Carchuna where **CALAHONDA** is another small resort with a good beach, the Playa de Carchuna, often full to the gunwales in summer. In the centre, the

West of Almería, and stretching from beneath the hills of the Sierra de Gador to the sea, lies the **Campo de Dalías**, a vast plain of salt flats and sand dunes which has become a shining sea of *plasticultura* – the forced production of millions of tons of tomatoes, peppers, cucumbers, strawberries and exotic flowers. This industry has wrought quite a revolution in impoverished Almería, covering a once-barren wilderness with a shimmering sea of 64,000 acres of polythene canopies (producing 20,000 tons of plastic waste annually) propped up by eucalyptus supports.

The boom is all due to the invention of drip-feed irrigation and it has led to phenomenal increases in the year-round production of crops, allowing cheap tropical fruit and flowers to fill the supermarket shelves of northern Europe throughout the year. The future of this miracle, however, may be precarious. Scientists have serious worries about the draining of the province's meagre water resources through the tapping of countless artesian wells – many as deep as 100m. A plan hatched by the Partido Popular government in 2002 to solve this problem by diverting water from the Río Ebro in northern Spain met with outraged resistance from the inhabitants and farmers of the Ebro delta and the plan was dropped by the incoming PSOE regime in 2004. The Almerian farmers have now placed their hopes in the construction of a mammoth seawater desalination plant at Carboneras.

The centre of the *plasticultura* zone is **El Ejido**, a conurbation that has multiplied from a modest population of two thousand, twenty years ago, to some fifty thousand today, making it second in the province only to the capital itself. Like some Wild West town, El Ejido has grown up for a dozen kilometres along the main highway with little or no planning restraints and with the free market in almost total control. The town's wealth explosion has also funded a football team – Polideportivo Ejido – which has charged up the divisions and is currently holding its own in Division Two with games against the likes of Real Madrid and Barcelona now a real possibility.

The lack of facilities for this enormous population growth has led to serious problems and the social cost has been high: the suicide rate has risen sharply as those who don't make the easy money anticipated get deep into debt, and the twelve- to fifteen-hour days worked in jungle humidity all year long inside the *invernaderos* (plastic tents) often lead to breakdowns. Besides illness and alcoholism, gambling and drug addiction are also taking their toll.

More depressingly, the high demand for workers willing to toil in the terrible conditions has led to the arrival of over 10,000 **immigrants** (mostly illegal) from Morocco and other African countries, who have built squalid shanty settlements on the edges of town. Despite the threat of high fines if farmers are found to be using these "*sin papeles*" (without papers) workers, many farmers still take the risk and the authorities often turn a blind eye. Early in 2000 simmering local resentment at the immigrant "invasion" erupted into violence when a two-day riot followed the fatal stabbing of a local woman by an immigrant (and mentally unstable) thief. The furious townspeople attacked the shops, bars and support centres of the immigrant population, setting some hostels ablaze and covering others with racist slogans. It took six hundred of the Guardia Civil to quell the disorder and the government's interior minister described it as "a disgrace for Spanish society". But tension between immigrants and locals remained and in the autumn of 2008 further violent disturbances took place at nearby Roquetas de Mar where a huge number of mainly African *invernadero* workers are quartered. When a street argument between some locals and immigrants resulted in the fatal stabbing of a Senagalese man by a local youth, the outraged immigrant *barrio* embarked on a three-day orgy of violence and arson during which cars, shops and apartment blocks were set ablaze. The Guardia Civil were once again called upon to restore order and it remains to be seen whether any long-term lessons have been learnt.

fish restaurant *El Ancla* is the best of the eating places, and a pleasant beach bar and *chiringuito*, *El Farillo*, is to be found by a toppled old watchtower at the western end of the strand. Next comes the unremarkable **TORRENUEVA**, where there's a reasonable beach but little else to stop for, before the road crosses a dreary plain planted with sugar cane, to the north of which lies the large and ugly chemical and industrial town of **MOTRIL**, and to the south its equally unappealing port-resort. The beaches to the west of Motril are described in Chapter One.

The Costa de Almería

The **Costa de Almería**, east of Almería, has a somewhat wild air, with developments constrained by lack of water and roads and by the confines of the **Parque Natural de Cabo de Gata**, a protected zone since 1987. If you have transport, it's still possible to find deserted beaches without too much difficulty, while small inlets shelter relatively low-key resorts such as **San José**, **Los Escullos**, **Las Negras** and **Agua Amarga**.

Further north is **Mojácar**, a picturesque hill village, which has become a beach resort of quite some size over the past decade. It is easiest – and most speedily – approached on the inland routes via Nijar (the A7-E15) or the "desert" road (N340A) through Tabernas and Sorbas.

Almería to Mojácar

The coast between Almería and Mojácar is backed by the **Sierra del Cabo de Gata**, which gives it a bit of character and wilderness. **Buses** run from Almería to all the main resorts, though to do much exploring, or seek out deserted strands, transport of your own is invaluable. The heat is blistering here throughout the summer, and you should bear in mind that during July and particularly August accommodation in the park is at a premium – try and book ahead if possible.

El Cabo de Gata and Las Salinas

Heading east along the main AL12, a turn-off to the right, 3km beyond the airport, heads south to **CABO DE GATA** (aka El Cabo). This is the closest resort to the city with any appeal: a lovely expanse of coarse sand, best in the mornings before the sun and wind get up. Six buses a day run between Almería and El Cabo, making an intermediate stop at Retamar, a retirement/holiday development.

Arriving at El Cabo, you pass a lake, the **Laguna de Rosa**, a protected locale that is home to flamingos and other waders. Nearby there's a **campsite**, *Camping Cabo de Gata* (⊕950 16 04 43). In the village itself there are plentiful bars, cafés and shops, plus a fish market. The seafront has a rather listless air and no places to stay meaning that for **rooms** you'll need to head inland to the friendly but pricey *Hostal Las Dunas* (⊕&⊕950 37 00 72; ❸), 100m back from the beach at c/Barrionuevo 58, offering a/c en-suite rooms with TV. The modern three-star *Hotel Blanca Brisa*, c/Las Joricas 49, on the edge of town (⊕950 37 00 01, ⊛www.blancabrisa.com; ❹ with breakfast) is not a great step up in price.

Just south of the village is another area known as **Las Salinas** – The Salt Pans – and it is exactly that, with a commercial salt-drying enterprise at its southern end. In summer **flamingos** and other migrants are a common sight here

CABO DE GATA
NATURAL PARK

Parque Natural de Cabo de Gata

Protected since 1987, the 71,500 acres of the **Parque Natural de Cabo de Gata** stretch from Retamar to the east of Almería across the cape to the Barranco del Honda, just north of Agua Amarga. The Sierra de Gata is volcanic in origin and its adjacent dunes and saltings are some of the most important wetland areas in Spain for **breeding birds** and **migrants**. At Las Salinas alone more than eighty species can be sighted throughout the year, including the magnificent pink flamingos as well as avocet, storks and egrets during their migrations. And there have been rarer sightings of Andouin's gull, as well as Bonelli's eagle and eagle owls around the crags.

Other **fauna** include the rare Italian wall lizard (its only habitat in Spain), with its distinctive green back with three rows of black spots, as well as the more common fox (sporting its Iberian white tail tip), hare and grass snake. Among the **flora**, the stunted dwarf fan palm is mainland Europe's only native palm and the salt marshes are home to a strange parasitic plant, the striking yellow-flowering *Cistanche phelypaea*, which feeds on goosefoot.

The best times for sighting the fauna here are at **dawn and dusk** as, with temperatures among the highest in Europe and rainfall at 10cm a year the lowest, energy has to be conserved. There are three official **Puntos de Información** in the park: at the Cabo de Gata lighthouse (see below), Pozo de Frailes (near San José; p.555) and the main centre at Rodalquilar (see p.557). There is also a private information office in the resort of San José (p.555). The three official offices should have free copies of *Cuaderno de Senderos* (in Spanish) detailing eighteen walks in the park of between two and twelve kilometres. Any hiking in the park is greatly assisted by using the Editorial Alpina 1:50.000 *Cabo de Gata Nijar* map which accurately marks trekking routes, tracks and campsites.

(see box above), so take binoculars if you have them – just before dusk is a good time. The park authorities have now installed **hides** here (signed off the road). The hills of salt are a striking sight in the bright sun, too, and the industry here has a pedigree dating back to the Phoenicians who first controlled the seawater which entered through the marshes to create pools for the extraction of salt in the first millennium BC. The park authorities like to cite the modern industry as an example of resource extraction and environmental conservation working hand in hand. Certainly the flamingos seem perfectly happy with the arrangement.

Almadraba de Montelva and the Cabo de Gata lighthouse

Four kilometres to the south of El Cabo village, just beyond Las Salinas, is **ALMADRABA DE MONTELVA**, more a continuation than a separate place, but altogether more pleasant for hanging around. You'll find a few bars and a couple of **restaurants** here: the seafront *La Almadraba* is the friendlier and more down-to-earth, whilst the nearby *Hotel-Restaurante Las Salinas* (T 950 37 01 03, W www.lasalinascabodegata.com; ❸) has a terrace restaurant and prices to reflect it; its rather kitschy hotel also has some decent rooms (with a fifty-percent surcharge in Aug).

Another 4km south, past a hill known as the Pico de San Miguel, the **Faro de Cabo de Gata** (lighthouse) marks the cape's southern tip. In the lighthouse car park a **Parque Natural information cabin** (June–Sept daily 10am–2pm & 6–8pm; Oct–May Sat & Sun 10am–3pm) has maps and information on the park. There's also a friendly tapas bar here, *El Faro*, serving up tasty locally caught fried fish and paella, as well as a *mirador* from where you can get a great view of the rock cliffs and – on clearer days – a sight of Morocco's Rif mountains.

Beyond the lighthouse a track leads to two of the finest **beaches** in the province, and to the resort of San José beyond. This track is closed to cars, which is all to your advantage for it makes for a fine walk through the Natural Park. Starting out as a paved road, climbing up from the lighthouse, this soon degenerates into a dirt track, passing prickly pear cactus plantations grown for their fruit, and access tracks to the wonderful fine sand beaches of **Monsul** (6km out) – with freshwater springs and a track west to the even more secluded Media Luna cove – and further east, **Los Genoveses** (10km from the lighthouse). A couple of kilometres further, and beyond another spur, you'll sight the sea and the resort of San José.

To reach San José **by car**, you'll need to double back to El Cabo de Gata and follow the signed road further inland. Passing Pozo de los Frailes 4km from San José, you'll find a **Punto de Información** kiosk (June–Sept daily 10am–2pm & 6–8pm) for the natural park on the main road through.

San José

The attractive little resort of **SAN JOSÉ** (served by three daily buses from Almería) has a sandy beach in a small cove, with shallow water, while more fine beaches lie within walking distance. Only a few years ago it was almost completely undeveloped, though things are changing, with a rash of apartments and a new yacht harbour.

If you've followed the walk from the lighthouse to San José (see above) and want to continue along the coast there's another **track**, running 12km north to Los Escullos and La Isleta. To start the walk take the road north out of San José, along which you'll shortly come to a turn-off along a dirt track on the right that heads around a hill – Cerro del Enmedio – towards the coast. The track branches at various points and you'll have to decide whether to follow the coastal tracks (which can be impassable) or the surer inland route. The first track off to the coast provides access to a beautiful and secluded cove. Further on, the route skirts the 500m-high Cerro de los Frailes, beyond which lie the inlets of Los Escullos and La Isleta.

Information

On San José's main street, Avenida de San José, near the centre of the village you'll find a privately run **Centro de Información** (daily 10am–2pm & 5–8pm; ☏950 38 02 99, ⊛www.cabodegata-nijar.com) for the natural park, which has lots of information on activities such as guided walks and horse treks in the area; they also have a complete list of accommodation and information on apartments to rent which may be a cheaper option for a longer stay. **Internet** access is available at Bla Bla Bla (daily 9am–midnight), Pasaje Curry, close to the Centro de Información. Near the main street's central junction, and up some steps almost opposite the *Hostal Costa Rica*, David the Bookman (daily 11am–2pm & 4.30–9pm) is an amiable source of paperback **books** in English and will exchange any books you wish to offload. **Horses** can be hired for exploring the park from the *Hotel Cortijo El Sotillo* (see p.556). Alpha (☏950 38 03 21, ⊛www.alphabuceo.com) is a PADI-certificated **diving centre** located in the Puerto Deportivo (yacht harbour) for courses in snorkelling and scuba diving. Along Avenida de San José there's a **bank** with ATM cash machine, plus a couple of well-stocked **supermarkets** for picnic supplies.

Accommodation

Rooms are usually easy to come by outside high season (July & Aug), and during this period some places want stays of at least five days (applying a surcharge for shorter durations). During high season it's essential to ring ahead and advisable at other times of the year, too. San José's good **campsite**, *Camping Tau* (☎ 950 38 01 66; April–Oct), is reached via a signed road on the left as you enter the village.

Albergue Juvenil c/Montemar s/n ☎ 950 38 03 53, ⓦ www.alberguesanjose.com. Reached by the same road leading to the campsite (see above) this privately run youth hostel has 86 places divided between rooms sleeping from two to eight persons. It is usually booked solid at Easter and in Aug. €12 per person.

Cortijo El Sotillo Ctra. San José s/n ☎ 950 61 11 00, ⓦ www.cortijoelsotillo.es. To the left on the main road in and a kilometre from the centre, this is a refurbished eighteenth-century ranch-house converted into a four-star country hotel with elegant rustically furnished rooms, excellent mid-priced restaurant, bar, pool, tennis courts, and stables with horses for hire. ➏

Hostal Aloha c/Cala Higuera s/n ☎ 950 38 04 61, ⓦ www.hostalaloha.com. Recently refurbished *hostal* with excellent a/c en-suite balcony rooms and the bonus of a fine palm-fringed pool at the rear; they also have a very good tapas bar below. ➌

Hostal Brisa del Mar c/Ancla s/n ☎ 950 38 04 31, ⓦ www.brisamar.com. Over the road from *Las Gaviotas*, (see below) this is a recent arrival with bright and airy a/c en-suite balcony rooms with TV and a pretty garden. ➌

Hostal Las Gaviotas c/Córdoba s/n ☎ 950 38 00 10, ⓦ www.hlasgaviotas.com. Almost next door to *Hotel Agades* this is a more economical (outside high season) option for en-suite rooms with a/c and TV. ➍

Hostal San José c/Las Olas s/n ☎ 950 61 10 80, ⓦ www.servimar.net. Perched on a hill overlooking the harbour, this is an upmarket *hostal* with a/c en-suite rooms equipped with kitchenette and balcony terraces with fine sea views. ➏

Hostal Sol Bahía c/Correos 5 ☎ 950 38 01 14, ⓦ www.solbahiasanjose.es. Near the main junction in the centre of the village, this is one of the better-value central places, offering spacious a/c en-suite balcony rooms with TV. ➍

Hotel Agades Agidir c/Córdoba s/n ☎ 950 38 03 90, ⓦ www.hotelagades.com. Very pleasant option with a/c en-suite balcony rooms with satellite TV, plus garden pool, bar and restaurant. Sited on the right-hand side of the main road as you come in (a 5min walk from the village). ➎

Hotel Doña Pakyta c/Correo s/n ☎ 950 61 11 75, ⓦ www.hotelpakyta.es. One of the swishest places in town at the western end of the bay offering light and airy terrace balcony rooms with stunning sea views. ➐ with breakfast.

Hotel La Posada de Paco c/Correo s/n ☎ 950 38 00 10, ⓦ www.laposadadepaco.com. On the main street and slightly east of the main junction, this is a stylish small hotel with pool and a/c terrace rooms with satellite TV. ➎ with breakfast.

Eating and drinking

There are numerous **bars** and **restaurants** on the central Plaza de Génova and facing the nearby beach on c/del Puerto Deportivo, offering everything from fast food and pizzas to excellent fresh local fish. Try the *salmonetes* (red mullet fried with garlic) at *La Cueva*. Next door to the latter, the equally good *El Tempranillo* does tasty paellas and treats its clientele to some excellent – and cheap – Láujar wines from the Almerian Alpujarras. The nearby *Mediterráneo* is also worth a try. Just around the corner from these and overlooking the Puerto Deportivo, the *Taberna del Puerto* is another good – if slightly pricier – place for fish and has a small terrace. Near the main junction, the friendly and good-value *Bar-Restaurante El Emigrante* (opposite the *Hostal Sol Bahía* above) prepares good fish and *platos combinados* and has a *menú* for €10. For a splurge, apart from *Cortijo El Sotillo* (see above) the area's only place with any pretensions is *La Gallineta*, 4km back along the entry road at Pozo de los Frailes (☎ 950 38 05 01; main dishes €12–22; closed Mon); it offers sophisticated Mediterranean meat and fish dishes in an elegantly furnished traditional house beside a restored Moorish waterwheel.

Los Escullos and La Isleta

Next along this rugged coastline is the isolated and peaceful **LOS ESCULLOS**, 8km north by road, with a good if rather pebbly beach and a formidable once ruined – but recently refurbished – fort, the eighteenth-century **Castillo de San Felipe**. The pleasant beachfront *hostal-restaurante*, *Casa Emilio* (℡950 38 97 61, 🅦www.hostalcasaemilio.com; ❸), offering a/c en-suite rooms with terrace balcony is the best of a couple of options here with a good bar and restaurant below. There's also a **campsite**, *Camping Los Escullos* (℡950 38 98 11), set back from the sea with limited shade. **LA ISLETA**, 2km beyond, is a slowly expanding fishing village which still manages to retain a sleepy atmosphere and has a rather scruffy pebble beach, although there's a better one – Playa la Ola – to the east backed by a car park. A **hostal**, *Isleta del Moro* (℡950 38 97 13, 🅕950 38 97 64; ❸), overlooks the harbour, has reasonably priced en-suite sea-view balcony rooms plus a decent **bar-restaurant** serving tapas and a good-value *menú* for around €12. The best tapas bar in these parts, however, is the nearby 🍴 *Bar-Restaurante La Ola*, set back from the beach with a shady terrace, serving seafood tapas and *raciónes* plus great fish and *bogavante* (lobster).

Rodalquilar

The road north of here climbs over the cliffs above Isleta and heads inland before descending to a pleasant valley, passing after 4km the desert hamlet of **RODALQUILAR** surrounded by scrub, palms and cactuses. Once a centre of gold mining initiated by the Romans, the nineteeth-century workings scar the crags behind the village where a daunting edifice still bears the inscription in English "Guard Block B." You will also pass the lines of ruined miners' dwellings from this era along the entry road leading to a **Natural Park information office** (June–Sept daily 10am–2pm & 5–8pm, Oct–March Sat & Sun 10am–3pm; ℡950 38 98 20), c/Fundición s/n, opposite the church in the centre. On on the village's eastern edge the attractive desert **inn** *Hotel Rodalquilar* (℡950 38 98 38, 🅦www.hotelrodalquilar.com; ❻ with breakfast) has comfortable rooms arranged around a sunken courtyard; a restaurant, pool, sauna and gym plus free loan of mountain bikes are just a few of the facilities on offer. Next door to here the *El Ajillo* is a very good mid-priced restaurant (main dishes €10–17) and also rents out modern stylish rooms at its own adjoining hotel (℡950 38 97 20, 🅦www.posadaelajillo.com; ❻). Rodalquilar is served by a single daily **bus** from Almería.

Las Negras and San Pedro

LAS NEGRAS, another expanding beach settlement 5km further, is situated in the folds of a beautiful cove, with an *atalaya* (watchtower) sited on the edge of the village as you approach. There's a pebbly beach, a few **bars** – including the pleasant *La Manteca* on the seafront which stays open all year – and a decent **restaurant**, *La Palma*, which overlooks the beach. A **campsite**, *La Caleta* (℡950 52 52 37), set in a tranquil location with its own bay, is reached via a 1km road just outside the village on the way in. For **rooms**, the friendly and excellent-value *Hostal Arrecife*, c/Bahía 6 (℡950 38 81 40; ❷), close to the *estanco* (see below), has a/c en-suite sea-view terrace rooms with TV. More possibilities aren't difficult to spot in summer as many shops and bars post signs offering accommodation to let. Another option for longer stays (five nights plus in high season) is the collection of **apartments and chalets** (❹) in coastal and country locations rented out by Estanco Piedra García (℡&🅕950 38 80 75, 🅦www.lasnegras.com), the main street tobacconist and information office whose proprietors speak good English. On the seafront, the PADI certificated Buceo de Las Negras (℡950 38 82 17) offers **scuba-diving** courses (beginners and advanced) and also hires out kayaks, mountain bikes and offers **internet** access.

For a change of beach the *estanco* should be able to arrange for someone to row you up the coast to the ruined village of **SAN PEDRO**. If you can't find an oarsman, you'll have to walk – no bad hike when it's cool – to visit the village with its caves and ruined castle; it lies 4km north on a poor track. The place was inhabited until a few years ago when the mainly elderly residents upped sticks to Las Negras, which had acquired a road, leaving their houses – sometimes occupied by north European pseudo-hippies – to crumble. If you are feeling really energetic, you could walk 7km on from here along the coast to Agua Amarga, via another pleasant beach at **Cala del Plomo**. If you attempt these walks in summer remember to take along drinking water as there is none to be had en route or at San Pedro.

Agua Amarga

AGUA AMARGA stands just before the Natural Park's northern boundary and is a delightful little fishing village cut off from the surrounding world by a long road and limited accommodation. To reach it from Las Negras (a route not served by public transport) you'll need to head inland to the village of **Fernan Pérez**, from where a new road heads east for 11km to reach the small resort.

Many of the summer visitors here are Italians who rent a tasteful crop of villas. The excellent, fine sand **beach** has outlets renting windsurf boards and canoes, and there are a number of bars and restaurants backing it. The PADI-certificated Centro de Buceo, c/Aguada s/n behind the beach (☏950 13 82 13) offers **scuba-diving** courses for beginners and experienced divers.

For **rooms**, there's the friendly French-run *Pensión Family* on c/La Lomilla (☏950 13 80 14, ⓕ34 950 138070; ❹ with breakfast) set back from the south end of the beach, where en-suite rooms are complemented by a small pool, garden and restaurant with a good-value €23 *menú*. Alternative accommodations include the *Hotel Las Calas*, c/Desagüe s/n, fronting the beach at the southern end of the village (☏950 13 80 16, ⓦwww.hotellascalas.com; ❹ with breakfast), offering pristine rooms with terrace and sea view, and, on a rise behind *Pensión Family*, *Hotel El Tío Kiko* (☏950 13 80 80, ⓦwww.eltiokiko.com; ❼ with breakfast), a luxury boutique hotel with terrace sea-view rooms arranged around a pool. *Hostal-Restaurante La Palmera* (☏950 13 82 08, ⓔhrlapalmera@terra.es; ❺

▲ The beach at Agua Amarga

with breakfast) has en-suite rooms behind the central beach. For longer stays (2 nights plus) renting a fully equipped sea-view **apartment with terrace** from the friendly ⚓ *Apartamentos Playa*, c/Aguada s/n (☎950 13 81 03, Ⓦwww .aguamarga.net; ❹), is another possibility. All the hotels and *hostales* above have their own **restaurants** and another place well worth a visit for seafood is the reasonably priced restaurant of the *Hotel Las Calas* (see p.558) with good fish and a pleasant terrace.

Towards Mojácar

Leaving the Natural Park behind, **CARBONERAS**, 11km north of Agua Amarga, is a large but easy-going fishing port with an average beach slightly marred by the shadow of a massive cement factory around the bay. North of here lies a succession of small, isolated coves, backed by a characteristically arid Almerian landscape of scrub-covered hills and dried up *arroyos*, or watercourses. The **Carboneras–Mojácar road** itself winds perilously – and scenically – through the hills and offers access to some deserted grey-sand beaches before ascending to the Punta del Santo with fine views along the coast. The descent from here brings you to the **Playa de Macenas**, another pleasant beach with wild-camping possibilities. There are a couple more beaches – **Costa del Pirulico** is a good one with a beach *chiringuito* – before the urban sprawl of Mojácar takes over.

Mojácar and around

MOJÁCAR, Almería's main and growing resort, is split between the ancient hill-top village – **Mojácar Pueblo** – sited a couple of kilometres back from the sea, a striking town of white cubist houses wrapped round a harsh outcrop of rock, and the resort area of **Mojácar Playa** which ribbons for a couple of miles along the seafront.

In the 1960s, when the main Spanish *costas* were being developed, this was virtually a ghost town, its inhabitants having long since taken the only logical step, and emigrated. The town's fortunes revived, however, when the local mayor, using the popularity of other equally barren spots on the Spanish islands and mainland as an example, offered free land to anyone willing to build within a year. The bid was a modest success, attracting one of the decade's multifarious "artist colonies", now long supplanted by package holiday companies and second-homers. These days something of a tourist trap, the hill village has a plush 150-room hotel as well as a parador in the beach resort below, both symbolic of the changing times.

Mojácar Pueblo

Mojácar's hill-top settlement goes back at least to prehistoric Iberian times, and became prominent during the Roman period when Pliny described it as one of the most important towns of *Baetica* – as the Roman province was called. Coins found from this era give the Roman name as *Murgis*, which the later Moors adapted to *Muxacra*. The village's **main fountain** (the Fuente Mora) – signed to the right off the road climbing towards the centre – has been newly restored with lots of marble and geraniums and was where forty years ago veiled women still used to do the family washing. A plaque nearby relates how keen the Moors were to hang on to their hill-top eyrie when challenged by the *Reconquista*. First declaring loyalty to the Reyes Católicos the Moorish mayor, Alabez, then stated that if the Catholic monarchs wouldn't accede to the request to be left in peace, "rather than live like a coward I shall die like a Spaniard. May Allah protect you!" The monarchs were impressed and, for a time at least, prudently granted Alabez's wish.

An ancient custom, no longer practised but parodied on every bangle and trinket sold in the tourist shops, was to paint an **indalo** on the doorways of the village to ward off evil. This symbol – a matchstick figure with arms outstretched, holding an arc – comes from the six-thousand-year-old Neolithic drawings in the caves at Vélez Blanco to the north, and anthropologists believe that it is a unique case of a prehistoric symbol being passed down in one location for numerous millennia.

Indalos apart, sights in the upper village are limited to strolling around the sinuous, white-walled streets, looking at the heavily restored fifteenth-century church of **Santa María**, and savouring the view over the strangely formed surrounding hills and coast to the north from the **mirador** in the main square, Plaza Nueva.

Practicalities

The **Turismo** (Mon–Fri 10am–2pm & 5–7pm, Sat 10am–1.30pm; ☎950 61 50 25, Ⓦwww.mojacar.es) is located just below Plaza Nueva – you'll need their free **map** to negotiate the maze of narrow streets – with the **post office** in the same building and an ATM next door. Places **to stay** include a handful of small *hostales*, all with some en-suite rooms, including *Hostal Arco Plaza* (☎950 47 27 77, Ⓔarcoplazam@yahoo.es; ❸) just off the main square and, west of the church, the friendly *Pensión El Torreón*, c/Jazmín 4 (☎&Ⓕ950 47 52 59; ❷), which has charming if slightly pricey rooms sharing bath. On the way into town, the more upmarket but good-value ⚑ *Mamabel's* at c/Embajadores 3 (☎&Ⓕ950 47 24 48, Ⓦwww.mamabels.com; ❹) has beautiful, individually styled en-suite rooms (no. 1 is a dream), some with stunning view, and a restaurant. The grand *Hotel El Moresco* (☎950 47 80 25; ❺), despite its pool, comes second best. Mojácar's **campsite** *El Quinto* (☎950 47 87 04) lies 2km below the village along the Turre road.

Places to **eat and drink** tend to be a bit pretentious and most of the overpriced restaurants are best avoided. The tapas bars around the main square are worth a try, and the nearby *Rincón de Embrujo*, with a terrace on the plazuela fronting the church, does inexpensive *platos combinados*. Moving upmarket, a place for carefully prepared Spanish standards is the mid-priced *Casa Minguito*, with an inviting terrace on the leafy Plaza Ayuntamiento at the heart of the village, next to the town hall. Nearby, ⚑ *El Palacio*, Plaza del Cano s/n, (June–Sept dinner only, ☎950 47 28 46) is one of the *pueblo*'s two best-value restaurants with a reasonably priced menu and wine list, creative dishes such as *mero a la naranja* (grouper with orange sauce) and a wonderful roof terrace for alfresco dining. An equally memorable meal is on offer at *Mamabel's* (see above) where a good-value €18 *menú* – often featuring couscous and paella – can be enjoyed with vertiginously spectacular views from their own terrace.

There's not much **nightlife** in the hill village but late-night drinking goes on at *Budu Pub* and the nearby *La Luna*, both on c/Estación Nueva north of the church, and at the oddball *El Loro Azul*, off the nearby Plaza Fronton.

Mojácar Playa

Down below on the seafront, **Mojácar Playa** is refreshingly brash: an excellent beach with warm and brilliantly clear waters, flanked by lots of fine beach bars and *discotecas*, rooms for rent, several hotels and *hostales*, and a good campsite, *El Cantal de Mojácar* (☎950 47 82 04). The beach resort's focal point is an ugly Centro Comercial, at the intersection – known locally as *El Cruce* – of the seafront highway with the road leading inland to Mojácar Pueblo. Hourly

buses from the beach up to Mojácar Pueblo run from a stop outside the Centro Comercial, or you can pick them up at various stops along the seafront. Just south of here, **internet** access is available at Indal-futur, Paseo del Mediterráneo 293 (Mon–Fri 9am–2pm & 5–10pm, Sat & Sun 11am–2pm & 6–11pm; ☎950 61 51 56). The Turismo's **map** (see p.560) also covers the coastal strip and is a useful aid to getting your bearings.

Among the **places to stay**, the sprawling seafront *Hotel El Puntazo* on the Paseo del Mediterráneo s/n, 1km south from *El Cruce* (☎950 47 82 29, ⓦwww .hotelelpuntazo.com; ❻), is one of the resort's top addresses and an obvious landmark; rooms come with sea views, lots of frills and there's a pool. In the same area, *Hotel Sal Marina* (☎950 47 24 04; ❹) has very pleasant a/c balcony rooms with sea views and drops prices by thirty percent outside August. Another hotel nearby doing similar price cuts is *Virgen del Mar* (☎950 47 22 22, ⓦwww.hotelvirgendelmar.com; ❺), a three-star place with sea-view balcony a/c rooms with TV. Nearby, the simpler *Hostal Bahía* (☎951 47 80 10; ❷–❸) has en-suite rooms ranged around a charming patio. Next door, *Hotel Marazul* (☎950 47 84 36, ⓦwww.marazulmojacar.com; ❺) rents out fully equipped sea-view studio apartments sleeping up to three; here also prices are almost halved outside high summer. Just south of *El Cruce*, Mojácar's nondescript parador, the modern *Parador de Mojácar* (☎950 47 82 50, ⓦwww.parador .es; ❻), with pleasant gardens and pool, also fronts the beach.

Food along the seafront is dismal, overpriced and standards fall markedly in high season; the sterile parador restaurant nevertheless has a reliable €30 *menú*. Most of the reasonable options lie to the south of *El Cruce* and places to try here include *Albatros*, close to the *Hotel El Puntazo* (see above) on the seaward side of the road, and *Sal Marina* attached to the hotel of the same name (see above); both do good fish and paella. A kilometre further south again, *Omega* and its neighbour *Casa Egea*, Playa Las Ventanicas 127, are a couple of other long-established and reliable seafront places.

More restaurants and fast-food outlets, mostly of indifferent quality, are to be found all along the seafront, where after dark you'll also find plenty of **nightlife** in throbbing beach bars and *discotecas*. Most of the action takes place along the coastal strip covering the 3km to the south of El Cruce. First on the left comes the huge *Mandila Beach*, with numerous bars and dancefloors, followed by *Maui Beach Bar* and – a couple of kilometres further south – *Buddha Bar*. All three are flanked by late-night *copas* and music bars that plug away till dawn in high summer.

North from Mojácar

North from Mojácar, there's a clutch of resorts – none of them much to write home about – and a few last sights of interest, before the road crosses Andalucía's border into Murcia. Inland, two small towns are worth an excursion: at **Vélez Rubio**, there's a cave with important **prehistoric paintings** depicting the *indalo* (see p.560), whilst at neighbouring **Vélez Blanco** there's a fine Renaissance **castle**. Although both are served by a single daily **bus** from Almería, transport of your own will make these detours much more rewarding.

North along the coast

North from Mojácar, and served by occasional buses, **GARRUCHA** is a lively, if undistinguished, town and fishing harbour with a sizeable fleet. When this comes home to port with its catch in mid-afternoon the ensuing auction at the port-side market is wonderfully entertaining. The fleet also lands a good supply of the seafood – the prawns are renowned – served at the numerous **fish restaurants** lining the seafront harbour promenade, El Malecón. The most celebrated place in town is the outstanding ⚓ *El Almejero*, (☎ 950 46 04 05) with its attractive terrace actually fronting the Puerto Pesquero harbourside, where the fish is landed – if what's caught doesn't meet their exacting standards they don't open. All the fish dishes are recommended (especially their renowned *arroz caldoso* – fish and rice soup; main dishes €12–22) and there's an excellent tapas bar attached, too – try the mouthwatering *calamares* and *boquerones fritos*. Pleasant en-suite **rooms** are available at *Hostal-Restaurante Cortés*, Paseo Marítimo 200 (☎ 950 13 28 13, ⓦ www.hostalcortes.net; ❸), overlooking the promenade and excellent beach.

From Garrucha, the road heads 9km inland, skirting the estuary of the Río Almanzora and the small farming town of Vera, to **CUEVAS DEL ALMANZORA**, 6km farther north. A town with a distinguished past, sights include a well-preserved sixteenth-century Gothic castle built to defend the settlement from piracy, and a handful of Guadix-style cave dwellings where evidence of habitation by Neanderthal and Cro-Magnon man was found. The castle – the splendidly restored **Castillo del Marqués de Los Vélez** – now houses an interesting archeological museum and the **Museo Campoy** displaying artworks by Goya, Picasso, Miró, Toral and Vásquez Díaz among others (both Tues–Sat 10am–2pm; €1).

Palomares and the H-bombs

Palomares was once at the centre of one of the world's biggest nuclear scares. Here, on January 17, 1966, an American B-52 bomber collided with a tanker aircraft during a midair refuelling operation. Following the collision in which many of the crew of both aircraft perished, three ten-megaton **H-bombs** (each one-hundred times more powerful than that used at Hiroshima) fell on land and a fourth into the sea, just off the village. Those that fell in the fields were recovered quickly, though one had been damaged, causing radioactive contamination nearby. Fifteen US warships and two submarines searched for many weeks before the fourth bomb was recovered. On March 19, thousands of barrels of plutonium-contaminated soil were transported by the USAF for disposal in South Carolina. Nobody has ever convincingly explained how the incident happened, nor is it known why the bombs didn't explode, for the damaged bomb had actually lost its safety catch.

The fourth bomb made a fortune for local fisherman Francisco Simó Orts (known ever after as **"Paco, el de la Bomba"**) who saw where the missile fell into the sea and aided the search to locate it. With the assistance of a lawyer he also – as the finder – claimed salvage rights under maritime law calculated at one or two percent of the value of the object salvaged. As each bomb was worth 2 billion dollars according to the Pentagon the sum claimed was twenty million dollars and Paco appeared at the New York Federal Court to make his case. The Pentagon duly settled out of court for an undisclosed sum. Palomares' world-famous fisherman died in 2003.

The story, however, is far from over and in 2004 when tests on plots designated for housing construction revealed significant **radioactive contamination**, the land was immediately expropriated by the Spanish government. In 2006 the Spanish and US governments agreed to sharing the cost of a further decontamination programme and a survey of the area to determine how this should be done revealed abnormal levels of radiation in snails and other wildlife indicating dangerous amounts of radioactive material still in the subsoil. In 2008 it was revealed that scientists had located two highly radioactive trenches – near where one of the bombs had fallen – used by the US Army to bury contaminated earth following the incident in 1966. The US government agreed to pay for the earth's removal and transportation to the US in addition to the decontamination of the surrounding area.

Slightly back from here, there's a road which returns you to the coast and the village of **PALOMARES**, of nuclear notoriety (see box, p.562). The rather curious feature of this otherwise dull hamlet is a church tower which resembles – with its rounded cone – an atom bomb. Near to where you rejoin the coast, Vera's **Parque Aquatico** (daily 10.30am–7.30pm; €16, kids €11) is a fun place to kill a couple of hours, especially if you're towing kids; it's got all the usual water features, and they allow you to take your own picnic inside.

Three kilometres on from Palomares, **Villaricos** is a humdrum resort with an uncomfortable black pebble beach. North again from here, the road cuts between the sea and the **Sierra Almagrera**, riddled with mine workings. The old mining settlements beyond these hills, in a landscape of scrub and desert cactuses, are eerie, godforsaken places where any strangers are regarded with suspicion. Back on the coast, **POZO DEL ESPARTO**, 12km from Villaricos, has a reasonable pebble beach with plenty of shade, and quite a few places where wild-campers can pitch their tents. Another 4km on, **SAN JUAN DE LOS TERREROS** straddles the seafront behind a narrow beach flanked by characterless *hostales* and mushrooming *urbanizaciones* and holiday apartments. Just to the north of here, however, the coast road passes a number of temptingly isolated coves and inlets with small beaches, before Andalucía's border with Murcia is reached.

Vélez Rubio and the Letreros cave

Inland from Cuevas del Almanzora, a rambling 60km detour along the A7-E15 and A327 will bring you out at the town of **VÉLEZ RUBIO**, surrounded by *sierras*, olive groves and fields of cereals. It's no great shakes as towns go (Vélez Blanco is a better proposition for an overnight stop), but the **Turismo** (April–Sept Tues–Sat 9am–2pm plus Sat 5–7.30pm, Oct–March Tues–Sat 9.30am–2pm plus Fri & Sat 4.30–7pm; ☎950 41 25 60, ⓦwww.turismolosvelez.com), housed in the town **museum**, c/Carrera del Carmen 19 (same hours), can provide information and a town map. The museum, itself located inside the eighteenth-century Hospital Real, contains an interesting collection of artefacts and ceramics from prehistoric to Moorish times and includes a section on the ancient cave paintings in this area.

▲ Los Letreros cave near Velez Blanco

The main monument of note here is the magnificent Baroque church (Almería province's biggest) of **La Encarnación** (Mon–Fri & Sun 10am–8pm; free) on the plaza of the same name. Constructed in the eighteenth century, this has an imposing carved facade which includes, above the entrance, the arms of the marquises of Villafranca y Vélez, who built it. Inside, the main altar has a superbly detailed, 20-metre-high carved wood **retablo** and there's also a splendid Baroque organ constructed in 1796.

What makes a trip here really worthwhile, however, is to see the prehistoric cave paintings of the **Cueva de los Letreros**, 4km out of town. To get there take the A317 north until you reach a petrol station on the left, next to which is a signed turning to the cave. Visits to the cave are now only possible with a guide who will meet visitors (daily July–Sept noon & 6pm, Oct–June noon & 4.30pm; €1) at the information kiosk near the campsite on the opposite side of the road to the petrol station. Any queries, or in case of bad weather, should be directed to the guide, Señora Milagro Navarro, on ☏mobile 617882808 (some English spoken). The tourist offices in Vélez Rubio or Vélez Blanco will be able to detail any changes to this arrangement.

The cave or *abrigo* (rock shelter) is sited beyond a secure fence on the side of the hill behind the petrol station, a good kilometre's walk. Once through the gate of the compound you will be able to see remarkably fresh-looking red and brown sketches of human figures, birds, animals, astronomical signs and not very well-preserved *indalos* (see p.560) which have been dated to around 4000 BC and are amongst the oldest representations of people and animals together. Unfortunately the local practice of touching the *indalos* and throwing water on the paintings in order to make them clearer has not helped their preservation, but what remains is still stunning.

Vélez Blanco

Nestling at the foot of a rocky outcrop, the whitewashed village of **VÉLEZ BLANCO**, 6km north of its neighbour, is a smaller and more attractive conurbation. Atop the hill is an outstanding **Renaissance castle** (Wed–Sun May-Sept 10am–2pm & 6–8.30pm, Oct–April 10am–2pm & 4–6pm; €1) – an extension of the original Moorish *alcazaba* – built by the marquises of Vélez Blanco in the early years of the sixteenth century. It is today something of a trompe l'oeil, with an empty shell behind the crenellated battlements: a gutting that took place as recently as 1904, after the castle was sold off by the impecunious marquis for 80,000ptas (€500) to an American millionaire, George Blumenthal, who tore out the whole interior including the **Patio de Honor** – a fabulous courtyard carved in white marble by Italian craftsmen – and shipped it off to the United States. After service as this plutocrat's Xanadu, it has since been reconstructed inside the Metropolitan Museum of Art in New York. The castle's interior, much of it now supported by steel girders, has fragments of the original decoration. Given the Met's reluctance to return its dubiously acquired prize exhibit, a complete and exact reconstruction of the original using marble from the nearby quarries of Macael has begun (which may temporarily close off parts of the castle over the coming years). A book on sale in the small shop at the entrance – *El Castillo de Vélez Blanco* by Alfonso Ruiz García – has an image of the reconstituted patio in the New York Met, plus a watercolour of what it looked like *in situ*. Make sure to take in the fine **views** from the tower, the Torre del Homenaje. If you can't get in during normal hours call ☏950 41 50 27 or mobile 607415055, or enquire at the Ayuntamiento (☏950 61 48 00) on c/La Corredera. At the opposite end of the town, the sixteenth-century **Convento de San Luís**, also built by the Vélez family, has a fine chapel (currently closed to visitors) which was damaged during the Civil War.

Practicalities

The Almacen del Trigo **information office** (Tues–Sat 10am–2pm & 4–6pm, Sun 10am–2pm; ☎950 41 53 54) at the far end of the town (follow the signs), has information on Vélez and the surrounding Parque Natural de la Sierra de María (see below). For a **place to stay** in Vélez Blanco, the *Hostal La Sociedad*, c/Corredera 14 (☎950 41 50 27; ❷), is central and friendly for pleasant en-suite rooms with TV, or moving upmarket there's the elegant and excellent-value ⚘ *Casa de los Arcos*, c/San Francisco 2 (☎950 61 48 05, ⓦ www.casadelosarcos .net; ❸), near the information office, a beautifully restored eighteenth-century *casa señorial* overlooking a gorge. The hotel also organizes daily guided visits to the Letreros cave which are open to non-guests. A **campsite**, *Pinar del Rey* (☎649901680, ⓦ www.pinardelrey.es), lies on the edge of town towards Vélez Rubio, close to the Letreros cave. For **meals** the *Hostal Sociedad*'s owners, *Bar Sociedad* over the road, serve decent tapas and *raciónes* on their lively terrace. More formal meals and good local cooking are on offer at *Restaurante El Molino*, up some steps opposite a tiled fountain at the west end of the main street, with a charming patio terrace (the fresh trout is good here). *Mesón Antonia* near the castle entrance with a *menú* for around €8, and the nearby *Barbacoa María Fernández* (aka *Mavi*), c/Al'qua-sid 10, are other good little local places to eat.

Sierra de María and Orce

Walkers – and those in need of greenery after endless desert landscapes – may be tempted to continue northwest from Vélez Blanco along the A317 to María, a small town set among pine woods and, incidentally, the highest settlement in Almería, which is also the jumping-off point for the **Sierra de María**, a recently declared natural park. Information about walking trails, and on the park in general is available from a **visitors' centre** (Fri–Sun 10am–2pm & 6–8pm; ☎950 52 70 05), 2.5km beyond María on the Orce road.

Beyond María the SE35 soon enters an extensive plain covered with wheat-fields and stretches arrow-straight and apparently endlessly to the distant mountains. In high summer this plain is a cauldron beneath vast cloudless skies and you'll be lucky to meet another vehicle. Apart from a couple of godforsaken hamlets and the occasional wheeling eagle overhead hunting for prey, there are few features to punctuate this desolate but beautiful panorama. The landscape takes on a doubly dramatic aspect when you realize that one and a half million years ago this plain was a great lake visited by elephants, hippos, rhinos, water buffaloes, musk oxen, giant bears and ferocious hyenas as well as lions, leopards and lynxes. Early humans were known to have been in the area as early as 500,000 years ago but recent finds seem to have pushed this back by an aston-ishing additional one million years which, if scientifically confirmed, would make it the earliest appearance of primitive humans on the continent of Europe by a long way. These Stone Age arrivals probably came from Africa and lived on a diet of wild plants and carrion supplemented by fracturing the craniums and bones of the dead beasts to extract the brains and marrow – they had not yet developed the technology to take on and hunt big game.

When you finally reach it, the dusty and impoverished little settlement of **ORCE** hardly lives up to the self-styled billing – now proclaimed on all its literature – as *Cuna de la Humanidad Europea* (Cradle of European Man). The heart of the village is a tree-lined main square, Plaza Nueva, with an eighteenth-century fountain fronted by the Ayuntamiento and, in one corner the village's main bar, *Bar Plaza*. Just behind the square (with a rear entrance onto it) lies the **Casa Palacio de los Segura**, c/Tiendas 18, a sixteenth-century *casa señorial* with an elegant tower. This now houses a **tourist office** (Tues–Sun 10am–2pm & 4–7pm;

T958 74 61 71, Wwww.orce.es) and the superbly presented **Museo de la Prehistoria** (same hours; €2) which exhibits the Orce discoveries. As well as impressive animal remains from the periods of the finds there are displays (in Spanish) reconstructing the lifestyle of these early humans. The star exhibit is a copy (the original is under lock and key in the Ayuntamiento) of the small million-and-a-half-year-old **fragment of human skull** that has brought worldwide celebrity to Orce. Whilst not accepted conclusively by many experts (a point made in the museum presentation), its discoverers claim it belonged to a child of unknown sex which is thought to have been devoured by a great hyena. Most archeologists and paleontologists working in the area are now fairly sure that the skull fragment is not human but the same experts are convinced that the dating *will* eventually be confirmed due to crucial evidence turned up in 1998–99 of remarkable **lithic artefacts** (stone tools; displayed in the museum) around 1.4 million years old; finding genuine human remains, they believe, is only a matter of time. Various free leaflets on the finds in Spanish and an informative book on the excavations, *El Hombre de Orce*, are on sale. ·

Orce's only other sights of note lie just off the main square. The first is the eleventh-century **Moorish alcazaba** (Sat, Sun & holidays noon–2pm & 4–6pm; free) with an impressive tower – the Torre del Homenaje – whilst the other, opposite across a square, is the eighteenth-century **Iglesia de Santa María** (open service times 7–9pm) with a fine *retablo*.

A wonderful **place to stay** in Orce is at the ⅃ *Cuevas de Orce*, Ctra. de María s/n (T958 74 62 81, Wwww.cuevasdeorce.com; ❹), passed on the way into the village coming from María which is, as its name tells you, a **cave hotel**. Cosy en-suite cave dwellings come with kitchen and curious cave bathrooms. The village's best **place to eat** is *Mesón La Mimbrera*, (T958 74 61 48) just off the main square which does tasty game and regional dishes with a lunch-time *menú* for €9. Along the Galera road, 1km out of Orce, the green valley of the Río Galera contains the Manantial de Fuen Caliente, a beautiful natural pond filled with fish which has become the local **swimming pool**, complete with *cafetería*.

At Cúllar Baza, 23km southwest of Orce along routes SE33 and A330, you can pick up the A92N *autovía* heading towards Granada, 130km distant.

Inland Almería

An alternative way of reaching the coast to the east of Almería is to take a trip through the weird lunar landscape of Almería's distinctive desert scenery. There are two possible routes: via **Níjar** along the A7–E15 *autovía* to Carboneras, or via the more interesting **Tabernas** and **Sorbas** route (along the N340A) to Mojácar. The latter more northerly route, described below, passes by Almería's old western film set, **Mini Hollywood**, and a detour off this road can also be made to the pottery centre of **Níjar**. A visit to the underground caves of **Sorbas** is also a great adventure.

The road to Tabernas

The main road to Tabernas heads north out of Almería along the valley of the Río Andarax and forks right at Benhadux – along the A340 – passing the village of **Rioja** before it enters a dramatic brown-tinged-with-purple eroded landscape which looks as if it should be the backdrop for a Hollywood western. Some 10km past Rioja, in a particularly gulch-riven landscape, at Mini Hollywood you discover that someone else had the same idea first.

A visit to **MINI HOLLYWOOD** (aka Oasys Parque Temático; daily: June–Oct 10am–9pm; Nov–May 10am–7pm; €19, under 12 €9) is hard to resist – especially if you're travelling with kids – although better value if timed with one of the daily shows. The old film set's most famous production was a *Fistful of Dollars*, a connection that its publicity flyers never tire of repeating. Once inside, you'll see a main street overlooked by a water tower, which you may just recognize from the 1960s classic, or from *The Good, the Bad and the Ugly*, another film made here along with countless other spaghetti and paella westerns. You can wander into the *Tombstone Gulch* saloon for a drink, and in summer there are daily shows (noon, 5pm and 8pm), when actors in full cowboy rig and blasting off six-guns stage such epics as the capture, escape and final shooting of Jesse James, whilst in between the saloon stages shows of cancan girls flaunting their frillies. There's also a somewhat incongruous **zoo** – with birds, reptiles and big cats prowling depressingly small cages – plus a **pool** and numerous **fast food** outlets. Regular **buses** (from Almería's Intermodal bus-train station) link the city with Mini Hollywood, but not the places mentioned below.

Further along the road towards Tabernas, on the left, is **Texas Hollywood** (April–Oct daily 9am–8pm; three shows morning and afternoon; €16.50, kids €9.50), the location for *Once Upon a Time in the West* among other productions, where a couple of less commercialized film sets in a much more spectacular setting have an Indian village complete with wigwams, a Mexican town and a US cavalry frontier fort as well as camels and buffaloes. A kilometre or so east on the same road, a third site, **Western Leone** (similar hours and prices to Texas Hollywood), offers more sets used in the making of many Sixties' and Seventies' westerns including a ranch used in the making of *Once Upon a Time in the West*.

As well as the landscape and cheap labour costs, the film-makers were also drawn to the same unpolluted crystalline air which has lured astronomers here, and to the north of Tabernas, at Calar Alto in the Sierra de Filabres, a series of high-powered telescopes enables the **Hispano–German observatory** to study the heavens.

Tabernas

Surrounded by torrid desert scrubland, **TABERNAS** lies at the foot of a hill dominated by an impressive-looking **Moorish castle** where Fernando and Isabel ensconced themselves during the siege of Almería. Unfortunately, closer inspection reveals it to be mainly ruined and there's little to hang around for, except a drink, in the searing summer heat. Just beyond the village a road on the left – followed after 1km by a right turn towards the hamlet of Senés – leads to the **Centro Solar**, one of Europe's biggest solar energy fields, where row upon row of mirrors reflect the powerful sunlight and generate energy. Still at the development stage, it's hoped that when the system is commercially viable it could power massive desalination plants to regenerate the desert. If you have your own transport and are looking for **food** the *Venta Compadre* on the N340, just beyond Tabernas, is an excellent stop for a hearty €10 *menú*. Four kilometres beyond Tabernas on the left the *Hospedería del Desierto* (☎950 52 53 08, ⓦ www .hospederiadeldesierto.es; ❷–❸) is a comfortable desert *hostal*-hotel with palms, yuccas and cactuses filling its gardens, where there's also a pool.

Across the Sierra Alhamilla

Beyond Tabernas there are more dramatic landscapes – badlands with naked ridges of pitted sandstone, cut through by twisted and dried-up riverbeds, all of which vary in colour from yellow to red and from green to lavender-blue depending on the time of day and the nature of the stone. After 9km a road on the right opens up the possibility of a wonderfully scenic trip south to Níjar **across the Sierra Alhamilla**. This road climbs through more Arizona-type landscape, first to the hamlet of **Turrillas**, and then turns east to **Lucainena de las Torres**, a cluster of white boxes surrounding its red-roofed church. Beyond Lucainena the road snakes over the rugged Sierra Alhamilla to descend into Níjar, 16km to the south.

Níjar

NÍJAR is a neat, white and typically Almerian little town, with – in its upper Moorish *barrio* – narrow streets designed to give maximum shade. Now firmly on the tourist trail due to the inexpensive handmade **pottery** manufactured in workshops around the town and sold in the shops along the broad main street – Avenida García Lorca – and c/Real to the west, it still retains a relaxed and tranquil air. Little remains of the Moorish fort here but the pottery tradition – dating back to when the Moors held sway and including attractive traditional patterns created with mineral dyes – lives on, as exhibits in the museum at Almería clearly demonstrate. The town is also known for its **jarapas**: bed-covers, curtains and rugs made from rags. The more authentic potters are located in the **barrio alfarero**, along c/Real running parallel to the main street, where the *talleres* (workshops; open 10am–2pm & 4–7pm) of Gongora, Granados, El Oficio and the friendly Angel y Loli (at no. 54) are located. Also here, off the bottom of the street in a bullishly named studio-shop called La Tienda de los Milagros, is resident English ceramic artist Matthew Weir (married to an *almeriense*) who has a more modernist approach. His wife Isabel is a skilled producer of *jarapas* and textiles in her own right.

Practicalities

Níjar's new **turismo,** c/Real 1 (Mon 9am–2pm, Tues–Sun 9am–2pm & 4–8pm; ☎950 61 22 43, ⓦ www.nijar.es) is sited at junction of c/Real with

---

Blood Wedding

An event that happened at Níjar in 1928 inspired one of Lorca's most powerful plays, *Bodas de Sangre* (*Blood Wedding*). A young woman named Francisca was about to marry a man named Casimiro at a farmhouse near Níjar. She was an heiress with a modest dowry and a reluctant bride, he a labourer pressured by his scheming brother and sister-in-law to make this match and thus bring money into the family. A few hours prior to the wedding taking place, Francisca eloped with her cousin, with whom she had been in love since childhood, but who had only realized his feelings when confronted with the reality of losing her. They were swiftly intercepted by Casimiro's brother, who shot her cousin dead. His brother was convicted of the murder, whilst Casimiro, the groom, was unable to overcome his humiliation and, it is said, never looked upon Francisca or even her photograph again. Francisca never married and lived as a recluse until her death in 1978.

Lorca avidly followed the story in the newspapers and had a knowledge of the area from time spent in Almería as a child. An interesting afterword is told by the writer Nina Epton, who, on a visit to San José in the 1960s, was dining at the house of a wealthy Spanish *señoron*, or landowner, while a group of farm labourers waited outside on a long bench, no doubt for payment. In her book *Andalusia* she describes what happened when eventually she accompanied Don José, her host, to speak to the men:

Among them was a wizened old man called Casimiro whom I would not have looked at twice before I was told that a dramatic incident in his youth had inspired Federico García Lorca to take Casimiro for his model of the novio in "Blood Wedding".

the Avda. García Lorca, and can provide a map and information on the town and region.

There are a number of small **hostales**, of which the best for en-suite rooms is *Montes* (T 950 36 01 57; ❷) at Avda. García Lorca 26; they also serve a *menú*. At the top of the same street *Hostal-Restaurant Asensio* (T 950 36 10 56; ❸) is another possibility. Other places along the main street serving **meals** include *Bar La Untá*, Avda. García Lorca 6, which does good tapas and *platos combinados* and has a small terrace. There are more **tapas** and **raciónes** bars in the upper town beyond the church where, on Plaza La Glorieta, the excellent *El Pipa* also does meals and *Bar La Glorieta* – with an elevated terrace – also does food as well as being a pleasant place for a nightcap.

Sorbas and the Paraje Natural de Karst en Yesos

Continuing 18km east from the turn-off to Lucainena de las Torres along the N340A, this corner of Almería has one last dramatic sight in **SORBAS**, an extraordinary place, surrounded by more moonscapes, whose cliff-top houses overhang an ashen gorge, best seen from the main road. Like Níjar, it is reputed for its **pottery** – although the designs are less original – which is sold at a trio of inconspicuous *alfarerías* (workshops, near one of which still stands a remarkable **Moorish kiln**) in the lower part of the village, near a white-walled *ermita* (chapel) and signed from the main square, Plaza del Ayuntamiento. This tidy little place is also on the tourist trail, especially on Thursdays when trippers flock in from Mojácar for the weekly **market** in the same plaza.

The main pull for visitors to these parts, though, is the astonishing scenery in the surrounding **Paraje Natural de Karst en Yesos** (just south of town and signed from the main N340A), where around six million years ago water erosion carved out subterranean chasms full of stalagmites and stalactites. Guided visits to the caves are a two-hour adventure – with helmets and flashlights and not a little scrambling and squeezing – organized by the Turismo (English and Spanish; April–Oct visits daily on the hour from 10am–1pm & 3–8pm, W www.cuevasdesorbas.com; €12, kids €8). A couple of more-challenging explorations lasting three to six hours are also on offer (see website for details). Above ground, the water's action has created flat-topped, volcano-like protrusions and deep gorges. These are visible from the main N340A, but for a closer look take the minor A8203 towards Los Molinos del Río Aguas east of Sorbas. At the crest of a hill, a track to the left leads to a peak above the gorge, where sweeping circular views extend over the lunar landscape as far as the snowcapped peaks of the Sierra Nevada; it's a great place to watch the sunset. Alternatively, you could follow the track descending through the tumbledown but picturesque hamlet of **Los Molinos** to follow the course of the dried-up river gorge.

Practicalities

Sorbas's small **Turismo** is at c/Terraplén 9, just off the main N340A on the way into town (July–Aug Mon–Fri 10.30am–2.30pm & 5.30–8pm, Sept–March Tues–Fri 10.30am–2.30pm; T 950 36 44 76, W www.sorbas.org). The Turismo lies 50m uphill from the interesting and informative **Centro de Visitantes** (April–Sept 11am–2pm & 4–7pm; ring for winter hours; T 950 36 44 81) for the Karst en Yesos caves.

For a **place to stay**, *Hostal Sorbas* (T 950 36 41 60; ❸), on the right as you enter the town from Tabernas, has tidy en-suite rooms but by far the nicest place to put up is *Hostal Rural Montelés* (T 950 36 46 35, W www.hostalmonteles.com; ❸), c/Calvo Sotelo 4, with pleasant a/c en-suite rooms in a striking mansion just off the main square, Plaza del Ayuntamiento. **Food** is available at *Cafetería*

Caymar, also on the main square, which does tapas and *raciónes*; for more elaborate fare visit their upmarket offshoot next door, *Restaurante El Rincón* (℡950 36 41 52), which prepares regional specialities with flair. On the main road to the east of town – where you'll get the best view of the cliff-top houses – the *Café-Bar El Suave* does substantial *platos combinados*.

To reach Sorbas from Níjar you could retrace your path back over the **Sierra Alhamilla** (there's a 4km short cut to the N340A from Lucainena) or, for a bit of variety, follow the A7-E15 east for about 23km, turning off along a minor road (the A8203) for the final 10km to Sorbas.

Travel details

Trains

Almería to: Granada (4 daily; 2hr 15min); Guadix (6 daily; 1hr 20min); Seville (4 daily; 4hr 30min).
Granada to: Algeciras (3 daily; 4hr 15min); Almería (4 daily; 2hr 15min); Córdoba (3 daily; 2hr 30min); Guadix (4 daily; 1hr); Málaga (5 daily; change at Bobadilla; 2hr 40min); Ronda (3 daily; 2hr 45min); Seville (4 daily; 3hr 30min).

Buses

Bus times are quoted for the fastest journey times, normally direct. There may be other buses to the same destination which make additional stops at towns and villages en route.
Almería to: Agua Amarga (2/4 daily; 1hr 30min); Aguadulce (every 30min; 20min); Almerimar (3 daily; 1hr 30min); Cabo de Gata via Retamar (6 daily; 55min); Carboneras (2/4 daily; 1hr 15min); Córdoba (1 daily; 5hr); Garrucha (4 daily; 1hr 15min); Granada (10 daily; 4hr); Guadix (4 daily; 2hr 15min); Jaén: (3 daily; 4hr); Láujar de Andarax (2 daily; 2hr); Las Negras (2 daily; 1hr 15min); Málaga (9 daily; 3hr 30min); María (2 daily; 3hr 15min); Mojácar (3 daily; 1hr 30min); Mini Hollywood (4 daily; 40min); Nijar (2 daily Mon–Fri; 35min); Rodalquilar (daily; 1hr 30min);

Roquetas de Mar (every 30min; 30min); San Jose (4 daily; 1hr 15min); Seville (3 daily; 5hr 45min); Sorbas (4 daily; 1hr); Tabernas (4 daily; 40min); Ubeda (2 daily; 3hr); Velez Blanco (1 daily; 3hr); Velez Rubio (1 daily; 2hr 50min).
Granada to: Almería (8 daily; 4hr); Almuñecar (15 daily; 1hr 40min); Baeza/Ubeda (9 daily; 2hr 15min); Baza (8 daily; 1hr 30min); Cádiz (4 daily; 5hr); Cazorla (2 daily; 4hr); Córdoba (4 daily; 2hr 45min); Guadix (15 daily; 1hr); Jaén (12 daily; 1hr 15min); La Herradura (8 daily; 1hr 50min); Madrid (13 daily; 5hr); Mojácar (2 daily; 4hr); Montefrío (3 daily; 1hr 15min); Motril (11 daily; 1hr 45min); Nerja (7 daily; 2hr 15min); Salobreña (7 daily; 1hr); Seville (9 daily; 3hr 40min); Sierra Nevada /Alpujarras: the following all pass Lanjarón and Órgiva, 1hr trip from the city; current departure times are 8.30am & 5.30pm to Ugíjar (also passing Albondón, Cádiar & Yegen); noon & 5pm to Berchules (also passing Pampaneira, Bubión, Capileira, Busquistar & Trevelez); Berja (2 daily; 4hr 10min).

Ferries

Almería to: Melilla (1/2 daily; 6–8hr); Nador (1/2 daily; 4–9hr).

Contexts

Contexts

History

A s the southernmost region of the Iberian peninsula, Andalucía has manifested throughout its history a character essentially different from the rest of Spain. Due to the variety of peoples who came and settled here, the region has always had an enriching influence on the territories further north. This meeting place of seas and cultures, with Africa only nine miles off the coast of its southern tip, brought Andalucía into early contact with the sophisticated civilizations of the eastern Mediterranean and a long period as part of the North African Moorish empire. The situation was later reversed when Andalucía sent out explorers to the New World and became the gateway to the Spanish American empire.

Prehistory

The first Europeans of whom we have knowledge lived in Andalucía. A recent series of spectacular discoveries at **Orce**, seventy miles northeast of Granada, rocked the archeological world as the date for the **arrival of early humans in Europe** was pushed back from c.700,000 years ago to perhaps a million years before this, making Orce – if the findings are scientifically confirmed – the earliest known site of human occupation in Europe for a long way. Arriving from Africa and crossing the straits by swimming or on rafts these Stone Age people colonized an area of now vanished lakeland near Orce. Here they hunted hippos, hyenas, mammoths and vultures and made tools from flint. Evidence of occupation by Stone Age societies stretching back some 400,000 years was already known about from discoveries at nearby **Venta Micena** where early inhabitants hunted elephant and rhino and left behind tools and camp fires. Archeologists have now started work on filling in the gaping prehistorical record between these two sites. Some of the earliest **human fossils** found on the Iberian peninsula were unearthed inside the **Gibraltar** caves with evidence of **Neanderthals** dating from around 100,000 BC. In the Paleolithic period, the first **Homo sapiens** arrived on the Iberian peninsula from southern France, settling around the Bay of Biscay as well as in the south. They were cave dwellers and hunter-gatherers and at the Pileta and Nerja caves in Málaga have left behind remarkable **cave paintings** depicting the animals that they hunted. During the later Neolithic phase, a sophisticated material culture developed in southern Spain attested to by the finds of esparto sandals and baskets as well as jewellery in the **Cueva de los Murciélagos** in Granada.

Subsequent prehistory is more complex and confused. There does not appear to have been any great development in the cave cultures of the north. Instead the focus shifts south – where **Neolithic colonists** had arrived from North Africa – to Valencia and **Almería**. Cave paintings have been found in rock shelters such as those at **Vélez Blanco** dating from around 4000 BC. Here also, not long afterwards, **metalworking** began and the debate continues as to the cause of this dramatic leap forward: a development by the indigenous inhabitants or the arrival of "technicians" – evidenced by many trading artefacts such as ivory and turquoise – from the eastern Mediterranean. The fortified site of **Los Millares** (c.2700 BC), in the centre of a rich mining area in Almería, with its Aegean-style "bee-hive" tombs is one of the most important remains from this era. In the same period, **dolmens** were being built such as those at **Antequera**, a building style which spread from here throughout the peninsula and into Europe. This dolmenic culture also influenced a ceramic style, typified by bell-shaped artefacts and giving rise to the name **Beaker folk**. More developments occurred in the same area of Almería about 1700 BC when the **El Argar** civilization started to produce bronze and worked silver and gold, trading across the Mediterranean. This culture fanned out across the south between 1700 and 1000 BC and, during the first millennium BC, the **Iberian civilization** fully established itself.

Tartessus and the Iberians

The **kingdom of Tartessus** appeared early in the first millennium BC and typifies the great strides forward being made by the Iberians of the south. Both the Bible (which names it Tarshish) and Greek and Latin texts refer to this important kingdom and trading centre. It was probably sited on the estuary of the Río Guadalquivir on the border of Huelva and Seville provinces; its precise location has yet to be identified, although its prowess as a producer and exporter of bronze, gold and silver as well as a creator of sophisticated **jewellery** is apparent from the finds displayed in Seville's archeological museum. The Tartessians were also a literate people but nothing of their literature survives apart from scattered inscriptions which have thus far defied translation. In the mid-sixth century BC Tartessus incurred the wrath of the rising power of Carthage through its friendship with the Greeks and not long after this appears to have been destroyed by them.

The Iberians at other centres in the south also developed sophisticated cultures based upon agriculture, stockbreeding, fishing, mining and iron production. When the Romans came into contact with them in the third century BC they found a literate people with written laws, and a vibrant culture which included music and dance. Their skills in the plastic arts – an enduring flair throughout the peninsula's history – are displayed in artefacts such as the splendid **Dama de Baza**, a dramatic fourth-century BC painted terracotta statue of a woman, discovered at Baza in Granada. The Iberian skill with masonry and stone sculpture can be seen at the necropolis at **Toya** in Jaén province, and other remarkable works from the fifth century BC are in the museum at Jaén itself.

The first colonists

The southern coast attracted colonists from different regions of the Mediterranean. The **Phoenicians** – founders of a powerful trading empire based in modern Lebanon – established the port of Gadir (Cádiz) about 1100 BC. This was obviously connected with their intensive **trading operations** in the metals of the Guadalquivir valley carried from Tartessus where they may even have had a factory. Their wealth and success gave rise to a Spanish "Atlantis" myth, based around Huelva. Besides metals, the Phoenicians also came for the rich fishing along the southern coast which stimulated industries for salting and preserving the catch. The salt itself was gained from beds such as those at the **Cabo de Gata** – still in commercial operation today – in Almería. Other operations, such as the **purple dyeing industry**, for which the Phoenicians were famous, exploited the large stocks of murex shellfish in coastal waters. The coastline of Andalucía is dotted with Phoenician **settlements** from this time such as those at Malaka (Málaga), Sexi (Almuñecar) and Abdera (Adra). Market rivalry also brought the **Greeks**, who established their trading colonies along the northeastern coast – the modern Costa Brava – before penetrating southwards into the Phoenician zone. They were encouraged by the Tartessians, no doubt in an attempt to break the Phoenician economic stranglehold on the region.

When the Phoenicians were incorporated into the Persian Empire in the sixth century BC, however, a former colony, **Carthage**, moved into the power vacuum, destroyed Tartessus and ejected the Greeks from the south. Carthage then turned the western Mediterranean into a jealously guarded trading monopoly, sinking ships of other states who attempted to trade there. This she tenaciously held on to, as the rising power of Rome forced her out of the central Mediterranean. In the course of the third century BC, Carthage built up Spain into a new base for her empire, from which to regain strength and strike back at her great rival. Although making little impact inland, the Carthaginians occupied most of Andalucía and expanded along the Mediterranean seaboard to establish a new capital at Cartagena ("New Carthage") in Murcia. The mineral wealth of Andalucía, particularly **silver**, was used to finance the military build-up as well as to recruit an enormous army of Iberian mercenaries. Under Hannibal they prepared to invade Italy and in 219 BC attacked Saguntum (modern Sagunto), a strategic ally of the growing Roman Empire. This precipitated the **Second Punic War**, bringing Roman legions to the Spanish peninsula for the first time. Heading south from modern Catalunya, the coastal towns were successively conquered and the **end of Carthaginian domination** of Spain was sealed in 206 BC at the battle of Ilipa (Alcalá del Río), just north of Seville. When Cádiz fell the following year, Rome became master of the southern peninsula and **Itálica** (near Seville) was founded as the first Roman city in Spain. A new and very different age had begun.

Romans and Visigoths

The **Roman colonization** of the peninsula was far more intense than anything previously experienced and met with great resistance from the Celtiberian tribes of the north and centre, although much less so in Andalucía where the Turditanian people, tired of Carthaginian oppression, welcomed the invaders. In the final years of the Roman republic many of the crucial battles for control of the Roman state were fought out in Spain, ending with Julius Caesar's victory at Munda, south of Córdoba, in 45 BC. After Caesar's assassination, his successor Augustus reorganized Spain into three provinces, the southernmost of which became **Hispania Baetica**, roughly modern Andalucía, with **Corduba** (Córdoba) as its capital.

In this period Spain became one of the most important and wealthiest centres of the Roman Empire and Andalucía was its most urbane heartland. Unlike the rugged and fractious Celtiberians further north, the sophisticated Iberians of the south had their own municipal traditions and took easily to Roman ideas of government. Indeed, their native languages and dialects had disappeared early in the first century AD as Latinization became complete. For four centuries Andalucía enjoyed a "**Golden Age**" with unprecedented prosperity based on the production of olive oil, wool, grain, wine and the highly prized *garum* fish sauce made at centres such as **Baelo Claudia** near Tarifa. Another important development was a massive expansion of mining at **Río Tinto** in Huelva. During this period, Baetica supplied **two Roman emperors**, Trajan (one of the greatest) and his adopted son Hadrian, along with the outstanding writers Seneca and Lucan. The finest monuments of the period were built in the provincial capital at Córdoba, and cities such as Cádiz, Itálica, Málaga and Carmona, linked by a network of superb roads and adorned with temples, baths, amphitheatres and aqueducts, were the equal of any in the empire.

In the fourth and fifth centuries, however, the Roman political framework began to show signs of **decadence and corruption**. Although the actual structure didn't totally collapse until the Muslim invasions of the early eighth century, it became increasingly vulnerable to **barbarian invasions** from northern Europe. Early in the fifth century AD, the Suevi (Swabians), Alans and Vandals swept across the Pyrenees leaving much devastation in their wake. The Romans, preoccupied with attempts to stave off Gothic attacks on Italy, bought off the invaders by allowing them to settle within the imperial borders. The Suevi settled in Galicia, the Alans in Portugal and Murcia, whilst the **Vandals** put down roots in Baetica, providing the origin of Andalucía's name. The resulting wars between the invaders only served to further weaken Rome's grip on the peninsula as a burgeoning Christian Church – its first Spanish council was held at Iliberis (Granada) – gained more influence over the population.

Internal strife was heightened by the arrival of the **Visigoths** from Gaul, allies of Rome and already Romanized to a large degree. The triumph of Visigothic strength in the fifth century resulted in a period of spurious unity, based upon an exclusive military rule from their capital at Toledo, but their numbers were never great and their order was often fragmentary and nominal, with the bulk of the subject people kept in a state of disconsolate servility and held ransom for their services in times of war. Above them in the ranks of the military elite there were constant plots and factions – exacerbated by the Visigothic system of elected monarchy and by their adherence to the heretical Arian philosophy. When **King Leovigild** attempted to impose this creed on Andalucía in the mid-sixth century, the region revolted with the king's son Hermenegild at its head, but the insurrection was brutally crushed. In 589 **King Recared** converted to Catholicism, which for a time stiffened Visigothic control, but religious strife was only multiplied: forced conversions, especially within the Jewish enclaves, maintained a constant simmering of discontent. The Visigoths precariously held on to their domain for a further century as plots and counter-plots surrounded the throne. This infighting led indirectly to the Moorish invasions of Andalucía when **King Witiza**, who died in 710, was thwarted by a usurper, Roderic, duke of Baetica, from handing over the throne to his son, Achila. Once **King Roderic** had installed himself on the throne the embittered family of Witiza appealed to the Muslims in North Africa for assistance to overthrow him. The North Africans, who had long eyed the riches of Andalucía with envy, now saw their opportunity.

The Moorish conquest

In contrast to the long-drawn-out Roman campaigns, the **Moorish conquest** of the peninsula was effected with extraordinary speed. This was a characteristic phenomenon of the spread of Islam – Muhammad left Mecca in 622 and by 705 his followers had established control over all of North Africa. Spain, with its political instability, wealth and fertile climate, was an inevitable extension of their aims. In 711 **Tariq**, governor of Tangier, led a force of seven thousand Berbers across the straits and routed the Visigoth army of King Roderic on the banks of the Río Guadalete close to Jerez. Two years later the Visigoths made a last desperate stand at Mérida and within a decade the Moors had conquered all but the wild mountains of Asturias. The land under their authority was dubbed **al-Andalus**, a fluid term which expanded and shrank with the intermittent gains and losses of the Reconquest. It was Andalucía, however, that was destined to become the heartland of the Moorish ascendancy and where the Moors were to remain in control for most of the next eight centuries.

The Moorish incursion was not simply a military conquest. The Moors (a collective term for the numerous waves of Arab, Syrian and Berber settlers from North Africa) were often content to grant a limited autonomy in exchange for payment of tribute; their administrative system was tolerant and easily absorbed both Spanish Jews and Christians, those who retained their religion being known as "Mozarabs". This **tolerant attitude** was illustrated when the Moorish army reached Córdoba where they found the large Visigothic church of St Vincent, now the fabulous Mezquita. Unlike previous invaders, they did not sack or burn the heathen temple but purchased half of it to use as a mosque whilst the Christians continued to use the other half for their own services.

Al-Andalus was a distinctly Spanish state of Islam. Though at first politically subject to the eastern caliphate (or empire) of Baghdad, it was soon virtually independent. In the tenth century, at the peak of its power and expansion, Abd ar-Rahman III asserted total independence, proclaiming himself caliph of a new **western Islamic empire**. Its capital was **Córdoba** – the largest, most prosperous and most civilized city in Europe. This was the great age of Muslim Spain: its scholarship, philosophy, architecture and craftsmanship were without rival and there was an unparalleled growth in urban life, trade and agriculture, aided by magnificent irrigation projects. These and other engineering feats were not, on the whole, instigated by the Moors who instead took the basic Roman models and adapted them to a new level of sophistication. In **architecture** and the **decorative arts**, however, their contribution was original and unique – as may be seen in the astonishingly beautiful monuments of Seville, Córdoba and Granada.

The Cordoban caliphate (and the emirate that preceded it) created a remarkable degree of unity, despite a serious challenge to their authority by the rebel leader **Ibn Hafsun** from his Bobastro fortress (north of Málaga) in the latter years of the ninth century. But its rulers were to become decadent and out of touch, prompting the brilliant but dictatorial **al-Mansur** to usurp control. Under this extraordinary ruler Moorish power reached new heights, using a professional Berber army to push the Christian kingdom of Asturias-León back into the Cantabrian mountains and sacking its most holy shrine, Santiago de Compostela, in 997. However, after al-Mansur's death the caliphate quickly lost its authority and in 1031 disintegrated into a series of small independent kingdoms or **taifas**, the strongest of which was Seville.

Internal divisions meant that the *taifas* offered less resistance to the Christian kingdoms that were rallying in the north, and twice North Africa had to be called upon for reinforcement. This resulted in two distinct new waves of Moorish invasion – first by the fanatically Islamic **Almoravids** (1086) and later by the **Almohads** (1147), who restored effective Muslim authority and left behind one of Moorish Spain's most elegant monuments, the **Giralda** tower in Seville. However, their crushing defeat by the Christian forces under Alfonso VIII in 1212, at the battle of **Las Navas de Tolosa** in Jaén, marked the beginning of the end for Moorish Spain.

The Christian Reconquest

The **Reconquest** of land and influence from the Moors was a slow and intermittent process. It began with a symbolic victory by a small force of Christians at Covadonga in the region of Asturias (722) in northern Spain and was not completed until 1492 with the conquest of Granada by Fernando and Isabel.

Covadonga resulted in the formation of the tiny Christian **kingdom of the Asturias**. Initially just 25km by 19km in area, it had by 914 reclaimed León and most of Galicia and northern Portugal. At this point, progress was temporarily halted by the devastating campaigns of al-Mansur. However, with the fall of the Cordoban caliphate and the divine aid of Spain's Moor-slaying patron saint, the avenging Santiago (St James the Apostle), the Reconquest moved into a new and powerful phase.

The frontier castles built against Arab attack gave name to **Castile**, founded in the tenth century as a county of León-Asturias. Under Fernando I (1037–65) it achieved the status of a kingdom and became the main thrust and focus of the Reconquest. In 1085 this period of confident Christian expansion reached its zenith with the capture of the great Moorish city of Toledo. The following year, however, the Almoravids arrived by invitation from Seville, and military activity was effectively frozen – except, that is, for the exploits of the legendary **El Cid**, a Castilian nobleman who won considerable lands around Valencia in 1095, thus checking Muslim expansion up the eastern coast.

The next concerted phase of the Reconquest began as a response to the threat imposed by the Almohads. The kings of León, Castile, Aragón and Navarra united in a crusade that resulted in the great victory at Las Navas de Tolosa. Thereafter Muslim power was paralysed and the **Christian armies** moved on to take most of al-Andalus. Fernando III ("El Santo", the saint) led Castilian soldiers into Córdoba in 1236 and twelve years later into Seville. By the end of the thirteenth century only the Nasrid **kingdom of Granada** remained under Muslim authority and this was to provide a brilliant sunset to Moorish rule in Andalucía. Its survival for a further two centuries whilst surrounded by its Christian enemies was due as much to skilful diplomacy as to payment of tribute to the monarchs of Castile.

Two factors should be stressed regarding the Reconquest. First, its unifying religious nature – the **spirit of crusade**, intensified by the religious zeal of the Almoravids and Almohads, and by the wider European climate (which in 1085 gave rise to the First Crusade). At the same time the Reconquest was a movement of **recolonization**. The fact that the country had been under arms for so long meant that the nobility had a major and clearly visible social role, a trend perpetuated by the redistribution of captured land in huge packages, or **latifundia**. Heirs to this tradition still remain as landlords of the great estates, most conspicuously in Andalucía where it has produced wretched conditions for the workers on the land ever since. Men from the ranks were also awarded land, forming a lower, larger stratum of nobility, the **hidalgos**. It was their particular social code that provided the material for Cervantes in *Don Quijote.*

Any spirit of mutual cooperation that had temporarily united the Christian kingdoms disintegrated during the fourteenth century, and independent lines of development were once again pursued. **Castile** emerged as the strongest over this period: self-sufficiency in agriculture and a flourishing wool trade with the Netherlands enabled the state to build upon the prominent military role under Fernando III.

Los Reyes Católicos

Los Reyes Católicos – the Catholic Monarchs – was the joint title given to **Fernando V of Aragón** and **Isabel I of Castile**, whose marriage in 1479 united the two largest kingdoms in Spain. Unity was in practice more symbolic than real: Castile had underlined its rights in the marriage vows and Aragón retained its old administrative structure. So, in the beginning at least, the growth of any national unity or Spanish – as opposed to local – sentiment was very much dependent on the head of state. Nevertheless, from this time on it begins to be realistic to consider Spain as a single political entity.

At the heart of Fernando and Isabel's popular appeal lay a **religious bigotry** that they shared with most of their Christian subjects. The **Inquisition** was instituted in Castile in 1480 and in Aragón seven years later. Aiming to establish the purity of the Catholic faith by rooting out heresy, it was directed mainly at Jews (despite Fernando's half-Jewish parentage) – resented for their enterprise in commerce and influence in high places, as well as for their faith. Expression had already been given to these feelings in a pogrom in 1391; it was reinforced by an edict issued in 1492 which forced up to 400,000 Jews to flee the country. A similar spirit was embodied in the reconquest of the Nasrid **kingdom of Granada**, also in 1492. During this long campaign Gonzalo Fernández de Córdoba, "El Gran Capitán," developed the Spanish army into a formidable force that was set to dominate the battlefields of Europe for the next century and a half. As Granada was the last stronghold of Muslim authority, the religious rights of its citizens were guaranteed under the treaty of surrender. Then the policy was reversed and forced mass conversions were introduced. The subsequent and predictable rebellions – particularly violent in **Las Alpujarras** – were brutally put down and within a decade those Muslims under Christian rule had been given the choice between conversion or expulsion.

The year 1492 was symbolic of a fresh start in another way: it was in this year that **Columbus** sailed from Huelva to make the **discovery of America**, and the papal bull that followed, entrusting Spain with the conversion of the American Indians, further entrenched Spain's sense of a mission to bring the world to the "True Faith". The next ten years saw the systematic conquest, colonization and exploitation of the **New World**, with new territory stretching from Labrador in modern Canada to Brazil, and new-found wealth pouring into the royal coffers. The control of trade with the New World was carried on through **Seville** where the Casa de Contración (House of Trade) was established in 1503. The city rapidly grew into one of the great cities of Europe during which it enjoyed two centuries of commercial monopoly. Paradoxically, Andalucía as a whole benefited little from this wealth, which was appropriated by the crown for its foreign campaigns and by absentee landlords. Over the succeeding two centuries the region languished as a backwater and the poverty of the peasants led many to emigrate to the New World in order to better themselves, turning much of the region into a vast, unpopulated desert.

The Habsburg Age

Carlos I, a Habsburg, came to the throne in 1516 as a beneficiary of the marriage alliances of the Catholic monarchs. Five years later, he was elected emperor of the Holy Roman Empire as Carlos V (**Charles V**), inheriting not only Castile and Aragón, but Flanders, the Netherlands, Artois, the Franche-Comté and all the American colonies to boot. With such responsibilities it was inevitable that attention would be diverted from Spain, whose chief function became to sustain the Holy Roman Empire with gold and silver from the Americas. It was only with the accession of **Felipe II** in 1556 that Spanish politics became more centralized and that the notion of an absentee king was reversed.

This was a period of unusual religious intensity: the **Inquisition** was enforced with renewed vigour, and a "final solution" to the problem of the Moriscos (subject Moors), who continued to adhere to their ancient traditions and practise Muslim worship in secret, resulted in a decree banning Arabic dress, books and speech. The result was another rising of Moriscos in Las Alpujarras that was fiercely suppressed with Muslims being forcibly deported to other parts of the country. Felipe III later ordered the expulsion of half the total number of Moriscos in Spain – allowing only two families to remain in each Alpujarran village in order to maintain irrigation techniques. The **exodus** of both Muslim and Jews created a large gulf in the labour force and in the higher echelons of commercial life – and in trying to uphold the Catholic cause, an enormous strain was put upon resources without any clearcut victory. Despite being a golden literary and artistic age, politically and economically the seventeenth century was a disaster for Spain. Lurching progressively deeper into debt, she suffered heavy defeats on the battlefield as her possessions in the Netherlands and France were lost, and recurring financial crises and economic stagnation engendered a deepening mood of disillusionment. **Andalucía** shared in this decline, exacerbated by the tendency of the mercantile classes to involve themselves only in entrepôt trade which left most of the profits in the hands of other countries. There was also no stimulus given to industrial production by the custom of merchants retiring from commerce and investing their profits in land, which created a landed gentry weighed down by honours and titles whose lifestyle came to be looked upon as being incompatible with commerce.

The Bourbons

The **Bourbon dynasty** succeeded to the Spanish throne in the person of Felipe V (1700); with him began the **War of the Spanish Succession** against the rival claim of Archduke Charles of Austria, assisted by British forces. As a result of the Treaty of Utrecht that ended the war (1713), Spain was stripped of all territory in Belgium, Luxembourg, Italy and Sardinia, but Felipe V was recognized as king. **Gibraltar** was seized by the British in the course of the war. For the rest of the century Spain fell very much under the French sphere of influence, an influence that given political definition by an alliance with the French Bourbons in 1762. This Gallic connection brought the ideas of Enlightenment Europe into the peninsula and during the reign of Carlos III (1759–88) a number of radically minded ministers attempted to deal with the nation's chronic problems. Along with a more tolerant attitude towards the **gypsies**, who had become victims of racial abuse and hostility, the king's minister, Pablo de Olavide, began an imaginative, if ultimately unsuccessful, scheme to **repopulate the Sierra Morena** in Andalucía with foreign immigrants (see p.312).

Contact with France also made involvement in the **Napoleonic Wars** inevitable and led eventually to the defeat of the Spanish and French fleet at the **Battle of Trafalgar** off the coast of Cádiz in 1805. Popular outrage was such that the powerful prime minister, Godoy, was overthrown and King Carlos IV forced to abdicate (1808). Napoleon seized the opportunity to install his brother, Joseph, on the throne, whilst French armies and generals ransacked and stole much of the country's artistic heritage.

Fierce local resistance in the form of guerrilla warfare was accompanied by armies raised by the various local administrations. Thus it was that a militia put in the field by the junta of Seville inflicted a resounding defeat on a French army at **Bailén** in Jaén in 1808, which forced Joseph, the "intruder king", to flee back across the border. This resistance was eventually backed by the muscle of a British army, first under Sir John Moore, later under the duke of Wellington, and the French were at last driven out in the course of the **War of Independence** (Peninsular War). Meanwhile, the **American colonies** had been successfully asserting their independence from a preoccupied centre and with them went Spain's last real claim of significance on the world stage. The entire nineteenth century was dominated by the struggle between an often reactionary monarchy and the aspirations of liberal constitutional reformers.

Seeds of Civil War

Between 1810 and 1813, whilst the war raged on across the peninsula, an ad hoc Cortes (parliament) meeting in **Cádiz** had set up a **liberal constitution** which stipulated a strict curtailment of the powers of the crown with ministers responsible to a democratically elected chamber. The first act of the despotic Fernando VII on being returned to the throne was to abolish this, and until his death in 1833 he continued to stamp out the least hint of liberalism. But the Constitution of 1812 was to remain a "sacred text" for a future democratic Spain, besides introducing the word "liberal" to Europe's political vocabulary. On Fernando's death, the right of succession was contested between his brother, Don Carlos, backed by the Church, conservatives and Basques, and his infant daughter, Isabel, who looked to the Liberals and the army for support.

So began the **First Carlist War**, a civil war that divided Spanish emotions for six years. Isabel II was eventually declared of age in 1843, her reign a long record of scandal, political crisis and constitutional compromise. Liberal army generals under the leadership of General Prim effected a coup in 1868 and the queen was forced to abdicate, but attempts to maintain a Republican government foundered. The Cortes was again dissolved and the throne returned to Isabel's son, Alfonso XII. The military began increasingly to move into the power vacuum left by the weakened monarchy. The **pronunciamiento** – whereby an officer backed by military force "pronounced" what was in the best interests of a city or region – was born in this period and was to plague the country into modern times.

The **nineteenth century** in Andalucía mirrored Spain's national decline. The loss of the American colonies had badly hit the region's trade, and this was compounded by the phylloxera plague from the 1870s onwards which wiped out most of the vineyards, brought the sherry industry to its knees, and fuelled the growth of strikes in the cities and popular uprisings on the land as the economy deteriorated. Parodoxically, this century also did more than any other to bestow on Andalucía the image it has held ever since. Writers, artists and travellers of the **Romantic Age** saw in its bullfights, flamenco, bandits and beguiling women a world of gaiety and colour, epitomized in the operas *Carmen* and *The Barber of Seville*, both works from this period.

The years preceding World War I merely heightened the discontent, which found expression in the growing **political movements** of the working class. The Socialist Workers' Party was founded in Madrid after the restoration of Alfonso XII, and spawned its own trade union, the UGT (1888). Its anarchist counterpart, the CNT (Confederación Nacional de Trabajo), was founded in 1911, gaining substantial support among the oppressed peasantry of Andalucía.

The loss of **Cuba** in 1898 emphasized the growing isolation of Spain in international affairs and added to economic problems with the return of soldiers seeking employment where there was none. In Andalucía a regionalist movement known as **Andalucismo** was born demanding land reform and greater Andalucian autonomy. A call-up for army reserves to fight in **Morocco** in 1909 provoked a general strike and the "Tragic Week" of rioting in Barcelona. Between 1914 and 1918, Spain was outwardly neutral but inwardly turbulent; inflated prices made the postwar recession harder to bear.

The general disillusionment with parliamentary government, together with the fears of employers and businessmen for their own security, gave **General Primo de Rivera** sufficient support for a military coup in 1923. Coming himself from Jerez de la Frontera, the paternalistic general backed the great **Ibero–American Exhibition of 1929** at Seville which, it was hoped, would calm the agitation for radical change by promoting a "rose-coloured" image for the troubled region; its most immediate effect was to bankrupt the city. Dictatorship did result in an increase in material prosperity, heavily assisted by a massive public works policy, but serious political misjudgements and the collapse of the peseta in 1929 made Rivera's voluntary resignation and departure into exile inevitable. The legacy of this dictatorship was to reinforce a belief on the Right that only a firm military hand would be capable of holding society together, and many of those who served in Primo de Rivera's administration were to back the Franco regime in the next decade. The victory of anti-monarchist parties in the 1931 municipal elections forced the abdication of the hopelessly out of touch King Alfonso XIII, and the **Second Republic** was declared.

The Second Republic

The Second Republic, which lasted from 1931 to 1936, was ushered in on a wave of optimism that finally some of the nation's fundamental ills and injustices would be rectified. But the government – a coalition of radicals, socialists and leftist republicans – struggling to curb the power of vested interests such as the army, the Church and the landowning class, was soon failing to satisfy even the least of the expectations which it had raised. Moreover it lost support when it got involved in activities identified with earlier repressive regimes, as happened at the village of **Casas Viejas** (modern Benalup de Sidonia) in Cádiz, when it ordered the troops to open fire on a group of starving workers who had been the victims of a lockout by the local landowner and who were attempting to raise the area in an anarchist revolt.

Anarchism was gaining strength among the frustrated middle classes as well as among workers and peasantry. The **Communist Party** and left-wing **socialists**, driven into alliance by their mutual distrust of the "moderate" Socialists in government, were also forming a growing bloc. There was little real unity of purpose on either left or right, but their fear of each other and their own exaggerated boasts made each seem an imminent threat. On the right the **Falangists**, basically a youth party founded in 1923 by **José Antonio Primo de Rivera** (son of the dictator), made uneasy bedfellows with conservative traditionalists and dissident elements in the army upset by modernizing reforms.

In an atmosphere of growing confusion, with mobs fighting on the streets and churches and monasteries being torched whilst landed estates were taken over by those impatient for agrarian reform, the left-wing Popular Front alliance won the general election of **February 1936** by a narrow margin. Normal life, though, became increasingly impossible: the economy was crippled by strikes, the universities became hotbeds for battles between Marxists and Falangists, and the government failed to exert its authority over anyone. Finally, on July 17, 1936, the military garrison in Morocco rebelled under **General Franco**'s leadership, to be followed by risings at military garrisons throughout the country. It was the culmination of years of scheming in the army, but in the event far from the overnight success its leaders almost certainly expected. Airlifting his troops into Seville by means of German transport planes, Franco ensured that the south and west quickly fell into Nationalist hands, but Madrid and the industrialized north and east remained loyal to the Republican government.

The Civil War

The ensuing **Civil War** was undoubtedly one of the most bitter and bloody the world has seen. Violent reprisals were taken on their enemies by both sides – the Republicans shooting priests and local landowners wholesale, the Nationalists carrying out mass slaughter of the population of almost every town they took. Contradictions were legion in the way the Spanish populations found themselves divided from each other. Perhaps the greatest irony was that Franco's troops, on their "holy" mission against a godless "anti-Spain", comprised a core of Moroccan troops from Spain's North African colony.

It was, too, the first modern war – Franco's German allies demonstrated their ability to wipe out entire civilian populations with their bombing raids on Gernika and Durango in the Basque country, and radio proved an important weapon, as Nationalist propagandists offered the starving Republicans "the white bread of Franco".

Despite sporadic help from Russia and thousands of volunteers in the International Brigades, the Republic could never compete with the professional armies and the massive assistance from Fascist Italy and Nazi Germany enjoyed by the Nationalists. As hundreds of thousands of refugees flooded into France, General Francisco Franco, who had long before proclaimed himself head of state, took up the reins of power.

Franco's Spain

The early reprisals taken by the victors were on a massive and terrifying scale. Executions were commonplace in town and village, and upwards of two million people were put in concentration camps until "order" had been established by authoritarian means. Only one party was permitted and censorship was rigidly enforced. By the end of World War II, during which Spain was too weak to be anything but neutral, **Franco** was the only fascist head of state left in Europe, and responsible for sanctioning more deaths than any other in Spanish history. Spain was economically and politically isolated and, bereft of markets, suffering – almost half the population were still tilling the soil for little or no return. The misery of the peasantry was particularly acute in Andalucía and forced mass emigrations to Madrid and Barcelona and Europe beyond.

When General Eisenhower visited Madrid in 1953 with the offer of huge loans, it came as water to the desert, and the price, the **establishment of American nuclear bases** such as those at Rota near Cádiz and Morón de la Frontera, was one Franco was more than willing to pay. Once firmly in the US camp the Franco regime (administered by the so-called *tecnocratas* group of ministers) rapidly transformed Spain into a market economy and in the late Fifties the country joined the International Monetary Fund, the International Bank for Reconstruction and Development and the OECD in quick succession. However belated, economic development was incredibly rapid, with Spain enjoying a growth rate second only to that of Japan for much of the 1960s, a boom fuelled by the tourist industry, the remittances of Spanish workers abroad and the illegality of strikes and industrial action at home.

Increased **prosperity**, however, only underlined the political bankruptcy of Franco's regime and its inability to cope with popular demands. Higher incomes, the need for better education, and a creeping invasion of Western culture made the anachronism of Franco ever clearer. His only reaction was to attempt to withdraw what few signs of increased liberalism had crept through, and his last years mirrored the repression of the postwar period. Franco finally died in November 1975, nominating **King Juan Carlos** as his successor.

The new Spain

On October 28, 1982, *sevillano* Felipe González's Socialist Workers' Party – the PSOE – was elected with massive support to rule a country that had been firmly in the hands of the right for 43 years. The **Socialists** captured the imagination and the votes of nearly ten million Spaniards with the simplest of appeals: "for change". It was a telling comment on just how far Spain had moved since Franco's death, for in the intervening years change seemed the one factor that could still threaten the new-found democracy.

Certainly, in the Spain of 1976 the thought of a freely elected left-wing government would have been incredible. **King Juan Carlos** was the hand-picked successor of Franco, groomed for the job and very much in with the army – of which he remains official commander-in-chief. His initial moves were cautious in the extreme, appointing a government dominated by loyal Francoists who had little sympathy for the growing opposition demands for "democracy without adjectives".

To his credit, however, Juan Carlos recognized that some real break with the past was now urgent and inevitable, and set in motion the process of **democratization**. He legitimized the Socialist Party and, controversially, the Communists. When elections were held in June 1977, the centre-right **UCD** Christian–Democrat party gained a 34 percent share of the vote, the **PSOE** (Spanish Socialist Workers' Party) coming in second with 28 percent, and the Communists and Francoist Alianza Popular both marginalized at nine percent and eight percent.

It was almost certainly a vote for democratic stability rather than for ideology. The king, perhaps recognizing that his own future depended on the mainte-nance of the new democracy, lent it his support – most notably in February 1981 when a tragicomic Civil Guard colonel named Tejero stormed the Cortes brandishing a revolver and, with other officers loyal to Franco's memory, attempted to institute an **army coup**. But the crisis, for a while, was real. Tanks were brought out onto the streets of Valencia, and only three of the army's ten regional commanders remained unreservedly loyal to the government. But as it became clear that the king would not support the plotters, most of the rest affirmed their support. Juan Carlos had taken the decision of his life and emerged with immensely enhanced prestige in the eyes of most Spaniards.

The new political system had successfully dealt with the first real challenge to its authority and following these events Spanish democracy – even in army circles where most of the old guard were gradually pensioned off – now became firmly institutionalized. And in the fourteen-year rule of the charismatic **Felipe González** (always known as "Felipe") and the PSOE the system found, at least until the Nineties' slide into the political mire and defeat, a party of enduring **stability** and to the left of exasperating **moderation**.

The swing to the right

The final years of González's and the PSOE's period in power were dogged by a series of **scandals**. As illegal financing of the PSOE and corruption and commission-taking on government projects by party officials and ministers were being exposed, the director of the Guardia Civil (appointed by González) jumped the country with millions of dollars of secret service funds, and the governor of the Bank of Spain was caught out making a private (and illegal) fortune. The most serious of all, however, was the **GAL affair** (Grupo Antiterrorista de Liberación) when it was discovered that a state-sponsored anti-terrorist unit had been fighting a dirty war against ETA that included kidnappings and even assassinations of suspected terrorists. The press – and a later judicial investigation – exposed police participation in these crimes and a clear chain of command reaching up to the highest echelons of the PSOE government. González narrowly avoided being hauled before the courts, but the nation's progressive disillusion with his government saw the rise to prominence of **José-María Aznar** as leader of the **Partido Popular** conservatives (a merger of the UCD and Alianza Popular).

A former tax inspector with little charisma, Aznar's dogged criticism of the PSOE government's incompetence and corruption nevertheless finally won the PP a narrow **victory** in the 1996 elections, following an equally narrow defeat in 1993. Having to do a deal with the smaller nationalist parties in order to form a government soured Aznar's triumph somewhat, whilst González, boosted by the avoidance of a predicted crushing defeat, hastily dismissed ideas of retirement. This merely delayed the inevitable and, unable to make any significant impact on changing public opinion and with the PSOE still in turmoil, early in 1998 González finally **resigned** from the leadership of the party he had led in government and opposition for 23 years.

González was replaced as PSOE leader and the party went into the 2000 election campaign under the leadership of uninspiring González crony **Joaquín Almunia**. Almunia cut little ice with the Spanish electorate, not helped by his refusal to criticize González's record in power. In an attempt to forestall a seemingly inevitable electoral defeat, Almunia stitched up a deal with the PSOE's bitter arch rival, the ex-communist Izquierda Unida (United Left) party, thinking that their combined votes could overturn a likely Aznar victory. However, many of the rank and file on both sides were unhappy about this "shotgun marriage" (each has long blamed the other for Franco's victory in 1939) and the disorganization on the ground was reflected in their leaders' lack of a coherent policy.

The outcome of the March 2000 **general election** was a stunning **victory for Aznar** and the PP in which – for the first time since the death of Franco – the right were in power with an overall majority, and no longer dependent on the whims of nationalist coalition partners. It seems that the great majority of the electorate were not willing to risk the economic gains of Aznar's period in office, while many on the left didn't bother to turn out to support a leftist coalition which smacked more of political opportunism than a government in waiting. Joaquín Almunia, the architect of this crushing defeat for the left, resigned on election night.

At the party convention that followed, and bearing parallels to Tony Blair's elevation to the Labour leadership in Britain, the PSOE's old guard were swept aside and delegates elected a relatively unknown young politician, **José Luis Rodríguez Zapatero** – a member of the moderate socialist "Nueva Via" (new way) group within the PSOE – as their new leader. After an unpromising start in which he struggled to get to grips with both Aznar and the party's powerful regional "barons", Zapatero embarked on a strategy of owning up to the PSOE's past mistakes, in particular distancing himself and the party from the sleazier activities of the González years. This seemed to go down well with public opinion and Zapatero's improved performance against Aznar in the Cortes (Spanish parliament) gave the party some hope of mounting a successful challenge to the ruling Partido Popular government in the elections to be held in 2004.

The return of the PSOE

In 2001, José María Aznar – ever an enigma to those around him – announced that he would lead the PP up to the general election of 2004 but would then resign, and that it must seek a new leader. As leader designate (to take over after the poll) the party chose Aznar's nominee, the less prickly, cigar-puffing **Mariano Rajoy**, minister for the interior and deputy prime minister. Despite the highest level of **unemployment** in the EU and a **general strike** in June 2002, caused by opposition to labour law and social security reforms intended to free up the labour market and slash social security benefits, the opinion polls still showed solid public support for the Aznar administration. Throughout 2003 Aznar relentlessly urged the electorate to back the party that had brought steady economic growth and low inflation. This strategy appeared to work, and early in 2004 all the indicators suggested the following March general election would deliver a comfortable victory for the ruling PP and its new leader, Rajoy.

Then, on March 11, and three days before polling day, a series of **bombs** exploded on rush-hour commuter trains travelling into Madrid, killing 192 people and injuring almost two thousand others. The nation was thrown into shock at the most savage attack seen in Spain since the Civil War. Despite the discovery by police within hours of a van connected to the bombings containing detonators and a Koranic audiotape, the PP leadership decided that the Basque terrorist group ETA had to be the culprits. This was a high-risk tactic for the government but it seemed convinced that by pinning the responsibility on ETA it would deflect attention away from its support for the Iraq war (ninety percent of Spaniards had been against it) just long enough for the votes to be counted. No mention was to be made of any possible link with Islamic militant groups and at the same time the blaming of ETA would conveniently vindicate Aznar's hardline stance against Basque terrorism and separatism.

For the three days prior to the election the heavily state-influenced media and Spanish diplomats around the world attempted to peddle the "ETA is responsible" line. But soon doubts began to surface and in the hours before the polls opened the electorate seems to have become highly suspicious of the government's tactic of using ETA as a scapegoat to save its skin, believing that the attack – as was subsequently proved – was the work of **Islamic terrorists** and a retaliation for Spain's participation in the unpopular Iraq war.

The nation turned out in force (turnout went up by a crucial eight percent over the 2000 poll) to give its verdict and Zapatero and the PSOE an **unexpected victory**. Two million new young voters angered by Aznar's unwavering support for the Iraq war seem to have been pivotal to the final result. In Catalunya and the Basque country the government's duplicity backfired spectacularly. The Catalans voted overwhelmingly for socialist and Catalan nationalist candidates, reducing the PP to a fringe party, and there was a similar fall in support in the Basque regions. The lies and distortion accusations hurled at the Partido Popular following the election result only intensified when it was revealed that the outgoing government had hired a specialist company to destroy all computer records dealing with the bombings before leaving office.

Contemporary politics

The first act carried out by Zapatero as government leader was to announce the immediate **withdrawal of Spanish troops from Iraq**, an election promise. This aligned him firmly with the German and French governments in Europe to whom Aznar had been hostile, but incurred the displeasure of US president George W. Bush, who shunned Zapatero for the rest of his presidency and turned down requests by the Spanish leader for a meeting at the White House or in Madrid.

In his first four years of office, leading up to the 2008 elections, Zapatero's record was competent if unspectacular. His government will probably be more remembered for being Spain's first in which half the cabinet seats were occupied by women and for legalising **gay marriages** rather than for any dramatic shifts of policy. He also enjoyed the benefit of favourable economic circumstances with consistently high economic growth figures and an economy producing more jobs than any other euro-zone member. International financial number-crunchers declared in 2007 that's Spain's GDP per head had overtaken that of Italy. But in the latter part of the same year the impact of the world **economic downturn** was also felt in Spain as one of the major drivers of the Spanish economy, the huge construction industry, went into meltdown. Unemployment figures started to rise as worried consumers put off making major purchases such as cars and homes. The **general election** of March 2008 took place against a background of economic uncertainty and although the result was another **PSOE victory** the reality was that they had scraped home seven seats short of the overall parliamentary majority that Zapatero had stated was the party's main campaign target. The fact that the PSOE had won at all was as much due to a lacklustre campaign fought by opposition leader Mariano Rajoy and the PP, as the PSOE's rather tame appeal to the voters that offered few new ideas. A further worry for the Zapatero government was that without a majority it must again rely on the votes of smaller parties to get its administrative programme through. It may end up regretting a decision not to seek a formal alliance with any of these minor parties. Comprised mainly of nationalist Basques and Catalans (with separatist agendas of their own), they will undoubtedly demand a high price for help in pushing through any unpalatable policies to deal with the nation's economic predicament.

Given the unstable economic climate it is a certainty that Zapatero's second term will be considerably tougher than his first. As he tries to cope with his first economic crisis he has still to define a coherent strategy capable of meeting Spain's economic and constitutional problems. The country's **economic problems** – accentuated by a decline in tourist income, a construction industry whose bubble has burst, rising unemployment and inflation figures and faltering consumer spending – are going to need a steady hand and some clearly thought out policies in the years ahead. The haemorrhaging of foreign investment as multinational companies quit the peninsula to cut costs by moving production to low-wage economies such as Poland, Hungary and the Czech Republic has also had a serious impact on Spain's economic fortunes. More worrying still is the fact that as a consequence of EU enlargement, Spain – until recently the largest recipient of EU aid – has lost around seven billion euros in annual grants.

In dealing with the **autonomous regions**, Zapatero has been confronted by the same intransigent nationalist demands as his predecessor Aznar. When the Basque regional president Juan José Ibarretxe announced early in 2005 that the Basque parliament had approved a blueprint for a "Basque free state" with its own court system, passports and international diplomatic representation, Zapatero demised the proposals as unconstitutional and the plan was thrown out by the Madrid Cortes. But the Basque autonomous government (run by nationalists) refused to accept this decision and in the spring of 2008 Ibarretxe announced plans to hold a **double referendum** in the Basque country on whether to start peace talks with ETA and "the right for Basques [rather than Spaniards] to decide" if the *autonomía* remains a part of the Spanish state. The government referred the case to the Spanish constitutional court which, predictably, ruled the referendum unconstitutional, therefore illegal. Ibarretxe condemned the ruling and announced that the Basque government would now take its case to the European Court of Human Rights. The Spanish government is only too aware that where the Basques lead the Catalans (and possibly the Galicians, too) will wish to follow which is why they are prepared to give no quarter on an issue that threatens the unity of the state. In October 2005 the Catalan parliament voted overwhelmingly for a similar charter to that of the Basques, defining Catalunya as a "nation" and seeking to distance itself from Spain. Not quite as intransigent as the Basques, in a **referendum in 2006** the Catalans approved a revision of their statute of autonomy which the Spanish government hopes will keep them satisfied for a few years until the engine of further decentralization is cranked up once more.

Despite the economic storm clouds currently gathering over the peninsula, the larger picture has many positives. Thirty years on from the 1978 constitutional referendum that effectively dispatched the Franco era to the political dustbin, Spain is a confident player on the world stage and a core member of the **European Union**. And while the nation is no longer as starry-eyed about the European project as it was two decades ago when it joined the then EC, most citizens are acutely aware of the benefits that have flooded into the country as a result of huge EU grants funding important infrastructure projects as well as subsidies channelled to the pivotal farming sector. As these funds now dry up a major challenge for the country is to continue to transform the economy as well as outdated educational and legal systems, all key factors in building the Spain of the new century. Another crucial test for the future is how the country comes to terms with **regional nationalism** which, if mishandled, could doom the state to disintegration. As with the transition to democracy, Spain often confounds its detractors by finding the inspiration and the energy to carry out necessary changes. There is no reason to believe that it will not do so again.

Modern Andalucía

Andalucía shared in the progressive decentralization of power in Spain throughout the post-Franco period and in 1980 became an **Autonomous Region** with a regional government based in Seville exercising a large amount of control over its own destiny for the first time. Largely because of its enduring social problems, Andalucía remained a socialist bulwark for the PSOE throughout the Eighties – the so-called *sartenilla* (frying pan) of the south which traditionally "fries" the right-wing votes further north. Throughout the 1990s this support enabled the discredited PSOE government of Felipe González to remain in power whilst denying Aznar's PP its longed-for majority when it finally did become the largest party. However, the tide was turning and in the **general election of 2000** there was a significant shift in voting patterns away from the left and towards Aznar and the PP that contributed significantly to the right's victory. In the **poll of 2004** Andalucía shared in the national fury at the PP government's attempts to shift the blame for the Madrid bombings onto ETA and they turned out once more to vote for Zapatero and the PSOE, increasing the number of votes for the Socialist Party by almost three million over the 2000 figure.

Despite a more fickle attitude to voting (or abstaining) in general elections that allowed the PP to win a majority in Andalucía, in the 2008 elections to Andalucía's **autonomous parliament** the region voted solidly to maintain this in the hands of the PSOE. This was the socialist party's eighth consecutive victory since regional elections were inaugurated in 1982, due in no small part to the PSOE's leader in Andalucía, **Manuel Chaves**. A canny and popular politician and president of the autonomous government since 1990, he has presided over a revolution in Andalucía which has seen rapid growth in tourism, a vast improvement in communications and the eradication of poverty in large parts of the region.

Still, and contradicting the sunny image presented to most of its visitors, chronic economic and social problems remain, and not for nothing is Andalucía known as the "workhouse of Spain". The regional **unemployment** level is among the European Union's highest at an alarming fifteen percent (compared with ten percent for Spain as a whole), and earnings per head are a third lower than the national average. The region has also been severely affected by Spain's **economic recession**. A major participant in the construction boom of the last decade, the recent collapse of this sector has led to construction companies going bust, estate agents filing for bankruptcy and tens of thousands of unemployed building workers swelling the dole queues. The position of Andalucía's 200,000 **agricultural workers**, who face nine months' unemployment each year and depend on patronage from the great landowners for work during the other three, also remains unresolved, despite the PSOE government having introduced a minimal unemployment benefit scheme in the 1980s. Industries such as fishing have also been affected by EU regulations limiting the size of catches to conserve dwindling fish stocks, with the consequent rise in unemployment in port towns throughout Andalucía.

All this has compelled a greater dependence on **tourism**, a sector which now faces stiff competition from low-cost holiday destinations such as Croatia, Tunisia and Turkey. At the same time tourism's decades of success has produced its own problems as many flocked to the coast in search of work leaving a mere twenty percent of the population in provinces such as Almería inhabiting the hinterland. The Junta de Andalucía regional government now mounts an annual "rural tourism" campaign to attract visitors inland in order to channel some of the tourist income away from the coast. Another area now receiving belated attention is the region's **educational system** where serious flaws have long been evident (in a 2006 Europe-wide survey of student achievement Andalucía came out bottom in Spain while Spain itself was placed in the bottom half of the European table). Higher education is no better and employers frequently grumble that universities do little to equip students for careers in business, while experts blame the sector for failing to provide the vocational courses to train the skilled workers necessary for a modern industrial economy. Other outstanding problems for the region to deal with include the waves of **illegal immigrants** who arrive (if they do not perish en route) almost daily on Andalucía's beaches packed into flimsy fishing boats and the spread of **crime and corruption** on the Costa del Sol, where many foreign criminal syndicates are based.

In spite of these challenges, however, today's Andalucía is wealthier than it has ever been in its history. It is no longer necessary for starving *andaluzes* to emigrate to other parts of Europe to earn a living, as happened in 1950s, and current standards of health care and welfare are equal or superior to most in the EU. A local saying asserts that God created Andalucía as a place to go if he ever got tired of heaven. Few *andaluzes* would probably go so far as to describe their region as heaven on earth, but most would doubtless agree that when the sun is shining there is no other place they would rather be.

Flamenco

Flamenco is undoubtedly the most important musical-cultural phenomenon in Spain, and over the past decade or so it has experienced a huge resurgence in popularity, and a profile that has reached out far beyond its Andalucian homeland. The sanitized kitsch flamenco, all frills and castanets, exploited as an image of tourist Spain during the Franco period, has been left far behind by a new age expressing the vitality and attitudes of a younger generation of flamenco clans.

In the 1980s, the Spanish press hailed **Ketama** (named after a Moroccan village famed for its hashish) as creators of the music of the "New Spain" after the release of their eponymous first album, which fused flamenco with rock and Latin salsa. Later they pushed the frontiers of flamenco further still by recording *Songhai*, an album collaborating with Malian kora player Toumani Diabate and British bassist Danny Thompson, followed by *De Aki A Ketama* developing more rock-fusion themes. *Blues de la Frontera* (Frontier Blues), the first disc of **Pata Negra** ("black leg" – the highest quality of cured ham – and an everyday term used for anything good), caused an equal sensation.

This flamenco revival of the 1980s and 1990s is no longer confined to the purists who kept old-time flamenco alive in their *peñas* or clubs. On radio and on CD-players blaring from market stalls right across the country you hear the typical high-pitched treble tones of commercial flamenco singers such as **Tijeritas**. The European success of the flamenco-rumba of the **Gipsy Kings**, a high-profile gypsy group from southern France, has further opened and prepared the ear of European popular audiences for something more powerful. Rumba, a Latin form, has come back to Spain from Latin America, and so is known as a music of *ida y vuelta* ("go and return"), one of the many fusions of the Spanish music taken to the New World with the *conquistadores* and their descendants, where it has mixed with African and other elements, before making its way back again. The impetus began at the end of the 1970s, with the innovations of guitarist **Paco de Lucía** and, especially, the late great singer, **El Camarón de la Isla**. These were musicians who had grown up learning from their flamenco families but whose own musical tastes had embraced international rock, jazz and blues. Paco de Lucía blended jazz and salsa with the flamenco sound. Camarón, simply, was an inspiration – and one whose own idols (and fans) included Chick Corea and Miles Davis, as well as flamenco artists. Latterly flamenco musicians are to be found playing in many different contexts, including rock and folk genres – the result is an exciting and dynamic scene.

Origins

The **roots of flamenco** evolved in southern Spain from many sources: Morocco, Egypt, India, Pakistan, Greece and other parts of the Near and Far East. How exactly they came together as flamenco is a source of great debate and obscurity, though most authorities believe the roots of the music were brought by **gypsies** arriving in the fifteenth century. In the following century, it fused with elements of Arab and Jewish music in the Andalucian mountains, where Jews, Muslims and "pagan" gypsies had taken refuge from the forced conversions and clearances effected by the Catholic monarchs and the Church. The main flamenco centres and families are to be found today in quarters and towns of gypsy and refugee origin, such as Alcalá del Río, Utrera, Jerez, Cádiz and the Triana *barrio* of Seville.

There are two theories about the origins of the name flamenco. One contends that Spanish Jews migrated through trade to Flanders, where they were allowed to sing their religious chants unmolested, and that these chants became referred to as flamenco by the Jews who stayed in Spain. The other is that the word is a mispronunciation of the Arabic words *felag* (fugitive) and *mengu* (peasant), a plausible idea, as Arabic was a common language in Spain at the time.

Flamenco aficionados enjoy heated debate about the purity of their art and whether it is more validly performed by a **gitano** (gypsy) or a **payo** (non-gypsy). Certainly, flamenco seems to have thrived enclosed, preserved and protected by the oral tradition of the gypsy clans. Its power, and the despair which its creation overcomes, has emerged from the precarious and vulnerable lives of a people surviving for centuries at the margins of society. Flamenco reflects a passionate need to preserve their self-esteem.

These days, there are as many acclaimed *payo* as *gitano* flamenco artists. However, the concept of an **active inheritance** is crucial. The veteran singer **Fernanda de Utrera**, one of the great voices of "pure flamenco", was born in 1923 into a gypsy family in Utrera, one of the *cantaora* centres. She was the granddaughter of the legendary singer "Pinini", who had created her own individual flamenco forms, and with her younger sister Bernarda, also a notable singer, inherited their flamenco with their genes. Even the members of Ketama, the groundbreaking Madrid-based flamenco-rock group who split up in 2004, came from two gypsy clans – the Sotos and the Carmonas.

Although flamenco's exact origins are obscure, it is generally agreed that its "laws" were established in the nineteenth century. Indeed, from the mid-nineteenth century into the early twentieth, flamenco enjoyed a legendary **"Golden Age"**, the tail-end of which is preserved on some of the earliest 1930s recordings. The original musicians found a home in the *café cantantes*, traditional taverns which had their own group of performers (*cuadros*). One of the most famous was the *Café de Chinitas* in Málaga (see p.81), immortalized by the Granada-born poet García Lorca. In his poem *A las cinco de la tarde* (At five in the afternoon), Lorca claimed that flamenco is deeply related to bullfighting, not only sharing root emotions and passions, flashes of erratic genius, but because both are possible ways to break out of social and economic marginality.

Just such a transformation happened in 1922 when the composer Manuel de Falla, the guitarist Andrés Segovia and the poet García Lorca were present for a legendary *Concurso de Cante Jondo*. A gypsy boy singer, **Manolo Caracol**, reportedly walked all the way from Jerez and won the competition with the voice and flamboyant personality that were to make him a legend throughout Spain and South America. The other key figure of this period, who can be heard on a few recently re-mastered recordings, was **Pastora Pavón**, known as *La Niña de Los Peines*, and popularly acclaimed as the greatest woman flamenco voice of the twentieth century.

In addition to *café cantantes*, flamenco surfaced – as it does today – at fiestas, in bars or *tablaos*, and at *juergas*, informal, private parties. The fact that the Andalucian public are so knowledgeable and demanding about flamenco means that musicians, singers and dancers found even at the most humble local club or festival are usually very good indeed.

The art of flamenco

It is essential for an artist to invoke a response, to know they are reaching deep into the emotional psyche of their audience. They may achieve the rare quality of **duende** – total emotional communication with their audience, and the mark

▲ Flamenco dancing, Seville

of great flamenco of whatever style or generation. *Duende* is an ethereal quality: moving, profound even when expressing happiness, mysterious but nevertheless felt, a quality that stops listeners in their tracks. And many of those listeners are intensely involved, for flamenco is not just a music, for many it is a way of life, a **philosophy** that influences daily activities. A flamenco is not only a performer but anyone who is actively and emotionally involved in the unique philosophy.

For the musicians, this fullness of expression is integral to their art, which is why, for as many famous names as one can list, there are many, many other lesser-known musicians whose work is startlingly good. Not every superb flamenco musician gets to be famous, or even to record, for flamenco thrives most in **live performance**. Exhilarating, challenging and physically stimulating, it is an art form that allows its exponents huge scope to improvise while obeying certain rules. Flamenco guitarist Juan Martín has remarked that "in microcosm it imitates Spanish society – traditional on the outside but, within, incredible anarchy".

There is a **classical repertoire** of more than sixty flamenco songs (*cantes*) and dances (*danzas*) – some solos, some group numbers, some with instrumental accompaniment, others *a cappella*. These different forms of flamenco are grouped in "families" according to more or less common melodic themes. The most common beat cycle is twelve – like the blues. Each piece is executed by juxtaposing a number of complete musical units called *coplas*. Their number varies depending on the atmosphere the *cantaor* wishes to establish and the emotional tone they wish to convey. A song such as a *cante por solea* may take a familiar 3/4 rhythm, divide phrases into 4/8 measures, and then fragmentally subdivide again with voice ornamentation on top of that. The resulting complexity and the variations between similar phrases constantly undermine repetition, contributing greatly to the climactic and cathartic structure of each song.

Songs and singer

Flamenco **songs** often express pain, and with a fierceness that turns that emotion inside out. Generally, the voice closely interacts with improvising guitar (*toque*), the two inspiring each other, aided by the **jaleo**: the hand-clapping *palmas*, finger-snapping *palillos* and shouts from participants at certain points in the song. This *jaleo* sets the tone by creating the right atmosphere for the singer or dancer to begin, and bolsters and appreciates the talent of the artist as they develop the piece.

Aficionados will shout encouragement, most commonly "*¡Olé!*" – when an artist is getting deep into a song – but also a variety of stranger-sounding phrases. A stunning piece of dancing may, for example, be greeted with "*¡Viva la maquina escribir!*" (long live the typewriter), as the heels of the dancer move so fast they sound like a machine; or the cry may be "*¡Agua!*" (water), as the scarcity of water in Andalucía has given the word a kind of glory.

An essential characteristic of flamenco is the singer or dancer taking certain risks, by putting into their performance feelings and emotions which arise directly from their own life experience, exposing their own **vulnerabilities**. Aficionados tend to acclaim more a voice that gains effect from surprise and startling moves than one governed by recognized musical logic. Vocal prowess or virtuosity can be deepened by sobs, gesticulation and an intensity of expression that can have a shattering effect on an audience. Thus pauses, breaths, body and facial gestures of anger and pain transform performance into **cathartic events**.

Flamenco dance

Most popular images of flamenco dance – twirling bodies in frilled dresses, rounded arms complete with castanets – are **Sevillanas**, the folk dances performed at fiestas, and, in recent years, on the nightclub floor. "Real" flamenco dance is something rather different and, like the music, can reduce the onlooker to tears in an unexpected flash, a cathartic point after which the dance dissolves. What is so visually devastating about flamenco dance is the physical and emotional control the dancer has over the body: the way the head is held, the tension of the torso and the way it allows the shoulders to move, the shapes and angles of seemingly elongated arms, and the feet, which move from toe to heel, heel to toe, creating rhythms. These rhythms have a basic set of moves and timings but they are improvised as the piece develops and through interaction with the guitarist.

Flamenco dance dates back to about 1750 and, along with the music, moved from the streets and private parties into the *café cantantes* at the end of the nineteenth century. This was a great boost for the dancers' art, providing a home for professional performers, where they could inspire each other. It was here that legendary dancers like **El Raspao** and **El Estampio** began to develop the spellbinding footwork and extraordinary moves that characterize modern flamenco dance, while women adopted for the first time the flamboyant **hata de cola** – the glorious long-trained dresses, cut high at the front to expose their fast moving ankles and feet.

Around 1910, flamenco dance had moved into Spanish theatres, and dancers like **La Niña de los Peines** and **La Argentina** were major stars. They mixed flamenco into programmes with other dances and also made dramatic appearances at the end of comic plays and silent movie programmes. **Flamenco opera** was established, interlinking singing, dancing and guitar solos in comedies with a local flamenco flavour.

In 1915 the composer Manuel de Falla composed the first flamenco ballet, **El Amor Brujo** (Love, the Magician), for the dancer Pastora Imperio. The celebrated dancer, **La Argentina**, who had established the first Spanish dance company, took her

Siguiriyas which date from the Golden Age, and whose theme is usually death, have been described as cries of despair in the form of a funeral psalm. In contrast there are many songs and dances such as *tangos*, *Sevillanas* and *fandangos* which capture great **joy** for fiestas.

The **Sevillana** originated in medieval Seville as a spring country dance, with verses improvised and sung to the accompaniment of guitar and castanets (which are rarely used in other forms of flamenco). **El Pali** (Francisco Palacios), who died in 1988, was the most well-known and prolific *Sevillana* musician, his unusually gentle voice and accompanying strummed guitar combining an enviable musical pace with a talent for composing popular poetic lyrics. In the last few years dancing *Sevillanas* has become popular in bars and clubs throughout Spain, but their great natural habitats are **Seville's April Feria** and the annual pilgrimage to **El Rocío**. It is during the Seville *feria* that most new recordings of *Sevillanas* emerge.

Among the best contemporary singers are the aforementioned **Fernanda** and **Bernarda de Utrera**, **Enrique Morente**, **El Cabrero**, **Juan Peña El Lebrijano**, the **Sorderas**, **Fosforito**, **José Menese** and **Carmen Linares**. However, one of the most popular and commercially successful singers of modern flamenco was the extraordinary **El Camarón de la Isla** (The "Shrimp of the Isle" of León, near his Cádiz home), who died in 1992. Collaborating with the guitarists Paco and Pepe de Lucía, and latterly, Tomatito, Camarón raised **cante jondo**, the virtuoso "deep song", to a new art. His high-toned voice had a corrosive, rough-timbred edge, cracking at certain points to release

version of the ballet abroad in the 1920s, and with her choreographic innovations flamenco dance came of age, working as a narrative in its own right. Another key figure in flamenco history was **Carmen Amaya**, who from the 1930s to the 1960s took flamenco dance on tour around the world, and into the movies.

In the 1950s, dance found a new home in the **tablaos**, the aficionados' bars, which became enormously important as places to serve out a public apprenticeship. More recently the demanding audiences at local and national fiestas have played a part. Artistic developments were forged in the 1960s by **Matilde Coral**, who updated the classic dance style, and in the 1970s by **Manuela Carrasco**, who had such impact with her fiery feet movement, continuing a rhythm for an intense and seemingly impossible period, that this new style was named after her (*manuelas*).

Manuela Carrasco set the tone for the highly individual dancers of the 1980s and 1990s, such as **Mario Maya** and **Antonio Gades**. These two dancers and choreographers have provided a theatrically inspired staging for the dance, most significantly by extending the role of a dance dialogue and story – often reflecting on the potency of love and passion, their dangers and destructiveness.

Gades has led his own company on world tours but it is his influence on film which has been most important. He had appeared with Carmen Amaya in *Los Araños* in 1963 but in the 1980s began his own trilogy with film-maker Carlos Saura: *Boda de Sangre* (Lorca's play, Blood Wedding), *Carmen* (a reinterpretation of the opera) and *El Amor Brujo*. The films featured Paco de Lucía and his band, and the dancers **Laura del Sol** and **Christina Hoyos** – the latter one of the great contemporary dancers. Hoyos has herself created a superb ballet, *Sueños Flamencos* (Flamenco Dreams) and has also been a force behind the founding of Seville's new Museo del Baile Flamenco (p.278).

Aside from the great companies and personalities of flamenco dance, there are an enormous number of local dancers all over Andalucía, whose dancing brings flamenco to life, and whose moves can be sheer poetry.

a ravaged core sound. His incisive sense of rhythm, coupled with almost violent emotional intensity, made him the quintessential singer of the times.

Flamenco guitar

The flamenco performance is filled with pauses. The singer is free to insert phrases seemingly on the spur of the moment. The **guitar accompaniment**, while spontaneous, is precise and serves one single purpose – to mark the *compas* (measures) of a song and organize rhythmical lines. Instrumental interludes which are arranged to meet the needs of the *cantaor* (as the creative singer is called) not only catch the mood and intention of the song and mirror it, but allow the guitarist to extemporize what are called *falsetas* (short variations) at will. When singer and guitarist are in true rapport the intensity of a song develops rapidly, the one charging the other, until the effect can be overwhelming.

The flamenco **guitar** is of lighter weight than most acoustic guitars and often has a pine table and pegs made of wood rather than machine heads. This is to produce the preferred bright responsive sound that does not sustain too long (as opposed to the mellow and longer sustaining sound of classical guitar). If the sound did sustain, particularly in fast pieces, chords would carry over into each other.

The guitar used to be simply an accompanying instrument – originally the singers themselves played – but at the end of the nineteenth century and in the early decades of the twentieth century it began developing as a **solo** form, absorbing influences from classical and Latin American traditions. The greatest of these early guitarists was **Ramón Montoya**, who revolutionized flamenco guitar with his harmonies and introduced tremolo and a whole variety of arpeggios – techniques of right-hand playing. After him the revolution was continued by Sabicas and Niño Ricardo and Carlos Montoya. The classical guitarist **Andrés Segovia** was another influential figure; he began his career playing flamenco in Granada. Then in the 1960s came the two major guitarists of modern times, **Paco de Lucía** (see below) and **Manolo Sanlucar**.

These days, solo guitarists have immediately identifiable sounds and rhythms: the highly emotive **Pepe Habichuela** and **Tomatito**, for example, or the unusual rhythms of younger players like **Ramón el Portugués**, **Enrique de Melchor** and **Rafael Riqueni**. Flamenco guitar has now consolidated its position on the world's great stages as one of the most successful forms of instrumental music.

Nuevo flamenco

One of flamenco's great achievements has been to sustain itself while providing much of the foundation and inspiration for new music emerging in Spain today. In the 1950s and 1960s, rock'n'roll displaced traditional Spanish music, as it did indigenous music in many parts of the world. In the 1980s, however, flamenco reinvented itself, gaining new meaning and a new public through the music of Paco de Lucía, who mixed in **jazz**, **blues** and **salsa**, and, later, groups like Pata Negra and Ketama, who brought in more **rock** influences. Purists hated these innovations but, as José "El Sordo" (Deaf One) Soto, Ketama's main singer, explained, they were based on "the classic flamenco that we'd been singing and listening to since birth. We just found new forms in jazz and salsa: there are basic similarities in the rhythms, the constantly changing harmonies and improvisations. Blacks and gypsies have suffered similar segregation so our music has a lot in common."

Paco de Lucía, who made the first moves, is the best known of all contemporary flamenco guitarists, and reached new audiences through his performance in

Carlos Saura's films *Blood Wedding* and *Carmen*, along with the great flamenco dancers, Cristina Hoyos and Antonio Gades. Paco, who is a non-gypsy, won his first flamenco prize at the age of 14, and went on to accompany many of the great traditional singers, including a long partnership with Camarón de la Isla, one of the greatest collaborations of modern flamenco. He introduced new harmonies, chord structures, scales, open tunings and syncopation that initiated the most vital renaissance of *toque* since Ramón Montoya, a remarkable achievement considering the rigid and stylized nature of this most traditional of forms. He started forging new sounds and rhythms for flamenco following a trip to Brazil, where he fell in love with bossa nova, and in the 1970s he established a sextet with electric bass, Latin percussion, and, perhaps most shocking, flute and saxophone from Jorge Pardo. Paco has also introduced into Spanish flamenco the Peruvian **cajón**, a half-box resembling an empty drawer played by sitting straddled across the top; this reintroduced the sound of the foot of the dancer. Over the past twenty years he has worked with jazz-rock guitarists such as John McLaughlin and Chick Corea, while his own regular band, featuring singer Ramón de Algeciras, remains one of the most original and distinctive sounds on the flamenco scene.

Other artists experimented, too, throughout the 1980s. **Lolé y Manuel** updated the flamenco sound with original songs and huge success; **Jorge Pardo** followed Paco's jazz direction; **Salvador Tavora** and **Mario Maya** staged flamenco-based spectacles; and **Enrique Morente** and **Juan Peña El Lebrijano** both worked with Andalucian orchestras from Morocco, while **Amalgama** worked with southern Indian percussionists, revealing surprising stylistic unities. Another interesting crossover came with **Paco Peña**'s 1991 *Misa Flamenca* recording, a setting of the Catholic Mass to flamenco forms with the participation of established singers such as Rafael Montilla "El Chaparro" from Peña's native Córdoba, and a classical academy chorus.

The more commercially successful crossover with rock and blues, pioneered by **Ketama** and **Pata Negra**, became known, in the 1990s, as **nuevo flamenco**. This "movement" is associated particularly with the label Nuevos Medios, and in Andalucía, and also Madrid, where many of the bands are based, is a challenging, versatile and musically incestuous new scene, with musicians guesting at each other's gigs and on one another's records.

The music is now a regular sound at nightclubs, too, through the appeal of young singers like **Aurora**, one of the first to crack the pop charts, and **Martirio** (Isabel Quinones Gutierrez), a flamboyant personality who appears dressed in lace mantilla and shades, like a cameo from a Pedro Almodóvar film, and sings songs with ironical, contemporary lyrics about life in the cities.

In general, the new songs are more sensual and erotic than the traditional material, expressing a pain, suffering and love worth dying for.

Martirio's producer, **Kiko Veneno**, who wrote Camarón's most popular song, *Volando voy*, is another artist who has brought a flamenco sensitivity to Spanish rock music, as has Rosario, one of Spain's top female singers. Other contemporary bands and singers to look out for on the scene include **La Barbería del Sur** (who add a dash of salsa), **Wili Giménez** and **Raimundo Amador**, and **José El Francés**. In the mid-1990s **Radio Tarifa** emerged as an exciting group who started out as a trio, expanded to include African musicians, and whose output mixes Arabic and traditional sounds onto a flamenco base. Flamenco is one of the most powerful popular traditions of music to be found in Europe today, distinguished by its ability to renew itself constantly.

Jan Fairley

Books

T he listings on these pages represent a highly selective reading list on Andalucía and matters Spanish, especially in the sections on history. Most titles are in print, although we've included a few older classics, many of them easy enough to find in secondhand bookshops, libraries or on secondhand-book sites such as ⓦwww.abebooks.co.uk. We have also included websites below for some publishers whose publications are not widely distributed and where it is possible to order from their website. Where the publisher has more than one entry the website appears in the details of the first publication listed in each section.

A reliable **specialist source** in the UK for out-of-print books on all aspects of Spain is Paul Orssich, 2 St Stephens Terrace, London SW8 1DH (ⓣ020/7787 0030, ⓦwww.orssich.com).

General accounts

Introductions

David Baird *Inside Andalusia, Back Roads of Southern Spain, East of Málaga* (Santana, Málaga; ⓦwww .santanabooks.com). *Inside* is a book that grew out of the author's series of articles published in the now defunct *Lookout* magazine, giving an anecdotal yet perceptive overview of the region with plenty of interesting and offbeat observations and glossy illustrations. *Back Roads* by the same author is a drivers' guide to Andalucía displaying the same erudition while *East of Málaga* is an in-depth guide to the Axarquía and its coastline.

Ian Gibson *Fire in the Blood: the New Spain*. Gibson is a Madrid-based

writer, resident since 1978, and a Spanish national since 1984. He is a passionate enthusiast and critic of Spain and the Spanish, both of which he gets across brilliantly in this 1993 book – the accompaniment to a gripping TV series – in all their mass of contradictions, attitudes, obsessions, quirks and everything else. Despite the lack of an updated edition, it's still hugely readable with strong pieces on Andalucía, but did receive flak from outraged Spanish reviewers.

John Hooper *Spaniards: A Portrait of the New Spain*. This excellent, authoritative portrait of

---

The Mercurio literary review

If you're a Spanish-speaker one magazine you should certainly look out for is **Mercurio** (ⓦwww.revistamercurio.es), an excellent monthly literary review carrying articles on Andalucía's literary figures past and present – Richard Ford and Ian Gibson have featured (see p.601 and above respectively for both) – as well as reviews of many new books (fiction and non-fiction) dealing with *andaluz* and broader Spanish themes. The best thing of all is that it's free and available from most good bookshops in the region's major towns and provincial capitals – such as Vértice in Seville or Proteo in Málaga. If you can't locate a copy, email them from their website for a list of stockists.

post-Franco Spain was originally written (by *The Guardian's* then Spain correspondent) in the 1980s. The revised second edition (2006) has already become somewhat dated, but despite only passing references to Andalucía, along with Giles Tremlett's book (see below), this is still one of the best possible introductions to contemporary Spain.

Michael Jacobs *Andalusia*. Well-crafted, opinionated and wide-ranging introduction to Andalucía. It covers everything from prehistory to the Civil War and manages to cram in perceptive pieces on flamenco, gypsies and food and drink. A gazeteer at the back details major sights. This

remains one of the best introductions to the region.

Allen Josephs *White Wall of Spain*. Intelligent series of essays on the mysteries of Andalucian folk culture from the origins of flamenco to the significance of Semana Santa and bullfights, by the former president of the Ernest Hemingway Foundation.

Giles Tremlett *Ghosts of Spain*. Tremlett (the Madrid correspondent of *The Guardian*) digs into the untold story of Spain's Civil War dead and the collective conspiracy of silence surrounding the war's terrors, and goes on to peel away the layers of the post-Franco era to present an enthralling and often disturbing study of contemporary Spain.

Recent travels and accounts

David Baird *Sunny Side Up* (Santana, Málaga Ⓦwww .santanabooks.com). A shrewdly and humorously observed homage to the village of Frigiliana in Málaga where Baird, a veteran Costa del Sol writer and journalist, has lived for over thirty years.

Alastair Boyd *The Sierras of the South: Travels in the Mountains of Andalusia*. A sensitively worked portrait of the Serranía de Ronda which describes one Englishman's continuing love affair with a region he knew as home for twenty years. His earlier *The Road from Ronda* (Collins, UK) is a Sixties' view of the same landscape – the *campesinos* are still struggling.

Adam Hopkins *Spanish Journeys: A Portrait of Spain*. Published in 1993, this is an enjoyable and highly stimulating exploration of Spanish history and culture, weaving its considerable scholarship in an accessible and unforced travelogue form, and full of illuminating anecdotes.

Norman Lewis *The Tomb of Seville*. This final work (before his death in 2003) by eminent travel writer Lewis draws on recollections of a journey to Seville's cathedral in 1934 to attempt to discover a family tomb. The often hazardous journey, through a Spain on the brink of civil war, is described with the writer's customary panache.

Nicholas Luard *Andalucía – A Portrait of Southern Spain* (Century, UK). English writer and naturalist Luard went off to live in Andalucía with his cookery-writer wife and kids for a decade that spanned the end of dictatorship and the early post-Franco years. The result is a closely observed and well-written account of the passing of the seasons in an isolated valley in the Campo de Gibraltar.

Elizabeth Nash *Seville, Córdoba and Granada: a cultural and literary history*. An eloquent, themed and multi-layered exploration of the literary and cultural history of Andalucía's three major cities by *The Independent's*

Madrid correspondent. Ideal reading for the plane or dipping into along the way.

Chris Stewart *Driving Over Lemons.* A contributor to this guide ploughs the same furrow as Luard (see p.599), only this time in Granada, where he describes – often with humour – his move with family to an Alpujarran farmhouse (El Valero) and the numerous adventures involved in setting up house there. The sequel, *A Parrot in the Pepper Tree*, has more stories from El Valero interspersed with accounts of some of the author's earlier adventures as a sheep shearer in Sweden, drummer with rock band Genesis, and greenhorn flamenco guitarist in Seville. The saga's latest episode, *The Almond Blossom Appreciation Society*, delivers another cocktail of hilarious, improbable and poignant tales.

Ted Walker *In Spain* (out of print). Until his death in 2004 the poet Ted Walker had lived and travelled in Spain on and off since the 1950s. This is a lyrical and absorbing account of the country and people, structured around his various sorties, a couple of them in Andalucía.

Jason Webster *Duende* and *Andalus*. In *Duende*, author Webster sets off on a Spanish odyssey to learn flamenco guitar, which takes him to Alicante, Madrid and finally Granada with quite a few emotional encounters along the way. *Andalus* relates a journey with an illegal immigrant whose precarious toe-hold in Spain inspires parallels with the current position of Islam on the peninsula. Interestingly told, but the "What the Arabs did for us" approach occasionally grates.

Earlier twentieth-century writers

Gerald Brenan *South From Granada* and *The Face of Spain.* *South From Granada* is an enduring classic. Brenan lived in a small village in Las Alpujarras in the 1920s, and records this and the visits of his Bloomsbury contemporaries Virginia Woolf, Lytton Strachey and Bertrand Russell. In 2002 the book was made into a film, *Al Sur de Granada* by Spanish director Fernando Colomo. *The Face of Spain* is a later collection of highly readable travel writings gathered on a trip through Franco's Spain in 1949 with a substantial chunk devoted to Andalucía.

Penelope Chetwode *Two Middle-Aged Ladies in Andalucía* (Century, UK). Poet John Betjeman's wife took to the roads of Andalucía with another middle-aged lady – her horse. A paean to "picturesque poverty", this is southern Spain seen from a quaintly English perspective.

Nina Epton *Andalusia* (Weidenfeld & Nicolson, UK). Sixties portrait of the region by a friend of Gerald Brenan. Contains interesting vignettes on people and places immediately prior to the arrival of mass tourism.

Laurie Lee *As I Walked Out One Midsummer Morning, A Rose For Winter, A Moment of War.* *Midsummer Morning* is the irresistibly romantic account of Lee's walk through Spain – from Vigo to Málaga – and his gradual awareness of the forces moving the country towards Civil War. As an autobiographical account, of living rough and busking his way from the Cotswolds with a violin, it's a delight; as a piece of social observation, painfully sharp. In *A Rose For Winter* Lee describes his return, twenty years later, to a very different Andalucía, while in *A Moment of War* he looks back again to describe a winter fighting with the

International Brigade in the Civil War – an account by turns moving, comic and tragic.

Alfonso Lowe *Companion Guide to the South of Spain.* A travel classic from the 1970s. Idiosyncratic account of southern Spain often recording an Andalucía long gone – packed with fascinating background.

James A. Michener *Iberia.* A bestselling, idiosyncratic and encyclopedic compendium of fascinating interviews and impressions of Spain in 1968 on the brink of the post-Franco years.

Jan Morris *Spain.* Morris wrote this in six months in 1960, on her (or, at the time, his) first visit to the country. It is an impressionistic account – good in its sweeping control of place and history, though prone to see everything as symbolic. The updated edition is plain bizarre in its ideas on Franco and dictatorship – a condition for which Morris seems to believe Spaniards were naturally inclined.

Walter Starkie *Don Gypsy.* The tales of a Dublin professor who set out to walk the roads of Spain and Andalucía in the 1930s with only a fiddle for company. The pre-Civil War world – good and bad – is astutely observed and his adventures are frequently amusing. Like Borrow earlier (see below), he fell for the gypsies and became an expert on their culture.

J. B. Trend *Spain from the South.* A classic look at the south in the 1920s by a well-travelled Hispanist who intermingles perceptive observations on the region's history, culture and landscape with shrewd and entertaining sketches of the contemporary scene.

Older classics

George Borrow *The Bible in Spain* and *The Zincali.* On first publication in 1842, *The Bible in Spain* was subtitled by Borrow "Journeys, Adventures and Imprisonments of an English-man"; it is one of the most famous books on Spain – slow in places but with some very amusing stories. *Zincali* is an account of the Spanish gypsies, whom Borrow got to know pretty well and for whom he translated the Bible into *gitano*.

Richard Ford *A Handbook for Travellers in Spain and Readers at Home* and *Gatherings from Spain.* The *Handbook*, first published in 1845, must be the best guide ever written to any country and stayed in print as a Murray's Handbook (one of the earliest series of guides) well into the last century. Massively opinionated, it is an extremely witty book and in its British, nineteenth-century manner, incredibly knowledgeable and worth flicking through for the proverbs alone. Copies of Murray's may be available in secondhand bookstores – the earlier the edition the purer the Ford. *Gatherings* is a filleted – but no less entertaining – abridgement of the Handbook produced "for the ladies" who were not expected to be able to digest the original. Also recommended is a recent biography *Richard Ford, Hispanophile, Connoisseur and Critic* by Ian Robertson (Michael Russell, UK ©michaelrussell @waitrose.com); a fascinating read, it illuminates the creation of Ford's great work and places him in the context of the Victorian world of arts and letters.

Washington Irving *Tales of the Alhambra* (originally published 1832; abridged editions are on sale in Granada). Half of Irving's book consists of Oriental stories, set in the Alhambra; the rest of accounts of his own residence there and the local characters of his time. A perfect read *in situ*. Irving also wrote *The Conquest of Granada* (1829; out of print), a description of the fall of the Nasrids.

Anthologies

Jimmy Burns (ed) *Spain: A Literary Companion*. A good anthology, including worthwhile nuggets of most authors recommended here, amid a whole host of others.

Lucy McCauley *Travellers' Tales: Spain*. A wide-ranging anthology slanted towards more recent writing on Spain; includes strong pieces on Andalucía by many of the authors mentioned in this section.

David Mitchell *Travellers in Spain: an Illustrated Anthology* (Ⓦwww .santanabooks.com). A well-told story of how four centuries of travellers – and most often travel writers – saw Spain. It's interesting to see Ford, Brenan, Laurie Lee and the rest set in context.

Customs and culture

🏃 **Edward Lewine** *Death and the Sun: A matador's season in the heart of Spain*. Bullfight aficionado Lewine takes on the perilous task of trying to make this Spanish blood-sport comprehensible to non-believers. He spends a year on the road in the company of top *matador* Francisco Rivera Ordoñez – whose great-grandfather was revered by Hemingway – and provides fascinating background on the gruelling routine of long road journeys between towns, often dingy hotels and the bitter recriminations when the "boss" has had a disastrous day in the ring.

Timothy Mitchell *Flamenco Deep Song*. Diametrically opposed to Woodall's work (see below), the author sets out to debunk the mystagogy of flamenco purists by arguing that they are shackling the form's development and ends up with an improbable defence of the Gipsy Kings. A well-researched and entertaining read whether or not you accept its iconoclastic premise.

Eamonn O'Neill *Matadors*. Subtitled "a journey into the heart of modern bullfighting" this is part autobiographical travelogue, part sociological study of the role of bullfighting in modern Spain, throwing light on a peculiarly Iberian industry worth a billion dollars annually.

Paul Richardson *Our Lady of the Sewers*. Presents an articulate and kaleidoscopic series of insights into rural Spain's customs and cultures, fast disappearing.

🏃 **James Woodall** *In Search of the Firedance: Spain through Flamenco*. This is a terrific history and exploration of flamenco, and as the subtitle suggests it is never satisfied with "just the music" in getting to the heart of the culture.

CONTEXTS | Books

History

General history

Juan Lalaguna *A Traveller's History of Spain*. A lucid – and pocketable – background history to the country, which spans the Phoenicians to Franco, Felipe González and the emergence of democratic Spain.

M. Vincent & R.A. Stradling *Cultural Atlas of Spain and Portugal.*

A deceptive, coffee-table format belies a formidable historical, artistic and social survey of the Iberian peninsula from ancient times to the present; excellent colour maps and well-chosen photos amplify the text.

Prehistoric and Roman periods

James M. Anderson *Spain: 1001 Archaeological Sites*. A good guide and gazetteer of Spain's archeological sites with detailed instructions of how to get to them.

Henri Breuil *Rock Paintings of Southern Andalucía*. Published in 1929, this is still the definitive guide to the subject.

Roger Collins *Spain: An Archeological Guide*. Covering around 140 sites, temples, mosques and palaces dating from prehistory to the twelfth century, this book devotes more space per entry to maps, plans and data, making it a more useful vade mecum to the major sites than Anderson's work (see above).

Maria Cruz Fernández Castro *Iberia in Prehistory*. A major study of the Iberian peninsula prior to the arrival of the Romans which includes extensive coverage of early Andalucian sites such as Los Millares as well as the later Iberian settlements encountered by the Phoenicians and Greeks. This is

the first volume of the publisher's (Blackwells) important series on the history of Spain from the prehistoric era through to the Civil War.

S.J. Keay *Roman Spain* (British Museum Publications/California UP). Definitive survey of a neglected subject, well illustrated and highly readable.

John S. Richardson *The Romans in Spain*. A new look at how Spain came to be a part of the Roman world, which also examines the influences that flowed from Spain to Rome as well as vice versa.

Chris Stringer & Robin McKie *African Exodus*. If you want to grasp Spain's part in the Neanderthal story, this lively and accessible account by an expert in the field (aided by the science editor of *The Observer*) is the book. The account of the last of the Neanderthals hanging on in a cave above the Zaffaraya Pass in northern Málaga only adds to the drama of the landscape on the ground.

Visigothic Spain to the nineteenth century

J.M. Cohen *The Four Voyages of Christopher Columbus*. The man behind the myth; Columbus's astonishing voyages as described by the man himself in his log are

interwoven with opinions of contemporaries on the great explorer, including his biographer son Hernando. A fascinating collection, superbly translated.

Roger Collins *The Arab Conquest of Spain 710–97.* Cogently argued and controversial study which documents the Moorish invasion and the significant influence that the conquered Visigoths had on the formative phase of Muslim rule by a scholar uniquely expert in both fields. Collins's *Visigothic Spain* is a significant companion volume to the above and his earlier *Early Medieval Spain 400–1000* takes a broader overview of the same subject.

John A. Crow *Spain: the Root and the Flower.* Perceptive, highly readable and shrewdly observed cultural and social history from Roman Spain to the present by the late US hispanist, who was a friend of Lorca and who personally experienced many of Spain's twentieth-century triumphs and tragedies.

J.H. Elliott *Imperial Spain 1469–1716.* Best introduction to "the Golden Age" – academically respected and a gripping tale.

Richard Fletcher *Moorish Spain.* A fascinating, provocative and highly readable narrative with a suitably iconoclastic conclusion to the history of Moorish Spain. The best introduction to the subject.

L.P. Harvey *Islamic Spain 1250–1500.* Comprehensive account of its period – both the Islamic kingdoms and the Muslims living beyond their protection.

Henry Kamen *The Spanish Inquisition, Philip of Spain* and *Spain's Road to Empire. Inquisition* is a highly respected examination of the Inquisition and the long shadow it cast across Spanish history and development. *The Spanish Inquisition: An Historical Revision* returns to the subject in the light of more recent evidence, while Kamen's *Philip of Spain* is the first full biography of Felipe II, the ruler most closely associated with the Inquisition. In

Empire, Kamen skilfully dissects the conquest of the Americas and Philippines and concludes that the Spanish were ill-suited to the imperial role, displaying both organizational incompetence and little interest in the peoples they subjugated.

Elie Kedourie *Spain and the Jews: the Sephardi Experience, 1492 and after.* A collection of essays on the three-million-strong Spanish Jews of the Middle Ages and their expulsion by the Catholic monarchs.

John Lynch *Spain 1516–1598.* New interpretation of Spain's rise to empire with plenty of interesting detail on Andalucía's trading role – especially the cities of Seville and Cádiz – in the exploitation of the Americas. The same author's *Hispanic World in Crisis and Change 1598–1700* and *Bourbon Spain 1700–1808* carry the story forward to the critical crossroads that determined Spain's future for the ensuing century and a half.

Bernard F. Reilly *The Contest of Christian and Muslim Spain.* A fascinating and detailed study of the stresses and strains of the crucial tenth and eleventh centuries when Christians, Muslims and Jews were locked in a struggle for supremacy on one hand and survival on the other, by an acknowledged expert on the subject.

James Reston Jr *Dogs of God.* A alternative take on the Inquisition from that of Kamen (see above) connecting it with the epic year 1492 and linking religious intolerance to the final defeat of the Moors in Spain and Columbus' sudden widening of the Spanish crown's sphere of influence.

Adrian Shubert *A Social History of Modern Spain.* This accomplished first social history of Spain in English documents the turbulent history of post-1800 Spain from a people's perspective. An essential read to understand the origins of modern Andalucía's structural and social problems – such as *latifundismo* – in their Spanish and European context.

Colin Smith, Charles Melville & Ahmad Ubaydli *Christians and Moors in Spain*. A fascinating collection of documents by Spanish and Arabic writers from the Muslim conquest to the Christian supremacy which are intended for the lay reader as well as the academic. The bilingual parallel text (including Arabic) allows you to read firsthand not only the key historical, military and literary accounts but also the invariably fascinating views of Christians and Moors on each other. Recommended.

The twentieth century

Gerald Brenan *The Spanish Labyrinth*. First published in 1943, Brenan's study of the social and political background to the Civil War is tinged by personal experience, yet still an impressively rounded account.

Raymond Carr *Modern Spain 1875–1980* and *The Spanish Tragedy: the Civil War in Perspective*. Two of the best books available on modern Spanish history – concise and well-told narratives.

Ronald Fraser *Blood of Spain*, *In Hiding* and *The Pueblo*. Subtitled "An Oral History of the Spanish Civil War", *Blood* is an impressive – and brilliantly unorthodox – piece of research, constructed entirely of oral accounts. *In Hiding* is a fascinating individual account of a Republican mayor of Mijas (in Málaga) hidden by his family for thirty years until the Civil War amnesty of 1969. *Pueblo* is a penetrating and compelling study of the trials and struggles of one Costa del Sol mountain village seen through the eyes of its inhabitants which speaks for much of Andalucía today.

Ian Gibson *Federico García Lorca*, *The Assassination of Federico García Lorca* and *Lorca's Granada*. The biography is a gripping book and *The Assassination* a brilliant reconstruction of the events at the end of his life, with an examination of fascist corruption and of the shaping influences on Lorca, twentieth-century Spain and the Civil War. *Granada* explores Lorca's city by way of a collection of fascinating walks around the town.

Joe Monk *With the Reds in Andalucía* (out of print). One Irishman's eyewitness account of the optimism, hell, and finally despair, of fighting with the Irish Brigade of the international volunteers during the Civil War.

Paul Preston *Concise History of the Spanish Civil War*, *Franco* and *The Triumph of Democracy in Spain*. A formidable expert on the period, Preston has succeeded in his attempt to provide a manageable guide to the Civil War labyrinth – with powerful illustrations. *Franco* is a penetrating – and monumental – biography of the dictator and his regime, which provides as clear a picture as any yet published of how he won the Civil War, survived in power so long, and what, twenty years on from his death, was his significance. *Triumph* presents the absorbing story of the unravelling of the Franco years and the ultimate burial of the past with the election of the 1982 Socialist government.

Hugh Thomas *The Spanish Civil War*. This exhaustive 1000-page study is regarded (both in Spain and abroad) as the definitive history of the Civil War, but is not as accessible for the general reader as Preston's account (see above).

Paddy Woodworth *Dirty War, Clean Hands: ETA, the GAL and Spanish Democracy*. "Democracy is defended in the sewers as well as the salons" was Felipe González's retort to critics of his dirty and illegal 1980s war against the Basque terrorist organization ETA when the state employed assassination and kidnap squads to play the terrorists at their own game. This important and impeccably researched work analyses what happens when a democracy abandons the rule of law and shows how this shocking policy actually strengthened rather than defeated revolutionary terrorism.

🏃 Gamel Woolsey *Málaga Burning* (Pythia Press, US) and, under its original title *Death's Other Kingdom* (Eland, UK). A long ignored minor classic written in the late 1930s and recently reprinted (and retitled) by a US publisher in which the American poet and wife of Gerald Brenan vividly describes the horrors of the descent of their part of Andalucía into civil war. The Eland edition includes an interesting biographical afterword by Michael Jacobs.

Art and architecture

Marianne Barrucand and Achim Bednoz *Moorish Architecture*. A beautifully illustrated guide to the major Moorish monuments.

Bernard Bevan *History of Spanish Architecture*. Classic study of Iberian and Ibero-American architecture which includes extensive coverage of the Mudéjar, Plateresque and Baroque periods.

🏃 **Titus Burckhardt** *Moorish Culture in Spain* (out of print). An outstanding book which opens up ways of looking at Spain's Islamic monuments, explaining their patterns and significance and the social environment in which, and for which, they were produced.

Godfrey Goodwin *Islamic Spain*. Architectural guide with descriptions of virtually every significant Islamic building in Spain, and a fair amount of background. Small enough to take along.

🏃 **Michael Jacobs** *Alhambra*. If you've fallen under the

Alhambra's spell then this sumptuously produced volume with outstanding photographs and expert commentary will rekindle the memory. Authoritatively guides you through the history and architecture of Andalucía's emblematic monument, placing it in its Islamic context, and concludes with a fascinating essay on the hold that the palace has had on later artists, travellers and writers from Irving and Ford to de Falla and Lorca.

George Kubler and Martin Soria *Art and Architecture in Spain and Portugal 1500–1800* (Pelican, UK). Provides an alternative to, if not a vast improvement on, the Sitwell book (see below).

David Talbot Rice *Islamic Art* (Thames & Hudson, UK). A classic introduction to the whole subject.

Sacheverell Sitwell *Spanish Baroque*. First published in 1931, this is interesting mainly for the absence of anything better on the subject.

Fiction and poetry

Spanish fiction

Pedro de Alarcón *The Three-Cornered Hat and Other Stories* (out of print). Ironic nineteenth-century tales of the previous century's corruption, bureaucracy and absolutism by a writer born in Guadix. He also wrote *Alpujarra* (out of print), a not very well-observed tour through the Sierra Nevada.

Miguel de Cervantes *Don Quijote*. *Quijote* (or *Quixote*) is of course the classic of Spanish literature and remains an excellent and witty read, especially in J.M. Cohen's classic Penguin translation or a new version by Edith Grossman.

Juan Ramón Jiménez *Platero and I*. Andalucía's Nobel Prize-winning poet and writer from Moguer in Huelva paints a lyrically evocative picture of Andalucía and its people in conversations with his donkey, Platero.

Antonio Machado *Eighty Poems* and *Juan de Mairena* (out of print). The best-known works in English of this eminent *sevillano* poet and writer. The latter novel draws on his experience as a schoolteacher in Baeza.

Modern fiction

Arturo Barea *The Forging of a Rebel*. Superb autobiographical trilogy, taking in the Spanish war in Morocco in the 1920s, and Barea's own part in the Civil War in Andalucía and elsewhere. The books were published under the individual titles *The Forge*, *The Track* and *The Clash*.

Arturo Pérez Reverte *The Seville Communion*. An entertaining crime yarn by one of Spain's leading writers involving a hacker in the pope's computer, a stubborn old local priest up against rapacious bankers eager to bulldoze his church, a number of corpses, and an investigator dispatched by the Vatican. All is played out against the colourfully described backdrop of Seville. *The Dumas Club*, an engrossing tale about a bibliophile's search for a book on black magic, *The Fencing Master*, a political thriller set in nineteenth-century Spain, and *The Nautical Chart*, a search for treasure in a galleon sunk off the coast of Andalucía, are other translated works by Pérez Reverte. His recent novel, *The Queen of the South* took the Spanish bestseller lists by storm and relates the story of a woman drug trafficker running narcotics between Morocco and Cádiz.

Plays and poetry

A.J. Arberry (trans.) *Moorish Poetry* (Cambridge UP, UK). Excellent collection of Hispano-Arab verse.

Cola Franzen (trans.) *Poems of Arab Andalusia* (City Lights, US). Sensitively rendered collection of verse by some of the best poets of Moorish al-Andalus.

Federico García Lorca *Five Plays: Comedies and Tragicomedies*, *Selected Poems* and *Poem of the Deep Song*. Andalucía's great pre-Civil War playwright and poet. The first two volumes have his major theatrical works and poems, whilst the latter is a moving poetic paean to *cante jondo*, flamenco's blues, inspired by his contact with *gitano* culture. Arturo Barea's *Lorca: the Poet and His People* is also of interest.

San Juan de la Cruz *The Poetry of Saint John of the Cross.* Excellent translation by South African poet Roy Campbell of the poems of this mystical confessor to Teresa of Ávila who died at Úbeda.

Foreign fiction

Douglas Day *Journey of the Wolf.* Outstanding first novel by an American writer, given the seal of approval by Graham Greene ("gripping and poignant"). The subject is a Civil War fighter, "El Lobo", who returns as a fugitive to Poqueira, his village in the Alpujarras, forty years on.

Ernest Hemingway *Fiesta/The Sun Also Rises* and *For Whom the Bell Tolls.* Hemingway remains a big part of the American myth of Spain. *Fiesta* contains some lyrically

beautiful writing while the latter – set in Civil War Andalucía – is a good deal more laboured. He also published an enthusiastic and not very good account of bullfighting, *Death in the Afternoon.*

Amin Maalouf *Leo the African.* A wonderful historical novel, re-creating the life of Leo Africanus, the fifteenth-century Moorish geographer, in the last years of the kingdom of Granada, and on his subsequent exile in Morocco and world travels.

Specialist guides

Phil Ball *Morbo – The Story of Spanish Football.* Excellent account of Spanish football from its nineteenth-century beginnings with the British workers at the mines of Río Tinto to the golden years of Real Madrid and the dark days of Franco, with the ever present backdrop of the ferocious *morbo* – political, historical, regional and linguistic rivalry – that has driven it since.

Bob and Ruth Carrick *Made in Andalucía – the Arts and Crafts of Southern Spain.* Informative guide to the crafts workshops and artisans of rural Andalucía (the larger towns and provincial capitals are not covered), organized by province with suggested routes enabling tours of a specific area, with maps, directions and

contact details for all the artisans and workshops mentioned.

Christopher Turner *The Penguin Guide to Seville.* A set of interesting guided walks around Andalucía's capital city.

Sandy Walker *Campo – A Guide to the Spanish Countryside* (@www.santanabooks.com). On one level a how-to book on planting and cultivating trees, on another a vade - mecum to almost every kind of fruit tree grown in Andalucía (where the author has her farm). All kinds of trees from almonds and olives to carobs and pomegranates are covered and there's fascinating detail on the history, local background, and medicinal potential of each species – she even throws in the odd recipe.

Hiking and cycling

David and Ros Brawn *Sierra de Aracena* (Discovery UK ⓦwww .walking.demon.co.uk). Excellent walking guide to this magnificent Sierra by two experienced walkers. Covers 27 walks (from 3–14km) with an accompanying map (sold separately) and all routes are GPS waypointed.

Matt Butler *Holiday Walks from the Costa del Sol* (Sigma, UK ⓦwww .sigmapress.co.uk). Holiday walks within reach of a Costa del Sol base, covering the coast from Cádiz province in the west to Granada province in the east. Free internet updates available.

Chris Craggs *Andalusian Rock Climbs*. Introductory guide to one of Andalucía's fastest-growing sports. Has descriptions of all the major climbs plus details of how to get there.

Charles Davis *Costa del Sol Walks* (ⓦwww.santanabooks.com). Well-written guide to 34 walks – between 4 and 8km – along the Costa del Sol between Nerja and Estepona; each walk has its own map. The same author's *Walk! the Axarquía* (Discovery, UK) is a reliable guide to this picturesque region describing thirty walks between 5 and 22km, all GPS waypointed. Davis has also published *34 Alpujarras Walks* (Discovery, UK) with a similar format detailing 34 GPS waypointed treks between 4km and 25km. In both the latter books each walk has its own map or there are waterproof 1:40,000 *Axarquía/Alpujarras Tour and Trail* maps (sold separately) with all walks (and GPS points) marked.

Harry Dowdell *Cycle Touring in Spain*. Well-researched cycle touring guide which describes eight touring routes of varying difficulty in the north and south of Spain. Plenty of practical information on preparing

your bike for the trip, transporting it, and what to take.

Guy Hunter-Watts *Walking in Andalucía* (ⓦwww.santanabooks .com). First-rate walking guide to the Natural Parks of Grazalema, Cazorla, Los Alcornocales, Aracena and La Axarquía as well as the Alpujarras and the Sierra Nevada, comprising thirty-two walks between 8 and 17km in length, each with its own colour map.

John & Christine Oldfield *Andalucía and the Costa del Sol*. This addition to the popular *Landscapes* walking guide series has 23 clearly described walks (with maps) ranging from 5 to 22km in Las Alpujarras, Sierra Nevada, Axarquía and Grazalema, as well as the areas bordering the Costa del Sol.

Guías Penthalon (Penthalon, Spain). Detailed and generally reliable – although some need updating – series of walking guides (in Spanish) to various regions of Andalucía including the Sierra de Aracena and Sierra Nevada.

Jeremy Rabjohns *Holiday Walks in the Alpujarra* (Sigma, UK). Excellent walking guide by Alpujarras resident Rabjohns describing twenty-four walks between 3 and 22km in length with clear maps (including many village street maps) and background information. Free updates and corrections available on the internet.

Alison Raju *Via de la Plata – The Way of St James*. A walker's guide to the lesser-known pilgrim route – much of it following ancient Roman roads – to Santiago de Compostela which started out from Seville. Gives clear route directions, plus information on sights en route, places to stay and practicalities.

Kirstie Shirra & Michelle Lowe *Walking the GR7 in Andalucía.*

CONTEXTS | Books

A well-described guide to hiking the 700km long GR7 from Tarifa to the fringes of the Cazorla natural park in Jaén. Both the northern (via Cazorla) and southern (via Las Alpujarras) routes are covered and there's plenty of background detail. The route can easily be broken up into shorter walks of a day's duration, taking a bus or taxi back to the start point.

Andy Walmsley *Walking in the Sierra Nevada* (Cicerone, UK). Forty-five walks of varying distance and difficulty from three-hour strolls to the seriously arduous Tres Mils (3000m-plus) peaks.

Wildlife

John R. Butler *Birdwatching on Spain's Southern Coast* (🌐www .santanabooks.com). A guide to the major – and many minor – birdwatching sites of Andalucía including the Costa de Almería, Costa de la Luz and the Doñana national park. The author – who lives in Málaga and leads birdwatching tours – includes maps and the usual bird calendars as well as the highly unusual (and laudable) information concerning sites accessible (the vast majority are) to wheelchair-using and disabled twitchers.

Teresa Farino and Mike Lockwood *Travellers' Nature Guides: Spain*. Excellent illustrated wildlife guide to the peninsula by two Spanish-based experts; conveniently divided into regional groupings with detailed maps, it covers many of Andalucía's major habitats for spotting flora and fauna.

🏃 **Ernest García and Andrew Paterson** *Where to Watch Birds in Southern Spain*. A well-planned guide to bird watching sites throughout Andalucía with location maps and reports detailing species to be seen according to season.

🏃 **Frederic Grunfeld and Teresa Farino** *Wild Spain*.

A knowledgeable and practical guide to Spain's national parks, ecology and wildlife with a section on Andalucía. Particularly recommended.

Heinzel, Fitter and Parslow *Collins Guide to the Birds of Britain and Europe*. Alternative to the *Collins Bird Guide* (see below). Also includes North Africa and the Middle East.

John Measures *The Wildlife Travelling Companion: Spain*. Clearly laid-out field guide to specific wildlife areas complete with an illustrated index of the most common flora and fauna.

Oleg Polunin and Anthony Huxley *Flowers of the Mediterranean*. Useful if by no means exhaustive field guide.

Oleg Polunin and B. E. Smythies *Flowers of South-West Europe*. Covers all of Spain, Portugal and southwest France; taxonomy is old, but still unsurpassed for its plates, line drawings and keys.

🏃 **Svensson, Grant, Mullarney and Zetterstrom** *The Collins Bird Guide*. The best bird field guide yet published covers (and illustrates) the birds of Europe including almost everything you're likely to encounter in Spain.

Food and wine

Vicky Benninson *A Taste of Place: Andalucía*. A cornucopia of a book covering all aspects of food and drink in Andalucía: what to buy, where to buy it, and what to do with it in the kitchen; plus – if you prefer to dine out – where to eat *andaluz* cuisine at it's very best throughout the region.

Nicholas Butcher *The Spanish Kitchen* (Macmillan, UK). A practical and knowledgeable guide to creating Spanish – including *andaluz* – dishes. Lots of informative detail on tapas, olive oil, *jamón serrano* and herbs.

Bob Carrick *Ventas Within a Short Drive of the Costa del Sol*. Useful guide to some of the best *ventas* – Spain's bargain roadside restaurants – within easy reach of the Málaga coast. Widely available at bookshops in major resorts.

Penelope Casas *The Foods and Wines of Spain* and *Tapas: the little dishes of Spain*. An excellent overview of classic Spanish and Andalucian cuisine, plus the same author's guide to the tapas labyrinth.

Jon Clarke *Dining Secrets of Andalucía* (@www.santanabooks.com). Excellent guide to many up-and-coming (as well as established) quality restaurants in Andalucía with selections from all eight of the region's provinces.

Alan Davidson *The Tio Pepe Guide to the Seafood of Spain and Portugal*. An indispensable book that details and illustrates every fish and crustacean you're likely to meet in Andalucía. His *Mediterranean Seafood* is another classic worth trying to get hold of.

Julian Jeffs *Sherry* (Faber, UK). The story of sherry – history, production, blending and brands. Rightly a classic and the best introduction to Andalucía's great wine.

The same author's *Wines of Spain* is an erudite guide to traditional and emerging wine regions with details of vineyards, grape varieties and vintages.

Jean Claude Juston *The New Spain – Vegan and Vegetarian Restaurants* (copies available from @www.vegetarianguides.co.uk or @www.ivu.org/atelier). Very useful guide to vegetarian restaurants throughout Spain by the owner/chef of a vegetarian restaurant in the Alpujarras. Catering also for vegans, each listing has its own review and there's lots of background information on Spanish veggie websites and magazines plus details of animal-friendly organizations.

Elisabeth Luard *The La Ina Book of Tapas* and *Flavours of Andalucía*. Once you're hooked on tapas, this is the bible for all classic recipes. The Andalucía volume parades the major dishes of the region province by province.

Maite Manjon *Gastronomy of Spain and Portugal*. Useful, wide-ranging and alphabetical guide to food and drink on the peninsula.

John Radford *The New Spain* and *The Wines of Rioja*. Lavish coffee-table format disguises *New Spain*'s serious content: a detailed region-by-region guide to Spanish wine with colour maps, *bodega* and vintage evaluations and fine illustrations. *Wines of Rioja* is a comprehensive survey of the wines and producers in this emblematic Spanish wine region.

Jan Read *Guide to the Wines of Spain*. Regularly updated, encyclopedic (yet pocketable) guide to the classic and emerging wines of Spain by a leading authority. Includes maps, vintages and vineyards.

Paul Richardson *Late Dinner*. A joyous dissection of the food of Spain, region by region, season by season, nibble of ham by shoot of asparagus. A celebration of culture and cuisine, this is the best general introduction to what Spanish food – and life – is really all about.

Learning Spanish and living in Spain

Breakthrough Spanish. The best of the tape- and book-linked home-study courses which aims to give you a reasonable fluency within three months. The same series has advanced and business courses.

Collins Spanish Dictionary. Recognized as the best single-volume bookshelf dictionary. Regularly revised and updated so make sure to get the latest edition.

Get by in Spanish (book and cassette). One of the BBC's excellent crash-course introductions which gets you to survival level (bars, restaurants, asking the way, and so on) Spanish in a couple of weeks.

David Hampshire *Living and Working in Spain* (Survival Books, UK ⊛www.survivalbooks.net). An information-packed comprehensive guide to moving to, and setting up home in, Spain.

Guy Hobbs & Heleina Postings *Live and Work in Spain and Portugal* (Vacation Work, UK). Well-researched handbook full of useful information on moving to the peninsula, buying property, seeking work, starting a business, finding schools and lots more.

David Searl *You and the Law in Spain* (Santana, Málaga ⊛www .santanabooks.com). Invaluable, lucid and remarkably comprehensive guide to the Spanish legal and tax system (now in its nineteenth updated edition) and an essential read if you are thinking of buying property, working or setting up a business in Spain.

Learn Spanish Now! (Transparent Language UK/US ⊛www .transparent.com). CD-ROM based interactive language course incorporating all kinds of gadgets and gizmos enabling you compare your pronunciation with a native speaker, take part in conversations, access web-based additional learning resources and play skill-improving interactive games. Works on either Mac or PC systems.

Spanish Dictionary Phrasebook (Rough Guides). Good pocket-size dictionary that should help with most travel situations.

Language

Language

Spanish

Once you get into it, **Spanish** is one of the easiest languages to learn – and you'll be helped everywhere by people who are eager to try and understand even the most faltering attempt. English is spoken, but only in the main tourist areas to any extent, and wherever you are you'll get a far better reception if you at least try communicating with Spaniards in their own tongue. Being understood, of course, is only half the problem – getting the gist of the reply, often rattled out at a furious pace, may prove far more difficult.

The rules of **pronunciation** are pretty straightforward and, once you get to know them, strictly observed. Unless there's an **accent**, words ending in d, l, r, and z are stressed on the last syllable, all others on the second last. All **vowels** are pure and short; combinations have predictable results.

A somewhere between the "A" sound of back and that of father

E as in get

I as in police

O as in hot

U as in rule

C in castellano (standard Spanish) is lisped before E and I, hard otherwise: cerca is pronounced "thairka". However, many parts of Andalucía pronounce as an "s" – "sairka" or even "Andalusia".

G works the same way, a guttural "H" sound (like the ch in loch) before E or I, a hard G elsewhere – gigante becomes "higante".

H is always silent

J the same sound as a guttural G: jamón is pronounced "hamon".

LL sounds like an English Y or LY: tortilla is pronounced torteeya/torteelya.

N is as in English unless it has a tilde (accent) over it, when it becomes NY: mañana sounds like "manyana".

QU is pronounced like an English K.

R is rolled, RR doubly so.

V sounds more like B, vino becoming "beano".

X has an S sound before consonants, normal X before vowels.

Z (in castellano) is the same as a soft C, so cerveza becomes "thairvaitha", but again much of Andalucía prefers the "s" sound – "sairvaisa".

A list of a few essential words and phrases follows which should be enough to get you started, though if you're travelling for any length of time, a dictionary or phrasebook is obviously a worthwhile investment. If you're using a dictionary, bear in mind that in Spanish CH, LL, and Ñ count as separate letters and are listed after C, L, and N respectively. For recommended books and tapes on learning Spanish, see the "Books" section, p.612.

Useful words and phrases

Basics

Yes, No, OK	Sí, No, Vale	With, Without	Con, Sin
Please, Thank you	Por favor, Gracias	Good, Bad	Buen(o)/a, Mal(o)/a
Where, When	Dónde, Cuando	Big, Small	Gran(de), Pequeño/a
What, How much	Qué, Cuánto	Cheap, Expensive	Barato, Caro
Here, There	Aquí, Allí	Hot, Cold	Caliente, Frío
This, That	Esto, Eso	More, Less	Más, Menos
Now, Later	Ahora, Más tarde	Today, Tomorrow	Hoy, Mañana
Open, Closed	Abierto/a, Cerrado/a	Yesterday	Ayer

Greetings and responses

Hello, Goodbye	Hola, Adiós	Do you speak English?	¿Habla (usted) inglés?
Good morning	Buenos días	I don't speak Spanish	(No) Hablo español
Good afternoon/ night	Buenas tardes/ noches	My name is ...	Mi llamo ...
See you later	Hasta luego	What's your name?	¿Como se llama usted?
Sorry	Lo siento/disculpéme		
Excuse me	Con permiso/perdón	I am English/ Australian/ Canadian/ American/Irish	Soy inglés(a)/ australiano(a)/ canadiense(a)/ americano(a) irlandés(a)
How are you?	¿Como está (usted)?		
I (don't) understand	(No) Entiendo		
Not at all/You're welcome	De nada		

Hotels and transport

I want	Quiero	It's fine, how much is it?	¿Está bien, cuánto es?
I'd like	Quisiera		
Do you know ...?	¿Sabe ...?	It's too expensive	Es demasiado caro
I don't know	No sé	Don't you have anything cheaper?	¿No tiene algo más barato?
There is (is there)?	(¿)Hay(?)		
Give me ... (one like that)	Deme ...(uno así)	Can one ...?	¿Se puede ...?
		camp (near) here?	¿acampar aquí (cerca)?
Do you have ...?	¿Tiene ...?		
... the time	... la hora	Is there a hostel nearby?	¿Hay un hostal aquí cerca?
... a room	... una habitación		
... with two beds/ double bed	... con dos camas cama matrimonial	How do I get to ...?	¿Por dónde se va a ...?
		Left, right, straight on	Izquierda, derecha, todo recto
... with shower/bath	... con ducha/baño		
It's for one person (two people)	Es para una persona (dos personas)	Where is ...?	¿Dónde está ...?
		... the bus station	... la estación de autobuses
... for one night (one week)	... para una noche (una semana)	... the railway station	... la estación de ferrocarril

... the nearest bank	... el banco mas cercano	I'd like a (return) ticket to ...	Quisiera un billete (de ida y vuelta) para ...
... the post office	... el correos/la oficina de correos	What time does it leave (arrive in ...)?	¿A qué hora sale (llega a ...)?
... the toilet	... el baño/aseo/servicio	What is there to eat?	¿Qué hay para comer?
		What's that?	¿Qué es eso?
Where does the bus to ...leave from?	¿De dónde sale el autobús para ...?	What's this called in Spanish?	¿Como se llama este en español?
Is this the train for Seville?	¿Es este el tren para Sevilla ?		

Numbers and days

1	un/uno/una	80	ochenta
2	dos	90	noventa
3	tres	100	cien(to)
4	cuatro	101	ciento uno
5	cinco	200	doscientos
6	seis	201	doscientos uno
7	siete	500	quinientos
8	ocho	1000	mil
9	nueve	2000	dos mil
10	diez		
11	once	first	primero/a
12	doce	second	segundo/a
13	trece	third	tercero/a
14	catorce	fifth	quinto/a
15	quince	tenth	décimo/a
16	diez y seis		
20	veinte	Monday	lunes
21	veintiuno	Tuesday	martes
30	treinta	Wednesday	miércoles
40	cuarenta	Thursday	jueves
50	cincuenta	Friday	viernes
60	sesenta	Saturday	sábado
70	setenta	Sunday	domingo

Food and drink

Andaluz cuisine reflects its history and climate: many of the spices used, like cumin, coriander and saffron, were introduced by the Moors, and the variety of cold dishes such as gazpacho are intended to cool you down as much as to nourish. The list below should cover most of your needs, and local specialities are mentioned in the body of the *Guide*. Other things you'll simply see people eating. "Quisiera uno asi" ("I'd like one like that") can be an amazingly useful phrase.

Restaurant terms

Almuerzo	Lunch	Cuchillo	Knife
Botella	Bottle	La cuenta	The bill
Menú	Set meal	Desayuno	Breakfast
La carta	Menu	Mesa	Table
Cena	Dinner	Tenedor	Fork
Cubierto	Set of cutlery	Vaso	Glass
Cuchara	Spoon		

Menu terms

a la brasa	(charcoal) grilled	cazuela, cocido	stew
a la Gallego/a	Galician style	cocina casera	homemade
a la Navarra	stuffed with ham	en salsa	in (usually tomato) sauce
a la parilla/plancha	grilled		
a la romana	fried in batter	escabeche/ escabechado	pickled or marinated
a la rondeña	Ronda style		
a la sal	baked in a salt crust	frito	fried
al ajillo	in garlic	guisado	casserole
al horno	baked	ibérico	superior meat from Spanish black pigs
alioli	with mayonnaise		
asado	roast	rehogado	baked

Basics

Aceite	Oil	Pan	Bread
Ajo	Garlic	Pimienta	Pepper
Arroz	Rice	Queso	Cheese
Azúcar	Sugar	Sal	Salt
Fruta	Fruit	Verduras/Legumbres	Vegetables
Huevos	Eggs	Vinagre	Vinegar
Mantequilla	Butter		

Soups and starters (sopas y entrémeses)

Ajo blanco	Creamy gazpacho with garlic and almonds	Sopa de cocido	Meat soup
		Sopa de gallina	Chicken soup
		Sopa de mariscos	Seafood soup
Caldillo	Clear fish soup	Sopa de pasta (fideos)	Noodle soup
Caldo verde/ gallego	Thick, cabbage-based broth		
		Sopa de pescado	Fish soup
Gazpacho	Cold tomato and cucumber soup	Sopa de picadillo	Chicken and vegetable broth garnished with egg
Migas	fried breadcrumbs		

Salad (ensalada) and starters

Arroz a la cubana	Rice with fried egg and home-made tomato sauce	Pimientos rellenos	Stuffed peppers
Ensalada (mixta/verde)	(Mixed/green) salad	Verduras con patatas	Boiled potatoes with greens

Fish (pescados)

Anchoas	Anchovies (tinned)	Merluza	Hake
Anguila	Eel	Mero	Grouper
Angulas	Elvers (baby eel)	Mojama	Salted blue-fin tuna
Atún	Tuna	Pez espada	Swordfish
Bacalao	Cod (often salt)	Rape	Monkfish
Besugo/Pargo	Red bream	Rodaballo	Turbot
Bonito	Tuna	Salmón	Salmon
Boquerones	Anchovies (fresh)	Salmonete	Mullet
Chanquetes	Whitebait	Sardinas	Sardines
Dorada	Gilt head bream	Trucha	Trout
Lenguado	Sole	Urta	Member of the bream family
Lubina	Sea Bass		

Seafood (mariscos)

Almejas	Clam	Langostinos	Giant king prawns
Calamares	Squid	Mejillones	Mussels
Cangrejo	Crab	Ostras	Oysters
Centollo	Spider crab	Percebes	Goose barnacles
Chipirones	Small squid	Pescadilla	Small whiting
Cigalas	King prawns	Pulpo	Octopus
Conchas finas	Large scallops	Puntillitas	Baby squid
Erizo de mar	Sea urchin	Sepia	Cuttlefish
Gambas	Prawns/shrimps	Vieiras/Conchas	Scallops
Langosta	Lobster	Zamburiñas	Baby clams

Meat (carne) and poultry (aves)

Albóndigas	Meatballs	Cochinillo	Suckling pig
Cabra	Goat	Codorniz	Quail
Callos	Tripe	Conejo	Rabbit
Carne de vaca	Beef	Cordero	Lamb
Cerdo	Pork	Criadillas	Testicles
Chorizo	Spicy sausage	Escalopa	Escalope
Choto/Cabrito	Kid	Faisán	Pheasant
Chuletas	Chops	Hamburguesa	Hamburger
Ciervo	Deer	Hígado	Liver

Jabalí	Wild boar	Rabo de toro	Stewed bull's tail
Lengua	Tongue	Riñones	Kidneys
Lomo	Loin (of pork)	Salchicha	Sausage
Mollejas	Sweetbreads	Salchichón	Cured salami-type sausage
Morcilla	Blood sausage		
Pato	Duck	Sesos	Brains
Pavo	Turkey	Solomillo	Pork tenderloin
Perdiz	Partridge	Ternera	Veal
Pollo	Chicken		

Vegetables (legumbres)

Aguacate	Avocado	Judías verdes, rojas, negras	Green, red, black beans
Ajo	Garlic		
Alcachofas	Artichokes	Lechuga	Lettuce
Berenjenas	Aubergine/eggplant	Lentejas	Lentils
Calabaza	Pumpkin	Nabos	Turnips
Cebollas	Onions	Palmitos	Palm hearts
Champiñones/ Setas	Mushrooms	Patatas (fritas)	Potatoes (chips/french fries)
Coliflor	Cauliflower	Pepino	Cucumber
Espárragos	Asparagus	Pimientos	Peppers
Espinacas	Spinach	Puerros	Leeks
Garbanzos	Chickpeas	Repollo	Cabbage
Guisantes	Peas	Setas	Mushrooms
Habas	Broad beans	Tomate	Tomato
Judías blancas	Haricot beans	Zanahoria	Carrot

Rice dishes

Arroz a banda	Rice with seafood, the rice served separately	Paella a la catalana	Mixed meat and seafood sometimes distinguished from a seafood paella by being called paella a la valenciana
Arroz a la marinera	Paella: rice with seafood and saffron		
Arroz negro	"Black rice", cooked with squid ink		

Desserts (postres)

Many desserts in Andalucía are customarily served with a dollop (or squirt) of whipped cream. Ask for "*sin nata*" (without cream) when ordering if you would prefer your *postre* without this garnish.

Alfajores	Honey and almond pastries	Flan	Crème caramel
		Helados	Ice cream
Arroz con leche	Rice pudding	Melocotón en almíbar	Peaches in syrup
Crema catalana	Crème brûlée		
Dulces	Tarts or cakes	Miel	Honey

Nata	Whipped cream (topping)	Pudin	Pudding
Natillas	Custard	Tarta de Santiago	pastry tart with almond filling
Pastel	Cake or pudding	Tocino de cielo	Andalucía's rich crème caramel
Peras al vino	Pears cooked in wine		
Pestiños	Anís or wine fritters	Yemas	Egg-yolk cakes
Polvorones	Almond cakes	Yogur	Yogurt

Fruit (frutas)

Albaricoques	Apricots	Manzanas	Apples
Almendras	Almonds	Melocotónes	Peaches
Castañas	Chestnuts	Melón	Melon
Cerezas	Cherries	Membrillo	Quince
Chirimoyas	Custard apples	Naranjas	Oranges
Chumbo	Prickly pear	Nectarinas	Nectarines
Ciruelas	Plums, prunes	Peras	Pears
Dátiles	Dates	Piña	Pineapple
Fresas	Strawberries	Plátanos	Bananas
Granada	Pomegranate	Pomelo	Grapefruit
Higos	Figs	Sandía	Watermelon
Limón	Lemon	Uvas	Grapes

Tapas and snacks

The most usual fillings for *bocadillos* are *lomo* (loin of pork), *tortilla* and *calamares* (all of which may be served hot), jamón (York or, much better, serrano), chorizo, *salchichón* (and various other regional sausages – such as the small, spicy Catalan *butifarras*), *queso* (cheese), or *atún* (tuna – probably canned). Standard tapas and *raciónes* might include:

Aceitunas	Olives	Champiñones	Mushrooms, usually fried in garlic
Albóndigas	Meatballs, usually in sauce		
		Chipirones	Whole baby squid
Anchoas	Anchovies	Chorizo	Spicy sausage
Banderilla	Tapa on a cocktail stick	Cocido	Stew
		Croqueta	Fish or chicken croquette
Berberechos	Cockles		
Boquerones	Fresh anchovies	Empanadilla	Fish/meat pasty
Calamares a la romana	Squid, deep fried in rings	Ensalada malagueña	Málaga salad with salt-cod oranges and potato
Calamares en su tinta	Squid in ink		
		Ensaladilla	Russian salad (diced vegetables in mayonnaise)
Callos	Tripe		
Caracoles	Snails, often served in a spicy/curry sauce		
		Escalibada	Aubergine (eggplant) and pepper salad
Carne en salsa	Meat in tomato sauce		
Cazón en adobo	Marinated and deep fried dogfish	Espinacas con Garbanzos	Spinach with chickpeas

Flamenquines	Ham or veal in breadcrumbs, deep fried	Patatas alioli	Potatoes in garlic mayonnaise
Gambas (al ajillo)	Shrimps (fried with garlic)	Patatas/Papas a lo pobre	Potatoes cooked with garlic and parsley
Habas con jamón	Broad beans with ham	Patatas bravas	Fried potato cubes topped with spicy sauce and mayonnaise
Hígado	Liver		
Huevo cocido	Hard-boiled egg		
Jamón ibérico	Top-quality black pig mountain cured ham	Pimientos	Peppers
		Pincho moruno	Kebab
Jamón serrano	Mountain (or factory) cured ham from white pigs	Pulpo	Octopus
		Puntillitas	Deep fried baby squid
		Riñones al Jerez	Kidneys in sherry
Jamón York	Regular ham	Salchichón	Cured sausage
Judias	Beans	Sardinas	Sardines
Mejillones	Mussels (either steamed, or served with diced tomatoes and onion)	Sepia	Cuttlefish
		Tabla	Tapa served on a wooden board
Montadito	Tapa served on bread	Tortilla de camarones	Fritters with small prawns
Morcilla	Blood sausage (black pudding)	Tortilla española	Potato omelette
Navajas	Razor clams	Tortilla francesa	Plain omelette
Pan con tomate	Bread, rubbed with tomato and oil		

Drinks

Café	Coffee	Agua mineral	Mineral water
Café solo	Espresso coffee	...(con gas)	... (sparkling)
Café con leche	White coffee	...(sin gas)	... (still)
Descafeinado	Decaff	Leche	Milk
Té	Tea	Limonada	Lemonade
Chocolate	Drinking Chocolate	Zumo	Juice
Agua	Water	Horchata	Tiger-nut drink

Alcohol

Anís	Aniseed liqueur	Fino (de Jerez)	Sherry
Brandy	Coñac/brandy	Pacháran	Sloes-based liqueur
Cerveza	Beer	Ron	Rum
Champán	Champagne	Vino	Wine

Glossary

Acequia irrigation channel.

Alameda park or tree-lined promenade.

Albariza type of soil in wine-growing zones with high chalk content enabling retention of moisture.

Alcalde mayor of town or village.

Alcazaba Moorish castle.

Alcázar Moorish fortified palace.

Almohads Muslims originally of Berber stock, who toppled the Almoravids and ruled Spain in the late twelfth and early thirteenth centuries.

Almoravids fanatical Berber dynasty from the Sahara who ruled much of Spain in the eleventh and twelfth centuries.

Artesonado wooden coffered ceiling of Moorish origin or inspiration.

Atalaya watchtower.

Autovía/autopista dual carriageway or highway/motorway or expressway.

Ayuntamiento town hall (also Casa Consistorial).

Azulejos glazed ceramic tiles (originally blue – hence the name).

Balneario spa.

Barrio suburb or quarter.

Bodega cellar, wine bar or warehouse.

Bracero landless agricultural worker.

Calle street.

Camarín shrine (inside a church) with a venerated image.

Campiña flat stretch of farmland or countryside.

Cante jondo deeply-felt flamenco song.

Capilla mayor chapel containing the high altar.

Capilla real royal chapel.

Carmen Granadan villa with garden.

Carretera highway or main road.

Cartuja Carthusian monastery.

Casa forestal woodland hunters' house/hotel.

Casa rural rural guesthouse or villa for rent.

Casa señorial/palacio aristocratic mansion.

Casco antiguo the old part of a town or city.

Casino social and gaming club.

Castillo castle.

Centro comercial shopping centre/mall.

Chiringuito beachfront restaurant.

Churrigueresque extreme form of Baroque art named after José Churriguera (1665–1725) and his extended family, its main exponents.

Ciudad town or city.

Ciudadela citadel.

Colegiata collegiate (large parish) church.

Comunidad autónoma autonomous region with significant powers of self-government. Andalucía is one of seventeen autonomous regions set up following the return to democracy in the 1970s.

Convento monastery or convent.

Converso Jew who converted to Christianity.

Copa/copas alcoholic drink(s).

Coro central part of church built for the choir.

Coro alto raised choir, often above west door of a church.

Corral type of patio or yard.

Correos post office.

Corrida de toros bullfight.

Cortes Spanish parliament in Madrid.

Cortijo rural farmhouse in Andalucía.

Coto de caza hunting reserve.

Cuesta slope/hill.

Cueva cave.

Custodia large receptacle or monstrance for Eucharist wafers.

Desamortización (Disentailment) nineteenth-century expropriation of church buildings and lands.

Duende to have soul (in flamenco).

Embalse artificial lake, reservoir or dam.

Ermita hermitage.

Esparto grass used for mats, window blinds and olive presses.

Feria annual fair.

Finca farm.

Fogón stove.

Gitano gypsy.

Huerta vegetable garden.

Isabelline ornamental form of late Gothic developed during the reign of Isabel and Fernando.

Jarra wine jug or pitcher.

Jornalero landless agricultural day-labourer.

Judería Jewish quarter.

Juerga (gypsy) shindig.

Junta de Andalucía government of the Autonomous Region of Andalucía.

Latifundio large estate.

Locutorio telephone office.

Lonja stock exchange building.

Marismas marshes.

Matanza pig slaughter.

Medina Moorish town.

Mercado market.

Mezquita mosque.

Mihrab prayer niche of Moorish mosque facing towards Mecca.

Mirador viewing point (literally balcony).

Monasterio monastery or convent.

Morisco Muslim Spaniard subject to medieval Christian rule – and nominally baptized.

Movida the (nightlife) scene; where the action is.

Mozarabe Christian subject to medieval Moorish rule; normally allowed freedom of worship. Mozarabic is the architectural style evolved by Christians under Arab domination.

Mudéjar Muslim Spaniard subject to medieval Christian rule, but retaining Islamic worship; most commonly a term applied to architecture which includes buildings built by Moorish craftsmen for the Christian rulers and later designs influenced by the Moors. The 1890s–1930s saw a Mudéjar revival, blended with Art Nouveau and Art Deco forms.

Palacio aristocratic mansion.

Panadería bakery.

Pantano reservoir held by a dam.

Parador luxury state-run hotel, often converted from minor monument.

Parroquia parish church.

Paseo promenade; also the evening stroll thereon.

Paso float bearing tableau carried in Semana Santa processions.

Patio inner courtyard.

Piscina swimming pool.

Plateresco/plateresque elaborately decorative Renaissance style, the sixteenth-century successor of Isabelline forms. Named for its resemblance to silversmiths' work (platería).

Playa beach.

Plaza square.

Plaza de toros bullring.

Plaza mayor a town or city's main square regardless of its name.

Posada old name for an inn.

Pueblo village or town.

Puerta gateway, also mountain pass.

Puerto port.

Rambla dry riverbed.

Reconquista the Christian reconquest of Moorish Spain.

Reja iron screen or grille, often fronting a window or guarding a chapel.

Retablo carved or painted altarpiece.

Río river.

Rociero adhering to the traditions of the El Rocío pilgrimage.

Rococo late-Baroque style with a profusion of rock-like forms, scrolls and crimped shells. From the French rocaille – "rock-work".

Romería religious procession to a rural shrine.

Sacristía, sagrario sacristy or sanctuary of a church.

Sacristía (ii), wine cellar in sherry bodega.

Saeta passionate flamenco song in praise of the Virgin and Christ.

Sebka decorative brickwork developed by the Almohads (eg, Giralda).

Semana Santa Holy Week, celebrated throughout Andalucía with elaborate processions.

Señoritismo behaving in a condescending manner; generally applied to rich landowners.

Sevillana rhythmic flamenco dance.

Sierra mountain range.

Sillería choir stall.

Solar aristocratic town mansion.

Solera blending system for sherry and brandy.

Tablao flamenco show.

Taifa small Moorish kingdom, many of which emerged after the disintegration of the Córdoba caliphate.

Tajo gorge.

Tetería Arabic tearoom.

Trascoro end-wall of the choir.

Torno dumbwaiter used by convents to sell their cakes and pastries.

Urbanización residential housing estate.

Vega cultivated fertile plain.

Venta roadside inn.

Yeso/yesería plaster/plasterwork.

Political parties and abbreviations

ETA Basque terrorist organization. Its political wing is the banned Batasuna.

Falange Franco's old fascist party; now officially defunct.

Fuerza Nueva Descendants of the above, also on the way out.

IR Izquierda Republicana, left-wing republican party.

IU Izquierda Unida, broad-left alliance of communists and others.

MC Movimiento Comunista (Communist Movement), small radical offshoot of the PCE.

OTAN NATO.

PA Partido Andalucista, the Andalucian Nationalist Party.

PASOC Partido de Acción Socialista, "traditional" socialist group to the left of the PSOE.

PCE Partido Comunista de España (Spanish Communist Party).

PP Partido Popular, the right-wing party formed by a union of Alianza Popular and the Christian Democrats led by Mariano Rajoy; currently the main oppostion party in the Cortes.

PSOE Partido Socialista Obrero Español (Spanish Socialist Workers' Party). Currently the government party led by prime minister José Luis Rodríguez Zapatero.

UGT Unión General de Trabajadores, Spain's most powerful trade union.

We speak English, German and Spanish!!!

B E S T * P R I C E S * S E R V I C E * C A R S

N O Q U E U E S * N O W A I T I N G * N O S H U T T L E B U S

Costa del Sol

BVQi

PRIMA RENT A CAR

Prima Service · Prima Preis · Prima Autos

Our deliver services:

- Airport
- Bus and train station
- Delivery to the Málaga Harbour
- Delivery to your hotel

Large variety of high quality vehicles.

Attractive prices and hospitality
Personal Service
Reductions for long terms rental

Reservations:

☎ Phone: ....+ 34 952 310 975
🖨 Fax: ....+ 34 952 359 936
🕐 Mobile: ....+ 34 608 840 401
✉ E-mail:...........................prima@rentacarprima.com
🖥 Web:...................................www.rentacarprima.com

Address:

C/ Idelfonso Marzo, 9. Málaga 29003
C/ Alemania, 3. Málaga .29001
C/ Hegel, 2. Pol. Ind Villarrosa. Málaga 29004

- ➢ **SPECIAL DISCOUNT TO ROUGH GUIDE READERS**
- ➢ **Large range of high quality vehicles.**

Small print and

Index

A Rough Guide to Rough Guides

Published in 1982, the first Rough Guide – to Greece – was a student scheme that became a publishing phenomenon. Mark Ellingham, a recent graduate in English from Bristol University, had been travelling in Greece the previous summer and couldn't find the right guidebook. With a small group of friends he wrote his own guide, combining a highly contemporary, journalistic style with a thoroughly practical approach to travellers' needs.

The immediate success of the book spawned a series that rapidly covered dozens of destinations. And, in addition to impecunious backpackers, Rough Guides soon acquired a much broader and older readership that relished the guides' wit and inquisitiveness as much as their enthusiastic, critical approach and value-for-money ethos.

These days, Rough Guides include recommendations from shoestring to luxury and cover more than 200 destinations around the globe, including almost every country in the Americas and Europe, more than half of Africa and most of Asia and Australasia. Our ever-growing team of authors and photographers is spread all over the world, particularly in Europe, the USA and Australia.

In the early 1990s, Rough Guides branched out of travel, with the publication of Rough Guides to World Music, Classical Music and the Internet. All three have become benchmark titles in their fields, spearheading the publication of a wide range of books under the Rough Guide name.

Including the travel series, Rough Guides now number more than 350 titles, covering: phrasebooks, waterproof maps, music guides from Opera to Heavy Metal, reference works as diverse as Conspiracy Theories and Shakespeare, and popular culture books from iPods to Poker. Rough Guides also produce a series of more than 120 World Music CDs in partnership with World Music Network.

Visit www.roughguides.com to see our latest publications.

Rough Guide travel images are available for commercial licensing at www.roughguidespictures.com

SMALL PRINT

Rough Guide credits

Text editor: Emma Gibbs
Layout: Ajay Verma
Cartography: Jasbir Sandhu
Picture editor: Emily Taylor
Production: Rebecca Short
Proofreader: Amanda Jones
Cover design: Chloë Roberts
Photographer: Georgie Scott
Editorial: **London** Ruth Blackmore, Andy Turner, Keith Drew, Edward Aves, Alice Park, Lucy White, Jo Kirby, James Smart, Natasha Foges, Róisín Cameron, Emma Traynor, James Rice, Kathryn Lane, Christina Valhouli, Monica Woods, Mani Ramaswamy, Alison Roberts, Harry Wilson, Lucy Cowie, Joe Staines, Peter Buckley, Matthew Milton, Tracy Hopkins, Ruth Tidball; **New York** Andrew Rosenberg, Steven Horak, AnneLise Sorensen, Ella Steim, Anna Owens, Sean Mahoney, Paula Neudorf; **Delhi** Madhavi Singh, Karen D'Souza, Lubna Shaheen
Design & Pictures: **London** Scott Stickland, Dan May, Diana Jarvis, Mark Thomas, Nicole Newman, Sarah Cummins; **Delhi** Umesh Aggarwal, Jessica Subramanian, Ankur Guha, Pradeep Thapliyal, Sachin Tanwar, Anita Singh, Nikhil Agarwal
Production: Vicky Baldwin

Cartography: **London** Maxine Repath, Ed Wright, Katie Lloyd-Jones; **Delhi** Rajesh Chhibber, Ashutosh Bharti, Rajesh Mishra, Animesh Pathak, Karobi Gogoi, Alakananda Roy, Swati Handoo, Deshpal Dabas
Online: **London** George Atwell, Faye Hellon, Jeanette Angell, Fergus Day, Justine Bright, Clare Bryson, Áine Fearon, Adrian Low, Ezgi Celebi, Amber Bloomfield; **Delhi** Amit Verma, Rahul Kumar, Narender Kumar, Ravi Yadav, Debojit Borah, Rakesh Kumar, Ganesh Sharma, Shisir Basumatari
Marketing & Publicity: **London** Liz Statham, Niki Hanmer, Louise Maher, Jess Carter, Vanessa Godden, Vivienne Watton, Anna Paynton, Rachel Sprackett, Libby Jellie, Laura Vipond, Vanessa MacDonald; **New York** Geoff Colquitt, Nancy Lambert, Katy Ball; **Delhi** Ragini Govind
Manager India: Punita Singh
Reference Director: Andrew Lockett
Operations Manager: Helen Phillips
PA to Publishing Director: Nicola Henderson
Publishing Director: Martin Dunford
Commercial Manager: Gino Magnotta
Managing Director: John Duhigg

Publishing information

This 6th edition published May 2009 by
Rough Guides Ltd,
80 Strand, London WC2R 0RL
345 Hudson St, 4th Floor,
New York, NY 10014, USA
14 Local Shopping Centre, Panchsheel Park,
New Delhi 110021, India
Distributed by the Penguin Group
Penguin Books Ltd,
80 Strand, London WC2R 0RL
Penguin Group (USA)
375 Hudson Street, NY 10014, USA
Penguin Group (Australia)
250 Camberwell Road, Camberwell,
Victoria 3124, Australia
Penguin Group (Canada)
195 Harry Walker Parkway N, Newmarket, ON,
L3Y 7B3 Canada
Penguin Group (NZ)
67 Apollo Drive, Mairangi Bay, Auckland 1310,
New Zealand

Cover concept by Peter Dyer.

Typeset in Bembo and Helvetica to an original design by Henry Iles.

Printed and bound in China

© Geoff Garvey and Mark Ellingham

No part of this book may be reproduced in any form without permission from the publisher except for the quotation of brief passages in reviews.

640pp includes index

A catalogue record for this book is available from the British Library.

ISBN: 978-1-84836-037-2

The publishers and authors have done their best to ensure the accuracy and currency of all the information in **The Rough Guide to Andalucía**, however, they can accept no responsibility for any loss, injury, or inconvenience sustained by any traveller as a result of information or advice contained in the guide.

1   3   5   7   9   8   6   4   2

Help us update

We've gone to a lot of effort to ensure that the sixth edition of **The Rough Guide to Andalucía** is accurate and up to date. However, things change – places get "discovered", opening hours are notoriously fickle, restaurants and rooms raise prices or lower standards. If you feel we've got it wrong or left something out, we'd like to know, and if you can remember the address, the price, the hours, the phone number, so much the better.

Please send your comments with the subject line "**Rough Guide Andalucía Update**" to ® mail@roughguides.com. We'll credit all contributions and send a copy of the next edition (or any other Rough Guide if you prefer) for the very best emails.

Have your questions answered and tell others about your trip at
® community.roughguides.com

Acknowledgements

On our sixth edition grateful thanks must once again go to Josép Vergés, Angela García and Josefina del Castillo for help in Almería. Special thanks also to Pau for her help in Seville and to Chris and Ana Stewart for the lowdown on the western Alpujarras. We'd also like to say "muchísimas gracias" to Pam for all her help in Granada and also to Lindsay Vick for assistance with Seville nightlife. We are also indebted to Pedro Martín and Ana Fernandez at the Alhambra, Granada, Javier Andrade at the Museo del Baile Flamenco, Seville and Pepa Babot at the Museo Picasso, Málaga. A big thank you also goes from Geoff to Han for her untiring help and support in producing another edition.

Valuable assistance on the ground was also rendered by Christine Hofer in El Chorro, Paco Moyano & Lola Maiztegui in Alhama de Granada, Alicia Jiménez and Bienvenido Luque in Málaga, Julie Hetherington and Rafael Calzado Reca in Andújar, James Stuart and Carmen Atkins García in Vejer, Vicente Sousa in Aracena, Jean-Claude Juston in Mecina Fondales, Ignacio Muñiz García in Almedinilla, Angelica Romero in Huelva, Gina de los Santos in Sevilla, Manuel Amigo García in Aroche, Juan Carlos Ábalos Guerrero and Clive Jarman in Zuheros, Jesús García in Benarrabá, Elma Thompson in Nerja, Juan Manuel Pérez in Salobreña, María Angeles Rodríguez in Antequera, Rosa, González in Conil, Raquel Ahedo in La Linea, Juan Carlos Raths Aznar in Mojácar, Francisco Serrano in Mijas, Mercedes Galvez in Jaén, Anton Peer in Segura de la Sierra, Raquel Pasqual in Córdoba, Pepe Morales in Punta Umbría, Polly Rodger Brown and Juan María Luna Moreno in La Axarquía and Pasqual Rovira and Quica Caballero Mata at the donkey sanctuary in Rute.

Special thanks are also due to Tony Wailey for Civil War background, Bienvenido Martinez Navarro for updates on excavations at Orce, Paul Winstanley for modern art information, Hugh Broughton for architectural suggestions and to Mark Honigsbaum for surfing tips. We were greatly helped with advice on birdspotting from Huw Morgan, Anthony Winchester and Martin Bott. We would also like to thank Raquel Fonseca Cambeiro and the staff of the Spanish National Tourist Office in London for their help with numerous queries, as well as the staff of the Sherry Institute in London.

Readers' letters

Thanks to all the readers who have taken the time to write in with comments and suggestions (and apologies if we've inadvertently omitted or misspelt anyone's name):

Luis Miguel Aguilera & Aurora Damigo, Nir Aides, Sue Ashcroft, Susan Ashcroft, Bill Bain, John Bainbridge, Alexandra Balkwill, Michael van Beinum, Amanda Bekker, Gordon Bell, Anita Bijer & Walter Michels, Tony Bishop, Caroline Bowman, Finola Brady, Ann Bresnihan, Nancy Brinton, Alan Burchard, Valerie Cameron, David Chadwick, Steve & Anne Chandler, Clare & Gerald Chapman, Sarah Chatwin & Mark Unwin, Mike Coleman, Paul Connell, Christine Cox, Elizabeth Cox, Dave Craig, Jan Davies, Jill & Anthony Davies, Gina Day, Tom Delaney, Brenda Dixon, Sonia Dominguez Alcañiz, Louise Dominian, Ian Donnely, Rona Dunbar, Graham Dunning & Vicky Oxby, Margaret Ecclestone, Jack Edwards, Kathrin Engels, Dror Etzion, Huw Evans, Marian Fairley, Jan Field, Derek Fitzpatrick, Linda Fletcher, Edna Gallagher, Ella Garner, John Gill, Barry Gant, Sarah Godfrey, Carey Grey, Carmen Guardeño, Angela Hague, Andrew Halliwell, Patrick Hannet, Sue Harding, Steve Hardwick, Tom Harrison, Liz Hatherley, Barbara Hauch, Camilla Victoria Hellern, Clive Henman, Saskia Hens, Jim Heron, Valerie Hilton, Tim Holt & Keith Tennyson, Peter Hudson, Anita Hummel, Kathrin Hunger, Claire Hunt, Gordon Hunter, Katherine Jamieson, Edmund Janowski, John Johnstone, Neil Jones, Simon Jones, Eileen Kerr, Alice Kildsgaard & Lau Mølgård, N.J. King, Truusja Kofflard, Carmen Ladrón de Guevara, Elizabeth Lancaster, Kerstin Lange, Linda Lashford & David Lanfear, Fiona Lawson, John & Carole LeBrun, Howard Little, F. McDonald, Javier y Manuela, Nichole Martinson, Joan Marc Mas, Joy Mayglothling, Vicky McGhee, Tim Mercer, Jo Miles, Matt & Debbs Miles, Helen Minnaar, Nina Mittendorf, Christian Most, W K Muir, Denis Murphy, Ian Murray, David Nash, Fatima Norat, Barry North, Mike North, David Nuyen, Bernie O'Reilly, Harry Palmer, Tim Parker, Chris Pearce, John Percy, Jean

Pitt, Robert Pittam, D. Potter, Anne Price, Mike Purdue, Carole Rankin, David Razzell, Allan & Zena Reedie, Alex Richardson, Noel Richardson, Koen de Rijcke, Alan Roberts, John Roberts, Howard Rogers, Dietmar Roth, Esteban Rovira, Simon Rowe, Eric Rowland, Moira Janet Salt, Julian Sanders, Lucia Sanou, Janet Scott, Carola Scupham, Jeremy Seal, Ben Searle, Seb Sheppard, Julia Simpson, Kate Skelton, Andy Smith, Maja Stone, Martin Stone, Torsten Ström,

Pat Swinbanks, Dawn Taylor, Rita Thompson, Eddy Tomlinson, Vicki Trott, Barry Troy, Luis Velasco, Andres Velez-Guerra, Tony Walker, Catherine Walkley, Roisin & Quinn Wallace, Sarah Walpole, Ian Walsh, Anna Ward, Laura Warner, Ellen Weaver, Ruth Weaver, Rudi Wesselius, Ken Westmoreland, Zoë Weston, Mary White, Graham Williams, Kate Williams, Terry Wilson, Colin Wing, Matthew Woodcock, Nicola Wright, Gavin Yates, Andrew Young, Clifton Young, Marta Zamorano.

Photo credits

All photos © Rough Guides except the following:

Introduction
Osbourne Bull, Cadiz © Geoff Garvey
Traditional Spanish Costumes at Feria de Córdoba © Hanneke Sanou
Oranges in the gardens of the Real Alcazar, Seville © Robert Harding/Jupiter Images
Street Performers During Cadiz Carnival © Geoff Garvey
Kite Surfing, Tarifa, Costa De La Luz © Timothy Allen/Axiom
A hiker pauses to drink from a stream, Trevelez Valley © O. Alamany & E. Vicens/Corbis

Things not to miss
01 Salt marshes in the Natural Reserve of Cabo de Gata-Nijar © Thomas Dressler/Photolibrary
04 Flamingos in Donana national park © Nardi/ Tips Images
09 Hiker on the Pinsapar trail in the Sierra de Grazalema © Roberto Soncin Gerometta/DRR. Net
10 Picasso's work on paper © Courtesy of The Picasso Museum
12 Gibraltar © Gibraltar Tourist Board
15 Village encierro (bull run) Benaocaz, Cádiz © Geoff Garvey
16 Ronda © Andres Aguayo/Ronda Tourist Board
17 Flamenco Dancing © Courtesy of Museo de Flamenco, Seville
19 Waterfall near Cazorla town © Geoff Garvey
22 Museo Ballas Arts © Keith Drew
29 Albaycin, Granada © Graham Heywood/iStock Photos

Andalucian cuisine colour section
Sardines Drying On A Beach © Keith Drew
Tapas Bar Jerez de la Frontera © Renaud Visage/ Alamy

Semana Santa colour section
Semana Santa procession, Puente de Triana, Sevilla © Geoff Garvey
Sevilla Semana Santa © Hanneke Sanou
Sevilla Semana Santa © Geoff Garvey

Moorish architecture colour section
Ruins of the Palace of Abd al-Rhaman III © Javier Larrea/Photolibrary

Black and whites
p.68 Picasso Museum © Courtesy of The Picasso Museum
p.131 Relaxing in Marbella © AlexValent/iStock Pictures
p.146 Apes in Gibraltar © Gibraltar Tourist Board
p.161 Arco de Felipe V © Andres Aguayo/Ronda Tourist Board
p.310 Ejilca, Sevilla © Geoff Garvey
p.319 Puerta del Buey at the walled town of Niebla © JD Dallet/Photolibrary
p.334 El Rocio © Stephane Frances/Tips Images
p.432 Arab baths (11th century) © JD Dallet/ Photolibrary
p.453 Castillo La Yedra, near Cazorla town © Geoff Garvey
p.506 Alhama De Granada © The Travel Library
p.536 Cave Dwelling in Guadix © Bowater/Tips Images
p.544 Port and Alcazaba, Almeria © Charles Bowman/Robert Harding/DRR.Net
p.558 Agua Amarga; small resort in Cabo de Gata natural park © Geoff Garvey
p.563 Los Letreros cave near Velez Blanco © Juan CarlosMunoz/Photolibrary

Selected images from our guidebooks are available for licensing from:

ROUGHGUIDESPICTURES.COM

Index

Map entries are in colour.

INDEX

Map symbols

maps are listed in the full index using coloured text

----··	International boundary	⊠—⊠	Gate
----··	Provincial border	◆	Point of interest
---	Chapter division boundary	ℂ	Telphone office
	Motorway	ⓘ	Tourist office
	Major road	⊠	Post office
	Minor road	@	Internet access
	Pedestrianized street	ℂ	Telephone office
ⅢⅢⅢ	Steps	⚡	Skiing
	Railway	⚠	Campsite
●---●	Cable car	🅿	Parking
-----	Footpath	▣	Restaurant
— —	Ferry route	◉	Accommodation
	Coastline/river	)(	Bridge
	Wall	⊙	Statue
▲	Mountain peak	✡	Synagogue
/|\	Hill shading	🏛	Monastery
𝘈𝘈𝘈𝘈	Cliff	♖	Castle
⌒	Rocks	∴	Ruins
><	Pass	▥	Mosque
🌙	Dunes		Building
⬗	Cave	+—	Church
⬇	View point		Park/forest
⊥	Lighthouse	+⁺+	Cemetery
✈	Airport		Beach
⊥	Gardens	−	Saltpan

We're covered. Are you?

ROUGH GUIDES Travel Insurance

Visit our website at www.roughguides.com/website/shop or call:

COLUMBUS DIRECT
Travel Insurance

ROUGH GUIDES

📞 UK: 0800 083 9507

📞 Spain: 900 997 149

📞 Australia: 1300 669 999

📞 New Zealand: 0800 55 99 11

📞 Worldwide: +44 870 890 2843

📞 USA, call toll free on: 1 800 749 4922

Please quote our ref: **Rough Guides books**

Cover for over 46 different nationalities and available in 4 different languages.